CHRIST IN CHRISTIAN TRADITION

VOLUME ONE

CHRIST
IN CHRISTIAN
TRADITION

VOLUME ONE

From the Apostolic Age to Chalcedon (451)

SECOND, REVISED EDITION

by

ALOYS GRILLMEIER, S.J.

translated by
JOHN BOWDEN

JOHN KNOX PRESS
ATLANTA

Imprimi potest: Nik. Junk, s.j., *Praep. Prov. Germ. Inf. Coloniae,*
die 20 Iulii, 1964

Joh Günter, Gerhartz, S.J., *Praep. Prov. Germ. Inf. Coloniae,*
die 25 Novembris, 1974, *pro editione altera*

Nihil obstat: Ricardus J. Foster, s.t.i., l.s.s., *censor deputatus*
Imprimatur: ✠ Franciscus, *Archiepiscopus Birmingamiensis*
Birmingamiae, die 21a Augusti, 1964

Published in Great Britain by A. R. Mowbray
& Co. Limited and in the United States by
John Knox Press. ⓒ A. R. Mowbray & Co.
Limited. First edition 1965, second edition
1975.

Library of Congress Cataloging in Publication Data

Grillmeier, Aloys, 1910-
  Christ in Christian tradition.

  Bibliography: v. 1, p.
  CONTENTS: v. 1. From the apostolic age to Chalcedon
(451)
    1. Jesus Christ—History of doctrines—Early church,
ca. 30-600. I. Title.
BT198.G743 1975   232   75-13456
ISBN 0-64-22301-x
10 9 8 7 6 5 4

Printed in the United States of America

IN GRATITUDE TO
THE LATE PROFESSOR F. L. CROSS
TO WHOM THIS WORK
IS MUCH INDEBTED

AUTHOR'S PREFACE

THIS book is a full revision of my article 'Die theologische und sprachliche Vorbereitung der christologischen Formel von Chalkedon', which was published in A. Grillmeier–H. Bacht, *Das Konzil von Chalkedon I,* Würzburg 1951, 1959², 1962³, 1973⁴, 5–202. The original plan, suggested by the Rev. John Bowden, was simply for a translation of this study and an expansion of the bibliographical notes on the basis of the corrected reprint of 1959. Mr Bowden also took upon himself the troublesome task of translation, which steadily increased as the scope of the revision enlarged. I am especially grateful for his help.

I have been particularly concerned to describe the transition from the apostolic age to the time of the emergence of the christological problem proper, i.e. to give an account of the christological development of the second century. This calls for still greater consideration and more adequate treatment than can be offered here. On the whole, I have tried to understand and to describe each stage of the development in its own particular character and to avoid introducing later dogmatic concepts. In my opinion, however, this does not exclude the stressing of the rudiments of later developments where these rudiments are really present.

As far as is possible, this investigation is to be continued, first of all as far as the end of the patristic period; the preliminary work is already quite far advanced.

My thanks are also due to the publishers, John Knox Press, who undertook to publish the work and have waited with great patience for its completion.

Finally, I should like to take this opportunity of expressing my gratitude to Dr F. L. Cross and the Oxford International Conference on Patristic Studies, to which this work is much indebted.

FRANKFURT, 24 MAY 1964

PREFACE TO THE SECOND EDITION

MORE than a year's work has been devoted to the preparation of this new edition of *Christ in Christian Tradition* (Vol. 1). As far as possible, details have been given of the literature which has appeared since 1965, and the results of research have been incorporated into the text. I have been particularly concerned to give a new account of the theological development between Origen and the Council of Nicaea (325). The council itself now has a chapter of its own. There is an extended account of the christology of Marcellus of Ancyra which, thanks to research into the Marcelliana, can now rest on a relatively broad foundation. In this connection I am particularly grateful to Dr Martin Tetz of Bochum, for a great deal of advice. In this new section it has been possible to give a more clear-cut and more reliable account of the history of the Logos-sarx christology. The section on Didymus of Alexandria has also been reworked. The account of Origenism has been expanded as far as Aponius. Finally, the christological development between Ephesus and Chalcedon has been enlarged and made more precise. There are still some gaps, but these can only be filled at a later stage. Work is needed above all on the christology of Pelagius and the Pelagians.

Further work, however, must first be done on christology after Chalcedon. The second volume of this work will cover the period from 451 to the death of Gregory the Great (604). The third volume will then describe developments as far as the iconoclastic dispute and Spanish adoptionism.

I am grateful for help on this second edition from Dr Gerbert Brunner, who has been awarded a grant for his collaboration from the Deutsche Forschungsgemeinschaft. Particular thanks must go to Mr Bowden, who has undertaken the demanding task of translation for the new edition with great patience. Thanks are also due to the publishers, A. R. Mowbray & Company, for venturing on so considerably enlarged an edition of my work. I am especially obliged to my friends Richard Mulkern and John Stockdale.

A.G.

FRANKFURT-MAIN, 21 MARCH 1974

TRANSLATOR'S PREFACE

MEETING old friends again is always a pleasure. *Christ in Christian Tradition* was the first book I ever translated, and that the late Dr Cross, Mr Neville Hilditch of Mowbrays and Professor Grillmeier himself should have encouraged an inexperienced young graduate who knew less German than he imagined to embark on what has since proved a highly enjoyable career of translating is one of the immense pieces of good fortune which has come my way and over which I shall always be surprised as well as grateful. Certainly I never expected to return to the book again, but when the first edition sold out and a revised edition was planned, the prospect of sharing in the new work was irresistible.

English readers of *Christ and Christian Tradition* are perhaps luckier than they know. It is certainly the only book to my knowledge written by a German-speaking author living in Germany to have appeared first in England; moreover, we now have a second edition before German readers have even had one. The revision has been very thorough indeed: bibliographical details in the notes have been completely updated, and large sections of the text have been completely rewritten to take new research into account. The equivalent of a small book has been added to the length. In its new form, *Christ in Christian Tradition* now seems good for at least another decade. The paean of praise which greeted its first appearance certainly deserves to be repeated.

Once again, Dr Grillmeier has proved the most helpful of all authors for a translator to work with, and he has been indefatigable in pursuing the revision through all its stages. Margaret Lydamore did not know quite what she was letting herself in for when she agreed to help with the indices, but persevered to the end with her usual determination and thoroughness. Finally, in these competitive and economically difficult days it has been a delight to work for another publisher and to pass on problems to a good friend, Richard Mulkern of Mowbrays, who has probably had more sleepless nights over this revision than I have.

JOHN BOWDEN

SCM PRESS LTD, ST VALENTINE'S DAY 1975

ABBREVIATIONS

AAA	Acta Apostolorum Apocrypha, post C. Tischendorf denuo edd. R. A. Lipsius–M. Bonnet
AAS	Acta Apostolicae Sedis, Romae 1909ff.
AbhGöttGW	Abhandlungen der Gesellschaft der Wissenschaften zu Göttingen, philosophisch-historische Klasse, Göttingen
AbhMünchAkW	Abhandlungen der Bayrischen Akademie der Wissenschaften, philosophisch-philologisch-historische Klasse, München
ACO	Acta Conciliorum Oecumenicorum, ed. E. Schwartz, Argentorati–Berolini–Lipsiae
ACW	Ancient Christian Writers, ed. J. Quasten–J. C. Plumpe, Westminster, Maryland
AnalBibl	Analecta Biblica, Romae
AnalBoll	Analecta Bollandiana, Paris–Bruxelles
AnalGreg	Analecta Gregoriana, Romae
Angel	*Angelicum*, Romae
AnLovBiblOr	Analecta Lovanensia Biblica et Orientalia, Louvain
Anton	*Antonianum*, Romae
Aug	*Augustinianum*, Romae
AugMag	*Augustinus Magister, Congrès International Augustinien 1954*, Vols. I and II Communications, Vol. III Actes, Paris 1954–55
BGBE	Beiträge zur Geschichte der biblischen Exegese, Tübingen
BGBH	Beiträge zur Geschichte der biblischen Hermeneutik, Tübingen
BHistTh	Beiträge zur historischen Theologie, Tübingen
BJRL	*Bulletin of the John Rylands Library*, Manchester
BLE	*Bulletin de Littérature Ecclesiastique*, Toulouse
Byz	*Byzantion*, Paris–Liège
ByzZ	*Byzantinische Zeitschrift*, Leipzig–München
BZ	*Biblische Zeitschrift*, Freiburg im Breisgau
BZNW	Beihefte zur *Zeitschrift für die Neutestamentliche Wissenschaft*, Berlin
CCL	Corpus Christianorum, series Latina, Turnholti
COD	Conciliorum Oecumenicorum Decreta. Edidit Istituto per le scienze religiose—Bologna, curantibus J. Alberigo, J. A. Dossetti, P. P. Joannou, C. Leonardi, P. Prodi, consultante H. Jedin, Bologna 1973³
CQR	*Church Quarterly Review*, London
CSCO	Corpus scriptorum christianorum orientalium, Paris–Louvain
CSEL	Corpus scriptorum ecclesiasticorum latinorum, Wien
DictAL	*Dictionnaire d'Archéologie Chrétienne et de Liturgie*, ed. F. Cabrol–H. Leclercq, Paris 1924ff.
DictBibl(Suppl)	*Dictionnaire de la Bible*, ed. F. Vigouroux, 5 vols., Paris 1895–1912, 1926³ff.; Supplément 1920ff.
DictHGE	*Dictionnaire d'Histoire et de Géographie Ecclésiastiques*, ed. A. Baudrillart, Paris 1912ff.
DictSpirit	*Dictionnaire de Spiritualité, Ascétique et Mystique, Doctrines et Histoire*, ed. M. Viller, Paris 1932ff.

DomStud	*Dominican Studies. A Quarterly Review of Theology and Philosophy*, Oxford
DOP	*Dumbarton Oaks Papers*, Cambridge, Mass.
DTC	*Dictionnaire de Théologie Catholique*, ed. A. Vacant–E. Mangenot–E. Amann, Paris 1909ff.
DThP	*Divus Thomas*, Piacenza
EO	*Echos d'Orient*, Paris–Constantinople
EphThLov	*Ephemerides Theologicae Lovanienses*, Louvain
ET	English translation
EtBibl	Études Bibliques, Paris
EvTh	*Evangelische Theologie*, München
Folia	*Folia. Studies in the Christian Perpetuation of the Classics*, New York
FrancStud	*Franciscan Studies*, New York
FRLANT	Forschungen zur Religion und Literatur des Alten und Neuen Testaments, Göttingen
GCS	Die Griechischen Christlichen Schriftsteller der ersten drei Jahrhunderte, ed. Kirchenväter-Kommission der Preussischen Akademie der Wissenschaften, Leipzig, now: Kommission für spätantike Religionsgeschichte der Deutschen Akademie der Wissenschaften zu Berlin
GÖK	Geschichte der Ökumenischen Konzilien, ed. G. Dumeige–H. Bacht, Mainz
GOTR	*The Greek Orthodox Theological Review*, Brookline, Mass.
Greg	*Gregorianum. Rivista di studi teologici e filosofici*, Romae
HCO	Histoire des Conciles Oecuméniques, ed. G. Dumeige, Paris
HDG	Handbuch der Dogmengeschichte, Freiburg–Basel–Wien
HistJb	*Historisches Jahrbuch der Görres-Gesellschaft*, München–Freiburg
HZ	*Historische Zeitschrift*, München
ITQ	*Irish Theological Quarterly*, Maynooth
JAC	*Jahrbuch für Antike und Christentum*, Münster i. W.
JBL	*Journal of Biblical Literature*, Boston–New Haven
JEH	*Journal of Ecclesiastical History*, London
JLH	*Jahrbuch für Liturgik und Hymnologie*, Kassel
JTS	*Journal of Theological Studies*, London–Oxford
Kyriakon	Festschrift J. Quasten I–II, Münster 1970
LitJb	*Liturgisches Jahrbuch*, Münster i. W.
LThK	*Lexikon für Theologie und Kirche*2, ed. J. Höfer–K. Rahner, Freiburg im Breisgau 1957ff.
Mansi	*Sacrorum Conciliorum nova et amplissima Collectio*, Florence 1759ff.; Venice 1769ff.; Paris–Arnhem–Leipzig 1901–27
MiscF	*Miscellanea Franciscana*, Romae
MSR	*Mélanges de Science Religieuse*, Lille
Mus	*Le Muséon*, Louvain

NF	Neue Folge
NGött	Nachrichten von der Gesellschaft der Wissenschaften zu Göttingen, philosophisch-historische Klasse (until 1940); Nachrichten der Akademie der Wissenschaften in Göttingen, Göttingen 1941ff.
Nov Test	*Novum Testamentum*, Leiden
NRT	*Nouvelle Revue Théologique*, Tournai
NS	New series
NTAbh	Neutestamentliche Abhandlungen, Münster i. W.
NTS	*New Testament Studies*, Cambridge
NTT	*Nederlands Theologisch Tijdschrift*, Leiden
OC	Orientalia Christiana, Romae
OCA	Orientalia Christiana Analecta, Romae
OCP	*Orientalia Christiana Periodica*, Romae
OrChr	*Oriens Christianus*, Leipzig 1901–41; Wiesbaden 1953ff.
PG	Patrologiae cursus completus, ed. J. P. Migne, Series graeca, Paris 1857–66
PL	Patrologiae cursus completus, ed. J. P. Migne, Series latina, Paris 1844–55
PLS	Patrologiae Latinae Supplementum, ed. A. Hamman: I, Paris 1958; II, 1960; III, 1963
PO	Patrologia Orientalis, ed. R. Graffin–F. Nau, Paris
PRE	*Realencyklopädie für protestantische Theologie und Kirche*[3], ed. A. Hauck, Leipzig
PS	Patristica Sorbonensia, Paris
PSyr	Patrologia Syriaca, Paris
PTSt	Patristische Texte und Studien, Berlin
PWK	Pauly–Wissowa–Kroll, *Realencyclopädie der klassischen Altertumswissenschaft*, Stuttgart
RAC	*Reallexikon für Antike und Christentum*, ed. T. Klauser, Stuttgart 1950ff.
RAM	*Revue d'Ascétique et de Mystique*, Toulouse
RB	*Revue Biblique*, Paris
RevBén	*Revue Bénédictine*, Maredsous
RevEtAug	*Revue des Études Augustiniennes*, Paris
RevEtByz	*Revue des Études Byzantines*, Paris
RevEtGrec	*Revue des Études Grecques*, Paris
RevEtLat	*Revue des Études Latines*, Paris
RevHistRel	*Revue d'Histoire des Religions*, Paris
RevOrChr	*Revue de l'Orient Chrétien*, Paris
RevSR	*Revue des Sciences Religieuses*, Strasbourg–Paris
Rev Thom	*Revue Thomiste*, Paris
RGG	*Die Religion in Geschichte und Gegenwart*[3], ed. K. Galling, Tübingen 1957ff.
RHE	*Revue d'Histoire Ecclésiastique*, Louvain
RivStorLittRel	*Rivista di Storia e Letteratura Religiosa*, Florence
RSO	*Rivista degli Studi Orientali*, Roma
RSPT	*Revue des Sciences Philosophiques et Théologiques*, Paris
RSR	*Recherches de Science Religieuse*, Paris
RTAM	*Recherches de Théologie Ancienne et Médiévale*, Louvain
RömQ	*Römische Quartalschrift für christliche Altertumskunde und für Kirchengeschichte*, Freiburg im Breisgau

SBGesGött	Sitzungsberichte von der Gesellschaft der Wissenschaften zu Göttingen, philosophisch-historische Klasse, Göttingen
SBMünchAk	Sitzungsberichte der Bayrischen Akademie der Wissenschaften, philosophisch-philologisch-historische Klasse, München
SBT	Studies in Biblical Theology, London-Naperville
SC	Sources Chrétiennes, Paris
Schol	*Scholastik*, Freiburg im Breisgau
SPT	*Les sciences philosophiques et théologiques*, Paris
ST	Studi e Testi, Roma-Città del Vaticano
StudPat	*Studia Patristica*, ed. K. Aland-F. L. Cross, I-VI (TU 63-4, 78-81), Berlin 1957-62ff.
SymbOsl	*Symbolae Osloenses*, Oslo
TD	Textus et Documenta, series theologica, Romae
TDNT	*Theological Dictionary of the New Testament*, ed. G. Kittel-F. Gerhard, ET by G. W. Bromiley, Grand Rapids 1964ff.
TG	*Theologie und Glaube*, Paderborn
Theo-Phil	*Theologie und Philosophie, Vierteljahresschrift*, Freiburg im Breisgau
TheolStud	*Theological Studies*, Woodstock, Maryland
ThLZ	*Theologische Literaturzeitung*, Leipzig
ThR	*Theologische Rundschau*, Tübingen
TQ	*Theologische Quartalschrift*, Tübingen
TR	*Theologische Revue*, Münster i. W.
Trad	*Traditio. Studies in Ancient and Medieval History, Thought and Religion*, New York
TThZ	*Trierer Theologische Zeitschrift*, Trier
TU	Texte und Untersuchungen zur Geschichte der altchristlichen Literatur, ed. O. V. Gebhardt-A. von Harnack et al., Leipzig-Berlin
TZ	*Theologische Zeitschrift*, Basel
VC	*Vetera Christianorum*, Bari
VigC	*Vigiliae Christianae. A Review of Early Christian Life and Language*, Amsterdam
VoxT	*Vox Theologica*, Assen, Nederland
ZKG	*Zeitschrift für Kirchengeschichte*, Gotha-Stuttgart
ZkTh	*Zeitschrift für katholische Theologie*, Innsbruck-Wien
ZNW	*Zeitschrift für die neutestamentliche Wissenschaft und die Kunde der älteren Kirche*, Berlin
ZRelGG	*Zeitschrift für Religions- und Geistesgeschichte*, Marburg
ZThK	*Zeitschrift für Theologie und Kirche*, Tübingen

CONTENTS

SECTION TWO
FROM EPHESUS TO CHALCEDON

SECTION THREE
THE COUNCIL OF CHALCEDON

INTRODUCTION

CHRISTIANITY takes its name from Christ (Acts 11. 26). At the beginning of its history stand the Christ-event, Christ's revelation and, above all, Christ himself as a person. From the very beginning, an intellectual struggle set in over this event and this person which is to be counted among the most profound of all human controversies, within Christianity or outside it. It is essential to understand this struggle, which can only happen completely on the level of faith, if we are to understand how Christianity and mankind appropriated the *mysterium Christi*. We do not understand the present condition of our faith in Christ unless we have taken the measure of this faith as it was in the past. We may not be indifferent to any age in this past. Each generation of Christian history has contributed something towards the appropriation of the *mysterium Christi* which deserves the consideration of posterity. To allow only those questions which are live issues for the present—and perhaps only for the present—to determine the interpretation of the *mysterium Christi* would be a dangerous limitation to our understanding of Christ. But at the same time, the problems of our day are of the utmost value in understanding history. They teach us that we must show how a consideration of the past is relevant to the present. This is not difficult for us in the particular case of the history of ancient christology. For ancient christology puts Christ in the middle of time and sees in the development of faith in him a process which will only end with the Second Coming of the Lord. There has often been a feeling of deep suspicion towards ancient christology, and it has been said to have no value for our age because it made use of a technical language and a Hellenistic presentation, both of which must be rejected. But if we are to proclaim the *mysterium Christi* in the language of our time, we must first have understood what the Fathers wanted to say in the language of their time. The inward, intellectual struggles of the ancient church testify that the christological writers of that church were concerned with something vital, namely the very nature of Christianity.

PART ONE

THE BIRTH OF CHRISTOLOGY

CHAPTER ONE

BIBLICAL STARTING-POINTS FOR PATRISTIC CHRISTOLOGY

1. THE PRESENT SITUATION

THE nineteenth century used all its energy to work out a purely historical picture of Jesus by means of the techniques of historical investigation. In this investigation, the dogma of the incarnation was not to be accepted as a basic presupposition: the life of Jesus was to be treated as a purely human life which developed in a human way. The attempt came to nothing.[1] Thereupon there followed a return to the theological treatment of the New Testament statements about Christ. Martin Kähler[2] stood at the beginning of the new movement; he brought to German Protestant theology the recognition,

> that the Christian faith is related to Jesus of Nazareth as he was preached in the apostolic proclamation as the crucified and the risen one. The message of the apostles is the proclamation of a *kerygma* for which they have been commissioned by the appearances of the risen one.... The reminiscences of the Jesus of history were preserved, shaped and interpreted within the framework of the proclamation of the risen one and this interpretation is the right and legitimate one for the Christian faith.[3]

The pendulum has now swung in the opposite direction: whereas the slogan used to be 'the pure Jesus of history', it is now 'the pure Christ of faith'. To this effect, Bultmann pursues Kähler's views to their conclusion. As one of the founders of 'dialectical theology' he breaks with an isolated liberal scholarship, though he incorporates its results extensively in his programme of 'demythologization'. The picture of Christ offered by Bible and church, which represents Christ as *Kyrios* and *Theos*, is declared to be a myth the roots of which lie partly in Hellenism, partly in Jewish apocalyptic. It is impossible, he argues, for modern man with his unmythological view of the world to accept the Chalcedonian Definition as a final result. While the 'Christ myth' of the New Testament is not, of course, to be excluded, as it was in the elimination-work carried on by the Liberals, it should be utilized for a Christian self-understanding by means of 'existential interpretation'. This existential interpretation is to be independent of any objective and affirmative statement about Christ and

[1] A. Schweitzer, *The Quest of the Historical Jesus*, London 1954[3].
[2] M. Kähler, *The So-Called Historical Jesus and the Historic, Biblical Christ*, Philadelphia 1964.
[3] N. A. Dahl, 'Der historische Jesus als geschichtswissenschaftliches und theologisches Problem', *Kerygma und Dogma* I, 1955, 112. Cf. T. W. Manson, 'The Life of Jesus. Some tendencies in present day research', in *The Background of the New Testament and its Eschatology*, ed. W. D. Davies–D. Daube in honour of C. H. Dodd, Cambridge 1956, 211–21.

the acceptance of it in faith, such as, say, Paul demands in 1 Cor. 15. It is to be pure self-understanding before God in Christ, the crucified one, and therefore pure faith which is not directed towards a content believed objectively. As a result, the problem of the 'Jesus of history' is bracketed off from 'theology', and the latter is made dependent on itself.

To illustrate this theological position, occupied by a part of German Protestant scholarship, the words of one of its best representatives may be quoted, Hans Conzelmann writes:

> We (i.e. the representatives of this radical *kerygma* theology) are accustomed to begin our thinking with the *gap* which lies between the Jesus of history and the community, marked by his death along with the Easter experiences, and with the difference between Jesus' preaching of the Kingdom of God and the *kerygma* that has *him* as its subject, between Jesus the proclaimer and the proclaimed Christ. Yet self-evident as this viewpoint may seem to us, we must be clear that outside central Europe it convinces only a few. The majority of English theologians either do not react to form criticism at all, or they acknowledge it merely as a formal classification of literary types and contest that it leads to historical or systematic judgements. They thus reserve for themselves the possibility of drawing a continuous line from Jesus' understanding of himself to the faith of the community. Easter is in no way ignored, but the content of the Easter faith, and with it the basic christological terms and titles, is traced back to Jesus' own teaching. The theology of the community appears as the working out of the legacy of the Risen Christ on the basis of his appearance. ... To the representatives of this position the form-critical reconstruction seems to be a rationalistic abstraction, foreign both to history and to reality, and from a practical point of view a reduction of Christianity to a general religious consciousness, a formal dialectic of existence.

But Conzelmann himself has to recognize that:

> The advantage of this solution is that an established continuity is in itself historically more probable than the assertion of a discontinuity which is hardly able to explain the formation of the categories of the faith of the community. Furthermore, it can make plausible the transformation that the christological concepts (Servant, Messiah, Son of Man) have undergone between their Jewish (biblical and apocalyptic) origin and their Christian usage: they received their present concrete meaning in Jesus' interpretation of himself. The way from here to the formation of the gospels also becomes clear: the material deriving from Jesus received its shaping in the teaching work of the community; the proof from scripture, for example, may have been a formative factor. And as Jesus used to work on the same basis, a substantial agreement is assured.[4]

So today—and in a part of German Protestant theology too—a synthesis is being sought between the extremes (pure Jesus of history—pure Christ of faith); the Jesus of history is taken as a presupposition of the Christ of faith. There is a recognition that the primitive community itself already achieved this conjunction. It identified the humiliated Jesus of

---

[4] H. Conzelmann, 'Gegenwart und Zukunft in der synoptischen Tradition', *ZThK* 54, 1957, 279f.; cf. W. R. Matthews, *The Problem of Christ in the Twentieth Century. An Essay on the Incarnation*, London–New York–Toronto 1950, 1951; G. V. Jones, *Christology and Myth in the New Testament*, London 1956. The NT is interpreted in accordance with the continuity mentioned above especially by Vincent Taylor, *The Names of Jesus*, London 1953; *The Life and Ministry of Jesus*, London 1954; *The Person of Christ in New Testament Teaching*, London 1958. Worth noting is the conclusion of

Nazareth with the exalted *Kyrios*. With this twofold recognition it was in a position to withstand the error of docetism on the one hand and the denial of the transcendence of the *Kyrios* on the other. Indeed, it was just this tension, this war waged on two fronts by the New Testament authors, that demanded clarity of expression in talking about Jesus and hence depth in theological interpretation. They knew that the earthly, crucified Jesus was to be seen only in the light of Easter day. But it was also realized 'that the event of Easter cannot be adequately comprehended if it is looked at apart from the earthly Jesus'.[5] It follows from this that for the understanding of the primitive church 'the life of Jesus was constitutive for faith, because the earthly and the exalted Lord are identical'.[6] Recent scholarship also understands the special position of the Fourth Gospel from this tension. Its special character lies in the fact that 'it portrays the story of the exalted Lord as one and the same with that of the earthly Lord. . . . It is precisely the Fourth Gospel, originating in the age of the anti-docetic conflicts, which neither can nor will renounce the truth that revelation takes place on earth and in the flesh.' According to Käsemann there is a consequence for us as well: 'We also cannot do away with the identity between the exalted and the earthly Lord without falling into docetism and depriving ourselves of the possibility of drawing a line between the Easter faith of the community and myth.'[7]

This problem of the 'Jesus of history' and the 'Christ of faith' has been posed, both terminologically and methodologically, in a more exact and fruitful way in recent discussion. From the results achieved we can draw a few conclusions for our interpretation of patristic christology as well.

First of all, the concept of 'the historical Jesus' has itself been clarified, after its somewhat vague usage proved to have unfortunate consequences for New Testament theology.[8] The following definition has recently been suggested and has found acceptance: the phrase 'historical Jesus' refers to 'Jesus, in so far as he can be made the object of critical historical research'.[9] This formulation brings into consideration, along with the question of historical content, the historical consciousness of the modern researcher,

B. Gerhardsson, *Memory and Manuscript. Oral Tradition and Written Transmission in Rabbinic Judaism and Early Christianity* (Acta Sem. Neot. Upsal. 22), Uppsala 1961, 325: 'This high Christology (of the synoptic tradition) cannot be disconnected from the impression made by Jesus on his disciples, and furthermore it must have some original connection with Jesus' own view of his work, of his position, and of himself. The opinion expressed by so many scholars, that the Christology of the N.T. is essentially a creation of the young Church, is an intelligent thesis, but historically most improbable.'

[5] Cf. E. Käsemann, 'The Problem of the Historical Jesus', in *Essays on New Testament Themes*, London 1964, 25.

[6] Ibid., 38.

[7] Ibid., 34.

[8] For the following, cf. F. Hahn, 'Methodologische Überlegungen zur Rückfrage nach Jesus', in *Rückfrage nach Jesus. Zur Methodik und Bedeutung der Frage nach dem historischen Jesus* (Quaest. Disp. 63), ed. K. Kertelge, Freiburg 1974, 11–77; id., 'Methoden-Probleme einer Christologie des Neuen Testaments', *Verkündigung und Forschung* 2, 1970, 3–41.

[9] P. Biehl, 'Zur Frage nach dem historischen Jesus', *TR* 24, 1956/7, 55; quoted by F. Hahn, op. cit., 61.

as well as the recently developed array of tools and methods at his disposal. G. Ebeling once put it this way: ' "Historical Jesus" is therefore really an abbreviation for Jesus as he comes to be known by strictly historical methods, in contrast to any alteration and touching up to which he has been subjected in the traditional Jesus picture.'[10] To speak of the 'historical Jesus', then, is not only to refer to a thoroughly undogmatic wandering preacher of Galilee—to the Jesus characterized historically in this concrete way—but also to a certain way of considering him, from our side. F. Hahn has recently recommended a more detailed range of expression: (1) if one is discussing problems in the history of biblical traditions, he suggests a distinction between the 'pre-Easter Jesus' and the 'post-Easter community'; (2) if one is referring to the specifically christological interest of primitive Christian preaching, it would be better to speak of 'the earthly Jesus' and 'Jesus, the risen Lord'. Along these lines, the earliest community was interested in the 'earthly Jesus' to varying degrees which were articulated more or less clearly, but not in the 'historical Jesus' in the sense of modern criticism. So Hahn urges that we follow the suggestion of R. Slenczka[11] and choose a way of speaking which shows that by 'historical Jesus' we always mean our own modern range of questions as well. Thus we shall avoid speaking of the 'historical Jesus' when we simply mean the earthly Jesus of primitive Christian preaching, and at the same time we can make it clear that we are interested in the very same Jesus of the time before Easter, if in a different way. So we shall bring to expression both the sameness of our point of view and its difference from that of the first Christians, in that we are concerned with the same 'object', but are using a mode of 'observation' which depends on modern presuppositions.[12]

The method which exegetes have worked out for specifying the relation between the 'pre-Easter, earthly Jesus', and the 'post-Easter community' (in discussing the traditions behind the biblical text) and the 'earthly Jesus' and 'Jesus, the risen Lord' (in investigating the content of the early Christian preaching) can be important, too, *mutatis mutandis*, for the post-apostolic patristic age and for our interpretation of it. This is surely true of the three terms which F. Hahn has coined to characterize the transition from the pre-Easter Jesus to post-Easter reflection: (1) *selection* in the tradition about Jesus; (2) the *forming* and *re-forming* of this tradition within the New Testament; and (3) *reinterpretation*.[13] The whole process is one of transformation, within which we must expect—in accordance with the

---

[10] G. Ebeling, 'The Question of the Historical Jesus', in *Word and Faith*, London 1963, 294.
[11] R. Slenczka, *Geschichtlichkeit und Personsein Jesu Christi: Studien zur christologischen Problematik der historischen Jesusfrage* (Forschungen zur systematischen und ökumenischen Theologie, ed. E. Schlink, 18), Göttingen 1967, 22–4, 137–75.
[12] F. Hahn, op. cit., 63.
[13] F. Hahn, op. cit., 14–18 (selection); 19–23 (forming and re-forming); 23–6 (reinterpretation).

first term—both the loss and the elaboration of traditional material. After Easter, in fact, we can even observe a 'narrowing of focus', in that a keryg-matic tradition comes to be developed—largely independent of the individ-ual traditions of the story of Jesus which already existed—which refers almost exclusively to his death and resurrection, and to his being sent, or being made man. The church deliberately concentrates on certain main lines in Jesus' preaching, and on events and controversies in his life which have lasting relevance.

Let us apply this to the patristic period. Alongside the reception of the total picture of Christ there takes place (1) a *selection* or special highlighting of certain features in this picture. We can observe this (a) in the use of scripture. However much the whole of Scripture continued to be read, theological polemics, precisely in trinitarian and christological discussion, restricted themselves to a certain number of important or disputed scriptural texts. We shall present most of this selection of texts in the course of this book. (b) Beginning with the question of the function and meaning of Jesus for us and our salvation, christology undoubtedly concentrates its efforts more and more on the narrower question of his nature: on whether he is true God, whether he is true man, whether he is one and the same in true Godhead and true manhood. In its original context, however, this question of Jesus' nature was precisely the question of his soteriological function and meaning. (c) The process of selection also includes the different 'christologies', which come more and more to be distinguished as 'orthodox' or 'heretical'. A great deal seems to lie unused alongside the path of tradition. Some have even seen in its progress decided traces of a power-struggle, in which the stronger party, not necessarily the truth, has usually carried the day. Still, in forming judgements on this process we ought not to fasten our attention upon individual names, such as those of the early Christian monarchians and adoptionists, Theodotus of Byzantium or Noetus of Smyrna, or later those of Paul of Samosata, Photinus of Sirmium or even Nestorius. Just such a series of names as this shows that the theological concern they represent does in fact keep reappearing in the church, if always on a new level of reflection. Their concern did indeed penetrate more or less unnoticed into the history of the Christian interpretation of Christ, even though their names remained a source of horror. It can be shown that the opposed extremes of christo-logical heresy have, in the end, decisively influenced what came to be, in the tension between them, the church's middle road. Chalcedon was to preserve the authentic kernel of what both Monophysitism and Nestorian-ism wanted to say, and hand it on to the future.

The second century after Christ is especially instructive on this process of selection. The truly endless stream of popular anonymous and pseudo-nymous literature seemed to be aiming at one thing: reversing the 'selection' given by the New Testament. The life of the pre-Easter Jesus was filled out again with all sorts of purported information about words and deeds and events. The most notable feature in all of this was that the inflation of information could not call forth a deeper faith than the New Testament had already done, even through the sayings of Jesus in the Gospel of Thomas. On the contrary, in many ways these writings distracted the reader with trivialities. The 'selective' New Testament stands far above the inflated picture of Jesus given in the apocrypha. Of course, the interpretation of the events of Jesus' death given by the *descensus*-theology should not be included in this 'inflationary' christology; it belongs already to reflection on the post-Easter Jesus.

(2) The patristic period continues the process of *transformation* which F. Hahn assumes for the time of the New Testament. This process, which leads first of all from lived experience to the preached gospel, the *kerygma*, then leads further from *kerygma* to dogma, without implying any opposition between them. Dogma is, after all, nothing other than a more reflective *kerygma*, clarified by theology and borne by a deepened consciousness of the reality of the church. We can see here, if we are properly cautious, a kind of analogy: just as the post-Easter *kerygma* always orientates itself by the earthly pre-Easter Jesus and incorporates him— selectively, forming and interpreting what it takes—so patristic christology always remains dependent on the *kerygma* and on the earliest Christian experience, which remains present, in its own peculiar way, in the liturgy and the sacraments. Arius is as much a witness of this as is Nicaea, the Chalcedonian controversy as much as the Nicaean. One of our aims here will be to keep directing attention to this kerygmatic foundation.

(3) As the *kerygma* was handed on, a *new interpretation* of the tradition which had gone before, as well as of the New Testament itself, took place necessarily at every step. As the Septuagint and the New Testament themselves had done, the church assimilated language and concepts from the world around—language which was of increasing philosophical intensity, but not such that the theological nature of the interpretation would be lost in the process. Even so, the danger that theology might be overgrown by philosophy became acute from time to time, as Arius himself and the second generation of Arians show. Doubtless, too, there was a disadvantage in the fact that precisely christology and the trinitarian interpretation of Christian monotheism tended to end in formulas whose biblical and kerygmatic origin was no longer apparent. Still, as we hope to show, this emphasis on isolated formulas *in re trinitaria et christologica* is more the product of scholastic selection and abstraction than the real centre of the church's thinking in the patristic period.[14]

[14] Cf. A. Grillmeier, ' "Piscatorie"-"Aristotelice". Zur Bedeutung der "Formel" in den seit Chalkedon getrennten Kirchen', *Mit ihm und in ihm* (*Christologische Forschungen und Perspektiven*), Freiburg 1975.

Just as New Testament exegesis must face the problem of accurately specifying the relationship between the pre-Easter Jesus and the Christ preached by the early Christian community, so patristic studies and all theology have the task of specifying with the same accuracy the relationship between the New Testament *kerygma* and theology, and of keeping the tension between them always in mind. Nicaea and Chalcedon did not see their formulations as a distortion of the *kerygma*, but as its defence and its confirmation. The content of the *kerygma*, however, was always the person of Christ and his uniqueness.[15] The theological struggles of the patristic period are nothing else than an expansion of this central question; this gives them their continuity. For from the gospel of Jesus Christ as Son of God, and of his subsequent history (as pneuma, *en pneumati*), grew the question of Christian monotheism (of the one God as Father, Son and Holy Spirit). And this expanded theological horizon remained contained within yet another: the question of the peculiar nature of the salvation God has given us in Christ and in the Holy Spirit. Soteriology remained the actual driving force behind theological inquiry, even—as we shall see especially in the period from the third to the fifth century—behind reflection on the identity of Christ and the Holy Spirit.

It will not be possible, nor even necessary, always to demonstrate this connection between soteriology and the theology of the Trinity in the same way at every phase of their development. Nevertheless, we must never lose sight of it. If even the New Testament has managed to concentrate its attention on the person of Christ, it must be legitimate to go on making the question of his person the focal point of our investigation. But just as the Christ of the New Testament can only be understood in his relationship to the Father who sends him and to the Spirit, so he can never be discussed, even for the period that follows, wholly apart from them.

As a starting-point, then, for the history of the christological *kerygma* in the patristic period, we must sketch the basic christological features of the most important groups of documents in the New Testament. With this as our goal, we can omit an investigation of the relationship of the earthly, pre-Easter Jesus to the Lord of Easter—and leave that task to the exegetes.[16]

2. NEW TESTAMENT OUTLINES

(a) The christology of the primitive community

The earliest christology must be sought in the primitive Jewish-

---

[15] Cf. F. Hahn, op. cit., 63–7, 'Das ursprüngliche Interesse an der Geschichte Jesu'.

[16] Cf. besides the study of F. Hahn the following other studies in the collection *Rückfrage nach Jesus*: F.-L. Lentzen-Deis, 'Kriterien für die historische Beurteilung der Jesusüberlieferung in den Evangelien', 78–117; F. Mussner and colleagues, 'Methodologie der Frage nach dem historischen Jesus', 118–47; R. Schnackenburg, 'Der geschichtliche Jesus in seiner ständigen Bedeutung für Theologie und Kirche', 194–220.

Christian community. It derived from the resurrection of Jesus, which was understood as his appointment to heavenly power. In his resurrection, Jesus was made 'both Lord and Christ' (Acts 2. 33–36). In other words, Jesus is now 'Messiah' in the full sense of the Jewish expectation. He is the redeemer king who rules in the name of God (cf. Matt. 28. 18). The use of the language of Ps. 2. 7 in Acts 13. 33 to say that he is the 'adopted Son of God' is not necessarily an indication of a strict adoptionism.

On the contrary, only the career of Jesus, which, while always messianic, leads through humiliation to exaltation, is here approximated to Jewish thought. The ignominious death of the Messiah, inconceivable to Jewish sentiment, is the necessary prelude to his saving dominion which offers even to blinded Israel one more opportunity for repentance and the forgiveness of sins (cf. Acts 3. 18ff.; 5. 31). Neither the baptism of Jesus nor his resurrection is the basis for an 'adoptionist' christology in the later sense.[17]

The career of Jesus is regarded as a revelation of the divine work of salvation. Two stages or periods, however, were seen in it—one earthly, in the flesh, and one heavenly, in the spirit (Rom. 1. 3f.; 1 Pet. 3. 18; 1 Tim. 3. 16a). Whenever Jesus is described according to his earthly descent as Son of David, his transcendence is also being emphasized at the same time, in contrast to his ancestor (cf. Mark 12. 35ff.; Acts 4. 25ff.). This title is in any case important for Matthew (1. 1; 9. 27; 12. 23; 15. 22; 20. 30f.; 21. 9, 15) and for Luke (1. 32, 69; 2. 4, 11). Even the Apocalypse still knows it (3. 7; 5. 5; 22. 16). Jesus is the fulfilment of the Messiahship promised in David.

As well as this title 'Son of David', the earliest christology also knows another, 'Servant' (Matt. 12. 18 = Isa. 42. 1; Acts 3. 13, 26; 4. 27, 30). A reference to the servant songs may justifiably be assumed here. The designation of Jesus as 'prophet' was only short-lived; it had a reference to Deut. 18. 15, 18 and served to explain Jesus' mission to Jewish audiences (Acts 3. 22; 7. 37; John 6. 14; 7. 40). And even if the Fathers are right later in emphasizing that the transcendence of Christ is something more than a heightened prophetical office, this title nevertheless embraces his mission as revealer of the Father and teacher of men.[18] In any case, it has a high soteriological significance. Finally, the relation of the exalted Lord to the church and to the world is further expressed through the idea of the *parousia*. It is of great importance in the Christian picture of history, even

[17] R. Schnackenburg, art. 'Jesus Christus' in *LThK* V, 1960, 933, which provides a selective bibliography; T. De Kruijf, *Der Sohn des lebendigen Gottes. Ein Beitrag zur Christologie des Matthäus-evangeliums* (AnalBibl 16), Romae 1962, 25–40 (Die Christologie der ältesten Tradition); B. M. F. van Iersel S.M.M., *'Der Sohn' in den synoptischen Jesusworten*, Leiden 1961; G. Strecker, *Der Weg der Gerechtigkeit. Untersuchung zur Theologie des Matthäus* (FRLANT 82), Göttingen 1962, 86–188 (Christology); 189–242 (Ecclesiology); F. Hahn, *Christologische Hoheitstitel. Ihre Geschichte im frühen Christentum* (FRLANT 83), Göttingen 1963. The relative sections from this important study are as follows: Menschensohn, 15–53; Kyrios, 67–125; Christos, 133–225; Davidssohn, 242–79; Gottessohn, 280–333.

[18] L. Goppelt, *Typos*, Gütersloh 1939, 70ff.; O. Cullmann, *The Christology of the New Testament*, London 1963[2], 13–50; F. Gils, *Jésus Prophète d'après les Évangiles Synoptiques*, Louvain 1957.

though at first, in the apostolic preaching, it stands in the background. For of course the exaltation of the crucified one had first to be proclaimed (cf. Acts 3. 20f.). But a strong belief in the *parousia* (Matt. 24. 3) was alive in the primitive community, and found its liturgical expression in the Aramaic cry of longing *Marana-tha* (1 Cor. 16. 22; Rev. 22. 20; 1 Cor. 11. 26). It is at the same time evidence of worship offered to Jesus as 'Lord'.

(b) The synoptists

By now, faith in Christ has already found expression in several different ways in the individual writings of the New Testament. The synoptists are the interpreters of the faith of the primitive church in the career of Jesus the Messiah through humiliation to exaltation, in accordance with the will of the Father and the witness of Holy Scripture. Their purpose is furthered by the stressing of the threefold announcement of the passion (Mark 8. 31; 9. 31; 10. 32ff. par.) and the whole interpretation of the course of the passion (Luke 24. 25f., 45f.). The unity of this course is demonstrated in the structure and the special linking of the passion and resurrection accounts. This is particularly pronounced in Matthew.[19]

Now the one who follows this course is the 'Son of God', a title which, while affording a special insight into the primitive church's understanding of Jesus (cf. Mark 1. 1, 11; 9. 7; 14. 61; Luke 1. 35; 22. 70; Matt. 2. 15; 14. 33; 16. 16; 27. 40, 43), nevertheless has its basis in the unique consciousness of divine Sonship in Jesus himself. This consciousness (Mark 12. 6; 13. 32; 14. 36), together with Jesus' claim to be the only saving way to the Father (Matt. 11. 25–27), is the decisive starting point not only for the confessions of primitive Christianity and the early church, but also for the christology which developed from them and led up to Chalcedon.[20]

It is recognized that within these common basic features each of the synoptists forms his own picture of Christ. The concept of the Son of Man stands as the central feature of Mark. Jesus' earthly work is interpreted from the Messianic secret, which the disciples do not understand (cf. 6. 52; 8. 17; 9. 10). In this way special emphasis seems to be laid on the darkness of his sufferings, but at the same time the light of the resurrection, ascension and *parousia* (Mark 8. 38; 14. 61f.; 16. 19) breaks through. Matthew is the 'Book of the Church' in a special way. The reason for this is not the occurrence of the word *'ecclesia'* (16. 18; 18. 17), but the ecclesiology of the

---

[19] See K. H. Schelkle, *Die Passion Jesu in der Verkündigung des Neuen Testamentes*, Heidelberg 1949; K. Stendhal, *The School of St. Matthew and its use of the Old Testament*, Uppsala 1954. The prevalent verdict today on the description of the synoptic gospels as 'a passion narrative with a detailed introduction' (M. Kähler) is that this holds only for Mark. With Dahl, Marxsen and Bornkamm, J. Schreiber, 'Die Christologie des Markusevangelium', *ZThK* 58, 1961, 154–83, sees in Mark 'the book of hidden epiphanies' and finds in it the christology of the Hellenistic communities.

[20] Cf. R. Schnackenburg, art. 'Jesus Christus' in *LThK* V, 1960, 934; id., 'Sohn Gottes, Gottessohnschaft' (I. NT) in *LThK* IX, 1964, 851–4, with a good survey of all interpretations of the title 'Son'. S. stresses the distinction between 'Son of God' and the absolute use of 'Son', esp. after F. Hahn, op. cit., 328f., 380–404.

gospel itself, which has its basis in the christology.[21] At the climax of this gospel, which has already spoken earlier of the kingdom that has come in Jesus, there also rings out the famous confession 'You are the Son of the living God' (16. 16). In the view of the evangelist this is without doubt an adequate expression of the mystery of the person of Jesus. The figure of Jesus is raised to divine transcendence, which was already a concern of the first chapters. The picture of Christ, the bringer of salvation, is drawn, as in the other gospels, in three particular figures: those of 'Son of God', 'Servant' and 'Son of Man'. In each of these titles the close conjunction of expressions of exaltation and expressions of humiliation should be noted. 'Son of God', say, is no more to be taken simply as a description of transcendence than 'Servant' as an indication of humiliation. For it is just this Son of God who is at the same time the 'Ebed Yahweh' and the 'Ebed Yahweh' who is at the same time the 'Son of God'. The title 'Ebed Yahweh', which is here understood from its Old Testament, patriarchal background, is well capable of expressing the inward relationship of Jesus to God, his Father.

It is in this relationship to the Father that the sayings about Jesus, the revelation brought by him (Matt. 11) and his church (Matt. 16. 16) have their foundation. In Matt. 11 the 'Son of Man' and 'men' are deliberately contrasted. The grace and salvation inherent in the 'heavenly mystery' of the Son of Man are derived from Jesus' relationship with the Father. Only God, only the Father 'knows' the Son. The twofold γινώσκειν is not to be given an intellectual interpretation: precisely in this twofold form it represents the mutual relationship between the Father, who chooses the Son in love, and the Son, who in love entrusts himself to the Father. In this section (Matt. 11. 25–30), the statements about the Son, who extols the Father's plan of salvation, are intrinsically bound up with the interpretation of the saving history. In ch. 11, Jesus, who is compared with the Baptist, is represented as the turn of the ages. For he brings in the dominion of God, because he is the bearer of the spirit, the conqueror of Satan, the beloved Son of God. In concepts deriving from apocalyptic language (cf. Dan. 2. 2, 3) and perhaps also from wisdom literature, Jesus is proclaimed as Son of Man (cf. Dan. 7. 14), Wisdom and Servant (after Isa. 52. 14; 53. 2). In his words and actions, in his person and his conduct, the revelation of the kingdom of God, the new world of God, is already present, but revealed only to the little ones and to the poor who treasure the work of God. It is, then, in this context that the words describing the whole unique relationship between Father and Son stand. True, in the first place they concern only the ordering of revelation and salvation. Jesus ascribes to himself a

[21] G. Bornkamm, 'End-expectation and Church in Matthew', in Bornkamm–Barth–Held, *Tradition and Interpretation in Matthew*, London 1963, 15–51; T. De Kruijf, *Der Sohn des lebendigen Gottes*, 150–68, and G. Strecker, op. cit. (for details of these n. 17 above).

special knowledge of the mysteries of salvation. But they can and must be carried back further to a transcendent relationship which is the basis of this special knowledge. Jesus himself stresses this unique relationship by distinguishing clearly between the address to the Father which he himself uses and that which he allows to men. At no time does he associate himself with men in this form of address—a fact which can be noticed more frequently in Matthew than elsewhere. In using 'Abba', an address impermissible to a Jewish man, as an intimate name for the Father, he is expressing a filial relationship that surpasses all Old Testament precedent.[22] The relationship of the 'Son of God' to the 'Father' is therefore not just a more or less technical circumlocution for a special election of Jesus, say, to be Messianic king: it means a real relationship of Son to Father.

But that is not to say that the eternal generation of the Son and the unity of substance of Father and Son already find explicit expression here (Matt. 11. 25–7). It is not the metaphysical relationship between Father and Son but their personal relationship—one might almost say their moral relationship—that is described. Indeed, it would be better if we said 'is suggested'. For the intimacy of Father and Son is not considered in itself; it is revealed as a mysterious reality because of its relationship to the mystery of the kingdom. . . . Like the Son of Man in Daniel, the Son has received 'all' from the Father. This 'all' includes kingly might, ἐξουσία, but even more than that: the kingdom itself is given to the Son. The kingdom is, however, no substantial earthly reality; it is realized by the Son on earth in his powerless, yet authoritative, proclamation and in the revelation of its mystery to the disciples. As revealer, the Son is mediator between God and a number of elect, but he is this precisely by virtue of his uniquely intimate relationship to the Father, which is more than that of a prophet, a king, or a faithful servant: the Son of God really is the beloved Son, to whom the Father can give all things.[23]

In Matt. 16. 13–19, too, Peter's confession is more than a confession of the Jewish Messiah. This is above all clear from the Old Testament background once more presupposed here, as in ch. 11—again Daniel, but also Num. 11–13. The Son (of Man), to whom all was given by the Father, is not only the revealer of the kingdom; in his revelation he also realizes the kingdom. The *basileia* is the kingdom of heaven, the kingdom of God. In so far as the Son realizes it, it is the kingdom of the Son (of Man—cf. Matt. 13. 41). In so far as the kingdom is realized on earth, it is the ἐκκλησία, the people of the saints. The Son is mediator between the kingdom of heaven and the ἐκκλησία upon earth. Just as the Father has given 'all' to him, including precisely this position as mediator, so too the Son gives to Peter the 'keys of the kingdom of heaven' on the strength of the latter's confession of faith in him as the Son. So there is a reciprocal relationship between the confession of faith and the promise given to Peter. Peter's

[22] J. Jeremias, 'Characteristics of the *ipsissima vox Jesu*', *The Prayers of Jesus*, SBT II 6, London 1967, 108–15.
[23] T. De Kruijf, *Der Sohn des lebendigen Gottes* (see n. 17 above), 75–6; for what follows cf. ibid., 80–8 (Matt. 16. 16); 112–15 (Matt. 28. 19); 142–9. See too A. M. Hunter, 'Crux criticorum—Matt. 11. 25–30—A Re-appraisal', *NTS* 8, 1961–62, 241–9.

confession of faith is in fact a confession of the 'Son' as the mediator between God and the people, between the kingdom of heaven and the coming kingdom on earth, the church. But again, as in 11. 27, Jesus can only be this unique mediator on the basis of his unique relationship to the Father. So here too we already have another indication that Jesus has more than a purely functional significance.

Matthew 11. 27 already points us on to Matt. 28. 18, with Dan. 7. 13ff. once again standing in the background: 'All power (ἐξουσία) is given to me in heaven and in earth.' The eschatological realization of the kingdom has taken concrete form in the church, which already exists *in nuce* in the disciples and now receives the commission to extend itself. The command to baptize εἰς τὸ ὄνομα is an intimation of the saving work of the Father, the Son and the Holy Spirit. It expresses the living unity of Father, Son and Spirit, particularly their common concern in the saving work. Just as this saving work had its beginning in the baptism of Jesus, so too it begins in the faithful through baptism as the saving work of the church. So in the confession of the 'Son' (εἰς τὸ ὄνομα . . . τοῦ υἱοῦ) we are to think of the whole richness of the Son of God sayings in Matthew, and particularly Matt. 3. 17 and 11. 27 (the absolute use of the 'Son'). The role of Jesus in the realization of the kingdom and the unique relationship of the Son to the Father is thus summed up in the one word 'Son'.

In contrast to Matthew and Mark, the christology of the evangelist Luke is moulded more by Hellenistic thought. Jesus is the 'Saviour' (2. 11), who still in the works of his messengers 'proclaims salvation' to all the world (εὐαγγελίζεσθαι is a favourite word of Luke's). He is the helper of all (7. 13), doctor to the sick, the friend of sinners (7. 36–50; 15; 18. 9–14; 19. 2–10; 23. 43), the succour of the poor (6. 20f.; 14. 12f.; 16. 19–31). He respects women (8. 1ff.; 10. 38–42; 23. 27f.) and attacks the powerful (13. 31ff.; 23. 8f.). He is the living embodiment of goodness, of piety and of patience in suffering (22. 44; 23. 34, 46).

All these synoptic statements about Jesus are related to the concrete situation of salvation history[24] in which he stands. The background of the synoptic christology is the history of God's doings with men. Jesus always begins from the Old Testament concept of God. But in the Old Testament God is a God of history. For this reason Jesus also begins his preaching with the comprehensive announcement πεπλήρωται ὁ καιρὸς καὶ ἤγγικεν ἡ βασιλεία τοῦ θεοῦ (Mark 1. 15), that is, the decisive point in history has now arrived. The rule of God is breaking in. But Jesus goes on to show that in these historical acts of God he himself has a special, indeed, the one

---

[24] Cf. H. Conzelmann, *The Theology of St. Luke*, London 1960; O. Cullmann, *Christ and Time*, London 1962². Cf. G. Strecker, *Der Weg der Gerechtigkeit* (see n. 17 above), 186: 'The synoptists have in common a salvation-historical motivation for the life of Jesus.' On the idea of salvation history see J. Frisque, *Oscar Cullmann. Une théologie de l'histoire du salut* (Cahiers de l'Actualité Religieuse 11), 1960, 7–279.

decisive, place. After God had sent 'his servants', i.e. the prophets, to the Jewish people to recover his 'fruit', he now last of all sent 'his beloved Son' (Mark 12. 1–12 par.). With this, the climax of the history of Israel has arrived, and for the last time the 'time of visitation' is offered to this people (Luke 19. 44). This history even becomes a time of preparation for Jesus Christ; what the scriptures prophesied about the Messiah has been fulfilled in his person (Luke 4. 16–30; Matt. 11. 2–6 par.; Luke 24. 25–27, 44–49; Mark 12. 35–37 par.). With Jesus, the acts of God cease to limit themselves to the sphere of Israel; they now extend to the whole history of mankind (cf. Luke 4. 18f.). In this Jesus of Nazareth, earthly and human as he was, who died a criminal's death, the Son of Man and Messiah and so the judge of the world has appeared among men.

(c) Pauline christology

The central christological ideas of Paul are the notion of pre-existence (though this is more presupposed than explicitly taught) and the worship of Christ as *Kyrios*. Both, however, were already at hand for him to use. He simply deepened the ideas and adapted them for preaching in the Hellenistic communities, at the same time composing them into a universal vision of the history of salvation. The notion of pre-existence already had strong roots in Judaism, not only in apocalyptic, but also among the rabbis and in wisdom speculation.[25] The visionary speeches of Ethiopian Enoch attribute a heavenly pre-existence to the Son of Man, sometimes the 'Elect One' (39. 6ff.; 40. 5; 48. 2f., 6; 49. 2; 62. 6f.). According to other conceptions, the Messiah is first in a condition of concealment, later to 'reveal' himself (4 Esd. 7. 28; 12. 32; 13. 25f.; Syr. Apoc. Bar. 39. 3; 39. 7; Sibyll. V. 414f.). Among the rabbis, a pre-existence of the Messiah is assumed only as an idea in the thought of God, though at the same time a real pre-existence of his soul is held (Strack-Billerbeck II, 339–352). The Jewish-Hellenistic wisdom literature is more important for Paul than apocalyptic and the rabbis. Here 'Wisdom' is extolled as something existing before the world and already working in creation (Job 28. 20–28; Bar. 3. 32–38; Prov. 8. 22–31; Ecclus. 1. 4, 9; 24. 3–22; Wisd. 7. 25f.; 9. 9f.). Paul begins from here (1 Cor. 1. 18–2. 16; 10. 1–5. In 10. 4 the 'rock that followed' is the pre-existent Christ. Philo had already interpreted this rock as Wisdom: *Leg. all.* II, 86; *Deter.* 115–18). The link with the wisdom teaching is particularly close where Paul speaks of the work in creation of the pre-existent Logos, now made manifest in Christ. This happens in the ancient formula of 1 Cor. 8. 6 (. . . καὶ εἶς κύριος Ἰησοῦς Χριστός, δι' οὗ τὰ πάντα καὶ ἡμεῖς δι' αὐτοῦ), further in Col. 1. 15ff. (see below), in Heb. 1. 2f. and finally in John 1. 1ff. (see below).

---

25 See E. Schweizer, 'Zur Herkunft der Präexistenzvorstellung bei Paulus', *EvTh* 19, 1959, 65–70 (speaking about 1 Cor. 8. 6; 10. 4; Rom. 10. 6f.; Gal. 4. 4).

In addition, Paul also has his own way of expressing pre-existence, in that he speaks of the 'sending' of the 'Son of God' into the world (Gal. 4. 4). It is in this title 'Son' that Paul expresses his own conception of Christ. For him Jesus Christ is quite simply *'the* Son of God' (2 Cor. 1. 19 and often), he is 'God's own Son' (Rom. 8. 32). In speaking of the coming of this Son, Paul can survey the whole of his career, which leads to incarnation and crucifixion (Rom. 5. 10; 8. 32), but goes on to resurrection, exaltation, and finally the second coming (1 Thess. 1. 10).

In describing Christ as *Kyrios*, Paul is understandably influenced by the ideas of the Septuagint. He does so whenever he speaks of the redemptive work of Christ towards his believers (Rom. 10. 12f.; 2 Cor. 3. 18) or celebrates his status as ruler over the cosmos (Phil. 2. 11; 1 Cor. 2. 8; cf. 15. 25f.; Eph. 1. 20ff.). But this *Kyrios* is also described on the lines of a Hellenistic cult-deity—by means of a contrast. Christ as the only *Kyrios* is set over against the 'gods' and 'lords' that are worshipped in the world (1 Cor. 8. 5f.). As the community of Christ, the Christian worshipping community has nothing to do with the pagan sacrificial cultus (1 Cor. 10. 21). Paul can therefore talk of 'our' Lord Jesus Christ, as he is so fond of doing. To Christ the community of believers belongs: he is its Lord and Saviour (σωτήρ, Phil. 3. 20) and its inner unity (Eph. 4. 5). This is the way in which Paul has expounded the *Kyrios* concept as legitimate for the Greek world.

The establishment of the 'cosmic christology' in Col. 1. 15ff. represents a new step. It is directed against the so-called στοιχεῖα speculation (Col. 2. 8, 20) which threatens to leave no place for the mediation and redemptive work of Christ; the Jewish–Gnostic angel cult (Col. 2. 18) and the worship of 'principalities and powers' seem to be taking up his place (Col. 1. 16). The space between God and the material world is occupied by these powers which have the rule and government of the world. In the light of the Pauline doctrine of redemption, subservience to these powers represents voluntary slavery and loss of Christian freedom. The primacy of Christ in creation and history (the church) is therefore displayed with full force (see below). Similar terms and ideas are used to advance this cosmic christology in Ephesians. The divine plan of salvation reaches its climax in Christ. Through him the whole cosmos is being returned to its original ordering. Here the concept of *anakephalaiosis,* so important for the christological theology of history to come, is introduced (Eph. 1. 10). The whole of the past and the future, the earthly and the heavenly, is to be contained in Christ, the sovereign head. He is also peace among mankind, between Jew and Gentile (Eph. 2. 14–18). Serious attention is being paid to this combination of a cosmic and salvation-historical christology again only in modern times (O. Cullmann, J. Daniélou and others).

If predominantly Hellenistic thought is to be detected in the interpretation of Christ outlined above, Paul also has ideas that are determined more by Judaism. The most important of these is his description of Christ as 'Second Adam'. This Adam–Christ typology is significant as much in the anthropological[26] as in the theological and historical sphere. The ruin incurred by Adam is abundantly made good again in Christ. The 'last Adam', himself a 'lifegiving spirit', will change us at the resurrection from 'earthly, adamitic' men into the image of the 'heavenly' and spiritual, as he himself has already been changed in his resurrection (Rom. 5. 12–21; 1 Cor. 15. 44–49). Christ as the perfect image of God (Col. 1. 15) will in this way again restore in us the original likeness of God. The 'new man' is inaugurated (Col. 3. 10; cf. Eph. 4. 24). The Fathers have here a firm starting point for their soteriological emphasis on the true and complete manhood of Christ.

Now that we have attempted to describe the Pauline picture of Christ in a broad sweep, we must move on further and investigate some of the most important christological formulas.[27]

(d) Pauline christological formulas

Romans 1. 3, 4. The character of this inexhaustible passage can be seen to some extent just from its ordered construction.

(a)	v. 3 περὶ τοῦ υἱοῦ αὐτοῦ		
	I		II
(b)	τοῦ γενομένου	v. 4	τοῦ ὁρισθέντος
(c)	ἐκ σπέρματος Δαυὶδ		υἱοῦ θεοῦ ἐν δυνάμει
(d)	κατὰ σάρκα		κατὰ πνεῦμα ἁγιωσύνης
			ἐξ ἀναστάσεως νεκρῶν
	(a) Ἰησοῦ Χριστοῦ τοῦ Κυρίου ἡμῶν		

The symmetrical and antithetical arrangement of the clauses is unmistakable.

The subject of all the statements stands out quite clearly: it is the 'Son of God, Jesus Christ our Lord'. Like a pair of brackets it encloses two sets of clauses of which it is the exclusive concern. This Son of God is the whole Christ.

Paul is not concerned here to put the divinity and the humanity of Christ over against each other in the same sort of way as the later doctrine of the two natures. His two formulas '*kata sarka—kata pneuma*' were soon understood in this sense. Certainly there is here, as elsewhere in Paul, belief in the pre-existent Son of God and at the same time recognition of the true humanity of Christ. Phil. 2. 5–11 and also 2 Cor. 8. 9; Col. 1. 16; Gal. 4. 4 show this with sufficient clarity. They presuppose that Christ's

---

26 W. D. Stacey, *The Pauline View of Man*, London 1956. Here the Christian character of Pauline anthropology is emphasized.

27 On what follows cf. L. Cerfaux, *Le Christ dans la Théologie de Saint Paul*, Paris 1951; E. Schweizer, *Lordship and Discipleship*, SBT I 28, London 1960.

career has already begun before he enters into history, in a 'being' without
beginning, since he already *is* in the form of God when he sets out upon
the historical part of his life. According to Rom. 8. 3; Gal. 4. 4, he who is
sent is already Son, and, moreover, Son of God in contrast to all those
who are to become sons after him and with him (cf. ὁ υἱὸς αὐτοῦ 1 Thess. 1.
10; Rom. 1. 9; 5. 10; 8. 29; τὸν ἑαυτοῦ υἱόν Rom. 8. 3; τοῦ ἰδίου υἱοῦ
Rom. 8. 32, etc.). We are not therefore compelled to say that Christ,
originally only the Son of David, became the Son of God through the
miraculous events at his birth, baptism, resurrection and ascension. On the
contrary, all this happens to one who is already the Son of God, but now
after the flesh is born of the seed of David (Rom. 1. 3; Gal. 4. 4). In other
words, Paul is not concerned to set the divine nature and the human
nature in Christ side by side and to describe them. Rather, he is concerned
with two historical events which God has brought about in Christ so as
to show him forth as bringer of salvation. The first event—an event of
humiliation—is his birth of the seed of David. Seed here means the same
as 'house' (Luke 1. 55; Mark 12. 22; John 8. 33; Rom. 4. 13, 16). 'After
the flesh' need not be regarded, as in Gal. 4. 23, 29, as the way in which
or the cause through which Christ comes to be descended from the house
of David, that is to say, it need not mean 'in a fleshly, natural or human
way' as opposed to a more exalted mode of conception. The two 'modes
of conception' are contrasted in Gal. 4. 23, 29. Here, in Rom. 1. 3, 4, Paul
is concerned to represent the birth from the seed of David as a first saving
event brought about by God, a saving event which, however, means a
humiliation for Christ. Paul is probably not thinking here in the first place
of the conception by the Holy Spirit (Luke 1. 35), though this is certainly
included. The coming of Christ in the flesh is brought about by God
because it is in fact the Son of God who comes in the flesh. It is a humiliation
because the Son of God appears as man. With the coming of this Son in
the flesh, the basis of salvation is already laid. The order of sons has already
come into being (cf. Rom. 8; Gal. 4. 4–6).

For this order of 'sons' to be set up completely, however, Christ,
humbled in his fleshly birth and in this fleshly nature crucified, had to be
shown to be Son of God in his existence in the flesh. This is stated in the
second series of expressions.

They are concerned with the exaltation of Christ in the resurrection by
the power of God in the Holy Spirit. There has been much debate about
the meaning of ὁρίζειν.[28] The Greek expedient of taking the word to
refer not to the actual constituting of the Sonship but to its revelation is
possible, but does not fully reproduce the apostle's thought. 'Ορίζειν need
not be limited to a 'revelation'. Originally it means to 'bound', 'circum-
scribe', 'define', hence to give a clearer definition to what is already there.

[28] M.-E. Boismard, 'Constitué Fils de Dieu (Rom. 1. 4)', *RB* 60, 1953, 5–17.

It can refer to a real 'elevation to the Sonship of God'. From its opposition to the γενομένου of the first series we must assume that ὁρισθέντος too describes a fundamental event in the history of the Son of God. As in the first section we have a description of the beginning of his early existence, after the flesh, so here we have the beginning of his heavenly existence, but again 'after the flesh'. Both are predicated of one who is already Son before he starts on this career. Nevertheless, we have here a real 'exaltation' to dominion which is accomplished in the Son by the Father. But this is an exaltation of the incarnate Christ (cf. Acts 10. 42, 'appointed by God to be judge'). Christ is appointed not merely Son of God, but 'Son of God in power'—unless ἐν δυνάμει refers to the power of the Father in the resurrection, as in Eph. 1. 19 (cf. Rom. 6. 4). But even in this case it would mean the establishment of the incarnate Christ in his place of dominion through the resurrection and the ascension, as in Ps. 110 (109). 1 (Sit thou at my right hand), cf. Mark 16. 19; Eph. 1. 20f.; Heb. 1. 3. This 'Son of God in power' is contrasted with the 'Son of God in weakness'. In other words, Paul here uses basically the same features to describe the historical career of the supra-historical Son of God as he does in Phil. 2. 5–11. The elevation to be Son of God (also after the flesh) and the elevation from the form of a servant to the dominion of *Kyrios* and Son—these titles correspond one with the other—was accomplished 'according to the spirit of holiness, by the resurrection of the dead'. Κατὰ σάρκα is opposed to κατὰ πνεῦμα, and it is just because of this opposition that Rom. 1. 3, 4 exerted a powerful influence in history, as in a similar way did John 1. 14.

But what is the christological significance of the opposition? This becomes clear from what has been said earlier. Rom. 1. 3, 4 is not intended to contrast soul and body in Christ as anthropological factors. That would be to mistake the sense of the whole passage. Does it then simply contrast the human and the divine nature in Christ? It is quite biblical to use *sarx* to describe the human nature. But is *pneuma* in Paul Christ's divine nature? This interpretation is certainly possible, but is not valid for Rom. 1. 3, 4. Paul is here contrasting not so much the two *natures* (in the same way as the diphysitism of later christology) as two conditions under which Christ exists and the effects which these conditions have on one and the same kind of existence in Christ, that is, his fleshly nature. The condition of humiliation, which is governed by the mere fact of the incarnation, is contrasted with the condition of exaltation, which is determined by the power of the Spirit. To be servant in the flesh, then, is contrasted with having dominion as *Kyrios* in the flesh. Being exalted, being Lord, even 'partaking in the Lordship of the Son after the fleshly nature', all are synonymous. This view of Christ as humiliated because of the incarnation, and exalted and in his exaltation declared to be Son, also after the flesh, is truly Pauline. But at this point it would be totally un-Pauline not to go behind the conditions under which Christ exists and to see there, as a background, what he actually is, both God and man. It then follows that while *sarx-pneuma* does not mean a formal opposition of Godhead and manhood in Christ in the sense of the later terminology, this opposition nevertheless underlies all the assertions in Rom. 1. 3, 4, because the divine Son of the Father is born of the house of David after the flesh.

Alongside Rom. 1. 3, 4 and Col. 1. 15ff., the most powerful and most concentrated expression of the christology of Paul's letters is to be found in *Phil. 2. 5–11*. It is thought today by many scholars that the passage is a hymn, and is, moreover, pre-Pauline. According to J. R. Geiselmann,[29] who draws largely on E. Lohmeyer, there are here three strophes which depict the 'course of events in the salvation history': pre-existence, kenosis and the 'super-exaltation' of Christ, which has its foundation in the kenosis:

5 τοῦτο φρονεῖτε ἐν ὑμῖν ὃ καὶ ἐν Χριστῷ ᾿Ιησοῦ
(I) 6 ὃς ἐν μορφῇ θεοῦ ὑπάρχων
οὐκ ἁρπαγμὸν ἡγήσατο τὸ εἶναι ἴσα θεῷ
7 ἀλλὰ ἑαυτὸν ἐκένωσεν
μορφὴν δούλου λαβών
(II) ἐν ὁμοιώματι ἀνθρώπων γενόμενος
καὶ σχήματι εὑρεθεὶς ὡς ἄνθρωπος
8 ἐταπείνωσεν ἑαυτὸν
γενόμενος ὑπήκοος μέχρι θανάτου
θανάτου δὲ σταυροῦ.
(III) 9 διὸ καὶ ὁ θεὸς αὐτὸν ὑπερύψωσεν
καὶ ἐχαρίσατο αὐτῷ τὸ ὄνομα τὸ ὑπὲρ πᾶν ὄνομα
10 ἵνα ἐν τῷ ὀνόματι ᾿Ιησοῦ
πᾶν γόνυ κάμψῃ ἐπουρανίων καὶ ἐπιγείων καὶ καταχθονίων
11 καὶ πᾶσα γλῶσσα ἐξομολογήσηται ὅτι Κύριος ᾿Ιησοῦς Χριστὸς
εἰς δόξαν θεοῦ πατρός.

In the first strophe, the hymn contains the idea of the pre-existence of Christ, as has already been indicated: ὃς ἐν μορφῇ θεοῦ ὑπάρχων. Now this μορφή should not be taken in the classical (Aristotelian) sense as meaning *essentia, forma*. The term is intended to define the sphere in which the pre-existent Christ stands, the sphere which determines him like a field of force. That is the way in which mode of being is defined in Hellenism.[30] Käsemann therefore translates 'a mode of existence in divine

[29] J. R. Geiselmann, *Jesus der Christus*, Stuttgart 1951; P. Henry, art. 'Kénose', *DictBibl*(Suppl) V, 1950, 7–161; E. Käsemann, 'Kritische Analyse von Phil. 2.5–11', *ZThK* 47, 1950, 313–60; G. Bornkamm, 'On Understanding the Christ-hymn (Phil. 2. 6–11)', in *Early Christian Experience*, London 1969, 112–22; E. Schweizer, 'Die Herkunft der Präexistenzvorstellung bei Paulus', *EvTh* 19, 1959, 65–70.
[30] E. Käsemann, op. cit., 330f.

power and substance'.[31] But even if such a Hellenistic influence can be conceded, the content of ἐν μορφῇ θεοῦ is still primarily to be defined from its opposition to ἐν μορφῇ δούλου. This servant-idea is fundamental to the hymn and points back to Isa. 53 (cf. esp. vv. 3, 8, 12). On the other hand, the appeal to the Adam–Christ typology (with the *anthropos*-myth as an alleged background) makes interpretation more difficult instead of making it easier. It cannot be demonstrated that οὐχ ἁρπαγμὸν ἡγήσατο is meant to refer to Adam's aspiration to be like God. Nor is there any indication that the pre-existent Christ had to resist a temptation that would have seduced him into grasping after the Godhead (as a *res rapienda*). Indeed, he is already ἐν μορφῇ θεοῦ.

The most natural interpretation of the passage yields the following meaning: he who was found in a divine mode of being did not wish to cling to his position in selfish exploitation. Instead he gave himself up to the condition of kenosis (cf. 2 Cor. 8. 9: δι' ὑμᾶς ἐπτώχευσεν πλούσιος ὤν). But this kenosis is defined in the same sentence by a participle, λαβών! This means that by becoming man, the pre-existent Christ, who exists in a divine mode of being, chooses a mode of existence which is a concealment of his proper being. Historical existence as man can never express what the pre-existent Christ is in himself. Because this kenosis is a 'taking', or better an 'adding', the first kind of being is not done away with. He who is on an equality with God adds something to his divinity, the form of a servant. The being which he assumes serves more to conceal than to reveal him. The ἐκένωσεν ἑαυτόν is expressed from a human, not a divine, stand-point. For him it is a humiliation before us, but in accordance with the will of God. This humiliation can already be seen in his acceptance of the form of a servant, i.e. in the incarnation as such.

But it is not the intention of the hymn to isolate the incarnation and to regard it by itself. It contains no reflection on the fact of the pre-existent Christ's equality with God in relation to God, nor does it say anything about how this 'equality with God' is related to manhood in a concrete way. We have here neither a description of two kinds of being nor even a description of two conditions of being; attention is directed rather towards the *course* of Christ's self-humiliation. The hymn portrays a drama of salvation history, 'the redeeming course which the pre-existent Christ has traversed through his self-surrender and self-humiliation until that particularly significant event in salvation-history, his death, and his exaltation as *Kyrios* of the whole world'.[32] For this reason, the main stress lies on the second strophe, v. 8, i.e. on the depth of the self-surrender achieved by obedience in suffering until death. The μορφὴ δούλου there-

---

[31] J. Dupont, 'Jésus-Christ dans son abaissement et son exaltation d'après Phil. 2. 6–11', *RSR* 37, 1950, 500–14, translates 'condition divine'. M. Meinertz, *Theologie des Neuen Testamentes* II, Bonn 1950, 64, 'Erscheinungsweise in göttlicher Majestät und Herrlichkeit'.

[32] J. R. Geiselmann, op. cit., 140.

fore does not just embrace the plain fact of the incarnation but in v. 7b already points clearly towards the death of the one who assumes human nature. But it would be false to overlook this plain fact of the incarnation. Any docetic understanding of the incarnation is quite excluded by the first two verses of the second strophe (ἐν ὁμοιώματι . . .). Käsemann sees in καὶ σχήματι '. . . even a sharpening of "being made in the likeness of men" ' (ἐν ὁμοιώματι ἀνθρώπων γενόμενος) and a protection against any qualifying of the incarnation.[33] The pre-existent Christ has assumed a true μορφή of manhood to offer the obedience refused by men.

Now that the lowest point of this course has been reached with Christ's death on the cross, the ascent begins (third strophe). In form, the presentation of this exaltation has the style of an enthronement, with the individual acts of mounting the throne, proclaiming the new dignities, *proskynesis* and acclamation. Exaltation, described as an enthronement, means sitting at the right hand of God. There is no mention here of the resurrection, as the 'humiliation-exaltation' framework does not require it to be stressed, but it is not, of course, excluded. It is here that we have the foundations of the *Kyrios* cult, the biblical derivation of which is at the same time demonstrated by the passage, as it is clear that v. 11 has been governed by Isa. 45. 23: 'for every knee shall be bowed to me (Yahweh)'. The divine name Yahweh, translated ὁ Κύριος by the LXX, was transferred by the primitive church to the σύνθρονος of God, to whom the rule of the world has been entrusted. The church, which unites itself with the spiritual powers, worships Jesus as God.

This third strophe, then, betrays a connection with the ancient 'exaltation-christology'. According to R. Schnackenburg, this is also an indication that the first strophe does not presuppose the *anthropos* myth, but reflects on the pre-existence which precedes the humiliation.[34] The Christhymn of Phil. 2 depicts the 'super-exaltation' of the Christian redeemer whose 'humiliation' is all the more inconceivable because of his heavenly origin. Recent scholarship rightly emphasizes that this hymn is not in the first place concerned with Christ's *being*, with the unfolding of the *mysterium Christi* in accordance with the framework of the doctrine of two natures, but looks towards the salvation event. On the other hand, however, it would be false to refuse the later theology of the church the right to reflect upon the being of Christ with the help of this hymn. As the pre-existence of Christ is included or at least pre-supposed in its approach, since the name *Kyrios* must be understood as a divine predicate, while nevertheless the true manhood of the pre-existent Christ is being discussed, this reflection can find a legitimate starting point here.

That Paul should depict Christ in such a way is of tremendous importance for the whole tradition of the church. It is a 'katagogic' christology,

---

[33] E. Käsemann, op. cit., 339.   [34] R. Schnackenburg, *LThK* V, 935.

which makes any 'anagogic' christology such as the adoptionist spirit-christology impossible. And because everything that happens to the historical Christ has its essential resting-place in pre-existence, a clear place in the framework can be accorded to the 'exaltation'.

Colossians 1. 15–20 (with 2 Cor. 4. 4):

(I)   (13 ... εἰς τὴν βασιλείαν τοῦ υἱοῦ τῆς ἀγάπης αὐτοῦ)

    15 ὅς ἐστιν εἰκὼν τοῦ θεοῦ ἀοράτου
         πρωτότοκος πάσης κτίσεως

    16 ὅτι ἐν αὐτῷ ἐκτίσθη τὰ πάντα
         ἐν τοῖς οὐρανοῖς καὶ ἐπὶ τῆς γῆς,
         τὰ ὁρατὰ καὶ τὰ ἀόρατα
         εἴτε θρόνοι εἴτε κυριότητες εἴτε ἀρχαὶ εἴτε ἐξουσίαι
         τὰ πάντα δι' αὐτοῦ καὶ εἰς αὐτὸν ἔκτισται

    17 καὶ αὐτός ἐστιν πρὸ πάντων καὶ τὰ πάντα ἐν αὐτῷ συνέστηκεν

    18 καὶ αὐτός ἐστιν ἡ κεφαλὴ τοῦ σώματος, τῆς ἐκκλησίας,
         ὅς ἐστιν ἀρχή
         πρωτότοκος ἐκ τῶν νεκρῶν
         ἵνα γένηται ἐν πᾶσιν αὐτὸς πρωτεύων

(II) 19 ὅτι ἐν αὐτῷ εὐδόκησεν πᾶν τὸ πλήρωμα κατοικῆσαι

    20 καὶ δι' αὐτοῦ ἀποκαταλλάξαι τὰ πάντα εἰς αὐτόν,
         εἰρηνοποιήσας διὰ τοῦ αἵματος τοῦ σταυροῦ αὐτοῦ, δι' αὐτοῦ
         εἴτε τὰ ἐπὶ τῆς γῆς εἴτε τὰ ἐν τοῖς οὐρανοῖς.

According to E. Schweizer (see n. 27 above) we probably have here a hymn which was used by Christians. In it, Hellenistic–Jewish ideas are used to explain the status of Christ. The hymn stands within a thanksgiving for the mystery of our election in Christ with the saints through the Father; the connection between this and the hymn is the mention of Christ. In the second strophe (18b–20), in contrast to the ordering of creation (15–18a), the ordering of salvation is considered, that ordering which is brought about through the death and resurrection of Jesus Christ. This antithesis is intentional and is also emphasized in the construction of the verses. The first and second strophes are joined by an interlude (17, 18a), which in its first verse echoes Stoic terms and concepts, while being in the second half a wholly Pauline theological composition.

(i) *The subject of the christological expressions of Col. 1. 15f.* The question considered is: 'What sort of a Christ is it who has received the kingdom from the Father (v. 13)?' Concern, then, is with the exalted Christ and therefore with the God-man. In addition, the statements about the pre-existent Christ are intended to strengthen faith in the exalted Christ among the Colossians. For this faith is in danger of being constrained by their belief in the spiritual powers. Attention is therefore drawn to the incarnate

Christ from the very beginning, in the glory of his exaltation. To divide the expressions into those which concern only the pre-existent Christ, independently of the incarnation, and those which concern the incarnate *qua* incarnate is quite unjustifiable. The discussion is concerned not so much with the relationship of Christ to the Father as with his relationship to the world, though, of course, the latter derives from his relationship to the Father. (ii) *The content of the christological expressions.* Here the expression εἰκών, which also occurs at 2 Cor. 4. 4, is of particular significance.[35] According to this latter passage the glory of God is visible 'in the face of Christ'. For Christ is the εἰκών τοῦ θεοῦ. The phrase τῆς δόξης τοῦ Χριστοῦ, ὅς ἐστιν εἰκών τοῦ θεοῦ in v. 4 corresponds to the phrase τῆς δόξης τοῦ θεοῦ ἐν προσώπῳ Χριστοῦ in v. 6. The glory of Christ is none other than the glory of God which becomes visible in the face of Christ; this is only a paraphrase of what the predicate 'image of God' means: Christ as εἰκών of God is the one who makes possible knowledge of God. *God* himself becomes visible in Christ, his image. Christ as image of God is therefore the revelation and the representation of God. (In this the influence of Jewish teaching about Sophia can be traced. 'Sophia' bears the title εἰκών of God and represents a heavenly being. But the expressions which Hellenistic Judaism applied to Sophia—still probably conceived of as impersonal—are in Paul applied to the historical Christ in his total status: cf. 1 Cor. 8. 6 and Col. 1. 15 where Christ is described as mediator of creation. In Paul the pre-existent Christ and the divine wisdom of the Jews are one and the same figure.) In Col. 1. 15ff. the cosmological significance of Christ as the image of God comes to the forefront. The church is to be shown by the emphasis on this status of Christ as image of God that in him she has something which no angel can be and which needs no completion by another revealer and bringer of salvation. But this making visible of God who is himself invisible does not mean that he is made visible for human eyes here and now; rather, it refers to that vision of the glory of Christ which according to 2 Cor. 3. 18 is the possession of all Christians in so far as they have a part in the *oikonomia* of the *pneuma*. In Christ his εἰκών, God, the ἀόρατος, becomes visible, ὁρατός, i.e. is manifest not only through the person and work of Jesus (cf. 1 John 1. 1ff.), but also through preaching and proclamation accepted in faith. Thus ἀόρατος is, as Chrysostom already recognized, an expression of the incomprehensibility of God.

In addition, a second expression became significant for christology, πρωτότοκος πάσης κτίσεως. It is used to describe the pre-eminent position of Christ in the whole world (τὰ πάντα). Christ's office as revealer, as image of God in the world, gives him a special status in the cosmos. He is

[35] Cf. W. Eltester, *Eikon im Neuen Testament*, Berlin 1958, especially 130–52; J. Jervell, *Imago Dei, Gen. 1. 26f. im Spätjudentum, in der Gnosis und in den paulinischen Briefen*, Göttingen 1959.

the firstborn. Πρωτότοκος should not be read as a temporal definition. It says in biblical language that a factual 'pre-' corresponds to the temporal 'pre-' of the firstborn (Ps. 89. 28; Exod. 4. 22; Heb. 12. 23). It simply indicates a 'dignity'. Christ the firstborn is to be displayed in his lordship over the angelic powers and here a 'temporal' existence before the angels is not the point in question. True, the Fathers of the fourth century, and later still John of Damascus, interpret Col. 1. 15 of the Son of God who is of one substance with the Father. This was because they wished to deprive the Arians, who made a contrast between εἰκών, an inferior copy, and the original, and saw in πρωτότοκος an indication of the createdness of the Logos, of the right to refer to these passages. In this way they were able to make what is contained implicitly in this passage into an explicit assertion. But at the same time, this interpretation did not allow the particular christology of the passage to make itself felt later. Marcellus of Ancyra, however, had already interpreted the Colossians passage as referring to the incarnate Christ as the image of the Father (cf. GCS *Eusebius-Werke*, Vol. 4, frags. 90–7). But Paul does not mean to speak explicitly of pre-existence in the pure Godhead; he presupposes it. In πρωτότοκος, there-fore, he is not stressing the difference between the being and existence of Christ and that of men and spirits. 'Firstborn' has been chosen because of the πρῶτος and expresses the element of Christ's dignity and Lordship. Christ enjoys absolute primacy over all creatures (comparative genitive) among which, as the context indicates, are included spiritual beings, angels and men. For in him (ἐν αὐτῷ) and through him (δι' αὐτοῦ) and for him (εἰς αὐτόν) all things have been created. Without distinction between his ideal pre-existence (Christ foreseen by God as a creature) and his personal pre-existence as the eternal Son, Christ is described as the 'firstborn' of the whole creation.

This primacy of Christ in creation is the basis of his primacy in redemp-tion (second strophe). Christ alone is lord of the church. It was the ordin-ance of God that 'he' (αὐτός!), he and no other, should have the rank of 'firstborn' in the church also. Since Christ has received this rank and fullness (cf. Col. 1. 19; 2. 9) from his Father, he is, by virtue of his pre-eminence over creation, capable of redeeming the universe from the dominion of the powers. God's decision 'to re-establish all things in Christ' (Eph. 1. 10) has laid all things under his feet (Eph. 1. 22). A new and living bond comes into being between Christ and that part of the universe which accepts his Lordship: Christ and the church take on the unity of head and body. Christ pours out the whole fullness of life and grace (*pleroma*, Eph. 1. 23) over this his church, as he himself is the fullness, the *pleroma*, of the Father (Col. 1. 19; 2. 9). Of the universe, only the church may call itself the body and fullness of Christ. In it he therefore also remains present in the world.

All the Pauline letters regard christology from this salvation-historical viewpoint. In Christ, the rule of God becomes event and reality and at the same time the salvation of the world. To such an extent is God active in Christ that the name of God, which is elsewhere reserved for the Father, is, in one text concerned with the salvation history, Titus 2. 13, applied to Jesus Christ (cf. Phil. 2. 11).

We will just mention briefly the introduction to the Epistle to the Hebrews, which shows some affinity to the Colossians hymn. Here, too, creation and redemption are closely linked together. Christ, sitting at the right hand of the Father and inheritor of the kingdom of God (cf. Col. 1. 12f.; Heb. 1. 3), could receive this rank and become universal redeemer because he is the brightness of the Father and mediator of creation. Christ fulfilled his mission as redeemer through *kenosis*. He became lower than the angels and tasted of death, and has therefore also been crowned with glory and honour (Heb. 1. 9; cf. Ps. 8). He now sits at the right hand of God, exalted above the angels. In this way of humiliation and exaltation he has fulfilled the function of the true high priest who alone could bring about eternal redemption (2. 17, 18; 2. 14–5. 10; 9. 1–10, 18).

(e) The 'Word made flesh'

The climax in the New Testament development of christological thought is reached in John. His prologue to the Fourth Gospel is the most penetrating description of the career of Jesus Christ that has been written. It was not without reason that the christological formula of John 1. 14 could increasingly become the most influential New Testament text in the history of dogma.

The Johannine christology[36] has a dynamism all of its own. Christ appears as the definitive Word of God to man, as the unique and absolute *revealer*, transcending all prophets. As αὐτόπτης he and he alone can bring authentic tidings from the heavenly world (John 1. 18; 3. 11, 32ff.; 7. 16; 8. 26, 28, etc.). He is not only lawgiver, as Moses, but also giver of grace and truth. In him God is present: 'He who sees me sees the Father also' (14.9). His revelation therefore has as its theme not only the Father, but also the person and mission of Christ. 'He himself' belongs to the content of his message. This is expressed in the many 'I' sayings, in which he describes himself in particular as 'Light' and 'The Life of the World' (8. 12; 9. 5; 11. 25; 14. 6; cf. 1. 4), but most strongly in the absolute ἐγώ

---

[36] P.-H. Menoud, *L'Évangile de Jean d'après les recherches récentes*, Neuchâtel–Paris 1947²; J. Behm, 'Der gegenwärtige Stand der Erforschung des Johannes-Evangeliums', *ThLZ* 73, 1948, 22–30; W. F. Howard, *The Fourth Gospel in Recent Criticism and Interpretation*, revised by C. K. Barrett, London 1955⁴; F. M. Braun, 'Où en est l'étude du quatrième évangile', *EphThLov* 32, 1956, 535–46; R. Schnackenburg, *BZ*, NF 2, 1958, 144–54 (Eng. lit.); James M. Robinson, 'Recent Research in the Fourth Gospel', *JBL* 78, 1959, 242–52.

εἰμι (8. 24, 28, 58; 13. 19).[37] This last is a theophany formula. The wonders ('*signa*') also play their part in Jesus' revelation of himself (2. 11; 11. 4). But this activity of revelation is directed completely towards the *salvation* of men, for it brings life. Whoever believes on the Son of Man (9. 35) or the Son (μονογενής, υἱός) as the eschatological ambassador of God has (eternal) life (3. 15, 36; 5. 24, etc.). For this Son is the true God (οὗτός ἐστιν ὁ ἀληθινὸς θεός, I John 5. 20).

In John, Christ's activity of revelation and redemption is represented as a dramatic descent and ascent.[38] The course traversed by Christ begins in the heavenly world (1. 1ff.) and leads to the earthly world (1. 11, 14), to the cross (19. 17ff.). The return then follows in the re-ascent of the risen one into his earlier glory (3. 13, 31; 6. 62; 13. 1; 14. 28; 16. 28; 17. 5). Thither Christ also leads those who become his own from 'this world' and who therefore can participate in the world of life and light. For he is to all 'the Way' (14. 6), the sole access to the life to come ('the door', 10. 7, 9). The way in which John marks the turning points on the course of redemption, the 'becoming flesh' (1. 14) and the 'being exalted' (= 'being glorified', cf. 3. 14; 8. 28; 12. 23, 32; 13. 31f.; 17. 1f.)[39] is of extraordinary significance for future theology. It is principally the incarnation of the Logos which occupies the centre of theological reflection. What is the reason for this? It is surely the tension which is present in the Johannine formula 'Logos-sarx'. Let us attempt to measure its force.

1. *Logos:* Christ is here for the first time in Christian literature described by a name which is to be repeated countless times. First of all, let us try to paraphrase its content from John himself. The first element which underlies the Johannine Logos concept is the idea of 'revelation' and the 'revealer'. Christ is the Word of God, already existing before the world, and spoken into the world. The office of 'revealer' is so closely bound up with the person of Jesus that Christ himself becomes the embodiment of revelation. Not only his words, but the very fact of his coming and of his being are in themselves a divine self-revelation. In Rev. 19. 11–16, the office of the divine ambassador is described in the imagery of the rider on a white horse. His name, ὁ Λόγος τοῦ Θεοῦ, is quite explicit. It is his task to bring to man the 'Word' of God. This he can do because he is this Word. In John, 'Logos' is primarily the spoken word in contrast to the

---

[37] E. Schweizer, *Ego Eimi*, Göttingen 1939; H. Zimmermann, 'Das absolute 'Εγώ εἰμι als die ntl. Offenbarungsformel', *BZ* 4, 1960, 54–69, 266–76; id., 'Das absolute "Ich bin" in der Redeweise Jesu', *TThZ* 69, 1960, 1–20; A. Feuillet, 'Les *ego eimi* christologiques du quatrième évangile', *RSR* 54, 1966, 5–22, 213–40.

[38] Cf. M.-E. Boismard, *Le Prologue de s. Jean*, Paris 1953; this dynamic consideration of the Logos in the prologue is not confused by Boismard with a mere 'functional' christology, i.e. the Logos being a mere 'function' of the Godhead. See L. Malevez, 'Nouveau Testament et Théologie fonctionelle', *RSR* 48, 1960, 258–90 (on Cullmann, *Christology of the New Testament*, who takes Dupont and Boismard as representatives of such a functional theology).

[39] Cf. W. Thüsing, *Die Erhöhung und Verherrlichung Jesu im Johannesevangelium*, second edition—enlarged by Part V, NTAbh XXI, 1–2, Münster 1970.

Logos as reason (*ratio*). This also forms the basis for the close relationship between Logos and revelation. A further description of the intrinsic and essential relationship between the person of Christ and his office occurs in 1 John 1. 1–3, though it is a disputed point whether 'Logos' here is to be understood of the *person* of Jesus Christ or of his *teaching*. Both are certainly included. Christ is the personal 'Word of Life' which comes from eternity and is sent to men. These are themes from the prologue.

Essential as the idea of the revealer is for the Logos concept, it does not exhaust it. The associated expressions θεός and μονογενής serve to deepen and clarify the concept decisively. The content of the teaching and the authority have their particular source in the conjunction of the activity of the revealer and the status of the Son of God (1. 18; P 66 and P 75 now show that μονογενὴς θεός in this verse is almost certain, so at the beginning and at the end of John (cf. 20. 29) we have a declaration of Christ's divinity). True, the two concepts Logos and Son are not to be equated formally. But in fact λόγος, θεός, μονογενής at the least imply one and the same subject who is to be understood as pre-existent, beyond time and beyond the world. The Logos is God in God, mediator of creation and bringer of revelation—and this in the full sense by virtue of his appearance in the flesh. He 'is' the Word of God in the flesh.

The sources of a theology of this kind have often been sought all too far from the material revealed in the Old and New Testaments—scholars have been misled in particular by the Logos concept.[40] Yet the obvious course would seem to be to begin from the spiritual home of a disciple of John the Baptist and Christ, such as John is, i.e. from the Old Testament. The Old Testament 'Theology of the Word' gives us a first point of contact. This theme of the Word of God recurs constantly. It contains not only the idea of the revelation of God but also the conception of the Word as power and wisdom, which are made manifest in the cosmic workings of God.[41] But it is impossible to derive the Johannine Logos concept from the Old Testament 'Theology of the Word' alone. The idea of cosmic power and revelation is still insufficiently developed, and, above all, the notion of the 'Word' as personal is missing.[42]

The Old Testament *Wisdom teaching*[43] takes us considerably further.

---

[40] See R. Schnackenburg, art. 'Johannesevangelium', *LThK* V, 1960², 1101–5, especially II (intellectual milieu; special tendencies); relations to the Qumran texts are mentioned there. For John and Qumran see F. M. Braun, *EphThLov* 32, 1956, 540f.; id., *Rev Thom* 54, 1954, 22–42, 259–99, 523–58; id., *RB* 62, 1955, 5–44; id., *Recherches bibl.* 3, Louvain 1958, 179–96; O. Cullmann, *NTS* 5, 1958–59, 157–73.

[41] Cf. Gen. 1. 1; Ps. 107. 20; Wisd. 18. 14–16; these passages describe the sending out of the Word and its work in the world. Ps. 33. 9 (32. 9), 'He spoke, and they were made', shows the connection between Word and event. See L. Dürr, *Die Wertung des göttlichen Wortes im AT und im antiken Orient. Zugleich ein Beitrag zur Vorgeschichte des ntl. Logos-Begriffes*, Leipzig 1938.

[42] M. J. Lagrange, *Évangile selon Saint-Jean*, Paris 1936⁵, 29.

[43] Cf. C. Spicq, 'Le Siracide et la structure littéraire du prologue de S. Jean', in *Mémorial Lagrange*, Paris 1940, 183–95.

The Wisdom of the Old Testament and the Logos of John have many features in common. Both exist from the beginning (Prov. 8. 22; Ecclus. 24; John 1. 1; cf. Gen. 1. 1) and dwell with God (Ecclus. 24. 4 LXX; Prov. 8. 23–25, 30). Common to both is their work in the world, though this is emphasized more strongly in Proverbs and Ecclesiasticus than, for example, in John 1. 3, 10. Wisdom and Logos come to men (Ecclus. 24. 7–22 LXX; Prov. 8. 31) and 'tabernacle' with them (Ecclus. 24. 8 LXX– John 1. 14). So strong is the similarity between the Johannine prologue and Prov. 8 and Ecclus. 24 that one can speak of a literary dependence. But in that case, why did John not retain the name 'Wisdom'? His choice of the name Logos may have been influenced by the rabbinic identification of Wisdom and Torah.[44] Moreover, the feminine form 'Sophia', and her place in Gnostic speculations, would be no recommendation in the Greek cultural sphere.[45]

A further influence on the evangelist John will have been the New Testament formulas and ideas which had already taken shape before him. In Paul, moreover, the Old Testament confronts him once again. True, 1 Cor. 1. 24 (Christ as the 'Power of God' and the 'Wisdom of God') may be not so much a christological expression as a definition of Christ's part in the economy of salvation, and in this way may refer more to the work than to the person of Christ. But Col. 1. 15; 2 Cor. 4. 4 and Heb. 1. 3, which speak of 'effulgence' and 'image', certainly refer to Wisd. 7. 26 and contain an expression of Christ's essential being. The cosmological status of Wisdom in Prov. 8. 22–31 and Wisd. 7. 22–28 may have had an influence on Col. 1. 15ff. But the Pauline expressions themselves, such as the formula of 'equality with God' (ἴσα εἶναι θεῷ) and 'form of God' (μορφὴ θεοῦ) or even Heb. 1. 3 (ἀπαύγασμα τῆς δόξης καὶ χαρακτὴρ τῆς ὑποστάσεως αὐτοῦ) already point in the direction of the Johannine concepts and terminology and stand on the same theological plane as John does.

Finally, however, if the apostle chooses a particular word and a parti-

---

[44] G. Kittel, *TDNT* 4, 138ff., and H. Strack–P. Billerbeck, *Kommentar zum NT aus Talmud und Midrasch*, München 1922–28, III, 126–33, 353, are perhaps to some extent right in attempting to understand the Logos concept in the Johannine prologue as an antithesis to the rabbinic Torah-speculation. But the attempt as such must be rejected. The Torah-speculation extracted only subsidiary features from the Old Testament Wisdom teaching, and these were certainly the less significant ideas. The same is true of the comparison of the rabbinic Memra teaching with the Johannine Logos. Cf. P. Borgen, 'Observations on the Targumic Character of the Prologue of John', *NTS* 16, 1970, 288–95; id., 'Logos was the True Light. Contributions to the Interpretation of the Prologue of John', *NovTest* 14, 1972, 115–30.

[45] F. M. Braun, *EphThLov* 32, 1956, 540f., stresses the relations to Qumran: 'Entre l'Évangile de Jean et les documents de l'Alliance, les affinités littéraires et spirituelles sont aujourd'hui trop connues pour qu'il faille les démontrer longuement. On en peut conclure que l'évangéliste avait non seulement l'esprit saturé des Écritures proto- et deutérocanoniques, mais qu'il était également familiarisé avec la littérature apocalyptique et pseudoépigraphique en honneur parmi les sectaires de la mer Morte. Il n'est pas certain que l'auteur du quatrième Évangile ait été en relation directe avec la Communauté de l'Alliance ni qu'il ait eu connaissance du *Manuel de discipline*, du *Document de Damas*, ou du recueil des *Hymnes*. Mais ce que l'on peut affirmer sans exagération, c'est que l'arrière-fond de ces écrits et celui du *Quatrième Évangile* est sensiblement le même.'

cular concept which is borrowed from Greek philosophy, there must be some connection between the two. Do John and his Logos concept, then, already point in a direction in which the history of the dogma of the incarnation is to lead us again and again—to Alexandria? The Epistle to the Hebrews indicates that there is already some connection between the New Testament and Alexandrian theology and exegesis. Alexandrian influence on John goes hand in hand with the place given to Old Testament Wisdom teaching in his theology. According to Irenaeus, the Fourth Gospel is directly opposed to Cerinthus, a Jew from Alexandria, who comes to Ephesus to preach his gnosis there, a gnosis in which Hellenistic theosophy plays a predominant role. There can be no doubt that we have in John a witness of the encounter between Christianity and the spirit of Hellenism at this early date, and it would be most remarkable if no trace of this manifested itself in his gospel, not only in a positive way by the recognition that Christianity and Hellenism were connected, but also in a negative way by repudiating the baleful influences of the latter.[46]

It can certainly be assumed that the prologue to the gospel is directed primarily, if not exclusively, towards the Greeks. It stands apart, like a Greek façade to the Jewish-Christian building that is behind—the gospel. It was the Logos concept that moulded this façade. The analogy should not be pressed, for the façade too is essentially of the Old Testament, and Christian, even though Hellenistic influence is unmistakable. This Logos concept is certainly more than a mere frontage, put up on the outside; it is intrinsically bound up with the gospel. But at the same time it represents a real acceptance of ideas from the Greeks, even though the content assigned to them by John gives back to the Greeks infinitely more than they were able to bring to him. The Greek view of the Logos is in itself by no means sufficient explanation of the Johannine concept.[47] While Heraclitus and the Stoics make the Logos the principle governing the cosmos, they allow that it is immanent. The Logos of the prologue, on the other hand, is at the same time both personal and transcendent. Nor, despite the great similarity of many of his formulas, is Philo sufficient to explain the heights reached by John.[48] Granted the Philonic Logos is already a being distinct from God, with divine properties and a function embracing the creation of the world and God's relationship with men; in the two writers the relationship between God and the Logos is completely different,[49] and, most of all, in Philo the idea of incarnation is missing.

[46] See F. X. Monse, *Johannes und Paulus*, NTAbh 5, 2. 3, Münster 1915, 85–96; 176–200.

[47] From the Catholic side, the relationship of the Johannine Logos concept to Hellenism, and in particular to the philosophy of Heraclitus, has been emphasized by A. Dyroff, 'Zum Prolog des Johannesevangeliums', *Pisciculi, Festschrift für F. J. Dölger*, Münster 1939, 86–93. The essentials are in H. Kleinknecht, *TDNT* 4, 76–89. Similarly M. Pohlenz, *Stoa* I, Göttingen 1948, 405f.; see C. H. Dodd, *The Interpretation of the Fourth Gospel*, Cambridge 1954, 263–85.

[48] This despite the 'kaleidoscopic variety of meanings' (H. Kleinknecht, in *TDNT* 4, 87).

[49] John places Christ as Logos clearly on the side of God, and as man equally clearly on the side of men. Philo, on the other hand, says of the Logos οὔτε ἀγένητος ὡς ὁ θεὸς ὢν οὔτε γενητὸς ὡς ὑμεῖς,

2. *The Logos in the flesh*. John now says of the divine Logos that 'He was made flesh and dwelt among men'. The personal presence of the revealer is a presence in the flesh. The Word of God has appeared *visibly* (1 John 1. 1ff.). The Logos of God *is* man. The peculiarly Johannine contribution lies in the sharpness of the *antithesis* and the depth of the *synthesis* of Logos and sarx.

In no book of the New Testament is the christological opposition of pre-existent being and fleshly nature so sharply drawn out as in John. Divine though the Logos may be in his abode with God, beyond the senses, beyond time and beyond the world, his presence in true fleshly nature is none the less absolutely real. The apostle 'in his tripartite introduction in 1 John 1. 1, 2, 3 can never be satisfied in stressing over and over again that he who has appeared (ἐφανερώθη) has done so in the concreteness of time and space'.[50] A statement on the incarnation in these terms must have made an unimaginable contrast to the background of the Hellenistic Logos concept in its different forms. The expression 'sarx', 'flesh', would, it is true, emphasize the visibility and genuineness of the divine and immortal Logos, but in so doing would point to the mortality of his human nature. A Greek could certainly think of no greater opposition than that of 'Logos' to 'sarx', especially if the idea of suffering and death was associated with it. For this reason, the Christian proclamation saw ever-repeated attempts of a docetic kind to deny the reality of Christ's flesh or to loosen the unity of Logos and sarx. These two factors were those which Irenaeus stressed against Cerinthus. It is precisely to meet such attacks that the apostle chooses the strong expression the 'flesh' of the Logos, by which he surely understands a complete human nature. He deliberately mentions what is most visible in man to demonstrate that the coming of Christ, the God-Logos, was visible.[51]

It is hardly a fault of John's that such an emphasis could turn into heresy again and again. We will, however, see how it was that this pointed antithesis gave occasions for far-reaching misrepresentations of the nature of Christ, just as it inspired the theology of the church to its deepest expressions. In view of the later misrepresentations it is important to point out how John represents his Christ as a real man, with body and soul, and therefore capable of spiritual feeling and inner emotion. The apostle who has an unparalleled vision of the Logos in Jesus always sees him as having a human psychology (11. 33; 12. 27; 13. 27). The Logos concept has not been able to obliterate the true picture of Christ's humanity. The reality

---

ἀλλὰ μέσος τῶν ἄκρων (*Quis rer. div. her.* 42, ed. Cohn-Wendland III, 206: on Deut. 5. 5: *Ego . . . medius fui inter dominum et vos*).
[50] *TDNT* 4, 130.
[51] 1 John 4. 2: 'Ιησοῦν ἐν σαρκὶ ἐληλυθότα. On the question of docetism cf. A. Grillmeier, art. 'Doketismus', *LThK* III, 1959, 470f.—R. Schnackenburg, *LThK* V, 1960, 939, says of this Johannine christology: 'This opened the door to the later two-natures doctrine; this christology is no longer purely "functional", even if it does not separate the person of Christ from his work.'

of his life stands too clearly in view. The Greek thought-world will experience the same idea as a temptation and will largely succumb to it.

This attempt to obtain a general view of New Testament christology has—as far as possible—taken the present state of exegesis as its starting point. The transition from the apostolic age to the post-apostolic and patristic period confronts us with other conditions. The study of the use and understanding of scripture would be of the greatest significance for the whole of patristic christology. Up to now, however, there have been very few studies of the subject,[52] and these differ both in method and in results. The mere position of the gospel of John in the church and among the Gnostics during the second century throws particular light on the spiritual state of the early church.

[52] Cf. E. Massaux, L'influence de l'Évangile de saint Matthieu sur la littérature chrétienne avant saint Irénée, Louvain–Gembloux 1950; H. Köster, Synoptische Überlieferung bei den Apostolischen Vätern. TU, Berlin 1957, arrives at somewhat different results; he does not appear to know Massaux's work. On John, see: W. v. Loewenich, Das Johannesverständnis im zweiten Jahrhundert, Giessen 1932; J. N. Sanders, The Fourth Gospel in the Early Church. Its origin and influence on Christian Theology up to Irenaeus, Cambridge 1943; F.-M. Braun, Jean le théologien et son évangile dans l'Église ancienne (EtBibl), Paris 1959; id., 'Le quatrième Évangile dans l'Église du second siècle', Sacra Pagina II, Paris–Gembloux 1959, 269–79; J. S. Romanides, 'Justin Martyr and the Fourth Gospel', GOTR 4, 1958–59, 115–34; T. E. Pollard, Johannine Christology and the Early Church, Cambridge 1970; A. Laurentin, Doxa. Études des Commentaires de Jean 17. 5 depuis les origines jusqu'à S. Thomas d'Aquin I–II, Paris 1972. On Paul: E. Aleith, Paulusverständnis in der alten Kirche, Berlin 1937; M. F. Wiles, The Divine Apostle. The Interpretation of St Paul's Epistles in the Early Church, Cambridge 1967. The title of a collective work like La Bible et les Pères (Travaux du Centre d'Études Supérieures specialisé d'Histoire des Religions de Strasbourg. Colloque de Strasbourg 1er–3 octobre 1969), Paris 1971, is significant. For individual studies see below.

CHAPTER TWO

FIRST GROWTH: THE CHRISTOLOGY OF
THE SECOND CENTURY[1]

WITHIN the limits marked out on the one hand by the synoptists and on the other by John and Paul, the christology of the New Testament itself already displays considerable diversity. We have, for example, the contrast between a messianic christology (the Acts speeches, the synoptic gospels) and the Johannine idea of the Logos; the factors which determine a portrayal of Christ may be salvation history (synoptics; Rom.; Gal.), cosmology (Eph.; Col. 1. 15ff.), liturgy (Heb.) or apocalyptic (Rev.). The picture of Christ given by the New Testament already shows sometimes predominantly Judaistic, elsewhere predominantly Hellenistic features. It would, however, be a mistake to remain completely sceptical about the essential unity of the christological tradition because of such differences. Common to all sources is a firm recognition of Jesus' transcendence and his central position in the salvation history. This clearly rests on living experience (primarily of the resurrection, but also quite simply of the words and actions of the Lord) and finds its climax in belief in the lordship of God and the divinity of Christ. This single recognition, or this single experience, is also the bond which links the post-apostolic and the apostolic age. The general tendency of contemporary scholarship is to regard the possession of Holy Scripture as the only psychological bridge between the two epochs. With regard to the Old Testament and the way in which it is used, this is to some extent correct. The role of the canonical books of the New Testament, and particularly the position of the synoptic tradition, which may lay prime claim to transmitting the words and deeds of the Lord, is a question all on its own.

At the time of the Apostolic Fathers, the New Testament writings, even the synoptic gospels, did not yet have the normative character which they were to acquire in the course of the second century, when the canon was being formed. A detailed examination of the use of the synoptic gospels by the Apostolic Fathers has produced the following conclusion: 'In this period, even our three synoptic gospels play a completely subordinate

---

[1] On the whole of this and the following parts see J. A. Dorner, *Entwicklungsgeschichte der Lehre von der Person Christi* I, Stuttgart 1845; Berlin 1851²; 2, Berlin 1853; R. V. Sellers, *Two Ancient Christologies*, London 1940; A. Michel, 'Jésus-Christ', 'Incarnation', 'Hypostase', *DTC* 8, 1108–1411; 7, 369–568, 1445–1539; J. Lebreton, *Histoire du dogme de la Trinité* 1, Paris 1927⁹; 2, 1928⁴; G. L. Prestige, *God in Patristic Thought*, London–Toronto 1956²; J. N. D. Kelly, *Early Christian Doctrines*, London 1960²; A. Vögtle, R. Schnackenburg, A. Grillmeier, K. Rahner, W. Pannenberg, 'Jesus Christus', *LThK* V, 1960, 922–64; Per Beskow, *Rex Gloriae. The Kingship of Christ in the Early Church*, Uppsala 1962; K. Baus, *Von der Urgemeinde zur frühchristlichen Grosskirche*, Handbuch der Kirchengeschichte, ed. H. Jedin, Vol. 1, Freiburg–Basel–Wien 1962, with a good bibliography.

role as a source for the citing of synoptic sentences.'[2] We are still in a period when the real motive force behind the tradition was the all-pervading influence of a great reality of experience,[3] the Christ event, that is, the life and teaching of Jesus Christ. The written synoptic gospels were not the only expression of this event nor were they the only way in which the reality might be possessed. The church knew that she was in full possession of the words and deeds of the Lord and of his whole history, even independently of the written gospels. In the apostolic age, this full possession formed the basis of teaching and preaching, the basis of the church's formulation of her proclamation of Christ, even the basis of the written gospels, themselves meant as an expression of the 'one gospel'. This phase of the Christian tradition was therefore dominated by the living, oral proclamation. If this was accompanied by a consciousness of the scriptures—as was, in fact, the case from the very beginning—prime concern was with the Old Testament. Thus in the immediate post-apostolic age there was a Christ-tradition, but this was as direct a source for the Apostolic Fathers as it had been for the written gospels.

If this oral tradition is also an integral part of the nature of the church, the consciousness of the position of scripture in it can develop further. This was the case from Justin onwards. 'He already "uses" the gospels to a great extent. In Justin's writings, the sources of the synoptic tradition are almost exclusively our gospels, and therefore the history of the tradition is in Justin for the first time a history of the exposition of our gospels.'[4] A multilinear development now begins. In combating Gnosticism and its 'traditions' the church increasingly reflected upon its 'one' tradition. This meant being committed to the canon of New Testament writings, though not of course simply to the written word, and in addition the formation of the creed and the stress on the *regula fidei* in teaching and in preaching. Thus even the didactic formulas acquired a special significance, although it was precisely this age which still permitted a considerable variation in them. The special position of the formula, which is already evident in the New Testament (1 Cor. 15), meant that the *auditus fidei* played a great part. 'Faith from hearing' (cf. Rom. 10. 9–15) corresponds to the clearly defined word, the formula, the formulated tradition, and makes a link reaching back to the revelation which was completed in Christ. The place

[2] H. Köster, *Synoptische Überlieferung bei den Apostolischen Vätern*, TU, Berlin 1957, 257. E. Massaux (p. 32, n. 52 above), however, asserts that the Fathers of the second century used a distorted text of the New Testament and thus restricts the part of oral tradition. Investigating the Didache, J.-P. Audet achieves a similar result to Köster: *La Didachè, Instructions des Apôtres*, Paris 1958, 166–86; cf. F.-M. Braun, *Jean le théologien*, Paris 1959.

[3] B. Gerhardsson, *Memory and Manuscript*, 325 (see the quotation on pp. 4f., n. 4); cf. J. Daniélou, *RSR* 47, 1959, 65.

[4] H. Köster, *Synoptische Überlieferung*, 267; F. E. Vokes, *The New Testament Today*, Oxford Conference 11–15 September 1961, sees the same situation reflected in the Didache and therefore dates it after 150. See now B. Gerhardsson, op. cit., 194–207, 324–35; J. Beumer, *Die mündliche Überlieferung als Glaubensquelle* (HDG I, 4), Freiburg-Basel-Wien 1962, 15–22.

of the *auditus fidei* is catechesis, the sermon coming within the framework of the liturgy which, through its holy signs, actions and rites, is itself a powerful support to tradition and the source of a particular tendency towards conservatism.[5] Here it fulfils another special function which cannot be valued highly enough for the life of the church: if the formulated tradition runs the risk of historicizing the picture of Christ and the whole reality of faith and objectifying it so that it becomes too impersonal, the living liturgy has the task of providing and bringing alive a direct link with the Lord of glory, the *Christus praesens*, which transcends all history. It is pecularly well suited for achieving the transition from the formula to the inner, spirit-governed faith which must support everything.

Throughout the early Christian period we notice a great simplicity in formulas. It was this simplicity alone which could secure uniformity of preaching amidst the deficient theological education of most of the church's spokesmen and, above all, could keep heresy away from the church. It is astonishing how the church of the 'illiterates' was able to cope with the powerful onslaught of Gnosticism in the second century. Hippolytus gives us an example of an encounter between faithfulness to the formula of the church and newly emerging heresy which would certainly apply to Christian preaching in preceding years as well. Noetus of Smyrna came forward and declared that the words of scripture concerning Father, Son and Spirit are really said only of One, of one person. Therefore in Christ the Son of the Father did not take the form of a servant. This constituted an attack on the fundamentals of the Christian proclamation. The matter was brought before the presbyters of the church of Smyrna. They were confronted for the first time with a difficulty towards the solution of which centuries were to labour. But the presbyters did not resort to high theology; they contented themselves with the simple formula which they had heard:

> We too worship only one God, but as we understand it. We too hold Christ to be the Son of God, but as we understand it—who suffered as he suffered, died as he died, and rose again the third day and ascended into heaven and sits at the right hand of the Father, and will come to judge the living and the dead. This we say as we have learned (ἐμάθομεν). Thereupon they convicted him (Noetus) and expelled him from the church, because he was carried to such a pitch of pride that he founded a sect.[6]

From this we see that already at this time the simple framework of a christological confession forms, so to speak, the backbone of the church's tradition about Christ, something in which she can find support. We must always take into consideration the presence of such a christological confession with belief in the Godhead and manhood of the one Lord, if

---

[5] Cf. H. E. W. Turner, *The Pattern of Christian Truth*, London 1954, 361.
[6] Hippolytus, *Antinoetus* 1: ed. P. Nautin, *Hippolyte, Contre les hérésies*, Paris 1949, 235[18]–237[3]; C. H. Turner, 'The blessed presbyters who condemned Noetus', *JTS* 23, 1922, 28–35.

we are to understand the development of the church's teaching about Christ.[7] The author of the 'Little Labyrinth', transmitted to us in extracts by Eusebius, includes even the Apologists, who certainly signify a new departure in theology, the emergence of a *théologie savante*, without further ado among the first simple witnesses of the church's belief. They too describe Christ as God (θεολογεῖν) and acknowledge him as God and man.[8] We should also notice the hymns of the early Christian period, the *carmen Christo quasi Deo dicere secum invicem*, which is referred to by Pliny[9] as a mark of the primitive church.

Certainly the massiveness of the *mysterium Christi* continued to remain the source of impulses leading to new formulas and efforts to give new expression to the inexpressible. Men were conscious that the *mysterium* was something beyond words. We will further find that the church grasped the totality of the picture of Christ more in a kind of spiritual intuition than in words and formulas. For this reason expressions could vary even to the point of formulas which apparently contradicted each other. The church measured newly emerging doctrines as much by her intuition as by her formula and made from them new fixed forms for her proclamation.

The incentive for this came less from within than from without, not least from the church's encounter with the pagan world and its philosophy. The need to construct a *théologie savante* emerged from this encounter with pagan philosophy.[10] Both the concepts and the language with which Christian doctrine was presented had to be developed further. The first aim was a clarification of the relation of Father and Son in the *mysterium Christi*. Thus the second century introduced the great task of the patristic period, that of achieving a better grasp of the data of revelation with the help of pagan philosophy. This proved to be both a powerful driving force to theological progress and a favourite starting point for heresies. It had important consequences for christology: the dynamic presentation of the mission of Christ in the economy of salvation was impregnated more and more with a static-ontological awareness of the reality of Christ as God and man. This is shown by the later creeds, as for example in the *homoousios*

---

[7] It is not our task here to sketch the history of the creed in itself. See the excellent chapter in H. E. W. Turner, *The Pattern of Christian Truth*, London 1954, 309–86; J. N. D. Kelly, *Early Christian Creeds*, London 1972³. A good survey of the creeds is available in the new edition of H. Denzinger, *Enchiridion Symbolorum*, revised by A. Schönmetzer, 1963, 1–76. V. H. Neufeld, *The Earliest Christian Confessions* (New Testament Tools and Studies, V), Leiden 1963, investigates the confessional formulas (*homologiai*) of the New Testament. Cf. most recently the article by P. Smulders, 'Some Riddles in the Apostles' Creed', *Bijdragen* 31, 1970, 234–60; 32, 1971, 350–66.

[8] Eusebius, HE, V, 28, 4, 5. Mention is made of Justin, Miltiades, Tatian and more especially of Melito of Sardis and Irenaeus.

[9] C. Plinius Sec. Min., *Epist.* 10, 96, 7.

[10] Cf. J. Lebreton, 'Le désaccord de la foi populaire et de la théologie savante', *RHE* 19, 1923, 481–506; 20, 1924, 5–37. Lebreton, of course, lays too much stress on the opposition of the two factors mentioned. Cf. A. Grillmeier, 'Vom Symbol zur Summa', *Kirche und Überlieferung* (in honour of J. R. Geiselmann), Freiburg 1960, 124–41.

of Nicaea, but also in formulas as early as Melito of Sardis and Tertullian. We can see, and it will become still clearer as we proceed, that here there was a special opportunity for metaphysics and therefore for the Greek way of thinking.

In this way the first phase of the oldest tradition was developed into something new, which has two main characteristics: the shaping of formulas and of a canon, and theological reflection. The post-biblical era of Christian theology, viewed as a whole, is a typical period of transition. Subsequent ages are inclined to value such periods lightly. The witnesses of the second century have not indeed yet the brilliance of the great names of the third, fourth and fifth centuries, the patristic age proper. But their nearness to life is all the more valuable, as later we have the danger of abstract teaching.

We shall now attempt to describe the christological characteristics of the second century. The first feature on which we shall lay stress will be the archaic character of its christology, which for the most part is to be attributed to Jewish–Christian influences. We will then be concerned with the popular image of Christ in the second century. Its problems are revealed even in the first christological heresies. The christology of the great church, however, finds its real expression in the defenders of the divinity and manhood of Jesus against docetism and Gnosticism, Judaism and paganism. Here we are on the way from economic to ontological christology, or the doctrine of two natures, but at the same time we also find the first influential examples of a christocentric salvation history. Simple christological formulas stand alongside the first contacts of Christian theologians with pagan philosophy. No epoch of christology displays such numerous and so different currents of thought as the second century.

1. CHRISTOLOGICAL VARIANTS

(a) An archaic heritage: Christ and Jewish–Christian theology

A special feature of post-apostolic christology is its archaic character, and this must be defined more closely. It is a result of the influence which Jewish Christianity had on the early Christian period. Jewish–Christian theology is part of the pattern of the second century, but only within the last twenty years has the written history of dogma consistently concerned itself with it.[11]

11 Cf. A. Grillmeier, 'Hellenisierung-Judaisierung des Christentums als Deuteprinzipien der Geschichte des kirchlichen Dogmas', *Schol* 33, 1958, 321–55, 528–58, with a survey of recent scholarship and a bibliography. J. Daniélou, *The Theology of Jewish Christianity*, London 1964 (= Daniélou I); id., *Gospel Message and Hellenistic Culture*, London 1973 (= Daniélou II), esp. 197–300; M. Simon and A. Benoit, *Le Judaisme et le Christianisme antique d'Antiochus Epiphane à Constantin*, Nouvelle Clio 10, Paris 1968; S. Lyonnet, 'Ellenesimo giudaismo nel Nuovo Testamento', and R. Cantalamessa,

There is, of course, as yet no complete agreement on what is to be understood by the term 'Jewish–Christian theology'. J. Daniélou, along with L. Goppelt,[12] means by it neither Ebionite nor yet heterodox Jewish–Christian theology.[13] Nor does he mean the closed community of Jerusalem, which came to an end in the year 70, though it had played a special part in carrying out missionary work in Egypt and was still to be encountered in Eastern Syria (Jude, *Evangelium sec. Hebr.*). By Jewish Christianity he means rather that spirituality which did not lead to the formation of special communities and did not call for a connection with Jewish communities, but still betrayed in its expression Jewish patterns of life and liturgy. This Jewish Christianity, taken in the broader sense, was so to speak omnipresent and quite influential in the Mediterranean, at least until the middle of the second century. Indeed, we find traces of such influence even in the fourth century, and particularly in the region of Antioch.[14] Judaism had two completely conflicting effects on early Christianity. The Gnostic Judaism of Corinth[15] markedly menaced the community of that place with syncretism. On the other hand, Jewish nomism was in certain measure assimilated in the early Christian period precisely so that it would be some protection against the disintegrating tendencies of Gnosticism. The strongest testimony of this is the Didache, whose Jewish character is manifest above all in the doctrine of the Two Ways, which is also presented by the Manual of Discipline of Qumran.[16]

What sources allow us to assume a Jewish–Christian concept of Christ?[17] First, the writings of the Jewish Old Testament Apocrypha, in so far as they are either Jewish–Christian revisions or even actually Chris-

---

'Cristianesimo primitivo e filosofia greca', both in *Il cristianesimo e le filosofie a cura di Raniero Cantalamessa* (Pubblicazioni della Universita Cattolica del Sacro Cuore, ScRel 1), Milano 1971, 8–25, 26–57.

[12] L. Goppelt, *Apostolic and Post-Apostolic Times*, London 1970.

[13] Cf. H. J. Schoeps, *Theologie und Geschichte des Judenchristentums*, Tübingen 1949, 71–116; id., *Aus frühchristlicher Zeit*, Tübingen 1950; id., *Urgemeinde, Judenchristentum, Gnosis*, Tübingen 1956; id. 'Die ebionitische Wahrheit des Christentums', in W. D. Davies–D. Daube, *The Background of the New Testament and its Eschatology*, Cambridge 1956, 115–23. Against these, Daniélou I, 55–64; G. Strecker, *Das Judenchristentum in den Pseudoklementinen*, Berlin 1958, 23–6.

[14] In this connection, continually developing contact with Judaism proper should be noted. Cf. M. Simon, *Verus Israel*, Paris 1948, 356–93; R. V. Sellers, *The Council of Chalcedon*, London 1953, 158–81; G. Downey, *A History of Antioch in Syria from Seleucus to the Arab Conquest*, Princeton 1961. See his index s.v. Jews.

[15] W. Schmithals, *Die Gnosis in Korinth, Eine Untersuchung zu den Korintherbriefen*, Göttingen 1956; for criticism, see H.-M. Schenke, *Der Gott 'Mensch' in der Gnosis*, Göttingen 1962.

[16] Cf. A. Seeberg, *Die Didache des Judentums und der Urchristenheit*, Leipzig 1908, 5–41; J.-P. Audet, *La Didachè, Instructions des Apôtres*, Paris 1958: he would see in Didache 1–6 a purely Jewish tractate, but this is to minimize the Christian elements; id., 'Affinités littéraires et doctrinales du "Manuel de Discipline" ', *RB* 59, 1952, 217–38 (part 1). It should, however, be noted that a Hellenistic nomism also developed, probably under the particular influence of the Stoa.

[17] The following is based on Daniélou I, 7–85. It is remarkable that Philo has found no place in this sketch. Daniélou excludes him because of his Hellenistic exegesis. We will indicate Philonic influence at the most important points.

tian works utilizing Jewish materials (Ascension of Isaiah, II Enoch, Testaments of the Twelve Patriachs). To these must be added some of the Sibylline books (Books 3 and 4 are Jewish; Book 5 is Jewish but revised by Christians; Books 6 and 7 are Jewish–Christian work). With these we should consider as a second group the Apocrypha of the New Testament, so far as we possess them either whole or in fragments (the gospels of Peter, of James, according to the Hebrews, the Egyptians, etc.; or apocalypses, e.g. that of Peter; and the *Epistula Apostolorum*). In these works there is already a theological reflection upon the gospel message, the Jewish–Christian 'Gnosis'. We have already referred to a third group, concerned with liturgy, morality, asceticism and catechesis—in this the Didache occupies a central place. The Odes of Solomon,[18] the Epistle of Barnabas and the Shepherd of Hermas[19] deserve a special mention. It is especially noteworthy that the epistles of Ignatius of Antioch can also be mentioned in this connection, although they use the language of the Jewish synagogue and the primitive community significantly less than the Shepherd of Hermas and therefore even at this stage have a noticeably more Hellenistic tendency.[20] They show traces of Syrian influence, which points to a Judaism of Gnostic character, having orthodox and heterodox forms. The Syrian-Antiochian character of these epistles lies, according to J. Daniélou, chiefly in their special attitude to the divine mystery, in the accent which they place on transcendence. There are signs that I Clement belongs to the same group as the epistles of Ignatius. Though Hellenistic-Stoic influences cannot be denied, the real theological milieu of I Clement is Jewish–Christian. We do not, of course, find here an Antiochene mystical approach, nor do we have any form of esoteric Gnostic Judaism. I Clement is rather part of that Jewish didactic literature with a tendency to moralize which was formed in Palestinian Judaism and is evidenced in the Midrashim.

In addition to these written relics of Jewish–Christian theology we have the oral traditions (recorded at a later stage) such as we find in the 'Presbyters', cited by Papias, Irenaeus and Clement of Alexandria.[21] Whereas Papias and Irenaeus testify to an Asiatic tradition, Clement points to another source which W. Bousset was anxious to trace back to Pantaenus

[18] According to Daniélou I, 30–3, this is a Jewish–Christian work intended for the great church composed in Eastern Syria but having affinities with Bardesanes. Cf. recently *Papyrus Bodmer* X–XII; XI: *Onzième Ode de Salomon*, Bibl. Bodmeriana 1959, 49–69.

[19] J.-P. Audet more than any other scholar emphasizes in the second part of his article mentioned above, *RB* 60, 1953, 41–82, the Jewish character of this book, which he holds might derive from an imperfectly converted Essene whose parents could have had contact with the Qumran community. He affirms that no reference of Hermas to the Holy Spirit, good and evil spirits, the Son of God and the church could be adopted by the general tradition without the strictest reservations. His verdict is perhaps too harsh (see below).

[20] H. Schlier, *Religionsgeschichtliche Untersuchungen zu den Ignatiusbriefen*, Giessen 1929; cf. also Daniélou I, 39–43.

[21] Daniélou I, 45–54.

and hence to an Alexandrian school tradition. With Casey and Munck, Daniélou, would stress the Judaistic colouring of these traditions, which indicates a Palestinian Jewish teaching rather than a Hellenizing Judaism of the Philonic type. In view of *Strom.* I, 1, 11–12 and Eusebius, HE VI, 13, 8–9, we must conclude that Clement knew an oral tradition which came not in fact from the apostles but from an apostolic milieu, and hence was typically Jewish–Christian.[22]

An important characteristic of Jewish Christianity is its attitude to the Bible. While during the course of the second century the great church fell back on a strict canon of scripture, Jewish Christianity based itself on the sources described above and on Judaistic exegesis, particularly the exegesis of later Judaism in opposition to the Hellenistic exegesis of Philo (though this does not imply that no Philonic influence is perceptible in Jewish Christianity). It seems that the Septuagint was the principal text. There was no special Jewish–Christian translation of the Old Testament, but there were perhaps revisions of the Septuagint.[23] This reveals an exegesis created out of apologetic or liturgical interests, which worked by means of association of texts, changes, additions and omissions. It was of very archaic character. Besides such Targumim, it seems that the existence of Jewish–Christian Midrashim, paraphrases of the Old Testament, can also be proven. It is further claimed that the early Christian sources, whether Jewish–Christian or from the great church, demonstrate that a selection of texts of the Old Testament existed in the form of *Testimonia*,[24] and these would be regarded as material for christological proof. From them, it is claimed, the Old Testament prophetical proof for the person of Jesus Christ whether as Messiah or as Son of Man was to be drawn. Christ and the church, the *Testimonia* are meant to show, are in accordance with the eternal plan of God.

One feature of the content of Jewish–Christian exegesis is its interest in Genesis.[25] This is also to be found, however, in Philo (who is primarily a Hellenist), in Late Judaism (Kabbala) and in the Hermetic writings. Finally the cosmology, the elements of which are as yet perhaps not quite exclusively drawn from Jewish apocalyptic writings, also belongs to the theological categories of Jewish Christianity. We find cosmology even in the New Testament. But there it is not an end in itself, but is made an

[22] Daniélou I, 51f.

[23] Cf. K. Stendhal, *The School of St Matthew*, Uppsala 1954, 169–82.

[24] Cf. R. Harris, *Testimonies* I–II, Cambridge 1916–20. For the whole problem of the Testimonies see P. Prigent, *Les Testimonia dans le christianisme primitif. L'épître de Barnabé I–XVI et ses sources* (EtBibl), Paris 1961, 16–28 (Les Testimonia. État de question); G. T. Armstrong, *Die Genesis in der Alten Kirche* (BGBH 4), Tübingen 1962, 3–6.

[25] Cf. G. T. Armstrong, op. cit. (on Justin, Irenaeus, Tertullian). The Psalms in particular underwent a christological revision and interpretation after the church's reaction against the luxuriance of the hymns had been overcome, and they became to a special degree the songs of the church (this, though, was the concern of the great church). Cf. B. Fischer, *Die Psalmenfrömmigkeit der Märtyrerkirche*, Freiburg 1949.

auxiliary to christological or theological statement. 'As the Ascension of Isaiah demonstrates, the situation is different in post-canonical writings.'[26] The cosmology is a part of the Jewish-apocalyptic *kerygma*, though this remains orientated upon God. 'The Ascension of Isaiah went on to try to create a christocentric cosmology.'[27] Jewish apocalyptic writings finally had great influence in offering images which were significant for christology: the idea of the heavenly book (as a guarantee of God's eternal plan with Christ), of the unveiling of a sacral cosmos (with good and evil spirits), of the revelation of a saving history, of the *mysterion* which was approachable through 'Gnosis'. These images could also be of value to the universal church. But the determinative characteristic of Jewish Christianity which marked it off from the great church was a total attitude which can be described as prophetic and apocalyptic. This tendency, which can also be regarded as a basic theological structure, is especially evident in a preference for the apocryphal and particularly the apocalyptic literature rather than for the canon of the great church. As is well known, Revelation had particular difficulty in obtaining recognition in the latter. Daniélou speaks of a visionary tendency. In extremes this could easily lead to a mythologizing of Christianity.

This general description of the sources and contents of Jewish–Christian theology is, of course, still rather vague and inadequate. 'The presentation and realization of Christianity in the forms of late Judaism' is perhaps the most appropriate definition.[28] But do we not find this already in the New Testament, in Paul, in James, in Peter and finally in Jesus himself? This need not be denied. But in so far as the great church and Judaism are definable entities, it must be possible to establish to some degree what Jewish elements there are in certain presentations of Christianity. A specific analysis will demonstrate this by indicating the archaic features in the early Christian picture of Jesus Christ even if their derivation from Jewish sources cannot always be proved.

The first archaic element we encounter is a pre-Pauline and pre-Johannine 'name-christology'.[29] The old-established Shem-theology of the later books of the Old Testament appears to have been continued and applied to Christ. In Ethiopian Enoch 48. 2f. we find this name-theology primarily associated with the concept 'Son of Man'. The Son of Man is brought before God 'and his name before the Ancient of Days'; his name was 'named before the Lord of spirits' before the creation of the stars. 'The

[26] H. Bietenhard, *Die himmlische Welt in Urchristentum und Spätjudentum*, Tübingen 1951, 67, cf. 51, 214–21 and passim. See too the index s. v. Jesus; Daniélou I, 173.

[27] H. Bietenhard, ibid., 263.

[28] Cf. Daniélou I, 9. With Goppelt, Daniélou means in particular the Judaism of the Pharisees, the Essenes and the Zealots.

[29] Cf. Daniélou I, 147–63. We cannot accept as evidence all the passages which Daniélou cites here. Cf. J. Ponthot, *La signification religieuse du 'NOM' chez Clément de Rome et dans la Didachè* (AnLov BiblOr III, 12), Louvain 1959.

pre-existence of the name paraphrased in this way probably describes in this passage the pre-existence of the Son of Man himself, for name and person are very closely linked together.'[30] A further step would have been taken when the word 'name' became a description of the Godhead of Christ and thus took the place of 'Logos' or 'pneuma'. Christ would thus be, so to speak, the incarnate 'Name' of God, in the same way as he is the 'incarnate Logos' or the 'divine pneuma (= Godhead) in the flesh'.

There is some support for such an idea. In Philo (*Conf. Ling.* 146) the Logos is called the 'name of God'. According to the Shepherd of Hermas, the name of the Son of God has a divine honour and function: 'The name of the Son of God is great and incomprehensible (ἀχώρητον) and it (the name) supports the whole cosmos.'[31] The second half of the quotation may remind us of Heb. 1. 3: 'upholding all things by the word of his power'. The difference is, of course, clear. In Heb. 1. 3, God is the subject and the word (ῥῆμα) is the instrument. In the Shepherd of Hermas the 'name' is the subject of the world-sustaining activity, the βαστάζειν. This is surely the expression of the mediation of the Son of God in creation. Name is simply identical with 'Son of God', as is clear from the following extract:

> If then the whole creation is supported by the Son of God, what do you think of those who are called by him, who bear the name of the Son of God and walk in his commandments? Do you see then the people whom he supports? Those who bear his name with their whole hearts. He himself became their foundation and he supports them gladly, because they are not ashamed to bear his name.[32]

The Shepherd of Hermas seems Christian here in so far as it assumes a distinction within God and thus with some degree of clarity allows the foundations of a trinitarian or at least a binitarian (Father–Son) belief to be established. Its idea of God cannot be derived from a Jewish monotheism.[33] The idea of the 'Son of God' has already progressed too far. The 'name of the Son of God' here implies complete transcendence and pre-existence. This, however, leaves the question of the incarnation completely untouched. It is not yet possible to establish the view of the Shepherd of Hermas on the incarnation. The 'name' means merely 'the invisible part of Jesus, the only-begotten Son', to use the language of the *Excerpta ex Theodoto*.[34] Nevertheless, different features hint that the Son sent into the world is the subject of the discussion. This name is indeed already present in the Christians by virtue of their being sealed in baptism and their

---

[30] H. Bietenhard, Art. 'Onoma' in *TDNT* V, 266[39–41].
[31] Past. Herm., *Sim.* IX, 14, 6; ed. Whittaker, GCS 48, 91[5].
[32] Past. Herm., *Sim.* IX, 14, 5–6; ed. Whittaker 91[5–6].
[33] As attempted by J.-P. Audet, *RB* 60, 1953, 68–76. But he has to posit a number of textual alterations, which counts against his thesis.
[34] Clem. Al., *Excerpta ex Theod.* 26, 1 (GCS 17, 115[17]) τὸ δὲ ἀόρατον ⟨τὸ⟩ ὄνομα ὅπερ ἐστιν ὁ υἱὸς ὁ μονογενής See also Daniélou II, 244.

confession[35] of Christ. Therefore the mediacy of the Son in creation also becomes the means of salvation both for Christians and for the angels: the Shepherd of Hermas expresses this in the rather awkward similitude of the old rock and the new door (*Sim.* IX, 2ff.). Hermas sees in a plain a great shining rock, higher than the hills, so large that it could hold the whole world:

> The rock was old, and a door was cut in it. It appeared to me that the door had been cut quite recently. The door shone so much in the sun that I marvelled at the brightness of it (*Sim.* IX, 2, 2).

The explanation interprets the picture:

> 'The rock and the door is the Son of God.' 'But how, sir (Hermas asks the Shepherd), is it that the rock is old but the door is new?' The Shepherd replies: 'The Son of God is older than all his creation, so that he was counsellor to the Father about his creation. Therefore he (the rock) is also old.' 'But why is the door new, sir?' 'Because he (the Son) was manifested in the last days of the consummation; for this reason the door is new, so that those who are to be saved may go through it into the kingdom of God' (*Sim.* IX, 12, 1–3).

Note that the rock and the door together represent the Son of God. The 'old rock' means the pre-existence of the Son before the creation and his mediacy at the creation as counsellor of the Father. But the 'door' means the revelation of the Son to the world and his exclusive mediation of salvation, providing the way to the Father. He is the only door, 'the only entrance to the Lord'.[36] The reference to Christ is not to be doubted, even though there is no mention of the incarnation here either. The mediation of salvation is clearly distinguished from the mediation at creation. This too, however, is linked with the 'name' of the Son of God: 'Whoever does not receive his name (be he man or angel) will not enter into the kingdom of God' (*Sim.* IX, 12, 8b). Thus the Shepherd of Hermas associates with the name-theology quite a clear recognition of the pre-existence and mediatory position of the Son of God. The foundation of its soteriology is by no means objectionable. Its concrete presentation of Christ, however, poses us many questions, as we shall see. The names 'Jesus', 'Christ', do not occur in the work. The picture of God (and his relationship to Christ and the Christians) seems dominated by Jewish thought-patterns. God is more frequently represented as the *Kyrios* of the Christians than as their Father. The Christians are slaves of God. In *Sim.* V even the Son of God is described as a slave, whom his master then frees and adopts. In *Sim.* V, 5, 5 Hermas himself is surprised at this description and attempts to correct it in what follows. The cult of the almighty master

---

[35] The confession of the name of the Son of God 'had particular significance during the time of persecution'. Cf. Daniélou I, 156f. with reference to Acts 5. 41; Past. Herm., *Vis.* III, 1, 9; 2, 1; *Sim.* IX, 28; Ign., *Eph.* 1, 2; 3, 1; 7, 1.

[36] Past. Herm., *Sim.* IX, 12, 5 and 6. Christ as the door see John 10. 7ff.; Ign., *Ad Phil.* 9, 1; I Clem. 48, 2.

(δεσπότης) conceals the picture of the heavenly 'Father' and puts Son and Spirit in the background. The church is described in *Vis.* I, 3, 4 as the creation of God, with no mention of Christ. The second coming, too, is described as the coming of God and not of Christ, a real Jewish tradition (*Sim.* V, 5, 3). *Sim.* IX, 7, 6 of course differs. There it is the Son of God who will come again. The way in which the Shepherd of Hermas understands this will be described at the end of this section, where the archaic Jewish concept of Christ is to be compared with the picture of Christ in the great church. The work will occupy us quite frequently as we proceed with the investigation.

A further way of expressing the transcendence of Christ, and most obvious to Judaism, is the identification of Jesus with the law (νόμος) or with the covenant (διαθήκη).[37] In Judaism, the same characteristics were ascribed to the law as are given by John to the pre-existent (and incarnate) Logos. It has therefore quite properly been asked whether the prologue of the Gospel of John was not composed as an answer to Jewish speculations on the Torah.[38] Among the Jews, the Torah is the incarnation of the wisdom of God, among the Jewish Christians it is Jesus. Philonic language and Pauline ideas (1 Cor.) may lie behind such doctrines. Jewish apocalyptic ideas are, however, probably the direct source. Once again we encounter the Shepherd of Hermas: 'This great tree, which overshadows plains, mountains and the whole earth, is the law of God (νόμος θεοῦ) which was given to the whole world. And this law is the Son of God who is preached to the ends of the earth' (*Sim.* VIII, 3, 2). Clement of Alexandria refers to the *Kerygmata Petri*, which call the Lord law and Logos (νόμον καὶ λόγον) (*Strom.* I, 29, 182, 2). As Clement expressly states (*Eclog. Proph.* 58), the saying in Isa. 2. 3, 'Out of Zion shall go forth the law, and the word of the Lord from Jerusalem,' underlies this. Part of the quotation recurs in Melito's *Easter Homily*[39] and here the theme leads to lengthy discussions about Logos and Nomos, though in a way different from our Jewish-Christian sources: the Logos which has appeared in Christ annuls the Nomos. These terms acquire special significance in Justin, as will become evident. He calls Christ at the same time law and covenant: 'It was prophesied that Christ, the Son of God, was to be an eternal law and a new covenant for the whole world.'[40] This description of Christ as law and covenant refers primarily to his significance in salvation history. The New Testament already depicts Christ as the bringer of the final law.[41] But our texts mean more. They identify the Son of God with the law and the

---

[37] Daniélou I, 163–6; J. Lebreton, *Origines du Dogme de la Trinité* II, Paris 1928, 648–50. For the Nomos in Philo see H. A. Wolfson, *Philo*, Camb., Mass. 1948, I, 184–94; II, 165–200.
[38] See above, p. 29, n. 44.
[39] Melito, *Peri Pascha* 7.
[40] Justin, *Dial.* 43, 1; cf. 11, 2; 51, 3.
[41] Cf. P. Bläser, *Das Gesetz bei Paulus*, Münster 1941, 234–43.

covenant. Christ is all this in his existence, as hypostasis, in his all-embracing divine reality which is present in the man Jesus in the world. Here Christian theology works with the post-biblical Jewish idea of the hypostasis, applying it to the Son of God in his pre-existence and his incarnation: 'He who disposes all things and is true law and ordinance and external word is in reality the son of God.'[42]

Just as the Johannine prologue already refers back to Gen. 1. 1 and reads from the term ἀρχή the role of the Logos with God and in the creation, so ἀρχή retains its significance in primitive Christian theology. Once again the term is sharpened in a typical way. The Son is not merely 'in the beginning', but 'beginning' *par excellence*, as, for example, Clement of Alexandria says in his *Eclogae propheticae*.[43] Of course, most of the patristic statements about Christ as ἀρχή are connected with the Logos,[44] and this goes beyond the circle of Jewish-Christian ideas. But in addition to the reference in Clement of Alexandria to the Jewish-Christian *Kerygmata Petri*, Theophilus of Antioch in particular guarantees the archaic Jewish character of this connection. In referring to Gen. 1. 1 he hypostasizes the '*bereshith*' and understands it of the Logos as mediator at the creation:

Thus God produced with his Wisdom his Word, which he bore within himself, by letting it come forth from him before all things. This Word he used as the means in all his creations and he created all through it. This Word is called 'the beginning', because it is the principle and the Lord of all things which have been created through it (*Ad Autol*. II, 10).

The Gnostics too take the *arche* of Gen. 1. 1 as a personal hypostasis, in that they regard God, the *arche*, heaven and earth as a quaternity (Iren., *Adv. Haer*. I, 18, 1). A rabbinic tradition, which may be traced through Irenaeus, Tertullian, Jerome and Hilary, even translates *reshith* (Gen. 1. 1) as 'son', which in its turn is synonymous with 'only-begotten'.[45]

The designation 'Day' for Christ is also to be explained from Gen. 1. Jewish speculations seem to lie behind it. According to Eusebius of Caesarea, this title for the incarnate Christ still occurs in Marcellus of Ancyra, though here the whole context is permeated with the Logos idea:

It is therefore clear in every respect that there is no other name suitable for the eternal Logos than that which the holy disciple of the Lord and apostle John has given at the beginning of the gospel. Often though he may be called after the assumption of the flesh Christ and Jesus, Life and Way and *Day* and Resurrection and Door and Bread—and whatever other names there are elsewhere in the divine scriptures—we may not overlook the first name, that he was the Logos.[46]

---

[42] Clem. Alex., *Strom*. VII, 3, 16: GCS 17, 12[18–19]: νόμος ὢν ὄντως καὶ θεσμὸς καὶ λόγος αἰώνιος.
[43] Clem. Al., *Eclog. proph*. 4, 1: ὅτι δὲ ἀρχὴ ὁ υἱός. Cf. *Strom*. VI, 7, 58 with a reference to the *Kerygmata Petri*. Ἀρχή is frequent in Philo. See H. Leisegang, *Indices*, s.v. ἀρχή 1.
[44] Justin, *Dial*. 6, 1, 1; Tatian, *Or. ad Graecos* 5; Origen, *Hom. Gen*. I, 1; *Comm. Io*. I, 19.
[45] Perhaps the christological expressions of Col. 1. 15ff. (πρὸ πάντων, κεφαλή, πρωτότοκος) are also nothing more than the different interpretations of ἀρχή; cf. Daniélou I, 168.
[46] Marcell. Anc., frag. 43, in: Eus. Caes., *C. Marcell*.; GCS 14, 192. W. Gericke, *Marcell von*

One of the attempts of the primitive Christian period to express the transcendence of Christ is the so-called 'angel-christology' or the designation *Christos angelos*. It is so significant that attempts have been made to prove that it was the original christology, at least in Jewish-Christian circles. Jesus, it is held, was understood as an angel in the strict sense, i.e. as a heavenly creature sent by God into the world.[47] With the condemnation of Arianism this legitimate and original conception was stamped as heresy. It had to give place to the strict doctrine of two natures. According to M. Werner, the messianic title Son of Man is best interpreted if we assume 'that this Messiah belonged to the (highest) celestial realm of the angels. This view is expressly confirmed by the sources.'[48] As early as the synoptic gospels, the Son of Man is depicted as an angelic prince. 'He appears with the host of his "holy angels" (Mark 8. 38; Matt. 13. 41f.; Mark 13. 26ff.; 1. 13; Luke 22. 43; 1 Thess. 4. 16). The Messiah–Son of Man is chosen by God to execute a special mission and, accordingly, he was set over the celestial world of angels.'[49] Although Christ may be given the title *Kyrios* by Paul, this is merely a 'particular instance of the general, but too-long-neglected fact, that Late Judaism and primitive Christianity designated and invoked the angels as κύριοι'.[50] Indeed, in the New Testament κυριότης usually just means a class of angels. It was because of the according of this status to Christ, Werner claims, that no approach to the question of the Trinity could be made in primitive Christian times (the real reason for this deficiency was, however, the prevalence of the economic view of the relationship between Father, Son and Spirit). This alone could have been the cause of the early Christian subordinationism which Jesus had himself most decisively advocated (Mark 10. 18; 13. 32; 14. 36). The subordination only became a co-ordination of Christ with God during the process of 'de-eschatologizing'. Even the angel-christology did not, of course, by-pass the problem of the relationship of this *Christos angelos* to the historical Jesus of Nazareth. The idea of 'transformation' (of the one into the other) formed the bridge between the two. Phil. 2. 5–11 and Rom. 1. 4 bear witness to this. The pre-existent Messiah gave up his divine, i.e. heavenly, form and ' "substituted" for it the "form" of a slave (sc. of the angelic powers which ruled the world), i.e. he appeared in

Ancyra, Halle 1940, 205; cf. Daniélou I, 111, 168–72; II, 262 (Hippolyt., *Bened. Moys.*, ed. Mariès 170: Christ as Day, Sun and Year).

[47] M. Werner, *Die Entstehung des christlichen Dogmas*, Bern–Tübingen 1954², 302–88; in an abridged version, Stuttgart 1959, 74–100; ET, *The Formation of Christian Doctrine*, London–New York 1957, 120–61. This edition will be quoted in what follows. Against this W. Michaelis, *Zur Engelchristologie im Urchristentum*, Basel 1942. On the whole question: J. Barbel, *Christos Angelos* (Theophaneia 3), Bonn 1941; id., 'Zur "Engel-Trinitätslehre" im Urchristentum', *TR* 54, 1958, 49–58; 103–12 as a comment on G. Kretschmar, *Studien zur frühchristlichen Trinitätstheologie*, Tübingen 1956, and J. Daniélou, *RSR* 45, 1957, 5–41 and I, 117–47.

[48] M. Werner, *The Formation of Christian Dogma*, 120.

[49] Ibid., 121–2.

[50] Ibid., 123.

a form like that of a man, he had in his whole manner (σχῆμα) resembled a man'.[51] Such a transformation was only possible if the subject was not 'God unchangeable', but merely a created angelic being.

(Here Werner's argument is no longer exegetical but dogmatic. The later development of christology will give him the dogmatic answer that it is more easily possible for the omnipotent God to take upon himself a human existence while preserving his transcendence than it is for an angelic being to change into a human form. God alone can have the power over his being which, in the view of the Fathers, is necessary for the incarnation. The Fathers, too, saw the problem of the divine transcendence very clearly, and in their struggle against Arianism, Apollinarianism and Monophysitism they achieved a complete solution without renouncing belief in the incarnation. They are thus, unlike the angelic transformation of Werner's view, a long way separated from myth.)

On the other hand, Jesus, the prophetic man, revealed himself through his mighty deeds and signs as the one chosen for future elevation to the rank of the heavenly Messiah.

The history of the Primitive Christian doctrine of Christ as a high angelic being pursued its way in the post-apostolic period through successive stages. At first the view gradually subsided of its own accord and became problematical. Then, already profoundly shaken within, it had to endure finally a decisive assault during the Arian dispute of the fourth century. In that conflict it was bitterly attacked by the representatives of the new doctrine of Christ, which had emerged in the interval, and at last it was proscribed and suppressed as erroneous doctrine.[52]

It is quite true that the *Christos angelos* theme is a very real one and that it had an important position in the early Christian period, but Werner has failed to evaluate its historical characteristics accurately. He overestimates what is meant to be an aid towards christological thought. The fact that the synoptists make Jesus of Nazareth, who is to come again in all his glory, an angel-prince, does not mean that Christ himself is an angel, but just that he is the Lord of the angels and the powers. The position of Jesus among the good powers is to be understood in a way analogous to his relationship with the evil powers whom Paul at any rate includes among the κυριότητες. Werner forgets to find a place for Christ in the total picture of all the powers (both good and evil). Christ transcends all powers. We are as little forced to conclude from his Lordship over the good powers that he shares their nature as we are able and entitled to draw a similar conclusion from his Lordship over the evil powers.[53] The nature of the transcendence of Jesus at the least remains open. One basic fact should be noted, that Jesus' lordship, his κυριότης, is predicated of

[51] Ibid., 127.
[52] Ibid., 131.
[53] Cf. H. Schlier, *Mächte und Gewalten im Neuen Testament* (Quaestiones Disputatae 3), Freiburg 1958, 37–49.

him as man. The Lord of the powers is he who has gone through death and the resurrection (cf. Col. 1. 15–18). The extent of his exaltation is first evident from the fact that although man, he is raised *above* all powers (Eph. 1. 21; cf. Heb. 1. 3f.). The terms which express the difference between the natures are here 'man' and 'spirit-powers'. The comparison of natures here is purely negative (Christ, although man, is set over the powers); the positive element of the comparison is the difference between Christ, the man, and the spirit powers. These powers did not recognize the wisdom of God working itself out in Christ and therefore they crucified the 'Lord of Glory' (1 Cor. 2. 8). They did not bow themselves before the humble Jesus of Nazareth who himself overcame the powers through his obedience. There is no hint that Jesus owes his victory over these powers to his angelic nature or that the messianic title Son of Man is best explained from the angelic nature of Christ. That would be to make a sad mistake. In Phil. 2. 5–11, too, Christ's lordship is not essentially derived from his angelic nature, though at the same time it is said that the exalted one rules over all realms of creation and thus over the powers also. To say that this exalted one had previously transformed himself by abandoning his angelic nature for human form is an inapposite mythologizing of the Pauline passage. The σχῆμα is true human nature which is assumed by the pre-existent one of whom it is said that he is in the form of God. We are not justified in seeing in him an angelic being.

We may point out the over-estimating of the *Christos angelos* idea, but within limits it is not to be denied as a historical fact. The sources testify that Christ was given the name 'angel' right up until the fourth century.[54] A first reason behind this will have been the idea of the *mal'akh Yahweh*, the angel of Yahweh. If this was transferred to Christ, it needed a special interpretation. It was therefore the practice of the Fathers of the second century to interpret the theophanies of the Old Testament, in which the angel of the Lord was the central figure, as theophanies of the Logos. This gave rise to the equation 'Logos = *mal'akh Yahweh*'. In doing this, however, these Fathers do not force down the Logos to the status of a created angel, however much subordinationist ideas may have crept in. The Logos concept remains dominant, and the angel concept is given a new significance. With this interpretation of the appearances of the Logos we have not yet, however, reached the Jewish–Christian realm. We first come into this latter when the late Jewish doctrine of angels is used to interpret the nature and mission of Christ. Prime concern is with the interpretation not of the nature, but of the mission of Christ. Judaistically conditioned christology is predominantly functional, not ontological. It is possible to transfer the name 'angel' to Christ as a functional category as long as the

---

[54] For what follows see J. Barbel, *Christos Angelos*, 181–311; Daniélou I, 117–47; F. Stier, *Gott und sein Engel im Alten Testament*, Münster 1934, 1–3.

way lies open for a full definition of his transcendence and the way in which, in the view of the tradition, it corresponds to his nature. But the insufficiency of this teaching in this respect was soon felt.

The Shepherd of Hermas already shows us the whole position of the angel christology. It is fond of talking of the 'glorious' or the 'most reverend' angel (ἔνδοξος, σεμνότατος ἄγγελος, *Sim.* IX, 1, 3; *Mand.* V, 1, 7) who sends the 'shepherd' or the 'angel of repentance', thus revealing himself as someone different from the latter. The angel of repentance is merely guardian of those who are made righteous by the 'most reverend' angel (*Mand.* V, 1, 7). The latter, in fact, decides the penance which Hermas has to undergo (*Sim.* VII, 1–3). He sends the Shepherd to Hermas (ibid. 4). According to *Sim.* VIII, 1, 1–2 (the parable of the willow) this 'glorious angel', depicted as a surpassingly tall figure, decides about righteous and sinners in their acts of repentance. He bestows the seal and grants admission to the company of the holy ones, the church, which is symbolized by the tower. Everything indicates that this high angelic figure is meant to be Christ. Now we suddenly learn that the glorious angel is Michael:

And a glorious angel of the Lord, very tall, stood by the willow tree; he had a great sickle, and he kept cutting branches from the willow tree and giving them to the people who were in the shadow of the tree (*Sim.* VIII, 1, 2). This great tree, which overshadows plains and mountains and all the earth, is the law of God, which is given to all the world. And this law is the Son of God preached to the ends of the earth. And the people who are under its shadow are those who have heard the preaching and have believed in it. The great and glorious angel is *Michael*, who has power over this people and governs them, for it is he who put the law into the hearts of those that believe . . . (*Sim.* VIII, 3, 2–3).

There is much that is Jewish in this parable. The law is likened to a tree. We already know the origin and significance of the equation 'Son-law.' The interpretation of Michael as the leader of the chosen people is also Jewish. Here Hermas is either duplicating his figures (the Lord of the church would be first Christ and then Michael) or he is identifying the two, so that either the Son of God would have to be understood as Michael or Michael as the Son of God.

Hermas usually makes his parables complicated in this way. He works with traditional material and does not completely achieve the transposition to a new level of understanding. But there can be no question of a substantial reduction of the Son of God to Michael. For the Son is in the end quite clearly distinguished from the archangel, even though the latter stands in the place usually occupied by the Son of God. The elements of transcendence in the picture of the 'most reverend' angel, by which is meant the Son of God, go far beyond the Jewish picture of Michael. For the Jewish tradition Michael is indeed the supreme leader of the heavenly hosts (ἀρχιστράτηγος), but it is not certain that he is also the chief of the seven archangels in the sense that the other six are his subordinates.[55] The Shepherd of Hermas, however, quite clearly leaves this place free for Christ and in such a way as to correspond to the new figure:

'Have you also seen the six men and the glorious and great man in their midst, who is walking round the tower and who rejected the stones from the building?' 'Yes, sir.' 'The glorious man is the Son of God, and those six are the glorious angels who support him on the right and on the left. Of these glorious angels none can enter the presence of God without him. Whoever does not receive his name will not enter the kingdom of God' (Sim. IX, 12, 7–8).

Here it is quite clear that the Son of God is meant and that as such he is superior to the six chief angels. These angels are his entourage. He does not stand like Michael as *primus inter pares*, for he is the way to God even for the angels! Michael is not given such a role among the archangels, even in his capacity as escort of souls. For this is merely an incidental mediation of salvation, which is in no way comparable to that of the Son of God. As a visible symbol of this transcendence, the figure of the Son of God is given superhuman dimensions, so that he even overtops the tower (Sim. IX, 6, 1). We find this symbolism quite frequently in early Christian writing, especially in connection with the angels. According to V Esdras, hostile to Judaism as it is, the elect are assembled around Christ on mount Sion and 'in their midst stood a young man of exceptional height who overtopped them all. On the head of each one of them he set a crown and grew upwards still more. . . .' 'It is the Son of God, whom they confessed in the world,' is the answer given when the identity of this person is sought.[56]

The Gospel of Peter, limited to small circles in Syria, is particularly concerned to defend the divinity of Christ against pagan and Jewish attacks. So the suffering of Christ is idealized and the resurrection in particular is transformed:

And whilst they (the soldiers of the governor) were relating what they had seen (the descent of two men from heaven to the sepulchre of Jesus), they saw again three men come out from the sepulchre, and two of them sustaining the other, and a cross following them, and the heads of the (first) two reaching to heaven, but that of him who was led of them by the hand overpassing the heavens.[57]

The extraordinary size of the figure of Christ is meant to be a palpable sign of his transcendence which (as in the Shepherd of Hermas) makes him tower even above the angels. Heavenly beings, including angels,

[55] Cf. J. Barbel, *Christos Angelos*, 224–35, esp. 233.
[56] E. Hennecke–W. Schneemelcher–R. McL. Wilson, *New Testament Apocrypha* II, London 1965 (cited as *New Test. Apoc.* II), 695. The scene is reminiscent of Rev. 14.1.
[57] *Evang. Pet.* 39, 40: ed. L. Vaganay, *L'Evangile de Pierre*, Paris 1930, 207–300, ET in Hennecke–Schneemelcher–Wilson, *New Testament Apocrypha* I, London 1963 (cited as *New Test. Apoc.* I), 186; a similar scene *Ascension of Isaiah* III, 16, 17, in *New Test. Apoc.* II, 647–8.

reach above everything earthly.[58] But Christ is still higher than all heavenly spirits. His head is higher even than heaven itself. The fact that the
risen one is led is not a sign of weakness, but a feature borrowed from the
ceremonial accorded a ruler and suitable for Christ, the *Kyrios*. The
representation of the transfigured Christ as a giant is in accordance with a
pattern common among orthodox and heretics alike. According to
Hippolytus, the Elkasaites represented Christ after this fashion.[59] It is also
known to the Gnostic Acts of John and many acts of the martyrs.[60] There
was a special standard for the divine form upon earth, as Celsus testifies
by demanding an expression of the Godhead of Christ even in the form
of Jesus of Nazareth, an expression which he does not discover in the
description of Christ given by Christians.[61] Here we are in the realm
of Hellenistic ideas, though of a popular kind. Later a similar but more
sublime approach will be evidenced by the Antiochenes. Of course, the
figure of the 'great Son of Man' cannot guarantee a description of the
transcendence of Christ as it is meant by the dogma of the church, i.e.
true Godhead. It remains perforce a quantitative distinction. The theological approach remains decisive. Individual ideas must be investigated
to determine their respective values as theological expressions.

The Christ–Gabriel and the Christ–Michael–Gabriel relationships
deserve special attention. The *Epistula Apostolorum* makes the angel Gabriel
the angel of the annunciation, into a form of the Lord himself, who of his
own power forms a body in the Virgin. Gabriel is not the Lord himself; he
merely gives him his form.[62]

> The view that the Logos formed himself in the womb of his mother does not imply
> any identification of Christ and Gabriel. Nor does the idea that the conception took place
> during the salutation of the angel prove this identification. . . . The only time that the
> voice of the angel (or even the angel himself) has greater significance, this idea is sharply
> repudiated by a representative of the great church.[63]

Tertullian, who fought against the denial of the incarnation of Christ by
the docetists, shows that even at this stage there could be a reflex dis-
avowal of the angel-christology. He allows the validity of only one
parallel between Christ and the angels out of six possibilities: Christ is an
angel as the messenger of the Father to redeem the human race.

---

[58] See also the great resurrection angel of the *Anaphora Pilati* A 9; ed. C. Tischendorff, *Evangelia
Apocrypha*, 440f.
[59] Hippolytus, *Elenchus* 9, 13, 2: GCS 26, 51; J. Barbel, *Christos Angelos*, 278, n. 410.
[60] *Acta Ioann.* 90: Lipsius-Bonnet, II, 1, 195; *Acta Perpet. et Felic.* 4, 5 and 10, 4: Krüger, 37, 39;
Passio Mariani et Iacobi 7, 3: Krüger, 70.
[61] Origen, *Contra Celsum* 6, 77: GCS II, 146.
[62] *Epist. Apost.*. 13, 14, ed. H. Duensing, *New Test. Apoc.* I, 198–9; C. Schmidt, *Gespräche Jesu mit
seinen Jüngern nach der Auferstehung*, Leipzig 1919, 50ff.
[63] J Barbel, *Christos Angelos*, 261; he refers to Ps. Athan., *Sermo in annuntiat. Deiparae* 7f.: PG 28,
925D–928C; Barbel, op. cit., 247–8, 235–62.

Dictus est quidem (Christus) magni consilii angelus, id est nuntius, officii, non naturae vocabulo. Magnum enim cogitatum patris, super hominis scilicet restitutione, adnuntiaturus saeculo erat.[64]

His distinction that angel is a name descriptive of a function and not of a nature will remain decisive for Latin theology. Thus the name 'angel' can be applied to Christ, just as he can also be given the name 'prophet'. For Christ is the last and absolute revealer of the Father, quite simply his Logos sent out into the world. Of course, some of the other five possibilities which Tertullian enumerates and rejects have been held in numerous circles. Origen, for example, goes further than Tertullian. Certainly he recognizes the incarnation of the Logos. But he also acknowledges a process of becoming an angel similar to that of the scheme of descent in the *Ascensio Isaiae*. He derives his idea from his understanding of the Old Testament theophanies:

> But observe that according to the account in Scripture the angel spoke to Abraham and that in what follows this angel is evidently shown to be the Lord. Therefore I believe that just as his appearance among men is that of a man, so too his appearance among angels is that of an angel.[65]

Origen is concerned with the universality of redemption. Here the soteriological principle '*quod non est assumptum non est sanatum*', which we are to meet in his writings, is applied not merely to men but to the world of spirits. Surely, apart from Philo,[66] the neo-Platonic view of the world which Origen followed lies behind such an idea. But it should be noticed that in becoming man and becoming angel the Logos remains what he is. He merely assumes a different figure in each case. Nevertheless, Jerome is extremely incensed about Origen: 'He is wrong about the resurrection of the body, he is wrong about the condition of souls and the repentance of the devil, and more grave than all this, he testifies that the Son and the Holy Spirit are Seraphim.'[67] Is Origen then on the threshold of an angel-christology in the strict sense? It is true that for him the two seraphim of Isa. 6 are 'my Lord Jesus and the Holy Spirit'.[68] He refers to Jewish sources. Surely here too the Philonic interpretation of the two winged beings on the ark of the covenant as two 'powers' of God has been of influence. For Origen these two powers become the Logos and the Holy Spirit, understood in a markedly subordinationist sense. For the Logos himself prays to the Father and is not himself the focus of worship: 'We may not pray to him who himself prays.'[69] Theologically speaking, the greatest danger here is that of an equation of Logos and angel *secundum naturam*, and not

---

[64] Tertullian, *De carne Christi* 14; in Barbel, *Christos Angelos*, 286, n. 439. Cf. ibid., 284–8.
[65] Origen, *In Gen. hom.* 8, 8; quoted by Barbel, op. cit., 288; cf. 288–97.
[66] Philo, *De somniis* I, 232, 238f. In this chapter we examine the idea of a change of form only briefly. Barbel, op. cit., 293.
[67] Jerome, *Ep. 71 ad Vigilant.*: CSEL 54, 577$^{1-6}$.
[68] Origen, *In Is. Hom.*: GCS VIII, 244$^{22-28}$; *De Princ.* I, 3, 4: GCS V, 52^{17}–53^4.
[69] Origen, *De orat.* 15, 2: GCS II, 234^{19}.

merely *secundum officium*, to use the language of Tertullian. But Origen did not take this step (see below under 'Origen'). Nevertheless, the fact that this path, by way of the angel-christology, could lead to Arianism is not to be denied. Methodius of Olympus, Lactantius and an unknown preacher on the 'three fruits of the spiritual life' would seem to be much nearer to the suspicion of Arian heresy.[70] The play on the monogram ΧΜΓ, which in many cases is meant to be solved as Christ–Michael–Gabriel, threatens to become a play with heresy.[71] But even if these three names stand together, we are not necessarily to conclude that Christ is held to have the nature of an angel.[72]

Although the *Christos angelos* idea was extremely popular through the centuries and has real theological value as an expression, its limitations became recognized more and more. The idea was incapable of expressing the whole force of the picture of Christ present in the church's faith.

In the post-apostolic period, then, in the second and beginning of the third centuries, we discover an archaic christology which has its own, surely to great extent Jewish, way of expressing the transcendence of Christ. Christ is the present 'name' of God and the realization of the divine 'law', the 'beginning' and the new 'day' for the world, the 'angel of mighty counsel'. All these expressions still belong to the Old Testament, biblical way of talking about God, which in the case of God or of Christ is concerned more with their works, their revelation and the demonstration of their power than with the understanding of their essential being. Nevertheless, a view of the nature of Christ also emerges here. It is a matter of his person. In essentials his relationship to God, to the world and to the church are described in a way which is not essentially different from that in the other traditions of the period, as will become plainer in what follows.

We shall now attempt to interpret the second-century picture of Christ from a different point of view, namely the popular character of early Christian theology. There we shall have the opportunity of indicating Jewish–Christian material still more frequently, especially in connection with the theology of the mysteries of the life of Jesus.

(b) A popular picture of Christ

In the second century, the Christian tradition is like a young stream, coming down from the mountains, which can now for the first time spread itself on a broad landscape and extend into a lake. The landscape becomes wider and more varied, but at the same time less noble. The lake

---

[70] Cf. Barbel, *Christos Angelos*, 181–92, 192–5.

[71] Ibid. 262–9.

[72] We may perhaps pass the same judgement on this monogram as on the picture which Werner gives as evidence for angel-christology in his work *The Formation of Christian Dogma*. Christ is shown as the 'angel of mighty counsel' and is winged (North Greek Fresco). But has Werner noticed that in the nimbus of this *Christos angelos* ὁ ῾ѠN is written? Christ is thus clearly meant as God.

threatens to lose itself at the edges and to form stagnant water. But then at last the river again re-forms, to go on its way more strongly and more swiftly than before. This is the picture which meets us if we investigate the christological beliefs of the many anonymous and pseudonymous and apocryphal[73] writings of the second century, and after moving round the periphery of the tradition eventually end among the great witnesses of the second century, Clement of Rome, Ignatius of Antioch and Polycarp. Even so, we will have seen only a part of the christological landscape of the second century. It has still more surprises in store.

The writings with which we are concerned here are almost all known to us from the previous section. Our present examination of them with respect to their popular nature is particularly important for any understanding of the tradition of the second century, for in this unlearned and unconsidered writing we trace the direct effort of early Christian catechesis. We see the form in which the Christian faith was alive in the hearts of the wider, uneducated classes. As has often been said, it was of these people that Christianity was at first predominantly composed.[74] The Jewish, Judaizing and Hellenistic milieu of the second century is characterized by the traces of widespread popular influence and popular ideas. For this reason, the writing of the period is spread still wider, and is more variegated, than in the age of the theologians. This is also the reason for its open tone. Everywhere the heart and the imagination speak more loudly than the mind, while in the apocryphal writings we have above all 'le désir d'émouvoir par le pathétique ou d'intéresser par le merveilleux'.[75] This has implications for the description of the transcendence of Jesus.

We shall now first outline the picture of Christ and the views of the person of Jesus as they appear in some characteristic writings of the early period, and then pay particular attention to the so-called mysteries of the life of Jesus, which were the favourite preoccupation of the time. The Shepherd of Hermas is an example of the embarrassment over christological problems (see above). The contradictions in the interpretation of the incarnation which occur in this work are probably to be attributed to different stages of editing.[76] In addition, the christology is at the service of parenesis. Presumably inspired by the parable of the vineyard in the gospels

---

[73] New Test. Apoc. I, 21–8; II, 79–87; A. de Santos, Los Evangelios Apocrifos (Biblioteca de Autores Cristianos), Madrid 1956, 1–27.

[74] Cf. Athenag., Suppl. 11; Minucius Fel., Octav. 14, 1, where the Christians are described as a lot of 'miller's workers' (miller's workers and bakers were regarded as the lowest class), cf. ibid. 8, 4; 12, 2, 7, where reference is made to the low standard of education among the Christians, something for which they were despised by the pagans. Galen includes the Christians among those who can follow no 'connected argument and so need to be instructed by parables' (in E. Hennecke, Ntl. Apokryphen, Tübingen 1924[2], 476, n. 1). But the social distribution of Christians differed according to regions and had already changed by the second century. Cf. Minucius Fel., Octav. 31, 6; Euseb., HE V, 24, 1.

[75] A. Puech, Histoire de la littérature grecque chrétienne jusqu'à la fin du 4e siècle II, Paris 1929, 4.

[76] There are completely contradictory assessments of the trinitarian teaching and christology of the Shepherd of Hermas: (a) Those who maintain that it corresponds with the teaching of the church

(cf. Mark 12. 1–12; Luke 20. 9–19), in *Sim.* V, 2 Hermas proceeds to clarify the advantage of fasting and works of supererogation by using as an example Christ (whose name is not mentioned), the worker in the vineyard of the Lord.

A faithful servant is chosen and commissioned by God, the lord of the vineyard, to look after the property. He is just to put a fence round it while his master is abroad. But the servant does more than he has to, digs over the vineyard and clears it of weeds. On his return the lord is pleasantly surprised, grants the servant his freedom in return for the work which was asked of him and for the work over and above what was asked proposes to make him joint heir with his son. The son gives his consent. Because the servant proves himself further by passing on to his fellow servants food which has been sent to him from the master's feast (in fact, the commandments of God), the decision which has been made is further confirmed, especially as the fellow servants make intercession for the faithful servant.

Now what does this image of the servant signify for Christ? For we must assume that it is he who is meant. A clear adoptionist christology seems to underlie the passage.[77] But in *Sim.* V, 5 the Shepherd of Hermas itself gives an explanation which in contrast to the parable contains important statements and goes some way towards vindicating the writer. The servant himself, in fact, appears to be described as the Son: 'And the servant is the Son of God . . . the food which he sent him from the feast are the commandments, which he gave to his people through his Son' (*Sim.* V, 5, 2–3). In the explanation, many decisive features of the parable are, in fact, passed over: the adoption, which is stressed so much in the parable; the intercession of the fellow servants, which is so shocking, and finally the counsel of the 'first created angels'. In V, 6 the interpretation is further deepened. Chapter 5 ends with the significant question why the Son of God in the parable is given the form of a servant. Now in ch. 6 the servant is openly designated Son. To him the people are entrusted, and to protect them, the Son, who appears 'in great might and glory', appoints the angels. He himself cleanses the sins of the people and shows them the path of life through the law. But once again everything is made doubtful, for alongside the Son, in the form of a servant, there appears a further 'Son', the Holy Spirit. To him the incarnation is now ascribed (*Sim.* V, 6, 5–7):

are: T. Zahn, *Der Hirt d.H*, 1868; R. Seeberg, *Dogmengeschichte* I, 1920, 126ff.; Dorner, *Entwicklungsgeschichte*, 190–205; (*b*) Those who maintain that it does not correspond: Lipsius, Baur, Harnack, Loofs, Funk, Bardenhewer; (*c*) Those who explain it from the point of view of historical development: J. Lebreton, *Trinité* II, 346–87. Cf. M. Dibelius, *Der Hirt des Hermas*, Tübingen 1923, 572–6; R. Joly, *Hermas le Pasteur* (SC 53), 1958, 31–3; (*d*) S. Giet, *Hermas et les Pasteurs*, Paris 1963: three authors!

[77] Harnack and Hilgenfeld detect adoptionism. Lebreton (*Trinité* II, 368) and Dibelius (op. cit., 573) are milder in their judgements.

The Holy Spirit, which was there beforehand, which created all creation, was made by God to dwell in the fleshly nature (*sarx*) which he willed. Now this fleshy nature, in which the Holy Spirit dwelt, served the Spirit well, walking in holiness and purity, and in no way defiling the spirit (V, 5). The fleshly nature lived a good life, with purity, toiling with the Spirit and working with it in every deed, behaving with power and bravery, and so (the Lord) chose it as a companion with the Holy Spirit; (God) took pleasure in the conduct of this flesh because it was not defiled with this world while it was bearing the Holy Spirit (V, 6). He took his Son and the glorious angels as counsellors so that this fleshly nature also, having served the Spirit blamelessly, should have some dwelling place and not seem to have lost the reward (for its service; for all flesh) in which the Holy Spirit has dwelt (will receive its reward) if it be found undefiled and spotless (V, 7).

Here we get glimpses of the christology and the trinitarian faith of the great church, but the confusion is great and cannot completely be put right. Now the body, the *sarx*, appears in the place of the 'appointed servant'. This makes the adoptionist tone of the parable milder. The Holy Spirit 'which was there beforehand, which created all creation' is surely none other than the pre-existent Godhead which is elsewhere predicated of the Logos. Here the Shepherd of Hermas lapses into a terminological equivocation of the early church. It was customary to designate the Godhead quite simply as *pneuma* (cf. Rom. 1. 4), but also to use this for the person of the Holy Spirit. Just as in Johannine terminology (as we shall see), Christ could be described as Logos-sarx, so the other formula 'pneuma-sarx' could also take its place.[78]

The Shepherd of Hermas can find no way out of this terminological confusion. First of all it distinguishes Father and pneuma and the in-dwelling of the pneuma in the flesh, i.e. Christ (here we surely have the primitive Christian belief that Christ is God incarnate). But then occurs the other line of tradition, that the pre-existent Son, the mediator of the Father at the creation of the world (*Sim.* IX, 12, 2!) and his revealer (ibid., 3!) has entered the world (see (*a*) above). Remarkably enough, the Shepherd of Hermas no longer speaks of the incarnation in this context. So the incoherence of the ideas remains. We have, moreover, seen that the confusion is heightened by a third factor: an angel-christology in addition to the Son- and Spirit- christologies. Of the christology of the Shepherd of Hermas, we may say that it is a reflection of the christology of the church, not clearly understood, and not a creation of the Shepherd of Hermas itself. In any case it found no appreciation in later years: attention

---

[78] On the pneuma-sarx formula see below on Ignatius, esp. p. 88, n. 183; Melito of Sardis; F. Loofs, *Theophilus*, 101–210. 2 Clem. 9. 5 (ed. Bihlmeyer, 75) is typical. A variant text has Logos instead of pneuma. Here we see the orthodox use of this formula. Like the Shepherd of Hermas, the Acts of Paul also succumb to the equivocation. Cf. L. Vouvaux, *Les Actes de Paul et ses lettres apocryphes*, Paris 1913, 72–6. There are also misunderstandings in Ps.-Cyprian, *De montibus* 4 (ed. Hartel, app. 108[17ff]) and in Victorinus of Pettau (cf. ZNW 36, 1937, 38–41). See now J. P. Martin, *El Espiritu Santo en los origenes del cristianismo. Estudio sobre I Clemente, Ignacio, II Clemente y Justino Martir*, Zürich 1971; M. Simonetti, 'Note di cristologia pneumatica', *Aug* 12, 1972, 201–32. Simonetti produces further evidence going beyond that in Martin.

was paid only to its most original teaching, on morals and on repentance. The christology was not found interesting in itself. This is in accordance with the assessment which has been made of it.

In the Epistle of Barnabas we have a witness from groups of common people in Alexandria.[79] Its teaching is simpler and less rich than that of the other writings which are numbered among the Apostolic Fathers. 'Barnabas' fights against the Jews, perhaps because of the danger of a restoration of the city of Jerusalem and the temple. The Old Testament is made relative, even devalued. In the first part of the letter (chs. 1–17) the whole light of the promises is concentrated on Christ, the only Son of the Father, to prove his Godhead and his absolute transcendence. Speculations on the mysteries are alien to the writer (6. 5). Nevertheless, we find in his work—on Alexandrian soil—the significant distinction between simple faith and complete knowledge, *gnosis*. The believers are to be led to the *teleia gnosis* (1. 5), to the art of the allegorical interpretation of scripture (13. 7). God has indeed revealed himself in the incarnation, but at the same time he has also concealed himself. For our eyes, incapable of looking upon him as God, now see him clothed in the flesh (5. 10). This, then, is one significance of the incarnation—the second leads towards the redemption. Christ willed to die in order that he might destroy death and show forth the resurrection from the dead (5. 6). A remarkable word appears in this context—for the only time between Paul and Irenaeus: ἵνα τὸ τέλειον τῶν ἁμαρτιῶν ἀνακεφαλαιώσῃ . . . Now the 'Son of God came in the flesh for this reason, that he might recapitulate (complete, fulfil) the total of the sins of those who persecuted his prophets to death' (5. 11). For the whole of three chapters the letter again and again leads up to the question of the significance of the incarnation, but without solving it (5–7). The incarnate one is the Son of God who is not just Son of God through the incarnation but is already Son of God before his advent in the flesh, indeed, before the creation of the world (6. 12). Perhaps the epithet 'the Logos' in 6. 17 applies to him. Again and again 'Barnabas' speaks of this Son of God (5. 9; 5. 11; 6. 12; 7. 2; 7. 9; 12. 8, 10; 15. 5). It is not clear whether the Son is also given the title 'God' (21. 5?). In any case, Christ is the *Kyrios*, the Lord of the whole world (5. 5), and has a divine nature. For the body is the 'vessel of the spirit' (7. 3 and 11. 9), an expression which, despite all its ambiguity in the time when it was written, is here to be understood of the divine nature. For the body, as the vessel, and the spirit are sharply contrasted. Only in stressing such an opposition is there any point in speaking of an 'appearing in the flesh' (5. 6; 6. 7, 9, 14; 12. 10)

---

[79] *Epist. Barnabae*, shortly before 130–1. Cf. H. Veil, in Hennecke, *Handbuch der ntl. Apokryphen*, 1904, 206–38; H. Windisch, *Der Barnabasbrief*, Tübingen 1920, 374ff. (on christology); J. Lebreton, *Trinité* II, 332–45; K. Wengst, *Tradition und Theologie des Barnabasbriefes* (Arbeiten zur Kirchengeschichte 42), Berlin 1971, 82–9 (on christology). Text: T. Klauser, *Doctrina duod. apost. Barn. epist.*, Floril. Patr. 1, Bonn 1940.

or of a 'coming in the flesh' (5. 10, 11). 'Barnabas' allows the tension in Christ, the *scandalum crucis*, to stand untouched. Godhead is predicated precisely of the suffering Christ, as the mystery of the cross leads Christians to regard the extent of the humiliation (5. 5). Thus in this writing the person of Christ occupies an absolutely central position. The letter is meant to be directed towards a comprehension in faith. Its sources and in particular the sources of its teaching on Christ and its attitude towards the old covenant lie in the Epistle to the Hebrews, to which it is akin in thought. In its evaluation of the Old Testament 'Barnabas' stands midway between the Epistle to the Hebrews and the Antitheses of Marcion.

With the so-called Second Epistle of Clement, a homily (17. 3; 19. 1), we are brought perhaps to Rome, to the environment of the Shepherd of Hermas, and see—in a very different light—the communal belief of the Roman church about 120–150.[80] The homily is of the synoptic, prophetic, late Jewish type. It is in every respect more facile than John and only in the first chapter does it attain 'the heights of a Johannine experience of Christ'.[81] The beginning of the homily already contains a clear recognition of the Godhead of Christ: 'Brethren, we must think of Jesus Christ as of God (ὡς περὶ θεοῦ), as of the judge of the living and of the dead; and we may not think little of our salvation. For if we think little of him we also hope to attain but little' (1. 1–2a). In 9. 5 there is one of the finest christological statements of the period: εἰ Χριστὸς ὁ Κύριος ὁ σώσας ἡμᾶς, ὢν μὲν τὸ πρῶτον πνεῦμα, ἐγένετο σάρξ . . . 'If Christ the Lord who saved us, who was first Spirit, became flesh and so called us, so also will we receive our reward in this flesh.' We are already familiar with 'Spirit' as an early Christian expression for the Godhead of Christ. As has already been said, a textual variant directly replaces this with the word Logos, of which the next words are also reminiscent. 'Spirit (= Logos)—man'; this is Christ. This union of God and man is the type and cause of our calling. In Christ God also becomes the Father of Christians (1. 4; 3. 1). In Christ appears God (12. 1; 17. 5) who has made us of nothing (1. 8) and has redeemed us. In 2 Clement we can see an already far-reaching christocentricity, particularly in the doctrine of redemption, which is more clearly apprehended and described than in Hermas. As the Gnostic scorn for the body and for the resurrection spreads wider, the mystery of the incarnation is the point which is put forward as the dogmatic foundation for the valuation of human nature. Christ, the divine pneuma being made man, becomes the pledge of our calling to the resurrection in the flesh. He is the reason for prizing the body as the temple of God, in the Christian and in

---

[80] So J. Lebreton, *Trinité* II, 388 (in spite of 7. 3), with Knopf, A. Puech, Harnack. For Corinth: Funk, Krüger, Altaner. For Alexandria: Harris, Streeter.
[81] W. v. Loewenich, *Johannesverständnis*, 7.

his neighbour (chs. 9 and 12, and often). Around Christ is built up the church, which is his body. Its nature is even understood in a way completely analogous to the twofold nature of Jesus Christ, as the homily, like Hermas, knows of a pre-existent church.

> Now I imagine that you are not ignorant that the living church is the body of Christ. For the scriptures say, 'God made man male and female.' The male is Christ, the female is the church. Moreover, the books and the Apostles say that the church is not of the present, but is from above (ἄνωθεν); for she was spiritual (πνευματική) as was also our Jesus; but (He) appeared at the end of days to save us. Now the spiritual church appeared in the flesh of Christ to show us that each of us who guards her in the flesh and does not corrupt her will receive her back in the Holy Spirit. For this flesh is an anti-type of the Spirit. No one therefore who has corrupted the anti-type shall receive the reality. This means, brethren, guard the flesh that you may receive the Spirit. Now if we say that the flesh is the church and the Spirit Christ, of course he who has abused the flesh has abused the church. Such a one will not receive the Spirit, which is Christ.[82]

Without realizing it, the preacher has here come very close to a Gnostic idea. For the idea of the pre-existent spiritual church, which preceded even the synagogue, is condensed by the Valentinians into the aeon of the Ecclesia.[83] The distinction 'the male is Christ, the female is the church' is reminiscent of the pair of aeons 'man–church' (ἄνθρωπος καὶ ἐκκλησία) among the Valentinian Gnostics. But the purpose of the homily is anti-gnostic. It deals with the value of the flesh through its relation to Spirit, church and Christ. In any case, here the preacher takes the divine element and the human element in Christ seriously and treats both as a type of our manhood and our calling, which comprises both flesh and spirit. 'Were we to press the words of this fiery speaker, we would have here already the whole order of recapitulation. The human body is symbolically likened to the church which becomes visible at the incarnation,' and which here, as in Hermas (*Mand.* XII, 4, 2), is regarded as the goal of creation. Irenaeus will carry through the line to Christ still more strongly.[84]

Popular writing and hence the popular picture of Christ in the early Christian period perhaps finds its most characteristic expression in the *Sibylline books*. The collection of these fourteen (twelve extant) books[85] represent a maze of voices of many centuries, of pagans, Jews and Christians, of orthodox and heretics, who speak through one another and against one another. The Christian parts of this work may quite justifiably be described as a mirror of the Christian thought of the second and early

---

[82] 2 Clem. 14. 2–4; ed. Funk, *Patres Apostolici* I, 1901, 200–2; see the excellent commentary by A. Orbe, *La uncion del Verbo. Estudios Valentinos*, Vol. III (AnalGreg. 113), Roma 1961, 14–20.

[83] Note the similarity with Pastor Herm., *Vis.* I, 1, 6; 3, 4; II, 4, 1. Cf. J. Krüger, *ZNW* 31, 1932, 204–5 (mythic-gnostic interpretation). The Platonism of 2 Clement is evident.

[84] E. Scharl, *Recapitulatio Mundi*, Freiburg 1941, 118–19.

[85] Text: J. Geffcken, GCS, 1902; also A. M. Kurfess, *Sibyllinische Weissagungen*, Urtext und Übersetzung, München 1951. A. Rzach, art. 'Sibyllin. Orakel', *PWK* 2. R. 5, 2103–83; A. Kurfess, *TQ* 117, 1936, 351–66; id., 'Christian Sibyllines' (with bibliogr.), *New Test. Apoc.* II, 703–44. Bard Thompson, 'Patristic Use of the Sibylline Oracles,' *Review of Religion* 116, 1952, 115–36 (not available to me).

third centuries. We hear the talk of ordinary Christians, which often
sounds clumsy, but still is often laden with deep anxieties and hopes. The
pressure of persecution and the consciousness of their inability to get
redress at law overburdens their hearts. In these verses they struggle to
justify their existence in the face of heathenism and are recognized and
slandered by the pagans as the perpetrators of such sayings.[86] With
deep-felt, Cassandra-like cries the Christians seek to preserve themselves
from the dangers of persecution and suppression by promising to the
Roman authorities the return of their powerful king and lord, the God
Jesus Christ, the judge of all beings. They place their Christian faith in the
mouth of the Sibyls of an earlier age, so as to produce the support of
antiquity for their teaching and thus vindicate their cult. Because even in
pre-Christian times acrostic verses were considered genuine and particularly safe against falsification because of their association with a sequence
of letters from the alphabet, the Christians began to construct acrostics of
this kind. These were, in fact, so successful that they were soon regarded
as genuine even among the Christians themselves. By the time of Lactantius and Constantine the Great, in whose speech *ad Coetum Sanctorum* the
great acrostic of Book VIII occurs and is given as the prophecy of the
Erythraean Sibyl, there is no longer any doubt about their authenticity.[87]
Augustine produces a translation—which does not stem from him—and
passes on to the Middle Ages his delight in these verses.[88] The Roman
emperor attached the death penalty to the reading of such books. But in
vain. The passionate struggle of the Christians of the time of the Apologists
kept making progress. Whereas the Jews gradually gave up the spiritual
battle against Rome, the Christians kept it up until their final victory. The
Sibylline books were, moreover, quoted eagerly by the Fathers (see n. 85
above).

The Christian poems in, or additions to, these books largely concern the
figure of Christ, his life and work, and his *parousia*. Book VIII, which in
its essentials (including the great acrostic) belongs to the second century,
is particularly important. A hymn is composed on the last judgement and
the second coming using as an acrostic the letters of the credal saying
IHCOYC XPEICTOC ΘEOY YIOC CⲰTHP CTAYPOC (vv. 217–50). If we
read the initial letters of this first acrostic by itself, the result is a second, the
well-known ICHTHYS. After the letters of the word ICHTHYS (fish) another
poet soon afterwards added vv. 244–50. These in their turn are followed by
a new, didactic, really un-Sibylline prophecy on the being of Christ (251–
323). His birth is then described in an imitation-pagan way in vv. 456–79,
a high point of the whole collection, after the pre-mundane existence of

---

[86] So Celsus in Origen, *Ctr. Cels.* VII, 53; V, 61.
[87] Lactant., *Div. Inst.* 4, 15, 26; Euseb., *Constant. Orat. ad sanct. coet.* 19, 1.
[88] Augustine, *De civ. Dei* XVIII, 23; A. M. Kurfess, *HistJb* 77, 1958, 328–38.

the Logos and his creative might have been celebrated (429–55). These verses contain the most important aspect of the 'Sibylline' christology, in so far as it belongs to the second or the early third century. The other christological parts (VI; VII, 64ff.) are less important here. The Christian additions to I derive from the middle of the third century.

The poet of the acrostic is concerned to paint an impressive picture of Christ as king and lord. 'From heaven will descend one who is future king to eternity, who is to judge all flesh and the whole world. Believing and unbelieving men will look upon God, Him, the Highest, with the saints at the end of time' (VIII, 218–21). 'All will come to the judgement-seat of God, the king' (242). The poet of the CTAYPOC acrostic has clothed his christological proclamation in an artificial verse-form. At the last judgement the cross will also be the seal and sign of believers, the longed-for horn (full of) grace, which pours out its blessings in baptism through the twelve apostles (VIII, 244ff.). Christ, 'the iron shepherd's crook, will rule' (VIII, 248, cf. Ps. 2. 9; Rev. 2. 27). Therefore the Roman rulers are to know that they will share the fate of those in Ps. 2 who make an uproar—this is evidently the thought which the poet has in mind. He summarizes the theme of his Sibylline saying once again: 'He who has now been made known through the acrostic is our God, the saviour, the immortal king, who has suffered on our behalf' (249f.). The oppressed Christian souls of that time found their comfort in the crucified one and the lowly earthly appearance of Christ. This is clear from the next verses, which are inspired by scripture. For Moses already foretold the crucified one 'when he stretched out his holy arms and conquered Amalek in faith'. For so too will Christ, by the stretching out of his hands upon the cross, be accepted by the Father, the rod of David and the promised stone (Isa. 11. 1; 8. 14; 28. 16).[89] Laden with the cross he stands before these Christians: 'For he will come into the creation not in glory, but like a man, wretched, dishonoured, unsightly, to give to the wretched hope' (VIII, 256f.). This is the Christ of the period of persecution.[90]

But it is only one aspect of Christ. This man of poor appearance is the hope of the oppressed because he has a hidden being within himself, he is 'the counsellor of the Almighty', the type of created man (VIII, 264f.). He already is before all creation, but is entrusted by the Father with the care of the men created by them both. Here, of course, the relationship of the 'Son' to the Logos is not obvious. It seems as if the Logos were some-

[89] On the favourite and frequent motif of the 'Stretching out of the hands' see A. Grillmeier, Der Logos am Kreuz, München 1956, 67–80, and E. Stommel, 'Σημεῖον ἐκπετάσεως (Didache 16, 6)', RömQ 48, 1953, 21–42.

[90] On this idea of the 'unsightly and hateful Christ' cf. A. Grillmeier, op. cit., 42–7; H. W. Wolff, Jesaja 53 im Urchristentum, Berlin 1952. This idea would also be prompted by anti-docetic and anti-Gnostic tendencies. It contrasts with the idea of the 'fair Christ'. Cf. A. Grillmeier, op. cit., 47–9. In all this we have a popular, pictorial idea of Christ, which was of course also utilized for theological purposes.

one else alongside the Son: 'Now will I with my hands[91] and you with the Logos care for our form (i.e. the man formed by God). . . . Now mindful of this decree will he come into creation, bearing an image of the same likeness in the Holy Virgin' (VIII, 267ff.). But in what follows the Son and the Logos and the incarnate one are one and the same: 'For he himself is all hearing, sense and Logos, whom all obeys' (284), he who walks visibly among men, so visibly that 'the reprobate and unbelievers strike "God" on the back with impious hands and spit upon him venomously from loathsome mouths' (288). Whatever happens to the man Jesus happens to the Son of God. The poet sees quite clearly 'who he is and whose son, whence he came to speak to the dead' (293). Come down from heaven, descended into hell, spanning the whole world with his outstretched hands (302), he can also rise again 'in the flesh, as he was before, and will show on hands and feet the four marks which have been branded on his members, east and west, south and north; for so many kingdoms of the world will complete the godless, shameful act on our image' (319ff.). In short, the suffering Christ as the Son of God who embraces the whole world, the creator, redeemer and judge of men, will make even the Roman authorities tremble.

With Christ, the church too will come triumphantly out of persecution:

Rejoice, holy daughter of Sion, who hast endured much (suffering); thy king himself comes on a gentle colt, to take away the yoke, the yoke of slavery so hard to bear, from our necks, and to free us from impious ordinances and powerful fetters. Recognize him as thy God, the Son of God. Praise him, cherish him in thy heart, love him with all thy soul and bear his name. Lay aside the former (gods) and wash thyself with his blood; for he will be reconciled not with thy songs, nor through entreaties, nor does he heed the transitory sacrifice, unchanging as he is. But if a prudent mouth lets the song of praise sound forth it recognizes who he is and then wilt thou see the Creator (324–36).

Book VIII again sets out to describe the Godhead and manhood in Christ, his double nature. 'For he is the Logos, who counselled thy heart[92] before all creation, the maker of man and the creator of life' (439). In a way rare for the 'Sibyl', the divine acts in the incarnation are described with great solemnity: 'But in the last times he (the Logos) went down to earth and appeared small and emerged from the womb of the Virgin Mary as a new light, and, coming from heaven, he assumed human form' (456ff.). The message of the angel is depicted as though by the Minne-singers (459–69) and the conception is described in a very profound way: 'The Word flew into her body, gradually became flesh and, gaining life

---

[91] 'The hands of the Father' are the Logos and Spirit as mediators of creation, in Irenaeus, *Adv. Haer.* IV, 20, 1; IV, Preface 4; V, 5, 1; see A. Orbe, *Greg* 43, 1962, 451–6.
[92] The Logos and the heart of the Father was a favourite conjunction particularly about the turn of the second and third centuries: *Od. Sol.* 41, 10: 'For his abundance has begotten me and the thought of his heart.' Tertull., *Adv. Prax.* 7: *proprie de vulva cordis ipsius.* Hippol., *Comm. on Song of Songs* 2, 4; 13.

in a mother's womb, gave itself human form[93] and became a boy through being born of a virgin; among men this is indeed a great miracle, but nothing is a great miracle for God the Father and God the Son' (469–73). Through God's ordinance and choice Bethlehem was 'named the home of the Logos' (478). The poet has probably been stimulated in many ways by the apocryphal writings and describes the birth (γοναί) of his God Jesus Christ in a Hellenistic way. But such influences are completely subordinate to the faith of the great church, which says, 'The Word was made flesh and dwelt among us, in Bethlehem.' The Christian interpolator of the otherwise Jewish book I (II), who probably writes about AD 150, produces a formula of the Logos christology which is not far distant from the title Theotokos, Mother of God, which emerged about the middle of the third century. He speaks of the 'young maiden' who 'will bear the Logos of the Highest God' (323a). Of Book VI, with its Gnostic-inspired hymn to Christ (1–28), which describes the incarnation, the work and the suffering of Christ, only the conclusion need be mentioned. This is a glorification of the wood of the cross: 'O blessed tree, on which God was hung! No longer will the earth contain thee, but thou wilt look upon the house of Heaven. . . .' Here again there is a clear formulation of the *communicatio idiomatum* such as became frequent about this time: 'O blessed tree, on which God was hung!' (26).[94]

So from these heterogeneous poems of the Sibylline Oracles we are faced with authentic and inauthentic matter. Nevertheless, the Sibyllines formed their characteristic, even powerful picture of Christ. The persecuted Christians found considerable comfort in it. Book VIII in particular is a valuable book of devotion from the second century and a witness of a living faith in Christ already deeply rooted in the people. The poets know scripture and tradition well and have done well in adapting the pictorial theology, the knowledge of the christological symbols of the second century.[95] The figure of Christ has been created from a living grasp of the times. Many verses already proclaim a better future for the beliefs for which they fight. In Book XII (28–34), the poet or interpolator of the third century already guesses at a different relationship between Christendom and Rome: 'But when the star (the star of the Magi) appears from heaven at midday shining like the sun, then the Word of the Most High will come secretly, bearing flesh like to the mortal; yet with him will grow the might of Rome and the illustrious Latins.' Why then are the Christians

---

[93] For the Logos as creator of his own humanity see: Justin, *Apol.* 23, 32; *Dialog.*, c. 105; *Epist. Apost. Copt.* VII, 10; Tertull., *Adv. Prax.* 26; Clem. Al., *Exc. ex Theod.* 60; *Strom.* V, 3, 16, 5. Similarly, but with typical Gnostic illustrations, cf. Hippol., *Elench.* VI, 35, 3–4; 35, 7. Cf. Barbel, *Christos Angelos*, 241–7.

[94] See the paraphrase in Andrew of Crete, PG 97, 1033. See n. 89 above.

[95] The christological characteristics of the early period of the church are especially reflected in its love for pictorial symbols. See my detailed description in *Der Logos am Kreuz*, München 1956, 33–66; also the theological symbolism of the sign of the cross: ibid., 67–96.

suspect as enemies of state? This is the question of this 'Apologist', who perhaps already envisages a Christian empire.[96]

(c) Myth, legend and belief: the popular theology of the mysteries of the life of Jesus

There was an extraordinary interest in the life of Jesus in the period of the apocryphal writings.[97] This is no historical interest, like that of the 'Quest of the Historical Jesus' in the nineteenth century. Quite the opposite. There is no trace whatsoever of historizing. Myth and legend and faith in an objective reality stand side by side. But all is subordinate to a theological expression, albeit an expression in a popular form. Orthodoxy and heresy alike declare their interest in this form of elaborating the life of Jesus. Today we too have discovered that mythical forms of expression can have their own theological content.[98] Even orthodoxy need not therefore renounce mythical and legendary statements. It can express a great deal by means of them. But the bounds within which myth, legend and saga may be accepted must be drawn very carefully and in accordance with the inner meaning of Christian reality. Demythologization may not be extended to the point at which it does away with any of the substance of Christianity. If it does this, it has a deadly effect. Such would be the case if the appearing of God in our world, the incursion of the transcendent into our realm and the presence of the eternal in our time were on *a priori* grounds interpreted as myth, without objective reality. It is well known that Bultmann makes the primitive Christian proclamation so dependent upon the old two-storied view of the universe ('above' and 'below') that any objective saving presence of God in our history and any objective reality of salvation is dissolved along with the modern dissolution of this view of the universe.

Mythology is the use of imagery to express the other worldly in terms of this world and the divine in terms of human life, the other side in terms of this side. For instance, divine transcendence is expressed as spatial distance. It is a mode of expression which makes it easy to understand the cultus as an action in which material means are used to convey immaterial power.[99]

Were this the case, then the whole of the Christ-event as understood by the Bible and the early church would be 'myth', and would only have validity for us in so far as it could be reinterpreted as an existential self-understanding before God in Christ. For Christ is the presence of God in our world and in our history. Now Bultmann evidently presupposes a

---

[96] Cf. A. M. Kurfess, *ZRelGG* 7, 1955, 270-2. 6 Esdras is a similar book of devotion for the period of early Christian persecution (second-third century), but has nothing relevant for christology.

[97] Cf. W. Bauer, *Das Leben Jesu im Zeitalter der neutestamentlichen Apokryphen*, Tübingen 1909.

[98] Cf. W. Stählin, *Symbolon. Vom gleichnishaften Denken*, Stuttgart 1958, 40-53 (mythological thought in Holy Scripture).

[99] R. Bultmann in *Kerygma and Myth*, London 1953, 10, n. 2. Cf. *Kerygma und Mythos* II, 180, n. 2.

Gnostic-mythical concept of incarnation and not the spiritual, refined understanding which became more and more clear in the course of the discussion of christological dogma. The Gnostic redeemer-figure is a mythical figure in so far as a pre-existent being traverses the spheres in a real, physical way, is present in the lower world and again vanishes from it after fulfilling his task (see (d) below).

The incarnation as understood by Christians presupposes no physical journeyings of the pre-existent one, but the acceptance of a human existence in the world by God's Word of power. It presupposes no two-storied view of the universe, but simply the two entities God and the world. God acts no differently in the incarnation from the way in which he acted at creation. He is concerned with his world as he always has been. But *this* act of creation results in a new relationship between God and the world. From the creation God appropriates for his eternal Logos a human existence in the world, through a human birth, but without the necessary consequence of a physical descent of the Logos *qua* Logos. Bultmann rightly demands that the transcendence of God be not violated. But it was precisely the significance of the discussions over the incarnation with Arianism, Apollinarianism and Monophysitism that they made it clear how a true unity of God and man could be achieved without the violation of this divine transcendence and without the physical journeying of the pre-existent one into this world. In the face of docetism and Gnosticism the church insisted on a real presence of the incarnate God in the world and thus on an objective history of the acts of God which cannot be allowed to dissolve into merely an existential self-understanding. The church's concept of incarnation is the personal, objective unity of God and man in Christ and is here already demythologized when compared with the Gnostic conception of the descent of a redeemer. True, even Scripture speaks in a way of the descent and ascent of the redeemer (John 3. 13; 6. 41; Eph. 4. 9). It was, however, the aim of the orthodox christology to interpret these statements in an ungnostic way.

Now the literature of the early Christian period shows us that a mythical understanding of the incarnation gained a footing in the same way as the legends which adorned and expanded the gospel narratives about Jesus of Nazareth. It will be our task to extract the genuine nucleus from early Christian myth and apocryphal legends. We are therefore not concerned to compile all the individual details which the apocryphal age added to the life of Jesus.[100] Our interest is in the theological expression.

The *conception and birth of Jesus* from Mary are the first mysteries of the life of Jesus.[101] According to the scriptural understanding, the virgin

---

[100] This is done in W. Bauer, *Das Leben Jesu im Zeitalter der neutestamentlichen Apokryphen*, Tübingen 1909; he summarizes the most important points in E. Hennecke, *Ntl. Apokryphen* 1924, 75ff.
[101] Cf. W. Bauer, *Das Leben Jesu*, 29–87.

conception means that God appoints the beginning of the messianic life of Jesus and prepares the salvation of men in Jesus, the Messiah, the Son of the Most Highest (Luke 1. 26–38). The narrative is theocentric and christocentric and looks towards a Messiah and a theology of salvation. In the Protevangelium of James emphasis is on the virginity of Mary.[102] The annunciation itself falls into two scenes: Mary goes to the well. There she hears a voice, 'Hail, thou that art highly favoured (the Lord is with thee, blessed art thou) among women' (Luke 1. 28 and 42). It is only in the house, to which Mary has rushed trembling to pray, that the angel appears in visible form. His message is already framed in more theological terms than that in Luke, Συλλήμψῃ ἐκ Λόγου αὐτοῦ (11. 2). The Logos is the power which effects the conception. Mary's question is formulated in such a way that the real aim of the Protevangelium emerges clearly, a defence of the virginity of Mary: 'Shall I conceive of the Lord, the living God (and bear) as every woman bears (ibid.)?' To put this virginity above all suspicion, great emphasis is placed on the physical separation of Joseph and Mary. When on Joseph's return Joseph makes the discovery described in Matt. 1. 18ff., manifest evidence of the innocence of the two must be produced. Both are given a cup with the 'water of the conviction of the Lord' (Num. 5. 11–31), and the decision from heaven is awaited (16. 1; Ps.-Matt. XII). Ps.-James sends both into the hills, Ps.-Matt. has them compass the altar seven times. Finally their innocence is confirmed in the sight of all the people.[103]

The birth of Jesus, like his conception, is also described as a miraculous event. According to the Ascension of Isaiah (11. 7–14), the Acts of Peter (24), II Enoch (an imitation of the Ascension of Isaiah) and the Odes of Solomon, stress is laid on the inviolateness of Mary, and the painlessness of the birth, which needs no human assistance. The Protevangelium of James describes all this vividly. Attempts are made to demonstrate the greatness of the new-born child by a whole series of miraculous events. Tertullian perceived in this a danger of docetism and therefore gave a very matter-of-fact and realistic picture of the birth of Jesus.[104]

We are led back to the messianic theology through the depicting of the wonderful star, which shines either at the birth of Jesus or at the coming of the Magi. Matt. 2. 2 and Num. 24. 17 (a star shall come forth out of Jacob) are the basis of this messianic feature.[105] Justin goes on to link these

---

[102] Protev. Iacobi, hereafter New Test. Apoc. I, 370–4 (Introduction), 374ff. (text). E. de Strycker, S.J., La forme la plus ancienne du Protévangile de Jacques (Subsidia hagiogr. 33), Bruxelles 1961, 147–67, 467–9.

[103] Cf. the description of the annunciation in Epist. Apost. (Coptic) VII, 6ff. (TU 43, 51f.); see New Test. Apoc. I, 198–9. The archangel Gabriel is the visible manifestation of the Logos, who speaks to Mary. The Logos himself forms his own body. In the Gnostic Pistis Sophia (ch. 8), in a similar way Christ himself appears in the form of the angel and 'thrusts' the divine power into Mary. For the theological question of the conception of Christ by the Logos see n. 93 above.

[104] Tertullian, Adv. Marcion. 4, 21; De carne Chr. 23.

[105] Ign., Eph. 19. 2–3; Protev. Iacobi 21, 2; Orac. Sibyll. XII, 30–3; Daniélou I, 239–47.

two passages with Zech. 6. 12 (LXX: *anatolē, oriens* is his name) or even with Isa. 11. 1.[106] For Origen, the star which appeared at the birth and was prophesied by Balaam becomes the symbol of deity.[107] Recourse was at one time made to Hellenistic astrology to explain the ring of stars in Ignatius (*Eph.* 19. 2),[108] but perhaps there are more Jewish ideas in it than appear at first sight. Perhaps, in fact, Gen. 37. 9, the dream of Joseph ('the sun and the moon and eleven stars were bowing down before me'), a passage which has been given a christological interpretation by Hippolytus, had some effect here.[109] Joseph saw Christ beforehand. According to Justin and Origen the Magi were subjects of evil powers. They served them by their magic and astrological practices.[110] But now Jesus in the guiding of the Magi by the star appears as the conqueror of the evil powers even before his birth.

Luke 2. 41–52 seemed to provide the justification for shaping stories of Jesus' *childhood*. Following Gnostic patterns, the Childhood Gospel of Thomas creates the picture of the precocious boy Jesus with his downright impertinent and dangerous use of his omnipotence.[111] Jesus as a moral figure is abandoned in favour of demonstrating this omnipotence. 'The acts of the apocryphal Jesus are destructive and, indeed, morally reprehensible. He places his power at the service of his greed for revenge and his impiousness, and if he feels slighted, spares neither health (ch. 3; 5. 2) nor life (ch. 4).'[112] The Gnostics manifestly strive to reveal Jesus quite simply as a Gnostic. He 'alone knew the unknown' (Iren., *Adv. Haer.* I, 20, 1). Of course, the majority of these Gnostics, like the Valentinians and Cerinthus, the Gnostics of Irenaeus (I, 30, 13 and 14), showed no interest in the childhood of Jesus. Christ as a man is superior to any human limitations. Others, like the heretic Justin and the *Pistis Sophia* (ch. 61), abundantly elaborated the childhood of Jesus with manifestations of his deity. Because for the adoptionists Jesus' acceptance as Son only took place at his baptism, they were, of course, unable to make use of his childhood. It is passed over, as the Gospel of the Ebionites shows.[113]

The *baptism of Jesus* by John is eminently significant for the interpretation of the mission, life and person of Jesus. The Jewish Christians as such and not merely the Ebionites seem to have been particularly interested in it. The events at the baptism are interpreted with the aid of mythological ideas. The descent of Jesus into the water is a *descensus* into the realm of

---

[106] Justin, *Dial.* 106, 4; 126, 1; *Apol.* 32, 12–13.
[107] Origen, *Hom. in Num.* 18, 4.
[108] So H. Schlier, *Religionsgeschichtliche Untersuchungen zu den Ignatiusbriefen*, Giessen 1929, 14–15.
[109] Hippolyt., *Bened. Is. et Iac.*, PO 27, 3; after Daniélou I, 220.
[110] Cf. I Enoch 8. 3; evil angels teach men magic arts: *Hom. Ps.-Clem.* VIII, 12–24; IX, 13–19.
[111] *New Test. Apoc.* I, 388–401.
[112] W. Bauer, *Leben Jesu*, 91.
[113] On *Theodot.* cf. Hippolyt., *Elenchus* VI, 35; for the view of the great church see Justin, *Apol.* I, 35; *Dial.* 88.

death and of the dragon, who is thereby destroyed. Thus the baptism of Jesus is connected with the descent into hell. It achieves the purification of the waters, which are ruled over by demons, and thus frees the baptized from their domination. At the same time, baptism by water is associated with baptism by fire (cf. Matt. 3. 11). It has a messianic-eschatological significance. According to Justin, the Jordan is on fire as Jesus ascends from it.[114] According to the Sibylline Oracles this occurrence means that Jesus escapes this fire of wrath for us and in the dove sees the God of grace coming to meet him. According to the *Excerpta ex Theodoto* (76, 1) there is a threefold soteriological parallel: the mystery of the Magi's star frees us from fate, the baptism from the fire of judgement and the passion of Jesus from suffering.[115] In addition, the baptism becomes the manifestation of Jesus, an interpretation which is permitted by the biblical scene and which is now developed in greater detail. As well as the appearance of the dove and the sound of the voice, a light shines out. The baptism of Jesus is made into a scene parallel to the transfiguration.[116]

Against the bright background of the baptismal theophany, the encounter of the Messiah with Satan, depicted by the gospels in the report of the *temptation* (Matt. 4. 1–11 par.), appears all the more gloomy. According to Matthew the tempter only appears after Christ has already fasted and prayed for forty days. Mark and Luke do not exclude the possibility that Satan already approached Jesus during this period (Luke 4. 2; Mark 1. 13). The Pseudo-Clementine homilies make the whole event a forty-day testing: 'Our Lord and Prophet, who sent us out, told us that the Evil One disputed (διαλεχθείς) with him for forty days.'[117] Origen too assumes a forty-day temptation.[118] The Gospel of the Hebrews completely mythologizes the event: 'Even so did my mother, the Holy Spirit, take me by one of my hairs and carry me away on to the great mountain Tabor.'[119] According to the *Excerpta ex Theodoto* (85), the wild beasts of Mark 1. 13 are made Satan's entourage. In Irenaeus, Clement of Alexandria, Origen and Ambrose, Satan is kept in ignorance of the true nature of Christ, in fact, through ambiguous answers given by Jesus himself.

---

[114] Justin, *Dial*, 88. 3. Even two MSS of the Old Latin Version know of the shining of a great light over the water. Cf. Huck–Lietzmann–Cross, *Synopsis of the First Three Gospels*, 13; also the Gospel of the Ebionites (4) and the Sibyllines (VI, 6; VII, 84). See W. Bauer, *Leben Jesu*, 132–9.

[115] Cf. Justin, *Dial*. 88, 2, 4; Daniélou I, 228.

[116] Daniélou I, 231, finds the connection between light and baptism, which also influences the naming of the baptized as 'enlightened' (Heb. 6. 4; 10. 32), reminiscent of the Jewish–Christian linking of the baptism of Christ and the feast of Tabernacles (cf. John 7. 1–10, 21); J. Daniélou, 'Les Quatre-Temps de septembre et la Fête des Tabernacles', *Maison Dieu* 46, 1956, 125–30. The way in which the initiation rite into Gnostic circles was fashioned in accordance with this is shown by F. J. Dölger, 'Die Sphragis als religiöse Brandmarkung im Einweihungsakt der gnostichen Karpokratianer', *Antike und Christentum* 1, 1929, 73–8.

[117] From the Clementine homilies XI, 35; XIX, 2; GCS 42, 171, 253.

[118] Origen, *Hom. XXIX in Luc.*: Lommatzsch 5, 194f.; see M. Steiner, *La Tentation de Jésus dasn l'interprétation patristique de saint Justin à Origène*, Paris 1962.

[119] *New Test. Apoc.* I, 164. Mount Tabor was also taken as the mountain of the temptation. Cf. W. Bauer, *Leben Jesu*, 146.

Because Satan had no right to discover the true being of Christ, such conduct could imply no imperfection in Christ, as the Acts of Thomas expressly emphasize: 'And the despot asked who and whence he was, but he did not declare the truth, for he (Satan) is a stranger to the truth' (ch. 143).

According to the biblical accounts of the *transfiguration* (Matt. 17. 1–8 par.) the scene is a messianic attestation of Jesus by God, the law (Moses) and the prophets (Elijah) in the presence of the future witnesses of the Word ('Hear ye him', Matt. 17. 5). Early Christian, Gnostic or Gnostic-inspired writings make speculations from it concerning the being of Jesus. The Acts of John are purely docetic in expression (ch. 90). The Acts of Thomas, worked over by the great church but not fully free of Gnosticism, which in the original text go back to the beginning of the third century, say that the form of Jesus was more than the disciples could apprehend. They looked merely at the form of lowliness, in faith they knew his majesty, but on the mountain could not perceive his 'heavenly type' with their eyes (ch. 143; AAA II, 2, p. 250). Ps.-Thomas assumes that on the mountain the essential Godhead of Christ was displayed. In the Acts of Peter, too, the so-called '*Actus Petri cum Simone*', Christ has two forms (*figura*), one in which the disciples can see him, each according to his capabilities, another in which they are unable to look upon him. 'Our Lord wished to let me see his majesty on the holy mountain, but when with the sons of Zebedee I saw the brightness of his light, I fell down as dead and closed my eyes and heard his voice in a way which I cannot describe.'[120]

The texts describing the transfiguration show that in early Christianity the question of the 'form' of Christ was put in an unhistorical way. No one thought perhaps to resort to the sources and accounts of the appearance of Jesus; they made their decisions on this from ideal standpoints: Christ wretched and unsightly—Christ shining and beautiful. Origen is the witness of a tradition which knew of a Christ in many forms, and even found this credible:

> Now this much was handed down to us about him: there were not just two ways in which he appeared (*duae formae*) (the one in which all saw him and the other after which he was transfigured on the mountain before his disciples, so that 'his countenance shone like the sun'); rather he appeared to men in so far as they deserved to see him (*sed etiam cuique apparebat secundum quod fuerat dignus*), (as the Jews in the wilderness found that the manna suited every taste) . . . For myself, I find no difficulty in believing the tradition (*traditio*), whether I interpret it of Jesus in the body, showing himself to men in different ways, or whether I understand it of the nature of the Logos, which is not revealed to everyone in the same way.[121]

The gospels make the scene on Mount Tabor an isolated event, which has no effect on the earthliness of the appearance of Jesus. The mode of

120 Cf. W. Bauer, *Leben Jesu*, 153; 2 Pet. 1. 16b–18.
121 Origen, *In Matt. comment. ser.* 100; GCS XI, 2, 218–9.

existence in lowliness is a law which stands over the life of Jesus right up until his death (Luke 24. 26, 46; 1 Pet. 1. 11), even though at the same time there are hints at the resurrection and his glorification. Where Gnostic and docetic tendencies are in play, the firm framework of the historical life of Jesus is loosened. Even in his earthly life, the figure of Jesus no longer stands firmly upon the earth. Thus in the early Christian period we find visions of Christ in numerous forms.[122] According to Origen it is naturally quite understandable that from a spiritual point of view Christ is a 'plurality'. It is clear to him from the transfiguration and from the fact that only three disciples could witness it 'that with regard to the actual seeing he did not show himself in the same way to all who saw him but showed them only what they could comprehend'.[123] There was a difference in the eyes with which Jesus could be perceived 'and this was a difference not just of the spirit, but also, as I believe, of the body'.[124]

The difference in the way in which Christ was seen lay not merely subjectively on the side of men, in their mind and in their perceptual abilities of body and soul, but also objectively, in an actual variation in the bodily appearance of Jesus. For Origen, the proof of this lies in the necessity of the kiss of Judas. The enemies of Jesus had to have a sign 'because of the way in which Jesus transformed himself' (propter trans-formationes eius). Through his lengthy association with Jesus, Judas had acquired such a knowledge that he knew the forms in which Jesus used to appear to his disciples (ut intelligeret transformationes eius, secundum quam suis apparere solebat).[125] This picture of Christ is far different from that of the synoptists. The historical Jesus appears to each 'in the form . . . which was appropriate to his ability and his state of salvation'.[126] The material body is by nature changeable, and the Logos can play what he will on his instrument. Now the 'traditiones' to which Origen refers are to be sought among the Gnostic groups. This is clear from the Acts of John. At the calling of the sons of Zebedee by Jesus the following conversation between James and John develops:

James: 'What would this child have that is upon the sea shore and called us?' John replies: 'What child?' And James says again: 'That which beckoneth to us.' John answers: 'Because of our long watch we have kept at sea, thou seest not aright, my brother James; but seest thou not the man that standeth there, comely and fair and of a cheerful counte-nance?' But James is unable to see him. Hardly have they reached land when another figure appears to them. John sees a bald-headed man with a thick, flowing beard, but James a 'youth whose beard was newly come'. The beloved disciple moreover now sees

---

[122] Cf. Past. Herm., Sim. IX, 2ff.; Martyrium Perpetuae et Felicitatis IV; the Acts of Thomas describe the (exalted) Christ as πολύμορφος: 48 and 153: AAA II, 2, 164, 262. Photius censures the abstruse visions of Christ in the Acts of the Apostles by Lucius Charinus: Bibliotheca cod. 114: PG 103, 389B.
[123] Origen, C. Celsum II, 64: GCS I, 185f.
[124] Ibid.: GCS I, 186¹⁶ᶠ.
[125] Origen, In Matt. comment. ser. 100: GCS XI, 2, 219.
[126] Origen, C. Celsum VI, 77: GCS II, 146.

'a small man and uncomely, and then again as one reaching unto heaven'. When he touches Jesus his body is sometimes immaterial and unreal, then again 'smooth and tender, and sometimes hard like unto stones'. Finally, the form of Jesus is quite unearthly, hovering free over the earth: 'And oftentimes when I walked with him, I desired to see the print of his foot, whether it appeared on the earth (for I saw him as it were lifting himself up from the earth). And I never saw it.'[127]

Relics of such 'traditions' also occur in the 'acts' of other apostles. Perhaps the Hellenistic–Egyptian Horus-speculations have some influence upon this idea of the varying form of Jesus. We are on the borders of the Christian tradition and in the sphere of an acute 'Hellenizing' of the figure of Christ.

According to I Cor I. 24 the 'son of God' who *suffered* and finally ended on the *cross* was to the Jews a stumbling-block and to the Greeks foolishness. Celsus and Julian the Apostate were not the only mockers at the crucified God. Can we blame those who were attacked in this way if they sought to retouch the image of the cross, to obviate the *scandalum crucis*? Christ sweating blood for fear and having to be strengthened by an angel (Luke 22. 43f.) was already found particularly objectionable and a number of biblical manuscripts in fact omit this 'shameful' event. Jesus might not be portrayed otherwise than in Matthew and Mark where, however bitter the struggle, he gains the victory through his own strength. How could Jesus still be above the angels if one of them had to give him aid? If the angel was to be left in as he was, then he would have to be given another significance. An old scholion thus alters the 'strengthen' into 'declare that he was strong'. Moreover, the angel's help had explicitly to be explained as unnecessary in a solemn doxology, 'for he did not need the might of the angel who is adored and glorified by all supernatural powers with fear and trembling'.[128] It was also felt permissible to sacrifice some of the verses in the Lucan account or at least to alter their meaning. Origen reports that the words 'my soul is troubled . . .' were interpreted by many as of the apostles. For the Lord had named them his 'heart'.[129] He himself tries to find a way out by referring to the phrasing 'he began' to tremble (*nihil amplius tristitiae et pavoris patiens, nisi principum tantum*).[130] Moreover, Christ, he says, suffered in his human nature and not in his divine power.

If even the *initia passionis* were weakened in this way, then the biblical picture of the *crucified one* was threatened all the more.[131] The writer of the Gospel of Peter is one of the typical exponents of a counterfeit theology of the cross which need not, however, be properly Gnostic. True, he has a

<hr />

[127] Acts of John 88–93: AAA II, 1, pp. 194–7. ET after M. R. James, *The Apocryphal New Testament*, Oxford 1953, 251–3. Cf. the polemic against such ideas in *Epist. Apost.* 11 (22).

[128] W. Bauer, *Das Leben Jesu*, 171.

[129] Origen, *De princ.* II, 8, 5: GCS V, 163.

[130] Origen, *Comment. in Matt. ser.* 90: GCS XI, 2, 206[29–30].

[131] The numerous smaller deviations from the interpretation of the passion given by the canonical gospels are listed in W. Bauer, *Das Leben Jesu*, 173–243. We indicate here only what is important for a christological understanding.

serious concern. As far as we can conclude from the remains of the work, it is the writer's purpose to defend the lordship (or the Godhead) of the suffering Christ against pagans and Jews and to awaken the conviction that despite the death on the cross our redemption is a divine work. But this seems possible to him only if he deletes and strikes out everything which in his view and in that of his opponents is a sign of weakness and excessive humanity. One revealing feature is that he veils his Christ in the majesty of sorrowful silence. 'And they brought two malefactors and crucified the Lord in the midst between them. But he held his peace, as if he felt no pain' (v. 10). All the words of Jesus are, in fact, omitted except for the final cry of dereliction, and this is altered: 'And the Lord called out and cried, "My power, O power, thou hast forsaken me!" And having said this he was taken up' (ἀνελήφθη, v. 19; *New Test. Apoc.* I, 184). According to the canonical gospels (Matt. 27. 46; Mark 15. 34) the cry of dereliction sounded like the cry of a helpless man against God, who now does not testify to his Messiah as on Mount Tabor, but abandons him to his enemies and to death. This appeal to God is now replaced by 'my power', the significance of which of course remains obscure (natural power of life? the power to work miracles? the divinity of Christ, which according to quite widespread ideas separated from the body at death?).[132] Here the superiority of Christ to suffering—while not volatilized in a Gnostic or docetic way—is stressed at the expense of the seriousness of the passion and death and its significance for our salvation. The gospel picture of the crucified Son of God (Mark 15. 39) and the suffering Messiah and redeemer has not become richer and deeper, but more feeble and superficial. There is a better balance elsewhere in the second century from Ignatius of Antioch to Melito of Sardis, leaving aside, of course, all forms of Gnosticism and docetism, which still lack proper expression. There is still no Gnosticism in the Gospel of Peter, but it already presages it. Even the *Epistula Apostolorum* (Copt. 24. 12) is better at preserving a proper mean than the apocryphon we have been discussing. The Testaments of the Twelve Patriarchs speak—almost in Ignatian language—of the 'suffering of the Most Highest' (II, 4). Thus they dare to stress both poles of the passion and of the incarnation in the interpretation of the second century: 'For God assumes a body and eats with men and he redeems them' (II, 6, 7). The Sibylline Oracles account the silence of Christ in suffering one of the features of his lowliness and concealment, not of his revelation: 'And when smitten upon his back he will keep silent, that none may see who and whose Son he is, whence he came to speak to the dead' (VIII, 292f.).[133]

---

[132] A. Grillmeier, 'Der Gottessohn im Totenreich', *ZkTh* 71, 1949, 1–53, 184–203.

[133] We here pass over the staurology, the interpretation of the cross as the symbol of redemption and also of the doctrine of two natures. Here there was a special field for Gnostic speculations on the

If the early Christian writers omit to give a deeper interpretation of the death of Christ and the circumstances of it, they largely fall into the same error in explaining *the descent of Christ into hell*. Now this is very closely connected with the resurrection and the ascension, particularly in Jewish Christianity.[134] We will begin there. The Old Testament and Judaism contributed to the concrete Christian picture of the descent of Christ into hell by their idea of the underworld and by traces of a general doctrine of a descent.[135] This religio-historical idea of the descent of a 'God' could not, however, have any influence because Yahweh, although Lord of the underworld, remained absolutely transcendent in relation to it. On the other hand, the idea of the resurrection of the flesh was particularly significant for the concept of the descent into hell. For now the eschatological, messianic hope was extended to the world of the dead. The Jewish Christians needed only to put the saving death of the Messiah into this framework, for which the Enoch literature is especially remarkable, to produce the idea of the descent into hell.

I Peter 3. 18–20; 4. 6 provides a typical Jewish-Christian idea of this occurrence.[136] We hear of a passing of Christ (πορευθείς). This passing need not be death as such, but it can presuppose death and also include the resurrection and the ascension. The one who descends to death and to Sheol (or who is already raised and now goes up to heaven) goes to a place where the spiritual powers or also the souls of men are lodged. This place can be either below (Sheol) or above. Peter describes what happens there with the word ἐκήρυξεν. This is to be understood as referring to a proclamation or a demonstration made by Christ before these powers or souls, a proclamation of the lordship of God which has now been extended over all powers and authorities by virtue of the death on the cross. In the light of the Enoch traditions we can describe this proclamation as a preaching in Hades. It is directed to the spirits (souls) of the time of the flood as types of paganism and as patterns of the Christian confession. Christ fulfilled it 'in the spirit', i.e. as a messianic work. If we take this journey to hell as a confrontation of the risen and ascending one with the spiritual powers which inhabit the spheres, it is also easy to understand a Jewish–Christian interpretation of the journey to hell which sees Christ descend 'in the body'.[137]

The teaching on the descent in the early Christian period remains in this soteriological framework delineated by I Peter, but refers the journey to

cross. Cf. Daniélou I, 265–92, and further literature in A. Grillmeier, *Der Logos am Kreuz*, München 1956, 67–96.

[134] On the *descensus* see A. Grillmeier, art. 'Höllenabstieg', *LThK* V, 1960, 450–55, with bibliography; H. J. Schulz, 'Die "Höllenfahrt" als "Anastasis" ', *ZkTh* 81, 1959, 1–66.

[135] Cf. Isa. 14. 9–15; Exod. 32. 17–32; Isa. 45. 2 with Ps. 107. 16; 2 Sam. 22. 5ff.; Deut. 32. 39.

[136] So E. Schweizer, *TZ* 8, 1952, 154.

[137] It occurs only in a few texts, such as Ephraem, *Sermo de Domino nostro*, and in the Arabian parallels of the Mystagogia of the Testamentum Domini, *Didascalia arabica*, ed. F. X. Funk.

hell simply to the underworld. The individual themes of the descent are richly elaborated in three ways: Christ is at work in the underworld: (1) in preaching salvation (preaching theme),[138] the oldest theme known to us; (2) in administering baptism to the righteous (of the old covenant) (baptism theme);[139] and (3) in the complete subjugation of hell and the ruler of the underworld (battle theme).[140] In the first two themes it becomes clear that salvation is held attainable only through faith and the sacrament of baptism. The righteous of the old covenant are not to be excluded from the salvation of Christ. Hence the saving message is preached in Sheol and baptism is administered. In this way the doctrine of the descent of Christ becomes an expression of the universality of the mission of Christ which also reaches back right to the beginning of the human race. Here we have a theology of history, however primitively it may be expressed.

One principal element of the work of Christ is his victory over the powers of the underworld who are depicted in three figures, Hades, Death and Satan. Here there was an opportunity for richly developed myth and dramatization, which perhaps reaches its climax in the Gospel of Nicodemus.[141] In Hippolytus' *anaphora*, which dates from about 218, we have an example of the incorporation of this soteriological doctrine of the descent into the liturgy. Nothing was more natural than an association of the eucharist (as the commemoration of the death of the Lord and the redemption achieved by him) with the recollection of the descent to the underworld:

> We render thanks unto thee, O God,
> through thy beloved child Jesus Christ . . .
> who is thy word inseparable . . .
> who when he was betrayed to voluntary suffering
> that he might abolish death
> and rend the bonds of the devil
> and tread down hell
> and enlighten the righteous,
> and establish the ordinance
> and demonstrate the resurrection,
> taking bread and giving thanks to thee, said. . . .[142]

With the progress of reflection on the being of Jesus Christ, the doctrine of the descent too was given a more narrowly christological orientation. It was asked what relation there was between the Godhead, the soul and the body of Christ at his death. The peculiarity of this phase of the doctrine

---

138 As well as 1 Pet. 3. 19 also Past. Herm., *Sim.* IX, 16, 5–7; Gospel of Peter 41; Sibylline Oracles VIII, 310–12; *Epist. Apost.* 27 (38); Iren., *Adv. Haer.* IV, 27, 2; Hippol., *Bened. Moys.* VII, νεκρῶν εὐαγγελιστής; Clem. Al., *Strom.* II, 9, 44, 1–2; VI, 6, 445–52; Origen, *Contr. Cels.* II, 43; *In Matt. serm.* 132.

139 Past. Herm., *Sim.* IX, 16, 3, 5; *Epist. Apost.* (Eth.) 27 (38); *Od. Sol.* 42, 20.

140 *Od. Sol.* 17, 9; 42, 11; *Test. Dan* 5, 11; Acts of Thomas 143; 32; 10. Melito of Sardis, *Hom. Pasch.* 68, 102. Cf. A. Grillmeier, 'Der Gottessohn im Totenreich', *ZkTh* 71, 1949, 1–23.

141 *Evang. Nicodemi* II, 4 (XX), 3, ed. Tischendorf 1876, 327.

142 G. Dix, *The Apostolic Tradition of St Hippolytus*, London 1937, 7f.

of the descent lay in the acceptance of the so-called 'descent of the Logos'. But this development belongs to the late third and early fourth century.

So in the view of the church in the early period, the sombre picture of Hades belongs closely with the bright images of the 'exaltation christology', which comprises the resurrection, the ascension and the session at the right hand of the Father. From the point of view of 1 Pet. 3. 19–20, the action of Christ, which is elsewhere described as a *descensus ad inferos*, is probably already taken up into his ascent. In any case, as a victory over Hades, Death and Satan, the *descensus* has an Easter character. But the connection between *descensus* and *doxa* is not always so close. The later phase of the *descensus* doctrine, which regards Christ as being in a state of the separation of (Godhead,) soul and body, and reflects on this, lets the thought of Easter sink into the background. It is the *descensus in triduo mortis*.

The exaltation christology has as its proper content the *resurrection, ascension* and *session at the right hand of God*. These Christ-events were originally closely connected. In the writings of Paul, resurrection and ascension are certainly a unity. The appearances of the risen one at the same time testify to his exaltation.[143] This unity also remains in a number of early Christian writings. The ascension expresses the theological content of the resurrection, at least as far as the event of the resurrection concerns Christ. The act of the raising of Christ has, of course, a special significance as a mighty act of the Father worked in Christ. The *doxa Christi* certainly only becomes fully visible in the ascension. The 'session at the right hand of the Father' is at first the consummation of the Easter glory. There is still a clear unity in the Gospel of Peter. Thus the angel at the tomb says to the women: 'Wherefore are ye come? Whom seek ye? Not him that was crucified? He is risen and gone . . . he is not here. For he is risen and is gone thither whence he was sent.'[144] Other early Christian writings, however, make a clearer distinction between resurrection and ascension, in a temporal respect too. The starting point is most likely the 'forty days' of the Acts of the Apostles.[145] Just as in the post-canonical period the accounts of the appearances of the risen one were expanded and the number of the witnesses of the resurrection was increased, so too the time of the stay of the risen one on earth was lengthened. The Ascension of Isaiah (9. 16), for example, puts it at 545 days. It is the Gnostics, however, who have the greatest interest in such lengthening of the time. They transfer to this period the impartation of their secret doctrines, which they cannot put in the mouth of the historical Jesus of the canonical gospels. They go up to twelve years, so as to substantiate the fullness of the

---

[143] Cf. Rom. 1. 4; 8. 34; Phil. 2. 9–11; 1 Thess. 1. 10; 1 Cor. 15. 4ff.; also Matt. 28. 18.

[144] *Evang. Pet.* 56; *New Test. Apoc.* I, 187.

[145] On the biblical relationship between resurrection and ascension see 'Himmelfahrt', *LThK* V, 1960.

revelations which they have been vouchsafed. The twelfth year brings the last and highest mysteries. As is well known, Clement of Alexandria and Origen have also been influenced by such views of the existence of a secret tradition.[146] But revelations of this kind are to be found most abundantly in the Coptic-Gnostic writings, the *Pistis Sophia*, the books of Jeu, the Gospel of Mary and the *Sophia Jesu Christi*. In these writings the biblical picture of Christ is fundamentally perverted. The risen one appears as a 'great magician, to whom all spirits and all worlds are subservient'.[147] Here myth has prevailed. The Christ event is made subordinate to cosmological preconceptions and is overlaid with Hellenistic ideas.

(d) Solvere Christum (*1 John 4. 3*): *on the christological heresies of the second century*

Christianity, with its message of Christ, the Son of God, well suited the contemporary religious longing for transcendent figures and in particular the Greek idea of 'sons of God', and therefore while it had to guard against misunderstanding it could also reckon on a certain prior understanding. In the original Jewish milieu of Christianity, however, everything spoke against such a teaching. The first contests over the new message therefore took place in the sphere of Judaism. Even in Jewish Christianity, because of its leanings towards Judaism, the idea of Jesus as Son of God was felt as a greater or lesser stumbling block. Hence the tendency to look on the transcendence of Christ exclusively in the light of the idea of the Messiah, thus placing Christ in the ranks of the prophets and the men specially endowed by God.

The Jewish–Christian circles usually included together under the name 'Ebionites' eventually succumbed to this temptation. The origin of the name has still not been fully explained. Several explanations were given in antiquity. They were called Ebionites, (a) because of the poverty of their intelligence; (b) because of the poverty of the law which they followed; (c) because of the poverty of the opinions they had of Christ; (d) because they were 'poor in understanding, hope, and deeds'.[148] Like the views held about the name 'Ebionites', opinions on the Ebionite writings differ widely. The attempt by H. J. Schoeps to prove the so-called *Kerygmata Petri* in the Pseudo-Clementines to be an Ebionite writing must be regarded as unsuccessful in view of the detailed analysis by G. Strecker.[149]

---

[146] Cf. Clem. Al., *Hypotyp.* 19; Euseb., HE II, 1, 4; Origen, *C. Cels.* V, 58.

[147] Cf. W. Bauer, *Leben Jesu*, 274. For the whole, ibid., 258–79.

[148] J. A. Fitzmyer, 'The Qumran Scrolls, the Ebionites and their Literature', in: K. Stendhal, *The Scrolls and the NT*, New York 1957 (208–31, reprinted, in slightly abridged form, from *TheolStud* 16, 1955, 335–72), 209. Fitzmyer holds it probable that 'the name "Ebionite" actually does mean "follower of Ebion" ' (op. cit., 210). H. J. Schoeps, *Theologie und Geschichte des Judenchristentums*, Tübingen 1949, 9 and Excursus II, differs.

[149] H. J. Schoeps, op. cit., 45–61. This view is taken over by J. A. Fitzmyer, J. Reuss, 'Ebioniten', *LThK* III, 1959, 633f. Against this G. Strecker, *Das Judenchristentum in den Pseudoklementinen*, Berlin 1958, 214–18. Strecker stresses that the Gnosticism and Hellenism of the *Kerygmata* excludes a direct

In fact, there are only the scant remnants of the so-called Gospel of the Ebionites[150] and, as secondary sources, the reports of the church Fathers.[151] There can be no doubt that the Ebionites to some extent recognize a transcendence of Jesus and do not simply regard him as a 'mere man'. For them, Christ is the 'elect of God' and above all the 'true prophet' (not, of course, priest), as Epiphanius (*Haer.* 30, 13, 7f.) testifies. But they delete the early history of Jesus, Matt. 1 and 2, from their gospel. They deny the virgin birth and also that Jesus is the Son of God, thus rejecting his pre-existence: 'They say that he (Christ) was not begotten of God the Father, but created as one of the archangels . . ., that he rules over the angels and all the creatures of the Almighty . . .' (frag. 6 in Vielhauer). The fact that at Christ's baptism the Holy Spirit descends upon him and enters into him and that the voice of the Father declares him to be the Son is not to be taken, as in the faith of the church, as an indication of the divine Sonship of Christ. Nor is it probable that we should think of an adoption as understood by classical adoptionism or even of a prophetic inspiration. We will probably be more correct in seeing here the Gnostic idea of the union of a heavenly being with the man Jesus, resulting in the Christ, the Son of God.[152] His mission is to do away with Jewish sacrifice (frag. 6) and thus to bring to an end the Old Testament priesthood. According to Hippolytus and Epiphanius, the Jesus of the Ebionites first earned the name Christ by fulfilling the law. For them, therefore, Jesus is no real way of salvation. Despite their New Testament framework they remain deeply rooted in Judaism. Epiphanius' further ascription of docetic tendencies and the denial of Christ's true manhood to them is surely the exaggeration of a heresiologist.[153]

We know little more about the first exponents of a proper adoptionist christology than about the Ebionites. Theodotus the Elder (the tanner) is

relationship with the primitive community. The early Christian ideal of poverty is no longer present. 'Nor does the author term himself an "Ebionite". This term degenerated in heresiological literature and the church historians to the title of a sect, so that it does not even appear to be applicable to the PsC, which in fact give no indication of a sectarian situation . . .' (op. cit., 215). J. L. Teicher's interpretation of the new Qumran texts as Ebionite writings has also found no support. Cf. J. A. Fitzmyer, op. cit.—K. Schubert, 'Die jüdischen und judenchristlichen Sekten im Lichte des Handschriftenfundes von 'En Feščha', *ZkTh* 74, 1952, 1–62, would assume a strong influence of the Zadokite sect on Jewish Christianity, which 'eventually . . . (with other factors) led to the splitting off of dissident Jewish Christianity, Ebionitism, from the church' (op. cit., 41). Thus K. Schubert, with H. J. Schoeps, assumes that the Ebionites are offshoots of the Essenes. Against this G. Strecker, op. cit., 216–18: 'The influence of the Essenes and the Zadokites on the picture of Jesus in the *Kerygmata* is improbable. Even the most elementary terminological presupposition, that Jesus is described as the "teacher of righteousness", is missing. Instead, the *Kerygmata* call Jesus the "true prophet" and the "Christ". The sect, on the other hand, does not give the Teacher of Righteousness this title, but independently of the fact that it believes in the future resurrection of its teacher . . ., awaits the Messiah . . .' (217). See now the important remarks of K. Rudolph, *Die Mandäer, I, Das Mandäerproblem* (FRLANT, NF 56), Göttingen 1960, 239–45, esp. 244, n. 3.

[150] Ed. P. Vielhauer in *New Test. Apoc.* I, 153–8.

[151] Passages in J. Reuss, op. cit. J. A. Fitzmyer, op. cit., 292f. (notes), gives a well-arranged analysis of the contents of these heresiological reports.

[152] So P. Vielhauer, *New Test. Apoc.* I, 155.

[153] See frag. 5, *New Test. Apoc.* I, 158.

the first of these. According to Epiphanius, he justified his apostasy from the Christian faith in Rome with the claim that in Jesus he had not denied God, but merely a man.[154] He seeks to demonstrate with passages from the Old and New Testaments that Christ was a 'mere man' (ψιλὸς ἄνθρωπος), who was, of course, specially gifted with the grace of God (GCS, Ep. II, 317–23). Theodotus the Younger (the money-changer), with his disciples, the Melchisedekians, puts Melchisedek, the mediator of the angels, above Christ, whom he claims to have been merely the mediator of men.[155] Artemon will renew such adoptionist tendencies in the third century. Nothing can be discovered about their origins. The presence of Judaistic influences in the background could perhaps be assumed from the Shepherd of Hermas. The concept of the Son of God and of the Holy Spirit which is developed in Sim. V, 5 is probably to be explained from them. The pneuma which God makes to dwell in the flesh of Jesus is regarded not as a divine person, but as a divine power, in some way analogous to the biblical sophia, with the result that a similarity has also been concluded between it and the Manual of Discipline (J. P. Audet). The 'Son of God' in Sim. V, 5 emerges as the servant chosen by God, in whom the spirit of God has dwelt and who because of his faithfulness is permitted to share in the privileges of the divine spirit. The themes of christologies of 'indwelling' and 'merit'[156] begin to make themselves felt. These words were later used as labels to denote heresy, although some of their basic concepts could have maintained their significance in the context of the whole of the church's picture of Christ and within the framework of belief in Christ as the true Son of God. We have already shown how the Shepherd of Hermas produces new nuances in Sim. VIII and IX. But it becomes clear in Sim. V that an absolutely closed Judaistic monotheism necessarily brings adoptionism in its train. We have reached the point where church teaching had to develop trinitarian and christological dogma side by side if it was to maintain the divine Sonship of Christ in the true sense. This connection first becomes fully clear in the third century, and at the same time the difficulties which accompany it are revealed.

Whereas adoptionism has more of a rationalistic basis, with docetism[157] we are transported into a completely different religious climate. It is the attempt to solve the problem of the incarnation and the suffering of the Son of God on a dualistic-spiritualistic basis. The humanity and suffering of Jesus become mere semblance. The name δοκηταί is not to be taken as the name of a definite sect. Serapion of Antioch (190–211) applies it to the

---

[154] Epiphan., Haer. 54. 1: GCS, Ep. II, 318[11].

[155] Ibid. 324–37: ZKG 66, 1954–55, 131.

[156] German 'Bewährungschristologie'. There is no exact English equivalent; it is the doctrine that Christ earned his exaltation to Sonship through his obedience and virtue (see below on Theodore of Mopsuestia and Nestorius).

[157] P. Weigandt, Der Doketismus im Urchristentum und in der theologischen Entwicklung des zweiten Jahrhunderts, Diss. Heidelberg 1961.

supporters of those who circulate the Gospel of Peter (Eusebius, HE VI, 12, 6). Clement of Alexandria accuses his δοκηταί of certain special teachings, without naming them (*Strom.* VII, 17, 108). Their head is the Encratite, Julius Cassian (*Strom.* III, 13, 91–4), whose doctrine Jerome expounds as real docetism (*Comment in Gal.* 6. 8: PL 26, 46). The *Philosophumena* (of Hippolytus) see in docetism a 'many-sided and fickle heresy', which loves Gnostic speculations about the aeons (VIII, 8–11; X, 16). In Theodoret, the name δοκίται includes Marcion, Valentinus, Manes and others (*Ep.* 82: PG 83, 1264). The false teachers of the Johannines (1 John 4. 2; 5. 6; 2 John 7) and those of Colossians and the Pastoral Epistles are not docetists in the strict sense. In other words, it cannot be demonstrated that they already denied the reality of Christ's flesh. Thus there was still no christological docetism in the narrower sense of the word. It was rather a matter of a false docetist doctrine in the wider sense, which is, however, none the less a real dissolving of Christ (*solvere*, according to the Vulgate and some textual witnesses who have the word λύει for the μὴ ὁμολογεῖ of 1 John 4. 3).

The theological character of the second and early third century was, however, in the end most deeply influenced by the encounters with early Christian Gnosticism.[158] This grew up like a twin brother alongside early Christianity, almost like Esau with Jacob.[159] In the account of the second century until now, we may have had the feeling that the Christian message contained merely a number of individual truths placed in simple juxtaposition, though, of course, these were ordered more and more

[158] Only the most important recent works are mentioned here. There are, of course, the well-known earlier works by W. Anz, W. Bousset, E. de Faye, H. Leisegang and the lexicon articles in *PWK*, *RGG*³, *LThK*²; L. G. Rylands, *The Beginnings of Gnostic Christianity*, London 1940; A. Festugière, *La révélation d'Hermès trismégiste*, 4 vols., Paris 1950–54 (for the pagan Hermetic Gnosis); G. Quispel, *Die Gnosis als Weltreligion*, Zürich 1951; H. Jonas, *Gnosis und spätantiker Geist*: I *Die mythologische Gnosis*; II, 1 *Von der Mythologie zur mystischen Philosophie* (FRLANT, NF 33 and 45), Göttingen 1954, Vol. I in 2nd edition; id., *The Gnostic Religion*, Boston 1958; H. Schlier, 'Das Denken der frühchristlichen Gnosis', in *Neutestamentliche Studien für Rudolf Bultmann*, BZNW 21, 1954, 1957², 67–82; id., 'Der Mensch im Gnostizismus', in *Anthropologie religieuse*, Numen, Supplement II, 1955, 60–76; A. Orbe, *Los primeros herejes ante la persecucion* (Estudios Valentinianos V), Roma 1956; R. McL. Wilson, *The Gnostic Problem*, London 1958; R. M. Grant, *Gnosticism and Early Christianity*, New York 1959; C. Colpe, *Die religionsgeschichtliche Schule. Darstellung und Kritik ihres Bildes vom gnostischen Erlösermythus* (FRLANT, NF 60), Göttingen 1961 (with bibliography); H.-M. Schenke, *Der Gott 'Mensch' in der Gnosis*, Göttingen 1962. On the finds at Nag Hammadi: J. Doresse, *Les livres secrets des gnostiques d'Egypte*, I–II, Paris 1958 and 1959; revised English edition, *The Secret Books of the Egyptian Gnostics*, London 1960; H.-M. Schenke, *Die Herkunft des sogenannten Evangelium Veritatis*, Berlin 1958, Göttingen 1959; Robert M. Grant–David N. Freedman, *The Secret Sayings of Jesus*, New York 1960; B. Gärtner, *The Theology of the Gospel of Thomas*, London 1961; W. C. van Unnik, *Evangelien aus dem Nilsand*, Frankfurt 1960; R. McL. Wilson, *Studies in the Gospel of Thomas*, London 1960; R. Roques, *Structures théologiques de la Gnose à Richard de Saint-Victor*, Paris 1962, 1–39. On the literature: H. Quecke, 'L'évangile de Thomas: État des recherches', in *La Venue du Messie* (Recherches Bibliques VI), Bruges–Paris 1962, 217–41; *Le origini dello gnosticismo. Colloquio di Messina 13–18 aprile 1966. Testi e discussioni pubblicati a cura di Ugo Bianchi* (Studies in the History of Religions XII), Leiden 1967. M. Simonetti, *Testi Gnostici Cristiani*, Bari 1970, gives an excellent introduction to Christian Gnosis (with texts).

[159] Cf. H. Schlier, 'Das Denken der frühchristlichen Gnosis', 81. He points to W. Bauer's *Orthodoxy and Heresy in Earliest Christianity*, London 1972, an important study in this respect, and to the special role played by Rome in combating heresy.

within the creed. Now, however, Christian theologians begin to feel the necessity of developing a general 'Christian' religious view. Christianity now becomes a *Weltanschauung*, i.e. a teaching which attempts to answer the great human questions, God, man and the world; the cosmos and history; death and the beyond; body, matter and spirit, on the basis of the Christian revelation. True, Gnosticism too was regarded more under a material viewpoint in earlier scholarship. For most scholars it was an accumulation 'of pseudo-mythological fantasies, an omnium–gatherum of rudimentary theories from all the principal religions, associated with doubtful cultic and moral practices'. Such a Gnosticism could 'not have embarrassed the faith and life of early Christianity. That could have been done only by an experience of approximately the same form and the same importance as Christianity and a thought which explained this experience'.[160] More recent scholarship has recognized that behind the 'material' of Gnostic doctrines and traditions, which were often no longer understood in their original sense, and behind the elaborate myth of redeeming Gnosis, there stood a new experience of God, man and the world which had not emerged in antiquity hitherto. This experience stirred the world of the time more and more, pagans and Christians alike. 'This thought was so intensive that it even produced a new, radical attitude and gave rise to new forms of life in which such thought and such an attitude could be realized. Only in this way does it become comprehensible how Gnosticism became a great danger to the church.'[161] Both these aspects of Gnosticism, the 'material' and the 'existential', are not, however, to be separated. Otherwise, by placing the essence of Gnosticism in this 'existential' element alone, we would arrive at a pan-Gnosticism. The Gnostic experience of the world and of man is based on Gnostic dualism as a specific religious doctrine and on Gnosis as a way of salvation. Within the one Gnostic experience different systems were possible: a pagan, a Jewish, a Jewish–Christian and a Christian Gnosticism.

The theologians of the church were concerned on the one hand to preserve the doctrine as handed down, but on the other hand to represent this doctrine as the true answer to the problems raised by Gnosticism. In so doing, however, they did not introduce any alien element into Christianity, but elucidated its innermost nature, that of being a religion of revelation and redemption.

It is not our present concern to give a detailed description of the matter of Gnostic christology.[162] We will merely show briefly how the christology

---

[160] Cf. H. Schlier, op. cit., 68.

[161] Ibid., 67f. In this connection Schlier notes the pioneering studies of H. Jonas (see n. 158 above) The still unfinished study by C. Colpe must also be mentioned. A good description of 'Gnosis' is to be found in W. C. van Unnik, *Evangelien aus dem Nilsand*, Frankfurt 1960, 32–8. See the excellent remarks of K. Rudolph, *Die Mandäer, I, Das Mandäerproblem* (FRLANT, NF 56), Göttingen 1960, 141–76.

[162] Cf. W. Völker, *Quellen zur Geschichte der christlichen Gnosis*, Tübingen 1932; R. McL. Wilson,

and soteriology of the church was also confronted by these vital questions as a result of the Gnostic problematic. It will not be misleading to represent Gnosticism primarily as a soteriological anthropology. Gnosticism is primarily concerned with man, a position that could also be shared by Christianity, but only with an important displacement of the focal point. In Gnosticism, man occupies the central position. Man's nature derives from the world above. This is the presupposition of all Gnostic systems. Recent scholarship has been able to make the enigmatical figure of the God 'Man' in Gnosticism clearer than it was previously.[163] According to the oldest and most valuable sources, the God 'Man' was originally the supreme God. He is the antitype of the 'Man' Adam and is therefore called the 'first man' in the *Apocryphon Johannis*. The background to this view is Gen. 1. 26f., which is expounded in accordance with the 'antitype-type' thought pattern. If man has been created in the image of God, it must follow that God is the first man. God and man, or rather the 'inner man', are of the same nature. As far as one can see, two variants of this doctrine of the God 'Man' are to be distinguished.[164] According to the first variant, God is the '*Urmensch*'. In his image there arises the earthly '*Urmensch*', the ancestor of the earthly man. On the earthly '*Urmensch*' is laid the image of the divine '*Urmensch*', which is the divine and essential element in the earthly man. According to the second variant (Poimandres, Zosimus, the Naassene sermon, 'The Essence of the Archons'), there are three '*Urmenschen*': God, the heavenly '*Urmensch*' and the ancestor of earthly man. There is in the earthly man a power of light which joins him with the world above. It consists in the second heavenly man, enclosed in the body, and formed after the image of the supreme God (the first *Urmensch*). H.-M. Schenke thinks that this doctrine of the God 'Man' in its two variants is a product of Jewish or Samaritan Gnosticism, whether in the pre-Christian or the Christian era. He rightly sees here a key to the solution of the whole problem of Gnosticism.[156] The origin of the Gnostic myth of the God 'Man' is, however, an allegorizing of the *imago* passage, Gen. 1. 26f., which was current in the writings of Philo and generally in the more or less orthodox Judaism of Philo's time.[166]

According to Philo, the Logos (also = Nous) is the likeness of God. The human *nous* is the likeness of this superior Nous. For Philo there is no difference between the Heavenly Man and the Logos (*Conf. Ling.* 146; II,

The Gnostic Problem, 211–28 (salvation, the redeemer). For the christology of the newly discovered Gnostic sources see H.-M. Schenke, op. cit., on the so-called *Evangelium Veritatis*; B. Gärtner, op. cit., 118–58, on the Gospel of Thomas, H. Quecke, art. cit., pp. 226f. Cf. Hippolytus, *Elenchus* V–VII: see below under Irenaeus.

163 On what follows we are indebted to the study by H.-M. Schenke, *Der Gott 'Mensch' in der Gnosis*; cf. J. Jervell, *Imago Dei: Gen.* 1. 26f. im *Spätjudentum, in der Gnosis und in den paulinischen Briefen* (FRLANT, NF 58), Göttingen 1960.

164 H.-M. Schenke, op. cit., pp. 65–8.

165 Ibid., 71.

166 Ibid., 120–43.

257, 1–5, where the Logos is entitled ὁ κατ' εἰκόνα (θεοῦ) ἄνθρωπος). According to him, Gen. 1. 27 speaks of the heavenly antitype of the earthly man and Gen. 2. 7 of the creation of the earthly man. The Logos is meant in Gen. 1. 27. He is a perfect, heavenly being, a heavenly man, who has been created as antitype, the idea of the earthly man. In the same way as this Logos, the heavenly Nous, is the antitype of the whole world, so too is it the antitype of the chief element in man, the human *nous*.

It is clear from this that anthropology can stand in the centre of the Gnostic system. It is, of course, incorporated in a concept of God and the world, to which theogony and cosmogony are to some extent conjoined.[167] The creation of the world is an indication of the incompetence or clumsiness or displeasure of God. Life in the body in the world is a permanent violation of God. But God is not overthrown. The divine element is hidden in man as a spark of the Father above,[168] as a spark of the divine self-consciousness, and must be redeemed. Man must free his own self, thrown into need and lust and almost overwhelmed, and so realize the original conception of God. In the encounter of Simon and Helena in the spiritual and the sexual sense, there is brought about a new encounter of the primal divine principles, Dynamis and Ennoia, which cannot be prevented by the powers hostile to God. Among the Simonians God comes to himself, through man, by means of a 'conscious' *libidinose vivere*, in Saturninus by means of asceticism and complete continence.[169] Both libertinism and encratism rest on the same understanding of the relationship between God and the world. Both are ways of redemption.

The conceptions of this redemption are, as is already clear with Simon and Saturninus, very different. The chief difference—if we survey the Gnostic systems briefly—lies in whether a redeemer figure (mythological) is considered necessary or not.[170] A first group needs no such redeemer figure: the Ophites in Origen's Celsus, the Nicolaitans, the Archontics and the Antitactae. The Hermetica also belong here. Among this group Gnosis, i.e. redeeming knowledge, is sufficient. For the revelation of this knowledge there is need only of a prophet, who can be called or sent in different ways. The opposite type knows a Gnostic redeemer, who descends, though only through the firmaments, into the realm of the powers, without reaching the earth (second type).[171] Between the two stands a third type: a redeemer walks on the earth, but only in a phantom

---

[167] Cf. the interpretation of Simonian Gnosticism in H. Schlier, *Das Denken der frühchristlichen Gnosis*. Also J. Frickel, *Die 'Apophasis Megale' in Hippolyt's Refutatio (VI 9–18): Eine Paraphrase zur Apophasis Simons* (OCA 182), Rom 1968. See Barbara Aland, *TheolPhil* 48, 1973, 410–8.

[168] H. Schlier, op. cit., 72, points to Hippolytus, *Elench.* VII, 28, 5ff.; Epiphan., *Pan. haer.* 23, 2².

[169] H. Schlier, op. cit., 79, n. 26, 75, on the encratism and libertinism of the Gnostics.

[170] On what follows see R. McL. Wilson, *The Gnostic Problem*, 211–28; C. Colpe, *Die religionsgeschichtliche Schule*, 194–208.

[171] Colpe, op. cit., 198; H. Schlier, *Christus und die Kirche im Epheserbrief*, Tübingen 1930, 18–26.

body. In Manichaeism (according to C. Colpe), all three types occur side by side, the first and second types in several expressions. The second type is most richly developed among the Mandaeans and the Valentinians, but with important differences. (The chief point is that in the Valentinian systems there were three Christs: 'the Christ produced by Nous and Aletheia with the Holy Spirit, the common fruit of the Pleroma, the consort of the exiled Sophia who is itself named the Holy Spirit . . .; and the third, born of Mary to better our creation.'[172]) The Christian-Gnostic systems in the narrower sense on the other hand develop the third type.

There is still debate in contemporary scholarship as to how the redeemer figure came into Gnosticism. One thesis runs that Gnosticism only took over this figure under Christian influence (G. Quispel, E. Schweizer, R. McL. Wilson). The counter-thesis runs that the redeemer figure does not derive from Christianity (H. Schlier, P. Vielhauer, C. Colpe). The first thesis finds support in the tremendous significance of Christ for Gnosticism. It should not, however, be overlooked that the redeemer can have other names (*The Hymn of the Pearl*) or that there are other redeemer-hypostases instead of or alongside Christ (Sophia redemption).[173]

As is well known, scholars of the history of religions have sought to sum up the Gnostic doctrine of redemption under the catchword 'the redeemed redeemer'. They have even spoken of the *dogma* of the 're-deemed redeemer'. This catchword is subjected to strict criticism by C. Colpe. While it does rough justice to a certain state of affairs, it is basically a modern interpretation, which does not occur in the sources. The real problem of redemption in Gnosticism is better dealt with in the categories brought together by H. Jonas.[174] One could at most speak of the *Salvator salvandus*, as Augustine (*C. Faustum* II) insinuates. In fact, the concern of Gnosticism is that a heavenly part, the spark of light, the Nous, embodied in man must again be made free from matter. Now this spark of light is identical in substance with the Nous or Logos, the redeemer of the world above, from which the soul has fallen. Each is separated from the other and must be reunited. This means the dissolution of the world and of man to a condition which corresponds with pre-existence, but makes a new cosmogony impossible.

Gnosticism is thus concerned with a physical redemption, which is, moreover, understood in a dualistic way, i.e. a sense hostile to the body and to matter. In Christianity, redemption is primarily a freeing from sin and its consequences. It includes the body along with the rest of the physical world. This redemption is built on the figure of the historical

---

[172] Hippolytus, *Elench.* VI, 36, 4; further examples from the sources in H.-M. Schenke, *Die Herkunft des sogenannten Evangelium Veritatis*, 24, n. 22.

[173] Cf. C. Colpe, *Die religionsgeschichtliche Schule*, 207. He means to clarify these questions further in the continuation of his work.

[174] Ibid., 174, 186–9; Hans Jonas, *Gnosis* I, 94–140; id., *Gnostic Religion*, 48–97.

Jesus, who is true man, and yet comes from God. Even though his coming into the world is understood under the image of a descent, this pictorial representation of the incarnation is not to be confused with the descent of the Gnostic redeemer. With the progress of theology, Christianity conceived its redeemer more and more by the exclusion of all images, and mythologies, but nevertheless continued to hold ever more strongly to the reality of the incarnation of God in Christ. This is achieved particularly in the christological councils. Gnosticism stems from the real experience of human existence—which is also immediately accessible to the Christian. To interpret this experience it takes refuge in mythical aetiologies and in magic, which are enriched partly with Christian, Jewish and other elements. In this it does not succeed in transcending the limits of a naturalistic doctrine of redemption. Thus Christianity differs from the Gnostic redeemer-myth in two ways:

1. On the basis of the biblical doctrine of creation it has a well-balanced relationship between the transcendence of God and the immanence of God. The one, ever-transcendent God remains in a constant relationship to the spiritual and material world that he has created. Only sin, not matter, means separation and falling away from this God. The fall is a historical and not a mythological event. And to overcome sin, God intervenes in the world in historical action with the aim of bringing the whole man (body and soul) and the whole world to God.

2. This action of God culminates in the incarnation of the Son of God, who by his moral obedience before God lays the foundation for the spiritual and physical restoration of man to God, which he already accomplishes in a figure in his own resurrection.

Gnosticism, then, has in common with Christianity its experience of man and the world and a longing for freedom from death, fate and sorrow, in short, for redemption. The peculiar element in Christianity, in contrast with Gnosticism, is, however, the clear historical founding of this experience on the sin of the spirit. Also peculiar to it is a consciousness of the act of redemption carried out by God in Christ which, while resting on a revelation, in the last resort rests on a spiritual and moral act of Christ. This act is rooted in the person of Christ and in his nature as the God-man. The interpretation of the person of Christ therefore increasingly becomes the central problem of the Christian doctrine of salvation.

The completion of this clarification of the Christian understanding of salvation in the face of Gnosticism, Judaism (the law) and paganism (the mysteries, magic) was, however, the task of the second and early third century, once Paul and John had already introduced the process.

(e) Martyrdom and apology

Our picture of belief in Christ in early Christianity would not be complete if we did not make reference to two special ways of bearing witness to Christ: martyrdom and apology. They arise out of the encounter of Christianity with paganism, its philosophy and anti-Christian polemic, and above all its conception of the state. In their juxtaposition, the testimony of blood and the testimony of the writings addressed to the pagans show the tension there is in the development of belief in Christ in this early period. With the Apologists, whose main representatives have still to be discussed, the question of the Hellenization of the picture of Christ becomes acute in a new way. As we have seen, this problem was already raised with the New Testament and the mere encounter of Christianity with Hellenistic culture. But with the Apologists, the attempt to press pagan philosophy into the service of Christianity begins to a special degree, an attempt which brought both positive and negative results. The whole of our investigation must concern itself with this question.

The dispute with paganism which was sealed in the witness of the Christian martyrs is of quite a different nature. Here there is no place for reflection or speculation, but only for simple witness, such as has encountered us time and again in the popular piety of the second century. It is, however, a witness which is consummated in action. We need not therefore attempt a description of the christology of the acts of the martyrs. We have already come across some christological motifs of the time of the martyrs in the Sibylline books: the spirit of discipleship of Christ, the breath of a passion-mysticism. The extant acts of the martyrs do, however, testify to something very important, which the liturgical sources of the early period, for example, could not tell us. Whereas in the liturgy prayers are offered above all to Christ, seen as mediator, and *through* Christ (*per Christum*) to the Father, the prayers of the Acts of the martyrs are to an astonishing extent addressed to Christ himself, whether they be praise, thanksgiving or intercession,[175] as indeed Pliny has already shown us (see n. 9 above). So prayer *to* Christ was made even before the Arian disputes. Precisely this practice reveals the 'tremendous christocentricity' of the Acts of the martyrs (and of their age). They show themselves to be 'almost drunk with a christocentric piety' (Baus). To worship Christ, the true man, as God, is the joy and comfort of the early Christian period.

2. THE TESTIMONY OF PASTORS AND TEACHERS OF THE CHURCH FROM CLEMENT OF ROME TO IRENAEUS

Hitherto we have been listening for most of the time to fairly wide sections of early Christianity or even to anonymous and apocryphal

[175] Cf. B. Fischer, *Die Psalmenfrömmigkeit der Märtyrerkirche*, Freiburg 1949; K. Baus, 'Das Gebet der Märtyrer', *TThZ* 62, 1953, 19–32; id., *Von der Urgemeinde zur frühchristlichen Grosskirche*, Freiburg–Basel–Wien 1962, 340–7; Baus here enlarges on the investigations of J. A. Jungmann, *Die Stellung Christi im liturgischen Gebet*, Münster 1925; photographic reprint with author's additions, 1962. On pp. 146–51, Jungmann asserts that the apocryphal acts of the apostles already know of prayer *to* Christ.

writings. Beyond these, there emerge individual writings, and above all individual figures, in whom the development of early belief in Christ is crystallized: Clement of Rome, Ignatius of Antioch, Justin, Melito of Sardis and Irenaeus.

(a) Clement of Rome

According to the testimony of Irenaeus (*Adv. Haer.* III, 3, 3), Clement o Rome handed on the apostolic teaching intact in his letter to the Christian community at Corinth. Nevertheless, personal characteristics are not lacking. Clement is restrained and averse to any speculation. There is, however, a clear Judaistic and Stoic tone to his letter.[176] He is very familiar with the Old Testament and therefore with the Old Testament picture of God the Creator. With pregnant sentences he describes the nature of the ordering of salvation established by the Father in Christ and the Spirit, and entrusted to the apostles (42. 1–3). His picture of Christ has probably been developed in particular along the lines of Paul (2 Cor. 8. 9; Phil. 2. 5–11) and the Epistle to the Hebrews (12. 2). 'The sceptre of the majesty of God, the Lord Jesus Christ, appeared not with pomp of pride or arrogance, though well he might, but in humility' (16. 2). *Kyrios*, Lord, is the proper name of Christ, just as 'God' and 'Ruler' are titles of the Father. The emphasis on the figure of Christ gives a New Testament colouring to the letter, which it might otherwise be found to lack (especially chs. 36 and 49). The pre-existent Son of God, the brightness of the Father, was sent into the world as man, and is the high priest of mankind and their way to blessedness (ch. 36). As such, he is exalted above all creatures, the king of the world, the giver of all divine gifts, light, knowledge and immortality. After his exaltation he is united with the Father in glory and receives divine honour.[177]

(b) Ignatius of Antioch

Ignatius of Antioch is one of the few early Christian authors who proclaimed faith in Christ in such a way that believers had to make this faith into a question about Christian existence. Once again we can hear Paul and John speaking. He detected the climate brought about for Christian preaching by the docetists and the emergence of Gnosticism. His message of Christ speaks of an objective reality and a historical, cosmic event, and yet at the same time it is a message of man and his salvation. 'The thought that dominates Ignatius' mind is not the striving for righteousness (as in Paul) but the longing for life; and in so far as this is so, he is more closely related to John than to Paul.'[178] Like Paul, Ignatius lives in

---

[176] Cf. G. Bardy, *RSR* 12, 1922, 73–85; L. Sanders, *L'hellénisme de Saint Clément de Rome et le Paulinisme*, Louvain 1943. Cf. I Clem. 19, 20, 28, 33.

[177] See the doxologies in 1 Clem. 32, 4; 38. 4; 43. 6; 58. 2; 61. 3; 65. 2.

[178] R. Bultmann, 'Ignatius and Paul', in *Existence and Faith*, ed. Schubert M. Ogden, London 1960, 271. See too W. v. Loewenich, *Johannesverständnis*, 25–38.

the hope of a future salvation, of the *anastasis*. He can call Christ our hope, just as he can call him our *zoe*. Ignatius is aware of an act of the eschatological drama to come, but the eschatological event of the *parousia* has already taken place in the historical appearance of Jesus (*Philad.* 9. 2; cf. *Magn.* 9. 2). For Jesus appeared at the end (of time) (*Magn.* 6. 1). Christ means a new existence for the faithful, for they are 'members' of Christ (*Eph.* 4. 2; *Trall.* 11. 2), 'branches of the cross' (*Trall.* 11. 2) and, as those who are united in the *ekklesia*, the body (*Smyrn.* 1. 2) whose head is Christ (*Trall.* 11. 2). The whole life of faith is 'in Christ'—a formula which still has original force in Ignatius. Through Jesus Christ, death is already overcome and life has been made present. Through the God who has appeared as man, the old kingdom has been destroyed and the newness of eternal life has been put in its place (Eph. 19. 3). What is peculiar about Ignatius' thought is 'that the whole life of the Christian is drawn into a sacramental unity with Christ and thereby receives a sacramental character—namely, as participation in Christ's passion, death and resurrection'.[179] This is the theme as a result of which Ignatius attaches such significance to the divine and human reality in the one Christ in the face of any possible falsification. The doctrine of the one Christ, God and man, is saving doctrine.

As in John, the unity of the two kinds of being in Christ, Logos and sarx, is full of tension. There is strong emphasis on both these poles, particularly in the face of the separationist tendencies of the docetists and all those heretics who were already during the lifetime of the apostle John striving to 'dissolve' Christ (1 John 4. 3). To counter them, the Bishop of Antioch inserts into the apostolic expressions of the incarnation a 'complete'[180] or a 'genuine', to exclude all hint of 'semblance' (τὸ δοκεῖν). Three times in John we find the designation 'God' for Christ, in Ignatius it is already quite frequent.[181] Out of the tendency to hold in tension Christ's Godhead and manhood in the one statement, there arises the antithetic, two-membered formula, so well loved in the later history of the dogma of Christ, which emphasizes the distinction between the kinds of being in the *one* Lord. In *Eph.* 7. 2 Ignatius says:

$$\text{εἷς ἰατρός ἐστιν}$$

σαρκικός τε	καὶ πνευματικός,
γεννητὸς	καὶ ἀγγένητος,
ἐν σαρκὶ γενόμενος	θεός,
ἐν θανάτῳ	ζωὴ ἀληθινή,
καὶ ἐκ Μαρίας	καὶ ἐκ θεοῦ,
πρῶτον παθητὸς	καὶ τότε ἀπαθής,

$$\text{Ἰησοῦς Χριστὸς ὁ Κύριος ἡμῶν.}$$

---

[179] R. Bultmann, op. cit., 275.　　　　[180] Ign., *Smyrn.* 4, 2.
[181] Texts in J. Lebreton, *Trinité* II, 297f.; W. v. Loewenich, *Johannesverständnis*, 28–9; H. Kraft, *Clavis Patrum Apostolicorum*, München 1963, s.v.

This fine passage[182] contains two series of statements about the one Christ: on the left are clearly those which concern Christ in the flesh, as man; on the right are those which are made of him as the pre-existent Son of God. In the first antithesis of *Eph.* 7. 2 there is without doubt an allusion to Rom. 1. 3, 4. Thereafter, this contrast that Christ is pneuma and sarx, flesh and spirit, i.e. God and man, became very popular until under the influence of the Logos doctrine of the Apologists it retreated well into the background in favour of the Johannine phraseology 'Logos-flesh'. It did not, however, vanish completely. With Ignatius and the majority of its other representatives it is so firmly embedded in a recognition of the two kinds of being *in Christ* that it runs no serious risk of being suspected of an association with 'spirit-christology' (as understood by F. Loofs).[183] As the two kinds of expression refer in holy scripture to one and the same reality, so also do they in the Christian tradition.

The contrast of γεννητός καὶ ἀγέννητος caused particular difficulties at the time of the Arian controversy. The former became a characteristic of the pre-existent Son with the significance 'begotten'; the latter, on the other hand, became a characteristic of the 'Father' and meant 'unbegotten' (in contrast to the Son). Thus when it was applied to the same Christ in a post-Nicene sense, Ignatius' statement caused difficulties for the Nicenes: 'begotten' in his manhood (of Mary, though this did not mean being begotten through a man), 'unbegotten' in his Godhead (though in Nicene language this would not be a characteristic of the Son, but of the Father). Theodoret sought to avoid the difficulty by replacing ἀγέννητος with καὶ

---

[182] *Eph.* 7. 2; ed. J. A. Fischer, *Die Apostolischen Väter*, Darmstadt 1966⁵, 146–8ᵣ Here we assume the authenticity of the middle recension (= M) of the seven letters of Ignatius. It has again been doubted in a study, *Les Lettres d'Ignace d'Antioche. Étude de critique littéraire et de théologie par R. Weijenborg*, O.F.M., mis en français par B. Heroux, O.F.M., Leiden 1969. Weijenborg sets out to demonstrate that M is dependent on the longer recension (= L), which was only made after 360. He also argues that the shorter recension (= C), known only in a Syriac translation, also came into being after 360, as it arises out of M. Weijenborg's study has been contested by both A. Wenger, *RevEtByz* 29, 1971, 315, and O. Perler, 'Die Briefe des Ignatius von Antiochien', *Freiburger Zeitschrift für Philosophie und Theologie* 18, 1971, 384ff. (on *Eph.* 7. 2). Perler also refers (p. 383) to the newly discovered Arabic translation which is an important witness to the tradition of the seven genuine letters (*Melto* IV, 2, 1968, 107–91). Cf. also M. Perry Brown, *The Authentic Writings of Ignatius. A Study of Linguistic Criteria*, Durham, NC 1963. For the christology of the Ignatian epistles see now R. Berthousoz, 'Le Père, le Fils et le Saint-Esprit d'après les Lettres d'Ignace d'Antioche', *Freiburger Zeitschrift für Philosophie und Theologie* 18, 1971, 397–418, esp. 398–410.

[183] On the pneuma-Sarx formula see (*b*) above (n. 78). How the two christological formulas pneuma-sarx, Logos-sarx are identical in point of content of ideas appears especially in Justin, Hippolytus and Tertullian; cf. A. D'Alès S. J., *La Théologie de Tertullien*, Paris 1905, 96–8. The more Christianity, in the person of its theologians, came into contact with philosophy, and especially with the Stoa, the more the language which described the divine element in Christ as pneuma had to retreat. For in Stoic thought, pneuma did not exclude a material nature. Clement of Alexandria avoids calling God a pneuma; only 'once in a while' does he apply the word to Christ (M. Pohlenz, *Stoa*, 416; examples in supplementary volume p. 200). Origen, on the other hand, defends the Christian use of pneuma against the Stoa. Celsus knows the pneuma-soma-sarx formula as a Christian confession: Origen, *C. Cels.* 6, 69, ed. Koetschau 139: (ὁ θεὸς), πνεῦμα ἴδιον ἐμβαλὼν εἰς σῶμα ἡμῖν ὅμοιον. On Melito of Sardis see below.

ἐξ ἀγεννήτου ('begotten and of the unbegotten', but this then ceased to be a true antithesis). The contradiction is removed once the Nicene terminology and view of the problem is abandoned in favour of the early Christian and Hellenistic meaning of the word (this would be even more the case if it could be demonstrated that the original form was γενητός–ἀγένητος).[184] 'Born' here means 'coming into being in time' (or in the visible order of things); its antithesis is 'unbegotten' in the sense of 'not having to come into being' in the eternal (invisible) order, i.e. as Godhead.

Ἐν σαρκὶ γενόμενος θεός is to be preferred to Lightfoot's ἐν ἀνθρώπῳ θεός (2. 1, pp. 47–8, as later in Athanasius, Theodoret, Gelasius and Severus of Antioch).[185] It is not, however, to be seen in the perspective of Apollinarian christology, i.e. as a denial of the soul of Christ. Here there is simply a contrast between the reality of the flesh and of the Godhead in Christ in the Johannine sense. This theological understanding of the unity in Christ finds its clearest expression in Ignatius in his use of the so-called 'exchange of predicates', where the divine is predicated of the man Christ and the human of the Logos, while the distinction between the two kinds of being is clearly maintained. This way of speaking is possible only because the unity of the subject is recognized.[186] Though the static character of a 'two nature' christology may become visible as early as Ignatius, a full, living dynamic is evident throughout his writings. This has its source in his all-pervading view of the economy of salvation and the basic soteriological-anthropological tone of his christology.

(c) Justin, philosopher and martyr

At the height of the second century we see the proclamation of Christ fully engaged in debate with Judaism and paganism. This debate finds its expression most clearly in the person and work of Justin, the 'philosopher and martyr' (Tertullian, Val. 5).[187] In his (first) Apology it is his intention to prove the divinity of Christ to the heathen from the prophecies of the

[184] Cf. Lampe, art. γεννητός or ἀγέννητος, and γενητός (with which it is frequently confused in MSS).

[185] Instances in J. B. Lightfoot, The Apostolic Fathers, London 1885, I, 141, 163.

[186] Ign., Eph. 1. 1: ed. Fischer, 142: αἷμα θεοῦ—Rom. 6. 3; ed. Fischer, 188: πάθος τοῦ θεοῦ μου —Eph. 18. 2: ed. Fischer, 156: ὁ . . . γὰρ θεός . . .ἐκυοφορήθη ὑπὸ Μαρίας. Ignatius reveals a delicate understanding of the divine subject in Christ when he speaks of the 'flesh-bearing Lord' (κύριος . . . σαρκοφόρος) but not of the 'God-bearing man'. The latter will meet us later. Cf. Smyrn. 5, 2: ed. Fischer, 208.

[187] (a) For bibliography on Justin see E. R. Goodenough, The Theology of Justin Martyr, Jena 1923, 295–320; N. Hyldahl, Philosophie und Christentum. Eine Interpretation der Einleitung zum Dialog Justins, Kopenhagen 1966, 301–8; L. W. Barnard, Justin Martyr. His Life and Thought, Cambridge 1967, 180–3, with supplementary material to Hyldahl.

(b) Studies on the philosophical and historical background to Justin: in addition to (a) above see J. M. Pfättisch O.S.B., Der Einfluss Platos auf die Theologie Justins des Märtyrers, Paderborn 1910; G. Bardy, 'Saint Justin et la philosophie stoïcienne', RSR 13, 1923, 491–510; 14, 1924, 33–45; C. Andresen, 'Justin und der mittlere Platonismus', ZNW 44, 1952/53, 157–95; id., Logos und Nomos, Berlin 1955; in addition especially R. Holte, Logos Spermatikos, Christianity and Ancient Philosophy according to St Justin's Apologies (Studia Theologica 12), Lund 1958, 109–68; important new additions to Andresen and Holte are N. Hyldahl, op. cit.; J. C. M. van Winden, An Early Christian Philosopher.

Old Testament (30–53). In the *Dialogue with Trypho*, he shows that the worshipping of Christ is no contradiction to monotheism (48–108). For his christological proof, Justin searches out to a hitherto unparalleled extent new types in Genesis which proclaim beforehand Christ and his suffering. What the *regula fidei* means for Irenaeus and Tertullian the christological intention is for Justin—mutatis mutandis—in his exposition of scripture. He is one of the first exegetes to use belief in Christ consistently as a basic hermeneutical principle in expounding the Old Testament (G. T. Armstrong).[188]

Adolf von Harnack sums up Justin's christology in the classical formula 'Christ is the Logos and Nomos'. The Apologists, in using these central concepts of Greek philosophy, wished to show the Greeks that Christianity was the true philosophy.[189] Justin, however, incorporated these concepts into a theology of history and completely transformed them. 'Wherever Christ is called Logos and Nomos as mediator of divine revelation, this is done within the context of a historical understanding of revelation.'[190] This is evident in Justin's teaching on creation and eschatology, but most of all in his teaching on the incarnation. Here he goes back both to the synoptics and to John, in whom he finds proof for the identity of the Word made flesh with the pre-existent Logos, who is also the mediator of creation and revelation. As the eternal Dynamis of God, the Logos can himself beget his earthly existence from the Virgin (*Apol.* I, 33, 1ff.). Justin sets great store on stressing the historical data of this earthly existence of the Word made flesh (*Apol.* I, 13, 3; 35, 9 and often). But this incarnation is the last link in a chain of events, during which the Logos had earlier already appeared on earth in other circumstances to reveal the will of the Father (*Dial.* 75, 4). The Logos maintains this function of being mediator of revelation until the end of the world. It comes to an end in the 'second parousia'—a phrase which Justin coined (*Apol.* I, 52, 3; *Dial.* 14, 8 and often). Through the uninterrupted work of revelation of the Logos the history of mankind becomes a carefully-planned construction with beginning, purpose and end.

Justin Martyr's Dialogue with Trypho, Chapters One to Nine (Philosophia Patrum I), Leiden 1971; H. Mühl, 'Der λόγος ἐνδιάθετος und προφορικός von der älteren Stoa bis zur Synode von Sirmium', *Archiv für Begriffsgeschichte* 7, 1972, 7–56 (on Justin, pp. 46f.); W. Pannenberg, 'The Appropriation of the Philosophical Concept of God as a Dogmatic Problem of Early Christian Theology', in: *Basic Questions in Theology* II, London and Philadelphia 1971, 119–83; G. T. Armstrong, *Die Genesis*, 18–51.

(c) Justin's christology and theology: A. Feder, *Justins des Märtyrers Lehre von Jesus Christus*, Freiburg 1906; R. Cantalamessa, 'Cristianesimo primitivo' (see note 11 above); J. Howton, 'The Theology of the Incarnation in Justin Martyr', *StudPat* IX (= TU 94), 1966, 231–9; see the works cited in the next note.

[188] See now P. Prigent, *Justin et l'Ancien Testament* (EtBibl), Paris 1964; W. A. Shotwell, *The Biblical Exegesis of Justin Martyr*, London 1965. Note pp. 320–32 in Prigent, 'Le plan du Dialogue', which is compared with the 'plan du Syntagma' (*Apology*, 26).

[189] See also N. Hyldahl, op. cit., 233–55, and 256–95, 'Philosophie und Christentum'. In addition, the remarks by J. C. M. van Winden and his thorough commentary should be noted.

[190] S. C. Andresen, op. cit., 312; for what follows see ibid., 312–44.

Now in this way Christ also becomes the 'Nomos' of the human race (after Ps. 1. 2 and Isa. 2. 3f.; *Apol.* I, 40, 5ff.; 39, 1; *Dial.*, 11-25). By him order is brought into a world in which everything has been in confusion. The advent of this Logos-Nomos in the flesh also breaks the influences which the demons had exerted in history through the '*nomoi*' of the peoples. Herein lies the significance of the expansion of Christianity. 'For now that we have believed in the Word, we too have withdrawn from them (i.e. the demons), and now follow the only unbegotten God through his Son' (*Apol.* I, 14, 1). Because a new Nomos of the world has thus been created in Christianity through the Logos as the 'power of God', his incarnation perpetuates itself. The new ordering of the world has its centre in Christ. In this way, Justin's Logos doctrine has taken over from the Greeks the two main concepts of Logos and Nomos, but has incorporated them into a historical-theological approach.[191] Justin finds his framework for this in Rev. 1. 8; 4. 8, where there is mention of him 'who is and was and is to come' (cf. *Dial.* 111, 2). It is Justin's intention to show by this theology that Christians do not think of the Logos after the manner of the pagan myths (*Apol.* I, 53, 1ff.). In so doing he also dismisses Jewish modalistic speculations. These make the Logos merely a form in which the Father is manifested and rob the Logos of the character of mediator of divine revelation (*Apol.* I, 63, 15; *Dial.* 128, 1f.). (In Melito's *Peri Pascha*, the relationship between Logos and Nomos differs from that in Justin.) Finally, Justin's conception of history gives him the opportunity of rejecting the Stoic teaching of world-periods and the Platonic transmigration of souls (*Apol.* II, 7, 3).

By his christocentric theology of history, therefore, Justin was able to stress clearly the Christian character of the Logos doctrine. Nevertheless, he was subject to stronger influence from Stoicism and from Middle Platonism, particularly in his doctrine of the *Logos spermatikos* (*Apol.* II, 8, 3; 13, 3). The expressions σπέρμα τοῦ Λόγου and σπερματικὸς Λόγος derive from Stoicism. For the Stoics, the Logos, as immanent fire, is the principle of all reason (*ratio*). Reason in the individual man is merely an aspect of it. By virtue of the activity of the Logos, all men are capable of forming certain moral and religious concepts. They are called φυσικαὶ ἔννοιαι or κοιναὶ ἔννοιαι or even σπέρματα. Therefore the Logos as an active principle can also be called σπερματικὸς Λόγος. In the light of the Stoic origin of these terms, some scholars felt that an identity between human reason and the divine Logos should be assumed in Justin's Logos doctrine. This was done in Harnack in a rationalistic sense, in J. M. Pfättisch in a supernaturalistic sense.[192]

191 See Daniélou II, 159.
192 A. von Harnack, *History of Dogma* I, London 1900, photographic reprint New York 1961, 179–90; J. M. Pfättisch O.S.B., *Der Einfluss Platons auf die Theologie Justins des Märtyrers*, Paderborn 1910, 110, 115f. See Daniélou II, 41–8.

C. Andresen has shown new ways of interpreting Justin and has shown that despite his Stoic vocabulary, Justin's thought here is Platonic, or rather Middle Platonic. R. Holte has made some corrections here.[193] He has shown that the expression σπερματικὸς Λόγος does not occur in Middle Platonism, but in Philo (as a description of the activity of the Logos, which is transcendent to the human spirit). In Justin, a distinction must be drawn between the σπερματικὸς Λογός and the σπέρματα τοῦ Λόγου. These σπέρματα are a participation in the Logos by the human spirit. They derive from the activity of the Logos, which therefore sows knowledge in the human reason in this way. This, however, is only the lower degree of knowledge, which must be brought to fulfilment by the incarnate Logos himself. Where there are only the 'seeds of the Logos', the Logos is present only 'in part' (ἀπὸ μέρους). Now as the Logos is the source of all partial knowledge of the truth in all men, he must also in the end be the subject and norm of this knowledge. So when Justin assumes of the ancient philosophers, like Heraclitus or Socrates, that they lived in accordance with the Logos, he understands by this Logos not reason (ratio), but the divine Logos. But these philosophers knew this Logos only obscurely and partially (ἀπὸ μέρους). In this respect their philosophy is incomplete and false. Thus one and the same divine Logos is known by philosophers and Christians, but by the former only in a deficient way, while the latter have full and complete knowledge. The way in which the Logos spermatikos works in human reason is to be understood in Justin in the light of the Platonic presuppositions of his theory of knowledge. He does, however, recognise for the ancient philosophers a special way of participating in the revelations of the Logos in the world, namely by way of the Old Testament. The philosophers borrowed from the prophets and from

---

[193] C. Andresen, op. cit., 340–3; R. Holte, Logos spermatikos, 144, 145. The researches of C. Andresen and R. Holte have been taken further by J. H. Waszink, 'Bemerkungen zu Justins Lehre vom Logos Spermatikos', Festschrift Theodor Klauser, JAC supplementary vol. 1, Münster 1964, 380–90, and especially by Salvatore R. C. Lilla, Clement of Alexandria. A Study in Christian Platonism and Gnosticism (Oxford Theological Monographs), Oxford 1971, 21–6. Lilla stressed Holte's distinction between the λόγος σπερματικός of Apol. II, 13, 4 and 8, 4 and the λόγου σπορά or the σπέρμα τοῦ λόγου in Apol. II, 13, 6, and 8, 1: 'Whereas the λόγος σπορά or σπέρμα τοῦ λόγου represents what is dropped by the Logos, the λόγος σπερματικός is nothing but the divine Logos himself engaged in a special activity. Both Holte and Waszink have rightly pointed out that the expression λόγος σπερματικός must be interpreted in an active sense: the Logos, in the three passages quoted above, is represented in the act of "sowing" philosophical doctrines; the Greek philosophers are the object of this activity, i.e. they receive what the Logos sows' (op. cit., 24). For criticism of Holte see Lilla, 22f., n. 4. With Pfättisch and Waszink, Lilla stresses that Justin assumed the presence of a portion of the Logos in man, a matter which Holte has questioned. Lilla himself remarks (ibid., 23): 'The terms σπέρμα and σπορά must necessarily hint at something which is dropped by the divine principle and which, before being dropped, is part of it.' According to Lilla, it is important to note the connection between σπερμά, μίμημα, μετουσία and μίμησις: 'Human reason is represented as a "seed", i.e. as a particle of the divine Logos, and, in this sense, it also partakes of him (μετουσία) and is his imitation (μίμημα, μίμησις). The underlying idea of Justin's sentence recalls both Philo's interpretation of the expression κατ' εἰκόνα of Gen. 1. 26 and 27, according to which human reason is a copy or image of the divine Logos, and the Platonic teaching which regarded the human νοῦς as a divine fragment.' This connection with Philo is true especially for Apol. II, 13, though according to Lilla the fact has been missed by Holte and Waszink.

Moses (*Apol.* I, 59, 1; 60, 1, 5–8). Moses is the first of the prophets, more ancient than all the writers of the Greeks (*Apol.* I, 59, 1). But the knowledge of the philosophers always remains a partial knowledge (*Apol.* I, 44, 9–10; II, 10, 2). This is all the more the case if the philosophers participated in revelation by way of the demons (*Apol.* I, 54, 2–4).[194]

From this point we can go on to investigate Justin's conception of the person of Jesus Christ.

The Apologist finds in all men, even in pagans, part of the power of the divine seed; the prophets of the Old Testament shared in it to an exceptional degree. The Christian is endowed with the whole, personal Logos; it dwells with him in the freedom of grace. Finally, in Christ we have the supreme example of the conjunction of Logos and man. But just at the point where Justin wishes to make clear the difference between the presence of the Logos in Christ and all the previous stages, different possibilities of interpretation seem to throw us up once more against the unresolved dilemma. This is the case in this much-debated passage:

> Our religion is clearly more sublime than any teaching of man for this reason, that the Christ who has appeared for us men represents the Logos principle in its totality (τὸ λογικὸν τὸ ὅλον), that is both body and Logos and soul. For all that the philosophers and legislators at any time declared or discovered aright they accomplished by investigation and perception in accordance with that portion of the Logos which fell to their lot. But because they did not know the whole of the Logos, who is Christ, they often contradicted each other.[195]

Some have found the wording here remarkable, and have made speculations from it which would already presuppose a developed christology in Justin.[196] But C. Andresen points to the right way of interpreting the passage.[197] He stresses that the subject of the sentence is a neuter (τὸ λογικὸν τὸ ὅλον), and translates 'the whole Logos principle'. This principle is Christ, 'who has appeared for us men'. Justin means to give the Logos the status of a cosmological principle. In this, he takes up the speculations of the Platonist school about the Platonic world-soul and uses them as a foundation for his teaching on the *Logos spermatikos*. According to the Platonists, the world-soul is the principle at work in ordering the world, both at creation and in sustaining the world. It has a rational element which is termed Nous, Logos or even ἡ λογική. Now, according to Justin, Christ as Logos has taken over the working of this cosmological principle. In his incarnation he has appeared in history, as 'body and reason and soul'. This division, which is made after the same pattern as the trichotomy of the Platonist school, expresses no more than the reality of the Logos as

[194] Cf. N. Pycke, 'Connaissance rationelle et connaissance de grâce chez s. Justin', *EphThLov* 37, 1961, 52–85.

[195] Justin, *Apol.* II, 10, 1: διὰ τοῦ τὸ λογικὸν τὸ ὅλον τὸν φανέντα δι' ἡμᾶς Χριστὸν γεγονέναι, καὶ σῶμα καὶ λόγον καὶ ψυχήν.

[196] A. Feder, *Justins Lehre*, 169, similarly G. Bardy, *DTC* 8, 2264.

[197] Op. cit., 336–44.

a man in history. It as yet contains no speculation on the relationship of Logos, soul and body in Christ. But in using the phrase Justin certainly deliberately wishes to go beyond the contemporary teaching on the Logos. The doctrine of the *Logos spermatikos* is not merely taken in a cosmological sense, but is incorporated in Justin's framework of the history of revelation in Christ. Whether with this framework he was successful in obviating completely the danger of a Hellenization of the Logos doctrine is another question. Hellenistic cosmology and the Christian theology of history are hard to unite in a valid synthesis. Justin's honourable intention of assigning first place in this synthesis to the Christian element is not to be doubted. Not only does he put Christ in the Old and New Testament perspective of prophecy and fulfilment, but he makes the Greek world and the history of its thought into a prelude and a preliminary to Christianity.

Justin takes one further step forward as a theologian. He is to be of great significance for the future of christological and trinitarian doctrine. He lays the first foundations of the Logos theology and christology.[198] This will be examined further below.

(d) Melito of Sardis

Between Ignatius and Irenaeus there stands another significant figure for the theology of the second century—Melito of Sardis.[199] According to a remark of Bishop Polycrates quoted in Eusebius (HE V, 24, 5), he was one of the 'great stars of Asia' and was regarded as a notable champion of the Godhead and manhood of Christ (HE V, 28, 5). The God-man Jesus is, according to the sources available to us, the dominant point of the theology of the Bishop of Sardis. The struggle against Gnosticism, and especially against Marcion, must certainly be taken very much into account here. The divine-human being of Jesus Christ is the guarantee of

---

[198] See Daniélou II, 345–57.

[199] Cf. Otto, *Corpus Apolog.* IX, 374–5; 497–512; O. Perler, *Méliton de Sardes, Sur la Pâque, et fragments*, SC 123, Paris 1966; C. Bonner, *The Homily on the Passion by Melito Bishop of Sardis*, London–Philadelphia 1940; B. Lohse, *Die Passa-Homilie des Bischofs Melito von Sardes*, Leiden 1958; M. Testuz, *Papyrus Bodmer XIII. Méliton de Sardes. Homélie sur la Pâque*, Bibl. Bodmer. 1960; H. Chadwick, 'A Latin Epitome of Melito's Homily on the Pascha', *JTS* 11, 1960, 76–82; P. Nautin, *Le dossier d'Hippolyte et de Méliton*, Paris 1953, 43–56. Nautin is against the authenticity of the Peri Pascha; so already *RHE* 44, 1949, 429–38; for its authenticity, in addition to Bonner and Testuz (p. 21), E. Peterson, W. Schneemelcher, F. L. Cross, *The Early Christian Fathers*, London 1960, 104. Especially as a result of the *Papyrus Bodmer*, there is no need to raise further doubts. There is now a Coptic and a Georgian version; the latter is edited by J. N. Birdsall, 'Melito of Sardis ΠΕΡΙ ΤΟΥ ΠΑΣΧΑ in a Georgian Version', *Mus* 80, 1967, 121–136 (the first half) and by M. van Esbroeck, 'Le traité sur la Pâque de Méliton de Sardes en géorgien', *Mus* 84, 1971, 373–94 (the second half). Further important new contributions to the *corpus Melitonianum* are: M. van Esbroeck, 'Nouveaux fragments de Méliton de Sardes dans une homélie géorgienne sur la croix', *AnalBoll* I 90, 1972, 63–99 (Cod. A-144 de Tiflis); M. Richard, 'Témoins grecs des fragments XIII et XV de Méliton de Sardes', *Mus* 85, 1972, 309–36. According to M. Richard le cod. Tiflis A-144, fol., 208v and 212r–v 'donnent le début et la fin d'une homélie sur la Croix attribuée à S. Athanase, mais dont le style est tout à fait semblable à celui de Méliton' (loc. cit., 311, n. 15). Of a special importance is the history of frag. XIII: 'Ce fragment s'est conservé en version syriaque dans la partie du cod. Londres, British Museum, Addit. 12. 156 connue sous le titre "Florilège d'Édesse", depuis sa publication sous ce titre par I. Rucker en 1933 [*Florilegium Edessenum anonymum*

our salvation and of man's return to his original home with God. Beginning with the Exodus account of the passover feast in Egypt and the freeing of Israel (Exod. 12. 1–42), the newly discovered work (homily?) develops a view of salvation history as comprehensive as that of Irenaeus. The differences are, of course, unmistakable. Melito achieves his universal view by beginning the history of man in the height of paradise and making it end once again with God. From *soteria*, the divine security in the height of paradise, man has fallen into the *apoleia* of this world and under the tyranny of *hamartia*, both of which deliver him to death and to the depths of Hades. Israel's servitude in Egypt is a real sign of this reality. But the turning point comes through Christ, in that the mystery of the new passover was fulfilled in the body of the Lord (no. 56). Now this mystery was already unfolding in the old covenant, in the patriarchs, the persecuted prophets and in the whole people of Israel as the type of the suffering Messiah, in the Easter lamb, and in the destroying angel which smote Egypt and delivered Israel (nos. 57–60). So Christ was foreshown in 'type'. The prophets proclaimed the coming Christ in 'word' (nos. 61–5). Finally, by taking to himself a body that could suffer, Christ has brought salvation (no. 66). This all-prevailing christocentricity is exhibited in a whole series of new attempts, and the preparation for the coming of Christ is pointed out in all the events and persons of the salvation history. In the end, Christ appeared as true man and died the death of the cross (nos. 67–71). In this death we have the new passover mystery (nos. 72–100): ὁ θεὸς πεφόνευται. 'God' himself has been killed at the hand of Israel (no. 96).[200]

(syriace ante 562): SBMünchAk, 1933, 12–16]. Il est intitulé *Melitonis episcopi Sardium ex tractatu De anima et corpore* et se compose de deux parties séparées par *Et post Alia*. Il est maintenant bien établi qu'il fait partie de la descendance littéraire du traité Περὶ ψυχῆς καὶ σώματος de Méliton mentionné par Eusèbe, *Hist. Eccl.* IV, 26, 1. [See W. Schneemelcher, 'Der Sermo "*De anima et corpore*" ein Werk Alexanders von Alexandrien?', *Festschrift f. Günther Dehn*, Neukirchen 1957, 119–143; O. Perler, 'Recherches sur le Peri Pascha de Méliton', *RSR* 51, 1963, 407–21.] Les autres témoins dérivés du texte original perdu sont une homélie syriaque *De anima et corpore deque passione Domini* attribuée à Alexandre d'Alexandrie [= A. Mai, Nova Bibliotheca Patrum, 2, Rome, 1884, 531–9 = PG 18, 586–604, avec version latine, d'après le cod. Vat. syr. 368; . . . E. A. Wallis Budge, *Coptic Homilies in the Dialect of Upper Egypt*, London 1910, 407–15, Coptic text; 417–24, English version], l'*Additamentum* anonyme qui suit cette homélie dans le cod. Vat. syr. 368 et se retrouve dans le florilège d'Édesse, cette fois sous le nom d'Alexandre, une homélie copte "concerning the soul and the body" attribuée à Athanase d'Alexandrie et éditée par E. A. Wallis Budge [op. cit., 115–32, avec version anglaise, 258–74], et une homélie grecque sur la resurrection attribuée tantôt à S. Épiphane, tantôt à S. Jean Chrysostome, dont le texte original a été publié pour la première fois par M. P. Nautin [op. cit., 155–59]. Enfin le R. P. M. van Esbroeck vient de découvrir dans le cod. Tiflis A-144, fol. 209r–211v, la version géorgienne d'une homélie apparentée aux précédentes et directement traduite du grec [*AnalBoll*, loc. cit.]. Celle-ci est malheureusement mutilée au début et à la fin, mais semble être le meilleur témoin du texte original de Méliton. Le début, lignes 1–29, et la fin, lignes 191–235, sont entièrement nouveaux et certainement authentiques. La partie médiane, malgré quelques lacunes, permettra de mettre de l'ordre dans les autres témoins . . .' (M. Richard, loc. cit., 31of.). For the christology of Melito see R. Cantalamessa, 'Méliton de Sardes. Une christologie antignostique du IIᵉ siècle', *RevSR* 37, 1963, 1–26. For bibliography see R. Mainka, 'Meliton von Sardes. Eine bibliographische Übersicht', *Claretianum* 5, 1965, 225–55; for later publications see *Kyriakon*. Festschrift Johannes Quasten, ed. P. Granfield and J. A. Jungmann, Münster 1970, 236–65.

200 C. Bonner, op. cit., 19, sees modalism already expressed in such expressions. But there is nothing more than the *praedicatio idiomatum*, which was already very widespread in the second century. R. Cantalamessa, art. cit., 4–11, deals with the question of modalism (monarchianism) at length (Melito

What Israel refused its king, unreasoning nature, the earth, with its quakings, supplied (nos. 93–9). In conclusion, the peroration shows Christ's victory over Death, Hades and Satan. Man is led by Christ to the heights of heaven from which he had once been cast down. There Christ himself sits at the right hand of the Father. So the mystery of redemption has been fulfilled (nos. 101–5).[201]

Melito's doctrine of redemption is based on his conception of the divine-human being of Jesus. In it, strong emphasis is laid on the reality of the incarnation and the completeness of Christ's human nature. This presentation is certainly governed by an anti-docetic, anti-Gnostic tendency.[202] According to Anastasius Sinaita, Melito wrote against Marcion under the title περὶ σαρκώσεως Χριστοῦ (PG 89, 229). Marcion denied that either the birth or the flesh of Christ was real. For him it was a 'phantasma'.[203] Against this Melito asserts an 'aphantaston' (= no 'phantasma' = real), and does so in the very work mentioned by Anastasius Sinaita, the De incarnatione (PG 89, 228). Here Melito even speaks of the 'perfect man' (ἄνθρωπος τέλειος), an expression which, of course, only becomes frequent later, in the anti-Apollinarian controversy. It does, however, already occur in Hippolytus (C. Noetum 17) and does so in the same connection as in Melito. When Melito stresses the birth from the womb of the virgin (in virgine incarnatus), his intent is also anti-Gnostic. He is possibly thinking of Valentinus, who ascribed a spiritual body to Christ, and, while allowing it to go through the virgin, did not allow it to be begotten of her (trans-meatorio potius quam generatorio more, as Tertullian, Adv. Valent. 27, 1, put it).

To give clear expression to his conviction of the real incarnation of Christ, Melito also enriches christological terminology.[204] He takes up biblical imagery and (like the two anti-Gnostics, Tertullian and Hippolytus) is fond of talking about 'induere (indutus) hominem', presumably to avoid the possibility of a false interpretation of the Johannine 'Verbum caro factum est'. The Logos 'wove' (texuit) himself his garment (frag. XIV). Most significant of all is the shaping of words and concepts like incarnatus-incarnatio (σαρκωθείς-σάρκωσις), corporatio-corporatus. Almost at the same time, Justin forms the expression σαρκοποιηθείς (Apol. I, 32) surely in connection with John 1. 14. Hippolytus too speaks of the 'testimonies of the incarnation of Christ' (περὶ σαρκώσεως τοῦ λόγου μαρτυρίαι, C.

fits completely into the framework of the doctrine of the Apologists concerning the functions of the Logos and his issuing from the Father); ibid. 24–5 (ref. to fragm. in Anastas. Sin., PG 89, 197); ibid., 24–6 on the praedicatio idiomatum in Melito.

201 Cf. O. Perler, Ein Hymnus zur Ostervigil von Meliton, Fribourg 1960. If the hymn discussed here can be accepted as original, there would be an interesting continuation of Melito's doctrine of redemption in ecclesiology (bride-mysticism).

202 As R. Cantalamessa well indicates from the sources, art cit., 14–18.

203 Cf. Tertullian, De carne Christi 1, 2; Adv. Marcion. III, 10, 11; IV, 7, 1–5; III, 8, 1 (passages in Cantalamessa, 16f.; also for the following details).

204 Cf. R. Cantalamessa, art. cit., 18–24.

Noetum 16). If the doctrine of the corporeality of God could have been ascribed to Melito, as Tertullian assumed under Stoic influence, this would be because the title of his work περὶ ἐνσωμάτου θεοῦ was translated '*De deo corporeo*' or was understood to refer to the corporeality of God (Origen, in Theodoret, PG 80, 113). In fact, Melito uses *corporatus* for *incarnatus*. So the title which Eusebius (HE IV, 26, 2) gives has been better translated *De Deo corpore induto* (PG 5, 1202). Melito's very doctrine of the incarnation is enough to rob the charge made against him, that he taught the corporeality of God, of any force: '*Propter haec venit ad nos, propter haec cum sit incorporeus* (ἀσώματος), *corpus ex formatione nostra texuit sibi*' (frag. XIV). A quotation from Melito in Ps. Cyprian, *Adv. Iudaeos*, says the same thing: *Hic est qui in virgine corporatus est.*

Melito's anti-docetism also led to an antithetical stressing of the divine and human reality of Christ similar to that which we have already noticed in Ignatius. The terms used are *corpus* (*caro*) and *Spiritus*. Papyrus Bodmer offers us a new example of this:

Etant arrivé des cieux sur la terre en faveur de celui qui souffrait, et ayant revêtu celui-ci même par la Vierge Marie, et étant apparu comme un homme, il prit sur lui les souffrances de celui qui souffrait, par son *corps* capable de souffrir, et mit fin aux souffrances de la chair. Et par son *Esprit* qui ne pouvait mourir, il tua la mort tueuse d'hommes.[205]

On the basis of a certain textual tradition Melito could be credited with a significant step in the direction of a more technical terminology for the doctrine of the two natures. This would only be the case, however, if the text transmitted by Anastasius Sinaita (= frag. VI, Otto and Perler) were genuine. In reality, however, it comes from the time of the Diphysite controversies. Nevertheless, the text is worth mentioning, insofar as it was possible to attribute it to Melito:

θεὸς γὰρ ν ὡόμοῦ τε καὶ ἄνθρωπος τέλειος
ὁ αὐτὸς τὰς δύο αὐτοῦ οὐσίας ἐπιστώσατο ἡμῖν.[206]

More in keeping with Melito's time is a sentence which he wrote in the *Peri Pascha* and which can be regarded as a summary of the second-century doctrine of the divine-human being of Christ: 'Buried as a man, he rose

---

[205] Melito, *Peri Pascha* 66: Perler, SC 123, 96–7; Testuz, 38f.; Bonner, 131 (lacuna). This text is important, because it proves that Melito belongs to the type of 'pneuma-sarx-christology'. See M. Simonetti, 'Note di cristologia pneumatica', *Aug* 12, 1972, 201–23; R. Cantalamessa, 'La primitiva esegesi cristologica di "Romani" I, 3–4 et "Luca" I, 35', *Rivista di Storia e Letteratura religiosa* 2, 1966, 69–80. If the above-mentioned Georgian, Syriac and Coptic derivations of the Melitonian *Tractatus de anima et corpore* retain genuine formulas of Melito himself, then the interpretation of the descent into hell would be a confirmation of this 'pneuma-sarx-christology'. The three versions have the idea of a 'pneuma-descensus', that is of a descensus of the Godhead of Jesus. There is no mention of Christ's human soul. This is an important prelude to the idea of the 'Logos-descensus'. For a full discussion of this descensus text, with an interpretation of the Georgian text different from that given by M. van Esbroeck in *AnalBoll* 90, 1972, 78–9, §12, see A. Grillmeier, *Mit ihm und in ihm*, Freiburg 1975, Part I, 2: 'Der Gottessohn im Totenreich'.

[206] In Anastas. Sin., *Viae dux* 13: PG 89, 229AB; O. Perler, SC 123, 126–7, regards the text as genuine. Against A. von Harnack, P. Nautin, *Le dossier* (see above, n. 199), 84, denied its authenticity; so too now does M. Richard in *Mus* 85, 1972, 310.

from the dead as God, being by nature God and man (φύσει θεὸς ὢν καὶ ἄνθρωπος)'.[207] 'Nature' (*physis*) still, of course, has no philosophical sense; it simply means 'real', 'true', like the *alēthōs* in Ignatius of Antioch.

(e) Irenaeus of Lyons

Now that Irenaeus scholarship has once again come back to recognizing the inner unity of the theology of the Bishop of Lyons[208] after the separatist source-criticism of F. Loofs,[209] the recognition of his significance for the history of early Christian theology is also increasing. O. Cullmann could write:

> Down to the theologians of the 'redemptive history' school in the ninteenth century ... there has scarcely been another theologian who has recognized so clearly as did Irenaeus that the Christian proclamation stands or falls with the redemptive history, that this historical work of Jesus Christ as Redeemer forms the mid-point of a line which leads from the Old Testament to the return of Christ.[210]

Only through such a universal view could he be a match for the Gnostics and set up against the fantasies of his Gnostic-docetic opponents as successfully as Ignatius of Antioch an interpretation of Christian doctrine understood in the light of the whole of Christian experience. The Valentinians, too, knew of a planned ordering of salvation, an '*oikonomia*'. But they excluded the flesh from it. So it was not the whole man that was the object of the saving work from above. Nor is it an ordering of salvation that could comprehend the whole of human history. The Gnostics reject the Old Testament. They falsify Christian eschatology. By holding fast to the historical revelation of the Old Testament, which for him is fulfilled in the New Testament, Irenaeus avoids the fantasies of Gnostic speculations.[211]

Three figures among the Gnostics stand out especially: Basilides, Valentinus and Marcion, though, of course, completely different influences were at work among them. In *Valentinus'* system, God above is separated from the world below by the Pleroma, a mid-world built up in a complicated way. Between the lower and the upper world (Pleroma), a drama of salvation is played out, a drama which is to liberate the divine

[207] Melito, *Peri Pascha* 8: Bonner, 89, 168; Testuz, 33f.
[208] See the surveys of the present state of Irenaeus scholarship: W. Völker, *ThLZ* 72, 1947, 170–3; A. Benoit, *Saint Irénée. Introduction à l'étude de sa théologie*, Paris 1960, 9–44; cf. the bibliography, 257–62.—G. N. Bonwetsch, *Die Theologie des Irenaeus*, Gütersloh 1925; A. Houssiau, *La christologie de St. Irénée*, Louvain 1955; M. Widmann, 'Irenäus und seine theologischen Väter', *ZThK* 54, 1957, 156–73; A. Bengsch, *Heilsgeschichte und Heilswissen. Eine Untersuchung zur Struktur und Entfaltung des theologischen Denkens im Werk 'Adversus Haereses' des hl. Iren. v. L.*, Leipzig 1957; G. Wingren, *Man and the Incarnation*, Edinburgh and London 1959; G. T. Armstrong, *Die Genesis*, 52–92. For Gnosticism and Irenaeus: F. Sagnard, O.P., *La Gnose Valentinienne*, Paris 1947, 55–80; E. C. Blackmann, *Marcion and his Influence*, London 1949; A. Bengsch, op. cit.
[209] F. Loofs, *Theophilus von Antiochien Adversus Marcionem und die anderen theologischen Quellen bei Irenaeus* (TU 46, 2), Leipzig 1930.
[210] O. Cullmann, *Christ and Time*, London 1962², 56–7.
[211] Cf. G. T. Armstrong, op. cit., 60.

spark imprisoned in man. Christ is an aeon, who descends to redeem man.[212] This Christ of the upper world unites himself to the Jesus of the lower world, who is not, however, the Christ of the gospels. For any union of the divine with the material is unthinkable, as the latter is radically evil. The words and actions of the earthly Christ are no more than signs of the realities which are being played out in the upper world of 'middle-beings'. Salvation does not consist in the return of the earthly and visible world and of fallen man, body and soul, to God, but only in the return of the fallen divine 'fragment' to divinity. This return is effected by knowledge. The *Ptolemaeans*, who developed from the Valentinians, wished to make a complete fragmentation of Christ by assigning different subjects to the different sayings of the Johannine prologue. One was the Logos, one the Only-begotten, another the Saviour, another the Christ. *Marcion* is characterized by an extreme dualism. In his '*Antitheses*', in complete contradiction to the Christian tradition from which he came, he assumed the existence of two gods, one of the Old Testament and another of the New. Jesus Christ is the Son of the God of the New Testament, but is seen by Marcion in an almost modalistic nearness to the Father. Jesus is the good God in person, clothed in the form of a man. He need only lay this aside to become once again pure Godhead. If we take into consideration Marcion's condemnation of marriage and intercourse, corporeality and matter, it is possible to understand his christological docetism. This, however, is not carried through to its logical conclusions. For finally Jesus dies a real death on the cross, by which he redeems men from the Creator God and his domination—the God whose work Christ had come to destroy.

Against these powerful new attacks on the '*substantia domini nostri*', as Irenaeus puts it, it was his task not so much to put forward anything new as to preserve the *depositum fidei*. This means above all the emphasizing of the true incarnation of Jesus Christ and the true historicity of his act of redemption. But at the same time this true Christ, God and man, must be made the embodiment and the real centre of 'unity' against all dualism in the cosmos and in history. This all had to be proved from scripture (that is from the Old Testament, read from a christological standpoint,[213] and from the New Testament) and from tradition.

After this brief description of the material and formal characteristics of Irenaeus' theology, both must be discussed in rather more detail. We turn first to the formal means with which Irenaeus works.

With the theologians of the second century, and above all Justin, Irenaeus seeks to utilize the Old Testament in accordance with the content of the church's *regula fidei*.

212 F. M. M. Sagnard, *Gnose Valentinienne*, 387–415.
213 A. Benoit, *Saint Irénée*, 74–102; G. T. Armstrong, *Die Genesis*, 52, 60.

The most varied passages from Genesis are expounded in a Christian way and find an appropriate place in Irenaeus' thought. The chief emphasis is placed on Gen. 1–3, three chapters which are fundamental for Irenaeus' doctrine of redemption. In comparison with Justin, these chapters are given a very full, independent treatment, whereas for the exposition of the later chapters many thoughts are taken over directly from Justin.[214]

The choice of the chapters and passages to be discussed is governed by the struggle against the Gnostics. Thus those passages of Genesis became most important which could serve to lay a basis for the theological conception which Irenaeus wanted to advance against these opponents. So, for example, all the individual details of the Fall are expounded, although not all serve as the starting point for theological reflection in the same way. Irenaeus is also associated with Justin in his rich use of typology. Through the express subordination of this typology to the idea of a plan of salvation, however, his work takes on a special character in comparison with that of his exemplar. Both have the basic principles of typological exposition in common: '*Nihil enim vacuum, neque sine signo apud Deum*' (*Adv. Haer.* IV, 21, 3 fin.). If anyone reads the scriptures carefully, he will find in them mention of Christ and the prefiguration (*praefigurationem*) of the new calling. '*Hic est enim thesaurus absconsus in agro . . ., absconsus vero in Scripturis thesaurus Christus, quoniam per typos et parabolas significabatur*' (ibid., IV, 26, 1).

Irenaeus' christology, moreover, shows how firmly he is tied to tradition, especially to the tradition of Asia Minor and of Rome, because the church of Lyons and Irenaeus himself were closely connected with them.[215] A clear attempt can certainly be found in his work at a distinction between simple belief and theological speculation. In his struggle against the Gnostics he does not go nearly so far as to reject any investigation into the truth or any attempt at the deepening of belief, but he understands more clearly than do the Apologists and the Alexandrians that investigation into the truth must be illuminated by the light of Christ.

'Autrement dit, Irénée ne conçoit pas le travail du théologien comme une réflexion personelle sur le contenu de la révélation ou même comme une critique de la prédication de l'Église à partir de cette révélation, mais il conçoit le travail du théologien comme un exposé de la foi avec l'aide de toutes les données traditionelles, de tout l'apport du passé chrétien.'[216]

For him this was especially Justin, Papias, Theophilus of Antioch, the Presbyters and John (the prologue of his gospel!). Non-Christian elements find no place in his understanding of Christ (cf. *Adv. Haer.* I, 10, 1–3). He is not a philosopher as his master Justin was, but above all a biblical theologian, 'the first deliberately biblical theologian of the Christian church',[217] and an interpreter of the traditional creed. Precisely for his

[214] G. T. Armstrong, *Die Genesis*, 89.   [215] A. Benoit, *Saint Irénée*, 47–73.
[216] Benoit, op. cit., 218.
[217] G. T. Armstrong, *Die Genesis*, 52 (after H. Frhr. v. Campenhausen); see J. Lawson, *The Biblical*

main themes, the unity of the Father, the unity of Christ and the unity of the *oikonomia*, he begins directly from the credal formulas, which he knew particularly in their Eastern forms.[218] So as witness to the 'one' faith he could become the starting point for further development.

Against the Gnostic dissolution and separation of God and the world, against the division of Christ, of man and of salvation history, Irenaeus now resolutely sets the idea of the unity of God, Christ and salvation.[219] In this connection, he develops the idea of a universal *oikonomia*. Presumably tradition already provided him with this concept, as a concept fundamentally orientated on the coming of Christ. Irenaeus preserves the christocentricity of this traditional concept, but extends it so that it has universal scope. *Oikonomia* now embraces both creation and the end, and puts the Christ-event in the middle.[220] Creation, the incarnation of Christ, redemption and resurrection belong together as different parts of the one all-embracing saving work of God. The significance of *anakephalaiosis* in Irenaeus must also be assessed in the light of the idea of the *oikonomia*. The *anakephalaiosis* as an act of Christ is the special contribution which Christ makes to the realization of the one *oikonomia* of the Father in Christ and the Spirit. True, Christ is already revealed and prefigured in the Old Testament and is thus already an object for the faith and hope of the men of the Old Testament. And in the New Testament, something new has been brought by the real coming of Christ, which enriches the knowledge of faith: '... *in novo Testamento ea, quae est ad Deum, fides hominum aucta est, additamentum accipiens Filium Dei, ut et homo fieret particeps Dei*' (*Adv. Haer.* IV, 28, 2). Nevertheless, this new thing of the New Testament is only really there as a result of the *recapitulatio* brought about in Christ, as *Adv. Haer.* III, 16, 6 shows. The whole order of salvation, which finds its climax in the incarnation of Christ (with his passion, his resurrection, his coming again and the resurrection of the flesh and the revelation of salvation) is said to lead to this *recapitulatio* in Christ:

> There is therefore ... one God the Father, and one Christ Jesus our Lord, who came by means of the whole dispensational arrangements and gathered together all things in himself. But in every respect, too, he is man, the formation of God: and thus he took

---

Theology of Saint Irenaeus, London 1948, 115–291 (for critics see A. Benoit, op. cit., 4, n. 5); G. Bentivegna, 'Criteriologia de S. Ireneo per una indagine sul mistero della Salvessa', OCP 26, 1960, 5–28.

[218] Benoit, op. cit., 209–12 (*Adv. Haer.*); 234–50 (*Epid.*).

[219] See the good collection of texts in Benoit, op. cit., 204, n. 1.

[220] Ibid., 219–27; A. D'Alès, 'Le mot οἰκονομία dans la langue théologique de Saint Irénée', *RevEtGrec* 32, 1919, 1–9; T. L. Verhoeuven, *Studien over Tertullianus' Adversus Praxean*, Amsterdam 1948; O. Lillge, *Das patristische Wort* οἰκονομία; *seine Geschichte und seine Bedeutung bis auf Origenes*, Theol. Diss. Erlangen 1955; M. Widmann, *Der Begriff* οἰκονομία *im Werk des Irenäus und seine Vorgeschichte*, Theol. Diss. Tübingen 1956; J. Reumann, *The use of* oikonomia *and related terms in Greek sources to about* AD 100, *as a background for patristic applications*, Theol. Diss. Univ. of Pennsylvania, Univ. microfilms, Ann Arbor, Michigan 1957; id., ' "Stewards of God"—pre-Christian religious application of *Oikonomos* in Greek', *JBL* 77, 1958, 339–49; H. Thurn, *OIKONOMIA von der frühbyzantinischen Zeit bis zum Bilderstreit*, Phil. Diss. München 1960, 36–126.

up man into himself, the invisible becoming visible, the incomprehensible being made comprehensible, the impassible becoming capable of suffering, and the Word being made man, thus summing up all things in himself: so that as in super-celestial, spiritual and invisible things, the Word of God is supreme, so also in things visible and corporeal he might possess the supremacy, and, taking to himself the pre-eminence, as well as consti- tuting himself head of the church, he might draw all things to himself at the proper time.

Just as in the invisible world the Logos is already the head of all being created through him, so now in the incarnation he becomes head of the visible and corporeal world, and above all the head of the church, so drawing everything to himself. This represents at the same time a recapitu- lation of creation and above all of fallen Adam, i.e. a renewing and saving permeation of the whole history of the world and of mankind by 'Christ the Head', from its beginning to its end.[221] In this way the world, history, man are all brought to their climax, but at the same time they are also brought back by Christ to their principle, to God. The whole of God's previous work through the Logos in the world and to men is concentrated (ἐν συντόμῳ) in the incarnation of Christ; it reaches its fullness and now in Christ fills the whole of the world and the whole of history.[222]

We have now shown to some degree the theological framework into which Irenaeus inserts his picture of Christ. It is with Ignatius above all that he is agreed in emphasizing the unity of Christ. He uses a phrase which will occur some seven times even in the Chalcedonian Definition, 'Christ, one and the same' (εἷς καὶ ὁ αὐτός).[223] The support of its strength is to prove itself over and over again in disputes over the description of the unity of person in Christ. Over against the fourfold 'ἄλλος' of the Ptole- maeans Irenaeus puts a sevenfold 'τοῦτον' to emphasize the self-sameness of the one subject of all the names which the Johannine prologue gives to Christ.[224] The Gnostic struggle may not have been concerned with the same inner problems of the unity of Christ's person as were at the root of the dispute with Nestorius—the Gnostic destruction of unity in Christ is much more radical and is taken into the context of a much larger system— but as the church makes her defence, formulations already emerge which are to be re-echoed in the later struggles.[225]

---

[221] On the concept of *anakephalaiosis* in Irenaeus see: G. T. Armstrong, *Die Genesis*, 63–7 (the pres- ent state of scholarship); A. Houssiau, *La Christologie de Saint Irénée*, Louvain–Gembloux 1955, 216– 24; Benoit, op. cit., 225–7; B. Reynders, *Lexique comparé du texte grec et des versions latine, arménienne et syriaque de l' 'Adversus haereses' de saint Irénée* (CSCO, Subsidia 5–6), s.v. *recapitulatio, recapitulo*.

[222] Cf. Houssiau, op. cit., 220f. (la 'concision').

[223] Cf. Benoit, op. cit., 212–14.

[224] Iren. *Adv. Haer.* I, 9, 2: III, 16, 2: *sed et Matthaeus unum et eundem Jesum Christum cognoscens . . .*; III, 16, 8.

[225] Iren., *Adv. Haer.* III, 16, 9: *si enim alter quidem passus est, alter autem impassibilis mansit; et alter quidem natus est, alter vero in eum, qui natus est, descendit, et rursus relinquit eum, non unus, sed duo mon- strantur.* Because of his clear recognition of the unity in Christ despite a differentiation of the natures, Irenaeus can make a good distinction between the two births (III, 19, 2), interpret the name Christ (III, 18, 3), and keep apart Logos, humanity, and the grace of the Spirit given to the assumed human nature (III, 9, 2–3).

In his fight to describe the unity in Christ, Irenaeus developed a singularly concrete kind of language which has therefore a remarkably 'Nestorian' ring. Such a mixture of 'unitive' and 'devisive' christology is to meet us still more frequently. It should arouse no suspicions of adoptionism or 'Nestorianism'. Theological language is still for a long time to lack the more refined means of expression of a later age.[226]

Now the unity which Irenaeus defends is the conjunction of Logos and flesh in Christ. As might be expected, it stamps his teaching as a christology concerned with the Logos and with unity. Yet his Logos concept betrays less of the influence of the Greek philosophers than does that of the Apologists before him and, still more, that of the Alexandrians after him. Nevertheless, all the delight in the Logos which characterizes the second century, and above all Justin, lives again in him. In his view, the incarnation is merely the conclusion in an immense series of manifestations of the Logos which had their beginning in the creation of the world.[227]

Irenaeus, however, sees the incarnation as a unity of Logos and flesh held together in a tension similar to that which will appear later, in an intensified form, in Athanasius. There is surely some dependence here. The concern in the one writer as in the other is with the resurrection of the human body, which in Christ has become a participant in the life-giving divine power through its union with the Logos. For this reason it is the flesh in particular which is mentioned as being that part of man which is in need of redemption, though in Irenaeus, as in Athanasius, the whole man is understood to be destined for salvation.[228] But because in the struggle with Gnosticism the flesh of man stands so much in the foreground, Irenaeus frequently speaks as though Christ consisted only of Logos and sarx. Yet he certainly does not deny the soul of Christ.[229] His is a theology of antithesis, which lets the glory of the divine Logos become visible simply by joining it to its most extreme opposite, the sinful

---

[226] Iren., *Adv. Haer.* V, 14, 1: Paul frequently speaks of the flesh and blood of Christ *'uti hominem eius statueret'*; V, 21, 3 (on the redeemer's struggle with Satan) *'fugitivum eum homo eius et legis transgressorem, et apostatam Dei ostendens, postea iam Verbum constanter eum colligavit'*. This sentence bears the strongest resemblance to a 'divisive' theology. But even F. Loofs, *Theophilus*, 352, n. 5, concedes that there is no more behind this than a concrete way of speaking which does not as yet know the abstracts 'Godhead', 'manhood'. Cf. Tertullian, *Adv. Praxeam* 30 (on Matt. 27.46)—on the other hand the exchange of predicates (*communicatio idiomatum*) in Irenaeus shows that he quite clearly maintains the unity of subject in Christ: *Adv. Haer.* III, 19, 1, λόγος σαρκωθείς.

[227] Iren., *Adv. Haer.* III, 18, 3: cf. J. Lebreton, *Trinité* II, 590–601, on the relationship between Irenaeus and the Apologists. In Irenaeus, unlike the Apologists, the theology of the theophanies is not meant to show the distinction between Father and Son, but to prove against Marcion the unity of the divine plan of revelation which culminates in the incarnation. Cf. *Adv. Haer.* IV, 20.

[228] Iren., *Adv. Haer.* V, 9, 1: *'perfectus homo constat, carne anima et spiritu: et altero quidem salvante et figurante, qui est Spiritus; altero quod unitur et formatur, quod est caro; id vero quod inter haec est duo, quod est anima. . . .'* The *'Spiritus'* is the spirit of grace which is lacking in those who walk by earthly lusts. This anthropology is opposed to the Gnostic teaching of *semen spirituale*, i.e. that 'fragment' by virtue of which they thought themselves superior to others. The significance of the Logos made flesh for the whole Irenaean anthropology is noticeable.

[229] Iren., *Adv. Haer.* III, 22, 1. There only the human soul is explicitly mentioned, but it implicitly refers to the soul of Christ also.

corruptible flesh of man. Coming generations of the church's writers are to take more and more notice of this conjunction of Logos and flesh begun by Irenaeus, already following in the footsteps of the Apologists. We find ourselves at the first beginnings of a great soteriological concept, whose developments in the christological sphere are to make further special demands on our attention.[230] The essential point is, however, that the Logos is in a living relationship to the flesh he has assumed.[231] The coming periods of christology were to be deeply concerned in this unity of life. The Apologists and Irenaeus laid the foundations for their results.

CONCLUSION

This survey of the growth of christology in the second century could certainly have probed deeper. It has, however, been made as wide as it is to show how the second century is a link between the apostolic age and the emergence of the christological problem proper and to make clear its theological significance. This significance seems to us to lie in the following characteristics:

1. Nourished completely by the tradition of the primitive church, its interpretation of the Old Testament, and more and more too by the express use of the writings of the New Testament, this century made belief in Jesus Christ as true God and true man and belief in the *one* Christ prevail with equal weight in totally different strata of church life. Jewish Christians and Gentile Christians, popular christology and already more eminent spirits like Ignatius of Antioch, Justin and Irenaeus, put forward the same faith in Christ, despite all the differences. This faith sought expression in doctrine, in creed and in picture.[232] The struggle against the docetists and the adoptionists gives rise to stronger stress on the Godhead and the manhood in Christ. The dispute with Gnosticism brings quite clearly into sight the basic features of the salvation history and the Christian redeemer-figure.

[230] Note the richness of the language which Irenaeus uses to describe the circumstances of the conjunction of God and man in Christ. IV, 33, 4, θεὸς ἐχωρήθη εἰς ἄνθρωπον; cf. later Methodius of Olympus, *Symposium* 3, 4; III, 16, 6: the only-begotten Logos, united and interspersed in his creation (*consparsus*, Greek perhaps συνεσπαρμένος); III, 20, 2 '*Verbum Dei quod habitavit in homine*'; IV, 20, 4 '*Commixtio et communio Dei et hominis*'; IV, 33, 11 ἕνωσις τοῦ λόγου τοῦ θεοῦ πρὸς τὸ πλάσμα αὐτοῦ. The double phrases, like *commixtio et communio, communio et unitas, adunitio et communio*, are used both of Christ and of Christians to express their union with God. This is a typically Irenaean way of thinking (teaching a mystical-real redemption). Cf. III, 18, 7 '*haerere itaque fecit et adunivit . . . hominem Deo*'.

[231] Iren., *Adv. Haer.* III, 19, 3: the humanity in Christ is the target for temptation and suffering, the Logos is the source of glorification. The Logos must 'quiesce' so that the human nature of Christ can suffer, just as on the other hand it 'comes to the rescue' in victory, in the resurrection and the ascension (ἡσυχάζοντος τοῦ Λόγου–συγγινομένου). We will see how strongly Athanasius piles up such clauses, but unlike Irenaeus, we must in his case take Stoic ideas of the work of the Logos into account.

[232] Cf. A. Grillmeier, *Der Logos am Kreuz*, München 1956 (with bibliography); F. M. Braun, *Jean le Théologien et son Évangile dans l'Église ancienne*, Paris 1959, also refers to iconography.

2. Despite this emphatic delineation of the God-manhood of Jesus Christ, there is still no doctrine of two natures in the technical sense. Only Melito makes the first timid beginnings. The simple language of the church's proclamation is retained, although it is in fact expressing just what the technical language of the doctrine of two natures is to say later. It is for precisely this reason that the second century, seen from the point of view of the history of tradition, is so valuable. Because the love of the mysteries of the life of Jesus and the view of salvation history is still so much alive, because the unity of history is supported by typology and exegesis of the Old Testament, the portrait of Christ in the second century still seems dynamic, and not static, despite all the stress on Godhead and manhood and an often monotonous antithetical way of making christological statements.

3. Nevertheless, the second century is already brought up against the christological problem proper in two ways:

(a) The problem of the relationship between the Father and the Logos emerges (Justin; the Apologists), as we shall now see.

(b) Already round about 178, Celsus was putting quite pointedly the question how Godhead and manhood could be united in the one Christ. He confronted the theology of the church with a dilemma—either docetism or a change in the Godhead. In other words, either the incarnation of Christ is only a semblance, or it means that the Godhead is changed: 'Either God really changes himself, as they say, into a mortal body . . . or he himself is not changed, but makes those who see him think that he is so changed (ποιεῖ δὲ τοὺς ὁρῶντας δοκεῖν). But in that case he is a deceiver and a liar.'[233]

So the second century is already confronted with problems as difficult as any generation of Christian theologians had to solve. The doctrine of the 'one person in two natures', much abused because of its technical terms, was the only way out of the dilemma raised by Celsus. The question was whether God had really entered history while still remaining God, the same problem with which contemporary theology is still engaged, though in a different way, in its debate with Bultmann. The substance of Christianity was at stake.

[233] Cf. Origen, C. Celsum IV, 18: GCS Orig. I, 287.

FROM HIPPOLYTUS TO ORIGEN: THE FOUNDATION OF CHRISTOLOGY AS SPECULATIVE THEOLOGY AND THE EMERGENCE OF HELLENISM

THE foundations for the further development of christology were laid in the East (by Origen) and in the West (by Tertullian) during the first half of the third century. Justin had, of course, already done some preliminary work. The controversy with Gnosticism had made the church all the more conscious of the value of a closed biblical and apostolic tradition within the framework of the *regula fidei*. This consciousness is to become a constant corrective in the trinitarian and christological struggles of later times, and is further strengthened by the introduction into theology of the 'argument from the Fathers'. At the same time, the church found herself driven to thinking through the traditional material of her belief more deeply, whether from an inward interest in the Christian revelation or from the demands of the controversy with Judaism and paganism. The hour had come for the birth of speculative theology, of theological reflection, of *théologie savante*. The confession of Jesus Christ as the Son of God, the *novum* of the Christian faith (cf. Irenaeus, *Adv. Haer.* IV, 28, 2), demanded of Christian theology a twofold demonstration, first that it was compatible with Jewish monotheism, and secondly that it was different from pagan polytheism. The solution of this problem depended on the possibility of combining in God a true unity with a true distinction (between Father, Son and Spirit). At the same time, Christians became more and more conscious of what it meant to assert that God had been made incarnate.

As a result of Gnosticism, Christian theologians also saw themselves compelled both to show how their belief in God the Father and God the Son incarnate fitted into the whole pattern of the relationship between God and the world and to construct a Christian picture of the world and of history. Here christology had its chance of becoming the cardinal point of a *Weltanschauung*. And here Christian theologians made a contribution which can and must be placed alongside the great cosmological systems of Platonism, Stoicism and Neo-Platonism. As a result of these systems, above all Stoicism, Middle Platonism and finally Neo-Platonism, the theologians were also stimulated to make speculations, and they began to see the possibility of making a first attempt at solving the problems mentioned above. The Gnostic doctrine of emanation must not be forgotten in this context.[1]

[1] There is a good discussion in H. Dörrie, 'Was ist "spätantiker Platonismus"? Überlegungen zur Grenzziehung zwischen Platonismus und Christentum', *ThR* 36, 1971, 285–302, of the question

The procession of the Son and the procession of the world, creation and incarnation: for all this the acknowledged systems offered some help, but it was only very limited. The Christian problems burst the bounds of any one system. If this was not realized, if an attempt was made to apply any of these systems to the Christian revelation without correction, the result was of necessity a false one. An identification of the Neo-Platonic triad of *Hen*, *Nous* and *Pneuma* with the Christian triad of Father, Logos and Spirit inevitably led to a denial of the transcendent-immanent character of this Christian triad, i.e. to Arianism. A transference of the Stoic teaching of expansion and contraction to the procession of the Son and the Spirit led to no less dangerous consequences. So the history of Christian theology, now beginning, was often like a movement made up of two steps forward and one back. Hardly any speculative attempt at interpretation succeeded at once. Corrections had to be made continually in the light of the church tradition. If these were refused, the result was a real paganizing and Hellenizing, and thus a debasing, of the Christian revelation. Where the analogical character of the speculative concepts or even of the popular pictures with which this revelation was expressed was not consciously borne in mind, the peculiar element of a transcendent reality could never be preserved.

Over against this, the church's dogmas of the Trinity and the incarnation are an attempt to maintain the mystery inherent in the basic data of the Christian revelation by a limited use of Hellenistic or contemporary concepts and language and to avoid the distortions of Hellenization. To see the chronic Hellenization of Christianity in these dogmas themselves

whether in this context one should speak of the 'Platonism of the Church Fathers' or (better) only of 'Platonizing Fathers'. Further comments are added by E. P. Meijering, 'Zehn Jahre Forschung zum Thema Platonismus und Kirchenväter', ibid., 303–20. On the theme of 'emanations' see H. Dörrie, 'Emanation. Ein unphilosophisches Wort in spätantiken Denken', *Parusia. Studien zur Philosophie Platons und zur Problemgeschichte des Platonismus* (Festgabe f. Johannes Hirschberger, ed. K. Flasch), Frankfurt 1965, 119–41; J. Ratzinger, 'Emanation', *RAC* 4, 1959, 1219–28; Dörrie explains the different position of 'emanation' in Plato. 'After Plato notions of emanation have no more place in the now dominant philosophy than in higher literature' (128f.). However, Clement of Alexandria and Eusebius sought to characterize the Platonist doctrine of the *Nous*—apparently unintentionally—with the word ἀπόρροια (137). 'Plotinus virtually avoided the notion of emanations. . . . He persistently contested . . . the notion that the One expanded to become the many by emanation. The Gnostics were the real representative of a doctrine of emanation. They wanted to use it to explain how a God outside the world could come into contact with man, and indeed with a God who stood over against the world. If emanations of God can be demonstrated in this world, then a bridgehead has been established which is all-important to Gnosticism, despite its pessimism' (130). Despite the fundamentally anti-Gnostic thought of Christianity, for a time ἀπόρροια became a fashionable word. Cf. Tertullian (see below; further instances in Dörrie, 137f.). But emanation models (like those involving springs or rivers) could only characterize processes from the lower levels of nature. The idea that the 'source' may lose something of its substance does not necessarily arise at first. Even Plutarch does not introduce the notion of emanation into the central areas of philosophy (ibid., 135). Once Nicaea and Nicene theology had made a sharp distinction between the begetting of the Son within the Godhead and the 'procession' of the Spirit in God on the one hand, and the 'creation' of all things outside God on the other, a doctrine of emanation was quite unnecessary. For the interpretation of Plotinian and Neo-Platonic philosophy see K. Kremer, *Die Neuplatonische Seinsphilosophie und ihre Wirkung auf Thomas von Aquin* (Studien zur Problemgeschichte der antiken und mittelalterlichen Philosophie 1), Leiden 1966, 1971², 2–7, 321–3, 343, 471.

(A. v. Harnack) is to mistake the first intention of the dogmatic statements.[2]

The process thus described begins with the Logos doctrine of the Apologists and reaches its first heights in Tertullian, Clement of Alexandria and Origen.

1. THE LOGOS DOCTRINE OF THE APOLOGISTS

We do not consider it our task to develop this doctrine in all its details. We will expound it only briefly, in so far as it forms the background for the doctrine of the incarnation. There are two sources for the Logos doctrine of the Apologists: Christian tradition (the prologue of the Gospel of John) and Hellenistic philosophy (of the Middle Platonic and Stoic types); a Judaistic exegesis is sometimes combined with both of these. Philo is significant here, above all else, different though the verdicts on his influence may be. A common concern links him with the later Apologists. His aim is to convince the Gentiles of the universal validity of Judaism and its monotheism, and to this end he represents the law of Moses as the true philosophy. The Logos doctrine of the philosophers is for him a welcome means of explaining the relationship between God and the world. His own Logos speculation shows a strange synthesis of Old Testament, Platonic and Stoic features.[3] The wisdom literature of the Bible had given him a good foundation for his theological attempt, and the allegorical method of scriptural exegesis made it considerably easier to bridge the gap between two different thought-worlds. In connection with the Apologists it is important to note that Philo's Logos speculation is the most far-reaching attempt at the hypostatization of Wisdom (or of the Logos) within the Hebrew tradition.[4]

We may compare Justin, who considered it his task to convince Jews and pagans of the truth of the Christian message; here the Logos doctrine has a new lease of life. Where Justin represents an advance on Philo and the Stoa, however, is in the proclamation that the Word had become flesh. In the light of this substantial expansion of the Logos doctrine, there was from the outset only a limited possibility for the influence of Philo to make itself felt on the Apologists. Nor should the philosophical influence be over-estimated.

Although throughout the Apologies Christianity is more or less placed under the protection of ancient philosophy, the superiority of Christianity over the latter is stressed

---

[2] On the whole problem see A. Grillmeier, 'Hellenisierung-Judaisierung des Christentums', Schol 33, 1958, 321–55, 528–58.
[3] R. Holte, Logos spermatikos, 123.
[4] Ibid. For what follows, note L. W. Barnard, Athenagoras. A Study in Second Century Christian Apologetic (Théologie historique 18), Paris 1972. Barnard stresses that Athenagoras is able to avoid any appearance of subordinationism.

consistently, and the Second Apology closes with Justin, in spite of the partial agreement, abandoning all philosophical systems and confessing his wish to be considered solely as a Christian.[5]

But Greek philosophy also had an influence on the Apologists by way of the Gnostic writings. The Logos is also mentioned in them. He has a cosmic role in creation, as an intermediate being or as an emanation. Or he emerges as a mythical figure, as the redeemer of the soul. Valentinian Gnosis, with its doctrine of syzygies and emanations, provides the richest material for this. The *Evangelium Veritatis* (16, 23, 26, 37, 41) and the *Apocryphon Ioannis*[6] also speak of the Logos as an emanation of creation, as revealer and saviour. The Odes of Solomon (12. 10ff.; 16. 19; 41. 11–14) also bear witness to the same Logos myth. It is quite possible that through Gnosticism an earlier myth has been enriched by the Christian doctrine of the redeemer, and not vice versa. The early history of the Nicene *homoousios* shows us that the theologians of the church were probably made aware of this concept, and thus of the doctrine of emanation, by the Gnostics. At the same time, however, we can see how these theologians immediately make important corrections to this doctrine of emanation, so as not to make the Logos a creature.[7]

In any case, whatever the sources may have been, the Apologists already made something special out of the Logos doctrine and gave it a key position in Christian theology. They regarded the Logos:

(1) In its cosmological aspect as creative Word;
(2) In its noetic aspect as the basis of knowledge and truth;
(3) In its moral aspect as the basis and embodiment of the moral law (cf. Justin: *Logos–Nomos*);
(4) In its psychological aspect as the original form of thought (*verbum mentis*);
(5) In its saving-historical aspect as Word of revelation and mediator of salvation.

Aspects (1) and (5) were particularly suitable for interpreting the work of God outside, in the creation of the world and the incarnation of the Logos. Aspects (2) and (4) represented a special way of solving the relationship of Logos and Father within God. All the aspects of the Logos doctrine together in any case show that the Fathers were concerned with the totality

---

[5] Ibid., 111. The relationship of tradition to speculation in Justin is well described by R. Holte. On what follows see too J. Lebreton, *Trinité* II, 395–516; M. Pohlenz, *Stoa*, 400–65; M. Spanneut, *Le stoicisme des Pères de l'Église de Clément de Rome à Clément d'Alexandrie*, Paris 1957; G. Aeby, *Les missions divines. De saint Justin à Origène*, Fribourg 1958.

[6] Ed. W. Till, TU 60, 1955, 40, 103 (31, 15); M. Krause–P. Labib, *Die drei Versionen des Apokryphon des Johannes im Koptischen Museum zu Alt-Kairo*, Wiesbaden 1962, 62f., 126f., 209.

[7] Cf. A. Grillmeier, art. 'Homoousios', *LThK* V, 1960, 467–8. For what follows see C. Huber, art. 'Logos III. dogmengeschichtlich', *LThK* VI, 1961, 1125–8.

of God, the world and history. Greek philosophy, and above all Middle Platonism, offered a model for this striving after an overall understanding of reality. In it, the Logos was regarded as the reasonable principle of the cosmos, the knowledge of truth, and morality. In the controversy with Hellenism, the cosmological, noetic and moral aspects had to be put in the foreground. In transferring the anthropological distinction between the '*logos endiathetos*' and the '*logos prophorikos*' from man to God, however, the Apologists bring the psychological element into play. Remarkably enough, the first attempts at the idea of the '*generatio verbi per intellectum*', which would have been found in Plato (*Phaedrus* 276f.) and in Aristotle (*noesis noeseos*), remain unnoticed. Only Origen seems to have become aware of them (cf. *Frag. in Io.* 13).

This new step forward in Christian theology had important consequences. The positive side is not to be mistaken. The great history of theological reflection had begun. We may not see in this without further ado an unjustified rationalization of the revealed truth. For if the right bounds are observed, there is here only an *intellectus fidei*, which can leave the *mysterium fidei* intact. In the writings of *Justin*, for example, the danger of a rationalization of the Christian revelation was avoided by his feeling for tradition, in the face of which his philosophical inclinations took only second place. This is also evidence of his philosophical eclecticism.[8] Contact with contemporary philosophy was finally necessary because it was the only way in which Christianity could speak to the leading intellectual circles and unfold all its riches. Nevertheless, the new step remained a risk, and one cannot say that the Apologists were completely successful. The coming Arian struggles are no more than the consequences of the error which was introduced at the time of the Apologists. The error lay in the fact that the Stoic Logos was essentially monistic, and was understood in relation to the world. As Middle Platonism and also Alexandrian Judaism overstressed the absolute transcendence of God, his invisibility and his unknowableness, the Logos was too much restricted to the role of subordinate mediator. God the Father was thought to have such an absolute transcendence that he could not possibly deal actively with men (R. Holte). The danger of subordinationism was not far off. This danger was increased by the idea which linked too closely together the procession of the Logos and the creation of the world, the creation and redemption of man.

In calling the Logos the servant, the apostle, the angel of the absolutely transcendent Father, Justin gives him a diminished transcendence, even if he does not make him a creature. He compares the Logos with Hermes, the Logos-interpreter of Zeus (λόγον τὸν ἑρμηνευτικόν: *Apol.* I, 21, 2; 22, 2). There is a *deus inferior* subordinate to the *theos hypsistos*.

8 Cf. R. Holte, *Logos spermatikos*, 117-19.

Ce fils qui naît de la volonté du Père en vue de la création est véritablement Dieu, mais c'est un Dieu inférieur au Père: il vient en second lieu (δευτέραν χώραν), après (μετὰ) le Père qui l'a engendré, il est au-dessous (ὑπό) de lui. En un mot, 'il y a et il est dit qu'il y a un autre Dieu et Seigneur au-dessous du Créateur de toutes choses (θεὸς καὶ κύριος ἕτερος ὑπὸ τὸν ποιητὴν τῶν ὅλων)' (*Dial.* 56. 4).[9]

Justin's disciple, *Tatian*, also makes the procession of the Logos from the Father dependent on the creation.[10] 'The Lord of all, who is himself the ground of everything, was alone, in so far as the creation had not yet come to pass' (5. 1). There was no eternal pre-existent Logos in a distinct existence. But the oneness of God is to be regarded as 'structured unity'. The Logos is in God as Logos-power (*dynamis*). He proceeds from the oneness of God by an act of will. Thus he is the 'firstborn work' of the Father and the 'origin of the world' (ibid.). A bridge has now been made between the 'one' and the 'many'. We can see the intention of providing through the idea of the procession of the Logos an interpretation of the unity and diversity of God and the world. Now this procession of the Logos does not represent a separation. It is merely a disposition of the divine, or a voluntary, real self-unfolding of the one God. But it only takes place in respect of the creation of the world. Tatian, as a Platonist, thus sees the Logos only within this cosmological function and gives him no historical or saving-historical significance.

Hippolytus too makes God in his oneness and transcendence and complete independence the starting point of a movement which leads by way of the Logos to the world.[11] Logos and Spirit are in this God as *ratio* and *sapientia*, as *dynamis* and decision, and through the Logos and the Spirit so too are all things that are to be created. For through the Logos and the Spirit God both conceives and concludes creation. Hippolytus, however, takes the line further than Tatian. In creation, the Logos manifests an existence distinct from that of the Father, and this becomes increasingly clear in the law, the prophets, and finally in the incarnation. The consequences for the understanding of the *Logos incarnatus* himself are to be investigated later (see below). Here we are concerned solely with the fact of this connection between the procession of the Logos within God and creation and incarnation. Life within God, creation and history are closely linked.

Something similar is true of *Tertullian*. Like Hippolytus, he fights against the different anti-Trinitarian heresies which occupied the West at

9 Cf. G. Aeby, *Les missions divines*, 14. Cf. 12–15; B. Studer, *Zur Theophanie-Exegese Augustins. Untersuchung zu einen Ambrosius-Zitat in der Schrift* De videndo Deo (Ep. 147) (Studia Anselmiana 59), Roma 1971, 153–6: the theophany testimonies of pre-Nicene theology are discussed here, and the subordinationism in the pre-understanding of the Old Testament theophanies is discussed on pp. 56–69.
10 Tatian, *Or. ad Graec.* 5: Goodspeed, 272; on the whole subject see the good remarks of M. Elze, *Tatian und seine Theologie*, Göttingen 1960, 70–83.
11 Cf. *C. Noet.* 10: P. Nautin, *Hippolyte, Contre les Hérésies, Fragment, Étude et Édition critique*, Paris 1947, 251; G. Aeby, *Les missions divines*, 86–102.

the beginning of the third century. Hippolytus' *Contra Noetum* and Tertullian's *Adversus Praxean* spring from the same theological concern. Over against unitarian modalism they set their doctrine of the one God, who is yet threefold according to his *oikonomia*. Here the word and concept of *oikonomia* takes on a new application.[12] Tatian (*Or. ad Graec.* 5. 1) had already made use of this word to interpret the procession of the Logos. The Valentinian Gnostics had used it similarly to describe the internal organization of the *pleroma*.[13]

Among the Valentinians, the *oikonomia* embraces the whole providence or the gracious dispensation of God, from his primeval will in showing himself to the aeons to the complete fulfilment of the final consummation. In its origin and its history, the *pleroma* enters into the *oikonomia* of God, as 'upper *oikonomia*' (ἡ ἄνω οἰκονομία: *Adv. haer.* I, 16, 2) or 'pattern', according to the image and similitude of which the *dispensatio salutis* must run through the sensible world. Furthermore, the origin of the sole Only-Begotten (νοὸς μονογενοῦς), which precedes the constitution of the *pleroma*, represents one phase of the *oikonomia*. The whole Gnostic theory is centred on 'salvation'. The '*probolē*' represents an element in the mechanism of the divine dispensation. By virtue of it, the Godhead unfolds itself (*se administra*) in aeons, by projecting the leading ideas which have to introduce the descent of God into the world and the return of man to God. Incarnation (= *Humanación* = origin of man), redemption . . . and cosmogony are merely other phases of the one single *oikonomia*, which runs its course on two parallel planes: the upper plane of the *pleroma*, which ends in the salvation of the aeons in the sight of the Father, and the lower plane of the cosmos, which finds its consummation in the salvation of the spiritual church, in the union (*fusión*) of men with angels and in the unity of the universe with the Son for the vision of the Father. It would be a mistake to want to set the '*oikonomia*' of the first centuries over against '*theologia*', just as the incarnation stands over against the Trinity or the life of the Trinity. Neither Justin nor Irenaeus, still less Tertullian, knew a distinction of this nature. According to Tertullian, the Trinity itself develops within the *oikonomia*. In distinction from the '*monarchia*' of the modalists, the African stresses the Trinity by means of the unity of '*substantia, status, potestas*', which goes from one divine person to the other by means of the '*probole*', for the salvation of the world (= the church). The *oikonomia* is the drama of mediation (*mediación*) between God and man. Or, and this comes to the same thing, it is the saving history whose origin is to be found in the free decision of God, and whose end will lead to the Son giving back his '*auctoritas*' to the Father in the consummation of the ages.[14]

It is impossible to give a precise description of the historical position of Tertullian and of his trinitarian doctrine here. The point with which we are concerned in this context is sufficiently explained. The *oikonomia* within God and the *oikonomia* outside him are extremely closely connected. Creation and history threaten to become factors in the inner procession

---

[12] See p. 101, n. 220; on this, R. Braun, '*Deus Christianorum*'. *Recherches sur le vocabulaire doctrinal de Tertullien* (Publications de la Faculté des Lettres et Sciences Humaines d'Alger XLI), Paris 1962; bibliography, ibid., 158f.; cf. S. Otto, '*Natura*' *und* '*dispositio*'. *Untersuchung zum Naturbegriff und zur Denkform Tertullians* (Münchener Theologische Studien II, 19), München 1960; K. Wölfl, *Das Heilswirken Gottes durch den Sohn nach Tertullian* (AnalGreg 112), Rome 1960, 35–117. See now J. Moingt, *Théologie trinitaire de Tertullien* I–IV (Théologie, vols. 68–70, 75), Paris 1966, 1969, especially 45–8, 851–932, 1019–24.

[13] Cf. R. Braun, op. cit., 160, n. 2.

[14] A. Orbe, S.J., *La Uncion de Verbo. Estudios Valentinianos* III (AnalGreg 113), Rome 1961, 211–12.

of God. The neat distinction between the *processiones* within God and the *missiones* outside him must be developed in a careful process without the two being separated. Only in this way can the danger of pantheism, and also of subordinationism, be avoided. The tremendous attempt to make the doctrine of the Trinity and the incarnation into a *Weltanschauung* had to come to grief on this idea of *oikonomia*. Nevertheless, the attempt had to be made to see God, the world and history in a unity and to see all this in the light of the figure of Christ. It was the task of the following centuries to correct this attempt and to obviate the danger of the Hellenization of Christianity.

We now turn to the doctrine of the incarnation or the idea of the person of Christ for the time between Hippolytus and Origen.

2. Hippolytus

The writings of Hippolytus[15] represent a Logos theology which in its emphasis on the history of revelation directly recalls the second century, and above all Irenaeus, who was perhaps his mentor.[16] His love of christological antitheses points to the same background.[17] He is akin to Justin and to Tertullian in respect of his Logos-christology (see above). Here chief weight is laid on the idea of the incarnation and of the redemption achieved in it. This redemption is grounded in the revelation of the divine *oikonomia*. Now this has its unity in the one God, in the Father, Son and Spirit, distinct, but united in their ordering:

Il y a en effet un seul Dieu, car il y a le Père qui ordonne, le Fils qui obéit et le Saint Esprit qui fait comprendre: le Père qui est sur tout, les Fils par tout, et le Saint-Esprit en tout.[18]

---

[15] For the sources see B. Altaner, *Patrology*, London 1960, §31; J. Quasten, *Patrology* II, Antwerpen–Utrecht 1953, 165–98; for bibliography, ibid. and: M. Richard, PO 27, 1954, 271–2; G. Kretschmar, *JLH* 1, 1955, 90–5. Only the most important studies are cited here: P. Nautin, *Hippolyte et Josipe*, Paris 1947 (cited as Josipe); id., *Hippolyte, Contre les hérésies, Fragment*, Paris 1939 (cited as *Hippolyte*); id., 'Le dossier de Hippolyte et de Méliton dans les florilèges dogmatiques et chez les historiens modernes', *Patristica* I, Paris 1953. Nautin would assign the works of Hippolytus to two writers. To one, named Josippus, and depicted in the well-known Lateran statue, he would ascribe the *Elenchus*, *De Universo* and the *Chronicle* (of 235); to the other, a Hippolytus of unknown nationality but of Eastern rather than Western origin, the other works, *Commentary on Daniel*, *Blessing of Jacob*, *On the Antichrist*, *Antinoetus* (= frag. of *Contra omnes haereses*), *Apostolic Tradition*. Opposed are: G. Bardy, 'L'énigme d'Hippolyte', *MSR* 5,1948, 63–88; M. Richard, ibid., 294–302; id., 7, 1950, 237–68; 8, 1951, 19–50; B. Capelle O.S.B., 'Hippolyte de Rome', *RTAM* 17, 1950, 145–74. On christology see A. D'Alès, *La théologie de saint Hippolyte*, Paris 1906; E. Lengeling, *Das Heilswerk des Logos-Christos beim hl. Hippolytos von Rom*, Rome 1947, Dissertation; A. Hamel, *Die Kirche bei Hippolyt von Rom*, Gütersloh 1951; L. Bertsch, *Die Botschaft von Christus und unsere Erlösung bei Hippolyt von Rom. Eine materialkerygmatische Untersuchung*, Dissertation, Innsbruck 1962, published Trier 1966—with special consideration of Hippolytus' christological typology.
[16] Photius, *Bibliotheca Cod.* 121: PG 103, 401D—404A, speaks of the associations between Hippolytus and Irenaeus; cf. G. Bardy, 'L'énigme d'Hippolyte', 75, n. 5.
[17] P. Nautin, *Josipe* 50f., sees a difference between the *Syntagma* (*Antinoetus*) and the *Elenchus* in that the former stresses the Godhead and the manhood of Christ to the same extent, whereas the latter places special emphasis on the manhood. This will be because of its anti-docetic character. Cf. B. Capelle, 'Hippolyte', 161–2.
[18] Hippol., *Haer.* 14: Nautin, 257⁵⁻⁷.

Over against Noetus, Hippolytus is concerned to demonstrate the distinction in the unity of Father and Logos. That is why the fact of the incarnation is stressed so much. For here there is convincing proof that the Father and the Logos are distinct from each other, as the Logos now stands visibly over against the Father as 'Son'. This does not mean that the Logos first comes fully to himself (*qua* Logos) in the incarnation. It is that now the invisible procession of the Logos becomes visible to the world. Both are inwardly related. We shall demonstrate this from some texts taken from the *Syntagma* (*Adv. omn. haer. = Haer.*):

> Et sa Parole (Verbe) qu'il tenait en lui-même et qui était invisible au monde créé, il la rend visible. L'enonçant d'abord comme voix et l'engendrant lumière issue de lumière, il émit comme Seigneur pour la Création sa propre Intelligence, et celle-ci qui était d'abord visible à lui seul et invisible au monde créé, il la rend visible, afin que le monde en la voyant grâce à cette épiphanie puisse être sauvé.[19]

Now the incarnation is understood as the unity of the procession of the Logos from the mouth, heart and loins of the Father[20] and from David or the Virgin Mary. It is not just a matter of the Logos coming into the world, but of a procreation in respect of the world. So Hippolytus (*Cant.* 2, 23) can say: 'From him (= David) and from the heart of the Father (the Son—i.e. the incarnate Logos) came forth by birth.' In connection with Gen. 49. 25 he speaks of the 'twofold birth of the Word, from God and from the Virgin',[21] as Ignatius of Antioch had already written (Eph. 7. 2). He expressly emphasizes that Genesis sees this twofold birth in a unity: 'Showing both in one as though showing one, that we may know spiritually of him, both spiritually and physically.'[22] The Logos is begotten of the Father as it were in the corporeality which the Virgin supplies. By this he is first fully revealed as 'Son':

> Quel est donc ce propre Fils que Dieu a envoyé dans la chair, sinon le Verbe, qu'il appelait Fils parce qu'il devait devenir homme? Et c'est le nom nouveau de l'amour pour les hommes, qu'il a pris en s'appelant Fils, car sans chair et en lui-même le Verbe n'était pas vrai Fils, bien qu'il fût vrai Monogène. . . . Il s'est donc manifesté seul vrai Fils de Dieu.[23]

The Logos made flesh in this way, by his birth of the Spirit and the Virgin shown to be Son, has offered himself as Logos to the Father, and has done so through the flesh:

> Le sens était donc, frères, que le Mystère d'Economie c'était bien le Verbe, qui s'est montré par sa naissance de l'Esprit Saint et de la Vierge le seul vrai Fils de Dieu . . . [John 3. 13 follows] . . . Maintenant certes il y a de la chair, celle qui a été offerte par le

---

[19] Ibid., 10: Nautin, 253[4-8].
[20] Hippol., *Cant.* 13, 1, 3: TU 23, 46[16-17]; 47[6]; *Ben. Mos.* 15. 4: TU 26, 67[8]; cf. PO 27, 169.
[21] Hippol., *Ben. Iac.* 27, 3: TU 26, 44[20-1]; the Greek text, PO 27, 112-13, already uses post-Chalcedonian language: 'que le Verbe est engendré de deux substances (ἐκ δύο οὐσιῶν γεγενῆσθαι) de Dieu et de la Vierge'.
[22] Ibid., 27, 1: TU 26, 44[1-2] = PO 27, 109, 111.
[23] Hippol., *Haer.* 15: Nautin, 259[14-21].

Verbe au Père en don (car) celui qui par sa naissance de l'Esprit et de la Vierge s'est montré vrai Fils de Dieu s'est évidemment offert lui-même au Père, mais auparavant dans le ciel il n'y avait pas de chair. Qui donc était dans le ciel, sinon le Verbe sans chair, qui a été envoyé pour montrer qu'en étant sur la terre il était aussi dans le ciel?[24]

So the incarnation is firmly incorporated in the *oikonomia*, in a falling and rising line which begins in God himself, through the procession of the Logos and the Spirit. Hippolytus sees the 'one' Christ in two stages of his existence, as the pre-existent λόγος ἄσαρκος (first stage), who as λόγος ἔνσαρκος makes his way into history (second stage) by being born of the Virgin Mary: ὁ λόγος τοῦ θεοῦ, ἄσαρκος ὤν, ἐνεδύσατο τὴν ἁγίαν σάρκα ἐκ τῆς ἁγίας παρθένου.[25] The theophanies of the Old Testament also belong to this historical revelation of the Logos: they are a prelude to the incarnation, the beginning of the process of the incarnation in the full sense. Here τέλειος acquires a new significance in referring to the perfectness of the appearance in the world. First of all the Logos appeared only 'in part' (μερικῶς; *In Dan.* 4, 39, 4), ἐν σχήματι ἀνθρώπου, but not yet in full human form (τελείως ἄνθρωπος). This he first assumed in the incarnation. This approach via a 'historical theology' has at the same time its soteriological aspect; Christ experiences in turn every age of man (*Elenchus* 10, 33), he takes upon himself all the reality of man's sufferings (ibid.). Here, in fact, we come across the pattern of a soteriological principle put forward by the Gnostics (Iren., *Adv. Haer.* I, 6, 1), Tertullian, Origen, the Cappadocians and patristic theology in general: 'That which is not assumed (by Christ) is not healed (by him)' (see below).

Whereas Hippolytus lays so much stress on the two stages of the Logos as ἄσαρκος and ἔνσαρκος, he makes no explicit mention of the problem of the conjunction of the two states of being. Apart from one or two tentative beginnings, we still do not find any technical language from the doctrine of the two natures. The combination Logos-sarx in particular indicates the two poles between which Hippolytus' christological language tends to move. On the other hand, he excludes the pneuma-sarx framework of contemporary modalists. It is his purpose to speak of the pneuma Christi only in the traditional biblical sense. His Logos-sarx antithesis should not, however, be regarded as equivalent to the explicit Logos-sarx theology which was to be constructed later. Hippolytus has simply taken over the Johannine and early Christian statements about the incarnation. There is still no more explicit emphasis that the flesh itself is also possessed of a soul, as in a dispute with the Gnostics and the docetists the most important thing of all is the reality of the flesh.[26] Even when the

---

[24] Ibid., 4: Nautin, 241[26]–242[8].   [25] Hippol., *De Christo et Antichr.* 4: ed. Achelis, 6.

[26] Anti-apollinarian writers have retouched the passage with interpolations at a later date. With others, P. Nautin, *Hippolyte*, 114–15 and 261[24–26] (text), assumes such an addition in *Haer.* 17. Nautin brackets as spurious . . . θεὸς λόγος . . . κατῆλθεν εἰς τὴν ἁγίαν παρθένον Μαρίαν, ἵνα σαρκωθεὶς ἐξ αὐτῆς (λαβὼν δὲ καὶ ψυχὴν τὴν ἀνθρωπείαν, λογικὴν δὲ λέγω, . . .) σώσῃ τὸν πεπτωκότα ᾿Αδάμ . . .

phrase τέλειος ἄνθρωπος occurs, this is interpreted in a way which in the first place does not go beyond the problems raised in the struggles of the early church against the Gnostics. As a christological expression, 'perfect man' merely affirms the true reality of Christ's incarnation.[27]

Nevertheless the language of the future emerges; the Logos clothes himself with the flesh (ἐνδύομαι, ἐπενδύομαι), he dwells in the body as in an ark, as in his temple.[28] There is another striking passage, which already seems to produce the explicit terminology of the great christological controversies, but its language can fully be explained from premises with which we are already familiar, as far as an actual development of christological language is not perceptible. It is certainly surprising to find for the first time in Christian literature the word ὑφιστάναι and the concepts which underlie it, especially when it is in close proximity to an equally important term σύστασις. The latter, of course, was to have only a limited significance in the development of christological dogma. The passage in question occurs in the fragment against Noetus:

And he has taken for humanity the new name of love by calling himself Son; for neither was the Logos before the incarnation and when by himself yet perfect Son, although he was perfect Logos, only begotten, nor could the flesh exist by itself apart from the Logos, as it had its existence in the Logos. Thus, then, was manifested one (single) perfect Son of God.[29]

Even assuming that the *Antinoetus* is to be regarded as a *retractio*, no one should mistake the Hippolytean colouring of the passage. In this respect, it is especially important to pay attention to the idea that the 'Sonship' of Christ is to be associated with the incarnation.[30] This idea is of considerable antiquity, as it seems already to have been advanced before Hippolytus. Alongside this there is yet another reference to the Logos-sarx antithesis. Both Logos and flesh now become bound together in Christ in a special way, first through the idea, expressed above, that the Logos needs the incarnation for perfect Sonship, but further through a similar link on the part of the flesh—the *sarx Christi* cannot exist by itself, without the Logos, as it has its 'systasis' in the Logos.

[27] Hippol., *Haer.* 17: ed. Nautin, 263[8-10], Οὗτος (ὁ λόγος) προελθὼν εἰς κόσμον θεὸς ἐνσώματος ἐφανερώθη, ἄνθρωπος τέλειος παρελθών, οὐ γὰρ κατὰ φαντασίαν ἢ τροπήν, ἀλλὰ ἀληθῶς γενόμενος ἄνθρωπος.
[28] Hippol., *De Christo et Antichr.*, loc. cit.; *Bened. Is. et Iacob.* 6, PO 27, 20; *In Dan.* 4, 39, 5.
[29] Hippol., *Haer.* 15: ed. Nautin, 259[18-21], οὔτε γὰρ ἄσαρκος καὶ καθ' ἑαυτὸν ὁ λόγος τέλειος ἦν υἱός, καίτοι τέλειος (λόγος) ὢν μονογενής, οὔθ' ἡ σὰρξ καθ' ἑαυτὴν δίχα τοῦ λόγου ὑποστᾶναι ἠδύνατο διὰ τὸ ἐν λόγῳ τὴν σύστασιν ἔχειν. οὕτως οὖν εἷς υἱὸς τέλειος θεοῦ ἐφανερώθη.
[30] See above and the passages in P. Nautin, *Josipe*, 49; id., *Hippolytus*, 157–69. For the extension of this concept, with which the recognition of the divinity of Christ is closely connected, cf. H. J. Carpenter, *JTS* 40, 1939, 31ff. This theological concept does not, however, occur in the *Elenchus*, as A. D'Alès, *Hippolyte*, 27, also establishes. Cf. e.g. *Elenchus* X, 33, 1–17. For the second century cf. *Ascensio Isaiae* 8, 25, in E. Hennecke–W. Schneemelcher–R. McL. Wilson, *New Testament Apocrypha* II, 1965, 656. Cf. also B. Capelle, 'Le Logos Fils de Dieu dans la théologie d'Hippolyte', *RTAM* 9, 1937, 109–24. Against this P. Nautin, *Hippolyte*, 143–4, n. 2. Cf. again B. Capelle, 'Hippolyte', 172.

If a foreign hand can be detected anywhere in the passage, then surely the following clause has first claim to be attributed to it: οὔθ' ἡ σάρξ καθ' ἑαυτὴν δίχα τοῦ λόγου ὑποστᾶναι ἠδύνατο διὰ τὸ ἐν λόγῳ τὴν σύστασιν ἔχειν. But before anyone seeks to deprive Hippolytus of his right to authorship, he must first attempt to defend it. Perhaps the correct translation and interpretation will be of assistance in this task. It would be wrong to wish to read into the passage the precise idea of *subsistence*. It would be centuries too early for this. Ὑφιστάναι here has its root meaning of 'to exist'.[31] This will also meet us time and again later on. Now if we work with this original meaning 'existence', the word loses much of its strangeness. It occurs not infrequently in Hippolytus in this significance, though usually in the context of cosmological descriptions.[32] In any case, the word is already familiar in theological language. The relation of this passage to the genuine works of Hippolytus can be established still more clearly by its use of the term σύστασις, which appears to have an intrinsic connection with the other, ὑποστᾶναι. From the ὑποστᾶναι of the flesh in the Logos there arises a σύστασις, a *con-stitutio*. One comes across this term frequently in the theological language of the third century, especially in Clement of Alexandria and later with Methodius of Olympus. Hippolytus uses it quite often. It occurs with a christological application in the acts of the Synod of Antioch of 268, if these can be regarded as genuine. In the fourth century Apollinarius introduces it again. Elsewhere it finds no firm footing, particularly as a christological term. Its hey-day was in the third century.[33] Is it then too early for Hippolytus to make an attempt at the christological usage of these two terms ὑποστᾶναι and σύστασις? In time they lie extremely close to him. All the other christological thought and language which we find in Hippolytus give us good grounds for assuming the whole passage to be genuine, especially as it takes over the Johannine Logos-sarx formula (and derivatives such as the expressions λόγος ἄσαρκος and ἔνσαρκος). All in all we have the ingredients for a particularly close realization of the unity in Christ.

3. TERTULLIAN

In the opinion of many writers, the older Western christology finds its consummation in Tertullian, particularly in the formulation of his christology. As a result of his contribution—so this view has it—Western theology had a start of some centuries over the East. It will be our task to make an objective criticism of this African's contribution and also to

[31] Hippolytus, *Elenchus* I, 8, 2: (ὑφιστάναι synonymous with ὑπάρχειν); cf. P. Nautin, *Hippolyte*; 181f.
[32] Hippol., *Elenchus* VII, 21, 4; I, 9, 2.
[33] Σύστασις in Hippol., *Elenchus* VII, 19, 3 (cosmological); VII, 31, 1; VII, 15, 3; IV, 8, 5; VI, 29, 25; V, 26, 13. Cf. Methodius Olymp., *De Resurr.* I, 34, 4; *De lepra* 9.

determine his influence, which, of course, according to Hilary, was not great: 'consequens error hominis detraxit scriptis probabilibus auctoritatem'.[34] Certainly much of his influence remained alive, even if his name is often passed over in silence.

Tertullian grasped very well that the truth of Christianity is an unalterable word of God, spoken into the world, which has been transmitted by the apostles to the church. He therefore often speaks of the regula and the lex fidei, and refers to the traditio and the praescriptio, the specific limits of the apostolic message over against all heretical novitates. Now this phrase 'regula fidei' includes above all else the christological kerygma, which forms its content (see Prax. 2). In christology Tertullian remained completely faithful to this rule.[35] Had he of course taken christological speculation further than he in fact did, he would have realized the tension between his own view and the formula which he had taken over.

(a) Tertullian's christology in its historical context[36]

Tertullian has to defend the church's tradition of the incarnation of Christ on two different fronts: against pagan polytheism and against monarchianism[37] within the Christian church. In addition to this he has to fight against the disruptive and divisive tendencies of Marcion and Valentinus.[38] To combat these forces—from within the church's tradition —Tertullian forms his christological terminology. The Bible, Judaism, Gnosticism, popular and legal language—the latter only to the degree in which it was familiar to educated Romans of that time: these were the sources of his theological formulas.[39] Stoicism was particularly helpful to him for theological reflection.[40]

As apologist to the pagans, it is his task to 'probare Christum', i.e. to 'probare divinitatem Christi' (Apol. XXI, 14). He begins to answer this demand by making clear the Christian conception of God and particularly the notion of the singleness of God (ibid., X–XVII). Here he puts forward the idea of monarchia, the singleness of God—a concept introduced into Christian theology by the Apologists, which was made native to the doctrine of God by the Hellenistic Jews of Alexandria.[41] The historical

---

[34] So Hilary on Tertullian in Comment. in Matt. 5, 1: PL 9, 913.

[35] For the importance of the regula fidei see R. Braun, op. cit., 26f.; 424–6, 446–53. The whole chapter (407–73) is on revelation.

[36] For Tertullian's christology see n. 12 above, especially R. Braun, op. cit., 207–42, 242–326; R. Cantalamessa, O.F.M.Cap., La Cristologia di Tertulliano (Paradosis XVIII), Fribourg 1962.

[37] On the concept of trinitarian monarchianism see G. Bardy, art. 'Monarchianisme', DTC 10, 2193–209; E. Evans, Tertullian's Treatise against Praxeas, 6–18; R. Cantalamessa, op. cit., 126–31 (La Cristologia monarchiana).

[38] A collection of christological heresies in Tertullian, De carne Christi 24: CCL II, 915–16.

[39] Cf. R. Braun, op. cit., 547–54; R. Cantalamessa, op. cit., 119–25.

[40] R. Braun, op. cit., 554; M. Spanneut, Le stoïcisme des Pères, 305–9.

[41] T. Verhoeven, 'Monarchia dans Tertullian, Adversus Praxean', VigC 5, 1951, 43–8; R. Braun, op. cit., 71–4; K. Wölfl, op. cit., 41–9; cf. Tertullian, Apol. XVII, 1. The concept of monarchia is directed against either polytheism or philosophical dualism (instances in E. Evans, op. cit.).

revelation of this God has already begun in Judaism, and is also recognized by Christians (*Apol.* XXI, 1). In this revelation of God which the Jews have received, the advent of the Son of God was also prophesied, and indeed it has taken place. 'Thus there came he who by God's prior proclamation was to come, to renew the teaching and bring it to light namely Christ, the Son of God' (ibid., 7). But Tertullian has to explain two things if he is not to give any assistance to heathen polytheism: how this Son of God does not, as Son, destroy the singleness of God, and how it happened that he could become man, and become man in a way different from the heathen mythologies. In 197 Tertullian already adopts the course he is to follow years later in his *Against Praxeas* (probably written in 213).

For Tertullian, the deepest mystery of Christianity is expressed in the word *monarchia*, namely that God has a Son. This Son exercises the whole power of the one God in the world and for this period of world-time. Tertullian sees the *monarchia* first of all within the framework of the economic Trinity. God the Father remains ruler and he retains the sovereignty. But the administration of the rule is handed over to the Son. The *monarchia* is further guaranteed by the inner unity in substance of Father, Son (and Spirit). By the concept *substantia, una substantia,* Tertullian means above all to exclude any division in God. *Substantia* means first of all the character of the reality of both the Father and the Son. Both are *spiritus,* πνεῦμα. The Son has his *substantia* from the whole spiritual substance of God, but in accordance with a definite order of origin.

> The unity constitutes the triad out of his own inherent nature, not by any process of sub-division, but by reason of a principle of constructive integration which the Godhead essentially possesses. In other words, his idea of unity is not mathematical, but philosophical; it is an organic unity, not an abstract, bare point.[42]

By the substance of God, Tertullian understands a light, fine, invisible matter which while being a unity is differentiated within itself. Father, Son and Spirit are in the one total reality of God. The Son proceeds from this one *substantia* as it is in the Father and thereby receives his own reality, without being separated. Son and Spirit are distinguished through the order of their origin. Tertullian also describes the character of the Son (and the Spirit) by the word *portio*. This does not properly mean 'part' (*pars*). The Son is not a 'part' of the divine substance, but has a 'share' in it. The Father possesses the *substantiae plenitudo,* the Son is a *portio* and as such has a share in this fullness. The divine substance is essentially one; the Son is, as it were, an effluence of this one substance: *Pater enim tota substantia est, filius vero derivatio totius et portio (Prax.* IX, 2).

> With regard to him (the Logos), we are taught that he is derived from God and begotten by derivation so that he is Son of God and called God because of the unity of substance (*Apol.* XXI, 11).

Tertullian makes this community of substance clear by a number of similes. Just as a sunbeam, the extension of the substance of the sun, remains one in substance with the sun and yet is different from it, so too the Son of God is 'Spirit of Spirit and God of God' (cf. *Apol.* XXI, 12). The divine substance is thus not divided, but extends itself, and does so for a special task which the Son has to fulfil in the creation and redemption of the world. From the divine *substantia* there comes about a special form of existence, the *status* in which God finds himself. He is Father, Son and Spirit together: '*tres autem non statu, sed gradu, nec substantia sed forma, nec potestate sed specie, unius autem substantiae et unius status et unius potestatis, quia unus deus . . .*' (*Prax.* II, 4). By this *status* of God, Tertullian understands God's essential properties which guarantee his constancy, his inner coherence, his *monarchia*. The *una potestas*, finally, is the keystone of this unity of God. The *monarchia* of God is preserved because the Son exercises only the one rule of the Father and gives it back to the Father at the end of this world period. The will of God towards salvation is an expression of the unity of God, the guarantee of the *monarchia*, and, indeed, so much so that it is not only the norm of the Son's work but also the ground of the existence of the Son and the Spirit.[43]

It is not our task to show how Tertullian attempts to envisage the threeness in God.[44] To help in this attempt there are concepts like *oikonomia* (*dispositio, dispensatio*), the names 'Father, Son and Spirit', expressions like *alius, numerus, trinitas, modulus, gradus, forma, species* and finally the important word *persona*. In this context it is sufficient to indicate the thought-pattern which underlies Tertullian's interpretation of the unity and the distinction in God. He begins his thinking from the unity, the origin. The Father is the guarantee of the unity of God, of the *monarchia*. The Son is assigned the second and the Spirit the third place. Here Tertullian is thinking not of a purely static threeness within God, the metaphysical Trinity, but of an economic, organic, dynamic threeness. I.e. for him the second and the third persons proceed from the *unitas substantiae* because they have a task to fulfil. Only the Father remains completely transcendent. Because Tertullian thus has the unfolding of the divine threeness already happening with a view to creation and redemption, the step from trinitarian doctrine to the doctrine of the incarnation is easily taken. Suppose we return once more to the picture of the sunbeam[45] with which he explains the procession of the Logos:

---

[43] Cf. K. Wölfl, op. cit., 64–7; R. Braun, op. cit., 167–99: La notion de substance; 199–207: La notion de *status, gradus.*

[44] Cf. K. Wölfl, op. cit., 68–106; R. Braun, op. cit., 151–242, where the above-mentioned expressions are examined in detail. Cf. also B. Piault, 'Tertullien a-t-il été subordinatien', *RSPT* 47, 1963, 181–204.

[45] Cf. F. J. Dölger, 'Sonne und Sonnenstrahl als Gleichnis in der Logos-theologie des christlichen Altertums', *Antike und Christentum* 1, 1929, 271–90.

This ray of God, as had always been prophesied long before, descending into a virgin and made flesh in her womb is in his birth God and man united (*homo deus mixtus*). The flesh, formed by the Spirit (*caro spiritu structa*), is nourished, grows, speaks, teaches, works and is Christ.[46]

The Greeks, the Roman authorities and the Jews, who know only the *humilitas conditionis humanae* in Christ, will not be deceived when he comes at his second coming 'in the exaltation of bright shining Godhead', that Godhead which is the property (*res propria*) of Christ.

(b) Sermo in carne[47]

The controversy with monarchianism and patripassianism carried on in the *Praxeas* introduces us to Tertullian's characteristic christological ideas and terminology. The tri-personality of the one God is an unconditional presupposition for his understanding of the mystery of the incarnation. He has defended this in the first 26 chapters against Praxeas, the monarchian. Though he was himself a defender of the *monarchia*, he had now in some respects become an anti-monarchian. Praxeas had exaggerated the idea of the monarchy and now sought to bring his trinitarian modalism into his teaching on the incarnation as well, and to interpret Christ as a manifestation of the Father. On the one hand he wants to say that the Father became man and suffered (hence the name patripassianism), but on the other he must concede that scripture ascribes the incarnation to a 'Son'. So as not to have to give up his ideas of the exaggerated *monarchia*, he helps himself by describing the 'flesh' as the new subject to which the title of Son pertains.[48] Then the relationship between Father and Son described in the scriptures is only an apparent relationship which knows no real difference of the persons.[49] The 'flesh' and the '*spiritus*', which is the Father, i.e. the unipersonal God of Praxeas, together make up the Christ of patripassianism; a very rare christological framework '*spiritus-caro*'.

Tertullian begins from trinitarian presuppositions and introduces the Logos as a person, thus providing the proper subject of the incarnate.[50] The Logos, or as Tertullian says, the '*Sermo*'[51] or even the '*spiritus*', the

---

[46] Tertullian, *Apol.* XXI, 14: CCL I, 125.

[47] See R. Braun, op. cit., 298–326; R. Cantalamessa, op. cit., 65ff.; 94–6.

[48] Tertullian, *Prax.* XXVII, 4: CCL II, 1198: *Ecce, inquiunt (haeretici = Praxeas) ab angelo praedicatum est: Propterea quod nascetur sanctum uocabitur filius dei. Caro itaque nata est, caro itaque erit filius dei.*

[49] Ibid., XXVII, 1: CCL II, 1198: *Filium carnem esse, id est hominem, id est Iesum, Patrem autem spiritum id est Deum, id est Christum.*

[50] Ibid., XXVII, 4–6: CCL II, 1198f.: *Immo de spiritu Dei dictum est* (namely the word 'angel'). *Certe enim de Spiritu sancto virgo concepit, et quod concepit id peperit. Id ergo nasci habebat quod erat conceptum et pariundum, id est spiritus, cuius et vocabitur nomen Emmanuel . . . caro autem deus non est ut de illa dictum sit: Vocabitur sanctum Filius Dei, sed ille qui in ea natus est Deus, . . . quis Deus in ea natus? sermo et Spiritus qui cum sermone de Patris voluntate natus est. Igitur sermo in carne. . . .*

[51] On the description of the Logos as *sermo* and *ratio* see C. Mohrmann, 'Les origines de la latinité chrétienne', *VigC* 3, 1949, 166–7; Tertullian prefers the word '*sermo*' to describe the Logos, especially in *Prax.* Mohrmann shows that in Tertullian *Prax.* V and VII there is a neat distinction between *ratio* (*Logos immanens; nativitas imperfecta*) and *sermo* (*Logos procedens; nativitas perfecta*): see the analysis of R. Braun, op. cit., 264–72 (concurrence de '*uerbum*' et de '*sermo*').

spirit in Christ, is the only subject of the incarnation. In the preceding chapters, Tertullian has already shown that he is distinct from the Father as person, but is one in *substantia*. '*Spiritus*' is the same way of describing the divine nature of Christ as the 'pneuma' which we already know from the Greeks. This word *spiritus* often occurs when Tertullian wants to describe the divine nature of Christ.[52] Like Praxeas, he also speaks of the flesh as the other factor which is concerned in the union in Christ. The Johannine character of this language is obvious. Tertullian does not assume that anything special lies behind Praxeas' antithesis of '*spiritus-caro*'. His primary concern is with the Godhead. Thus in many sections of his writings he himself speaks in the terms of a christology which appears to recognize only Logos and flesh, although no one had hitherto spoken so clearly about the soul of Christ.[53]

So close a unity is achieved between the Son of God and the 'flesh' that it is possible to describe the Son of God as the incarnate. Tertullian also engages in the early Christian practice of the *communicatio idiomatum*. This is illustrated in a very vivid way in the *De carne Christi*:

> There are, to be sure, other things quite as foolish which have reference to the humiliations and sufferings of God. Or else, let them call a crucified God wisdom. But Marcion will apply the knife to this also, and even with greater reason. For which is more unworthy of God, which is more likely to raise a blush of shame, that he should be born, or that he should die? That he should bear the flesh, or the cross? Be circumcised, or be crucified? Be cradled, or be coffined? Be laid in a manger, or in a tomb? You will show more of wisdom if you refuse to believe this also. . . .
>
> The Son of God was crucified; I am not ashamed because men must needs be ashamed. And the Son of God died; it is by all means to be believed, because it is absurd. And he was buried, and rose again; the fact is certain, because it is impossible.[54]

Although this language is checked somewhat later, in *Prax.*, Tertullian stands by his christological expression, once chosen, but is now fond of adding the basis or the justification for it. In so doing, however, he remarkably enough does not refer back to the unity of person in Christ, but rather to the duality of the natures (in *De carne Christi* this is done by stress on the human nature of Christ, in *Prax.*[55] by the accentuation of the two natures). This is to be explained from his particular conception of the unity in Christ or of the conjunction of the two natures.

What is the relationship of the '*Sermo*' to the flesh? Does the incarnation represent a transition, a change and transfiguration (*transfiguratio*) of the

---

[52] E. Evans, *Against Praxeas* 63–70 (on Luke 1. 35); A. D'Alès, *La théologie de Tertullien*, Paris 1905, 96–8; R. Braun, op. cit., 189–92, cf. esp. *Prax.* XXVI; *Apol.* XXI, 11.

[53] On Tertullian's doctrine of the soul of Christ see R. Cantalamessa, op. cit., 88–90.

[54] Tertullian, *De carne Chr.* V, 1–4: CCL II, 880–1. See R. Cantalamessa, op. cit., 178.

[55] Tertullian, *Prax.* XXIX, 2: CCL II, 1202: *Quanquam cum duae substantiae censeantur in Christo Iesu, divina et humana, constet autem immortalem esse diuinam, cum mortalem quae humana sit, apparet quatenus eum mortuum dicat, id est qua carnem et hominem et filium hominis, non qua Spiritum et sermonem et Dei Filium.* See R. Cantalamessa, op. cit., 179.

Spirit (= Godhead) into flesh? Or does he remain what he is and is he merely 'clothed' (*indutus*) with the flesh? These are the two possibilities which Tertullian sees.[56] His grasp of the problem is not very deep, and his answer reveals itself to be no more than a first venture into the mystery of the incarnation.

At first glance, Tertullian's particular contribution to the problem of the unity of Christ is the introduction of the concept of person into christology, and the christological formula thus formed, which already seems to point to the formula of Chalcedon. If we are to be on the right lines here, we must attempt to work out an accurate understanding of this formula. It sounds like the result of long reflection and the consequence of a bilateral consideration:

Videmus duplicem statum, non confusum sed coniunctum in una persona, Deum et hominem Iesum—de Christo autem differo—et adeo salua est utriusque proprietas substantiae, ut et Spiritus res suas egerit in illo, id est virtutes et opera et signa, et caro passiones suas functa sit, esuriens sub diabolo, sitiens sub Samaritide, flens Lazarum, anxia usque ad mortem, denique et mortua (est.)[57]

Writers disagree in the translation and exposition of this important text, just as they disagree in the punctuation of it. First of all Tertullian stresses the twofold *status*, which is given with the duality of the substance in Christ. This duality must form the starting point. Whereas there is in God only 'one substance', even if it is divided, and thus also only 'one status' (*Prax.* II), in Christ there is a twofold *status* by virtue of the twofold substance. In the language of his time Tertullian could also have said that there was in Christ a twofold *natura* or *condicio* or *qualitas*. In choosing the word *status*, he is not seeking a juridical expression but making the concept *substantia* more precise both philosophically and theologically. In colloquial language *status* meant 'state of being', 'situation', 'condition'. But that is not enough here. Without doubt the Stoic notion of the *ens physicum concretum* is presupposed here—and from this point we will also be able to explain his concept of *persona*. *Substantia* is first of all seen as ὑποκείμενον, round which the οὐσία lies. This οὐσία forms the basis of the κοινὴ ποιότης, the 'common quality' of the substance, in our case the Godhead and the manhood in Christ. For this 'common quality' or even ἕξις, Tertullian chooses the word *status*. In popular language, *stare* had become an equivalent of *esse*, 'be'. *Status* is another expression for *quod quid est*. It can therefore be translated 'state of being'. In fact it is also elucidated in

---

[56] Tertullian, *Prax.* XXVII, 6: CCL II, 1199: *Igitur sermo in carne; tum et de hoc quaerendum quomodo sermo caro sit factus, utrumne quasi transfiguratus in carne an indutus carnem. Immo indutus. . . .* See R. Cantalamessa, op. cit., 72–8, on the importance of this '*induere carnem*'.

[57] Tertullian, *Prax.* XXVII, 11: CCL II, 1199f. Editions differ in the position of the comma in the first sentence. Oehler and Kroymann put: *statum, non confusum, sed coniunctum, in una persona, deum.* See R. Cantalamessa, op. cit., 171, n. 2, who mentions Bakhuizen van der Brink as supporting our position: CCL II, 1199; Scarpat.

Tertullian's writing by the word *esse*. So Tertullian could have been led to make his choice by this equation *stare = esse*. Perhaps we should say with R. Braun:

> Cependant, croyons nous, c'est plutôt au sens étymologique qu'il est attaché (*esse* à *status*): l'idée de 'stabilité' de 'presence immuable' du radical *stare*, est la ligne par laquelle il a été conduit à utiliser le dérivé nominal pour le *certum quid* des caractères essentiels et distinctifs de l'être concret.[58]

Status is thus meant to stress the 'permanent reality' of Godhead and manhood in Christ, or as Tertullian says, *deus et homo Iesus*.

This 'permanent reality' is only preserved because Godhead and manhood are not mixed, but merely united or conjoined, and are united or conjoined *in una persona*. Before we go on to expound and assess this statement more fully, we must first describe its wider context. If, in fact, says Tertullian, the unity of Christ were to be understood as a confusion and a new *tertium quid* arose, then the expressions of the two substances[59] would not appear so neatly distinguished (*non tam distincta documenta parerent utriusque substantiae: Prax.* XXVII, 12). A divine-human confusion, so to speak, would have appeared in the actions as well. Each of the two substances would then have been mortal, the flesh immortal. But because the two substances acted differently each according to its nature, each retained its way of acting (*opera*) and its own destiny (mortality, immortality).[60] Tertullian sums it all up in a scriptural quotation:

> Learn therefore with Nicodemus that what is born in the flesh is flesh and what is born of the Spirit is spirit (John 3. 6). Flesh does not become spirit nor spirit flesh. Evidently they can (both) be in one (person) (*in uno plane esse possunt*). Of these Jesus is composed, of flesh as man and of spirit as God: and on that occasion the angel, reserving for the flesh the designation Son of Man, pronounced him the Son of God in respect of that part in which he was spirit.[61]

The conjunction·between the two substances and permanent realities, the Godhead and the man Jesus, happens *in una persona*. It is worth noticing at this stage how the transference of trinitarian conceptuality to the incarnation proved as easy for the African as it was hard for the Greeks. It can hardly be by accident that precisely in his *Against Praxeas* Tertullian's formula for the incarnation closely follows the development of trinitarian conceptuality; here there is an analogous use of the same language and concepts. The triune God is different in person, one in substance: 'You

[58] R. Braun, op. cit., 207.
[59] For the important '*duae substantiae*' formula, see R. Cantalamessa, op. cit., 105–10.
[60] See R. Cantalamessa, op. cit., 181–6: Il '*distincte agere*' e le proprietà delle due nature.
[61] Tertullian, *Prax.* XXVII, 14: CCL II, 1200. For the anti-Marcionite character of the christology of Tertullian see A. D'Alès, *Tertullien*, 162–200; G. Quispel, *De Bronnen van Tertullianus adv. Marcionem*, Leyden 1943; E. C. Blackman, *Marcion and his Influence*, London 1949, passim; R. Cantalamessa, op. cit., 119–25 (Valentinus–Marcion); Barbara Aland, 'Marcion', *ZThK* 70, 1973, 420–47.

have two (Father–Son), one commanding a thing to be made, another making it. But how you must understand "another" I have already professed, in the sense of person, not of substance.'[62] Person and substance stand, then, one over against the other as the two planes on which distinction and unity are to be sought in the triune God. Both terms in Tertullian are accompanied by a number of secondary and explanatory expressions: 1. *nomen, species, forma, gradus*; 2. *deitas, virtus, potestas, status* and also *res*. The second series expresses the ground of the unity in God, the first series gives the ground of distinction. To this *persona* also belongs.[63] What does this word mean in Tertullian's theology? We will give briefly its etymology, its use in Tertullian, the sources of this usage and finally its theological significance.

The etymology of this word is still not finally explained, and the history of its interpretation is very complicated.[64] The latest attempt (with F. Altheim) is to derive the Latin *persona* from the Etruscan word *phersu*, and in turn to bring this into connection with the cult and rites of the goddess Persephone. According to this explanation, the name of the goddess was used to describe the 'mask', because masks were used on the festival of the goddess. Perhaps an adjectival formation lay at the root, e.g. (*larva*) *persona*—Phersonian mask. The substantive fell out, and the adjective remained as the word for mask. This resulted for the Romans in a remarkable mixing of stems, as '*personus*' (from *personare* = resound) and '*persona*' = mask fused into a unity. It was possible for the word *personare* to be associated with the completely different etymological formation '*persona*' = mask (from *Persepona* or (*larva*) *persona* = belonging to Phersu) because of the psychological and technical effect of the mask. The history of the meaning of the word *persona*, then, began with Etruscan rites and from there was extended to the stage. As the style of the Roman theatre clearly shows signs of Etruscan influence, it is probable that this was the way in which the word *persona* acquired for itself the meaning 'mask'. By the time of the Second Punic War *persona* had already taken on different meanings—theatre mask, character in a play or 'theatre role', perhaps also as early as this 'person' in the grammatical sense. Thus the meaning of the word developed very quickly, and by Cicero's

---

[62] Tertullian, *Prax.* XII, 6: CCL II, 1173. Cf. ibid., II, 4: CCL II, 1161: *Unius autem substantiae et unius status et unius potestatis, quia unus deus ex quo et gradus isti et formae et species in nomine Patris et Filii et Spiritus sancti deputantur.* Similarly ibid., VII, 9: CCL II, 1167: '*quaecumque ergo substantia sermonis fuit, illam dico personam et illi nomen Filii vindico, et dum Filium agnosco secundum a Patre defendo.*'

[63] In describing the Logos as '*res et persona*' in *Prax.* VII, 5 (CCL II, 1166), Tertullian only means to say against Praxeas that the Son is not a mere mode, but divine substance, *res*. For he explains how he understands the Son, '*substantivus in re per substantiae proprietatem*'. Tertullian's concept of *persona* should therefore not be reduced to a technical legal level as it is by A. v. Harnack. See E. Evans, 'Tertullian's theological terminology', *CQR* 139, 1944–45, 56–77; *Against Praxeas* 38–75; R. Braun, op. cit., 181–2 (*res-substantia*); 188–94 (L'application de *substantia* à la théologie).

[64] The following after M. Nédoncelle, 'Prosopon et persona dans l'antiquité classique', *RevSR* 22, 1948, 277–99; H. Rheinfelder, *Das Wort Persona*, Halle 1928; R. Braun, op. cit., 207–42 (!); R. Cantalamessa, op. cit., 150–76.

time it revealed all its riches at once.[65] How does Tertullian use the word?[66]

Persona is rarely used to mean 'mask' or 'theatre role' (*Nat.* I, 16, 5; *Spec.* XXIII, 5; *Carn.* XI, 5). But it occurs frequently (about thirty times) in Tertullian's writings with the meaning 'person'. Tertullian had no difficulty in transferring to the Godhead the designation for human individuality. Along with the rest of Western Christendom he also laid claim to and made use of a biblical expression to describe 'individuality', 'personality', which as a result of its Hebrew origin and Greek usage came very near to the meaning 'countenance'. This was *acceptio* (*exceptio, respectus*) *personae* (*personarum*), πρόσωπον λαμβάνειν, προσωποληψία. One particular stimulus towards the theological use of *persona* was the expression *ex persona*, ἀπὸ (ἐκ) προσώπου, 'through the mouth of . . .'.[67] This phrase was allotted a special role by the Christian exegetes who were, however, probably influenced by the rhetoricians and grammarians. Philo appears to have pioneered this 'prosopographic exegesis' (*Vita Moys.* II, 23). Christian theologians like Justin and also Hippolytus, Clement and Origen used phrases like '*ex persona Patris*', '*ex persona domini*' to give a dramatic description of the inner life of God and so to stress the distinction within God against the monarchians and against the Jews. The biblical use of *persona* itself or of πρόσωπον in the LXX further favoured a theological specialization of this expression. Tertullian's writings provide seven places in which he begins from the biblical usage of *persona*, viz. πρόσωπον.[68] In *Marc.* III, 6, 7 (CCL I, 515: *persona spiritus nostri Christus dominus*) and *Marc.* V, II, 12 (CCL I, 698: *persona autem dei Christus dominus*) Tertullian describes Christ as the (visible) *facies* of the (invisible) Father. Behind this there stands the biblical usage of *prosopon*. *Persona* with this content, however, occurs only in a few places. The other texts give *persona* with the meaning 'individuality'. Here the Greek *prosopon* is wrongly interpreted in the sense of the Latin concept of *persona*.

Now if *persona* was to receive a technical significance in theology, it needed to be made more precise. *Adv. Prax.* shows us this process, which

[65] Collection of the evidence from Cicero, Nédoncelle, op. cit., 297–8. It is significant for us that *persona* can mean: person in law—as opposed to case—personality or concrete character of an individual. Finally, the philosophic concept of person is already apparent. Thus Nédoncelle, op. cit., 298, can say in summing up the development of the term *persona*: 'Un peu avant l'ère chrétienne, il pouvait déjà exprimer l'idée d'individualité humaine avec plus de fréquence que ne le faisait πρόσωπον.'

[66] The following after Braun, op. cit., who, of course, does not go sufficiently into the Stoic analysis of the *ens concretum physicum* and thus does not fully define the breadth of the concept of *persona* in Tertullian from the point of view of the history of theology.

[67] R. Braun obviously does not know C. Andresen's important study 'Zur Entstehung und Geschichte des trinitarischen Personbegriffes', *ZNW* 52, 1961, 1–39, which makes a more detailed investigation of the prosopographic exegesis of scripture.

[68] These are collected in Braun, op. cit., 216–17 (*Herm.* XVIII, 2 = *Prax.* VI, 2; *Marc.* III, 6, 7 is to be compared with *Prax.* XIV, 10 and *Marc.* V, 11, 12; *Marc.* III, 22, 5 is to be compared with *Scor.* VIII, 2; *Marc.* V, 11, 11 with *De res. mort.* XLIV, 2; *Marc.* V, 11, 12; *De res. mort.* XXIII, 12; *Pud.* XIII, 2). The underlying scriptural passages are Prov. 8. 30; Lam. 4. 20 (LXX); Isa. 57. 1; Ps. 4. 7; 2 Cor. 4. 6, 10; Acts 3. 20.

consists essentially in the provision of a link between *substantia* and *persona*. The way to this seems to have been pioneered by the Gnostics. On the basis of Tertullian's *Adv. Valentinianos* IV, 2, R. Braun points out that Ptolemy regarded the aeons as *personales substantiae* existing outside the Godhead, while Valentinus himself included them in the Godhead as *sensus et affectus (et) motus*. Tertullian did not give an interpretation of Gnostic doctrine with this expression; it was the Gnostics themselves who had already created it for him. It seems that the concept of the 'divine person' already had a part in the Valentinian system. Whereas Valentinus was here conscious of the meaning 'countenance' and *manifestatio*, in the West the meaning 'individuality' became predominant as a result of the contact with the Latin *persona*. Perhaps, however, the two meanings are not so far apart as Braun seems to suppose. We must come back to this. In any case, it is fairly certain that *persona* had penetrated the theological realm even before Tertullian,[69] as is clear from 'prosopographic exegesis', the Bible itself, and the Gnostics. The formula 'two prosopa' already occurs in Hippolytus, *C. Noet.*, before *Prax.* was written.[70] The concept of the 'divine person' was already the common property of a number of theologians at the end of the second century. Thus Tertullian needed only to make clear to Praxeas a concept which had already been introduced, and the already existing conjunction of *substantia* and *persona*. In addition, however, he had a special incentive for this. Praxeas will not ascribe reality or personality to the Logos. He will not concede that the Logos has his own *prosopon*.[71] To prove the contrary, Tertullian begins with popular ideas of 'person' which he finds evidenced for the Logos in scripture. A person is a being who speaks and acts. Now God the Father and the Son speak one with the other (*Prax.* XI, 7). Besides, the Bible uses the plural for God (*Prax.* XII, 4, with reference to Gen. I. 27). There are also reports of different *voces*, which must have been uttered by different persons (*Prax.* XXIII, 4 with reference to the transfiguration and other scenes). Finally, the different names refer to different persons. Thus—Tertullian concludes—the Logos is substance and person: *quaecumque ergo substantia sermonis fuit, illam dico personam* (*Prax.* VII, 9). Person is only realized in a substance and is a special reality in the substance.

This now leads us to the last question. What speculative content does

69 H. Rheinfelder, op. cit., would see in Tertullian and particularly in his work *Prax.* the beginning of the theological-technical use of *persona*.

70 Cf. Hippol., *Haer.* 7: Nautin, 247[12-13]; 14: Nautin, 255[30]-257[3].

71 Tertullian, *Prax.* VII, 5: CCL II, 1166: *Ergo, inquis, das aliquam substantiam esse sermonem . . .? Plane. Non vis enim eum substantivum habere in re per substantiae proprietatem, ut res et persona quaedam uideri possit et ita capiat secundus a deo constitutus duos efficere, Patrem et Filium, Deum et Sermonem.* The author of the *Philosophoumena* bears witness to the same thing for Noetus (*Elenchus* 9, 12, 18-19; GCS 26, 249[7ff.]); Origen for the modalistic patripassians (frag. *in Tit.*: PG 14, 1304). Cf. Braun, op. cit., 230.

Tertullian give to his theological use of *persona*? We can pass over the meaning *facies*, 'countenance', here. It was already given him by the Bible and is associated with no particular philosophical content. The meaning 'individuality' is another matter. It is, as has already been indicated, to be conceived of philosophically along the lines of the analysis of the *ens concretum physicum*, as it occurs among the Stoics.[72] From this aspect we can understand why *substantia* and *persona* can have something in common and why they are finally opposed. We said earlier that in the Stoic idea the *ens concretum* is built up from the *hypokeimenon*. This is first made concrete by the κοινὴ ποιότης so that it becomes a κοινῶς ποιόν. The individual being is only finally completed by the ἰδία ποιότης. Only on the basis of properties, *proprietates*, ἰδιότητες, can a being act and move. These properties are also described as *species*, εἶδος, as *forma*, μορφή, as *character*, by which the individuality is made complete. Now this individuality is described as πρόσωπον, as *persona*. We have some indications that *prosopon* and *persona* have already penetrated theological language with this significance. Irenaeus thus describes the relationship of the four written gospels to the one gospel which is the message of Jesus Christ:

> *Vani omnes et indocti et insuper audaces, qui frustrantur speciem evangelii* (τὴν ἰδέαν τοῦ εὐαγγελίου), *et vel plures quam dictae sunt, vel rursus pauciores inferunt personas evangelii* (εὐαγγελίων πρόσωπα) (*Adv. haer.* III, 11, 9).

It is clear that *persona*, *prosopon*, here has the meaning of concrete, ultimate form, of ultimate individualization, over against a single generality existing not in itself but precisely only in concrete manifestations. The one gospel exists as 'quadriform' (*quadriforme*, τετράμορφον; *Adv. Haer.* III, 11, 8). Tertullian, too, regards the relationship of *persona* to *substantia* as being of this kind, or knows of it. The Gnostics did not want to describe the relationship of soul and body as a relationship of two different substances but wanted to see in the body only another form, manifestation or shape of the soul and to regard it as another power.[73] While Tertullian rejects this explanation of the relationship of body and soul, he sees in it a possible interpretation of the Trinity and then also of the relationship between Godhead and manhood. The one *substantia* in God has three figures, forms, *species*, *gradus*, *personae*, by virtue of a division of the one divine substance—again understood in a Stoic way. So in God there are

---

[72] See E. Zeller, *Die Philosophie der Griechen*, Leipzig 1920⁶, III, 1, 95; Pohlenz, *Die Stoa* I, 64 ff.; H. Dörrie, 'Ὑπόστασις. Wort- und Bedeutungsgeschichte (NGött 1955, 3) 35–92, esp. 61 ff.; E. Schendel, *Herrschaft und Unterwerfung Christi* (BGBE 12), Tübingen 1971, 30–73, esp. 48–51.

[73] Tertullian, *De anima* XL, 3: CCL II, 843: *adeo nulla proprietas hominis in choico, nec ita caro homo tanquam alia uis animae et alia persona, sed res est alterius plane substantiae et alterius condicionis.* Cf. R. Braun, op. cit., 227, n. 2, who rightly says that *persona* here has the meaning 'forme, présentation d'une réalité qui a une individualité, aspect particulier d'un être'. Note the reference to the '*uis*', the *dynamis*, which for the Stoic is only given when the final stage of concreteness has been reached. Cf. *Prax.* VI, 1 (*persona—uis*).

three persons. But what is the position in the case of Christ? Is the Stoic understanding of *persona* also presupposed here?

It should be noted that Tertullian is not concerned with the *explanation of the unity* of Godhead and manhood in Christ. He merely means to put right the christology of the monarchians. For them, Christ was a composite being made up of God the Father and the man Jesus, in one person.[74] The Father is the Godhead, the Son is the manhood (*Pater* = *deus; Filius* = *homo*). The one is named 'Christ', the other 'Jesus'. Over against them Tertullian asserts that Godhead and manhood may not be divided between Father and Son in this way. The Son is not the 'flesh',[75] but unites both realities, Godhead and manhood, in himself without confusion. The Logos (*Sermo*) already has a peculiar reality, a *status*, a *persona* in God. As a result of his assumption of human nature, however, this person of the Son has a twofold status, Godhead and manhood. Tertullian's intention is to express this fact of the constitution of Christ thus composed and its relationship to the Father. In this he does not mean to bring the question of the unity of the two substances in Christ into the foreground. He is more concerned to stress against Praxeas the Son's own character as 'person' and against Marcion the distinction of the natures. So we find the statement: '*Videmus duplicem statum, non confusum sed coniunctum in una persona, deum et hominem Iesum.*' The '*coniunctum in una persona*' may not therefore be interpreted in such a way that '*in una persona*' already provides the explanation of the manner of the conjunction of God and man in Christ. The way in which Tertullian conceives of this unity is to be discovered from other expressions. As a result of these it transpires that Tertullian has not yet considered what unity of person in Christ means, whether the 'man' in Christ has his own *prosopon*. In other words, the Chalcedonian problem of the relationship of nature and person has yet to present itself. Tertullian does not yet in fact have the explicit christological formula of the future '*una persona, duae naturae, duae substantiae*', though he seems to be only a step from it. He is primarily the theologian of the two natures or the two substances. This he says of Christ, whom he means to have clearly distinguished from the Father as a person.

If Tertullian does not interpret the unity of Christ in the light of the concept of 'person', he has nevertheless a definite conception of the unity of the two substances in the incarnate one. Here he remains within the framework of the Stoic *krasis* doctrine,[76] which knows of a *mixtio* or total mutual penetration (*compenetratio*) of solid bodies which retain their co-

---

[74] Tertullian, *Prax.* XXVII, 1: CCL II, 1198: *Undique enim obducti distinctione Patris et Filii quam manente coniunctione disponimus . . ., aliter eam ad suam nihilominus sententiam interpretari conantur, ut aeque in una persona utrumque distinguant, Patrem et Filium.*

[75] Ibid., 15: CCL II, 1200: *Novissime, qui Filium Dei carnem interpretaris, exhibe qui sit filius hominis, aut numquid Spiritus erit?*

[76] This has been demonstrated by R. Cantalamessa, op. cit., 135–50.

natural characteristics in the process. He also understands the unity of body and soul in man in the same way, ascribing a 'corporeality' to the soul. Thus he defines man as 'concretio sororum substantiarum' (De anima LII, 3). 'Concretio' is a rendering of the Stoic κρᾶσις.[77] He now also applies this doctrine of the mixtio to Christ by speaking of the homo deo mixtus and of Christ as miscente in semetipso hominem et deum.[78] As Prax. XXVII, 8 and 12 show, he first of all excludes in the case of Christ the mixing of the two substances in a third (a transfiguratio et demutatio substantiae, a mixtura ut electrum ex auro et argento; a tertium ex utroque confusum; a tertia aliqua forma ex confusione). It is the mixture 'secundum confusionem' (κατὰ σύγχυσιν) which the Stoics know. On the other hand, they also recognize a purely external union of bodies, a iuxtapositio (παράθεσις); for the Stoics, between the confusio and the iuxtapositio there lies the mixtio (μῖξις),[79] i.e. the total mutual penetration of solid bodies which preserve their co-natural characteristics, and the concretio (κρᾶσις), the complete mutual penetration of fluid bodies which preserve the corresponding properties. Since the confusio of Godhead and manhood is now excluded, the question remains which other of the ways of conjoining indicated above Tertullian means by his 'coniunctus'. Tertullian speaks of a 'coniunctio corporis animaeque' (De anima XXVII, 2) which for him, however, is a concretio, a κρᾶσις δι' ὅλων. In trinitarian doctrine he knows the 'personarum coniunctio' which is given on the basis of the one substance. This shows that in christological doctrine also the coniunctio is not to be explained as a iuxtapositio[80] but on the lines of this κρᾶσις δι' ὅλων. Tertullian confirms this himself in saying in Prax. XXVII, 4: caro et Spiritus (i.e. flesh and Godhead) in uno esse possunt. This duo in uno esse is for Tertullian, as for the Stoics, the technical expression for the physical union of the κρᾶσις δι' ὅλων. In choosing for this the more obscure coniunctus he was governed by the fact that in his controversy with Marcion the demonstration of the reality of the two natures or substances in Christ stood in the foreground. He could not stress the unity too much.

By this it is clear that Tertullian has not yet grasped the full depth of the christological problem of how the unity and the distinction in Christ are to be envisaged. He drew some basic lines for the solution, which could be enlarged in later tradition. Whether his first beginnings here were really

---

[77] Demonstration, ibid., 139–40. Cantalamessa rightly points out that Tertullian allows himself certain freedoms in the application of the Stoic krasis doctrine because of the demands of polemic. The same is also true of the analysis of the ens physicum concretum.

[78] Tertullian, Apol. XXI, 14; Marc. II, 27, 6; De carne Chr. XV, 6, and esp. 18: CCL II, 906. Tertullian appears to understand the union of God and man in Christ here on the lines of the union of the semen virile with the materia uterina: 'vacabat semen viri apud habentem Dei semen . . . sic denique homo cum Deo dum caro hominis cum Spiritu Dei.' Tertullian here forgets to stress the role of the soul of Christ, which he does not overlook elsewhere.

[79] When Tertullian, Prax. XXVII, 8, excludes a mixtura, he means by this word confusio, σύγχυσις or μίγμα, not μῖξις, cf. Cantalamessa, op. cit., 145–6.

[80] This is shown by a comparison with Novatian. Cf. R. Cantalamessa, op. cit., 147–8.

appreciated is, however, another question. The most striking thing in his writings seemed to be the formula of the *una persona* in Christ. But tradition up to Augustine is silent about it. Augustine himself (see below) seems to have discovered it independently of Tertullian. Had Tertullian thought his Stoic beginnings right through to the end, he would have been thrown up against the same problems as Nestorius—according to the interpretation of the latter advanced here. In the time of Nestorius the problem of the unity and distinction in Christ is fully raised and in his writings we see how unsatisfactory Tertullian's first beginnings prove. Despite the way in which individual concepts of Tertullian's—not his formula—already seem to point towards Chalcedon, his speculative understanding is still far removed from it.[81] But in that he regards the unity of subject in Christ, along with tradition, in the light of the Logos (*Sermo*) and holds to the *communicatio idiomatum*, his christology is preserved from the crisis to which his speculation would have had to lead him.

4. Novatian

Although Tertullian's formula *una persona* might have aroused attention, pointing so much as it did towards Chalcedon, it is noticed little, either by Latins or by Greeks, in the next two centuries. The christological problem is not yet seen from the viewpoint of the concept of person. Only at the end of the fourth century (in the writings of Jerome) and finally from 411 in the writings of Augustine does *una persona* acquire a new christological significance.[82] Though Novatian[83] strengthens the terminological link between christology and trinitarian doctrine,[84] though he speaks of the 'person' of Christ, he does so always in a trinitarian sense. Like Tertullian, in so doing he is still stressing the distinction between Father and Son.[85] Like Tertullian, and even more than Irenaeus and Hippolytus, he is set on distinguishing the natures in Christ, those of the 'Son of man' and the 'Son of God', going on to speak of a '*permixtio*' and '*connexio*', a *concordia*, a *concretum* and a *confibulatio*.[86] The union in

---

[81] In my account in *Chalkedon* I, 48, I have over-estimated the significance of the christology of Tertullian.

[82] See R. Cantalamessa, op. cit., 168f. However, Cantalamessa, op. cit., 94ff., 126ff., has been criticized for his thesis that *una persona* in Tertullian should be understood in trinitarian and not christological terms. Cf. H. Karpp, *ZKG* 75, 1964, 369–71; M. Simonetti, ' "*Persona Christi*" Tert. Adv. Prax., XXVII, 11', *RivStor LettRel* I, 1, 1965, 97f.

[83] Novatian, *De Trinitate*: On the threefold God. Text and German translation with introduction and commentary edited by H. Weyer, Düsseldorf 1962; A. D'Alès, *Novatien*, Paris 1925; R. Favre, 'La communication des idiomes dans l'ancienne tradition latine', *BLE* 37, 1936, 130–45; J. Barbel, *Christos Angelos*, Bonn 1941, 80–94; cf. F. Scheidweiler, 'Novatian und die Engelchristologie', *ZKG* 66, 1954–55, 126–39.

[84] R. Cantalamessa, op. cit., 169. Cf. especially Novatian, *Trin.* X, XI, XXIV: Weyer, 78–89, 156–61.

[85] Novatian, *Trin.* XXI, XXVI, XXVII: Weyer, 142–6, 166–8, 168–74.

[86] Ibid. XXIV: Weyer, 156–61; cf. R. Cantalamessa, op. cit., 147–8.

Christ is thus understood and explained along the lines of the Stoic κρᾶσις δι' ὅλων. Novatian is able to express both the unity of subject and the duality of natures in Christ in an advanced formula, as when he speaks of Christ, the Son of God, as the *Verbum Dei incarnatum*[87] or already introduces the distinction that Christ is '*qua homo ex Abraham*', '*qua Deus ante ipsum Abraham*'.[88] And yet Christ is 'one and the same'.[89] Novatian's criticism of the docetism, modalism and adoptionism of his time, which he bases firmly on biblical arguments, leads to some confusion of two christological frameworks. On the one hand he sets the 'Son of God' over against the 'Son of Man' to combat the tendency of these heresies to dissolve Christ's manhood, while on the other hand he speaks in the 'Word-flesh' framework so as to stress the Godhead. Here his starting point is John 1. 14.[90] His formulation of the mystical-sounding expression the '*sponsa caro*', which the Son of God has assumed (*Trin.* XIII, 68), stems from the resting on each other of the Word and the flesh (*caro Verbum Dei gerit, et Filius Dei fragilitatem carnis assumit*, ibid.). He finds no difficulty in fitting together the two frameworks of christological thought when he says:

> And how is he the firstborn of every creature except by being that divine Word which is before every creature; and therefore, the firstborn of every creature, he becomes flesh and dwells in us, that is, assumes that man's nature which is after every creature, and so dwells with him and in him, in us, that neither is humanity taken away from Christ, nor his divinity denied?[91]

Here he is not thinking expressly of the soul of Christ, even when he is explaining the death of Christ.[92] There is, of course, no particular reason why he should mention it at this point, as he is merely preserving the clause 'God has died' (*Trin.* XXV) against misinterpretation. Death affects only the flesh, the body, the man. It concerns the Godhead in Christ as little as it concerns the soul of the ordinary man. So over and over again we find the two contrasting pairs 'body-soul' (in the ordinary man) and 'Word-flesh' (in Christ) placed side by side. Even if it is legitimate to use this comparison in the argument, the neglect of the soul of

---

[87] Novatian, *Trin.* XXIV, 138: Weyer, 158: *principaliter autem filium dei esse verbum dei incarnatum . . . hic est enim legitimus dei filius, qui ex ipso deo est, qui, dum sanctum istud assumit et sibi filium hominis annectit et illum ad se rapit atque transducit, conexione sua et permixtione sociata praestat et filium illum dei facit, quod ille naturaliter non fuit, ut principalitas nominis istius filius dei in spiritu sit domini, qui descendit et venit, ut sequela nominis istius in filio dei et hominis sit, et merito consequenter hic filius dei factus sit, dum non principaliter filius dei est.* Novatian thus clearly recognizes in some degree that Christ's constitution is to be understood as '*verbum dei incarnatum*' and that the Son of God is the subject of the incarnation. The description of the assumption of the '*filius hominis*', however, shows Antiochene features. The union itself happens by way of the Stoic *conpenetratio* between the descending 'Spirit' (= Logos) and the assumed Son of Man. The impermissibility of speaking of a spirit christology in the same way as F. Loofs is rightly stressed by H. Weyer, 158, n. 92.
[88] Novatian, *Trin.* XI, 60: Weyer, 88. Cf. already Tertullian, *Prax.* XXIX, 2: CCL II, 1202.
[89] Novatian, ibid., '*hunc eundem*'.
[90] Ibid., XIII, 67–71; Weyer, 94–9.   [91] Ibid., XXI, 123: Weyer, 144.
[92] Ibid., XXI and esp. XXV: Weyer 144–6, 160–5; A. Grillmeier, *ZkTh* 71, 1949, 31f.

Christ is nevertheless striking. Novatian's christology therefore represents a remarkable mixture in which the old Roman Logos-sarx christology put forward by Hippolytus still plays a large part. There are, however, at this stage growing traces of the *Verbum-homo* framework characteristic of later Latin theology.

5. THE ALEXANDRIANS

The special centre of christological reflection in the Greek-speaking world of the third century is Alexandria. It is to maintain its leading role for a long while. Wherever Alexandrian theology penetrated, the picture of Christ has been lastingly influenced by it. For in it the doctrine of the Logos and the incarnation occupy a central position, even if they are at the same time seen through a special Alexandrian prism, in Clement from a Gnostic and ethical point of view, in Origen from the viewpoint of the *imago* doctrine and mystical knowledge. This distinction should not be taken in an exclusive sense.

(a) Clement of Alexandria

A masterly investigation has recently been made into the subjective conditions or the 'pre-understanding' of the christology of Clement of Alexandria, taking account of previous scholarship.[93] The idea of 'Gnosis' is the deciding factor for him. In Clement it contains the following elements: (1) an esoteric character, which is given to it by the acceptance of symbolism in scripture and the existence of a secret tradition; (2) the role of the Logos as the source and the teacher of 'Gnosis'; (3) the ideal of contemplative life in close conjunction with the idea of separation from the sensible world and communion with its intelligible realities; (4) the role of the encyclical disciplines and philosophy in the construction of 'Gnosis'; (5) the allegorical interpretation of the Jewish tabernacle and the entry of the high priest into the holy of holies; (6) the journey of the 'Gnostic' soul to heaven and its divinization.[94] Lilla stresses that the first four points concern the first stage of 'Gnosis', i.e. the Gnosis which can be attained in earthly life. Point (6) on the other hand, concerns the second stage, i.e. the 'Gnosis' to which the soul attains after its separation from the body. Point (5) concerns both stages.

In dependence on Jewish–Alexandrian philosophy, Middle Platonism, Neo-Platonism and also the Gnostics, Clement has a tendency to describe the esoteric character of 'Gnosis' with terms from the teaching of the

---

[93] The reference is to the study by S. R. C. Lilla, *Clement of Alexandria*, Oxford 1971, 142–89, which has already been mentioned above (p. 193). In the following, particular reference is made to ch. III, 'Pistis, Gnosis, Cosmology, and Theology', 118–22.

[94] Ibid., 143.

mysteries. This tendency to stress the esoteric character of 'Gnosis' is reinforced by his understanding of scripture: scripture needs to be interpreted allegorically because it is veiled in symbols. This makes comprehensible the assumption of a 'secret tradition' in contrast to the common Christian tradition. This secret doctrine also came to Clement from Christ—by the apostles. It is impossible to follow J. Daniélou in deriving this view of Clement's from Jewish–Christian apocalyptic; rather, we must go back to Gnosticism,[95] or more specifically to Valentinian Gnosticism.

In the present context, the role of the Logos in communicating secret doctrine should be noted. 'Just as in ethics the Logos acts both as a metaphysical principle and as a historical person, so also in *gnosis* he has the same dual role.'[96] Knowledge of the supreme deity can be attained only through the intermediary of the Logos, the second hypostasis. Hence there arises the position of the Logos as the 'teacher' in Gnosticism, and also as the high priest. As he may enter the innermost sanctuary of the holy of holies, he has full knowledge of the first principle. We are reminded of Philo and his doctrine of the priesthood of the Logos, and indeed of Gnosticism.[97]

But the Logos cannot remain purely on the level of a pure metaphysical principle; he must have a relationship with history. Clement already bridges the gap by regarding the Logos, as *pneuma* and *Logos spermatikos*, as the source not only of philosophy but also of the prophecy of the Old Testament.[98] But the Logos intervenes in history above all in Jesus Christ.

Like Justin, Clement begins with the Old Testament theophanies, in which he sees a preparation for the incarnation.[99] The incarnation

[95] Lilla, op. cit. 155–7. Lilla refers to a letter of Clement which has only been discovered recently by Morton Smith in the library of the Syrian monastery of Mar-Saba, and also mentions W. Jaeger, *Early Christianity and Greek Paideia*, Cambridge, Mass. 1965, 56–7 and 132, n.22. In this letter Clement speaks of a secret tradition which also came to the sect of the Carpocratians, but which they handed on with many errors. Lilla comments, 157f.: 'It is important to notice that Clement does not reject at all the Carpocratian conception of the secret tradition but, on the contrary, accepts it entirely, limiting himself to expressing some reservations on its content. The conception of the secret, esoteric tradition of *gnosis* is the same both in Clement and in Gnosticism.'

[96] Ibid., 158, with many instances from the *Stromata*.

[97] Ibid., 158 and 173, with reference to P. Heinisch, *Der Einfluss Philos auf die älteste christliche Exegese*, Münster 1908, 233–9 ('the high priest'); 240–9 (the tabernacle); C. Montdésert, *Clément d'Alexandrie. Introduction à l'étude de sa pensée religieuse à partir de l'Ecriture*, Paris 1944, 172–82; id., 'Le symbolisme chez Clément d'Alexandrie', *RSR* 26, 1936, 158–80. For Gnosticism see ibid., 160–3, with instances.

[98] Ibid., 9–59 (Clement's views on the origin and value of Greek philosophy).

[99] See G. Aeby, *Les missions divines de Saint Justin à Origène*, Fribourg 1958, 120–46; H. A. Wolfson, *The Philosophy of the Church Fathers* I, Cambridge, Mass. 1956, 193–256; A. Mehat, 'L'hypothèse des Testimonia à l'épreuve des Stromates. Remarques sur les citations de l'Ancien Testament chez Clément d'Alexandrie', *La Bible et les Pères* (*Colloque de Strasbourg 1ᵉʳ–3 Octobre 1969*), Paris 1971, 229–42. Some remarks which describe Clement well might be cited: 'Non seulement donc Clément a conservé des *Testimonia*, mais encore il en a conservé l'ésprit, il en a au moins l'intention. . . . On a exagéré l'hellénisme de Clément. Mais enfin il est assurément le plus hellénisant des Pères de l'Eglise avant Nicée' (233). 'Il est le dernier des Pères, on l'a dit, qui soit encore au contact vivant de la tradition

itself, however, is something completely new, just as there are also a new people of God and a New Testament (*Paed.* I, 59, 1). The incarnate Logos as Logos retains his transcendence, which he has in common with the Father—an advance on Justin and the Apologists, who had exaggerated the transcendence of the Father and based the possibility of a mission of the Logos on his diminished transcendence. His entry into history, however, makes him its centre and completes the Old Testament theophanies. His coming is the sign of the Father's love for men (*Paed.* I, 8, 2; *Protr.* 116, 1). In him a new sun rises on the world (*Paed.* I, 88, 2), the sun of the revelation of the Father which alone brings us the true light of the knowledge of God (*Protr.* 113, 3). The incarnation is the Son's step into visibility (*Strom.* V, 39, 2; 16, 5). The Logos begets himself—Clement applies Luke 1. 35 to the Logos—without thereby becoming twofold. He remains identical with himself (ἐν ταυτότητι).[100] He is one and the same who is begotten of the Father in eternity and becomes flesh (*Exc. Theod.* 7. 4; 8. 1). The Gnostic multiplicity of Logoi and redeemer figures is thus strictly repudiated. Clement stands by the Johannine prologue. This gives his christology a clear line and focus in contrast to the Gnostic dissolution. Of course in Clement the relationship between the inner begetting of the Logos in God and the incarnation is as unexplained as in the early theologians considered hitherto. The starting point of the mission of the Son into the world is the begetting of the Logos as the *Imago* of the Father, as his *prosopon* (*Strom.* V, 34, 1). 'The prosopon of the Father is the Logos, by whom God is made visible and manifest' (*Paed.* I, 57, 2).[101] The Son as incarnate is thus the *prosopon* of the Father, but is so because he is already the *Imago* of the invisible God from eternity (*Strom.* V, 38, 7). By virtue of his being begotten of the eternal *Nous* he is already 'revealer' by nature. So closely, however, do eternal begetting and incarnation seem to be linked together that the first only takes place because the second lies in the purpose and the love of God (*Q. div. salv.* 37, 1–2).

S. R. C. Lilla, in accord with the majority of modern scholars, has again stressed the development of the inner 'three different stages of existence' of the Logos; at the same time, however, he points to the contacts between Clement and Jewish–Alexandrian philosophy, Middle Platonism and Neo-Platonism:

> The Logos is, first of all, the mind of God which contains his thoughts; at this stage, he is still identical with God. In the second stage, he becomes a separate hypostasis, distinct from the first principle; in this stage, he represents the immanent law of the universe or, in other words, the world-soul.[102]

apostolique. Il vaut donc la peine de voir comment il cite l'Ancient Testament' (238; cf. ibid., 238–41). See id., *Etude sur les Stromates de Clément d'Alexandrie* (PS 7), Paris 1966.

[100] See G. Aeby, op. cit., 125f.; R. P. Casey, *JTS* 37, 1924, 43–56 (on the rejection of a doubling of the Logos).

[101] For the Logos doctrine of Clement see S. R. C. Lilla, op. cit., 199–212.

[102] Ibid., 201, with numerous examples of the origin of these ideas.

The inner *oikonomia* of God is coupled with the outer one, just as cosmos and salvation are conjoined. Clement progresses from the idea of creation and incarnation to the idea of the church (*Paed.* I, 27, 2). In the church, the school of the divine pedagogue, Christ is our father, mother, guardian and nourisher (cf. *Paed.* I, 42, 1–3). In that the Christ becomes the abode of the Logos through the baptism, he is made like to the Logos and God (*Paed.* III, 1, 5). Risen like the sun in the incarnation, he will become the sun of the soul (ἥλιος ψυχῆς) and escort it on his chariot to the Father (*Protr.* 121, 1; cf. *Protr.* 118, 4: picture of Odysseus' ship).

The fact that in contrast to the Logos concept of Middle Platonism, which is defined predominantly in personal and cosmological terms, Clement identifies the personal pre-existent Logos with the historical person Jesus Christ, shows his essential distinction from all non-Christian Logos and pneuma doctrines, however much they may have influenced him.[113] As Clement is so enamoured of the Logos idea, the emphasis on the descent of this Logos into the flesh is especially marked (*Strom.* V. 105, 4: τὴν εἰς σάρκα κάθοδον τοῦ κυρίου). This *katabasis* becomes a presence which can be comprehended by the senses (*Strom.* V, 38, 6: αἰσθητή παρουσία), as being bound to the flesh.[104] We shall now look at this picture of Christ as a unity of Logos and sarx rather more closely.

The unity in tension between the Logos and the flesh is the predominant factor.[105] It is true that Clement has repeatedly been suspected of docetism, but he consistently maintains the reality of the human nature of Christ, though at the same time his tendency to spiritualize seems to make the reality of the incarnation merely relative.[106] Attempts have also been made to interpret the figure of Christ which Clement presents as the union of the Logos with a mere unsouled fleshly nature, a position where the special significance of the Logos in Alexandrian christology would become manifest.[107] Put in these terms, however, such an interpretation is mistaken. The tradition of Christ's soul is clearly still so vigorous that even the teaching of animation through the Logos cannot obscure it.[108]

Nevertheless, we find in Clement precisely that element of the non-Christian Logos doctrine which leads to the total obscuring of the distinction between Logos and soul in his christology. His teaching on πάθη

---

[103] P. B. Pade, *Logos Theos. Untersuchungen zur Logos-Christologie des Titus Flavius Clemens von Alexandrien*, Rome 1939, 60–3; M. Pohlenz, *Stoa*, 415–23; G. Verbeke, *L'évolution de la doctrine du pneuma du stoïcisme à saint Augustin*, Paris-Louvain 1945, 429–40; S. R. C. Lilla, op. cit., 201ff.

[104] Clem. Al., *Protr.* 111, 2: GCS I, 79.

[105] After P. B. Pade, *Logos Theos*, where the Logos-concept is specially developed, also T. Rüther, 'Die Leiblichkeit Christi nach Clemens v. Alexandrien', *TQ* 107, 1926, 231–54.

[106] T. Camelot O.P., *Foi et Gnose, Introduction à l'étude de la connaissance mystique chez Clemens d'Al.*, Paris 1945, 80, 88f. Cf. the fine formula in *Protrept.* 7, 1: νῦν δὴ ἐπεφάνη ἀνθρώποις αὐτὸς οὗτος ὁ λόγος, ὁ μόνος ἄμφω, θεός τε καὶ ἄνθρωπος.

[107] See *Chalkedon* I, 61, n. 28.

[108] Demonstrated in T. Rüther, *Leiblichkeit Christi*, 235, 247. Cf. also the testimony of Socrates on Clement, HE 3, 7: PG 67, 392A.

is an indication of this. Clement distinguishes two kinds; the one is necessary for the preservation of the body (*Strom.* VI, 9, 71), the other is a suffering of the soul. The latter in particular must be subdued in a Christian if he is to be a Gnostic; in Christ, πάθη of the soul are quite unthinkable. On the other hand, bodily sufferings are necessary for the ordinary man (κοινὸς ἄνθρωπος) because of the 'economy', to maintain bodily life. But from either point of view Christ is without suffering. He does not need the automatic, bodily impulses to maintain his (always real) bodily life. On the contrary, these are replaced by the indwelling 'holy power'.[109] In him, therefore, *apatheia* is complete because the indwelling Logos can itself perceive those necessities which are brought to the notice of the ordinary man by the impulses which the creator Logos imparts. Without doubt we can trace here a strong Stoic element—the doctrine of the ἡγεμονικόν. Clement knows it, and knows it, moreover, in its original Stoic form, even though he expands it by adding biblical concepts. The λογιστικόν and ἡγεμονικόν is the fundamental basis for the organic unity of a living being, its σύστασις (*Strom.* VI, 135, 1–4), the seat of free will, decision and the power of thought. It is so to speak the soul of the soul.[110]

Now if the ἡγεμονικόν in its inmost being is none other than the Logos, or that part of man's being which has the greatest participation in the Logos, the christological significance of this Stoic anthropology is immediately clear, as too is the indication of the danger to the traditional christology. Clement speaks of the 'governing power' of the Logos.[111] Now if this Logos, entire and personal, has taken up its dwelling in Christ, according to Clement's Stoic–Philonic doctrine of the soul it must also be the predominant ἡγεμών of Christ's human nature. When the original appears, the copy must lose its place and function. The lower soul of Christ, then, remains throughout an instrument in the service of the λόγος ἡγεμών, as it is also the mediatrix between ἡγεμονικόν and body, and lies like a covering around the inmost kernel, the 'inner man'.[112] But

109 Clem. Al., *Strom.* III, 6, 49; GCS II, 218. Cf. T. Rüther, *Die sittliche Forderung der Apatheia in den beiden ersten christl. Jahrhunderten und bei Clemens von Alexandrien*, Freiburg 1949, 58–60.

110 See the index in O. Stählin (GCS), 447. Further on the anthropology of Clement in F. Rüsche, *Blut, Leben und Seele*, Paderborn 1930, 402–12; id., *Das Seelenpneuma*, Paderborn 1933; G. Verbeke, *Pneuma*, 429–40. Important for the history and significance of the *hegemonikon* is E. v. Ivanka, 'Apex Mentis', *ZkTh* 72, 1950, 129–76; on the Stoa, 147–60. This is a field of particular Philonic influence, through which Stoic and Platonic ideas worked upon the Alexandrians. On Philo, see F. Rüsche, *Blut, Leben und Seele*, 364–401.

111 Clement Al., *Paed.* I, 7, 58, 1: GCS I, 24, cf. Index, 447.

112 Ibid., III, 1, I, 2: GCS I, 236: 'Seeing now that the soul consists of three parts, the power of thought (τὸ νοερόν), which is also called λογιστικόν, is the *inner man*, which here governs the visible man.' The expression 'inner man' (ὁ ἄνθρωπος ὁ ἔνδον) should be noted. Henceforward it is to play a great role. Clement, like other representatives of the christological use of 'outer' and 'inner' man, goes right back to Paul, who for his part speaks in the language of his time. From this, an anthropological framework develops in the writers of the church. Cf. 2 Clem. 12, 4: καὶ τὸ ἔξω ὡς τὸ ἔσω, τοῦτο λέγει. τὴν ψυχὴν λέγει τὸ ἔσω, τὸ δὲ ἔξω τὸ σῶμα λέγει. Origen frequently speaks of the ἔσω ἄνθρωπος. In the newly discovered Διάλεκτος πρὸς Ἡρακλείδαν, ed. J. Scherer, *Entretien d'Origène avec*

in Christ, the 'inner man' is the Logos, which in Clement's christology becomes the all-predominating physical principle. The power of the Logos makes a transforming intervention in the physical body of the Lord. Clement takes over a curious point of view from the Gnostic Valentinus, that no true digestion and elimination of food took place in the Lord (*Strom.* III, 7, 59, 3). A still more suspicious idea occurs in the Gnostic 'Acts of John', which Clement uses for the exegesis of 1 John 1. There the apostle speaks of a tasting of the 'Word of Life'. Clement reports 'traditions' according to which John could thrust his hand into the inside of the Lord's body and there directly feel the divine power.[113] The Logos is the 'sunbeam' in the depths which must be distinguished from the bodily nature, the *corpus quod erat extrinsecus*, and it is certainly regarded as the real 'inner man' that is within Christ. In such a christology the human soul of Christ can achieve no theological significance, though to claim that 'a positive understanding of the redemptive meaning of the incarnation in Jesus is completely lacking in Clement'[114] seems to us to be too harsh. His whole christology is not to be identified with a number of speculations influenced by Gnosticism and philosophy.

(b) Origen

Our consideration of Origen—as earlier that of Justin, Tertullian and Clement—must begin from the church's tradition, and more particularly from Holy Scripture. Only in this way can we form a right appreciation of his *theologoumena*.[115] There is a real traditional basis to his christology

---

Héraclide et les évêques ses collègues sur le Père, le Fils, et l'âme (Textes et Documents 9), Le Caire 1949, 144–6 (new ed. SC 67, 76–80), he devotes a whole section of his arguments to the distinction between 'outer' and 'inner' man. The christological significance of an application of this distinction to the person of Christ is evident. If the 'inner man' is taken as man's proper being, it seems probable that in Christ the Logos should be regarded as this inner man. To fit in with the basic anthropological framework this can happen either with or without the inclusion of the (higher) soul of Christ. There are already examples of such conceptions in Gnosticism; cf. the *Pistis Sophia*, which has the power of the great Sabaoth, the Good, entering into Mary in place of the soul of Jesus: ch. 8, ed. K. Schmidt, *Koptisch-gnostische Schriften* I, Berlin 1959³, 8–9. For Valentinian Gnosis see G. Quispel, 'The original doctrine of Valentine', *VigC* 1, 1947, 66.

[113] Clem. Al., *Adumbrat.* (in 1 John 1): GCS III, 210: '*Et manus,*' inquit, '*nostrae contractaverunt de verbo vitae*'; *non solum carnem eius, sed etiam virtutes eiusdem filii significat, sicut radius solis usque ad haec infima loca pertransiens, qui radius in carne veniens palpabilis factus est discipulis . . .* Exegesis in T. Rüther, *Leiblichkeit Christi*, 251–3.

[114] A. Wintersig, *Die Heilsbedeutung der Menscheit Jesu in der vornicänischen griechischen Theologie*, Tübingen 1932, 72.

[115] This 'Origen the churchman' is developed particularly in J. Daniélou S.J., *Origen*, London–New York 1955; more strongly in H. de Lubac, *Histoire et Esprit*, Paris 1950; cf. H. Crouzel, *Théologie de l'Image de Dieu chez Origène*, Paris 1956; id., *Origène et la 'connaissance mystique'*, Desclée de Brouwer 1961; id., *Origène et la philosophie* (Théologie 52), Paris 1962. Against, M. Harl, *Origène et la fonction révélatrice du Verbe Incarné*, Paris 1958 (with extensive bibliography); R. P. C. Hanson, *Allegory and Event*, London 1959; and now F. H. Kettler, *Der ursprüngliche Sinn der Dogmatik des Origenes*, Berlin 1966. For criticism of Kettler see M. Simonetti, *I Principi di Origene*, Torino 1968; id., 'Note sulla teologia trinitaria di Origenes', *VC* 8, 1971, 273–307; H. Crouzel, *Bibliographie critique d'Origène* (Instrumenta Patristica VIII), Steenbrughis 1971, ad ann. 1966, sub nom. K. For Origen's methods, reference may again be made to M. Simonetti, 'Eracleone e Origene', *VC* 3, 1966, 3–75.

which is, moreover, expressed particularly clearly, as for example in his recognition of the two natures of the Lord.[116]

More important than the question of the relationship between Godhead and manhood in Christ, as far as Origen is concerned, is the overall framework into which his picture of Christ is inserted. He is said to be the first Christian systematic theologian, even if no agreed view has yet been reached on his theology.[117] The more the fundamental principles of his theology are recognized, the more profound a view of his christology is possible. But precisely here is the point at which contemporary theology is in dispute. Only a few points of current concern need be mentioned, but once again the question of 'Origen the churchman' comes to the fore. Hal Koch has sought to understand Origen from outside, i.e. from his context in the history of thought.[118] Origen is the Christian philosopher of 'educative providence'. He appears as a thinker who more than any other understood the problems of his time and gave a Christian answer to them.[119] W. Völker seeks an answer from within, by studying the mysticism of Origen's spiritual experience.[120] By contrast, A. Lieske rightly emphasized that Origen was a theologian and mystic of the Logos; nor did he forget the trinitarian bearing of Origen's theology and his ecclesiology.[121] In this study, however, Origen may be seen too little as a theologian of the saving economy of the Trinity, and too little attention may be paid to the role of the Holy Spirit. The concern of a more recent investigation is to understand Origen's doctrine of the Trinity completely as a function of his 'spiritual teaching'.[122] The dynamism, the passion in the Alexandrian's reflection on the Trinity, reflect his questioning about the soul's (re-)ascent to God. To this intent, the various tasks of the Logos and the spirit in the divinization of the rational creature must first be demonstrated. The Logos has a twofold role: it is the source of

[116] Origen, *Comm. in Io.* 19, 2; ibid., 10, 6: GCS IV, 176; E. Corsini, *Commento al Vangelo di Giovanni di Origene*, Torino 1968, 386, where Corsini also refers to *Hom. in Jer.* XV 6. Origen describes the christological heresies which have emerged up to his time and which deny either the Godhead or the manhood. He means to maintain the recognition of the two. According to Christian teaching Christ is a 'composite being' (σύνθετόν τι χρῆμα): *Ctr. Cels.* I, 66. If we can trust Rufinus' translation, he is also the first to introduce the expression *Deus-homo*: *De princ.* II 6, 3: GCS V, 142, 13. Cf. M. Simonetti, *I Principi di Origene*, 287.

[117] Cf. Hugh T. Kerr, *The First Systematic Theologian, Origen of Alexandria*, Princeton, N.J. 1958; see also the work by F. H. Kettler mentioned above.

[118] Hal Koch, *Pronoia und Paideusis. Studien über Origenes und sein Verhältnis zum Platonismus*, Berlin–Leipzig 1932.

[119] H. Dörrie, *Die platonische Theologie des Kelsos in ihrer Auseinandersetzung mit der christlichen Theologie auf Grund von Origenes c. Celsum 7,42ff.* (NGött 1967), however, finds that Origen has not adequately understood Celsus' thinking.

[120] W. Völker, *Das Vollkommenheitsideal des Origenes. Eine Untersuchung zur Geschichte der Frömmigkeit und zu den Anfängen christlicher Mystik*, Tübingen 1931.

[121] A. Lieske, *Die Theologie der Logosmystik bei Origenes*, Münster 1938. For Origen's ecclesiology see J. Chenevert, S. J., *L'Eglise dans le Commentaire d'Origène sur le Cantique des Cantiques* (Studia 24), Bruxelles–Paris–Montréal 1969.

[122] J. Rius-Camps, *El dinamismo trinitario en la divinisazión de los seres racionales segun Origenes* (OCA 188), Roma 1970.

creaturely *ratio*, but also of supernatural *sapientia*. The pneuma inserts itself between these two functions. It provides a new substratum, which makes it possible to receive 'the wisdom of Christ'. The Spirit appears as *'materia spiritualis'* which is informed by the 'Logos-wisdom'. To these different functions of the Logos and the Spirit in the economy of salvation correspond their different constitutions within the Trinity. The Logos, which proceeds from the will of the Father, needs the anointing of the Spirit to be constituted. The Word spoken by the Father still does not have a numerically different existence from the Father by virtue of being spoken. But the Spirit also needs the Logos. It pre-exists primarily as so to speak an amorphous *'materia spiritualis'*. To achieve full existence the pneuma needs to be informed by the Logos. The Holy Spirit is neither unbegotten like the Father, nor begotten as is the Son, nor is it created like other creatures. It issues from the Father and becomes a subsisting hypostasis by means of the Logos. Thus it belongs on the side of God, but is in third place after the Father and the Son. Rius-Camps believes that the different constitutions of the Son and the Spirit have their foundation in two basic dispositions of God the Father, i.e. in his Fatherhood and in his Motherhood. Here Origen is said to refer back to an anthropomorphic conceptuality (that of bi-sexuality), used by the Gnostics to interpret the intelligible world. Rius-Camps accords these Gnostic notions no more than the role of a catalyst in Origen; they are not a real source. Origen's starting points are—it is claimed—genuinely biblical, but have been given particular emphasis by the Gnostics.

Does this stress on pneumatology in Origen produce a new picture of the place of Christ in the Alexandrian's system? M. Simonetti has made some important comments on the impressive researches of the Spanish theologian.[123] Here we extract some remarks about the position of his christology:

Lo schema fondamentale, in base al quale Origene considera il rapporto fra Dio e il mondo, è uno schema impostato in senso radicalmente cristocentrico, nel senso che nella figura di Cristo Logos egli vede realizzata ed esaurita nella forma più autentica e piena ogni possibilità di mediazione fra il Padre ed il mondo nel doppio aspetto di azione providenziale di Dio nei confronti del mondo e di ritorno del mondo a Dio. In tale semplicissimo schema non resta margine apprezzabile per inserire in maniera organica e distintiva l'opera dello Spirito santo. D'altra parte la tradizione affiancava, nella professione di fede, lo Spirito santo al Padre ed al Figlio; in ossequio ad essa Origene non ha avuto difficolta ad affiancare lo Spirito santo al Figlio nell'opera di mediazione, e lo introduce *longe lateque* in tutte le sue opere come Spirito di Dio e di Cristo; ma ha trovato evidenti difficolta ad assegnarli un ruolo specifico nell'opera di mediazione fra il Padre e il mondo, sopratutto in rapporto alla soverchiante prevalenza del Figlio in tale opera di mediazione (295-6).

123 M. Simonetti, 'Note sulla teologia trinitaria di Origene', *VC* 8, 1971, 273-307; id., *I Principi di Origene* (Classici delle Religioni), Torino 1968: Introduzione 45-55.

In altri termini, mentre Origene ha avuto ben chiaro il concetto che tutto quanto il Padre fa, lo fa attraverso l'opera del Figlio, solo parzialmente cioè nella sanctificazione e nella inspirazione scritturistica, ha inserito in tale unità d'azione lo Spirito santo: l'ambito operativo del Padre e del Figlio coincide perfettamente e abbraccia l'ambito operativo dello Spirito santo; l'ambito dello Spirito santo invece ha comprensione minore rispetto a quello commune al Padre e al Figlio (298).

Thus christology retains its central place in the system of the Alexandrian, for all the importance of pneumatology.

Origen, however, is not primarily interested in the ontological constitution of Christ. He sees Christ above all as mediator of the mystical union of the soul with the hidden God, as mediator between church and God, and all this from the viewpoint of the union in knowledge and in love. Logos, soul of Christ, the humanity of the Lord, are seen in the service of that movement in which God goes out from himself and returns to himself. The Platonic pattern of antitype-type shows the poles between which this movement takes place and in addition helps to make clear the tension there is between them. The whole drive is from symbol to reality (truth). Despite the extent to which Origen's christology incorporates the traditional doctrine of Christ, his Godhead and manhood, and of body and soul, it is completely moulded by his subjective interests and thought-patterns and hence by his mysticism. This is why his doctrine of *epinoia* could become so central for his interpretation of Christ.[124] The *epinoia* is typical of Origen in so far as it has a subjective and an objective side. It is 'title', 'expression', and at the same time objective reality. The titles or names have a corresponding objective reality. From a christological point of view the *epinoiai* are the objective perfections of Christ which display a hierarchy within themselves. Whereas strictly speaking there is no plurality of such *epinoiai* to be found in God the Father because of his absolute simplicity, Christ as *multiplex in constitutione* has room for a number of such titles, not only from a soteriological point of view, but also in respect of his very constitution.[125] Christ is called wisdom, might or power of God, Logos, life, etc., and receives these names already in his divine nature. Merely by virtue of the supreme and first *epinoia*, i.e. in so far as he is simple wisdom,[126] he is a multiplicity:

---

[124] Cf. H. Crouzel, *Connaissance mystique*, 389–91; esp. A. Orbe, *La Epinoia*, Romae 1955, 16–32; F. Bertrand, *Mystique de Jésus chez Origène*, Paris 1951, 15–46; J. Rius-Camps, *El dinamismo trinitario*, 118–61.

[125] Origen, *Comm. in Io.* I, 20: GCS IV, 24, 23ff.; E. Corsini (see above, p. 139) 154f. and n. 42: 'Anche il Nous plotiniano diventa molteplice (πολύς). . . . Sia pure con intendimenti e con impostazione molto diversi, l'esigenza tanto in Plotino quanto in Origene è la stessa: risolvere il problema della mediazione dall'Uno al molteplice, il problema che era stato posto dal *Parmenide* platonico, interpretato in un certo modo. Su questo punto Origene ritorna sovente, in senso più squisitamente metafisico: il Logos è il complesso multiforme degli intelligibili, delle ragione degli esseri: cf. I, 243–44; XIX, 146–7; *De princ.* I, 2, 2 (V, 28, 13ff.) ecc.'

[126] On this important concept see H. Jaeger, 'The Patristic Conception of Wisdom in the Light of Biblical and Rabbinical Research', *StudPat* IV (TU 79), Berlin 1961, 90–106.

Nos nihil purum et humanum de Christo sentiamus, sed Deum pariter atque hominem fateamur, quia et 'sapientia' Dei 'multiplex' dicitur, uti per haec mereamur participium sumere 'sapientiae Dei' qui est 'Christus' Iesus Dominus noster.[127]

Most instructive of all is the 'Father–Son' contrast. Although Origen can also describe the Father by many names, he regards the nature of the Father as being utterly incomprehensible and transcendent (*De princ.* IV, 14 [26]). It is another matter with the Son. In him the transcendent properties of the Father take form. The Father can be described as the 'Father' of truth, wisdom, the Logos, but this way of speaking does not comprehend the real transcendent properties of the Father. If the Son is spoken of as truth, wisdom, etc., the expressions are not relative ones, but real descriptions of his being. So in the Father the *epinoiai* are not objectively manifold; this is because of his simplicity and his transcendence. In the Son, however, there is an objective multiplicity. According to scripture he bears many names.[128] All must be considered with equal care. Some (the Gnostics) give too great predominance to the name Logos—wrongly, in Origen's opinion. The names of Christ are partly independent of Adam's sin (wisdom, Logos, life, truth), partly dependent on it (light of men, firstborn of the dead, shepherd, physician, priest, etc.). The *epinoiai* of Christ are partly absolute, partly relative ('for us', as our sanctification, our righteousness, our redemption). Another arrangement distinguishes three classes of names: (1) those which are given to Christ alone; (2) those which are proper to Christ and others; (3) those which describe Christ only in relation to others, e.g. shepherd, way, etc.

The Son, then, is the revelation of the Father and his mediator towards the world. From his begetting onwards he exists for mankind.[129] In him the transcendent properties of the Father take form, as the expression of an objective, inexpressible reality. By means of participation, Christians too for their part can express the perfections of Christ and further the unfolding of the *epinoiai*. By means of the knowledge of the perfections of Christ they themselves ascend to the Father. That is why Origen works so hard to discover a hierarchy of these names. Here, too, lies for him the solution of the problem of unity and multiplicity in the tension between God and the world—a problem which has been making itself felt in Christian theology ever since Justin, Tatian and the Apologists. He bases his cosmology and his soteriology, exegesis as a method and mysticism as the ascent of the soul to God, all on the doctrine of the *epinoiai*.[130] Above all, the *epinoiai* show the fullness of being in Christ, they show him as the fullness of good things. 'For this reason Origen continually points out that

---

[127] Origen, *In Lib. Iesu Nave Hom.* VII, 7: GCS VII, 335.
[128] F. Bertrand, *Mystique de Jésus*, enumerates 34 names.
[129] *Catena fragment* 2: GCS IV, 484[4ff.]; cf. A. Orbe, *Epinoia* 29.
[130] Cf. G. Gruber, *ΖΩΗ. Wesen, Stufen und Mitteilung des wahren Lebens bei Origenes* (Münchener Theologische Studien II 23), München 1962, 241–67: Das Leben als Epinoia Christi.

"Jesus is many in accordance with the *epinoiai*".'[131] The different titles, i.e. the designation of Christ according to his benefits and his virtues, do not, however, dissolve the unity of Christ.[132]

Origen now also takes up his interpretation both of the relationship between the Godhead and the manhood of Christ and of the place of the soul of Christ into his doctrine of the mystical ascent of the soul. The Logos is the image of God, but the soul of Christ is the image of the Logos. It is worth noting that 'Logos' stands as a personal name for the 'bridegroom of the soul':

> The soul is the bride of the Logos . . . she takes him to herself, him, the God-Logos who was in the beginning with God, who of course does not always remain with her . . . but sometimes visits her, sometimes leaves her so that she will long for him still more.[133]

As the embodiment of all being, the Logos comprehends all the titles of Christ in so far as they give definitions of Christ's nature. So the title Logos enjoys a certain pre-eminence (i.e. as the embodiment of all these names, not regarded by itself in isolation as with the Gnostics). The Logos is the Only-Begotten in whom all other titles have substantial being.[134]

But the way to the Logos-God is by means of the 'Logos incarnatus'. Christ's manhood is the starting point of the ascent. It is not that the ascending one has to leave it completely behind. Even Christ in his ascension into heaven did not leave behind his manhood, as some assume. These are combated by Origen.[135] With the progress of the ascent of the soul, the manhood of Christ merely becomes more and more (and finally in the eternal vision completely) transparent for the Godhead. In the Logos, of course, all the secrets of God are first contained. He reveals the Father. The manhood of Christ, like Holy Scripture, is like a filter through which the Godhead is imparted in accordance with the receptive capability of man. Christ is a spiritual nourishment appropriate for all. Hence the doctrine of the different forms under which Christ is perceived.[136] This may not be interpreted as docetism.

> Le thème des différentes formes du Christ ne concerne pas directement le corps humain, mais le rayonnement de la divinité à travers lui. Il n'y a pas là ombre de docétisme. De soi la divinité transparait toujours à travers l'humanite de Jésus: il y a union de personne entre le Logos, son âme et son corps; l'humanité est signe de la divinité et la porte.[137]

---

131 Ibid., 246.

132 Instances in G. Gruber, op. cit., 259–63, where reference is also made to the significance of the conceptual framework *hypostasis-epinoia* in Origen's controversy with the monarchians.

133 Origen, *Cant*. III: GCS VIII, 218$^{9-15}$; in G. Gruber, op. cit., 263, with other instances.

134 Cf. G. Gruber, op. cit., 263–4.

135 Cf. H. Crouzel, '*Connaissance mystique*', 460–5.

136 Examples, ibid., 470–4. Here the doctrine of the *epinoiai* is associated with the idea of the change in the form of Jesus. 'La multiplicité du Logos s'exprime donc aussi par son incarnation: chacun le voyait de la façon dont il était capable' (ibid., 471); cf. G. Lomiento, 'Cristo didaskalos dei pochi e la communicazione ai molti secondo Origene', *VC* 9, 1972, 25–54.

137 Ibid., 474. In this context H. Crouzel also deals with the question of the '*simplices*' and their restriction to the manhood of Christ (476–82). Cf. *Ser. in Matt*. 27: GCS XI, 45$^{19\mathrm{ff}}$: the fleshly men see only the external appearance of Christ's body, the spiritual men do not notice it, so as to focus their whole attention on the works of his divine power.

The relationship between the Son of God and the man Jesus Christ on the one hand and the various anthropological elements already existing in man on the other is expressed particularly clearly in the *Commentary on John* I, 28. In connection with Ps. 44. 8, Origen points out the difference between the titles 'Christ' and 'king'. The title 'king' has its basis in the status of the *firstborn* of all creation, that is, in his divine nature (cf. Col. 1. 15)—a saying which Origen interprets in a different way from that later adopted by the Arians. To the manhood of Christ, or the 'assumed man', he assigns the name 'son of the king' which is introduced in Ps. 44. 8. However, he immediately issues a warning that the unity of Christ must not be surrendered in this distinction. Thus in Christ there is a twofold rule, that of the Son of God and that of the man Christ. In accordance with this, men are led in different ways:

> Whereas some are led by Christ as the 'shepherd' because they are capable of being guided and the part of their soul which is outside reason is tranquil, others come to him as the 'king', who rules over the rational spirit and raises it up to worship God. But there are also differences among those who are under his sovereignty, depending on whether a man is ruled over mystically and with inexpressible mystery, according to God's fashion, or in a lesser way. I would say that those who attain to the sight of incorporeal things . . . are removed outside all matters of the senses by the 'Word'. They are ruled royally by the guidance of the Only-Begotten. However, those who only penetrate as far as the word of sensual things and reverence the Creator through these, are also ruled by the Word and to the same degree stand under the Lordship of Christ. But let no one take offence if we distinguish aspects of the Redeemer in this way, and think that as a result we are transferring a division into his very being.[138]

This is where the whole problem of the appreciation of the incarnation in Origen is raised. Even in Origen, the incarnation is the real new element of the New Testament, as is shown above all by his interpretation of the wedding at Cana.[139] The Fathers before Origen have also seen the coming of the Logos in the Old Testament theophanies without thereby diminishing the significance of the incarnation.[140] So for Origen also the incarnation means the real arrival of the Logos.[141] Even if the corporeality of Christ has in some respects the more negative function of a filter[142] and appears to lose its positive significance as medium of revelation in the

138 Origen, *Comm. in Io.* I, 28: GCS IV, 35–36; cf. E. Schendel, *Herrschaft und Unterwerfung Christi* (BGBE 12), Tübingen 1971, 86–8.

139 Book IX of the *Commentary on John* with the interpretation of Cana is lost. His ideas may be deduced from other texts. See H. Crouzel, op. cit., 185–6. For the understanding of the doctrines of incarnation and redemption in Origen see also M. Simonetti, 'La morte di Gesù in Origene', *Rivista di Storia e Letteratura religiosa* 8, 1972, 3–41.

140 For the theme of theophanies see the comprehensive study by B. Studer, *Zur Theophanie-Exegese Augustins*, cited above, especially from p. 53: 'Zur Vorgeschichte der Theophanie-Exegese'; for Origen see 84f.

141 Cf. G. Aeby, *Les Missions divines de saint Justin à Origène*, Fribourg 1958, 146–83.

142 Corporeality necessarily means concealment of the Godhead. But Origen shows in his interpretation of the transfiguration scene (Matt. 17. 1–8 par.) how the Godhead becomes transparent precisely in the corporeality of Jesus. Cf. H. Crouzel, '*Connaissance mystique*', Index, 608 (Matt. 17. 1–8).

view of eternity,[143] nevertheless the whole possibility of this view and the ascent to it even in Origen depend on the fact of the incarnation. It thus remains for ever valid and remains so above all in the reality of the church. Although Origen's symbolism and his doctrine of the ascent seem to make the incarnation (and the corporeality) of Christ relative, it still has true saving significance and truly brings about salvation and thus also has true historicity.[144]

At all events, the conjunction of the Logos with the human soul which he has assumed remains a permanent one, even if it could be demonstrated that Origen supposed that at some point corporeality would cease. 'For Origen, the οἰκονομία τῆς ἐνανθρωπήσεως (*Comm. in Io.* II, 11: 66, 20) is the basic datum of soteriology (Andresen).'[145] In the manhood of Christ the

---

[143] But cf. Origen, *Comm. in Io.* II, 8 (4): GCS IV, 62²⁴ᶠᶠ, where the Logos rider of Revelation is mentioned and the manhood of Christ is represented as the object of the sight of the blessed.

[144] The controversy between R. P. C. Hanson (n. 115 above) and the works on Origen by H. U. v. Balthasar and H. de Lubac centres on this point above all else. Hanson, op. cit., 259–88. Cf. R. Crouzel, 'Origène devant l'Incarnation et devant l'Histoire', BLE, 1960, 81–110 (on R. P. C. Hanson and M. Harl). Origen has again been censured for denying that the body continues in the final state by F. H. Kettler, *Der ursprüngliche Sinn der Dogmatik des Origenes*, Berlin 1966, as also by E. Schendel, *Herrschaft und Unterwerfung Christi* (BGBE 12), Tübingen 1971 (81–110 about Origen), esp. 106ff. It is a constant argument of Kettler that Origen only makes a distinction between doctrine and investigation to avoid the church's intolerance. Origen's system goes back to the eclectic Platonism of his time. Cf. H. Crouzel, *Bibliographie Critique d'Origène*, 555f. M. Simonetti, *I Principi di Origene*, Introduzione 64–69, and in the commentary on *De princ.* II, 3 and III, 6, vigorously rejects Kettler's basic argument and his remarks on an *apokatastasis* without the body. He claims that Origen puts forward two arguments: the first is for a corporeality which becomes increasingly subtle and in the end is completely dissolved at the moment of union with God; the second is the thesis of a changeable body which can adapt itself to all the conditions in which the soul may be, even that of the vision of God. At that point the body changes into a *corpus spirituale* (cf. 1 Cor. 15. 35–49). Rufinus has altered the text of Origen in order to be able to present the second argument as Origen's own. Jerome and Justinian, on the other hand, want to present Origen as an advocate of ultimate incorporeality. Kettler insists especially on the independence of the tradition of the witness handed down by Jerome and Justinian which censures Origen. But Simonetti stresses that Origen did not mark out any fixed position; he was tossed to and fro between the Platonic conviction that nothing corporeal can attain to the vision of God and the Christian tradition about the resurrection. The agreement between Rufinus and Jerome over *De Princ.* II, 3, 7 and III, 6, 9 bears witness to this (cf. the texts in Koetschau, 125 and 290f.; Simonetti, 260f. or 479f.). Here Simonetti also challenges the argument of W. Völker (op. cit., 109), according to which for Origen 'la mediazione di Cristo avrà termine alle fine del perfezionamento dei beati, che perciò potranno contemplare il Padre senza bisogno di intermediario. . . . In realtà la funzione di Cristo a questo punto non viene soppressa ma cambia aspetto: i beati saranno ormai completamente incorporati (ma non spersonalizzati . . .) in lui, constituiranno le membra del suo corpo, si che vedranno il Padre come lo vede lui, saranno un solo Figlio con lui.' Of course the different conclusions of Rufinus and Jerome in III, 6, 9 should be noted (Koetschau, 291): (Rufinus) *Tunc ergo consequenter etiam natura corporea illum summum et cui addi iam nihil possit recipiet statum*; (Jerome, in the apparatus) *Et erit 'Deus omnia in omnibus', ut universa natura corporea redigatur in eam substantiam, quae omnibus melior est, in divinam videlicet, qua nulla est melior.* M. Simonetti, op. cit., 480, n. 63: 'Allo stato attuale delle nostre conoscenze non è possibile ammettere in Origene questa concezione panteistica (as is expressed in the Jerome letter), che contrasta con tanti altri luoghi delle sue opere.' In his criticism of Origen's doctrine of the resurrection, Methodius does not raise this charge of pantheism. At the end, it is stressed again by Origen himself that he is leaving the judgement on these two opinions to the reader. For Jerome see M. Simonetti, op. cit., 480, n. 64. F. Refoulé, 'La christologie d'Evagre et l'origénisme', OCP 27, 1961, 221–66, also tends towards a critical view of Origen's christology, looking back from Evagrius. Refoulé does not, of course, mean to say that the one-sidedness of Evagrius is all Origen, 'mais il est difficile de refuser à Origène la paternité du système d'Evagre et des origénistes' (ibid., 264). On Evagrius see below.

[145] E. Schendel, *Herrschaft und Unterwerfung Christi*, 102, with reference to C. Andresen, in *RAC* VI, 142.

fullness of the Godhead is present, even if hidden in the kenosis. Origen
felt this tension on the basis of the New Testament (Phil. 2. 5–8 and Col.
2. 9), though at the same time he does not seem to preserve a complete
balance because of his Platonism.

Origen is, above all, the theologian of the soul of Christ. Here he takes
up genuine biblical traditions and helps in a number of ways to guarantee
their continuance.[146] At the same time, however, he subjects these selfsame
traditions to a heightened danger. His teaching on the soul of Christ was
overloaded with peculiar anthropological and christological concepts
which were at a later date either given up or at least strongly contested.
The soul of Christ has a special function in Origen's reflections on the
conjunction of Godhead and manhood.

Unity in Christ is achieved through the mediacy of the soul of Christ
between sarx and Logos, which the Platonic dualism of Origen is otherwise unable to unite. This soul, however, has already been united from
eternity with the divine Logos in complete understanding and love of
God. Indeed it has already existed from eternity, before the body was
created.[147] But what is the relationship between soul and Logos? The two
are directly conjoined through direct vision in love (De Princ. II, 6, 3). The
soul is related as spirit to spirit. By complete union with the Logos the
soul of Christ becomes, as it were, the living view of God and the perfect
love of God.[148] This provides for Origen the highest and most inward
mode of union, in which the human soul of Christ becomes fully divinized and is aglow throughout as iron in the fire (De Princ. II, 6, 6). From
Origen's metaphysic of the action of the spirit we must conclude that the
unity so formed is meant as a really ontic unity, a conjunction which does
not merely rest on the power of the subjective moral act, as, say, with the
adoptionism which he has described earlier.[149] But the fact is that the
unity of the God-man is only meant to be an ontic unity, and is not really
proved to be such. Basically, this explanation of Origen's leads along a
false trail and confuses essential being with its (spiritual) actions. When

---

[146] Cf. De princ. IV, 4 (31): GCS V, 353–5; M. Simonetti, I Principi di Origene, 548–51, with important remarks on 'tristis est anima mea', which may not be understood of the Word, but only of the
soul of Christ. Origen makes particular mention of the soul of Christ in chs 4 and 5 cited above. See
R. Gögler, 'Die christologische und heilstheologische Grundlage der Bibelexegese des Origenes', TQ
136, 1956, 1–13.

[147] Origen, De princ. II, 6, 3: GCS V, 142⁵⁻¹⁵ (see M. Simonetti, Principi, 287 and notes: Illa anima . . .
ab initio creaturae et deinceps inseparabiliter et atque indissociabiliter inhaerens, utpote sapientiae et verbo dei et
veritate ac luci verae, et tota totum recipiens atque in eius lucem splendoremque ipsa cedens, facta est cum ipso
principaliter unus spiritus . . . Hac ergo substantia animae inter deum carnemque mediante (non enim possibile
erat dei naturam corpori sine mediatore misceri) nascitur, ut diximus, deus-homo, illa substantia media existente,
cui utique contra naturam non erat corpus assumere.

[148] A. Lieske, S.J., Die Theologie der Logos-Mystik bei Origenes, Münster 1938, 125.

[149] Origen, De princ. IV, 4, 31: GCS V, 354⁶⁻⁸: Nec tamen ita dicimus fuisse filium dei in illa anima,
sicut fuit in anima Pauli vel Petri ceterorumque sanctorum, in quibus Christus similiter ut in Paulo loqui creditur.
The presence of the Logos ensures the sinlessness of Christ. In De Princ. IV, 3, 30; GCS V, 352²⁸⁻⁹: Jesus
is distinct in that the whole Son of God dwells in him, though he was at the same time everywhere 'in
corpore totus et ubique totus aderat filius dei'. The same thought will meet us again in Athanasius.

all is said and done, Christ is in danger of being still only a 'quantitatively' different exceptional case of the universal relationship of the 'perfect' to the Logos, however mystically deep Origen may wish to make the relationship between Logos and soul in the God-man. Incidentally, it is interesting to see that the problem of unity in Christ is stated quite explicitly as such, and is described as being a mystery. John the Baptist is not worthy to loose the thong of Jesus' sandal, because the loosing of the sandal signifies the mystery of how the Logos has assumed human nature.[150] Even as a Platonist Origen is none the less conscious of the Christian *mysterium*.

Though Origen spoke above all as a Platonist in his explanation of the mediacy of the soul of Christ, it is as a Stoic that he goes on to talk of the ἡγεμονικόν. He, too, knows of it, and transfers it to the heart.[151] This ἡγεμονικόν, i.e. the νοῦς or the πνεῦμα λογικόν is the 'interior homo' qui et rationabilis dicitur (De princ. IV, 4, 9). Has Origen brought this 'inner man' and the Logos in Christ so near together that the latter now becomes the ἡγεμονικόν in the human nature of Jesus? The final grounds on which a difference is to be assumed between the indwelling of the Logos in 'Peter' or 'Paul' and in Christ is this—that in Christ the Logos is completely in control. With Origen's Christ this control is exercised primarily in the moral sphere.[152] But once the Stoic term ἡγεμονικόν has been taken over and has been associated with the Logos terminology which has likewise been enriched from the Stoics, the final result must be a picture of Christ in which unity is based on the working of the divine ἡγεμών. Here Origen could ultimately be on the way to a metaphysical interpretation of the unity of Christ by means of the concept of 'person'. For the real personality of a man is rooted in his ἡγεμονικόν. On the other hand, this conception of the Logos-Hegemon together with his doctrine of the soul of Christ was logically to lead Origen to assume a double personality of Christ. For the soul of Christ was conceived as a centre of activity. The lack of the concept of 'person' is a clear fact.

At the same time he could well debar himself from an approach to the understanding of the unity of person in Christ because this unity is transferred into the sphere of physical action and finally is not really anything more than a 'natural' unity, that is to say, a unity like the unity between two constituent parts which go together to form one reality. Origen

---

[150] Cf. Origen, *Comm. in Io.* 1, 23: GCS IV, 498[20-7].

[151] See E. v. Ivánka, 'Apex mentis', 155-9; F. Rüsche, *Blut, Leben, Seele*, 420-1; G. Verbeke, *Pneuma*, 456-69. But as a rule Origen will have nothing of the idea which Celsus attributes to the Christians, that Christ is 'divine pneuma in a body'. For this is a Stoic-materialistic attitude, *Ctr. Cels.* 6, 69f.

[152] Origen, *De Princ.* IV, 4 (31): GCS V, 354[13-15]: 'Oleo ergo laetitiae unguitur (anima Jesu), cum verbo dei immaculata foederatione coniuncta est et per hoc sola omnium animarum peccati incapax fuit, quia filii dei bene et plene capax fuit. . . .' As the Father and the Son are one, so also are the Logos and the soul of Jesus one. Ibid., 354: 'anima . . . totam in se sapientiam dei et veritatem vitamque receperat . . . Christus qui in deo absconditus dicitur . . . id est substantialiter deo repletus.'

himself, it is true, did not draw these consequences; nevertheless, he exposed himself to the charge that his system left no room for a full appreciation of the humanity of the Lord.[153] Even the essential act of the human Christ, his redemptive death, has been said to be devalued.[154] It is thus possible to note two opposed tendencies in this christology. One would follow the path of the church's tradition towards a distinction of the two natures, so that even the idea of indwelling emerges as a theological interpretation of the unity in Christ.[155] The other would urge the obliteration of the human element in the Lord.[156]

Be this as it may, Origen is himself a key witness to the traditional teaching of the soul of Christ, even though he has mixed it with strong philosophical elements.[157] The newly discovered *Dialektos* (ed. Scherer) is of great importance for Origen's christological anthropology.[158] He distinguishes in Christ body, soul, spirit, and in addition to these the divine pneuma. Moreover, Origen already advances that argument which is to play a great part in the anti-Apollinarian controversy, and which we have already noticed in Tertullian, 'The whole man would not have been redeemed had he not assumed the whole man' (εἰ μὴ ὅλον τὸν ἄνθρωπον ἀνείληφει).[159] His interpretation of the death of Christ (ed. Scherer 138, 2ff.) is also remarkable, and in some respects is reminiscent of the *Easter Homily* of Ps.-Chrysostom and its explanation of the event.[160] This christological anthropology of the *Dialektos* and the other works of Origen needs a more detailed investigation than is here possible. The teaching on the soul of Christ is one of those points in Origen's system which received least attention in subsequent Alexandrian theology. Tendencies opposed to this tradition were able to exert the stronger influence.

CONCLUSION

It is clear from this survey that the rise of christological reflection was a very slow process. The main emphasis was laid on the theological interpretation of the relationship of Father and Son, though this was seen to be closely connected with the incarnation. Over against the Gnostics and the

---

[153] A. Wintersig, *Menschheit Jesu*, 73–85; M. Harl, *Origène*, 198–200, further 139–218.

[154] A. Wintersig, op. cit., 82.

[155] Origen, *Ctr. Cels.* 2, 9 (with reference to 1 Cor. 6. 17).

[156] Cf. A. Wintersig, op. cit., 114, n. 31.

[157] Cf. the verdict of Socrates, HE 3, 7: PG 67, 362AB.

[158] On this see now J. Boada, S.J., *El Hombre segun el Comentario de Origenes a los Romanos*, Diss. Pont. Univ. Gregoriana 1971, partly published Madrid 1971; Boada pays special attention to the newly discovered Greek portions of Origen's *Commentary on Romans*, ed. J. Scherer, *Le Commentaire d'Origène sur Rom. III. 5–V.7 d'après les extraits du Papyrus No 88748 du Musée du Caire et les Fragments de la Philocalie et du Vaticanus Gr. 762*, Le Caire 1957.

[159] *Dialektos*, ed. Scherer 136[16ff.]; SC 67, 70[17–19]. Cf. L. Früchtel, *ThLZ* 75, 1950, 504–6.

[160] PG 59, 744; P. Nautin, *Homélies pascales 1: Une homélie inspirée du Traité sur la Pâque d'Hippolyte* (SC 27), Paris 1950, 183.

docetists, the theologians of the church had above all to stress the duality of the two natures in Christ and their reality. True, the first reflections on the problem of the unity of Godhead and manhood are made. The Fathers know that the incarnate Logos is 'one and the same'. But this unity is more intuitively seen than speculatively interpreted. It can—with the sublimity of the Mysterium Christi in the Christian faith—also be no more than a matter of the first repulse of the attacks which, for example, Celsus had made against the Christian doctrine of the incarnation (see above). For the interpretation of the unity in Christ, the Fathers fall back on the Stoic *krasis* doctrine. Here they bequeathed posterity a legacy which was to burden theology for a long time. In fact, in this way the path of a *unio secundum naturam*, the Monophysite solution, was trodden. Even if the concept of person emerges for the first time, it is not yet made the basis of the solution of the problem of Christ. And where in addition 'person' is sought metaphysically in 'individuality', the centring of theological reflections on this concept will first go on to create the real difficulties which are later manifest in the Nestorius dispute. So about 250, we have merely a first, confused beginning of speculative christology. But this also has a very positive side: the foundation of christology is the tradition and the simple proclamation of the church. It still shines clearly through the different speculative attempts at interpretation.

PART TWO

THE FIRST THEOLOGICAL INTERPRETATIONS OF THE PERSON OF CHRIST

From Origen to Ephesus (431)

INTRODUCTION: TOWARDS FOURTH-CENTURY
CHRISTOLOGY

THE interpretation of the basic christological truths in the tradition, begun by the Apologists and continued by the Alexandrians Clement and Origen, without doubt exerted a far-reaching influence. At first, however, it is difficult to ascertain. What happened between the death of Origen (253/4) and Nicaea (325)? Here there are many blank patches on the patristic map. Measured in terms of Origen, there was a shift in the line of questioning and an intensification of it in two respects: (i) whereas with the Alexandrians we have a clear acknowledgment of the three hypostases in God, and especially a clear distinction between Father and Son in God, Sabellius and his followers represented the opposite pole. Once again the problem of Christian monotheism became acute. We can say that this already marked the immediate prelude to Nicaea, even if we have to go on to distinguish several phases. (ii) Whereas the soul of Christ had a special place in Origen's picture of Christ as *anima mediatrix* between Logos and sarx, soon after Origen's death there came about a tacit 'inclusion' or even a deliberate 'exclusion' of the soul of Christ.

Some more concrete information should be given about the development of these two complexes of questions. In the year 231 Origen left Alexandria. His place as leader of the Didaskaleion was taken by *Heraclas*, but in the following year—after the death of Demetrius—Heraclas was elected bishop of Alexandria. This made room in the Didaskaleion for Origen's pupil Dionysius, but in 247 he ascended the throne of St Mark and occupied it until 265.[1] It was in his pontificate that two men emerged who were to arouse momentous reactions for centuries afterwards: Sabellius in Libya or the Pentapolis, and Paul of Samosata, with whom several synods of Antioch were concerned. We know little about the emergence of Sabellius. After the unrest of the persecution and the confusion over Novatian, a time of peace arrived, as Dionysius reports in a letter to Stephen I of Rome (died 257).[2] But in the same year his attention was drawn to the new heresy, as Eusebius indicates in a quotation from a letter of Dionysius to Pope Sixtus II:

---

[1] For Dionysius of Alexandria see C. Lett Feltoe, ΔΙΟΝΥΣΙΟΥ ΛΕΙΨΑΝΑ. *The Letters and other Remains of Dionysius of Alexandria*, Cambridge 1904; W. A. Bienert, *Dionysius von Alexandrien, Das erhaltene Werk* ΔΙΟΝΥΣΙΟΥ ΛΕΙΨΑΝΑ (Bibliothek d. Griech. Lit. 2), Stuttgart 1972; E. Boularand S.J., *L'hérésie d'Arius et la 'foi' de Nicée, I: L'hérésie d'Arius*, Paris 1972, 135–43; L. W. Barnard, 'The Antecedents of Arius', *VigC* 24, 1970, 172–88, esp. 176–9; for what follows, reference should also be made to the same author's *Athenagoras. A Study in Second Century Christian Apologetic* (Théologie historique 18), Paris 1972.

[2] Eusebius, HE VII, pref. 4–5; text in C.L. Feltoe, op. cit., 44–5; German translation in W. A. Bienert, op. cit., 37–8.

In Ptolemais in the Pentapolis in our time a godless teaching was proclaimed which contains many blasphemies against Almighty God, the Father of our Lord Jesus Christ, many unbelieving statements about his only-begotten Son, the firstborn before all creation, the Logos made man, and ignorance about the Holy Spirit. As declarations came from both sides and brethren sought me out to discuss the matter with me, I have, to the best of my ability and with the help of God, written some letters for your better instruction. Copies of them I am sending to you.[3]

Dionysius had already shown that he was zealous in fighting against heresies, in a letter to Pope Stephen I:

If there is anyone who makes unfitting statements about God, like those who call him unmerciful, or if anyone wishes to introduce the worship of strange gods, then he should be stoned, as the law commands. But we should 'stone' these people with powerful words of faith. Or if anyone will not completely accept the *mysterium Christi* or changes it or falsifies it; or (if he says) he is not God or he is not man or he did not die or he did not rise again or he will not come to judge the living and the dead, then—Paul says—let him be cursed.[4]

The struggle against Sabellianism was all the more urgent since, according to the evidence of Athanasius, some bishops from the Pentapolis had espoused this doctrine.[5] Perhaps these were the men to whom Dionysius had already written about Sabellius, as Eusebius records: Ammon of Berenice, Telesphorus, Euphranor and Euporus.[6] When these letters had evidently proved fruitless, Dionysius again wrote to Euphanor and Ammonius:

In this way at any rate the Father is Father and not Son, not because he came into being, but because he is; he does not derive from another, but remains in himself. The Son is not Father, not because he was, but because he came into being; he received the status of Son not of himself, but of the one who made him.[7]

With this, strife broke out. In the eyes of those to whom he was writing and of some believers in Alexandria and the Pentapolis, Dionysius had evidently gone too far and advocated tritheism.

According to Athanasius, they went to Rome, to Pope Dionysius.[8] The five errors with which they charged Dionysius of Alexandria may best be reproduced in the summary given by L. W. Barnard:[9]

[3] Eusebius, HE VII, 6: C.L. Feltoe, op. cit., 51–52; W. A. Bienert, op. cit., 39 (2); H. Kraft, *Kaiser Konstantins religiöse Entwicklung* (BHistTh 20), Tübingen 1955, 322–3. Sabellius seems to have come to Rome shortly before 217, where he became the head of the monarchian party which was already in existence there (Praxeas, Epigonus, pupil of Noetus, Cleomenes). He was excluded from the church by Pope Callixtus. Cf. Hippolytus. *Refut.* 9, 12; R. Lachenschmid, 'Sabellianismus, Sabellios', *LThK* 3, 1964, 193–4; C. Andresen, 'Die Enstehung und Geschichte des trinitarischen Personbegriffes', *ZNW* 52, 1961, 1–39.
[4] Dionysius Al., letter to Stephen I of Rome: C.L. Feltoe, op. cit., 45–8; W. A. Bienert, op. cit., 42; I, 6, 1.
[5] Athanasius, *Sent. Dion.* 5: Opitz, AW II, 1, 4, p. 49.
[6] Eusebius, HE VII, 26, 1: Schwartz GCS, *Eus. W.* II, 2, p. 700.
[7] W. A. Bienert, op. cit., 75 (3. 1). On this see p. 118, n. 205.
[8] Athanasius, *Sent. Dion.* 13: Opitz, AW II, 1, 4, p. 55.
[9] L. W. Barnard, *VigC* 24, 1970, 77; quotations in W.A. Bienert, op. cit., 78–84.

(1) He separated the Father and the Son (διαιρεῖ καὶ μακρύνει καὶ μερίζει τὸν υἱὸν ἀπὸ τοῦ πατρός) De Sent. Dion. 16, 3 (Opitz, AW II, 1, 4, p. 58);

(2) He denied the eternity of the Son (οὐκ ἀεὶ ἦν ὁ θεὸς πατήρ, οὐκ ἀεὶ ἦν ὁ υἱός, ἀλλ᾽ ὁ μὲν θεὸς ἦν χωρὶς τοῦ λόγου, αὐτὸς δὲ ὁ υἱὸς οὐκ ἦν πρὶν γεννηθῇ, ἀλλ᾽ ἦν ποτὲ ὅτε οὐκ ἦν· οὐ γὰρ ἀίδιός ἐστιν ἀλλ᾽ ὕστερον ἐπεγέγονεν) De Sent. Dion. 14, 4 (Opitz, p. 56);

(3) He named the Father without the Son and the Son without the Father (πατέρα λέγων . . . οὐκ ὀνομάζει τὸν υἱὸν καὶ πάλιν υἱὸν λέγων οὐκ ὀνομάζει τὸν πατέρα) De Sent. Dion. 16, 3 (Opitz, p. 58);

(4) He virtually rejected the term ὁμοούσιος used of the Son (προσφέρουσιν ἔγκλημα κατ᾽ ἐμοῦ ψεῦδος ὂν ὡς οὐ λέγοντος τὸν Χριστὸν ὁμοούσιον εἶναι τῷ θεῷ) De Sent. Dion. 18, 2 (Opitz, p. 59);

(5) He spoke of the Son as a creature of the Father and used misleading illustrations of their relationship (ποίημα καὶ γενητὸν εἶναι τὸν υἱὸν τοῦ θεοῦ, μήτε δὲ φύσει ἴδιον, ἀλλὰ ξένον κατ᾽ οὐσίαν αὐτὸν εἶναι τοῦ πατρός, ὥσπερ ἐστὶν ὁ γεωργὸς πρὸς τὴν ἄμπελον καὶ ὁ ναυπηγὸς πρὸς τὸ σκάφος· καὶ γὰρ ὡς ποίημα ὢν οὐκ ἦν πρὶν γένηται) De Sent. Dion. 4, 2 (Opitz, p. 48).

We know of various reactions to these charges and to the Dionysius affair generally. The most important may be mentioned briefly: the answer given by Dionysius of Rome, the self-defence of his namesake in Alexandria, Arius' appeal to his teaching, the interpretation of the *sententia* of Dionysius by Athanasius and the attitude of Basil of Cappadocia.

Dionysius of Rome seems to have called a synod which condemned these dangerous statements.[10] Thereafter the Pope wrote two letters, one to his namesake in Alexandria, which is no longer extant, in which he asked him to reply to the charges made against him.[11] Dionysius of Rome wrote a second letter to the church of Alexandria, in which he rejected the errors under discussion, without naming the bishop of the city. He sought a *via media* between Sabellianism and tritheism.[12] In accord with the Western tradition, the Pope wanted to defend the 'monarchia' against those who,

in some way tear apart, dismember and destroy God in three forces and three separate hypostases and deities . . . (Sabellius) blasphemes God in saying that the Son is the same as the Father and *vice versa*; but they (the followers of Dionysius) to some degree proclaim three gods, by tearing apart the holy Unity into three alien and completely separate hypostases. It is necessary that the divine Logos be united with the God of the universe and that the Holy Spirit also dwell and abide in God. It is also unconditionally necessary

10 Athanasius, De Syn. 43, 4; 45, 1; Opitz, AW II, 1, 9, p. 269.
11 Athanasius, De Syn. 43, 4; see also Sent. Dion. 13, 2: Opitz, AW II, 1, 3, p. 55.
12 Athanasius, Decr. Nic. Syn. 26: Opitz, AW II, 1, 3, p. 21³⁰–23¹⁶; C. L. Feltoe, op. cit., 176–82; W. A. Bienert, op. cit., 75–7; see the notes by Opitz on Sent. Dion. 13: p. 55.

that the divine Triad be so to speak composed and assembled around a summit—I mean
the God of the universe, the ruler of all. . . . No less, however, should one censure those
who take the Son to be a work and believe that the Lord came into being like one of the
entities of the universe (τοὺς ποίημα τὸν υἱὸν εἶναι δοξάζοντας, καὶ γεγονέναι τὸν κύριον ὥσπερ
ἕν τι τῶν ὄντως γενομένων νομίζοντας), although the divine words expressly bear witness
that what is appropriate for him and in accord with him is conception, albeit not as an
act of formation or creation. . . . If the Son were created, there would be a time when
(all) this was not so; in that case there was a time when God was without these (powers).
But that is complete nonsense.

Dionysius then challenges the false exegesis of Prov. 8. 22: 'The Lord
created me as the beginning of his ways,' and again stresses:

Everywhere among the divine words we find that the Son is said to have been begotten, not created. . . . Thus we may neither divide the wonderful and divine unity into
three Godheads nor impair the honour and towering greatness of the Lord by the idea of
making (ποιήσει κωλύειν τὸ ἀξίωμα καὶ τὸ ὑπερβάλλον μέγεθος τοῦ κυρίου),[13] but must believe
in God, the Father, the Ruler of all, and in Jesus Christ, his Son, and in the Holy Spirit—
albeit in such a way that the Logos is united with the God of all. For he says 'I and the
Father are one' (John 10. 30), and 'I am in the Father and the Father is in me' (John 14.
10–11). For only in this way can the divine triad and the holy doctrine of the monarchia
be fully preserved.

The decisive points in the discussion about the 'divine triad and the
holy doctrine of the monarchia' are these: Son and Holy Spirit belong on
the side of God, indeed they are in God; the Son is not created, but the
Holy Scriptures bear witness to his γέννησις, which here must be translated
'begetting'. Father, Son and Spirit do not represent three completely
separate hypostases, but remain a 'monad'. However, there is no explanation of what hypostasis means here, nor does Dionysius of Rome get
beyond the subordinationist understanding of the relationship of the Logos
and the Spirit to the Father. He speaks of a 'summit' in the Godhead, the
God of all and ruler of all. Christ is declared to be God's Logos, wisdom
and power, so that his eternal divine reality is assured, but the idea of a
subject different from the Father is expressed too weakly. Nevertheless,
that the Son (and the Spirit) are created is decisively rejected.

Dionysius of Alexandria answered with a defence which consisted of
four books.[14] What did he say to the five charges?

(1) He denies that he separates Father and Son. His argument proceeds
from the terms 'Father' and 'Son', which mutually determine each other.
He is clearer about the pneuma than Eusebius or Lactantius are to be later:
'I have added the Holy Spirit, but at the same time I have also stated

---

[13] The translation in W. A. Bienert, op. cit., 75, is not quite correct here. He says, 'One may
neither divide the wonderful and divine unity into three Godheads, nor impair the honour and
towering greatness of the Lord through a creature.' It should be noted that the Greek is ποίησις and
not ποίημα. C. L. Feltoe, op. cit., 182, n. 1, interprets it rightly: 'to hinder (or impair) by the idea of
making'.

[14] Eusebius, HE VII, 26, 1: Schwartz, GCS, Eus. W. II, 2, p. 700; C. L. Feltoe, op. cit., 182–98;
W. A. Bienert, op. cit., 77–84 (3, 3).

whence and through whom he comes.' According to a fragment of the second letter about 'refutation and defence' addressed to Dionysius of Rome, handed down by Basil, the letter ended with a doxology: 'To God the Father, and the Son, our Lord Jesus Christ, together with the Holy Spirit, be honour and glory to all eternity. Amen.' Dionysius describes this formula as the 'form and rule' taken over 'from the presbyters before us'.[15]

(2) He sees the eternity of the Son grounded in the fact that he is Logos, wisdom and power of God, and also in the fact that he is termed the 'reflection of the eternal light' (Wisd. 7. 26; Heb. 1. 3). 'For if the light is always there, it is clear that the reflection is also always there.' Again he returns to the correlation of 'Father' and 'Son'. If the Father is eternal, so too is the Son.[16] This is also an answer to the third charge.

(4) The answer to the charge that he rejected the *homoousios* is an interesting one.[17] He makes a distinction between the use of the word and acceptance of the matter to which it refers.

> For if I also say that this word cannot be found or read anywhere in Holy Scripture, my conclusions on the matter do not depart from this view, a fact about which they (his opponents) have kept silent. I introduced the comparison with human descent because here was evidently a (relationship) of the same kind, and said that parents differ from their children only in one thing (relationship); for they themselves are not their children; were this not so, there would necessarily be neither parents nor children.[18]

Thus Dionysius sees that the *homoousios*, which he evidently did not use himself, but did not reject either, achieves only in a limited way what he wished to state with similar terms[19] and certain comparisons: it was necessary to express at the same time both the unity of and the distinction between those who are *homoousioi*, the Father and the Son. If he has stressed the distinction between Father and Son, he has not denied their homogeneity. If one plant derives from another, they are indeed different plants, but they nevertheless remain 'related by nature' (ὁμοφυής). We should not demand too much of Dionysius here. There is still to be a long struggle before the Fathers clarify to some degree what is meant by 'unity of substance' in God.

(5) Perhaps Dionysius had compromised himself most by the expression that the Son was a ποίημα of the Father and by his comparisons between

[15] On the Holy Spirit: W. A. Bienert, op. cit., 81 (7); Basil, ibid., 83 (frag. 14); C. L. Feltoe, op. cit., 192, n. 198.

[16] C. L. Feltoe, op. cit., 185-7 (3); W. A. Bienert, op. cit., 78-9 (3).

[17] W. A. Bienert, op. cit., 79, frag. 4 from Athanasius, *Sent. Dion.* 18: Opitz, AW II, 1, 4, p. 59¹-60⁹; C. L. Feltoe, op. cit., 187-90. W. A. Bienert, op. cit., 119, n. 217: 'The text in Feltoe is partially enlarged in comparison with that of Opitz, and is corrected according to the parallel tradition of these texts in Athanasius: Ath., *Decr.* 25, 4-5 [Opitz 21¹⁶⁻²⁹] and Ath., *Syn.* 44 [Opitz 269⁶⁻¹⁹].' Bienert refers to the explanation of the *homoousios* in Opitz, *Dion.* 18 (p. 59 in the apparatus).

[18] C. L. Feltoe, op. cit., 188-9: W. A. Bienert, op. cit., 79-80.

[19] Dionysius uses ὁμογενής to describe the relationship of parents and children (Feltoe, op. cit., 189⁵) and ὁμοφυής to describe the relationship of plants (ibd., 189¹⁴).

'shipbuilder and ship' or 'farmer and vine', and their application to the relationship between Father and Son in God. In their defence he insists that for him the terms 'Father' and 'Son' have pre-eminence, and that the other terms and comparisons are only used by way of addition:

> Because I do not regard the Logos as a work, I do not call God his maker, but his Father. That when I was discussing the Son, I referred in passing to God as his maker is defensible in this particular case. The wise men of the Greeks call themselves 'makers' of their own books, although they are fathers of their own books. . . .[20]

Here Athanasius is in some difficulty over defending his 'client'. He already applies to the texts of Dionysius the stratagem which is later to become a hermeneutical principle in the controversy with the Arians: those sayings about Christ in Scripture which concern his exaltation are true of his Godhead, and those which concern his humiliation refer to his manhood. Thus, Athanasius says, Dionysius spoke of the Son as a work of the Father only in respect of Christ's manhood.[21] But this was not the case. It was the purpose of Dionysius to clarify the relationship between Father and Son in God in this way, and to make a distinction between the two.

This gave Arius some footholds, some 'slogans' which—once they were isolated—could make Dionysius an authority for the Arians. And as we shall see, Arius was concerned to have authorities and tradition. Athanasius cannot wash Dionysius clean of the charge laid against him, and when he tries to do so, he 'interprets' him according to later distinctions. At any rate, he wants to prevent the Arians from being able to appeal to the Alexandrian. Here Basil is more critical about the bishop over whom the controversy raged, and expresses his criticism in a letter to the philosopher Maximus, who asked him about Dionysius' orthodoxy:[22] he is not surprised at all that he says, and in some respects he must refute him strictly. 'Above all he is, so far as we know, the first person to have sown the now rampant seed of godlessness in respect of the ἀνόμοιον.' Probably he had no evil intention, and was merely concerned to combat Sabellius as vigorously as possible. But Dionysius met the same fate as a gardener trying to make a crooked tree straight again: he bent it too far over the other side.

> The result is that he has exchanged one evil for another and has surrendered the ὀρθότης τοῦ λόγου. He is therefore very changeable in his writing, because he sometimes rejects the ὁμοούσιον, since his opponents used it to object to the ὑποστάσεις, and sometimes accepts it, when he is replying to his namesake. He has also made inappropriate remarks about the spirit, as he has banished him from the Godhead that is to be worshipped and assigned him to a lower order together with created and subject nature. That is the case with this man.

[20] W. A. Bienert, op. cit., 82 (9) and 81 (9); C. L. Feltoe, op. cit., 193–5.
[21] Athanasius, Sent. Dion. 21, 2; Opitz, AW II, 4, p. 624⁻¹⁴; C. L. Feltoe, op. cit., 194–5.
[22] Basil, Ep. IX 2 ad Maxim. phil.: Courtonne, Lettres I, Paris 1957, 38–9.

Even here, Basil does not do full justice to the historical situation of Dionysius. The personal declarations of the Alexandrian do not amount to a formal and literal rejection of the *homoousion*. The Bishop of Caesarea in Cappadocia also concedes that when he wrote to Maximus he did not have the 'books', i.e. the written defence,[23] in which Dionysius went into the criticisms made by Dionysius of Rome. There was a turning-point in the theology of the Alexandrian, but this could not take him decisively beyond the sphere of subordinationism. Arius referred to the earlier Dionysius; important Arian slogans are to be found in the charges laid against the Alexandrian, especially in the second charge (see above). Basil knew only the earlier Dionysius, Athanasius overestimated the later Dionysius and interpreted him in line with his own teaching. At all events, the Arians could not commandeer him, even in respect of his view of the incarnate Christ, which we have still to consider.

Unfortunately, nothing is known of the writing of *Theognostus*, the head of the Didaskaleion from 247/8 to 282, apart from four fragments and a report by Photius, *Bibl. cod.* 106. According to this, the Alexandrian wrote seven books of *Hypotyposes*, or sketches of Christian doctrine.[24] Book I, according to Photius, discussed the Father, the Creator (with a discussion of the question of the eternity of matter). Photius does not give the title of Book II, but it must have been 'On the Son'. According to Photius' account, Theognostus wanted to introduce conclusive proof that the Father has a Son and that this Son is a creature, a *ktisma*, and has to do only with those who are endowed with reason (υἱὸν δὲ λέγων κτίσμα αὐτὸν ἀποφαίνει καὶ τῶν λογικῶν μόνον ἐπιστατεῖν). Book III dealt with the Holy Spirit, Book IV with angels and demons, Books V and VI with the humanity of the Redeemer. According to his wont, he sought to prove that the incarnation of the Son was possible, but found himself in difficulty, especially when he boldly asserted that while the Son was restricted by space, there were no limits to his activity. Photius is happier with Book VII (On the Creation, i.e. on the created world), because it evidently contained no heresies (unlike the books about the Father and the Son). By and large he sees the Alexandrian caught in the net of Origenist heresies. The reason for this is that Theognostus seeks to defend Origen and makes use of half some of his sayings, which do not express his own view. Or perhaps he is coming down to the level of his audience and is content that they should acquire some knowledge of the Son, instead of remaining in complete ignorance about him. Photius was particularly concerned over the use of the expression *ktisma* for the Son; he interpreted this in accord-

---

[23] Basil, loc. cit.: οὐ πάρεστί γε μὴν τὰ βιβλία.

[24] Photius, *Bibl. cod.* 106: Henry II, 72–4. Fragments of and about Theognostus have been collected and commented on in A. v. Harnack, *Die Hypotyposen des Theognost* (TU, NF 9, 3), Leipzig 1903, 73–92; see F. Diekamp, below, and also L. B. Radford, *Three Teachers of Alexandria: Theognostus, Pierius and Peter*, Cambridge 1908; L. W. Barnard, *VigC* 24, 1970, 179–82.

ance with his later understanding, and not in terms of the understanding of Theognostus. 'κτίσμα for Theognostus meant what ποίημα did for Dionysius. It was a metaphor, capable of being used in various senses, which was used of the basic relationship of the Father and the Son. Arius took up this term in describing the relationship between the οὐσία of the Father and the οὐσία of the Son. The Son was essentially the expression of the Father's will, and κτίσμα-κτίζω expressed this.'[25] In Arius, of course, *ktisma-ktizein* were understood in such a way that to use these words of the Son clearly put him among the sphere of created things.[26]

We cannot make out much of the teaching of Theognostus from the four extant fragments. In the second fragment, handed down by Athanasius[27]—the first refers to the Holy Spirit and warns against putting the Spirit above the Son—we have, according to Athanasius, proof that Theognostus too had the Son issuing from the substance of the Father. So the Son could not be regarded as 'created':

> The nature of the Son is not derived from outside, nor was he produced out of nothing (ἐκ μὴ ὄντων), but issued from the nature of the Father like radiance from light and like vapour from water. Radiance and vapour are not sun or water, nor is the one alien to the other; so too (the nature of the Son) is not the Father, nor is it alien to him, but is an outflowing of the nature of the Father, without the Father's nature being divided. The sun is not diminished by the rays which it sends out, nor does the nature of the Father undergo any change in having an image of itself, the Son.[28]

Theognostus has certainly used the comparisons he cites in order to express both the similarity and the difference between Father and Son. But one might be tempted to describe the talk of the issuing of the Son 'from the nature' of the Father as an 'interpretation' of Athanasius, if we did not already have the same formula in Origen. Of course, the comparisons indicated point to a subordinationist understanding of the relationship between Father and Son, as in the rest of Alexandrian theology of the time. But in Theognostus we do not have Arianism *avant la lettre*.

The third fragment, which is handed down by Gregory of Nyssa, points clearly in the direction of subordinationism:

[25] L. W. Barnard, *VigC* 24, 1970, 180.

[26] Any definition of *ktizein* in Arius has to take note of his understanding of the divine 'monad' (see below).

[27] Athanasius, *Decr. Nic. Syn.* 25, 2: Opitz, AW II, 1, 3, pp. 20–21 with reference to A.v. Harnack, op. cit.; see L. W. Barnard, *VigC* 24, 1970, 180f.

[28] Athanasius, loc. cit.: Opitz, p. 21¹⁻⁷. For the earlier history of 'from the substance of the Father' see G. C. Stead, ' "Eusebius" and the Council of Nicaea', *JTS* NS 24, 1973, 85–100, esp. 88–92. He points to Tertullian (*Prax.* 4, 7, 8), Novatian (*Trin.* 31), and above all to Origen. The latter seeks to avoid materialistic conceptions (*John Commentary* XX, 157–8; *De princ.*), though the expression 'from the substance of the Father' is not used. But Origen, according to Stead, speaks expressly of it in three passages: *Comm. in Io.*, frag. 9 (Preuschen, 490²⁰⁻²³): Τὸ » 'Ως μονογενοῦς παρὰ τοῦ πατρός« νοεῖν ὑποβάλλει ἐκ τῆς οὐσίας τοῦ πατρὸς εἶναι τὸν υἱόν. οὐδὲν γὰρ τῶν κτισμάτων παρὰ πατρός, ἀλλ' ἐκ θεοῦ διὰ τοῦ λόγου ἔχει τὸ εἶναι. Also in *Comm. Rom.* IV, 10, and in a fragment from *Comm. Heb.* preserved for us by Pamphilus. For Theognostus see G. C. Stead, op. cit., 90.

When God desired to create all things, he first prepared the Son as a measure for the creation of the world.[29]

Here the emergence of the Son is connected with the creation of the world. Of course, this need not be interpreted as 'creation' of the Son, but the emergence of the Son is only mentioned in connection with creation. The fourth fragment from the *Hypotyposes*, discovered by F. Diekamp,[30] discusses the names (predicates) which are given to the Son of God in Scripture: Logos, image, wisdom.

. . . (They call him) Logos because he comes forth as the *nous* of the Father of the universe. For it is clear that the finest product of the *nous* (the understanding) is the Logos (the word). For Logos (the word) is also image (εἰκών). For he (the Logos, the word) alone of all that is in the understanding finds a way outside. Words in us are only a partial expression of things that could be expressed, others remain unspoken and hidden in the understanding. But it is reasonable that the essential word of God is ⟨the interpretation⟩ of all ⟨the ideas of God⟩. For that reason (the scriptures) also named him (the Logos) wisdom, as this name can show the fullness of the ideas hidden in him.[31]

Theognostus then discusses Col. 2. 9: 'in him dwells the fullness of the Godhead'. He explains what this dwelling means in the following way:

As he (the Son) has similarity with the Father according to his being (ἔχων τὴν ὁμοιότητα τοῦ πατρὸς κατὰ τὴν οὐσίαν, so too he also has similarity according to number (as the only one). Therefore there is only one Logos and only one Sophia, for the Father needs no other ⟨wisdom⟩; nor did he need to give any other image of his nature (alongside the Son), as though the first were deficient. For in this way it (i.e. the image) would have full similarity, if it were also sufficient in number (i.e. if only a single image were necessary to represent the Father completely). Thus he is the only (Logos) and preserves complete similarity with the One. So too he is unalterable (ἀναλλοίωτος), as he is the image of the unalterable Father; for it is impossible for what is directed towards similarity with the One to experience change (ἀδύνατον γὰρ μεταβολῆς ἐν πείρᾳ γενέσθαι τό γε ἀκριβῶς πρὸς τὴν τοῦ ἑνὸς ὁμοιότητα νενευκός).[32]

What is said about the Logos here may be summed up as follows:

(1) As Logos, the Son is associated with the idea of revelation. We have the beginning of a theology of the Word.

(2) This Word issues from the understanding of the Father, from his *nous*.

(3) As this Word can express all the thoughts of the *nous* of the Father, it becomes the *eikon*, the image.

---

[29] Greg. Nyss., *C. Eunom. orat.* III 2 (not 3, as in Barnard, see n. 25 above): Jaeger II, 2, Leiden 1960, 92[11-12]; A. v. Harnack, op. cit., 77.

[30] F. Diekamp, 'Ein neues Fragment aus den Hypotyposen des Alexandriners Theognostus', TQ 84, 1902, 481–94; text 483f.; A. v. Harnack, op. cit., 77f.

[31] F. Diekamp, op. cit., 483, with a supplementation of the text which is also recognized by Harnack: τὸν δὲ οὐσιώδη τοῦ θεοῦ λόγον ἁπάντων ⟨τῶν τοῦ θεοῦ θεωρημάτων ἑρμενέα λέγειν εἰκός⟩.

[32] F. Diekamp, op. cit., 483[6-7]; A. v. Harnack, op. cit., 77–78; on p. 80 Harnack rejects Diekamp's theory that Book VII of the *Hypotyposes* had a special title and was composed as a retraction of the six earlier books; nor did the didactic writing by Dionysius of Rome have any influence on it, as Diekamp assumes.

(4) Because it is a perfect image, the uniqueness of the Logos-Son is guaranteed.

(5) Because of the abundance of ideas which can be and are interpreted in this way in the essential Logos of the Father, he is also called Wisdom, Sophia.

How near to or how far from Arius is Theognostus at this point? How strongly has he interpreted Origenism in terms of Arianism? A controversy has arisen here, above all in English scholarship.[33] Two points may probably be made:

(1) In Theognostus, the Son is still on the side of God, despite all the subordination to the Father. Even the use of the word *ktisma* does not assign him to the creaturely realm. One thing above all clearly distinguishes Theognostus' Logos from that of Arius, as we shall see: because it is a perfect image, the Logos shares in the unalterability of the Father. This is an essential difference, which can only be fully clarified with reference to a fragment from Arius himself.

(2) The Logos is a mediator between the 'one' and the 'many'. But this 'one' whom the Logos interprets through his fullness is not the 'Hen' of Plotinus, which is fully undifferentiated in itself. If Diekamp's elaboration is correct, the fullness of ideas is already present in the *nous* of the Father.[34] The strong stress on the 'uniqueness' of the Logos as the one perfect image brings about a greater approximation of the 'one' to the 'one Logos'. In Arius, matters are quite different. The extant fragments of Theognostus do not allow us to make him already a heretical predecessor of Arius himself.

Pierius, presbyter of the church of Alexandria under Theonas (Bishop of Alexandria from 281/2 to 300),[35] was called the 'new (i.e. the younger) Origen'.[36] He kept the memory of the great master alive, according to Photius, by teaching the pre-existence of souls, but above all by the extent of his work, his talent and the charm of his manner of speaking. Photius adds the telling comment: 'At that time Origen still belonged to the men

[33] T. E. Pollard, 'Logos and Son in Origen, Arius and Athanasius', *StudPat* 2 (TU 65), Berlin 1957, 282–7; id., 'The Origins of Arianism', *JTS* 9, 1958, 103–11; for criticism, M. F. Wiles, 'In Defence of Arius', *JTS* 13, 1962, 339–47; G. C. Stead, 'The Platonism of Arius', *JTS* 15, 1964, 16–31. There is a short summary of the various positions in L. W. Barnard, *VigC* 24, 1970, 172f. In TU, NF 9, 3, 83, Harnack stresses the way in which the content of Theognostus' teaching corresponds with that of Origen, a fact which Photius, *Bibl. cod.* 106 (Henry II, p. 73) already noted, albeit in a deprecatory way. Cf. L. W. Barnard, op. cit., 182: 'In some ways, Arius is nearer to Theognostus than to Origen and may have found support for his views in Theognostus' use of κτίσμα, his idea of the Son as the 'standard of creation', and in his use of Logos as a title of the Son and, in that sense, derivative. However, there is much in Theognostus which does not fit into Arius' system. Nevertheless, it is possible that, as with Dionysius, Arius picked up one strand in Theognostus' thought and developed it with remorseless logic within his own philosophical scheme.'

[34] F. Diekamp, *TQ* 24, 1902, 483[1–4]. See n. 31 above.

[35] Cf. L. W. Barnard, *VigC* 24, 1970, 182–3; L. B. Radford, op. cit.: on Pierius p. 303.

[36] Photius, *Bibl. cod.* 119: R. Henry II, 94[24–5]: ὥστε καὶ νέον ἐπονομασθῆναι 'Ὠριγένην. Jerome, *De vir. ill.* 76: E. C. Richardson, TU 14, 1896: *ut Origenes Iunior vocaretur*. As has now been established, Pierius, like Asterius, weakened in the persecution. Cf. H. Chadwick, *JTS* 24, 1973, 446f. and n. 2.

of repute.'[37] Of his teaching, Photius can only say that it was orthodox in respect of the Father and the Son, 'with the exception that he speaks of two substances and two natures; for he uses these words "ousia" and "physis" instead of the word "hypostasis", and not as it is used by the followers of Arius. As regards the Holy Spirit, his teaching is very bold and heretical; in fact he declares his status to be lower in comparison with the Father and the Son.'[38] We may probably conclude from this that Pierius took over the subordinationism of Origen. One other interesting detail about Pierius may be mentioned. His pupil was the famous Pamphilus, with whom Eusebius of Caesarea felt special ties. C. de Boor discovered that Pierius composed a 'Logos on the Life of St Pamphilus', about which Eusebius lets slip no word. According to C. de Boor it is not improbable that a teacher should set up a monument to his pupil. But the silence of Eusebius could be caused by rivalry.[39]

(a) THE INTERPRETATION OF THE INCARNATION

If we are to understand the decline in the development of doctrine between Origen and Arius (Nicaea), we must also pay attention to the question of the incarnation of the Logos and its interpretation. About this time theological thought—for all the reflection about the Logos—primarily moved within the economy, i.e. within the *kerygma* of the incarnation. At all events, concern was with the whole Christ, the whole *kerygma*, as we can see especially from Dionysius of Alexandria. However, a momentous change begins to set in within the doctrine of the incarnation. Alongside one set of problems, the Father and his Logos, another develops: the Logos and his flesh.

The immediate followers of Origen evidently kept in his footsteps, at least as far as the doctrine of the soul of Christ was concerned. We find no doubt about it in Gregory Thaumaturgus (died *c.* 270). Dionysius of Alexandria mentions it expressly in a fragment—assuming that the fragment is genuine. The passage concerns the longer text at Luke 22. 42ff. In his interpretation of Luke 22. 44 ('And being in an agony he prayed more earnestly; and his sweat became like great drops of blood falling down upon the ground'), he mentions John 10. 18, and says:

However, the (saying) 'I have power to lay down my soul and I have power to take it again'—with this he shows that the suffering is voluntary, and further that the soul given and received is to be distinguished from the Godhead given and received. And just as he voluntarily took death upon himself in the flesh and planted incorruptibility in the flesh, so according to his own will he took the sorrow of slavery upon himself (Phil. 2. 5–11)

[37] Photius, *Bibl. cod.* 119; R. Henry II, 94[25–6].
[38] Ibid., 93.
[39] C. de Boor, *Neue Fragmente des Papias, Hegesippus und Pierius in bisher unbekannten Excerpten aus der Kirchengeschichte des Philippus Sidetes*, TU 5/2, Leipzig 1889, 165–84; on Pierius: 170–71.

and sowed in it courage and boldness, through which he strengthens those who believe
in him for the great struggles of martyrdom. . . .[40]

Yet despite the clear assumption of a human soul in Christ, this soul
does not seem to be the seat of the free acts which are decisive for salvation.
The seat of these acts is rather the Godhead of Christ, which is represented
as 'giving and receiving' in relationship to the soul of Christ. The will of
the Godhead of Christ is also discussed right at the beginning of the long
fragment (Bienert I), in the interpretation of Christ's prayer on the Mount
of Olives (Matt. 26. 39). The comment reads:

> Thus he, the beloved, knew his *will*, which was *perfect* (Rom. 12. 2), and he says often
> that he was come to accomplish this—not his own, i.e. that of men. [It should be noted
> that the mention here is not of the individual human willing of the soul of Christ but of
> universal human willing! The former was to be a problem for the seventh century.] For
> he assumed the *prosopon* [Bienert, 'the character'] of man when he became man. For that
> reason then he also refused to do his own will, the lesser, and rather asked that the will of
> the Father, the greater, the divine will, might be done; of course, in keeping with the
> Godhead his will and that of the Father are wholly and utterly one. For it was the Father's
> will which enjoined him to go through all the temptation, in which the Father preserved
> him in a wonderful way from falling into temptation. He was not involved in it, but
> stood high above temptation and left it behind him. However, it is neither impossible
> nor to no purpose that the Redeemer should pray with his will set over against that of the
> Father. . . .[41]

The soul of Christ is recognized as a reality, but it does not come to the
fore in the interpretation of the suffering on the Mount of Olives. The
presuppositions to be found in Origen are no longer used. Furthermore,
Pierius' pupil, the presbyter *Pamphilus*, makes an important observation
in his *Apology for Origen*. Origen's doctrine that Christ had assumed a
human soul became a stumbling block for a number of people. Of course,
the presbyter does not waste any words on the extent of such a 'scandal';
but at all events we have here a remarkable, open opposition, which was
probably connected with hostility to Origen's doctrine of the pre-
existence of souls.[42]

There can be no doubt that the 'Affair of Paul of Samosata' is a distinctive event in the history of christology. Unfortunately the necessary
critical conditions for its interpretation have not yet been created.[43] Paul
appears to have represented a 'divisive' christology, and his opponents in

---

[40] Dionysius Al., C. L. Feltoe, op. cit., 242–3; W. A. Bienert, op. cit., 99: . . . ἐν τούτοις δηλοῖ
ἑκούσιον εἶναι τὸ πάθος· καὶ ἔτι, ὡς ἄλλη μὲν ἡ τιθεμένη καὶ λαμβανομένη ψυχή, ἄλλη δὲ ἡ τιθεῖσα
καὶ λαμβάνουσα θεότης. For the whole text (C. L. Feltoe, op. cit., 231–50; W. A. Bienert, op.
cit., 95–102), cf. Bienert, p. 122, n. 266. This section could be genuine, unlike the last section of V,
44 (Bienert p. 100), where there is a clear allusion to the monothelitic controversy. Here, however,
pre-Nicene problems can still be discovered.
[41] Dionysius Al., C. L. Feltoe, op. cit., 233⁵–234³; W. A. Bienert, op. cit., 96.
[42] Pamphilus, *Apol. pro. Orig.*: ed. C. H. E. Lommatzsch, Berolini 1846, 24, 373f.: *Si quis sane
offenditur, quod dixit Salvatorem etiam animam suscepisse: nihil de hoc amplius respondendum puto, nisi quod
huius sententiae non Origenes auctor est, sed ipsa sancta scriptura testatur, ipso Domino et Salvatore dicente
. . .* (there follow John 10. 18; Matt. 26. 38; John 12, 27).

the church, among whom the presbyter Malchion played a leading role, a 'unitive' christology. According to the synodal letter preserved in part by Eusebius (HE 7, 30), Paul denied the divinity of Christ which he had earlier allowed. Christ had not 'come down from heaven' but was 'from below'. According to witnesses of a later period (*Contestatio Eusebii* of 428, *Timothy Aelurus, Severus of Antioch*) Paul put forward a christology of the indwelling of the 'Logos' in a man (with body and soul). Malchion, on the other hand, appears to have put forward a christology the terminology of which had already progressed quite considerably. He saw in Christ a unity of Logos and sarx corresponding to the unity between body and soul in a human being. The Logos is in Christ what the soul is in man. Malchion would see that this guaranteed a strict unity in Christ. If Paul on the other hand allowed a soul in Christ, Malchion would have felt him to be renouncing the possibility of assuming a strict unity in Christ. Thus the Apollinarian solution of christology would be anticipated as early as the third century. If (as de Riedmatten sees it) we can accept the tradition about Paul of Samosata as genuine, it would be possible that we had here the common root of Arianism, Apollinarianism and some aspects of the christology of the Alexandrian church. Naturally the different development of the three branches of this Logos-sarx christology would have to be taken into account. In any case, their mutual relationship is an important problem in the history of the dogma of the third and fourth centuries. We will attempt to draw attention to this in what follows. Scholarship, however, has so far been unable to agree on the authenticity of the fragments and so if we take them into consideration in this study at all it can only be conditionally.

We can already establish a negative attitude towards Origen in *Peter of Alexandria* (died 311), especially towards Origen's teaching of the pre-existence of the soul. Does this influence the actual picture of Christ? Peter was a renowned witness of the Christian faith and was even quoted at the Council of Ephesus, but we are unable to answer the question because of the regrettably few remains of his writings.[44] It is nevertheless striking that in two of the best known of Origen's opponents, *Methodius of Olympus* (died *c.* 311) and *'Adamantius'*, as, perhaps, in Athanasius' teacher *Alexander of Alexandria* (died 328), a more or less pronounced form of the 'Word-flesh' christology may be discerned.[45] It is probably

---

[43] Cf. P. Nautin, *École Pratique des Hautes Études, Sec. Sc. Rel. Annuaire* 1953–54, 56–8, on H. de Riedmatten O.P., *Les Actes du procès de Paul de Samosate, Étude sur la Christologie du III e et IV e siècles*, Fribourg 1952; further G. Bardy, *Paul de Samosate*, Louvain 1929[2]; F. Loofs, *Paulus von Samosata*, Leipzig 1924. Nautin promises a new edition of the fragments and a new description of Paul's teaching.

[44] ACO I, 1, 2, p. 39. On the christology of Peter of Alexandria: M. Richard, 'Pierre I er d'Alexandrie et l'unique hypostase du Christ', *MSR* 3, 1946, 357–8. Further L. B. Radford, op. cit., 56–8, esp. 61–70. Another significant article is: J. Barns–H. Chadwick, 'A Letter ascribed to Peter of Alexandria', *JTS* 24, 1973, 443–55.

[45] 1. Methodius OP.: *Symposion* 3, 3–7: ed. Bonwetsch, 29–34.—*Ctr. Porphyrium* 3: ibid., ed. B.

because of his opposition to Origen that Methodius, who fought against Origen's doctrine of the pre-existence of souls and in particular of the soul of Christ, was occasioned to leave Christ's soul unnoticed in his picture of Christ. He maintains a complete silence over it, though in view of his dependence upon Origen elsewhere he must have known of the teaching of the *Peri Archon* (cf. *Symposion* 7, 8 with *De Princ.* II, 6, 4). Some formulas seem to combine a Logos-anthropos and a Logos-sarx framework:

> For this was Christ: man filled with the pure and perfect Godhead, and God comprehending man (3, 4). . . . And so God, moistening His clay once again and modelling the same man again unto honour, fixed and hardened it in the Virgin's womb, united and mingled it with the Word, and finally brought it forth dry and unbreakable into the world . . . (3, 5).

At the conclusion of this introduction, we return once again to the starting point of the period which we have been describing. Here we meet the figure of *Gregory Thaumaturgus*, but now outside Alexandria, at Caesarea in Palestine, soon after 231–233: that is, after the flight of Origen from Alexandria to his Palestinian friends Theoctistes and Alexander. If we are right, no theologian in this period produces a confession of the triad in God which comes so near to Nicaea as does Gregory, above all in his *Expositio fidei*. Interestingly enough, its place in the history of doctrine is best illuminated by Arius. Indeed, in his *Thaleia* Arius perhaps makes a direct allusion to it. For this reason, we shall only be considering it within the framework of the Arian doctrines of the Logos and the incarnation. Whereas in some Alexandrians, as we have seen, subordinationism becomes more marked than that of Origen, Gregory Thaumaturgus 'almost'—this word can be substantiated from the texts—establishes the equality of Father, Son and Spirit in the triad. In effect, in Gregory Thaumaturgus and Dionysius of Alexandria it is possible to see a 'twofold' Origen, that is, the ambivalence of his teaching in respect of Nicaea and Arius.

506²³–507⁷. Cf. G. N. Bonwetsch, *Die Theologie des Methodius v. Ol.*, AbhGött GW 7 1, Berlin 1903, 87–96; H. Musurillo, S. J., *St Methodius, The Symposion. A Treatise on Chastity* (ACW 27). Introduction, esp. 19. J. Montserrat Torrents, 'Los titulos cristológicos en la obra de Metodio di Olimpo', *Scriptorium Victoriense* 16, 1969, 135–40. 2. There is a Logos-sarx christology in 'Adamantius' which is wholly based on Rom. 1. 3 and John 1. 14. The antithesis Logos (pneuma)-sarx occurs quite frequently in the christological section of the *Dialogus* (written about 300): ed. De Sande Bakhuyzen, 168¹⁹–202²⁴. The descriptions (ibid. 184²¹) of the 'complete man' in Christ and of his 'rational soul' are, according to J. Liébaert, certainly to be assumed a later interpolation. 3. *Alexander of Alexandria* is not, however, the author of the *Sermo de anima et corpore* . . . (PG 18, 585–608), which belongs to the tradition of the *Melitoniana* with its pneuma-sarx christology. See above pp. 94–8; cf. *Sermo de anima* 5.6: PG 18, 598C, 600.

SECTION ONE

THE 'ONE GOD' AND HIS 'LOGOS', THE 'LOGOS' AND HIS 'FLESH', THE 'LOGOS-SARX' CHRISTOLOGY

CHAPTER ONE

THEOLOGICAL TWILIGHT

Towards the end of the fourth century the Fathers were aware that the Council of Nicaea in 325 marked the starting-point of a new development in Christian faith. However, the first general council only acquired this significance in the course of the bitter struggles over its validity. Nicaea became a turning-point, but did so only in the course of a long history leading to its acceptance. However, since Nicaea is a 'turning-point', it is extremely important to study the state of christology immediately before the Council through men who—partly, at any rate—also wrote after the Council. Lactantius is the only exception among those who concern us here. Eusebius of Caesarea shows us that it was possible to put forward the same doctrine before and after the Council, and not to take any new steps. Asterius the Sophist is an obscure figure. Aphrahat the Persian sage seems to know nothing of Nicaea, or rather to take no notice of it. Without doubt the most significant figure is Eusebius of Caesarea who, together with Lactantius, is the last great non-heretical subordinationist. He is the link backwards to Origen. He acquires great significance for the future of christology not so much as a 'christologian' as by the incorporation of his Logos christology in a political theology. He laid the spiritual foundations for the theology of the imperial church, which was to be influential for many centuries to come.

1. EUSEBIUS OF CAESAREA

Eusebius (c. 260–339) interests us primarily as a theologian and christologian.[1] To do justice to his particular characteristics, it would be necessary

---

[1] A. Bigelmair was probably the first to discover Eusebius the 'theologian' (in addition to Eusebius the church historian) in his contribution to the *Festschrift* for Georg von Hertling: 'Zur Theologie des Eusebius von Caesarea', Kempten–München 1913, 65–85, here following the special printing of 1914. A study which is still useful even today is M. Weis, *Die Stellung des Eusebius von Cäsarea im arianischen Streit. Kirchen- und dogmengeschichtliche Studie*, Trier 1919; H.-G. Opitz, 'Euseb von Caesarea als Theologe', *ZNW* 34, 1935, 1–19, offers new suggestions, as does H. Berkhof, *Die Theologie des Eusebius von Caesarea*, Amsterdam 1939. G. Bardy, 'La théologie d'Eusèbe de Césarée

to pay more attention to various presuppositions than is possible within the framework of the present book. More would have to be discovered about the intellectual background from which Eusebius came. Three or more factors are at work in him: (a) the tradition of the church to which he often appeals, but which is refracted by the subordinationism of the Apologists and especially by the influence of Origen; (b) Scripture; (c) writers from Middle Platonism. It would be necessary to investigate,

whether the influence of Middle Platonism has been corrected by statements from Scripture ⟨and the creeds⟩, or whether on the contrary the Middle Platonist pattern of hypostases has largely determined the choice of scriptural passages. Still, in assessing Eusebius it is important not to overlook the starting-points which were offered him by earlier tradition, and especially by the Apologists, for his picture of the Logos. Special attention should be paid to the question how far in Eusebius the doctrine of the divine persons is still a theological doctrine of God's saving action, his economy, and how far it appears in the philosophical perspective of the problem of immanence and transcendence which so preoccupied Middle Platonism.[2]

d'après l'Histoire Ecclésiastique', RHE 50, 1955, 5–20. The christology of Eusebius is discussed in: H. de Riedmatten O.P., Les actes du procès de Paul de Samosate. Étude sur la christologie du IIIᵉ et IVᵉ siècle (Paradosis VI), Fribourg 1952, 68–81; A. Weber, ΑΡΧΗ. Ein Beitrag zur Christologie des Eusebius von Cäsarea, München 1965; id., 'Die Taufe Jesu im Jordan als Anfang nach Eusebius von Cäsarea', TheolPhil 41, 1966, 20–9; F. Ricken, 'Die Logoslehre des Eusebios von Caesarea und der Mittelplatonismus', TheolPhil 42, 1967, 341–58; G. C. Stead, '"Eusebius" and the Council of Nicaea', ƒTS NS 24, 1973, 85–100. There are also long sections on the Logos doctrine or christology of Eusebius in D. S. Wallace-Hadrill, Eusebius of Caesarea, London 1960, esp. chs. V and VI; J. Sirinelli, Les vues historiques d'Eusèbe de Césarée (Univ. de Dakar, Publ. de la Sect. de langues et littérature 10), Dakar 1961; R. Farina, L'Impero e l'Imperatore Cristiano in Eusebio di Cesarea. La prima teologia politica del Cristianesimo, Zürich 1966, esp. 'Parte prima. I fondamenti teologici della concezione di Eus. sull'Impero e l'Imperatore Cristiano', 25–106 (for further literature on political theology see below); Per Beskow, Rex Gloriae. The Kingship of Christ in the Early Church, Uppsala 1962, 261–8; Marie-Josèphe Rondeau, 'Une nouvelle preuve de l'influence littéraire d'Eusèbe de Césarée sur Athanase: l'interprétation de psaumes', RSR 56, 1968, 385–434; id., 'Le "Commentaire des Psaumes" de Diodore de Tarse I–III', RevHistRel 176, 1969, 5–23, 153–88; 177, 1970, 5–33. Here we follow the dating of the works of Eusebius worked out by D. S. Wallace-Hadrill, op. cit., 39–58; cf. R. Farina, op. cit., 11–12. Compare the various articles on Eusebius in the lexica: E. Schwartz, PWK VI, 1370–439, here following the reprint in: Schwartz, Griechische Geschichtsschreiber, edited by the Kommission für Spätantike Religionsgeschichte bei den Deutschen Akademie der Wissenschaften zu Berlin, Leipzig 1959², 495–598; J. Moreau, DictHGE 15, 1963, 1437–60; id., in RAC 6, 1966, 1052–88; M.-J. Rondeau and J. Kirchmeyer, Dict. de Spirit. 4, 1961, 1686–90; J. Quasten, Patrology III, 1963, 309–45.

   Works relevant for the christology of the pre-Nicene period are above all the various parts of the Historia Ecclesiastica (HE), the Eclogae Propheticae (EP), the two works Praeparatio Evangelica (PE) and Demonstratio Evangelica (DE) (both from the years 312–18); important individual documents are the Panegyric of Tyre (315–16 or 316–17) and the letter to Euphration of Balneae (c. 318). Important Nicene/post-Nicene works are: the letter to the community of Caesarea (about Nicaea) with his creed (June 325); on this see J. N. D. Kelly, Early Christian Creeds, London 1972³, 182, 217–26. Also Contra Marcellum (CM) (335), De Ecclesiastica Theologia (ET) (335), Laus Constantini (LC) (335), Commentaria in Psalmos (CP) (after 330; for the various datings see M.-J. Rondeau, RSR 56, 1968, 420, n.60); Theophaneia (Greek frag. = TG; Syriac text = TS; for the dating see M.-J. Rondeau, RSR 56, 1968, 386, n.2); cf. Wallace-Hadrill, op. cit., 55. 'The work (Theophany) as a whole reads like a retractatio, a last word in which Eusebius is recapitulating the best of what he has had to say over forty years of writing.' According to Wallace-Hadrill, the Theophaneia is later than LC 11–18, in which others see an 'outline' of the Theophaneia. See the various views in M.-J. Rondeau, loc. cit.

   [2] F. Ricken, 'Die Logoslehre des Eusebios', TheolPhil 42, 1967, 358. Ricken was the first to make a thorough investigation of the philosophical presuppositions of the Logos doctrine of Eusebius, and establishes noteworthy relationships. R. Farina has not noted this study. Ricken makes some references to the state of scholarship: 'In Berkhof's work the influence of the scheme of hypostases on Eusebius' thought comes clearly to the fore, but the biblical influences on the terse and systematic account are

In the foreground of the thought of the historian and theologian Eusebius we seem to find a reference to the Origenist tradition, which he understands to be the tradition of the church. As far as he differs from Origen in important points, he is influenced by the Alexandrian school of the period after Origen, of course with the exception of Arius.[3] In what follows we shall present the main features of his Logos doctrine and his interpretation of the incarnation, above all in the period before Nicaea. Where it seems appropriate, we shall also refer to his works after Nicaea. The separation of these two phases is more important for his political theology than for his christology.

(a) The Logos doctrine of Eusebius before Nicaea

In his earliest works, Eusebius asserts that it is the practice of Scripture to name the Logos of God Lord and God after the Father above and the God of all things.[4] It is good to refer at the beginning of our investigation to the confession which he presented to the Synod of Nicaea to demonstrate his orthodoxy, and above all to recognize the guideline to which he kept, while making clear how confession and reflection could go different ways.

We believe in one God, the Father, almighty, maker of all things visible and invisible; And in one Lord Jesus Christ, the Logos of God, God from God, light from light, life from life, Son only-begotten, first-begotten of all creation, begotten before all ages of

---

discussed less. Weber is largely oriented on the scriptural exegesis of Eusebius (esp. on Prov. 8. 22–31), but unfortunately does not go sufficiently into the philosophical and theological dependencies . . . so that apart from allusions in APXH, 163–5, the question which we have posed is not discussed' (op. cit., 358, n.148). It is important to note not only the positive content of the *tradition* present in Eusebius but also what it declares to be 'heresy'. In this twofold perspective, Origen is particularly significant for Eusebius. The negative canon which Origen sets out in his commentary on Titus 3. 10f. can be traced clearly in Eusebius. Cf. *Apologia pro Origene* I of Pamphilus (handed down in the translation by Rufinus, Lommatzsch 24, 314–19). The following characteristics of heresies are enumerated: 'Anyone who regards himself as a Christian but nevertheless claims that there is a fundamental difference between old and new covenants (the Old Testament and the New Testament), and who therefore separates the God at work in the Old Testament from the God in the New Testament, who regards Jesus Christ as only a man and refuses to give him exalted and divine attributes, who puts forward an adoptionist or patripassian view, who assumes that human souls are of different substance, who denies free will, who rejects the resurrection of the dead, who puts forward false teaching about devils and angels, is a heretic.' Thus F. Winkelmann, 'Grosskirche und Häresien in der Spätantike', *Forschungen und Fortschritte* 41, 1967, 245. Also important are the studies by M. Weis, A. Bigelmair, G. Bardy and H. de Riedmatten. Weis compares Origen (62–8) and the post-Origenistic Alexandrians (68–73); cf. G. Florovsky, 'Origen, Eusebius and the Iconoclastic Controversy', *Church History* 19, 1950, 3–22.

[3] M. Weis, op. cit., mentions three decisive differences from Origen, but is only thinking of the Logos doctrine here. The question of the 'soul of Christ' should be added. He makes Dionysius of Alexandria, Theognostus and Pierius responsible for the differences which he stresses; he finds that their influence on Eusebius was communicated principally by his teacher Pamphilus. Cf. HE VI and VII; PE VII, 19; XIV, 23–7 on Dionysius of Alexandria, to whom the Arians appealed; cf. Athanasius, *De sent. Dion.*: H.-G. Opitz, AW II, 1, 4, pp. 46–67; Gennadius, *Liber Eccles. Dogm.* 4: C. H. Turner, *JTS* 7, 1906, 90; W. A. Bienert, *Dionysius von Alexandrien, Das erhaltene Werk*, Stuttgart 1972, 17–18; E. Boularand, 'Denys d'Alexandrie et Arius', *BLE* 67, 1966, 161–9; id., *L'hérésie d'Arius et la "Foi" de Nicée I: L'Hérésie d'Arius*, Paris 1972, 135–43.

[4] Eusebius, EP: PG 22, 102,9B: ὁ τοῦ θεοῦ λόγος, ὃν μετὰ τὸν ἀνωτάτω πατέρα καὶ θεὸν τῶν ὅλων κύριον καὶ θεὸν ἀποκαλεῖν ἔθος τῇ ἱερᾷ γραφῇ.

the Father, through whom all things came into being, who because of our salvation was incarnate, and dwelt among men, and suffered, and rose again on the third day, and ascended to the Father, and will come again in glory to judge living and dead. We believe also in one Holy Spirit. (He adds the explanation: We believe that each of these exists and exists independently, the Father truly as Father, the Son truly as Son and the Holy Spirit truly as Holy Spirit. As also our Lord said when he sent out his disciples to preach: Go and teach all peoples and baptize them in the name of the Father and of the Son and of the Holy Spirit.)[5]

Eusebius' assertion that the Logos and the Son have their own hypostasis acquires a key position.

For he (the Logos of God) has in himself his own entirely divine and rational hypostasis, which exists for itself and also works for itself, but is immaterial and incorporeal, and in every respect is similar to the nature of the first and unbegotten and only God; it (this hypostasis) bears within itself the Logoi of all that is made and the incorporeal and invisible ideas of all that is visible. Therefore the divine sayings also name it wisdom and God's Logos.[6]

When Eusebius speaks here of a 'similarity', and also stresses that the Logos has its own hypostasis, we can see the tension that arises with the *homoousios* of Nicaea. This also emerges in the fact that he is unwilling to use the simile of the ray of light for the relationship of Father and Son, which according to Athanasius expresses the *homoousion* between them.[7]

In the post-Nicene *Ecclesiastical Theology* he uses the comparison of the emperor and the picture of the emperor to express the relationship between Father and Son in God. This is meant to express not only the *similitudo* but also the *dissimilitudo*.[8] In his sermon on the feast of the consecration of the church of Tyre he compares the Father, Son and Spirit with the three gateways of the basilica. The middle gateway, which represents the Father, is greater than the two side gateways:

The whole temple he (Bishop Paulinus of Tyre) adorneth with a single, mighty gateway, even the praise of the one and only God, the universal King; and on either side of the Father's sovereign power he provideth the secondary beams of the light of Christ and the Holy Spirit.[9]

In his interpretation of the relationship of Father and Son in God, Eusebius adopts a very difficult position. In no way does he wish to endanger the singleness of God or monotheism. Therefore the Father is

---

[5] J. N. D. Kelly, *Early Christian Creeds*, London 1972³, 182. Greek in the letter of Eusebius to his community, Opitz, AW III 1, 2, document 22, p. 43.

[6] DE V, 5, 10: Heikel, 228²⁹⁻³⁶; cf. also HE I, 1, 14: Schwartz, I, 18¹²⁻¹⁵: καὶ ὅτι γέ ἐστιν οὐσία τις προκόσμιος ζῶσα καὶ ὑφεστῶσα, ἡ τῷ πατρὶ καὶ θεῷ τῶν ὅλων εἰς τὴν τῶν γενητῶν ἁπάντων δημιουργίαν ὑπηρετησαμένη. λόγος θεοῦ καὶ σοφία χρηματίζουσα. . . .

[7] Cf. DE V, 1, 19: Heikel, 213¹⁷⁻²⁶; IV, 3, 4–7: 153¹⁻¹⁶. The ray is σύμφυτος, of one nature with its source, but not the Logos *vis-à-vis* the Father. The ray is indivisible from the light, but the Logos has his own hypostasis.

[8] ET II, 23: Klostermann–Hansen, 133³⁴–134⁴.

[9] HE X, 4, 65: Schw. II, 88¹⁷⁻¹⁸; translation here from Kirsopp Lake, *Eusebius: The Ecclesiastical History* II, 1957, 439f. Cf. X, 4, 41; Schw., 874²⁹–875.

designated 'the God' (ὁ θεός), and clearly set over the Son.[10] According to the passage quoted above, the basis of this pre-eminence is the fact that the Father is the only God, who has received his Godhead by nature, i.e. from no one else. Thus the Logos-Son necessarily occupies second place; the Logos has received his Godhead from the Father; this Godhead is in the same relationship between Father and Son as that of the original to a representation; it is to be understood in the framework of Middle Platonic hypostasis-speculation. The problem which the confession of the divinity of Christ (and of the Holy Spirit) poses for Christian monotheism is therefore solved by Eusebius in terms of ante-Nicene, Origenist subordinationism. But in contrast to Origen, this subordination is made more acute as the result of certain important nuances.[11] The nature of Eusebius' Logos becomes clear when his place in the picture of God and the world is defined. There is a supreme hypostasis, the 'first God' (DE V, 4, 11; cf. IV, 2, 2; 3, 3). It is the 'one Father' (DE IV, 5, 13; cf. 6, 2), the divine monad (αὐτὸ τὸ ἕν or αὐτὸς ὁ εἷς) (DE IV, 3, 1 and 8; cf. LC III, 6: Heikel 201[14-31]; for the important word monad or henad cf. DE IV, 6, 1: Heikel 158[21]; TE II, 6: Klostermann-Hansen 103[9f.]). The Father is 'wisdom unbegotten and without beginning' (DE IV, 3, 5; IV, 1, 2; 6, 6; V, prooem. and V, 1, 4). It should be noted here that Eusebius does not distinguish between ἀγένητος and ἀγέννητος, i.e. between 'not coming into being' (uncreated) and 'unbegotten' (not born). Only the Father is the 'true being' (LC VII, 2) and the 'first, powerful and only true good' (DE V, 1, 24; ET III, 18; 179[11f.]), 'the wholly good', who is 'good of himself, by nature' (LC XI, 5; XII, 2). The transcendence of this monad is so heightened that it is seen 'beyond the universe' (LC I: 196[18]: ἐπέκεινα τῶν ὅλων; DE IV, 7, 4), 'beyond and far above all being' (LC XI: 227[7]: πάσης ἐπέκεινα καὶ ἀνωτάτω οὐσίας).

On the other hand, the Son is 'the second' (PE VII, 15, 9; I, 7, 9; DE V, 3, 9); or 'the second God' as in Origen (DE V, 30, 3; cf. PL 23, 37). 'Being the second' is so to speak the nature of the permanent state of the Logos, as is indicated by the participle in the phrase δευτερεύων θεῖος λόγος (HE I, 2, 5). The Logos is the 'second ousia' (PE VII, 15, 6; DE VI, prol. 1), the 'second cause' (HE I, 2, 3; EP I; III, 1: PG22, 1025D; 1121B; PE XI, 15, 7; DE V, prol. 20, 23), the 'second Lord' (HE I, 2, 9; EP I, 12: PG 22, 1068C); 'the second light' (DE IV, 3, 7). Whereas the Father has the absolute primacy in rule, the Son is allotted only the second role in his reign and as ἀρχή (τὰ δευτερεῖα τῆς κατὰ πάντων βασιλείας καὶ ἀρχῆς) (HE I, 2, 11; EP I, 5: PG 20, 1037C). Thus this essential subordination is expressed in the order of sovereignty, which makes the Son the

[10] DE V, 11-14: Heikel, 225[26]-226[16]: the Son, although by nature Son and our God, is not the first God; he is God only because he is firstborn Son.
[11] For what follows cf. F. Ricken, TheolPhil 42, 1967, 343-8, where fuller information is given; R. Farina, op. cit., 42-69.

servant and living organ and minister of the Father in the service of man.[12]
It can be seen especially in the designation of the Son as 'servant of God'
(παῖς τοῦ θεοῦ) (DE V, 11, 9).

This gradation in Eusebius' doctrine of God and the Logos becomes
more marked when it is seen against a background of Middle Platonism.
This background can in fact be demonstrated.[13] The Logos is reduced to
the role of mediator between the uncreated God and the *ousia* of what is
created.[14] The Logos is the demiurge (DE IV, 5, 13: 10[1]; ET I, 9: 67[19];
II, 7: 105[31]; cf. HE I, 2, 3; PE XI, 14, 4),[15] the governor (ὕπαρχος) (LC III:
202[2]), the helper (ὑπουργός) (DE IV, 10, 16; V, 1, 17), the servant (ὑπηρετι-
κόν) (ET I, 20: 81[17]; II, 14: 116[2]; cf. Justin, *Dial.* 61, 1) and living instrument (ὄργανον ἔμψυχον καὶ ζῶν) (DE IV, 4, 2). The difference between
the Logos and the Father is stressed so strongly that the Logos can be
described as the helmsman who stands on the ship of the world and directs
the rudder in accordance with the indications of the Father—the latter
being one who stands high above him (DE IV, 2, 1; 4, 2; ET I, 13: 73[12];
II, 17: 121[20]; LC VI, 9; XI, 11; XII, 8). It is unnecessary to cite all the
individual functions of this mediation.[16] The Logos administers everything
throughout the realm of the visible and the invisible; he binds all together
(δεσμός) and thus arranges the ordering of the world. In this way the Logos
is given the function assigned to the world-soul in Middle Platonism.[17]

The position of the Logos as mediator, as the instrument of the Father,
is maintained so consistently that it is hardly allowed any initiative of its
own. From the early writings (EP) on, it merely carries out the plans of
the Father, 'plus acteur que l'auteur'.[18] J. Sirinelli finds in the HE the first
and probably the only mention of the Logos' own activity and initiative:

> Then, indeed, when the great flood of evil had come nigh overwhelming all men, like
> a terrible intoxication overshadowing and darkening the souls of almost all, the first-
> begotten and first-created Wisdom of God, the pre-existent Logos himself, in his exceed-
> ing kindness appeared to his subjects, at one time by a vision of angels, at another person-
> ally to one or two of the God-fearing men of old, as a saving power of God, yet in
> no other form than human, for they could not receive him otherwise.[19]

At all events, the activity of the Logos is always that of an instrument
to carry out or restore the order of the Father. His chief tasks are to 'reveal'

[12] DE IV, 2, 2: Heikel, 152[11-13]: ὑπηρέτης . . . ζῷον ὄργανον; DE V, 10, 5. Heikel, 233[12-13]: οὐ
μὴν ἐπὶ πάντων, ἀλλ' ὁ ἐκείνου δεύτερος, τὰ τοῦ πατρὸς εἰς ἀνθρώπους διακονούμενος καὶ διαγγέλλων.
[13] See F. Ricken, op. cit., 344-8.
[14] Cf. DE IV, 6, 3; Heikel, 159[1-3]; LC XI, 12: Heikel, 227[15-17]; PE VII, 12, 2: Mras, 386[11-14];
cited in F. Ricken, op. cit., 348.
[15] For the cosmological functions of the Logos cf. R. Farina, op. cit., 47-49; DE IV, 5, 13: Heikel,
158[3-5]; V, 1, 6-7: H., 211[10-19]; v. 5, 7: H., 228[1-15].
[16] Cf. F. Ricken, op. cit., 348-51; J. Sirinelli, *Les vues historiques*, 278-80.
[17] F. Ricken, op. cit., 350; cf. the depiction of the cosmological function of the Logos in DE IV,
13, 2-3: Heikel, 171[3-15].
[18] J. Sirinelli, *Les vues historiques*, 298.
[19] HE I, 2, 21; translation in Kirsopp Lake I, 1953, 23f.; J. Sirinelli, op. cit., 299, stresses the exceptional character of this passage.

the truth about God and to 'educate' all men to morality. The ordering of the cosmos, the leading of men to knowledge of God and morality—these tasks seem to penetrate deeply into human happenings,

> mais cette fonction ne lui (the Logos) donne aucune prise sur l'Histoire. Tout le reste de son activité, qu'il s'agisse de cette révélation permanente qui émane de lui en tant qu'il est la raison de l'univers, ou qu'il s'agisse de cette révélation épisodique par quoi il redresse constamment les erreurs des hommes et les achemine vers le verité, tout en lui est activité pédagogique et révélatrice.[20]

With this view of the relationship between God, the Logos and the world, Eusebius finds himself on the same ground as Philo, Origen and those Middle Platonists of which he made use, especially in the PE.[21] However, he differs from the whole of Middle Platonism.

> Designating not the first, but the second God as δημιουργός. Here he agrees with Numenius, with the system of the Chaldaean oracles, which is closely related to him in both content and chronology, and with Plotinus. However, Eusebius differs from the latter in that he has only two stages in the divine realm and not the system of three hypostases (hen–nous–psyche) which is to be found in Plotinus. Moreover, his supreme God is the bearer of ideas in contrast to Plotinus' hen. Eusebius identifies the Logos with the demiurge in the same way that Numenius identifies the world soul with it. . . .[22]

The way in which Eusebius restricts his doctrine of God so closely to the Middle Platonic distinction between the first and the second hypostasis explains why the Holy Spirit retreats into the background in his writings, and is even removed from the divine sphere. The Holy Spirit is to be regarded as the first of creatures,[23] and in Eusebius is in some respects assigned the place which Arius gives to the Logos.[24]

What does the Bishop of Caesarea say about the *origin* of the Logos or the Son? It is incomprehensible to the human mind and even to higher spiritual beings, as we have here the genesis of the Only-Begotten of

---

[20] J. Sirinelli, op. cit., 299f.

[21] Cf. Books XI–XV and the index in Mras II, 439–65; É. des Places, 'La tradition patristique de Platon (spécialement d'après les citations des Lois et de l'Epinomis dans la Préparation évangélique d'Eusèbe de Césarée)', RevEtGrec 80, 1967, 385–94. Ibid., 392: 'Eusèbe, après Justin, croyait trouver chez Platon le Verbe, le Logos, et bien des pages qu'il a reproduit, touchant Dieu ou l'âme, pouvaient entrer dans la philosophie chrétienne.'

[22] F. Ricken, TheolPhil 42, 1967, 355–6, who makes particular mention of the relationships to Numenius. For comparison with Plotinus see C. Sorge, La dottrina delle ipostasi. Antologia delle Enneadi, Società Editrice Internazionale 1959; J. L. Fischer, 'La signification philosophique du néoplatonisme', in: Le Néoplatonisme. Colloques Internationaux du CNRS, Royaumont 9–13 juin 1969, Paris 1971, 147–50.

[23] F. Ricken, op. cit., 358, with reference to H. Berkhof, Die Theologie des Eusebius v. Caesarea, 87; cf. ET III, 4–6: Klostermann-Hansen, 157²⁹–164³⁶; cf. ibid., 6: 164¹⁸⁻²⁰: τὸ δὲ παράκλητον πνεῦμα οὔτε θεὸς οὔτε υἱός, ἐπεὶ μὴ ἐκ τοῦ πατρὸς ὁμοίως τῷ υἱῷ καὶ αὐτὸ τὴν γένεσιν εἴληφεν, ἐν δέ τι τῶν διὰ τοῦ υἱοῦ γενομένων τυγχάνει. . . .

[24] Cf. M. Weis, Die Stellung des Eusebius von Cäsarea, 75–9. In the heightening of Origen's subordinationism Eusebius is here probably dependent on Theognostus and Pierius, who according to Photius, Bibl. cod. 106 and 119, ed. R. Henry, Photius Bibliothèque II, Paris 1960, 72–4, and 92–4, had heretical doctrines on the Holy Spirit.

God.[25] At the Council of Nicaea, the bishop after long delay subscribed to the formula 'begotten of the substance of the Father'. In his letter to the Christians in his diocese he justified this step by saying that in its statement the Council was not making the Logos 'part' of the Father and was not accepting any 'division' of God.[26] Even before 325 he had made a decisive distinction between divine spiritual conception and human corporeal conception:

It is not right to say that the Son proceeded from the Father in the way that living beings are begotten among us, nature from nature with suffering and extreme separation. For the divine is wholly and utterly indivisible (ἀμερές καὶ ἄτομον), cannot be split, taken apart, cut up, put together or diminished.[27]

We may suppose that he only rejects the 'from the substance of the Father' to the degree that he believes a materialist conception to be associated with it. For shortly after (in the DE), he takes up a rather more positive attitude:

Beginning from the familiar text 'Who shall explain his generation?', he continues: 'But if anyone ventures to go further and compare what is totally inconceivable with visible and corporeal examples, perhaps he might say that the Son came forth from the unoriginate nature and ineffable substance of the Father (ἐκ τῆς τοῦ πατρὸς ἀγενήτου φύσεως καὶ τῆς ἀνεκφράστου οὐσίας) like some fragrance and ray of light...,' v. 1, 18; but he almost immediately points out the limitations of all such metaphors, and once again associates the phrase ἐξ οὐσίας with the notion of change and division: οὐδὲ γὰρ ἐξ οὐσίας τῆς ἀγενήτου κατά τι πάθος ἢ διαίρεσιν οὐσιώμενος. οὐδὲ γὰρ ἀνάρχως συνυφέστηκεν τῷ πατρί etc., ibid., 201. It must be said that Eusebius looks on the phrase 'from the substance' with marked disfavour, even though he does not reject it consistently, like his namesake of Nicomedia; so that his reluctant acceptance of it at Nicaea has some support in what he had previously written.[28]

Eusebius prefers to limit himself to the ἐκ τοῦ πατρός, 'of the Father', which he proposes. On the other hand he does not want to accept that the Son is 'created'. Before and after Nicaea he completely avoids the *homoousion*, although he too has subscribed to it. According to him the Son does not have the *same* substance as the Father, although he is 'begotten'. The activity of the Father in bringing him forth is a φύειν (ET II, 14), προβάλλειν (I, 8), ἀποτίκτειν (I, 10) and especially a γεννᾶν. Κτίζειν, found, create, can indeed be used of founding a city, but not of the action of a father, whether in the human or in the divine sphere.[29] It is a matter of

25 DE V, 1, 25: Heikel, 214²⁶⁻³¹; cf. HE I, 2, 2: Schwartz I, 10. In both passages Eusebius refers to Matt. 11. 27. Cf. J. Sirinelli, *Les vues historiques*, 278.
26 Eusebius to his community: Opitz, AW III, 1, 2, document 22, 7, p. 44.
27 DE V, 1, 9–10: Heikel 211³⁰–212¹. G. C. Stead presents further passages in JTS 24, 1973, 91.
28 G. C. Stead, op. cit.; ET I, 12: Klostermann-Hansen, 72¹⁵⁻²⁵, should especially be noted for the period after Nicaea. It develops a negative theology in respect of the emergence of the Son.
29 ET I, 10: Klostermann-Hansen, 68¹⁷⁻²². He interprets the *ktizein* of Prov. 8. 22, the chief passage of the Arians, in terms of an 'appointment' to rule. Cf. ET III, 2: Klostermann-Hansen, 140⁸⁻⁹. See index, 219. For Prov. 8. 22 in the prehistory and history of Arianism see M. Simonetti, *Studi sull' Arianesimo*, Roma 1965, 9–87; 'Studi sull'interpretazione patristica di Prov. 8. 22'. For Eusebius, ibid., 48–56: A. Weber, ΑΡΧΗ, 127–31.

'being begotten *of* the Father, not *from* the Father (ἐκ τοῦ πατρός, not ἀπὸ τοῦ πατρός)' as the Arians assume.[30]

The Son does not have divinity in his own right (ἰδιόκτητον); it is not without beginning and without begetting in him, but it does not come from anywhere outside the Father. Consequently it comes through participation in the nature of the Father, which bubbles over him as from a fountain and fills him.[31] In this way, Eusebius believes that he has safeguarded the interests of a strict monotheism:

> There is only a single God, Father of the one perfect and only-begotten Son and not of several gods and sons, as one may assume only one substance of light which brings forth from itself the perfect ray.[32]

Thus determining Eusebius' position in respect of the begetting of the Son and the Logos doctrine in general, and its relationship to Origen, Arius and Nicaea, is something of a theological jig-saw puzzle:

(1) With Origen and Nicaea he assumes a 'begetting' of the Son, but not a 'begetting *from the substance*', because he sees this to involve a division of the divine nature. With Origen, and above all against Marcellus of Ancyra, he assigns the Son his own hypostasis (post-Nicene theology later takes over this terminology, but understands it differently). To preserve this 'hypostasis' of the Son, he believes that he must reject the *homoousios*. In order to avoid all difficulties, he says that the Son is (begotten) 'of the Father'.[33]

(2) He does not follow Origen and Nicaea in assuming an 'eternal begetting'.[34] Just as the Godhead in the Son himself is diminished, so too the pre-temporality of the procession of the Son is not the 'eternity' of the Father. The begetting is not an act without beginning; it is therefore

---

[30] ET I, 11: Klostermann-Hansen, 70²¹⁻²³: (the church) οὐδένα μὲν ἄλλον τῶν γενητῶν ἀναγορεύειν θεὸν ἀξιοῖ, μόνον δὲ τοῦτον οἶδεν θεόν, ὃν μόνον ὁ πατὴρ ἐξ ἑαυτοῦ ἐγέννα. . . . This begetting takes place from the monad. Cf. ET II, 6: Klostermann-Hansen, 103²³⁻⁴: μονὰς δὲ ὢν ἀδιαίρετος ὁ θεὸς τὸν μονογενῆ αὐτοῦ υἱὸν ἐξ ἑαυτοῦ ἐγέννα. . . . The *Arians*, on the other hand: (a) Eusebius Nicomed., *Ep. ad Paulin. Tyr. ep. (c. 320/1)*: Opitz, AW III, 1, 1, document 8, p. 162⁻³: . . . ἀλλ'ἐν μὲν τὸ ἀγέννητον, ἓν δὲ τὸ ὑπ'αὐτοῦ ἀληθῶς καὶ οὐκ ἐκ τῆς οὐσίας αὐτοῦ γεγονός. . . . (b) The confession of faith of Arius to Alexander of Alexandria (c. 320): Opitz, AW III, 1, 1, document 6, p. 13⁸⁻¹⁰: . . . ὁ δὲ υἱὸς ἀχρόνως γεννηθεὶς ὑπὸ τοῦ πατρὸς καὶ πρὸ αἰώνων κτισθεὶς καὶ θεμελιωθεὶς οὐκ ἦν πρὸ τοῦ γεννηθῆναι ἀλλ' ἀχρόνως πρὸ πάντων γεννηθείς, μόνος ὑπὸ τοῦ πατρὸς ὑπέστη.

[31] ET I, 2: Klostermann-Hansen, 63²¹⁻⁶: καθ'ἣν τὸ πλήρωμα τῆς πατρικῆς θεότητος καὶ αὐτὸν υἱὸν θεὸν ὑπεστήσατο, οὐκ ἰδιόκτητον καὶ τοῦ πατρὸς ἀφωρισμένην οὐδ'ἄναρχόν τινα καὶ ἀγέννητον οὐδὲ ἀλλοθέν ποθεν ξένην καὶ τοῦ πατρὸς ἀλλοτρίαν ἐφελκόμενον θεότητα, ἐξ αὐτῆς δὲ τῆς πατρικῆς μετουσίας ὥσπερ ἀπὸ πηγῆς ἐπ'αὐτὸν προχεομένης πληρούμενον. For Eusebius' views on the birth of the Son see A. Weber, ΑΡΧΗ, 49–53.

[32] DE IV, 3, 1–2: Heikel, 152²³⁻⁶. Eusebius has two comparisons for the emergence of the Son: (1) ray/light: (2) anointing oil/fragrance. Cf. A. Weber, op. cit., 49–51.

[33] Cf. ET I, 10: Klostermann-Hansen, 68–9. Cf. M. Weis, *Die Stellung des Eusebius von Caesarea*, 45–51.

[34] Cf. Origen, *De princ*. III, 5, 3; I, 2, 2: GCS V, 291¹¹–30²: *Propter quod nos semper deum patrem novimus unigeniti filii sui, ex ipso quidem nati et quod est ab ipso trahentis, sine ullo tamen initio, non solum eo, quod aliquibus temporum spatiis distingui potest, sed ne illo quidem, quod sola apud semet ipsam mens intueri solet et nudo, ut ita dixerim, intellectu atque animo conspicari. Extra omne ergo quod vel dici vel intellegi potest initium generatam esse credendum est sapientiam.*

also a single act, whereas according to Origen it happens 'timelessly for ever'.[35]

(3) As A. von Harnack rightly sees,[36] Origen regards the act of divine begetting as an act which is inwardly necessary to the nature of the Godhead. Eusebius denies this necessity and regards the begetting as an act of the Father which is free in every respect.[37] But this makes the existence of the second hypostasis dependent on the decision of the first. This dependence heightens Eusebius' subordinationism, even more than the assumption of a diminished Godhead or a weakened eternity of the Logos. At this point he is only a step away from Arianism.

(4) What does decisively separate him from Arius is his denial that the Logos or the Son is created from nothing (ἐξ οὐκ ὄντων).[38] He sees clearly that Arian 'monotheism' is incompatible with the church:

[35] Origen, *Hom. in Jerem.* IX, 4: Klostermann-Hansen, 70[17-25]: τὸ ἀπαύγασμα τῆς δόξης οὐχὶ ἅπαξ γεγέννηται καὶ οὐχὶ γεννᾶται· ἀλλὰ ὅσον ἐστὶν τὸ φῶς ποιητικὸν τοῦ ἀπαυγάσματος ἐπὶ τοσοῦτον γεννᾶται ὁ σωτὴρ ὑπὸ τοῦ πατρός. For Eusebius, on the other hand, according to R. Farina, *L'Impero e l'Imperatore*, 39: 'L'eternità dunque del Logos non è la stessa eternità del Padre: questo ha l'eternità in senso proprio, il Logos, come γενόμενον, l'ha derivata.'

[36] A. von Harnack, *Lehrbuch der Dogmengeschichte* I, Tübingen 1931[5], 672, with reference to a fragment from Origen's commentary on Hebrews.

[37] DE IV, 3, 7: Heikel 153[12-16]: καὶ πάλιν ἡ μὲν αὐγὴ οὐ κατὰ προαίρεσιν τοῦ φωτὸς ἐκλάμπει, κατά τι δὲ τῆς οὐσίας συμβεβηκὸς ἀχώριστον, ὁ δὲ υἱὸς κατὰ γνώμην καὶ προαίρεσιν εἰκὼν ὑπέστη τοῦ πατρός. βουληθεὶς γὰρ ὁ θεὸς γέγονεν υἱοῦ πατήρ, καὶ φῶς δεύτερον κατὰ πάντα ἑαυτῷ ἀφωμοιωμένον ὑπεστήσατο. Cf. A. Weber, APXH, 53: 'Thus God becomes Father through his counsel and through his *dynamis*, i.e. through his will, and not *vi naturae*, like the ray from the light and the fragrance from the oil.' Nevertheless, the Son is not a creature and is 'in all things like' the Father. Eusebius is resolutely concerned to preserve the predominant place of the Son: ἐν ἑνὶ γὰρ μόνῳ τῷ μονογενεῖ αὐτοῦ Λόγῳ ἡ τοῦ Πατρὸς ὁμοιότης σώζεται. Διὸ καὶ εἰκὼν χρηματίζει θεοῦ, καί, θεὸς ἦν ὁ Λόγος, ὡς ἐν αὐτῷ μὲν σώζεσθαι μόνῳ τὴν τοῦ Πατρὸς ὁμοίωσιν, οὐκέτι δὲ καὶ ἐν τοῖς πολλοῖς θεοῖς (CP, in Ps. 85. 10: PG 23, 1036B). Cf. DE V, 1, 21: Heikel, 213[35]: αὐτοουσίᾳ τῷ Πατρὶ ἀφομοιούμενος and frequently. An investigation would have to be made into the question how far the later semi-Arians go back to Eusebius with their ὅμοιος κατὰ πάντα. Cf. J. Gummerus, *Die homöusianische Partei bis zum Tode des Konstantius. Ein Beitrag z. Geschichte des arianischen Streites in den Jahren 356–61*, Leipzig 1900, 8–35, esp. 18f. (relationships between Eusebius and his follower Acacius); 19–21 (Eusebius of Emesa); 21–4 (Cyril of Jerusalem).

[38] Nevertheless Eusebius was from time to time in danger of going over into Arian teaching. G. Bardy sums up the position in this way in *RHE* 50, 1955, 9f.: 'On sait par contre qu'Eusèbe, malgré sa prudence, dut être l'un des premiers à se déclarer en faveur des idées nouvelles (d'Arius). Une lettre adressée par lui à l'un de ses collegues, Euphration de Balanée, déclare que le Père est antérieur au Fils et lui est aussi supérieur. Une lettre d'Arius à Eusèbe de Nicomédie signale parmi ses partisans, qui nient la coexistence éternelle du Père et du Fils, Eusèbe de Césarée, Théodote de Laodicée, Paulin de Tyr, Athanase d'Anazarbe, Grégoire de Beryte, Aetius de Lydda. Une autre lettre encore, d'Eusèbe de Césarée à Alexandre d'Alexandrie, justifie ceux qu'on accuse à tort d'avoir enseigné que le Fils a été fait de néant comme toutes les autres choses [cf. Opitz, AW III, 1, 1, document 7: Alexander is accusing Arius and his companions ὡς λεγόντων ὅτι ὁ υἱὸς ἐκ τοῦ μὴ ὄντος γέγονεν ὡς εἷς τῶν πάντων (14. 5f.). Here Eusebius refers to document 6, Arius' confession of faith.] Une lettre de Nicomédie, écrivant à Paulin de Tyr, justifie Eusèbe de Césarée des accusations portées contre lui [Opitz, ibid., document 8]. Un synode de Palestine mentionne une députation envoyée par Arius à Paulin de Tyr, à Eusèbe de Césarée, à Patrophile de Scythopolis, pour leur demander d'organiser des réunions en sa faveur [Opitz, ibid., document 10]. Enfin le concile d'Antioche, réuni quelque temps avant le concile de Nicée déclare excommuniés Théodote de Laodicée, Narcisse de Néronias et Eusèbe de Césarée [Opitz, ibid., document 18]et nous savons qu'il a existé une lettre adressée par Narcisse de Néronias à Chrestus, futur évêque de Nicée, Euphronius, prêtre de Césarée, et Eusèbe de Césarée, pour les avertir qu'Ossius l'avait interrogé sur la foi d'Eusèbe' [Opitz, AW III, 1, 2, document 19]. For the Synod of Antioch, according to Opitz held in the first weeks of the year 325, see Kelly, *Early Christian Creeds*, 208–11, with reference to the history of the investigation of this synod; most recent and careful criticism of these results in D. L. Holland, 'Die Synode von Antiochien (324/325) und ihre

Those who assume two hypostases, the one uncreated, the other created from nothing, indeed establish 'one God'. But for them the Son is neither the only-begotten, nor the Lord, nor God, as he no longer partakes of the divinity of the Father in any way, but is thrown together with the rest of creation, insofar as it exists (having been created) from nothing. But this is not what the church believes.[39]

(5) Eusebius' acknowledgment of the hypostasis of the Son, who is begotten of the Father and distinct from him (a legacy of Origen), rightly separates him from Marcellus and the latter's understanding of 'monotheism'. But his understanding of the hypostasis of the Son as being lower or diminished in relationship to the Father in fact amounts to a surrender of true monotheism. There was no possibility of an intermediate solution between Arius and Nicaea. Eusebius never recognized this.

(6) In common with *Nicaea*, he never saw the assumption of a Son begotten of the Father (i.e. not created), and therefore clearly on the side of God rather than creation, to be a danger to 'monotheism'. But he differs from the Council in his hesitation over the *homoousios*, which grows increasingly strong; in his refusal to name the Son 'true God of true God', a point at which he follows Origen;[40] in his assumption of a less than eternal existence of the Son and a begetting which is dependent on the freedom of the Father; and in his fear of the Council's formula 'from the substance of the Father', as he sees here a division of this substance. Thus Eusebius is farther from the Nicene creed than Origen.

As a result, Eusebius increased the confusions of the Logos doctrine before Nicaea rather than diminished them. Because he could not accept the theology of Nicaea and remained between all fronts—between Sabellius, Origen, Arius, Nicaea and Marcellus—he could not exercise any influence within theology proper, but was restricted to the realm of political theology. Before we go into that, however, we must present a brief account of Eusebius' doctrine of the incarnation.

(b) The incarnate Logos

What significance can the incarnation of the Son have in view of the

Bedeutung für Eusebius von Caesarea und das Konzil von Nizäa', *ZKG* 81, 1970, 163–81. Holland thinks that there was not such a difference between the theology of Eusebius and the teaching of this synod that an excommunication of Eusebius would have been instituted. This coincides with our conclusions here. Nevertheless, the close contact of Eusebius with the Arians may have been the motive for the 'precautionary excommunication' (Kelly). Holland supposes that the name of Eusebius was inserted later. Eusebius maintained contact with the leading groups of Arians even after Nicaea, but without adopting their teaching. We shall have to return to this behaviour and the motives for it (cf. below on J.-M. Sansterre). Montfaucon regards Eusebius as a true Arian in the *Praeliminaria in Eusebii Commentaria in Psalmos*, cap. VI: PG 23, 28–48: here there are numerous passages on the subordinationism of Eusebius.

39 ET I, 10: Klostermann-Hansen, 69⁶⁻¹¹. Cf. I, 9: 67–8; III, 2: 140⁵–141¹⁴, a passage which is already introduced by Socrates, HE II, 21 (Hussey, I, 237–9), to demonstrate the orthodoxy of Eusebius.

40 Cf. Origen, *Comm. in Io.* II, 3: Preuschen, 55⁹⁻¹⁵. Eusebius, *Letter to Euphration*, is very illuminating: Opitz, AW III, 1, 1, p. 5, no. 3 (document 3), also ET I, 10: Klostermann-Hansen, 68¹⁴⁻¹⁶: Christ is indeed 'true Son', but not 'true God', he is only 'God'. Cf. below on the interpretation of the Nicene creed. See further ET II, 7, 14 (106²⁰, 118⁸); I, 9 (68¹¹); DE V, 1 (210³¹).

stress on the mediatory function of the Logos in cosmology, revelation and teaching? In the HE and in practice in all the works of Eusebius, the incarnation is introduced as the supreme instance among the theophanies of the Logos.[41] But was it really necessary in his theology? Eusebius gives the following reasons for the incarnation of the Son of God in the *Theophaneia*, which has been preserved in Syriac:

But as it is clear that there was by no means one, but were many reasons why the Redeemer caused all his theophanies among men, it is necessary also to say briefly after these (things) why he needed a human vessel and entered into converse among men. How else could the divine οὐσία, hidden, invisible and intangible, the bodiless and incorporeal understanding, the Logos of God, display itself to corporeal men, who were sunk in the depths of evil, who were coming into being and seeking God on earth? There was no other way in which they could or would see the Creator or the creation of the universe and his master workman. It had to be in human composition and form, in a way which was made known to us as by an interpreter. How otherwise could bodily eyes see the incorporeality of God? How otherwise could the mortal nature discover the hidden, the invisible, him whom it had not recognized from a myriad works? So for this reason he needed a mortal instrument and an appropriate expedient for converse among men, because this was agreeable to them. For it is said that *all* love that which is like them.[42]

The law of adaptation to corporeal men requires the incarnation as the last of the ways taken by the Logos which manifests itself in theophanies. In visible form Christ could become the teacher of knowledge of God and the victor over death and the devil in a special way.[43] In the incarnate Christ there is a new beginning of his Lordship, and the direct guidance of men by the Logos is resumed. It is in accord with the doctrine of the Logos mediator that the incarnate Christ is regarded as instrument, interpreter, image, vehicle of the indwelling Logos.[44] The body is the clothing, the temple, the abode of the Logos. So much is the Logos the decisive element in the total reality of the incarnate Christ that Eusebius is taken a considerable distance from Origen's picture. The *anima mediatrix* between Logos and sarx has disappeared. Eusebius cannot use any human soul in his Christ. Here we come across the first clear trace of a proper Logos-sarx christology in the fourth century. The chief passages for this doctrine do in fact come from the late works.[45] But in view of the conservatism of Eusebius (which is still to be differentiated), an inference to the pre-Nicene period is permissible.[46] Even there, however, we come

---

[41] For the following see R. Farina, *L'Impero e l'Imperatore*, ch. III: 'Il Cristo', 75–106; H. Berkhof, *Die Theologie des Eusebius von Caesarea*, 119–26; also in the excellent index by J. A. Heikel in *Eusebius-Werke* VI. 531–5.

[42] TS III, 39: Gressmann, 141[17–25]; R. Farina, op. cit., 79, n. 17.

[43] CP XCII, 1: PG 23, 1184CD.

[44] Cf. H. Berkhof, op. cit., 120, n. 1–3, where numerous instances are given.

[45] Chief texts are: ET I, 20: Klostermann-Hansen, 87[12]–89[5], which is here analysed in more detail; III, 10: 167[10–20]; II, 25: 136[22–3]; CM II, 2: 43[21–7].

[46] Thus R. Farina, op. cit., 80, 85, speaks quite naturally of this Logos-sarx christology of Eusebius, as do A. Bigelmair, op. cit., 13, 17, 18; H. Berkhof, op. cit., 120; H. de Riedmatten, op. cit., 75–81. He also explains the texts which apparently speak of a soul of Christ. Cf. also A. Weber, ΑΡΧΗ, 18.

across further signs which point in the same direction, above all the interpretation of the death of Jesus.

The Logos-sarx framework is an obvious choice for Eusebius to make in interpreting the person of Jesus, because he is concerned to achieve the greatest possible immediacy in the efficacy of the Logos among men and in mankind as a whole. To include a human, created reason here in the actions of the revealing and teaching of the Logos would be an intolerable weakening of the basic notion held by Eusebius. He builds fundamentally on the presence of the Logos-Son in the sarx, and indeed on his immediately tangible presence and efficacy. Jesus' body is completely illumined and divinized by the Logos:[47]

Of course, there would be nothing to prevent us saying that they too (mire and loam, etc.) are illuminated by the splendour of the light (of the sun) and the light is not obscured, nor is the sun made impure, by being mixed with matter, although this would not be alien to the nature of the matter. But the Logos of God, without ὕλη and without matter, which is life itself and the intelligent light itself: all that it touches with incorporeal divine power must live and be in rational light. So too the body which it touches is healed and at the same time illuminated, and every illness, every grief and every suffering departs; whatever is deficient receives an abundance. Therefore he spent his whole life in such a way that he now showed his image (body) in suffering similar to us, and now revealed the Logos God in deeds of power and marvellous works like those of God. Moreover, he foretold by prophecies what was to come, and displayed the Logos of God, which many cannot see, in wonderful works, signs and wonders, and in special powers and further in divine doctrines, which have been prepared to guide men's souls to the heavenly city above, that they may hasten to the citizens there as brothers and kinsmen, and come to know their Father in heaven . . ., so that they might make their journey from here to there easily and without hindrance, and might be ready to receive eternal life with God, the king of all, and light inexpressible and the kingdom of heaven with the hosts of the holy angels.

This text shows very well the whole tendency to a christology of glorification which we found in Clement of Alexandria. In view of the position of the Logos in Eusebius' picture of Christ, it is only consistent that he should place in the foreground even in the incarnate Christ those functions which are proper to the Logos *qua* Logos: Christ is Sophia incarnate and is therefore a 'philosopher' and the 'first of the philosophers', the 'philosopher and God-fearer'. By virtue of this holiness which is peculiar to the Logos (ἀγίων ἅγιος), and by virtue of his wisdom and piety, Christ is the teacher of all the pious and the model for all the virtues. Names like Christ 'the light' refer wholly to his Godhead, as it reveals itself in the human body. Therefore the Logos made flesh is the 'rational light which shines through a mortal and corruptible body'.[48] So this body

---

[47] TS III, 39: Gressmann 144²³–145¹⁶; partly in R. Farina, op. cit., 85⁶⁹, who also refers to DE IV, 13, 1–3, 6–10: Heikel 170²⁸–171¹⁸, 172¹⁰–173¹².

[48] *Commentary on Luke* XXII, 20: PG 24, 568C: εἴη δ' ἄν καὶ σαρκωθεὶς λόγος τοιοῦτος, φῶς νοερὸν διὰ θνητοῦ καὶ ὑγροῦ σώματος ἐκλάμψαν. For this work see E. Schwartz, 'Eusebius', 588–9; D. S. Wallace-Hadrill, 51.

is called a 'lamp', the 'rational light' itself, the 'light of the world', 'light of the nations'.[49] For that reason it can also be compared with the sun, a theme which could easily be taken up again in the political theology of Eusebius.

Although Eusebius predominantly interprets the coming of Christ in terms of the function of the Logos as revealer, other themes of soteriology are not lacking. Thus we find, with reference to Paul, statements that Christ reconciled the Father through his death,[50] by the sacrifice of his body. The Logos, as high priest, took this body from us, the flock as 'lamb and sheep', in order to offer it to the Father as the first-fruits of the human race.[51] The body of Christ suffered a martyr's death for our sins.[52] We shall have to go into a special peculiarity of this soteriological act later, but only when the structure of Eusebius' Logos-sarx Christ has been made rather clearer.

Eusebius speaks most clearly of the relationship between Logos and sarx in the controversies with Marcellus of Ancyra. In these he outlines all the possible interpretations of the picture of Christ which seem to him to be either possible or impossible in the light of his tradition.[53] Marcellus took the idea of monotheism as seriously as Eusebius and Arius and the rest of the tradition of the church, but in interpreting the relationship of Father and Logos he took a diametrically opposed course to Eusebian (and Arian) subordinationism. For him, the *homoousios* of Nicaea meant that it was impossible to accept the Logos as a second hypostasis alongside he Father. He thus found it difficult to define the subject of the incarnation and to assign it to the Logos *qua* Logos. Over against this, Eusebius ascribes the incarnation to the second hypostasis in God, which—as has been shown—is divine, but subordinate to the Father. The incarnation takes place when this hypostasis of the Son is sent into the sarx assumed by the Virgin and dwells in it. Eusebius collects from scripture those sayings of the incarnate Christ which demonstrate that the Father is truly other, and those which he believes make Marcellus' understanding of the incarnation impossible. For example, when Jesus of Nazareth describes the Father as teacher (cf. John 8. 28), the distinction between the (divine)

[49] There is a lengthy soteriological text in DE X, prooem. and chs. 1–8. Heikel, 445¹–492¹².
[50] For the propitiation of the Father: 445¹²⁻¹³. ἱλεούμενος τὸν πατέρα. The death of Christ for our sins: prooem.: 446¹⁻².
[51] Sacrifice as high priest: ibid., 446²⁻⁴: ἔδει γὰρ τὸν ἀμνὸν τοῦ θεοῦ, τὸν ὑπὸ τοῦ μεγάλου ἀρχιερέως ἀναληφθέντα ὑπὲρ τοῦ τῶν λοιπῶν συγγενῶν ἀμνῶν καὶ ὑπὲρ πάσης τῆς ἀνθρωπίνης ἀγέλης, θυσίαν τῷ θεῷ προσαχθῆναι. It should be noted that the 'high priest' is the Logos *qua* Logos, whereas the lamb is the human sarx. Cf. ibid., 445¹¹⁻¹³: μέγας τε καὶ αἰώνιος ἀρχιερεὺς ὑπὲρ τῆς τῶν γεννητῶν ἁπάντων οὐσιώσεώς τε καὶ σωτηρίας ἱερώμενος καὶ ἱλεούμενος τὸν πατέρα. For a closer definition of the priesthood of Christ see R. Farina, *L'Impero e l'Imperatore*, 91f.; A. Orbe, *La Unción del Verbo* (Estudios Valentinianos II), Roma 1961, 543–58, 569–76 (Origen, Eusebius).
[52] See DE X, prooem.: Heikel, 445²⁶⁻⁸; DE X shows that the death of Christ was prophesied.
[53] Cf. ET I, 20: Klostermann-Hansen, 87¹²–89⁵.

teacher and the (divine) pupil is clarified. Marcellus' Logos, who is thought to be identical in substance with the Father, could not describe the Father as his teacher, even in his incarnation. He would declare himself to be his own teacher. Nor, according to Marcellus, could the Logos, who is inseparable from the Father (ἀχώριστος ὤν), 'be sent' into the flesh (ἀπεστάλθαι). Another argument against Marcellus is even more significant: if the incarnate Logos—thus Eusebius—were not a true counterpart (ἕτερος) of the Father, he could not prove himself morally before the Father, i.e. do what was well-pleasing to the Father.[54] This comment, which is repeated soon afterwards,[55] is important for Eusebius' understanding both of the person of Christ and of its soteriological actions. The Logos-Son, dwelling in the flesh and thought of in subordinationist terms, lives in our midst before the Father and achieves the acts of obedience which are decisive for our salvation. Marcellus cannot indicate any instrument by which this obedience is achieved. Eusebius can. However, it is no human instrument, but the Logos indwelling the flesh *qua* Logos. This is even the case when Eusebius stresses the voluntariness of the death of Jesus. Its seat is this Logos, or the Son sent into the flesh, and not a human soul:[56]

He suffered a violent end, but voluntarily handed over his body to his persecutors as all that was his own . . . the Logos freely separated himself from the body (αὐτὸς ἀφ'ἑαυτοῦ τὴν ἐκ τοῦ σώματος ἀναχώρησιν ἐποιεῖτο). On the third day he took the body back to himself, he who had formerly willingly separated himself from it (ὁ πρὶν ἀναχωρήσας ἑκών).

Thus the resurrection is like a new assumption of the flesh, a new incarnation (καὶ δείκνυσίν γε πάλιν αὐτὸς ἑαυτὸν ἔνσαρκον, ἔνσωμον, αὐτὸν ἐκεῖνον οἶος καὶ τὸ πρὶν ἦν). In this new assumption of the body, the transfiguration of the risen Christ can be overlooked.[57] Indeed, in essence it is already present at the beginning.

That the divine Logos is the organ of the moral proving of the incarnate Christ is also clear from another consideration: because the *divine* Logos is the instrument of free decision, Eusebius does not face the problem that

---

[54] ET I, 20: ibid., 87[18]: πῶς δὲ ἓν καὶ ταὐτὸν ὑπάρχων (numerical and specific identity of the Logos with the Father according to Marcellus) τῷ θεῷ τὰ ἀρεστὰ πράττειν. Cf. John 8. 29.

[55] Ibid., 88[13-14].

[56] DE III, 4, 27-9: Heikel, 114[29]-115[9]: βίαιον ὑπέμεινε τελευτήν, ἀλλ' ὡς αὐτὸ μόνον ἑκὼν παρεδίδου τοῖς ἐπιβουλεύουσι τὸ σῶμα. . . . In the passages of the psalm commentary that has already been mentioned, in Ps. XCII: PG 23, 1184CD, the incarnation is described as the assumption of the body as a 'mortal instrument' by the Logos of God, 'who is the life itself', in order to be able to hand it over to death as a demonstration of its own nature and then to raise it to life again. In this way the rule of death and the tyranny of the devil, who has ruled over men by means of demons, is destroyed. In the same way, the divine life also comes to reign in man.

[57] But it is mentioned in DE III, 2, 24: Heikel, 100[21f.]: εἰς τὴν θεότητα μεταβολή. Cf. H. de Riedmatten, op. cit., on this whole complex of problems: 'Eusèbe songe si peu à une humanité intégrale pour le Christ qu'il éprouve le besoin de justifier la résurrection et surtout l'immortalité de son corps.' Cf. LC XV: Heikel, 244-6: TS III, 42-4, 57: Gressmann 148*-9*, 153f*. Eusebius repeats the ideas of the DE. The whole of the third book of TS develops this soteriology.

it could be 'mutable', i.e. morally fallible. Thus in contrast to Arius, as we shall see, the words τρεπτός or ἄτρεπτος do not appear in his work in connection with the (incarnate) Logos.[58] The problem of the immutability of the divine nature of the spirit or the mutability of *created* spiritual nature is only discussed briefly where the origin of demons or their fall is explained. If the demons had to be understood as the issue of a higher nature, then they could not have fallen from their native lot or status.[59]

The essential basis of Eusebius' doctrine of the incarnation is thus that the Logos-Son, understood in subordinationist terms, dwells in the flesh, taken from the Virgin, in the place of a human soul. According to Eusebius, Marcellus of Ancyra, on the other hand, cannot explain the incarnation at all. For in his case it would be necessary to assume that the Logos, of one substance and identical with the Father, dwelt in the flesh. But this leads to a fourfold dilemma:[60]

(1) Marcellus must allow that the Father himself dwells in the flesh. If he is unwilling to do this, there remain:
(2) that the Son has an independent subsistence and works in the flesh (which is the teaching of Eusebius), or
(3) that a human soul is to be assumed in Christ. And if (2) and (3) are impossible for Marcellus, then
(4) the flesh of Christ must be animated automatically, as it would be without either soul or reason (ἄψυχον οὖσαν καὶ ἄλογον).

The first solution, Eusebius stresses, means that the Father begets himself, suffers in the flesh himself (i.e. patripassianism) and takes all human characteristics on himself. This would be Sabellianism, which the church has condemned. In that case, according to Eusebius, it is necessary to assume a subject or hypostasis which is different from the Father, viz. the Son, to whom the incarnation and the passion can be ascribed. This Logos-hypostasis dwells in the flesh. Thus this is Eusebius' conception of the incarnation.[61] But if Marcellus will not allow this 'Son' any subsistence, there remains only the third expedient which, like the first, leads to heresy: he must assume that Christ is a 'mere man' (ψιλὸς ἄνθρωπος), who consists of soul and body and is in no way different from human nature in general![62] But this too is rejected by the church's dogma. It is the doctrine

[58] Cf. the indices in GCS, *Eusebius-Werke*.
[59] PE XIII, 15, 1–10, esp. 7: Mras II, 233[8–13].
[60] ET I, 20: Klostermann-Hansen, 87[29]–88[22]; cf. ET II, 6, 4: 164[23–6]. Marcellus has only the choice between Sabellius and Paul of Samosata (and his Judaism). Cf. ET I, 1; 5; 14: 63[11–13]; 64[19–20]; 74[10–13], 23–4; II, 4: 102[34–6].
[61] ET I, 20: Klostermann-Hansen, 88[2–4]: εἰ δὲ τὸν πατέρα λέγειν οὐ θεμιτὸν ἐνανθρωπήσαντα, τὸν υἱὸν ὁμολογεῖν ἀνάγκη μαθητευομένους τοῦτο διδάσκοντι.
[62] Cf. CM II, 3: Klostermann-Hansen, 49[6–9]: if Marcellus allows Col. 1. 15 (Christ the image of the invisible God) to be said of the flesh of Christ, the flesh of all men and the prosopa of the body would also have to be called 'image' of God, 'so that there would not be anything extraordinary about the Redeemer'. ET I, 20: Klostermann-Hansen, 88[4–7]: εἰ δὲ τοῦτον ἀρνοῖτο Μάρκελλος ὑφεστάναι, ὥρα

of the Ebionites and recently of Paul of Samosata, whose associates are called Paulinians and have to suffer the punishment of the blasphemer.

All this shows what Eusebius thinks about the reality of a human soul in Christ. He does not need it and cannot need it, because in it he scents a heretical christology. To adopt the fourth possible course, a flesh without Logos and without soul in Christ, is ridiculous from the start.[63] Let us once again allow Eusebius to give the answer to the decisive question in his own words:

> So who was this (Christ)? Either the Logos (who abides) in God, who according to Sabellius is God (i.e. the Father) himself, or, as is said in true holiness, the living and subsisting only-begotten Son of God. But if he (Marcellus) will say none of this, he must necessarily assume a human soul (in Christ), and Christ will be a mere man: and our innovating writer will no longer be a Sabellian, but a Paulinian.[64]

Thus for Eusebius, Christ is:

(1) The Son dwelling in the flesh, distinct from the Father but begotten of him and similar to him.

(2) By this unity of Logos-Son and sarx, Christ transcends the *usual, universal* human nature. Thus he is no 'mere man', but a naturally higher being, as a synthesis of God-man. The stress on this transcendence once again indicates that for Eusebius Christ is only Logos and sarx. In contrast to Arius, Eusebius wishes to confess this Logos as God, But in fact he too is in danger of making this Logos-sarx synthesis into a *mythical* being, which hovers between divinity and the created world.

(3) The Logos dwelling in the sarx physically accomplishes the spiritual acts by which he achieves God's good pleasure. It is he who is the moving element in the sarx. All the significant soteriological acts which Eusebius knows are to be derived from this Logos. They pertain to him not only as subject, in the terms of the *communicatio idiomatum*, but also as the executive natural principle. In the flesh the Logos proves himself before the Father and gains his good-pleasure, even in the voluntary acceptance of death, i.e. in voluntarily separating himself from his body and taking it up again. But because he is God, the Logos is not exposed to mutability and sin (like angelic beings).

(4) Despite his katagogic Logos christology, then, Eusebius also puts forward an 'anagogic' christology in which Christ truly stands over against the Father—but only as the Logos in the flesh, seen in subordinationist terms. At any event, here—in the stress on his freedom—the Logos (in the

---

ψιλὸν ἄνθρωπον αὐτὸν ὑποτίθεσθαι ἐκ σώματος καὶ ψυχῆς συνεστῶτα, ὡς μηδὲν τῆς κοινῆς ἀνθρώπων διαλάττειν φύσεως. ἀλλὰ καὶ τοῦτο τῆς ἐκκλησίας ἀπελήλαται ⟨τὸ⟩ δόγμα. Thus for Eusebius Christ is a synthesis of sarx and Logos (in place of a soul), which represents a physical plus over against man elsewhere on the level of nature.

63 ET I, 20: 889-11: τί δὴ οὖν λείπεται μετὰ ταῦτα ἢ τὴν σάρκα μόνον εἰσάγειν δίχα παντὸς ἐνοίκου δίκην τῶν παρὰ τοῖς θαυματοποιοῖς αὐτομάτων κινουμένην;

64 ET I, 20: 8816-22.

flesh) is ascribed his own initiative.[65] Nevertheless, this 'Christ' cannot be allowed any real *human* obedience. The soteriological acts are pure acts of the Logos *qua* Logos. The flesh is only passively involved in this action.

(5) The evaluation of the human element in Eusebius' picture of Christ is considerably hindered by fear of the doctrine that Christ is 'a mere man'. His christology is developed in opposition to Paul of Samosata on the one hand and Marcellus of Ancyra on the other. The former had the greater influence. Only Eusebius' argumentation, and not his picture of Christ, was influenced and extended by Marcellus of Ancyra. Paul of Samosata aroused the anxiety that the Logos might be associated too closely with the flesh. So he can also talk of indwelling.[66] The Logos remains at a superior level and at an inner distance from the flesh which he animates. In the HE, Eusebius compares the divine element in Christ with the head and the human element in him with the feet of a body.[67] In the ET he stresses the difference in substance between the 'Son' and the 'body which is assumed',[68] which he names the 'Son of Man'. Nevertheless, one cannot speak of two natures in Eusebius.[69] Nor, however, can one speak of the *mia physis*, which Apollinarius has at a later stage as the basis of his christology, although an essential element of this approach is present: the Logos is the only *kinetikon* of the sarx. H. Berkhof is right to speak of an Apollinarian and Nestorian trend in the teaching of Eusebius.[70] He also

[65] J. Sirinelli, *Les vues historiques*, 299, finds HE I, 2, 21 the only passage in which Eusebius ascribes to the Logos *qua* Logos a different autonomous activity from that of the Father: in view of the great fallenness of the human race, 'la Sagesse de Dieu, sa première née et sa première créature, le Verbe préexistant lui-même, par un excès d'amour pour les hommes, se manifeste aux êtres inférieurs tantôt par l'apparition d'anges, tantot directement comme pouvait le faire une puissance salvatrice de Dieu'. In addition, however, attention should be paid to the idea of 'proving' the Logos *in statu incarnationis*, in that he did what was well-pleasing to the Father and above all voluntarily gave up his body as a sacrifice. According to Eusebius, this too is part of the direct physical initiative of the Logos, and not just by reason of the *communicatio idiomatum*.

[66] ET I, 6, 7: Klostermann-Hansen, 65[1, 18, 30]; I, 20: 93[24ff.]: Logos-indwelling and pneuma christology are here associated in an interesting way. To the indwelling christology of Eusebius there also belong the important expressions which H. Berkhof, *Theologie des Eusebius*, 120, has collected: organ, vessel, temple, dwelling, garment, vehicle.

[67] HE I, 2, 1: Schwartz I, 10[1-4]; Kirsopp Lake I, 11: 'Now this nature was twofold: on the one hand like the head of the body, in that he is recognized as God, on the other comparable to the feet, in that he put on for the sake of our own salvation, man of like passions with us. Therefore to make our description of what follows complete we should start the whole narrative concerning him by the most capital and dominant points of the discussion.'

[68] ET I, 6: Klostermann-Hansen, 65[7-9]: ἀλλ' οὔτε ὃ ἀνείληφεν σῶμα ταὐτὸν ἦν τῷ ἀνειληφότι υἱῷ τοῦ θεοῦ, οὔτε αὐτὸς ὁ υἱὸς τοῦ θεοῦ εἷς καὶ ὁ αὐτὸς ἂν νομισθείη τῷ γεγεννηκότι. In this context Eusebius speaks of three, or a 'first', a 'second', and a 'third': namely of (1) God the Father, (2) the Son proceeding from him, (3) καὶ τρίτος ὁ κατὰ σάρκα υἱὸς ἀνθρώπου, ὃν δι' ἡμᾶς ἀνείληφεν ὁ υἱὸς τοῦ θεοῦ (ibid., 65[4-7]). By this 'Son of Man' he understands the sarx of Christ.

[69] The translation of the passage cited above (in n. 67) from HE made by R. Farina, *L'Impero e l'imperatore*, 84, with 'due sone le nature in Cristo' is probably too strong. διττοῦ δὲ ὄντος τοῦ κατ' αὐτὸν τρόπου is not meant to be technical language, but is merely meant to stress the duality of the modes of being in Christ. But cf. n. 2 in Kirsopp Lake, *Eusebius: Ecclesiastical History* I, on HE I, 1, 5, which precedes the text cited above: 'οἰκονομία and θεολογία are semi-technical terms. The οἰκονομία or "dispensation" with regard to Christ was the incarnation of the divine Logos; the θεολογία was the ascription of divinity to him. Hence this passage might almost be rendered freely as "the divine and human natures of Christ, which pass man's understanding".'

[70] H. Berkhof, *Die Theologie des Eusebius von Caesarea*, 120: 'All (the Fathers before the fifth century) are agreed in rejecting the doctrine that Christ was a mere man (ψιλὸς ἄνθρωπος); the

differs from the Arians in his loosening of the unity of Logos and sarx. They require that the Logos should be affected *qua* Logos through his synthesis with the flesh, so as to be able to demonstrate his mutability and creatureliness. However, much as Eusebius seems to be at one with the Arians and Apollinarians in his acceptance of the Logos-sarx framework, he differs from them through his conception of the inner relationship between Logos and sarx. Above all, there is lacking that apparently ontological terminology which is to be found in the fragments ascribed to the presbyter Malchion[71] from the trial of Paul of Samosata[71] and then in Apollinarius and his followers (see below).

(c) The historical influence of Eusebius

Once again, attention should be drawn to the distinction between the personal theology and the 'political' theology of the Bishop of Caesarea. The latter will concern us again and again. The 'theological' Eusebius is of shorter duration. His influence has still not been investigated adequately, and it is perhaps considerably greater under the surface than can be demonstrated from direct quotations and kindred ideas. The following points should be borne in mind in assessing this theological significance.

(1) The intrinsic uncertainty of Eusebius' doctrines of the Logos and the incarnation meant that these could only exercise a limited influence. His thought about the Logos and the incarnation, which, while being orthodox, was nevertheless dangerous at certain important points, inevitably compelled a decision. The quicker this was made, the quicker the typical (theological) Eusebius was ruled out of court.

(2) His theological influence was endangered by the fact that politically he was too involved with the Arian group of bishops centring on Eusebius of Nicomedia. According to a recent hypothesis which still remains to be

church had discovered and condemned this heresy in adoptionism and Samosatenism. Therefore the favourite course was to limit Christ's humanity to his corporeality. At the same time the Logos was not to be thought of as being subject to the destiny of his body (suffering and death). In that case, the Godhead would be done away with. The compulsion was therefore to a sharp separation between the Logos and his body. So in the same writings one can see forerunners of both Apollinarius and Nestorius. . . . This sharp separation is necessary for the history of Jesus to be given its due and at the same time for the Logos to be elevated above any suffering and death. The manhood manifested its nature in the birth, suffering and death; the Godhead in birth from a virgin, in the miracles, in the heavenly teaching, in the prophecies and in the resurrection. . . . The divine assumes the human in such a way that it is not changed and not even affected. The Logos is not bound to the body in the same way as is a human soul.' On p. 122 Berkhof refers to DE IV, 13, 6–7: Heikel, 172[6–24]. For the controversy between Eusebius and Paul of Samosata cf. H. de Riedmatten, *Les actes du procès*, 71–3; he cites the following texts: ET I, 20 (see above); HE V, 28, 1; EP III, 19 and IV, 22 (Gaisford, 219[11] and 205[10–14]); HE VII, 27–30 (Schwartz I, 702–14: translation Kraft, see n. 3 above, 346–51).

71 Compare the fragments which have been newly collected in H. de Riedmatten, *Les actes du procès*, 136–58, especially S., 14a; S., 14, 22–4, 33, 36. In view of the relationship between Eusebius and the acts of the trial of Paul of Samosata, the question arises: did Eusebius not find the Apollinarian-sounding terminology in the acts, or did he deliberately pass over it because he could not use it? In view of his positive attitude to the Alexandrian tradition between Origen and him one would be inclined to the former alternative. That would increase the suspicion that the Malchion fragments have only come down to us in a later revision.

discussed, he was even in danger of seeking a revision of the Nicene creed with the aid of imperial authority. This necessarily meant that the supporters of the Council had considerable reserve towards him. But because he was the dominant writer of his time, even his opponents could not escape his influence, as can be demonstrated in the case of Athanasius.

(3) One danger which lay in the background, and was perceived especially by the Eastern church of his time, gave a special opportunity to the christology of Eusebius, or the direction which he was paramount in demonstrating: this was the generally prevailing fear of treating Christ as a 'mere man' (ψιλὸς ἄνθρωπος), which was provoked by Paul of Samosata. Even the Arians took the other side here.

(4) The central point of Eusebius' immediate and more extended influence, however, is probably the fact that the position opposed to Paulianism can be described with some degree of clarity as a 'Logos-sarx christology' (as a christology 'without a soul in Christ'). This can be clearly demonstrated in his writings. As Eusebius presents this christology, he seems to have inherited it. But his doctrine of the Logos has intensified his heritage. It is doubtful whether there was any serious discussion during his lifetime on the matter, at least such as would have compelled him to adopt a particular position. We shall have to consider the position of Eustathius of Antioch at a later stage. Marcellus of Ancyra—too obscure as a theologian and too much under the suspicion of Sabellianism—could not manage to get the Bishop of Caesarea to reconsider his own weak points; indeed, it was Marcellus who confirmed him in his inadequate views, in his subordinationist Logos doctrine and his Logos-sarx christology. Even a weak theologian, Eusebius, was enough to compromise a still weaker Marcellus in certain points, without himself being compromised.

(5) The only opponent who could take Eusebius further was Athanasius. But at first the much younger Alexandrian—even in the years when he was on the opposite side in church politics—was more the pupil. Here we come to a decisive point in the influence of Eusebius' christology and Logos doctrine. At this point, it is necessary to make a brief allusion to the history of scholarship and its contemporary state.

As early as 1913, T. Kehrhahn[72] had demonstrated that Eusebius' *Theophaneia* was a source for Athanasius' two apologies, *Contra Gentes* and *De Incarnatione*. In 1935, H.-G. Opitz took this starting point further and created a new basis for the discussion of questions of authenticity and date for Athanasius' two works.[73] This also raised important questions for the date of Eusebius' works. Marie-Josèphe Rondeau gives an excellent

---

[72] T. Kehrhahn, *De sancti Athanasii quae fertur Contra gentes oratione*, Berlin 1913.
[73] H.-G. Opitz, *Untersuchungen zur Überlieferung der Schriften des Athanasius* (Arbeiten zur Kirchengeschichte 23), Berlin and Leipzig 1935, 192–200. Cf. E. Gentz, *RAC* I, 1950, 862; W. Schneemelcher, *RGG* I, 1957, 1669–70.

survey of this history of scholarship.[74] The chief results are these: (a) Opitz established numerous parallels between the *Theophaneia* of Eusebius and the *De Incarnatione* of Athanasius, especially between T III, 57 (TG 9, 4ff.; TS 153[25ff.] Gressmann) and ch. 22 of the short recension of DI, which J. Lebon had discovered.[75] (b) In his inaugural lecture as Lady Margaret Professor of Divinity, Oxford, on 1 December 1944,[76] F. L. Cross returned to this question of the literary relationship between Eusebius and Athanasius. As in his view a literary exchange of ideas between the two men in and after the crisis of Nicaea was impossible, since before Nicaea the dependence of the old and learned (bishop!) Eusebius on the young and unknown Alexandrian deacon was improbable, F. L. Cross reversed the relationship: the young Athanasius had come under the influence of the old Eusebius, on the occasion of a journey of the Bishop of Caesarea to Alexandria, probably in the year 311. Athanasius had taken up the ideas of the famous man and then reproduced them more clearly than Eusebius himself. Thus there was an influence from man to man which worked further in the two and expressed itself on the one side in the *Theophaneia* and on the other in the CG and DI, without it being necessary for literary relationships to be assumed. In the discussion of this lecture W. Telfer pointed to the youth of the Alexandrian in the year 311.[77] He conjectured a common dependence of Athanasius and Eusebius, particularly in view of the apologetic methods usual at the time, specifically perhaps on the then director of the Didaskaleion, who could have been Achillas. H. Nordberg sought once again to take the course pioneered by T. Kehrhahn (direct influence of the *Theophaneia* on CG and DI). To prove it possible, he dated CG-DI in the year 362/3.[78] To that point the question of the relationship or the affinity between Eusebius and Athanasius had been limited to the realm of apologetic.

The investigation of Marie-Josèphe Rondeau led to new insights in that it also included the realm of exegesis.[79] Strikingly, it proved that Athanasius' *Expositiones in Psalmos* display 'a systematic, sometimes literal use'

---

[74] Marie-Josèphe Rondeau, 'Une nouvelle preuve d'influence littéraire d'Eusèbe de Césarée sur Athanase: l'interpretation des psaumes', *RSR* 56, 1968, 385–434; id., 'Le "Commentaire des Psaumes" de Diodore de Tarse I–III', *RevHistRel* 176, 1969, 5–33, 153–88; 177, 1970, 5–33; for Eusebius–Athanasius: II, 173–7.

[75] H.-G. Opitz, op. cit., 195; J. Lebon, 'Pour une edition critique des oeuvres de S. Athanase', *RHE* 21, 1925, 524–30; cf. C. Kannengiesser, *Athanase d'Alexandrie Sur l'Incarnation du Verbe* (SC 199), Paris 1973: Introduction 21–34, where the further discoveries on the short recension of DI by Opitz, Kirsopp Lake, Robert P. Casey and the Syriac translation (Lebon; ed R. W. Thomson) are introduced. An important comment on Casey is to be found in M. Tetz, 'Athanasiana', *VigC* 9, 1955, 159–75.

[76] F.-L. Cross, *The Study of S. Athanasius*, Oxford 1945.

[77] W. Telfer, *JTS* 47, 1946, 88–90.

[78] H. Nordberg, *Athanasius' Tractates Contra Gentes and De Incarnatone. An attempt at redating* (Scient. Soc. Fennica, Commentationes human. litt. t. 28, f. 3), Helsinki 1961; id., 'A Reconsideration of the Date of S. Athanasius' Contra Gentes and De Incarnatione', *StudPat* 3 (TU 78), Berlin 1961, 262–6; id., *Athanasiana* I, Helsinki 1962.

[79] See n. 74 above.

of Eusebius' *Commentaria in Psalmos*. After investigating the question of the state of the text of the two commentaries, the author indicates an affinity in the so-called 'hypotheses'. At the beginning of each psalm there is a 'hypothesis', 'c'est-à-dire une introduction fournissant brièvement le thème du poème, le plus souvent en fonction de son *Sitz in Leben*. Or ces hypothèses presentent une indéniable parenté avec les *Comm. in ps.* d'Eusèbe de Césarée.'[80] In his edition of Eusebius' 15 *Hypotheses*, at the beginning of his explanations of the psalms of ascent, G. Mercati had already drawn attention to the similarity between these and the corresponding *Hypotheses* of Athanasius.[81] Of course Athanasius is much shorter— although he takes over individual words. Some significant omissions which are particularly concerned with christology need to be investigated in detail, as M.-J. Rondeau indicates.

The affinity between the two psalm commentaries also extends to the corpus of the explanations, sometimes even becoming an 'identité littérale',[82] though this is certainly not servile. Only in a few cases is it impossible to derive the exegesis of Athanasius from Eusebius.[83] There is an alternation between spectacular instances of Athanasius' dependence and passages which M.-J. Rondeau describes as 'des recoupements au niveau de l'interprétation, des coïncidences verbales, parfois trop caractéristiques pour relever du hasard, mais limitées'.[84] This leads to an assured result:

Les deux commentaires sont donc parents, d'une parenté précise qui se noue certainement au niveau des textes, car dire qu'Eusèbe et Athanase respiraient le même air du temps, ou ont pu avoir vers des entretiens dont ils auraient ensuite consigné de part et d'autre le fruit, ou se sont peut-être souvenus l'un et l'autre du lointain enseignement du même maître, est tout à fait insuffisant devant l'exactitude de certaines correspondances. Deux explications seulement peuvent rendre compte de celle-ci: ou bien les deux commentaires sont frères, dependant d'une même source commune *écrite*, qui ne peut être que l'exegèse psalmique d'Origène; ou bien leurs rapports sont ceux de père à fils, la dépendance ne pouvant être que d'Athanase vis-à-vis d'Eusèbe, puisque le discours

---

[80] M.-J. Rondeau, *RSR* 56, 1968, 394f. Cf. Rondeau–Kirchmeyer, art. 'Eusèbe', in: *DictSpirit* 4, 1961, 1689–90 (important for the exclusion of interpolations). Euseb. Caes., *Commentaria in Psalmos*: PG 23 (Pss. 1–118) (Montfaucon); PG 24, 9–76 (Pss. 119–50) (Pitra); fragments J.-B. Pitra, *Analecta Sacra* 3, Venetiae 1883, 365–520.

[81] G. Mercati, *L'ultima parte perduta del Commentario d'Eusebio ai Salmi* (Rendiconti del Real Istituto Lombardo di Scienze e Lettere, ser. 2, t. 31), Milano 1898, 1036–45; reprinted in id., *Opere minori* II (ST 77), Vaticano 1937, 58–66.

[82] M.-J. Rondeau, *RSR* 56, 1968, 398–409, with numerous examples; ibid., 399 characterizes the way in which Athanasius took it over as follows: '. . . la confrontation des *Comment. in ps.* (= Euseb.) et des *Exp. in ps.* (= Athanas.) révèlent tout un dégradé insensible depuis ces plagiats caractérisés (rares) jusqu'à l'absence de correspondance et à la divergence d'interprétation, en passant par une gamme importante d'emprunts plus ou moins librement remaniés, la similitude consistant souvent en ce qu'un developpement tel que nous le lisons chez Eusèbe est substantiellement assumé par Athanase, qui le condense en gardant ça et là le repère de certains mots caractéristiques ou d'expressions particulièrement bien venues, à la manière d'un lecteur qui prend des notes.' Attention should now be called to two further studies on the place of the psalter in Athanasius: M.-J. Rondeau, 'L'Epître à Marcellinus sur les psaumes', *VigC* 22, 1968, 176–97; H. J. Sieben, 'Athanasius über den Psalter. Analyse seines Briefes an Marcellinus', *TheolPhil* 48, 1973, 157–73.

[83] J.-M. Rondeau, *RSR* 56, 1968, 401f., where only Pss. 54–5 are in question; cf. 403–9; Ps. 140.

[84] Ibid., 410–13 with examples.

continu, logiquement articulé de ce dernier prêtait à ce qu'on en tirât des notes plus ou moins résumées, tandis qu'on ne voit pas que la poussière de gloses allusives d'Athanase pût fournir à quelqu'un d'autre le noyau de développements qui coulent avec tant d'abondance et de facilité.[85]

This offers a new basis for a comparison between Athanasius and Eusebius. The relationship seems to point back to a common source for both, to Origen. But the *catenae* hardly offer any possibility of bringing the three great men together. Only fragments of the explanation of Ps. 37 in Origen and Eusebius give an unqualified possibility of investigating a triangular relationship between Origen, Eusebius and Athanasius. It can be shown that while Eusebius is dependent on Origen for Ps. 37, the elements of this explanation to be found in Athanasius (with ideas taken over and omitted) show that the latter did not make immediate use of Origen, but of Eusebius. How far this is true for further parts of the psalter or for the whole of Athanasius' expositions must remain an open question.[86]

In a short but comprehensive investigation, M.-J. Rondeau also goes into the theological dependence or independence of Athanasius on Eusebius. Only hints may be given here, since the matter is so complex: certain dependencies can be established in respect of christology, especially as far as the vocabulary in the *Expositiones in psalmos* and in CG and DI is concerned.[87] Nevertheless, even in this early writing Athanasius is no blind copyist, but avoids two weaknesses or dangers in Eusebius' christology: he leaves out anything that might smack of *subordinationism*.[88] Furthermore, in interpreting the unity of God and man in Christ he avoids those expressions which might seem to be 'Nestorian', but were chosen by Eusebius above all to ensure the transcendence of the Logos over his sarx.[89] To the end Eusebius remains a homoiousian; Athanasius is a man of Nicaea and a homoousian.[90]

These indications may be sufficient to show that most recent scholarship has already created a solid basis for building a bridge between Eusebius and Athanasius. Further investigation is needed as to how far the similarity extends and where the dissimilarity sets in. But it should not be forgotten that Athanasius was not only a positive (albeit a critical) mediator of Eusebius' ideas; he was also a *katechōn*. For in the end the Alexandrian contributed towards stamping the Caesarean an 'Arian', an epithet which was to dog him throughout the whole of the Byzantine period. It was only the church historian and encomiast of the emperor Constantine to whom more understanding was given. But this

---

[85] Ibid., 413f.
[86] Ibid., 414–19.
[87] Ibid., 427–34; C. Kannengiesser in SC 199, 67–162.
[88] Cf. the Praeliminaria (VI) of B. Montfaucon in PG 23, 28–48, on the CP of Eusebius.
[89] M.-J. Rondeau, RSR 56, 1968, 429f. Further references below on Athanasius.
[90] Cf. above on Eusebius; M.-J. Rondeau, op. cit., 433.

related to the 'political theology' of Eusebius, which we have still to discuss.[91]

2. 'SAPIENS RELIGIO—RELIGIOSA SAPIENTIA':
ON THE CHRISTOLOGY OF LACTANTIUS

Lactantius (*c.* 250–after 317), the contemporary of Eusebius, similarly had a relationship with the emperor Constantine in that he was the tutor of the emperor's son Crispus. With him we have a new attempt to present Christian doctrine in a firm system. He is a witness to both the African–Western and the Asian–Eastern tradition, which later he either found in Gaul or took there himself. It was there, too, that he put the final touches to his *Divinae Institutiones.* If one also adds the lines which associate him with Victorinus of Pettau, and the general cultural and intellectual background to his writings, there are grounds for astonishment at the extent of the philosophical, theological and religious intercommunion which existed at that time. The disappointment is, of course, that Lactantius did not succeed in making a homogeneous whole of his mass of information and his sources. In the very area that interests us particularly, the doctrine of the Trinity and christology, the inadequacy of his powers of assimilation is most evident. He seems most consistent when one considers the framework in which he incorporated Christian doctrine: his Platonic–Hermetic–Gnostic doctrine of redemption.[92]

(a) The historical and intellectual background

Lactantius came from North Africa and before his conversion to Christianity had moved to Asia Minor, where he lived at Nicomedia in Bithynia. He was a Christian during the time of persecution there.[93] In Africa he was a pupil of Arnobius the Elder,[94] but was especially influenced by Tertullian, Minucius Felix and Cyprian. According to A. Wlosok,

---

[91] See the informative study by F. Winkelmann, 'Die Beurteilung des Eusebius von Caesarea und seiner Vita Constantini im griechischen Osten', *Byzantinische Beiträge*, ed. J. Irmscher, Berlin 1964, 91–120.

[92] For what follows, see now R. Pichon, *Lactance. Étude sur le mouvement philosophique et religieux sous le règne de Constantin*, Paris 1901; J. Stevenson, 'The Life and Literary Activity of Lactantius', *StudPat* 6 (TU 63), 1957, 661–77; Antonie Wlosok, *Laktanz und die philosophische Gnosis* (Abh-HeidelbergerAkWiss 1960, 2), Heidelberg 1960, with bibliography (cited hereafter as Wlosok I); id., 'Zur Bedeutung der nichtcyprianischen Bibelzitate bei Laktanz', *StudPat* 1 (TU 79), 1961, 234–50 (cited hereafter as Wlosok II); V. Loi, *Lattanzio nella storia del linguaggio e del pensiero pre-niceno*, Zürich 1970, with bibliography 281–92; esp. ch. IV: 'La pneumatologia' (155–99); ch. V: 'La cristologia' (203–32); ch. VI: 'La soteriologia' (235–73). Sources: *Divinae Institutiones* (cited hereafter as *Inst.*); *Epitome* (cited hereafter as *Epit.*): CSEL 19, 1, Wien 1890. For *Inst.* see D. R. Shackleton Bailey, 'Lactantiana', *VigC* 14, 1960, 165–9; for *Epit.* see J. Stevenson, 'The *Epitome* of Lactantius, *Divinae Institutiones*', *StudPat* 7 (TU 92), 1966, 291–8.

[93] Jerome, *De vir. ill.* 80: Richardson, 42; V. Loi, *Lattanzio*, xivf.; Wlosok II, 247.

[94] Jerome, *De vir. ill.*, loc. cit; id., *Ep.* 70, 5: CSEL 54, 707; id., *Chronicon*, GCS Eusebius-Werke 7, Berlin 1956, 230 *ad ann.* 318/9: *Quorum Crispum Lactantius Latinis litteris erudiuit, uir omnium suo tempore eloquentissimus, sed adeo in hac uita pauper, ut plerumque etiam necessariis indiguerit.*

before his conversion to Christianity Lactantius had adopted a Platonism combined with Hermetic doctrines. The theory of the impossibility of knowing God which this would involve, and the strong stress on his transcendence, would inevitably have been strengthened by the subordinationism which he inherited from Justin and Tertullian. Here he was primarily concerned to defend and interpret Christian monotheism. The strong emphasis on a theology of revelation in Lactantius is also to be ascribed to the Platonic *Hermetica*. A. Wlosok has convincingly demonstrated that Lactantius did not acquire his concept of religion from Christianity, but brought it over from his pagan period.

The framework of Platonic–Hermetic doctrine was sufficiently wide to allow the acceptance of important Christian elements which Lactantius probably first came to know in the East; on the other hand, it was so narrow, that there were elements of Christianity which could not be fitted into it, as with the vigorous figures of the baroque artists which seem to burst out of the settings of their paintings. In other words, in addition to the Platonic–Hermetic 'theory' there was now a demand for 'practical' piety as a pledge of salvation, which could in this way be regarded as a reward. 'The divine revelation, the sending of Christ the redeemer, the appropriation of revelation in the mystery of baptism, in short the whole event of redemption and salvation, has the significance of making possible this new service of righteousness.'[95] In Lactantius' view the Hermetic teaching was already so near to Christian belief in revelation that the reader of his works or his hearer could rightly ask why it was necessary to become a Christian at all. However, Hermetic theory lacked a decisive element, 'historical reality'. However clearly it might speak of the spiritual transcendent God, of his revelation through the 'Son', of human lostness and immortality as man's destiny; however much it might promise redemption and future reward for the service of righteousness, this element was missing.[96] With a *tour de force* Lactantius sought to create a link between Christian reality and Hermetic theory: the Hermetic doctrine of revelation is declared to be a 'prophecy' of Christianity.[97]

Marginal mention should be made of some theological themes which can derive neither from classical philosophy, from Hermetic Gnosticism nor from the church, especially the doctrine of the two hostile spirits and of cosmological–anthropological dualism in Lactantius.[98] We are directed towards Jewish and Jewish–Christian sources. The 'two hostile spirits' are mentioned in the Qumran Manual of Discipline (3. 18). According to

[95] Wlosok I, 228.
[96] Ibid., and 229. In Lactantius, as in Justin, in the end it is a question of the one extra element in Christianity, the incarnation.   [97] Ibid.
[98] Cf. V. Loi, 'Problema del male e dualismo negli scritti di Lattanzio', *Annali delle Facoltà di Lettere, Filosofia e Magistero dell'Università di Cagliari* 29, 1961–65, 42–55, 58–61, 71–4, esp. 89–94, quoted in Loi, *Lattanzio* xvii and 15, 189. Ibid., 189–99.

Philo's *Quaestiones in Exodum* (I, 23) they enter into a man's soul at birth and from then on fight for the ascendancy.[99] The combination of 'two spirits' and 'two ways' directs us to Jewish–Christian literature,[100] say to Ps. Barnabas (*Ep. c.* 18. 1–2), to the Didache (I, 1: here only the 'two ways'), to the Shepherd of Hermas (*Mand.* V, 1, 2–4; VI, 2, 1: 'two spirits'; *Mand.* VI, 1, 2–4; 'two ways'). Lactantius was especially influenced by the pseudo-Clementines (*Homiliae* and *Recognitiones*), especially in respect of the dualism which is so characteristic of him: the one divine will brings the two antagonistic spirits under control and dominates them.[101]

Significant for the Asian milieu in which Lactantius found himself is the millenarianism which he took over from Jewish–Christian apocalyptic. He could have been all the more influenced by it as he experienced the first years of Diocletian's persecution in Asia.[102] His high regard for the (Jewish–Christian parts of the) Sibylline books may also come from a similar situation of distress and the expectations which it nourished—quite apart from their apologetic usefulness. He defends their authenticity.[103] A. Wlosok was able to show that the quotations from the *Odes of Solomon* in particular are a demonstration of the significance of Lactantius' stay in Asia for his thought. For these *Odes* were not in the African Bible.[104] Here we are pointed towards Eusebius of Caesarea. For it can be demonstrated that he used Odes of Solomon 19, the very one that is cited in Lactantius, in his christological exegesis of Psalm 21.

This exegesis has its setting in the theological controversy with Judaism, in face of which Eusebius attempts to demonstrate the messianic character of the psalm. In *Demonstratio Evangelica* X (499cd), v. 10 of the psalm is interpreted in terms of the miraculous birth of the redeemer, in which the activity of the midwife is assigned to God the Father, an unusual idea which appears in this form in Od. Sal. 19. 9.[105]

It is noteworthy here that Eusebius never mentions the Odes by name, nor does he ever quote them properly. Nevertheless,

he bears witness to a biblical-apologetic theology which is influenced by the Odes. In view of this fact, it may no longer be thought to be a coincidence when Ode 19 is also cited in Lactantius in the context of christological exegesis, and when this exegesis is related to vigorous polemic from the synagogue which challenges the messiahship of Jesus. Thus both Eusebius and Lactantius, who can hardly be set in direct relationship at this time, must go back to a common tradition.[106]

---

[99] Philo, *Quaest. in Exod.* I, 23: commentary Wlosok I, 107–11; there is a comparison there with the text of the Manual of Discipline.

[100] Cf. V. Loi, *Lattanzio*, 190–3.

[101] Ibid., 194.   [102] Ibid., 193f.

[103] *Inst.* I, 6, 6–15; 20–2; *Epit.* 5: 679f.; *De Ira Dei* 22, 4–23, 2: CSEL 27, 2, 1: 123–5. Cf. the index in Brandt, CSEL 27, 2, 2: 259–61.

[104] Cf. Wlosok II, 242–4.

[105] Ibid., 243: cf. Eusebius, DE X, 8, 56–8 on Ps. 21. 10 (ὥσπερ μαιούμενος says Eusebius); *Od. Sal.* 19, 8: A. v. Harnack–J. Flemming, *Ein jüdisch-christliches Psalmbuch* (TU 35, 4), 1910, 50, conj. Flemming.

[106] Wlosok II, 243–4.

According to A. Wlosok, the Odes of Solomon are especially informative on Lactantius' understanding of redemption, as is shown by a comparison of *Od. Sal.* 15, 1–6 and *Inst.* VI, 9, 13ff.[107] We shall finally be concerned with this Asian background in connection with Lactantius' 'spirit christology' and his 'binitarianism'.

Despite all these different influences, however, the most significant fact is probably that 'Lactantius applies to the Christian doctrine of salvation the same historical categories as those by which Hermetic Gnosticism understood itself. For him, Christianity is a religion of the redemption of the spirit and as such the true synthesis of philosophy and religion.'[108] This is expressed in the motto which is prefixed to these remarks about Lactantius: *sapiens religio—religiosa sapientia*.[109] We may follow A. Wlosok in seeing this as a summary of the apologetic and missionary programme of Lactantius. He means to proclaim,

> that *sapientia* and *religio*, the knowledge of the truth and religious service, can only truly be in synthesis, as such a unity is only to be found in Christianity, and that once they are isolated, human philosophy (= *falsa sapientia*, Book III) and divine religion (= *falsa religio*, Book I) must be perverted. The way in which Lactantius sees this synthesis coming about is that worship of God necessarily builds up revelation of God and, conversely, that the search for truth must be wholly directed towards the knowledge of God and his will. Thus Lactantius, like Hermetic anthropology, extends pious behaviour into knowledge and action, in such a way that the pious man is solely and simultaneously both *sapiens* and *religiosus*. The origin of both *sapientia* and *religio*, right knowledge of God and true worship of him, is the one divine source of revelation, and it is this which gives this particular attitude the character of a piety like that of the mysteries.[110]

We have now had some hints of the perspectives in which Lactantius' doctrine of God and his Son are to be seen.

(b) The one God and his Son

From now on we can keep to Book IV of the *Divinae Institutiones* and the corresponding passages from the Epitome. Two problems of the early

---

[107] Ibid., 244, n. 2. [108] Wlosok I, 211; cf. ibid., 210–15.

[109] Ibid., 212–14: Christianity as a synthesis of *sapientia* and *religio*. Our motto: *Epit.* 36, 4: 712. Wlosok I, 215 should be noted: 'In his own concern to systematize the various terms and to associate them by definitions, Lactantius later inserts the formula *sapientia/religio* (also in the version *sapientia/iustitia*) into the two basic frameworks which he had applied to the constitution of man, that from salvation history and the anthropological tradition which he had taken over with orthodox tradition.' Note here the constant play with the verses from Ovid., *Metamorph.* I, 84ff., which are quoted in *Inst.* II, 1, 15 (p. 98):

> pronaque cum spectent animalia cetera terram
> os homini sublime dedit caelumque uidere
> iussit et erectos ad sidera tollere uultus.

This is applied to the physical structure, the moral and spiritual attitude and the eternal destiny of man, even to the point of the vision of God. Cf. *Inst.* VII, 5, 22; cf. Wlosok I, 215, 216–22; II, 244–6.

[110] Wlosok I, 213, with reference to *Inst.* IV, 3–4. Cf. ibid., 214 (and n. 112): 'Before Lactantius no one . . . used the Hermetic writings to such a degree for apologetic purposes. Indeed, he was the first really to introduce them into the apologetic literature.' Cf. Wlosok I, 261f., for the Hermetic citations and allusions in Lactantius.

Christian Apologists are also pressing for Lactantius: (1) How can Christianity confess monotheism, when it believes in the Word or the Son of God? (2) How can Christianity, as a new philosophy and religious gnosis, speak of the incarnation of God? Lactantius raises the first question in matter-of-fact words: 'Perhaps someone may ask how we can affirm "two", God the Father and God the Son, when we claim to worship only one God. This assertion leads many into great error.'[111] So the unity of God[112] is an unavoidable theme: 'When we speak of God the Father and God the Son, we do not speak of different things and do not separate the two, as neither can the Father be separated from the Son nor the Son from the Father. There is no name of the Father without the Son, and the Son cannot be begotten without the Father.'[113] The solution of this great and oppressive riddle does not go far beyond the position already reached by Tertullian. In both Father and Son there is one understanding (*mens*), one spirit (*spiritus*), one substance (*substantia*). But the Father is like the spring and the Son the brook that flows from it; or the relationship between the two is like that of sun and ray.[114] The word *portio* also appears.[115] It is easy to see the Stoic doctrine of the spirit behind these remarks. It has an advantage over the strong stress of the moral interpretation of the unity of Father and Son in pointing to the unity of substance in God, however incomplete the ideas associated with it may have been.

When Lactantius uses the analogy of the *paterfamilias* to express the unity in God, he is probably betraying his 'Roman' connections. Whereas Tertullian makes considerable use of the idea of the *monarchia*, and explains the relationship of Father and Son on this basis (see p. 119 above), the word has only minor significance in Lactantius.[116] In this context Tertullian had used the example of a ruler and his many officials to explain the unity of the divine rule over the world and the unity in God himself (cf. *Apol.* 34, 2). Lactantius seems to be more 'domestic', whether one thinks of the smaller or the larger family (the *paterfamilias* with his sons and slaves). This family or *domus* is so fixed for him, *civili tamen iure*,[117] that it can serve as an analogy for the unity in God. So he has no difficulty in speaking of two 'persons' in God. Taking up the words of the prophet Isaiah, he contrasts the transcendent Father and the incarnate Son (Christ) under this nomenclature:

---

[111] *Inst.* IV, 29, 1: 391f.   [112] Ibid., IV, 29, 2: 392. 4: *nunc de unitate doceamus.*
[113] Ibid., IV, 29, 3: 392.
[114] Cf. *Inst.* IV, 29, 4: 392; Tertull., *Prax.* VIII, 5–6; XXII, 6; XXVII, 1: CCL II, 1167f.; 1190; Tertull., *Apol.* XXI, 11: CCL I, 124; Cyprian, *Test.* II, 3: CSEL III, 1, 64f.
[115] *Inst.* IV, 29, 6: 392: *cum igitur a prophetis idem manus dei et uirtus et sermo dicatur, utique nulla discretio est, quia et lingua, sermonis ministra, et manus, in qua est uirtus, indiuiduae sunt corporis portiones.*
[116] Cf. V. Loi, *Lattanzio*, 49–50: the term *monarchia* only appears twice in connection with Platonic theism: *Inst.* I, 5, 23; *Epit.* 4, 1: (Plato) *monarchiam adserit, unum deum dicens, a quo sit mundus instructus (et) mirabili ratione perfectus.* Loi points to Tertull., *Prax.* III, 2: *monarchiam nihil aliud significare scio quam singulare et unicum imperium.*
[117] *Inst.* IV, 29, 7: 392–3; 8: 393: *sic hic mundus una dei domus est et filius ac pater, qui unanimes incolunt*

Finally, Isaiah has shown that one God can be both Father and Son when he says, 'They will bow down to you and make supplication to you, saying, "God is with you only, and there is no other, no god besides him" ' (Isa. 45. 14). In another place, he says similarly: 'Thus says the Lord, the king of Israel and the eternal God his Redeemer: "I am the first and I am the last; besides me there is no god" ' (Isa. 44. 6). Since he has introduced two persons, that of God the king, which is Christ, and that of God the Father, who has raised him from the underworld after suffering, as the prophet Hosea has shown according to our words: 'And I will deliver him from the hand of the underworld' (Hos. 13. 14), so he (Isaiah) observes in referring to each of the two persons, 'and besides *me* there is no God', as he could say 'besides us' (*praeter nos*): but it was not right to allow a separation of such a close conjunction by using the plural. There is only one God, the free, supreme God, without origin, as he himself is the origin of things, and in him the Son and all else is contained. So because the understanding and will of the one is in the other, or better, is one in both, so the two can rightly be called one God; for what is in the Father over-flows into the Son, and what is in the Son descends from the Father. The one who wishes only to worship the Father does not worship even the Father unless he also worships the Son. And the one who accepts the Son and bears his name, worships the Father along with the Son, because the Son is the ambassador and messenger and priest of the supreme Father.[118]

Thus a distinction must be made between Father and Son in the one God. The Son belongs on the side of God and not among created things or beings. He, too, participates in the transcendence and unknowability of the Father—he is really known only to the Father.[119] The Son issues from the Father. But here we hear strange things. For as 'spirits', the angels also issue from God.[120] What is the difference between them and the Son in this respect? Very anthropomorphic notions must be used to solve this riddle:

For the Word (= *sermo*, as in Tertullian) is a breath (*spiritus*), but it is produced with a voice that is loaded with meaning. But because breath and word are produced by different (parts of the body)—the breath comes from the nose, the word from the mouth —so there is a great difference between this Son of God and the rest of the angels (*inter hunc dei filium ceterosque angelos!*). They came forth from God as dumb breath (*taciti spiritus*), because they were not created to communicate a divine doctrine, but only to

mundum, deus unus, quia et unum est tamquam duo et duo tamquam unus. For a correct understanding note Wlosok I, appendix 232–46. 'Die Gottesprädikation *pater et dominus* bei Laktanz. Gott in Analogie zum Römischen *pater familias*.' Cf. ibid., 180–92; 212ff.; 229ff. The designation '*pater familias*' under-lies the '*pater et dominus*'. *Pater familias* represents an official (Ulpian); it is a double term, which com-bines the idea of the *pater* and that of the *dominus*. For its Roman antecedents see ibid., 236ff. Tertullian also knows this double function, *Orat.* II, 4; *Marc.* I, 27, 3; II, 13, 5; *Apol.* XXXIV, 2, but he makes a distinction, see Wlosok I, 241: 'Thus in Tertullian the analogy between God and *pater familias* is not carried through consistently, and above all is not evaluated further in terms of the doctrine of God. Lactantius was the first to do this; he deliberately and consistently built up his new concept of God on the two-sidedness of the conception of the *pater familias*. . . .'
118 *Inst.* IV, 29, 10–15: 393f. Cf. *Epit.* 45, 4–5: 723. Here the ground for the unity between Father dan Son is that in them *substantia et uoluntas et fides una est*. In respect of the cult, we find here: *unus esthonos utrique tribuendus tamquam uni deo et ita diuidendus est per duos cultus, ut diuisio ipsa compage inseparabili uinciatur* (45, 5).
119 *Epit.* 37, 9. 713²⁰ᶠᶠ· (with reference to Rev. 19. 12).
120 *Inst.* IV, 8, 6: 296: *primum nec sciri a quoquam possunt nec enarrari opera diuina, sed tamen sanctae litterae docent, in quibus cautum est illum dei filium dei sermonem itemque ceteros angelos dei spiritus esse. nam sermo est spiritus cum uoce aliquid significante prolatus.*

serve (*ministerium*, cf. Heb. 1. 14, 7). But the Son came forth from the mouth of God aloud and with a voice, like a word, for a purpose, to use his voice towards all people, that is because he was to be the coming teacher of divine doctrine and the divine mystery that was to be brought to men. God first spoke him (the *sermo*, the *spiritus*), so as to be able to speak to us through him and so that he could reveal God's voice and will to us. He is therefore rightly called *sermo* and Word of God, because God has formed the vocal breath (*uocalem spiritum*) which proceeds from his mouth, which he conceived, not in the womb but in the understanding (*mente*), to be an image in the inconceivable power and might of his majesty, an image which enjoys his own senses (*sensus*) and his own wisdom. Our breath (*nostri spiritus*) blows away because we are mortal: but God's breath (*spiritus*) lives and remains and feels because he himself is immortal and the giver of feeling and life (*sensus ac vitae dator*). . . .[121]

This text, with its very anthropomorphic flavour and its parallels, gives us some idea of Lactantius' notion of the relationship of Father to Son in one God. But it should be noted that he speaks as an apologist and descends to the level of his audience and their presuppositions. The anthropomorphisms are comparisons and analogies. Of course, they would be all the more open to misinterpretation the more we were able to assume Stoic materialism in the Apologists' doctrine of the spirit.[122] But he clearly stresses the incorporeality of God, who for him is an '*incorporalis mens*' (Greek probably ἀσώματος νοῦς).[123] If one also considered the term *spiritus* in Lactantius, as does G. Verbeke, one would have to assume that even Lactantius does not get beyond the idea of the sublime corporeality of God (*corpus sui generis* in Tertullian). But he will have none of Stoic materialism, and rather switches on to the Platonic–Pythagorean line when he talks of the '*incorporalis mens*' in God.[124] This becomes rather clearer when one notes the relationship between Lactantius and Novatian.[125] But one only does justice to the corresponding texts in Novatian by using not only 'spirit' to translate '*spiritus*' but (as with the Hebrew *rūaḥ*) also breath or wind, depending on the context. *Trin.* VI, 33–VII, 39 is concerned with explaining pictorial statements about God, as when scripture speaks of the eyes, ears, fingers, hands, arms and feet of God. In this context Novatian makes very elevated statements about God and what we would call his 'spiritual nature', but does not use the word 'spirit' in our sense. Rather he speaks of the 'simplicity' of God:

[121] *Inst.* IV, 8–10: 296–7.
[122] G. Verbeke, *L'évolution de la doctrine du pneuma du stoïcisme à S. Augustin*, Paris–Louvain 1945, 469–85, stresses Lactantius' Stoic materialism too much. Cf. against this V. Loi, *Lattanzio*, 155–99. On p. 156 Loi challenges especially Verbeke's statement on p. 516: 'Lactance . . . fait procéder tout ce qui existe de l'être suprême par une espèce d'émanation matérielle, basée sur une interprétation étymologique de certains termes scripturaires.' See the polemic of Lactantius against the Stoa in *Inst.* VII, 3, 11: 589.
[123] Cf. V. Loi, *Lattanzio*, 33–35, 158f.
[124] Ibid., 35, 156 with reference to E. Bréhier, *La théorie des incorporels dans l'ancien Stoïcisme*, Paris 1928, 1–13, 60–63; E. Evans, *Tertullian's Treatise against Praxeas*, London 1948, 234–6.
[125] Cf. V. Loi, *Lattanzio*, 164–7. Ibid., 165, n. 31, has further references to the term *spiritus* in Novatian and Tertullian.

That which is simple does not have different parts. The latter is what happens with something that is divided into individual members, whose existence moves between coming to be and passing away. But whatever is not composite is one in itself and simple and eternal, whatever its nature might be. And because it is one in itself, it cannot be dissolved into parts and pass away, because, whatever it may be, it has no possibility of dissolution and is not subject to the laws of death.[126]

But when Novatian comes to speak of the word *spiritus*, he introduces qualifications. 'God is "spirit" ' is a metaphorical and not a substantive statement (VII, 39). When John 4. 24 says that God is *spiritus*, this does not describe God's being, as all *spiritus* is created.[127] According to him, 'God is "spirit" ' must be set alongside other metaphorical statements like the assertion that the substance of God is love, or light, or breath (*spiritus*) or fire (cf. *Trin.* VII, 38). But the real nature of God is above all these statements (*Trin.* VII, 38).[128] In other words, the highest statements about God cannot be made in terms of the word *spiritus*.

In Lactantius we find a similar situation. Suppose we return to the statement: 'He is therefore rightly called *sermo* and Word of God, because God has formed the vocal breath which proceeds from his mouth, which he conceived, not in the womb but in the understanding (*mente*), to be an image in the inconceivable power and might of his majesty. . . .' (*Inst.* IV, 8, 9). We shall understand this sentence if we begin from his definition of *sermo*: '*sermo est spiritus cum uoce aliquid significante prolatus*',[129] i.e., 'the Word is a breath which is produced by the voice giving it a meaning'. The origin of the word is the *mens*, and the *spiritus*, the breath, is the vehicle to which the voice, formulated through the mouth, gives a meaning. This is how the word is produced. But we can also breathe (*spirare*) through the nose. This does not produce a word. By means of this human analogy Lactantius explains the difference between the *sermo spiratus* or the *uocalis spiritus*, i.e. the Word of God or the Son, and the other 'breaths' (*spirationes*), the angels (and human souls). Because they are *spirationes* of God, they are immortal, but because they are mere *spirationes*, they are not the 'Word', nor are they the expression or the 'image' of God. So they cannot be the bearers of revelation; they are only effective forces which God uses in the world to serve him.

Because Lactantius claims the word *spiritus* so much for the issuing of the Son from the Father, and uses it in the way that has been described, two conclusions follow for him. First, his Logos doctrine is a 'spirit christology', and instead of a 'doctrine of the Trinity' he has a 'binitarianism'.

---

[126] Novatian, *Trin.* VI, 36: Weyer, 64–66.

[127] Novatian, *Trin.* VII, 39: Weyer, 66–68: *Denique si acceperis spiritum substantiam dei, creaturam feceris deum—omnis enim spiritus creatura est, erit ergo iam factus deus. . . .*

[128] Cf. V. Loi, *Lattanzio*, 166, with reference to Origen, *De Princ.* I, 1, 1; *Comm. in Io.* XIII, 21.

[129] *Inst.* IV, 8, 6: 296. A. Orbe, *Hacia la primera teologia de la procesión del Verbo*, (*Estud. Val.* I, 1), Roma 1958, 451; I, 2, 534, n. 14; 545–6, has demonstrated its Stoic origin. Details of sources in Loi, *Lattanzio*, 169, n. 43.

These two definitions are so important that we need to illuminate them briefly from the theological situation before and after Nicaea.[130]

(c) Lactantius and spirit christology

M. Simonetti distinguishes three forms of spirit christology:

(1) *Spiritus, pneuma*, when used of Christ, denotes his divine nature, or the divinity of Christ.

(2) *Pneuma* denotes the 'person' of the pre-existent Christ.

(3) In certain Fathers or authors, as a result, the pre-existent Christ and the Holy Spirit can be identified. The consequence is binitarianism.

For the first form of spirit christology Simonetti introduces the following evidence (with a reference to the influence of Rom. 1. 3–4, which we have already discussed): Ignatius, *Eph.* 7. 2; II Clem. 9. 5; Melito of Sardes, *Peri Pascha* 66 (Perler, 470ff.); Ps.-Hippolytus, *In S. Pascha* (= IP) (SC 27), 45; Clement of Alexandria, *Paed.* II, 19, 4. It should be noted that Origen is against the use of *pneuma* as a designation of the divine nature, unlike Athanasius, *Ad Serap.* 4, 19 (4, 23). Marcellus of Ancyra, *De Incarnatione et c. Arianos* 11 and *Sermo maior de fide* 13 (Schwartz, frag. 76), of course takes up an opposing position to Origen (see below under Marcellus).

From the Latin sphere Simonetti cites the *Epitome* of Lactantius (38, 43: *Primum de Deo in spiritu ante ortum mundi, postmodum in carne ex homine, Augusto imperante*); Hilary, *Comm. in Matt.* (written before his stay in Asia) 2, 5; 4, 14; 16, 9; 27, 4. Also Marius Victorinus, *Adv. Arian.* I, 44; III, 12 and 14.

The evidence for the second form of spirit christology (*pneuma, spiritus* as a designation of the person of the pre-existent Christ) is as follows: Ignatius, *Magn.* 15, 2; especially, however, IP 45–7. It is somewhat difficult to demonstrate that Tatian, *Adv. Graec.* 7 belongs here, and the same is true of Theophilus of Antioch.[131] Although Hippolytus clearly stresses the trinitarian structure of the deity in comparison with Theophilus (*C. Noet.* 12, 14), he can use *pneuma* specifically of the Son of God: 'What issued from the Father, if not the Logos? What was begotten by him if not the *pneuma*, that is, the Logos?' (*C. Noet.* 16; cf. 4). Clement of

130 In what follows we make use of M. Simonetti, 'Note di cristologia pneumatica', *Aug.* 12, 1972, 201–32; J. P. Martin, *El Espiritu Santo en los origenes del cristianismo*, Zürich 1971; R. Cantalamessa, 'La primitiva esegesi cristologica di "Romani" I, 3–4 et "Luca" I, 35', *RivStorLettRel* 2, 1966, 69–80. See above the references to F. Loofs. For 'Logos-Sophia' in pre-Christian and early Christian times, cf. Wlosok I, 157f.

131 M. Simonetti, loc. cit., 212f.: 'In altri termini, Teofilo da una parte in ossequio alla formula di fede, tende ad affiancare al Figlio (= Logos) lo Spirito Santo (= Sapienza) come persona distinta; ma d'altra parte tende a riportare al solo Figlio i vari nomi di facoltà e potenze divine (sapienza, potenza, spirito): questa seconda tendenza mi sembra prevalente. E in questo senso anche pneuma è adoperato appunto come appellativo specifico del Logos, come nome personale (*Ad Autol.* 2. 10). Questo dunque (cioè il Logos), che è Spirito di Dio e sapienza e potenza dell'Altissimo, scendeva sui profeti e per mezzo loro raccontava com'era avvenuta la creazione del mondo e di tutte le altre cose.' For this terminology of Theophilus cf. also M. Simonetti, 'La Sacra Scrittura in Teofilo d'Antiochia', *Epektasis*, 197–207.

Alexandria writes to the same effect: '. . . The Lord is *pneuma* and Logos.
. . . The Lord Jesus Christ, that is the Logos of God, is *pneuma* made flesh,
hallowed, heavenly flesh.'[132] Irenaeus says in *Demonstr.* 71: 'Scripture in-
forms us that Christ, although the *pneuma* of God, had to subject himself
to suffering as man', cf. *Adv. haer.* IV, 31, 2. Tertullian certainly has a
broader spectrum of remarks (some of which belong to the first form of the
use of *spiritus*). In *De Oratione*[133] and *Prax.* 26,[134] however, *spiritus* is used as
a proper name of the pre-existent Christ. Lactantius is not so significant
for the identification of *Logos* and *Spiritus Dei* (only *Inst.* IV, 9 is relevant).
Phoebadius of Agen, *C. Arian.* 20, is clearer,[135] although he too knows of
the person of the Holy Spirit (22). Finally, mention should be made of
Gregory of Elvira (*De fide* 8, 93, where, however, the second redaction
should be noted as well as the first: CCL 69, 245).

It was the ambivalence of the exegesis of Luke 1. 35, above all, which
contributed to the identification of *spiritus* (*sanctus*) and the pre-existent
Christ. According to M. Simonetti, three groups should be distinguished
here:

(1) Especially in the reading πνεῦμα κύριον for πνεῦμα ἅγιον, Luke 1.
35 is referred to the pre-existent Christ, without a formal identification of
the Logos with the Holy Spirit.[136]

(2) The same terminology contains, among other things, precisely this
identification.[137]

(3) But there is also an identification of the pre-existent Christ and the
Holy Spirit without reference to Luke 1. 35.[138] This is the context of
Lactantius, with Victorinus of Pettau and Hilary's commentary on

---

[132] Clem. Al., *Paed.* II, 19, 4: M. Simonetti, 'Note di cristologia pneumatica', *Aug* 12,
1972, 213.

[133] Tertullian, *Orat.* I, 1: CCL I, 257: *Dei spiritus et Dei sermo et Dei ratio, sermo rationis et ratio
sermonis et spiritus utriusque, Iesus Christus, dominus noster.*

[134] Tertullian, *Prax.* 26, 4: CCL 2, 1196-7: *Hic spiritus Dei idem erit sermo. Sicut enim Iohanne dicente:
sermo caro factus est* (*Io* 1, 14), *spiritum quoque intelligimus in mentione sermonis, ita et hic sermonem quoque
agnoscimus in nomine spiritus. Nam et spiritus substantia est sermonis et sermo operatio spiritus, et duo unum
sunt.*

[135] Phoebad. Agen., *C. Arian.* 20: PL 20, 28CD: *Nam idem spiritus Sermo et sapientia Dei est. . . .
Denique cum eadem sapientia et Verbum Dei, et spiritus Dei sit, singulorum tamen nominum officia nuntiantur.
. . . Apparet ergo unum eundemque venisse nunc in nomine spiritus, nunc in appellatione sapientiae.* Phoebadius is dependent on Tertullian, *Adv. Prax.* (cf. ch. 20), and acknowledges three persons in God (cf.
ch. 22: PL 20, 29-30). M. Simonetti, loc. cit., 216f.

[136] Thus attested in the Greek sphere by Justin, *Dial. c. Tryph.* 100; *Apol.* I, 33; Iren., *Haer.* V, 1, 3;
in the Latin sphere by Tertullian, *Prax.* 26, 3-4; Lactantius, *Inst.* IV, 12, 1: 309: *Descendens itaque de
caelo sanctus ille spiritus dei sanctam uirginem cuius utero se insinuaret elegit. at illa diuino spiritu hausto
repleta concepit et sine ullo adtactu uiri repente uirginalis uterus intumuit.* Gregor. Illib., *De fide* 8, 92: CCL
LXIX, 245: *Vides ergo ipsum Spiritum, id est filium dei, venisse ad(in) virginem et inde (in) dei et hominis
filium processisse.* Thus the first recension. A second recension, demonstrated by M. Simonetti (loc.
cit. 222, n. 48) from *Oxon. Laudian. misc.* 276 has instead: *ipsum Verbum, ipsum Dei Filium,* which is
not indicated in CCL, loc. cit. For Novatian see Simonetti, ibid. (in controversy with V. Loi, *Lattanzio,* 196).

[137] The Holy Spirit is the subject of the assumption of the flesh from Mary, especially in the West,
and in some works which are ascribed to Cyprian: *Quod idol.* 11; *Mont. Sina* 4; Victorinus of Pettau,
Fabrica mundi 9; *In Apoc.* 12, 1; Hilary, *Trin.* II, 26. Cf. M. Simonetti, loc. cit., 223.

[138] Cf. Past. Herm., *Sim.* IX, 1, 1; V, 6, 5; Ps. Cyprian., *Ad Vigil.* 7. M. Simonetti, loc. cit., 225.

Matthew.[139] These are therefore almost exclusively Western witnesses. M. Simonetti explains this by saying that in the West the accent lay more on the stress on the unity in God, and not on the distinction of persons. Novatian had already weakened the clear distinction of the three persons in God as it was to be found in Tertullian. The letter of Dionysius of Rome to Dionysius of Alexandria also shows that in Rome there was more concern for a stress on the unity than for an elucidation of the Trinity which Origen had so carefully produced in the East. Of course, the dispute over Marcellus of Ancyra will show that there were also theologians in the East who were primarily concerned to safeguard the unity in God, even to the point of endangering the distinction.

(d) Lactantius as a binitarian

Our examination of pre-Nicene 'spirit christology' makes it possible for us to mark out Lactantius' place among the representatives of this pneumatology, which does not accept any third hypostasis in the Godhead. Jerome also asserts that in the letters to Demetrianus, which are no longer extant, Lactantius denied the personal subsistence of the Holy Spirit.[140] However, he could not bypass the biblical and patristic doctrine of the *pneuma* which regards the spirit as a charisma of sanctification and above all as a force of prophetic inspiration.[141] Above all, a closer investigation is needed of Lactantius' doctrine of baptism and its background, the Asian baptismal catechesis of his time. A. Wlosok shows that it has a great significance for him:

> Sin, the state of lostness, is an ignorance which has its basis in the obscuration of the human capacity for understanding. So redemption by the communication of revelation consists in an inner illumination and the bestowal of knowledge. This is achieved by the influx of divine wisdom, which is thought of as a pneumatic substance, like light, and

---

[139] Lactantius, *Epit.* 38 (43), 9: 715: *renatus est ergo ex uirgine sine patre tamquam homo, ut quemadmodum in prima natiuitate spiritali creatus [est] ex solo deo sanctus spiritus factus est, sic in secunda carnali ex sola matre genitus caro sancta fieret, ut per eum caro, qua subiecta peccato fuerat, ab interitu liberaretur.* Victor. Poetov., *In Apoc.* VI, 4: CSEL 49, 74; Hilar. Pict., *Comm. Matt.* 12, 17 (the sin against the Holy Spirit, Matt. 12. 31–2, is interpreted in terms of denying the divinity of Christ): *Quid enim tam extra veniam est quam in Christo negare quod Deus sit et consistentem in eo paterni Spiritus substantiam adimere?* (PL 9, 989B).

[140] Jerome, *Ep.* 84, 7, reproduced in CSEL 27, 1, 157: *Lactantius in libris suis et maxime in epistulis ad Demetrianum spiritus sancti omnino negat substantiam et errore iudaico dicit eum vel ad patrem referri vel filium et sanctificationem utriusque personae sub eius nomine demonstrari.* Cf. Jerome, *Comm. in Ep. ad Galat.* II, 4, 6: CSEL 27, 1, 156f., where there is mention of the eighth book of letters to Demetrianus, and it is also said of other authors: *asserunt spiritum sanctum saepe patrem, saepe filium nominari.* For what follows see *V.* Loi, *Lattanzio*, 174–6.

[141] For the theme of 'spirit and prophetic inspiration' cf. *Inst.* IV, 18, 30–1: 358–9. David made a prophecy in Ps. 21. 17–19 (*effoderunt manus meas . . .*), but not about himself, as he did not suffer as king. The spirit of God spoke through him, indeed the one who was to suffer a thousand and fifty years later. These are the number of years to be counted from the reign of David to the cross of Christ. The *spiritus divinus* is the Logos. But apart from this passage, *spiritus divinus* denotes the spirit of inspiration in *Inst.* IV, 5, 5 (284); IV, 6, 6 (290); V, 9, 6 (425: poetic inspiration of a quasi-divine kind): VI, 1, 1 (479) (by Lactantius related to himself); VII, 24, 9 (660). Cf. V. Loi, *Lattanzio*, 176.

coincides with the Holy Spirit. In this way the original state of man, as it was desired by his Creator, is restored.[142]

Lactantius also transfers to the act of baptism the process of restoration, which he understands as restoring man to his *rectus status*.[143] When we add to this the way in which the apologist speaks of the baptism of Christ[144] and the equipping of the apostles to preach in the whole world and to perform miracles,[145] it is clear that in the background of his teaching and speculation we can still find the biblical and early Christian *kerygma* of the Father, who communicates himself for the redemption of men in his Son Jesus Christ and in the Holy Spirit. The constriction of this to a binitarianism, and in conjunction with this to a subordinationism, about which we shall soon have to speak, is a result of the serious concern of the church after the middle of the second century (Justin), down to the period before Nicaea, to think through the kerygma of Father-Son-Spirit, presented in terms of the economy of salvation, in a theological manner. The problems which Lactantius finds are no greater than those of his other contemporaries, even if in some statements he comes suspiciously close to an Arian-type christology.

(e) Lactantius as a subordinationist

The weakest part of his teaching is the interpretation of the way in which God brings forth the good and evil spirits:

> Before God took in hand this work of (the creation of) the world . . . he brought forth a spirit similar to him who was to be equipped with the powers of God the Father . . . then he created another in which the divine character (*indoles divinae stirpis*) did not abide.[146]

---

[142] Wlosok I, 7.

[143] Wlosok I, 7 and 185. It would be worth investigating not only the effects of baptism in Lactantius but also the problem of grace. Cf. *Inst.* VII, 5, 22 (600): *quae ratio docet mortalem nasci hominem, postea uero inmortalem fieri, cum coeperit ex deo uiuere id est iustitiam sequi, quae continentur in dei cultu, cum excitauerit hominem deus ad aspectum caeli ac sui. quod tum fit, cum homo caelesti lauacro purificatus exponit infantiam cum omni labe uitae prioris et incremento diuini uigoris accepto fit homo perfectus ac plenus.*

[144] Cf. V. Loi, *Lattanzio*, 174–6, with an analysis of *Inst.* IV, 5, 3 (baptism of Christ and the interpretation of Luke 3. 22, with reference to the parallels in Hilary). J. Doignon, 'La scène évangélique du baptême de Jésus commentée par Lactance (*Diuinae institutiones* 4, 15) et Hilaire de Poitiers (*In Matthaeum* 2, 5–6)', *Epektasis*, 63–73, does not agree with drawing this parallel. Hilary is not oriented on the extant commentaries of Origen on Matthew and Luke, but is primarily inspired by the pages which Tertullian devoted to the scene of the baptism by the Jordan. 'Cependant, dès cette première interprétation hilarienne du Baptême, se dessine un effort de pensée théologique, qui, en dépit de sources communes, comme les *Testimonia* de Cyprien, crée un écart profond entre la manière dont Hilaire sait faire saisir les dimensions mystérieuses de la scène évangélique du Jourdain et la manière encore très apologétique dont Lactance entend réfuter une interprétation thaumaturgique de la naissance du Christ à la "puissance celeste" ' (73). Hilary goes more deeply into the specifically christological problems.

[145] For the theme of the Holy Spirit and the sending out of the disciples see *Epit.* 42, 3 (720–1): *profectus igitur in Galilaeam post resurrectionem discipulos suos . . . ordinata euangelii praedicatione per totum orbem inspirauit in eos spiritum sanctum ac dedit eis potestatem mirabilia faciendi, ut in salutem hominum tam factis quam uerbis operarentur.*

[146] *Inst.* II, 8, 3–4: 129.

To one he gave his love as a good son, whereas he rejected (*abdicauit*) the other as wicked.[147] He returns to this doctrine in *Institutiones* IV:

> God, who brings about things and gives them their being (*machinator constitutorque rerum*), as we said in our second book, brought forth a holy and incorruptible spirit (*sanctum et incorruptibilem spiritum genuit*) before he took in hand this glorious work, and named him Son. And although later he created numerous other (spirits), whom we name angels, he thought only this firstborn (*primogenitum*) to be worthy of the divine name, as he delighted in the power and majesty of the Father.[148]

As witnesses to the supreme authority of this 'highest Son of God' (*summi dei filius*), he introduces not only the testimony of the prophets, but also his favourite authors, Hermes Trismegistus and the Sibyllines. The text of Hermes tells the whole story:

> The Lord and Creator of the universe, whom we rightly call God, when he had made the second visible and perceptible God ... when he had made this as the first and only one, he appeared to him to be good (beautiful) and full of all goodness, so he loved him completely and utterly as his only child.[149]

With the Sibyllines, Lactantius calls him 'Son of God, leader and commander of all'. Finally, there follows the quotation from Prov. 8. 22–30 which the Arians were so fond of using in their arguments.[150] This may be sufficient to show the subordinationist doctrine of Lactantius. His doctrine of the incarnation will supplement it in some important ways. One suspicious peculiarity of his teaching is the connection between the emergence of the firstborn and the second spirit, who is to turn to evil. The connection between the birth of the Son and the creation of the world is also clearer than in the other Apologists.[151]

(f) The second birth of the Son of God

The element in Lactantius' teaching which goes beyond a Hermetic and Gnostic doctrine of revelation is the incarnation of Christ. To defend it is as much Lactantius' concern as to interpret Christian monotheism, which seemed to Gentiles and Jews to be infringed by the acceptance of a

---

[147] *Inst.* II, 8, 7: 130–1 (see apparatus p. 131). This text has only been transmitted in certain codices (R, S, g). Cf. V. Loi, *Lattanzio*, 203, n. 2. §7 expresses the conjunction of the emergence of the Son and the work of creation especially clearly: *exorsus igitur deus fabricam mundi illum primum et maximum praefecit operi uniuerso eoque simul et consiliatore usus est et artifice in excogitandis ordinandisque perficiendisque rebus, quoniam is et prouidentia et ratione et potestate perfectus est. ...*

[148] *Inst.* IV, 6, 1–2: 286.

[149] *Inst.* IV, 6, 4: 286–8 (Greek text); *Epit.* 37, 4–5: 713 (Latin text). The translation here is introduced by the note that Plato spoke of the first and second God (δεύτερος θεός), not as a philosopher but as a prophet, possibly following the Trismegistus. Cf. Asclepius ch. 8: Nock–Festugière 3, 304²⁰–305³. Cf. lines 6–12. For this text, which speaks of man (and the world) as the image of God, but is interpreted by Lactantius in terms of the Son of God, cf. R. P. Festugière, *La révélation d'Hermès Trismégiste* 3: *Les doctrines de l'âme*, Paris 1953, 36f. R. P. Festugière, *La révélation* 1, Paris 1950, Introduction 1–44, shows how Greek rationalism was transformed into a doctrine of revelation even in Middle Platonism.

[150] *Inst.* IV, 6, 6: 290–1; M. Simonetti, *Studi sull'Arianesimo*, Roma 1965, 32–7. Prov. 8. 22ff. occurs with variations in Cyprian, *Test.* II, 1: CSEL III, 1, p. 62.

[151] Cf. the text cited above from *Inst.* II, 8, 7.

For he is born twice (*bis enim natus est*), first of God in the spirit (that is, according to the Godhead) before the origin of the world, and then in the flesh of men under the rule of Augustus. This is a great and profound mystery which contains the salvation of man, the worship of the supreme God and all truth.[162]

In his birth from God and by his birth from the virgin Jesus appears as 'heavenly man' (*homo caelestis*). Again this statement has a soteriological point:

> But so that his being sent from God might be secure, he could not be born as other men, compounded from two mortal elements (*ex mortali utroque concretus*); so that he might be seen by men to be heavenly, he (i.e. the manhood of Jesus) was created without a begetter. He had God as his spiritual (i.e. divine) Father, and just as God (i.e. the Father) is father of his deity without a mother, so the mother of his body is the Virgin, without a father. So as God and man he was set in the midst (*medius*) between God and man, wherefore the Greeks call him μεσίτης, so that he could lead men to God, i.e. to immortality. For had he only been God ... he would not have been able to give men the example of virtue; if he had only been man, he could not have led (*cogeret*) men to righteousness; in addition there had to be superhuman authority and virtue.[163]

The following soteriological considerations provide a parallel: man consists of body and spirit (and the body involves the spirit in death). So redemption has to come through Christ, composed of a divine spirit and (earthly) body.[164] This soteriology is thus based on an implicit Logos-sarx framework. Had Lactantius reflected here on the problem of a human soul, his picture of Christ and his soteriology would have broken down. But his picture is in fact a simple one: 'Therefore (the mediator) clothed himself with flesh so that he might tame the lusts of the flesh and thus teach that man does not sin of necessity, but with deliberate will.'[165] The one who proved himself in the struggle against the lust of the flesh is clearly not, for Lactantius, the human will, but the spirit come down from above, the *sermo* of the Father, garbed in human flesh. Granted, this spirit proceeded from God before the creation, but this was in connection with the creation and not from eternity; Lactantius does not say whether his emergence is dependent on the free decision of the Father, though he does stress freedom explicitly in his definition of the supreme God.[166] This freedom could also be related to the production of the *spiritus-sermo*.

---

162 *Epit.* 38, 2: 714: *Idem est dei et hominis filius. bis enim natus est: primum de deo in spiritu ante ortum mundi, postmodum in carne ex homine Augusto imperante. cuius rei praeclarum et grande mysterium est, in quo et salus hominum et religio summi dei et omnis ueritas continetur.*

163 *Inst.* IV, 25, 3–5: 376: cf. *Epit.* 38, 8–9: 715. In *Inst.* IV, 24, 1–19, Lactantius so to speak sets out the *a priori* conditions which a *doctor perfectus* must fulfil for mankind: *fingamus aliquem de caelo esse mittendum, qui uitam hominum rudimentis uirtutis instituat et ad iustitiam formet.* Neither a purely earthly nor a purely heavenly teacher is enough. The long paragraph ends in 19 (375): *liquido igitur apparet eum qui uitae dux et iustitiae sit magister corporalem esse oportere nec aliter fieri posse ut sit illius plena et perfecta doctrina habeatque radicem ac fundamentum stabilisque aput homines ac fixa permaneat, ipsum autem subire carnis et corporis inbecillitatem uirtutemque in se recipere cuius doctor est, ut eam simul et uerbis doceat et factis; item subiectum esse morti et passionibus cunctis, quoniam et in passione toleranda et in morte subeunda uirtutis officia uersantur. quae omnia ut dixi consummatus doctor perferre debet, ut doceat posse perferri.*

164 *Inst.* IV, 25, 6–8: 376f. 165 *Ibid*, no. 8: 377.

166 *Inst.* IV, 29, 12: 393f.: *unus est enim, solus, liber, deus summus, carens origine, quia ipse est origo rerum et in eo simul et filius et omnia continentur.*

When the *spiritus*, understood in a subordinationist way, becomes man, the result is indeed a superhuman being, a *homo caelestis*, but he is still only a 'middle being' between the supreme God and the creation. The designation μεσίτης for the incarnate Christ also introduces some incidental obscurities. Although this Christ has many traditional features, he is dangerously near to becoming a mythical being. Arianism is only a step away.

3. ASTERIUS THE SOPHIST

One especially complex figure from the time immediately before and immediately after Nicaea is Asterius the Sophist (died soon after 341). He is complex, in that on the one hand it can be demonstrated that he put forward strictly Arian teaching, particularly in his *Syntagmation*, which was written before Nicaea, while on the other hand homilies on the Psalms and a series of Easter sermons are ascribed to him which evidently must be put after 335 and display throughout a pre-Nicene, orthodox christology, which is archaic in many of its features.[167] In comparison with Eusebius of Caesarea, his friend, Asterius is heretical in the *Syntagmation*, but in his homilies he is more a man of the church and more orthodox than Eusebius. Philostorgius records a change in Asterius' attitude to Arianism,[168] but can an author change from a decided advocacy

---

[167] For what follows see M. Richard, *Asterii Sophistae Commentariorum in Psalmos quae supersunt. Accedunt aliquot homiliae anonymae*, SymbOsl Fasc. Suppl. XVI, Oslo 1956; also E. Skard, *Index Asterianus (Index de l'édition d'Asterius le Sophiste établie par Marcel Richard ...)*. SymbOsl Fasc. Suppl. XVII, Oslo 1962. For the history of research and the various editions see: (1) G. Bardy, 'Astérius le Sophiste', *RHE* 22, 1926, 221–72; id., *Recherches sur S. Lucien d'Antioche et son école*, Paris 1936, 316–57; (2) M. Richard, 'Les homélies d'Asterius le Sophiste sur les psaumes IV–VII', *RB* 44, 1935, 548–58; id., 'Une ancienne collection d'homélies grecques sur les psaumes I–XV', *SymbOsl* 25, 1947, 54–73; id., 'Le recueil d'homélies d'Astérius le Sophiste', *SymbOsl* 29, 1952, 93–8; id., 'Nouveaux témoins des homélies V et XX d'Astérius le Sophiste sur les psaumes', *SymbOsl* 34, 1958, 54–7; id., 'L'homélie XXXI d'Astérius le Sophiste et le Codex Mosquensis 234', *SymbOsl* 36, 1960, 96–8. (3) E. Skard, 'Asterios von Amaseia und Asterios der Sophist', *SymbOsl* 20, 1940, 86–132; id., 'Bemerkungen zu den Asterios-Texten', *SymbOsl* 27, 1949, 54–69; id., 'Zu Asterios', *SymbOsl* 34, 1958, 58–66. (4) S. Eitrem, 'Zu Asterios Sophistes, Hom. XXII', *SymbOsl* 36, 1960, 127. Studies: H. Auf der Maur, *Die Osterhomilien des Asterios Sophistes als Quelle für die Geschichte der Osterfeier* (Trierer Theol. Studien 19), Trier 1967; further literature on p. xv. Also Marie-Josèphe Rondeau, 'Le "Commentaire des Psaumes" de Diodore de Tarse I–III', *RevHistRel* 176, 1969, 5–23, 153–88; 177, 1970, 5–33. In the studies listed above there has been a discussion between M. Richard and E. Skard over the authenticity of Homilies VI–XI (on Ps. 5), also Homilies X and XXII. Richard still has doubts over Hom. I (pp. 1–4) and Hom. XXIV (182–7), and reservations on Homilies X and XXVII. Research is not yet complete.

[168] Philostorgius, HE II, 15: Bidez–Winkelmann, 25²⁵⁻⁷: ἀλλὰ δὴ καὶ τὸν Ἀστέριον παρατρέψαι τὸ φρόνημα ἀπαράλλακτον εἰκόνα τοῦ πατρὸς οὐσίας εἶναι τὸν υἱὸν ἐν τοῖς αὐτοῦ λόγοις καὶ γράμμασι διαμαρτυρούμενον. Asterius changed his mind and in his discourses and writings designates the Son as the identical image of the substance of the Father. Granted, this expression cannot be demonstrated in the texts edited by Richard, but it occurs in the fragments produced by Marcellus of Ancyra (according to Eusebius, CM frag. 96: Klostermann–Hansen, 205³⁰). Cf. G. Bardy, *Recherches*, 349f., who takes up the same fragment from Acacius, *Contra Marcellum*, according to Epiphanius, *Haer.* LXXII 8 (not 6) (Holl, *Epiphanius* III, 262f.). Cf. below on the so-called second creed of Antioch. Of course, it should be noted that in the text of Philostorgius it is possible that Noominius or Numenius should be read instead of Asterius. Cf. loc. cit., apparatus and Winkelmann, 347, with reference to Koetschau and Bidez.

of Arianism to so naive an orthodox and pre-Nicene christology, at the time of the vigorous disputes surrounding Nicaea, without displaying some of the spiritual struggles he has been through? This psychological dilemma is all the more acute, as Asterius the Sophist maintained the closest links with his Arian friends right until his death.[169]

The riddle remains insoluble when one considers the various expedients which have been adopted to reach some answer:

(1) Were the Easter homilies really written between 335 and 341? Not all the reasons advanced for this late dating are compelling.[170] However, various passages from Jerome seem to be decisive support for a late dating.[171]

[169] Cf. Athanasius, *De Synod.* 18, 2–3: Opitz AW II, 1, 9, p. 245, where there is an account of Asterius' origin in Cappadocia, his many-headedness (πολυκέφαλος σοφιστής), his place in the group around Eusebians of Nicomedia, and then his travels through Syria and other churches (always in association with the Eusebians), where he delivered his *Syntagmation.* Socrates, HE I, 36: Hussey I, 164–5, has an abbreviated résumé of this report.

[170] Cf. H. Auf der Maur, *Die Osterhomilien,* 8–10. He takes the years 325–41 as the approximate period of the origin of the Homilies on the Psalms (in distinction to the Easter homilies which are contained in them). As the author takes Philostorgius' report of Asterius' abandonment of Arianism seriously, he thinks that he must limit the time of the origin of these writings to the period between 335 and 341. Hom. II, 21 (Richard, 13³⁻¹⁰) then gives him a special point of contact for dating. He thinks that he can read out of the homily that the feast of Easter was recognized as ἑορτὴ πάνδημος by the heads of state. But it should first be noted that the mention of royal usages in 'popular festivals' is only in very general terms, especially as regards the freeing of prisoners, which could also take place in pagan times. A conclusion is then drawn from this to Christ's liberating actions on the feast of the (redemptive) passion. The author's statements (p. 13, n. 3) are therefore probably too strong when he says: '. . . before Constantine it was inconceivable that the heads of state would have recognized the feast of Easter as ἑορτὴ πάνδημος, much less that they would have taken notice of it in practice.' However, even if a connection between the 'feast of Easter' and a 'general popular festival' cannot be read out of this text of Asterius, Auf der Maur is right in suggesting that with Constantine a new relationship begins between the emperor and his officials and Christian festivals. In our text special mention of the governor is made in connection with Easter: 'Christ has anticipated what the governors do among us at Easter: they strike no one, and free those who are fettered in prison' (Richard, 13⁸⁻¹⁰). It is unnecessary to suppose that such conditions could only obtain in the period after 325, much less in the period after 335. As early as the year 321 we have a decree of Constantine about rest on the *dies solis,* which is incorporated in the *Cod. Iust.* (3, 12, 2), and has been interpreted in terms of the Christian Sunday (see the early history of this in Coleman-Norton, 83f.). However, more weighty and clearer evidence than this decree is the fact that Eusebius, *Vita Const.* IV, 23 (Heikel, 126³⁻⁶) associates this document with a statute of Constantine whose wording is no longer extant, but whose content is reproduced in Eusebius. In it, the Archontes mentioned by Asterius are commanded to observe the feasts of martyrs and to honour the feasts of the church: καὶ τοῖς κατ' ἔθνος δ' ἄρχουσιν ὁμοίως τὴν κυριακὴν ἡμέραν νόμος ἐφοίτα γεραίειν· οἱ δ' αὐτοὶ νεύματι βασιλέως καὶ μαρτύρων ἡμέρας ἐτίμων καιρούς τε ἑορτῶν ἐκκλησίας ἐδόξαζον, πάντα τε βασιλεῖ καταθυμίως τὰ τοιαῦτα ἐπράττετο. Among these can be included the feast of Easter, as the chief Christian feast. All this only means that in the light of the legislation of Constantine, Hom. II, with its reference to the observance of Easter, could even be ante-Nicene.

[171] Jerome, *De vir. ill.,* 94: Richardson, TU 14, 1896, 46: *Asterius, Arianae philosophus factionis, scripsit, regnante Constantio,* In epistulam ad Romanos *et* In Evangelia *et* In Psalmos *commentarios et multa alia, quae a suae partis hominibus studiosissime leguntur.* Id., *Ep.* 112, 20: CSEL 55, 390: *. . . maxime in explanatione psalmorum, quos apud Graecos interpretati sunt multis uoluminibus primus Origenes, secundus Eusebius Caesariensis, tertius Theodorus Heracleotes, quartus Asterius Scythopolita, quintus Apollinaris Laodicenus, sextus Didymus Alexandrinus. Feruntur et diuersorum in paucos psalmos opuscula, sed nunc de integro psalmorum corpore dicimus.* Cf. H. Auf der Maur, *Die Osterhomilien,* 6. There are two striking things in *Ep.* 112: (1) that Jerome enumerates the psalm commentaries in chronological order. Asterius comes after Eusebius of Caesarea. For the dating of Eusebius' commentary, Marie-Josèphe Rondeau, 'Le "Commentaire des Psaumes" de Diodore de Tarse et l'éxegèse antique du Psaume 109/110 (II)', *RevHistRel* 176, 173: 'oeuvre difficile à dater, certainement postérieure aux Eclogae, à la *Préparation*

(2) If one accepts the late dating of the homilies edited by M. Richard, some other way must be found of solving the dilemma:

(a) Perhaps the homilies were in fact delivered in the period before Nicaea and 'edited' after Nicaea, without being revised in an Arian direction.

(b) Perhaps the homilies, too, were originally permeated with Arian ideas, and were then 'purged' in the course of the tradition. At any rate, the question of manuscripts and the textual history outlined by M. Richard raises grounds for doubt. But would such a 'revision' of the homilies, which to our eyes have a quite uniform christology, not be more decisively along the lines established by Nicaea? Would not the last trace of subordinationism be blotted out?[172]

(c) Finally, one could point to the very different literary genres of the *Syntagmation* and the homilies. The *Syntagmation* is a brief account of the chief Arian doctrines, so to speak, for theological discussion. What was said and written here did not need to be presented to the people in worship. We do in fact have various analogous instances of such a discrepancy during the Arian struggle: namely between quite orthodox sounding Credos (say in Eusebius, Arius, Marcellus of Ancyra)[173] and the general *theology* of these men. It was therefore possible to speak in quite orthodox terms and to 'interpret' in quite a different way—an art which has been cultivated in the history of theology right down to modern times. In the psalm homilies, which have been ascribed to Asterius the Sophist, we have 'sermons that were really given', and not a 'commentary on a school'.

> The rhetorical style itself is decisive. The author often turns to his audience. . . . The term 'commentaire' which Richard uses is probably to be understood in a wider sense: these are sermons which comment on Psalms 1–20. In contrast to the Easter homilies, which are also psalm homilies, we shall use the term psalm commentary in the sense described above.[174]

---

et à la *Démonstration*, mais malaisée à situer par rapport au *Contra Marcellum* (vers 336) et à la *Théologie ecclésiastique*.' Cf. id., 'Une nouvelle preuve de l'influence littéraire d'Eusèbe de Césarée sur Athanase: l'interprétation des psaumes', *RSR* 56, 1968, 385–431, esp. 420, n. 60 (enumeration of the various opinions) and 420ff., further discussion of the dating. In Jerome, *Ep.* 112, Asterius and Theodore of Heracleia in Thrace (bishop there from 335–55) should probably be interchanged. Cf. Jerome, *De vir. ill.*, 90: Richardson, 45; J. Reuss, *Matthäuskommentare aus der griechischen Kirche* (TU 61), Berlin 1957, XXVI–XXIX. (2) For Asterius' nickname 'Scythopolita', which is probably derived from a lengthy stay there (Palestine), see G. Bardy, *Recherches*, 329f. The evidence of Jerome, especially *Ep.* 112, suggests that Asterius' psalm commentary should be put in the years 336–41. We could, however, at least ask whether '*in Psalmos* commentarii' refers to the *Homilies* on the psalms. The title of M. Richard's edition (see above), suggests that he at least is of this opinion. On this cf. Auf der Maur, op. cit., 7.

[172] Interestingly, M. Richard brackets off a *homoousios* which occurs in *Hom.* XVII (132[10f.]), and suggests instead ἀγαπητός as a possible reading. In *Hom.* XXXI, 5 (244[16]), he would like to replace it by συνεργός ἐστιν, following the corrigenda in *Index Asterianus* by E. Skard, 14.

[173] Cf. H. G. Opitz, AW III, 1, 1: document 6 (creed of Arius, etc.); III, 1, 2: document 22 (Eusebius of Caesarea). For Marcellus of Ancyra see below.

[174] H. Auf der Maur, *Die Osterhomilien*, 8.

But could so close a friend of the Arians take such a course of action, speaking in such a 'conservative' way and inwardly thinking in very different terms? It should also be noted that the last influence of Asterius of which we hear concerns the literary genre of a creed, in the framework of the Synod of Antioch in 341.

> Bardy ascribes to the influence of Asterius and to that of Eusebius of Constantinople, who was also present, the two last surviving representatives of the Lucianic circle, the fact that the Synod accepted the Lucianic Creed instead of the Nicene Creed, a creed moreover which corresponds completely with fragments of works of Asterius from his extreme Arian period.[175]

In short, the great difficulties have not been resolved. Was Asterius really 'converted' from Arianism to the (relative) orthodoxy of the homilies on the Psalms? Are these homilies preserved with their original text? Has the question of authenticity been satisfactorily resolved for the bulk of these homilies? Despite this doubt, it is interesting to examine the christology of the homilies on the Psalms. We shall take it as evidence of a complex person and a still more complex century; we shall take it as it is, as the expression of a Christian proclamation which is ante-Nicene in spirit, chiefly inspired by scripture and the liturgy, and it will remind us once again of the church's kerygma before and around Nicaea.

Asterius the Sophist was first a non-Christian orator in Cappadocia.[176] After his conversion to Christianity, he was given the title of 'the Sophist'. In the persecution of Maximian he weakened and offered sacrifice. This

---

[175] Ibid. 5–6, with reference to G. Bardy, *Recherches*, 125–7. See now J. N. D. Kelly, *Early Christian Creeds*, London 1972³, 268–72. For the connection with Lucian, ibid., 268: 'There is an ancient tradition that the creed of Lucian of Antioch underlies this formula, and the possibility that it has some link with him cannot be dismissed.' Reference to G. Bardy, *Recherches*, 85ff. But Kelly, op. cit., 270, stresses: 'Arianism proper is excluded, and the creed piles up descriptions of the Son as UNALTERABLE AND UNCHANGEABLE and WHO WAS IN THE BEGINNING WITH GOD, as well as putting a ban on several Arian doctrines in the concluding section of the anathemas.' But Kelly also rightly shows that the Arians could have digested this creed of Antioch by their own interpretation. He also shows the connections with Asterius and stresses the anti-Sabellian and anti-Marcellian character of the creed. The best explanation of the relationship of this creed to Lucian, Eusebius, Asterius and their views is that it comes from a common root, which Kelly, 271, describes as follows: 'Positively it has a markedly Origenist flavour, as indeed its use of Col. 1, 15 shows. Its guiding conception is of three quite separate hypostases, each possessing its own subsistence and rank and glory, but bound into a unity by a common harmony of will. This reproduces exactly what Origen had taught when he spoke of the Father and the Son as being "two things in subsistence, but one in agreement and harmony and identity of will". . . . The synod was working with a theology which, while by no means sympathetic to Arianism, was subordinationist and pre-Nicene.' The more we assume that Asterius had a hand in the formation of this creed, the more the pre-Nicene (Origenistic) character of his theology is confirmed, even after 335. For the idea of the harmony of the three hypostases in God according to Asterius cf. the index in Klostermann-Hansen, 254, συμφωνέω, συμφωνία.

[176] Cf. Socrates, HE I, 36: Hussey I, 164–5: *Asterius quidam in Cappadocia artem rhetoricam docens, ea relicta, Christianam religionem profiteri coepit. Libros etiam scribere aggressus est qui etiamnum habentur; quibus Arii dogma asserebat: Christum dicens esse virtutem Dei eodem modo, quo locusta et brucus apud Moysem virtus Dei esse dicitur: aliaque his similia. Versabatur autem assidue idem Asterius cum episcopis, ac praecipue cum illis qui opinionem Arii minime reiiciebant. Quin etiam ad synodos frequens ventabat, ad episcopatum cuiuspiam civitatis studens arrepere. Verum ille sacerdotium quidem minime est assecutus, eo quod persecutionis tempore sacrificasset. Urbes autem Syriae peragrans, libros quos composuerat, publice recitabat.* Cf. above Athanasius, *De synod.* 18, 2–3.

was held against him all his life by his opponents, and prevented him from being ordained or becoming a bishop.[177] Under the influence of his teacher, Lucian of Antioch,[178] he retracted his apostasy and repented. From this Antiochene circle he came into contact with the Alexandrian presbyter Arius and his friends. He himself became an Arian, as his *Syntagmation*, on which Athanasius had designs, and the scanty fragments transmitted by Marcellus of Ancyra, show.[179] These texts will be discussed in connection with Arianism. For the moment we shall attempt to demonstrate the christology of the homilies on the Psalms edited by M. Richard. In some respects they recall the tradition from Asia Minor which we already know, and in individual formulas they even recall the rhetoric and christology of Melito of Sardes. But we must pay closer attention to this context and justify it.[180]

In the first homily, over whose authenticity there is, of course, some doubt, we find the *testimonium* from Isa. 2. 3 which is often quoted in early christology, with a contrast of Nomos and Logos:

> And who else is this Nomos but Christ, the one who is inexpressibly begotten of the Father, who is not written on carved tables? For out of Sion goes forth the law and the Word of the Law from Jerusalem (Isa. 2. 3). He is called 'law' because he bears the Father's will in himself, and 'Logos' as the one who is inseparable from the Father.[181]

The statement about the inexpressible begetting of the Word is significant here, as it is surely quite un-Arian. Even if this text could not be attributed to Asterius, it has a parallel in Homily XVI, 8, which is regarded as genuine. In connection with Jer. 2. 21 (the planting of the fruitful vine) it reads: '. . . there came the only-begotten vine, which the Father had begotten above in an expressible way, who caused the virgin land below to spring forth without seed'.[182] This is an allusion to the begetting of the Son from the Father and the virgin birth of Jesus from Mary. In the continuation of this important sentence the soteriological and ecclesiological dimension of the incarnation is well expressed, in a thorough interpretation of the image of the vine and what happens to it:

[177] HE I, 36, further Athan., *De decr. Nic. syn.* 8: Opitz, AW II, 1, 3, p. 7²⁰ ('Αστέριος ὁ θύσας); *C. Arian.* II, 24: PG 26, 200A; *De synod.* 18; Opitz, AW II, 1, 9: pp. 245–6; Epiphan., *Haeres.* 76, 3: Holl, p. 343²³⁻⁴: apostasy under Maximian; Philostorgius, HE II, 14: Bidez–Winkelmann, 25.
[178] Philostorgius, HE II, 14: Bidez–Winkelmann, 25, where it is reported that Asterius came into the circle of Lucian of Antioch, whose members were Eusebius of Nicomedia, Maris of Chalcedon, Theognis of Nicaea, Leontius, later Bishop of Antioch, Antonius of Tarsus in Cilicia, Menophantus, Noominius and Eudoxius, and finally Alexander and Asterius: what follows seems to refer to the two latter: οὓς καὶ ἑλληνίσαι φησὶν ἐνδόντας τῇ τῶν τυράννων βίᾳ, ὕστερον δὲ ἀνακαλέσασθαι τὴν ἧτταν, συλλαβομένου πρὸς τὴν μετάνοιαν τοῦ διδασκάλου. See further G. Bardy, *Recherches*, 193–216.
[179] Cf. G. Bardy, op. cit., 341–54.
[180] In what follows we keep to the text of the edition of M. Richard; there are references to the teaching in G. Bardy, op. cit.; H. Auf der Maur, op. cit.; M.-J. Rondeau, 'Le "Commentaire des Psaumes" de Diodore de Tarse I–II', *RevHistRel* 176, 1969, 14, 161–5; III, 1970, 5f.
[181] *Hom.* I, 4: Richard, 28¹⁻¹³; for what follows cf. E. Skard, *Index Asterianus*, s. v. γεννάω, with reference to *Hom.* XVI: 1198: ἀφράστως ἐγέννησε.
[182] *Hom.* XVI, 6: Richard, 1197⁻⁹.

The vine came and brought forth the apostles as branches, the redeemed as shoots; he was pruned in suffering, received a cross as a stake (for support), was dug round with nails, pierced with the lance; he wept for the corruption of the Jews, was laid in the grave, sprouted forth again in the resurrection, bore the nations as grapes and filled the wine press of the church.[183]

This Hom. XVI is full of the early church's confession of Christ as the *Kyrios* of all realms of creation and all phases of history, just as the confession of 'God in the flesh' is expressed in Hom. II:

As indeed the crucified one was God in the flesh (θεὸς ἐν σαρκί) and the invisible one was mocked in his visible form, so the demons dealt with men, the bodiless ones with the fleshly nature against him together.[184]

On the other hand, the robber crucified with Christ was 'not disturbed that he had been nailed to the wood, but that the Son of God was crucified with robbers'. Therefore 'he also prayed to Christ as God'.[185] In the passion, Christ,

did not lose his divine power. Even when he hung on the cross, (as God) he bore heaven and earth (οὐρανὸν καὶ γὴν ὑπερεστήριξε).[186] Though he hung alongside robbers, he was marvelled at by the angels. Though he was derided by the Jews, he handed over the spirit to the Father. Though he was laid in the tomb, he emptied the rooms of Hades. And though he bore the fetters of the dead, he shattered the bonds of death. Though he was condemned by unbelievers, he will come as judge of the living and the dead. So what use was it for the godless, mere men, to fight against God?[187]

In these homilies, then, there lives on a tendency different from that of the Arianizing co-Lucianist Asterius. The gospel statements about Christ's humiliation, so carefully collected by the Arians, are not exploited so that the Godhead of Christ can be denied; rather, they are used to show that all that was human in Christ was borne by him as God.

When you hear that the creator of Adam was crucified, hung, nailed in the flesh, do not for that reason call him a 'mere man' (ψιλὸν ἄνθρωπον) but God, who took to himself in the flesh the suffering and death of the flesh.[188]

Throughout Hom. XXII Asterius is still fighting with the 'heretic' who says: the crucifixion cannot be predicated of the creator of Adam, i.e. of Christ as God, but only of a man. Asterius explains the teaching of

[183] Ibid., 119[9-15].
[184] *Hom.* II, 6: Richard, 6[17-20]; cf. II, 10 (8, 3) 'God entombed'; II, 16 (11[6]) 'Christ the transcenden king'.
[185] *Hom.* V, 19: Richard, 41[18-24].
[186] *Hom.* II, 19: Richard, 12[14-15]. This text is reminiscent of a homily influenced by Hippolytus' *Tractate on the Pasch*, ed. P. Nautin, *Homélies pascales* (SC 27), Paris 1950, no. 51, 177[21]-179[6]. The tree of the cross is στήριγμα τοῦ παντός; cf. ibid., no. 55, 3: p. 182: 'Toutes choses en effet étaient épouvantées et agitées par un tremblement de peur, tout était secoué, mais, quand à nouveau monta le divin Esprit (in the death of Christ: Luke 23. 46), l'univers en quelque sorte animé, vivifié et affermi (στηριζόμενον πάλιν ἔστη τὸ πᾶν) retrouva la stabilité.' Similarly Cyril Al., *Or. ad Augustas de fide* 17: ACO I, 1, 5, p. 34[21] (on Matt. 27. 46: στερεοῖ μὲν οὐρανοὺς τῷ ἰδίῳ πνεύματι).
[187] *Hom.* II, 19: Richard, 12[13-20].
[188] *Hom.* XXII, 3: Richard, 173[17-20]. This crucified one is ποιητὴς καὶ δημιουργὸς τοῦ Ἀδάμ (ibid., 172[25]).

the *communicatio idiomatum* completely in accord with the early Christian tradition (though without having a theory about it), and assigns all statements of humiliation, suffering and death to the body of Christ as the instrument of the suffering, but he allows God in Christ to be the subject of all suffering.[189]

The Sophist's confession clearly runs: '(In contrast to the Jews, who only look on the flesh and come to grief in the flesh) we look on God in the flesh and will rise for ever.'[190] Here we can probably detect the atmosphere of the struggle against Judaism and the doctrine of the 'mere man', which was ascribed to Paul of Samosata.[191] Equally clear is Hom. VIII, 10, where it is said of the burial and resurrection of Christ:

> Though he was buried as man, he rose as God. The grave was not able to hold God . . . Angels are at the grave, for God was laid in the grave. . . . Just as soldiers are not placed at the grave of a common man (ἰδιότης) (but only watch over the grave of a king), so angels do not sit at the tomb of a mere man.[192]

The resurrection is therefore the revelation of the deity of the crucified Christ—a connection with the earliest christology! Hom. X, 10 may be taken as the theme of such an understanding: 'In the morning the only-begotten God rose from the dead.'[193] In the Asterius of the Homilies, this title 'only-begotten Son' or above all 'only-begotten God' represents a clear confession of the Godhead of Christ, as far as it corresponded to the tradition of the pre-Arian period.[194] The same theme is expressed by the interpretation of the appearance of the risen Christ to Thomas and the doubter's confession:

> 'My Lord and my God' (John 20. 28). It was not enough simply to say 'My Lord', as a man would have been honoured by this address (reference to Gen. 18. 12; 33. 13). . . . None of the saints said to a man 'my God'. . . . With this 'my God', Thomas shows that

[189] Hom. XXII, 5: Richard, 172[1-2]: Κἂν τὸ σῶμα ἐσταυροῦτο, ἀλλ᾽ ὁ κύριος τῆς δόξης ἐκρέματο. This is amplified still further.

[190] Ibid., 7: 174[21-2].   [191] Cf. Hom. VIII, 10: Richard, 68[6].   [192] Ibid., 67[22]-68[7].

[193] Hom. X, 10: Richard, 74[13-14]: ὁ μονογενὴς θεὸς ὄρθρου ἐκ νεκρῶν ἀνιστάμενος. It is unnecessary to follow E. Skard, SymbOsl 20, 1940, 131, in supposing Arianism here: 'And now it has been demonstrated that this very reading—ὁ μονογενὴς θεός—corresponds to the Arian view, and indeed to the view of the Arian Asterius.' No significance can be attached to the choice of μ.θ. instead of μ. υἱός in this context. Cf. R. Schnackenburg, The Gospel according to John I, London 1968, 280: 'The weight of the testimonies is in favour of θεός. . . .'

[194] In Hom. II, 17: Richard, 11[26f.], Christ is named 'only-begotten king', against whom five kings had conspired to challenge his royal status. In Hom. VIII, 1: Richard 63[7], we find Christ named the 'only-begotten bridegroom and heir of the Father'. In Hom. XVI, 8: Richard, 125[26]: Christ is addressed as 'Kyrios, only-begotten Son'. Thus Asterius also knows the reading μονογενὴς υἱός (cf. n. 193 above). Hom. XVIII, 14: Richard, 132[10-11] is particularly clear: Καὶ τίς ὁ υἱός; Ὁ μονογενὴς θεὸς λόγος, ὁ τοῦ πατρὸς υἱὸς [ὁμοούσιος], ὁ τοῦ κόσμου ποιητής. According to the context, this Sonship is confirmed (mutually) by both the Father and the Son. For homoousios in this passage see n. 172 above. As in some readings of John 1. 18, the title μονογενής is also used absolutely in Asterius. The church of Christ is called 'the bride of the only-begotten' (Hom. XXX, 1: Richard, 239[18-19]). There are also connections with metaphorical statements. The 'only-begotten as the door to the Father, indeed the only gateway': Hom. XXVII, 1: Richard, 214[18-20]. Certainly the title 'only-begotten of God' could be interpreted among the Arians in the sense of 'the first creation of God'. But there is no evidence of this in the homilies.

he did not call Christ Lord as man, but as God. He does not just say 'my Lord', but 'My Lord and my God'; 'my Lord', because you have bought me with your own blood, me who was destroyed through sin. 'My God', as the one who has given me forgiveness of sins. No one can forgive sins but only God (εἰ μὴ εἷς ὁ θεός). 'My Lord and my God' instead of 'My Master and my Creator' (ὁ δεσπότης μου καὶ ὁ δημιουργός μου). Many people rule; of course only God creates.[195]

Could the author of these homilies speak in this way after he had been through all the problems of the Arian controversy and had even himself gone over to Arianism? Or would he not have been concerned to communicate Arian ideas secretly to his audience? If so, he would not have refrained from bringing Prov. 8. 22, that favourite Arian verse, into his explanation when he mentioned Prov. 8 in Hom. XXI, 12. But he is content with vv. 23 and 25. He explains why the day of the resurrection is counted as the eighth day, and gives an interpretation of the Christian week: the *first* day of Christ is his birth before time, 'not as though there was a day before the conception of Christ, but because this birth of Christ before time (ἡ τοῦ Χριστοῦ πρὸ αἰώνων γέννησις) was called "day", as he himself says, "I am the light of the world" (John 8. 12)'. Even if one could read out of these words a connection between the conception of Christ and God's decision to create the world, one could not speak here of the Logos being 'created' as the first of creatures, because v. 22 is passed over. The *second* day of Christ is his birth from the Virgin according to the flesh (in the mention of the first and second births the word γέννησις is used, and in both instances it must be translated 'conception' or 'birth'). The *third* day of Christ is his revelation in the miracles, the theme of the epiphany. The *fourth* day, in the middle of the ogdoad, is the raising of Lazarus. The *fifth* day is the institution of the eucharist. The *sixth* day—a counterpart to the day on which man was created in God's six days of labour—is the day of Christ's death upon the cross. The rest in the grave on the *seventh* day corresponds to God's day of rest in the hexahemeron. The *eighth* day, a *novitas Christiana*, is the day of the resurrection.[196]

This christology has a soteriological and eschatological orientation, and is set against a Jewish–Christian background.[197] With the Arian Asterius we are far removed from the problems which were introduced through Marcellus of Ancyra. An 'eternal significance' is accorded to the humanity of the risen Christ without special reflection. He, the 'heir of the Father', hands over his heritage, his *kleronomia*, to the church; indeed, in his own risen glory he is the most glorious part of this heritage:

---

[195] *Hom.* VI, 16: Richard, 52[17]–53[6].

[196] *Hom.* XXI, 12: Richard, 165[6]–166[9]. Cf. Auf der Maur, *Die Osterhomilien*, 24–8.

[197] For this background, cf. Auf der Maur, op. cit., 10f. But the reference to Athanasius, *Or. c. Arian.* III, 2: PG 26, 324C–325A, where Athanasius accuses Asterius of 'imitating the Jews' in his Arianizing interpretation of John 14. 20 ('I in the Father and the Father in me'), is unjustified. For it is common practice to accuse those who deny the Godhead of Christ of 'Judaism', e.g. Paul of Samosata as a follower of Ebion.

Christ, the only-begotten bridegroom and heir of the Father, showed to his bride the church after his death and burial his riches and his heritage in the resurrection, that is, the gospel and the kingdom.[198]

In Hom. VI, 1, the preacher asks who the 'heir' is, in accordance with the title of Ps. 5. 1 (Εἰς τὸ τέλος, ὑπὲρ τῆς κληρονομούσης). He answers: 'The church. And why did he (the Psalmist) not say: for the heiress (ὑπὲρ τῆς κληρονόμου)? Because she is always in the process of inheriting. And the queen (i.e. the church) inherits much, the souls of the faithful, the patriarchs, the prophets, Christ, heaven.'[199] Thus Christ is incorporated very well into the church of eternity, and also into the whole of salvation history. However, Irenaeus' idea of anakephalaiosis is missing.

This much is clear: the content and diction of the christology of these homilies points to the period before Nicaea. There is no indication that their author has gone through a difficult crisis of faith. They do not betray the fact that the kerygma of the church has entered the phase of critical reflection, unless there is some indication of the emergency that was called forth by the ψιλὸς ἄνθρωπος of Paul of Samosata.

4. APHRAHAT THE PERSIAN SAGE

Attention should be drawn to one further figure from the period of transition between the third and the fourth centuries, who does not otherwise fit into further developments during the fourth century. It is all the more significant that he belongs to the Eastern, Semitic circle of tradition, which retained relative autonomy in comparison with the Greek West and had virtually no contact at all with the still more distant Latin West. This figure is Aphrahat the Persian sage (born between 270 and 285 and died after 345).[200]

As can be seen from the studies of Ortiz de Urbina and A. Vööbus, Aphrahat's writing contains various efforts at christology. They need not and should not be brought forcibly under one heading, nor should they be treated in isolation or played off one against the other, say to the

---

[198] Hom. VIII, 1: Richard 636⁻¹⁰. For kleronomia cf. the index of E. Skard and Lampe, s.v. Melito developed the dark counterpart of the consequences of Adam's sin under the heading of the same word. Cf. A. Grillmeier, ' "Das Erbe der Söhne Adams" in der Homilia de Passione Melitos', Schol 20–4, 1944–49, 481–502.

[199] Hom. VI, 1: Richard, 45⁸⁻¹⁵.

[200] For the biography of Aphrahat and bibliography on him see A. Vööbus, 'Aphrahat', JAC 3, 1960, 152–5; id., 'Methodologisches zum Studium der Anweisungen Aphrahats', OrChr 46, 1962, 25–32; the chief tendencies of Aphrahat's christology are briefly discussed here. For more detail see I. Ortiz de Urbina, S.J., Die Gottheit Christi bei Afrahat (OC 31), Roma 1933; A. Hudal, 'Zur Christologie bei Afrahates Syrus', TG 3, 1911, 477–87; J. Neusner, Aphrahat and Judaism (Studia Post-Biblica 19), Leiden 1971, esp. ch. 7, 68–75: Dem. XVII, 'On the Messiah. That he is the Son of God'. For christological terminology cf. A. F. J. Klijn, 'The Word kᵉjān in Aphraates', VigC 12, 1958, 57–66. We follow the Syriac text with a Latin translation by I. Parisot, Aphraatis Sapientis Persae Demonstrationes: PSyr I 1 and 2, Paris 1894 and 1907. Cf. the German translation by G. Bert, Aphrahat's des Persischen Weisen Homilien (TU 3), Leipzig 1888.

effect that in Aphrahat we have a trustworthy witness to an independent
tradition alive outside the main Greek and Latin church,[201] which still
knows nothing of a 'Godhead' of Christ as understood by the early
councils or even by the teaching of the church before Nicaea. The occasion
for assertions of this kind is his 'Instruction' (*Demonstrationes* = *tahwiatē*)
XVII.[202] Though Christ is called God here, this designation should not be
taken in the strict Nicene sense. The Council of Nicaea is not mentioned
by Aphrahat, nor are its central statements like 'identical in substance' or
'true God of true God'. His opponents are not the Arians, but the Jews.
Their charge runs: 'You (Christians) worship and serve a human being
begotten and a crucified man; and you call a son of man "God". And
although God has no son, you say, "This crucified Jesus is the Son, the
Son of God . . ."'[203] The following section may indicate the ante-Nicene
manner of Aphrahat's answer:

> Against this, my dear people, I shall prove to you as well as I can, and as far as my
> weakness allows, that if we grant them that he (Jesus) is a child of man, and if we also
> worship him and call him 'God' (*Alahā*) and 'Lord' (*Maryā*), we do not give him these
> titles in any peculiar way, and we do not attach to him any strange names of which they
> (the Jews) do not make use. But it is certain for us that Jesus, our Lord, is God (*Alahā*),
> Son of God (*Bar Alahā*) and king, prince, light of light, creator (*Barē*) and counsellor and
> leader and way aud redeemer and shepherd and gatherer and gate and pearl and lamp;
> and with many names is he named. But we shall now leave all these on one side, and prove
> that he is Son of God, and that he is God, who has come from God.[204]

To demonstrate the justification of his presentation, Aphrahat
adduces examples from Holy Scripture in which God himself has used
such terminology towards men: 'We call him God like Moses, and firstborn and son like Israel, and a great prophet like all the prophets.'[205] This
is probably no more than an *argumentum ad hominem* against the Jews.
It is simply a 'manner of speaking'. It does not mean that Aphrahat will
have understood his own remarks on the same level.

Aphrahat's subordinationism, like his name christology, is also ante-
Nicene. It is quite clearly expressed in the typological explanations of
Jacob's vision of the heavenly ladder:

> *Sed et scala ipsa quam Iacob vidit, Salvatoris nostri mysterium est, per quem homines iusti ab
> imo sursum ascendunt. Mysterium insuper est crucis Salvatoris nostri, quae ad modum scalae
> erecta fuit, et in cuius summo Dominus ('God the Father' is meant) stabat. Nam* supra
> Christum *exstat Dominus omnium, quemadmodum beatus Apostulus dixit:* Caput Christi
> Deus est (I Cor. XI: 3).[206]

---

[201] This isolation of the East Syrian church is stressed especially by F. C. Burkitt, *Early Christianity
outside the Roman Empire*, Cambridge 1899.
[202] Cf. J. Neusner, op. cit., and also I. Ortiz de Urbina, op. cit., 48–69.
[203] *Dem.* XVII, 1: PSyr I, 784.
[204] *Dem.* XVII, 2: PSyr I, 785–88.
[205] *Dem.* XVII, 11: PSyr I, 813.
[206] *Dem.* IV, 5: PSyr I, 145–6; cf. A. Vööbus, OrChr 46, 1962, 26.

F. Loofs has taken Aphrahat as a witness to early Christian spirit christology.[207] He thinks that Aphrahat does not know of the deity of Christ as a divine hypostasis. In fact, there are statements which indicate a marked spirit christology.[208] It should be noted that the spirit which dwells in Christ has also been given to us. We surely have in part a complex of statements which coincide with the communication of the spirit to Christ and believers in the biblical economy of salvation. To want to argue from that that according to Aphrahat Christ is not 'God', but merely the dwelling-place of the spirit, would be to overlook other elements which Aphrahat shares with the tradition of the early church.[209] Within the framework of a christology of humiliation and exaltation we find the foundations which allow us to assume in Aphrahat belief in the pre-existence of Christ, in the incarnation and the exaltation. Here is the pre-existent Son of God who took the form of a slave and brought his manhood with him to the throne of glory. We are reminded of Phil. 2. 5–11, in the framework of an admonition to the monks:

> *Exemplum ergo accipiamus, carissime, a Vivificatore nostro, qui, cum dives esset, se ipsum pauperem effecit (cf. 2 Cor. VIII: 9): Altissimus maiestatem suam demisit; in excelsis habitans non habuit locum ubi caput reclinaret (cf. Matt. VIII: 20); in nubibus quondam venturus, pullo asinae insedit, ut Ierosolymam intraret; Deus et Dei Filius formam servi accepit (Phil. II: 7). . . . Cui in tabernaculo Patris sui ministrabatur, ipse hominum ministerium accepit. . . . Cunctorum mortalium Vivificator seipsum morti crucis tradidit.*[210]

The introduction of the word *k^ejān (kyanā)* in Aphrahat is significant for the history of christological language; all the more since—as has been asserted—he had little contact with Hellenistic culture. The sources from which Aphrahat seems to have taken this word are the NT and the Odes of Solomon. Where the Greek physis occurs in the NT it is regularly translated by *k^ejān* in Syriac.[211] For Aphrahat's non-theological christo-

---

[207] Cf. F. Loofs, *Theophilus von Antiochien adversus Marcionem* (TU 46, 2), Leipzig 1930, 257–99. There is a short summary in I. Ortiz de Urbina, op. cit., 8of. and 124–38. See M. Simonetti, 'Note di cristologia pneumatica', *Aug* 12, 1972, 201–32.

[208] Cf. *Dem.* VI, 14: PSyr I, 293/4; and on this the observations by Parisot, ibid., LVI–LVII; I. Ortiz de Urbina, op. cit., 124–38. We cannot go into Aphrahat's difficult doctrine of the *pneuma* here. Cf. especially *Dem.* VI, 14: PSyr I, 292–7.

[209] Cf. the texts which I. Ortiz de Urbina, op. cit., 110–11, has set in parallel: PSyr I, 276²³–281⁸ and 420¹⁵–421⁵, and II, 96⁹–100⁹.

[210] *Dem.* VI, 9: PSyr I, 275–8.

[211] So according to A. F. J. Klijn, 58, whose findings we presuppose here. Klijn notes on the etymology and the semantics: 'The word *k^ejān* is derived from the verb *kun*, to be translated by "to be" or "to exist". Thus literally the word *k^ejān* means "being", "existing", "existence". . . . *K^ejān* being taken in the sense of "existence" or "being" means a strikingly exact equivalent for the word φύσις. This word is derived from the root φυ–, meaning "to be" and may be translated by τὸ εἶναι.' In this connection Klijn points to the great breadth of variation in the significance of this word φύσις, following the study by D. Holwerda, *Commentatio de Vocis quae est ΦΥΣΙΣ Vi atque Usu Praesertim in Graecitate Aristotele Anteriore*, Groningae 1955. According to Holwerda, possibilities of translating φύσις extend from *condicio, status, compositio* to *sors* and *forma* (op. cit., 140–2). 'This summary of possibilities shows that the word φύσις may point to something existing within somebody or something which happens to be. Thus we are dealing with a word rendering the idea *essentia* in its widest sense' (Klijn, op. cit., 58–9). Klijn further remarks that the translators do not render *k^ejān* in Aphrahat consistently: Bert translated it with 'nature', not making any distinction;

logical terminology $k^e j\bar{a}n$ never means abstract substance, though this is possible for *physis* (as e.g. in 2 Peter 1. 3). Rather, it renders the 'empirical situation' or 'the thing observed by men'.[212] In theological and christological sections, on the other hand, $k^e j\bar{a}n$ is often used where there is mention of humility (e.g. in connection with Matt. 23. 22)[213] and also in texts which discuss 1 Cor. 15. For these passages we should not go back to the Greek meaning of *physis*: 'The Greek word φύσις, though varying in meaning, always shows a tendency to define the essence of somebody or something. The phenomena are deducted to reach the unchangeable reality, the things always present.'[214] In fact we should not look for any 'doctrine of two natures' in Aphrahat, in the technical sense of the controversy before and after Chalcedon. $K^e j\bar{a}n$ must be defined in the Semitic way of approaching the concept of being. 'In Aphraates $k^e j\bar{a}n$, the existence of somebody or something, is defined by the way it appears to men. . . .'[215] Nevertheless, in the end the being of a person or of something is affected. 'To fall in the dust' or 'to be glorified' are realities which affect most profoundly the corporeality of Adam and of Christ, to such an extent that the one is native ($k^e j\bar{a}n$) to sinful Adam and the other to the humbled Christ. But if 'glory' is 'native' to the corporeality of Christ

---

Parisot chose between *condicio, status* and *sors*: Ortiz de Urbina conjectured nature, property, state, mode of being and life, action, sphere of nature. 'His summary of possibilities, however, only shows a very limited picture of Aphraates' use of this word.' So Klijn investigates all individual meanings in non-theological (or christological) and properly theological and christological sections.

[212] See Klijn, op. cit., 59–61.

[213] Cf. *Dem.* VI, 10: PSyr I, 277/8: Christ's humility is taken as an example: *Cum Dominus noster extra naturam suam (men $k^e j\bar{a}neh$) venit, in nostra natura (bekjānan) ambulavit. Maneamus autem nos in condicione nostra naturali (bekjānan), ut in die iustitiae naturae suae (lakjāneh) consortes nos efficiat. Dem.* VI, 19: 279/80: *Quod nostrum est, in honore apud illum habetur* (i.e. our corporeality, in the exaltation of Christ), *quanquam non in nostra (sit) natura ($d^e al$ bakjānan); quod eius est, in ipsius natura (bakjan'ā) cohonestemus.* Ortiz de Urbina, op. cit., 100, translated $k^e j\bar{a}n$ here as 'manner of being', which certainly accords with Aphrahat's intention, but still does not meet with Klijn's approval: 'We may notice, however, that we are not dealing in these passages with a way of being, but with a situation in which Christ and men happen to be. On the analogy of what is said about the non-christological passages, we may translate "reality belonging to Christ and men" or "the existence belonging to Christ or men".' But perhaps 'state', *condicio*, would be a better word here. Our manhood is exalted in Christ to God; not, however, in the condition of our lowliness and transitoriness, but in the state of exaltation and glory which come to Christ. Thus the text which Klijn, p. 62, cites from *Dem.* IX, 6, 421–2. 'Situation' would be too external here. When in *Dem.* IX, 14, 439/40, Aphrahat speaks of Adam's unbecoming struggle and the punishment which follows it, he again mentions the opposed conduct of Christ and God's reward: *Adam exaltavit se et humiliatus est, ac pulveri naturae suae (l'afr'ā lakjāneh quadmāj'ā) pristinae redditus. Salvator noster gloriosus atque inclitus se humiliavit; exaltatus est autem, et ad naturam suam priorem (lakjāneh hu qadmāj'ā) evectus, gloriaque ampliatus et cuncta ei subiecta sunt. Salvator, quia seipsum humiliavit, gloriam suscepit et incremento auctus est* (we have cited the text in more detail than Klijn). Klijn's view is (p. 62): 'This is sufficient to get an insight of what is meant by $k^e j\bar{a}n$ here. Dealing with Christ and men we may discern two data, two phenomena, viz. heaven and earth. Adam's sin was his not abiding to his datum.' Here again Klijn takes $k^e j\bar{a}n$ in too external a way. Adam strove to be like God, although God would have given him a chance to reach a higher status through obedience (*ut, imperio perfecte servato, ad statum superiorem a Domino eveheretur*) (IX, 14: 439/40). But because of his sin he is *pulveri naturae suae pristinae redditus.* 'To become dust' corresponds to his real *condicio*, his natural status. Christ acted in the opposite way, and so he meets with the opposite destiny, that is, after his humiliation he receives the glory that is his own. In Adam and in Christ, returning to dust or being glorified profoundly affect their respective humanity, and this is in accord with their due from the beginning.

[214] A. F. J. Klijn, op. cit., 66.

[215] Ibid.

which he has taken from us, then also, according to Aphrahat, this is because it is a matter of the Son who comes from the glory of the Father, who has assumed our corporeality (*Dem.* VI, 9 and 10).

This archaic christology of Aphrahat, this fourth-century theologian, with all its differentiations, enriches the picture of the highly significant period of theology that we have been considering. In its main content it points backwards rather than forwards. But in its language it has taken up a word that was to make history in the region of Syria. Even in its own particular Semitic meaning, *kᵉjān* as a christological word bears witness that a bridge had to be built towards the Greeks.

The result of this short investigation of christology between Origen and Nicaea is to some degree disappointing or even confusing. We find quite different 'christologies', which can hardly be brought together under the same heading. But we should not forget that from the time of the Apologists we are really moving on two different levels: first on the level of preaching and catechetics, which is stressed especially by Origen and is still evident in Asterius and Aphrahat, and secondly on the level of a reflection which Origen also cultivated in a special way, and which we find above all in Eusebius of Caesarea.

Two forms of christology seem to have begun to develop between Origen and Nicaea: as a kind of working hypothesis we may name them Logos-sarx christology and Logos-anthropos christology. This contrast between Logos-sarx christology and Logos-anthropos christology does not entirely coincide with the usual distinction between 'Alexandrian' and 'Antiochene' christology. Useful as such a classification of christological views may be, it does only partial justice to the real state of affairs. The historical reality is far more complicated than the division between Alexandria and Antioch might suggest. When we pursue all the traces of the development we find that Antioch and its surroundings has a special part in the history of Logos-sarx christology. To avoid misunderstanding, let us state that we see the real classical period of christology without a soul of Christ in the time of the second generation of Arianism and in the time of Apollinarianism. But there are some clear indications that the beginnings of this christology lie earlier. At any rate, the presence and strength of such an interpretation of Christ will remind us of the particular views of a large body of theologians in the fourth century. No century was so multicoloured and so polymorphous in its theology as the fourth.

CHAPTER TWO

ARIUS AND ARIANISM

THE arrival of Arius (born in Libya, according to some about 256 and according to others about 260, died 336) in Alexandria inevitably led to a break in the theological twilight of the period after Origen.[1] He ventured to put forward a one-sided solution to the half-measures of the sub-ordinationism of the pre-Nicene *théologie savante*, and this in turn called forth a reaction from the church. Because of the intervention of Constantine and his imperial power, which had created a new situation for Christianity, for the first time, this dispute had dynamics which were to be paradigmatic for the future. This is something that we shall have to discuss. But here we are primarily interested in the significance of the controversy between Arians and anti-Arians for Christian monotheism, and especially for the doctrines of the Logos and the incarnation.

1. THE FATHER AND HIS LOGOS

To begin with, mention should be made of the problems of research into Arianism, as far as they are relevant here. A first group of questions relates to the time at which Arianism began and its development up to the time of Nicaea. Interpreting the content of Arian doctrine does not depend overmuch on an answer to this question. Here we shall use the chronology sketched out by W. Schneemelcher, in the steps of H. G. Opitz.[2] Both assume that the starting point for establishing the chronology

---

[1] For biographical information on Arius, cf. F. Loofs, 'Arianismus', *PRE* 2, 1897, 6–45, with earlier literature; F. Cavallera, 'Arianisme', *DictHGE* 4, 1930, 103–13 with lit.; R. Aigrain, 'Arius', ibid., 208–15; G. Gentz, 'Arianer', *RAC* 1, 1950, 647–51; T. Camelot, 'Areios', *LThK³* 1, 1957, 829–30 with details of the patristic sources; J. Liébaert, 'Arianismus', *LThK³* 1, 1957, 842–8; J. Quasten, *Patrology* III, 1963, 7–13; H. M. Gwatkin, *Studies of Arianism*, Cambridge 1900; G. Bardy, *Recherches sur saint Lucien d'Antioche et son école*, Paris 1936, 217–95 (hereafter cited as Bardy, *Lucien*); É. Boularand, S.J., *L'hérésie d'Arius et la 'Foi' de Nicée I: L'hérésie d'Arius*, Paris 1972, 9–37. For the 'Judas death' of Arius (analogous to Acts 1. 18), cf. Athan., *Ep. ad eppos Aeg. et Lib.*: PG 25, 580; Socrates, HE I, 38: Hussey I, 169–72. For a criticism of this tradition see O. Seeck, 'Untersuchungen zur Geschichte des Nicänischen Konzils', *ZKG* 17, 1897, 34–41; id., ' "Urkundenfälschungen" des IV Jahrhunderts 2', *ZKG* 30, 1909, 429; Alice Leroy-Molinghen, 'La mort d'Arius', *Byz* 38, 1968, 105–11, with a discussion of the different patristic evidence. Attention should also be drawn to the *Enarrationes breves chronographicae* of the eighth or ninth century with a description of the notable sights in the Forum Constantini at Constantinople (the death of Arius is said to have taken place in this neighbourhood). Among them mention is made of the marble bas-reliefs of Arius, Sabellius, Macedonius and Eunomius which were disfigured in all kinds of ways. Cf. T. Preger, *Scriptores origin. Constantinop.* I, Lipsiae 1901, 43¹⁶–44¹²; II, 173.

[2] W. Schneemelcher, 'Zur Chronologie des arianischen Streites', *ThLZ* 79, 1954, 393–400. For earlier discussion see L. Nain de Tillemont, *Memoires pour servir à l'histoire ecclésiastique* 6, Paris 1704, 239–633; C. W. F. Walch, *Entwurf einer vollständigen Historie der Kezereien* 2, Leipzig 1764, 385–700; O. Seeck, 'Untersuchungen zur Geschichte des Nicänischen Konzils', *ZKG* 16, 1896, 1–71, 319–62; also a partial retraction, id., 'Die Urkunden der *Vita Constantini*', *ZKG* 18, 1898, 321–45; E. Schwartz, 'Zur Geschichte des Athanasius', 6, SbGesGött. (Phil. hist. Kl. 1905), 257–99, now in: *Gesammelte*

of the dispute must be the date of Constantine's victory over Licinius, i.e. the year 324. Immediately after this victory, Constantine had written to Alexander of Alexandria and to Arius.

... When Constantine ... intervened in these disputes they were already in full swing. Various synods had taken place. Letters had been exchanged, and so on. All this could hardly have happened within the space of a few weeks or months. As Opitz has rightly pointed out, the *terminus post quem* can be discovered from the subscriptions to the synods of Ancyra and Caesarea, that is, after 314–7.[3]

A second group of questions is more significant for us. At the same time it is more difficult, because it is very complex. These questions involve the cultural background and leading influences on Arius: (1) The place of the Bible in his system and the origin of his exegetical method, whether this was the allegorical method of Alexandria or the literal method of Lucian of Antioch; (2) The influence of various theological traditions before him: Philo, the Alexandrians or even Paul of Samosata; (3) The place of theology in Arius; (4) The different weight to be attached to these various influences. What made up the real originality of Arius, if we are to suppose that he was original? These questions are difficult to solve because, quite apart from the scarceness of Arian texts, the various source-areas of Arian theology seem to be so interconnected that one cannot be separated from another.[4] But this was already a datum of the tradition before him. The

Schriften 3, Berlin 1959, 117–68; id., 'Das antiochenische Synodalschreiben von 325', SBGesGött. 1908, 305–74; extracts consisting of pp. 354–9, 365–74, are reprinted in *Gesamm. Schr.* 3, 169–87. For the discussion with Seeck see P. Snellman, *Der Anfang des arianischen Streites. Ein Beitrag zur Geschichte des Streites*, Helsingfors 1904; S. Rogala, *Die Anfänge des arianischen Streites*, Paderborn 1907. For more recent discussion see H. G. Opitz, 'Die Zeitfolge des arianischen Streites von den Anfängen bis zum Jahre 328', *ZNW* 33, 1934, 131–59; W. Telfer, 'When did the Arian Controversy begin?', *JTS* 47, 1946, 129–42; N. H. Baynes, 'Sozomen, *Ecclesiastica Historia* I 15', *JTS* 50, 1949, 187–91. For documentation see H. Opitz, *AW* III, 1, 1–2: *Urkunden zur Geschichte des arianischen Streites*; see the survey of the content of the documents between 318 and 333, pp. 75f.; H. Dörrie, *Das Selbstzeugnis Kaiser Konstantins*, AbhAkWissGött. (Phil.-hist Kl. 3.F.,no 34), Göttingen 1954; H. Kraft, *Kaiser Konstantins religiöse Entwicklung* (BHistTh 20), Tübingen 1955.

[3] W. Schneemelcher, op. cit., 394, where reference is made to Tillemont (see n. 2 above) who accepts about seven years for the controversy before Nicaea. E. Schwartz, *Ges. Schr.* 3, 167: all the documents relating to the Arian dispute can be brought 'without trouble' into the period between autumn 323 and the beginning of 325, that is, within eighteen months. W. Telfer conjectures a twenty-two month chronology (on the basis of a 'very negative interpretation of Sozomen I 15'). Another argument for Telfer was the fact that Athanasius, *C. Gentes, De Incarn.* contained no allusions to the controversy and therefore must have been written before it began. In between, 336 has been taken as a time for the composition of these writings. Cf. C. Kannengiesser, 'Le témoignage des Lettres festales de Saint Athanase sur la date de l'Apologie Contre les Païens—Sur l'Incarnation du Verbe', *RSR* 53, 1964, 91–100; id., 'La date de l'Apologie d'Athanase Contre Les Païens et Sur l'Incarnation du Verbe', *RSR* 58, 1970, 383–428. H. Nordberg, *Athanasius' tractates* Contra Gentes *and* De Incarnatione. *An attempt at redating* (SocScFenn. Comm. hum. litt. 28, 3), Helsinki 1961, had even proposed the year 362 for these writings, but that is unacceptable.

[4] In a number of writings T. E. Pollard has put forward the thesis that in his exegetical method Arius is dependent on the 'literalism' of Lucian of Antioch. Furthermore, the strong stress on the unity and absolute transcendence of God does not fit in with the trinitarian pluralism of Origen and the Alexandrians. The distinction made by Arius between the Logos immanent in God and the 'Son' who is not 'Logos' by nature, but only through participation, and indeed can only be given this title by an abuse of the word, is also claimed to be un-Alexandrian: 'Logos and Son in Origen, Arius and Athanasius', *StudPat* II, 1957, 282–7; 'The Origins of Arianism', *JTS* 9, 1958, 103–11; 'The Exegesis of Scripture and the Arian Controversy', *BJRL* 41, 1958/59, 414–29.

For a challenge to Pollard see M. Wiles, 'In Defence of Arius', *JTS* 13, 1962, 339–47; here Pollard's remarkable thing about Arius is that while he always began from the Christian kerygma, he was always concerned to clarify the tensions present in pre-Nicene theology and its subordinationism. He relaxed this tension, but did so in such a way that he made the existing tradition more pointed where it was in line with his own ideas (here the influence of philosophy was particularly virulent) or expressly refuted it where it was opposed to him. And here we come up against a piece of evidence which seems to have been a particular stumbling block for him.

When Arius was elevated to the priesthood, he was commissioned to expound the scriptures,[5] probably in the 'pastorate' of Baukalis in Alexandria. He was one of those people who are able to produce both vigorous supporters and vigorous opponents among their audience. This led to charges against him being laid with Bishop Alexander. The arguments of Arius which we find, for example, in a letter sent by him and

three arguments for his thesis are rejected, although Wiles also assumes that with Peter of Alexandria an anti-Origenistic reaction set in which also extended to the sphere of exegetical method. Nevertheless, the teaching of Arius can be explained from its Alexandrian milieu. G. C. Stead, 'The Platonism of Arius', *JTS* 15, 1964, 16–31; F. Ricken, 'Nikaia als Krisis des altchristlichen Platonismus', *TheolPhil* 44, 1969, 321–41: both authors point to (Middle) Platonism as a source of Arian philosophy. For Stead, Arian theology—with an ingredient from Methodius—can be explained in terms of the Origenist milieu, though the differences in this area should be noted: Arius made the subordinationism of Origen more radical. Ricken extends the historical background of Arius' philosophy in the direction indicated by Stead. L. W. Barnard, 'The Antecedents of Arius', *VigC* 24, 1970, 172–88; id., 'What was Arius' Philosophy?', *TZ* 28, 1972, 110–17: Athenagoras is important for Arius' monad doctrine, and he was of Alexandrian and not Athenian origin. Arius took his subordinationism from Origen, the doctrine that the Logos is a ποίημα and κτίσμα from Dionysius of Alexandria and Theognostus, his anti-allegorical views from Peter of Alexandria, and he combined all these predominantly Alexandrian influences into an organic whole, even if they were disparate. Over against his critics Wiles and Stead, Pollard stresses in *Johannine Christology and the Early Church*, Cambridge 1970, 141–6 that in Egypt Arius encountered a fundamentally hostile attitude, unlike that of the disciples of Lucian of Antioch; the special influences on Arian thought must therefore be sought in a tradition existing in the latter place, albeit not identical with that of Marcellus of Ancyra and Eustathius. For the whole debate see M. Simonetti, 'Le origini dell'arianesimo', *Rivista di Storia e Letteratura Religiosa* 7, 1971, 317–30. According to Simonetti, the anti-Origenist trend in Alexandria (with Peter of Alexandria) should not be pictured in too strong terms. As has already been stressed above, it can be found above all in connection with the pre-existence of souls. As we have already seen, despite his peculiarities Arius can be accommodated in the Alexandrian tradition. How he used it, sieved it or even distorted it, becomes clear against the background of what has been said and in the following account, which largely agrees with the results of the studies by M. Simonetti, G. C. Stead, M. F. Wiles and F. Ricken. We shall, however, examine the *Thaleia* for its (negative, contrary) relationship to Gregory Thaumaturgus. Another important work is É. Boularand, *L'hérésie d'Arius et la 'Foi' de Nicée* I, Paris 1972, 67–174, who investigates in turn: (1) the biblical starting point; (2) the connection between Arianism and the religion of the '*summus deus*' (which was also discussed by H. M. Gwatkin, A. Harnack, P. Batiffol, J. Zeiler, J. Carcopino, each in a different way); (3) the philosophical sources, which include Philo, the Stoic Logos, Plato's demiurge, Aristotle, Gnosticism; (4) the Alexandrian theologians (Origen, Dionysius of Alexandria); and finally (5) the Antiochene tradition. Boularand agrees with Pollard's argument that the doctrine of the oneness and transcendence of God is set over against the pluralism of Origen and is thus dependent on strict Antiochene monarchianism. See also H. I. Marrou, 'L'Arianisme comme phénomène alexandrin', a contribution to the *Seixième Centenaire d'Athanase d'Alexandrie 373–1973*, Paris-Chantilly 1973. He points to Epiphanius, *Pan.* 69, 2, and Socrates, HE, V, 22, and to the two positions of Dionysius of Alexandria (see above) to characterize the *Alexandrian* milieu of Arius.

[5] Theodoret, HE, I, 1: Parmentier 6¹⁵⁻¹⁶: . . . τὴν δὲ θείων γράφων πεπιστευμένος ἐξήγησιν (under Bishop Achillas). Cf. É. Boularand, op. cit., I, 86–93. For the exegesis of Arius, cf. M. Simonetti, *Studi sull'Arianesimo* (Verba Seniorum NS 5), Roma 1965, 9–87: 'Sull'interpretazione patristica di Proverbi 8, 22'; for Arius: 32–37.

Euzoius to the emperor Constantine indicate his biblical starting point. This letter contains a confession in which he derives his belief in the Father, the Son and the Holy Spirit from the gospels, and especially from Matt. 28. 19:

> We have received this belief from the holy gospels, as the Lord says to his disciples: 'Go and make disciples of all nations and baptize them in the name of the Father, the Son and the Holy Spirit.' But if we do not believe this and do not truly accept Father and Son and Holy Spirit as the whole Catholic church and the scriptures teach, which we believe in all things, then God (ὁ θεός = the Father) is our judge now and on the day to come.[6]

Although further explanation of this confession sounds very suspicious there can be no doubt that this forms the framework for all Arius' theological reflections. Later developments in the Arian dispute produced on either side a dossier of scriptural passages which were regularly discussed and interpreted by each party.[7] But the choice and interpretation of the scriptural passages was determined by a theological and philosophical premise, a particular understanding of monotheism. It is necessary here to go back beyond all the Christian theologians, especially the Alexandrians before Arius, and beyond Philo, to philosophical sources, especially to so-called Middle Platonism and the beginnings of Neo-Platonism.[8] What follows will be an attempt to point briefly to some points of contact which were certainly not discovered by Arius, but still had some influence on him.[9] Reference will be made to the various stages of the Plato renaissance which has been outlined by H. Dörrie in the article mentioned above.

Only the *Timaeus* played a role in the first phase of the revival of Platonism. As has been demonstrated above all by W. Theiler, the so-called doctrine of the three principles was inferred from it.[10] This doctrine answers the question: what, in Plato's view, are the primal grounds, the basic principles (*archai*) of the world? The answer is encoded in prepositional statements: three in the case of Plato and four in the case of Aristotle.

---

[6] Arius and Euzoius to the emperor Constantine: Opitz, AW III, 1, 2, p. 64, document 30, from the year 327. Other documents for the biblical starting point of Arius are given in É. Boularand, I, 86f.

[7] In addition to Prov. 8. 22 the chief passages are Heb. 1. 4; 3. 1; Acts 2. 36; Col. 1. 15. Athanasius censures the 'misuse' of scripture and individual scriptural passages by the Arians in *Or. I c. Arian.* 37ff.: PG 26, 88ff.

[8] In addition to the studies by Stead, Ricken and Barnard already mentioned in n. 4 above, cf. H. Dörrie, 'Die Erneuerung des Platonismus im ersten Jahrhundert vor Christus', in: *Le Néoplatonisme, Royaumont 9–13 juin 1969*, Ed. du CNRS 1971, 17–28. H. A. Wolfson, 'Philosophical Implications of Arianism and Apollinarianism', DOP 12, 1958, 5–9, makes too isolated a reference to Aristotelianism in Arius; J. de Ghellinck, *Patristique et Moyen Age* III, Bruxelles–Paris 1948, 245–310 ('Un aspect de l'opposition entre hellénisme et christianisme. L'attitude vis-à-vis de la dialectique dans les débats trinitaires') also stresses the Stoic influence (esp. pp. 282ff.), but speaks above all of the second generation of Arians.

[9] É. Boularand, op. cit., I, 11: between 275 and 285 Arius could have found in Alexandria 'les grammairiens, les philosophes, les médecins les plus réputés, des bibliothèques d'une richesse unique'. We should not, however, assume that particular philosophical schools existed.

[10] W. Theiler, *Die Vorbereitung des Neuplatonismus*, Berlin 1930, 13–35.

Platonic: ὑφ' οὗ   ἐξ οὗ   πρὸς ὅ
Aristotelian: ὑφ' οὗ   ἐξ οὗ   καθ' ὅ   δι' ὅ.

H. Dörrie terms this attempt 'didactically admirable' but 'false in content',
to the extent that it claims to be a valid description of the teaching of
Plato and Aristotle. For Plato would never have wanted to arrange
'God–idea–matter' (= these three principles) in such a way that each of
the three needed the co-operation of the two others. However, this was
meant to make Plato's teaching—read out of the *Timaeus*—readily understandable and communicable. It was so successful that it spread throughout the ancient world as valid knowledge.[11]

As early as 1930, W. Theiler (op. cit.) pointed out that these series
played a part in Arianism and in the controversy with it. Of course, he is
only referring to evidence from the second generation of Arians and to
Basil.[12] The series itself cannot be noted in Arius; all that can be seen is the
linguistic element contained in the series. This is clear from a verse from
the *Thaleia*, the language of which is very similar:

θεοῦ θελήσει ὁ υἱὸς ἡλίκος καὶ ὅσος ἐστί
ἐξ ὅτε καὶ ἀφ' οὗ καὶ ἀπὸ τότε ἐκ θεοῦ ὑπέστη.
The Son has age and magnitude from the will of God,
His origin from God has a 'from when', a 'from which' and a 'from then'.[13]

Thus in Arius we certainly do not have three parallel series, as might
easily be concluded:

1. from whom	from which	for which
2. God	idea	matter
3. Father	Logos (Nous)	Pneuma–Hyle.[14]

Nevertheless, with him too—taking other expressions into account—
in the final result his understanding of God and the world is reminiscent
of the gradations of the Middle Platonic world. What goes beyond
Middle Platonism is the incorporation of the biblical, Christian idea of
creation,[15] though this happens in a way which serves to distort the

[11] H. Dörrie, op. cit., 21, with reference to H. Diels, *Doxographi graeci*, Berlin 1919, 309–10:
Aetii Plac. I, 11, 2 and 4.

[12] W. Theiler, *Die Vorbereitung des Neuplatonismus*, Berlin 1930, 23f.; Basil, *De Spiritu Sancto* 3–4:
PG 32, 76–7. Basil expressly says that the Arians took over this series of *archai* from alien writers and
applied them to the relationship between Father, Son and Spirit. Thus the adoption of the (Middle
Platonic) series is attested in the case of the second generation of Arians.

[13] Athanas., *Syn.* 15: Opitz, AW II, 1, 9, p. 243[11–12]: PG 26, 705C–708C; G. Bardy, *Lucien*,
257[30–]. There are other instances of this prepositional language in F. Ricken, *TheolPhil* 44, 1969,
331–2.

[14] Cf. G. C. Stead, 'The Platonism of Arius', *JTS* 15, 1964, 16, with reference to P. Henry and his
Sarum Lectures in Oxford, where such a parallelism seems to have been suggested.

[15] For the relationship between neo-Platonism and the idea of creation cf. K. Kremer, *Die neuplatonische Seinsphilosophie und ihre Wirkung auf Thomas von Aquin* (Studien z. Problemgeschichte der
antiken und mittelalterlichen Philosophie 1), Leiden 1971 = 1966[1] with an appendix, 530–3 (discussion of his remarks on pp. 304f.). See also the observations of G. C. Stead in *JTS* 15, 1964, 25; ibid.,
28 for a reference to Methodius, *De creatis* IX: Bonwetsch, GCS 27, 498.

Christian kerygma of Father, Son and Spirit. This leads us to a deeper question about the dependence of the Arian concept of God on Platonism or Middle Platonism.

The second phase of the Plato renaissance was more significant for Christian theology than the first. Here H. Dörrie has drawn attention to the progress in method introduced by *Eudorus*[16] after the naive eclectic Platonism of the first phase.

(1) From theological discussions with Pythagorean circles, Eudorus drew the conclusion that the two summit positions (the '*archai*') of the table of opposites, the One and the Two, should be crowned by a higher One. His conclusion was that even the Platonic deity is to be conceived of in gradated form.[17] This achieved one thing for the interpretation of Plato: Plato's inconsistency could be explained by a demonstration that in various sayings he spoke now of one stage of the Godhead and now of another.

(2) The Plato concordance could be extended, and interpretation could become broader, deeper and more universal. A step had been taken towards a Plato theology. H. Dörrie stresses that in this way, by 100 BC, time was already ripe for a Plotinus. But then came the delay of three hundred years which is usually called Middle Platonism. It is part of the prehistory of Arianism, as has become increasingly clear in the analysis of subordinationist theology. But what produced the move from the tolerable (unclarified) subordinationism of the church to intolerable Arianism? Here there seems to be an indirect link in thought (it could hardly have been direct) between Arius and Eudorus, in the question of 'God as monad' in contrast to the 'dyad'.

In his *Thaleia*, Arius wrote the important verses:

ξένος τοῦ υἱοῦ κατ'οὐσίαν ὁ πατήρ, ὅτι ἄναρχος ὑπάρχει.

σύνες ὅτι ἡ μονὰς ἦν, ἡ δυὰς δὲ οὐκ ἦν, πρὶν ὑπάρξῃ.

The Father is alien in being to the Son, and he has no origin.
Know that the monad was, but the dyad was not, before it came into being.[18]

Here we meet the real (Middle) Platonic element of Arius' picture of God, which achieves its pointed form in contrast to all possible predecessors among earlier writers because of its place in the context of the church's kerygma of Father—(incarnate) Son—and Holy Spirit. In accepting gradations between God and the world into his Judaistic monotheism, Philo would feel less threatened than a Christian theologian

---

[16] H. Dörrie, 'Die Erneuerung des Platonismus', 23f.; art. 'Eudoros 10', *PWK* 6, 915–16; E. Zeller, *Die Philosophie der Griechen* III, 1, Leipzig 1923⁵, 633ff.

[17] Cf. H. Dörrie, op. cit., 24; E. Zeller, op. cit., 634, n. 1. For the Platonic doctrine of the gradation of the deity after Eudorus, Dörrie points to Arius Didymus Eudorus in Stobaeus, *Ecl.* II, 49, 17: there a separation is made between a θεὸς ὁρατὸς καὶ προηγούμενος and a higher hypostasis θεὸς νοητὸς καὶ ἁρμονικός.

[18] Athanas., *Syn.* 15: Opitz, AW II, 1, 9: 242²⁷–243¹; PG 26, 708A; G. Bardy, *Lucien*, 256.

who designated Christ (and the Pneuma) as God.[19] Arius was even more aware of the problem posed by the assumption of a true Son of God, and approached it through a contrast of monad and dyad. His supreme monad allows no kind of differentiation. It excludes any 'dyad', any duality. G. C. Stead has explained what this means.

Δυάς, of course, does not mean 'the Two', i.e. Father and Son, as Τριάς[20] means 'the Trinity'. Δυάς means 'the number two', implying both 'the Second' and 'the Twofold'. It is almost certainly uncomplimentary; in Platonic circles duality implies imperfection, matter, the world of the senses, the left hand, the female principle.[21]

We may leave aside Philo and the Chaldaean Oracles, which Stead cites as further examples,[22] but we cannot pass over his reference to Numenius, frag. 25 (Eusebius, PE 22, p. 544[b]): ὁ γὰρ δεύτερος, διττὸς ὤν, αὐτοποιεῖ τήν τε ἰδέαν ἑαυτοῦ καὶ τὸν κόσμον, δημιουργὸς ὤν. That is, 'The second (God), being (in himself) twofold, himself forms of himself the idea and the world, as he is the demiurge.'[23]

Arius himself set down the consequences of this doctrine of the monad for his picture of God in the confession which he included in a letter to Alexander of Alexandria about the year 320 (sent also in the name of his friends):

We know only one God, who alone is uncreated [increate, unbegotten = ἀγέννητον], who alone is eternal, who alone is without origin, who alone is true, who alone possesses

---

[19] For Philo's monotheism, cf. J. Daniélou, *Philon d'Alexandrie*, Paris 1958, 143–82: 'La théologie de Philo', a controversy with H. A. Wolfson, *Philo* II, Cambridge, Mass. 1948. Daniélou, 163: '... Philon a interprété le Logos biblique sous des influences philosophiques. ... Ce qui paraît important est que ces influences sont diverses. La conception du Logos comme pensée de la création par Dieu est platonicienne. Chez Aristote, il est un equivalent du νοῦς divin. Enfin, le Logos pénétrant et animant le monde est stoïcien. Wolfson a eu tort, semble-t-il, de distinguer ces trois aspects comme formant trois plans d'existence chez Philon. Il élimine par là la notion d'intermediaire, qui lui parait incompatible avec le monothéisme de Philon, mais il semble que c'est à tort. Par contre, il a eu raison de montrer que le Logos ne tenait jusque-là chez aucun penseur la place qu'il a chez Philon. C'est lui qui a substitué l'expression au νοῦς d'Aristote et à la ψυχή stoïcienne (I, 253). C'est pourquoi c'est chez lui que les théologiens chrétiens chercheront des éléments pour élaborer leur théologie du Verbe.' According to Daniélou, 162, two lines should be distinguished in Philo's Logos doctrine: (1) the opposition between substance and the *dynameis* of God, which is the doctrine of the divine attributes. (2) The opposition between being and the Logos, which leads to the doctrine of hypostases. This second line can be found in Justin and Origen. Philo anticipated Arius in working out the distinction between the knowable Logos and the unknowable Father.

[20] The passage quoted from the *Thaleia* (Athanas., *Syn.* 15: Opitz, AW II, 1, 9: 24[24–7]; Bardy, *Lucien*, 256[16–18]) says on the triad: ἤγουν τριάς ἐστιν δόξαις οὐχ ὁμοίαις, ἐνεπίμικτοι ἑαυταῖς εἰσιν αἱ ὑποστάσεις αὐτῶν, μία τῆς μιᾶς ἐνδοξοτέρα δόξαις ἐπ' ἄπειρον (see n. 65 below).

[21] G. C. Stead, *JTS* 15, 1964, 19.

[22] Ibid. Cf. É. des Places, *Oracles Chaldaïques*, Paris 1971, frag. 8, 68; R. P. Festugière, *La révélation d'Hermès Trismégiste* III, Paris 1953, 55. Cf. W. Theiler, 'Die chaldäischen Orakel und die Hymnen des Synesios', in: id., *Forschungen zum Neuplatonismus*, Berlin 1966, 252–301. Theiler stresses that a distinction must be made between the *vertical* hierarchy of hypostases in Plotinus and the *horizontal* articulation of the triads in the Chaldaean Oracles. But this distinction is far removed from the relationship between the Trinity of the saving economy and the immanent Trinity among the Nicenes of the second half of the fourth century. Further investigation should, however, be made of the doctrine of the Trinity in Synesius and Marius Victorinus—with Theiler's article, cited above, as a background—though this is not our task.

[23] Cited in Stead, *JTS* 15, 1964, 19.

immortality, who alone is wise, who alone is good; the sole ruler, the judge of all, the ordainer and governor, unchanging and immutable, righteous and good, the God of the Law and the prophets of the New Covenant, who brought forth the only-begotten Son before eternal times [γεννήσαντα: this expression should be translated 'neutrally' here, it is certainly not intended to express true begetting], by whom he created (πεποίηκε) the aeons and all things; he did not bring him forth (γεννήσαντα) in appearance only, but in truth, as being in his own will [his own freedom for decision, see below], as unchanging and immutable, as God's perfect creature, but not as one of the creatures; brought forth (γέννημα), but not as others are brought forth; not like Valentinus, who represented the one who was brought forth from the Father as an emanation (προβολή; see Lampe, s.v., no. 10); not like the Manichaeans who introduced what was brought forth as part of the Father, of the same substance; not like Sabellius, who divided the *monad* and called it 'Father–Son'. He was not, as Hieraclas [assumed], kindled as a torch from a torch or as a lamp [from a lamp], so that two would arise [in God himself] (λύχνον ἀπὸ λύχνοῦ ἢ ὡς λάμπαδα εἰς δύο). Nor [do we know the Son] as one existing in an earlier mode of existence [i.e. undifferentiated in God] and later begotten or created [in God himself] as Son, views which you, blessed Pope, have often condemned in the midst of the church and in the council. But we say, created (κτισθέντα) by the will of God before the times and aeons, who received life and being from the Father and (the designations of) honour, so that the Father exists together with him (συνυποστήσαντος αὐτῷ τοῦ πατρός). For the Father did not rob himself when he gave to him as a heritage all that he bears uncreated in himself. For he is the source of all. So there are three hypostases. And God (ὁ μὲν θεός, i.e. God the Father) is the cause of all, quite alone without origin, but the Son was brought forth (γεννηθείς) timelessly [i.e. before there was time] by the Father and created and founded before the aeons, and was not before he was brought forth. He was brought forth timelessly before all things, and he alone received his existence from the Father. For he is not eternal or as eternal or as uncreated as the Father, nor does he have identical being with the Father, as some say of 'that which is related to something' (ὡς τινες λέγουσι τὰ πρός τι), thus introducing two uncreated *archai*. Rather, as monad and *arche* of all, he (the Father) is God before all (ἀλλ' ὡς μονὰς καὶ ἀρχὴ πάντων, οὕτως ὁ θεὸς πρὸ πάντων ἐστί). So he is also before the Son, as we have also learned from you and as you have proclaimed in the midst of the church.[24]

Now as he has being and (the designations of) honour and life from God, and all things are delivered over to him, to this degree God (ὁ θεός) is his origin. He rules over him as his God and the one who was before him. But if 'from him' and 'from the womb' and 'I proceeded and came forth from the Father' (1 Cor. 8. 6; Ps. 109. 3; John 8. 42) is understood as a part or as an emanation of the same substance as him, then according to this view the Father is composite and divisible and changeable and corporeal, and accordingly the incorporeal God is both corporeal and capable of suffering.[25]

[24] For Alexander's conduct in the Arian question cf. P. Snellman, *Der Anfang des arianischen Streites*, Helsingfors 1904, 55–69. According to Sozomen, HE I, 15; Bidez-Hansen, 33, in several discussions Alexander 'allowed the two parties, led by Collutus and Arius, to express and defend their opposed views, but he himself maintained a reserved position. Thus to begin with we can imagine a theological disputation (ἅμιλλα)' (Snellman, op. cit., 58). Alexander seems at first to have felt that the assertions that were made and the concepts that were used 'were not completely at odds with one another or mutually exclusive opposites'. But he had to accept the charge of Arius' opponents that the latter had indulged excessively in dogmatic innovations (Sozomen I, 15, 4). 'Sozomen is perfectly right in showing the theologians as being unprepared to make their standpoint more precise at that moment. We might ask whether this was the first occasion on which the hidden duality in Origenistic christology first came unequivocally to the surface' (Snellman, 61).

[25] Confession of faith by Arius and his colleagues to Alexander of Alexandria (according to Opitz presumably written before the synod in Bithynia, about 320): AW III, 1, 1: document 6, 2–5, pp. 12f. G. Bardy, *Lucien*, 235–8.

Arius' true opinion is expressed here more clearly than in the confession of faith which he later presented to the emperor Constantine, along with his closer friends.[26] In this short formula of faith he succeeded in leaving out everything that was either markedly anti-Nicene or markedly Nicene. Some things were capable of being interpreted either way.[27] We need not assume that he had altered his opinion from earlier. So we may attempt to sum up his interpretation of the Christian kerygma of the Father, Son and Holy Spirit in a short synthesis:

(1) The decision has been taken with the interpretation of the monad, the first and only *arche*, or the first hypostasis in the triad. All duality is excluded from this monad. In the confession which has just been cited, Arius does not explain this in philosophical terms, but through his negative remarks about other interpretations of the relationship between Father and Son. He rightly recoils from Marcion and his assumption of a God of the Old Testament and a God of the New. Arius acknowledges the unity of the economy. Similarly, the interpretation of the Son as a Gnostic *probole* or an emanation is excluded. Nor does the doctrine of two stages of the Logos (ἐνδιάθετος–προφορικός) find any favour. Sabellius already has too much differentiation in the monad for him, so Arius makes himself the opponent of any differentiation in the 'monad' of God. His talk of 'three hypostases' (cf. also Athanasius, *Syn.* 15, 2: Opitz, AW II, 1, 9, p. 242$^{22-24}$ from the *Thaleia*) does not mean what Origen understood by this phrase (cf. *Comm. in Io.* II, 10, Preuschen, 65^{15ff}). For Origen understood the only-begotten to be subordinate, but nevertheless the Son of God in essence (p. 65^{22}). Moreover, according to Origen the Son does not proceed from the Father, but remains in his bosom as in his 'place', although in the incarnation he comes into this world with a human soul (*Comm. in Io.* XX, 18 [16]: Preuschen 350$^{24, 34}$). Gregory Thaumaturgus insists still more energetically on this indissoluble unity (see below). Arius differs: for him only the first hypostasis, the monad, is God in the real and unqualified sense. The hypostases of the Son and the Spirit are gradated and belong in the creaturely sphere. If they are called 'hypostases', this is to express their reality in the face of Sabellius or the Gnostics. Therefore in Arius the *Father* is also the *real and essential Logos*, essential wisdom and power. The Son—and all else through him—has existence, wisdom and power only *per participationem* and indeed *per creationem*. The Son does not arise from eternity *in* God, as Origen and Gregory Thaumaturgus have it, but *outside*.

---

26 Opitz, AW III, 1, 2; document 30, p. 64, according to Socrates, HE I, 26; Sozomen, HE II, 27; G. Bardy, *Lucien*, 274–8.

27 G. Bardy, *Lucien*, 276: 'Arius d'ailleurs semble avoir fait de grands efforts pour écarter de sa profession de foi tous les termes précis qui auraient pu le compromettre. Sur les relations du Père et du Fils, il est volontiers bref, sinon obscur, car on peut aussi bien rattacher les mots θεὸν λόγον à ce qui les precède qu'à ce qui les suit, et la signification de la phrase essentielle se trouve dès lors incertaine.'

(2) Thus the Son is the *participans primarius* in the Father, the real God. He is given the *epinoiai* 'God', 'Logos', 'Sophia', 'Dynamis', but only from grace, *per gratiam*:

> He (Arius) says that there are two *sophiai*, one which is peculiar to God (the Father) and one in existence with him; the Son was brought forth in this wisdom and is called wisdom and Logos only because he participates in it. ... So he also says that there is another Logos alongside the Son in God and that the Son participates in this and *by grace* is called Logos and Son.[28]

This sounds adoptionist. But this 'by grace' should not be confused with the adoptionism of Paul of Samosata, which speaks of the man Jesus. Here we are dealing with the 'pre-existent' Christ, so far as this expression can be allowed in Arius.

Now Arius has various definitions of the nature, the existence and the function of the Son:

(a) Because of the unavoidably narrow understanding of the divine monad, Son and *pneuma* must be removed from the divine sphere and put in the order of creatures. Although the Son is *'theos'* in an analogous sense, he is not true God (θεός ἀληθινός).[29] He is therefore 'alien' (ἀλλότριος)[30] to the Father and dissimilar from him (ἀνόμοιος)[31]. It follows from this difference and alien character that the Father himself cannot be truly known by the Son. Athanasius reports a number of remarks to be found in the *Thaleia*:

> Thus God himself, in so far as he is, is inexpressible for all (ἄρρητος). He is inexpressible (even) for the Son. For he (the Father) is what he is for himself, that is (he is) unutterable (ἄλεκτος), so that the Son cannot express any of the statements which encompass (God's being). For it is impossible for him to search out the Father who is in himself.[32]

Granted, negative predicates of God and the terminology of Middle Platonism are also to be found among the Apologists of the second century, in Origen and in Eusebius of Caesarea. But Arius transcends negative theology: the gulf between the creation and the transcendent God is unbridgable, because the 'Son' too is the other side of the gulf and therefore cannot know the Father as he is in himself, but only in the way

---

[28] Athanas., *C. Arian. or.* I, 5: PG 26, 21B: G. Bardy, *Lucien*, 264; ibid., ref. to I, 9: PG 26, 29B; *Decr. Nic. Syn.* 16, 4–5; Opitz, AW II, 1, 3, pp. 13f. Cf. G. Bardy, *Lucien*, 273, frag. XVIII (Marcell. Anc.). Arius makes a distinction in *dynamis* similar to that between the *sophia* which is of the one substance and the *sophia* which is obtained by participation: the one, eternal, infinite *dynameis* is exclusively identical with the substance of the Father; the Logos is one of the many *dynameis* outside God, an idea which often occurs in the Arian fragments of Asterius. Cf. frags. V–VII and VIII in Bardy, *Lucien*, 264f. According to Arius, the Logos outside God cannot properly be so called, but only καταχρηστικῶς. This is attested by Alexander of Alexandria, in Bardy, 271; Socrates, HE I, 6: Hussey I, 13–22, esp. 15. Also Marcellus of Ancyra, frag. 46 (and 45): Klostermann-Hansen, 193; Christ is also called λόγος κατ' ἐπίνοιαν: Bardy, *Lucien*, frag. XVI, 271, according to Athanas., *C. Arian. or.* II, 37: PG 26, 225A.
[29] Cf. Bardy, *Lucien*, frag. X, 266–7.
[30] Ibid., frag. XV.
[31] Ibid., frags. XIII–XV.
[32] Athanas., *Syn.* 15, 3: Opitz, AW II, 1, 9, p. 242[9] and p. 243[14–17].

in which he has the right (ὡς θέμις ἐστίν),[33] that is, only with creaturely knowledge. Arius would have found it difficult to lay the foundations for a theology of revelation. He sees the Son chiefly as the mediator of creation. Apart from one other element which has still to be mentioned, his Logos doctrine thus is determined cosmologically.

Like the Hellenistic philosophers, Arius probably came up against the problem of the 'one' and the 'many'. We already found a starting point in the relationship between the divine monad and the Logos–Son as dyad. At any rate, the Son is understood as a demiurge. In Middle Platonic philosophy, following Plato, Timaeus 27a–52b, a special place was accorded to the cosmological and its gradation. In the Didaskalikos of Albinus, the first Nous becomes the cause of a cosmic nous who—himself ordered by the Father—now becomes a principle of order for the whole world.[34] Numenius built up the intermediate sphere between the supreme God and hyle still more: above is the completely unknown, 'first God, being in himself, simple'; then there is the 'second God', the demiurge (= the 'world soul' of the Timaeus in Albinus). This 'second God' is good through participation in the 'first God'. Such conceptions can to some degree find their way into Arius' ideas.[35]

However, the crisis was brought about by a combination of this cosmological doctrine of God with the biblical doctrine of creation. If the idea of the monad was taken absolutely and the statements about the Logos were understood one-sidedly in a cosmological way, this idea of creation inevitably led to the conclusion that the Platonic middle sphere had to be assigned to the creaturely realm. This is already true of the Middle Platonic statements about the Logos as the bearer of the ideas, which had been taken over in two forms by ante-Nicene theology: (i) In the doctrine that God, being 'logikos' from eternity, first gives the Logos a subsistence of its own by a free decision of the will before the creation of the world. Was the bringing forth of this Logos already part of the process of creation? (ii) In Origen's doctrine, which accepted the begetting of this Logos but did not surrender its cosmological reference. Origen indeed assumed that God is creator from eternity, but because he refused to accept that the real creation is eternal like God, the Logos had to become from eternity the point of reference to which God's creative will and activity relate. This produced the danger that even in Origen the Logos might be assigned to the creaturely sphere, all the more as the Logos was spoken of as the 'world soul'. For 'an immanent principle of form, movement and order cannot belong to the sphere of the transcendent creator God'.[36]

---

[33] Ibid., p. 242[23].
[34] Cf. F. Ricken, 'Nikaia als Krisis des altchristlichen Platonismus', TheolPhil 44, 1969, 324–5.
[35] Ibid., 325.   [36] Ibid., 326.

(b) The temptation to this solution became stronger for terminological reasons. Before Nicaea no distinction was made between ἀγέννητος = unbegotten and ἀγένητος = uncreated.[37] For Greek thought, both words refer to the same thing: the uncreated, intransitory and ideal being with which the world of coming into being, passing away and *doxa* is contrasted. The Apologists follow this usage. They were concerned to show that only the transcendent Father God is ἀγέννητος, that is, without origin and without change. This 'being without origin' excluded both being created and being born. But there was no distinction made between the two. The word described the 'absolute' in contrast to that which 'came into being'. Now if only the divine monad was considered 'uncreated', the Son or the Logos (as mediator of creation) had to be transferred into the realm of that which had 'come into being'. But in that case the Son could no longer come forth from the Father as one who was in truth 'begotten'. Despite this, Origen had the courage to speak of an 'eternal begetting'.[38] But that no longer fitted the concept of the monad in Arius. In his *Oratio I contra Arianos*, Athanasius has handed down a text from the *Thaleia* which expresses the option which Arius chose:

Dieu (ὁ θεός) n'a pas toujours été Père, mais il fut un temps où Dieu était seul et où il n'était pas encore Père. Ensuite il devint Père. Le Fils n'a pas toujours été, car puisque toutes les choses ont été tirées du néant et que toutes sont des créatures et des oeuvres, le Verbe de Dieu lui-même a été tiré du néant, et il eut un temps où il n'était pas. Et il n'était pas avant de naître, mais il a eu, lui aussi, le commencement de la création. En effet, dit-il, Dieu était seul, et il n'y avait pas encore de Verbe ni de Sagesse. C'est ensuite, quand il voulut nous produire, qu'il fit un certain être et le nomma Verbe, Sagesse et Fils, afin de nous produire par lui.[39]

The ambiguity of ἀγέννητος–γεννητός has now been removed. For Arius the Son is clearly created or brought into being. This was also stated directly, as Arius' letter has shown us.[40] The fact that the Son is created is underlined by the reference back to the 'will of the Father'. In other words, the Son does not exist of necessity, but only in dependence on a decision by the Father.[41] The 'whence' (ἀφ' οὖ) of the Son is defined exactly in his mode of proceeding. For Arius, being begotten

[37] See instances and literature in Ricken, op. cit., 329, from which the following sentences have been quoted.
[38] F. Ricken, ibid., 328, with examples (see below).
[39] Athanas., *C. Arian. or.* I, 5: PG 26, 21AB; French translation here follows Boularand I, 57f.; cf. G. Bardy, *Lucien* 261f., frag. III, with parallel passages.
[40] Cf. Opitz, AW III, 1, 1: document 6, 2; it is said here that the Father 'brings forth' the only-begotten Son (γεννήσαντα υἱὸν μονογενῆ), who however is then called the 'perfect *creature* of God'. Cf. Bardy, *Lucien*, frags. III and IV, 261–4. Reference may be made once again to Origen, *Comm. in. Io.* II, 10 (Preuschen, 65). Cf. E. Corsini, *Commento al Vangelo di Giovanni di Origene*, Torino 1968, 220–2. Preuschen, 65[22f.], is translated by Corsini as follows: '. . . solo l'Unigenito è Figlio per natura fin dal principio.' Arius is the opposite of this.
[41] Arius, *Thaleia*: Opitz, AW II, 1, 9: 243[19]: υἱὸς γὰρ ὢν θελήσει πατρὸς ὑπῆρξεν ἀληθῶς. Cf. further frag. IV from *C. Arian. or.* I, 5 and II, 4: Bardy, *Lucien*, 262f. Ep. Alexandri Al., '*Cum unum*': Socrates, HE I, 6: Hussey, I, 16. See above Eusebius Caes., DE IV, 3, 7; A. Weber, ΑΡΧΗ, 53.

within the Godhead is a division in God himself. He therefore retreats from Origen. The 'whither' (δι' ὅ = δι' ἐκεῖνον . . . δι' ἡμᾶς), that is, the purpose of the creation of the Son, is also given exactly. He is only created when the Father wanted to create us.[42] According to Alexander of Alexandria, Arius can put the matter even more sharply:. 'He (the Son) was created *for our sake*, so that God might create us *through him* as through an instrument; and he would not exist if God had not wanted to create us.'[43]

This demonstrates yet again that when Arius talks of the 'Father–Son' relationship, he is already talking of the relationship between God and the world. We hear nothing of soteriology or a theology of revelation. The Son is typically understood as a cosmological intermediary:

When God wanted to create nature and bring it into being, he saw that it could not participate in the unmixed (ἀκράτου, i.e., purely absolute and infinite) hand of the Father and his creation (δημιουργίας); therefore first of all he created and made only the sole, unique one and called this Son and Logos, so that he might be the middle one (i.e. intermediary in a cosmological sense); in this way the rest and the universe could come into being through him.[44]

Thus the Son is the mediator of the creation and the instrument[45] of God's creative action. He can be counted among the creatures (cf. the expression 'the rest'), and the expression 'three hypostases' or 'Triad' can only be understood in Arius from that perspective.[46]

We now meet the Arianizing *Asterius*. For if we presuppose that Arius' Logos has a similar intermediary position between the *noeta* and the visible to the second hypostasis in Albinus and Numenius (the Chaldaean Oracles should only be mentioned with caution at this point),[47] we can understand a fragment handed down by Athanasius:[48]

He (the Logos) is the first of what has been made and one of the intelligible natures. And just as the sun is only one of the luminaries in the visible sphere, but lights the whole world according to the ordinance of the one who made it, so too the Son, who is one among the intelligible natures, appears and illuminates all that is in the *noetos kosmos*.

Thus it is the concern of Arius and Asterius to assign the Son to an intermediate sphere, in which, however, he occupies the supreme position. The entire universe is illuminated by him as by the one created sun.

[42] Cf. frag. IV, already quoted, in G. Bardy, *Lucien*, 262f.

[43] Alexander Al. Ep., 'Cum unum': Socrates, HE I, 6: Hussey, I, 169‑12. Cf. Ps. Athan., C. Arian. or. IV, 11. PG 26, 484A; A. Stegmann, *Die pseudo-athanasianische 'IVte Rede gegen die Arianer' als 'κατὰ Ἀρειανῶν λόγος' ein Apollinarisgut*, Rottenburg a. N. 1917, 54: οὐ γὰρ ἡμεῖς δι' ἐκεῖνον, φασίν, ἀλλ' ἐκεῖνος δι' ἡμᾶς γέγονεν, εἴγε διὰ τοῦτο ἐκτίσθη καὶ ὑπέστη, ἵνα ἡμᾶς δι' αὐτοῦ κτίσῃ ὁ θεός.

[44] G. Bardy, *Lucien*, frag. IV, 263, in the version from Athanas., C. Arian. or. II, 24: PG 26, 200A, words which are also ascribed to Eusebius of Nicomedia and Asterius as well as to Arius.

[45] Alexander Al. Ep., 'Cum unum': Socrates HE I, 6: Hussey, I, 16[10].

[46] Arius, *Thaleia*: Opitz, AW II, 1, 9; 24224‑26. The text is cited further below (cf. n. 65); cf. Lampe, s.v. τριάς B.

[47] See above, n. 22. Asterius is the first systematician of the Arians, and as such is not very original.

[48] Bardy, *Lucien*, 343; translation in F. Ricken, *TheolPhil* 44, 1969, 331.

With his creation time also appears, albeit in a way which corresponds to his degree of existence.[49] Thus one can say with some degree of truth that Arius and Asterius interpreted the baptismal kerygma of Father, Son and Holy Spirit in accordance with the descending cosmological pattern of the Middle Platonists, who inserted the *nous* (now identical and now not identical with the *pneuma*, the world-soul) between the supreme *hen* and the lowermost *hyle*. The biblical and Christian element here is, of course, that the idea of creation plays an explicit role (as it already does in Philo). The Son of the baptismal creed has become the created mediator of creation. His exclusive pre-eminence consists in the fact that he alone was created directly by the Father, the only true God.[50] Everything else was created through him. Furthermore, he alone of all the other creatures made good use of his freedom, although he too was by nature τρεπτός, i.e. was capable of making a morally bad decision—in this like all other rational creatures. But we shall discuss this further in connection with Arius' conceptions of incarnation so far as these can be made out.

(a) Gregory Thaumaturgus and Arius

In conclusion, we shall now attempt to shed some light on Arius' Logos doctrine from its context in the history of dogma. The characteristic element of this situation seems to be the opposition of Arius to Gregory Thaumaturgus. Before the Nicene creed there are no documents so opposed to each other in their picture of God as the *Expositio fidei* of Gregory Thaumaturgus and the *Thaleia* of Arius (along with a few other documents).

Gregory Thaumaturgus' *Expositio fidei* has been handed down in a biography written by Gregory of Nyssa. Gregory of Nyssa asserts that he has himself seen the autograph of this confession.[51] According to Caspari it was written between 260 and 270. The famous scholar has established numerous relationships between the *Expositio* and Origen

---

[49] Arius, *Thaleia*, after Athanas., *Syn.* 15, 3: Opitz, AW II, 1, 9: p. 242[13]: ἐν χρόνοις γεγαότα. From this it followed that ἦν ποτε ὅτε οὐκ ἦν. The passages for this are given in Bardy, *Lucien*, 262, on frag. III. This, then, is the context in which we find the saying that the Son 'was created from nothingness (those things which are not)': ἐξ οὐκ ὄντων ὑπέστη. Arius clarifies this in his letter to Eusebius of Nicomedia (c. 318): οὔτε ἐξ ὑποκειμένου τινός (Opitz, AW III, 1, 1: p. 3, 1; Bardy, *Lucien*, 228).
[50] Cf. Bardy, *Lucien*, 262f., frag. IV.
[51] Greg. Nyss., *Vita Gregorii Thaumaturgi*: PG 46, 912D–913A, where however our part IV, 2–4 is no longer treated as part of Gregory's confession. Our text here follows C. P. Caspari, *Alte und neue Quellen zur Geschichte des Taufsymbols und der Glaubensregel*, Christiania 1879, 10, with text-critical and historical notes, ibid., 10–17; authenticity and integrity, ibid., 25–64; cf. also H. Dehnhard, *Das Problem der Abhängigkeit des Basilius von Plotin*, Berlin 1964, 19–32; L. Froidevaux, 'Le symbole de Saint Gregoire le Thaumaturge', *RSR* 19, 1929, 193–247. For Gregory Thaumaturgus see V. Ryssel, *Gregorius Thaumaturgus*, Leipzig 1880; a partly very critical discussion by F. Overbeck, *ThLZ* 6, 1881, 283–6; over against Caspari, Overbeck seeks a tradition independent of Gregory of Nyssa for final proof of the authenticity of the *Expositio fidei*. This question has not been taken up again since then, although there is now a consensus on the authenticity. For the remaining writing of Gregory and for the literature see H. Crouzel, *Grégoire le Thaumaturge, Remerciement à Origène suivi de la Lettre d'Origène à Grégoire* (SC 148), Paris 1969, 9–92, and the further remarks here.

which we need not repeat here.[52] However, this dependence on Origen[53] left enough room for the development of Thaumaturgus. There are some differences and developments of doctrine, e.g. in that Gregory makes the *pneuma* the *eikon* of the Son and the 'perfect image of the perfect'.[54] For Origen the soul of Christ is the image of the Son. Does Gregory part company with his master here because he no longer accepts a 'soul of Christ'? In 264 or 265 he had taken part in the first synod against Paul of Samosata, whose doctrine of the soul of Christ was possibly interpreted falsely. The scanty remarks of Gregory on the incarnation do not allow us to say more here.[55]

In the foreground of his thinking is the holy triad: the *Expositio fidei* is the finest testimony to this. The most significant thing in it is the way in which the relationship between Father, Son and Holy Spirit is defined. It is evidently directed against a Sabellian understanding of the Trinity, following in the footsteps of Origen. Remarkably strong emphasis is laid on the unity and equality of the 'three' as well as on their reality. Any subordinationism seems already to have been overcome. The Christian picture of God is developed in a tension between unity and difference. The word 'monad' does not occur, but 'triad' does, with more stress on unity and equality than can be found earlier in Christian theology. The *Expositio fidei* is clearly constructed. The first article deals with the one God, Father, who is however immediately introduced in his relationship to the Son. The second article is a confession of the 'one Lord', and points back to the first hypostasis. The third article speaks of the Holy Spirit, who has his origin from 'God' (the Father) and has been manifested through the Son. This is perhaps the most likely place in which a subordinationist element might be seen, but we would do better here to speak of the 'perspective of the saving economy' which is already expressed in this third article. Of course there is no express mention here of the incarnation.

---

[52] C. P. Caspari, op. cit., 25–64.
[53] H. Crouzel, op. cit., points to this.   [54] C. P. Caspari, op. cit., 49f.

[55] Cf. H. Crouzel, op. cit., 53, on Gregory's panegyric on Origen: 'Grégoire ne fait dans son discours aucune allusion à l'Incarnation, pas une fois il ne prononce le nom de Jésus, ni même celui de Christ. Il n'y a là qu'un aspect partiel de la christologie d'Origène qui donne leur place à l'Incarnation et à la Croix et a pour le nom de Jésus une devotion si profondément affective.' Cf. also M. Simonetti, 'La morte di Gesù in Origene', *RivStorLettRel* 8, 1972, 3–41. Among the other works assigned to Gregory, the doctrine of the incarnation and of the death of God appears especially in *Ad Theopompum, De passibili et impassibili im Deo*, J. B. Pitra, *Analecta Sacra* IV, Paris 1883, Syriac 103–20; Latin 363–76; German in V. Ryssel, *Gregorius Thaumaturgus*, Leipzig 1880, 71–99. For the name of Jesus, Pitra, 376; Ryssel, 99; also in the disputed *Ep. ad Evagrium* (PG 46, 1101–8) 1105C. The first-mentioned writing *Ad Theopompum* surely does not belong to the author of the *Expositio fidei*. However, to whom it should be assigned remains uncertain. It will be edited by Professor Dr Luise Abramowski in the Syriac text of Brit. Mus. add. 12156. She also affirms the contrast between *Exp. fid.* and *Ad Theopomp.* (letter of 13.1.74), and draws the same conclusions for different authorship. The *Ep. ad Evagr.* mentioned above is put in the context of Marcellianism by F. Refoulé, 'La date de la lettre a Evagre,' *RSR* 49, 1961, 520–48. There are different views before and after from M. Simonetti, 'Gregorio Nazianzeno o Gregorio Taumaturgo?', *Atti dell'Istituto Lombardo de Scienze e Lettere*, 1953, 108ff.; id., 'Ancora sulla lettera ad Evagrio (PG 46, 1101–8)', *Rivista di Cultura Classica e Medievale* 4, 1962, 371–4.

Most interesting for a comparison between Gregory and Arius is the appendix which is added to the three articles. Father, Son and Holy Spirit are seen as a 'perfect triad', in their immanent connection within the Godhead—statements which are of the greatest significance in the history of the doctrine of the Trinity. In what follows we shall point to some points of comparison—mostly *e contrario*—between the *Expositio fidei* and the fragments from the writings of Arius. For this purpose we have divided the Greek text into verses and have added a French translation, made by J. Lebreton but not published by him.[56] To justify this comparison it may also be pointed out that Arius composed the *Thaleia* when he was living with Eusebius of Nicomedia after his excommunication by Alexander of Alexandria.[57] If he did not know the confession of Gregory Thaumaturgus from Alexandria, it is quite probable that he made its acquaintance during his stay with Eusebius of Nicomedia. At least it may have been fresh in his mind. Gregory's understanding of the Trinity does not seem to be envisaged in the confession of faith sent by Arius and his friends to Alexander of Alexandria (see above).

Expositio fidei of Gregory	Translation by J. Lebreton
I. Εἷς θεός,	Un seul Dieu
1 πατὴρ λόγου ζῶντος,	Père du Logos vivant,
2 σοφίας ὑφεστώσης	de la Sagesse subsistante,
3 καὶ δυνάμεως καὶ χαρακτῆρος ἀιδίου	de la Puissance, de l'Empreinte et image de la divinité
4 τέλειος τελείου γεννήτωρ,	qui a engendré parfaitement un Fils parfait,
5 πατὴρ υἱοῦ μονογενοῦς.	(–)
II. Εἷς κύριος,	Un seul Seigneur,
1 μόνος ἐκ μόνου,	unique de l'unique,
2 θεὸς ἐκ θεοῦ,	Dieu de Dieu,
3 χαρακτὴρ καὶ εἰκὼν τῆς θεότητος,	empreinte et image de la divinité,
4 λόγος ἐνεργός,	Logos actif,
5 σοφία τῆς τῶν ὅλων συστάσεως περιεκτικὴ	Sagesse qui maintient l'ensemble de l'univers
6 καὶ δύναμις τῆς ὅλης κτίσεως ποιητική,	et Puissance qui a fait la création universelle,
7 υἱὸς ἀληθινὸς ἀληθινοῦ πατρός,	Fils véritable, du Père véritable,
8 ἀόρατος ἀοράτου	invisible de l'invisible,
9 καὶ ἄφθαρτος ἀφθάρτου	et incorruptible de l'incorruptible
10 καὶ ἀθάνατος ἀθανάτου	et immortel de l'immortel,
11 καὶ ἀίδιος ἀιδίου.	et éternel de l'éternel.

---

[56] See L. Froidevaux, *RSC* 19, 1929, 194–5. Lebreton leaves one verse untranslated, which is here marked as (–).

[57] Cf. C. Kannengiesser, 'Où et quand Arius composa-t-il la Thalie?', *Kyriakon* I, 1970, 356–61. Kannengiesser refers to Athanas., *Syn.* 15: Opitz, AW II, 1, 9: 242[4–7]: 'Mais, jeté déhors et poussé par les Eusebiens, Arius consigna sa propre hérésie par ecrit et comme dans une *Thalie*, sans imiter aucun des sages, . . . il rédige beaucoup des choses.' I.e., Arius was given the impulse to compose the *Thaleia* from those around Eusebius of Nicomedia, that is, after the excommunication by Alexander of

III. Καὶ ἓν πνεῦμα ἅγιον,

1 ἐκ θεοῦ τὴν ὕπαρξιν
   ἔχον καὶ δι'υἱοῦ
   πεφηνὸς [δηλαδὴ τοῖς ἀνθρώποις],

2 εἰκὼν τοῦ υἱοῦ,
   τελείου τελεία,

3 ζωὴ ζώντων αἰτία,

4 πηγὴ ἁγία,

5 ἁγιότης ἁγιασμοῦ χορηγός,

6 ἐν ᾧ φανεροῦται θεός
   ὁ πατὴρ ὁ ἐπὶ πάντων καὶ ἐν
   πᾶσι, καὶ θεὸς ὁ υἱὸς
   ὁ διὰ πάντων.

Et un seul Esprit Saint,
ayant de Dieu l'existence
et ayant apparu par le Fils
(–),
image du fils,
parfait du parfait
vie principe des vivants
(–)
sainteté qui confère la sanctification,
en qui se manifeste Dieu le Père
qui est au-dessus de tous, et Dieu le
Fils qui est répandu en tous. (?)

IV. τριὰς τελεία,

1 δόξῃ καὶ ἀιδιότητι
   καὶ βασιλείᾳ μὴ μεριζομένη
   μηδὲ ἀπαλλοτριουμένη,

2 Οὔτε οὖν κτιστόν τι
   ἢ δοῦλον ἐν τῇ τριάδι,

3 οὔτε ἐπείσακτον,
   ὡς πρότερον μὲν οὐχ ὑπάρχον,
   ὕστερον δὲ ἐπεισελθόν.
   οὔτε γὰρ ἐνέλιπέ ποτε
   υἱὸς πατρί,
   οὔτε υἱῷ πνεῦμα,

4 ἀλλ'ἄτρεπτος καὶ
   ἀναλλοίωτος
   ἡ αὐτὴ τριὰς ἀεί.

Trinité parfaite
qui n'est ni divisée, ni aliénée
dans la gloire, l'éternité et le règne.

Il n'y a donc dans la Trinité rien
de créé, rien d'esclave,
rien d'introduit du dehors,
comme n'ayant pas d'abord existé
et étant ensuite arrivé (à l'existence),
car ni le Fils n'a jamais manqué au Père,

ni au Fils l'Esprit,
mais la même Trinité est
toujours restée sans transformation
ni changement.

On I: the 'one God' is presented as Father of the living Logos, who is at the same time existing, subsistent wisdom, and also *dynamis* and the image of the Father given from eternity. Arius could no longer agree that this Logos, this *sophia* and *dynamis* should be thought of as completely immanent in God and yet different from the Father. However, vv. 4 and 5 must have been the decisive factor: the perfect Father is the begetter of the perfect Son, the real Father of the Only-Begotten.

In the *Thaleia*[58] we find another account: 'Wisdom existed through wisdom, namely through the will of the wise God.' This means the 'created' wisdom which exists outside God. The wisdom that is immanent in God is for Arius identical with the Father. When Gregory describes the eternal and separate existence of the Logos as the *dynamis* and image of

Alexandria but before the civil exile from Alexandria. For Arius' tour of agitation see P. Snellman, *Der Anfang des arianischen Streites*, Helsingfors 1904, 75–91 (according to Sozomen I, 15).

[58] Athanas., *Syn.* 15, 3: Opitz, AW II, 1, 9: 243⁵: ἡ σοφία ὑπῆρξε σοφοῦ θεοῦ θελήσει. And V, 19: υἱὸς γὰρ ὢν θελήσει πατρὸς ὑπῆρξεν ἀληθῶς.

God, he of course speaks of the one Kyrios who is spoken of in II. Arius sharply opposes this view: 'Christ is not the physical and true *dynamis* of God (the one Father).'[59] At any rate, here in Arius as in Gregory, Christ is envisaged as God's wisdom and power (cf. I Cor. 1. 24). The impression has therefore probably rightly been gained that Arius directed his 'no' against the creed framed by Gregory.

On II: in this article Arius could affirm the wording in a different way. Its content must have spurred him to opposition. Whether there is literary acquaintance with Gregory's creed or not, we can find sentences in Arius which by their wording can be understood as counter-theses to Gregory.

For example, what looks like a variation of Gregory II, 1 can be found in Arius, frag. IV (Bardy),[60] though it is immediately connected with a clear dissociation: 'First of all the unique one created the one unique one—but only the Son came into being (directly) from the one God.' With Gregory, Arius too could regard Christ as 'God from God' (II, 2, see above). But some remarks of Arius in frags V–VII (Bardy) look like an angry refutation and clarification of this confession:[61] 'He (Christ) is not the true and only Logos of the Father himself', as does frag. III (Bardy):[62] 'Christ is not true God' (cf. on the other hand Gregory in II, 7). True, Arius assigns the created Logos the role of demiurge. But in his view—in contrast to that of Gregory—this demiurge is created. Consequently the Alexandrian cannot follow Gregory in combining statements about the *immanent* Logos as 'active Logos' as the 'wisdom which embraces the whole systasis of the universe' with statements about his part in the creation (v. 6). Arius blocks this conjunction with his thesis that the Son is the first creation of the Father. He is not the 'true Son of the true Father', as Gregory says in II, 7. Just as Arius assigns the Son to the sphere of creation, so too he assigns him to the sphere of the visible world (cf. Numenius, frag. 20, Leemans). Therefore it was impossible for the Alexandrian to accept II, 8 in Gregory. In the *Thaleia*, 'invisibility' is limited to the Father, so that the 'Son' necessarily belongs in the visible sphere.[63]

On III: it is striking that at first sight we cannot find any particular remarks in Arius about this section on the Holy Spirit. But this may not be so much because of Arius himself but because of our sources, i.e. his

[59] According to Bardy, *Lucien*, 265, this verse comes from the *Thaleia*: οὐκ ἔστιν ὁ Χριστὸς ἡ φυσικὴ καὶ ἀληθινὴ δύναμις τοῦ θεοῦ. . . .

[60] Bardy, *Lucien*, frag. IV, 263, following Athanas., *C. Arian. or.* II, 24: PG 26, 200: . . . καὶ κτίζει πρώτως μόνος μόνον ἕνα καὶ καλεῖ τοῦτον υἱὸν καὶ λόγον.

[61] Bardy, *Lucien*, 264, following Athanas., *C. Arian. or.* I, 9: PG 26, 29B: οὐκ ἔστιν ὁ ἀληθινὸς καὶ μόνος αὐτὸς τοῦ πατρὸς λόγος. . . . According to Athanasius these words are from the *Thaleia*.

[62] Athanas., ibid.: PG 26, 29AB (from the *Thaleia*): καὶ οὐκ ἔστιν ἀληθινὸς θεὸς ὁ Χριστὸς ἀλλὰ μετςχῇ καὶ αὐτὸς ἐθεοποιήθη; Bardy, *Lucien*, 262.

[63] According to Athanas., *Ep. ad eppos. Aegypti et Libyae* 12: PG 25, 565A; Bardy, *Lucien*, 268: καὶ τῷ υἱῷ ὁ πατὴρ ἀόρατος ὑπάρχει, καὶ οὔτε ὁρᾶν οὔτε γινώσκειν τελείως καὶ ἀκριβῶς δύναται ὁ λόγος τὸν ἑαυτοῦ πατέρα . . . and the other variations of the theme, ibid.

opponents. These were primarily interested in Arius' Logos doctrine.[64] They may not therefore have noted statements about the *pneuma*. For Arius himself, too, the question of a *Son* in God was paradigmatic. If he was excluded, the question of a *divine pneuma*-hypostasis no longer played any part. But we cannot exclude the possibility that the *Thaleia* also had some verses on the *pneuma*. For it is clear that the closest connections can be established between Gregory and Arius for section IV of Gregory's *Expositio*. So Arius will also have known section III.

On IV: Arius may well have been attracted in the first place by the remark about the 'perfect triad'. For we read in the *Thaleia*, 'There is one triad which is not equal in honour; for its hypostases (i.e. the hypostases of the triad) are not mixed with one another; one is higher in honour than the other, to an infinite degree.'[65] For only one of them belongs to the uncreated, infinite order. And even the two hypostases which belong to the created order are unlike each other. Just as Gregory lays the basis for his 'perfect triad' above all in v. 1, so Arius grounds his 'incomplete triad' in some remarks which Athanasius seems to have taken from the *Thaleia*: 'The substances (plural = hypostases) of the Father and of the Son and of the Holy Spirit are divided in nature and alienated from one another and separate from one another (ἀπεσχοινισμέναι), mutually different and without participation.'[66] The fact that there is no mention of the *homoousios* or of its rejection in this context either in Gregory or in Arius testifies to the ante-Nicene character of the two texts. For Arius the hypostases are ἀνόμοιαι, as we read in the text which has already been quoted.

In IV, 2 we find quite an un-Arian remark: 'There is nothing either created or slave-like in the perfect triad.' We can be sufficiently certain that over against this Arius stresses the created nature of the Son and the rule of his Father, as his creator, over him (see above, the conclusion of the confession of faith to Alexander of Alexandria). So he can take no pleasure at IV, 3: in the triad there is nothing that is 'added' later which was first non-existent and was then introduced afterwards. This is in fact an anticipated rejection of the 'there was once a time when he (the Son) was not'. For Gregory the Son had never lacked the Father, just as the *pneuma* had never lacked the Son. Arius' doctrine of the monad was the opposite of this.

Finally, Arius completely reversed the key words of IV, 4: because the triad is *always* Father, Son, Holy Spirit and because it does not come into

---

[64] As a representative only Nicaea need be named, which simply says, 'and in the Holy Spirit' Opitz, AW III, 1, 2: p. 52². But cf. Alex. Al., *Ep. ad Alex. Byz.*; Opitz, AW III, 1, 1, document 14 p. 28⁵³. For Alex. Byz. (not Thessalon.) see F. Scheidweiler, *BZ* 47, 1954, 91f.

[65] Athanas., *Syn.* 15, 3: Opitz, AW II, 1, 9: p. 242²⁴⁻⁶: ἤγουν τριάς ἐστιν δόξαις οὐχ ὁμοίαις, ἀνεπίμικτοι ἑαυταῖς εἰσιν αἱ ὑποστάσεις αὐτῶν, μία τῆς μιᾶς ἐνδοξοτέρα δόξαις ἐπ' ἄπειρον.

[66] Bardy, *Lucien*, frag. XIII, 268, following Athanas., *C. Arian. or.* I, 6: PG 26, 24B: μεμερισμέναι τῇ φύσει καὶ ἀπεξενωμέναι καὶ ἀπεσχοινισμέναι καὶ ἀλλότριοι καὶ ἀμέτοχοί εἰσιν ἀλλήλων αἱ οὐσίαι τοῦ πατρὸς καὶ τοῦ υἱοῦ καὶ τοῦ ἁγίου πνεύματος.

being *in succession*, Gregory cannot recognize any change or alteration in
it. There is no τρεπτόν and no ἀλλοιωτόν in it. But both can be found in
Arius' Logos, or created Son, and of course in the *pneuma*. Because both
are mutable and changeable, they are *extra deitatem*. We shall return later
to this stress on the mutability of the Son.

In his contestation of the earlier doctrine of a procession in God,
Arius makes the following remark in the confession of faith which he
sent, in company with his friends, to Bishop Alexander of Alexandria
(about 320): '(In the doctrine of a procession within God) the Father is
composite and divisible and changeable (τρεπτός) and corporeal, and
accordingly the incorporeal God is corporeal and capable of suffering'
(document 6, p. 13). In contrast, Gregory accepts a begetting in God and a
procession of the Spirit, yet still refuses to speak of a change and of
suffering in the Godhead.[67]

Is it coincidence that in Arius we find an antithesis to the confession of
Gregory Thaumaturgus, set out step by step? We can hardly assume that
Gregory's *Expositio fidei* was unknown to Arius. But if he did know it, he
must have been attracted by the idea of a refutation, and all the more since
he might have noted that the document was widespread in Asia Minor.
Arius matches ballad-monger's[68] verses against the articles of a creed!
Although this may not be conclusive proof, nevertheless the coincidence
is striking and noteworthy.

2. THE 'LOGOS' AND HIS 'FLESH'

In the creed which was sent to the emperor Constantine, Arius also
acknowledges the incarnation of the Son of God, his (created) Logos,
'who descended and assumed flesh and suffered and rose again and
ascended into heaven, to come again to judge the living and the dead'.[69]
We must now raise the question: how did Arius and his friends, the
Arians of the first generation, and then his supporters in the second
generation, view the relationship between the Logos and his flesh?

Despite the difficult state of our sources, Arianism, which stands nearest
in history to the Alexandrians, gives a reasonably certain indication of
what can be understood by 'Logos-sarx christology'. Such a christology,
at least in this first form, assumes that the Logos and flesh are directly conjoined in Christ and that Christ has no human soul. We should be clear
from the outset that the denial or the acceptance of a soul in Christ is not
a question of secondary importance; it affects the whole picture of Christ

---

[67] On this see Alexander Al., *Ep. ad Alex. Byz.* (324): Opitz, AW III, 1, 1: document 14, 27[47]:
ἄτρεπτον τοῦτον καὶ ἀναλλοίωτον ὡς τὸν πατέρα, ἀπροσδεῆ καὶ τέλειον υἱόν, ἐμφερῆ τῷ πατρὶ
μεμαθήκαμεν, μόνῳ τῷ ἀγεννήτῳ λειπόμενον ἐκείνου. Cf. also 28[52] end.

[68] Cf. Athanas., *C. Arian. or.*, I, 6 and 7: PG 26, 24BC; *Syn.* 15, 2: Opitz, AW II, 1, 9, p. 242.

[69] Arius and Euzoius to the emperor Constantine: Opitz, AW III, 1, 2, p. 64: document 30, no. 2.

and the nature of the redemptive act. The interpretation of the relationship between Godhead and manhood in Christ depends on it.

Epiphanius reports:

> Lucian[70] and all the Lucianists deny that the Son of God took a soul (ψυχή); they
> say that he had flesh only, so that he could naturally appropriate to the God-Logos the
> human suffering, thirst and hunger, weeping and weariness, sorrow and perplexity and
> everything else which comes with his presence in the flesh.[71]

According to this account, then, the Arians, whom we may take to be
identical with the 'Lucianists or Co-Lucianists', as they call themselves,[72]
professed a 'formal' denial of the soul of Christ. Whether, however, the
same is in fact true of Lucian himself and his immediate pupils need not
be assumed without further inquiry, despite the reports of the heresiolo-
gists. In their polemic the later Fathers could have made silence into a
positive denial. Nevertheless, about the time of Eustathius the point seems
to have made itself widely enough felt for him to be able to say: 'But
why do they (the Arians) take so much trouble to show that Christ took a
body without a soul (ἄψυχον σῶμα)?'[73] It may not be far off the mark to
suppose that this explicit denial—more than a mere silence—came about
as a result of the polemic of the Bishop of Antioch. In any case we must
allow a time for the ideas of the early Arian circle to spread unimpeded.
They would, however, have simply allowed the Logos to take the place
of the soul in Christ without saying anything further about this soul. The
overall situation of christology in the third and fourth centuries, which is
still to be examined further, indicates that the Logos-sarx framework led
its 'latent' existence until about 362, i.e. until the Synod of Alexandria,
and even beyond. Only Eustathius and his followers have become aware
of it, but they do not carry their point before 362.[74] An excerpt which
Athanasius quotes in the *Oratio III contra Arianos* from an unnamed
writer of the Arian circle, who may perhaps have been Asterius the
Sophist, may well give us a true picture of the situation.[75] No mention
is made of the soul of Christ, because it was not yet a factor in theological
discussion, so the denial of it does not yet seem to have been felt as a

---

[70] On what follows, G. Bardy, *Lucien*.

[71] Epiphanius, *Ancoratus* 33, 4: ed. K. Holl: GCS I, 42; PG 43, 77AB; *Panarion haer.* 69, 19: ed.
Holl 3, 169; PG 42, 233B; οὐ μόνον δὲ τοῦτο, ἀλλὰ καὶ ἀρνοῦνται ψυχὴν αὐτὸν ἀνθρωπείαν εἰληφέναι
Haer. 69, 49; ed. Holl 3, 195; PG 42, 277A–C; cf. *Chalkedon* I, 69, n. 3.

[72] Philostorg., HE 2, 14; G. Bardy, *Lucien*, 57, 201–4.

[73] Eustathius, *De anima adv. Arian. frag.*: ed. M. Spanneut, *Recherches sur les écrits d'Eustathe d'Antioche*,
Lille 1948, 100[1–6]; PG 18, 689B.

[74] Cf. the verdict of Severus of Antioch: *Ctr. imp. Grammat.* III, 2, 28: ed. and tr. J. Lebon, CSCO
syr. ser. 4, vol. 6, 55–6, '*Vigente luctatione Arianorum, cui Patres repugnabant, nullam tunc habitam esse
quaestionem de incarnatione Domini.*' Severus makes some qualifications to his statement in the Disputation.

[75] So M. Richard, 'Saint Athanase et la psychologie du Christ selon les Ariens' (cited as 'Athanase'),
MSR 4, 1947, 7–9; id., 'Une ancienne collection d'homélies grecques', *SymbOsl* 25, 1947, 54–73; id.,
Asterii Sophistae Commentariorum in Psalmos quae supersunt . . ., Oslo 1956; see also *SymbOsl* 34, 1958,
54–7, 58–66.

stumbling block against the tradition.[76] Augustine, who was probably
thinking more of circumstances in the West, observes that the question
of Christ's soul stood very much in the background.[77] As we are to see
later, we can almost certainly assume that the denial of Christ's soul was
not discussed at the Council of Nicaea. This, too, would seem to suggest
that the question as such had not yet made itself felt.

In the evidence hitherto we have not yet reached the original formulation in which the Arians summed up the being of Christ. It can probably
best be found in Ps.-Athanasius, *Contra Apollinarem*, though little can be
discovered of either the author or the date of this writing. In it we come
across an expression which shows signs of considerable antiquity and of
Alexandrian derivation.

> Arius owns the flesh (of Christ) only as a veil over the Godhead; instead of the *inner
> man* within us, that is the soul, he says that the Logos was present in the flesh and he
> ventures to attribute to the Godhead a susceptibility to suffering and the ascent from the
> underworld.[78]

The addition 'that is the soul' is certainly to be attributed to Ps-Athanasius, whereas the inserted 'he says' refers the rest of the first half of the
passage back to Arius. In the expression 'inner man' we doubtless have the
genuine Arian formula before us. Once again we have here the decisive
concept which we have already met in the Alexandrian spirituality of the
third century. It also occurs in the Acts of the Synod of Antioch of 268.
If we are to take it as being genuinely Arian and with its full meaning, as
developed especially by the Stoa, then it means that the Logos supplies
all the psychical vitality and spiritual life in Christ's human nature. Theodore of Mopsuestia, who was particularly concerned with Asterius the
Sophist, provides some interesting evidence which presupposes that a
similar notion was Arian teaching.[79] The Logos has taken over the place
and the function of the 'soul'.

---

[76] Athanasius, *C. arian*. III, 26: PG 26, 377A–380B.

[77] Augustine, *C. haer*. 49: PL 42, 39; *In eo autem quod* (*scl. Ariani*) *Christum sine anima solam carnem
suscepisse arbitrantur, minus noti sunt: nec adversus eos ab aliquo inveni de hac re aliquando fuisse certatum* (!).
*Sed hoc verum esse, et Epiphanius non tacuit, et ego ex eorum quibusdam scriptis et collocutionibus certissime
comperi.* Here he may well be referring to the later Arians. Cf. August., *C. serm. arian*. 9: PL 42,
689–90. Theodoret, *Demonstrat. per. syll*. 12: PG 83, 333B, too already includes the Eunomians in his
judgement. The christology remain the same as in the first generation of Arians. Ps.-Didymus (*De
Trin*. 3, 21), Hilary (*De Trin*. 10, 51), Ambrose (*De incarn. Dom. sacr*. 68), Theodore of Mops. (*De
incarn*., Sachau 88; *Hom. Cat*. 5, ed. Tonneau 111ff.) also know of the Arian denial of the soul of
Christ. See W. P. Haugaard, 'Arius: Twice a Heretic? Arius and the Human Soul of Jesus Christ',
Church History 29, 1960, 251–63.

[78] Ps-Athanasius, *C. Apollin*. 2, 3: PG 26, 1136C–1137A: Ἄρειος δὲ σάρκα μόνην πρὸς ἀποκρυφὴν
τῆς θεότητος ὁμολογεῖ · ἀντὶ δὲ τοῦ ἔσωθεν ἐν ἡμῖν ἀνθρώπου, τοῦτ' ἔστι τῆς ψυχῆς, τὸν λόγον ἐν τῇ
σαρκὶ λέγει γεγονέναι, τὴν τοῦ πάθους νόησιν, καὶ τὴν ἐξ ἅιδου ἀνάστασιν τῇ θεότητι προσάγειν
τολμῶν. Cf. ibid. 1, 15: PG 26, 1121A. Further mention will be made of the 'inner man' in connection
with Apollinarius.

[79] Theodore Mops., *Hom. Cat*. 5, 7–19: ed. R. Tonneau–R. Devreesse, *Les homélies catéchétiques de
Théodore de Mopsueste* (ST 145), Città del Vatic. 1949, 109–29. This important text is given closer
examination in connection with Theodore's christology. Cf. also Greg. Naz., *Ep*. 101: PG 37, 134A.

Perhaps we are coming somewhat nearer to Arius himself or to the first Arian generation. In his edition of the so-called *Sermo maior de fide* of Athanasius, E. Schwartz introduces a text which according to the findings of modern scholarship can be assigned—like the whole of the *Sermo maior de fide*—to the first great opponent of Arianism, Marcellus of Ancyra. This text has been taken from the *Doctrina Patrum* and could therefore be suspected of having been adapted for the monothelitic controversy. But in the seventh century there was no longer any need to fight against a christology which did not have a soul for Christ. The only thing is that there might have been a desire to show that monothelitism was in danger of becoming Arianism. The most important sentences may be quoted from the longer text in Schwartz:

> Since he (Arius) assigns to him (the Logos) flesh which is bereft of a rational soul, he shows him to be both mortal and capable of suffering as regards his (viz. divine) nature. The suffering itself is not of free will, as the flesh without a soul no longer has any free motivating principle.[80]

We might well suspect the argument to belong to the seventh century did we not have the discussion between Eusebius and Marcellus of Ancyra on the soul of Christ. It already points to a similar set of problems (see pp. 180ff above). A quotation from Arius which has been handed down in several forms brings us nearer to this text in both time and content.[81] According to Athanasius, Arius says:

> By nature the Logos itself is changeable (τρεπτός), like all (creatures); but of his own freedom of will he remains good (καλός) as long as he wills. But if he so wills, he can also change as we can (i.e. probably: also sin), as he has a changeable nature. But because God knew beforehand that he would be good, he gave him this glory by anticipation (προλαβών) which after that he also had from his virtue as man; thus from his works which God foresaw, he allowed him to become the (Logos) that he now is (i.e. unchangeable and in glory; cf. Phil. 2. 11).

According to the parallel text from the letter of Athanasius to the bishops of Egypt and Libya, this is the teaching of Arius himself, which does not emerge so clearly from *C. Arian.* I, 5. Arius probably posed the problem of the proving (or of the changeableness or unchangeableness) of his created Logos in a way reminiscent of Origen and the question of the proving of the pre-existent soul of Jesus Christ (in contrast to the fall of the other souls). For him this was probably a problem connected with the nature or creatureliness of the Logos. It was only secondarily a soteriological question: the Logos receives his glory right from the beginning through his prevenient goodness. Is Arius also thinking here of the man-

---

[80] E. Schwartz. *Der sogenannte Sermo maior de fide*: Sb MünchAk, 1924, 53, following F. Diekamp, *Doctrina Patrum*, Münster 1907, 298, frag. 40, 5; ibid., 64–5: PG 89, 1180.

[81] G. Bardy, *Lucien*, 265f., from Athanas., *C. Arian. or.* I, 5: PG 26, 21C and *Ep. ad eppos Aegypti et Libyae*: PG 25, 564BC. The Synod of Antioch in 325 also points to the doctrine expressed in these texts, as will be shown in more detail below. Cf. Opitz, AW III, 1, 1, 39f., no. 13.

hood to be redeemed? Does he see the Logos only as the cosmological climax of creation or also as the head of the men who are to be redeemed by him? The text says nothing about this. Nevertheless, it gives a good insight into the Arian understanding of Christ. We might well conclude from this text that Arius' Christ has no human soul. Its place is taken by the created higher spirit which is the seat of his freedom of choice, both for the condition before the incarnation and in the state of his humanity. His pre-existent goodness and the *arete* which is practised *in statu incarnationis* are achieved by one and the same instrument. For both conditions, which are distinguished by an 'after that' (μετὰ ταῦτα), i.e. the fact of the incarnation, it is a question of the moral proving of the Logos. This is foreseen by the Father for both stages of the existence of the one created Logos, before his incarnation and after it.[82]

Alexander of Alexandria attests that this is a doctrine of the first generation of Arians. In his letter to Alexander of Byzantium he outlines the inner consistency of the basic Arian thesis, that of the created nature of the Logos:[83]

They (the Arians) say that God created everything from nothing, among which they include the creation of all creatures who have reason and all who do not, including the Son of God. Consequently they also say that he has a changeable nature, capable of both virtue and wickedness, and through their thesis that he is created they also do away with the divine scriptures (which say) that he is eternal. This also means that the Logos is unchangeable (τὸ ἄτρεπτον τοῦ λόγου) and that the wisdom of the Logos, which is the Christ, is divine.

As these wicked men state the matter, we too could be sons of God like him. Indeed, scripture says: 'Sons have I begotten and brought up' (Isa. 1. 2; cf. document 8, p. 171). But when they were confronted with the saying which follows, 'But they have despised me' (ibid.), which does not accord with the nature of the Redeemer, as he is unchangeable by nature, they abandoned all restraint and said: As God knew and saw in advance that the Son would not despise him, he chose him out from all the rest. Not because he was something by nature and had a special advantage above the other sons (did he choose him). (For they say that there is no natural Son of God nor one who has properties which come near to that.) Rather, he too has a changeable nature; but because through his carefulness in conduct and his asceticism he did not turn to evil, he (God) chose him.

Here, too, we have concern with the first-created Logos, even if implicitly he is also considered in his incarnate condition. This alone—and not a human soul in Christ—is the principle of moral decision.

[82] Cf. Athanas., *C. Arian. or. I*, 35: PG 26, 84AB: Αὐτεξούσιός ἐστιν ἢ οὐκ ἔστι; προαιρέσει κατὰ τὸ αὐτεξούσιον καλός ἐστι, καὶ δύναται, ἐὰν θελήσῃ, τραπῆναι τρεπτῆς ὢν φύσεως· ἢ ὡς λίθος καὶ ξύλον οὐκ ἔχει τὴν προαίρεσιν ἐλευθέραν εἰς ς τὸ κινεῖσθαι καὶ ῥέπειν εἰς ἑκάτερα; a spirit must be allowed freedom of choice, in contrast to a stone or a piece of wood. This question could only be answered in the affirmative. But the Arians apply this affirmative to a created Logos to which they allow the freedom to sin or not to sin. This Logos remains good—a fact that God foresees. So we have an absence of sin *de facto*, not an *impeccabilitas de iure*, which is presupposed by Eusebius. Here we probably have the earliest instance of a *praevisio libere futurorum* by God. One more step and the Molinists could discover their *scientia media* in Arius.

[83] Alexander Al., *Ep. ad Alexandr. Byz.* (324): Opitz, AW III, 1, 1, document 14, p. 211[11-13]; cf. p. 24[29-30]; PG 18, 552B-C.

Thus it is possible to adduce texts from Arius himself or from witnesses of the ante-Nicene period to show that even the first generation of Arians did not know a human soul in Christ. Had they posited a human soul in Christ in addition to the created Logos, there would have been two competing spiritual principles in 'Christ'. From all this it becomes clear once again that Arius 'mythicized' the picture of Christ. Today it would be said that he made Christ a 'superman'. The ontological basis for this was that in Jesus of Nazareth a higher angelic being became incarnate. We recall Eusebius' argument about the pre-eminence of Christ (or Jesus of Nazareth). Even now it is clear that the Nicenes will be the better theologians—and philosophers. They rule out the middle sphere which Arius occupied with his created Logos and *pneuma*, and thus reject the Middle Platonic picture of the world.[84]

What we have inferred from the views of the first Arian generation, the Arian Logos-sarx christology, will now be confirmed by the direct testimony of the second generation.

Eunomius, it is true, touches only fleetingly on the doctrine of the incarnation in his '*Apologeticus*', which appeared about 360–1. His main aim was a demonstration of the creatureliness of the Son.[85] In 378, in reply to Basil's '*Three books against Eunomius*' (written 363–5), he had still less reason for embarking on the doctrine of the incarnation, as his opponent did not express himself on the matter either.[86] In 383, however, he presented a confession of faith to the emperor Theodosius I.[87] In this he repeats earlier observations on the incarnation and emphasizes the unity of person in Christ (Mansi 3, 648C). At the same time he finds an opportunity to present the old Arian christology—the one Logos did not take upon himself a man consisting of body and soul.[88]

According to the witnesses cited hitherto, Arian christology probably developed a special system of ideas step by step. Their 'theopaschism' is particularly noteworthy. Theodore of Mopsuestia, Gregory Nazianzus and Ps.-Apollinarius testify to it. For this phase of the Arian christology the *biblical* language was largely sufficient. The situation changed as the controversy developed. Witnesses, certainly of a later date, now stress the monophysitism of the Arians.[89] They are not actually talking of the Monophysites. They are looking for suspected ancestors for them—a

[84] Alexander of Alexandria also does not seem to be able to escape from an ontological intermediary. In his view, the Arians make too direct a juxtaposition between the uncreated Father and the things that are created from nothing. But he himself recognizes the μεσιτεύουσα φύσις μονογενής, which is begotten of the substance of the Father, between the Father and the creation. Opitz, op. cit., 26[44–5].
[85] Cf. Eunom., *Lib. apologet.*: PG 30, 836–68.
[86] Cf. Basil, *Adv. Eunom*: PG 29, 497–669. There is a summary of the dispute with Eunomius in Gregory of Nyssa: PG 45, 248–464, 909–1121; ed. W. Jaeger, *Gregorii Nysseni Opera* I, II, Leiden 1960; I, 22–225, 226–409.
[87] Mansi 3, 645–9. Refutation in Greg. Nyss.: PG 45, 465–572; ed. Jaeger II, 312–410.
[88] Greg. Nyss., *Ctr. Eunom.* 2: ed. W. Jaeger II, 384[29]–385[2]; PG 45, 545A; Mansi 3, 648C, where the negative is wrongly omitted; see *DTC* 5, 1507.
[89] So Theodoret, *Pro Diodoro et Theodoro*, ed. J. Flemming, 108.

procedure which is also evident in the anti-monothelitic fragments already mentioned. But it is not at all improbable that this corresponds to the historical development. The cause may, in fact, have been the dynamism of Arian christology or even of its sources. We are now to see an example of the more progressive Arian formula.

Eudoxius, from 357 to 359 Bishop of Antioch, from 360 to 369 Bishop of Constantinople, and friend of Eunomius, emphasizes in his confession of faith that the Son became flesh, but not man, and assumed no human soul. Thus there are in Christ not two natures, but only one composite nature.[90] In this way Eudoxius provided the clearest Arian formula of the incarnation. We will meet some further representatives of this christology in a group which stands close to Arianism and whose spiritual leader is Eusebius of Caesarea.

Eudoxius makes a good starting point for inquiring about the chief christological formula of the Arian system.

> We believe in . . . the one Lord, the Son, . . . who became flesh, but not man. For he took no human soul, but became flesh so that God was revealed to us men through the flesh as through a curtain; not two natures, since he was no complete man, but God in the flesh instead of a soul; the whole is one nature by composition.[91]

The Logos has become 'flesh', but not 'man', for he took no soul; this is the central Arian formula as Eudoxius framed it. It is already strongly reminiscent of Apollinarius of Laodicea. It is worth noting that Theodore of Mopsuestia was of the opinion that this Arian formula had already been condemned at the Council of Nicaea in 325, and there is some support for such an assertion in the wording of the Nicene creed. For Eudoxius has clearly done no more than reverse the Nicene formula. The fifth Catechetical Homily of Theodore runs, 'But our Holy Fathers warned us of all these (the Arians), by saying, "who was incarnate and was made man" (σαρκωθέντα, ἐνανθρωπήσαντα), by which we believe that that which was taken is a complete man in whom God, the Word, dwelt.'[92] But there is probably no need to understand Theodore's statement to mean that the Fathers of Nicaea had already expressly taken up a position against the christological formula of the Arians. Nor is it to be supposed that Nicaea already inveighed against the denial of Christ's soul by the Arians or

---

[90] J. P. Caspari, *Alte und neue Quellen zur Geschichte des Taufsymbols*, Christiania 1879, 179ff.; A. Hahn, *Bibliothek der Symbole* § 191, pp. 261–2. Also J. Lebon, *RHE* 23, 1927, 20, n. 2. See now M. Tetz, 'Eudoxius-Fragmente?', *StudPat* III (TU 78), 1961, 314–23. He dates this confession about 360 and considers it the first explicit Arian testimony to the Logos-sarx christology (letter of 17.11.63).

[91] A. Hahn, *Bibl. d. Symbole* § 191, pp. 261–2: σαρκωθέντα, οὐκ ἐνανθρωπήσαντα· οὔτε γὰρ ψυχὴν ἀνθρωπίνην ἀνείληφεν, ἀλλὰ σὰρξ γέγονεν . . . οὐ δύο φύσεις, ἐπεὶ μὴ τέλειος ἦν ἄνθρωπος, ἀλλ' ἀντὶ ψυχῆς θεὸς ἐν σαρκί· μία τὸ ὅλον κατὰ σύνθεσιν φύσις. . . .

[92] Theodore Mops., *Hom. Cat.* 5, 17: ed. Tonneau 123. H. M. Gwatkin, *Arianism*, 250, could have referred to this place when he says, 'It will be remembered that according to Arius the created Word assumed human flesh and nothing more. Eustathius of Antioch had long ago (he means before the emergence of Apollinarius) pointed out the error, and the Nicene council shut it out by adding "and was made man".'

against the Logos-sarx christology in general. In the Arian controversy
this point cannot have been much debated, as the Logos-sarx christology
seems to have been propagated far beyond the Arian circle. In the battle
between Eustathius and the christology of the Arians there is, at least in
the extant fragments, no reference to the council of 325. Nor can it be
concluded from Athanasius and Apollinarius that the christological
question as a whole was a subject for discussion in this so much disputed
council.[93] The Synod of Antioch, which was assembled under the presidency of Bishop Ossius at the beginning of 325 to deal with the Arian
question, saw no particular difficulty in the doctrine of the incarnation. In
some places it even speaks what is virtually the language of the Logos-sarx
framework.[94] If because of this preliminary synod the Council of Nicaea
inserted 'was made man' as well as 'was incarnate', there is no particular
reason for suspecting here a retort against Arian teaching on the incarnation. On the contrary, we are probably to assume that the formula of
Eudoxius was directed against the Council of 325.

Of similar significance to the Symbol of Eudoxius is a fragment by the
Arian Lucian, who was Bishop of Alexandria from 373 to 378.

> What need was there for a soul, for the worship of a perfect man alongside God? John
> too, loudly proclaims the truth, 'The Word was made flesh'. This means that the Word
> was compounded with the flesh (συνετέθη σαρκί) and certainly not with a soul . . .,
> rather did it unite itself with a body, so as to become one with it. For how else do we
> know Christ than as one Person, one composite nature (ἕν πρόσωπον, μία σύνθετος φύσις)
> (in composition) like a man, of body and soul? But if he also had a (human) soul, the
> impulses from God and from the soul would necessarily have conflicted. For each of the
> two is self-determining (αὐτοκίνητον γὰρ τούτων ἑκάτερον) and strives towards different
> activities.[95]

Here too the central formula of Arianism emerges clearly enough—the
'became flesh', borrowed from John 1. 14, but given a new interpretation.
A more technical terminology will be sought over and above this important Johannine formula; its main term is the word 'synthesis', of Logos and
sarx, univocally bound up with the unity of the human body and soul.

3. The Importance of Christology in the Arian System

This brief sketch of Arian christology can perhaps be made somewhat
clearer if we consider its relation to the whole of the Arian system, in

---

[93] I. Ortiz de Urbina S. J., *El símbolo Niceno*, Madrid 1947, gives no indication of such a specific
allusion for ἐνανθρωπήσαντα in his relevant section 234-44. Instead he gives a much clearer derivation
from an opposition to Gnostic-docetic influences, which were still active even then. J. N. D. Kelly,
Creeds, 231-54, does not go into the question.

[94] Synod of Antioch 325: Opitz, AW III, 1, 1-2, document 18, p. 39 (Syriac; Greek translation E.
Schwartz): ὁ υἱὸς θεὸς λόγος καὶ ἐν σαρκὶ ἐκ τῆς θεοτόκου Μαρίας τεχθεὶς καὶ σαρκωθείς. The
problems of this synod are discussed by David L. Holland, 'Die Synode von Antiochien (324/5) und
ihre Bedeutung für Eusebius von Caesarea und das Konzil von Nizäa', *ZKG* 8, 1970, 163-81.

[95] *Doctrina Patrum*, ed. Diekamp, 65[15-24].

which the trinitarian problem appears to stand in the foreground. For this reason, some scholars conclude that the Arian doctrine of the incarnation occupied only a subsidiary position.[96] We must, however, ask whether this is the right interpretation.

We first hear of the trinitarian peculiarities of the Arians in the period 318–323.[97] Had they been expressed earlier, much sharper opposition to them would immediately have made itself felt—as had already happened with Paul of Samosata. On the other hand, we must assume that the christological views in question go back, at least in part, as far as Lucian, who for his part was certainly influenced from elsewhere.[98] We are therefore justified in asking whether the doctrine of the incarnation was not rather the starting point for the whole Arian system. Could not the heresy of the creatureliness of the Logos have been occasioned by the doctrine of the incarnation, at least in so far as through it the Alexandrian subordinationism was extended to the teaching of the Logos as a creature (κτίσμα)? We must, of course, concede priority to this subordinationist element, which was taken over from the Apologists and especially from Origen. But subordinationism is still no Arianism, for which the teaching of the Logos as a 'ktisma' is essential. For further progress a special impulse would have been needed, and this would not necessarily have come easily. Moreover, at a later date the Arians were still proclaiming that they nevertheless had a great regard for the Word, and this, too, is not wholly obscured by their doctrine of his creatureliness.[99] May one not see in the concrete presentation of the unity in Christ, which saw Logos and sarx directly united, a stumbling block to further reflection on the being of the Logos himself? This would result in a particularly close association between teaching on the incarnation and the trinitarian ideas, an association

[96] G. Voisin, 'La doctrine christologique de saint Athanase', RHE 1, 1900, 234. In this view the Arian doctrine of the incarnation is merely a consequence of their trinitarian doctrine. A similar attitude to that of Voisin is shown by H. M. Gwatkin, Arianism, and S. Rogala, Die Anfänge des arianischen Streites, Paderborn 1907. For those holding this point of view the trinitarian slant of old polemic is conclusive.

[97] On these disputed dates see the controversy between W. Telfer (for 323) and N. H. Baynes (for 318) in JTS 47, 1946, 129–42; 49, 1948, 165–8; 50, 1949, 187–91. J. N. D. Kelly, Creeds, 230 (for 318); W. Schneemelcher, 'Zur Chronologie des arianischen Streites', ThLZ 79, 1954, 393–400.

[98] Opposition to the teaching of Paul of Samosata should probably be taken into account.

[99] M. Richard, 'Athanase', 10. On the question of how far a Logos-ktisma teaching already occurs in Origen, cf. C. W. Lowry in JTS 39, 1938, 39–42; in De Princ. IV, 4, 1 : Koetschau, 349[13], the word ktisma is used of the Logos, or Son, in a fragment introduced by Justinian. The authenticity of this word has often been discussed. Cf. H. Görgemanns, 'Die "Schöpfung" der "Weisheit" bei Origenes: Eine textkritische Untersuchung zu De Principiis Fr. 26', StudPat VII (TU 92), Berlin 1966, 194–209, who would deny its authenticity. M. Simonetti, I Principi di Origene, Torino 1968, 543, esp. n. 11, differs. He points to the influence of Prov. 8. 22 and Col. 1. 15 on the language of Arian theology in the Commentary on John I, 19 (22). See now W. Marcus, Der Subordinatianismus als historisches Phänomen, München 1963. This study, like that of A. Weber, APXH. Ein Beitrag zur Christologie des Eusebius v. C., see above, shows that the pre-Nicene concept of oikonomia (combining the development of the Trinity with creation and incarnation) is to be considered as the starting-point of Arian theology and the Nicene discussion. Nicaea, however, is a turning point in the history of oikonomia because now the distinction (but not a separation) between theologia (the trinitarian process) and oikonomia (creation and salvation history) is stressed. This is therefore confirmation of what follows.

which was dissolved by anti-Arian polemic, as the latter was concerned only with the trinitarian position. Some isolated Arian fragments which discuss the nature of the Logos do in fact give the impression that the Logos doctrine was fully self-contained, and had no intrinsic connection with teaching on the incarnation. This should not, however, mislead us. According to Marcellus of Ancyra, Asterius only arrived at a distinction of the *hypostases* of Father and Son, or in Nicene language, a subordination of the Son to the Father, on the basis of the doctrine of the incarnation.[100]

At one point in Athanasius the Arians ask the question, 'If he (the Logos) was very God of very God, how could he become man?'[101] There is a deep background to this question and it points to basic christological principles. Behind these words there clearly stands the thought that a real incarnation can only take place if the Word that comes from heaven really enters into a *substantial* conjunction with the flesh and becomes its life-principle. But for a 'divine' Logos the entry into such a conjunction was inconceivable, and so the Arians say to their Nicene opponents, 'How dare you say that the Logos shares in the Father's existence, if he had a body so as to experience all this?'[102] Nor is their question unjustified if one assumes that they consider the problem in the light of the Logos-sarx framework, in which the Logos takes the place of the soul and enters into a vital, i.e. natural, union with the body so as to form a human being. Viewed from this standpoint, an 'incarnation' of the Logos means that the Logos enters into a physical conjunction (not a confusion) with the body, in such a way that a *systasis*, a *con-stitutio*, one entity, arises from the two.[103] Notice how the Arians can presume that their opponents also argue from this premise and can therefore point so emphatically to the unbridgeable opposition between 'divine' Logos and human flesh which also exists in their thought. So behind their objection there is probably the notion that a really transcendent Logos cannot enter into a body-soul conjunction with the human *sarx* of Christ. If, then, the unity in Christ is to be explained in terms of such a conjunction, the Logos must be brought substantially nearer to the flesh. In this instance, the essential and substantial nature of the conjunction of Logos and sarx is made an argument against the divinity of the Logos. In fact, Athanasius also accuses the Arians of supposing that 'because of the flesh, he (the Logos) is subject to change and becomes another'.[104] So the taking of the flesh is the ground for

100 Frag. XXX: ed. G. Bardy, *Lucien*, 352: ἀπὸ τῆς ἀνθρωπίνης σαρκὸς ἦν δι' ἡμᾶς ἀνέλαβεν σκανδαλιζόμενος. Cf. ibid., frag. XXVII.
101 Athan., *C. arian.* III, 27: PG 26, 381A.
102 Athan., *C. arian.* III, 27: PG 26, 381A.
103 The acts of the Synod of Antioch 268, if genuine, speak of a σύστασις of Logos and sarx, which occurs in Christ. The Origenistic opponents of Paul of Samosata assert that Christ is the image of the conjunction of soul and body in a human being, the only difference being that the Logos takes the place of 'our inner man'. See *Chalkedon* I, 76, n. 9.
104 Athan., *C. arian.* I, 36: PG 26, 85C; ibid. III, 35: PG 26, 400A.

assuming a change in the Logos. The consequent elaboration of this attitude then leads to the intolerable one-sidedness of the Arian heresy, which goes on to trace the weakness of the Logos throughout the scriptures so as to be able to ascribe it to the Logos *qua* Logos.[105] Their argument is only tenable if they posit a physical unity of being between Logos and flesh in Christ.

[105] Alexander Al., *Ep. ad Alexandrum* 1, in Theodoret, HE 1, 4: ed. Parmentier 9[13-14]: πᾶσάν τε αὐτοῦ τῆς σωτηρίου οἰκονομίας καὶ δι'ἡμᾶς ταπεινώσεως φωνὴν ἐκλεξάμενοι. Alongside passages such as Prov. 8. 22 the biblical objections to the divinity of the Logos are from the most part drawn from teaching on the incarnation. Further fragments of Asterius in Marcellus of Ancyra point to the christological origin of the Arian heresies: frags. 63, 76 (in E. Klostermann: GCS 14, Leipzig 1906, 196, 200-1). Cf. W. Gericke, *Marcell von Ancyra*, Halle 1940, 212, 219-21. This interpretation is also put forward by C. W. Mönnich, 'De achtergrond van de Ariaanse Christologie', *NTT* 4, 1950, 387-412. T. E. Pollard, 'The Origins of Arianism', JTS, NS 9, 1958, 103-11, considers the Logos doctrine only. For him Arianism is a fusion of the opposed Antiochene and Alexandrian traditions of Logos interpretation. É. Boularand, 'Les débuts d'Arius', *BLE* 65, 1964, 175-203; id., 'Denys d'Alexandrie et Arius', *BLE* 67, 1966, 161-9; id., 'Au sources de la doctrine d'Arius. La théologie antiochienne', *BLE* 68, 1967, 241-72; his view is: 'Ce n'est pas à Antioche qu'Arius a trouvé les formules-clés de son hérésie, mais à Alexandrie même . . . Néanmoins il a herité du rationalisme antiochien . . .' (272). L. W. Barnard, 'The Antecedents of Arius', *VigC* 24, 1970, 172-88, gives pride of place to Alexandrian influence, but lays greater weight on the fact that 'Arianism was foremost a matter of philosophical dualism' (187). Note now the works by M. Simonetti, *Studi sull'Arianesimo* (Verba Seniorum, NS 5), Roma 1965, esp. I, 'Sull'interpretazione patristica di Proverbi 8, 22', pp. 9-87; id., 'Giovanni 14:28 nella controversia ariana', *Kyriakon* 151-61 (this passage of Scripture, *'pater maior me est'*, plays a role in the Arian controversy after the Second Council of Sirmium in 357 and in the *Apologia* of Eunomius, 361); id., 'Le origini del'Arianesimo', *RivStorLettRel* 7, 1971, 317-30.

CHAPTER THREE

THE COUNCIL OF NICAEA (325) AND ITS INTERPRETATION OF THE BAPTISMAL KERYGMA

AFTER Arius' one-sided resolution of the tensions dominant in Christian theology from the time of Origen, the first ecumenical council of Christendom did not produce an equally 'clear' and 'easy' counter-solution to the problem of monotheism. The work of this council consisted, rather, in interpreting the traditional Christian kerygma of the one God, Father, Son and Holy Spirit, in the sense of a *lectio difficilior*. With its thesis of the true divinity of the Son (and the Spirit), the *fides Nicaena* required a renewed strictness in theological reflection, to interpret both the relationship between Father and Son in the one God and that between the divine Logos and his flesh. For as Eusebius and Arius show, the incarnation of a completely transcendent Logos or a Logos understood in divine terms was more difficult to accept than that of a 'Son' understood in subordinationist terms or even as a creature. After Nicaea, the church of the fourth century went its way with this problem more acute. Its intellectual work was to be fundamental for all the further history of theology and the church. Ephesus and Chalcedon were already able to draw on the experiences of this epoch. The anti-Arian struggles became a theological college for the Fathers of the fourth century and beyond. Nicaea and the First Council of Constantinople in 381 (even if it was only recognized to be ecumenical in 451) established that faith in the one God, Father, Son and Holy Spirit, belonged to the form of Christian monotheism. This monotheism was the foundation for the preaching and the liturgy of the church, indeed for its entire life. It is the structure of God's all-embracing economy of salvation in Christ and the Holy Spirit. In 380 the emperor Theodosius I made this faith the law of the empire.

This leads us to another experience of the fourth-century church, to which sufficient attention has certainly not been paid: the establishment of the system of the imperial church. Galerius' edict of toleration, which he promulgated in Nicomedia on 30 April 311 (shortly before his death),[1] was soon to become the fundamental law for the tolerance of Christianity in the Roman empire. This was only a first step. More decisive was the personal intervention of the emperor Constantine in religious politics and in his profession of faith from the year 312.[2] A new development followed

[1] For the edict of Galerius: text in Lactantius, *De mort. pers.* 34: Moreau (SC 39), 117–18; Eusebius, HE VIII, 17, 3–10: Schwartz, GCS, Eusebius II, 2, 790–4; English in P. R. Coleman-Norton, *Roman State and Christian Church. A Collection of Legal Documents to AD 535*, I–III, London 1966 (hereafter cited as Coleman-Norton), I, no. 7, 18–22.

[2] (a) Surveys of research and the history of the Constantine question: J. Vogt, 'Constantinus d. Grosse', *RAC* 3, Stuttgart 1957, 306–79; K. Aland, 'Die religiöse Haltung Kaiser Konstantins', *Stud-*

in 324: Constantine himself took over direction of church matters. This was the most momentous decision on the way towards the imperial church.[3] We shall find it to be a continuing problem in the later history of christology. For the moment, we may simply point briefly to two preliminary questions: (1) What is the significance for christology of the idea of the 'imperial church'? (2) What follows from this for the independence of decisions made by councils?

1. NICAEA AND THE RISE OF THE IMPERIAL CHURCH

(1) Even before the time of Constantine, Christian apologists[4] had already been made aware of the coincidence of the advent of Christ, the founder of the Christian religion, and the *Pax Augusta*, the unification and pacification of the Roman empire and the *oikoumene*. For example, in his *Commentary on Daniel* (IV, 9) Hippolytus compares the church and the Roman empire,[5] though he does this in a spirit of mistrust rather than of confidence. For Hippolytus, although the unification of the empire and the preaching of Christ coincide, only Christianity has a truly ecumenical mission. Melito of Sardes already looks further ahead.[6] He presents 'the salvation offered to men in Christ in a context (. . .) which embraces the

---

Pat I (TU 63), Berlin 1957, 549–600; G. Kretschmar, 'Der Weg zur Reichskirche', *Verkündigung und Forschung* 13, 1968, 3–43; S. Mazzarino, ' "Politologisches" bei Jacob Burckhardt. Betrachtungen zu Burckhardts "Zeit Constantin's" und zu verwandten Problemen der historischen Begriffsbildung', *Saeculum* 22, 1971, 25–34; P. Wirth, 'Literaturbericht über byzantinische Geschichte. Veröffentlichungen der Jahre 1945–1967, in: *Historische Zeitschrift*, Sonderheft 3, 1969, 575–640.

(b) For the sources see Opitz, AW III, 1 and 2: documents 17 (year 324), 25, 27, 29, 33, 34; H. Kraft, *Kaiser Konstantins religiöse Entwicklung* (BHistTh 20), Tübingen 1955 (hereafter cited as Kraft): letters 16–18, 20, 22–5 etc.; Coleman-Norton I, no. 46 (Constantine in the year 324); 47 (Constantine on the Arian dispute); 48 (summoning of the Council of Nicaea); further documents on the Arian question: nos. 51, 53, 58, 66, 67, 71, 73; E. Barker, *From Alexander to Constantine*, Oxford 1966[2].

(c) Important monographs: E. Peterson, *Theologische Traktate*, München 1951, esp. 'Der Monotheismus als politisches Problem', 45–147; 'Christus als Imperator', 149–64; M. Vogelstein, *Kaiseridee, Romidee und das Verhältnis von Staat und Kirche seit Konstantin* (Historische Untersuchungen 7), Breslau 1930; H. Berkhof, *Kirche und Kaiser*, Zollikon–Zürich 1947; F. Dvornik, 'Emperors, Popes and General Councils', *DOP* 6, 1951, 3–23; id., *Early Christian and Byzantine Political Philosophy. Origins and Background* (Dumbarton Oaks Studies IX, I–II), Washington D.C. 1966; for Eusebius: II, 611–58; J. M. Hussey (ed.), *The Byzantine Empire, Government, Church and Civilisation* = The Cambridge Mediaeval History IV/II, Cambridge 1967; R. Farina, *L'Impero e l'imperatore cristiano in Eusebio di Caesarea. La prima teologia politica del cristianesimo*, Zürich 1966; G. Podskalsky, *Byzantinische Reichseschatologie*, München 1972; G. H. Williams, 'Christology and Church–State Relations in the Fourth Century', *Church History* 20, 1951, no. 3, 3–33; no. 4, 3–26; for the discussion over the chief works of research, especially Peterson, Dvornik, Berkhof, Farina and Williams, cf. J.-M. Sansterre, 'Eusèbe de Césarée et la naissance de la théorie "Césaropapiste" ', *Byz* 42, 1972, 131–95, 532–94. For further history, especially in the fourth century, cf. F. Winkelmann, 'Konstantins Religionspolitik im Urteil der literarischen Quellen des 4. und 5. Jahrhunderts', *Acta Antique Academiae Scientiarum Hungariae* 9, fasc. 1–2, 1966, 239–56; A. Grillmeier, 'Auriga Mundi', in: id., *Mit ihm und in ihm. Christologische Forschungen und Perspektiven*, Freiburg 1975. See further the literature on Eusebius mentioned at n. 1 above, esp. J. Sirinelli, ch. XI: 'La coincidence de l'Empire et de l'Incarnation', 388–411.

[3] Cf. Coleman-Norton I, nos. 44–8.   [4] Cf. E. Barker, op. cit., Part V.

[5] Cf. N. Bonwetsch, GCS, *Hippolytus* I, 206–9.

[6] W. Schneemelcher, 'Heilsgeschichte und Imperium. Meliton von Sardes und der Staat', *Kleronomia* 5, 1973, 257–75.

whole of history'.[7] In this *Homily on the Pasch* he gives a

comprehensive interpretation of history from creation to redemption. All is created
by God and all is called back to God. The *Imperium Romanum* also appears in this history
. . . (But) the synchronism of Christ and Augustus and the association of the well-being
of the empire with the growth of Christianity make it clear that at this point Melito is
not thinking of some kind of fortuitous coincidence, but is demonstrating a connection
which has its real ground in the divine plan of salvation.[8]

In his controversy over the work of Celsus, Origen similarly stresses
the idea of a deliberate coincidence of Christianity and the Roman
empire, but does this in only a very limited perspective: Augustus fulfilled
a task with which Christianity, as a messenger of peace, could not be
burdened: he unified the empire and excluded particularism. The new
religion now had a chance to introduce the state of affairs which existed
before the confusion of tongues at the tower of Babel; not immediately,
however, but with the arrival of the Last Judgement.[9] The theology of
history was from an early stage bound up with the patristic doctrine of
the divine economy.

Finally, Eusebius of Caesarea[10] is the real theologian of the association
of Christianity with the Roman empire; indeed he is its 'publicist' (E.
Peterson). However, this happens only after 313. In his writings a *political
theology* seems more and more to have gained the upper hand over a
doctrine of the economy and a *theology of history*. Eusebius primarily saw the
encounter between Christianity and Rome from a *moral* perspective:
Hellenistic–Roman civilization has brought about an undeniable moral
progress for mankind. The event of the incarnation takes place in a condition of humanity which has been prepared for in this way. A *political*
note intervenes in the Eusebius of the years 314 to 320: the incarnation is
put in the context of the civilization of the empire as the embodiment of
peace and order. A historico-political theology emerges: the appearance
of the Messiah and imperial peace, Christianity and the empire, are
bound together in an indissoluble unity by the idea of providence. We
already saw hints of this in Melito and Origen. Eusebius provides the
theory. In the first book of the *Praeparatio Evangelica* (I, 4, 1–6) he sees two
movements running alongside each other: polytheism, a diabolical
pluralism, is overcome by Christianity; the polyarchy which separates
the peoples is overcome by the Augustinian monarchy. Unity is now
fortified against multiplicity in two ways: in Christianity, which is
founded on the incarnation, and in the *Imperium Romanum*, which is
based on the monarchy. Moreover, the Roman monarchy becomes the
representation of the heavenly monarchy: the political union is matched
by the spiritual victory over polytheism. For Christ has overcome the

---

[7] Ibid., 272.   [8] Ibid., 273–4.
[9] Origen, *C. Cels.* II, 30: Koetschau, 157–8.
[10] See the studies by J. Sirinelli, R. Farina and J.-M. Sansterre mentioned in n. 2 above.

demons who were the real disrupters of both the religious and the political order. Of course, Eusebius has a limited horizon: he does not look beyond the boundaries of the *Imperium Romanum*. The fact of the incarnation already seems to have brought about something like a definitive state of affairs. In Eusebius, the world has already been 'saved', tangibly. The divine providence has gained such effective control of the world that no further change will be possible. History will run a peaceful course, if one can even talk of 'history'. For the divine Logos—embodied in Constantine's *monarchia*—sees to a universal and immutable order. This idea of Eusebius seems to have had so strong an influence that even after the bitter experiences of the church to the contrary, we can still find it among a series of bishops from the period after Chalcedon. Of course, Augustine breaks through the narrowness and rigidity of Eusebius' picture of the world and of history. The *harmonia praestabilita* between church and empire is replaced by the pressing question of the distinction between the *civitas dei* and the *civitas terrena*. Augustine keeps the whole of history in view— albeit from his perspective.

But which Eusebius created this ideal picture of the emperor and the world and—as will soon transpire—imprinted it at least to a certain degree on the memory of the church? It seems that at this point we must make a clear distinction between Eusebius before 335 and Eusebius after this year. Similarly, the ideas and conduct of Constantine himself should not be confused with what the Metropolitan of Palestine makes of the emperor and his position in the church. A number of clichés should also be tested in connection with the reactions of orthodoxy or the Arians to the claims of Constantine and his followers. We cannot go further into the question here. But one thing is important for us: certain results of more recent scholarship[11] in connection with the influence of the emperor Constantine on the Council of Nicaea and the foundations of so-called 'Caesaro-papism'. For the dogma of the church was immediately affected by this. Did Constantine manipulate the Fathers of Nicaea and force the *homo-ousios* on them? We may go part of the way with J.-M. Sansterre.

Head of the church, if not on the ground of priesthood, at least by virtue of a kind of supreme magisterium (souverain magistère)—that is the ideal emperor who is proclaimed by Eusebius of Caesarea from the year 335 on, that is, eleven years after Constantine's victory over Licinius and only twenty-two years after the end of the great persecution.[12]

So it seems that Eusebius developed his political theology only from 336 on. Immediately before this there had been the Synod of Jerusalem in September 335, on the occasion of the consecration of the Church of the Holy Sepulchre.[13] This synod was for the most part composed of bishops

---

[11] For what follows we refer especially to the study by J.-M. Sansterre, *Byz* 42, 1972, 131–95, 532–94.
[12] Ibid., 131.   [13] Ibid., 133–5.

belonging to the party of Eusebius of Nicomedia, and who were therefor hostile to the Council of Nicaea. At the emperor's desire, the Arians[14] who had been condemned at Nicaea were again received into the fellowship of the church. Only the bishops of Egypt under the leadership of Athanasius refused to recognize this restoration and to take part in it themselves. For this reason the members of the Synod of Jerusalem wrote to the bishops of Egypt.[15] In their letter they pointed out that the emperor Constantine had admonished them in a personal letter to accept the friends of Arius again, 'who for a long time have been kept outside the church by an immoral envy'.[16] Now the emperor himself is testifying to the orthodoxy of these men in his letter, as he has received their confession of faith. The bishops themselves had been able to be convinced of this by means of a formula attached to the emperor's letter. 'Thus the emperor has rightly invited us to accept these men into the community of the church of God.' Consequently the bishops of Egypt must also act now, as the faith made known by Arius and his friends clearly preserves the apostolic tradition accepted by all.[17]

Thus for the bishops of the synod of Jerusalem, Constantine's judgement is decisive. They accord the emperor the right to judge the orthodoxy of the clergy and communicate this in an official letter to other clergy. In this way they give the impression that the Synod of Jerusalem merely accepted this imperial decision. The historical situation of this document can be clarified from a comparison with the Tricennalia speech of Eusebius which the latter delivered soon afterwards before Constantine, in Constantinople, and the Basilikon Syngramma, which together with this speech is termed the Laus Constantini.[18] These two documents, together with the Vita Constantini, may rightly be adduced to indicate Eusebius' political theology against the background of his theological ideas.[19] According to Farina, in the works combined to form the Laus, Eusebius set out to describe the ideal emperor, after which he demonstrated in the Vita Constantini (cited hereafter as VC) that this ideal had been realized in the person of Constantine.[20] We shall outline this picture of the emperor briefly.

According to the Laus, ch. I, the emperor is the image (εἰκών) of the ruler of the world. At the same time he imitates the Logos-Christ. Thus we have a twofold mimesis: first between the emperor and God, and

[14] Athanas., Syn. 21, 3: Opitz, AW II, 1, 9, p. 247[33]–248[2]: ... ἡπλωμένῃ δὲ καὶ εἰρηναίᾳ ψυχῇ δέξασθαι τοὺς περὶ Ἄρειον, οὓς πρός τινα καιρὸν ὁ μισόκαλος φθόνος ἔξω γενέσθαι τῆς ἐκκλησίας εἰργάσατο.

[15] Athanas., Syn. 21, 2–7: Opitz, AW II, 1, 9, pp. 247–8.

[16] See n. 14.

[17] Athanas., Syn. 21, 5: Opitz, 248.

[18] See I. A. Heikel, GCS, Eusebius I, 195–259 (chs. I–X = Tricennalia speech; chs. XI–XVIII = Basilikon Syngramma).

[19] Cf. R. Farina and J.-M. Sansterre, op. cit., 135–46.

[20] J. M. Sansterre, op. cit., 146–56.

second in the imitation of the *mimesis* which is to be found between Father and Son. We may recall that Eusebius understands the *eikon-mimesis* relationship between Father and Son in subordinationist terms. By virtue of this twofold mimesis, the emperor enters into a kind of triadic relationship with the Father and the Logos. He occupies the position of a 'third person'.[21] It follows almost automatically that the emperor also participates in the functions of the Logos before the Father. Eusebius mentions in first place here the priesthood of the Logos. Like Christ, the emperor too is a priest; a priest, moreover, in a pure and immaculate sacrifice which is not to be understood as an imitation of pagan rites, but spiritually: the sacrifice is of the soul and spirit of the ruler, which he offers to God. With this he enters into the execution of the saving work of Christ. He becomes above all an instrument of the victory of the Logos over darkness. He acquires a messianic role (*Laus*, ch. II). The Logos drives all rebellious (demonic) powers from his flock; the emperor subjects the visible enemies of faith, and as the interpreter of the Logos leads men to knowledge of God. Thus he becomes a teacher (*didaskalos*) and proclaims the laws of truth (ἀνακηρύττειν).[22]

The *Basilikon Syngramma* gives a further description of this mission of the emperor as *didaskalos*: Eusebius reminds the emperor of his 'experience' of the saving activity of God. He has already had countless 'theophanies', and countless revelations through dreams. Those revelations which have been refused to men have been handed down by God in the spirit of the emperor. Thus he becomes the instrument of providence over the whole world.[23] However, Eusebius indicates a certain difference from the ministry of the church at this point: the emperor's *didaskalia* extends primarily to witnessing the truth in *action*, above all to soldiers and pagans, but also to all subjects of the kingdom. The emperor is to communicate the knowledge of God and to radiate love of a religious life and prayer.

Though this description of the teaching activity of the emperor is put in very general terms, according to Sansterre it does not exclude imperial action in respect of dogma; on the contrary, it leaves open the door for more concrete actions:

Il serait, en effet, étrange que le prince, didaskalos de la connaissance de Dieu, ne puisse l'être de celle de la relation entre le Père et le Fils, d'autant plus que l'évêque lui reconnaît explicitement la possession de la science des choses divines parmi lesquelles figure en bonne place cette même relation, et cette science n'est pas le fruit de l'enseignement d'un homme—comprenons d'un membre du clergé—mais elle est révélée.[24]

---

[21] Eusebius, *Laus*, ch. II, 1: Heikel, 199⁴⁻⁸: Ὁ μέν γε τοῦ θεοῦ μονογενὴς λόγος τῷ αὐτοῦ πατρὶ συμβασιλεύων ἐξ ἀνάρχων αἰώνων εἰς ἀπείρους καὶ ἀτελευτάτους αἰῶνας διαρκεῖ· ὁ δὲ τούτῳ φίλος, ταῖς ἄνωθεν βασιλικαῖς ἀπορροίαις χορηγούμενος τῷ τε τῆς θεικῆς ἐπηγορίας ἐπωνύμῳ δυναμούμενος μακραῖς ἐτῶν περιόδοις τῶν ἐπὶ γῆς κρατεῖ.

[22] Ibid., Heikel, 199²⁵.   [23] Eusebius, *Laus*, ch. XI: Heikel, 223f.

[24] J.-M. Sansterre, op. cit., 143. In argument with K. M. Setton, Sansterre stresses that this is a

One further question: how does Eusebius interpret the position of the emperor *vis-à-vis* the imperial councils in the VC? According to the VC, Constantine guides the debate, reconciles opponents, conciliates some, wins over others, urges all towards unanimity.

So when the emperor had spoken in Latin and another had interpreted his words, he handed over to the president of the synod. Then some began to accuse others, the latter defended themselves and raised counter-charges. And when much had been put forward on both sides, and a great dispute was beginning to break out, the emperor patiently gave a hearing to all and took note of what had been put forward with acute attention, and by declaring himself in favour of individual points put forward by each party, he gradually brought the disputatious men closer together. And because he turned to individuals in a mild and gentle way, making use of the Greek language which was also not unknown to him, he appeared friendly and pleasant; thus he was able to convince some, to put others to shame by his word, to praise those who spoke admirably and urge all towards harmony, until he finally succeeded in making them all of *one* sense and *one* opinion on all doubtful points.[25]

Who was really competent here in questions of faith? Who gave the decision when opinions conflicted? The VC makes Constantine the head of the council. The role of the emperor seems to be stressed even more strongly in the section of the VC which speaks of the intervention of Constantine in the life of the church of Egypt after Nicaea:

Now whereas all were living in peace, the Egyptians alone persisted in unreconciled dispute among each other, so that they again caused the emperor disquiet, though without being able to stir him to anger. Indeed he showed them all honour, as to Fathers or rather as to prophets of God, and even summoned them a second time[26] and again sought patiently to mediate among them; again he bestowed gifts on them. He gave his arbitration through a letter, confirmed and enforced the resolutions of the synod, and required that they should keep harmony and not divide and tear apart the church of God, but recollect in the spirit of the divine judgement. The emperor also made this known through his own letter.[27]

What is here ascribed to the emperor can at first be regarded as a confirmation of the decisions of the synod. These had earlier been worked out by the bishops themselves, but were given the force of law by the emperor, so that they had to be observed in all the provinces. The other expression which speaks of a written arbitration by the emperor seems to be more dangerous. The bishops evidently worked out their dogmata on the basis of this decision; the emperor then gave his approval, and they received the force of law. In the earlier report of the VC on the summoning of the Council of Nicaea (III, 6–22), Sansterre already sees

serious idea of Eusebius, and no mere flattery, thus esp. 146: 'Chez Eusèbe, au contraire, la *didaskalia* de l'empereur, rendue possible par sa science révélée des choses divines, apparaît fréquemment, et, qui plus est, elle s'intègre parfaitement dans une vaste théologie politique . . .'.

[25] Eusebius, VC III, 13: Heikel, 83: A. Bigelmair provides a German translation in BKV² 9, 104–5.

[26] A. Bigelmair, op. cit., 111, thinks that this means the second synod of Nicaea in 327. But only the Egyptian bishops are involved here.

[27] Cf. A. Bigelmair, BKV² 9, 111: in the original text the two main sentences run ἐδήλου τε τὴν δίαιταν δι' ἐπιστολῆς and τὰ τῆς συνόδου δόγματα κυρῶν ἐπεσφραγίζετο. Heikel, 88³⁴–89¹.

evidence that 'Eusebius' Constantine' in fact has greater significance than the bishops. The emperor plays the chief role at the council. The bishops remain in the background, although Constantine looks on them as 'Fathers and prophets'. This is also confirmed by the famous text of the VC (I, 44) which depicts Constantine's concern for the church—first no doubt in view of the Synod of Arles, but nevertheless with a general application:

> And so, when disputes broke out in various lands, he summoned assemblies of the servants of God, as though he had been set over all by God as bishop (οἷά τις κοινὸς ἐπίσκοπος ἐκ θεοῦ καθεσταμένος). He was not ashamed to appear in the assembled gathering and to sit in it; he took part in their deliberations and tried to bring to all the benefit of divine peace. So he sat in their midst like one of the many who were present. . . . Then he lavished his highest praise on all those whom he saw willing to agree with the better view and prepared to live in peace and harmony, and showed himself delighted that they were all of one opinion. But the mischief-makers he put behind him with repulsion.[28]

In this interpretation of Constantine's role by Eusebius, the emperor makes the decision. According to Sansterre, it is not said that he abides by the majority decision of the synod. He gives his verdict as arbitrator, but it is not said from what perspective. The dominant theme is the achieving of unity. But who decided what the 'better view' (ἡ κρείττων γνώμη) was? Who determined what 'mischief-making' was? Evidently the one who was regarded as the 'common bishop' of all. Here Eusebius seems to set imperial authority over the Council and thus make it the supreme authority in the church, even in matters of belief.[29] In all that Eusebius says about Constantine the picture of the ideal ruler is drawn, in a serious and coherent theory with a theological foundation.[30]

It is of the utmost importance for conciliar history and the history of Christian belief to ask whether this ideal picture corresponded with Constantine's own understanding of himself or not. To this end Sansterre investigates—after a critical examination of the sources—fourteen texts which come from the emperor between 325 and 335.[31] An evaluation of

[28] Eusebius, VC I, 44: Heikel, 28: German follows A. Bigelmair, BKV² 9, 35; see J.-M. Sansterre, op. cit., 149–50; J. Straub, 'Constantine as κοινὸς ἐπίσκοπος, Tradition and Innovation in the Representation of the First Christian Emperor's Majesty', DOP 21, 1967, 39–55; see J.-M. Sansterre, op. cit., 150, n. 4, who criticizes this study because Straub does not distinguish between the ideas of Eusebius and those of Constantine.

[29] J.-M. Sansterre, op. cit., 152.

[30] Ibid., 155.

[31] We cite here the list of documents which J.-M. Sansterre has established in more detail, op. cit., 162–8:

(1) Letter Πεῖραν λαβών, June 325: Opitz, document 26, pp. 54–7; Dörries, 66–8; Kraft, Letter 19, 220–5; Coleman-Norton I, 52, 143–9.

(2) Letter Χαίρετε, June 325: Opitz, document 25, pp. 52–4; Dörries, 68–70; Kraft, Letter 18, 218–20; Coleman-Norton I, 53, 150–2.

(3) Letter Τὸν δεσπότην: Opitz, document 27, pp. 58–62; Dörries, 70–4; Kraft, Letter 20, 225–9; Coleman-Norton I, 50, 135–41.

these documents shows a clear difference from Eusebius' picture of the emperor. Of course the decisive and fundamental thesis for the relationship between church and empire occurs in Constantine: there is an indissoluble bond between the well-being of the state and the unity of the church. But as far as Constantine was aware, this nexus had been created by experience of the power of the God of the Christians and his grace, for the unity of the kingdom. It remained decisive for all Constantine's further thinking in respect of empire and church. So the ecclesiastical disputes between Arius and Alexander caused him sleepless nights.[32] The only cure was an assembly of bishops as expressed by Constantine in his letter to the communities (document 1)—though here it was in connection with the date of Easter. This was the Council of Nicaea, in which the emperor stressed his own participation.[33] Only once in the documents that we have is this imperial participation connected with the dogmatic disputes, in Constantine's letter to the community of Eusebius of Nico-

(4) Letter ῞Οση τῆς θείας ὀργῆς, rather later than (3): Opitz, document 28, pp. 63; Dörries, 76–7; Kraft, Letter 21, 229–30; Coleman-Norton I, 51, 142.

(5) What is probably a genuine part of the letter Κακὸς ἑρμηνεύς (325–7) (?); Opitz, document 34, §42, pp. 74–5. Cf. Sansterre, 159–61; Kraft, Letter 23, 233–9, with an important commentary, 239–42.

(6) (a) Letter 'Ως κεχαρισμένη; (b) Letter 'Ανέγνων ἥδιστα; (c) Letter 'Ανέγνων τὰ γραφέντα; Dörries, 89–94; Kraft, Letters 29–30, 248–50; Coleman-Norton I, 61, 164–9 (years 326–35).

(7) Letter Καὶ νῦν (beginning of 328 or 335): Opitz, document 32, pp. 66; Dörries, 80; Kraft, Letter 25, 242–3; Coleman-Norton I, 71, 201–3.

(8) Part of a letter from Constantine to Athanasius (at the beginning of the latter's episcopate): Opitz II, 1, 6: 140; Dörries, 95–6; Kraft, Letter 32, 252–3; Coleman-Norton I, 72, 203.

(9) Letter Cum summi dei, 5 Feb. 330: Dörries, 40–3; Kraft, Letter 12, 198–201; Coleman-Norton I, 59, 159–63.

(10) Letter 'Αγαπητοί ἀδελφοί (before Easter 332): Opitz II, 1, 6, 141–2; Dörries, 96–99; Kraft, Letter 33, 253–4; Coleman-Norton I, 69, 198–200 (date 334 corrected by Sansterre).

(11) Letter τοῖς παρὰ τῆς σῆς συνέσεως: Opitz II, 1, 6, 146–7; Dörries, 99–102; Kraft, Letter 34, 255–6; Coleman-Norton I, 68, 194–8.

(12) Letter ῟Ην μὲν ἴσως ἀκόλουθον (before the opening of the debates in Tyre, July–August 335): Eusebius IV, VC IV, 42: 134–5; Dörries, 114–17; Kraft, Letter 36, 257–8; Coleman-Norton I, 73, 204–6.

(13) Digest of a letter of Constantine to the Synod of Jerusalem (probably September 335): Opitz II, 1, 9, 247; Sansterre, 167.

(14) Letter 'Εγὼ μὲν ἀγνοῶ (6 November 335): Opitz II, 1, 7: 164–5; Dörries, 119–24; Kraft, Letter 37, 258–9; Coleman-Norton I, 75, 208–13. The text in Gelasius, HE III, 18, 1–13, is probably genuine; cf. Sansterre 168, n. 1.

Appendix: Letter of Constantine to Sapor II: Eusebius, VC IV, 9–13: 121–3; Dörries, 125–7; Kraft, Letter 40, 261–2; Sansterre, 168, n. 4 (on the authenticity).

[32] Constantine, Letter to Alexander and Arius: Opitz, document 17, 15, p. 35; Dörries, 55–62, esp. 58; Kraft, Letter 16, 213–17; Coleman-Norton I, 47, 114–18; Kraft, 217; Coleman-Norton I, 117–18: 'Restore, then, to me serene days and nights free from care, that to me also may be preserved henceforth a certain enjoyment of pure light and gladness of tranquil life; but if not, it is necessary for me to lament and wholly to be confounded with tears and not even to sustain peacefully the period of life. For, while God's people—of my fellow-servants I speak—have been divided among one another by so unrighteous and injurious contention, how is it possible for me to be secure in mind for the future?'

[33] See above, document 1, §2: Kraft, 220–1; Coleman-Norton I, 52, 143: 'But since this could not possibly obtain both a steadfast and a constant establishment unless, when all or at least the majority of the bishops has assembled together in the same place, there would be an examination of each of the points pertaining to the most sacred religion; because of this, when as very many as possible had been convened (I myself, as one of you, was present—for I should not deny that I have been your fellow-servant, wherein particularly I rejoice), all matters received a competent investigation to such a degree until a decision, satisfactory to God, the overseer of all, was brought into the light for the harmony of unity, so that nothing still remains for dissension or dispute over faith.'

media.[34] The reason for his presence at the synod was to bring about unity and to end heresy in the church. Following this letter, he took part in the debates, though here they are portrayed as a search for the truth. The emperor wanted to be like a fellow-servant (συνθεράπων) of the bishops, although he himself had summoned the assembly. This became a judgement of God himself on Arius, as the bishops followed the will of God and the illumination of the Holy Spirit (which should be noted in respect of the emperor's view of the council).[35] In the same sense, the emperor felt himself obliged to watch over the dogmatic and disciplinary decisions of the council. In claiming to be able himself to judge the orthodoxy of Arius, he is only following the norm laid down by Nicaea.[36] In examining the creed presented by Arius and Euzoius—we already know its eclectic and meretricious character—Constantine comes to the conclusion that both men are orthodox. So he asks Alexander of Alexandria for them to be accepted into the church again.[37]

Of course, with the progress of the Arian disputes, the acts of imperial intervention increased. But certain nuances in their basis are important. When the emperor heard from Athanasius of the partisan character of the Synod of Tyre (335), he summoned the bishops to Constantinople so that he himself might pass judgement on the actions of the members of the synod.[38] In a letter written for a similar purpose he instructs the bishops to reach a unanimous verdict, not motivated by hate or partiality but by a desire to seek out the principles of the church and of the apostles. If anyone goes against the emperor's will and does not take part in the synod, he is to be expelled by the imperial command and taught 'that it is not proper to act against an emperor's decisions published in defence of the

---

[34] Constantine, Letter 20, 13; Kraft, 227; cf. Dörries, 70–4; Coleman-Norton I, 50, 138: 'But since it is meet to say a few words about Eusebius himself to your Loves, your Patiences remember that at the city of the Nicaeans has been held a synod, at which even I myself was present in a manner befitting the duty of my conscience, having no other desire than to produce unanimity for all persons and above all both to refute and to dispel this trouble, which had taken beginning through the madness of Arius the Alexandrian, but was strengthened forthwith through the absurd and destructive zeal of Eusebius.'

[35] Cf. document 2, §8: Sansterre, 170; Constantine to the Catholic Church of the Alexandrians: Kraft, Letter 18, 3, 218; Coleman-Norton, 53, 150: 'But that this might happen, by God's suggestion I convoked to the Nicaeans' city most of the bishops, with whom I, one of you, rejoicing exceedingly to be your fellow-servant, also myself undertook the investigation of the truth. . . . At all events, when three hundred and more bishops, admired for both prudence and sagacity, were confirming one and the same faith, which by the truths and the precisions of God's law has been begotten to be the faith, Arius alone, yielding to the Devil's activity, was observed as having disseminated by unholy intention this evil, first among you and then among the rest. . . . Therefore let us accept the verdict which the Almighty has provided.'

[36] J.-M. Sansterre, 163 and 170, refers here to the authentic part of Κακὸς ἑρμηνεύς of the years 325–27; for 'Nicaea as norm' see document 7: Kraft, Letter 25, 242–3; Dörries, 80; Coleman-Norton I, 71, pp. 201–3. Arius and Euzoius are to come to court and give account of their faith in accordance with the norm of Nicaea.

[37] Cf. J.-M. Sansterre, 171, with n. 2, who refers to the repetition and sharpening of this demand on Athanasius; also to the synod of Jerusalem 335, where Nicaea always serves as the norm of orthodoxy for the emperor.

[38] Cf. Kraft, Letter 236, 257–8; Dörries, 114–7; Coleman-Norton I, 73, 204–6.

truth'.[39] Here, too, it is primarily the task of the bishops to bring about the unity of the church in the truth and in discipline. For all that church and state belong together, the intervention of the emperor is still understood to be 'subsidiary'.[40] For the ultimate norms are the tradition and the canons of the church. So one cannot even speak of a *magisterium* of Constantine in the true sense. Nevertheless, as Sansterre rightly stresses, he sees his activity to be parallel to the teaching task of the bishops. But the emperor himself only has to intervene where they fail.[41]

Two texts seem to point more in the direction of the 'emperor as *didaskalos*':

(a) the first is the emperor's invitation to Arius to come to court, which had already been mentioned. There the emperor wishes to search out the secrets of the Alexandrian's heart.[42]

Come to me, I say to the man of God. Be convinced that with my questions I shall search out the deepest corners of your heart. And if any folly still seems to be in them, I shall heal you wonderfully by an appeal to God's grace. But if you seem to be sound in your soul, I will recognize in you the light of truth and rejoice with you over your piety.

It should be noted that in what is a public matter the emperor wishes to deal privately with an individual transgressor. This is something that a man may think himself capable of without wishing to play the part of a *didaskalos* in public. But if Constantine considers himself a 'man of God', he can offer his services to the whole church.

(b) A second document is a letter from Constantine to the bishops of Numidia.[43] At its conclusion, he says of the Donatists: 'If they were willing to follow our behest, they would be freed from all evil.' Here also, one cannot yet speak of a real *magisterium* of the emperor, but only of his consciousness of being called to be a doctor to confused souls. For emperor and bishops the 'precepts' and the 'divine commandments' are the ultimate norm for right action.

These few examples may be enough to demonstrate that in the time between 325 and 335 Constantine still pictured himself as the 'man of the church', a different portrait from that drawn by Eusebius after 335:

(1) According to his own account, Constantine felt himself to be an instrument of God in summoning the Council of Nicaea.[44] In participating

---

[39] Kraft, Letter 36, 3, 257: Coleman-Norton I, 73, 205.

[40] An instance of this subsidiary position is given in Kraft, Letter 33, 11, 253–4; Coleman-Norton I, 69, 198–200, who wrongly sets this letter to the community of Alexandria in 334 instead of in the period before Easter 332. See Dörries, 96–99.

[41] Cf. the letter to the Synod of Tyre: Kraft, Letter 37, 258–9; Coleman-Norton I, 75, 208–13; Dörries, 119–224.

[42] These are the genuine parts of Κακὸς ἑρμηνεύς = Opitz, document 34, §42, pp. 74–5; Kraft, Letter 23, 233–9. For the authenticity see Kraft, 239–42, though he is criticized by Sansterre, 160–1. Sansterre regards only the closing part of the letter, quoted above, as genuine.

[43] Kraft, Letter 12, 198–200 (our quotation p. 200); Coleman-Norton I, 59, 198–200; Dörries, 40–3.

[44] J.-M. Sansterre indicates how such a self-understanding was already prepared for in the Gallic period, with some references to the Latin panegyrics (175, nn. 1–2). At that time Constantine already

in the council, he is a fellow-servant of the bishops. In his own documents he does not claim to have directed the synod. On the contrary, the decisions were worked out by the bishops themselves, under the guidance of the Holy Spirit, in search of the will of God. The ultimate norm for the decision of the council is to be sought here, as in the apostolic traditions and the canons of the church.

(2) In the documents we have, Constantine seems to have gone beyond the famous saying which should perhaps be transferred to the conclusion of the Council of Nicaea and expresses a division of authority: ἀλλ' ὑμεῖς μὲν τῶν εἴσω τῆς ἐκκλησίας, ἐγὼ δὲ τῶν ἐκτὸς ὑπὸ θεοῦ καθεσταμένος ἐπίσκοπος ἂν εἴην.[45] In Sansterre's translation:

> Mais vous, certes, vous avez été établis par Dieu comme évêques de ceux qui sont à l'interérieur de l'Église; moi; j'ai été établi par Dieu, comme évêque de ceux qui sont à l'extérieur de l'Église (litt. vous êtes des évêques établis . . . je suis un évêque . . .).[46]

In the document between 325 and 335 Constantine betrays a wish to regard himself as a fellow-servant of the bishops, but also to watch over the dogmatic and disciplinary decisions of the Council of Nicaea (and also of other synods). This still would not amount to an involvement in the formation of doctrinal decisions, but would rather be a guarantee of their validity, in their function for the unity of the church. In this sense we may understand the saying coined by Eusebius for the emperor, that he is the κοινὸς ἐπίσκοπος, the inspector general, for the observance of the decrees of the council.[47] In the terms of the other saying quoted above (Eusebius, HE IV, 24), the emperor first of all distinguished between the two religious groups in the empire, the pagans and the Christians, and differentiated his conduct accordingly. He felt that his spiritual task towards the pagans corresponded to that of a bishop towards Christians. He is their *pontifex maximus*. As Sansterre observes, in our documents the emperor does not repeat these words again. After 325 his confidence in the bishops evidently disappeared. He probably recognized their particular function and above all the authority of the synods. But his attitude towards the Christians developed further:

> Sans doute, à la suite de l'opposition au *Nicaenum* qui se manifesta dès novembre-décembre 325, comprit-il la necessité de 'brider' les évêques, de leur faire sentir qu'il n'était pas seulement l'évêque des païens, mais qu'il était aussi le gardien des décisions du concile. . . .[48]

---

experiences the divine help which guided his actions and set at nought the efforts of his opponents, which were directed at both Constantine and his army.

[45] Cf. the observations of J.-M. Sansterre on this famous saying, op. cit., 176, n. 2. He follows closely a study by C. Masay, L'"episcopat" de l'empereur Constantin, Mémoire de licence, Univ. Libre de Bruxelles, Sect. Histoire, 1967–68, which was not accessible to us.

[46] J.-M. Sansterre, op. cit., 176, n. 2.

[47] Eusebius, VC I, 28: Heikel, 28[19–20]: οἷά τις κοινὸς ἐπίσκοπος ἐκ θεοῦ καθεσταμένος.

[48] J.-M. Sansterre, op. cit., 176, n. 2.

Even if a development can be seen in Constantine's own attitude—it was compelled by the disappointment of his expectations of the bishops' desire for unity—his own claim can still be clearly distinguished from that made for him by Eusebius after 335. Eusebius' Constantine stands *above* the council, even in questions of belief. The imperial 'teaching office' is conceived of in sharper terms: the emperor is the interpreter of God and of the Logos-Christ; since like this Logos-Christ he has revealed knowledge of divine things, he is a teacher. The real Constantine did not claim either capacity for himself. On the other hand, the bishop of Caesarea makes the Christian emperor the summit of a pyramid, whose cloak covers both state and church in the same way. He sacralizes his figure so that it becomes the supreme summit of the visible world understood in religious terms. We shall see how this conception accompanies us through the Byzantine era of church history and the history of doctrine.[49]

If the imperial documents of the years 325–35 suggest that the council's statements of faith were not really influenced by Constantine, this can also be underlined from the content of his christology. Constantine was not in a position to achieve intellectual mastery of the problems which arose at Nicaea. His understanding of Christ, especially as it can be seen in Letter 20, remains on a pre-Nicene level.[50] Constantine is even uncertain over the name Christ. He uses it for Father and Son. For him, God really has no name. 'As the name Christ is applied to the whole Godhead, the name Son is now absent in Constantine. The "aeon" takes the place of the name Christ used in a Christian way.'[51] This term 'aeon'

[49] See the continuation of the present work dealing with christology after Chalcedon; also the study 'Auriga Mundi', already mentioned, in *Mit ihm und in ihm*, Freiburg 1975. The hypothesis of J.-M. Sansterre, that Eusebius presented the emperor after 335 in so lofty a style to bring about a corrective to the Council of Nicaea, is still to be demonstrated. He himself concedes that there is no textual evidence for it. Had Eusebius striven for this goal, one would surely be able to find some traces between the lines. Did Eusebius really want such a revision? It is remarkable that precisely in the *Basilikon Syntagma*, that is, at the time of the greatest friendship between the Eusebians and Arius, Eusebius seems to be furthest removed from Arian doctrine. A created Logos is excluded by sayings like *Tricennal.* XII (= *Basilikon*): Heikel I, 230$^{2-26}$; 231^{27}–232^6. Eusebius is largely subordinationist (cf. Heikel, 231$^{10-15}$: the Logos as the steersman who always looks up to God). But Sansterre rightly sees the necessity of seeking a motive in Eusebius for the way in which he sharpens the picture of the emperor over against Constantine himself. Even if Eusebius did not strive to do away with Nicaea, he did strive for the unity of the church, because he was obsessed by the idea of unity. It is probably also correct that Eusebius could never regard the Nicene creed as a guarantee of the unity of the church. He probably believed that his own subordinationism could be the basis of this unity in the years after 335. The further the emperor was set above the church, the more he could settle those whom Eusebius believed to be the real disrupters of the peace of the church: Athanasius, Marcellus of Ancyra and Eustathius of Antioch.

[50] Cf. the good comments on Constantine's christological views in Kraft, 108–13, together with Letter 20, ibid., 225–9, with commentary (Br. 20, only partially genuine!); also the speech to the 'Holy synod', in Kraft, 263–8, following Gelasius, HE 2, 7, 1–41 (to be regarded as genuine; cf. commentary 268–71, mentioned as a 'proposal' in contrast to the *Oratio ad Sanctos* in Eusebius VC IV, 32; text Heikel I, 154–92).

[51] Kraft, Letter 20, 225: 'Dear brothers, you all know well that the Lord God and Saviour Christ is Father and Son: I name him Father as the one without beginning and end who begets his aeon, Son, i.e. the will of the Father, who is neither embraced by a thought nor led to complete his works by matter which has already been explored. . . . (2) But the Son of God, Christ, the demiurge of all things and guide towards immortality was begotten—as is said by the faith which we confess—

points to the *Hermetica*, as does the designation of this aeon as 'divine counsel or will'. Where the church Christian would have spoken of the Word of God (Logos), the emperor speaks of the 'divine will'. Further Gnostic influence is betrayed in the fact that according to Constantine the 'divine will' is not received through any *enthymesis*, nor is it 'maintained by any matter'. In Nicene terms: the Logos (= the divine will in Constantine) may not be thought of in any material way. For *enthymesis*, the thought which comprehends, is part of matter. H. Kraft derives the anti-Arian position of the emperor from this: when the Arians say that Christ could not be God in the strict sense because he suffered, whereas God is incapable of suffering, the emperor replies that in no circumstances may God be thought of in material terms and that he is therefore incapable of corporeal suffering. Similarly, the emperor rejects a 'division' even in the relationship of Christ to the Godhead—and does so in complete agreement with the Nicenes. For the division and *apotomē* can only be expressed of matter.

How does Constantine solve the problem of the way in which true Godhead and suffering can come together in Christ?

> For this he makes use of the Stoic conception of the coming into being of entities. According to this an entity consists of two principles, one active and one passive: the former is identical with the Godhead, the latter is identical with matter. This divine principle, which is only active, bears the name *physis*; it is the creator of the world, which gives the cosmos rational form and creates it from matter. (Here Kraft points to Zeno, to an Orphic hymn to Physis, and to Plotinus. Zeno's doctrine in turn entered the Hermetic writings, with which Constantine also shows some affinity at this point). . . . Constantine applies the opposition between *physis* and *hyle* to the humanity of Christ; the immaterial *physis*, the creator God, assumed a pure and honourable body from the Virgin in order to bring gnosis to men, without losing his Godhead in the process. Thus this body is the seat of the material *pathē*, the suffering of Christ; if this body suffers, then God is present without suffering with it. A parallel to this is of the human soul with the body in which it dwells and which it leaves on its death, in order to live on further.[52]

Without doubt there is a significant theological element in Constantine's remarks against the Arians: in effect he advances a solution which will be later used by Marcellus of Ancyra and others. All suffering is assigned to the corporeal element in Christ. The Godhead remains intact; indeed, on the contrary,

> God chose a quite honourable body (. . .) through which to proclaim the proofs of faith and the examples of his own power. He wanted to ward off the destruction which had already spread widely through the human race as a result of the perversion of corruption, and to give a new religious doctrine, to purify the unworthy deeds of the spirit by the example of holiness, and finally to relieve the torment of death and proclaim the prize of immortality.[53]

was begotten, or rather, he himself came forth, who was constantly in the Father, to administer that which had come into being through him. In other words, he was begotten by proceeding forth in a way which causes no division. For the will is at the same time contained in his housing.'

[52] Letter 20, 4, in Kraft, 226.   [53] Ibid.

It is not easy to make Constantine's picture of Christ more precise.[54] H. Kraft discusses an interesting problem.

It is difficult to give a clear answer to the question of the way in which Constantine thought of the indwelling of God in a human body. Perhaps we are given an indication in the statement: 'To purify the unworthy deeds of the *nous* by the example of holiness.' According to this, one might assume that the body which was honourable did not have a human *nous* of its own, but that the place of the *nous* was taken by the Godhead.[55]

This supposition seems correct. For evidently Constantine believed that the divine pneuma dwelt in the sarx of Christ; the force of this pneuma was particularly effective in the sarx in the miracles, and thus demonstrated the divinity in this unity of pneuma and sarx. The indwelling of the numen in the body does not involve the Godhead in any suffering, but it does not seem to leave any place for a human soul in Christ. So for this unity of pneuma and sarx 'death' was no more than a separation of the two constituent parts. This is clear from Letter 20:

Now is there something in the midst between God, who (is) both Father and Son? Evidently not. For the commandment of the will received the fullness of all things by perception and in no way separated the will from the substance of the Father. Consequently, is there anyone who fears the suffering of Christ my Lord—more from reverence than from folly?[56] Does the divine element (τὸ θεῖον, in Latin *numen*) suffer anything when the housing of the honourable body (i.e. the body as the housing of the deity) issues a summons to recognize its holiness? Is not that different which has been taken from the lowliness of the body or can that which is separated from the body be touched (Latin, *nonne distat hoc, quod e corporis humilitate ablatum est*)?[57]

[54] Cf. Dörries, 376–96: the picture of Christ. Of course Dörries regards the speech *ad Sanctos*, mentioned above, ed. Heikel, to be genuine. Thus he introduces inauthentic features into the christology of Constantine. Cf. esp. 129–61, and for criticism Kraft, 271–2.

[55] Kraft, 113; the quotation from Constantine comes from Letter 20, 5, but only has force if one adds the context: 'Do you not see that God selected a quite honourable body by which to show forth the proofs of faith and the examples of his own power. . . .' These examples of his power are a demonstration that God dwells in the 'honourable body'. Cf. the genuine *Oratio ad sanctum coetum* (Gelasius), Kraft no. 22, 265. Here Constantine praises 'the finest righteousness of all, exalted above all praise, as he had resolved to dwell in this most holy body of his own divine pneuma and thus to have a healing influence on the bodies of men'. Here we can see a pneuma-sarx christology which knows of only two realities in Christ: the most holy body, born of the Virgin, which the divine pneuma calls his own, as an instrument by which to heal men. The doctrine of the impassibility of the Godhead in Christ should also be added to the total picture; here the suffering is thought of purely in connection with the corporeal element. Cf. Letter 20, 4.

[56] The problem of the suffering or impassibility of God, as suggested by Constantine, evidently played a considerable role at that time. Reference may be made to Ps.-Gregory Thaumaturgus, *Ad Theopompum* (see above, p. 233). Constantine's teaching might be compared with that of the *Ad Theopompum*.

[57] Kraft, Letter 20, 4, 226. According to Kraft, this part is one of the genuine sections of Letter 20. In comparison with Kraft, the translation Coleman-Norton I, 50, 136 (below) is inaccurate. So part should be quoted in the Greek text of Gelasius, HE III, Suppl. 1: GCS, Loeschke-Heinemann, 193–4: ἆρ' οὖν πάσχει τὸ θεῖον, ἐπειδὰν ἡ τοῦ σεμνοῦ σώματος οἴκησις πρὸς ἐπίγνωσιν τῆς ἰδίας ἁγιότητος ὁρμᾷ, ἢ ὑποπίπτει θίξει τὸ τοῦ σώματος ἐκκεχωρισμένον; ἆρ' οὐχὶ διέστηκε τοῦθ' ὅπερ ἐκ τῆς τοῦ σώματος ἀφῄρηται ταπεινότητος; Coleman-Norton, loc. cit.: 'Does the Divinity, therefore, suffer? After the soul (this is not what is being talked about!), the habitation of the august body, hastens to the knowledge of its own holiness, does what has been separated from the body fall beneath a touch? Has not the Divinity separated this, the soul (but it is not being talked about!) which has been taken

The ideas which Constantine has about Christ are well-known and very old-fashioned. Some of them are reminiscent of Lactantius; it is difficult to discover the origin of others. We may be justified in asking what Constantine understood by the *homoousios* of Nicaea, if he had such a confused understanding of the relationship between Father and 'Christ'. One thing is certain: the interpretation of the relationship between Father and Son in the Nicene creed cannot derive from him. But this does not exhaust the possible ways in which the emperor might have influenced the council. The more his authority grew, the more the influence of his advisers, or of certain groups to which he lent an ear, grew also. At first he seems to have listened to the majority in the council. But in the course of discussion, the Eusebian party seems to have found increasing access to him.

2. THE 'FIDES NICAENA'

The new statements made by the Council of Nicaea on the relationship of the Logos-Son to the Father had been prepared for by earlier tradition, but had required the emergence of Arius and his friends to provide the acute stimulus which brought them into the creed of the church and the general consciousness of believers. As we know, this reception was itself a long process. As has already been remarked, the *Expositio fidei* of Gregory Thaumaturgus comes nearest in content to the central theme of the Nicene proclamation of the faith. If our assumption is correct, Arius showed particular aversion towards this 'creed'. Whether this aversion also brought it to the notice of the Fathers of Nicaea and how far this was the case is a matter which needs further investigation, which cannot be undertaken here. The answer must be left open. In addition to the synods and writing of Alexander of Alexandria, the Fathers of Nicaea saw particular importance in the synods of Antioch of the years 268 (against Paul of Samosata) and 325 (or 324/5).[58] Fifty-six bishops from Palestine, Arabia, Phoenicia, Coele Syria and Cappadocia are mentioned at the beginning

---

from the body's humility?' Coleman-Norton has evidently been led by the following sentence to talk already of the soul of Christ, although this last sentence is only meant to be an analogue of the untouchability of the 'Godhead' in Christ: 'Do we not live, even if the soul's glory shall summon the body to death?'

[58] For the synods before Nicaea see the short outline by Dom H. Marot, 'Vornicäische und Ökumenische Konzile', in: B. Botte et al. (eds.), *Das Konzil und die Konzile*, Stuttgart 1962, 23–51; *Le Concile et les Conciles*, Chevetogne–Paris 1960. For Antioch 325: text (Syriac, with Greek translation by E. Schwartz), in Opitz, AW III, 1, pp. 36–41, document 18; Kelly, *Creeds*, 1972³, 208–11; V. C. De Clercq, *Ossius of Cordova. A Contribution to the History of the Constantinian Period*, Washington D.C. 1954, 206–17, with a survey of the discussion of the historicity of this synod extending to 1954; see now D. L. Holland, 'Die Synode von Antiochien (324/5) und ihre Bedeutung für Eusebius von Caesarea und das Konzil von Nizäa', *ZKG* 81, 1970, 163–81. Holland does not exclude the historicity of the synod, but fails to find the ultimate proof of it and feels that all the difficulties have not been eliminated.

of the synodal letter. The president was probably Ossius of Cordova.[59] Granted, discussion has recently been revived on the questions whether the synod took place and whether the synodal letter can be regarded as genuine. But once again, a number of doubts can already be laid to rest.[60] Some of the chief points of the creed may therefore be enumerated.[61]

The faith is . . . as follows: to believe in one God, Father . . . and in one Lord Jesus Christ, only begotten Son, begotten not from that which is not but from the Father, not as made but as properly an offspring, but begotten in an ineffable, indescribable manner, because only the Father who begot and the Son Who was begotten know (for 'no one knows the Father but the Son, nor the Son but the Father'), Who exists everlastingly and did not at one time not exist.

(The creed then stresses that the Son alone is the true image of the Father; he was necessarily begotten, without depending on whether the Father willed to beget him or not; nor was he 'adopted'. It follows that he is unchangeable and immutable; he was not created from nothing, but 'begotten'. So here already the 'begetting' is contrasted with a procession from 'the things that are not'. There is no mere 'similarity' between the Father and the Son; nor does he confound himself with the things that were made through him. His coming forth is completely transcendent, above all understanding. The wording of the creed then continues:)

We confess Him to have been begotten of the unbegotten Father, the divine Logos, true light, righteousness, Jesus Christ, Lord and Saviour of all. For He is the express image, not of the will or of anything else, but of His Father's very substance (ὑποστάσεως). This Son, the divine Logos, having been born in flesh from Mary the Mother of God and made incarnate, having suffered and died, rose again from the dead and was taken up into heaven, and sits on the right hand of the Majesty most high, and will come to judge the living and the dead.

In this confession the most important Arian theses are taken up and rejected. The typically Nicene formulas 'of the substance of the Father' or 'of one substance with the Father', or the *homoousios*, are still missing. Yet all that is important has been said: the begetting of the Son from the Father, his completely identical nature to him. J. N. D. Kelly points to the close similarity with the confession which Arius had laid before Alexander. Here is the church's counterpart to it, just as in the *Thaleia* Arius seems to have developed a counterpart to the confession of Gregory Thaumaturgus. Kelly also notes that the anathemas at the end of the Antiochene creed take up problems of the *Thaleia* point by point and reject the Arian solution to them:

And we anathematize those who say or think or preach that the Son of God is a creature or has come into being or has been made and is not truly begotten, or that there was when He was not. For we believe that He was and is and that He is light. Furthermore,

---

[59] Cf. V. C. De Clercq, op. cit.; H. Chadwick, 'Ossius of Cordova and the Presidency of the Council of Antioch, 325', *JTS* NS 9, 1958, 292–304; Kelly, *Creeds*, 1972³, 208.
[60] Cf. G. C. Stead, ' "Eusebius" and the Council of Nicaea', *JTS* 24, 1973, 98–9.
[61] Kelly, *Creeds*, 209f.

we anathematize those who suppose that He is immutable by his own act of will,[62] just as those who derive His birth from that which is not, and deny that He is immutable in the way the Father is. For just as our Saviour is the image of the Father in all things, so in this respect particularly He has been proclaimed the Father's image.[63]

E. Schwartz already believed that this surely overloaded creed was a paraphrase of the Tome of Alexander of Alexandria,[64] i.e. of the confession which he had sent on to his namesake of Byzantium. According to J. N. D. Kelly, in this creed we have 'the forerunner of all synodal creeds'. The method applied here, to take an already existing creed and incorporate into it the new elements that needed to be said, became an example for Nicaea and other synods. The addition of anathematisms at the end also became paradigmatic for the future. Nicaea had its 'overture' (J. N. D. Kelly).

So, then, the Fathers of Nicaea took up a baptismal creed—a fact which was thought in the fifth century to be an advantage which the first council enjoyed over against Chalcedon—and inserted into it their clauses directed against Arius. Their intention was to exclude any equivocation in the kerygma of the church and its creed. For the Arians also made use of this language, but understood it in their own way. Despite H. Lietzmann and J. N. D. Kelly, there is still no agreement whether the foundation of the Nicene creed is the baptismal creed of the church of Eusebius of Caesarea (which was the view prevailing before these scholars) or the creed of Jerusalem or another Palestinian creed, as Kelly in particular would like to assume.[65] We need not decide this question here.

The chief concern of the council[66] was to confess in one God, without

---

[62] There is an allusion here to the interesting doctrine of Arius, discussed in Chapter 2 above, of the free self-determination of the (created) 'Son' and the foreseeing of him by God; cf. G. Bardy, *Lucien*, 265f. The reference to this doctrine is certainly also a point in favour of the authenticity of this text.

[63] See Kelly, *Creeds*, 210.

[64] See Kelly, *Creeds*, 210, n. 2; Opitz, AW III, 1, 1, p. 38, apparatus.

[65] Kelly, *Creeds*, 217–20; for criticism see D. L. Holland, *ZKG* 81, 1970, 177–80, esp. 179: 'Thus it can by no means be regarded as an assured result of scholarship that Caes must be ruled out as a basis for N because of the allegedly closer relationships of N to a hypothetical Syro-Palestinian confession. . . .' Here, too, Holland will not accept it as proven that Caes has been demonstrated to be the basis of N; he simply wishes to point out that the arguments of Lietzmann and Kelly have not been fully substantiated. He would adopt the position of A. von Harnack, that 'Caes is largely regarded as the basis for N, while at the same time allowing the possibility that many of the bishops assembled at Nicaea similarly presented their confessions of faith to the redactor or redactorial committee, and thus equally deserve to some degree the title "Father of the Nicaenum". For this reason N should perhaps be regarded as a compilation of confessions, the style of which is not all of a piece, the theology of which is incompletely trinitarian and with which no one could be completely content.' However, it should be noted here that Nicaea was concerned to clarify a particular point *vis-à-vis* Arius rather than to provide a complete trinitarian statement. In view of the relative novelty of the decisive point, it would be difficult to indicate creeds which could be exploited for this purpose. Cf. however, the *Expositio fidei* of Gregory Thaumaturgus, although this was not a baptismal creed. Still, there were Western and Eastern traditions that could be utilized.

[66] For the text cf. G. L. Dossetti, *Il Simbolo di Nicea e di Constantinopoli. Edizione critica*, Roma 1967, taken over in COD, 1973³, 5, with an introduction, pp. 1–4. On this see D. L. Holland, 'The Creeds of Nicea and Constantinople Reexamined', *Church History* 38, 1969, 248–61. For the Nicene creed, cf. O. Seeck, 'Untersuchungen zur Geschichte des nicaenischen Konzils', *ZKG* 17, 1897, 1–72, 319–63; F. Loofs, *Der authentische Sinn des Nicaenischen Symbols*, Leipzig 1905; id., 'Das Nicaenum', in:

prejudice to faith in the one God, the true Father and Creator of all things visible and invisible and his true Son. No more is said about the Holy Spirit than was offered by the creed which had been adopted. Christian monotheism is preserved from Arian Hellenization; the baptismal formula contains an interpretation of it which is decisive for the whole future of the church. An explanation is given of the saving economy of the Trinity which shows that the Father communicates himself to us in the true Son (and in the Holy Spirit), while at the same time showing the truly divine status of the Son and also his soteriological relevance. The relationship between Father and Son within the Godhead is left within the framework of the economy of salvation. Jesus Christ is the one true Son of the Father, not a creature. This is made clear by a series of statements which leave no way open for the Arians:

> We believe . . . in one Lord Jesus Christ, the Son of God, begotten from the Father, only-begotten, that is, from the substance of the Father, God from God, light from light, true God from true God, begotten not made, of one substance with the Father, through whom all things came into being, things in heaven and things on earth, Who because of us men and because of our salvation came down and became incarnate, becoming man. . . .

(1) The Son is 'only-begotten', and is indeed 'begotten' (γεννηθείς). The tension of the ante-Nicene period introduced with the terms ἀγεννητός-γεννητός and κτίζειν is now resolved, by assigning to the Son the fact of being begotten. If ἀγέννητος is also applied to the Father, it can mean both 'uncreated' and 'unbegotten' for him. From now on, it is impossible to translate γεννητός, when applied to the Son, as 'created', and to use it in this sense. Of course a strict distinction between ἀγέννητος (unbegotten) and ἀγένητος (uncreated)—note the orthography—will only make itself felt with Athanasius.[67]

(2) This Son is begotten 'from the substance of the Father'. This expression, together with the Nicene word 'of the same substance' ('of one substance'), probably entered the discussion with the Arians as a result of the following considerations: (a) according to the Arians the Father is necessarily above the Son and his status. (b) From the Arian perspective, the Son derives his existence from the Father by a pure act of will and not through physical begetting or separation or emanation. Coming forth as a result of the 'will' guarantees the divine immutability and indivisibility. For the Arians, this meant that the uniqueness of the archē was preserved,

Festgabe für Karl Müller, Tübingen 1922, 68–82; E. Schwartz, see the index of writings in *Gesammelte Schriften*, vol. 4, Berlin 1960, 333ff. (from the year 1904); A. d'Alès, *Le dogme de Nicée*, Paris 1926; I. Ortiz de Urbina, *Nicée et Constantinople* (Histoire des Conciles Oecuméniques, ed. G. Dumeige, I), Paris 1963; G. Langgärtner, 'Das Aufkommen des ökumenischen Konzilsgedankens. Ossius von Cordoba als Ratgeber Konstantins', *Münchener Theologische Zeitschrift* 15, 1964, 111–26; F. Ricken, 'Nikaia als Krisis des altchristlichen Platonismus', *TheolPhil* 44, 1969, 321–41; Kelly, *Creeds*, 324–54; É. Boularand, *L'hérésie d'Arius et la 'Foi' de Nicée, II: La "Foi" de Nicée*, Paris 1972.
67 See e.g. G. L. Prestige, *God in Patristic Thought*, London 1952², 37–54.

and also the strict monotheism which they felt to be required. It was only consistent to regard the 'Son' as created, and furthermore as 'not necessary', as 'alien in substance' to the Father. The Fathers countered all this with the confession of the begetting of the Son from the substance of the Father.[68]

(3) The Arians were certainly ready to accept the formula 'God from God, light from light', and they could vary it in a number of ways. But they reacted in a very hostile way when the Council made it more precise by the phrase 'true God from true God'.[69] Here a further play with the equivocal use of the word 'God' was no longer possible. The designation of the Father as ὁ θεός, which was common in the ante-Nicene tradition in the light of scripture, was not made impossible as a result, but it was protected from Arian misinterpretation. For that very reason the coming forth of the Son from the Father was interpreted in terms of 'begetting', because this implied that he was of the same nature as the Father. Of course the council did not reflect on the question how the Father, Son and Holy Spirit could be truly different and yet participate in the one undivided nature of the Godhead. Here Nicaea, like the early church decisions in general, was an *ad hoc* solution. The implications of a statement were still not taken into account. Language and thought were kerygmatic. This is the true and valuable element of this council.

(4) Now at this point a word was inserted into the creed which was to disturb the whole of the fourth-century church: ὁμοούσιος, the expression of the identity of the substance of the Son and the Father. We cannot outline either the development of this dispute in the fourth century or the history of modern scholarship and the many tasks which still confront it.[70] We can only go so far as is necessary for an understanding of the

---

[68] In connection with the 'coming forth from God', the Arians wanted to associate the Son completely with us and with all creatures. Cf. the remarks in Athan., *Decr. Nic. Syn.* 19, 1–5: Opitz, AW II, 1, 3, pp. 15–16: ... οἱ περὶ Εὐσέβιον ... ἐβούλοντο τὸ ἐκ τοῦ θεοῦ κοινὸν εἶναι πρὸς ἡμᾶς καὶ τὸν τοῦ θεοῦ λόγον μηδέν τε ἐν τούτῳ διαφέρειν ἡμῶν αὐτὸν διὰ τὸ γεγράφθαι (quot. 1 Cor. 8. 6 and 2 Cor. 5. 17, 18). According to Athanasius the distinction between the coming forth of the Son and our createdness is made by the Son's 'being from the substance of the Father'. On this cf. G. C. Stead, art. cit., *JTS* 24, 1973, 85–92.

[69] The Arians argue with John 17. 3, which speaks of the μόνος ἀληθινὸς θεός, against the 'true God from true God' of Nicaea. Cf. Athan., *Syn.* 39, 5: Opitz, AW II, 1, 9, p. 265³⁰⁻³²; ibid., 45, 7–8: Opitz, 270–1, esp. 271⁸⁻⁹ (on the hypocrisy with the confession of ἐκ τοῦ θεοῦ). Cf. Athanas., *Syn.* 36, 5: Opitz, 263²¹: οὐκ ἔστιν ἀληθινὸς θεὸς ὁ Χριστός. Athan., *C. Arian. or.* I, 9: PG 26, 29AB; cf. further frag. VIII in Bardy, *Lucien*, 265; Phoebadius, *C. Arian.* 8: PL 20, 18D. Even Eusebius of Caesarea was evasive here, although he rejected the creation of the Son. Cf. his letter to his community, where he accepts 'God from God', but adds that 'the Father is truly Father and the *Son* is truly Son and the Holy Spirit is truly Holy Spirit': Opitz, AW III, 1, 2, document 22, p. 43¹⁶⁻¹⁷. But this is not equivalent to the 'true God' which Eusebius rejected in his letter to Euphration. Cf. Opitz, AW III, 1, 1, document 3, 3, p. 5: ἐπεὶ καὶ αὐτὸς θεὸς μὲν ὁ υἱός, ἀλλ' οὐκ ἀληθινὸς θεός· εἷς γάρ ἐστι καὶ μόνος ἀληθινὸς θεὸς διὰ τὸ μὴ ἔχειν πρὸ αὐτοῦ τινα. Cf. Athan., *Syn.* 17. 3: Opitz, AW II 1, 9, p. 244²⁷⁻⁸; according to Athan., *Ep. ad Afros* 6: PG 26, 1839BC, Eusebius represented true Arianism before Nicaea. But no essential alteration took place. In his own confession of faith, in contrast to the Nicene creed (Opitz, document 22, 4–6), there is certainly 'God from God', but 'true God from true God' is missing. Cf. the comments by Opitz, AW III, 1, 2, p. 45 apparatus.

[70] F. Ricken, 'Nikaia als Krisis des altchristlichen Platonismus', *TheolPhil* 44, 1969, 333–9 gives a good account of the literature and problems of the *homoousios*. See the important n. 26, p. 334, with

development of christology (as the doctrine of the incarnate Logos). Above all, it should be stressed that the Fathers of Nicaea did not want to 'Hellenize' the concept of God in revelation and the kerygma of the church by the word *homoousios*, that is, they did not want to superimpose 'a philosophical and technical concept of *ousia*'. 'They were more concerned to clarify what the Scripture said about the Son.'[71] Of course, it is conceded today that *homoousios* had the first phase of its theological history in Gnosticism, as is clear from Arian fragments and from the proceedings of 325 themselves.[72] Among the Gnostics it meant 'similarity of being' between different beings or their 'belonging to the same mode or stage of being'.[73] It has been thought that perhaps the Arians themselves gave occasion for the insertion of *homoousios* into the creed of Nicaea. For to the degree that we are concerned with documents of the Arian controversy, we find this word for the first time in Arius' *Thaleia* and in his letter to Alexander of Alexandria. In a fragment of the *Thaleia* we read:

He (the Son) has no characteristic (ἴδιον) of God in his individual subsistence (καθ'ὑπόστασιν ἰδιότητος), for he is not like him (ἴσος), nor indeed is he ὁμοούσιος.[74]

On this, F. Ricken remarks:

What is meant by the negation of the *homoousios* is clear from the preceding verses (p. 242[10-14], Opitz): The Father alone is as he is. He has nothing like him (ἴσον) nor is there anything similar (ὅμοιον) nor is there anything to which the same honour is due (ὁμόδοξον). In contrast to the Son he is uncreated, without origin and eternal. So in the sense of the Gnostic term the Son does not have the same kind of being as the Father, nor does he belong to the same level of being as the Father. He is a middle-being, which once was not and which received its being through the will of God. He is not the real and own Logos of God, but he is the Logos only in bearing the name (καταχρηστικῶς).[75] the account and criticism of the so-called 'neo-Nicene theory of T. Zahn for the interpretation of the *homoousios*'. From the literature, particular stress should be laid on: H. Kraft, 'ΟΜΟΟΥΣΙΟΣ', ZKG 76, 1954/55, 1-24; A.-M. Ritter, *Das Konzil von Konstantinopel und sein Symbol*, Göttingen 1965, 270-93 (literature); A. Tuilier, 'Le sens du terme ὁμοούσιος dans le vocabulaire théologique d'Arius et de l'Ecole d'Antioche', StudPat 3 (TU 78), Berlin 1961, 421-30; G. C. Stead, 'The Significance of the Homoousios', StudPat 3, 397-412; Kelly, *Creeds*, 242-54. F. Loofs, 'Das Nicaenum', in: *Festgabe für Karl Müller*, Tübingen 1922, 68-82, is still useful. F. Ricken, op. cit., deals with the question of the Western (Ossius) or the Eastern derivation of the *homoousios*. On the 'Western' thesis of Kraft and Ritter, he remarks: 'But it would be difficult to prove from the extant reports on the proceedings at Nicaea that the Fathers of the Council understood the *homoousios* in the sense which is suggested by the use of οὐσία in the questions of Ossius in Antioch. The restraint of the East *vis-à-vis* the *homoousios* can perhaps be explained sufficiently by the Gnostic sound of the word and the materialistic conceptions which it suggested. In that case Nicaea adopted the word only of necessity, to fix clearly its opposition to Arius, while continually stressing throughout the proceedings that it was not to be understood materialistically in the same terms as Valentinian Gnosticism. Any use of *homoousios* without the addition of an explanation of the way in which it was *not* to be understood had inevitably to seem dangerous in the East.'

[71] F. Ricken, op. cit., 335.   [72] Ibid., 335f.

[73] Cf. A. Orbe, 'Hacia la primera teología de la procesión del Verbo', *Estudios Valentinianos* I, 1-2, Rome 1958, 660-2.

[74] Arius, *Thaleia*, according to Athanasius, *Syn.* 15: Opitz, AW II, 1, 9, p. 242[16-17].

[75] F. Ricken, ibid., 336f. According to a fragment from a letter of Eusebius of Nicomedia to the Synod of Nicaea which Ambrose, *De fide* III, 15, has handed down to us, for him the confession of Christ as the true Son is synonymous with the confession of identity of substance: *Si verum, inquit, dei filium et increatum dicimus*, ὁμοούσιον *cum patre incipimus confiteri*.

In rejecting the *homoousios*, Arius was certainly concerned to ward off an inadequate conception of God, above all the conception of the corporeality of God, as though the Son as part of the divine being were on the way to being an emanation or a separate part of God. But those who supported the *homoousios* decidedly wanted to exclude this also. Hence the stress on the incorporeality of the Logos, hence the rejection of any division of the *ousia* or a suffering of the *ousia* and *dynamis* of the Father. But the acceptance of a begetting within God and the true identity of substance and the real difference between Father and Son (and Spirit) raised the problem of Christian monotheism in sharp contrast to the understanding of God in Judaism and Middle Platonism. For the Fathers of Nicaea, the sense of Scripture allowed two ways of proceeding from God: the first is immanent within God; the second leads *extra deum* and does so in a twofold way: first as creation and then as the sending of the Son (and of the Holy Spirit) into the world. The Arians could only conceive of 'creatio extra deum' as the sole way of the Son's proceeding from the Father. For them a 'begetting' had necessarily to be understood in corporeal terms.[76]

Without having thought through all the implications and problems, the Fathers of Nicaea had the courage to maintain the tradition of the 'Son of God' to be found in Bible and church in all its strictness, in part with unbiblical words. The question how a Sonship (and a procession of the Holy Spirit, which was seen at Nicaea only in the context of the economy of salvation) in the one being of God could be expressed in philosophical conceptuality was secondary for them. And this was a truly kerygmatic course of action to take, in full accord with the tradition. So much did the Fathers of Nicaea wish to remain within the framework of the baptismal kerygma, that they did not add any explanation of the way in which they themselves wanted the *homoousios* to be understood. Their understanding must be worked out from a number of documents which were written after the council, e.g. the letter of Eusebius of Caesarea to his community,[77] and various reports of Athanasius.[78] Eusebius tells us that 'Son of God displays no kind of similarity to creatures which have been brought into being, but only to the Father who has begotten him, similar in every way. He is not of another *hypostasis* or *ousia*, but of the Father' (loc. cit., no. 13). Of course Eusebius does not derive this inter-

---

[76] Cf. Eusebius of Nicomedia, *Ep. ad Paulinum*: Opitz, AW III, 1, 1, document 8, p. 17⁴⁻⁵, on coming forth from the 'will' of God; ibid. 17f., document 9 (letter of Paulinus of Tyre), on the corporeality of the begetting.

[77] Opitz, AW III, 1, 2, document 22, pp. 42–7.

[78] Athanas., *Decr. Nic. Syn.* 20 (year 350/1): Opitz AW II, 1, pp. 16–17; id., *Syn.* 45: Opitz, AW II, 1, pp. 269–71; id., *Ep. ad Afros* 6 (year 369): PG 26, 1040 AC. According to the text from *Decr. Nic. Syn.* 20, 6 (Opitz, 17), the main theses of the Arians abolish the confession of the coming forth from the nature of the Father and the *homoousios*: τὸ ἐκ τῆς οὐσίας καὶ τὸ ὁμοούσιον ἀναιρετικὰ τῶν τῆς ἀσεβείας λογαρίων εἰσίν, ἅπερ ἐστὶ κτίσμα καὶ ποίημα καὶ γενητὸν καὶ τρεπτὸν καὶ οὐκ ἦν πρὶν γεννηθῇ.

pretation from the term *homoousios* but from other presuppositions, which include subordinationism. This is precisely what was excluded by the new word as the Nicenes understood it. The subordinationist phase of theology, initiated by the so-called Christian Platonism of the ante-Nicenes, is concluded, though its consequences have still by no means been overcome. Athanasius defines the significance of the *homoousios* in contrast to the 'godless talk' of the Arians: (a) summing up what Scripture says about the Son, it is meant to express the fact that the Son is not only 'similar' to the Father but, as one who has come forth from the Father, is quite equal to him (ὁμοούσιον εἶναι τῷ πατρὶ τὸν υἱόν, ἵνα μὴ μόνον ὅμοιον τὸν υἱόν, ἀλλὰ ταὐτὸν τῇ ὁμοιώσει ἐκ τοῦ πατρὸς εἶναι σημαίνωσι); (b) it says that the Son is not separate from the substance of the Father, a point over which Athanasius refers particularly to the nature of the Son as 'Logos' of the Father.[79] However, after Nicaea there was necessarily a hard struggle to see how both the oneness of substance of the Son and the Father and the distinction between them could go together. To pursue this development lies outside our terms of reference. It finally led to the formula of one *ousia* in three *hypostases*. But the real Christian concern of the Nicenes is well summed up by Athanasius in one passage of the *Or. III c. Arian.*:

> Thus we acknowledge (only) one origin; of the Creator-Logos we say that he does not have another mode of being from the unique God, as he came forth from him (πεφυκέναι, thus by nature). Rather, the Arians can be accused of polytheism or godlessness, in that they assert in an unskilful way that the Son is an extra (-godly) creature, and that the Spirit too was created from nothing. So they must either say that the Logos is not God, or they call him God for the sake of Scripture, but not in a way that would accord him the nature of the Father: thus it is clear that they introduce several (many) gods because of the difference of the natures (of the Father and the Son), unless they venture to say that even the Son can only be called 'God' by participation, like other things. If that is their view, they are godless in the same way, as they designate the Logos as one of all (i.e. of the creatures). We shall never be able to accept this. For there is only one manner of divinity (ἓν γὰρ εἶδος θεότητος), which is also in the Logos, and God the Father, who is in himself, is one, in that he is over all; but he appears in the Son, in that he rules over all, and he is in the pneuma, in that he achieves everything through the Logos that is in him. So we confess one God in triad; this, our view, corresponds much more to piety than the multiform and many-faceted deity of the heretics, as we confess the one Godhead in the Trinity.[80]

The Nicene triad is understood strictly within the Godhead, although here Athanasius sees it in equally close conjunction with the works and

79 Athanas., *Decr. Nic. Syn.* 20, 1–5: Opitz AW II, 1, 3, pp. 16–17; ibid., 17³⁻⁶: Opitz, 14: in §4 Athanasius assigns physical derivation to the concept of Son and the inseparability of Father and Son, together with the origin of the Son from the Father, to the Logos concept. According to 26, 1–3 (pp. 21–22), the Arian doctrine of the 'three hypostases' which are alien to each other is connected with the denial of the 'unseparated': εἰς τρεῖς ὑποστάσεις ξένας ἀλλήλων παντάπασι κεχωρισμένας διαιροῦντες τὴν ἀγίαν μονάδα. In the apparatus, Opitz refers back to *Sent. Dion.* 16–20 (AW II, 1, p. 58¹¹⁻¹⁵); cf. now W. A. Bienert, *Dionysius von Alexandrien. Das erhaltene Werk*, Stuttgart 1972, 9–10, 75–7, 77–84 (texts), esp. 81 (7).

80 Athanas., *C. Arian. or.* III, 15: PG 26, 353AB.

outward activity of the Father, i.e. as the foundation of the ordinances of creation and salvation—which is why this is an important passage for the original unity of the immanent Trinity and the Trinity of the economy of salvation. The Arian triad has quite a different structure: the monad is above, then come the nous and the pneuma outside the Godhead, both of which in gradation are part of the creaturely order. Thus it was also easy even for the Arians to talk of 'three (separate) hypostases'.[81] We can already guess how difficult it would be for the Nicenes to take over talk of 'three hypostases'. For Nicaea itself had understood 'hypostasis' and 'ousia' synonymously, and thus had entered upon a quite different course.[82] Only after this synonymity had been abandoned was a signpost erected, pointing to the linguistic distinction between where unity was to be sought in God and where there was difference. Biblical monotheism, already essentially 'Christianized' in the kerygma of the coming of the Father in the Son and in the Holy Spirit, and thus marked out from Jewish 'monotheism', was demonstrated by the Nicene controversy to involve even more an inwardly differentiated structure.

(a) Nicaea and the understanding of the incarnation

In the christological controversies over Ephesus and Chalcedon, the Nicene creed retrospectively acquired the reputation of being a fundamental statement in the church's interpretation of the incarnation. This was not because of an explicit doctrine or a newly introduced concept, but in regard to a scheme which was found in the text. As the event of the economy of the flesh was predicated of a Son of the same substance as the Father, the creed was also found to express a unity of subject in the sense of a 'christology from above'. Cyril and Nestorius adopted this presupposition, albeit each in his own way. The Monophysites and the Chalcedonians equally claimed the Nicaea creed for themselves. They all wanted to speak of one and the same Son, of the same substance as the Father, who became flesh.

In fact the statement in the Nicene creed about the Son also had an implication of which the Nicenes themselves only slowly became aware: if the identity of the substance of the pre-existent Son with the Father was taken as seriously as at Nicaea, then the necessary consequence was a clarification in the understanding of the relationship between the Logos and the world: in concrete terms, of the Logos and the flesh. The sort of 'symbiosis' between Logos and sarx which we find among the advocates of the strict Logos-sarx framework in the pre-Nicene period (probably already in Malchion, the opponent of Paul of Samosata, in Eusebius of

---

[81] Cf. the confession of faith of Arius and his friends to Alexander of Alexandria: Opitz, AW III, 1, 1, document 6, 4, p. 13: ὥστε τρεῖς εἰσιν ὑποστάσεις.

[82] Symb. Nicaen., addition: Dossetti, 238–9; DOC, 5.

Caesarea, Arius and also in other theologians) could no longer be presupposed. The transcendence of the Logos over the world and the flesh which he had assumed might not be vitiated—if the spirit of Nicaea was taken seriously—even presupposing the Nicene unity of subject in Christ. We shall see how difficult it was to draw this conclusion in the work of so decided a Nicene as Apollinarius of Laodicea. Indeed, in him it becomes clear how the symbiosis of the Logos, understood precisely in Nicene terms, with his flesh could be interpreted particularly effectively in a soteriological context. The Fathers of Nicaea did not think of all these implications. Although the Logos-sarx framework had demonstrably already found quite a footing in the East, it did not become a problem at the council.

CHAPTER FOUR

FROM THE NICENE SON AND LOGOS TO A DOCTRINE OF THE INCARNATION

WHAT effect did the decision of Nicaea have immediately after the Council? In what way did christology gain from it—as an interpretation of the incarnation? We shall attempt to answer these questions by considering two controversial figures of the period after Nicaea: Marcellus of Ancyra (died 374) and Eustathius of Antioch (died before 337). It is hard to describe their christology, especially their doctrine of the Logos and the incarnation, because only fragments of their most important writings have been preserved, and the authentic form of these—at least in the case of Eustathius—has not yet fully been clarified. Important additions have been made to the *Corpus Marcellianum*, and research into it and interpretation of it is in full swing.

The question we must ask of these two Nicenes is how far a Nicene doctrine of Son and Logos became a starting-point for a new interpretation of the incarnation. Do we find that they had a clear understanding of the Nicene creed—especially Marcellus? Had Nicaea already been sufficiently impressed on men's consciousness in 325 for it to form a dominant starting-point for discussion? We believe that this consciousness only dawned with Athanasius, towards 362. In the case of both Eustathius and Marcellus, it was the Arian positions which attracted attention to them. They were thus at first more anti-Arian than Nicene.

1. MARCELLUS OF ANCYRA

Against the Arians, and especially Asterius, Marcellus advanced above all his own theological conceptions, his own method and his own evaluation of the sources.[1] 'Neither in his first writing nor in his Letter to Julius

---

[1] The most thorough treatment of the present state of scholarship and edition of the *Corpus Marcellianum*, together with an introduction to Marcellus' teaching is to be found in M. Tetz, 'Zur Theologie des Markell von Ankyra I–III' (cited hereafter as Tetz, Markell I, II, III): I. 'Eine Markellische Schrift *De incarnatione et contra Arianos*', ZKG 75, 1964, 217–70; II. 'Markells Lehre von der Adamssohnschaft Christi und eine pseudoklementinische Tradition über die wahren Lehrer und Propheten', ZKG 79, 1968, 3–42; III. 'Die pseudoathanasianische *Epistula ad Liberium*, ein Markellisches Bekenntnis', ZKG 83, 1972, 145–94; id., 'Markellianer und Athanasios von Alexandrien. Die markellianische *Expositio fidei* ad Athanasium des Diakons Eugenios von Ankyra', ZNW 64, 1973, 75–121 (cited hereafter as Tetz, 'Markellianer und Athanasios'). I am grateful to Dr Tetz for his comments on this chapter. For the sources: (1) The fragments of Marcellus' first writing and the *Epistula ad Iulium* in GCS, Eusebius-Werke IV: ed. Klostermann, new edition Berlin 1972, 255–63. There is a German translation (very suspect in parts) by W. Gericke, *Marcell von Ancyra. Der Logos-Christologe und Biblizist. Sein Verhältnis zur antiochenischen Theologie und zum Neuen Testament* (Theol. Arbeiten z. Bibel-, Kirchen- und Geistesgeschichte 10), Halle 1940, with a survey of research into Marcellus from Rettberg to 1930, 28–70. (2) De sancta

nor in the *Epistula ad Liberium* had Marcellus expressly referred to the Nicene creed for a positive account of his confession: rather—apart from Scripture—he kept to the *regula fidei* and in one instance also to the Roman creed.' Shortly before this, M. Tetz writes: 'The use of the *regula fidei* can already be recognized in Marcellus, frag. 121. The main part of the Letter to Julius contains a combination of a presentation of the *regula fidei* with the Roman creed. And the confession which has been handed down as the pseudo-Athanasian *Epistula ad Liberium* keeps to the *regula fidei* in a similar form to that acknowledged by Tertullian.'[2] On Marcellus' side, the Nicene creed comes into play only in the *Expositio fidei* of Eugenius, which is a testimony from the last years of Marcellus' life and 'formulates the faith of the community in Ancyra who stand firmly behind their aged bishop'.[3] However, this development had already been prepared for in the letters of Marcellus to Pope Julius and Pope Liberius. But even after Athanasius had accorded pre-eminence to the Nicene creed at the Synod of Alexandria in 362 (*Tomus ad Antiochenos*),[4] the followers of Marcellus remained open for an appeal to a more general tradition of faith which is also demonstrated by the *Expositio fidei* of Eugenius, mentioned above, as a writing 'which clearly documents the development of theological argumentation in the direction of an explicit proof from the Fathers'.[5] Thus from the perspective of his method and his sources, Marcellus may

Ecclesia, ed. G. Mercati, 'Anthimi Nicomedensis episcopi et martyris de sancta Ecclesia' (ST 5), 1901, 87–98; assigned to Marcellus by M. Richard, 'Un opuscule méconnu de Marcel évêque d'Ancyre', *MSR* 6, 1949, 5–28. (3) Ps.-Athanasius, *Sermo maior de fide*, better *Epistula ad Antiochenos*, ed. E. Schwartz, *Der sogenannte* Sermo maior de fide *des Athanasius*, SBMünchAk 1924, 6, München 1924; R. P. Casey, *The Armenian Version of the Pseudoathanasian Letter to the Antiochenes and of the Expositio Fidei* (Studies and Documents 15), London–Philadelphia 1947; H. Nordberg, *Athanasiana, Part I: The Texts* (Soc. Scient. Fennica, Comm. Hum. Litt. XXX 2), Helsinki 1962. Arguments in F. Scheidweiler, 'Wer ist der Verfasser des sog. *Sermo Maior de Fide*?', *ByzZ* 47, 1954, 333–57; M. Tetz, Markell II. (4) Ps.-Athanasius, *Contra Theopaschitas* = second version of the *Epistula ad Liberium*: H. G. Opitz, *Untersuchungen zur Überlieferung der Schriften des Athanasius*, Berlin–Leipzig 1935, 210–12; F. Scheidweiler, 'Ein Glaubensbekenntnis des Eustathius von Antiochien?', *ZNW* 44, 1952/3, later accepted as a writing by Marcellus following M. Richard's proposal: *ByzZ* 47, 1954, 353–4; *ZNW* 46, 1955, 208f. Now Tetz III, 152–4 (ed.). (5) Ps.-Athanasius, *De incarnatione et contra Arianos*: PG 26, 984–1028; assigned to Marcellus in Tetz, Markell I. Ps. Athanasius, *Expositio fidei*: Nordberg, op. cit., 49–56; cf. F. Scheidweiler, *ByzZ* 47, 1954, 356f., also noted among the *Marcelliana* by G. C. Hansen, op. cit., 255, and Tetz, Markell I, 221, but according to Dr Tetz now no longer to be regarded as one of the works of Marcellus. For interpretation see T. Zahn, *Marcellus von Ancyra*, Gotha 1867; F. Loofs, 'Die Trinitätslehre Marcells von Ancyra und ihr Verhältnis zur älteren Tradition', *SBBerlAk* 33, 1902, 764–81; id., 'Marcellus von Ancyra', *PRE*[3] 12, 1903, 259–65; cf. Gericke, op. cit., 59–69; for Marcellus' christology, in addition to Gericke, see J. Fondevila, 'Ideas cristologicas de Marcelo de Ancyra', *Estudios Eclesiasticos* 27, 1953, 21–64 (considers only the texts in GCS); E. Schendel, *Herrschaft und Unterwerfung Christi*, Tübingen 1971, 111–43; R. Hübner, 'Gregor von Nyssa und Markell von Ankyra', in: Marguerite Harl (ed.), *Écriture et culture philosophique dans la pensée de Gregoire de Nysse. Actes du Colloque de Chevetogne (22–26 Sept. 1969)*, Leiden 1971, 199–229; id., *Die Einheit des Leibes Christi bei Gregor von Nyssa. Untersuchungen zum Ursprung der physischen Erlösungslehre*, Leiden 1974, has long sections on Marcellus. See also T. E. Pollard, 'Marcellus of Ancyra. A Neglected Father', *Epektasis*, 187–96. Tetz, Markell III, 151, n. 33, announces an edition of the *Marcelliana*. He will discuss the criticisms of A. Heron and M. Simonetti, *JTS* 24, 1973, 110f.; *RivStorLettRel* 9, 1973, 313–29.

[2] Tetz, 'Markellianer und Athanasios', 114.
[3] Ibid., 76.
[4] Athanas., *Tomus ad Antioch.* 3–5; PG 26, 800A–801B.
[5] Tetz, 'Markellianer und Athanasios', 115.

claim a prominent place in the development of fourth-century christology. In the first years after Nicaea the theological initiative lay with him. His work is 'the first highly commendable and effective attempt to refute the Co-Lucianists on the basis of extensive interpretation of scripture'.[6] Even Athanasius came under his influence, for all his reserve. In his *Oratio II contra Arianos* Athanasius seems to be dependent on the first writing of Marcellus from the year 335, especially in the interpretation of Prov. 8. 22ff.[7] If the Athanasian double writing *Contra gentes—De Incarnatione* can be seen as a 'classical example of the doctrine of redemption in the early church', here again we may suppose Marcellus to have been the mediator.[8] In a first sketch of the history of the tradition of *De incarnatione et contra Arianos*, a writing which has now been returned to Marcellus, M. Tetz was able to show the role that Marcellus' writing played among the Eustathians in Antioch.[9] Marcellus' theology is a theology between two fronts. His chief opponents were and remained the Arians.

But for Marcellus there was more than this one front. On the old Nicene side he was confronted by a dangerous opponent, Apollinarius of Laodicea, with a christological doctrine which was directly opposed to (Marcellus') doctrine of the Adamic sonship of Christ (which was particularly directed against the Arians) and in which the doctrine of the *Virgin Birth* occupied a central position. For Marcellus, it and its author inevitably incurred the judgement which had struck the Arians. For Apollinarian doctrine, too, was not able to make a proper distinction between the two prosopa of Christ, but declared the two as ἕνα καὶ τὸν αὐτόν (cf. *Epistula ad Antiochenos* 21).[10]

Is there a basis here for the increasing tensions between Marcellus and Athanasius? When the Synod of Sardica in 342/3 took Marcellus' side against the changes of the orientals,[11] Athanasius, the leader of the Nicenes, spoke only of the 'tatters of Sardica'.[12] Basil of Cappadocia fell out with the deposed bishop[13] and the Council of Constantinople finally condemned him.[14] But this did not put an end to his influence. A number of important impulses for soteriology and ecclesiology and particular insights into

---

[6] Tetz, Markell I, 238.
[8] Ibid., 238.
[10] Tetz, Markell II, 40f.
[12] Athanas., *Tomus ad Antioch.* 5: PG 26, 800C.
[7] Ibid., 236.
[9] Ibid., 231–47.
[11] Tetz, Markell III, 166f.

[13] Cf. R. Hübner, 'Gregor von Nyssa und Markell von Ankyra'.
[14] Cf. A.-M. Ritter, *Das Konzil von Konstantinopel und sein Symbol*, Göttingen 1965, 191f., 121–3; R. Hübner, op. cit., 212 (note): 'Marcellus' interpretation of I Cor. 15. 28 in his book against Asterius was felt to be heretical on all sides and brought him condemnation both by the synod and by individuals. Among those who rejected his teaching in the East were Athanasius, Basil, Epiphanius, and in the West Hilary and Sulpicius Severus. The expression of it was also generally rejected in the passage "his kingdom shall have no end", which appears in almost all the Eastern creeds after 341, including the Constantinopolitan creed, and in the condemnation of the heresy of the Marcellians and all other heresies in the first canon of this council . . . (cf. the sharp *Epistula syn. Sardicensis Orientalium* [Philippopel]: CSEL 65, 49f.); there can be no doubt that Marcellus only preserved his friendship with Julius of Rome by means of a skilful deception (frag. 129: Klostermann 215⁶⁻⁸)' (with reference to M. Richard, *MSR* 9, 1949, 27f.; F. Scheidweiler, *ByzZ* 47, 1954, 355). For the condemnation of Marcellus see W. Gericke, *Marcell von Ancyra*, 25–6. Apollinarius of Laodicea and Diodore of Tarsus may also be included among Marcellus' opponents. Cf. L. W. Barnard, 'Pope Julius, Marcellus of Ancyra and the Council of Sardica', *RTAM* 38, 1971, 69–79.

christology and the doctrine of God lived on not only in Athanasius but also in Gregory of Nyssa,[15] quite apart from Marcellus' own circles and the Eustathians of Antioch, to whom Theodoret in turn referred.[16]

In his struggle over belief in God and in Christ, Marcellus' constant concern was to preserve the divine unity and its indivisibility (frags. 67, 71, 77, 78, 129). According to Eusebius, Marcellus' first book had the motto, if not the title, διὰ τὸ ἕνα γνωρίζειν θεόν.[17] In other words, it was a book devoted to the *monarchia*. Marcellus shared this concern to defend monotheism with his opponents and all the theological parties of the time. For Arianism, Sabellianism, the supporters of the formulas of one hypostasis and three hypostases (cf. the *Tomus ad Antiochenos* of 362) all pursued the same goal: preserving the strict unity of God. What different courses they followed!

When Marcellus speaks of the 'one God' (εἷς θεός) or of the monad of the Godhead (τῆς θεότητος μονάς) (cf. frags. 75–8: Klostermann, 200–2), he means something different from the unity of God in Eusebius or the monad conceived of in strict Arian terms.

The problem is discussed by Eusebius in ET I, 5, a work which is quite appropriately divided into three books.[18] He contests the new 'Sabellian' doctrine of Marcellus, who introduces into the 'one God', i.e. strictly into the monad, Father and Son:

Marcellus rightly defines God as one; but he says that this same God has united and conjoined the Logos in himself; but then he names from the one God this Father and the other Son, as though there were a twofold and composite substance in him.[19]

Granted Eusebius is right to point out the difficulty, in so far as Marcellus seeks unity and distinction in God purely and exclusively on the level of substance. But does he do that? Eusebius has no doubt about it, and therefore believes that he must prefer the doctrine of Sabellius to that of Marcellus. For at least the former did not divide the 'unoriginate and unmade and divine dynamis' and only asserted the identity of God (viz. the 'Father') with his mere Logos. The Bishop of Caesarea prefers to Marcellus and Sabellius the Jew who does not divide the 'one God' into Father and Son like Marcellus and does not introduce him as υἱοπάτωρ like Sabellius.[20] Thus for Eusebius, ὁ θεός, or even the 'one and unmade and unoriginate God', or the 'one origin', means only the Father. On the other hand, the Son should not be designated as 'unoriginate' or 'unmade', as otherwise

[15] R. Hübner, op. cit., 199: Athanasius is inspired by Marcellus in his exegesis of Prov. 8. 22 in his *Or. II ctr. Arian.*, as is already stressed by M. Tetz, Markell I, 236; further T. Zahn, *Marcellus von Ancyra*, Gotha 1867, 118; M. Simonetti, *Studi sull'Arianesimo*, Roma 1965, 9–87.

[16] Cf. Tetz, Markell I, 234–7.

[17] Euseb. Caes., ET I, 5: Klostermann–Hansen, 59[12f.] = frag. 128; cf. E. Schendel, *Herrschaft und Unterwerfung*, 113.

[18] Cf. the dedication of ET, Klostermann–Hansen, 60.

[19] Euseb. Caes. ET I, 5: Klostermann–Hansen, 64[21–5]; cf. Tetz, Markell III, 165f.

[20] Tetz, Markell III, 166. Klostermann–Hansen, Index υἱοπάτωρ.

there would be two principles of origin (*archai*) or two gods.[21] However, Marcellus also introduces the Logos/Son and the Pneuma into the monad, as is shown for instance by the *Epistula ad Liberium* §9: 'We do not keep this (i.e. the Logos/Son) separate from the Father or the Holy Spirit'.[22] This saying is directed against Asterius, who according to Marcellus, frag. 63, designated Father and Son two hypostases and thus separates the Son from the Father, 'as one would separate a human Son from his natural (κατὰ φύσιν) Father'.[23] The fundamental understanding here of the divine monad in the unity of Father, Son and Spirit can be made rather clearer both from the confession of Sardica and through the terminology and a more detailed explanation by Marcellus. The confession of Sardica says, 'We confess that the Father does not come into being without the Son nor the Son without the Father, because the Logos is Pneuma.'[24] The passage of scripture adduced here, John 4. 24, plays a 'definite role' in Marcellus—in contrast to Athanasius, who does not cite it. As frag. 57 shows, this saying 'God is spirit' must be understood in Marcellus 'in respect of the unity in which God alone is conjoined with Logos and Spirit' (frag. 66).[25] Because the one 'pneuma-nature' of God is undivided in Father, Son and Spirit, their unity is guaranteed. Therefore, according to the *Epistula ad Liberium*, the predicates 'immortal, invisible, untouchable and—we would add—incomprehensible' (ἀθάνατος, ἀόρατος, ἀψηλάφητος, ἀχώρητος) apply equally to the 'one God' and to the Logos and the Holy Spirit.[26] The extent of the difference between Marcellus and Eusebius here can be seen from the fact that the *Epistula ad Liberium* §2 even ventures to attribute the ἄναρχος (without origin) to the Logos.[27]

In this way the author of the *Epistula ad Liberium* not only stresses the unity of God but also implicitly attacks a theological position which reserved this epithet most strictly for God the Father. Eusebius keeps taking it up in his writings directed against Marcellus.[28]

Marcellus puts in question a particular terminology and a prime source of subordinationist trinitarian doctrine. This also emerges from his use of the designation of God as *pantocrator*. In the understanding of Eusebius,

[21] Cf. the passages from Eusebius, ET II, 5–6, 1 cited in Tetz, Markell III, 166.
[22] See the commentary in Tetz, Markell III, 176–8.
[23] Marcell. Anc., frag. ·63: Klostermann–Hansen, 196f.
[24] In F. Loofs, 'Das Glaubensbekenntnis der Homousianer von Sardica', AbhBerlAk. Phil.-hist. Kl. 1909, Berlin 1909, 3–39; text p. 8[16–18], here with a correction from Tetz, 'Markellianer und Athanasios', ZNW 64, 1973, 82: ὁμολογοῦμεν μηδέ ποτε πατέρα χωρὶς υἱοῦ μηδὲ υἱὸν χωρὶς πατρὸς γεγενῆσθαι μηδὲ εἶναι δύνασθαι ὁ ⟨τι Tetz⟩ ἐστὶ Λόγος πνεῦμα. There is a survey of the problem of the synod of Serdica along with all the necessary source details in W. Schneemelcher, 'Serdika 342. Ein Beitrag zum Problem Ost und West in der Alten Kirche', Evangelische Theologie, Sonderheft Ecclesia semper reformanda, 1952, 83–104. W. Gericke, Marcell von Ancyra, 18f., also deals with the creed of Serdica and Marcellus.
[25] Tetz, Markell III, 162.
[26] Ibid., 163.
[27] Text in Tetz, Markell III, 152: for an explanation see pp. 163, 165f.
[28] Tetz, Markell III, 165, with reference to the index in Klostermann–Hansen, 226, and F. Loofs, op. cit., 33.

the subordinationists and Arius, and also of no less ancient symbols and even of the Nicene creed,[29] this title is peculiar to the Father. Even the Roman creed has the same terminology, though not in the form in which Marcellus inserts it into his letter to Pope Julius. For here we read: εἰς θεὸν παντοκράτορα.[30]

> Marcellus avoids an identification of Pantocrator and Father [or he refrains from making Pantocrator the attribute or proper name of the Father], because otherwise he would favour the Arian view that the Logos is to be included among the πάντα ruled over be the Pantocrator.[31]

He himself includes 'Pantocrator' among the statements about the inseparability of Father and Son both in the *Epistula ad Iulium* (Klostermann, 215[26–31]) and in the *Epistula ad Liberium* §§10 and 11. Because here he primarily names the 'one God' Pantocrator, he can also give this name to the Father and could even apply it also to the Son and the Holy Spirit.[32]

But what about the interpretation and description of the distinction between Father, Son and Spirit in one God, a distinction which Marcellus takes over from the kerygma according to the *regula fidei* and means to maintain?[33] He refuses to speak of a 'second God' (the Son) or of a second and third hypostasis,[34] although he uses the word 'triad' (trinity), albeit in a text which is hard to interpret and to which we shall return.[35] But because he always thinks in terms of a pneuma-*ousia*, of the one Godhead, which is Father, Son and Spirit from eternity,[36] he can only find a basis for a distinction within the triad-monad with great difficulty. Eusebius wrongly accuses him of a Sabellianism which distinguishes three *prosopa* in the one *ousia*. Eusebius wrongly finds in his opponent the doctrine of a

[29] For *pantokrator* in the early creeds see Denzinger–Schönmetzer, *Enchiridion Symbolorum*, Freiburg 1967, 1–76; for Eusebius cf. the index in Klostermann–Hansen s.v. πατήρ and παντοκράτωρ; for Arius see his creed, in Opitz, AW I, 1, 2, document 30, §2.

[30] *Ep. ad Iulium*: Klostermann–Hansen, 215[19].

[31] Tetz, Markell III, 179, with reference to the *Expositio fidei* 1, 4 (which is not ascribed to Marcellus), PG 25, 201[11–13], where in the confession on the Son we read: '*Pantokrator* from the *pantokrator*. For the Son also rules and exercises his power over everything over which the Father rules and exercises his power.'

[32] Text in Tetz, Markell III, 152§§10–11; explanation 178–9.

[33] Cf. Marcell. Ancyr., *De incarn. et ctr. Arian.* 19: Tetz, Markell III, 180; PG 26, 1017[11–24]: μία γὰρ δόξα πατρὸς καὶ υἱοῦ καὶ ἁγίου πνεύματος . . . οὐ γάρ ἐστι δεύτερος θεὸς ὁ υἱός, ἀλλὰ Λόγος τοῦ ἑνὸς καὶ μονοῦ θεοῦ θεολογούμενος ἐν πατρί· ὡς καὶ ὁ πατὴρ ἐν υἱῷ θεολογεῖται.

[34] Cf. frag. 38: Klostermann–Hansen, 191, though Hansen could have accepted a suggestion on the text by F. Scheidweiler, *ZNW* 46, 1955, 207: ταῦτα 'Ὠριγένης γέγραφεν, μὴ παρὰ τῶν ἱερῶν προφητῶν τε καὶ ἀποστόλων περὶ τῆς ἀϊδιότητος τοῦ λόγου μαθεῖν βουληθείς, ἀλλ' ἑαυτῷ δεδωκὼς πλεῖον δευτέραν ὑπόστασιν (for ὑπόθεσιν) διηγᾶσθαι τοῦ λόγου μάτην τολμᾷ. Cf. Tetz, Markell III, 181, with reference to frag. 66 and Creed of Sardica 4, 6 and 10 (Loofs 9, 33 and 10, 47).

[35] For the 'triad' cf. *Ep. ad Liber.* §§11–12: Tetz, Markell III, 152: καὶ διὰ τοῦτο ἡ πίστις ἡμῶν ἐστιν εἰς ἕνα θεόν, πατέρα παντοκράτορα, καὶ εἰς τὸν υἱὸν αὐτοῦ τὸν κύριον ἡμῶν Ἰησοῦν Χριστὸν καὶ εἰς τὸ ἅγιον πνεῦμα· ταῦτα δὲ ἐξ ἑνότητος μιᾶς θεότητος, μιᾶς δυνάμεως, μιᾶς ὑποστάσεως, μιᾶς οὐσιᾶς, μιᾶς δοξολογίας, μιᾶς κυριότητος, μίας βασιλείας, μιᾶς εἰκόνος τῆς τριάδος ὁμοουσίον, 'δι' οὗ τὰ πάντα ἐγένετο.' Cf. Tetz, Markell I, 260, where reference is made to Loofs' development of Zahn's pneumatology. For Marcellus' pneumatology see below.

[36] Cf. the text cited above; also *Ep. ad Iul.*: Klostermann–Hansen, 215[4–9] (only about the Father–Son).

Logos which is first 'immanent' and then 'comes forth'.[37] Nor is the reality of Sonhood and the being of the Holy Spirit lacking in the triad-monad, so that he could be accused of Judaism.[38] But how does Marcellus define the relationship between Logos and Father in the one God? Here he begins from what is for him a fundamental position, the 'one hypostasis of God'. The error of his opponents is that 'they teach another Logos and another Sophia and Dynamis alongside the real and true Logos and there-fore speak of another ὑπόστασις separate from the Father . . .'.[39] To such a degree does Marcellus set out to maintain the uniqueness of the true Logos of God that he even describes the incarnate Christ as identical with the divine Logos: 'This is Son, this is Dynamis, this is Sophia, this is God's own true Logos, our Lord Jesus Christ, God's inseparable Dynamis.'[40] The Logos in God is designated Son, and is so designated 'by nature', because he is 'by nature God'.[41] He is the 'true Son of God', a fact that the Arians deny.[42] Indeed, Marcellus finally says that 'the Logos above is eternally begotten from the Father in an inexpressible, unutterable, incomprehen-sible way, but the same is also begotten below, in time, from the Virgin Mary'.[43] But he is always in God as God's Dynamis and Sophia, as is also the Holy Spirit. Therefore, on the basis of the new textual situation, it is no longer possible to follow Loofs in saying: 'There is no place at all in Marcellus for the Spirit alongside the pre-existent Logos; the Logos is the δύναμις, the σοφία, the βουλὴ τοῦ θεοῦ' (reference to frags. 64, 86, 52).[44] Granted, within the Godhead the role of the Holy Spirit is hardly differ-entiated from that of the Son. But the confession of the Holy Spirit in God is clear, and it is from this that Marcellus derives his role in the divine economy.[45]

In summary, Marcellus remarks in his *Epistula ad Liberium*:

Therefore our faith is in the one God, the Father, the Ruler of all, and in his Son our Lord Jesus Christ and in the Holy Spirit. This (= these three) from the unity of the one

[37] Passages in W. Gericke, *Marcell von Ancyra*, 136, n. 41.

[38] Compare frag. 60 (Klostermann–Hansen, 196) and the *Ep. ad Iulium*: Klostermann–Hansen, 215[4-8]. πιστεύω δὲ ἑπόμενος ταῖς θείαις γραφαῖς ὅτι εἷς θεὸς καὶ ὁ τούτου μονογενὴς υἱὸς λόγος, ὁ ἀεὶ συνυπάρχων τῷ πατρὶ καὶ μηδέποτε ἀρχὴν τοῦ εἶναι ἐσχηκώς, ἀληθῶς ἐκ τοῦ θεοῦ ὑπάρχων . . . οὗτος υἱός, οὗτος δύναμις, οὗτος σοφία . . . Cf. also Creed of Sardica 4 and 7: Loofs 8, 16–21 and 9, 34–6.

[39] Tetz, Markell III, 164.

[40] Cf. Tetz, Markell III, 164; *Ep. ad Iulium*: Klostermann–Hansen, 215[8 9]; *Ep. ad Liber.* §§2–7; Creed of Sardica 7: Loofs, 9.

[41] Marcell. Ancyr., *De incarn. et ctr. Arian.* 8: 996BC: κατὰ φύσιν υἱός ἐστι τοῦ θεοῦ, just as in turn God is the Father of the Son 'by nature'.

[42] Ibid., 8: PG 26, 997A: Αὐτὸς οὖν ὁ ἀληθινὸς υἱὸς τοῦ θεοῦ. According to Tetz, Markell I, 244, καὶ φύσει in 997[5] should be treated as an interpolation.

[43] Marcell. Ancyr., *De incarn. et ctr. Arian.* 8: PG 26, 996A: ὁ γὰρ γεννηθεὶς ἄνωθεν ἐκ πατρὸς λόγος ἀρρήτως, ἀφράστως, ἀκαταλήπτως, ἀϊδίως, ὁ αὐτὸς ἐν χρόνῳ γεννᾶται κάτωθεν ἐκ παρθένου [interpol. θεοτόκου] Μαρίας. Cf. ibid., 4: 989C: derivation of the 'of one substance' from 'begetting of the substance'.

[44] Cf. F. Loofs, 'Die Trinitätslehre Marcell's v. A', 772 (9); M. Tetz, Markell I, 268, designates the pneumatology of *De incarn. et ctr. Arian.* as a central and comprehensive complex.

[45] Cf. Marcell. Ancyr., *De incarn. et ctr. Arian.* 19: PG 26, 1017A; chs. 9–10 and 13–17.

Godhead, the one Dynamis, the one hypostasis, the one substance, the one praise (δοξολογία), the one rule, the one kingdom, the one image of the triad which is one in substance (μιᾶς εἰκόνος τῆς τριάδος ὁμοούσιον) 'by whom everything came into being'.[46]

Thus Marcellus is concerned to present the one God, the Ruler of all (§10), as three in one, by understanding the triad as *homoousios* from a number of aspects. There is more stress on unity than trinity, though this trinity is not 'dissolved' prematurely, i.e. before the *telos*, into unity (M. Tetz). The confession of Sardica, a special expression of Marcellus' theology, states (probably with the Bishop's opponents in mind): 'We do not say that the Father is the Son nor that the Son is the Father, but the Father is Father and the Son Son.'[47] This lays a foundation in that the incarnation is not to be understood in patripassian terms, but is attributed to the Son *qua* Son. To characterize the larger framework in which the event of the incarnation should be seen, Marcellus speaks of the 'economy' which knows several phases. The 'first economy' corresponds to the time from the creation of the world to the incarnation. We may infer this designation of a 'first economy' from his talk of a 'second economy', the 'economy according to the flesh', or the 'new and younger economy of the flesh' (καινὴ καὶ νέα κατὰ σάρκα οἰκονομία) or the 'economy according to men'.[48] It is not completely clear whether we may talk of a 'third economy', as F. Loofs supposes.[49] The brief section on Marcellus in Theodoret, *Compendium of Heretical Fables* 2, 10, which Loofs cites, certainly points in this direction:

Like him (Sabellius), Marcellus from Galatia denied the threeness of the hypostases. But according to what he says, the Godhead of the Father was to some degree extended to Christ, and he (Marcellus) called this God Logos; in this way the whole economy was drawn together and brought back to God, from whom it had been extended. The Holy Spirit he terms a concomitant extension of the extension, in which the apostles had a part. In general, he believed that the triad is extended and drawn back in accordance with the difference in the economies.[50]

This interpretation of Theodoret's is misleading, in so far as the coming forth of the Logos is transferred completely to the economy, as is that of the Holy Spirit. But the designation of the coming of the Holy Spirit as a

---

[46] Marcell. Ancyr., *Ep. ad Liber.* §§11–12: Tetz, Markell III, 152; commentary ibid., 180–4. It is difficult to interpret the statement about the *eikon*. According to Tetz III, 183f., in the *Marcelliana* 'εἰκών is primarily to be understood as the σάρξ/ἄνθρωπος taken by the Logos'. The humanity of Christ is the *eikon* of the triad on the basis of the following consideration: as man, Christ is the image of the identity of substance of this triad, just as according to Gen. 1. 26 man as such is already the image of God, as a 'small example' of the realization of the unity of God. Possibly the birth of Christ from the Virgin is to be associated with the *eikon* in a special way. Cf. the passage from *De incarn. et ctr. Arian.* 8 cited above, and the remarks on the κυριακὸς ἄνθρωπος below.

[47] Creed of Sardica 6: Loofs, 8f.

[48] Cf. frags. 4, 9, 17, 19, 43, 70, 100, 117; W. Gericke, *Marcell von Ancyra*, 126f., though his interpretation is wrong.

[49] F. Loofs, 'Die Trinitätslehre Marcell's v. A.', 772–4.

[50] Theodoret, *Haer. fab. comp.* 10: PG 83, 396f.: τὸ δὲ πανάγιον πνεῦμα παρέκτασιν τῆς ἐκτάσεως λέγει.

παρέκτασις of the ἔκτασις of God in the Logos in connection with the incarnation is an interesting one. The sending of the Spirit runs parallel with the incarnation and the economy of the flesh. The long chapters on the Spirit in *De Incarnatione et contra Arianos* also present this picture.[51] The way in which Marcellus links together incarnation and the bestowal of the Spirit at the end of ch. 9 of this book is completely Pauline.[52] It is surely wrong to speak of a 'third' economy, an 'economy of the Spirit', *and* to understand by that the dissolution of the 'second' economy. For the history of the 'second' encompasses the eschaton up to the drawing back of the church into God and the return of the incarnation to the pure being of the Logos. But because the apostles—after the exaltation of the Lord—are bearers of the Spirit along with the whole church, something like a 'third' economy, the 'economy of the Spirit', does come into being, though it never has independent existence. In Marcellus' 'concordance approach' (especially in the exegesis of the Isaianic trishagion, Isa. 6. 3, and of Prov. 8. 22 and 25), the history of the economies is linked backwards with the coeternity of Father, Logos and Pneuma; and a special bracket is set round the whole order of redemption in the unity of prophets and apostles, in whom the one Spirit is at work.[53]

To understand the right relationship of God in the unity of Father, Logos and Pneuma to the economy in Marcellus, it is necessary to start from his distinction between *dynamis* and *energeia*. His understanding of the incarnation is also to be derived from here. T. Zahn had already referred to the significance of these two concepts.[54] He also put forward the correct interpretation of them in words which we shall set out briefly as they are quoted by M. Tetz:[55] it is illegitimate 'to understand the coming forth of the Logos as a transition from potentiality to reality. Marcellus indeed knows a movement within the Godhead, a change in the relationship between God and Logos which is occasioned by his relationship to the world; but he excludes from the Logos all coming into being in the sense of grounding or enriching being. Precisely because he *is* in the full sense of the word, he cannot be begotten. However, the decisive objection to this view is that Marcellus does not go on, as would be necessary, to

[51] Marcell. Ancyr., *De incarn. et ctr. Arian.* 9–10, 13–17: PG 26, 997–1001, 1005–13.

[52] Ibid., 8: 996C–997A: Καὶ διὰ τοῦτο ὁ λόγος καὶ υἱὸς τοῦ πατρὸς ἐνωθεὶς σαρκί, γέγονε, σάρξ (according to Tetz, Markell I, 244 the ἄνθρωπος τέλειος is interpolated), ἵνα οἱ ἄνθρωποι ἐνωθέντες πνεύματι, γένωνται ἐν πνεῦμα.

[53] Cf. the texts and the interpretation of them in Tetz, Markell I, 258–63. For the *trishagion* see at length G. Kretschmar, *Studien zur frühchristlichen Trinitätstheologie* (BHistTh 21), Tübingen 1956, 134–82.

[54] T. Zahn, *Marcellus von Ancyra*, Gotha 1867, 123–8.

[55] Tetz, 'Markellianer und Athanasios', 96f., n. 59. Here Tetz criticizes the remarks of E. Schendel, *Herrschaft und Unterwerfung Christi*, 117 and 125–8. R. Hübner, 'Gregor von Nyssa und Markell von Ankyra', 219 indicates that in his dissertation he sets out to prove that 'in all probability Marcellus uses the concept of Aristotelian potency in his trinitarian speculations also'. For the moment it is not possible to see how far Hübner takes issue with Zahn's interpretation, corrects it or develops it. Perhaps it is possible to note a development in Marcellus.

separate the two forms of existence so that in becoming ἐνέργεια the δύναμις ceased to be δύναμις and only continued as ἐνέργεια᾽ (127). 'Only in so far as he [viz. the Logos] leads a life as ἐνέργεια δραστική does he separate himself from God, unite himself with men and return to God having shown his purpose for the world. But during all this he remains united with God in so far as he is δύναμις, that is, in so far as he is the power which rests in God, the capability of what he achieves as ἐνέργεια δραστική᾽ (127). Zahn stresses that the Logos himself is both latent and effective power: 'He leads a double life, a divine life and one related to the world. But he himself does not lead the latter less than the former' (128).

Thus shortly after Nicaea we have in Marcellus a combined view of the Trinity immanent in God and the economic Trinity, and also of the economy of creation and salvation.[56] Father, Son and Spirit have a share in this. But the Logos of God becomes the subject of the incarnation in that he acts on the flesh with his 'active energy' (ἐνέργεια δραστική). What does this mean for Marcellus' conception of the incarnation? The *energeia* of the Logos first becomes active in creation (frag. 60), but this already takes place with a view to the incarnation.[57] Thus in the incarnation the creative power of the Logos, and the Logos alone, is at work in a specific way:

> For if the Pneuma were investigated by itself, the Logos would rightly appear as one and the same as God; but if the flesh that was bestowed on the Redeemer were investigated (in respect of this), the Godhead would appear to have extended itself only as an activating force, so that the monad is rightly quite undivided.[58]

In frag. 117 Marcellus speaks of a separation of the Logos from God for the sake of the flesh, but only as an active force,[59] or in frag. 121 of an emergence of the Logos in this active *energeia*.[60] Thus we have not merely an indwelling but a creative activity in the assumption of the body or the flesh. A first characteristic of this is the Virgin Birth, which is assigned great soteriological significance.[61] We may probably assume that the Virgin Birth of Jesus is related to the function of the humanity of Christ as *eikon*: 'Before the news of the accomplishment of these actions, who would have believed that the Logos of God, born of a virgin, would assume our flesh and would put the whole Godhead corporeally on view?'[62] Through being grasped by the divine *energeia*, in this way the man Jesus—

[56] Cf. Marcell. Ancyr., *De incarn. et ctr. Arian.* 13: PG 26, 1005AB.
[57] Cf. frags. 60, 71, 116, 117, 121, and Tetz, 'Markellianer und Athanasios', 110-2, who points to Heb. 4. 12 as a source for the distinction between δυνάμει and ἐνεργείᾳ.
[58] Frag. 71: Klostermann–Hansen, 198; Gericke, 215.
[59] Frag. 117: Klostermann–Hansen, 210[15–16].
[60] Frag. 121: Klostermann–Hansen, 212[10–13].
[61] In addition to frag. 16 see also 48, 54, 107, 110 and *Ep. ad Iul.*: Klostermann–Hansen, 215[18]: also *Ep. ad Liber.* 4: Tetz, Markell III, 152.
[62] Frag. 16: Klostermann–Hansen, 187; Gericke, 197.

not the Logos—becomes the *eikon* of the invisible God, indeed of the whole Godhead, even if it is said at one point that the flesh of Christ is the 'image of the proper Logos' (frag. 95).[63] The term *'eikon'* expresses something positive, the relationship of the image to the original, i.e. the whole Godhead or the Logos, and also something negative. Against Asterius, Marcellus stresses that the *eikon* is not the Logos *qua* Logos— because by that he would be made a creature—but the flesh of Christ.[64] This distinction will be shown even more clearly to be a central christo- logical principle of Marcellus. First of all, however, it should be pointed out that Marcellus elsewhere makes use of a traditional form of language to describe the incarnation:[65] he speaks of 'becoming man', 'assuming or taking upon himself the flesh', of 'assuming man' (frag. 108); the Logos 'unites himself with the human flesh' (frag. 10); the only-beloved Son of God is 'the man united with the Logos' (frag. 109). In Marcellus, as in Irenaeus, this view is immediately developed in soteriological and ecclesiological terms. For through this union of the true Son of God and the Logos there arises a 'koinonia' between the two, the fruit of which is immortality.[66] The human sarx is divinized (frag. 16) and we share in the Sonship (frag. 19). This flesh is assumed by the Son and Logos of God, 'so that through this he overcame the devil, who had earlier conquered man, and makes (man) not only incorruptible and immortal, but also the co- ruler with God in the heavens' (frag. 110). All this is Pauline and Irenaean, and is said of the individual fleshly nature of Christ and at the same time of the whole human nature.[67]

Where do we find the accents which are typical of Marcellus? Over against the Arians, his doctrine of the incarnation is largely determined by his concern to assign the christological statements concerned with exalta- tion to the Logos and those concerned with lowliness to the 'man' or the 'flesh'. Thus he already assigns the function of 'being the *eikon* of God' entirely to the flesh; he refers the title 'firstborn Son' above all to the man Christ.[68] Asterius had related both designations to the 'Logos', in order to demonstrate his creatureliness and the difference of his hypostasis from that of the Father. This is excluded for Marcellus because he divides the predicates in a different way.[69] The task becomes more urgent when the Arians refer to statements about the incarnate Christ like 'mortal',

[63] Cf. *Ep. ad Liber.* 11/12 (see above) and Tetz, Markell III, 152, 182–4.
[64] Cf. frags. 92–7: Klostermann–Hansen, 205f.
[65] For what follows see frags. 10, 42, 48f., 54, 56, 76, 108–11, 119; *Ep. ad Iul.*: Klostermann–Hansen, 215[18].
[66] Cf. frags. 20–21, 41, 117.
[67] Cf. Marcell. Anc., *De incarn. et ctr. Arian.* 20: PG 26, 1020C–1021A (head-members). For the question of the individual manhood of Christ and humanity in general see below.
[68] Cf. the references in Tetz, Markell III, 164 and nn. 95, 96, 99; also frags. 2–8, 90–6: Klostermann– Hansen, 185–6, 204–6.
[69] Frag. 96: Klostermann–Hansen, 205[27-31]; Tetz, Markell III, 164f.

'visible' and especially 'weak'.[70] The latter predicate is taken up by Marcellus in connection with Matt. 26, 41, to quote it in *De Incarnatione et contra Arianos*, 21, in the following context:

> When he says, 'Father, if it be possible, let this cup pass from me, yet not my will, but thine be done.' 'The spirit is indeed willing, but the flesh is weak.' Here he shows two wills: the human will, which is that of the flesh, and the divine will. Because of the weakness of the flesh the human (will) pleads to be spared suffering, but the divine will is prepared.[71]

This first beginning of a Nicene christological anthropology deserves to be looked at more closely. The Arians wanted to burden the Logos and the will of the Logos with the weakness of the flesh. They declared that he was 'changeable', and that he was made 'unchangeable' through grace only because God foresaw that the will of the Logos would indeed persevere in the good. To ward off all weakness of the Logos as Logos, Marcellus introduces a 'will of the sarx'. He makes this clear, as M. Tetz, observes, in *De incarnatione et contra Arianos* 21. There, Marcellus,

> explains that the Logos and Son of God was always Lord and God and that his Godhead made his manhood Lord and Christ. This is the context in which, *inter alia*, the doctrine of the two wills mentioned above is developed. At the same time it is said that Christ as a man wanted to avoid suffering, but that as God he was ἀπαθής, and therefore willingly took suffering and death upon himself. Elsewhere the Apostle says: 'He suffered out of weakness, but he lives from the power of God' (2 Cor. 13. 4); the power of God is the Son, indeed suffering out of weakness, that is because of his conjunction with the flesh (ἐκ τῆς σαρκικῆς συμπλοκῆς), praying as man (ὡς ἄνθρωπος) that suffering might pass by him, but living from his own power (PG 26, 1024⁹⁻¹⁴) ... In §5 (of the *Epistula ad Liberium*), the same sort of thing is said in summary fashion about πάθη. Both in the statement from *De incarnatione et contra Arianos* and in §5, suffering and God's power are set over against each other.[72]

We can hardly be wrong in seeing the assertion of 'two wills' in Christ as a contrast to the Arian doctrine of the mutable will of the Logos which marks him out as a creature.[73] In this context Arius talks unequivocally of the 'one' will in Christ, which is creaturely even if it is superhuman and existed in the Logos even before the sarx came into being. For Arius it must have been quite superfluous to accept a second created human principle of will in Christ. Thus he could ascribe everything to this one will of the Logos: the possibility of sinning and proving himself, resistance against suffering, but also the willing acceptance of it. This is a new step of Marcellus in christology, applying the distinction between the divine and the fleshly nature in Christ to willing and the will also. To avoid burdening

---

70 Tetz, Markell III, 169f.

71 Tetz, Markell III, 170 (PG 26, 1021²⁵⁻³²): ὅταν λέγῃ· 'πάτερ, εἰ δυνατόν, παρελθέτω τὸ ποτήριον τοῦτο· πλὴν μὴ τὸ ἐμὸν θέλημα γένηται, ἀλλὰ τὸ σόν·' 'τὸ μὲν πνεῦμα πρόθυμον, ἡ δὲ σὰρξ ἀσθενής·' δύο θελήματα ἐνταῦθα δείκνυσι· τὸ μὲν ἀνθρώπινον διὰ τὴν ἀσθένειαν τῆς σαρκὸς παραιτεῖται τὸ πάθος. τὸ δὲ θεϊκὸν αὐτοῦ πρόθυμον. Tetz points to the resemblance to frag. 73.

72 Tetz, Markell III, 171–2.

73 See pp. 228–32 above; for the texts see Bardy, *Lucien*, 265f.

the Logos with the suffering on the Mount of Olives, as happens in Arian argumentation, he contrasts the divine will of the Logos with the human will of the flesh in Christ. This already seems to introduce the beginnings of a Word-man christology. A new feature can be seen in christological anthropology over against that of the Arians. After a very long silence, the 'soul' of Christ seems to have been rediscovered. But have we come thus far? Marcellus' remark about the two wills does not quite answer this question in a decisive way. Marcellus does not speak expressly of a human soul in Christ.[74] This is all the more remarkable as he knows Origen and his *Peri Archon*, and is probably also influenced by it in his doctrine of *apokatastasis*. He could have introduced the soul of Christ in a very effective way, in order to protect the Logos from anguish and the fear of death.

But Marcellus was convinced that he had already achieved his task by combining the Logos with the flesh not as *dynamis* but as *energeia*. Now this *energeia* had to become effective in the flesh as directly as possible and in a completely divine fashion. His soteriology required a Logos-sarx framework, whereas his anti-Arianism had insinuated a Logos-man framework. He did not reconcile these two aspects of his christology. A human soul as principle of the sarx in Christ must have been a weakness for his basic soteriological conception. We are reminded of Athanasius when we see that soteriology has predominance over christological anthropology. In Marcellus, as later in Athanasius, we can take one thing to be certain: the soul of Christ has not yet become a theological factor. This emerges clearly from the text of *De incarnatione et contra Arianos* 21, cited above. The real redemptive act of the will in Christ does not come from the 'will of the flesh' but from the 'divine will', which is prepared to accept suffering and could accept suffering, because it was incapable of suffering. The soteriological act of obedience comes from the Logos and from the *energeia* with which he communicates himself to the flesh. Perhaps the confession of Sardica (§11) already represents a gentle corrective to this view, in the sentence which seems to have irritated Athanasius: 'And

---

[74] On two further occasions Fathers of the fourth century speak of the soul of Christ and then move in a quite remarkable direction. This happens in the explanation of Luke 23. 46: 'Father, into thy hands I commend my spirit.' Marcellus adds his own version: πάντας ἀνθρώπους παρατίθεται τῷ πατρὶ δι' ἑαυτοῦ, τοὺς ἐν αὐτῷ ζωοποιουμένους (cf. 1 Cor. 15. 22; *De incarn. et ctr. Arian.* 5: PG 26, 902²⁶⁻⁸), quoted following M. Tetz, Markell III, 174, who also points to ch. 12 of the same writing (PG 26, 1004³⁸⁻⁴¹): καὶ ὅτε παρατίθεται τὸ πνεῦμα αὐτοῦ εἰς χεῖρας τοῦ πατρός, ὡς ἄνθρωπος ἑαυτὸν παρατίθεται τῷ θεῷ, ἵνα πάντας ἀνθρώπους παραθῆται τῷ θεῷ. 'His spirit' in Marcellus is to be understood in the light of ch. 8: 'His Logos became flesh that men, united in the spirit, might become a *pneuma*.' If in the face of the Arians Marcellus was concerned to protect the Logos from statements about Christ's humiliation (in this case handing over the *pneuma*), why does he not introduce the most obvious factor here, 'the human spirit' of Jesus, his soul? After all, he was familiar with the Western tradition. Because neither he nor the Arians think of it. The Logos animates the body by his *energeia*. The second occasion for reflection on the soul of Christ was offered by the interpretation of Christ's descent into Hades. Again, in Marcellus the Logos occupies a central position. He does not interpret the *descensus* in christological and anthropological terms, as was frequently the case before him. Cf. Tetz, Markell III, 172–3. Cf. A. Grillmeier, 'Der Gottessohn im Totenreich', *ZkTh* 71, 1949, 23–53, 184–203, now in *Mit ihm und in ihm*, Freiburg 1975.

this (viz. the divine pneuma) did not suffer, but the man whom he assumed, whom he took to himself from Mary the Virgin, the man who was capable of suffering. For man is mortal, but God is immortal.'[75] The *Epistula ad Liberium* (§5) offers a similarly strong formulation in saying of the assumed flesh of Christ: 'This was hung (on the cross) and not he himself (the divine Logos); this was buried, not he himself; this bore all human suffering as man, not he himself. But he is the dynamis of God.'[76] Here we have a clear christology of distinction, which points to the Word-man framework, as M. Tetz observes. Thus too in §8 of this *Epistula*: 'He was called Jesus, after he had assumed the flesh, in so far as he is man, i.e. has assumed man to himself, "in whom the whole fullness of the Godhead dwells corporeally".'[77] Certainly this tendency towards the Logos-man framework was provoked by the Arian theses. But it does not yet go so far as being an anti-Apollinarian reflection, even if the talk of 'two wills' is already a clear step in this direction. Athanasius does not take the step, and avoids Luke 22. 42, which is a decisive passage for Marcellus.

In the context of Marcellus' anti-Arian concerns to protect the Logos of God from all statements about lowliness and to assign them to the assumed human nature, one formulation plays an important part which has presented some difficulty to interpretation: κυριακὸς ἄνθρωπος (Latin *homo dominicus*).[78] It appears in *De incarnatione et ctr. Arianos* (c. 360) and in the *Epistula ad Antiochenos*, now assigned to Marcellus. It seems to have had a relatively long life. We begin with the *Epistula ad Antiochenos*.[79] If we leave aside this expression for the moment, we can see that in this *Epistula* Marcellus used a variety of other designations for the subject of the statements about humiliation: the 'man assumed from Mary', the 'man of the Lord' (ὁ τοῦ κυρίου ἄνθρωπος), the 'man Jesus', the 'man of the Redeemer', or simply 'man' in contrast to 'God'. The designations mentioned here occur when there is talk either of the suffering or of the human weakness of Jesus, or of the whole career of Jesus including his humiliation and exaltation. For example, the *kyriakos anthropos* is clearly out of place when it is said in quite general terms to his opponents that 'they do not distinguish which statements fit the Godhead and which the

---

[75] Creed of Sardica 11: Loofs, 10, to be compared with §3, where the counter-theses of the Arians are put forward.

[76] Marcell. Ancyr., *Ep. ad Liber.* 5: Tetz, Markell III, 152: for explanation see ibid., 170.

[77] Ibid., §8: Tetz, 152, with commentary, 170–2. The contrast between the incarnate 'Jesus' and the God who is incapable of suffering also occurs in Pseudo-Gregory Thaumaturgus, *Ad Theopompum*; cf. V. Ryssel, *Gregorius Thaumaturgus*, Leipzig 1880, no. 32, p. 99.

[78] There is a collection of passages with this expression in F. Loofs, *Theophilus von Antiochien Adversus Marcionem und die anderen theologischen Quellen bei Irenaeus* (TU 46, 2), Leipzig 1930, 138–41, n. 11; in E. Schwartz, 'Der sogenannte Sermo maior', 55ff.; A. Gesché, *La christologie du 'Commentaire sur les Psaumes' découvert à Toura*, Gembloux 1962, 71f., 80–90 (see p. 328 below); Tetz, Markell I, 268f., n. 191.

[79] Here we follow the edition by Schwartz, nos. 54–80.

man whom he has borne'.[80] Only *cod. Vaticanus graecus* 1431 inserts it, and
did not establish itself.[81] The reason can be seen on closer inspection:
κυριακὸς ἄνθρωπος only relates to the man Jesus in his glory. This can be
expressed in two ways: attention is directed either to the beginning
(ἀρχή)[82] of the earthly existence of Jesus, whether from God or from the
Virgin Mary, or to its end, the glory after death. In this context Marcellus
speaks of the κυριακὸς ἄνθρωπος, i.e. of the 'glorious' or 'glorified' man.
We need not concern ourselves here whether this is a 'Word-man' or a
'Word-flesh' framework. We can use particular instances as a test. In
Epistula ad Antiochenos (frag. 56), Prov. 8. 22 ('The Lord created me as the
beginning of his ways, the first of his acts') is interpreted in terms of the
'creation of the *homo dominicus* from Mary'.[83] In the next section (57) there
is a discussion of Jesus the crucified one, whom God has made Lord and
Christ, in connection with Acts 2. 36. Because 'a finger is first pointed to
the crucified Christ', Marcellus can only speak 'of the man of the Lord',
and not of the 'glorified man', because this new condition is brought about
only after the completion of the way of suffering. In this fragment he also
keeps to the expression he has once chosen, because he is talking about the
creation and crucifixion of the author of our salvation.[84] Section 60, which
contains a discussion of the statements of the gospels about the 'words and
works of lowliness', is also instructive. These statements refer to the '*soma*
which he (Jesus) bore of Mary for our own sakes'; to the '*soma* of Jesus'
and not to the 'Godhead of the Son'.[85] '*Homo dominicus*' does not appear
here. Nor can it stand in the context of the next fragment: 'He who raises
all the dead has also raised the man from Mary, Christ Jesus, whom the
Logos of God himself assumed.'[86] For it is this which introduces the status
of the 'glorified man'. This is discussed immediately afterwards, as in
frag. 63 Marcellus interprets Heb. 3. 1, 2: 'Consider Jesus, the apostle and
high priest of our confession. He was faithful to him who appointed him.'
This is about the 'exalted Christ', 'the mediator between God and man,
the man Christ Jesus' (1 Tim. 2. 5). At the end of this section discussion
returns to the humanity of Christ as created by the Logos—and this is
described as 'the man whom he bore for us'.[87] When in frag. 65 Marcellus
returns to Heb. 3. 1, 2 and introduces the saying of Stephen, 'I see the
Son of Man standing on the right hand of the power of God', we find:
'He did not say that he had seen the Logos or the Wisdom of the Father,

[80] *Ep. ad Ant.* 78: Schwartz, 31[18-19].
[81] Cf. Schwartz, op. cit., 32, apparatus; id., *Codex Vaticanus gr. 1431* (AbhMünchAkW 32, 6),
München 1927, 36[19].
[82] Tetz, Markell I, 268f., n. 191 points to this connection with ἀρχή.
[83] *Ep. ad Ant.* 56: Schwartz, 18.
[84] Ibid., 57: Schwartz, 18f.
[85] Ibid., 60: Schwartz, 19–21.
[86] Ibid., 62: Schwartz, 22.
[87] Ibid., 63: Schwartz, 23[6-7]; 29–30.

but the Son of Man, the glorified body from Mary (. . . τὸ ἐκ Μαρίας κυριακὸν σῶμα), of which Paul also says "He sits at the right hand of God".'[88] A few lines later a quotation of Ps. 109. 1 ('Sit at my right hand until I set your enemies as a footstool under your feet') is introduced, and because this is a discussion of the exalted Christ, κυριακὸς ἄνθρωπος immediately appears and also brings the fragment to a close.[89] Fragment 66 states pregnantly, once again on Ps. 109. 1: 'We have set forward this about "Sit at my right hand" because it is said of the glorified man (ὅτι εἰς τὸν κυριακὸν ἄνθρωπον λέλεκται).'[90] This expression appears twice more, first in frag. 69 where the Micah prophecy of the origin of Jesus from the tribe of Judah (5. 2) is interpreted in terms of the κυριακὸν σῶμα and there is mention of the ἀρχή of the incarnate Christ; it then recurs, as there is discussion of the resurrection of Jesus according to 2 Tim. 2. 8.[91]

The test seems to work. There is a clear relationship between κυριακὸς ἄνθρωπος and the exalted Lord or his 'glorious' emergence from God at the beginning of the economy of the incarnation. The phrase is simply concerned with the 'glorified body' or the 'glorified man' or the 'body of the Lord'. Philippians 2. 11 is probably the starting point of this formulation.[92] We are not concerned here with whether the successors to Marcellus maintained this neat terminology or not.

We can also easily show how closely this expression 'the glorified man' in Marcellus comes to two other terms of great soteriological and ecclesiological importance: ἀπαρχή (deposit) and κεφαλή (head).[93] The 'glorified man'—in thoroughly Pauline terms—realizes both in himself: bringing redeemed mankind home to God. Those who are thus restored are members of the head. *De incarnatione et contra Arianos* shows the connection between all these conceptions. In interpreting John 7. 39, Marcellus remarks:

And when he says, 'The Holy Spirit was not yet given because Jesus was not yet glorified', he is speaking of his flesh as not yet glorified. For it is not the Lord of glory (i.e. the Logos) who is glorified, but the flesh of the Lord of glory itself assumes glory, as it ascends with him into heaven. For this reason also the spirit of sonship was not yet in men, because the firstfruits (ἀπαρχή) taken from men had not yet ascended into heaven.[94]

88 Ibid., 65: Schwartz, 24[17].
89 Ibid., 65: Schwartz, 25[4] and 52.
90 Ibid., 66: Schwartz, 26[8].
91 Ibid., 69 and 77: Schwartz, 28 and 31[10].
92 It is not simply a matter of a linguistic derivation of κυριακός from Κύριος, but in addition of a Kyrios christology. Precisely the same limited use of κυριακὸς ἄνθρωπος can be found in the *Expositio fidei* which is evidently influenced by the ideas of Marcellus: PG 25, 200–208. Cf. ibid., 1: 201C–202A (ascent of the *dominicus homo* as our forerunner into heaven); for the opposite comparison see ibid., 3: 205A; for the connection between the virgin birth and Christ as ἀρχή and the κυριακὸς ἄνθρωπος (κυριακὸν σῶμα) see 3 and 4: 205BC.
93 For ἀπαρχή cf. Marcell. Ancyr., *De incarn. et ctr. Arian* 3, 8 and 12: PG 26, 989B, 996C, 997A, 1004B. Κεφαλή: ibid., 20: PG 26, 1020C. The concept of mediator is associated with this, ibid., 22: 1024BC.
94 Ibid., 3: PG 26, 989B, cited in Tetz, Markell I, 256, where there is also a reference to Acts 2. 3–4.

The 'second economy' comes to fulfilment. Marcellus is very fond of maintaining this idea. The body, the church, receives what the glorified Christ receives. Just as the Lord ascends to God, so too the members ascend with him:

> Whatever Scripture says that the Son 'has received', it says because of his body, as the body is the firstfruits (ἀπαρχή) of the church. The firstfruit, he (Paul) says, is Christ (1 Cor. 15. 13). But as the firstfruit has received the name above every name, the dough (cf. 1 Cor. 5. 6) too was raised by that power and also set (on the throne), according to the saying: 'He has raised us up with him and made us sit with him in the heavenly places' (Eph. 2. 6).[95]

Above all in connection with Colossians and Ephesians, Marcellus seems to achieve a good blend of christology and ecclesiology. But the problems raised by this first become clear in his interpretation of 1 Cor. 15. 24-8, which was second only to his doctrine of the Trinity in arousing opposition against him. This passage of scripture was the occasion for him to develop his doctrine of the end of the rule of the incarnate Christ. The good beginning made by his exaltation christology inevitably shattered on the one-sidedness of his exegesis. His general outline of christological soteriology and ecclesiology inspired by the deutero-Pauline epistles and Irenaeus falls apart at the point which is meant to be both its conclusion and its end. We therefore return once again to his Logos doctrine, but now in the new perspective of its significance for his christology and ecclesiology. Marcellus first presents his exegesis of 1 Cor. 15 and the ideas derived from it in frags. 41 and 113-17; also in the *Epistula ad Antiochenos*, frag. 70, and in *De Incarnatione et contra Arianos* 20 and 21.[96] Is there a development?

Just as the second economy had a beginning, so too it will have an end (cf. frags. 111-21). Marcellus seeks to prove this from a number of scriptural passages (frag. 115). What this end is must first be decided from the fate of the earthly, though also exalted, corporeality of Christ:

> Now what do we learn about the human flesh which the Logos assumed for our sakes not quite four hundred years ago? Will the Logos also possess it in the coming ages of the world or only until the Day of Judgement? The prophet's words must be confirmed by action. He says, 'For they will look upon him whom they have pierced' (John 19. 37). Of course, it was the flesh that they pierced.[97]

As Marcellus relates looking on the one who has been pierced to the Day of Judgement, it seems that in his view the Logos will be united with the flesh at least until the Day of Judgement. But in frag. 117 he gives

---

[95] Marcell. Ancyr., *De incarn. et ctr. Arian.*, 12: PG 26, 1004B; Tetz, Markell I, 256.

[96] On this see Tetz, Markell I, 257-8; E. Schendel, *Herrschaft und Unterwerfung Christi*, Tübingen 1971, 111-43; M. Eckart, *Das Verständnis von I Kor. 15. 23-28 bei Origenes* (Diss. Pont. Univ. Gregoriana), Rome 1963 (unfortunately the partial printing, Augsburg 1966, is too abbreviated to be usable); R. Hübner, 'Gregor von Nyssa und Markell von Ankyra', 210-29.

[97] Marcell. Ancyr., frag. 116: Klostermann–Hansen, 209f.; Gericke, 236f. For the piercing of the flesh and not the Logos, cf. on Eusebius of Emesa (*CCT* I, 1965) 253, n. 1.

quite a detailed answer to the question whether the corporeality of Christ will have an end after the Last Judgement:

> The Logos did not assume our flesh in order to make use of it, but so that the flesh might achieve immortality through communion with the Logos. [Thus, one might add, if mankind enjoys communion with the Logos after the Judgement, the mediatorial function of the manhood of Christ is superfluous. Marcellus does not cite John 6. 61–3 in an arbitrary way: '. . . It is the Spirit that gives life, the flesh is of no avail.'] Now if according to his own testimony the flesh is of no avail, how can it remain united with the Logos in the ages of the world to come, as though it were useful, when it is in fact of the earth and is useless? It is for this reason that the almighty God, the Lord, seems to say to it: 'Sit thou at my right hand, until I put thine enemies under thy feet' (Ps. 110 [109]. 1). He seems merely to separate it as an effective force (*energeia*) because of the human flesh, and therefore he speaks to him as though he had appointed the sitting at the right hand for only a limited period of time: 'Until I set thine enemies under thy feet.' The holy apostle interprets this prophetic word of David to us more clearly when he says, 'For he must reign until he has put all his enemies under his feet' (1 Cor. 15. 25). Thus his human economy and reign seem to have an end. For the apostle's words, 'Until he has put all his enemies under his feet' mean nothing else. . . . [Marcellus also finds proof for his theory in Acts 3. 21: 'Whom heaven must receive until the time for establishing.']. This (Acts) also speaks as if it were appointing a term or a period over which the human economy is to be united with the Logos. For what does the phrase 'until the time for establishing' mean if it does not proclaim to us a coming age of the world in which all things will be established anew? [Finally Marcellus refers to Rom. 8. 21, which talks about the liberation of creation, and then asks] . . . how could the servant form (cf. Phil. 2. 7) which the Logos has assumed (for it is the form of a servant!) remain in communion with the Logos? Thus the noble Paul has said clearly and explicitly that the fleshly economy of the Logos which came about for our sake must be continued for a short period of the past and the future, and that just as it has a beginning, it will also have an end. That is why he says, 'Then comes the end, when he hands over the rule to God the Father' (1 Cor. 15. 24).[98]

Two considerations put the 'eternal significance' of Christ's humanity and the second economy in question: (1) The conception of the unity of God and man in Christ. This is achieved in the following way. The Logos, remaining as *dynamis* in God, is only separated (χωρίʒειν) as *energeia* (ἐνεργείᾳ μόνῃ) to be united with the manhood. This conception itself betrays a transitory character. As *energeia*, the Logos tends to be taken back into God's *dynamis* and thus to be integrated without remainder into the monad. Moreover, as Dr Tetz has pointed out to me, the mode of *energeia* for the Logos becomes superfluous if the ἀντικειμένη ἅπασα ἐνέργεια (frag. 121 in connection with the *regula fidei*) is removed. (2) As 'flesh', the human nature is no use for the *dynamis* or for the Godhead, the Logos. Once the whole of redeemed mankind has returned to God,

---

[98] Marcell. Ancyr., frag. 117: Klostermann–Hansen, 210f.; Gericke, 237–8; also F. Scheidweiler, *ZNW* 46, 1955, 214. That 'the short duration of the economy of the incarnation is stressed (ἐν βραχεῖ τινι χρόνῳ) is reminiscent of Ps. Gregory Thaumaturgus, *Ad Theopompum*', V. Ryssel, *Gregor Thaumaturgus*, Leipzig 1880, no. 14, p. 84[24–6]: 'He who through the unrestricted will of his own person, in order to communicate his gifts, took the form of mortal man for a short time.' This passage is unique in ante-Nicene literature.

the 'firstfruit' has lost his function. The economy has been fulfilled. At the same time, the function of Christ, the Incarnate, as 'head' also changes. After the Day of Judgement, the head of the new mankind will no longer be the man borne by the Godhead, the *homo dominicus*, but the 'Logos' himself.

Eusebius poses to the bishop of Ancyra the question of what happens to the human nature of Christ after the restoration in a penetrating way. At the same time he criticizes Marcellus' Logos doctrine:

> But you take the Logos from it (the body) and bind it (the Logos) to God. Will this body without the Logos subsist alone in immortal and incorruptible irrationality and immovability (οὐκοῦν ἄνευ λόγου μόνον τὸ σῶμα στήσεται ἐν ἀθανάτῳ, ἀλογίᾳ καὶ ἀκινησίᾳ)? And how will the Logos take himself back into God and be bound to him again after the separation from the flesh? Or was he not in God when he was together with the flesh? Or was he always in him (God), as he was eternal like God and one and the same with God? How then did he exist in the body?[99]

Marcellus himself had already posed the question, but at first he sought to avoid it, finally attempting the solution that has already been described:

> If anyone were to ask after the flesh which has become immortal[100] in the Logos, what would we say to him? We at least believe that it is an uncertain matter to set up dogmas about a subject of which we have not learnt enough from the divine scriptures. How is it that some people can overthrow the dogmas of others? Rather, to those who would like to learn more from us on the subject, we would say that, following the holy apostle, we know only that we should regard the hidden mysteries as he told us. 'Now we see,' he says, 'in a glass darkly, but then face to face' . . . (1 Cor. 13. 12). Therefore do not ask me about what I have not learnt clearly from the divine scriptures. Because of that I cannot make any clear statement about the divine flesh which participated in the divine Logos (τῆς τῷ θείῳ λόγῳ κοινωνησάσης σαρκός).[101]

Marcellus then refers to the *regula fidei*, and takes from it a statement which he formulates as his own confession:

> Now I believe the divine scriptures, that there is one God and that his Logos came forth from the Father so that 'all things' might be made 'through him' (John 1. 3). But after the Day of Judgement and the rectification of all things and the conquest of every hostile power, 'then he himself will be subject to the one who has subjected everything to him' (1 Cor. 15. 28, 24), the God and Father, so that the Logos may again be in God what he was earlier before the beginning of the world. For before this nothing existed but God; but when all things were to come into being through the Logos, the Logos came forth as effective power (*energeia*); this Logos was the Logos of the Father.[102]

Marcellus' starting-point, his understanding of Christian monotheism, here clearly seems to be the real reason why I Cor. 15. 24–8 could so determine his view of Christ's humanity. By his return to the *regula*

[99] Euseb. Caes, *C. Marcell.* II, 4: Klostermann–Hansen, 57[2-16].
[100] Tetz, Markell III, 187f., for the various understandings of immortality, depending on whether talk is of God or the redeemed Christian (*De incarn. et ctr. Arian.* 15).
[101] Marcell. Ancyr., frag. 121. Cf. Schendel, op. cit., 124.
[102] Frag. 121 end: Klostermann–Hansen, 212; Gericke, 240.

fidei, coupled with his reference to the silence of scripture, the Bishop of Ancyra 'escaped censure in the West. But in the East he came up against enraged rejection. We hear from Epiphanius the view of Athanasius that Marcellus had justified himself.'[103]

Some recent scholars are of the opinion that while Marcellus developed his theses, he kept the substance and merely changed the presentation of his views.[104] However, this charge of 'deception' cannot be upheld. In the course of a discussion, matters are always made more precise and new formulations appear. Marcellus presented his new interpretation in *De incarnatione et contra Arianos* 20–1. Here are the decisive sections:

> And again the apostle says: when he surrenders the kingly rule to God and the Father, after he has annihilated every rule and every authority and power, etc. But when he has subjected all things to him, the Son will also subject himself to the one who has subjected all things to him, so that God may be all in all. He says this of the subjection of the cosmos which takes place in his flesh. For Daniel says of his divine rule that his kingdom will have no end. . . . The apostle, however, says that his kingdom will have an end. He must rule, he says, until he has set all enemies under his feet. . . . But when he has subjected all things to him, the Son too will subject himself to the one who has subjected all things to him, that God may be all in all. But this means, he says, that when we are all subjected to the Son and made his members, and all become sons of God through him— for you are all one, he says, in Christ—then he himself will be subjected in our place to the Father, as head for his own members. For so long as his members have not yet all been subjected, he, as their head, has not yet been subjected to the Father, but awaits his own members. If he were only one of those who are subjected, he would be subjected to the Father from the beginning and not only at the end. For we are those who are subjected in him to the Father, and we are those who rule in him until he has set our enemies under our feet; for because of our enemies the ruler of the heavens became like us and received the human throne of David, his father according to the flesh, to rebuild it and restore it, so that when it was restored we might all rule in him and he might hand over the restored human rule to the Father, so that God might be all in all, ruling through him as through the Logos-God, after he had ruled through him as the Man-Redeemer.
>
> 21. And when Peter says, 'Now let the whole house of Israel know that God has made him Lord and Christ, this Jesus whom you have crucified', he is not speaking of his Godhead, that he has made it Lord and Christ, but *of his manhood, which is the whole church*, which rules in him after his crucifixion and holds sway and has been anointed to the rule of heaven, so that it may rule with him who emptied himself for its sake and for its sake assumed the form of a servant. For the Logos and Son of God was always Lord and God and was not made Lord and Christ after the crucifixion but, as I said before, his Godhead made his manhood Lord and Christ.[105]

We are justified in assuming that here there is a controversy with Eusebius' criticism of Marcellus' interpretation of 1 Cor. 15. To maintain his position, Marcellus develops his teaching further. As R. Hübner has noted, the fragments of the writing directed against Asterius (above all 41,

---

[103] Epiphanius, *Panarion* 72, 4: Holl III, 59, 18–22; Tetz, Markell I, 257.

[104] R. Hübner, 'Gregor von Nyssa und Markell von Ankyra', 210–22, which lies at the basis of the following remarks.

[105] Marcell. Ancyr., *De incarn. et ctr. Arian.* 20–1: PG 26, 1020A–1021B (the text here follows the translation by R. Hübner, op. cit., 212–14).

113–21) do not relate the subjection expressly to the church, 'but constantly to the manhood of Christ and to the swallowing up of the Logos in the Father'.[106] (We cannot entirely accept this way of putting matters, so far as the humanity of Christ is concerned. One cannot talk of a 'swallowing up of the Logos in the Father'. The Logos simply returns as 'energeia' into the 'one God' to which he always belongs as 'dynamis'.) In connection with the manhood of Christ, it should be noted that in the chapters from *De incarnatione et contra Arianos* which have just been cited, this position is 'not abandoned for a moment'.[107] For 'the Man and Redeemer forfeits his function as ruler in favour of the God Logos' (1021A).[108]

To disguise his real view [this phraseology might also be challenged], Marcellus interprets the subjection of the Son in terms of his body, the church. . . . Marcellus retreats, but only in form and not in content. He could well have received the stimulus to choose this form, interpretation in terms of the 'body of Christ', from his opponents, the Eusebians and Origenists, for they similarly interpreted the subjection in terms of the 'body of Christ'.[109] Thus without giving way on the matter, Marcellus took the wind out of his opponents' sails by a skilful manoeuvre [?].[110]

Some important observations follow from this conclusion. (1) In the light of Eusebius' criticism, this identification of the humanity of Christ with the church as the body of Christ could force the question of the continued existence of the humanity of Christ into the background. For now 'the body of Christ' exists for all eternity. This 'body' no longer exercises any rule. God alone rules, but now through the 'Logos God, after he had ruled through him (Christ) as the Man Redeemer' (see above). Thus this relationship of Logos-body of Christ = church appears as the final result of the second economy, in which the union of the Logos with the individual manhood of Christ has found its fulfilment. This new union of 'Logos-*soma* (= church)' assigns the members of the head, which was the man Christ as the exalted one, to the Logos *qua* Logos, who now exists only as *dynamis* in the Father. But can he be this Logos head without also coming forth from God again as *energeia*? There seems to be a gap here in Marcellus' system. But at this point his pneumatology should be inserted, especially as he developed it in *De incarnatione et contra Arianos*. There we find, specifically in connection with eschatology:

All who bear the Spirit of God bear the light, and those who bear the light have put on Christ, and those who have put on Christ have also put on the Father. 'This corruption

---

106 R. Hübner, op. cit., 214.
107 R. Hübner, ibid., in controversy with Tetz, Markell I, 257.
108 R. Hübner, ibid. However, with Tetz, Markell I, 261, it should be noted that the christological and *ecclesiological* aspect of Marcellus can already be seen in frag. 1.
109 Ibid.
110 Ibid. Hübner then shows how far Gregory of Nyssa took over the identification of the humanity of Christ with the church as the body of Christ.

must put on incorruptibility, and this mortal must put on immortality' (1 Cor. 15. 53). But those who bear the Spirit of God bear incorruptibility and God is incorruptibility.[111]

The mission of the manhood of Christ is fulfilled in the communication of the Spirit to those in Christ who have escaped the rule of the enemy and in the union of them with the Logos *qua* Logos and through him with God. Its exaltation was certainly important for the communication of the Spirit,[112] but it does not remain the eternal source and mediator of the Spirit. The sayings of Rev. 21. 22–3 about God and the lamb as the temple of the new Jerusalem and about the glory of God and the lamb as the lights of this city do not play any role in Marcellus. Indeed he does not use this last book of the New Testament at all.[113] Redeemed mankind, filled with the Spirit, now delivers the 'firstfruit' (the exalted mankind of Christ):

As often as scripture says that the Son has received (sc. the name above all other names), it says this of *his body*, which body is *the firstfruits of the church*: the firstfruits it says, is Christ (1 Cor. 15. 23). *Now in that the firstfruits received a name above every name*, the mass was also raised with the firstfruits *according to its capacity* (δυνάμει) and was also set on the throne (Eph. 2. 6). For this reason men received grace to be called gods and sons of God. Now first the Lord raised his own body from the dead [just as he had also, as Logos, created his own body in the Virgin] and exalted it in himself; so too he will also raise the members of his body to give them as God all that he himself received as man.[114]

With this text we are now looking back once again to the individual body of Christ, in which however 'the dough, the mass' was also already raised according to its capacity. By referring to a text from Valentinian Gnosticism, R. Hübner also involves the *homoousios* in ecclesiology: 'Thus after the rule of death, the great champion Jesus Christ, also taking to himself the church as far as it was capable, raised up what he had assumed and bore it away, and through it that which is of the same substance. "If the firstfruit is holy, so too is the mass; if the root is holy, so too are the shoots." '[115]

The Redeemer and the redeemed have become an organic, universal unity: for Gnosticism, in that 'all the elements of *pneuma*, being of identical substance (. . .) (are) incorporated in the one body,'[116] for Marcellus in that all men are made alive through the *pneuma* of Christ, have become his members and thus one body (= church).[117] It is possible that Marcellus took up a Gnostic pattern of redemption.[118] An investigation of parallel

---

111 Marcell. Ancyr., *De incarn. et ctr. Arian.* 15: PG 26, 1009C.
112 Cf. above on *De incarn. et ctr. Arian.* 3: PG 26, 989B.
113 The index in Klostermann–Hansen has no entry under 'Revelation'.
114 Marcell. Ancyr., *De incarn. et ctr. Arian.* 12: PG 26, 1004B, cited in R. Hübner, op. cit., 217.
115 *Excerpta ex Theodot.* 58, cited in Hübner, 220 and n. 1 after F. M. M. Sagnard, *La gnose valentinienne et le témoignage de saint Irénée*, Paris 1947, 142 = Iren., *Adv. haer.* I, 8, 3.
116 R. Hübner, op. cit., 221.
117 R. Hübner, ibid., and n. 4, *De incarn. et ctr. Arian.* 5: PG 26, 992B.
118 R. Hübner, ibid., 222, with reference to his discussion with Tetz, Markell II, who sets out to prove that with this doctrine of the Adamic Sonship of Christ (the assumption of the body of Adam

ideas in Gregory of Nyssa could also be an important chapter in the history of the influence of Marcellus.

A demonstration of the links between Gregory and Marcellus, which could also be supplemented by other observations, also makes it possible to discover the origin of the physical doctrine of redemption which has its foundation in the identification of the manhood of Christ and the church; for it can be demonstrated from Marcellus that this identification was achieved by following an orthodox counter-interpretation to Gnostic soteriology into the theology of the Fathers.[119]

We must now also add a note on Marcellus' pupil Photinus. The latter, of course, sharpens Marcellus' one-sided attempts both in trinitarian doctrine and in christology. According to the meagre accounts we have, Christ was a mere man, though miraculously born, endowed with special power (δραστικὴ ἐνέργεια) by the Father, and finally accepted as Son.[120] In this way the Logos-anthropos christology would become a denial of the incarnation. The conjunction of a Marcellian key phrase ('active energy') with this Logos-anthropos framework, interpreted here in an adoptionist way, is interesting.

2. EUSTATHIUS OF ANTIOCH

In Marcellus of Ancyra we have made a first observation which indicates the rise of a christological anthropology. Scriptural sayings about the humiliation of Christ are not loaded on to the Logos *qua* Logos, but are attributed to the human element in Christ. This method seems to be present in a sharper form in Eustathius of Antioch (died before 337). Because of it, he has been made a follower of Paul of Samosata and a precursor of Nestorius. Such a context is, however, unfair to Eustathius; the remark of Severus of Antioch is true of him as well:

Between Ebionites and Artemon, between Paul of Samosata and Photinus, between the supporters of Diodore and Nestorius and these (the Chalcedonians) there were some differences, and the one does not seem to correspond with the other in all respects, although they were ensnared in the one net of worshipping a man.[121]

We shall try briefly to draw out the essential elements of Eustathius' picture of Christ. The outline will serve at the same time as a contribution to the question of the place of the humanity of Christ in the struggle

---

by the Logos), Marcellus has taken over a pseudo-Clementine tradition about the true teachers and prophets. However, Dr Tetz can demonstrate that the pseudo-Clementine tradition stands within the Jewish–Christian, Gnostic tradition.

[119] R. Hübner, op. cit., 229.

[120] On Photinus see G. Bardy, *Paul de Samosate*, Louvain 1929, 407–14; id., art. 'Photin', *DTC* XIII; M. Simonetti, *Studi sull'Arianesimo*, Roma 1965, 135–59; B. Studer, *Zur Theophanie-Exegese Augustins*, Roma 1971, 9–17.

[121] Severus A., *Ctr. Grammaticum* III, 2, 28: ed. Lebon, 58.

against Arianism.[122] However, we cannot claim to present already assured results. Our distinction here between the older and the younger Eustathius needs further critical examination, which cannot be made here. For according to an important note in a letter from Dr M. Tetz, the fragments which present a Logos-anthropos framework may well be *Eustathiana*, but documents which have been edited by supporters of Eustathius. We therefore present our remarks in section (*b*) with some hesitation, until the possibility of a new investigation is realized.

(a) The older tradition

From a time before the beginning of the Arian struggles and even still in his polemical writings, Eustathius has a form of christology which is completely un-Antiochene—in the later sense of the word. The passages concerned are those in which antithetical christological language is chosen to describe the magnitude of the mystery of redemption.[123] Because of the reputation which the Eustathian christology had gained, it was hardly felt possible to credit him with full recognition of the so-called *communicatio idiomatum*, and so a question mark was put after many of his texts. Two statements, however, belong among the strongest christological formulations of the whole of the older tradition. The first instance is in the theological letter on Melchisedek and concerns John the Baptist:

'*Johannes autem ipsum Verbum corpus factum, quod est principium imaginis et sigilli, manibus suis complexus deduxit in aquas.*'[124] Likewise he says of the Jews, '*Manifeste deprehensi sunt, qui Verbum Deum occidissent et cruci affixissent.*'[125]

Eustathius made this last remark in a homily to the church on John 1. 14, probably at a time when he had not yet been obliged by controversy to make his thought more explicit. If this is the case, we must assume that

---

[122] M. Spanneut, *Eustathe*; F. Cavallera, *S. Eustathii episcopi Antiocheni in Lazarum, Mariam et Martham hom. christolog . . . cum comment. de fragmentis eustathianis accesserunt fragmenta Flaviani I Antiocheni*, Paris 1905. (The authenticity of the homily cannot be maintained.) R. V. Sellers, *Eustathius of Antioch and his place in the early History of Christian Doctrine*, Cambridge 1928; F. Zoepfl, 'Die trinitarischen und christologischen Anschauungen des Bischofs Eustathius', *TQ* 104, 1923, 170–201; cf. Tetz, 'Markellianer und Athanasios'.

[123] Cf. frag. 13 (*De anima adv. arian.*): ed. Spanneut, 99; frag. 21 (*Comment. in Prov.* 8. 22): ed. Sp., 101³⁴⁻⁵: τὸ ἀσώματον τῆς Σοφίας Πνεῦμα—ὁ τῷ Πνεύματι σωματοποιηθεὶς ἄνθρωπος. Frag. 30 (ibid.), ed. Sp., 104: — Σῶμα — τὸ θεῖον τῆς Σοφίας Πνεῦμα . . . εἴσω τῶν σωματικῶν ὄγκων ἡ ἀνωτάτω σοφία. This fragment develops the same thought as Ath., *De incarn.* 17: PG 25, 125; ed. Robertson, 25–6. In the first form of the Eustathian christology many similarities to Athanasius or to the Alexandrians in general can still be pointed out, as, for example, the identification of Logos and Sophia. This is usual since Clement of Alexandria (see the Stählin Index). In Irenaeus, Theophilus of Antioch, the pseudo-Clementine homilies and others, Sophia = the Holy Ghost. The Antiochene Eustathius then takes up the Alexandrian way of speaking here. Cf. E. Schwartz, 'Zur Geschichte des Athanasius'; NGött VII, 1908, 365–6, where Eustathius is described as a fanatic follower of Alexander of Alexandria. Schwartz judges this relationship, however, on church-political principles.

[124] Eustath., frag. 64 (*Ep. de Melchisedech*): ed. Sp., 114⁹⁻¹⁰.

[125] Eustath., frag. 70 (*Or. coram eccl.*): ed. Sp., 118¹³⁻¹⁴. These two passages are in *Florilegium Edessenum anonymum*, ed. I. Rucker, SBMünchAk., 1933, H.5, pp. 23–4. On frag. 70, Spanneut says on p. 79: 'On ne peut, pour ce seul motif'—that Eustathius usually strictly avoids this sort of language (frags. 26, 27)—'ranger parmi les apocryphes ce texte qui est présenté par trois documents'.

Eustathius here speaks in a derived form of christology, the presence of which on Antiochene soil is particularly interesting. One may also note that he uses the title θεοτόκος without hesitation.[126]

Some distinguishing marks of a 'unitive theology' are also evident elsewhere in Eustathius, particularly in his idea of the divinization of Christ's soul and body and their participation in the properties and being of the Logos. Here we feel reminded of Origen, who saw the soul of Christ completely steeped in the fire of the Logos, though it is just in this context that the opposition between the Antiochene and the Alexandrian becomes apparent. Eustathius is offended above all by the remarks about the soul of Christ in the underworld which Origen produces on the occasion of the question of the 'Witch of Endor'. These remarks seem to date from before the outbreak of the Arian dispute. The Alexandrian sees the difference between the soul of Christ and other spirits in the fact that while it was below in Hades with the others, by *will* it was above.[127] The Antiochene says that by doing this Origen makes Christ an ordinary man, just as he cannot show how the prophets were superior to other men. For all souls, even those of the most wicked men, have a longing to be above and not below. Origen does not take the divine nature of Christ into consideration (ἀλλ' οὐκέτι καὶ τῆς θείας αὐτοῦ στοχαζόμενος φύσεως). As God the Logos, Christ is by virtue of his ἀρετή, in his might and power, over all and above all. The soul of Christ, too, has a share in these properties, especially in the all-embracing power, indeed the omnipotence of the Logos, and because of this it has the power to lead the departed souls out of the underworld.[128] Complete control over space and participation in the omnipresence of the Logos, sinlessness, an inner transformation, intensification of the powers of Christ's manhood and a share in the rule of the world, all these are the gifts of the Logos.[129] This emphasis on the divine element in the features of Christ's humanity stamps the whole of the Eustathian picture of Christ.

And what, then, is there strange in saying that when he (the tempter) beheld Christ's countenance and saw indeed that within he was God, and by nature the true Son of God,

[126] Eustath., frag. 68 (*Hom. de tentat.*): ed. Sp., 116[11-12], with explanation p. 78. R. V. Sellers, *Eustathius*, 67, and F. Zoepfl, 'Eustathius', 195, n. 1, doubt the authenticity, whereas F. Cavallera, *Homilia Christologica*, 84f.; O. Bardenhewer, *Altkirchl. Lit.* 3, 234, n. 2, and M. Spanneut support it. Spanneut, 78: 'Le mot "theotokos" n'étonne pas dans la bouche d'un antiarien.' The evidence is transmitted by Alexander Al., *Ad Alex.* in Theodoret, HE, I, 4, 54: ed. Parmentier, 23[3]. But Eustathius was a zealous follower of Alexander, as has already been established. Θεοτόκος is already quite frequent in the writers under Alexandrian influence, such as Athanasius, Eusebius of Caesarea and Didymus. In the Acts of the Council of Antioch the title is accepted as authentic (H.-G. Opitz, *AW* 3, 38-40). It was used with some restraint by the Fathers only because of the misuse of it by the Arians.

[127] Origen, *In I Reg.* 28: ed. E. Klostermann, *Origenes, Eustathius v. A. und Gregor v. Nyssa über die Hexe von Endor*, Bonn 1912, in H. Lietzmann, *Kl. Texte* 83, p. 12. Eustath., *De engastrimytho* 17: ibid., 44[13ff].

[128] Eustath., *De engastrimytho* 17: ed. Klostermann, 45[9-11].

[129] Ibid., 18: ed. Kl., 45[28-31]. The omnipresence of the Logos and the relationship to the humanity of Christ, ibid., 45[32]-46[10].

and perceived the pure, undefiled, unstained man that surrounded him—a most beautiful, sanctified, inviolable (ἀσύλητος) temple—he none the less to test him out attacked without hesitation, fighting against God as is his wont.[130]

To this aspect of his christology we should probably add such phrases as πανἀγία σάρξ and ἅγιον σῶμα, which he supposes to be fully divinized by the indwelling Logos.[131]

That is one Eustathius. This side of his christology is quite different from the Samosatene–Syrian–Antiochene aspects—to pile up the descriptions which have been used on occasion to illustrate his basic tendency. In the form described above, his teaching has the stamp of a 'unitive christology', which is none the less quite well balanced, as it stresses not only the Godhead of the Logos but also his complete human nature. One most valuable recognition is his insight into the unity of subject in Christ. The Logos is the subject, so that all that Christ does or suffers in the flesh can be predicated of the Logos. It is particularly interesting to find this type of christology on Antiochene soil when we consider the doctrinal traditions which had been or were to be derived from there.

Eustathius first becomes important for our investigation in his dispute with the Arian Logos-sarx christology. This controversy also demonstrates the role played by christology in the Arian system in a way which was not fully evident in, say, Athanasius. At the same time, it also produces the 'other' Eustathius, whose chief characteristic is a 'divisive christology'.

(b) Eustathius as opponent of the 'Logos-sarx' framework

We have met Eustathius as the first of our witnesses to have noticed the character of the Arian christology:

Why do they (the Arians) think it so important to show that Christ took a body without a soul, fabricating such gross deceptions? So that if only they can induce some to believe this false theory, they may then attribute the changes due to the passions (πάθη) to the divine pneuma and thus easily persuade them that what is changeable could not have been begotten from the unchangeable nature.[132]

That is the Arian aim. Now of course in the extant fragments we have no passage in which the 'spiritual' sufferings of Christ are mentioned in anything like the completeness of detail which is given to the πάθη τῆς σαρκός in Athanasius' Contra arianos III. But Eustathius, in contrast to Athanasius, recognizes real 'spiritual' sufferings in Christ and their principle and subject, the soul of Christ.[133] Here we see the outlines of his

---

130 Ibid., 10: ed. Kl., 31[10-16].
131 Eustath., frag. 74 (In Samaritan.): ed. Spanneut, 121, also 80. One need not reject this text because of the πανάγιος, as does R. V. Sellers, Eustathius, 67, cf. frags. 17 and 24 (ed. Sp., 100 and 102).
132 Eustathius, frag. 15 (De anima adv. arian): ed. Sp., 100[2-6].
133 Eustath., frag. 41: ed. Sp., 108[22-5]: . . . Homini vero haec (= suffering unto death, weariness, etc.) adplicanda sunt proprie, qui ex anima constat et corpore; congruit enim ex ipsis humanis et innoxiis motibus demonstrare quia non phantastice et putative, sed ipsa veritate totum hominem indutus est deus perfecte adsumens. Cf. frag. 47: ibid., 109.

new position, which is concerned with two things—the recognition of the completeness[134] of the humanity of the Lord and the distinction of the natures. We must acknowledge that, in view of the great predominance of the Logos-sarx christology of his opponents, valuable features of the old tradition are fully stressed here.

When the soul of Christ is to be given its explicit place in the picture of Christ, Eustathius chooses another framework: Word-man. In comparison with his other christology, however, this picture appears loose and not so completely integrated. A characteristic emerges which is felt to be peculiarly Eustathian and a prelude to the 'divisive christology' of Antioch: the *distinction* of the two natures is so stressed that it threatens to become a separation of persons. Thus we have the exact counterpart of the Logos-sarx framework with its exaggerated interpretation of unity: a christology of the 'Logos-man' type which endangers unity. His opposition to the Arians and their efforts to make the Logos the subject of expressions of Christ's humiliation leads Eustathius either to retract his remarks about the *communicatio idiomatum* or to explain them with qualifications: 'The God dwelling in him was not led like a lamb to the slaughter nor killed like a sheep, since he is by nature invisible.'[135]—'For it is not right to say that the Word, or God, died.'[136] On the contrary, he requires a strict distinction between the natures, in which of course 'the man' appears to have been made independent to such a degree that the real unity of person is endangered. So we can already find in Eustathius a typical formula which is to become characteristic of the Antiochenes:

But the 'I am not yet ascended unto my Father' was not spoken by the Logos, nor by the God who came down from heaven and lives in the bosom of the Father, nor by the Wisdom which embraces all that is created, but it was uttered by a *man* formed of different members, who was raised from the dead and had not yet ascended to the Father.[137]

If Eustathius' immediate concern was to distinguish the natures,[138] the explanation of the unity must necessarily have been a particular problem for him. Like Col. 2. 9, Origen and Athanasius—to mention just this evidence—he begins with the simple idea of the 'indwelling of the Logos' in the 'man' Christ. The soul (!) of Christ lives with the Logos.[139] The body is the temple, the tabernacle, the house, the garment (περιβολή) of the Logos, in which he is concealed and through which he works as

---

[134] In this context Eustathius readily comes forward as an anti-docetist and accuses the Arians of docetism.

[135] Eustath., frag. 37 (*In Ps.* 92): ed. Sp., 107.

[136] Eustath., frag. 48 (*Or. ctr. arian.*): ed. Sp., 109: *neque dicere fas est quia Verbum mortuum est et Deus.*

[137] Eustath., frag. 24 (*In Prov.* 8. 22): ed. Sp., 102–3 (from the year 327 or 328).

[138] Cf. also frags. 18–20, 24, 25, 27–30. These passages in which the reality of the manhood is particularly stressed should also be added: frags. 22–3 and 26: similarly the immutability of the Word: frags. 26 and 31.

[139] Eustath., frag. 17 (*De anima adv. arian.*): ed. Sp., 100: συνδιαιτωμένη κυρίως ἡ ψυχὴ τοῦ Χριστοῦ τῷ Λόγῳ καὶ Θεῷ.

through an instrument.[140] This language is the common possession of a popular, unreflecting tradition, and it is also used by his opponents. In Eustathius, however, it had to be given a heightened, almost an exclusive significance. The history of the 'indwelling-framework' shows how hard it was to make clear the real character of the unity of person in Christ. The attempt was frequently made by referring to the 'fullness' of the indwelling. Eustathius refers to its 'length' and wishes to distinguish Christ from the prophets in this respect.[141] Both of these remain a distinction in degree only and cannot be developed into a substantial one.

In his effort to distinguish the natures, Eustathius eventually shapes formulas which are at the least open to misunderstanding. Whereas Ignatius of Antioch had only spoken of the θεὸς σαρκοφόρος, and in this way had achieved a very subtle expression of the unity of subject in Christ,[142] his successor in the see reversed the phrase: ἄνθρωπος θεοφόρος, *homo deifer*.[143] Naturally such expressions should not be pressed, but the contrast between them and the formulations of the Logos-sarx christology is evident. Eustathius' explanation of a statement by a preacher who had given the name Son to the dead body of Christ shows the looseness of his presentation of the unity in Christ. He allows the statement because God dwells in the dead body:

> *Sed potestatis maiestatem introducere volens et ipsum corpus mortificatum hic Filium dixit, ipsum quidem sublimitatis nomen imponens, id est habitantis in eo dei decibiliter.*[144]

Only if such remarks are isolated can one raise the suspicion, otherwise completely unjustified, that Eustathius teaches two persons or has an adoptionist conception of Christ's being.

---

[140] This terminology is collected in F. Zoepfl, 'Eustathius', 185.

[141] Eustath., frag. 9 (*In titul. inscript.*): ed. Sp., 98: διὰ τὸν οἰκοῦντα θεὸν ἐν αὐτῷ διηνεκῶς. Here the unity of Christ, who because of this 'lasting' indwelling is called the σύνθρονος of God, appears to be constructed in a very loose way.

[142] Ign. Ant., *Smyrn.* 5, 2: ed. Lightfoot II, 302.

[143] Eustath., frag. 42 (*Or. adv. arian.*): ed. Sp., 108[29]: '*prospiciens deiferum hominem*'; ibid., frag. 43: ed. Sp., 109[2]: '*homo autem Deum ferens*', likewise frag. 59 (*De fide ctr. arianos*): ed. Sp., 112[9-12].

[144] Eustath., frag. 45 (*Or. adv. arian.*): ed. Sp., 109.

CHAPTER FIVE

BETWEEN ARIANISM AND APOLLINARIANISM

1. INTRODUCTION

THE Logos-sarx framework found a first considerable group of exponents in the Arians, who always remained true to the approach, evidently because it was either necessary to, or conditional upon, their system. Now one of the most remarkable facts in the history of dogma is that a number of their opponents must also be counted as exponents of this same christological framework. Indeed, it is here that the christology first achieves its classical expression and begins to exert its influence in history, evidently in two forms, one within the church and the other heretical. The great names associated with these two forms are in the first case *Athanasius* (died 373) and in the second *Apollinarius* (died after 385).

However, the picture of the theological and especially the christological situation after Nicaea will be very much enriched if we preface these two names with another, that of *Eusebius of Emesa*. Certainly this homoiousian cannot be put on the same level as the two Nicenes Athanasius and Apollinarius, but he too is an anti-Arian and also an important link in the chain which binds various theological regions together. He has connections on all sides, not only to Alexandria but also to Caesarea and Antioch, and was in essentials concerned with the same problem as Athanasius. One may well be against putting the two names of Athanasius and Apollinarius side by side, but the historical and personal connections between them are too close[1] for them to be completely separable. It will not prove too difficult to make a sufficient distinction between Athanasius and the heresy of an Apollinarius, though a common element in the basic conception of their christology cannot be denied. This common element is, however, probably to be regarded as a legacy which both received, each developing it in a different way. In any case, in Athanasius the negative elements of a suspect christological framework appear only to a limited extent, as they are completely incorporated into a wider context of general church tradition, particularly in the doctrine of redemption. Athanasius can hand on to later theology a decisive and positive element from his interpretation of Christ's being—the particularly pronounced consciousness of the substantial unity in Christ, the knowledge that the Logos 'is' flesh. This

---

[1] Apollinarius is an admirer of his friend Athanasius, whom he describes as his teacher. Cf. *Ep. ad Diocaes. epp.*: ed. Lietzmann, 255–6: τῷ κοινῷ διδασκάλῳ ὑμῶν τε καὶ ἡμῶν. *Ad Sarap.*, frags. 159–161: ed. Lietzmann, 254: τὴν δὲ ἐπιστολὴν τοῦ δεσπότου μου τὴν εἰς Κόρινθον ἀποσταλεῖσαν σφόδρα ἀπεδεξάμεθα. On C. E. Raven, *Apollinarianism*, 105, see *Chalkedon* I, 93, n. 5.

recognition, which still needs to be defined more closely, emerges as the most valuable result of the Alexandrian Logos-sarx christology, particularly as represented in Athanasius. But first we must discuss Eusebius of Emesa.

2. EUSEBIUS OF EMESA[2]

When we investigate the sources of the thought of *Eusebius*, who was born about 300 at Edessa and died at the latest early in 359,[3] we are led into the sphere of Alexandrian theology. After leaving Edessa, Eusebius became a pupil of *Patrophilus of Scythopolis* and then of *Eusebius of Caesarea*, that is of men who were near to Arianism and closely connected with the older Alexandrian theology. He also went on to Alexandria and there made contact with the inner Arian circle. He was particularly friendly with *George*, later Bishop of *Laodicea*, who came from Alexandria and was likewise a supporter of Arius.[4] The thought-world of Caesarea and Alexandria in which the young Edessene grew up was an Origenism which had been weakened in some respects and intensified in others by Theognostus and Pierius.[5] Finally Eusebius came to Antioch as well, to study the theological and biblicist traditions which had been alive since the time of Lucian[6]—that is those which he did not already know from the Collucianists of Alexandria.

After the deep acquaintance which Eusebius made above all with Alexandrian thought, it is understandable if the characteristic christological ideas of this group live on in him. We can hardly be mistaken in attributing some part in this to his namesake of Caesarea, who gives new life to the christology of Origen, though without teaching about the soul of Christ.[7] This background to the thought of Eusebius of Emesa is noteworthy, and significant for the early history of Antiochene christology. The affinity of his christological thought with the ideas of his teacher is also confirmed by the remains of his extensive writings which have been handed on. These show us the dualism of sarx and pneuma—or sarx and

---

[2] E. M. Buytaert: (1) 'L'authenticité des dix-sept opuscules contenus dans le ms. T. 523 sous le nom d'Eusèbe d'Emèse', *RHE* 43, 1948, 5–89; (2) *L'heritage littéraire d'Eusèbe d'Emèse* (Bibl. du Muséon vol. 24), Louvain 1949 (Literary-historical investigation of the remaining work of Eusebius and edition of the texts transmitted in Greek, Syriac and Armenian); (3) *Eusèbe d'Emèse, Discours conservés en Latin. Textes en partie inédits.* T.I: *La collection de Troyes*; T.II: *La collection de Sirmond*, Louvain 1953, 1957. On christology see B., *RHE*, loc. cit.; A. Grillmeier, *Schol* 32, 1957, 583–5 (Latin sermons).

[3] E. Buytaert, *Héritage littéraire d'Eusèbe*, 61–96.

[4] Ibid., 47ff. Soon after the death of Eusebius, George composed a short biographical sketch of his friend, the *Enkomion*, which is partly preserved in Socrates, HE, 1, 24 and 2, 9: PG 67, 144–5, 197–200. On the relationship of Eusebius to Arianism, ibid., 17–23.

[5] Ibid., 70.

[6] Ibid., 71. Eusebius was in Antioch about the time of the deposition of Eustathius. On this date cf. H. Chadwick, *JTS* 49, 1948, 27–35. He conjectures 326 (not 330). Against, M. Richard, *MSR* 7, 1950, 305–7.

[7] See above, Introduction to Part Two.

dynamis, which are the terms preferred here—with which we are already sufficiently acquainted. We should not, however, think of the 'indwelling might' of Paul of Samosata, for Eusebius is quite understandably his opponent.[8] Even though he does not accept the Nicene ὁμοούσιος, he maintains the divinity of the Logos. He belongs among the Homoiousians, who were very close to the Nicene party, and even takes up a position opposed to Arius. This has a marked effect on his picture of Christ.

The main features of this picture are therefore moulded principally by the 'pneuma-sarx' or 'dynamis-sarx' antithesis. Only these two factors are mentioned. Whether we are dealing with the living or the dead Christ, the soul never becomes a really visible part of this picture. This is probably most noticeable in his explanation of the death of Christ;[9] it comes about through the separation of the 'power' from the 'flesh', dynamis being understood as the Godhead of Christ.[10] Christ's death cry, too, is interpreted in this way; it is uttered by him who 'has the power both to dwell within and also to depart'.[11] The death of Christ is equivalent to the departure of the divine dynamis or the divine pneuma.[12] The sacrifice of Christ, too, is interpreted—as in Athanasius—in such a way that the Godhead, the pneuma, offers up the body.[13] In any case, the dualism of this picture of Christ is clear: here, too, the soul of Christ is no theological factor, whether or not Eusebius eventually recognized its existence.[14]

The interesting and important point for the history of dogma is, however, that Eusebius is an opponent of Arian christology and a defender of some kind of 'divisive' theology within the framework of the Logos-sarx christology. His first and real concern is, in fact, to protect the indwelling dynamis from any suffering imposed from without and from any physical participation in the πάθη of the flesh. The association of such a concern with a basic Logos-sarx framework has the same consequence as in the thought of Athanasius; here, too, the sufferings 'of the soul' become those 'of the flesh'.[15] In complete contrast to his contemporary and opponent

---

[8] Euseb. Emes., De arbitrio, et voluntate Pauli et Domini passione (= De arbit.) 2, 4: ed. Buytaert, 15*, where Eusebius has Christ holding an inquisition of heretics. Paul of Samosata is the first to be introduced, and the next figure who emerges is Arius.

[9] Ibid. 1, 1: ed. Buytaert, 9*: τί γὰρ ἦν αὐτῷ θάνατος: οὐχὶ τὸ ἀναχωρῆσαι τὴν δύναμιν ἀπὸ τῆς σαρκός;

[10] Ibid. 2, 1: ed. B. 13*, where it is described as divine power.

[11] Ibid. 1, 2: ed. B. 10*: ὁ δὲ ἔχων ἐξουσίαν καὶ ἐνοικῆσαι καὶ ἀναχωρῆσαι.

[12] Ibid. 1, 4: ed. B. 11*: Πῶς ἀπέθανε; . . . Ἀνεχώρησε τὸ πνεῦμα, ἔμεινε τὸ σῶμα, ἄπνουν ἔμεινε τὸ σῶμα.

[13] See Chalkedon I, 132, n. 12.

[14] The Armenian fragments apparently show the opposite teaching. Euseb. Emes., De passione 19: ed. Buytaert, 87*: qui autem potestatem habebat ponendi animam et sumendi, sicut e virgine ultro et non invitus carnem accepit, ita in cruce ultro et non invitus separationem propriae animae a corpore operatus est. It should not be surprising that the biblical quotation has led to a mention of the soul (cf. John 10. 18). H. de Riedmatten, DomStud 3, 1950, 186, points out that in the further exegesis of this biblical text Buytaert's translation suggests that we have yet another mention of the soul. 'Propriae animae' is to be translated as 'proprii spiritus'; this refers to the Godhead. The Armenian has (h)ogi.

[15] Euseb. Emes., De arbit. 1, 3: ed. Buytaert, 10*. οὐκ ἀληθεύων λέγω, ὅτι ἡ δύναμις οὐκ ἠδύνατο δέξασθαι τῆς σαρκὸς τὰ παθήματα;

Eustathius, Eusebius does not think of introducing the soul of Christ as a created instrument of suffering. In fact he imagines the relationship between dynamis and sarx to be quite parallel to that between soul and body, an anthropology as unsatisfactory as his christology. He wishes to show by the example of soul and body that the dynamis in Christ is not the physical subject which endures the suffering, the blows, the nails, in short all the attacks on the life of Jesus. 'Strike a nail into a soul, and I will concede that a nail can be struck into the dynamis too.'[16] This mention of the soul does not refer to the individual soul of Christ, but is a quite general reference to the human soul for purposes of comparison.

Why does Eusebius take so much care that the Godhead of the Lord should not suffer? He is making out a case against Arius and his debasement of the Logos to a 'suffering soul'.[17] The divine dynamis is removed to a safe distance, away from any suffering. This is a completely justified and necessary concern, which Eusebius shares with Athanasius. But the Bishop of Emesa goes further than the Alexandrian. His picture of Christ is looser, and already displays typically 'Antiochene' features. The formulas of the 'indwelling of the *dynamis* in the flesh' and of 'the taking of flesh by the divine power' form the basis of his interpretation, which nevertheless remains within the Logos-sarx framework.[18] Such a unity between power and sarx is achieved by the 'indwelling' and the 'taking' that a certain exchange of predicates is permissible: what the 'flesh' suffers can be ascribed to the 'power', and what the pneuma does can be ascribed to the flesh.[19] But there is clearly some restraint towards the *communicatio idiomatum*.[20]

---

[16] Ibid., ed. B. 11*: (ἡ δύναμις) οὐκ ἐδέξατο ἦλον. Πῆξον εἰς ψυχήν, καὶ δέξομαι εἰς δύναμιν. The soul of Christ is not mentioned here, but merely the human soul, which is represented as being invulnerable. Eusebius uses this invulnerability of the human soul as an example of the untouchability of the Logos; cf. De arbit. 1, 1: ed. B. 9*: Μὴ γὰρ ἦλον ἐδέξατο ἡ δύναμις, ἵνα φοβηθῇ. Eusebius expresses his thoughts on the human soul in De arbit. 2, 2: ed. B. 13*: it is invulnerable, like an angel. Much less than a soul or an angel can the immaterial divine *dynamis* be wounded. Cf. *Schol* 32, 1957, 584, with passages from the Latin sermons.

[17] For this reason Arius too is arraigned before Christ's judgement seat. De arbit. 2, 4: ed. B. 15*.

[18] (1) *Indwelling formula*: De arbit. 1, 5: ed. B. 12*: ταῦτα πάντα παθήματα (they were mentioned before) περὶ σῶμα, ἀναφέρεται δὲ ἐπὶ τὸν ἐνοικοῦντα.

(2) *Taking formula*: ibid. 1, 4: ed. B., 12*: ἐπειδὴ ἀναλαβοῦσα ἡ δύναμις ἀπ' οὐρανῶν κατῆλθεν, ὃ ἔχει ἡ δύναμις, ἀναλογίζεται τῇ σαρκί.

(3) *Neutral formula*: ibid. 1, 4: ed. B., 12*: ἃ πάσχει ἡ σάρξ, ἀναλογίζεται τῇ δυνάμει. Had Eusebius already put forward teaching on the soul of Christ, the 'assumptus homo' formula would certainly have had to emerge here.

[19] Cf. Euseb. Emes., De arbit. 1, 4: ed. Buytaert, 12*: ὃ ἔχει ἡ δύναμις, ἀναλογίζεται τῇ σαρκί, or ibid. 1, 5: ὅσα εἰς τὸ σῶμα αὐτῷ (doubtless τῷ πνεύματι is meant) λογίζεται. Ibid.: ταῦτα πάντα παθήματα περὶ σῶμα, ἀναφέρεται δὲ ἐπὶ τὸν ἐνοικοῦντα. So, too, the Opuscula of T.523. Christ is '*virtus*' and '*caro*'. Cf. E. Buytaert, 'L'authenticité', 42–89.

[20] If one notices the restraint which Eusebius shows towards the *communicatio idiomatum* in the De arbit., the strong emphasis on it in the Syriac fragments seems suspicious. If this exchange of predicates is not consistently denied in the De arbit., at least reservations are made. The unity in Christ does not seem to be so firmly constructed as in the expressions of the fragments: frag. 1, ed. Buytaert, 69*: '*Ego autem valde beatum praedico illum uterum, qui dignus fuit ut portaret Deum*'; Frag. 4, ibid., 72*: '*Deus . . . ex Virgine natus*'. Frag. 5, ibid., 72*: '*. . . Deus ab hominibus condemnatus est. Deus pro nobis mortuus est*'. Frag. 8, ibid., 73*: '*Deus crucifixus est, o homines*'.

At all events, we have here an attempt to apply a corrective to the Logos-sarx christology, which had been so much misused by the Arians. It is the more remarkable because it was itself constructed within this framework. But it will be of even greater historical significance if we can accept that it exerted some influence on Diodore of Tarsus.

The newly discovered writings and the christology of Eusebius of Emesa now also seem to offer the possibility of determining rather more closely the origin of the *Pseudo-Ignatian epistles* and their place in history. In fact they belong in the sphere of the christological views of Eusebius.[21] In both writers the divinity of Christ is defended against the strict Arians, though a semi-Arian position is adopted. The chief christological concern is a resistance to the teaching of Christ as a 'mere man' (ψιλὸς ἄνθρωπος).[22] The opponents to whom the teaching is ascribed are probably Marcellus of Ancyra and Photinus. What is remarkable, however, is that the Pseudo-Ignatians already find teaching of Christ as 'mere man' wherever he is said to have had a human soul. The recognition that the humanity of Christ is complete, with body and soul, is equated with a denial of his divinity, or Ebionitism, or even adoptionism:

Si quis autem dicit unum Deum (a formula which probably includes the charge of modalism made against Marcellus and Photinus) confiteturque et Christum Iesum, hominem vero purum putans Dominum et non Deum unigenitum et sapientiam et verbum Dei, sed ex anima et corpore eum existimans, huiusmodi serpens est seductor, errorem praedicans ad perditionem hominum: huiusmodi pauper est sensu (an allusion to the name 'Ebion'), sicuti vocatur et adinventor ipsius erroris Hebion.[23]

According to Pseudo-Ignatius, the incarnation is the dwelling of the Logos in a human body, i.e. in a body without a human soul, and not a dwelling of the Logos in a man consisting of both body and soul. In any interpretation of the incarnation there are, he holds, only two possibilities, between which a choice must be made: either Christ is the true union of Logos and sarx which is expressed in John 1. 14 (but understood as Ps.-Ignatius required), or he is a 'mere man' in whom God dwells: *Verbum in homine.*[24]

So the incarnational formula of the Pseudo-Ignatian epistles represents a strict Logos-sarx christology which is intended as an answer to the Arians, the adoptionists and the docetists. 'The Logos, then, dwelt *in the flesh.*' Mary bore only the body in which God dwelt.[25] This whole con-

---

[21] Demonstrated by O. Perler, 'Pseudo-Ignatius und Eusebius von Emesa', HistJb 77, 1958, 73–82. Perler bases his comparison especially on the idea of the sinlessness of Christ, but at the same time he shows the whole background of their common christology which is to be sought not in Apollinarianism, but in the semi-Arian Logos-sarx christology (against F. X. Funk and F. Diekamp).
[22] Cf. Ps.-Ignatius, Trall. VI, 6: ed. Funk 2, 1901, 67; X, 4–8: F. 73–74; Magn. XI: F. 91–92; Ad Tarsenses II–VI: F. 97–101; Ad Philipp. III–XII: F. 109–119.
[23] Ps.-Ign., Philad. VI, 3: F. 135; cf. VI, 6; F. 135–136.
[24] Ps.-Ign., Philipp. V, 2; F. 111: Verbo (sic!) enim caro factum est, verbum homo, sed non in homine. We may recall the Arian formula for the incarnation.
[25] Ps.-Ign., Smyrn. II, 2: F. 145; Trall. X, 4: F. 73.

ception fits into the framework of the interpretation of Christ which is represented by Eusebius of Emesa. Although Christ consists only of Logos and 'flesh', he is still called 'only-begotten Son, God Logos and man' (*unigenitus Filius, Deus verbum et homo*).[26] Pseudo-Ignatius finds this formula and the ideas behind it potent in many directions. The recognition of the reality of the flesh excludes docetism, the recognition of the strict unity of Logos and sarx combats the adoptionism of Ebion, Paul of Samosata, Marcellus of Ancyra and Photinus, and the acknowledgement of Christ's true Godhead is a reply to Arianism.

Pseudo-Ignatius believes that he offers a satisfactory theory of redemption by rooting Christ's sinlessness in the Logos *qua* Logos.[22] Only in the school of Didymus will it become clear that to do this is to alter the structure of the church's doctrine of redemption completely. It was evidently thought that the Arian objections to the divinity of the Logos could be by-passed by the presupposition of the same neo-Platonic anthropology and psychology as can be found in Eusebius where the unity of Logos and sarx in Christ is involved. In this way, many christological errors of the time are rejected, but the decisive heresy is still retained: the Logos is involved in a natural union with the flesh. Even a Logos-sarx christology understood from a neo-Platonic position cannot escape the charge of injuring the transcendence of the Logos fatally and, moreover, of having a false understanding of the relationship between God and the world. The intention of maintaining the true unity in Christ as a unity of God and man must, however, be recognized. The fact that those who recognize Christ's humanity to be complete, with body and soul, already appear as betrayers of the true union of God and man is significant for the state of christology in the time before the beginning of the controversy with Apollinarius.[28]

At this point we may add a note on the christology of Cyril of Jerusalem (died 386).[29] He was a convinced opponent of classical Arianism. He did, however, have close connections with the semi-Arian group which we came across in connection with Eusebius of Emesa. Cyril was in contact with George of Laodicea and was an opponent of Marcellus of Ancyra (cf. *Cat.* 15, 27).[30] He had not quite overcome the subordinationism of the pre-Nicene period. He did not use the Nicene catch-word *homoousios*, because in his eyes the expression was foreign to Scripture.[31] Nevertheless,

[26] Ibid., *Philad.* IV, 2: F. 129.
[27] Cf. O. Perler, art. cit., 79f.
[28] O. Perler, ibid., 82, conjectures 360–70 as the date of the composition of the letters. He suggests the semi-Arian Silvanus of Tarsus as a possible author. He calls for a new investigation of the relationship of these epistles to the 'Apostolic Constitutions'.
[29] See M. Niederberger, *Die Logoslehre des hl. Cyrill von Jerusalem*, Paderborn 1923; J. Lebon, 'La position de saint Cyril de Jérusalem dans les luttes provoquées par l'Arianisme', *RHE* 20, 1924, 181–210, 357–86.
[30] See B. Niederberger, op. cit., 77–86; J. Lebon, art. cit., 181–97.
[31] B. Niederberger, op. cit., 82f.; J. Lebon, art. cit., 193, 385f.

he confessed the divinity of Christ, the Logos incarnate, without reservation. His conception of Christ fits into a framework of salvation history which is reminiscent of Irenaeus. This view of course came naturally to him along the lines of the creed which he expounded in his baptismal instructions (cf. *Cat.* 7–18). What distinguishes him from Eustathius of Antioch is the clear insight which identifies the incarnate redeemer with the Logos who existed before all time with the Father (*Cat.* 12, 4; 4, 9). His emphasis on the true humanity of Christ (*Cat.* 4, 9; 12, 1) arises from his anti-docetic, anti-Gnostic, and anti-Manichaean sympathies (*Cat.* 12, 33, 26). The single identity of Christ is maintained even in the clear distinction between the divinity and humanity (*Cat.* 10, 3). In spite of the many titles or names, Christ remains a single subject (*hypokeimenon, Cat.* 10, 4). So the title 'Theotokos' for Mary would occur quite naturally to him, because she had given birth to the incarnate Logos (*Cat.* 10, 19). In general he was a preacher not given to deep speculations on the person of Christ.

3. ATHANASIUS

(a) The problem

In discovering the particular views which Athanasius held on the being of Christ we start from a number of plain facts. It is probably undeniable that in his picture of Christ the soul of Christ retreats well into the background, even if it does not disappear completely. Does this retreat imply that the human *psyche* is really missing from the Athanasian picture of Christ?[32] We must distinguish two points of view here. It can probably be demonstrated quite easily that the soul of Christ plays no part in Athanasius' explanation of the economy of salvation, and that it is not even a factor in the inner human life of Christ. These assertions may be made with reasonable assurance. But over and above them there is a further question to be asked. Did Athanasius, in fact, know nothing of a human soul in Christ? Did he exclude it altogether? We can summarize briefly what is to follow by putting the last question in this way: did Athanasius advocate a merely *verbal* Logos-sarx framework or a *real* one? While the former framework would indeed ignore the soul of Christ it would in fact tacitly assume its presence. The latter, on the other hand, would regard the soul as non-existent. We shall now show quite simply and clearly that in the Athanasian picture of Christ the 'soul' of the Lord is no 'theological factor'. This is probably the decisive approach to his interpretation of Christ. We shall also point out in all honesty those elements

---

[32] M. F. Wiles, 'The Nature of the Early Debate about Christ's Human Soul', *JEH* 16, 1965, 139–51, gives a survey of the history of statements about Christ's soul from Justin Martyr to Cyril of Alexandria.

which can be interpreted in such a way as to suggest that the soul of Christ is also not a physical factor. Nevertheless, Athanasius himself here seems to draw a line which, however obscure, should not be overlooked.

First of all, it will not be out of place to say something about the method which is to be used to solve the question. Previous scholarship has already clarified this in one important respect. In demonstrating that Athanasius believed Christ to have had a human *psyche*, G. Voisin relied in particular on the analysis of a term like 'man' (ἄνθρωπος and derivatives) and the formulas which were built up from this word.[33] Contrary attempts were made to argue from the terms 'flesh', 'body', etc., which say nothing of a soul. On neither side does this terminological analysis lead to a solution, as Athanasius does not use these anthropological terms with the precision of Aristotle or of the Schoolmen, and as yet has no 'diphysite' terminology. Two historical points can, in fact, be made: Eusebius of Caesarea and Apollinarius, for instance, use the self-same terms, 'man', 'made man', etc., and yet at the same time deny Christ's soul. Cyril, on the other hand, will similarly use the language of the Logos-sarx framework in his early writings and yet expressly acknowledge a full human nature in the Lord (see below). Thus it is clear that an analysis of words cannot be conclusive.

We must therefore begin above all with theological notions. To judge what place the soul of Christ had in the Athanasian picture of Christ we must first attempt to outline this picture. We can give only a limited answer to the question here, marking out the narrower scope of inquiry by a look at previous investigations.

After the preliminary work of F. C. Baur, K. Hoss[34] and A. Stülcken[35] were foremost in advancing the theory that Athanasius knew nothing of a soul in Christ. G. Voisin countered them in the article already cited. In a thorough investigation M. Richard recently took up the question and decided in the negative.[36] He analyses only the section from Contra Arianos III, 35–7, and in so doing establishes several valuable standpoints for assessing the Athanasian christology. Where he does not analyse the inner structure of the christological arguments in Athanasius, Richard's main weapon is the *argumentum e silentio*. The Arian texts excerpted and criti-

---

[33] G. Voisin, 'La doctrine christologique de saint Athanase', RHE 1, 1900, 226–48, esp. 230–6. Similarly E. Weigl, *Untersuchungen zur Christologie des hl. Athanasius*, Paderborn 1914, 66–75. See the observations in J. Liébaert, *S. Cyrille*, 147–58; J. Roldanus, *Le Christ et l'homme dans la théologie d'Athanase d'Alexandrie. Étude de la conjonction de sa conception de l'homme avec sa christologie* (Studies in the History of Christian Thought IV), Leiden 1968, especially §4, 252–76; E. P. Meijering, *Orthodoxy and Platonism in Athanasius. Synthesis or Antithesis?*, Leiden 1968. Meijering provides an analysis of CG, De incarn. Verbi and the Orationes ctr. Arianos (5–113).

[34] K. Hoss, *Studien über das Schrifttum und die Theologie des Athanasius auf Grund einer Echtheitsuntersuchung von Athanasius, Ctr. gentes, und De incarnatione*, Freiburg 1899.

[35] A. Stülcken, *Athanasiana. Literatur- und dogmengeschichtl. Untersuchungen* (TU, NF 4, 4), Leipzig 1899.

[36] M. Richard, 'Athanase', 5–54.

cized in *Ctr. Arianos* III in fact presuppose that the Logos took the place of the soul. Any modern theologian, says Richard, would begin by criticizing this framework, particularly where the Arian 'Christ' is said to be neither God nor man, but a middle being of unique character. Athanasius takes a different attitude. Not once in the course of his long criticism does he accuse his opponents of having forgotten the human soul of the Lord. He does not accuse them of having made Christ into a special type of being, but simply of having made him into an ordinary man. This shows that from an anthropological point of view his view of the problem is completely different from ours. He had no quarrel with his opponents here. Nor does he ever resort to the expedient of giving Christ a human soul in order to solve the great difficulties raised by the Arians. So he knows nothing of one. His Christ is only Logos and sarx.

One must, of course, ask whether this *argumentum e silentio* is completely conclusive.[37] We shall in fact come to the conclusion that while in some authors the soul of Christ is not a 'theological' factor it is nevertheless a 'physical' factor. Thus positive proof must be added to a negative argument if the question of the soul of Christ in Athanasius is to be decided. First of all we intend to allow the conclusion as valid in so far as it asserts that Christ's human soul was no 'theological factor' in Athanasius, that is, that it was not a principle which he found necessary for his interpretation of the being and the work of Christ. But as Richard confined his investigation to a limited sphere of christological anthropology—this he conceded in his presentation of the text—we shall attempt to complete the picture. It will emerge that in every passage where he gives a positive interpretation of the person of Jesus Christ, his being and his redeeming work, Athanasius has refrained from including the human soul of the Lord in a really visible way.

(b) *The activity of the Logos in Christ's humanity*

There is no particular difficulty in finding elements in the Logos doctrine of Athanasius which associate him with Origen, Clement of Alexandria and even the Stoa. We may recognize philosophical influences, and indeed Athanasius himself concedes them. They certainly make their impression on the picture of Christ in early works like the *Contra Gentes* and the *De incarnatione*, though no one will deny the truly Christian substance. But the decisive feature of the Stoic–Alexandrian Logos doctrine comes right

---

[37] H. de Riedmatten draws my attention to this point. On the interpretation submitted here see F. Ortiz de Urbina, 'L'anima umana di Cristo secondo s. Atanasio', *OCP* 20, 1954, 27–43; P. Galtier, 'S. Athanase et l'âme humaine du Christ', *Greg* 36, 1955, 553–89; C. Konstantinidis, 'Εδίδασκεν ὁ Μέγας 'Αθανάσιος ὅτι εἶχεν ὁ Κύριος ἀνθρωπίνην ψυχήν;, ΟΡΘΟΔΟΞΙΑ 29, 1954, 286–93, 446–52; 30, 1955, 92–8; 31, 1956, 69–78, seeks to prove that the soul of Christ was a physical and a theological factor for Athanasius. As against these studies I abide by the interpretation given here. The soul of Christ was no 'theological factor' for Athanasius, but at the same time he may not have denied its 'physical' reality.

into the foreground. There is an endeavour to make the Logos the force from which all life and all movement comes.[38]

The world is created in the Logos; the Logos is its pattern, its support, its ordering and its life.

For as by his providence bodies grow and the rational soul is moved and possesses life and thought . . . so again the divine Logos with one simple nod by his own power moves and holds together both the visible universe and the invisible powers, allotting to everything its proper function.[39]

For all his transcendence and divinity, the Logos acts as a life-giving principle towards the world. Because of the manifest transcendence, this principle should not be identified with the Stoic world-soul. Athanasius has, however, taken over the Stoic concept of the world as a body, as σῶμα, and has admitted the Logos, which unlike the Stoa he understands as personal, as it were in the place of the soul.[40] Now the human, rational soul is the most perfect copy of the Logos within the earthly, corporeal creation. It fulfils towards the body the function which the Logos has in the cosmos. It is a Logos in microcosm, and therefore also a way to him and to the Father.[41]

These basic ideas of Logos and world, soul and body, and especially the affinity between Logos and soul, must be kept in mind if we are to form a true verdict on the relationship between the Logos and the humanity of Christ. Athanasius' view might be put in these words: where the original itself appears with all its power, the copy, with its secondary and derived power, must at least surrender its function, even if it does not give place altogether. Athanasius probably assigned to the human soul as such a substance of its own and maintained its immortality.[42] When he considers the being of Christ, however, his attention is immediately caught by the Logos and his relationship to the body of Christ. This relationship is regarded as being quite analogous to the other, that of Logos-world, soul-body.

The fleshly nature of Christ is only a part (μέρος) of the great cosmos-soma. Now if the Logos can give life to the whole world-soma, how much

[38] A. Gaudel, 'La théologie du Logos chez saint Athanase', RevSR 9, 1929, 524–39; 11, 1931, 1–26; L. Bouyer, L'incarnation et l'église—Corps du Christ dans la théologie de saint Athanase, Paris 1943, 52–8. On the place of Hellenism in Athanasius see H. Dörries, 'Die Vita Antonii als Geschichtsquelle', NGött 14, 1949, 359–410; W. Schneemelcher, 'Athanasius von Alexandrien als Theologe und als Kirchenpolitiker', ZNW 43, 1950–1, 242–56. See now Athanase d'Alexandrie, Sur l'incarnation du Verbe. Introduction, Texte critique, Traduction, Notes et Index par C. Kannengiesser (SC 199), Paris 1973. For christology, ibid., 139–56. The texts cited here from PG 25 have been checked against the new edition. Cf. R. W. Thomson, Athanasius, Contra Gentes and De Incarnatione. Edited and translated (Early Christian Texts), Oxford 1971.

[39] Athanasius, Ctr. gent. 44: PG 25, 88C; cf. 42 (84B): τὰ ὅλα ζωοποιῶν καὶ διαφυλάττων; cf. 40, 44: PG 25, 81A, 88B.

[40] Ath., De Incarn. 41: PG 25, 168D–169A. Ctr. gent. 36: PG 25, 72A–73A; cf. Tertullian, Apol. 10, 5. See A. Gaudel, 'Logos', RevSR 11, 1931, 1–26.

[41] Ath., Ctr. gent. 30–4, esp. 32: PG 25, 61–9. The same comparisons recur as in the description of the Logos-world relationship. Ibid., 33: PG 25, 68B; A. Gaudel, loc. cit., 14ff., 201.

[42] Ibid., 34: PG 25, 68C.

more can it to a part.[43] The Logos dwells in this his body as in a temple and, moreover, in all his fullness. Here again we have a most important point. Although the life-giving action of the Logos is present everywhere, it can be concentrated in one particular place. Indeed it is already gradated throughout creation. Athanasius, with his Christian–Stoic point of view, sees that if the Logos dwells in a single body which in addition is so completely his as to be 'his own' body, it must follow that he mediates life and power to it in full. The indwelling is perfect, intrinsic and substantial and must be, so as to effect the redemption of the body which he has inherited.[44] A dilemma which Athanasius puts forward shows how real he thinks the presence of the Logos in the body of Christ to be. 'But if the Logos is shut into the body, is not then the rest of the world bereft of his working power (ἐνέργεια) and foresight (πρόνοια)?' With a finite spiritual being that would indeed be the case, but despite the totality of the indwelling the Logos still preserves his transcendence.[45]

If the Logos-world relationship is applied primarily to the soul and body (as a type of the first relationship) and then to Christ, the Logos must be the principle which gives life and movement to the body of Christ, he must become the ἡγεμονικόν.[46] Is he then the sole life-giving principle? At this point we shall say no more than that Athanasius so often speaks of the life-giving functions of the Logos towards the flesh that he completely forgets the human soul of Christ. Indeed he seems to leave no place for it.[47] There can be no doubt that the Logos is not merely the personal subject of Christ's bodily life, but also the real, physical source of all the actions of his life. There is not always a clear distinction between the mediation of natural and supernatural life—as little as, say, in Origen, in the relationship between the natural and the supernatural view of the Logos. There is no doubt that Athanasius, influenced by the Logos doctrine of the Stoics and of Alexandria, includes the mediation of natural life here in speaking of the life-giving function of the Logos towards his body. Now this giving of natural life to the flesh imperceptibly becomes σωτηρία, which from a biblical point of view must be regarded

[43] Ath, De incarn. 17: PG 25, 125B: οὕτως (sc. ὁ λόγος) καὶ ἐν τῷ ἀνθρωπίνῳ σώματι ὤν, καὶ αὐτὸς αὐτὸ ζωοποιῶν, εἰκότως ἐζωοποίει καὶ τὰ ὅλα καὶ ἐν τοῖς πᾶσιν ἐγίνετο, καὶ ἔξω τῶν ὅλων ἦν (transcendence !). For the new way of salvation which results, cf. De incarn. 14: PG 25, 121AB. The Logos-flesh conjunction as Athanasius sees it (i.e. in connection with the idea of ἐλευθερία, ἀπάθεια, θεοποίησις) is the pattern for the Christian. In the Vita Antonii Athanasius has described the ideal of the Logos-Christian in a way which corresponds to the figure of the Logos-Christ. Cf. H. Dörries, 'Vita Antonii', 394–6.
[44] Ath., De incarn. 44: PG 25, 173C–176C; Ep. ad Epictet. 11: PG 26, 1086B. Cf. Origen, De princ. IV, 2, 30: reference to the fullness of the indwelling.
[45] Ath., De incarn. 17: PG 25, 125B.
[46] While Athanasius does not have this word, the cognates ἡγεμονεύω and ἡγεμών occur for νοῦς and λόγος. See G. Müller S. J., Lexicon Athanasianum (cited as Lex. Ath.), Berlin 1944ff., 605.
[47] Ath., De incarn. 17: PG 25, 125B says of the Logos αὐτὸς αὐτὸ ζωοποιῶν. This double αὐτὸς–αὐτό should be noted.

as supernatural.[48] But the fact none the less remains that Athanasius, in true Alexandrian fashion, first of all looks at the relationship of Logos to world, soul to body, Logos to flesh, which we would call natural, even though he then intends to progress further to the supernatural.[49]

If the Logos is really to be considered as the sole motivating principle in Christ, then the decisive spiritual and moral acts must be assigned to him above all, and in a way which appears to imply more than an appropriation after the manner of the *communicatio idiomatum*. Such an approach in Athanasius can in fact be proved, at least in part. Here his interpretation of the sacrificial act of redemption is particularly important. The question is: how does the Logos participate in this act? Athanasius obviously regards the Logos as the real personal agent in those acts which are decisive for redemption, the passion and death of Christ. In Alexandrian theology this is taken for granted. There is, however, a further question. How does Athanasius envisage the physical completion of this redeeming act? Here he appears to make the Logos not merely the personal agent in the act (the *principium quod* of later terminology), but also the physical principle of its achievement (the *principium quo*). There are already glimmerings of such an approach in those expressions which describe the redemptive activity of the Logos according to the rules of the *communicatio idiomatum*; it probably becomes clear enough in the description of Christ's suffering in Gethsemane in *Ctr. Arian.* III, 57.[50] There, in a typically Athanasian way, the power and immutability of the will of the Logos is emphasized in contrast to the weakness of the flesh. In any case, the nearness of the verbal Logos-sarx framework to the real is most striking at this point. The whole of the Athanasian picture of Christ is stamped with this immediacy of the Logos, which everywhere throws into relief the physical activity of the Logos, even though it is at the same time mediated through the bodily reality of Christ's humanity. Athanasius does not, of course, deny here that the human sarx of Christ performs its natural functions; these too are to be attributed to the Logos, but in a different way from those actions which are proper to the Godhead.[51] In any case, Athanasius allows the working of the Logos to become transparent as such in a more direct way than would be the case in a strict 'diphysite'

[48] Cf. A. Gaudel, 'Logos', *RevSR* 11, 1931, 20f.; J. B. Berchem, 'Le rôle du Verbe dans l'oeuvre de la création', *Angel* 15, 1938, 205, 211.

[49] In *Ep. ad Epictet.* 9, ζωοποιεῖν is to be understood as the giving of purely supernatural life; likewise for the resurrection, ibid. 10: PG 26, 1068A; cf. *Ad Adelph.* 8: PG 26, 1081C. Note that Athanasius brings the concept of 'life' into the forefront so that it takes over the place which 'knowledge' (γνῶσις) had in Clement and Origen, without completely excluding this latter.

[50] Ath., *Ctr. Arian.* III, 57: PG 26, 441BC: . . . θεὸς ἦν θέλων μὲν αὐτός, γενόμενος δὲ ἄνθρωπος εἶχε δειλιῶσαν τὴν σάρκα, δι' ἣν συνεκέρασε τὸ ἑαυτοῦ θέλημα τῇ ἀνθρωπίνῃ ἀσθενείᾳ—cf. *De incarn.* 16, 4: PG 25, 124CD; ibid. 25: 140C; *Ad Maxim.* 3: PG 26, 1088D; *Ad Epictet.* 6: PG 26, 1061A; *De sent. Dionysii* 11: PG 25, 496B; Marcellus of Ancyra, *De incarn. et ctr. arian.* 21: PG 26, 1021BC has a similar text: τὸ γὰρ ἀνθρώπινον διὰ τὴν ἀσθένειαν τῆς σαρκὸς παραιτεῖται τὸ πάθος· τὸ δὲ θεϊκὸν αὐτοῦ πρόθυμον. See M. Tetz, Markell I (above, p. 274, n. 1).

[51] Further in M. Richard, 'Athanase', 22–3.

theology. The Logos

did not immediately upon his coming accomplish his sacrifice on behalf of all, by offering his body in death and raising it again, for by this means he would have made himself invisible. But he made himself visible in his body, abiding in it and doing such works, and showing such signs as made him known no longer as man, but as God the Word.[52]

Such statements are surely still too imprecise for us to make a clear decision about the inner character of this picture of Christ, but it is quite probable that the Logos *qua* Logos was seen by Athanasius as the spiritual principle which effected the real act of redemption.

If Athanasius really makes the Logos the first and—as it seems—the sole physical subject of all Christ's life, he must find himself in great difficulty when he comes to explaining the sufferings in Christ. Here there is obvious need for a human spiritual principle, for it is clear that a supporter of Nicaea could not have the Logos as a subject of the physical sufferings of the passion and all the experiences which affected body and soul beforehand. If all ἀνθρώπινα are to be kept away from the Logos, a created subject of the suffering must be found. Here we touch on the real problem of Athanasian christology. It is at this point too that all the attacks of the Arians against the divinity of the Logos were concentrated. Athanasius himself gives an impressive summary of these attacks, which compel him to reveal the basic principles of his whole christology.[53] In the third discourse against the Arians he produces a lengthy Arian text with four main theses which are supported by specific scriptural quotations. A first argument against the identity in substance of the Logos with the Father lies in the witness of Holy Scripture that Christ *received gifts. Inward distress and suffering* in general show that the Son could not be the Father's own power. Moreover, if the Son in any way *advanced* he could not be the Father's own wisdom. Finally, *destitution, prayer and ignorance of the day of judgement* prove that the Son was not the Father's own word. The weaknesses and the heretical presuppositions of these Arian arguments are obvious. It was Athanasius' task to show that these 'human characteristics' of the redeemer did not prejudice his transcendence and immutability. He therefore had to find the subject of all suffering in the manhood of Christ, so as to put it as a protective shield before the inviolable Godhead. This would not have been very hard had it been merely a question of purely bodily weaknesses and limitations. But the Arians transferred their attacks to the human psychology of Jesus. Ignorance, prayer for help, weariness, in fact simply suffering, are eminently spiritual phenomena, even though they have physical connections. Now the Arians could speak of real 'sufferings of the soul' (as opposed to purely bodily suffering) because they

---

[52] Ath., *De incarn.* 16, 4: PG 25, 124CD: ed. Robertson, 24.
[53] Ath., *Ctr. arian.* III, 26: PG 26, 377A–380B.

had reduced the Logos to being a 'soul'. We know well enough that they built up all their attacks on the strict Logos-sarx framework.

Had Athanasius attacked this framework as such, a defence of the inviolability and immutability of the Logos could have followed naturally and without any particular difficulty. But no such attack is produced throughout the whole of his answer, though one might with some degree of certainty or at least probability assume that he knew of the christological basis of Arianism. It is further evident that the soul of Christ is not in Athanasius the theological factor which would have been necessary to explain any experiences which could be described as 'spiritual'. Indeed, at decisive points he quite strikingly refrains from appealing to this soul. This becomes particularly clear in his refutation of the second Arian thesis, which deals with the suffering in Gethsemane and the agony in Christ's soul.[54] Here 'we look in vain for an explicit mention of Christ's soul'.[55] We shall be discussing this text in a later context.

Athanasius displays a general tendency to weaken the character of certain of Christ's inner experiences which might be attributed to a human soul so as to dissociate the Logos from them from the start. Thus Christ's anguish was only 'feigned', and not real anguish; his ignorance was no real ignorance, but only an *ignorantia de jure*, which was proper to the human nature from the start.[56] Not only does such a qualification relieve the pressure on the Logos itself, but it also raises the possibility of representing the human *sarx* of Christ as the subject of such affections as we should properly ascribe to the soul. As a result, we have Athanasius' remarkable procedure of making the 'flesh' of Christ the physical subject of experiences which normally have their place in the soul.[57] He can speak of an 'ignorance of the flesh' in which the term 'sarx' clearly begs the whole question. From the whole of his explanation of the ignorance of Christ it follows that the thought of a human knowledge, a limited human consciousness in Christ, has not occurred to him. In any case, there is so small a basis for a human psychology in the Lord that such a psychology can be built up upon it only with difficulty. We regard this as an observation which is still independent of the question of the real lack or presence of a soul in the Athanasian picture of Christ.

(c) The death of Christ as a separation of the Logos

Christ dying, as pictured by Athanasius, shows as little trace of his soul as Christ living. The death of the Lord is explained in the light of the 'Logos-sarx' framework and is represented as a separation of the 'Logos' from the body. It is the Logos, too, who descends into the underworld. A

---

[54] Ath., *Ctr. arian.* III, 54–8: PG 26, 436B–445C.
[55] M. Richard, 'Athanase', 31–8, against G. Voisin.
[56] Ibid. 42–6. [57] Ibid., 43.

function which should by rights belong to the soul as the means by which
the Logos descends is thus assigned to the Logos. There is already quite
widespread evidence for this conception, but it has not as yet been fully
explored. More work still remains to be done on the place of the idea in
the history of dogma and on its theological significance.[58] Be this as it may,
the theology of the death of Jesus and his descent into the underworld
affords us a glimpse into the inner details of the Athanasian picture of
Christ from a new angle.

Athanasius was probably aware of the definition of human death as a
separation of body and soul.[59] It is therefore all the more significant that
in his interpretation of the death of Christ he prefers the explanation
relevant to the Logos-sarx framework. In this the writings of his old age
in no way differ from those of his youth. An outstanding example is his
exegesis of John 12. 27 and 10. 18, to which allusion has already been
made in the preceding section. Here the 'Godhead' of Christ imperceptibly
replaces the 'soul'. As man (ἀνθρωπίνως) Christ said, 'Now is my soul
troubled' (John 12. 27). As God, the Lord spoke the words 'I have power
to lay my soul down, and I have power to take it up again' (John 10. 18).
Then Athanasius continues:

> For to be troubled was proper to the flesh, and to have power to lay down his life
> and take it again, when he will, was no property of men but of the Word s power. For
> man dies, not by his own power, but by necessity of nature and against his will; but the
> Lord, being himself immortal, had power as God to become separate from the body and
> to take it again when he would.[60]

The text is without doubt most significant. If the 'soul' is mentioned,
this is in the biblical sense and means 'life'. It is remarkable how this
giving up of the soul and taking it again is interpreted as a separation of the
Logos from the body and a reunion of it with him. The Logos-sarx
framework, then, is sufficient to explain the death of Jesus. The soul has
no part to play in it. Some further texts help us to complete the picture.
The De Incarnatione of Athanasius' youth introduces the idea of the separation of the Logos in the context of the 'life-giving power' of the Logos
with which we are already familiar:

> If then once more his (Christ's) body had fallen sick, and the Word had been sundered
> from it (ἀπ'αὐτοῦ = ἀπὸ τοῦ σώματος) in the sight of all, it would have been unbecoming
> that he who healed the diseases of others should suffer his own instrument to waste in
> sickness.[61]

The connection of ideas is very strange. For Christ, death means the
separation of body and Logos. Athanasius certainly does not imagine that

[58] A. Grillmeier, 'Der Gottessohn im Totenreich', ZkTh 71, 1949, 23–53, 184–203.
[59] Cf. G. Müller, Lex. Ath., Θάνατος 1, esp. Ctr. Gent. 33: PG 25, 65C.
[60] Ath., Ctr. arian. III, 57: PG 26, 444B.
[61] Ath., De incarn. 22: PG 25, 136B. The shorter recension of De incarn. retains this idea. The
reading of ms. Athos Doch. 78 is striking. Text in T. Camelot, Athanase, 253.

the Logos himself becomes visible as he departs. His departure is recognizable only by its effect on the body, that is by the cessation of κίνησις, the sign of life.[62] This is a new indication that in the Athanasian christology the giving of physical life to the body really comes from the Logos.

This exclusive character of the Logos-sarx framework emerges still more sharply in the *Letter to Epictetus*, an indication, moreover, that Athanasius remained constant in his thought. In this letter he mentions a group who speak of a changing of the Logos into flesh. Athanasius dismisses this attitude by referring to the events which took place at the death of Christ and their interpretation. Had this 'change' taken place,

> ... then there would have been no need of a tomb. For the body would have gone by itself to preach to the spirits in Hades. But as it was, he (the Logos!) himself went to preach, while Joseph wrapped the body in a linen cloth and laid it away at Golgotha. And so it is shown to all that the body was not the Word, but the body of the Word.[63]

The theological argument is quite remarkable. It rests on a twofold assumption, that the 'Logos' effects the descent into the underworld and that Christ is nothing else but a visible body and the invisible Word. This is implicit in the dilemma which can already be observed in Alexander of Alexandria, the teacher of Athanasius:[64] either a descent of the Logos or a descent of the body. Neither here nor anywhere else does Athanasius think of the separation and descent of a soul. The more remarkable this argument against a change in the Logos, the more relevant it is for the interpretation of the Athanasian picture of Christ. Certainly the assumption of a descent of the Logos is still in itself no proof that its advocate knows nothing of a soul in Christ, just as on the other hand the mention of a *descensus ad inferos* should not be regarded as evidence of the recognition of a soul in Christ. By the dilemma which he puts forward, Athanasius makes one thing abundantly clear—the soul of Christ is no real factor in his interpretation of the death and descent of Christ. Even for this he found that the pure Logos-sarx framework was sufficient.

(d) The body as an instrument

Now whether we consider the body in its relationship to the Logos during Christ's life on earth or at his death it is in any case the instrument of the Logos. In the word ὄργανον Athanasius sums up the whole significance of the Logos-sarx relationship.[65] Here his deep insight into the conjunction of the divine Word with the flesh becomes particularly clear.

---

[62] Ath., *Ctr. gent.* 33: PG 25, 65C.
[63] Ath., *Ep. ad Epictet.* 5, 6: PG 26, 1060AB. The μὴ χωρισθεὶς αὐτοῦ in no. 5 is to be deleted.
[64] Ps-Alexander Al., *Sermo de anima* 5, 6: PG 18, 598C, 600.
[65] T. Tschipke O.P., *Die Menschheit Christi als Heilsorgan*, Freiburg 1940, 28–30, puts forward, without further substantiation, the traditional view that Athanasius assumed Christ to have had a human soul. If the opposite could be proved, the result would be a new way of explaining the organon-concept. In any case, the possibility of a twofold explanation must be discussed. Cf. J. Gross, *La divinisation du chrétien d'après les Pères Grecs*, Paris 1938, 201–18.

The organon-concept is, of course, too indeterminate to provide any information about the Logos-sarx relationship by itself. It is a soteriological concept which presupposes a prior clarification of christological anthropology for its full understanding. If, however, it is introduced into the problematic of the framework under discussion, it is deepened in a peculiar way. The flesh becomes an agent moved directly and physically by the Logos. It is in this sense that we should understand the summary sentence: 'He became man; for this cause also he needed the body as a human instrument.'[66] Athanasius wishes to make two points here: first the unity of subject in Christ, and secondly the difference between the instrument and the agent. The organon-concept allows him to stress the living power of the Logos in redemption and at the same time to emphasize his transcendence, without relinquishing any of the closeness of the community of Logos and sarx.

> These points we have found it necessary first to examine, that when we see him doing or saying anything divinely through the instrument of his own body, we may know that he so works, being God, and also if we see him suffering or speaking humanly, we may not be ignorant that he bore flesh and became man, and therefore he so acts and so speaks.[67]

Regarded in the light of other observations which we were able to make hitherto, this formula is in itself completely neutral. But if it is right that the Logos is the principle of all life in Christ—and Athanasius' treatment not only of the living but also of the dead Christ seems to lead to such a conclusion—then the organon-concept is, of course, to be put in this context of ideas and thus seems to be rather dangerously exaggerated.

(e) The Tomus ad Antiochenos of 362

The most significant event for our inquiry is the Synod of Alexandria in 362.

> When the death of Constantius on 3 November 361 freed the bishops of all parties from the burden of oppression and Julian's contemptuous tolerance permitted the exiles to return, only Athanasius was quick enough to make good use of the occasion. He summoned a synod at Alexandria to hold a review of those who had remained faithful to Nicaea and to show the way towards strengthening the party. Now was the time to exploit the divisions which had appeared in the anti-Nicene majority since the victory of Milan in 355 and to win over the leading section of the opposition, the Homoiousians.[68]

We need not go into the question of the two trinitarian formulas 'one hypostasis'—'three hypostases' here. It is important for us that the christological question was raised and that it has a special section to itself in the Tomus which Athanasius composed and addressed to the Antioch-

---

[66] Ath., De incarn. 44: PG 25, 173C; cf. ibid. 8: PG 25, 109C.
[67] Ath., Ctr. arian. III, 35: PG 26, 397B.
[68] H. Lietzmann, Apollinaris von Laodicea und seine Schule, Tübingen 1904, 6.

enes.[69] This is of great importance for any assessment of the christology of Athanasius.

There has recently been criticism of the form of the text printed in Migne.[70] We must begin with this, and consider the new state of the question, since a final conclusion has now in fact been reached. The criticism is made both of the list of parties represented at the synod, and of the agreed text. As is well known, Athanasius, after holding this synod of 362,

tried to reconcile the four factions into which the orthodox of Antioch had split. According to the actual text of the *Tomus* these factions were: first, a group headed by the priest Paulinus and characterized by their full acceptance of the Nicene creed; secondly, a group under the guidance of the bishop Meletius who, although orthodox in his ideas, declined to accept the Nicene key word 'homoousios'; thirdly, the Apollinarians who, although professing the Nicene dogma, constituted a special party, in so far as they held that Christ, in contrast with his fellow-men, had not a rational soul. . . . The fourth group consisted of former Arians, now wishing to return to the church. In the present text of the *Tomus* Athanasius first states the conditions under which the Meletians and the former Arians might be united with the Paulinians with whom he was already in communion, then he proceeds to show that some other differences between Meletians and Paulinians are of a merely verbal nature and should for neither party constitute a reason to refuse communion with the other; finally, he examines certain utterances of the Apollinarians and declares them to be orthodox.[71]

According to the investigation mentioned above, the sentence '*Aderant autem etiam quidam monachi Apollinarii Episcopi ab eo in hoc ipsum missi*', which speaks of the presence of Apollinarian monks at the synod of 362, has been interpolated.[72] Nevertheless, in view of the significance which this synod acquired, we must reckon with the presence of Apollinarian representatives. They will not have missed this opportunity of participating in the theological discussion of their time. More important, however, is the question of the christological text itself. This contains a section

---

[69] Athanasius, *Tomus ad Antiochenos*, PG 26, 796A–809C; the christological passages are nos. 7 and 11: ibid., 804A–805B, 809AB.

[70] R. Weijenborg, 'De authenticitate et sensu quarundam epistularum S. Basilio Magno et Apollinario Laodiceno adscriptarum', *Anton* 33, 1958, 402–9 (for the *Tomus*). In this article Weijenborg tries to show that the *Tomus* written by Athanasius in 362 incorporates in its present form certain passages interpolated by an Apollinarian between 373 and 375. In a second article Weijenborg tries to prove that this interpolator, in the main parenthesis which he inserted, made use of some letters of Athanasius certainly written after 369. 'Apollinaristic Interpolations in the *Tomus ad Antiochenos* of 362', *StudPat.* III (TU 78), 1961, 324–30. For the text of the *Tomus* see ibid., 324, n. 2. According to a letter from Dr M. Tetz to the author (17.9.63), 'the text of the *Tomus* prepared by Opitz for the second volume of the critical edition of Athanasius' works hardly differs from the Migne text, except for the emendation of printer's errors'. Fr Weijenborg is arguing purely from internal considerations. Dr Tetz can now also produce external arguments against Weijenborg's thesis: see his article 'Markellianer und Athanasios von Alexandrien', *ZNW* 64, 1973, 81 and 107. According to him, it was impossible for the Marcellians to appeal to an interpolated text against Athanasius, the author of the *Tomus*, in 371.

[71] R. Weijenborg, art. cit., *StudPat* III, 1961, 324–5.

[72] PG 26, 808A; R. Weijenborg, *Anton* 33, 1958, 405. Fr Weijenborg stresses that the monks are said to have been present, but not to have subscribed, though the beginning and the end of the *Tomus* give an exact list of names of members of the synod and subscribers to the *Tomus*. But PG 26, 796A explicitly says that there were others present at the synod, and the list of the subscribers is not as complete as that of the members.

which very much suited the Apollinarians and was even accepted by them as an account of their teaching. If it is genuine, it certainly tells strongly against Athanasius. The possibility of regarding it as an interpolation would be a fortunate solution of the difficulty. For any kind of judgement of the question the whole text must be cited:

> But since also certain seemed to be contending together concerning the fleshly economy of the Saviour, we enquired of both parties. And what the one confessed, the others also agreed to, that the Word did not, as it came to the prophets, so dwell in a holy man at the consummation of the ages, but that the Word himself was made flesh, and being in the form of God, took the form of a servant, and from Mary after the flesh became man for us, and that thus in him the human race is perfected and wholly delivered from sin and quickened from the dead, and given access to the kingdom of the heavens. *They confessed also* ὅτι οὐ σῶμα ἄψυχον, οὐδ᾽ ἀναίσθητον, οὐδ᾽ ἀνόητον εἶχεν ὁ σωτήρ (for the time being we must leave this phrase untranslated). *For it was not possible, when the Lord had become man for us, that his body should have been without reason; nor was the salvation effected in the Word himself a salvation of body only, but of the soul also.* And being Son of God in truth, he became also Son of Man, and being God's Only begotten Son, he became also at the same time 'firstborn among many brethren'. Wherefore neither was there one Son of God before Abraham, another after Abraham; nor was there one that raised up Lazarus, another that asked concerning him; but the same it was that said as man, 'Where does Lazarus lie?', and as God raised him up; the same that as man and in the body spat, but divinely as Son of God opened the eyes of the man blind from his birth; and while, as Peter says, in the flesh he suffered, as God opened the tomb and raised the dead. For which reasons, thus understanding all that is said in the gospel, they assured us that they held rhe same truth about the Word's incarnation and becoming man.[73]

The chief theme of this text is obviously directed at the Antiochenes, as the Paulinians, being supporters of Eustathius, were suspected of adoptionism. The dispute mentioned by Athanasius surely arose from the question of how the incarnation of Christ was to be regarded: whether the Logos had 'become' man or whether he had 'come into a man'. It will probably have been Athanasius himself who put the Alexandrian formula in the foreground here: 'The Logos himself has become man', and so the strict unity in Christ and the work of redemption is assured. If this was the chief point at dispute, then the sentence about the soul of Christ is clearly not in place. If we omit it (see the italic text), the text becomes more of a unity. 'And being Son of God in truth . . .' has a direct logical connection with the notion 'but that the Word himself was made flesh.'[74] But this seems to be the only argument which could be advanced in favour of the interpolation hypothesis. And it is insufficient, especially as the statement about Christ's soul has a completely Athanasian ring to it.[75] We shall

[73] Ath., *Tom. ad Antioch.* 7: PG 26, 804A–805A. The words regarded by Weijenborg as an interpolation are printed in italics. Compare no. 11, PG 26, 809AB. In B, what Weijenborg supposes to be an interpolation is repeated almost word for word.

[74] The logical connection is also disrupted in no. 11 by the insertion '*Neque enim inanimatum . . . caruerit*'. The sentence: '*Ideoque anathemate damno eos qui fidem Nicaeae promulgatum vilipendunt . . .*' connects directly with '*Verbum carnem factum esse . . . et ex Spiritu Sancto esse genitum.*'

[75] In *Anton* 33, 1958, 405, Weijenborg would assume that the interpolation made use of the letter of Apollinarius to the Egyptian bishops in Diocaesarea (see below); in *StudPat* III, 1961, he wants

define this rather more closely, distinguishing it from the typically Apollinarian interpretation.

Let us consider the decisive sentence, printed above in italics.[76] What is its significance? In some respects the whole interpretation of the Athanasian picture of Christ could depend on the answer to this question. It is not easy to explain the passage. But whatever our views, we should not succumb to the temptation of reading later positions into it without further ado. Our analysis[77] may be divided into two parts:

(a) Is the soul of Christ a *theological* factor in the phrase in question? At first glance it seems that the question must be answered in the affirmative, but first let us investigate more closely and see how far this is, in fact, the case. Two clauses must be distinguished, the proposition and its substantiation. The proposition is expressed in the clause οὐ σῶμα ἄψυχον, οὐδ᾽ ἀναίσθητον, οὐδ᾽ ἀνόητον εἶχεν ὁ Σωτήρ. As substantiation is added, 'for it was not possible, when the Lord had become man for us, that his body should have been without reason; nor was the salvation effected in the Word himself a salvation of body only but of the soul also'.[78] In the substantiation two clauses are once more to be distinguished. We begin with the final one, and then return to the actual proposition.

A clear indication of a soul in Christ as a theological (and as a physical) factor is seen in the clause 'nor was the salvation effected in the Word himself a salvation of body only, but of the soul also'. This immediately suggests the main argument of the anti-Apollinarian period, as expressed by Gregory of Nazianzus. 'That which is not taken is not healed, but whatever is united to God is saved.'[79] If Christ had no soul, then the human soul is not redeemed. Both Origen and Tertullian had already argued in this way.[80] But do we find in the *Tomus* this clear form of the classical soteriological and christological argument which directly mentions the soul of Christ? No; all is still in some obscurity. Note that in our form of this argument only the object to be redeemed is mentioned, that is man and 'his' soul. Moreover—in contrast to the formula of Origen and of Gregory—nothing is yet said about the being of Christ himself,

to prove that the interpolator 'made use of some letters of Athanasius certainly written after 369 (*Ep. ad Maximum: ad Epictetum*). The letter of Apollinarius is surely excluded as a source, for in that case the interpolation would certainly have taken another form. The affinity to the other letters merely shows that the text of the *Tomus* is typically Athanasian. Weijenborg further asserts that Paulinus of Antioch already had the transmitted text about 374, like all the textual witnesses preserved for us. The fact of an Apollinarian interpolation would surely not have escaped the notice of the Paulinians (*StudPat* III, 329). The articles by Weijenborg do, however, show us that we are on the right lines in explaining the Athanasian texts in accordance with the Logos-sarx framework.

[76] Ibid. 7: PG 26, 804B. The text is repeated almost word for word in 809B.

[77] Cf. R. Weijenborg, *StudPat* III, 1961, 327–8.

[78] Ath., *Tom. ad Antioch*. 7: PG 26, 804B.

[79] Greg. Naz., *Ep.* 101 *ad Cledon*.: PG 37, 181C–184A: τὸ γὰρ ἀπρόσληπτον, ἀθεράπευτον. ὃ δὲ ἥνωται τῷ θεῷ, τοῦτο καὶ σῴζεται.

[80] Origen, *Dialect*.: ed. Scherer, 136[16ff.]; Tertullian, *De carne Chr.* 10; Iren., *Adv. Haer.* I, 6, 1; I, 2, 5 (Gnostic principle!). I am obliged to J. Frickel for the last reference. See my article 'Quod non est assumptum', *LThK*[3] VIII, 1963.

nothing, at least, that is relevant to this soteriological argument. The way in which the redemption of the whole man, soul and body, does not derive here from the taking of a soul by the Logos but simply from the Logos as the cause of the redeeming work is, however, a typical feature of the Logos-sarx christology. 'The salvation of soul and body were worked out *in the Logos himself*.'[81] This reference to the Logos 'himself' is significant, and is an essential distinction between our argument and the other form which has been mentioned. The communication of the Logos is, then, the cause of the redemption of the whole man. Here, too, the 'soul' of Christ is no theological factor. At the same time, the first part of the substantiation seems to become clearer. But we are here already touching on a second question, which must now be put: in the *Tomus*, is the soul of Christ a *physical* factor? In our answer we shall be able to shed further light on the question discussed above, and more particularly, we shall have some information towards an assessment of the Logos-sarx christology as a whole.

(b) The second part of the substantiation of the total redemption of man, body and soul, runs as follows: 'for it was not possible when the Lord had become man for us, that his body should have been without reason'. The emphasis of the clause surely lies on the world 'Lord'. Because he, i.e. the Lord or the Logos, had become man, his body could not have been without reason. But does this already mean that the reason was communicated to and conferred upon this body through a created, rational soul? We must try to answer this question from the presuppositions present in the thought of Logos-sarx christology and not in the light of any of the later controversies. The construction of the sentence seems to point to something different, to a truly Alexandrian idea: the reason is derived from the Logos *qua* Logos and not primarily from a created soul. For such an approach we have some evidence, albeit none too clear, in the *Life of St Anthony* which Athanasius wrote in 357, not long before the Synod of 362. Here he makes the desert Father express thoughts which are certainly his own when he says

... the Word of God was not changed, but being the same he took a human body for the salvation and well-being of man, that having shared in human birth he might make man partake in the divine and *reasonable* nature.[82]

This is not, of course, primarily a description of the part played by the Logos and his effect on the individual human nature of Jesus Christ;

---

[81] Ath., *Tom. ad Antioch.* 7: PG 26, 804B.

[82] Ath., *Vita Antonii* 74: PG 26, 945BC; the human nature only becomes divine and 'reasonable' through the communication of the Logos. This is a truly Alexandrian position and makes clear what Athanasius could have meant in the *Tomus*. The Greek element emerges in the formula νοερὰ φύσις. H. Dörries, 'Vita Antonii', 360, n. 2, rightly observes 'that in its christology the *Vita* agrees with the rest of the Athanasian writings'. Moreover, the formula discussed here is so framed that both the

attention is focused rather on the significance of the incarnation for manhood as a whole. Through the communication of the Logos the incarnation brings about participation in the divine nature and 'reason'. The
question, then—as far as the redemption of man is concerned—is that of
the supernatural communication of the divine grace and spirituality. In the
true Alexandrian approach this, of course, includes the natural reason of
man, which is understood to be communicated by the Logos. The same
is almost certainly true of the human nature of Christ. For Athanasius it is
indeed the pattern for that natural-supernatural reason which exists in
Christians through the communication of the Logos. It would surely be
contrary both to the Athanasian and to the Alexandrian approach to
ground the 'reason' in Christ himself primarily and exclusively in a
created principle, in a creaturely soul alone. For Christ, the Logos is the
ultimate principle of reason. This is probably so in the quite remarkable
passage, 'For it was not possible, when the Lord had become man for us,
that his body should have been without reason.' (The argument here
would be interrupted if the stress lay on the 'had become man'.) But does
the fact that even in Christ the reason is ultimately grounded in the Logos
exclude a human soul? No. This already seems to follow from the parallels
between the individual human nature of Christ and human nature in
general, becoming still more clear and direct in the actual proposition on
the being of Christ put forward in the *Tomus* of 362.

'They (the members of the synod of 362) also confessed ὅτι οὐ σῶμα
ἄψυχον οὐδ' ἀναίσθητον, οὐδ' ἀνόητον εἶχεν ὁ Σωτήρ.' We have here the
statement which has hitherto been regarded as an unequivocal recognition
of the soul of Christ on the part of the author of this sentence, who was
supposed to be Athanasius. We have purposely avoided a translation up
till now, as this depends on the interpretation of the sentence. We have to
consider two possibilities here, both of which are primarily connected with
the word ἄψυχος and are particularly expressed in it. The first possible
interpretation is the traditional translation of οὐκ ἄψυχος by 'not without
a soul', 'not unsouled'. If we have to translate in this way, the sense is
quite clear: the passage expressly recognizes a created soul in Christ. But
we must also consider another possibility, which is not to be dismissed
without investigation. It would stem from the 'Alexandrianism' of the
Logos-sarx christology. If we are to trace it we must begin from the Logos.
We have already seen how even Athanasius thought 'reason' was transmitted to the body of Jesus. Now in the main clause of the *Tomus* here
quoted, three adjectives are put one after the other: ἄψυχος, ἀναίσθητος,
ἀνόητος. What is true of one could probably be taken as true of the two

Paulinians and the disciples of Apollinarius could agree with it and at the same time read into it their
own interpretation of the being of Christ. We have here the first tentative approach between two
parties which should not yet be judged from the standpoint of the later controversies.

others—they refer back to the Logos. From previous remarks it has emerged that even Athanasius sees the Logos as the centre of all life in Christ, though he does not exclude a human soul in Christ. If this idea is to be taken seriously, it follows that there is no sphere of life which is excluded from the communication and influence of the Logos. The idea of making the Logos the ἡγεμών and the ἡγεμονικόν of the flesh of Christ is inherent in the basic Alexandrian position from which Athanasius starts.[83] From this it is only one step to the Apollinarian position of making the Logos the final source of all forms of life in the human nature of Christ. If this argument is acceptable, then ἄψυχος should not be translated 'soulless', but 'lifeless'. As we shall see later, this is the interpretation which Apollinarius gives to the *Tomus ad Antiochenos*.

We have just pointed out the elements which could suggest this interpretation,[84] but they are not overwhelming. We stand here at the point where the ways of the Alexandrian and the Laodicean part. As we investigate further we shall see a clear distinction both in the terminology and in the whole mentality of the two theologians. The decisive factor is probably that the church's tradition which stands in direct proximity to the *Tomus ad Antiochenos* of 362 always understands ἄψυχος as 'without a soul'. So, when everything is considered, it is correct to see a recognition of the soul of Christ in the christological expressions of the *Tomus* of 362 as Athanasius or an orthodox theologian would understand them. The reality of this soul is not, however, stressed as it would have been by later adversaries of Apollinarius. This is confirmed by the Letter to Epictetus. Here the soteriological argument used in the synodal letter of 362 recurs, that is, if the letter was written after 362.[85] Here, as in the *Tomus*, the exact wording should be noted. The important clause speaks only of the object to be redeemed, man; on *his* side, the 'totality of redemption' is asserted. Where the cause of the redemption is given, again only the *Logos* is mentioned, and not explicitly the assumption of body and soul in Christ. Nor is Athanasius already arguing like the later anti-Apollinarians in the following clause, which says that the redeemer 'really in truth became man'.[86] The clause is directed against the docetists, who at that time also were still

[83] For the Logos as ἡγεμών see G. Müller, *Lex. Ath.*, 605, though here, of course, the context is the influence of the Logos upon everything. The hegemonic influence of the Logos on the body does, however, follow from the complete description.

[84] It should also be noted that in the whole of the text no noun occurs for the soul of Christ. No mention is made either of a *nous* or a *psyche* of Christ. Where the term *psyche* appears, man and his soul as the object of redemption are being discussed. οὐκ ἄψυχος need not necessarily be translated as 'not without a soul'; it can simply mean 'living', like the positive ἔμψυχος which is even used of the Logos *qua* Logos. Greg. Thaumaturg., *Panegyr. in Orig.* 4: PG 10, 1061B; Alexander Alex., *Ep. ad Alex.*, in Theodoret, HE, 1, 4: ed. Parmentier, 19³.

[85] Ath., *Ep. ad Epictet.* 7: PG 26, 1061AB: ἀλλὰ μὴν οὐ φαντασία ἡ σωτηρία ἡμῶν οὐδὲ σώματος μόνου ἀλλ' ὅλου τοῦ ἀνθρώπου, ψυχῆς καὶ σώματος ἀληθῶς, ἡ σωτηρία γέγονεν ἐν αὐτῷ τῷ Λόγῳ. R. Weijenborg, *StudPat* III, 1961, 327–8, tries to prove that the Apollinarian interpolators of the *Tomus* used the *Letter to Epictetus*.

[86] Ath., *Ep. ad Epictet.* 7: PG 26, 1061A: ὄντως ἀληθείᾳ ἀνθρώπου γενομένου τοῦ σωτῆρος.

propagating their teaching, as the Letter to Epictetus shows.[87] It does no more than stress the reality of the incarnation and especially of the body of Christ (PG 26, 1061B).

From all this, then, we see the significance of the *Tomus* of 362 and of the *Letter to Epictetus* for the Athanasian christology and its interpretation. First of all we notice how deeply the Logos-sarx framework is built into the Athanasian christology. Even here, where the problem has now come under open discussion, the human soul of Christ has not yet become a theological principle. No other interpretation can be put on either the soteriology or the christology of Athanasius, although in the latter case it can be assumed with some certainty that we have a statement on the soul of Christ as a physical factor. In this Alexandrian picture of Christ, the bright light of the Logos swallows up any created light.

The *Tomus ad Antiochenos* and its christology, however, eventually gives rise to a still more basic consideration. Should the *Tomus* be assumed to contain an express recognition of the soul of Christ, we have the material for a conclusion on the general character of the Athanasian christology. In the *Tomus*, two features stand side by side: the soul of Christ is a physical, but not a theological factor. Athanasius recognizes its reality and even here, as in the *Letter to Epictetus*, cannot make it a principle of theological interpretation. Could not these two features stand side by side in the whole of his theological life's work? Such an assumption, of course, faces not inconsiderable difficulties:

(1) There might be a development in Athanasius' thought. Perhaps through the discussions of 362 he came to see that the recognition of a soul in Christ was in accordance with tradition but did not immediately draw all the conclusions.

(2) His idea of the positive, vital, dynamic influence of the Logos on the flesh of Christ and his interpretation of the death of Christ seem to go beyond a mere silence about the soul of Christ.

(3) The debate with the Arians was of such a character that silence over the soul of Christ was tantamount to a denial.

These objections are serious. But when we see that later even Cyril of Alexandria can still at a certain period of his christology use the 'verbal Logos-sarx framework' as a basis and none the less recognize a soul, we should be very cautious in the face of an *argumentum e silentio*. For a real proof that Athanasius drew a picture of Christ in which Christ had no soul, positive indications must be found which exclude any created spirit in the humanity of Jesus. The direction in which these must be sought is clear from the preceding investigation: the idea of the positive, vital and dynamic influence of the Logos on the flesh of Christ, which Athanasius put forward from his early writings onwards, at the least tends not just to

[87] Ibid., no. 2: PG 26, 1053A.

conceal the soul of Christ, but also to exclude it altogether. If, however, we say 'tends', this does not mean that Athanasius himself drew the full and final conclusions. He himself attributes redemption to the work of the Logos, and contents himself with a strong emphasis on the two main factors, Logos and sarx. He never spoke with complete clarity either positively or negatively about what lies between. So despite his clear exclusion of the soul of Christ as a 'theological factor' we may still consider it possible that his picture of Christ knew a human soul as a 'physical factor'. The *Tomus* of 362 is an indication of this possibility, but the last word has probably not yet been spoken.

We can to some extent confirm our interpretation of the Athanasian position in a comparison with the language and concepts of Apollinarius of Laodicea. It is interesting and important that in a letter to the Egyptian bishops staying at Diocaesarea, Apollinarius cites the decisive part of the *Tomus* of 362 and expressly agrees with it, though he manifestly shifts the stress in the direction of his own teaching. He does this first by saying that the Logos did not assume a human, changeable *nous*, subject to earthly influences, but that he is the divine, unchangeable, heavenly *nous*.[88] As evidence of this he inserts the words of the *Tomus*: 'the redeemer also did not have a lifeless (so ἄψυχος should be translated here) body devoid of perception and reason . . .' He then concludes with a truly Apollinarian notion that '(he was) one perfect only-begotten of God, perfect in divine, not in human perfection'.[89] This is where Athanasius leaves his company. He never made an explicit denial of the soul of Christ and wrote no sentence suggesting the sense which Apollinarius has given to it. Precisely at this point it becomes abundantly clear that though some aspects of his Logos-sarx christology are akin to that of Apollinarius, his thought and his picture of Christ is essentially different. His Logos-sarx framework is certainly open for an explicit doctrine of the soul of Christ. That of Apollinarius is closed.

(f) Athanasius' christological formula

Now that we have tried to draw some of the important outlines of the Athanasian picture of Christ we must go on to ask how this picture was expressed in his christological formula. Here we can go no further than his main formula. From our previous discussion it is clear that John 1. 14 became the fundamental christological statement for Athanasius. His christology occupies a special chapter in the history of this Johannine passage. He takes it very seriously and makes it an expression of his recognition of the unity of being in Christ—as opposed to the 'divisive christology' of a Paul of Samosata.[90] Thus a remark which Athanasius makes in

[88] Apollin., *Ep. ad Diocaes. eppos.* 2: ed. Lietzmann, 256.
[89] Ibid.
[90] Ath., *Ctr. Arian.* III, 30–2: PG 26, 388A–392C.

his main work against the Arians is to be regarded as his central christo-logical formula: '(The Word) became man and did not come into a man.'[91] It should be regarded as the classic formulation of the theology of the 'Logos-flesh' type as opposed to the christology of the 'Logos-man' type. In its extreme form, such as we see with the Arian Eudoxius and with Apollinarius, and as we are still to hear from a monophysitically inclined bishop even at the Council of Chalcedon, it contains an implicit denial of the soul of Christ.[92] Athanasius does not go so far, and merely rejects the adoptionism of Paul of Samosata without clarifying his formula in the direction of the explicit Logos-sarx christology of the other group.

In Athanasius, to 'become' man, to 'become' flesh, probably has a special depth of meaning, but he immediately interprets it in the traditional Pauline sense as a 'taking' of the flesh, which is yet so intense that one can and must say that 'the Logos *is* man'. This statement should not, of course, be regarded as an ontology of the hypostatic union. Nor is a special warning needed against supposing that such a formula in Athanasius expresses a confusion of Logos and flesh. Both retain their characteristics, even when they are compounded in a living unity.[93] Of course, a stress on unity remains the basic trend of his christology. This is the nucleus around which all his other statements are to be arranged, as for example when he speaks of 'putting on human nature' or of 'entering into the flesh' or of 'clothing'. If he speaks of a 'taking' of the fleshly nature he has Phil. 2. 7 to support him, as he has Col. 2. 9 (1. 19) in the indwelling formula.[94] This indwelling framework, which goes on to become the distinguishing mark of the opponents of the Logos-sarx christology, is none the less basically the position from which Athanasius, like Origen before him, is fond of starting when expressing the unity in Christ. His christological thought veers from 'becoming flesh' to 'dwelling in the flesh' as in a temple.[95] It is, however, remarkable that all the expressions which seem to suggest an accidental relationship between the Logos and the flesh are im-mediately expanded by the intimation that the Logos really 'became' flesh. At the same time, Athanasius seeks to guard against the risk of the interpretation of this 'becoming' as being in any sense a change by his explanation that the 'becoming' is a 'taking'.[96] Thus the unity in Christ is a unity in tension, from which it clearly emerges that the unity and the duality in Christ are each to be sought under different aspects. Athanasius was not, however, able to make these aspects clear with the terminological

---

[91] Ibid., 30: PG 26, 388A; cf. 47 (428A); Ad Epictet. 2 (1053BC).
[92] Cf. Eudoxius: A. Hahn, Bibl. d. Symbole § 191, with Apollin., Tom. synod., ed. Lietzmann, 262-3.
[93] Further Chalkedon I, 1967⁴, 100, n. 4.
[94] Ibid., n. 5.
[95] On the image of the temple: Ath., Ep. ad Adelph. 7: PG 26, 1080C-1084B.
[96] E.g. Ath., Ctr. arian. II, 47: PG 26, 248A.

and conceptual means at his disposal, though he tried to do it in paraphrase.[97]

The special future significance of the christological formula of Athanasius and of the Logos-sarx framework in general lies in its clear presentation of the 'unity of subject' in Christ. The *Logos* is the all-dominating and
sole principle of all existence and therefore subject of all statements about
Christ. This is the superiority of the Alexandrian formula over the
Antiochene, which is weakest here. The Athanasian picture of Christ is
clearly centred on the Logos and in its inner structure is superior to any
symmetrical christological formula which puts Logos and man on the
same level and sees them compounded in a superior *tertium quid*. The
human element in Christ is governed by the Logos, and the Lord is
'flesh-bearing Logos', but not 'God-bearing man'.[98] The idea of the
divine subject is thus preserved without a hiatus.[99] A true conception of
the personality of Christ is certainly revealed here. It is an old Christian
legacy, which we were able to establish as early as Ignatius of Antioch and
his source, John 1. 14.[100]

[97] So against the Arians Athanasius works with the principle of 'distinguishing the times' (i.e. of the
Logos before and after the incarnation), so as to be able to counter the Arian attacks on the divinity of
the Logos: *Ctr. arian.* III, 28, 29, 43, 55: PG 26, 381C–388A, 413B, 437B, cf. M. Richard, 'Athanase',
13–15.

[98] This latter is in Eustathius (see above). Cf. Marcell. Ancyr., *De incarn. et ctr. arian.* 8: PG 26,
996C: αὐτὸς οὖν ἐστιν θεὸς σαρκοφόρος, καὶ ἡμεῖς ἄνθρωποι πνευματοφόροι. Athanas., *Ctr. arian.*
III, 40: PG 26, 409C–412A: ἡ σαρξ θεοφορεῖται ἐν τῷ Λόγῳ.

[99] The expression ὁ κυριακὸς ἄνθρωπος has played a role in this context. We have noted that it was
used precisely in Marcellus of Ancyra, especially of the 'glorified Christ.' However, this context was
later apparently dissolved. First, however, it should be noted that Athanasius uses the expression once
in the context of an explicit Logos christology. This is the case if we presuppose the reading which
according to Severus of Antioch is to be accepted for *Ep. encycl. ad eppos Aegypti et Libyae* 9: PG 25,
560A, as J. Lebon has demonstrated in *RHE* 31, 1935, 321: 'But they (the Jews) could not deceive the
κυριακὸς ἄνθρωπον, for the Logos was made flesh.' Thus he had the knowledge to see through men.
Gregory of Nyssa, *Altera laudatio S. Stephani*: PG 46, 725B, also comes close to Marcellus in the use of
this expression. For Christ is called *'homo dominicus'* as he hands over 'his spirit to the Father' (Luke 23.
46). According to the context this is the introduction to the glorification and not a surrender to the
power of death. The passages cited by F. Loofs, *Theophilus von Antiochien Adversus Marcionem und die
anderen theologischen Quellen bei Irenaeus* (TU 46), 1930, 138–41, n. 11 for Augustine are concerned
either with the return to judgement (PL 34, 1278) or with the 'new, spiritual man', whom the *'homo
dominicus'* has created by his death, and thus with the victory over the power of the law or the
fleshly man (PL 36, 66; PL 35, 2072). But Augustine seems to be no longer aware of the context to be
found in Marcellus, because he then retreats in the *Retractationes* I, 8 (PL 32, 616–7), probably because
some of his opponents interpreted the expression in terms of Nestorianism. In the discussion of
Antiochene christology the expression became suspect and receded into the background (cf. later
Severus). But it is still used by Leontius of Jerusalem and by Pamphilus. Cf. J. Lebon, art. cit., and
especially J. Gesché, *La christologie du 'Commentaire des Psaumes' découvert à Toura*, Gembloux 1962,
71–2, 80–90. But see the criticism of M. Tetz, Markell I, 268–9, n. 191. However, the new starting
point for Marcellus that we have worked out should be noted.

[100] The crisis for the explicit Logos-sarx christology had already been reached at the end of Athanasius' life. As well as Athanasius, books iv–v, *Ctr. Eunomium*, PG 29, 672–773 knows it. There is still
no mention of the teaching of the soul of Christ here. To this category also belong the three pseudo-
Athanasian homilies of the *Codex Ambros.* D 51 sup.; *De semente*: PG 28, 144–68; *In cant. cantic.*: PG
27, 1349–61; *De patientia*: PG 26, 1297–1309; likewise the long homily *In passionem et crucem Domini*:
PG 28, 185–249. 'La doctrine christologique de ces documents est du type Verbe-chair, mais à la façon
de saint Athanase', M. Richard, *MSR* 6, 1949, 129.

CHAPTER SIX

APOLLINARIANISM

WHEN Gregory of Nazianzus affirms in his *Second Letter to Cledonius* that the Apollinarian heresies had begun thirty years earlier,[1] he may be referring to the spreading of their propaganda. The origin of the ideas of Apollinarian christology may be put much sooner. It is probable from the history of Arianism that there was an Apollinarianism before Apollinarius. The contribution of the latter consisted in the further development and systematic evaluation of beginnings which had already been made long before him. Here, of course, he exerted a powerful influence, and even as a heretic still made an important contribution to the terminological shaping of the christological formula of Chalcedon.

A comprehensive investigation of the problem of the derivation of Apollinarius' christological thought has still to be made.[2] It is impossible, especially in view of the state of present scholarship, to examine all the implications of this question here. Some indication of the relationship between Arianism and Apollinarianism does, however, seem to be called for, because the source of the christological outlook of the latter is often seen in the former. Nevertheless, one may well wonder whether Apollinarius (or any of the Nicene representatives of the Logos-sarx framework in its explicit form) may be said to have had the necessary psychological presuppositions for taking over the christological peculiarities of the Arians. If the Arian circle had been the only place from which a christology which knew nothing of a soul in Christ might have been derived, then its christology would probably have aroused as much suspicion as its trinitarian teaching. Finally, even if Apollinarianism seems only to have emerged *after* Arianism in time, the inner relation of the two systems requires so to speak a reversal of this chronological order. Christology

[1] Greg. Naz., *Ep.* 102 *ad Cledon.*: PG 37, 200C. Cf. M. Richard, 'L'introduction du mot "hypostase" dans la "théologie de l'incarnation" ' (cited hereafter as 'Hypostase'), *MSR* 2, 1945, 189–90.

[2] G. Voisin, *L'Apollinarisme*, Louvain–Paris 1901, one of the best-known Apollinarian scholars, presupposes the originality of Apollinarius to such an extent that he does not put the question of the derivation of his teaching. According to him the Laodicaean was the first to bring up the christological problem (ibid., 9). E. Weigl, *Christologie v. Tode d. Ath.*, 9–13, points to Lucian and Arius. The more common approach treats Apollinarianism as a developed Arian christology: cf. B. Altaner, *Patrologie²*, 270; M. Richard, 'Hypostase', 6. According to the earlier approach the relationship with Arianism should explain everything: so in J. A. Dorner, *Person Christi* I, 986; similarly H. M. Gwatkin, *Arianism*, 250–4, according to whom Apollinarius meant to develop the Arian teaching on the incarnation and remained dependent upon it. C. E. Raven, *Apollinarianism*, 177–88, points to the Synod of 268 as the principal source of Apollinarianism, but his text-critical basis and his historical estimate of the development are insufficient. E. Mühlenberg, *Apollinaris von Laodicea* (Forschungen zur Kirchen- und Dogmengeschichte 23), Göttingen 1969, here stresses Apollinarius' soteriological concern over against Voisin and these remarks. For criticism see R. Hübner, 'Gotteserkenntnis durch die Inkarnation Gottes', *Kleronomia* 4, 1972, 131–61.

might well have made the transition from Apollinarianism to Arianism, but not vice versa. The latter is no more than a development of the basic principles of the former. The 'Apollinarian' view of the physical, vital conjunction of Logos and sarx already contains the germ of that vitiation of the transcendence of the Logos which Arianism developed consistently. The strict Logos-sarx framework, which makes the Logos the soul, necessarily tends towards the Arian devaluation of the Logos. Thus historical Apollinarianism can hardly be understood as Arianism reshaped with an orthodox Logos doctrine.

Instead, we must reach back before the rise of the Arian Logos doctrine to find the origin of 'Apollinarian' thought as well as the 'Arian' doctrine of the incarnation. In its undifferentiated form, the common ancestry of both these heresies may also have produced the Alexandrian Logos-sarx christology. This last, however, was able to preserve the orthodox mean. We prefer to leave as an open question the extent to which—alongside the probable influence of Eusebius of Caesarea—the Synod of Antioch of 268 may have played a part. This is the synod with whose pronouncements Apollinarius sought to support his assertions, as Gregory of Nyssa tells us.[3] Nor was his basic concern, and the concern of all the representatives of the Logos-sarx christology, different from that of the synod of 268—in other words opposition to the 'divisive christology' of Paul of Samosata. The idea of a merely external, accidental gift of grace to a 'mere man', which Apollinarius saw or thought to be advocated both by Paul of Samosata and by the Paulinians and finally by Flavian and Diodore, was the object of his lifelong hostility.[4] The Samosatene and Paulinian picture of Christ is constructed too loosely for him. It can fall apart at any time, as 'division' is already an element in its outlines. It is therefore his purpose to interweave and join together God and man essentially and inseparably in Christ. This great aim should not be mistaken. Fear of division and the effort to make the unity in the Word made flesh as close and as deep as possible are, if we leave aside individual details, the two main features of the Apollinarian view.[5] Apollinarius approaches his task with great linguistic dexterity and philosophical acumen. We shall now attempt to work out the basic thoughts and language of his christology.

1. The 'Heavenly Man'

The metaphysical framework from which Apollinarius seeks to interpret the being of Christ is a picture of the substantial unity of man as a

[3] Greg. Nyss., *Antirrhet.* 9: ed. Lietzmann, frag. 24, p. 210: to support his view of Christ, Apollinarius refers to the Synodal Acts against Paul of Samosata: μέμνηταί τινων καὶ δογμάτων συνοδικῶν τῶν τε κατὰ Παύλου τοῦ Σαμοσατέως συνειλεγμένων.

[4] Apoll., *Ep. ad Dionys.* A1: ed. Lietzmann, 256–7. Cf. *Ep. ad Diocaesar. eppos.* 1: ed. L., 256¹⁻²; *Apodeix.*: frag. 71, ed. L., 221; G. Voisin, *Apollinarisme*, 32–59.

[5] See, for instance, Apoll., *Apodeix.*: frag. 36, ed. L., 212.

synthesis of body and soul. For him, the God-man is a 'σύνθεσις ἀνθρωποειδής', a compound unity in human form.[6] His particular aim in this phrase is to describe the way in which God and man are conjoined in Christ. A mere 'God dwelling in man', he says, is no man. Incarnation, as it must be envisaged in Christ, only comes about if divine pneuma and earthly sarx together form a substantial unity in such a way that the man in Christ first becomes man through the union of these two components. The prior independent constitution of the humanity of Christ either temporally (as in Apollinarius' interpretation of Paul of Samosata) or ontologically should not be a presupposition for the realization of the incarnation. The 'humanity' of Christ is only constituted as such by the union of divine pneuma and earthly sarx. To 'become' a man is not the same as to 'take' a man.[7] Once again we meet the 'becoming-man' formula of the Logos-sarx framework, but this time there is a change from Athanasius: it is sharpened in a typically Apollinarian way. We quite understandably shrink from the idea that the necessary basis for true manhood is not a human soul, in other words a spiritual being which has been created beforehand for a body, but some spirit which unites itself with the flesh to form a complete unity.[8] According to this approach, then, the incarnation of Christ means that the Logos joins himself to a human, fleshly nature to form a substantial unity and through this union constitutes a human being, i.e. a being of body and spirit. No one has put this in such clear and simple terms as Apollinarius.[9] But it is clear, too, that Christ is 'man' in quite a singular manner, as is emphasized in the *Anakephalaiosis* (Lietzmann, 242–6).

Starting from this position, Apollinarius calls the incarnate a 'heavenly man'. Charges of teaching that the *flesh* of Christ came down from heaven have misrepresented his thought. Instead, he teaches that the human, fleshly nature of Christ is taken from the Virgin and only becomes divine through union with the Godhead.[10] Moreover, the difference between the flesh of Christ and real human flesh lies only in this union: διὰ τῆς ἑνώσεως ἔχουσαν τὸ διάφορον.[11] Christ is heavenly 'man' only because of the divine pneuma, i.e. the Logos,[12] in so far as this Logos enters into a real substantial conjunction with the sarx to make up a human being. Now whether this synthesis of pneuma and sarx is viewed in the light of a dichotomist or a trichotomist anthropology is of secondary

---

[6] Apoll., *Ep. ad Dionys.* A 9: ed. L., 260[1-2]. Apollinarius goes into this comparison most in the *Apodeixis*: ed. L., 208–32.

[7] Ps.-Felix, frag. 186: ed. L., 318.

[8] Apoll., *Anaceph.* 16: ed. L., 244.

[9] Apoll., *Apodeix.*, frag. 69: ed. L., 220.

[10] Apoll., *Ad Sarapion.*, frag. 160: ed. L., 254[6-7]; cf. H. J. Schoeps, *Von himmlischen Fleisch Christi*, Tübingen 1951, 9–14; A. Gesché, *La christologie du 'Commentaire sur les Psaumes' découvert à Toura*, Gembloux 1962, 106–115.

[11] Ibid., frag. 161.

[12] Apoll., *Apodeix.*, frag. 25: ed. L., 210[23-5].

importance: it is the basic conception of incarnation as such which is
decisive.[13] Of course, this already had a past behind it by the time Apollinarius emerged, so he cannot be regarded as its creator.

Now if a true compound unity in human form, consisting of one
heavenly and one earthly element, is to be achieved in Christ, then both
these two elements must be related as 'parts' of a 'whole'. We need not go
closer into the well-known maxim 'two complete entities cannot become
one'.[14] In the interests of an integral unity in Christ, Apollinarius holds
that the human nature of Christ is incomplete, i.e. without soul (the *nous*).
This principle was surely only invented or brought into the problem *post
factum* to provide a defence for the strict Logos-sarx framework which
had already been taken up beforehand. The idea of 'parts' rather introduces us to the inner structure of the Apollinarian picture of Christ. Apollinarius can speak quite simply of 'parts' because something new, a 'totality',
is produced when the Logos takes flesh. The basic thought of the Apollinarian system, which logically leads to Arianism, becomes clear in this
passage:

> A *physis* is made up of the two parts, as the Logos with his divine perfection contributes
> a *partial energy* to the whole. This is also the case with the ordinary man, who is made up
> of two incomplete parts which produce one *physis* and display it under one name.[15]

The parts of the man's being form a whole, and this whole can be called
either 'flesh' or 'soul'. Neither of the two parts thereby loses its proper
nature. So, too, the God-man is a 'whole', which is composed of 'parts of
being'. This idea of 'parts' is eventually brought to an absolutely intolerable pitch by Apollinarius and illustrated by quite trivial examples which
would however, have been understood easily enough by the people. As a
result, we find the feeble example of the 'middle-being', a composite being
of symmetrical construction, which is basically foreign to the whole
dynamic of the Logos-sarx framework and should also be regarded as an
element foreign to Apollinarius' christology.

> Middle-beings (μεσότητες) are formed when different properties (ἰδιότητες) are com-
> bined in one thing, for example the properties of ass and horse in a mule and the properties
> of white and black . . . in the colour grey; but no middle-being (μεσότης) contains the
> two extremes (ἀκρότητας) in full measure (ἐξ ὁλοκλέρου)—they are there only in part.
> Now in Christ there is a middle-being (μεσότης) of God and man; therefore he is neither
> fully man nor God (alone), but a mixture of God and man.[16]

---

[13] H. Lietzmann, *Apollinaris*, argues for original dichotomy and later trichotomy; C. E. Raven,
Apollinarianism, is for consistent trichotomy. See H. de Riedmatten, 'La christologie d'Apollinaire de
Laodicée', *StudPat* II (TU 64), Berlin 1957, 208–34; and now R. A. Norris, Jr., *Manhood and Christ*,
Oxford 1963, 86: 'The dichotomous formula in fact conceals a tripartite structure.' N. stresses the
Pauline pneuma-sarx scheme as a key to Apollinarius' christological outlook (90).
[14] Ps.-Ath., *Ctr. Apollin.* 1, 2: PG 26, 1096B.
[15] Apoll., *De unione* 5: ed. L., 1877¹⁰. Cf. Κατὰ μέρος πίσ τις (cited hereafter as *k.m.p.*), ed. L.,
173¹⁴⁻¹⁵; *Logoi*: frag. 153: ed. L., 248²⁰⁻²¹. For comment see *Chalkedon* I, 107, n. 15.
[16] Apoll., *Syllog. frag.* 113: ed. L., 234.

This is an example of the most extreme symmetrical christology. One might suspect the influence of the Aristotelian teaching about *mixtum*. Apollinarius himself feels the absurdity of his conception and so later seeks to correct it.[17]

In the end, the idea of *compositio* does not take us all the way towards the real Apollinarian thought. The 'synthesis', which is so reminiscent of the metaphysic of the Aristotelian *mixtum*, might suggest that in Christ there is a conjunction of two 'static' components, but Apollinarius has a completely different way of considering the question. It is only here that the religious force of his idea of Christ, described so enthusiastically[18] but with considerable exaggeration by A. v. Harnack, becomes evident. Once again we come up against ideas of Stoic derivation which we have already met.

2. 'MIA PHYSIS'

According to Apollinarius, the 'parts' of the God–man Christ cannot be regarded as equivalent. The divine pneuma maintains its pre-eminence throughout. It becomes the life-giving spirit, the effectual mover of the fleshly nature, and together the two form a unity of life and being. Here for Apollinarius is ultimately the real metaphysical basis of the unity in the God-man, which lies in the fact that the whole of the power which gives life to the God-man unity is concentrated in the Logos *qua* Logos. A man whose conjunction to God is only accidental is a man apart from God. He would retain his individuality chiefly by carrying within himself the principle of his physical life. As long as there is this independence of physical life the unity is, for Apollinarius, only accidental. Therefore it cannot be said that the Logos has become flesh unless he has complete control over all life *qua* Logos.[19] The radical consequences for the whole of his picture of Christ immediately become evident. This is the secret of the religious influence of Apollinarianism and its dynamic picture of Christ. In an unwarranted exegesis of 1 Cor. 15.45 (the last Adam was a life-giving spirit) Apollinarius sees in Christ only one life, exclusively controlled by the Godhead.[20] The whole of man's salvation rests on the fact that an invincible, divine Nous (νοῦς ἀήττητος), an inalienable will and a divine power, is ensouled in the flesh of Christ, thus making it sinless (ἀναμαρτήτως).[21] This influence may not come from outside; it must be as much an inner process as the means by which the human nature is given life.[22] Apollin-

---

17 So in the symbol of the *k.m.p.*: ed. L., 1781⁻³.
18 A. v. Harnack, *Dogmengeschichte* 2, 1931⁵, 330f.
19 Apoll., *Apodeix*, frag. 107: ed. L., 232; cf. frag. 133: ibid., 239; frag. 144: ibid., 242⁴.
20 Apoll., *Ep. ad Dionys.* A 10: ed. L., 261²: κατὰ τὴν μίαν ζωήν.
21 Apoll., *k.m.p.* 30: ed. L., 1781³⁻¹⁷; cf. *Ad Julian.*, frags. 150–1: ed. L., 247–8; *Logoi*, frag. 153: ed. L., 248²²⁻²³.
22 Apoll., *Anaceph.* 21: ed. L., 244.

arius distinguishes between a νοῦς αὐτοκίνητος such as a man also has, and a νοῦς ταυτοκίνητος, that is, a nous which is always moved in the same way and so is unalterable. Self-determination and immutability together are the necessary factors for redemption, but these are realized only in the divine pneuma of Christ.

From here, too, derives the original meaning which Apollinarius. attaches to the concept of *physis* and the notorious formula of *mia physis*. The best approach for understanding this much-debated central concept lies in Apollinarius' remarks in the *Letter to Dionysius*, which might be paraphrased as follows: if we speak of two *physeis* this gives the best possible foothold for anyone wishing to destroy the unity in Christ. For there can only be division where there is a duality. There is no such duality if we understand Christ's being properly. For the body by itself is not a *physis*, as it cannot of itself give life. Nor can it be separated at all from the life-giving Logos. No more is the Logos 'separate', i.e. he exists no longer merely in his fleshless nature, but only when united with the flesh does he dwell in the world. To speak of two *physeis* is therefore fallacious:

> The created body does not live in separation from the uncreated Godhead, so that one could distinguish a created *physis*, and the uncreated Logos does not dwell in the world in separation from the body, so that one could distinguish the *physis* of the uncreated.[23]

The concept *physis*, then, can only apply to something which is an αὐτοκίνητον, which contains the power which gives it life, which can be regarded as the real source of life in any sphere of being. Now if the Logos provides all the life-giving power in Christ, the body as such cannot be accorded the character and the title of a *physis*. The *mia physis* formula automatically follows.[24] A further expression, ἕνωσις φυσική, natural unity,[25] likewise derives its original meaning from this. It expresses the unity of the working principle in Christ. The peculiarly Apollinarian significance of the *mia physis* formula is, then, to be understood on these lines. It must be admitted that the concept and the way in which it is expressed have a powerful attraction, and one can easily understand how the Greek mind seized upon it.

In fact we already know all the decisive elements for this interpretation of Christ. They are the result of a Stoic–Alexandrian anthropology and its application to Christ, and have already become influential long before Apollinarius.[26] *Physis* is here by no means the static, abstract '*essentia*', nor

---

[23] Apoll., *Ep. ad Dionys.* A 8: ed. L., 259, cf. *Logoi*, frag. 153: ed. L., 248²²⁻³.

[24] It occurs in Apoll., *Ad Jovian.* ed. L., 251¹⁻³: (ὁμολογοῦμεν . . . οὐ δύο φύσεις), ἀλλὰ μίαν φύσιν τοῦ θεοῦ λόγου σεσαρκωμένην καὶ προσκυνουμένην. It is explained still more closely in *Ep. ad Dionys.* A 2: ed. L., 257¹⁵⁻¹⁹: there is *one* φύσις in Christ ἐπεὶ μηδὲ ἰδία φύσις τὸ σῶμα καὶ ἰδία φύσις ἡ θεότης κατὰ τὴν σάρκωσιν, ἀλλ' ὥσπερ ἄνθρωπος μία φύσις, οὕτω καὶ ὁ ἐν ὁμοιώματι ἀνθρώπων γενόμενος Χριστός. Note once again the starting point: the idea of Christ as a body-soul unity. Cf. frags. 10,119, 149: ed. L., 207, 236, 247.

[25] Apoll., *Ad. Flavian.*, frag. 148: ed. L., 247¹, ²⁻¹⁰.

[26] Origen, *Ctr. Cels.* 6, 48: ed. Koetschau II, 120²⁻³. Cf. also the Acts of the Synod of Antioch 268: *Codex Jan. gr.* 27, p. XI (*Biblioteca della missione urbana di San Carlo Cod.* 27 fol. 353r.): Πυνθάνομαι οὖν

is it the 'nature-person' which unites in itself the two elements of the Chalcedonian hypostasis and physis. *Physis* is the 'self-determining being' (3ῷον αὐτοκίνητον, αὐτενέργητον). Self-determination, which has its seat in the ἡγεμονικόν, is the decisive element in the *physis*.

If this formula is so closely associated with the Logos-sarx christology as such and stems from it quite naturally, the question then arises whether Apollinarius was in fact the first to apply the term *physis* to the *mysterium Christi* and to shape this language which was to prove of such enormous influence in later history. We cannot for the moment go beyond the realm of hypothesis. With the meaning outlined above, this formula can only occur within a christology with the explicit and exclusive Logos-sarx framework.[27] Yet it need not have had this purely Apollinarian sense, as Ephraem the Syrian (died 373), a contemporary of Apollinarius, shows us. He, too, already knows the 'one nature' formula, but understands it in the sense of one concrete nature, i.e. one person. At the same time he speaks of 'two natures' in Christ, the Godhead and the manhood. This usage is already reminiscent of Cyril of Alexandria.[28]

Another concept which is to be as important in the future, οὐσία, should be regarded as equivalent or approximate to the concept of *physis*. This, too, is incorporated into the truly Apollinarian interpretation of the substantial unity in Christ. The body and the flesh are joined to the Logos by being made his ὄργανον, into which the ἐνέργεια of the Logos, its sole and exclusive source, flows, in order to excite κίνησις there. It is a question not only of the energy of the will and purely spiritual impulses, but also of all the life-energy. One should not therefore simply equate

εἰ ὥσπερ ἡμεῖς τοῦτο τὸ σύνθετον 3ῷον οἱ ἄνθρωποι σύνοδον ἔχομεν ἔκ τε σαρκὸς καί τινος ὄντος ἐν τῇ σαρκί · οὕτως αὐτὸς ὁ λόγος, αὐτὴ ἡ σοφία ἦν ἐν ἐκείνῳ τῷ σώματι ὡς τῆς ἐν ἡμῖν ἐνταῦθα 3ωῆς (F. Loofs, *Paulus v. S.*, 335[10], here inserts (τὸ κινοῦν)).

[27] The μία φύσις formula is used in a real Apollinarian sense in Eudoxius, who is so important in the history of Arianism: A. Hahn, *Bibl. d. Symbole* §191, pp. 261–2. According to Philostorgius, Eudoxius would have been a disciple of Lucian of Antioch (HE 2, 14). Perhaps further investigation into the figure of the monk Marcian will lead to an extension of our knowledge of the early history of the μία φύσις formula. Cf. J. Lebon, 'Le moine saint Marcien', *Misc. de Meyer* 1, 181–93. See now J. Kirchmeyer, 'Le moine Marcien (de Bethlehem?)', *StudPat* V, Berlin 1962, 341–59; we are concerned with the monk who wrote between 362 and 381 and is to be sought in the region of Antioch. Cf. now J. Lebon, *Le moine saint Marcien. Étude critique des sources, édition de ses écrits*, ed. A. van Roey (Spicilegium Sacrum Lovaniense 36), Louvain 1968. The μία φύσις formula does not appear. These works, so far as they are authentic, seem to be part of a first controversy with Apollinarian christology. Cf. the text in Lebon 252[34]–253[1]: 'Mais si tu t'accordes avec les *doctrines* correctes, tu sera trouvé disant, toi aussi, de deux natures l'unique Fils, en confessant de la nature divine et de la nature humaine il y a un *seul* Fils de Dieu à cause de l'adhésion de l'humanité à la divinité.' For his christological position see ibid., 73, esp. n. 13. For criticism of Lebon's work see A. de Halleux, *Mus* 85, 1972, 293–5, who expresses doubts about the spiritual works which Lebon assigns to the monk Marcian.

[28] Cf. E. Beck, O.S.B., *Die Theologie des hl. Ephraem*, Rom 1949, 56–7: Ephraem uses the term *kyânâ (natura, persona)*: *Hymn*. 10, 3: *'cum natura tua sit una, interpretationes eius sunt multae. . . .'*; 11, 9: *'natura eius una est, potes videre eam; silentium eius unum est quod potes audire.'* Here *kyânâ* stands for the unity of the person. But it can also be used like our expression of the two natures in Christ: *'Duae naturae, sublimis et humilis'* (*Sermo de Domino nostro* in Beck, 57). In this sense also *Hymn*. 19, 2–3: Beck, 58: *'Duo vestimenta erant tibi, Domine, vestimentum et corpus. . . . Ecce corpus tegebat splendorem tuum, naturam terribilem* (the Godhead), *vestimenta tegebant debilem* (the manhood).' Ephraem also rejects the denial of Christ's soul by the Arians: *Hymn*. 51, 3 in Beck, 55. See J. Gribomont, *Melto* 3, 1967, 147–82; *Parole de l'Orient* 4, 1973, f.1–2 (*Ehhrem 373–1973*).

'unity of ἐνέργεια' with 'unity of person'.[29] In all this, the one οὐσία, the one substantial and functional unity in Christ, is formed. So Apollinarius explains the connection between the terms in his *Logos Syllogistikos* against Diodore.[30] The God-man, then, is *one physis, one ousia*, because *one* life-giving power, which completely permeates the flesh, goes out from the Logos and unites the two in a living and functional unity, in a καθ' ἑνότητα ζωτικὴν ἑνωθέν.[31] The Logos-sarx christology is carried through to its last principles.

Here we touch on an important point in the interpretation of Apollinarius which has only been noticed in recent scholarship.[32] Particularly since G. Voisin and C. E. Raven, the idea of one 'person' has been the starting point.[33] But if one approaches the *mia physis* formula too quickly with this concept, the first and essential, if not ultimately the only, view of Apollinarianism escapes notice—i.e. the physical vitality and dynamism in its picture of Christ. The key to the understanding of the system lies here. Christ is one because he is a 'living unity' of Logos and sarx. The Virgin Birth is clearly indispensable for Apollinarius because it was the divine spirit which set in train the living process of the growth of Christ's fleshly nature.[34] The natural and supernatural aspects of this living unity coalesce, as when, for example, Christ's saying 'I consecrate myself' is interpreted on a biological level.[35] Finally, the vital union of the divine and human in this Logos-sarx totality is the ground for the one worship. To limit the *adoratio* to the Logos would mean the limitation of the one divine life, which also flows through the body.[36] The *communicatio idiomatum*, the exchange of predicates, is not merely a logical-ontological matter, in which the divine and human predicates can be exchanged only because there is a single subject in Christ. It only acquires depth if the vital conjunction of the two kinds of being is observed as it is by Apollinarius.[37] These have indeed been 'neglected aspects' of the Apollinarian system. But we have not yet raised the question of 'person' in Apollinarius. It will be considered along with the interpretation of *hypostasis* and *prosopon*. Here once again we will discover a close connection with vitalistic dynamism.

[29] As C. E. Raven, *Apollinarianism*, 223, assumes. R. A. Norris, *Manhood and Christ*, 106–11, shows well how in the Apollinarian concept of the unity of Christ a Stoic doctrine of mixture is combined with a Neo-Platonic outlook, 'both in admitting the incorporeality of spiritual substances, and in insisting that such a substance, though mixed with body, nevertheless transcends it and is free in relation to it' (106f.). Cf. 122.

[30] Apoll., *Logos. Syllog.*, frag. 117: ed. Lietzmann, 235–6; ibid., frag. 119, ed. L., 236: οὐκ ἄρα ἄλλη καὶ ἄλλη οὐσία θεὸς καὶ ἄνθρωπος, ἀλλὰ μία κατὰ σύνθεσιν θεοῦ πρὸς σῶμα ἀνθρώπινον.

[31] Apoll., *Ad Diodor.*, frag. 144: ed. L., 242[4].

[32] H. de Riedmatten, O. P., 'Some neglected aspects of Apollinarist christology', *DomStud* 1, 1948, 239–60; id., 'La christologie d'Apollinaire de Laodicée', *StudPat* II, Berlin 1957, 208–34.

[33] R. Draguet, 'La christologie d'Eutychès', *Byz* 6, 1931, 449, also works with the personal category.

[34] H. de Riedmatten, 'Apollinarist christology', 240–5. Cf. especially the illustrative sections of *De unione* 12, 13: ed. L., 185–93.

[35] Apoll., *De unione* 12: ed. L., 190[17–19].

[36] Apoll., *De fide et incarn.*: ed. L., 197[21–22].

[37] H. de Riedmatten, 'Apollinarist christology', 248, with reference to teaching on the eucharist.

3. THE CONCEPT OF 'PERSON'

It was in any case no great step from the metaphysics and conceptuality which were used in the dogma of the incarnation during the early stages of the Logos-sarx framework to the introduction of the word and concept *hypostasis*, so important for the later history of christology.[38] In Apollinarius, *ousia*, *physis* and *hypostasis* are closely connected. The element they have in common helps us a great deal in their interpretation, as it also points to the fact that all the concepts were particularly native to the sphere of the Logos-sarx christology. *Ousia* and *physis* need not first have been introduced as christological terms. The successful use of *hypostasis* to interpret the unity of person in Christ does, however, seem to have been the work of Apollinarius,[39] though we were able to see a first appearance of the root of this very significant word as early as Hippolytus. Moreover, the concept of σύστασις, which we verified both in Hippolytus and in the Acts of the Synod of 268, as well as in the wider usage of Methodius of Olympus, already to some extent anticipated both the idea of *hypostasis* and the actual word.[40]

These three chief christological concepts of the Apollinarian system are closely connected. The common, original idea from which Apollinarius begins is the σύνθεσις ζωτική which has been achieved in Christ. This common element is so strong that it conceals the closer meaning of the individual terms. The *compositum* 'Christ' is *one physis* and *hypostasis* and *one ousia* because the Logos as determining principle is the sole source of all life. Through his *symbiosis* with the fleshly nature a ἕνωσις φυσική is achieved. For the same reasons and in the same sense *one* πρόσωπον also is to be assumed in Christ, a word which is certainly meant to express unity of *person*. But the explanation of the *way in which* this unity of prosopon comes about remains within the active-dynamic presentation which has been described above: 'The flesh and the "determining principle of the flesh" are one prosopon.'[41] Here too, then, the vitalistic element stands in the foreground, and in fact this is true of the whole Apollinarian interpretation of the unity of person in Christ.[42] We have here the theological vindication of the *communicatio idiomatum*. Its basis in Apollinarius does not lie in the purely personal, hypostatic realm (as in later christology), but is rooted in a union in Christ which is understood to be a natural one.

[38] For the history of this word in christology up to the Council of Chalcedon we use the valuable preliminary study by M. Richard, 'Hypostase', 5–32, 247–70. For the other literature see *Chalkedon* I, 113, n. 1.

[39] M. Richard, 'Hypostase', 6–17, demonstrates this and cites the following four texts: 1–3: *De fide et incarn.* 3, 6, 8: ed. Lietzmann, 194, 198–9, 201; 4: *k.m.p.* 28: ed. L., 177 (apparatus).

[40] Hippolytus, *Antinoet.* 15: ed. Nautin, 259. For the Synod of Antioch 268, cf. F. Loofs, *Paulus v. S.*, 232, n. 8; G. Bardy, *Paul de Samosate*, 327.

[41] Apoll., *Logoi*: ed. L., 248[16]: σάρξ καὶ τὸ σαρκὸς ἡγεμονικὸν ἐν πρόσωπον. Note the Stoic element.

[42] Apoll., *Ad Diodor.*, frag. 144: ed. L., 242[2–4]; frag. 154: ibid., 248[30–2]; *Ep. ad Dionys.*, B.: ed. L., 262[15].

This does not mean that Apollinarius did not grasp or at least have an inkling of the idea of 'person' and 'unity of person' in Christ. Whatever happens, 'person' (*prosopon, hypostasis*) in his writings should not be equated with ἐνέργεια. The way in which unity of person comes about is not to be confused with this unity itself. Apollinarius, as will immediately be evident, is fond of putting personal terms with expressions having an energetic-dynamic content. This juxtaposition should not mislead us into taking person and energy, or person and physis, as synonyms.[43] Apollinarius comes nearest to the idea of unity of person as he speaks of the 'unity of subject in Christ': 'The changeable νοῦς is not confused with the unchangeable in forming a substantial unity of one subject.'[44] What is here said to be the result of the union of Logos and fleshly nature is 'one ὑποκείμενον': 'one subject'. This surely points in the direction of what is later called a 'natural unity' as opposed to a 'unity of person'.

Widespread though the notion of 'person' may already have been, the concrete basis put forward for it by Apollinarius was such as to hide the notion once again and even to endanger it. In fact he reduces the 'unity of person' to a vitalistic 'unity of nature'. One need only look at the context in which the decisive terms which are meant to express unity of person occur. They are incorporated into a typical pattern of ideas:

Holy scripture makes no difference between the Logos and his flesh, but the same (αὐτὸς) is one physis, one hypostasis, one power (ἐνέργεια), one prosopon, fully God and fully man.[45]

The reference to the 'one power' is an indication of the concrete way in which the 'unity of person' is to be achieved. It means not only the volitional direction of the body of Christ by the Logos—the Logos being the subject of the rational will—but also his influence on every sphere of life. The designation 'fully God and fully man' suggests that Apollinarius is not so much concerned to stress the 'unity of person' as the 'natural unity' in the Apollinarian sense: Christ is a ὅλον σύνθετον determined by one life-giving power, the parts of which may bear the name of the whole.[46] In any case, the starting-point from which Apollinarius seeks to understand the unity in Christ is almost always the idea of a vital dynamism. On all sides, one can see the connection between those terms which in Apollinarius have some 'personal' application and his 'vitalistic' position, though once again it should be noted that there is no conceptual identification of 'energy' and 'person'. Apollinarius speaks of one prosopon in Christ because he sees in him one 'living being'.[47]

[43] Cf. H. de Riedmatten, 'Apollinarist christology', 252f., against the interpretation of the Apollinarian concept of physis (= person) by C. E. Raven.
[44] Apoll., *Ad Julian.*, frag. 151: ed. L., 248[2-3].
[45] Apoll., *De fide et incarn.* 6: ed. L., 198–9.
[46] Apoll., *Ad Diodor.*, frag. 145: ed. L., 242; cf. *Logoi*, frag. 154: ibid., 248[20-5].
[47] Thus Apollinarius connects all the important christological concepts with the concept ζῷον. See the instances in *Chalkedon* I, 115, n. 10. R. A. Norris, *Manhood and Christ*, 92f., rightly stresses that in

Finally, this physical, active basis for the unity of hypostasis in Christ is also evident from Epiphanius. He witnesses to the fact that the school of Apollinarius worked with the concept of hypostasis and gave it a place within christology.[48]

From Epiphanius' extremely obscure refutation of the ideas of Apollinarius, we can work out an Apollinarian argument which well reproduces the basic thought of this christology:

> Man is a hypostasis by virtue of his νοῦς, which is the principle of life. His anima soul (ψυχή) and his body have their hypostasis in and through this νοῦς. If then the Word as divine νοῦς and divine πνεῦμα has taken a human νοῦς, there are two hypostases in Christ, which is impossible. If, on the other hand, he took only a body and an animal soul, then they are necessarily hypostatized in him and Christ is only a single hypostasis.[49]

It would probably be wrong to work primarily with the idea of person here to explain the Apollinarian concepts of ὑπόστασις and ἐνυποστασία. The only correct starting point is the idea of vital unity which is achieved because the Logos is the determining principle of the whole of Christ's human nature, i.e. of his flesh and his lower soul, the ψυχή. The idea of a physical ἐνυποστασία in Apollinarius is interpreted and established on quite a different basis from that of the Byzantines in the sixth century.

If we understand the *mia physis* and *mia hypostasis* formulas in Apollinarius thus, it is not difficult to distinguish him sufficiently from the other great representative of this terminology, Cyril of Alexandria. If, on the other hand, we approach the conceptuality common to both with only the concept of 'person' or 'nature-person', we cannot stress either the common elements or the distinguishing elements sufficiently. It is also plain that the idea of 'monophysitism', so far as this is understood as contrasted to the later concept of 'diphysitism', cannot be attributed to Apollinarius. The Apollinarian system is rather a monergetic or monothelitic creation and exerted its great influence in this form. The decisive element is the vital, dynamic concept of *physis*. It was only possible for confusion to arise over the *mia physis* formula because the concept of *physis* underwent a change in the anti-Apollinarian disputes in the direction of being static, so that it eventually became almost identical with 'abstract nature' or '*essentia*'. The arguments over 'real-monophysitism', which was, of course, little represented in history, owe their origin to this change of concepts in which the active element of the *mia physis* formula was no longer noticed. It will be the task of the following era up to the Council

---

the later works of Apollinarius, 'his interest has shifted, one might say, to the *ethical* aspect of the spirit-flesh scheme, and in the forefront of his mind is the nature of "spirit" as free, rational substance which is related to flesh as a governing, informing agent. . . . Apollinaris understands the redemptive work of Christ in terms of the sanctification or vivification (the terms are almost synonymous) of the flesh.' Now the vivification of the flesh is interpreted in terms which are 'not merely biological, but plainly moral'. Cf. 117–19.

[48] M. Richard, 'Hypostase', 9–12, which is also used in what follows.

[49] Ibid., 9–10: on Epiphanius, *Ancoratus* 77–8: ed. Holl, 96–8: PG 43, 161B–164C.

of Chalcedon to clarify and change the concept of *physis*. We must now look back to see—as far as is possible—the general character of the Logos-sarx christology.

RETROSPECT

THE preceding pages have not been by any means sufficient to provide a complete historical survey of the spread of the christology of the Logos-sarx type—some of its aspects are still to be enlarged upon—but they may have suggested its character and its importance. At any rate, its existence cannot be denied. Of course, there were within its confines representatives of different, even essentially different groups. But the differences do not do away with a common 'framework'. Both differences and common elements must now be summed up in short sections to give us some idea of the wider significance of the Logos-sarx framework.

(1) If for the purposes of comparison we arrange the representatives and schools of the Logos-sarx christology in a straight line, the Arians and Apollinarians will stand at the two extreme ends. Both demonstrate how unorthodox this christology is and how little it can be united with the true and complete picture of Christ. The difference between them lies in their different attitude towards the Nicene ὁμοούσιος and their respective denial or acceptance of the Godhead of the Logos and his identity of substance with the Father. Common to both is the express denial of a human soul in Christ. Here, however, we have only the negative element. Positively, they agree in assuming a unity of life and being between sarx and Logos through which the Logos (be he thought of as divine or as a κτίσμα) is made the 'soul' of the flesh. These vital influences form the bond of unity in Christ. The πρῶτον ψεῦδος of this christology is, then, the essential conjunction of Logos and fleshly nature, which is understood as a natural unity analogous to that of body and soul. The union of the Logos and the body is so understood that the physical forces and energies of the Logos overflow into the bodily being in a 'physical' way, thus exciting all living activity. The chief christological formula is John 1. 14, but this is interpreted in a special way; the Logos enters as a part into the totality which is the man 'Christ'. The 'incarnation' of the Logos is effected by the conjunction of a spiritual being, i.e. the Logos, with the flesh, a process in which the 'man Christ' is first constituted physically as such. With regard to Christ, Apollinarius calls this composition a 'heavenly man'. In the teaching of the church, on the other hand, the constituting of Christ's humanity is logically distinguished from its union with the God-head of Christ, as it is made up of the union of body and soul. Of course, the Arian–Apollinarian interpretation achieves an extraordinary close conjunction of the Logos and the fleshly nature, but at the cost of the transcendence of the Logos. The Arians saw through the character of this conjunction and quite consistently made the Logos a creature and a soul.

Here their christological and their subordinationist tendencies met. The Apollinarians rejected this conclusion of the Arians, but did not attack their premises.

There is also an orthodox theology which came under the influence of the Logos-sarx idea. From the start its boundaries are drawn more closely. The characteristic of this group is that it maintains a silence on the soul of Christ, and delineates its picture of Christ in such a way that the soul does not appear. Even if its presence is tacitly to be assumed, it is neither a christological nor a soteriological factor.

We could call Athanasius a representative of this Logos-sarx framework within the church for the following reasons: he avoids any formal, emphatic mention of the soul of Christ just as he avoids any denial. He refrains from any further development of the christological implications of the Logos-sarx framework, and in so doing clearly distinguishes himself from Apollinarius. All is incorporated in a doctrine of redemption which, as it stands, needs to be developed, but which is completely orthodox in its basic features. His key christological formula too is restrained, though it clearly betrays its affinity to the Logos-sarx framework. If we compare his teaching with that of the Apollinarians, the clarification made by the latter is significant.

(2) The consequences of this interpretation of Christ are not to be mistaken. The two heretical forms of the Logos-sarx christology, Arianism and Apollinarianism, represent probably the most serious and dangerous influx of Hellenistic ideas into the traditional conception of Christ. But even in its modified forms, which are to be developed still further in individual details, this christological framework contains some suspect elements. It is an eclectic framework, which does not emphasize all the traditional features of the picture of Christ in the same way. Though the individual details may be represented rightly, there is always the danger of distortion, especially with any further addition of colouring foreign to the tradition.

Such a danger can certainly be seen in Alexandrianism, now taken in the widest sense of the word. There can be no doubt that the decline in teaching about the soul of Jesus had a detrimental effect on the picture of Christ in the Eastern church wherever the Logos-sarx framework came to occupy a dominant place. It represents—to comment on its more outspoken forms—a misunderstanding of the whole manhood and human psychology of Jesus Christ. The all-sufficiency of the redeeming act can no longer be given its proper emphasis[1] and as a result the place of Christ's manhood in theology and generally in the worship of believers must suffer.

[1] In a history of soteriology a complete investigation would have to be made of the christological ideas mentioned here. J. Rivière, *Le dogme de la rédemption*, Paris 1905, and H. Sträter, *Die Erlösungslehre des hl. Athanasius*, Freiburg 1894, are, as far as I can see, completely silent about them.

We must, then, make the Logos-sarx christology and not merely an anti-Arianism primarily responsible for the repression of the true and complete manhood of Jesus. Arianism itself does not have the right theological basis for interpreting the humanity of Christ. The slowness with which the Greek Fathers of the fourth century struggled through to a full recognition of the humanity of the Lord may well be a result of the struggle against Arianism, as the Logos question came very much into the foreground. But the decisive factor was something quite different. Some Fathers had an unsatisfactory picture of Christ, in which the manhood of Jesus was not given its due place.[2]

We may see as the positive side of the theology of the Alexandrian church the way it gave the decisive place in its picture of Christ to the Logos, making him the really final subject of the human nature. In so doing it made possible a deep insight into what is meant by an essential, substantial unity of being in Christ. Its particular explanation may have proved insufficient, but this element will remain preserved for ever in the theology of the church and is recognized as a genuine interpretation of the Johannine formula 'The Logos *is* flesh'.

The whole development of the great complex of the Logos-sarx christology shows the result of the influx of non-Christian, philosophic elements on Christian revelation and theology. Still greater and harder struggles were needed for this kernel of foreign matter to be removed.[3]

[2] Cf. J. A. Jungmann S.J., *Die Stellung Jesu im liturgischen Gebet*, Münster 1925. The author pays only brief attention to the christology of the Arians and their misunderstanding of the manhood of Christ (p. 142). Notice should be taken of the whole complex of the Logos-sarx christology and its significance for the history of piety. But see now the additions made in the reprint of 1962.

[3] Cf. E. v. Ivánka, *Hellenisches und Christliches im frühbyzantinischen Geistesleben*, Wien 1948; H. A. Wolfson, 'Philosophical Implications of Arianism and Apollinarianism', DOP 12, 1958, 3–28.

SECTION TWO

THE 'LOGOS-ANTHROPOS' CHRISTOLOGY

INTRODUCTION

APOLLINARIUS stands at the end of a christological tradition which had sought to give an interpretation of the being of Christ over and above the expressions of the popular kerygmatic formula by means of a learned theology. After these principles for a first theological explanation of the person of Christ had been influential for some time unbeknown to a considerable part of the theologically educated public,[1] they reached such acuteness and power in Apollinarius that the church was called upon to give her decision. The discussion now comes to a close in the clear light of history, though in the end it is only concerned with theological positions which had already been prepared from the time of the Apologists. In the extreme forms of Arianism (as a christology) and Apollinarianism, with their powerful propaganda, the Logos-sarx christology called for a reply.

Although the Fathers were already prepared for the controversy as a result of the long trinitarian struggles with the Arians, there was nevertheless little inclination to take up a new discussion, the magnitude of which could be guessed. When the first recorded contact on the christological front took place in the year 362, Athanasius sought to avoid a repetition of the unfruitful and even detrimental theological word-splittings of the previous decades:

> But counsel the others, who explain and think rightly, not to inquire further into each other's opinions, nor to fight about words to no useful purpose, nor to go on contending with such phrases, but to agree in the mind (φρόνημα) of piety.[2]

No occasion was to be given for the resurgence of anything like the Arian period. So no attempt was to be made to expand the Nicene creed, in order to prevent a return of the era of struggles over the *homoousios*. The Nicene creed was sufficient to solve all important questions. The verdict of Basil the Great on an attempt to expand the christological section of the creed, put forward by Epiphanius, is very interesting here. His words are an admirable illustration of the position of christological thought at the beginning of the dispute between Apollinarius and the church. Basil

---

[1] Cf. the verdict of Severus Antioch., *Ctr. Grammaticum* III, 2, 28; translated J. Lebon, 55–6.
[2] Ath., *Tom. ad Antioch.* 8: PG 26, 805B.
[3] More in H. Dörries, *De Spiritu Sancto. Der Beitrag des Basilius zum Abschluss des trinitarischen Dogmas* (AbhGöttGW 3. F. No. 39), Göttingen 1956, 116f., 132, 168f.

certainly concedes that a later insertion had already been made in the
Nicene creed (*Epp.* 159; 51; 92; 258), namely a 'Doxology to the Holy
Ghost', as that of the three hundred and eighteen Fathers had proved too
short. At the time of the council of 325, the heresy against the Holy Spirit
had not yet emerged. But any further expansion, especially christological,
would be firmly resisted:

> But the teachings (*dogmata*) which are added to that creed (the Nicene) about the
> incarnation of the Lord (in the formula submitted by Epiphanius[3]) we have neither
> examined nor accepted, as being too deep for our comprehension, knowing that when
> once we alter the simplicity of the creed we shall find no end of discussion. The disputation
> will lead us ever on and on, and we shall disturb the souls of the simpler folk by the
> introduction of what seems strange to them.[4]

Basil's misgiving was justified. A similar restraint and embarrassment
about christological problems can also be seen in Diodore of Tarsus, who
also condescended to engage in debate with Apollinarius in his old age,
though he had already played his part in the struggle against Julian the
Apostate on christological questions (see below). A fresh territory had
been opened up. The first pioneers for its conquest were hard to find.

But the problems became too pressing. The powerful influence of the
Apollinarian writings could not remain unnoticed and unanswered.[5] An
admonition from Pope Damasus, who bewailed the negligence of the
East in this important matter, may well have been of no small help in
stirring up the power of the church to opposition.[6] Yet if one reads how,
say, Epiphanius tries to solve christological problems, one can see the
devastating effect on the church of the blow from Apollinarius.[7]

Nevertheless, this very fear and restraint of the Fathers who really felt
for the church is most important. It enables us to see how at the beginning
of the great christological struggles everything once again ranged round
the simple, straightforward formula of the tradition. While the first
attempt of learned theology to expound christological dogma had achieved
considerable influence and finally even tore away considerable groups
from the church, it had not been able to obscure or alter the kerygma of
the church in any way. If the adherents to this kerygma now had to take
up the debate with a form of christology which could already look back
to quite a long development, the gulf between them and their opponents
must have seemed enormous. The Logos-sarx christology, as it was put

---

[4] Basil, *Ep.* 258, 2: PG 32, 949BC; cf. *Ep.* 244, 3: ibid. 916B and *Ep.* 263, 4: ibid. 980B–D. For the
fear of an expansion of the Nicene creed see also Ath., *De Decretis Nicaen. synodi* 32: PG 25, 476BC;
Tom. ad Antioch. 5, 9: PG 26, 800C–801A, 805C. In No. 5 Athanasius mentions the decree of Sardica,
that no additions should be made to the Nicene creed. But J. N. D. Kelly, *Creeds*[3], 323, shows that
expanded formulas could also be described as '*fides Nicaena*'.
[5] For this influence cf. Basil, *Ep.* 263, 4: PG 32, 980B. For the culture of the church at Laodicea and
of Apollinarius himself see H. Lietzmann, *Apollinaris*, 1–5: J. Lebreton, 'Le désaccord de la foi populaire et de la théologie savante', *RHE* 19, 1923, 11–13.
[6] Damasus, *Ep.* 3 *ad Paulinum*: PL 13, 356–7. In addition, see below, pp. 349ff.
[7] Epiphan., *Ancor.* 119–120: PG 43, 232C–236C: Holl, chs. 118–19, pp. 146–9.

forward in Apollinarianism, had at its disposal not only an already well-developed terminology but also a theological 'framework' which could offer a consistent explanation of the person of Christ. The Fathers, on the other hand, had significantly more limited opportunities.

Apollinarius, therefore, at first had the initiative. As far as we can still see from the tradition, he must be credited with having introduced into christology, or having brought to bear on the discussion, the three most important concepts which occur in the Chalcedonian Definition, φύσις, ὑπόστασις and πρόσωπον. These concepts were eventually taken over by the opposition as well, and finally by the Council of Chalcedon itself, but they were canonized in a refined and clarified sense. A christology with a 'Word-man' framework will now develop. Of necessity it seems to lead to a loosening of the unity in Christ and so it was vigorously opposed by its counterpart. The problem to be solved, then, was how to combine this 'Word-man' framework with as deep and inward a conception of the unity of Christ as was possessed by the other side. It only became really acute, however, when belief in the divinity of Christ (against the Arians) and his soul (against both Arians and Apollinarians) was brought out into the open.

The development took place in quite clearly distinguishable stages, and different groups contributed to the process. The so-called Antiochene christology developed from the struggle against the Logos-sarx framework, but its origins and early stages seem, remarkably enough, to lie within the sphere of this framework. It will be our task here to distinguish the different ideas and the circles in which they are produced, together with the valid formulas which are composed there. With the progress of christological reflection, the philosophical presuppositions of the Fathers and the theologians are most influential, particularly in the conception of the unity of Christ. First of all, the usual conceptions of and analogies to the unity of two substances are unconsciously applied to the unity of Christ. Here the different parties begin from different philosophical presuppositions (Platonic, Neo-Platonic, Stoic, Aristotelian) or even from a mixture of different systems. Their task should have been to uncover these different philosophical frameworks, but this kept on being neglected. The mistake became all the more deep-seated because for a long time there was no clear presentation of the christological problem. The more the question of the unity of God and man presents itself, even in the period which is now to be examined, the more the chief concern is to make clear the levels on which unity and distinction are to be sought in Christ. The important complexities of this period are a result of the difficulty of separating these two levels.

CHAPTER ONE

EARLIER ANTI-APOLLINARIANISM AND THE 'LOGOS-ANTHROPOS' CHRISTOLOGY

EUSTATHIUS' struggle against the Arian christology is continued after him by *Paulinus* and his followers. Their aim is to uphold the memory and the tradition of the deposed Eustathius. But now *Apollinarianism*, too, comes into the picture. The Paulinians had a special opportunity of opposing it at the Synod of Alexandria in 362, which we have already discussed. Both parties were represented there. We are already familiar with the compromise formula, which, though finally accepted by both parties, was understood by each according to its own particular presuppositions. The commentary which Apollinarius wrote to Diocaesarea (Lietzmann, 255–6) shows that the Apollinarians did not regard this formula as a repudiation of their christology. The action of the Paulinians at Alexandria could not therefore offer the powerful impulse needed to overcome Apollinarianism.[1]

1. THE ACTION OF EPIPHANIUS OF CYPRUS AND OF POPE DAMASUS

Under the leadership of the presbyter Vitalis, the heresy was also established at Antioch. But that energetic opponent of all heresies, *Epiphanius of Cyprus* (died 403), also appeared on the scene. Perhaps at the request of Paulinus, Epiphanius travelled to Antioch in 374. There was a keen discussion woth Vitalis, who now had to clarify his teaching. According to the report of Epiphanius (*Haer.* 77, 23), it ran thus:

> We call (Christ) perfect man, putting his Godhead in place of the *nous*; then too there are the flesh and the (lower) soul (ψυχή).

Epiphanius takes up this trichotomist anthropology and applies it to christology. The Logos has become man by taking a *body*, a *psyche* and a *nous* (*Ancoratus* 75, 76), and so has ensured complete salvation. No part of man need become the prey of the devil—an argument the tradition of which goes back to the second century. Here Epiphanius does not keep to the christology of Paulinus, but incorporates this teaching of the 'perfect man' into an emphatic 'unitive christology', thus achieving a synthesis

---

[1] A survey and investigation of the most important documents between 362 and 379 can be found in J.-P. Billet, *L'école d'Antioche et l'apollinarisme (362–379)* (Thèse de Doctorat en Théologie), Lille 1947 (duplicated).

between Athanasius and Paulinus. This seems the only possible explanation for the mixture of two different frameworks in the creed which he puts forward at the end of the *Ancoratus*. It represents an expansion of the Nicene creed, into which elements of both a 'homo-assumptus' and a 'homo-factus' christology have been inserted:

> He 'became man, that is he took a complete man, (animal) soul and body and rational soul, and all that is man, sins excepted: he was not of human seed, nor in a man, but fashioned for himself flesh to make a holy union, different from his moving, speaking and acting in the prophets, and so became perfect man. For the Word was made flesh, without his own Godhead being changed or transformed into manhood.'[2]

Developments took a speedy course through the intervention of *Pope Damasus* (366–84). Vitalis thought he could make good his defeat of 374 by Epiphanius in Rome, in 375. He first sought to deceive Damasus by a spurious credal testimony which contained the formulas of the Synod of Alexandria of 362 (Lietzmann, 273). But hardly had Vitalis left Rome than Damasus became suspicious and sought to save the situation by a letter to Paulinus (375). In this important letter, '*Per filium meum*', Pope Damasus gives a short account of contemporary christological problems (PL 13, 356B–357A).[3] Here he rejects not only Apollinarianism but also adoptionism (doctrine of two sons). Christ, the one Son of God, the Word and Wisdom of God, took our whole Adam with body, soul and reason (*sensus*), sins alone excepted.

What Damasus does not realize is that the Apollinarian teaching is intended to be a solution of the problem of unity in Christ. On his side he makes no attempt to answer this problem. The same is true with the other concern of the Apollinarians, the sinlessness of Christ, a question which they mean to solve in their christology together with that of his unity. Damasus merely stresses that for Christ to have taken a human rational soul does not mean that he was exposed to the sins of this rational soul. For the taking of a body by no means signifies subjection to its vices and passions. Here Western anthropology has its place in the picture of Christ and allows the problem of sinlessness to be put in a still more pressing way. No attempt is made at a solution. Despite this, the attitude of Pope Damasus is significant, as he puts forward a firm christology with a 'Word-man' framework, and yet none the less acknowledges the 'one' Christ (357A). In 376, in an answer to letters from Basil and Meletius, he once more stresses belief in the complete manhood of Christ and supports

---

[2] Epiphan., *Ancoratus* 119: ed. Holl, 148[13-19].

[3] For sources and chronology see Margaret Ann Norton, 'Prosopography of Pope Damasus', *Folia* 4, 1950, 13–51; 5, 1951, 33–55; E. Schwartz, *ZNW* 35, 1936, 19–23; F. Diekamp, 'Das Glaubensbekenntnis des apollinaristischen Bischofs Vitalis von Antiochien', *TQ* 86, Tübingen 1904, 497–511; P. Galtier, 'Le "Tome de Damase", date et origine', *RSR* 26, 1936, 385–418, 563–578; J. N. D. Kelly, *Creeds*, 334–7 (Apollinarius); M. Richard, AnalBoll 67, 1949, 201f.

it from the so-called soteriological argument: 'What is not taken is not healed' (PL 13, 352–3B; cf. ZNW 35, 1936, 21f.). Thus Western christology supported Eustathius' concern, though it did not know how to cure the weakness of the Eustathian interpretation. In the autumn of 377, a synod was held at Rome in which Peter of Alexandria and envoys of Basil took part. Apollinarius, Vitalis and Timothy of Berytus were condemned. Finally, in 382, this condemnation of Apollinarianism was reaffirmed at a new Roman synod.

To understand the development of the struggle against the extreme Logos-sarx christology we must now return once again to the Antiochene scene. The supporters of Eustathius and Paulinus should not be identified *tout court* with the Antiochene tradition. They represent a quite limited circle which, apart from its association with Epiphanius and Rome, was of no special influence in history.

The real stimulus to the formation of what is known as 'Antiochene' christology, as the antithesis to the Logos-sarx christology, appears rather to have come from an opposed group, the *Meletians*. We know little of the position of this group before the year 379. If it is permissible to argue from Basil and his restraint over christological problems to his friend Meletius, we may say that in 375 neither suspected Apollinarius of heresy.[4] But the situation altered in 379 at a synod in Antioch where Meletius and Diodore of Tarsus, along with about 150 bishops, took up a position against Apollinarius. Extracts from the documents of Pope Damasus (*Ea gratia, Illud sane, Non nobis*; cf. ZNW 35, 1936, 20–3) were included in the Acts of this synod. The council accepted his teaching. This meant much for the status of Latin christology and the approach which it represented. Its witness hitherto had been confined in the East to the adherents of Paulinus. It was not without cause that the Council of Constantinople in 381 referred to the Synod of Antioch (see below, n. 29). But to understand developments we must go back further, to influences which lie right outside this circle. The remarkable thing, however, is that in the search for the sources of the thought of this group we are once again led back to the sphere of the Logos-sarx christology. Indeed in the influence of Eusebius of Emesa on Diodore of Tarsus we discover a connecting link between Antioch and Alexandria.

---

[4] Basil, *Ep.* 129 (end of 375); *Ep.* 244 (middle of 376). See G. L. Prestige, *St Basil the Great and Apollinaris of Laodicea*, London 1956, 1–37; H. de Riedmatten, 'La correspondence entre Basile de Césarée et Apollinaire de Laodicée', *JTS*, NS 7, 1956, 199–210. These two studies argue for the authenticity of the correspondence between Basil and Apollinarius, now best available in de Riedmatten's work. Against this, R. Weijenborg, 'De authenticitate et sensu quarundam epistularum S. Basilio Magno et Apollinario Laodiceno adscriptarum', *Anton* 33, 1958, 197–240, 371–414; 34, 1959, 245–298. Despite some good points, Weijenborg's counter-arguments are not conclusive. For us, this question has only a psychological significance, in that the correspondence clarifies the relationship between the two bishops. Otherwise only the trinitarian question is concerned. For the situation as a whole, see F. Cavallera, *Le schisme d'Antioche*, Paris 1905, 211–231; M. Richard, AnalBoll 67, 1949, 201f.

2. Diodore of Tarsus

It is Jerome who mentions the connection between *Diodore* (died before 394) and the teaching, if not also the person, of *Eusebius of Emesa*.[5] According to him there was a spiritual teacher-pupil relationship between the two. Historically this contact is quite possible, as Eusebius frequently came to Antioch, where too he was eventually buried.[6] Can such an affinity of thought be established specifically for his christology? In answering this question we shall naturally stress the point which seemed so striking in Eusebius himself, his Logos-sarx christology. Previous interpretation of the theology of Diodore suggested that the presbyter of Antioch and bishop of Tarsus had to be put right outside this framework, and made him a representative of the Logos-man christology. Moreover, the *'alius et alius'* for which he was so persistently censured also seemed to point in this direction and was felt already to be a complete anticipation of Nestorianism. All the more striking, then, is the result of an inquiry into the place of the soul in the christology of Diodore, based on an examination of the extant fragments. First of all, however, some account of the historical context of his christology seems to be called for.

Diodore's christological ideas probably became known to a particularly wide public when he was led by the religious policies of Julian the Apostate to defend the divinity of Christ. From the end of June 362 until 5 March 363, the emperor and restorer of ancient paganism lived in a hostile Antioch and there 'in many vigils' worked at a large book against the 'Galileans', which he probably published before his departure to the Persian war.[7] The presence of so powerful an opponent of Christianity in the town on the Orontes must have made a powerful impression both there and in the East generally. Christian writers saw themselves occa-

[5] Jerome, *De viris illustr.* 119: ed. G. Herding, *Hieronymi De viris inlustribus liber*, Leipzig 1924, 62: *Diodorus, Tarsensis episcopus, dum Antiochiae esset presbyter, magis claruit. Exstant eius in Apostolum commentarii et multa alia ad Eusebii magis Emiseni characterem pertinentia, cuius cum sensum secutus sit, eloquentiam imitari non potuit propter ignorantiam saecularium litterarum.*

[6] Ibid., ch. 91, ed. Herding, 54: *Eusebius Emesenus . . . floruit temporibus Constantii imperatoris, sub quo et mortuus, Antiochae sepultus est.* Cf. E. Buytaert, 'Héritage litt. d'Eusèbe', 61–96, where the frequent visits of Eusebius to Antioch are reported. The following are used in this study: M. Brière, 'Fragments syriaques de Diodore de Tarse réédités et traduits pour la première fois', *RevOrChr* X (XXX), 1946, 231–83 (with Syriac text by P. de Lagarde); K. Staab, *Pauluskommentare aus der griechischen Kirche*, (NTAbh. 15), Münster 1933; R. Abramowski, 'Der theologische Nachlass des Diodor von Tarsus', *ZNW* 42, 1949, 19–69 (cited hereafter as 'Nachlass Diodors'). V. Ermoni, 'Diodore de Tarse et son rôle doctrinale', *Mus*, NS 2, 1901, 422–44; R. Abramowski, 'Untersuchungen zu Diodor v. T.' *ZNW* 30, 1931, 234–62; L. Mariés, 'Le Commentaire de Diodore de Tarse sur les Psaumes', *RevOrChr* IV (XXIV), 1924, 58–189; id., *Études préliminaires à l'édition du Commentaire de Diodore de Tarse sur les Psaumes*, Paris 1933; M. Richard, 'Les Traités de Cyrille d'Alexandrie contre Diodore et Théodore et les Fragments dogmatiques de Diodore de Tarse', *Mélanges F. Grat* t. 1, Paris 1946, 99–116. I had access to the unpublished MS of G. Brandhuber C.SS.R. (†), *Diodor von Tarsus. Die Bruchstücke seines dogmatischen Schrifttums, gesammelt, übersetzt und untersucht*, Gars/Inn 1949; M. Jugie, 'La doctrine christologique de Diodore de Tarse d'après les fragments de ses oeuvres', *Euntes Docete* 2, 1949, 171–91; F. A. Sullivan, *The Christology of Theodore of Mopsuestia*, Rome 1956, 172–96.

[7] Libanius, *Or.* 18, no. 178: ed. R. Foerster, *Libanii opera* 2, Lipsiae 1904, 313–14. H. Leclercq, 'Julien l'Apostat'. *DictAL* 8, 380–1.

sioned to write against Julian right into the fifth century.[8] The divinity of Christ, the worship of a 'man from Palestine' and the title *Theotokos* were the great scandals against which he fought.[9] The Christians had to defend themselves. The emperor Julian himself shows that Diodore, then still in Antioch, entered this battle. According to *Facundus of Hermiane*,[10] Julian wrote to *Photinus*:

> But Diodore, the sorcerer of the Nazaraean, has increased further his unreasonableness by deep-dyed witchcraft.[11] . . . If all the gods, goddesses, muses and Tyche (the guardian of pagan Antioch) lend their help, we will show . . . that this his new Galilean God, whom he declares eternal because of a fable, was by his ignominious death and burial destitute of that Godhead which Diodore invents.

The emperor thus sees his opponent as a defender of the true divinity of Christ and a representative of the faith of the church. This testimony may surely be regarded as an indication of Diodore's orthodoxy.[12] True, the emperor accuses certain unnamed opponents of an unjustified evasion of his attacks on the divinity of Christ, and it might be supposed that Diodore was included among them:

> Nevertheless, some among these godless ones think that Jesus Christ is not the same as the Logos preached by John. But that is by no means the case. For the evangelist says that the one whom he himself affirms to be the Logos was recognized by John the Baptist, and that he was Jesus Christ. . . . But if the only-begotten Son is other than the God Logos, as I have heard some of your sect say, then John would not have dared to speak thus.[13]

It is a curiosity of history that the anti-Christian Julian noticed the contradiction between this interpretation—from whomsoever it may have come—and the genuine exegesis of John. But may we really include Diodore among those who are said here to have represented a 'divisive' christology? We will see that Diodore introduced a loosening of the conception of the unity in Christ. Was he perhaps already compelled by the attacks of the pagan emperor to work out two subjects for christological sayings so as to minimize the danger to the Godhead caused by

---

[8] J. Bidez, *Julian der Abtrünnige*, Munich 1940[3].

[9] Cyril Al., *Apol. ctr. Julian*. 8: PG 76, 901C, 924D–925A; C.-J. Neumann, *Scriptorum graecorum, qui christianam impugnaverunt religionem, quae supersunt, fasc.* 3: *Juliani imp. librorum ctr. christianos quae supersunt*, Lipsiae 1880, 210–14.

[10] Facundus Hermian., *Pro def. trium cap.* 4, 2: PL 67, 621AB.

[11] 'pigmentalibus manganis' (to be read instead of *manganes*).

[12] L. Mariès, 'Diodore de Tarse', 148–9, emphasizes this orthodoxy of Diodore's in connection with the *Commentary on the Psalms*, which he believes must be put before 378, probably even before 372. Here he points to some fragments of the *Commentary*, as yet unedited, on Ps. 109. Cf. now the extensive investigation by Marie-Josèphe Rondeau, 'Le Commentaire des Psaumes de Diodore de Tarse I–III', *Revue de l'Histoire des Religions* 176, 1969, 5–33, 153–88; 177, 1970, 5–33. In the first article, pp. 9–14, the commentary on Ps. 109 is translated. The authenticity and early date of this commentary have been convincingly demonstrated. In the commentary on Ps. 109, Diodore is engaged in controversy with the Jews, with the Arians, especially with Eunomius, with the followers of Paul of Samosata, with Photinus, Sabellius and Marcellus of Ancyra. See below.

[13] Julian Ap. in Cyril Al., *Apol. ctr. Julian*. 10: PG 76, 1012D–1013A; ed. Neumann, 224–5, translated in appendix, 42–3.

the traditional expressions which exchanged predicates (*communicatio idiomatum*)? Does he perhaps stress the possibility of a twofold worship to avoid the charge of worshipping a man? Such a division would seem to limit the *communicatio idiomatum*, and especially the attribution of human weaknesses to the 'Logos',[14] against which Julian directed so much of his calumniation, to a degree tolerable even to pagan ears. In a similar way, the traditional title 'Mother of God' would have had to be given up or at least softened by the insertion of the title 'Mother of man'. This could certainly be regarded as a reply to the charges of the emperor Julian, which in turn could have come to the notice of the ruler, as he used to allow the Christian bishops to debate in his very presence, and admonished them to unity.[15] This expedient of Diodore's, who was consecrated presbyter of Antioch during these years,[16] would be understandable. The simplicity and clumsiness of his solution could be explained from his belief that he must defend the divinity of Christ against non-Christian attacks in such a way. One thing at least may be certain: Diodore must have been intent on making a distinction in Christ. This distinction might have become a 'separation'. Of course the extent of such a separation is hard to decide in the present state of the tradition.

At all events, the extant remains of Diodore's writing are sufficient to indicate a development. The *Commentary on Psalms*, especially the commentary on Ps. 109, shows that Diodore must be regarded as fundamentally orthodox.[17] Consequently, it is worth reproducing here an important passage from this commentary (in the translation of M.-J. Rondeau):

Le Psaume 109 est interprété diversement par les juifs, par les disciples d'Arius et d'Eunome, par les partisans de Paul de Samosate, de Photin, de Sabellius et de Marcel le Galate [the whole group around Paul of Samosata would suppose that the psalm referred to a 'mere man' (ψιλὸν ἄνθρωπον), which Diodore himself rejects!] ... Mais il faut laisser tomber les billevesées des hérétiques et les fanfaronnades des juifs, et dire la vérité: ce psaume vise Notre-Seigneur Jésus-Christ, Monogène et Premier-né. Car le même est à la fois Monogène et Premier-né, non selon le même point de vue toutefois, mais selon des points de vue différents. Il est Premier-né selon la chair [i.e. as incarnate Logos], Monogène selon la divinité; Premier-né selon qu'il est de notre race, Monogène selon qu'il est de Dieu. Les deux choses sont cependant un seul Fils et un seul Seigneur. Le psaume le vise non selon qu'il est Monogène, mais selon qu'il est Premier-né. Car il a reçu l'ordre de siéger à côté du Père selon qu'il est Premier-né et héritier. Selon qu'il est Monogène, il est évidemment coéternel et copartageant du trône, ayant par nature même honneur et même trône que le Père.[18]

[14] Julian Ap. in ibid. 8: PG 76, 900D–901A; 924D–925A: ed. Neumann, 210–14.
[15] J. Viteau, 'Julien l'Apostat', DTC 8, 1959.
[16] F. Cavallera, *Schisme d'Antioche*, 329, who puts forward 361–5 as a date.
[17] For M. Jugie, 'A propos du Commentaire des Psaumes attribué à Diodore de Tarse', EO 33, 1934, 190–3, this is the reason for moving this commentary into the sixth century (cf. M.-J. Rondeau I, *Revue de l'Histoire des Religions* 176, 1969, 8f.). For Jugie, Diodore is *a priori* suspicious because he is the founder of the school of Antioch, from which Nestorius emerged.
[18] Op. cit., 9–10. There then begins the explanation of the details of Ps. 109. The more important passages are also quoted in Greek by Marie-Josèphe Rondeau, as in the case of the text cited above.

Apollinarius of Laodicea is still not addressed in this section. Diodore is concerned to avoid the diminution of the divinity of the one Christ by the Arians and the interpretation of Christ as a mere man by Paul of Samosata and his 'disciples'. By and large, his own understanding of Christ is quite correct. But the opponents mentioned here do not yet compel him to interpret the 'one Christ' more closely. How does his picture of Christ appear in the light of the problems indicated by Apollinarius?

As a result, instead of concerning ourselves directly with the question it seems more useful in the present context to develop an unnoticed aspect of Diodore's christology which will be of indirect help in giving a more accurate description of the character of his 'Antiochene' christology.

Diodore's christology has probably been judged far too much merely in the light of its opposition to Apollinarius, and in consequence it has been characterized as being in every respect an antithesis to the Apollinarian conceptions. There has seemed to be little difference between Diodore, Theodore of Mopsuestia and Nestorius. Yet each of these three representatives of Antiochene christology deserves an individual evaluation— Diodore of Tarsus most of all. The christological framework upon which he builds up his theology of 'distinction', or even 'division', distinguishes him from Theodore of Mopsuestia. In Diodore, strange as it may seem, it is the 'Logos-sarx' framework, while Theodore uses the 'Logos-man' framework. We can assume Diodore's recognition of the soul of Christ as a 'physical factor' and must eventually regard it as certain. The deficiency in his picture of Christ is the lack of this soul as a 'theological factor'. Because we are only concerned with developing this last point we may dispense with the difficult question of the chronological arrangement of the extant fragments, as in these he seems to have undergone no real development.

On going through the fragments of Diodore's work one immediately notices a striking neglect of the church's tradition of the soul of Christ. It does not become a central point of discussion even in the controversy with Apollinarianism. The Bishop of Tarsus does not criticize this deficiency in his opponent—at least that is not his primary concern. This is the more remarkable because there were other traditions flourishing on Antiochene soil, of course among the opposing party, the Paulinians. Diodore, as a Meletian, would not have been much inclined to resort to the theological ideas of the other side. Moreover, his own party had played no part in the Synod of Alexandria.[19] Diodore could only have felt inclined to make an appeal to the formula of the *Tomus* of Alexandria vis-à-vis Apollinarius if he had thought the question of the soul of Christ to be the principal point for discussion. In the face of all these expectations it must be ob-

[19] Ibid. 103. Cf. Ath., *Tom. ad Antioch.* 9–10: PG 26, 805C–809A.

served, as has been said, that the soul of Christ is no theological factor in Diodore's picture of Christ.

This is at its clearest in his exegesis of the Lucan passage (2. 52) which describes the growth and progress of Jesus, a passage which had been discussed over and over again since Origen and had become a *crux Patrum* with the Arians:

> (a) Jesus, he (Diodore) says, increased both in age and in wisdom. But this cannot be said of the Word of God, because he is born perfect God of the perfect (Father), Wisdom of Wisdom, Power of Power. Therefore he himself does not increase; indeed he is not incomplete so as to need additions (*incrementis*) for his completion. (b) But that which grew in age and wisdom was the flesh. (c) And as this had to be created and to be born, the Godhead did not immediately impart to it *all* wisdom, but *bestowed it upon the body in portions* (*particulatim*).[20]

We find ourselves firmly in the thought-world of the Logos-sarx framework. For an 'Antiochene' and an 'anti-Apollinarian', such as Diodore tends to be termed, two things are especially surprising. First, he here opposes the Logos to the 'flesh' and not to the 'man Jesus of Nazareth', who would perhaps be regarded as an adoptionist Christ. Secondly, he makes the Logos himself the direct source of the increase in wisdom and power. (Diodore's further mention of 'power' may be a reminiscence of Eusebius of Emesa, as the biblical texts give him no occasion for it.) Few ideas could be more 'un-Antiochene'. We are directed to the followers of the two Eusebii.

A separation of the Logos from the flesh in Christ occurs still more frequently.

> But how do you have one worship? Perhaps as with the soul and body of a king? For the soul by itself is not king and the body by itself is not king. (The two, then, cannot be separated in honour and are the subject of one action. But not so Christ.) But the God-Logos is king before the flesh and therefore what can be said of body and soul cannot be said of the God-Logos and the flesh.[21]

Fragment 17 describes an objection by Diodore's opponents. He maintained that only the 'flesh' in Christ was crucified and not the Logos. They ask: How then could the wonders, the darkening of the sun and so on, take place?[22] Logos and body stand over against each other in

---

[20] Diodore, frag. 36: trans. Abramowski, 51–3, with details of sources. Cf. frag. 35 (ibid., 51) and Cyril's polemic, ibid., 65, no. XVIII. Fragment 36c is also in Severus of Antioch, *Ctr. Grammaticum* III, 1, ch. 15: trans. Lebon, 178[10-12], where the translation runs '*paulatim dabat illam corpori*'.

[21] Diodore, frag. 39: trans. Abramowski 53, 55; Severus Antioch., *Ctr. Grammaticum* III, 2, 25: trans. Lebon, 33[30]–34[1]. Apollinarius attributes to Diodore a phrase in which the same comparison occurs: Οὐκέτι μένει τὰ ἴδια τοῦ θεοῦ καὶ τὰ ἴδια τῆς σαρκὸς ἐὰν ἕνωσις ᾖ, ed. Lietzmann, frag. 140: 241[11-13]. The translation made by M. Brière partly reveals the same antithesis, e.g. frag. 2, but frags. 11, 13, 15 differ. In frag. 2 (Brière, 260) the soul of Christ is probably not mentioned; the unity in Christ is compared with man's nature as a composition of body and soul. This comparison is not very clear in Brière's translation. The meaning of the fragment seems to be: 'Just as the one man is immortal as regards his soul, but mortal as regards his body, so is Christ, as one and the same, both before the worlds and also of the seed of David.'

[22] Brière, op. cit., 265; R. Abramowski, 'Nachlass Diodors', 35.

Diodore's explanation of the dereliction on the cross.[23] Pointing to Christ's knowledge of his resurrection and exaltation, he denies that there was a real dereliction. Here he displays a tendency like that of Athanasius, weakening the 'spiritual' sufferings of Christ so as to dissociate the Logos from them. The reason for his efforts can only be that he has not yet discovered the significance of Christ's human spirit as a theological factor and with it the whole complex of the psychology of Christ. The passage about Christ's descent makes no mention of the Lord's soul.[24] Finally, the 'body' is also the subject of that title which cannot be given to the Logos *qua* Logos, 'Son of David'.[25]

These are without doubt features which suggest that there is a real connection between Diodore and the Logos-sarx christology. It is a connection which must be taken extremely seriously. The mediating figure is Eusebius of Emesa. He is an important element in the history of dogma, making possible a better explanation of the link between Antioch and Alexandria. It will, of course, be argued that Diodore must eventually have come to recognize the soul of Christ in the anti-Apollinarian controversy. This must certainly be conceded, as will be shown. Nor do we deny that in Diodore's writings the majority of expressions are taken from the 'Word-man' framework. But it is not our concern here to assess the relative strengths of the 'Logos-sarx' and 'Logos-anthropos' frameworks in Diodore. We would merely point out traces in his writings of the former framework as well.[26] This was just a transitory phenomenon, as the mixture of the two frameworks shows.

Nevertheless, this does not alter the fact that he comes from a Logos-sarx christology and that although he recognized a soul in Christ he was not able to make it an element of his christology, a 'theological factor'. We shall still see traces of this rare mixture in the pre-Ephesine writings of Cyril—an indication of how deeply Alexandrianism was rooted in the East. The discovery of such 'un-Antiochene' features in Diodore contradicts the traditional historical picture of his christology. It was thought that an advocate of a 'divisive' theology must necessarily be a representative of the 'Logos-man' christological framework. Eusebius of Emesa and

---

[23] Cf. R. Abramowski, 37, whose translation does not, however, correspond with that given by Brière. The corresponding section of frag. 18 in the latter runs: 'En effet, ce (cri): Mon Dieu! Mon Dieu pourquoi m'as-tu abandonné? (Matt. 27. 46) non seulement n'appartient pas à Dieu le Verbe, mais encore, moi, je ne conteste pas qu'il appartienne au corps, ainsi qu'à celui qui a crié parce qu'il avait été abandonné.'

[24] Frag. 16, trans. M. Brière, 264; Abramowski, 33. Had Diodore referred to it, the problem which he poses, i.e. how Christ as a dead man could lead the thief into Paradise, would have been solved.

[25] Diodore, frags. 31–2: Brière, 271; Greek text, Abramowski, 46.

[26] Whereas in *Chalkedon* I, 135ff., too little stress was laid on the occurrence of the 'Word-man' framework in Diodore (though this was by no means denied), F. A. Sullivan, *The Christology of Theodore of Mopsuestia*, 181–96, tends to obscure the unquestionable derivation of Diodore from the 'Logos-sarx' christology; cf. Luise Abramowski, 'Diodore de Tarse', *DictHGE* 14, 496–504. To solve the problem completely an accurate chronological arrangement of the fragments of Diodore would be necessary.

Diodore of Tarsus are, the former completely, the latter in part, representatives of a divisive christology of the 'Logos-sarx' type—a theology which had little historical opportunity as it was eventually replaced in the theology of the church by the old 'Logos-man' framework. In this they are in certain respects akin to Athanasius who, while defending the divinity of the Logos, as they did, still remained an advocate of the 'unitive' theology and in so doing found the better synthesis. Some correction should also be made in respect of Diodore's anti-Apollinarianism; the battle was not waged over the term 'soul', a matter of 'Logos-man' against 'Logos-sarx', but simply on the theme 'union or division?' (as F. A. Sullivan, op. cit., 182, concedes).

We now have a remarkable confirmation of this interpretation of Diodore's theological attitude from no less a person than his later opponent, *Cyril of Alexandria*. The striking nature of Diodore's language did not escape him, and he replies thus:

> Diodore should also listen to this: If you now call (that) flesh which you once described as the *man* from Nazareth *taken* (by the Logos), then show yourself to us without any disguise and mask, say clearly what in your opinion a man should think and do not seek to deceive (simple) listeners by *speaking simply of a soulless flesh*.[27]

This remark is significant. It is a confirmation of what we have already noticed. Diodore, at least for a long period, built up his 'divisive' theology within the 'Logos-sarx' framework, and Cyril is surprised that it is not the 'Logos-man' framework. Of course Diodore's tendency towards division need only be joined to the last-mentioned framework to give rise to the real problem of the Antiochene christology. Nevertheless, as long as Diodore really remains within the explicit Logos-sarx framework, *Barhadbešabba* may with some justification seek to defend him against the charge of 'teaching two persons':

> And whereas blessed Diodore directs his attention to the natures of the Logos and of the *flesh*, this reviler (he means Cyril) reprimands him for a duality of sons.[28]

A similar conclusion may also be drawn from the words of Cyril quoted above.

It may be assumed that Diodore's christology was completed in the anti-Apollinarian controversy, especially after 379 and 381. At the Council of Constantinople in 381 Meletius, who died during the Council, and Diodore played a special role, and the definitions of the canons of the Council are surely also the personal view of the Bishop of Tarsus. Of course Apollinarius was condemned only in quite general terms in the first canon. We have a short extract from the Tome of the Council from

---

[27] Cyril. Al., frags. passim: ed. P. E. Pusey, *Cyrilli Archiep. Alexandrini in D. Joannis Evangelium* 3, 494. For their authenticity cf. G. Joussard, 'L'activité littéraire de saint Cyrille d'Al. jusqu'à 428', *Mélanges E. Podechard*, Lyon 1945, 164–6.

[28] Barhadbešabba, *Kirchengeschichte*, trans. R. Abramowski, *ZNW* 30, 1931, 241.

a later Nestorian synod. In an *apologia* in which they are defending their faith against Monophysite accusations before the Persian king Chosroes bar Hormizd (since 21 June 612), Nestorian bishops make the following report:

> The synod of 150 Fathers at Constantinople says in its letter on the faith to the Western bishops: 'The God-Logos is perfect God before all worlds and times. But at the end of the world for the salvation of us men he took from us a complete man and dwelt in him' (Mansi 3, 560A, 566B).[29]

According to the Nestorians, the Synod of 381 had helped to bring into the centre of the discussion a pattern of christology which forms the antithesis to the Logos-sarx framework: the idea of indwelling, associated with a christology of the 'Logos-man' type. The Nestorian tendency here is to be noted. It is not surprising that Diodore himself was familiar with the indwelling formula.[30]

We may find some confirmation of this interpretation of Diodore's christological thought from his christological formulas. Had he always been concerned to emphasize the soul of Christ, he could not have composed such formulas as ἔνσαρκος παρουσία[31] or ὁ σωτὴρ ἡμῶν Ἰησοῦς Χριστὸς ἐν σαρκὶ ἐπιδημήσας τῷ κόσμῳ[32] alongside those which have already been mentioned. Now it is particularly important for the history of the christological formula that Diodore clashed with the 'one hypostasis' formula. In the extant fragment we unfortunately have only texts which Diodore quotes from his opponents. His own attitude and the reasons for it are absent.[33] Nevertheless, one can deduce what he really rejects from the way he quotes. He rejects not only the confusion of the two natures in Christ, but also substantial, essential unity in Christ, unity between Word and flesh after the manner of a *compositum humanum*. One

---

[29] On the Nestorian citation: C. A. Kneller, S.J., 'Zum 2. allgemeinen Konzil vom Jahre 381', *ZkTh* 27, 1903, 794; O. Braun, *Das Buch der Synhados*, Stuttgart–Wien 1900, 326. Kneller thinks that the original form of the passage stood in the writings of the Synod of 382 at which roughly the same bishops were present as in 381: Theodoret, HE V, 9, 19: ed. Parmentier, 293[1-3]: 'We know that the God Logos is absolutely perfect and before all time, but that in the last days he became a complete man for our salvation.' For the relationship of Constantinople 382 to 381 see J. N. D. Kelly, *Creeds*, 325f. As early as 379, at the Synod of Antioch, subscription was made to a document submitted by Pope Damasus to the Eastern bishops. Diodore was the sixth to sign (H. Lietzmann, *Apollinarius*, 54). The text for subscription ran: '*Eundem (Dei Filium) redemptionis nostrae gratia processisse de virgine, ut perfectus homo pro perfecto qui peccaverat homine nasceretur*', Mansi 3, 486: PL 13, 354A. On the Synod of 379: G. Bardy, *RevBen* 45, 1933, 196–213. Id. in A. Fliche–V. Martin, *Histoire de l'Église* 3, Paris 1936, 283–4. Further literature in M. A. Norton, *Folia* 5, 1951, 54–5.

[30] Like Eustathius, Diodore appeals to the length of the indwelling as the distinguishing mark between the gift of grace in Christ and that in the prophets. Cf. frag. 35 after Severus Antioch., *Ctr. Grammaticum* III, 1, 15: trans. Lebon, 178[2-9].

[31] Diodore, on Rom. 14. 7–9: ed. K. Staab, *Pauluskomment.*, 109–10. On this cf. F. A. Sullivan, op. cit., 182; he stresses that Diodore also speaks of the 'complete man', which we do not deny.

[32] Diodore, frag. 26: trans. R. Abramowski, 43–5. His work, however, is very vulnerable. In comparison see Brière, 269–70. The translation of this important fragment by Brière was published earlier in M. Richard, 'Hypostase', 13–14. For an interpretation, ibid., 12–17. M. Richard cites the Apollinarian work *Quod unus sit Christus* (ed. Lietzmann, 294–302), in which he sees in turn the reaction to Diodore's position. In *ZNW* 30, 1931, 256, R. Abramowski had seen this frag. 26 as belonging to Diodore. This leads to a false description of Diodore's theological system (ibid., 253–62).

[33] Diodore, on Rom. 16. 25, 27: ed. Staab, 112.

should not, however, condemn the Bishop of Tarsus harshly for that reason. The only possibility he saw of saving the Godhead of Christ was to loosen the conjunction as it had been described by Apollinarius. In comparison with the Laodicaean he was largely right here, but he surely went too far. In the passage we have just discussed, the whole of Diodore's position once again becomes clear. If the opponent attacked by the Apollinarian of the *Opusculum 'Quod unus sit Christus'* is in fact Diodore, then it is evident that Diodore criticizes only the endangering of the Godhead of the Logos in the Apollinarian system. He is not concerned with the diminishing of the humanity of the Lord.[34] But he sees the Godhead endangered by the μία ὑπόστασις formula because in his opinion it makes a natural unity of Word and flesh—and as far as Apollinarius is concerned, he is right. It is therefore this special kind of union which he contests, and does so only because he is concerned about any diminishing of the Godhead. Diodore is unable to construct an effective christology with a 'Word-man' framework, but he nevertheless prepares the ground in important ways for another Antiochene who is to carry on the task, Theodore of Mopsuestia.[35]

[34] M. Richard, 'Hypostase', 15, makes this observation. The features of Diodore's christology which are worked out here, as yet insufficiently recognized among scholars, may well be regarded as an indication of the relative accuracy of the tradition of the fragments of his writings. His opponents, through whose hands they are for the most part transmitted, could have had no interest in allowing the basic elements of a Logos-sarx christology to emerge in his writings. Forgers would doubtless have preferred the 'Logos-man' framework for him. The astonishment of Cyril at the 'Logos-sarx' terminology in Diodore says a great deal here.

[35] See F. A. Sullivan, op. cit., 184-96 (with the qualifications which we have made above).

CHAPTER TWO

NEW TRENDS AFTER ORIGEN

With the anti-Apollinarian controversy we are able to establish a more or less general trend towards teaching about the soul of Christ. That is not to say that this particular point of Christian doctrine only then gained general acceptance and recognition. Often it may merely have been that the language was clarified and the question brought out into the open. Of course the new recognition was not always organically integrated into the total picture of Jesus Christ. Even now, the stress on Christ's human soul sometimes made comparatively little difference. Nor did everyone succeed in grasping all the theological implications of a human spiritual life in Christ. The anti-Arian and anti-Apollinarian arguments of the period are an example of this failure to think through the idea of the 'complete humanity' of the Lord, as we can still see from Cyril's pre-Ephesine christology. Nevertheless, a change is unmistakable.

We shall now study first of all some groups of theologians who were particularly involved, either as friends or as foes, in the controversy over Origen's legacy.[1] There are surprises here for fourth-century christology. Some of the results worked out by these groups could already have helped to solve, or even to avoid, the debates at Ephesus. No use was made of them. In any case, our study will reveal a great variety of christological views: among the Alexandrians, the Cappadocians and some outsiders, who are also examined here.

1. THE ALEXANDRIAN DEVELOPMENT OF A CHRISTOLOGICAL PSYCHOLOGY

Didymus of Alexandria (313?–398) is one of the most significant examples of the new trend of fourth-century christology. At first one might suppose that like Athanasius he belonged among those who thought and spoke in the framework of the Logos-sarx christology. But this was possible only as long as it was felt that *Ctr. Eunomium* IV and V, ascribed to Basil, could be attributed to him. This assumption is no longer tenable.[2]

[1] For the omnipresence of Origen's basic ideas in Greek theology see J. Kirchmeyer, 'Grecque (Eglise)', *Dictionnaire de Spiritualité* 6, 1967, 808–72 (*imago-similitudo*: role of the incarnation).
[2] *Ctr. Eun.* IV, V are to be found in PG 29, 672–773. Against the attribution of these books to Didymus are: C. Bizer, *Studien zu den pseudathanasianischen Dialogen. Der Orthodoxos und Aëtios*, Diss. Bonn 1966, Rotaprint 1970, revised, 213ff.; B. Pruche, 'Didyme l'Aveugle est-il bien l'auteur des livres Contra Eunomium IV et V attribués à Saint Basile de Césarée?', *StudPat* X (TU 107), 151–5; W. A. Bienert, *'Allegoria' und 'Anagoge' bei Didymos dem Blinden von Alexandria*, Berlin–New York 1972, 10–12; ibid., 5–31 on the person and work of Didymus. To him should be attributed only *De spiritu sancto*, the writing against the Manichees and (with reservations) the *catena* fragments, and now

During the dispute with Arianism, Apollinarianism and docetic, dualistic Manichaeism, he clearly acknowledges the teaching of the full reality of Christ's humanity. There is evidence of this in his *In Zachariam* found at Toura in 1941.[3]

Its significance for the development of christology may be briefly summarized as follows:

> Didyme insiste sur la réalité de l'Incarnation, qui n'a pas eu lieu en apparence (contre les docètes) (III, 306; IV, 125). Le Verbe de Dieu fait chair et sang (I, 27) a assumé l'homme complet, âme, corps, esprit, ψυχή, σῶμα, νοῦς (IV, 235), âme et corps (I, 193), âme et chair (I, 280), âme d'un homme parfait (IV, 92). La chair est toute sainte, puisqu'elle est formée à partir du Saint-Esprit survenu en Marie (I, 177). L'âme de Jésus est sans péché ni aucune souillure (I, 177, 281; II, 361).[4]

The soul of Christ in the texts quoted is considered particularly as a physical factor. But Didymus is reaching for a stronger evaluation of Christ's soul in its theological aspect. Its functions of bearing the original image of God and of offering complete obedience to God are recognized.[5] On the other hand, the soteriological argument *quod non est assumptum non est sanatum*, well known elsewhere since the time of Irenaeus, Tertullian and Origen, plays hardly any part. It is in contrast to the Arians that Didymus insists on the reality of the soul of Christ. The human spirit is now made the 'changeable' principle of Christ's spiritual suffering, temptation and being proved.[6]

above all the Old Testament commentaries on Genesis, Job, Zechariah, Psalms and Ecclesiastes found at Toura in 1941. It was not possible to make use of A. Heron, *Studies in the Trinitarian Writings of Didymus the Blind: His Authorship of the Adversus Eunomium IV–V and the De Trinitate* (dissertation of the Protestant Faculty of the University of Tübingen, 1972, and not yet published).

[3] L. Doutreleau, *Didyme l'Aveugle, Sur Zacharie I–III* (SC 83–5), Paris 1962. Ibid. I, 17–22, on the literary work of Didymus. Also available are: (1) A. Kehl, *Der Psalmenkommentar von Tura Quaternio IX (Pap. Colon. Theol. 1)* (Sonderreihe Papyrologica Coloniensia Vol. 1), Köln–Opladen 1964; (2) *Didymos der Blinde Psalmenkommentar (Tura-Papyrus)*, Teil I: *Kommentar zu Psalm 20–21* (L. Doutreleau–A. Gesché–M. Gronewald), Bonn 1969; Teil II: *Komm. z. Psalm 22–26, 10* (M. Gronewald), Bonn 1968; Teil III: *Komm. z. Psalm 29–34* (in conjunction with A. Gesché and M. Gronewald), 1969; Teil IV: *Komm. z. Psalm 35–39* (M. Gronewald), Bonn 1969; (3) *Kommentar zu Hiob*: Teil I. *Komm. z. Hiob Kap. 1–4* (A. Henrichs); Teil II: *Komm. z. Hiob 5, 1–6, 29* (A. Henrichs); Teil III: *Komm. z. Hiob 7, 20c–11* (Ursula Hagedorn–L. Hagedorn–L. Koenen), Bonn 1968; (4) *Didymos der Blinde Kommentar zum Ecclesiastes* (Tura-Papyrus 9): Teil VI: *Komm. z. Eccl. Kap. 11–12* (G. Binder–L. Liesenborghs), Bonn 1969.

[4] L. Doutreleau, op. cit., 1, 78, see 77–9. For the following see A. Gesché, 'L'âme humaine de Jésus dans la christologie du IVe siècle', *RHE*, 54, 1959, 385–425, especially 416–18 (cited hereafter as Gesché I); id., *La christologie du 'Commentaire sur les psaumes découvert a Toura'* (cited hereafter as Gesché II).

[5] Gesché I, 396, 399.

[6] A passage from Ps.-Didymus, *De Trinitate* III, 21: PG 39, 904AB, may be cited as a parallel: *Quomodo praeterea nosse potuissemus, eum factum esse carnem animatam vere, non vero imaginarie, cum ipsum putent Manichaei quidem, corpus apparenter habuisse, Ariani vero, fuisse inanimatum; nisi dixisset: 'Tristis est anima mea,' et timorem ostendisset, et cibum, ac potum, et somnum cepisset? Haec enim neque deitati conveniunt, neque carni inanimatae. Nam quod spectat quidem ad corpus, eae tantum in ipso passiones intelliguntur, quae corpus ipsum labefactare valent atque corrumpere, non vero animae passiones, quae ob penuriam rerum necessariarum aut utilium in nobis exoriuntur. Quod vero spectat ad animam, in ea deprehenduntur curae ac sollicitudines ob ipsas passiones susceptae* ... Cf. 2 (797A); 4 (829D); 21 (900A); 30 (949B); *In Ps.* 15 (1232C); *In Ps.* 23 (1297B); others in J. Liébaert, *S. Cyrille*, 152–3. Ps.-Didymus, *De Trinitate*, written after 379; cf. G. Bardy, *Didyme l'Aveugle*, Paris 1910, 30–1; cf. L. Béranger, *Etudes sur la christologie du De Trinitate, attribué à Didyme d'Alexandrie* (Thèse de doctorat), Lyon 1959–60

Of considerable interest for a psychology of Christ are the remains of a *Commentary on the Psalms* which were also found at Toura in 1941. Of course the authenticity of this commentary has not yet been fully established.[7] It does, however, certainly derive from the same environment as Didymus. Here we surely have the deepest recognitions of the significance and activity of Christ's human soul to appear in the fourth century. The commentary improves on the Antiochenes by incorporating its insights in an Alexandrian picture of Christ, centred on the Logos. In this way the danger of a 'divisive christology' is avoided. Only its Origenism, the best features of which are used here, once more somewhat jeopardizes what has been gained. The proper reply to the Arians, who would ascribe the spiritual sufferings of Christ to the Logos, indeed to a created Logos, is now clear. The gap left by Athanasius is filled:

> Now as the soul which Jesus took is something other than the Trinity (ἄλλη ἐστὶν παρὰ τὴν Τριάδα), it is by nature created to endure *propatheia* and the beginning of amazement (πέφυκεν δέχεσθαι προπάθειαν καὶ ἀρχὴν τοῦ θαμβεῖσθαι).[8]

Christ's soul, endowed with a true human understanding (*nous*), does not therefore share the immutability[9] and impassibility of the Godhead. By nature it is completely subordinate to the laws of creatureliness and also in fact experienced the natural weaknesses, like fear and anguish. Christ's human spirit, of the same nature as ours (ὁμοούσιος), can even be in a state of real, though only incipient, crisis, in προπάθεια.[10] This state is called *propatheia* because it occurs *before* the onset of a real *passio* (πάθος) in which the soul leaves a state of equilibrium and is subject to sin.[11] Eusebius of Emesa found it hard to interpret the sufferings of the soul (see above) and Cyril of Alexandria will have his difficulties, both because they start from a neo-Platonic anthropology. A more Aristotelian conception of the body-soul relationship coupled with a clear idea of the relationship between the divine Logos and the human soul in Christ now make possible a better answer to the difficulties raised by the Arians. Even the Apollinarian demands for Christ to be incapable of sinning are to

(dactylographié). This study was not available to me. For the question of the authenticity of *De Trinitate* see L. Doutreleau, 'Le *De Trinitate* est-il de Didyme l'Aveugle?', *RSR* 45, 1957, 514–57, and above W. A. Bienert. For its authenticity, Gesché II, 353–4.

[7] Cf. Gesché II, 322–417; L. Doutreleau, *Didyme l'Aveugle, Sur Zachariam* I 22, n. 1, who refers to the editor of Vol. 8 of the *Papyrus in Psalmos*, A. Kehl of Cologne. The latter suggests that the *Commentary* was edited by a pupil of Didymus.

[8] Text XVIII, 10⁴⁻⁵: Gesché II, 135.

[9] Incarnation is conceived of as an 'alteration', ἀλλοίωσις (cf. *Pss.* 33. 1; 44. 1; 76. 11). This idea is to be found in Origen, Eusebius of Caesarea, Gregory of Nyssa (*Vit. Moys.* II, 28) and Cyril of Alexandria: the divine nature remains unchanged, but by condescension it changes into our form. Cf. Gesché II, 249–66; J. Daniélou, *RSR* 52, 1964, 133–5.

[10] See Gesché II, 148–99.

[11] Gesché II, 181–3, has the following description of *propatheia*: 'Un émoi passager, instantané, non délibéré, inhérent à la nature de l'âme raisonnable, une épreuve, un état critique, à ne confondre avec la passion (πάθος).' The *Commentary on the Psalms* deals with *propatheia* in eight places, mostly from a christological point of view. Cf. Gesché II, 150–81, 198f.

some extent satisfied. The idea and concept of *propatheia* plays an important role here. An old legacy of Philo and Origen again makes its presence felt though Origen himself did not use the concept of *propatheia* christologically.[12] Remarkably enough, Jerome does just this.[13]

As has been intimated, the *Commentary on the Psalms* also goes into the problem of Christ's sinlessness, the special concern of the Apollinarians. Of course it does not advance as far as the idea of the impossibility of Christ's sinning (*impeccabilitas*), which even now is hard to envisage theologically; it simply recognizes an actual lack of sin (*impeccantia de facto*). This is, however, open to a deeper understanding in the direction of that *impeccabilitas* which later theology asserts more nearly of Christ's human nature in the light of the unity of person with the Logos.

Thus the *Commentary on the Psalms* connects the *propatheia* and hence the possibility of temptation and testing with this sinlessness of Christ. Only in this way can Christ's soul be said to remain truly human. Only in this way can there be any basis for merit there.[14] This is a theological insight which stands with the best of the christology of its time. Even modern interpretations have advanced little beyond it.

The doubtful element in the *Commentary* is the typically Origenistic explanation of Christ's sinlessness. The soul of Jesus is pre-existent and its freedom is already proved in this state. It alone of all created spirits did not descend by a fall into the land of death.[15] It alone has always remained bound up with the Logos.[16] Without knowing it, the author of the *Commentary* has thus already opened the way towards a speculative explanation of the unity in Christ, albeit a false one. For this unity is really built upon the moral conduct of Christ's soul[17]—an interpretation which had already been given by Origen (see above). With a fortunate inconsistency, however, the *Commentary*, like Origen, compensates for this mistake by understanding the whole picture of Christ in the light of the Logos, in good Alexandrian fashion. Christ is the Logos made flesh.

The passages used by the *Commentary* to interpret Christ are Phil. 2. 7

---

[12] Origen, *Selecta in Psalmos*, in Ps. 4. 5: PG 12, 1141D-1144B; Gesché II, 191-7, where texts from Didymus, from the *Commentary on the Psalms*, and from Jerome are cited.

[13] Jerome, *Comm. in Ev. Matt.* IV, in Matt. 26. 37: PL 26, 197AB: *Illud quod supra diximus de passione et propassione, etiam in praesenti capitulo ostenditur, quod Dominus, ut ueritatem probaret assumpti hominis, uere quidem contristatus sit, sed ne passio in animo illius dominaretur, per propassionem coeperit contristari. Aliud est enim contristari, et aliud incipere contristari.* Cf. Gesché II, 197, n. 1.

[14] Cf. Text XIV, 147[ff.]: Gesché II, 164: if no *propatheia* is ascribed to the soul of Christ, ἄλλην οὐσίαν εἰσάγεις ψυχῆς, καὶ οὐδὲ κλέος ἔχει, οὐδὲ ἀξία ἐστὶν ἐπαίνων καὶ στεφάνων, μὴ κλονηθεῖσα.

[15] Cf. Gesché II, 201.

[16] Text III, 119-17: Gesché II, 139: Μονογενὴς οὖν αὐτῷ ἐστιν αὕτη ἡ ψυχὴ παρὰ τὰς ἄλλας, ὅτι μόνη ἔχει τὸ ἀεὶ συνεῖναι αὐτῷ· οὐ χωρίζει αὐτὴν οὐ λογισμός, οὐκ ἐνθύμημα, οὐ ταραχή.

[17] Cf. Text XIV, 136-7: ibid, 209: οὐδέποτε ἄλλου τινὸς γέγονεν ἢ τοῦ ἀναλαβόντος αὐτήν. Διὰ τοῦτο μονογενῆ αὐτὴν ἑαυτοῦ λέγει, as though the preservation of the unity with the Logos depended on the free decision of Christ's soul. The freedom of Christ's soul is thus referred not merely to the undergoing of moral proving in an earthly existence but also to the preservation of the divine-human unity itself.

and Heb. I. 3.[18] In a comment on Ps. 30. 17, the Logos is introduced speaking to the Father. He says of himself that he is the image of the substance of the Father and has taken the form of a servant. The question of the unity of God and man in Christ is not made a theme of the *Commentary*, which is above all concerned to make clear the two realities in Christ, his divinity against the Arians and his humanity against the Arians and the Apollinarians.[19] To designate this twofold reality the author chooses a significant concept which has been familiar to us since the time of the Apologists and which will later be the stumbling block in the Nestorian controversy: Jesus had two 'prosopa', one human and one divine.[20] 'Prosopon' here has its old meaning, 'manner of appearance' (*mode de manifestation*). The twofold reality of Christ reveals itself in the two prosopa. There is still no suggestion of the content of 'person' in the later sense. This is important for the understanding of the preliminary history of Nestorianism. The acceptance of 'two prosopa' in Christ can—as the *Commentary* shows—go with an Alexandrian christology. In the time of Cyril and Nestorius the two will be felt to be utterly irreconcilable. It is also worth noticing that in this context the concepts of μορφή and χαρακτήρ also appear alongside 'prosopon', as a result of the biblical texts in question, Phil. 2. 7 and Heb. I. 3.[21] The same connection occurs in Theodore of Mopsuestia and will meet us again in the Cappadocians and eventually in Nestorius. Finally, the Stoa stands in the background. If we are to understand the significance of this christology, we must remember the influence which emanated for a full half century from Didymus as director of the Catechetical School at Alexandria.

It is interesting to see how other Alexandrians developed teaching on the soul of Christ and a christological psychology in the time between Athanasius and Cyril of Alexandria. Certainly no one reaches the heights of the Toura *Commentary on the Psalms*. *Peter II of Alexandria*, the successor to Athanasius, professed an acknowledgement of the complete manhood of Jesus Christ when a delegate to the anti-Apollinarian Synod held at Rome in 377.[22] His confession of 'two persons' in Christ is to be noted. Facundus of Hermiane has preserved a passage of his *Letter to the Egyptian Bishops banished for the Faith*, where Peter distinguishes between the Son of Man born of Mary and the Word who, according to the Old Testament (Proverbs), is Son of God. There the Holy Spirit is '*duas personas significans, de homine quidem ex Maria creato et plasmato, de illo vero,*

---

[18] Cf. Text X, 5[14-18]: Gesché II, 270-4 (with comment).

[19] Cf. Text XIX, 9[17-22]: Gesché II, 318: οὐχ εἷς ἐστιν (i.e. he does not have merely one reality) ἄνθρωπος καὶ θεός ἐστιν. Or on Ps. 30. 18, Gesché II, 319: οὐ μόνος ἄνθρωπός ἐστιν οὐδὲ μόνος θεός.

[20] Cf. Text X, 7[22]: Gesché II, 316: Δύο πρόσωπα εἶχεν Ἰησοῦς, ἀνθρώπου καὶ θεοῦ.

[21] Thus in Text X, 5[14-18]: Gesché II, 271. Like the *Commentary*, Didymus uses biblical language in christology which avoids the technical expressions and concepts which are already used very frequently by the Apollinarian opponents.

[22] Theodoret, HE V, 10: ed. Parmentier, 297. On the dating of the Synod see the survey: M. A. Norton, 'Prosopography of Pope Damasus', *Folia* 5, 1951, 46-9.

qui ante saecula est sine principio, et aeternae nativitatis.'[23] In this quotation, 'persona' implies no more than the reality of the two natures. We found the same terminology in the *Commentary* of Toura. Alexandria therefore has the formula of the 'two persons' in Christ as early as Antioch or even earlier.

In acknowledging the complete manhood of Christ, later Alexandrian tradition takes the same course as Didymus, the *Commentary* and Peter II, though some after-effects of the Logos-sarx christology are still apparent for a long time. In his 17th Easter Festal Letter, Theophilus (385–412) Cyril's uncle, is an energetic defender of belief in the true manhood of Jesus.[24] In his polemic against Apollinarius (esp. nos. 4–8) he demonstrates the reality of Christ's soul particularly from the so-called 'soteriological argument' which we know from Irenaeus, Tertullian and Origen and which we shall find above all in Gregory of Nazianzus: that alone is redeemed which is taken by Christ in the incarnation. Though Theophilus well describes the acts of Christ's manhood and their appropriation by the Logos (on the basis of the *communicatio idiomatum*, Mansi 10, 1092D), he is not as successful as the *Commentary* of Toura. The basis for a human psychology of Christ has once again become narrower.

His other opponent is, of course, Origen. He charges him with teaching that it was not the Godhead, but the soul of Christ, which took flesh:

> He dared to say that the soul of the Saviour emptied itself and took the form of a servant, so that John, who said 'The Word became flesh', may be deemed a liar . . . since it is not the Word himself who emptied himself and took the form of a servant, but his soul.[25]

As a result, for Origen the Godhead and the soul of Christ, indeed even human souls themselves, are identical: '*in forma enim et aequalitate dei animam saluatoris affirmans.*'[26]

Perhaps Theophilus was thinking of the texts from the *Peri Archon* (II, 6, 3) which describe the inward conjunction of Logos and pre-existent soul.[27] As we shall see, however, he reads Origen through Evagrius Ponticus.[28] It is a remarkable shift of positions: because of his subordinationism and his teaching about the soul of Christ, Origen is, in fact,

---

[23] Peter II Ep. Al., *Ep. ad Eppos. Aeg.*: PG 33, 1291D–1293A.

[24] Theophilus Al., *Ep. Paschalis* 17—Ep. 98 in Jerome: ed. Hilberg, CSEL 55, 185–211 (a. 402); cf. H. Lietzmann, *Apollinaris*, 76; R. Delobel—M. Richard, 'Théophile', *DTC* 15, 523–30; A. Favale S.D.B., *Teofilo d'Alessandria* (Biblioteca del 'Salesianum' 41), Torino 1958, 5–34 (works of Th.); 199–205 (christology).

[25] Theophilus Al., *Ep. paschalis* 17: ed. Hilberg, CSEL 55, 198.

[26] Ibid., 199 (with 198).

[27] See above on Origen. Cf. Theophilus, *Ep. paschalis* 16: ed. Hilberg, CSEL 55, 152: *praeterea in libris Περὶ Ἀρχῶν etiam hoc persuadere conatur, quod . . . non fuerit uerbum dei, sed anima de caelesti regione descendens et se de forma aeternae maiestatis euacuans humanum corpus adsumpserit. . . .* Cf. A. Guillaumont, *Les 'Kephalaia Gnostica' d'Evagre le Pontique et l'histoire de l'origénisme chez les Grecs et chez les Syriens* (Patristica Sorbonensia 5), Paris 1962, 96–101.

[28] Cf. A. Guillaumont, op. cit., 119.

ranked with Arianism and Apollinarianism. Theophilus' own arrival at a clear doctrine of the soul of Christ is not in the end a legacy of Origen himself. Once again it is evident that the history of fourth-century christology cannot be explained along the lines of 'Alexandria here'— 'Antioch there'. There are internal developments on both sides which reveal considerable conflicts. Only the supremacy of Cyril of Alexandria and his opposition to the Antiochenes will produce united fronts on both sides.

2. CAPPADOCIAN CHRISTOLOGY

Outside Alexandria, we find traces of a similar development on all sides. *Epiphanius* is a zealous promoter of orthodoxy (see above). The movement does not, however, progress everywhere with the same speed. In about 374, the Bishop of Cyprus tried in vain to interest Basil in the question.[29] But once the urgency of the theological problem was recognized, Cappadocian theology too made its own positive contribution towards the solution of the outstanding questions. *Basil* (died 379) himself naturally maintains his attitude of restraint. He does not comment on christology as an opponent of Arianism or Apollinarianism but rather as a critic of local errors, such as a partial resurgence of docetism, shown by his *Epistle* 261 to the people of Sozopolis and *Epistle* 262 to the monk Urbicius (PG 32, 968–72, 973–6). In these letters he has nothing striking to say about the nature of the incarnate Logos. His language remains within the customary limits (ἐνανθρώπησις, σάρκωσις, ἐνσωμάτωσις) and his illustrations and similes are in no way unusual. One sentence, however, shows how Cappadocian christology is approaching 'Antiochene' conceptions: 'The flesh of Christ is "bearer of the Godhead" made holy by union with God.'[30]

Basil's christology is more concerned to distinguish the divine and human characteristics in Christ than to stress the unity of person (in the language of the *communicatio idiomatum*).[31] Christ's humanity, with a created soul, becomes the subject of human suffering, of growth and progress and of ignorance of the day of judgement (*Ep.* 236, 1–2; PG 32, 876–80). In his letter to the people of Sozopolis, Basil gives a clearer explanation of the actual extent of such human suffering in Christ. There is no suffering in the Godhead itself. The subject of the πάθη is either the flesh, the flesh endowed with a soul, or just the soul, in so far as it makes

---

[29] Cf. Basil, *Ep.* 258: PG 32, 948–53. See the chapter on Apollinarianism. For the whole question see B. Otis, 'Cappadocian Thought as a Coherent System', *DOP* 12, 1958, 95–124.

[30] Basil, *Hom. in Ps.* XLV, 4: PG 29, 424 B: Τάχα τὴν σάρκα λέγει τὴν θεοφόρον, ἁγιασθεῖσαν διὰ τῆς πρὸς τὸν θεὸν συναφείας.

[31] Id., *Ep.* 236, 1: PG 32, 877BC: *Atque is quidem qui petebat (da mihi bibere), non erat caro inanimata, sed divinitas carne animata utens.*

use of the body (as an instrument). The flesh may be destroyed; flesh endowed with a soul may be weary and suffer, feel hunger and thirst; the soul that has made use of a body is subject to griefs, anxieties and cares. Of these, some are natural and necessary to the living being, others are brought on by a perverse will and lack of training in virtue. Whereas Christ took upon himself the former group to show the reality of his incarnation, the latter group, which contaminates the purity of our lives, has no place in him (*Ep.* 261, 3: PG 32, 972AB). It is thus sufficiently clear that Basil considers the soul of Christ as a 'theological factor' such as would answer Arianism and save the 'Logos' and his transcendence. This way was not found by Athanasius. But Basil does not appreciate all the implications of the presence of a human soul in Christ. He is only concerned to protect it from all sinful emotions, and does not think to transfer to it the spiritual decisions which are decisive for our redemption. The high point of the *Commentary* of Toura, which was not known to Basil, is not reached by him. It is very hard for the fourth-century Fathers to achieve a psychology of Jesus and a theology of the humanity of Christ, or a full christological anthropology, as we would say today. But are we better than the Fathers?

The christological position of *Gregory of Nazianzus* (died about 390) is at first very similar to that of his friend Basil. As late as 379 he regards the problems raised by Apollinarianism as a domestic quarrel.[32] But once it is realized that Apollinarianism not only raises the question of Christ's soul but also, at least *de facto*, puts forward a theory about the unity of God and man in Christ, both Gregory of Nazianzus and Gregory of Nyssa[33] attack the problem in their own way. While laying stress on the two natures in Christ, they are able to emphasize the unity more strongly and to develop it in their teaching. But their formulation of the problem and their theory of the unity in Christ are both very incomplete. Whereas in trinitarian doctrine, as we shall see, they clearly recognized that unity and distinction in the Godhead are to be sought through different approaches, they only dimly grasped a corresponding insight into christology. Nestorius will be the first to put the problem more clearly. But his solution will not do. So far as one can see, he is strongly dependent on the Cappadocians in his explanation of the christological problem. There are two failings in the Cappadocian christology: in the first place, it seeks to explain the unity and distinction in Christ with the help of Stoic theories about the mixing of two natural things which completely permeate each other without either losing its nature. True, the fact of this Stoic back-

---

[32] Greg. Naz., *Or.* 22, 13: PG 35, 1145B. See *Ep.* 202 *ad Nectar.*: PG 37, 332A. J. Lenz, *Jesus Christus nach der Lehre des hl. Gregor von Nyssa*, Trier 1925, 61, gives some suggestions to explain the position of the Orientals.

[33] But one feels Gregory of Nyssa's embarrassment about the christological problem particularly in the writing *Ad Theophilum Adv. Apollinaristas*; ed. Jaeger III, 1 (Mueller), 124¹²–125¹⁰.

ground shows that the Cappadocians wanted to maintain both true unity and true distinction in Christ. But it also shows that they seek the interpretation of the unity on a 'natural' level. At least, that is true of this doctrine of 'mixture'. The second failing is its insufficient definition of the relationship between substance and hypostasis (prosopon). Granted that the Cappadocians' deliberations mark one phase in the history of the definition of 'nature' and 'person', in effect they still remain in the realm of material categories as a result of their philosophical starting point, as we shall see. The Cappadocians have seen something, but neither their path nor their goal is stated clearly. As a result, the solution of christological problems is made much more difficult, as will be evident in the case of Nestorius.

From this standpoint, the place of the Cappadocians in the history of christology is to be defined in a slightly different way. We shall attach rather more importance to this definition. Of course it will not be possible here to outline the full theological content of the christology of the Gregories, even to a limited degree.

Gregory of Nazianzus inherited a clear doctrine of the soul of Christ from Origen,[34] as is already clear from his sermon of 362 (*Or.* 2, 23; PG 35, 432f.). In opposition to Gregory of Nyssa, he takes over Origen's idea of the soul as mediator between Godhead and flesh (ibid.).

His letters, which were intended to protect *Cledonius* from Apollinarian influences and to stir him to action, have acquired a great reputation. The basis of his doctrine of two natures becomes particularly significant against the background of the Apollinarian physis-concept: 'There are two natures, God and man (in Christ), as (there are in him) both soul and body.'[35] Thus the humanity of Jesus is a physis, because it consists of body and soul. So Gregory seems to take the Apollinarian physis-concept into account, to draw from it the consequences for his own christological formula, which sounds very 'Antiochene'. He expressly sets the two frameworks, '*Deus carnifer*' and '*homo deifer*', one against the other and declares himself for the latter (*Ep.* 102; PG 37, 200BC). This opposition presupposes the Apollinarian understanding of 'Logos-sarx'.

There is yet another significant element in his teaching, an element which can be understood in the light of the special Cappadocian interest in trinitarian speculations. For the first time in Greek theology, trinitarian

[34] For Gregory's christology see K. Holl, *Amphilochius von Ikonium in seinem Verhältnis zu den grossen Kappadoziern*, Tübingen–Leipzig 1904, 178–96; E. Weigl, *Christologie v. Tode d. Athanasius bis zum Ausbruch des nestorianischen Streites*, München 1925, 53–79; L. Stephan, *Die Soteriologie des hl. Gregor von Nazianz*, Wien 1938. For further literature see J. Barbel, *Gregor v. Nazianz, Die fünf Theologischen Reden* (Testimonia III), Düsseldorf 1963, 24–8; D. F. Winslow, 'Christology and Exegesis in the Cappadocians,' *Church History* 40, 1971, 389–96.

[35] Greg. Naz., *Ep.* 101 ad Cledon. I: PG 37, 180A; cf. *Ep.* 102 ad Cledon. II: ibid. 201B. On the date of the second letter see P. Galley, *La vie de saint Grégoire de Nazianze*, Lyon–Paris 1943, who suggests 386. Against this, M. Richard agrees with H. Lietzmann for 382: *MSR* 2, 1945, 189–90.

concepts are applied to the christological formula, though only within the limits of a popular terminology. Difficult concepts are not yet used. Gregory uses a most illuminating distinction, which describes the unity in Christ and the difference of the natures by extremely simple linguistic means, producing a parallel with trinitarian dogma: in Christ there is no 'ἄλλος καὶ ἄλλος' but 'ἄλλο καὶ ἄλλο'. In the Trinity, on the other hand, the relationship is reversed: Ἐκεῖ μὲν γὰρ ἄλλος καὶ ἄλλος, ἵνα μὴ τὰς ὑποστάσεις συγχέωμεν, οὐκ ἄλλο δὲ καὶ ἄλλο, ἓν γὰρ τὰ τρία καὶ ταυτὸν τῇ θεότητι (PG 37, 180AB). The interchange between masculine and neuter is a first step towards a conceptual distinction of 'person' and 'nature'.

The christology of Gregory of Nazianzus, however, springs not so much from speculative theological reflection as from his spiritual disposition. For his attention is taken up with the idea of the divinization of man, an idea for which the divinization of Christ's human nature is to supply the theological foundation:

And that (the cause of his birth) was that you might be saved who insult him and despise his Godhead, because of this, that he took upon him your denser nature (τὴν σὴν παχύτητα) having conjunction with the flesh by means of the mind. While his inferior nature, the humanity, became God because it was conjoined with God and became one (with him). In this the stronger part (sc. the Godhead) prevailed in order that I too might be made God so far as he is made man (Or. 29, 19: PG 36, 100A).

The christology of *Gregory of Nyssa* (died 394) is to be found in its finest form in the *Great Catechetical Oration* (*Or. cat. m.*: PG 45, 9–105). Here we have an outline of the church's dogma which has a true stamp about it. 'Theology' and 'economy' are clearly distinct, yet are involved together. Like a catechism, as the title of the work suggests, the whole makes up a theological triptych; the 'economy' is divided into the description of the historical realization of salvation in Christ and its appropriation in the sacraments and in faith in the triune God.[36]

---

[36] Cf. A. Grillmeier, 'Vom Symbolum zur Summa', in: J. Betz-H. Fries (ed.), *Kirche und Überlieferung*, Freiburg–Basel–Wien 1960, 150–2 (*Or. cat. m.*). For Gregory's christology: J. Lenz, *Jesus Christus nach der Lehre des hl. Gregor von Nyssa*, Trier 1925 (more a description of the material); K. Holl, *Amphilochius v. Iconium in seinem Verhältnis zu den grossen Kappadoziern*, Tübingen–Leipzig 1904, 196–235: J. Rivière, *Le dogme de la rédemption*, Paris 1905², 151–9, 384–7 (death of Christ); J. Daniélou, *Platonisme et Théologie mystique*, Paris 1944; for Gregory's spirituality: A. Lieske, 'Zur Theologie der Christusmystik Gregors v. N.', *Schol* 14, 1939, 485–514; id., 'Die Theologie der Christusmystik Gregors v. N.', *ZkTh* 70, 1948, 49–93, 129–68, 315–40; W. Völker, *Gregor v. N. als Mystiker*, Wiesbaden 1955, 8–22, critical survey of work done on Gregory; 219–24, Christ-mysticism. Cf. now J.-R. Bouchet, O.P., 'Le vocabulaire de l'union et du rapport des natures chez saint Grégoire de Nysse', *RevThom* 68, 1968, 533–82; a good analysis of Gregory's terminology, but without taking into account *Ep.* 38 by Ps.-Basil; he also indicates the philosophical presuppositions (Stoics, Aristotle, Philo, Neo-Platonists) and Greek medicine (pp. 553–60); id., 'La vision de l'économie du salut selon s. Grégoire de Nysse', *RSPT* 52, 1968, 613–44 (analysis of *Sermo in diem natalem Christi*, PG 46, 1128A–1148B, and the *Oratio catechetica magna*, chs. VIII–XXII); on this see *Gregor v. Nyssa, Die grosse katechetische Rede, Oratio catechetica magna*, with introduction, German translation and commentary by J. Barbel (Bibliothek der griechischen Literatur 1), Stuttgart 1971, with good christological commentaries. R. Hübner, 'Gregor von Nyssa als Verfasser der sog. Ep. 38 des Basilius. Zum unterschiedlichen Verständnis der beiden kappadozischen Brüder', *Epektasis*, 463–90, is an important

Here Gregory speaks as preacher of the *mysterium Christi*. In his other works he becomes the speculative interpreter of it. In comparison with his namesake of Nazianzus, Gregory's language is much more diphysite in tone. The reason for this lies in his dispute with the *Apodeixis* of Apollinarius. Flesh and Logos are described each as a separate physis to combat the Apollinarian 'one physis' doctrine.[37] The *'homo assumptus'* formula occurs frequently in his writings. He takes great trouble to think out the theological significance of the soul of Christ as a real redemptive principle.[38] The cause of Christ's death on the cross is the separation of soul and body, not that of Godhead and manhood.[39] Despite this strong emphasis on the distinction of the natures in Christ, which sometimes inspired Gregory to Nestorian formulas,[40] the unity is explained basically in categories of 'mingling'.[41] Again, we also find the idea of the divinization of Christ's manhood through the Logos. As the 'power of the most High', he takes 'servant form', the substance (*hypostasis*) which is born of the Virgin, to raise it to his own exalted status and to transform it into the pure and divine nature.[42] The famous simile of the absorption of the flesh in the Godhead 'like a drop of vinegar in the sea'[43] is extremely bold theological language. Gregory nevertheless attempts to mark out the correct limits. He cannot be completely successful, as he builds up the unity in Christ on the relationship of nature to nature, both taken as such. The flesh mingled with the Godhead does not remain within its own limitations and properties,[44] but is taken up into the heights of the overwhelming and transcending nature. Careful consideration can distinguish the proper-

---

study; of course, Hübner does not know the study by A. B. Fediuk (see below). In addition see R Hübner, 'Gregor von Nyssa und Markell von Ankyra', *Écriture et culture philosophique dans la pensée de Grégoire de Nysse. Actes du Colloque de Chevetogne (22–26 Sept. 1969)*, ed. Marguerite Harl, Leiden 1971, 199–229; ibid., 207, n. 2, also a short summary of the question of *Ep.* 38 among the letters of Basil (for this there is also a reference to Y. Courtonne, *Saint Basile. Lettres* I, Paris 1957, 81–92, with a French translation); Hübner, op. cit., 210, refers to his dissertation *Die Einheit des Leibes Christi bei Gregor von Nyssa. Untersuchungen zum Ursprung der physischen Erlösungslehre*, 1969, published Leiden 1974. See also P. Zemp, *Die Grundlagen heilsgeschichtlichen Denkens bei Gregor von Nyssa* (Münch-TheolStud II, 38), München 1970, esp. ch. 7: 'Die Zeit der Menschheit als Heilsgeschichte', pp. 209–45.

[37] Greg. Nyss., *Ant. adv. Apoll.* 18–19: ed. Jaeger III, 1 (Mueller), 154–8 : PG 45, 1157A–1164A.

[38] Greg. Nyss., ibid. 32, cf. 24: ed. Jaeger (Mueller), 180–2, 166–8: PG 45, 1192D–1196A, 1173–1176.

[39] Cf. Greg. Nyss., ibid. 30: ed. Jaeger (Mueller), 179¹⁻⁷: PG 45, 1189D; ibid. 55: ed. Jaeger (Mueller), 226¹³ᶠᶠ.: PG 45, 1260AC. Cf. A. Grillmeier, *ZkTh* 71, 1949, 184–7, where Ps-Athanasius, *C. Apollinarium*, is also quoted. See id., *Mit ihm und in ihm*, Freiburg 1975, I, 2.

[40] Greg. Nyss., ibid. 58: ed. Jaeger (Mueller), 231¹²⁻¹⁴: PG 45, 1265C (Lat.: *Si unus cum Patre factus est Christus, quomodo unus cum Deo qui in ipso est non evasit? Ita et homo Christus, alius existens* [ἕτερος ὤν], *Deo qui in ipso est coniunctus fuit*).

[41] Greg. Nyss., ibid. 21, 26, 51, 55: ed. Jaeger (Mueller), 161, 171, 217, 225: PG 45, 1165CD, 1180C, 1245C, 1257BC.

[42] Greg. Nyss., ibid., 25: ed. Jaeger (Mueller), 169f.: PG 45, 1177C.

[43] Greg. Nyss., ibid., 42: ed. Jaeger (Mueller), 201: PG 45, 1221C–1224A; id., *Ad Theoph. Adv. Apoll.*: ed. Jaeger (Mueller), 126¹⁷⁻²¹: PG 45, 1276D; id., *C. Eunomium* III, 4: ed. Jaeger II, 1960, 150, no. 43: PG 45, 728D.

[44] Greg. Nyss., *Ant. adv. Apoll.* 42: ed. Jaeger (Mueller), 201¹¹⁻²⁴; PG 45, 1124AB; ibid. 53: ed. Jaeger (Mueller), 222²⁷⁻⁹: PG 45, 1253B: οὔτε μετὰ τὴν εἰς οὐρανοὺς ἄνοδον ἔτι ἡ σὰρξ ἐν τοῖς ἑαυτῆς ἰδιώμασιν.

ties of the flesh and of the Godhead in an unmingled state only when each of the natures is examined by itself.[45] This transformation of manhood into Godhead already begins with Christ's conception in a virgin.[46] The divine formation of Christ's body is a unique instance. After his earthly life and passion there follows a still more far-reaching transformation.[47] Christ's second coming does not therefore take place in human form.[48] His manhood seems to be done away with. Gregory's Origenism is particularly evident here.[49] He himself seems to feel the dangers in his explanation. Then he is even led to posit some independence for Christ's human nature. Occasionally he assigns it a separate prosopon or hypostasis.[50]

In assessing this christology of Basil's brother, we must examine rather more closely one of the metaphysical presuppositions common to all three Cappadocians. These are not, of course, as developed for christology as they are for trinitarian doctrine. What is involved is an analysis of *ousia*, *hypostasis* and *prosopon* as used to explain the Unity and Trinity in God. In the Arian controversy it was important to show the different levels on which the Unity or Trinity in God was to be sought. This was the only way in which at least the contradiction in the doctrine of the Nicenes, so stressed by the Eunomians, could be removed, though at the same time the Cappadocians were quite aware that the divine mystery cannot be expressed and fully clarified.

We shall probably not be far wrong if we derive this speculative attempt by the Cappadocians from the explanation of the relationship between nature and hypostasis (prosopon) in Stoic philosophy,[51] or, more accurately, from its analysis of concrete, 'physical' being (after the example of Posidonius and Plutarch). Of course, a philosophical syncretism or even eclecticism is predominant in the fourth century. The Cappadocians remain Platonists, above all, in their analysis of 'spiritual' being.

In their analysis of concrete individual being, the Stoics begin from undetermined matter (οὐσία ὕλη), the ultimate subject (πρῶτον ὑποκείμενον) which—while undetermined in itself—is defined and characterized by a quality, ποιόν. On one side there is the undetermined, the ὑποκείμενον,

[45] Greg. Nyss., *C. Eunom.* 5: ed. Jaeger II, 1960, 129f., nos. 62, 63.
[46] Greg. Nyss., *Ant. adv. Apoll.* 54–5: ed. Jaeger (Mueller), 223²⁵ᶠᶠ·; 225¹⁸⁻²¹: PG 45, 1256B–D, 1257C.
[47] Greg. Nyss., ibid. 53: ed. Jaeger (Mueller), 221²⁵ᶠᶠ·: PG 45, 1252CD (*post passionem eadem unctione unitum sibi hominem decorans*).
[48] Greg. Nyss., ibid. 57: ed. Jaeger (Mueller), 227–30: PG 45, 1261–1265. Cf. ibid. 59: ed. Jaeger (Mueller), 233¹¹¹: PG 45, 1268D: 'If (Christ) is not in the body for us who are in the body, then he is not in the body for the heavenly ones either.' Cf. PG 45, 1253, n. 25. For an explanation of these conceptions of Gregory's, see below.
[49] For Gregory's Origenism see W. Völker, op. cit., 283–95.
[50] Greg. Nyss., *Ant. adv. Apoll.*, 44 and 45: ed. Jaeger (Mueller), 204³⁰–205¹⁹: PG 45, 1128C–1229A; cf. 58: ed. Jaeger (Mueller), 231¹⁸⁻²⁵: PG 45, 1265D–1268A.
[51] Cf. L. I. Scipioni O.P., *Richerche sulla Cristologia del 'Libro di Eraclide' di Nestorio. La formulazione e il suo contesto filosofico*, Fribourg 1956, 45–67, 98–109; A. Grillmeier, 'Das *Scandalum oecumenicum* des Nestorius in kirchlich-dogmatischer und theologiegeschichtlicher Sicht', *Schol* 26, 1961, 340–3.

as substantial, passive, indeterminate and undefined matter; on the other side is what determines, τὰ ἄλλα, i.e. quality, form, whatever can be designated as a characterizing element. Among the Stoics, 'substance' is first determined by the κοινὴ ποιότης, the specifying quality. Through this it becomes a species, a κοινῶς ποιόν, e.g. the substance of a horse, say, or of a man. When the particular character, the ἰδία ποιότης, is added, it becomes ἰδίως ποιόν, an individual, Socrates, or Diogenes. Now it is worth noting that the concepts σχῆμα and χαρακτήρ, which will become very important for theology, are both already used by the Stoics to paraphrase ποιόν or the particular character.[52]

Epistle 38 of Basil, which scholars now hold to be by Gregory of Nyssa, is most important for any theological analysis of the Cappadocians.[53] In it, Ps.-Basil develops his doctrine of ousia and hypostasis. He too begins with the universal nature (κοινὴ φύσις or κοινότης τῆς φύσεως) which is proper to the different particulars of a species. Mention of the 'universal substance' does not, however, describe the particular, which is characterized through its 'particularizing characteristic' (ἴδιον, ἰδίαζον). Κοινόν and ἴδιον, κοινότης and ἰδίαζον are constantly interchanged in this work (Ps.-Basil, *Ep.* 38). The particularizing characteristic, the ἴδιον, pertains to the hypostasis, whereas 'universality' (the κοινόν) is attributed to the physis (PG 32, 328AB). The 'particularizing characteristics' (ἰδιώ-ματα) make the 'universal' a hypostasis. To these 'particularizing characteristics' belong all inward and outward properties which, say, a particular man can have: position, or the identifying peculiarities of his character (τὰ τοῦ ἤθους γνωρίσματα, PG 32, 328C). (This will be very important for the understanding of Antiochene christology. The moral conduct of a particular man is not kept apart, but is here incorporated into the ontological analysis of concrete being.) Ps.-Basil then transfers the result of his philosophical exposition to the doctrine of the Trinity (from 328C). The doctrine of the *proprietates individuales* becomes the doctrine of the persons. In the Trinity, the 'community of substance' (κατὰ τὴν οὐσίαν κοινότης) stands over against the particularizing characteristic of the identifying peculiarities (the ἰδιάζον τῶν γνωρισμάτων, PG 32, 333A). In this way, Ps.-Basil believes that he has interpreted both the unity and the distinction in the Trinity.

[52] L. I. Scipioni, op. cit., 105, mentions Simplicius, who puts σχῆμα among the ποιά with reference to the Stoics: σχήματα . . . ὥσπερ καὶ τὰ ἄλλα ποιά (*In. Aristot. Categ.* 8, 271, 20). 'E che il valore di σχῆμα riguardi direttamente il ποιόν preso nel suo senso specifico . . . lo dimostra riprendendo l'argomentazione sul ruolo essenziale della qualità nella specificazione dell'ousia: εἰδοποιοῦνται αἱ ἕξεις κατ' αὐτούς, ἰδιότητί δέ τινι καὶ χαρακτῆρι (Simplicio, *In Arist. Categ.* 8, 238, 12). Dove σχῆμα si allaccia a ἰδιότης e a χαρακτήρ.' For examples of the gradation in concrete being in the Stoic sense (ὑποκείμενον, ποιόν, κοινῶς ποιόν, ἰδίως ποιόν), see ibid., 98–101.

[53] Cf. A. B. Fediuk, *Un Commentario de San Gregorio de Nísa o bien la Carta 38 atribuida a S. Basilio Magno. Estudio sobra la tradición manuscrita*, Roma 1963, dactylogr. This study, which makes use of the works of C. Cavallin, S. Y. Rudberg, J. Gribomont, etc., was made available to me by P. A. Orbe, Pont. Univ. Gregoriana, Rome.

He now gives an example from nature to make clear this difference between nature and hypostasis. Here his special understanding of the two becomes clear. The seven-coloured rainbow with the *one* sun in the centre is an illustration of the Trinity, the three persons in one substance (PG 32, 333B–336A). The three hypostases are like a three-coloured iris which is laid over the common sun (substance). This comparison recurs in the *C. Eunomium*:

> As the body of the sun is represented (χαρακτηρίζεται!) by the whole circle which surrounds it . . . so he (the apostle) says that the might of the Father is characterized in the magnitude of the might of the Son.[54]

Hebrews 1. 3 and Phil. 2. 5–11 provide the biblical basis for this hypostasis terminology and theology (so too in PG 32, 336C).

Hypostasis, then, is the conflux of the particularizing characteristics of each member of the Trinity (εἰ γὰρ ὑπόστασιν ἀποδεδώκαμεν εἶναι τὴν συνδρομὴν τῶν περὶ ἕκαστον ἰδιωμάτων, PG 32, 336C). This *concursus* is significant: the hypostasis is formed by a whole complex of *idiomata*. Here Ps.-Basil is particularly fond of the expressions χαρακτήρ and σχῆμα (337C) to express the particularizing characteristic (the ἴδιον) of each of the three persons in the one Godhead. The term εἰκών is also suggested by Colossians (340B). Finally, *Ep.* 38 finds the term πρόσωπον to bring the whole together and to express the relationship between Father and Son along the lines of Heb. 1. 3 and Col. 1. 15:

> Thus the hypostasis of the Son becomes as it were form (μορφή) and face (πρόσωπον) of the knowledge of the Father, and the hypostasis of the Father is known in the form of the Son, while the proper quality (ἰδιότητος) which is contemplated therein remains for the plain distinction of the hypostases (PG 32, 339–40C).

The hypostasis is visible and recognizable like a countenance, a *prosopon*. That is, the identifying peculiarities make it possible to contemplate, to see, to distinguish the hypostasis. There are clearly pictorial expressions here which appear alongside Heb. 1. 3; Col. 1. 15 and probably also Phil. 2. 5–11 in the metaphysical analysis.[55]

---

[54] Greg. Nyss., *C. Eunom.* III: ed. Jaeger II, 190, no. 13. Note that this passage, like Ps.-Basil, *Ep.* 38, deals with the relationship between Father and Son. In the latter, of course, the relationship between hypostasis and nature in the Godhead is developed more fundamentally. There are some consequences from this for an assessment of the so-called Neo-Nicene theory, developed by T. Zahn and A. Harnack, that the Cappadocians merely accepted a generic identity of the divine ousia. In the light of the above analysis this theory is untenable. Further remarks in A. Grillmeier, *Schol* 36, 1961, 355, n. 98.

[55] Heb. 1. 3 also plays a part in Basil. Cf. *Hom.* 24: PG 31, 608B. Hypostasis is held to be determined by δόξα, χαρακτήρ, ἀπαύγασμα. In *Ep.* 236, 6: PG 32, 884A–C the same complex of concepts appears: εἰκών, χαρακτήρ, ἴδιον, ἰδιάζον. The particularizing characteristic is combined with the universal in the Godhead to produce the divine person, τῶν προσώπων ἰδιάζον (884C). This gives Basil the formula: one ousia, three hypostases. Basil then speaks of the other formula in which ousia and hypostasis are taken to be synonymous. He cannot accept it on his definition of the terms. In that case one would have to assume one hypostasis and three prosopa in the Godhead and this would be almost Sabellianism (32, 884C). The teaching developed here becomes very important in the iconoclastic

Prosopon, then, here has its old meaning of 'countenance', already established in Irenaeus. Gregory demonstrates the same relationship between substance and hypostasis in the composition of a work of art[56] or in the comparison of individual human beings. Peter, James and John, who are one in substance, are distinguished by the particularizing characteristics of their hypostases (ἐν δὲ τοῖς ἰδιώμασι τῆς ἑκάστου αὐτῶν ὑποστάσεως).[57] Of course, Gregory also uses prosopon for hypostasis more frequently than Basil. He is not concerned about the word.[58] He stresses the importance of these *idiomata* for the constitution of the hypostasis as the completion of the substance. If the *idiomata*, which complete the substance, are missing, a thing is denied the '*tota substantiae* (= *essentiae*) *illius ratio*'.[59] The substance as such is first completed in its reality by its particularizing characteristics or its identifying peculiarities. Only then is it visible and recognizable. This is also true for Gregory of Nazianzus.[60]

Only in the writings of Nestorius, and even in some of the Fathers up to John of Damascus, will it become apparent what the Cappadocians have and have not achieved with their hypostasis-prosopon doctrine. Although they make it clear in their analysis that the Unity and Trinity in the Godhead are to be sought on different 'levels', their doctrine of hypostasis or person is incomplete. In fact, they almost completely neglect the 'personal' element. Only in their inclusion of moral properties among the *idiomata* do they transcend the realm of material categories. Otherwise their analysis concerns the 'thing' more than the 'person'. But above all they remain fast in a realm which we may describe as individuality. It is here that they make the difficulties which Nestorius and some Fathers of the sixth century are to feel when they transfer to christology the conceptual analysis which the Cappadocians apply to the Trinity. Gregory of Nyssa, in fact, himself began this transference, though without making his readers or his hearers conscious of it. The distinction between the universal substance and the particularizing characteristics is applied to Christ's human nature so as to rob of its force the Apollinarian charge that Gregory (and all those who believe in a soul of Christ and a complete manhood of the Lord) teaches a twofold Sonship of the Lord, or two Sons. In his letter to Theophilus of Alexandria he excludes the 'two Sons'

controversy for the foundation of the theology of the icon. Cf. A. Grillmeier, 'Die Herrlichkeit Gottes auf dem Antlitz Jesu Christi. Zur Bildtheologie der Väterzeit', *Christus und die Heiligen im künstlerischen Ausdruck der Gegenwart* (Studien u. Berichte d. Kath. Akademie in Bayern, H. 22), Würzburg 1963, 55–84, esp. 745. Now in id., *Mit ihm und in ihm*, Freiburg 1975, I, 1.

[56] Cf. Greg. Nyss., *C. Eunom.* III, 2: ed. W. Jaeger II, 74, no. 68: PG 45, 641D.

[57] Ibid. I: ed. Jaeger I, 93, no. 227. Cf. no. 228: PG 45, 320. This last comparison would support the Neo-Nicene theory mentioned above, but only if it were taken in isolation from Gregory's other explanations.

[58] Cf. S. González, *La formula* MIA 'ΟΥΣΙΑ ΤΡΕΙΣ 'ΥΠΟΣΤΑΣΕΙΣ *en San Gregorio de Nisa*, Romae 1939, 12–15.

[59] Greg. Nyss., *C. Eunom.* I: ed. Jaeger I, 80–1, no. 184; PG 45, 305D.

[60] Greg. Naz., *Or.* 42, 16; PG 36, 477B; *Or.* 39, 11: ibid., 345CD.

precisely by allowing a human physis in the exalted Christ while denying it the human particularizing characteristics which make a hypostasis:

> The first fruits of human nature which were taken by the omnipotent Godhead are mingled in the Godhead like a drop of vinegar in a vast sea, but not in its own particular properties (οὐ μὴν ἐν τοῖς ἰδίοις αὐτῆς ἰδιώμασιν). For if the Son were to be known in the ineffable Godhead in a nature of a different kind, identified by its own peculiar characteristics (ἑτερογενής τις φύσις [ἐν] ἰδιάζουσι σημείοις ἐπεγινώσκετο), in such a way that the one were infirm, or small, or corruptible, or transitory, and the other were powerful, and mighty, and incorruptible, and eternal, this would be to postulate two Sons.[61]

Christ's humanity, then, is not simply dissolved in the Godhead. It has reality, but no longer its earthly *idiomata*. Everything that makes the 'universal human physis' the human hypostasis or the human individual or the 'person' is done away with and replaced by the divine characteristics, wisdom, power, holiness, impassibility.[62] As there are only divine *idiomata* in Christ (i.e. in the humanity of Christ), there is no longer any cause to speak of two Sons. The human element in Christ is no longer shown in natural properties (*quod humanum est, non in proprietatibus naturae esse ostenditur*). All is filled with the glory of the Godhead.[63]

Gregory has a slight suspicion that this explanation leads to great difficulties. In the first place, Christ was indeed capable of suffering. His glory and power were revealed only after his passion.[64] Gregory's theory does not fit this side of Christ's lowliness. But he resorts to the expedient of changing the names, which is possible because of the 'inner conjunction of the flesh which is taken and the Godhead which takes':

> On account of the union achieved between the flesh which is taken and the Godhead which takes, names are communicated and given to each mutually in such a way that the divinity is spoken of in human terms and the humanity in divine terms. Thus Paul calls the crucified one the Lord of glory (1 Cor. 2. 8); and he who is adored by the whole creation, above, below and upon the earth, is called Jesus.[65]

Here Gregory does not altogether avoid begging the question. His whole interpretation of the unity in Christ therefore remains unsatisfactory. In many respects it already anticipates the explanation given by Nestorius (see below), though without endangering the traditional christology (*communicatio idiomatum*) as he does. It is interesting to note that this first theory of the unity of Christ is addressed to an Alexandrian, the uncle of Cyril of Alexandria. We have devoted some space to it to clarify the progress of theological development. Of course, the result has been only so to speak the skeleton of Gregory's christology. The picture of Christ in

61 Greg. Nyss., *Ad Theoph. adv. Apoll.*: ed. Jaeger (Mueller), 126[17]–127[4]: PG 45, 1275CD.
62 Greg. Nyss., ibid.: ed. Jaeger (Mueller), 127[8]: PG 45, 1276D.
63 Greg. Nyss., ibid.: ed. Jaeger (Mueller), 128: PG 45, 1277BC.
64 Greg. Nyss., ibid.: ed. Jaeger (Mueller), 127[11–15]: PG 45, 1277A.
65 Greg. Nyss., ibid.: ed .Jaeger (Mueller), 127[15]–128[3]: PG 45, 1278A(Lat.).

his preaching and in his Christ mysticism transcends his theory. His christology is at the same time saving doctrine. The whole man was taken in the manhood of Christ.[66] The whole being in nature and grace is Christ's gift, now in this time and in the life to come. With Origen, Gregory speaks of the birth of Christ within us. With Methodius of Olympus, he stresses the significance of the virginity of the soul for this birth, which found its pattern in Mary. All virtue is a growth of Christ in the baptized person, corresponding to the growth of Christ himself. He does not, however, dwell in everyone in the same way, but in each according to the measure of his moral standing. The contact between the God-man and the perfect man becomes closer and closer, until the purity of paradise and the image of God are completely restored. The relationship between Christ and the (virgin) soul is 'painted in the colours of Christ-mysticism'.[67] Here Gregory is more restrained than Origen. Through its communion with Christ, however, the spirit penetrates ever more deeply into the mystery of the vision of God.

Along with the Cappadocians we may mention their friend Amphilochius of Iconium (died about 394), the cousin of Gregory of Nazianus. It is remarkable that he remained untouched by their influence in the christological sphere. He lacks the typical Cappadocian features: strong emphasis on Christ's soul after Origen's example and the idea of 'mingling' and the 'transformation' of the manhood into the Godhead. His christology fluctuates. Sometimes it shows marked dualistic traits, especially in the course of anti-Arian and anti-Apollinarian polemic; at others there is a strong emphasis on the *communicatio idiomatum*. For this reason Amphilochius does not occupy the place in the history of christology which some have wanted to accord him. Above all, it cannot be claimed that he introduced the one hypostasis or one prosopon formula; the texts which appear to attest this are spurious.[68]

3. EVAGRIUS PONTICUS

Despite some one-sidedness, the Origenism of the Cappadocians was quite moderate—particularly in the case of Basil. Above all, they revealed the positive fruits of Origen's legacy. This is no longer true of Evagrius Ponticus (c. 345–399 or 400), who was introduced to the work of Origen

[66] Greg. Nyss., *Refut. Confess. Eunomii*: ed. Jaeger II, 312–13, nos. 1–3: PG 45, 465–8; a very fine christological passage.

[67] Cf. W. Völker, *Gregor. v. N. als Mystiker*, Wiesbaden 1955, 221, whom we follow here. Cf. the articles by A. Lieske mentioned at the beginning of this section.

[68] Cf. E. Weigl, *Christologie vom Tode des Athanasius bis zum Ausbruch des nestorianischen Streites*, München 1925, 49f., 56–67; K. Holl, *Amphilochius von Iconium in seinem Verhältnis zu den grossen Kappadoziern*, Tübingen-Leipzig 1904, with an edition of the fragments, 91–102. For criticism, M. Richard, 'Le mot "hypostase" au IVᵉ siècle', MSR 2, 1945, 29–32; id., 'Le fragment XXII d'Amphiloque d'Iconium', *Mélanges E. Podechard*, Lyon 1945, 199–210. The formula of the hypostasis of Christ occurs neither in John Chrysostom nor in the Cappadocians.

in the school of Basil and more particularly by Gregory Nazianzus. He certainly learnt from his masters, the authors of the *Philocalia*, in which Origen was to be cleared of Arianism, to hold fast to the Nicene faith. But he went beyond his master Gregory in taking over typically Origenistic theses such as the doctrine of the pre-existence of the soul. Other friends came after the Cappadocians, the elder Melania, Rufinus and the Origenistic monks of Egypt, among them Ammonius, who forced him along the path of a consistent Origenism. Only recently has it become possible to outline this spiritual development of Evagrius and to make clearer his place in the struggles over Origen. The discovery of a second Syriac translation of the *Kephalaia Gnostica* has made possible for the first time a more exact knowledge of the characteristic theology and christology of the most influential of all the Origenists.[69] It seems that important statements in Origen's christology, condemned at the Second Council of Constantinople in 553, were not in fact the actual work of Origen, but were taken from Evagrius' *Kephalaia Gnostica*.

We are chiefly interested here in any insights Evagrius may give us into the christology of the late fourth century, particularly that of the Origenistic tradition. Evagrius completely overcame the subordinationism of Origen, who was regarded by Jerome and Theophilus of Antioch as the father of Arianism.[70] He rejected both rationalistic Eunomianism and Apollinarianism. According to Palladius' *Historia Lausiaca*, three demons cross-questioned Evagrius, one as an Arian, one as a Eunomian and one as an Apollinarian.[71] In christology, however, he develops towards an exaggerated and eventually heretical Origenism.

In Ps.-Basil, *Ep.* 8, there are, of course, only a few traces of an Origenistic tendency. His opponents are the Eunomians. Gregory of Nazianzus is the inspiration of the realistic portrayal of Christ's humanity. Here the doctrine of the soul of Christ fades into the background. There is no longer a place for the great conception of Christ's freedom, such as is found in the *Commentary* of Toura (PG 32, 261B, on John 5. 19). Most reminiscent of Origen is the place assigned to Christ's manhood in the

---

[69] (1) Sources for the christology of Evagrius: (a) Ps.-Basil, *Ep.* 8: PG 32, 245–68; (b) *Selecta in Psalmos*, ed. De La Rue, printed in PG 12, 1054ff. (cited hereafter as R) and J. B. C. Pitra, *Origenes in Psalmos: Analecta Sacra* II, 444–83; III, 1–364 (cited as P); (c) *Kephalaia Gnostica*, ed. A. Guillaumont, *Les Six Centuries des 'Kephalaia Gnostica' d'Evagre le Pontique*: PO 28, fasc. 1–2, Paris 1958, with twofold critical edition of the familiar Syriac text (cited as S1) and the new complete one (cited as S2), together with two French translations.

(2) Studies: on (a) R. Melcher, *Der 8. Brief des hl. Basilius, ein Werk des Evagrius Pontikus*, Münster 1923; W. Bousset, *Apophthegmata: Studien zur Geschichte des ältesten Mönchtums*, Tübingen 1923, 335–41; on (b) M.-J. Rondeau, 'Le Commentaire sur les Psaumes d'Evagre le Pontique', OCP 26, 1960, 307–48; on (c) A. Guillaumont, *Les 'Kephalaia Gnostica' d'Evagre le Pontique et l'histoire de l'origénisme chez les Grecs et chez les Syriens* (Patristica Sorbonensia 5), Paris 1962, with bibliography 339–47. On the christology: F. Refoulé O.P., 'La christologie d'Evagre et l'origénisme', OCP 27, 1961, 221–66.

[70] Jerome, *C. Ioann. Hieros. ad Pammach.*: PL 23, 360B–D; Theophil. Al., *Ep. pasch. anni* 400, apud Jerome, *Ep.* 92: CSEL 55, 147–55; A. Guillaumont, *Les 'Kephalaia Gnostica'*, 90, 96f.

[71] C. Butler, *The Lausiac History of Palladius* (Texts and Studies VI, 1–2), Cambridge 1898–1904, 121⁹–122¹.

realm of knowledge: as the incarnate one, the Son is only the *primitiae*, the earnest, and not the end (*telos*) of blessedness. For here it is a matter of empirical knowledge (no. 7: PG 32, 256–60). Only as Logos is the Son the end and the fulfilment of blessedness, known in a way which is not empirical. In essentials, the christology of the Scholia on the Psalms is shaped along the same lines, for even here Evagrius does not intend to disclose the typically Origenistic doctrines. They are reserved for those who have progressed along the spiritual path. Once again there is unqualified recognition of Christ's divinity. The doctrine of the Lord's soul is now stressed more strongly. '. . . they are heretics who speak ill of the soul of Christ and deny it' (Ps. 108: P, 19). As with Didymus, the soul has become a physical and a theological factor, the seat of moral decisions and of sinlessness.[72] Of course this latter quality is explained in a fully Origenistic way and is already transferred to the decision of the pre-existent soul.

The interests at work here are not always purely theological. Origen's Platonism (*Peri Archon* II, 6, 3) exercises considerable influence. Together with Origen, Evagrius requires an *anima mediatrix* between Logos and sarx: 'The flesh by itself cannot assume God; for our God is Wisdom (i.e. he can only be assumed spiritually). . . . No being composed of the four elements is capable of receiving him' (Ps. 131: P, 7). It is worth noting that despite the strong emphasis on knowledge and spirituality, Evagrius still stresses Christ's humanity, or more accurately, the possibility of seeing it. This is probably to be explained from an old anti-docetic tradition which the Cappadocians may have passed on to him (Ps. 49: R, 3). The question, however, remains: is Christ's humanity sufficiently stressed, and is it given an 'eternal significance'? According to Evagrius, only the Godhead seems to have any significance for the heavenly spirits and the holy ones, a view which Gregory of Nyssa is very near to holding. Christ's humanity is perceived only by earthly knowledge: 'The spiritual powers and the holy ones recognize the Lord as *Lord* (ὡς Κύριον; Pitra read ὡς ἦν); men also recognize the Lord as man' (Ps. 113: P, 11; cf. Ps.-Basil, *Ep.* 8, no. 7).[73]

At this point, the first suspicions about the orthodoxy of the christology of Evagrius are awakened. In the first place, he sees everything in the light of the idea of knowledge: Christ is described in accordance with the hierarchy of physical or spiritual knowledge. This intellectualism is crystallized in four definitions of the person of Christ which are to be found in the Scholia on the Psalms.[74] In contrast to the heavenly powers, who are anointed by knowledge of the creation, Christ is anointed beyond

---

[72] As in Origen, *Peri Archon* II, 6, 5–6: GCS 22, 144–6; cf. Evagrius, Ps. 10 (Hebr.): R, 5 (2); Ps. 87: P, 4–6; Ps. 88: R, 23; Ps. 118: R, 109.

[73] Marie-Josèphe Rondeau kindly pointed out to me this false reading in Pitra. The Greek text reads: τὸν μὲν κύριον ὡς κύριον αἱ νοεραὶ καὶ ἅγίαι δυνάμεις ἐπίστανται, τὸν δὲ κύριον ὡς ἄνθρωπον γινώσκουσιν καὶ οἱ ἄνθρωποι. Pitra expanded the abbreviation κ̄ν wrongly.

[74] F. Refoulé, art. cit., OCP 27, 1961, 246; (a) Ps. 44: P, 3 (2); (b) Ps. 104: R, 15; (c) Ps. 118: R, 3; (d) Ps. 131: P, 7 (1).

all his followers through knowledge of the Monad (cf. *Cap. Gnost.* III, 3;
IV, 2)—a distinction which Evagrius evidently regards as the realization
of the session at the right hand of the Father (*Ps.* 44: P, 3; cf. *Cap. Gnost.*
II, 89). Evagrius' real conception of Christ is evident in these texts: 'I name
Christ the Lord who is come (into the world) with the Word God (Θεὸς
Λόγος)': Text 1–3 is to the same effect. Origen's conception of Christ is
now sharpened in two respects: first, the unity of God and man in Christ
is built up still more exclusively than in Origen on the spiritual acts of
Christ's pre-existent soul, more precisely, on its knowledge. The 'anointing' which makes Christ Christ is understood in a strictly intellectual way.
Origen at least made use of the whole realm of spiritual action, of willing
and loving, to describe the anointing, i.e. the binding of the soul of Christ
to the Logos (*Peri Archon* 4, 4). In Evagrius, the interpretation of the unity
in Christ is built on a much narrower basis. It is now also more difficult
to explain to the Gnostics the difference between the union of Christ's
soul with the Monad and their view of unity with God. For in the end
the perfect can also participate in this essential knowledge of Christ's soul
(Ps. 138: P, 7) and so become heirs of Christ (cf. *Cap. Gnost.* IV, 4, 8).

A further danger to the church's picture of Christ—still controlled in
Origen, but rampant in Evagrius—is the false conception of the subject
of the incarnation. The one who becomes flesh is not so much the Logos
as the pre-existent soul in which the Logos dwells: 'Here I name Christ
the spiritual *soul* which came into the life of man with the God-Logos'
(Ps. 131: P, 7).

Involuntarily, Evagrius does to some extent fall back into the Arian
interpretation of Christ and even makes it more acute by ascribing the
incarnation to a created spirit, to a (pre-existent) human soul. The Arians
had at least seen a higher spiritual being in the incarnate Christ. The one,
but important, difference in Evagrius is his recognition of the God-Logos
and his indwelling in the soul of Christ.[75]

'Christ', then, is first and foremost the pre-existent soul, though, of
course, only in so far as it is anointed with the God-Logos, i.e. is united
with him through supreme knowledge. The *anima mediante* has become the
centre of the picture of Christ. The danger of a Nestorian interpretation
of Christ is equally acute. For Christ is God only by participation. He is
to be worshipped only because of this participation and because of the
indwelling of the Logos (Ps. 98: R, 5; Ps. 131: P, 7; *Cap. Gnost.* V, 48),
not because of his status as a divine person. True, Origen had led up to

---

[75] It is possible that Evagrius makes this incarnate soul, united with the Logos, into the demiurge,
i.e. the mediator of creation. In that case the Evagrian picture of Christ would be still more like that
of the Arians, and the reaction of the sixth anathema of the Second Council of Constantinople would
be understandable. Cf. F. Refoulé, art. cit., OCP 27, 1961, 250. He points to Ps. 89: P, 4; Ps. 135: R,
23, where Christ is described as 'demiurge'. But these passages could be interpreted in an orthodox
way, and other texts are orthodox, as Refoulé observes.

this distortion of the picture of Christ. There is a text in the *Commentary on John* which Evagrius may have had in mind when he produced his own formulas: 'Perhaps the soul of Jesus was in God in its perfection and its fullness; it came forth, sent by the Father, and then took a body of Mary.'[76] But the Alexandrian elsewhere outlined the features of the 'incarnate Logos' so powerfully that any idea of the 'incarnation of souls' seemed to be excluded (see above, Part One).

The form of the Evagrian picture of Christ as hitherto depicted becomes still clearer with the newly discovered translation of the Urtext of the *Gnostic Centuries*.[77] Evagrius now speaks to the initiated who have progressed beyond πρακτική to θεωρία. Comparison of the two Syriac translations S1 and S2, moreover, suggests particular conclusions for the history of christology which are, of course, of prime concern for the sixth century. The traditional outlines of the church's belief in Christ are indeed present in the *Gnostic Centuries*. Christ is of like substance, his body to ours, his soul to ours, the Logos to the Father (VI, 79). Arianism and Apollinarianism are rejected. In truly Origenistic fashion, however, the soul of Christ is held to be pre-existent, united with the Logos from eternity (VI, 18, a passage which has been strongly altered in S1 to bring it in line with church doctrine). Above all, the intellectualism and spiritualism of Evagrius is now accentuated. 'Christ' is defined as the *nous* which is united with knowledge of the Unity (I, 77). The anointing consists in this purely spiritual knowledge of the divine Monad (IV, 18), which Christ possesses to a special degree. That is the meaning of the session at the right hand of the Father:

> L'onction ou bien indique la science de l'Unité ou bien désigne la contemplation des êtres [S1 ends here]. Et si plus que les autres le Christ est oint, il est évident qu'il est oint de la science de l'unité. A cause de cela, lui seul est dit 'être assis à la droite' de son Père, la droite qui ici, selon la règle des gnostiques, indique la Monade et l'Unité (IV, 21).

In the *Gnostic Centuries*, too, the centre and focal point of the picture of Christ lies in his pre-existent soul—in fact this thought is expressed most strongly here. Evagrius likes to describe the soul as the '*nous*', which is elevated to the knowledge of the Monad even before its creation. The great threat which such a view posed to the church's christology was recognized at the second Council of Constantinople.[78] Precisely this *nous* is the subject of the incarnation. It bears the name Christ because it is anointed with the knowledge of the Monad:

> L'onction intelligible est la science spirituelle de l'Unité sainte, et le Christ est celui qui est uni à cette science. Et si cela est ainsi, le Christ n'est pas le Verbe au début, en sorte

---

[76] Origen, *Comm. in Io.* 20,19: GCS, Orig. IV, 351$^{25-8}$.

[77] F. Refoulé, art. cit., *OCP* 27, 1961, 251–5; A. Guillaumont, *Les 'Kephalaia Gnostica'* (see n. 72 above), 117–19, 133–59.

[78] Cf. A. Guillaumont, *Les 'Kephalaia Gnostica'*, 133–70, esp. 156–9. He points out that the *Kephalaia Gnostica* are the main source for the fifteen anathemas against Origen in 553.

que celui qui a été oint n'est pas Dieu au debut, mais celui-là à cause de celui-ci est le
Christ, et celui-ci à cause de celui-là est Dieu (IV, 18).

The name of Christ, then, is primarily given to this *nous* united with
the Logos. The incarnation is no longer constitutive for the name. The
'anointing' happens to the pure *nous*, as an 'onction intelligible'.
The Logos and the flesh are approached only through the *nous*. Thus the
subject of the incarnation is shifted, as we have already established in the
case of the Scholia on the Psalms. It is no longer a matter of the 'incarnate
Logos', but of the 'incarnate *nous*'. 'Christ' is called 'Logos' and 'God'
only obliquely, just as the Logos is given the name 'Christ' only because
of his conjunction with the *nous* through the vision of God. So Evagrius'
picture of Christ clearly bears features which are usually said to be
'Antiochene'. It is, however, still essentially different from the Antiochene
picture of Christ because the latter lays the right stress on the incarnation,
whereas Evagrius' picture of Christ is one-sidedly spiritualistic and mystical. For the Antiochenes, Christ is above all 'Logos-anthropos'.

Christ's redemptive work, too, is seen by Evagrius in the light of this
pre-existent *nous*, anointed in the vision of God. He creates the material
world and secondary beings to redeem the fallen souls (I, 14; II, 2; III, 26).
The theophanies of the Old Testament are also ascribed to him:

Le Christ, avant sa venue, a montré aux hommes un corps angélique; et au derniers
ce n'est pas le corps qu'il a maintenant qu'il a montré, mais il a révélé celui qu'ils doivent
avoir (IV, 41).[79]

This created *nous* in Christ is therefore the real mediator in creation.
The Platonism or even Neo-Platonism which led the Arians to their
interpretation of the 'Logos' causes Evagrius to make Christ's soul the
demiurge. It has all the functions which the Arians ascribed to the subordinate Logos. When God created the spiritual beings (λογικοί), he was
in 'nothingness', but when he created bodily nature and the worlds he
already had his demiurge, his *nous-Christus*: not the Logos, but the *nous*
united with the Logos (IV, 58).[80] Even the descent into the underworld
and the ascension into heaven are ascribed to this *nous-Christus*. The death
of the incarnate Christ and the taking of flesh are both without significance.
For 'le corps grossier, en effet, n'est pas susceptible de la science, et Dieu
est connu' (IV, 80).[81] As all souls are in principle the same, all the redeemed
become another 'Christ' or co-heirs of Christ.

'Le cohéritier du Christ' est celui qui arrive dans l'Unité et se délecte de la contempla-
tion avec le Christ (IV, 8). L'héritage du Christ est la science de l'Unité; et si tous devien-
nent cohéritiers du Christ, tous connaîtront l'Unité sainte . . . (III, 72).

[79] This text is much weakened in S1.
[80] This text too is much weakened in S1.
[81] Once again, compare S1, which completely alters Evagrius' thought.

The result is the equality of all spirits, even with Christ, in the vision of God (IV, 51). For all are bound up with the Monad in this vision in the same way. The *apokatastasis* does away with all differences. For there are differences only in the world of bodies and of matter.

The christology which was influenced by Origen thus reached its final development. Evagrius was, of course, influenced by a particular part of Origen's teaching, taken in isolation and exaggerated. If we are to appreciate the full extent of the latter's influence we must take into consideration the Cappadocians, Didymus of Alexandria and even Athanasius, perhaps to some degree all the christological trends of the fourth century. In Evagrius, the christology of the doctrine of two natures, centred in the Logos—which is still clearly recognizable in Origen—has been transposed. Mystical union is the pattern of his interpretation of Christ. An ontology of Christ which, despite its presence since the second century, is, of course, only fully established at Chalcedon, now becomes a spiritualistic *nous-Christus* doctrine. The formula is neither Logos-sarx nor Logos-anthropos, but Nous-Logos. The order of the words is to be noted. Everything is now seen in the light of the unity in knowledge with the Monad. Knowledge is the real power of union between Logos and *nous*. In accordance with the Platonic interpretation, it completely transforms the knower into the known. In other words, the soul, and any created spirit, is transformed by mystical conjunction into the Logos and into God. Evagrius here looks only at the *nous Christi*. Gregory of Nyssa sought to depict the same transformation for the realm of Christ's corporeality and transferred here the interpretation of the unity in Christ. He too came suspiciously near to doing away with Christ's corporeality, but in the end he demanded an absorption only of the *idiomata* or particularizing characteristics of the bodily nature, and not of the ultimate corporeal substance. Evagrius goes further. Corporeality no longer has any significance for the restored world. It is merely the temporal manifestation of the *nous-Christus* for us (VI, 16). Only the spirit has significance, and knowledge, of all the spiritual acts. The whole unity of Christ is built on knowledge. Because there is this vision of God, there is only one Christ, only one Son: '. . . et celui qui dit deux Christs ou deux fils resemble à celui qui appelle le sage et la sagesse deux sages ou deux sagesses' (VI, 16). Through the union, the *nous Christi* becomes 'essential knowledge' (science essentielle, VI, 14, 16). Evagrius stresses this oneness of Christ and every soul so strongly that there is a thread of monism, as is clear, for example, in the letter of Evagrius to Melania.[82] He sees the whole creation as a sea, with which all the rivers were originally one, later to separate and to acquire for themselves

---

[82] Evagrius, *Ep. ad Melaniam*: W. Frankenberg, *Euagrius Ponticus*, Berlin 1912, 612–19; part of the letter is translated into French in I. Hausherr, *De Doctrina Spirituali Christianorum Orientalium*, OC 30, 3, 1933, 190–1. There is no mention of the soul of Christ in the letter.

different colours and different savours. But when they flow back into the
sea they become one with it:

> ... dans son unicité sans fin ni distinction, par suite de leur union de leur mixtion
> avec lui! ... de même dans la mixtion des intellects avec le Père, il n'y aura pas non plus
> ni dualité de natures, ni quaternité de personnes [better 'hypostases'], mais tout comme la
> mer est une dans sa nature dans sa couleur et dans sa saveur avant que les fleuves se mêlent
> à elle et encore après qu'il se sont mêlés à elle; ainsi la nature divine est une dans les trois
> personnes [better 'hypostases'] du Père et du Fils et de l'Esprit Saint, même quand se
> seront mêlés à elle les intellects, tout comme avant qu'ils ne fussent mêlés à elle.

Here Evagrius still seems to maintain a last boundary between created
and uncreated. This is also evident from the close of the letter, where he
speaks of the eternal praise which he and Melania will offer through the
Son and the Spirit to the Father for all eternity, without the mediation
of any creature (of course as *'noes gymnoi'*).[83] But the corporeality of
Christ has no place here, and indeed even the *nous Christi* seems to have
no function towards the other spiritual beings.

As far as the person of Christ is concerned, then, Evagrius occupies a
unique position between Arianism, Apollinarianism, even Nestorianism,
and orthodoxy. In his acute Origenism he regards the creation of matter
and the taking of a body by the *nous Christi* as nothing better than a
troublesome incident with all its sorry consequences.[84]

4. ORIGENIST CHRISTOLOGY IN THE WEST

At the beginning of the fifth century, an Origenist christology also
seems to have been put forward almost imperceptibly in the West, with
its sources in the East. It is to be found in the commentary by Aponius
on the Song of Songs.[85] There are significantly close connections here
between christology, soteriology and ecclesiology.[86] Most striking of all,

[83] Cf. W. Frankenberg. op. cit., 619. F. Refoulé, art. cit., OCP 27, 1961, 260, gives further texts
which clear Evagrius of the charge of monism.

[84] Cf. W. Frankenberg, op. cit., 619, no. 191. I. Hausherr, op. cit., 191.

[85] Cf. H. Bottino–J. Martini, *Aponii scriptoris vetustissimi in Canticum Canticorum Explanationis libri
duodecim*, Romae 1843, reprinted now in PLS I, 799–1031, with a new bibliography. A new edition
is in preparation for SC. For the christology of Aponius see J. Witte, *Der Kommentar des Aponius zum
Hohenlied*, Erlangen 1903, 50–6. Witte dates the commentary in the period between 405 and 415; he
pleads for a Syrian–Jewish origin for the author, although he wrote in Latin. A thorough analysis
would have to take note of earlier commentaries and homilies on the Song of Songs, especially those
of Origen and Gregory of Nyssa. Cf. O. Rousseau, *Origène, Homélies sur le Cantique des Cantiques* (SC
37 and 37 bis), Paris 1953¹, 1966², who prefaces the commentary with a saying of Aponius; R. P.
Lawson, *Origen, The Song of Songs. Commentary and Homilies*, Westminster–Maryland–London
1957; *Gregorii Nysseni in Canticum Canticorum*, ed. H. Langerbeck (Gregorii Nysseni Opera, ed. W.
Jaeger, VI), Leiden 1960; C. van den Eynde, *La version syriaque du Commentaire de Grégoire de Nysse sur
le Cantique des Cantiques*, Louvain 1939, discusses a *'pervetusta'* Syriac translation of this work. Cf. B.
Studer, 'Zur Frage des westlichen Origenismus', *StudPat* IX (TU 94), Berlin 1966, 270–87.

[86] Cf. L. Welsersheimb, 'Das Kirchenbild der griechischen Väterkommentare zum Hohenlied',
ZkTh 70, 1948, 393–449; the remarks on Aponius, which stress his good understanding of the
theology of Gregory of Nyssa, are brief and general. For the background, note should be taken of J.
Chenevert, S. J., *L'Eglise dans le Commentaire d'Origène sur le Cantique des Cantiques* (Studia 24),
Bruxelles–Paris–Montréal 1969.

however, is the stress on the soul of Christ and the human soul generally, against the background of a Platonic anthropology. No author from the time when Apollinarius began to be challenged to such a degree, speaks so often and in so much detail as Aponius about the soul of Christ. Against the Arians, he insistently confesses the equality in substance of the Trinity and the divinity of the Word, and against the Gnostics the true manhood of Christ.[87] But when he talks about the question of the unity in Christ, he uses the striking expression 'homo assumptus'.[88] This, however, is not to be interpreted simply in the current 'Antiochene' sense. True, the divine Word (the Logos) is the ultimate bearer of this homo assumptus, who is 'complete man' (homo perfectus) with soul and body; but in the picture of Christ as a whole the accent is clearly on the 'soul' of Christ. The work of redemption rests on its free decision; indeed, in this freedom it adheres to the 'Word' and remains conjoined with it, instead of turning to earthly, transitory, lower things. This recalls the idea of the pre-historical fall of the pre-existent souls in which one soul did not share, the soul of Christ. The idea of a pre-existence of souls and of the soul of Christ is not stated explicitly. Perhaps the idea of pre-existence has been replaced by that of God's foreknowledge of the behaviour of Christ's soul (p. 179: praescita cognoscitur). But echoes of Origen are so strong that one may with some degree of justification say that Aponius, too, is playing with the idea of the pre-existence of the soul. This is shown by a lengthy paragraph in Book IX:

Our king, the Lord and God, found among the countless thousands of souls which rejoiced and glorified him, which he created for his praise [the quotation is from Isa. 43. 21], one unstained and one perfect dove in the whole mass of souls which is the queen among queens, the mistress of all lords. [The following sentence seems to express creation in pre-existence most clearly.] It remained fixed at the stage of its formation by a free decision of the will (quae fixa in gradu plasmationis suae per arbitrii libertatem stans), and never opened the gates of its spirit to the enemy, the devil. It developed this gift of (free) will which it received from the Creator in the works of the will: it filled the storehouse of the heart, and kept this abundance enclosed and sealed for ever with great watchful-ness. . . . It was to despise all the glory of present things, never to give its assent to the corporeal delights of every kind, and incessantly to turn the acuteness of its spirit to the good things to come. All its desire was to be directed, not to any praise of the world, not to any transitory thing, not to any worldly action, but only to union with the word of God (nisi in sola verbi Dei glutatione poneret); thus it is recognized in foreknowledge (!) alone on earth, more humble than all other souls and more perfect than they. Just as the one God in heaven is manifestly above all powers of rules, thrones, seats, angels, in short

[87] Cf. Lib. V, p. 90. Quicumque enim solum hominem credit Christum (where Aponius has Photinus particularly in mind), non invenit eum. Et quicumque solam deitatem credit in Christo, vocat quidem in noctibus perversorum sensuum suorum Dominum Dei Filium; sed non respondet ei, sicut non respondit Sauli regi, a quo recesserat Deus. Cf. p. 92 middle.

[88] Cf. V, p. 99: Et quis alius potest intelligi pacificus, nisi Christus redemptor noster? Qui secundum Apostolum Paulum pacificavit quae in caelo sunt, et quae in terra, et reconciliavit Deo Patri humanum genus per sanguinem assumpti hominis sui. This sui should be noted. It is reminiscent of certain phrases used by Theodore of Mopsuestia (see below).

is Lord and Creator of all powers, so it (the soul of Christ) is the head of all holy souls. It is united to the Word of God not only through adoption in place of the Son (*verbo dei non adoptive*), or for a time, but also in a real corporeal way, in that the matter which has become one with it is preserved.[89] It avoids all works of sin and is free from every evil; thus it is called the perfect dove, by which the Word of God the Father has condemned sin in the flesh and has redeemed the world from the pronouncement of the flesh. . . . Through it all the souls of its race that are to be redeemed rejoice over their Redeemer, in whom there is true flesh and a true soul. In his resurrection from the dead he will raise the flesh and at the same time gather the souls to judgement, so that the true God may grant the immortal glory of his kingdom for the future. This is without doubt the one soul, the queen of queens, who has assumed and borne the word of God in exemplary fashion, by which he has shattered the underworld and released the souls imprisoned there; on taking his body again in the resurrection he has led them out with himself from the underworld. Through it and in it, against the nature of things, human frailty has also miraculously entered heaven; through it, after the expulsion of the devil, the fleshly nature became the abode of God. It is the Word made flesh which has united itself with the flesh and has dwelt among us; he has taken flesh of our nature from the womb of the Virgin, according to the word of the evangelist, 'And the word was made flesh and dwelt among us'.[90]

Much in this text is reminiscent of Origen and his understanding of the incarnation. Above all, there recurs the idea that the soul of Christ was free to decide either to attach itself to the Logos or to turn to earthly things. Here there is a 'proving' which is predicated purely of the soul as such and which could take place before the assumption of the flesh. The phrase *anima mediatrix* also recurs literally in the continuation of the text (on the saying, '*una est columba mea, perfecta mea. Unica est matris suae. Electa est genitrici suae*', Cant. VI, 8, we find):

(This) shows that from the abundance of souls one was chosen to be *mediatrix* between the power of the Godhead and the weakness of the flesh. In itself it displays the true God and the true flesh united, one person. It was sent into the body (created by the Creator, not produced by the power of the body, like all other human souls), came forth with the body and left the intact womb of the Virgin. . . . It continually attached itself to the Word of God and became completely fire, like a coal of fire.[91]

All this can be found in Origen (see above). Indeed, the soul of Christ comes into the centre of the picture of Christ to such a degree that one is reminded of the *nous* christology of Evagrius, though of course only in the perspective which is expressed in the following sentence (Christ's

---

[89] IX, p. 179: the meaning of this last sentence is difficult to elucidate. The Latin is: *Quae ut caput omnium animarum sanctarum, verbo Dei non adoptive, aut ad tempus, sed corporaliter unita, materia manente, unum cum eo effecta.* . . . The opposite to *adoptive* (θέσει) would be *naturaliter* (φύσει). '*Corporaliter*' possibly means this '*naturaliter*'. '*Materia manente*' does not mean the preservation of physical material, but the preservation without confusion of the reality of the soul, including its physical element.

[90] IX, p. 178 bottom to p. 180 top. The text on the soul of Christ as the central point for believers is taken still further. Some important statements will be noted below.

[91] IX, p. 181: . . . *sed ostendit inter multitudinem animarum, unam esse electam*, mediatricem *inter robur divinitatis, et carnis fragilitatem. Quae in se verum Deum, veramque carnem adunatam unam personam ostendit.* Note the ecclesiological continuation: *Et ut ignitus carbunculus inter multitudinem mortuorum carbonum coniunctus omnes accendit; ita in medio animarum vitae aeternae mortuarum, sola, unica, electa, omnes credentes in se animas vivificavit, et sibi similes fecit, et ad suam pulchritudinem adduxit.*

promise of peace and his peace-bringing mission according to Luke 2. 14;
John 14. 27 and Eph. 2. 14):

It (the soul of Christ) found a fore-ordained peace by concealing omnipotence, displaying weakness, displaying the form of the Godhead clad in the form of a slave; it found
peace as a mediatrix between God and man, as *on the one hand* it is united with God the
Word of the Father, and *on the other* with the unstained flesh, as on the cross it lives truly
in the Godhead and in the manhood goes gladly to death.[92]

Here the soul of Christ can be seen flanked on the one hand by the
Godhead and on the other by the flesh. Two pictures of Christ overlap:
the Word made flesh of John and Nicaea, and the soul-christology of
Origen and Evagrius. However, Evagrius' *nous* christology is kept in
check. Aponius is no spiritualist like Evagrius. He knows of the attempts
of the Arians to make the Logos *qua* Logos the physical instrument of
Christ's suffering, so as to be able to exclude his Godhead. So he makes
the flesh and soul the physical principle of all human experiences, of joy
and sorrow. But he knows that the Word is the ultimate bearer of all
'suffering':

Just as God, the Word of God, takes as happening to himself all the sorrow borne by
the flesh and the soul which it has assumed, so the aforesaid soul considers to have happened to itself all the joy that has been conferred on the Jewish people.[93]

We find a similar comment at the beginning of Book XII:

Thus this soul, often mentioned before, underwent tribulation through the mystery
of suffering for the salvation of the mortal, through that bitter death brought upon it by
the godless in fearful martyrdom; it is manifest that the threat brought on by suffering
was not experienced by the Godhead, which is incapable of suffering, but by the soul,
which suffers along with the flesh.[94]

The picture of Christ may be determined by the approaches of Origen
and Evagrius (though, as has been said, the latter is influential only to a
limited extent), but in addition there are Antiochene features: Christ is
the '*assumptus homo*', who by the achievement of an unstained life and the
torments of bitter suffering has earned 'a thousand silver pieces', i.e. the
honour of (divine) majesty; through this honour, however, which is
achieved in the resurrection and exaltation, the 'man assumed' shows
himself to be inseparably united to the Word of the Father.[95] There is no
mention of laying down the body, as in Evagrius.

92 XII, p. 237: . . . *reperit pacem, inter Deum et homines* mediatrix *existens, cum ex altero latere Deo
Verbo Patris, ex altero immaculatae carni coniungitur.* . . .
93 XI, p. 213 in connection with Cant. VIII, 2: *Sicut enim quidquid triste a carne animaque assumpta
agitur, sibi factum applicat Deus Dei Verbum, ita et memorata anima, quidquid gaudii collatum fuerit in
plebem iudaicam, sibi asserit provenisse.*
94 XII, p. 216.
95 XII, p. 241 (on Cant. VIII, 12): *Pro qua vinea excolenda, pacificus Christus assumptus homo, doctrina
vitae immaculatae et amarissimae passionis labore, mille argenteos, honorem maiestatis accipit, per quem
honorem cum Verbo Patris unitus indivisibiliter comprobatur.* This recalls the Shepherd of Hermas, *Sim.* V,
2 (pp 54f. above). Then follows a remark on Dan. 7. 13 (*Ecce sedes positae sunt, et vetustus dierum sedit, et*

This proving ended in the death of the cross (and here reference is made to Isa. 53. 11, 12). Only from this moment on does the union of God and man seem to have been indissoluble.[96] With this strong stress on the 'crucified' Christ, a Western element enters the christology of Aponius, though it can be derived from his Origenist presuppositions. It is not the *Christus gloriae* who is to accompany the Christian through his life, but the idea of the 'crucified one':

> If the soul wishes to overcome the evil of the adversary (it is necessary that) the crucified one should always be in the thoughts of the hearts and the actions of the hands.[97]

This christology of suffering and the soteriological perspective of the whole of Aponius' commentary give it a 'Western' character which in some respects is already reminiscent of Anselm. He sees the world devastated by men's wars against God. Only Christ, his elect soul, has brought peace:

> For unbroken peace does not prevail, not the fullness of peace, where countless old wars still rage day by day, where it is said, 'Woe to the world because of hindrances', where believers are still at war, where no crowns are given unless the battle is waged legitimately (*legitime*), where the warriors daily ask for allies. Rather, it is a matter of that peace of reconciliation between God and man through which he has taught us that from Adam, the first man to be created,[98] to the virgin birth, war has prevailed between the Creator and creation. . . . And in the whole time over which the Creator has been offended by such crimes (*et tanto tempore in his tantis sceleribus* offenso[99] *Creatore*), no man would have been found among men who was completely (*omnino*) free from his own guilt, to appease through his entreaty the God of human nature in his towering rage, had that soul not been created anew in a new order, the only one proceeding from the aforesaid mother, chosen to bear it, miraculously for heaven and earth. When it appeared on earth, the powers of heaven praised it; when it was exalted in the mystery of suffering (on the cross) (they praised) the rock that was riven. Through the greatness of its humility it found peace, it alone, between the Creator God and man, both of which it bore.[100]

Aponius may have approached Western thought with his soteriology and ecclesiology, but not with his understanding of the person of Christ as such. This did not exercise any further demonstrable influence in the West.

adductus est in conspectu eius filius hominis, et usque ad vetustum dierum pervenit). Idest usque ad Deitatis potentiam, et dedit ei potestatem, et iudicium fecit, et millia millium serviunt ei. Haec utique de assumpto homine praedicta sunt, eum usque ad statum indivisibilem Deitatis honorem exaltandum.

[96] Aponius, ibid., XII, p. 242, where the 'iam' should be noted: *Propter quod (inquit) laboravit anima eius, videbit et satiabitur, quia tradidit in mortem animam suam, et cum iniquis deputatus est, hoc est inter duos latrones ut sceleratus ab impiis crucifixus est. Hic est proculdubio argenteorum splendoris millenarius numerus collatus pacifico, ut solus, quidquid perfecti hominis est, quidquid perfectae Divinitatis, plenus esse probetur, quod dividi a sua iam unione nullatenus potest.* Thus the 'iam' indicates the point in time from which the eternal union of God and man in Christ is guaranteed.

[97] XII, p. 221: the text continues (pp. 227f.): . . . *et nec posse aliter transiri de morte ad vitam, nisi qui Christum eiusque crucem in conscientiis praetulerit pro signaculo semper.* . . .

[98] It should be noted that here the sin of Adam is taken as the beginning of the state of war, and not the fall of the pre-existent souls.

[99] This saying is reminiscent of Anselm's *Cur Deus Homo?*

[100] XII, p. 236. The conclusion is again significant for the picture of Christ: . . . *sola inter Creatorem Deum, et hominem,* quem utrumque gestabat, *pacem reperit.* . . . The 'soul' appears as the means of bearing the incarnate Word.

5. NEMESIUS OF EMESA

We end this survey of Origen's christological heritage with Nemesius, one of the successors of Eusebius of Emesa, with whom we are already acquainted. Werner Jaeger has shown that Nemesius is one of the most important sources for a knowledge of Neo-Platonism. The Bishop of Emesa became acquainted with it by way of Galen, and the Christian exegesis of Genesis, above all through Origen's commentary on Genesis which is, of course, lost except for a few fragments.[101] So we have good reason to add Nemesius, probably writing c. 400, at this point.

In his writings we find a clear repudiation of Apollinarianism, and an interpretation of the unity of the God-man which is intended to preserve a mean between Apollinarius and, evidently, the Antiochenes:[102]

> But the divine Logos, in no way changed as a result of the fellowship which he has with the body and the soul, without sharing in their weakness, nevertheless imparts to them his Godhead. He becomes one with them and continues in that state in which he was before his entry into the union. This manner of mingling and union is entirely new. The Logos mixes himself and yet remains always unmixed, unconfused, incorrupt and unchanged;[103] he does not share in suffering, but only in action (PG 40, 601 AB).

The union between the Logos and the whole manhood is a 'substantial' conjunction (κατ' οὐσίαν). It is significant that we find this expression in an opponent of Apollinarianism and the Logos-sarx christology. Nemesius, then, feels that it is quite possible to combine the 'Logos-man' framework with the idea of a substantial, essential unity. Of course, he makes little progress in presenting this approach in a detailed way. His polemic is chiefly aimed at Eunomius, who will not have the 'substances' (οὐσίαι, the Godhead and manhood) but only the 'powers' (δυνάμεις) of the divine and human natures conjoined in Christ. In his view, Christ's divine nature unites itself with the body by itself (οἰκεία φύσις), though remaining unmixed.[104] The union finally takes place through a complete permeation of the bodily nature by the spiritual nature of the Logos,[105] without the Logos himself being in any way confused. In this attempt at an explanation, Nemesius wishes to dissociate himself from the opinion of 'certain men of note', who hold that the union in Christ was 'an act of divine favour'. For him the 'nature' itself is the ground of union. For it is the substances themselves which are united and not merely their powers, just as the resultant relationship is not simply an accidental one.[106] The

---

101 W. Jaeger, Nemesios von Emesa, Berlin 1914, 94, 118, 142f.

102 Nemesius Em., De natura hominis, esp. ch. 3: PG 40, 592A–608A.

103 Ibid., 601B: μένει παντάπασιν ἄμικτος καὶ ἀσύγχυτος καὶ ἀδιάφθορος καὶ ἀμετάβλητος.

104 Ibid., 605B: βέλτιον οὖν . . . κατὰ τὴν οἰκείαν φύσιν τῶν ἀσωμάτων ἀσυγχύτως τὴν ἕνωσιν γίνεσθαι τῶν οὐσιῶν. . . .

105 Ibid., 605B–608A: ἡ καθαρῶς ἀσώματος φύσις, χωρεῖ μὲν ἀκωλύτως διὰ πάντων, δι' αὐτῆς δὲ οὐδέν· ὥστε τῷ μὲν χωρεῖν αὐτὴν διὰ πάντων, ἡνῶσθαι.

106 Ibid., 608A: οὐκ εὐδοκία τοίνυν ὁ τρόπος τῆς ἑνώσεως . . . ἀλλ' ἡ φύσις αἰτία. We should not assess what the Antiochenes mean by 'union by favour' solely from what their opponents say. The

background to this christology is the Neo-Platonic interpretation of the unity of soul and body, but this is taken over by Nemesius only when he has made considerable modifications.

First of all, he rejects the idea of grades of souls (PG 40, 608A; against Origen). Secondly, he has a different interpretation of the unity of soul and body from that of Plotinus and Porphyry (PG 40, 592–608). According to them, the composite being made up of body and soul forms a third element over and above the two components, an element in which these are included. The individual soul is the extension of the universal soul, with the body as a limiting factor. It is the composite being, and not the soul, which is the subject of the emotions. Here Nemesius introduces a first distinction; the soul, and not the composite being, is the responsible principle of all actions. The logical significance of this is that in the end the emotions of the composite being must be attributed to the soul itself. But if this is the case, the idea of the soul as an 'intelligibile immutabile, impassibile' must be abandoned. Together with the Neo-Platonists, Nemesius sees the union of soul and body as an extension of the universal soul to the extreme limits. This represents a trend towards the material (PG 40, 600AB). Now he wants to incorporate two basic principles into this approach; he wants to keep the complete lack of confusion between soul and body, but at the same time to hold the two together in a real unity. This real unity must be neither confusion (with a consequent alteration to each of the two components), nor a mere juxtaposition, as for example when two stones are laid side by side, not yet a blending as of water and wine (PG 40, 593A). The unity must be understood more as in Plotinus' picture of the sun, which gives light to all and from which too the illuminated air has its being, or as in the way in which two who love each other are one (ibid., 597B). The soul is disposed towards, it tends to, the body. But how can we still speak of a real unity here? According to the Neo-Platonists there is a 'great chain of being'. Everything, even the material world, stems from the One and is connected in absolute unity. But Nemesius has deprived himself of this link. For him the body is a reality independent of the soul and not confused with it. The example of the light which illuminates everything and brings it forth no longer applies. All that remains is the unity 'of two who love one another'.

If Nemesius is going to take this body-soul unity as a pattern for the unity in Christ, the consequences for his doctrine of the incarnation are manifest. However much he may continue to stress the conjunction of substance with substance he can achieve no more than a 'co-actio'. The measure of the union of Logos and man is the extent to which the Logos

---

Antiochenes reject the *physis* as the foundation of unity because they see the quality of grace in the incarnation endangered by the formula of physical union. It is interesting to find as early as Nemesius intimations of a problem which will meet us again in Theodoret and Nestorius.

pervades the bodily element in Christ without himself being affected by it. The union comes completely from the side of the Logos. It is based on the possibility that the Logos can wholly embrace the human element in Christ without being changed by the body. Here the unity in Christ transcends the unity of soul and body, as in the latter the soul is affected because it is not completely free from material and corporeal elements (PG 40, 601AB).

We have here an attempt to give philosophical clarification to the body-soul comparison and to apply it to the doctrine of the incarnation. The problem of the unity in Christ is approached in such a way that a philosophical theory of union is not only presupposed (as with the attempted interpretation of the Arians, Apollinarians and even members of the church, including Gregory of Nyssa) but prepared for at the end of the line of argument. Has Nemesius achieved much more than Origen?[107]

107 Cf. R. Arnou, *Nestorianisme et Néoplatonisme*, 116–131. Nemesius certainly knows the term 'hypostasis', but he does not make any christological use of it: *De natura hominis* 3: PG 40, 592A; E. Skard, 'Nemesiosstudien', *SymbOsl* 15–16, 1936, 23–43; 17, 1937, 9–25; 18, 1938, 31–41; 19, 1939, 46–56; 22, 1942, 40–8; id., 'Nemesios', *PWK*, Suppl VII, 562–6; L. I. Scipioni O. P., *Ricerche sulla cristologia del 'Libro di Eraclide' di Nestorio*, Fribourg 1956, 15–24; see E. Wyller, 'Die Anthropologie des Nemesios von Emesa und die Alkibiades I Tradition', *SymbOsl* 44, 1969, 126–45.

CHAPTER THREE

THE WESTERN CONTRIBUTION

It has become clear from the preceding history of the christological tradition that from Origen onwards the important developments took place in the East. This is partly because of the significance of the Alexandrians, but also because Arianism, Apollinarianism and finally Nestorianism all arose in the East. It was there primarily that the controversy had to be carried on, even if the whole church felt itself more or less to be affected. Nevertheless, after the first Christian centuries, which were characterized by a close communion between East and West, the Latin West began to have a more marked life of its own, beginning with Tertullian and Novatian, i.e. with the development of a Latin theological language. Tertullian was not, of course, so strong an impulse to development in the West as was Origen in the East. Augustine is the first Western theologian comparable with Origen—in fact his influence even exceeds Origen's. Despite the independent development of Eastern and Western theology, there was at the same time a constant interchange between the two theological language areas. This interchange was furthered in a number of ways: by the great 'displaced persons' of church history, like Athanasius, Hilary, Eusebius of Vercelli and Lucifer of Calaris; by the great pilgrims and travellers like Rufinus, Jerome, and Cassian, who did not, of course, all familiarize themselves with the East to the same extent, as Cassian is soon to show us; by significant church politicians like Ossius of Cordova; and by individual Roman Popes, above all, Damasus and Leo I.

In this exchange, the East usually, but not always, gave more than the West. The ways of giving and receiving were different. Hilary passed on Eastern christology (as far as he did) by a theological treatise; Jerome, above all, by translating exegetical works. Ambrose used Origen and Didymus without ever having seen the East. This is not the place to investigate the details of these connections between East and West.[1] Nor is it possible here to present a comprehensive picture of Latin christology from the time after Novatian until Augustine. As a line must be drawn somewhere, only the most important theologians of the period before the Council of Ephesus and their contribution to christology will be selected. We shall not be able to give an account of the Latin preaching

---

[1] Cf. P. Courcelle, *Les lettres Grecques en Occident*, Paris 1948, 37–115 (Jerome); 137–209 (Augustine); A. Siegmund, *Die Überlieferung der griechischen christlichen Literatur in der lateinischen Kirche bis zum 12. Jahrhundert*, München 1949; various investigations by B. Altaner are listed in his bibliography: *HistJb* 77, 1958, 576–600.

of Christ. *Maximus of Turin* (died between 408 and 423) could serve as an example. He

occupies only a modest place alongside his great contemporaries Ambrose, Augustine and Jerome. Whereas these three exercised a lasting influence on their environment through their writings and their work in the church, an influence which is testified to by many witnesses, the life and work of Maximus seems to have found no response during his lifetime.[2]

He did not further christological doctrine or christological formulas. His illustrations were of a popular character. He finds images in which to celebrate Christ and his work everywhere: in the cosmos, in ancient sagas (Odysseus tied to the mast, an idea which Jerome also knows),[3] and in the cultural life of his time. In this way he makes the theological picture of Christ into the sort of colourful mosaic which is loved by a popular audience. Of course, even the great theologians do not disdain popular expression like this, as, say, Ambrose shows us.

For a complete picture of Latin belief in Christ in the time before the Council of Ephesus, we should also note the hymnology which flourished particularly at that time, and all the liturgical and extra-liturgical devotion to the person of Christ. There is evidence of a far-reaching correspondence between the Eastern[4] and Western churches during the fourth century precisely in the sphere of hymn-writing (cf. Augustine, *Conf.* IX, 7). The Arians introduced the combination of strophic hymn and dogmatic refrain sung by the people, which was so important for their propaganda. There is something similar at the climax of the christological struggles in the interchange of a versicle—spoken by an individual—and a response given by the people (cf. *Chalkedon* III, Index s.v. 'Akklamationen'). It was Hilary of Poitiers who brought the knowledge of church hymnody from Phrygia to Gaul. But his poems were so theological that they seldom found their way into the liturgy. Ambrose may be regarded as the creator of Latin hymnody.

A climax is already reached with his contemporary, the Spaniard Aurelius Prudentius Clemens (died after 405). We shall make use of him for a brief account of the christological significance of this hymnody. He sets out in consummate form the theological controversies over trinitarian and christological dogma. In his *Apotheosis* he writes against the Patripassians (1–177), the Sabellians (178–320), the Jews (321–551), the Ebionites

---

[2] A. Mutzenbecher, *Maximi Episcopi Taurenensis collectionem sermonum antiquam . . . edidit*, Turnholti 1962, CCL 23, p. XV.

[3] P. Antin, 'Les sirènes et Ulysses dans l'oeuvre de s. Jérôme', *RevEtLat* 39, 1961, 232–41; H. Rahner, *Greek Myths and Christian Mystery*, London 1962, 328–86.

[4] Cf. W. Christ-M. Paranikas, *Anthologia graeca carminum christianorum*, Leipzig 1871; also H.-G. Beck, *Kirche und Theologische Literatur im Byzantinischen Reich*, München 1959, 262–6 and often; id., 'Hymnendichter, byzantinische', *LThK* V, 1960, with further literature. Ed. H. Auf der Mauer, 'Der Osterlobpreis Asterius' des Sophisten. Das älteste bekannte Loblied auf die Osternacht', *LitJb* 12, 1962, 72–85.

(552–781) and the docetic Manichaeans (952–1061). His *Hamartigenia* (origin of sin), probably under the influence of Tertullian's *Adversus Marcionem*, combats Marcionitism. As the preface and epilogue of his books show, his poetry is dominated by the figure of Christ:

> *Hymnis continuet dies*
> *nec uox ulla uacet, quin dominum canat;*
> *pugnet contra hereses, catholicam discutiat*
> *fidem* . . . (CSEL 61, 4).

In his *Kathemerion* we find some hymns of Christ taken into the church's hours of prayer, so that the whole day's work is referred to Christ. The *Hymnus omnis horae* (CSEL 61, 50–6) is a fine account of the life and miracles of Jesus. The hymns on Christmas (ibid., 63–8) and Epiphany (ibid., 68–76) are also significant. According to *Apotheosis* 309–11, Christ dominates history from the creation of man, when man, the image of God, is created in the fashion of Christ, the likeness of the Father, until the second coming of the Lord:

> *Christus forma patris, nos Christi forma et imago;*
> *condimur in faciem domini bonitate paterna*
> *uenturo in nostram faciem post saecula Christo* (CSEL 61, 94).

Our destiny is accomplished in Christ's fleshly destiny, as *Apotheosis* 1046–8 relates:

> *Christus nostra caro est, mihi soluitur et mihi surgit;*
> *soluor morte mea, Christi uirtute resurgo.*
> *cum moritur Christus, cum flebiliter tumulatur,*
> *me uideo* (CSEL 61, 122).

Prudentius has a skilful account of the doctrine of the two natures of Christ in the same book (1053–6):

> *si non uerus homo est, quem mors hominem probat ipsa,*
> *nec uerus deus est, operis quem gloria prodit*
> *esse deum, uel crede mori uel adesse refelle*
> *et gemina uerum Christum ratione negato!* (CSEL 61, 123).

Only educated Christians, who were perhaps the intended audience, will have understood this language.[5]

We now turn to the great Latin theologians of the time before Ephesus.

---

[5] For other christological hymn-writing see: B. Altaner, *Patrology*, ET §87; W. Bulst, *Hymni Latini antiquissimi LXXV, Psalmi III*, Heidelberg 1956; M. Manitius, *Geschichte der christlich.-latein. Poesie bis z. Mitte des 8. Jahrhunderts*, Stuttgart 1891; A. S. Walpole, *Early Latin Hymns*, ed. A. J. Mason, Cambridge 1922; J. Kroll, *Gott und Hölle*, Leipzig 1932, 1–182 (above all for the *Descensus*); F. J. R. Raby, *A History of Christian-Latin Poetry from the Beginnings to the Close of the Middle Ages*, Oxford 1953², 44–71 (Prudentius); there are some references with texts in PLS I, 1958, e.g. for Hilary, 273–81 (three authentic hymns and the probably spurius *Hymnus de Christo*). For the christology of the Latin hymns: J. Kroll, op. cit.; C. Blume, *Unsere liturgischen Lieder*, Regensburg 1932. On the whole subject see: John Julian, *A Dictionary of Hymnology I–II*, reprinted New York 1957; 'Hymnendichter', etc., *LThK* V, 1960.

Western theology runs parallel to the first Eastern attempts to oppose the Arian christology. The pressure of Arianism now leads to a stricter distinction of the 'natures' or the two 'substances' in Christ and in particular to a very concrete conception of his manhood. In his conflict with the Arians, *Hilary* (died 367) has a special contribution to make. His doctrine of the incarnation is fully incorporated into the great framework of his trinitarian doctrine.[6] For him, the incarnation is a revelation of the threefold God, and especially of the Sonship in God. This is clear from the pattern of the last five books of his work on the Trinity (PL 10, 234–472). True, the Arians recognize his struggle against Sabellianism, but they accuse him of violating Christian monotheism by his doctrine of the 'Son' in God. Because the Arians contest his belief in the pre-existent and true Son of God by referring to the human weaknesses of Christ, Hilary's debate with them leads him to christology. Hilary finds a better starting point than Athanasius. Even before the Apollinarian controversy he developed a quite explicit teaching on the soul of Christ. So he achieves a doctrine of the incarnation which is relatively complete by fourth-century standards. In trinitarian doctrine he occupies a position midway between Sabellianism and Arianism, in christology he comes between Arian 'monophysitism' and the 'Ebionitism' of Photinus.[7]

Hilary follows the main lines of the traditional christology of the church.[8] He acknowledges the full manhood of Christ and his true Godhead. Nevertheless, Christ is still only 'one' in the duality of Godhead and manhood: '*Non alius filius hominis, quam qui filius Dei est; neque alius in forma Dei, quam qui in forma servi perfectus homo natus est*' (*Trin*. X, 19: PL 10, 357AB). He attacks the '*tripartientes Christum*', i.e. those who separate the Logos, body and soul in Christ (*Trin*. X, 61–2: PL 10, 391A–392A) and also those who simplify him too much and make him a mere man (ibid.). He means to take Christ completely seriously as the great mystery of the revelation of God in the flesh, on all the levels of his reality (ibid., with reference to 1 Tim. 3. 16). Nevertheless, a distinction in Christ is necessary, into his constitutive, ontic elements and into the times before and after the incarnation. Christ's existence does not begin with the incarnation; he is preexistent as the true Son of God. He does not cease to be God when he becomes man (*Trin*. IX, 6; PL 10, 285AB). We may recall the distinction of the times in Athanasius. It serves to stress the

---

6 For Hilary's christology see P. Smulders, *La doctrine trinitaire de S. Hilaire de Poitiers*, Rome 1944, 195–206; P. Galtier, *Saint Hilaire de Poitiers*, Paris 1960, 108–58; E.-R. Labande (ed.), *Hilaire et son temps* (*Actes du Colloque de Poitiers 1968*), Paris (EtAug), which includes: J. Moingt, 'La téologie trinitaire de S.H.', 159–73; P. Smulders, 'Eusèbe d'Emèse comme source du *De Trinitate* de H. de P.', 175–212.—J. Doignon, *Hilaire de Poitiers avant l'exil*, Paris 1971: J. M. McDermott, 'Hilary of Poitiers: The Infinite Nature of God', *VigC* 27, 1973, 172–202.
7 Cf. H. de Riedmatten, *Les actes du procès de Paul de Samosate*, Fribourg 1952, 116–18.
8 Cf. P. Galtier, op. cit., 112–21.

distinction of the natures in Christ: '*Ut cum aliud sit ante hominem Deus, aliud sit homo et Deus, aliud sit post hominem et Deum totus homo, totus Deus. . . .*' (ibid., 285B).

Hilary distinguishes three times: pre-existence, kenosis and exaltation. He prefers this historical approach, which is of course closely bound up with an ontic one, to a static view of the two natures in Christ. He describes the kenosis of Christ with such strong words that some have asked whether he did not assume that the divine nature disappeared (cf. *Trin.* VIII, 45: PL 10, 270B).[9] But this kenosis or *evacuatio*, which consists in the renunciation of the *forma Dei* and the acceptance of the *forma servi*, presupposes in Hilary's writing that in fact the subject remains in his divine nature. For by this '*in forma Dei esse*' he expresses what the Antiochenes, especially Nestorius and Theodoret, and even Alexandrians like Didymus, understand by '*prosopon*' in its relationship to '*physis*': an emanation, a manner of appearance, a visible representation of a nature, of a being.[10] In the kenosis, then, Christ abstained from '*showing*' himself completely in his identity of substance with the Father, in the '*splendor gloriae*', although the fact that he was God shone through the servant's form in the miracles (*Trin.* IX, 51: PL 10, 323A: *Deum se virtutibus agens*). The divine nature, the being in the ontic sense, and the divine *virtus* are preserved in the kenosis; there is only a '*habitus demutatio*' (*Trin.* IX, 38: PL 10, 309B; cf. esp. 310). Did Hilary take this view of the concepts of '*natura*' and '*forma*' from the Fathers of the East? It is possible that he did, but Tertullian might also have been his starting point.

If Hilary stresses so strongly the permanence of the divine nature and its *virtus* in Christ's kenosis, what about the *virtus* and the nature of Christ's humanity? Has he here given way to Arian pressure and excessively weakened the lowliness and the reality of Christ's human nature? His opponents say that the church's theology does not attribute our human body and our human soul to Christ (*quod Christum dicamus esse natum non nostri corporis atque animae hominem*: PL 10, 358B–359A). Thus Hilary has reason to discuss Christ's soul and his bodily nature. This is Hilary's concern: he means to save the Logos from being made into the natural principle of suffering by the Arians.

Although Hilary had an advantage over Athanasius in that he clearly

---

[9] Cf. ibid., 122, n. 38.

[10] Cf. Hilary, *Tract, in Ps.* 68, 25 (PG 9, 456B: CSEL 22, 335$^{2-3}$): '*Forma et vultus et facies et imago non differunt.*' Hilary does not work with the word *persona*. Cf. P. Smulders, op. cit., 196, n. 74. It should be noted that '*in forma Dei*' 1. is equivalent to '*in natura Dei*' in the strict sense. Cf. P. Galtier, op. cit., 128, n. 64. In that case, 2. *forma* is distinct from *natura*: '*evacuatio formae non est abolitio naturae . . .*' (thus *Trin.* IX, 14: PL 10, 293A). Ambrosiaster, too (*In Ep. ad Phil.*, in 2, 6: PL 17, 408C–409D), takes '*forma*' in this sense, as 'manner of appearance', 'way of working' (*opera enim formam significabant*, 409B). '*Forma servi*' does not mean human nature. Ambrosiaster thus keeps to the one meaning of *forma*, whereas Hilary allows two. Cf. the exposition of Phil. 2. 6 in Pelagius, *In Epist. ad Phil.*: PLS I, 1312–13; id., *De Trin.*: PLS I, 1557–60 (*de Apollinario*); cf. PLS I, 1683–5 as evidence of Pelagian christology.

recognized the soul of Christ, he did not exploit this advantage sufficiently to answer the Arians. He still does not know how to make the soul of Christ into a full theological factor. Even in his *Commentary on Matthew* he seeks to keep sorrow and grief from Christ's soul. He has to take refuge in forced exegesis. Christ is not afraid of suffering and death for himself, but because of the stumbling block it could prove to the disciples. If the Lord prayed for the cup to pass from him, he was praying to the Father to give the cup to his disciples that they too might drink it with the same fearlessness (*In Ev. Matt.* XXXI, 4–7; PL 9, 1067B–1069A). In *De Trinitate* X he claims impassibility not only for the Logos but also for Christ's body and soul. So strongly does Hilary emphasize the influence of the Logos on his human nature that in his view the body and soul of Jesus are capable of suffering only by a divine miracle. There has to be a conscious decision of the Logos for his human nature to be laid open to suffering:

> ... how can we judge of the flesh conceived of the Holy Ghost on the analogy of a human body? That flesh, that is, that bread, is from heaven; that humanity is from God. He had a body to suffer, and he suffered: but he had not a nature which could feel pain. For his body possessed a unique nature of its own; it was transformed into heavenly glory on the mount, it put fevers to flight by its touch, it gave new eyesight by its spittle (*Trin.* X, 23: PL 10, 363A). ... the flesh he assumed, that is his entire manhood, was exposed to the nature of our passions (ibid., 24: 364A).

Thus the real 'natural' condition of Christ's body and soul is complete freedom from the usual human needs, even those of eating and drinking. Here we have not so much an insufficient elimination of docetism (as with Clement of Alexandria), as a transfiguration-theology which, in contrast to the Arians, stresses the divinity of Christ. It must be made impossible for the Arians to refer to the humiliating weaknesses of human existence.

True, the passion and death of Christ are a reality. But they are no grief to him, as the true reality of his body and soul is the state of transfiguration. This is also attested by his birth from the Virgin, of the Spirit, which acquires a special significance for Hilary in this context:

> It was above the weakness of our body, because it had its beginning in a spiritual conception (*Trin.* X, 35: PL 10, 371BC; cf. 44: 377C–378B).

Hilary seems to speak another language in the *Commentary on the Psalms* and the *De Synodis* and to recognize the workings of grief on Christ's body (cf. esp. *Tract. in Ps.* 53. 7: PL 9, 341A–C: CSEL 22, 140 and often; *De Synodis* 49: PL 10, 516B–517A). But he does not seem to have given up the basic features of his idea of the naturalness of the state of transfiguration for Christ's body. Is this a dependence on Eastern theology, or is it his own way out of the difficulties created by Arian objections? It is difficult to decide.

In any case, Hilary does not achieve a complete and satisfactory solution of the christological problem, although he made a good beginning with his clear distinction of the natures, strong emphasis on the soul of Christ and clear recognition of the unity (of person) in Christ. Compared with his contemporary Athanasius he has made tremendous progress in the way in which he analyses the sorrow of Jesus and his weeping at Lazarus' grave. He asks about the natural principle of this sorrow and this weeping: '*Quid sit deinde, quod in eo fleverit? Deusne Verbum, an corporis sui anima . . . ?*' And he finally replies. 'The soul, which is sorrowful, weeps' (*Trin.* X, 55: PL 10, 387AB; cf. 56: 387f.). The debate with the Arians gives him this insight. But because of this selfsame apologetic situation he again weakens the connection of suffering and sorrow with the humanity of Christ so as to protect the Logos from suffering in every respect. Like the Arians, Photinus too argues from the physical and spiritual suffering in the biblical picture of Christ, but while they do it to ascribe this suffering to the Logos *qua* Logos, he does it to show Christ to be a mere man. So Hilary fights on two fronts and stresses both the unity and the distinction of the God-head and manhood in Christ. He has the courage to take the earthly, human events seriously, but immediately displays a divine side to each earthly feature of Jesus' life. Only in this unity of earthly and divine, he feels, is belief in Christ whole and secure:

> Christ was born of the Virgin, but conceived of the Holy Ghost according to the Scriptures. Christ wept, but according to the scriptures; that which made him weep was also a cause of joy. Christ hungered: but according to the scriptures, he used his power as God against the tree which bore no fruit, when he had no food. Christ suffered: but according to the scriptures, he was about to sit at the right hand of power. He complained that he was abandoned to die: but according to the scriptures, at the same moment he received in his kingdom in Paradise the thief who confessed him. He died: but according to the scriptures, he rose again and sits at the right hand of God (*Trin.* X, 67: PL 10, 395B).

This tendency to stress the divinization of Christ's human nature eventually leads him above all to emphasize and expound Christ's exaltation.[11] The incarnation is not so much God's loss for men as in the last resort a gain, an ascent of man to God (*ut non defectio Dei ad hominem sit, sed hominis profectus ad Deum sit*: *Trin.* X, 7: PL 10, 348A). In the exaltation, the Godhead now has a total influence on Christ's humanity. Just as in the incarnation God becomes man, so in the exaltation man becomes God: '*ut caro potius hoc inciperet esse quod Verbum*' (*De Syn.* 48: PL 10, 516A). Hilary presses the idea of the divinization of Christ's manhood almost to the point of paradox. The '*susceptus homo*' is '*in naturam divinitatis acceptus*' (*Tract. in Psalm.* 68. 25: PL 9, 486B: CSEL 22, 335[9, 10]). The *forma servi* is

---

[11] Cf. P. Galtier, *Saint Hilaire de Poitiers*, Paris 1960, 141–58; J. F. McHugh, *The Exaltation of Christ in the Arian Controversy, The Teaching of St. Hilary*, Shrewsbury: Pont. Univ. Gregoriana 1959; and esp. A. Fierro, *Teologia de la Gloria en San Hilario* (AnalGreg 144), Roma 1964.

now taken up into the *forma Dei* (*Trin.* IX, 41: PL 10, 314B). We know
the temptation which 1 Cor. 15. 24–28 has been to theologians: the Arians
found in it their thesis of the inferiority of the Son to the Father, and
Marcellus of Ancyra, Evagrius and the Origenists wanted to derive from
it the abolition of the incarnation and the separation of the Logos from
the flesh, so that in the return of the Logos to the Father the latter became
all in all.[12] Hilary does not resort to this interpretation. Christ's humanity
has an eternal existence: *regnat autem in hoc eodem glorioso iam suo corpore*
(*Trin.* XI, 39–40; PL 10, 424B–426A). But it now becomes completely
incorruptible, eternal, spiritual (*quod carnale ei est, in naturam spiritus
devoratur: Trin.* XI, 49: PL 10, 432B). Over and above this, the manhood
of Christ is exalted to the glory of God, just as it earlier took the lowliness
of the servant form. True, God already glorified the Son of Man on earth
through this lowliness, by signs and wonders. In the resurrection, God's
glory is given to the body of Christ in all its fullness (*Trin.* XI, 42: PL 10,
427AB). But Hilary means something even higher by the final glorification, namely that the risen one enters into the glory of God himself:
ut . . . ipse exinde in Dei gloriam transeat (*Trin.* XI, 42: PL 10, 427A). In
its human reality this nature may now participate in the glory of God
and bear 'the name above all names'. Now we understand the drama which
Hilary has developed in *Trin.* IX, 6 with its individual acts: in the first act,
Christ is merely God (*ante hominem Deus*); in the second, Christ is God
and man (*homo et Deus*) and above all *in forma servi*. In the third, Christ is
still wholly man, but above all wholly God (*post hominem et Deum, totus
homo, totus Deus*). That, then, is the '*Deus omnia in omnibus*' for Hilary.
For this Christ it means '*Deus totus*'.

Hilary thus relieves the divine-human nature of Christ on two sides:
he often uses the expression '*assumptus (susceptus) homo*', so that it has been
inferred that he teaches two persons in Christ. On the other hand, as
P. Galtier observes, he seems to have anticipated the extreme basic
principle of the theologians of the Middle Ages which states: '*Anima
Christi habet per gratiam, quae Deus habet per naturam*'.[13] So Hilary has a
christology of divinization and union within the context of the 'Word-
man' framework and in this respect comes close to Gregory of Nyssa.
But the mystical element is subordinate or even lacking in his writings.
He is forced to his synthesis so as to be able to answer his opponents. He
would have been able to accomplish his task more easily had he seen more
clearly the levels on which unity and distinction are to be sought in Christ.
Despite his clear insight into the fact that the Logos has become man in
Christ and that therefore there is only 'one' in him,[14] he tries to explain

12 Cf. E. Schendel, *Herrschaft und Unterwerfung Christi. 1 Korinther 15, 24–28 in Exegese und Theologie der Väter bis zum Ausgang des 4. Jahrhunderts* (BGBE 12), Tübingen 1971, 158–67.
13 Cf. A. Grillmeier, 'Jesus Christus', *LThK* V, 1960, 949–51; P. Galtier, op. cit., 157f.
14 Cf. R. Favre, 'La communication des idiomes dans les oeuvres de s. Hilaire de P.', *Greg* 17, 1936,

this unity in the same way as all the Fathers of the time: in the light of the inward conjunction of the *natures* qua natures, in the manner of a 'mixing' such as, say, Gregory of Nyssa has shown us. Hilary did not, of course, put forward any theory on the subject and only expressed his view in descriptive fashion. He sees this mixing of divine and human in all of the earthly activity of Christ, until finally the Godhead is fully revealed and the humanity of Christ is virtually overwhelmed by the Godhead:

> Taking upon himself the weakness of our flesh, and remaining both his and ours, he performs, prays, professes, looks for all those things that are ours in such a way that those things which are his own are also *commingled* with them: at one time he speaks as a man, because he was born as a man, suffered and died as a man; at another time he speaks completely as God the Word. . . .[15]

Hilary has worked out his own picture of Christ. Latin christology has found its first comprehensive description. An advance has been made on both Athanasius and Tertullian.

It seems best to move on from Hilary directly to *Jerome* (died 419 or 420) and his friend and eventual opponent *Rufinus* (died about 410), because they too had personal acquaintance with the East. Jerome had direct contact with two Eastern theologians who occupied diametrically opposed christological positions, Apollinarius and Didymus:

> The doctrines of Apollinarius and of Didymus are mutually contradictory. The squadrons of the two leaders must drag me in different directions, for I acknowledge both as my masters.[16]

More than almost all the Latin Fathers, he made a special study of Origen, inspired to it by Gregory of Nazianzus. He does, however, protest that he had never been an Origenist (*si mihi creditis, Origeniastes numquam fui; si non creditis, nunc cessaui*).[17] The ardent admirer of the Alexandrian finally even concedes that the Council of Nicaea condemned Origen along with Arius (*quam quam latenter et Origenem, fontem Arii percusserunt* . . .).[18] Jerome puts forward his christological formula taking a middle course between Apollinarian-Arian monophysitism and the 'rationalistic'

481–514; 18, 1937, 318–36; J. J. McMahon, *De Christo Mediatore doctrina S. Hilarii Pictaviensis*, Mundelein 1947, 50–3.

[15] Hilary, *Tract. in Ps.* 54: PL 9, 348B: CSEL 22, 147–48. The term *persona* is taken from prosopographic exegesis rather than used in a technical sense. Cf. the anonymous *In symbolum Nicaenum* (end of the fourth century): PLS I, 234: *ostendit hominis personam deum dei filium baiulare*. Hilary avoids technical language. The words cited above recall Leo's interpretation of Christ's activity: *agit enim utraque forma* (see below). Many examples can be taken from the Latin Fathers examined here to show the division of Christ's work between Godhead and manhood. It has become a christological *topos*. See the selection of passages in B. M. Xiberta, *Enchiridion de Verbo Incarnato*, Matriti 1957, no. 18, 264–96.

[16] Jerome, *Ep.* 84, 3: CSEL 55, 123[10–12]. Rufinus does not think much of this pupil-relationship to Didymus: *Apol. c. Hieronym.* II, 15, 13–14: CCL 20, 94 (*et omnis eius iactantia in uno mense quaesita est*).

[17] Jerome, *Ep.* 84, 3: CSEL 55, 124[12–13]; cf. id., *Contra Joannem Hieros. ad Pammachium*: PL 23, 355–96 (1883: 371–412); also A. Guillaumont, *Les 'Kephalaia Gnostica' d'Évagre le Pontique* . . ., Paris 1962, 65–9, 89–92; L. Sanders, *Études sur S. Jérôme*, Bruxelles–Paris 1903, 345–82.

[18] Jerome, *Ep.* 84, 3: CSEL 55, 125[21]–126[1].

christology of the old adoptionists and Photinus. It does not, however, achieve the completeness and clarity of the other Latins:

> [The Saviour] is crucified as man and glorified as God. . . . We do not say this because we believe that God is one (person) and man another, and make two persons in the one Son of God, as falsely does the new heresy. Rather, one and the same is both Son of God and Son of Man, and whatever he says we refer on the one hand to his divine glory and on the other to our salvation.[19]

Jerome has not yet found his way to the Latin formula of the 'one person of Christ in two natures'. We find it—if the attribution can be maintained—before Augustine in the writing *Fides Isatis ex Iudaeo* (IV), the accuser of Pope Damasus who was converted from Judaism and later returned to it, in other words, in the circle of Jerome's acquaintances: '*quia unigenitus et primogenitus duae naturae sunt, diuina et humana, sed una persona*' (CCL 9, 343). The context, of course, shows that the christological conceptions have not kept pace with the formula. In comparison with this advanced formula Jerome still uses *persona* in an archaic way, as is shown by his play on words: '*Omnia Evangelia personant de persona hominis*' (i.e. of the humanity of Christ).[20] This strong stress on the humanity of Christ, with body and soul, is certainly interesting in someone who has sat under Apollinarius. The body of the Lord, too, has its sufferings and its desires. Hilary did not dare to draw so realistic a picture of Christ as does Jerome in the *Tractatus sive homiliae in psalmos*, on Psalm 108. The text is significant:

> If he had sorrow and pain, he also had feelings. For pain is a feeling. So if anyone wants to say to us, 'We say that he did not have feelings (*sensus = nous*) so that he may not be seen to have had sin', we reply, 'Did he have a body like ours or not?' If they say, 'Yes', we reply, 'In that case, he had the feelings of our body.' Everyone will understand what I say. And if they say that he did not have feelings or the desires of the body, we shall reply that he did not have a body. Let us say to them: 'He had a body like ours, yet did not have the sins of the body; he had a true soul and did not have the sins of the soul. For if the Lord did not take upon himself all that is of man, he did not save man. If he took a body and not a soul, he saved the body but he did not save the soul. But we would wish our soul to be saved rather than our body. Therefore the Lord took both body and soul that he might save both, that he might save the whole man, as he made him.' Thus if they say that the Lord did not take to himself feelings (i.e. the *nous*) in order that he might not sin, and yet themselves have human feelings, their ignorance is invincible. . . .[21]

Jerome dares to speak of *passiones* and *libidines corporis* in Christ, and in

---

[19] Jerome, *Ep.* 120, 9: CSEL 55, 497²²–498¹⁰. Cf. *Commentarioli in psalmos*, ed. Morin, *Anecdota Maredsolana* III, 1, 59⁹⁻¹³; id., *Tract. in libr. Psalm.*, *De Ps.* 109: ibid., 198: *non alius filius et alius filius, non facio duas personas in Deo et homine, sed ipse qui filius Dei est, ipse est et filius David. Comm. in Zach.* II, 7: PL 25, 1458A: '*Non Iesum dividimus, nec duas personas in unam possumus facere personam.*' *Comm. in Hieremiam* III, 52: CCL 74, 148¹⁵⁻¹⁷: '*non quo diuidamus personas . . . sed quo unus atque idem filius dei nunc iuxta carnem nunc iuxta uerbum loquatur dei.*' *Comm. in Ev. Matt.* II, in 14, 23: PL 26, 102A: '*non quod personam Domini separemus, sed quod opera eius inter Deum et hominem divisa sint.*'

[20] Cf. Morin, op. cit., 198²⁴⁻⁵.

[21] Morin, op. cit., 196³⁰–197¹⁷⁽²²⁾. Cf. *Comm. in Esaiam* XIV, in 53, 1–4: CCL 73A, 589⁵⁷⁻⁶¹.

this he is very modern. But he also knows of Christ's victory. The Apollinarians cheat Christ, and humanity, of this victory because they transfer the decision to the Logos *qua* Logos. 'If the Lord did not take all of man, he did not save man': we know the already well-established tradition of this christological-soteriological argument. The special stress laid on 'saving the soul' is unique. In his *Commentary on Matthew*, however, Jerome makes this picture of Christ rather more precise. He takes over the idea of *pro-patheia*, of *pro-passio*, which we have already noted (p. 363 above), from the tradition of Origen and the *Commentary* of Toura. He also stresses in his *Commentary on Isaiah* that the soul of Christ really felt grief for us:

Thus his soul truly suffered for us, lest Christ be thought to be part truth and part a lie.[22]

Nevertheless, this was only in '*incipere contristari*', so that the suffering, the *passio*, does not gain the mastery over Christ. Jerome does not go as far as Hilary: in his writings, the suffering remains a natural state of the soul and body of Christ and is not made an exception.

Even in Jerome, however, there are some features of a transfiguration-christology. In his *Commentary on Isaiah* he sees Christ with the prophets first of all as '*despectus . . . et ignobilis quando pendebat in cruce*'.[23] But the glory of the Godhead still broke through on the cross at the earthquake, and it also showed itself elsewhere during the earthly life of Jesus:

Truly that splendour, and the majesty of the hidden Godhead which also shone forth in his human face, was able to draw those who saw him by a glance (*Comm. in Ev. Matth.* in 9. 9: PL 26, 56A).

The stress on the suffering, unsightly Christ recalls ancient motives from the time of the persecution. The picture of the shining face points forward to Theodoret and his interpretation of the *prosopon* of Christ. Perhaps the Gospel of the Nazaraeans, of which Jerome gives his own interpretation, is also a source.[24]

It is clear from all this that Jerome did not treat christology in such detail and at such a depth as Hilary. There is still no consideration of the way in which God and man are one in Christ. But the picture of Christ's humanity and its activity is truer than that in the writings of the Bishop of Poitiers. Christ means much more for his devotion than for his theology. F. Cavallera has given an unsurpassable description of the devotion which this monk of Bethlehem had to Christ:

Dès son entrée dans la carrière de la vie parfaite, il a voué au Christ, à Jésus, une dévotion exclusive: c'est à Lui qu'il pense quand il sacrifie le monde, Lui qu'il a sous les

[22] Jerome, *Comm. in Esaiam* c. 53. 5, 7: CCL 73A, 590[29–30].
[23] Jerome, *Comm. in Esaiam* c. 53: CCL 73A, 588[45–6].
[24] See Hennecke–Schneemelcher–Wilson, *New Testament Apocrypha* I, London 1963, 150, no. 25.

yeux pour le soutenir dans les moments difficiles, Lui dont il rappelle les exemples et le dévouement pour encourager les âmes à se montrer généreuses. On ne trouvera pas beaucoup avant lui et autour de lui, depuis saint Ignace d'Antioche, d'échos semblables d'une dévotion aussi intime et personelle pour le Sauveur, ni qui ressemble de si près à celle du Moyen Age et des temps modernes. Ils évoquent l'intimité de la vie à deux avec Jésus, le dévouement passioné et absolut qui met en commun les joies et les peines et habitue à considérer le Sauveur comme le chef et l'ami. Sa pensée est toujours présente, son amour exalte tous les sacrifices. Sans oublier la perspective des récompenses éternelles avec les satisfactions qu'elles comportent, saint Jérôme s'élève ainsi jusqu' aux régions de l'amour désinteressé et ici encore est un écho fidèle de celui qui proclamait que rien ne pouvait le séparer de la charité du Christ.[25]

Jerome is also one of the witnesses of extra-liturgical prayer to Christ.[26] Anti-arian motives may have been at work in his stress on the worship of Christ, but its main source was surely the popular piety of the early church, as we have already pointed out (pp. 64–75 above), and above all that of Origen.

In this school, devotion to Christ became the centre of his religious life, as he himself said in exemplary fashion: 'Christ is all, that he who has left all for Christ may find one in place of all, and may be able to proclaim freely, "The Lord is my portion"' (Ps. 72. 26).[27]

In comparison, *Rufinus of Aquileia* (died about 410) does not have so much to offer. His own works show the strongly soteriological attitude of his christology. Certainly his theme, the exposition of the creed, written in his *Expositio Symboli*, led him firmly in this direction. The *Catechetical Lectures* of Cyril of Jerusalem may also have influenced him here. His view is cosmic, and not free from mythologizing elements. The cross of Christ is the '*tropaeum*', the sign of victory over Satan. The vertical beam of the cross draws lines upwards into the kingdom of the powers of the air and downwards into the underworld. The transverse beam points into the world of Christ's enemies on earth. The crucified himself, as man, is a bait for Satan. The Godhead is hidden in him like a hook; it becomes fatal to Satan: '*cui ipse carnem suam uelut escam tradens, hamo eum diuinitatis intrinsecus teneret inserto*'.[28] Rufinus also testifies to the varied tradition of the '*descendit ad inferna*', which does not occur in the Roman creed and is also absent in the East. But he explains this *descensus* in all too facile a way as being synonymous with the burial (*sepultus*) (no. 16: CCL 20, 152–3). Everything is directed towards the Lordship of Christ over all the realms of the world. Nevertheless, the features of Origen's Christ-mysticism are not lacking. With John, all the faithful rest on Christ's breast.[29] The whole

[25] F. Cavallera, 'Saint Jérôme et la vie parfaite', *RAM* 2, 1921, 110, with detailed examples.
[26] Cf. K. Baus, 'Das Gebet zu Christus beim Heiligen Hieronymus', *TThZ* 60, 1951, 178–188.
[27] K. Baus, ibid., 188. Jerome, *Ep.* 66, 8, 5: CSEL 54, 658[12–15].
[28] Rufinus, *Exp. Symb.* 14: CCL 20, 151[12–13].
[29] Rufinus, *Bened. Patr.* II, 13, 12–13: CCL 20, 211.

church is the bride of the Lord.[30] A rich typology is used to unfold the idea of Christ.[31] Thus Rufinus thinks more in the pictorial forms of the early Christian period, here too a pupil of his spiritual master, Origen. From Origen, too, he takes the sole speculative element of his christology, the idea of the *anima mediatrix* between Logos and sarx.[32] In its purely spiritual part, in '*secreta rationabilis spiritus arce*', in the '*apex mentis*', the soul grasps the Logos of God. Rufinus simply keeps to Origen, *Peri Archon* IV, 4, and to the speculations developed there.

Through its contact and debate with Apollinarianism, Western christology eventually consolidated further the Word-man framework which it had inherited. We have already described the influence which the West exerted even in Eastern disputes through the person of Pope Damasus (see above, pp. 349ff.). Later Western theologians, too, depended primarily upon Damasus; they took over his formulas without developing them into a christology of their own. *Ambrose* (339–97), of course, sees the problem of Apollinarianism in the East through Latin terminology, which has a strictly monophysite interpretation of the 'one physis' teaching:

> The authors of these things are those who say that the Godhead and the flesh of the Lord were of one nature. For I have read things that I would not believe had I not read them myself, namely that in some books it is argued that the instrument and that by which the instrument was moved were of one nature in Christ (*De Incarn.* 6, 51; PL 16, 866C).

Now the 'nature of the complete man' is emphasized even more decisively (ibid., 7, 76: PL 16, 873C). Christ has a body with a perfect soul and spirit (*sensus*); this without arousing suspicions that he is subject to his human desires (ibid., 7, 69: 871B). The soul of Christ here becomes both a physical and a theological factor, as it is the real principle of suffering, of progress and of our redemption, not separated from the Godhead but in union with it (ibid., 68–78: 871–4). An acute question in the Middle Ages about Christ's knowledge, often based on a spurious quotation from Ambrose, could not have arisen from Ambrose's genuine writings. They make a clear distinction between divine and human knowledge:

> But you say that we should take care lest, in assigning Christ two principal senses or two wisdoms, we divide Christ (ibid. 7, 75: 873B).[33]

For despite the clear distinction both remain 'one and the same' (*ipse igitur utrumque unus*), God and man. There is not one who is of the Father and another who is of Mary, but he who is of the Father took flesh (*non*

---

[30] Rufinus, ibid. II, 5, 18: *Apol. c. Hieron.* II, 38, 18f.: CCL 20, 206, 113.

[31] See CCL 20, Index s.v. 'Christus'.

[32] Rufinus, *Exp. Symb.* II: CCL 20, 148f.

[33] On the medieval controversy over Christ's knowledge cf. L. Ott, *Chalkedon* II, 916–21; E. Gutwenger, *Bewusstsein und Wissen Christi*, Innsbruck 1960, 79ff.; further references in T. J. Van Bavel, *Recherches sur la christologie de Saint Augustin*, Fribourg 1954, 158, no. 30.

enim alter ex Patre et alter ex Maria sed qui erat ex Patre carnem sumpsit ex virgine . . .). The duality in Christ becomes manifest in his works, which are divine or human (*operis distinctione*), and not in a difference of person (*non varietate personae*: in Ps. 61, 5: CSEL 64, 380). Ambrose builds up his interpretation of Christ within the simple, yet clear framework provided by this formula. And it is precisely because the formula already distinguishes the levels on which unity and distinction in Christ are to be sought that we find the Bishop of Milan completely unconcerned to make any speculative examination of the christological question.[34]

It is only when *Augustine* (354–430) has found out for himself the inadequacy both of his own ideas and of the traditional solutions that Latin christology is made aware of a wider set of problems.[35] One might perhaps expect that Augustine's picture of Christ would be particularly orientated on the christology of another great compatriot, converted before him, *Marius Victorinus Afer* (died after 362). The astonishment and joy of the church over the latter's conversion can still be felt in Augustine's time (*Conf.* VIII, 2, 4). Would not his own philosophical career have made it difficult for the admirer of Victorinus to accept the fact of the incarnation of God, a visible cult and sacraments, as was the case with his older exemplar (ibid.)? Similarly, the speculative strength of Victorinus and his particular vision of Christ could have restricted him and led him to interpret Christ in the same way. Would not Augustine have subscribed wholeheartedly to what Victorinus wrote?

Il fallut, pour notre libération, que l'universel, divin, c'est-à-dire la semence de tous les esprits qui subsistent selon un mode universel, c'est-à-dire l'être premier, c'est-à-dire le *Logos* universel, soit fait chair par le contact avec la matière inférieure et toute la corruption, pour détruire tout la corruption et tout le péché. Car les ténèbres de l'ignorance de l'âme, déchirée par les puissances matérielles, avaient besoin du secours de la lumière éternelle: *Logos* de l'âme et *Logos* de la chaire, après la destruction de la corruption, par le mystère de la mort qui mène à la résurrection, pourraient ainsi élever les âmes et les corps, sous la tutelle de l'Esprit-Saint, jusqu'aux pensées divines et vivifiantes grace à la connaissance, à la foi et à l'amour.[36]

---

[34] On the christology of Ambrose see: F. H. Dudden, *The Life and Times of St Ambrose* 2, Oxford 1935, 591–605; K. Schwerdt, *Studien zur Lehre des hl. Ambrosius von der Person Christi*, Bückeburg 1937; W. Seibel, *Fleisch und Geist beim hl. Ambrosius*, München 1958, 152ff., 174ff. (with a good connection of christology and soteriology). See now A. Morgan, *Light in the Theology of Saint Ambrose*, Diss. Pont. Univ. Gregoriana 1963; G. Matt, *Fons Vitae*, Diss., ibid. 1964.

[35] Selections from Augustine's christological texts are collected in: *Pages dogmatiques de Saint Augustin*, ed. Grand Séminaire Orléans, 1932, T. 2, 303–596; B. M. Xiberta, *Enchiridion de Verbo Incarnato*, Matriti 1957, no. 19, 296–340; on the christology itself: O. Scheel, *Die Anschauung Augustins von Christi Person und Werk*, Tübingen–Leipzig 1901; E. Schiltz, 'La christologie de S. Augustin', *NRT* 63, 1936, 689–713; T. J. Van Bavel, op. cit. (with criticism of the work by Scheel); J. A. Goenaga, *La humanidad de Cristo, figura de la Iglesia. Estudio de teologia espiritual agustiniana en las Enarrationes in Psalmos*, Madrid 1963; B. Studer, *Zur Theophanie-Exegese Augustins* (Studia Anselmiana 59), Roma 1971.

[36] Marius Victorinus, *Adv. Arium* I, 58, 14–24, tr. P. Hadot (SC 68), 371. For the christology of Marius Victorinus see P. Séjourné, 'Victorinus Afer', *DTC* 15, 2887–954, no. VII; also the excellent commentary by P. Hadot, *Marius V., Traités Théologiques sur la Trinité* II (SC 69), 1960.

Marius Victorinus understood clearly the soteriological significance of the taking of the body and the soul and the whole of man's fate by the Logos. Two ideas are closely connected in his writings: (1) the Logos takes the whole man, with body and soul; (2) the Logos takes the 'Logos' of the soul and the 'Logos' of the flesh, i.e. not merely an individual spiritual and fleshly nature, but the whole Logos of soul and flesh, i.e. the totality of all souls and all bodies. In this way Christ delivers all souls and all bodies. Here the orator stands in the larger tradition of the so-called mystical doctrine of redemption, which is represented in Irenaeus and Hilary.[37] At the same time, however, he also points forward to Augustine's idea of the *Christus totus* (see below). Victorinus unites with this a cosmic vision. Through the incarnation, Christ's first descent, and the resting of his soul in the underworld, his second descent, all realms of the world come into contact with the power and the activity of the divine spirit:

> Donc, lorsque l'Esprit assume l'âme, il projette, pour ainsi dire, sa puissance vers les inférieures et vers les actes, lorsqu'il remplit le monde et les choses du monde. . . . (*Adv. Arium* III, 12, 26–8).

Victorinus' christology could be described by the phrase *essence et présence*.[38] He is not satisfied with the adoptionist interpretation of Christ which he ascribes to Marcellus of Ancyra and finds in Photinus. He rejects the *homo assumptus* formula and firmly advocates an essential unity of Logos and man in Christ: '*Non igitur adsumpsit hominem, sed factus est homo*' (ibid., I, 22, 27–8: SC 68, 246). Certainly he was not afraid of talking of the complete reality of the incarnation and even of the taking of the emotions and sufferings of the soul.[39] But he arrives at formulas which leave the correct distinction of the natures obscure. They sound monophysite and would lead to a pan-Christism if they were measured against traditional christology:

> Car nous confessons que c'est le Logos lui-même qui a été dans la chair et non pas que le Logos est différent de l'homme dans lequel ils disent que le Christ habite (*dicimus* . . . *non aliud logon esse et aliud hominem*).[40]

---

[37] Cf. P. Hadot, on Mar. Vict., *Adv. Ar.* III, 3, 30–46: SC 69, 937–9. But it seems doubtful whether this is an answer to Apollinarianism, as Hadot assumes, if one observes how late the struggle against Apollinarius began in the East. One might rather imagine that Victorinus was acquainted with the Arian denial of Christ's soul, which was also known to Augustine.

[38] Cf. Mar. Vict., ibid., I, 13, 21–8; 18, 15–21: SC 68, 216, 228. P. Hadot, SC 69, 772: 'La théorie propre de Victorinus (cf. P. Henry, 'Kénose', p. 115) sur l'Incarnation du Logos et sa kénose utilise les notions néo-platoniciennes se rapportant à la *parousia* (= *praesentia*) de l'Incorporel dans le sensible . . .' H. points to *Adv. Ar.* III, 3, 27ff. and especially IV, 32, 14 and III, 12, 21ff.; A. Ziegenhaus, *Die trinitarische Ausprägung der göttlichen Seinsfülle nach Marius Victorinus* (MünchTheolStud II, 41), Munich 1972, esp. VII C: 'Das Bedeutungsfeld von Logos', 190–219.

[39] Mar. Vict., *Adv. Ar.* I, 22, 14f.: SC 68, 244: *Numquid enim* formam *solum accepit hominis, non et* substantiam *hominis?* Ibid., III, 3, 27–52: SC 68, 446–8. He points to Christ's sorrow and his wrath.

[40] Mar. Vict., *Adv. Ar.* I, 45, 8–10: SC 68, 324. He still does not distinguish between the masculine

But Victorinus maintains Christ's human nature. Indeed, he even has formulas which sound adoptionist.[41] Nevertheless, they only *sound* adoptionist. For he knows full well that Christ is the Son of God by nature, while we have that status only through adoption. So despite his neo-Platonism, which finds special expression in his interpretation of the Pauline description of Christ in the *forma Dei* and the *forma servi* (Phil. 2. 6, 7),[42] he has appropriated the essential outlines of the church's belief in Christ.

In some respects the development of Augustine's own thought is a recapitulation of earlier christological discussion. For Augustine before his baptism Christ was not yet the '*persona Veritatis*' of the church's faith, but merely a man, completely human and partaking of 'wisdom' to the full (*Conf.* VII, 19, 25). His original way of expressing the fact of the incarnation is still so unsatisfactory that an ill-disposed interpretation could read completely opposed christological errors into his writings. To this stage belong such formulas as '*hominem suscipere, hominem agere, corpus agere, susceptio inferioris personae*' (cf. espec. *Serm.* 119, 7). But his *Explanation of the Epistle to the Galatians*, written between 394 and 397, already draws a sharp distinction between the unity of God and man in Christ and the gift of grace to other men who do not happen '*naturaliter habere et agere personam Sapientiae*' (*Explan. Ep. ad Gal.* 27: PL 35, 2125). This '*naturaliter*' is reminiscent of Cyril's conception of the unity in Christ which is termed ἕνωσις κατὰ φύσιν, φυσική or οὐσιώδης. The substitution of abstract expressions for concrete ones is a further indication that he continues to gain a deeper insight into the unity and distinction in Christ: after his ordination as priest *natura humana* and *humanitas* become more frequent (see Van Bavel, 14, n. 4). Like Novatian, he learns to apply a rule for making a distinction within Christ: *qua Deus, qua homo* (PL 40, 87). Finally, even in Augustine's earlier christology there occurs a comparatively comprehensive formula whose affinity to the most moderate Antiochene theology is striking:

The whole of man was taken by the Word, that is, a rational soul and body, that the one Christ, the one God, the Son of God, should not only be Word, but Word and man. He is Son of God the Father on account of the Word, and Son of man on account of the man . . . And at the same time as being man he is Son of God, but on account of the Word, by whom the man was taken; and at the same time as being the Word he is Son of man, but on account of the man who has been taken by the Word (*Serm.* 214, 6; PL 38, 1069).

and neuter usage of *alius* and *aliud*, which we found in Gregory of Nazianzus. Victorinus understands his expressions in the sense of his Platonism or as substitution: Christ's manhood stands for all manhood. Christ has '*catholicum corpus ad omnem hominem*' (*Ad Gal.* VI, 14: PL 8, 1196D).
    [41] Mar. Vict., *Adv. Ar.* I, 10: SC 68, 208–9. *Ad. Gal.* II, 6–8: PL 8, 1207B has: *Christus . . . servi sumpsit personam*.
    [42] Cf. Mar. Vict., *Ad. Phil.* II, 6–8: PL 8, 1207A–1209C; SC 69, index s.v. 'forme'.

It was while in Milan that Augustine made acquaintance with Arian and Apollinarian christology, either through personal meetings or in his reading (PL 40, 93). His friend Alypius was himself an advocate of this position (*Conf.* VII, 19, 25). Augustine, however, was vigorous in emphasizing the wholeness of Christ's human nature. But he found it hard in the face of all the disparaging interpretations of Christ's person (e.g. those of the Manichaeans: PL 42, 177; CSEL 25, 200) to maintain his full transcendence. The reason for this is the lack of a deeper concept of person. At first, the significance of '*persona*' for Augustine is similar to that of *prosopon* for the Antiochenes; it means, 'tenir la place de quelqu'un, être pénétré de celui-ci, en être comme le reflet, la manifestation extérieure, le vêtement, l'aspect, l'apparence' (Van Bavel, 7). This is also still the case in the passages from his *Explanation of the Epistle to the Galatians* which have already been quoted. Christ's pre-eminence lies in the role of his manhood '*ad habendam naturaliter et agendam personam Sapientiae*' (see above). Of course, Augustine's recognition of the unity of subject in Christ and of the distinction of the natures continues to become clearer. It is not any man who appears in Christ, but the very Wisdom of God:

(Jesus Christ the man) was so taken, according to the catholic faith, that he might be Son of God, that is, so that in him the Wisdom of God might appear to heal sinners (PL 42, 177; cf. 425; CSEL 25, 200 and 633).

The real metaphysical significance of the 'concept of person', however, has still not yet been discovered.

The first approaches in this direction are made in trinitarian rather than christological investigations. We find a first reasonably acceptable definition of the difference between nature and person in Augustine's work *De Trinitate* (VII, 6, 11; cf. XV, 7, 11: PL 42, 943-4 and 1065). Nature is something which is had in common, person on the other hand is '*aliquid singulare atque individuum*' (943). This is reminiscent of the Cappadocians. But quite independently of finding terms to embrace the meaning of 'person', Augustine described the unity of subject in Christ in paraphrase, a method which had also enabled theologians before him to reach the crux of the matter without having terminological means at their disposal. As examples we have the formulas '*idem ipse et homo Deus—Deus homo*' (cf. Van Bavel, 19, 24); from this it is clear that for Augustine the unity of person in Christ was not merely the result of a synthesis of two natures. It is rather the pre-existent person of the Word who is the focal point of this unity and who 'takes up' the human nature 'into the unity of his person' (*in unitatem personae suae, Unigeniti, Verbi assumere*, ibid., 23 and n. 34). In this way Augustine eventually comes to make a definitive improvement in the Latin christological formula: *Persona una ex duabus substantiis constans; una in utraque natura persona.*[43]

At the same time keener attention is paid to the adequacy of christological expression. Formulas which could imply an accidental relationship between God and man in Christ are excluded. Any mention of 'God in mEn' or of 'having the Godhead' is recognized to be insufficient. God '*is*' man; this man Jesus Christ '*is*' the Son of God. Because of the substantial character of the union of Godhead and manhood, because of the impossibility of dissolving this conjunction, Christ is raised far above any prophet on whom the spirit has descended (*In Joh. Ev. tr.* 99, 2: CCL 36, 583: PL 35, 1886). In the famous letter on the presence of God, which had a great influence on medieval theology, Augustine points out the deep distinction between the presence of God in the world, in inspired 'saints' and in Christ (*Ep.* 187, 2ff.: PL 33, 833ff.: CSEL 57, 83ff.). Here Col. 2. 9, which speaks of the indwelling of the fullness of the Godhead in Christ, is not for a moment sufficient to describe the difference between Christ, the head, and his members (*Ep.* 187, 13, 40: PL 33, 847: CSEL 57, 117).

Not only do we find Augustine struggling with a christological formula, we also find him trying to gain an inner understanding of the unity of God and man in Christ. Here the famous analogy of the 'unity of body and soul' becomes particularly significant, and of course Neo-Platonic anthropology begins to exert some influence.[44] Augustine has different ways of describing the relationship between soul and body. One set of expressions presupposes an accidental framework, conceived more after the Platonic manner, as for example in the writing *De moribus ecclesiae catholicae* (I, 27, 52; PL 32, 1332): '*Homo igitur, ut homini apparet, anima rationalis est mortali atque terreno utens corpore.*' Here man is defined as 'soul', whose instrument the body is. But then another framework reveals a closer conjunction: '*Homo est animal rationale mortale*' (*De Ordine* II, 11, 31: PL 32, 1009: *De quantitate animae* 25, 47–9; ibid., 1062–3). The occurrence of these two frameworks in this christology does not necessarily mean that Augustine wavered between a substantial and an accidental unity in Christ. It has even been asked whether he did not define the unity of body and soul by considering the incarnation.[45] This would mean

---

[43] Augustine, *In Joh. Ev. tr.* 99, 1: CCL 36, 582⁴²⁻³; PL 35, 1886; *Serm.* 294, 9; PL 38, 1340. The formula *una persona geminae substantiae* also occurs (*C. Max.* II, 10, 2; PL 42, 765, cf. Van Bavel, 24). We may recall the formula of the *Fides Isatis ex Judaeo*: CCL 9, 343.

[44] Cf. T. J. Van Bavel, op. cit., 30–2; E. Schiltz, 'La comparaison du Symbol Quicumque vult', *EphThLov* 24, 1948, 440–55; F. M. Young, 'A Reconsideration of Alexandrian Christology', *JEH* 22, 1971, 103–23; L. I. Scipioni O. P., *Ricerche sulla cristologia del 'Libro di Eraclide' di Nestorio*, Fribourg 1956, 15–44; E. L. Fortin A. A., *Christianisme et culture philosophique au cinquième siècle. La querelle de l'âme humaine en Occident*, Paris 1959, 111–61; here with reference to C. Couturier, 'La structure metaphysique de l'homme d'après saint Augustin', in *AugMag* I, Paris 1954, 543–50.

[45] C. Couturier, op. cit., 544–50, is of this opinion: according to Augustine, the unity of a human being is 'ni accidentelle, ni substantielle, mais hypostatique'. It finds its real metaphysical expression in the analogy to the mystery of the incarnation. Also E. L. Fortin, op. cit., 112ff., who thinks that Augustine's interpretation of the body-soul relationship is still defined in primarily philosophical terms.

that he had achieved a thoroughly theological, and at the same time personal, interpretation of man and his body-soul unity. But if we make a
closer investigation of the relationship between Augustine's anthropology
and his doctrine of the incarnation it becomes clear that he already had the
body-soul unity at his disposal as a current analogy. This is at least the
case in his famous letter to the pagan Volusian, which he wrote at the
request of Marcellinus.[46] In it he wishes to remove any objections which
Volusian may make to the Christian proclamation of the incarnation of
God (cf. *Ep.* 137, 2). Is the incarnation not ruled out from the start because
of the impossibility of the union of God and man? Augustine, as is often
his custom, replies to this question by indicating a still more mysterious
instance, which occurs in the realm of nature and so can be used as an
analogy of the unity of God and man, the union of body and soul·

Some insist upon being furnished with an explanation of the manner in which the
Godhead was so united with a human soul and body as to constitute the one person of
Christ, when it was necessary that this should be done once in the world's history, with
as much boldness as if they were themselves able to furnish an explanation of the manner
in which the soul is so united with the body as to constitute the one person of a man, an
event which is occurring every day. For just as the soul is united to the body in one person
so as to constitute man, in the same way is God united to man in one person so as to
constitute Christ. In the former personality there is a combination of soul and body; in
the latter there is a combination of the Godhead and man. Let my reader, however,
guard against borrowing his idea of the combination from the properties of material
bodies, by which two fluids when combined are so mixed that neither preserves its
original character; although even among material bodies there are exceptions, such as
light, which sustains no change when combined with the atmosphere. In the person of
man, therefore, there is a combination of soul and body; in the person of Christ there
is a combination of the Godhead with man; for when the Word of God was united to
a soul having a body, he took into union with himself both the soul and the body. The
former event takes place daily in the beginning of life in individuals of the human race;
the latter took place once for the salvation of men (*Ep.* 137, 11: PL 33, 520: CSEL 44,
109f.).

It is, then, the make-up of man which forms the starting point for a
solution of the christological problem. In Augustine's view, however, the
gap to be bridged in the union of soul and body is greater than that in
the conjunction of God and man; in the former case the gap is between the
spiritual and the corporeal, while in the latter case, in Christ, spirit is
united with spirit. For it is the Godhead and the soul which are directly
united in him. The body is only joined to the Godhead by means of the
soul, '*anima mediante*'. So in Christ we have an easier case of union, that is
the unity of two rational beings, the Godhead and the soul.

And yet of the two events, the combination of two immaterial substances ought to be
more easily believed than a combination in which the one is immaterial and the other
material. For if the soul is not mistaken in regard to its own nature, it understands itself

[46] Augustine, *Ep.* 137 *ad Volusianum*: PL 33, 515–25: CSEL 44, 96–125. Marcellinus' letter, *Ep.* 136,
and Augustine's answer to it, *Ep.* 138, also belong here.

to be immaterial. Much more certainly does this attribute belong to the Word of God; and consequently the combination of the Word with the human soul is a combination which ought to be more credible than that of soul and body. The latter is realized by us in ourselves; the former we are commanded to believe to have been realized in Christ. But if both of them were alike foreign to our experience, and we were enjoined to believe that both had taken place, which of the two would we more readily believe to have occurred? Would we not admit that two immaterial substances could be more easily combined than one immaterial and one material; unless, perhaps, it be unsuitable to use the word combination (*mixtionis uel mixturae nomen*) in connection with these things, because material things usually have quite another behaviour by nature? (ibid.).

In this discussion with Volusian, Augustine gives us an extremely clear view of what lies behind his formulas. He shows us how far advanced is his speculative understanding of the unity in Christ. Although the word 'persona' occurs here, he still does not work with the concept of 'person'; he does not advance beyond a 'unity of natures' as a result of which the 'one person' first comes into being. But this 'unity of naturet' is understood from Neo-Platonic presuppositions. Here the assumption of the inner relationship, indeed the consubstantiality, of the divine and the human soul is of paramount importance (cf. *De civ. Dei* X, 29, 34). Both are as it were 'made of the same stuff'. And homogeneous things can be united. The unity, however, is not a 'κρᾶσις' as in the blending of material stuffs which together form a third new substance, nor is it an (accidental) *parathesis* as was assumed by Plato; it is something midway between the two; to use Greek terms, a ἕνωσις ἀσύγχυτος, ἄμμικτος. But what is achieved by this? How can a genuine unity be obtained if the Aristotelian explanation of the unity of body and soul is excluded? If all the details of the body-soul comparison which do not fit the unity of God and man are struck out, what is there left? Augustine tries to find a way out with the key phrase 'anima mediante', which had already provided Origen and Rufinus with a solution: '. . . (Verbum) particeps carnis effectum est rationali anima mediante' (*Ep.* 140, 4, 12: PL 33, 542: CSEL 44, 163). But how is this 'cohaerere' of Godhead and soul brought about? As Augustine is concerned with a 'unity without confusion', he is driven here to the solution which we found earlier in Nemesius. No longer is the original Neo-Platonic relationship between the Godhead, the soul and the world an underlying factor;[47] it is replaced by the conception of a 'unity of behaviour' such as occurs in Origen and Nemesius. Augustine, however, does not express himself further on this; he has not yet seen the real purpose which the body-soul comparison could have served once the Neo-Platonic anthropology had been transformed. The inadequacy of this speculation emerges still more clearly in his dispute with the Manichaeans. To show that the Godhead is not polluted through its conjunction with the material body,

[47] Cf. L. I. Scipioni, *Ricerche*, 20-2.

he lays great stress on the mediatory role of the soul. Not only is it made
a connecting-link; it almost becomes a protective screen between the
Godhead and the body:

> Nor should our faith be lessened by any reference to 'a woman's internal organs', as
> if it might appear that we must reject any such generation of our Lord, because sordid
> people think that sordid. . . . Those who think this ought to observe that the rays of the
> sun . . . are poured over evil-smelling drains and other horrible things and do their natural
> work there without being made foul by any contamination, though visible light is by
> nature more closely related to visible filth. How much less could the Word of God, who
> is neither visible nor corporeal, have been polluted by the body of a woman when he
> assumed human flesh along with a human soul and spirit, within which the majesty of the
> Word was hidden away from the weakness of the human body? (*De fide et symbolo* IV,
> 10: CSEL 41, 13).

So, clearly as Augustine recognizes the unity of subject and the uniqueness of the conjunction of Godhead and manhood in Christ, he has still to
find an adequate basis for his ideas in speculative theology. Moreover, his
imagery and comparisons readily point beyond the narrower christological problem to the association of Christ with the church. This happens
when he speaks of the mystical wedding between the Word and the
humanity[48] which took place with Mary's womb as the bridal chamber.
Augustine's teaching on the incarnation is in no way free from the
difficult problems of interpretation which confront us elsewhere when we
try to discover what he really means. The relationship between the
historical and the mystical Christ (Van Bavel, 110–18) and eventually the
problem of the knowledge of Christ (ibid., 149–61) are certainly cases in
point. Augustine does not always distinguish between the 'historical' and
the 'mystical' person, between the individual and the total Christ. This
gives his statements about the historical Christ the characteristic inconsistency which is also a feature of his picture of the *Christus totus*. He
frequently makes use of this distinction merely to attribute to the *Christus
totus* what he will not predicate of the historical Christ. But we should not
therefore take the statements which refer to the *Christus totus* as 'symbolic',
'non-real' predicates of Christ and see in them a dissolution of the historical
incarnation. The problem also arises in interpreting the experiences of
Christ's soul, especially in connection with the temptation, the dereliction
and the whole of the passion. Although Augustine always looks towards
the *Christus totus* and shows that it was he who bore our suffering, this
does not in any way imply that Christ did not suffer truly in his person.
Here, then, Augustine develops some sort of a psychology of Christ.
Christ's soul becomes a 'theological factor'. But here, too, he leaves us in
an uncertainty which has still not completely been resolved. Ambrose
saw more clearly what was involved (cf. Van Bavel, 149–61).

[48] Cf. *In Joh. Ev. tr.* 8, 4: CCL 36, 83f.: PL 35, 1452; *Enarrat. in Psalmos*, In. Ps. 44, 3: CCL 38,
494–6: PL 36, 494–6. Cf. T. J. Van Bavel, *Recherches*, 74–85, 110–18.

Latin christology gained much from Augustine.[49] But he could not provide what was needed to bring the crisis which had broken out in the East at the end of his life to a successful outcome.

[49] Unfortunately it is impossible to include an account of the christology of Pelagius and the Pelagians here. This would require still more preliminary work, especially in connection with their significance for the doctrine of grace. Some of the important literature which must serve as the starting point for such an investigation is as follows: G. de Plinval, *Pélage. Ses écrits, sa vie et sa réforme*, Lausanne 1943, 123–7 (clear distinction between Pelagius and Arian and Apollinarian christology); id., 'Pelagio e Pelagianismo', *Enciclopedia Cattolica* IX, Roma 1952, 1071–7; id., 'Points de vue récents sur la théologie de Pélage', *RSR* 46, 1958, 277–36; id., 'L'heure est-elle venue de recouvrir Pélage?', *RevEtAug* 19, 1973, 158–62. Here de Plinval discusses G. Greshake, *Gnade als konkrete Freiheit*, Mainz 1972; G. makes some remarks on the christology of Pelagius, 125–34. There is also an extensive bibliography. Cf. also R. Hedde–E. Amann, 'Pélagianisme', *DTC* XII, 675–715. For the problem of Pelagianism, Nestorius and Ephesus cf. M. T. Didier, 'Le pélagianisme au Concile d'Ephèse', *EO* 34, 1931, 314–33; J. Plagnieux, 'Le grief de complicité entre erreurs nestorienne et pélagienne d'Augustin à Cassien par Prosper d'Aquitaine', *RevEtAug* 2, 1956, 391–402; J. Speigl, 'Der Pelagianismus auf dem Konzil von Ephesus', *Annuarium Historiae Conciliorum* 1, 1969, 1–15.

CHAPTER FOUR

THE EVE OF EPHESUS

By the end of the fourth century the battle against the heretical Logos-sarx christology seems already to be abating in a number of places, for example, Alexandria, whereas in others, for example round Antioch, it only now seems to be coming to a climax. The younger Cyril of Alexandria, bishop since 412, seems to know nothing of the whole christological controversy between the time of Athanasius and his own. For Theodore of Mopsuestia, it is still a living reality. So in the first decades of the fifth century we find once more a Logos-sarx christology of an archaic kind, and, over against it, a developed Logos-anthropos framework. The representatives of these two interpretations of Christ are, respectively, Cyril and Theodore. There is no dispute between them. This in itself is a characteristic of the last two decades before Ephesus. But in both writers the positions are being prepared from which the fateful battle between Antioch and Alexandria is to be fought.

1. THE YOUNGER CYRIL AND THE 'LOGOS-SARX' CHRISTOLOGY

Cyril[1] may be most easily understood if we return once more to the classic figures of orthodox and heretical Logos-sarx christology, to Athanasius and Apollinarius, and attempt to describe his thought and language with reference to them. He reaches the final form of his picture of Christ by retaining some elements from these two writers and deleting others, to replace them with new ideas. Without doubt Athanasius is his chief tutor.

If we examine the characteristics of the christology of the earlier works of Cyril, we find nothing but Athanasius. The whole controversy with

[1] J. Liébaert, *La doctrine christologique de saint Cyrille d'Alexandrie avant la querelle nestorienne*, Lille 1951, who criticizes earlier introductions to Cyril's christology, especially: A. Rehrmann, *Die Christologie des hl. Cyrillus v. Al.*, Hildesheim 1902; E. Weigl, *Christologie vom Tode des Athanasius bis zum Ausbruch des Nestorianischen Streites*, Munich 1925, 123–203; R. V. Sellers, *Two Ancient Christologies*, London 1940; H. du Manoir, *Dogme et spiritualité chez saint Cyrille d'Alex.*, Paris 1944; J. Mahé, 'Cyrille', *DTC* 3, 2509–16. More recently: G. Jouassard, 'Un problème d'Anthropologie et de Christologie chez saint Cyrille d'Alexandrie', *RSR* 43, 1955, 361–79; id., 'Saint Cyrille d'Alexandrie et le schéma de l'Incarnation Verbe-Chaire', *RSR* 44, 1956, 234–42; B. Lavaud–H. M. Diepen, 'Saint Cyrille d'Alexandrie, court traité contre ceux qui ne veulent pas reconnaître Marie Mère de Dieu', *RevThom* 56, 1956, 688–712; R. L. Wilken, *Judaism and the Early Christian Mind. A Study of Cyril of Alexandria's Exegesis and Theology* (Yale Publications in Religion 15), New Haven and London 1971; the relevant chapters of this study are 'The Second Adam' (93–142); 'Moses and Christ' (143–61); 'The New Man' (181–200). Cf. also E. Nacke, *Das Zeugnis der Väter in der theologischen Beweisführung Cyrills von Alexandrien nach seinen Briefen und antinestorianischen Schriften*, Münster 1964. This last work also contains criticism of the works by J. Liébaert and H. du Manoir cited above. There is an important reconsideration of methods and subject-matter in the dispute between Cyril and Nestorius in L. I. Scipioni, *Nestorio e il concilio di Efeso. Storia dogma critica* (Studia Patristica Mediolanensia 1), Milano 1974 (see below and in the appendix).

Apollinarianism waged by Antiochenes, Cappadocians and even by the Alexandrians themselves seems to have passed without leaving any traces on his theology. Once again we find the Athanasian Logos-sarx christology in its pure form.[2] Like his predecessors, Cyril has only the Arians in view in writing the christological chapters of his *Thesaurus* (chs. 22–4 and 28). They are merely a paraphrase of the decisive section of the *Contra Arianos* III (35–57), but in a weaker and milder form. Cyril certainly makes alterations to the argument of his spiritual ancestor, but in doing so he has no intention of making any inner changes in it. He is merely bent on making it acceptable. Here, as also in *Dialogue* VI, the Athanasian setting of the problem and the solution go together.[3] From time to time, however, the copy frees itself from the original and produces independent formulas, though of course no new trend of christology emerges.

In the way in which the problem is put we still find ourselves firmly in the period before the Council of Ephesus. The christological question as such, how God and man are one in Christ, is not yet acute. One element in particular has yet to make an appearance—the soul of Christ. Even if Cyril recognizes it—and this must surely be assumed after the previous controversies[4]—he never considers it a 'theological factor' right up to the emergence of Nestorius. In the theology of the Greek church, Christ is once again only Logos and sarx. The *Thesaurus* and the *Dialogues* give no indication that Cyril recognizes a human *knowledge* in Christ and the *development* of a human understanding.[5] The Logos is the spiritual power of Jesus, and the progress of the Lord is no more than a gradual revelation of the wisdom of the Logos. Cyril thinks as little as Athanasius of repudiating the difficulties advanced by the Arians against the immutability of the Logos by referring to the soul of Christ. Both Alexandrians recognize the reality of the sufferings, and both attribute them to the 'sarx'. There are only πάθη τῆς σαρκός, sufferings of the flesh, *and no real sufferings of the* ψυχή.

---

[2] The sources of Cyril's earlier christology are: (1) the *Thesaurus*: PG 75, 9–656; (2) *Dialogi de s. Trinitate* (VI): PG 75, 657–1124; (3) *Homilia* VIII 4–6: PG 77, 565B–577A (= Easter Festal letter of 420); (4) *Commentary on John*: PG 73–4. On the chronology of the sources: G. Jouassard, 'L'activité littéraire de saint Cyrille d'Al. jusqu' à 428. Essai de chronologie et synthèse', *Mél. E. Podechard*, Lyon 1945, 159–74; N. Charlier, 'Le "Thesaurus de Trinitate" de saint Cyrille d'Al. Questions de critique littéraire', *RHE* 45, 1950, 25–81 differs slightly. For the *Commentary on John*: J. Mahé, 'Le date du Commentaire de S. Cyrille d'Al. sur l'Evangile selon S. Jean', *BLE* 9, Toulouse 1907, 41–5. Charlier (p. 56) regards the *Thesaurus* as the first major theological work of Cyril and dates it at the beginning of his episcopate (about 412). The *Commentary on John* is regarded as his first exegetical work (Charlier, 60–2). G. Jouassard, on the other hand, would put the *Thesaurus* between 423 and 425 and make the *Commentary on John* Cyril's last exegetical work (after 425). N. Charlier's arrangement seems to suit Cyril's christological development best.

[3] J. Liébaert, *S. Cyrille*, 82ff. Independently of this N. Charlier, 'Thesaurus de S. Cyrille', 51, also establishes that about a third of the *Thesaurus* is a reproduction of Ath., *Ctr. arian.* III.

[4] Cyril mentions the soul of Christ only twice in the pre-Ephesine period: in the Easter Festal letter of 420: PG 77, 573B and in the *Glaphyra in Gen.* 6: PG 69, 297C. If with N. Charlier, 'Thesaurus de S. Cyrille', 56, we put the *Thesaurus* soon after 412, both mentions of the soul of Christ occur after the discussions in the *Thesaurus*.

[5] J. Liébaert, *S. Cyrille*, 144.

The 'flesh' is also the recipient of *gifts*, of *holiness* and of *glory*.[6] Throughout his argument, which is directed against the Arians, Cyril never once thinks of attacking the basic christological principle on which they rely, that the Logos is the soul of Christ. He only disputes the consequences which the heretics draw from it for the nature of the Logos. Apollinarianism and the church's struggle against it seem to be virtually unknown to the author of the *Thesaurus* and the *Dialogues*.[7]

Hence the younger Cyril is no 'diphysite' in the later sense of the word, nor is he intent on the ontological interpretation of the two natures in Christ. We have not yet reached the classical period of the 'doctrine of the two natures'. The interpretative principle of the distinction of the 'two times', which Athanasius had developed in his struggle against Arius, must still help Cyril to preserve the transcendence and immutability of the Logos.[8] The statements of the gospels are to be divided between the Logos before the incarnation and the Logos after the incarnation: a dynamic, historical approach which is to be replaced by a more static, ontological one. Now because the latter is not to be found in Cyril, he is also not concerned to make a closer definition of the character of the nature that has been taken in Christ. True, even in the earlier writings the means of christological expression at his disposal is richer than that of Athanasius: Christ took 'flesh' or 'what is of man' (ἀνθρώπινα), finally even 'man'[9] and 'human nature'. But this last word should not lead us to assume the presence of the ontological approach mentioned above. For Cyril, as for Athanasius, this word signifies primarily the sum of all that is meant by humanity, human states in all their totality. To be sure, we find some Aristotelian definitions of man with reference to Didymus, but these do not signify any transference of an Aristotelian anthropology to christology.[10] For this reason, none of the christological formulas of the earlier writings (*Thesaurus* and *Dialogues*) allow us to conclude quite simply that in Cyril's picture of Christ the soul has already become a 'theological factor'.

Liébaert makes a detailed investigation of the christological formulas

[6] *Thesaurus* 24: PG 75, 396D does not contradict this. Cyril has recourse to the life of the human soul as an analogy for his interpretation of Christ. From this it may be inferred that the πάθη in Christ are movements of the flesh which are sensed by the spiritual principle that is in the flesh. But Cyril does not say what is to be understood by this spiritual principle. Cf. J. Liébaert, *S. Cyrille*, 210–11. *Dialog.* 4: PG 75, 868B uses the term *psyche* in the biblical sense, to mean life.

[7] J. Liébaert, *S. Cyrille*, 210–11.

[8] Ibid., 117 for a comparison of Cyril and Athanasius: *Thesaurus* 20, 22, 24 (PG 75, 337B–D, 369BC, 392D) = *Ctr. arian.* I, 54–5; III, 43, 55 (PG 26, 124B–128C, 413BC, 437B). Both have the same basic principle for the distinction of the natures in Christ: τὸν καιρόν, τὸν χρόνον ἐξετάζειν. Cf. further *Thesaurus* 10: PG 75, 120D; *Dialog.* 4: PG 75, 877D. *Ctr. arian.* III, 29, 30 also has some influence on the *Dialogues* and gives them their Athanasian colouring.

[9] J. Liébaert, *S. Cyrille*, 184–6, describes it as a concession to the 'Word-man' framework. But such formulas occur only in *Thesaurus* 15, 21: PG 75, 281D, 361D. Cf. Ath., *Ctr. arian.* II, 7, 67: PG 26, 161B, 289B. On the whole question see Liébaert, 182.

[10] Cf. ibid., 59. These definitions occur in the dispute with Eunomius, who was trained as an Aristotelian. Cf. *Thesaurus* 2, 34: PG 75, 29C, 32A, 596; *Dialog.* 2. 7: PG 75, 728A, 729CD, 1081C.

of Cyril's early period, to see how far they can be regarded as an expression of the Logos-sarx theology. Consequently we shall be content with the indications which have already been given and make only a brief examination of Cyril's christological terminology before Ephesus. But the points which have been made so far are sufficient for us to draw an important conclusion: Cyril can move completely within the limits of the Logos-sarx christology and still recognize a soul in Christ. He advances a verbal Logos-sarx framework in which the soul of Christ is certainly a *physical* factor, even if it is not yet a theological one. Here he is exactly like Athanasius, but differs from him in one very important respect: in Cyril, the idea of the vital, dynamic relationship between Logos and sarx, as it was developed in the early writings of Athanasius, could no longer attain its old significance.

It is especially significant that the chief formula of the Athanasian interpretation of Christ recurs, the formula which has become the basic expression of the whole of the Logos-sarx christology of all types: 'The Word *became* man and *did not come into a man.*'[11] Cyril also takes over the two frameworks which were to give a first, unconsidered explanation of the relationship between God and man in Christ, the frameworks of 'indwelling' and 'appropriation'. The Word is 'in' the body—and the body is 'appropriated' by the Word.[12]

In the *Thesaurus* and in most texts of the *Dialogues* Cyril limits himself to repeating the formulas of Athanasius. If he goes beyond them, this does not mean that there is any basic reorientation of his christology.[13] Christ, in the theological interpretation given by the young Cyril, is no more than Logos and sarx.

2. THE ANTIOCHENE PICTURE OF CHRIST

In the Cyril of the period before Ephesus, then, we do not yet find that classical type of Alexandrian christology which is usually put at the

---

11 Ath., *Ctr. arian.* III, 30: PG 26, 388A; Cyril. Al., *Dialog.* 1: PG 75, 681C. For Cyril's dependence on Athanasius cf. Liébaert, *S. Cyrille*, 163-4.

12 'Indwelling' framework: *Thesaurus* 23, 24, 28: PG 75, 389A, 392A, 393C, 428A; *Dialog.* 5: PG 75, 944C. παρουσία ἐν σαρκί, μετὰ σαρκός, ἔνσαρκος γέννησις or οἰκονομία, ἐν σαρκὶ κένωσις—and the corresponding terms such as 'temple' and 'house' are quite frequent in the earlier works of Cyril. For a collection see J. Mahé, 'Comm. de Cyrille d'Alex. sur S. Jean', 43-4, and N. Charlier, 'Thesaurus de S. Cyrille', 59-60. Later, however, these formulas will either be rejected or explained as implying a substantial unity. Mahé makes use of this change for his studies in the date of the *Commentary on John.* Cf. G. Jouassard, 'L'activité litt.', 159ff. For the 'appropriation' framework cf. the Athanasian concept ἴδιος; e.g. *Thesaurus* 21, 28: PG 75, 361C, 429A. Further in Liébaert, *S. Cyrille*, 197ff. Here too belong such expressions as ἀναλαμβάνειν, ἰδιοποιεῖσθαι, οἰκειοῦν.

13 Such new formulas are, for example: ἐνωθῆναι σαρκί, σαρκί συμφέρειν. Liébaert, *S. Cyrille*, 200-3. The ontologically deepened expressions in *Thesaurus* 32: PG 75, 504A-C may not be interpreted in the sense of the *unio physica* of the later Cyril (against E. Weigl, *Christol. v. Tode d. Ath.*, 147). It should be noted that Cyril speaks of Christ here as 'Mediator', who in his twofold nature participates both in God and in man: φύσει καὶ οὐσιωδῶς θεῷ τε καὶ ἀνθρώποις συναπτόμενος. We have here, then, not the *unio physica* of the two natures one with another, but the unity of Christ with both God and mankind.

opposite pole from Nestorianism. The whole Alexandrian tradition is not integrated, and what is to come is not yet visible. The Cyril of the early period takes a great deal, indeed almost everything, from Athanasius. But the further development of the Alexandrian tradition is, so to speak, included. The young Cyril surely knew the blind teacher of Alexandria, Didymus. The two belong to the same thought-world. Nevertheless, we cannot say that Didymus exercised a real influence.[14] The anti-Origenistic movement about 400 was probably to blame for that. Other elements are to shape Cyril's definitive Alexandrianism. On the other hand, the classical type of christology which is usually described as 'Antiochene' has not yet arisen. Those who are generally termed representatives of this type (Eustathius of Antioch, Diodore of Tarsus—who in fact had an advocate of an explicit Logos-sarx christology as his teacher—Theodore of Mopsuestia and their other partisans) are so very different from each other that it is only to a limited extent that they can all be included under a common designation. How little an Antiochene can represent an 'Antiochene' christology can perhaps be seen most clearly in John Chrysostom (died 407).

(a) John Chrysostom and his picture of Christ

If we begin from the usual a priori judgement, we would expect Chrysostom quite naturally to be openly opposed to Apollinarius and as a result to stress the soul and the complete human nature of Christ. To our surprise, we discover a christology which is very like that of the younger Cyril of Alexandria and his model, Athanasius. Chrysostom was a pupil of Diodore of Tarsus, a further confirmation that the teacher too should not simply be counted as a classical Antiochene in his christology. 'Chrysostom seems to have been singularly unpreoccupied with the Apollinarist heresy.'[15] He quotes Apollinarius only once.[16]

Equally rare is any express mention of Christ's soul. 'In the homily on Phil. 2. 7 which follows upon this reference to the heretic (Apollinarius), Chrysostom clearly affirms the existence of a soul in Christ, and attacks those who deny it'[17]—but he does this only after he has been made Bishop of Constantinople. In his Antiochene period there does not seem to be any direct attack on the Apollinarians. Chrysostom's christology is governed

---

[14] Cf. L. Doutreleau, 'Vie et survie de Didyme l'Aveugle', Les Mardis de Dar El-Salam; Sommaire 1956-7, Paris 1959, 43.

[15] Cf. C. Hay, 'St John Chrysostom and the Integrity of the Human Nature of Christ', FrancStud 19, 1959, 301. We shall follow this study and merely insert some additional details of Chrysostom's historical position. C. Hay makes an examination of earlier studies of Chrysostom's christology, particularly that of J. H. Juzek, Die Christologie des hl. Johannes Chrysostomus, Breslau 1912. Cf. now also F. M. Young, 'Christological Ideas in the Greek Commentaries on the Epistle to the Hebrews', JTS, NS 20, 1969, 150-63; Paul W. Harkins, 'Chrysostom the Apologist: on the Divinity of Christ', Kyriakon I, 441-51.

[16] Chrysostom, In Phil. 6, 1: PG 62, 218.

[17] Ibid., 7, 2-3: PG 62, 231-2; C. Hay, ibid., 301-2. The soul of Christ is mentioned once again, In Ioann. 27, 2: PG 59, 159 (ὁ ἔμψυχος ναός).

entirely by his defence against the Arian denial of Christ's soul. 'The transcendence and the consequent immutability of the divine essence' is his chief christological concern here. Even when he is stressing the reality of the body of Jesus against the docetists and the Manichaeans, the stronger emphasis always lies on the Godhead of the Lord. 'Our doctrine is this, namely, that God has prepared for Himself a holy temple (ναὸν ἅγιον)'— here we have an 'Antiochene' element—'through which He has transported the life of Heaven into our life.'[18] Chrysostom is interested not in the natural life of Christ, the human spiritual life inspired and supported by the divine spirit, but in the life which the Logos unfolds *qua* Logos in his humanity. Once again, on the threshold of the fifth century, we find a theologian in whose writings the soul of Christ, while being a physical reality, is not a theological factor in the interpretation of Christ. This is also clear from the way in which Chrysostom hardly notes, or even parenthesizes, the acts of Christ's intellect and his will. He supposes the existence of so close a communication between the Logos and the spiritual soul of Christ that he will allow no limitation to Christ's human knowledge because this seems to endanger his divinity. Because the Logos dwells in Christ, there is no need for knowledge to be mediated to Christ's human spirit by human sense experience: 'In the (divine) nature he possessed all.' 'Nowhere in his writings does Chrysostom give any indication that Christ possessed a distinct human knowledge.'[19] Chrysostom's interpretation of the activity of Christ's will corresponds with this.[20] The decision to accept the redemptive suffering stems from the divine will of the Logos. In the writings of Chrysostom, no human act of Christ's will is involved here—as in the Alexandrian Athanasius! This interpretation of Christ's spiritual activity seems to have come easily for him. Knowing and willing are indeed spiritual acts for which there seemed to be an adequate principle in the spiritual Logos.

Chrysostom never realized how little this answered the Arians and how much he had excluded the spiritual element of Christ's humanity. An interpretation of the feelings and purely physical experiences of Jesus' human nature is now even more difficult.[21] These have considerable significance for the soteriology of the great preacher. For he means to acknowledge the reality of the *oikonomia*, i.e. the incarnation, however much he may have to stress Christ's divinity. But he does not succeed very well in reconciling his two aims:

I have never left the assumed humanity unharmonized with the divine operation (οὐδαμοῦ τὴν ἀναληφθεῖσαν ἀνθρωπότητα τῆς θείας ἐνεργείας ἄμικτον ἀπολέλοιπα), (acting) now as man, now as God, both indicating the nature, and bringing faith to the economy;

18 Chrysostom, *In diem natal.* 6: PG 49, 359.
19 C. Hay, art. cit., 305.
20 Ibid., 305-9.
21 Ibid., 309-14.

teaching that the humbler things are to be referred to the humanity, and the nobler to
the divinity, and by this unequal mixture of actions, interpreting the unequal union of
the natures (διὰ τῆς ἀνίσου ταύτης τῶν ἔργων κράσεως τὴν ἄνισον τῶν φύσεων ἔνωσιν ἑρμηνεύων),
and by (my) power over sufferings, declaring that my own sufferings are voluntary; as
God, I curbed nature, supporting a fast for forty days, but afterwards, as man, I was
hungry and tired; as God, I calmed the raging sea, as man I was tempted by the devil;
as God, I expelled devils, as man I am about to suffer for men.[22]

The 'unequal mixture of actions' corresponds to the 'unequal union of
natures'.

We can hardly go far wrong in seeing behind formulas like this the
Stoic principle of 'predominance' and also a Stoic *krasis*-doctrine. We are
far from a picture of Christ like that given by Theodore of Mopsuestia.
Chrysostom, then, does not deny the human activity of Christ.

Christ acts as man, but these human actions are controlled by the Divine Person in
such a way that they bring faith to the economy without overshadowing the divine
nature.[23]

Here the human activity is noticed only in a limited field, namely in
the sub-rational sphere. Thus the purely spiritual, divine activity of the
Logos and the sub-rational activity of the emotions and the senses are
opposed in this particular picture of Christ. This may be illustrated by a
fairly lengthy text which deals with Christ's prayer in Gethsemane:

Consequently, in saying, 'If it be possible let this cup pass from me,' and, 'Not as I
will, but as Thou wilt,' He indicates nothing else than that He is truly clothed with flesh
which fears death; for to fear death, and to hesitate and have a horror of it, is a property
of this (i.e. the flesh). Sometimes, therefore, He leaves it destitute and deprived of His
own operation (γυμνὴν τῆς οἰκείας ἐνεργείας) in order that, having shown its weakness,
He might bring faith to its nature; sometimes He hides this same weakness in order
that you may learn that He is not a mere man. . . . Therefore He varies and mingles both
words and actions, that no pretext may be given to the disease and madness of Paul of
Samosata, nor of Marcion nor of Manes: therefore He predicts what is to be, as God, and
again He trembles (before death) as man.[24]

In the natural field of the sub-rational feelings and reactions of Christ's
human nature, the divine *energeia*, then, is, in Chrysostom's view, always
in command, in accordance with the principle of predominance. There is
no sign of a decision by Christ's human spirit.

It is significant that Chrysostom never speaks of the human activity of Christ as that
of a distinct human nature acting simply because it is human. Whenever Christ acted ὡς
ἄνθρωπος or ἀνθρωπίνως, He did so for either of two reasons: to prove the reality of the
economy, or out of condescension (συγκατάβασις) to His hearers.[25]

[22] Chrysostom, *In quatrid. Lazarum* 1: PG 50, 642-3; quoted in Hay's translation, 310.
[23] C. Hay, art. cit., 310.
[24] Chrysostom, *In eos qui ad synaxim non occurrerunt* 6: PG 48, 766; C. Hay, ibid., 306, n. 43, who points
out that Maximus Confessor used this passage to prove two wills in Christ, but was unjustified in so
doing.
[25] C. Hay, art. cit., 311. For this whole idea of 'condescension' see 311-13.

The sub-rational forces and *passiones* of this human nature seem, in Chrysostom's view, to work only in so far as the higher principle of the nature and person of the Logos wills it and only to the extent that he wills it.

When speaking of Christ's fast in the desert, Chrysostom remarks that Christ did not fast longer than forty days for fear that through the excess of the miracle 'the truth of the economy might not be believed'.[26]

Like Hilary, Chrysostom says of Christ: 'when he permits the flesh, then it shows its feeling'.[27] This picture of Christ is quite different from the 'Antiochene' one—taking this word in its usual sense. It is conceived more as the Alexandrian picture, and is governed by the same anti-Arian interests which moved Athanasius and Hilary. Like the former, Chrysostom is fond of talking about the 'flesh' of Christ when he is dealing with the activity of Christ's human nature. He is not excluding Christ's soul here, but merely leaving it out of the question.

Chrysostom argues from the physical and emotional activities of Christ to the reality of the flesh. He never argues from the spiritual activity of Christ to the reality of the flesh. In effect, Chrysostom nowhere affirms an intellectual or volitional activity of Christ, nor does he ever explicitly indicate the presence of a human intellect and will in Christ.[28]

The whole way in which Chrysostom's picture of Christ is drawn accords with this: everything is conceived of in the light of the Logos and of the unconditioned predominance of the divine nature.[29] The typically Antiochene difficulties in the interpretation of the unity in Christ do not exist for Chrysostom. It is not very significant that he says on one occasion: '(The apostle Paul) asserts against Marcellus that there are (in Christ) two persons distinct in substance.'[30] This is that concept of *persona* which is meant to prove, not the duality of subjects, but the reality of the two natures. We have also found it on the Alexandrian side. This Antiochene, so persecuted by the Alexandrians, is far more Alexandrian than Antiochene in his christology—a new indication of the care with which we must use a word like 'school'. Only with Theodore of Mopsuestia (died 428) does 'Antiochene' christology properly begin.

(b) Theodore of Mopsuestia and classical Antiochene christology

Under the influence of the passionate polemic of the Apollinarians and the Monophysites, and also through Cyril of Alexandria after the outbreak of the Nestorian controversy and the disputes over the 'Three Chapters' in the sixth century, Theodore's reputation has suffered considerably—not

26 Chrysostom, *In Matt.* 13, 2: PG 57, 210; quotation after Hay, 313.
27 Ibid. 67, 1: PG 58, 633.
28 C. Hay, art. cit., 315.
29 See Chrysostom, *Cat. Bapt.* I, 21: SC 50, 160–4.
30 See C. Hay, art. cit., 314, n. 73.

that he himself did not give occasion for this. But only his negative significance has been seen, and his positive contribution to the history of the Christian faith has been misunderstood. Recent scholarship has made different attempts at a more favourable exegesis of his christology, and it is to be judged right in many of its findings.

In the present discussion there is room for a word on the methods to be used for investigating Theodore's christology. Some modern investigations rightly stress that an examination should be made not only of Theodore's interpretation of Christ in the narrower sense, but also of his whole attitude to the Christian faith and its cult. A total picture of Theodore's faith will make it easier to establish his ideas in any specific section of that faith, e.g. in christology. So good attempts have been made to describe Theodore's theological system in the light of his notions of immortality and the rôle of the other heavenly realities.[31]

Christianity, so Theodore teaches his catechumens, is essentially directed towards heaven. This gives his theology its unity. His argument is above all based on typology. Theodore divides human history into two *katastaseis* or ages, the present and the future. The Old Testament contains the symbols for the life of the church, and the life of the church and of Christians is the pattern of life in heaven. The second *katastasis* is introduced by the redeeming work of Christ. Therefore Christ's work, more than anything else, reveals the way in which the whole *oikonomia* of God is orientated on immortality. In Christ, God shows us the first-fruits of the immortality which he has prepared for us. The various mysteries of the life of Christ offer us an anticipatory vision of the mysteries of the church. By baptism the Christian participates in the death and resurrection of the Lord. By adoption as child of God he participates in the true Sonship of the Son of God (the Logos). This participation is again realized and shown forth to us in a quite unique way in Christ as man. The whole *oikonomia* of God is present in the eucharistic feast. It already gives a share in the world of

---

[31] I. Oñatibia, 'La vida cristiana tipo de las realidades celestes', *Scriptorium Victoriense* I, 1954, 100–33 (quoted here from an offprint); Luise Abramowski, 'Zur Theologie Theodors von Mopsuestia', *ZKG* 72, 1961, 263–93. This article also refers to the first one. Both challenge W. de Vries, 'Der "Nestorianismus" Theodors v.M. in seiner Sakramentenlehre', *OCP* 7, 1941, 91–148; id., 'Das eschatologische Heil bei Th.v. M.', *OCP* 24, 1958, 309–38. Rowan A. Greer, *Th. of M. Exegete and Theologian*, London 1961 (he stresses the importance of biblical-christological terminology for Th. of M.; see 48–65); U. Wickert, *Studien zu den Pauluskommentaren Th's von M.*, Berlin 1962; G. Koch, *Die Heilsverwirklichung bei Theodore von Mopsuestia*, München 1965; Koch also challenges de Vries and studies Theodore's soteriology and ecclesiology in connection with his christology; the results are similar to those in the first two studies; in summary fashion the methods used in the examination of Theodore's writings and christology are given in R. A. Norris, Jr, *Manhood and Christ. A Study in the Christology of Theodore of Mopsuestia*, Oxford 1963. But R. A. Norris has not yet made the acquaintance of the above-mentioned studies. His special contribution is his demonstration of the anthropological presuppositions of Theodore's christology. I was unable to have access to G. H. M. Posthumus Meyjes, 'De Christologie van Theodorus van M.', *VoxT* 25, 1954–5 (cited in L. Abramowski, art. cit., 264). For newly discovered sources see William F. Macomber, S.J., 'Newly Discovered Fragments of the Gospel Commentaries of Theodore of Mopsuestia', *Mus* 81, 1968, 441–7. For the fundamental christological conception of the *Commentary on John* see K. Schäferdiek, 'Th.v.M. als Exeget des vierten Evangeliums', *StudPat* X (TU 107), Berlin 1970, 242–6.

heavenly realities. Redemption, then, does not merely consist in (the hope of) immortality, incorruption and immutability (in a future life), but already in a present, inner participation in the divine spirit:

> So too in the birth which is here made ours through baptism, which is the type of the resurrection, we shall receive grace through the same Spirit, but partially and as a first instalment. Then, however, we shall receive it completely, when we rise in truth, and incorruptibility is in reality communicated to us.[32]

This participation must be matched by moral life. The life of the future must already be lived in the community of the church, the pattern of the *civitas caelestis* to come. It is important for us to see this total picture of Theodore's view of Christianity, which in one of the studies already mentioned is characterized thus:

> This conception of our author, far from breaking with tradition, continues the line begun with St Paul. It would be easy to cite the Pauline passages which provide Theodore with a starting point for those concepts (*conceptos*) which we have investigated in this study. We have found nothing which could not be interpreted in an orthodox and traditional sense. Theodore's unique service consists in his ability powerfully and boldly to group a synthesis of all the truths of dogma and all the duties of morality round a principal idea and to offer a unified and imposing vision of Christendom, the elements of which are all harmoniously directed towards a final destiny which is bathed in light.[33]

But it should be clearly understood that in his doctrine of baptism and in his description of the condition of the Christian at baptism, Theodore is concerned to preserve the transcendence of God. The idea that comes into play here is not so much that of divinization as the idea of 'conjunction', *coniunctio*, and moral obedience, always with reference to Christ. It is quite clear that Theodore himself measures our participation in the divine life, achieved in baptism, by Christ, which means, in his own language, by the conjunction of the man who is taken with the Logos and his divine nature. The Logos makes the human nature of Christ (the *susceptus homo*) participate in the worship which is offered to him on the grounds of the *synapheia*, the conjunction. Through this, the man who is taken also participates in the other divine persons, the Father and the Spirit. For the Logos is *homoousios* with them. The glory of the man who is taken consists in his being accepted as Son. Through Christ, we too will share in this acceptance, though not in the same unique way.

---

[32] Theodore M., *In Ev. Joh.* III, 29: Vosté 56, here cited in the translation by R. A. Norris, *Manhood and Christ*, 162. I. Oñatibia and L. Abramowski stress strongly against the view of W. de Vries that Theodore knows of this inner participation in the life of the spirit already happening in the present life of Christians and that it is not just a hope of praeternatural gifts in eternity. The future condition is certainly already taken to be real in baptism: '. . . he who is born in baptism possesses in himself all the power of the immortal and incorruptible natures and he possesses all (its faculties); being incapable of using them, of putting them into action . . . until the moment which God has fixed, when we shall rise from the dead' (*Hom. cat.* XIV, 10: ed. Tonneau, 423, quoted in R. A. Norris, 162). He also shows (ibid., 186–8) that Theodore knows a true and actual grace, without detriment to human freedom.

[33] I. Oñatibia, art. cit., 34; cf. L. Abramowski, art. cit., 273f., which makes an excellent investigation of the concept of participation in Theodore (274–6).

Theodore characterizes the redeemed state of man in terms of assimilation to Christ, as in the following prayer which the Lord himself is made to speak: '. . . all of them . . . let them be in the likeness of my own glory, and let them possess conjunction with me, by which they may be exalted to the honour of intimacy with the divine Nature'.[34]

Even in eternity, the humanity of Christ is given a great significance as mediator of this conjunction. Whether we consider the unity of God and man in Christ or our conjunction with God formed on the pattern of this unity of God and man. Theodore is always moved by the one concern: to deprive the Arians of any occasion of violating the divine transcendence. However much he considers the immanence of God in our history, or our participation in God, or finally the decisive realization of this immanence and this participation in Christ, he is always concerned not to confuse the Godhead with the creature.

It is understandable that as a result the closeness of the conjunction of God and man, whether in Christ, or in us as imitators of Christ, might seem to be loosened. But it would be unjust to represent this loosening of the unity in Christ as Theodore's prime concern and to relate it to a false motive. Theodore is searching for a new interpretation of the participation of man in God and the conjunction of God and man in Christ, so as to be able to achieve a synthesis between the immanence and the transcendence of God in us and in Christ in the face of the Arians and the Apollinarians. This immanence of the Logos in Christ is to be such that both the divinity of the Logos and the integrity of the manhood in Christ are preserved.

Thus Theodore's christology is put in the framework of the whole of his theology, and his real concern is made clear. There is now just a word to be said on the way by which he means to reach his goal. A twofold approach is also to be distinguished in him: his attitude towards the traditional kerygma of the church and his own speculative attempts. Since Justin, the history of the dogma of Christ has been full of the tension between the *auditus* and the *intellectus fidei*. Origen was particularly conscious of it. To see the character of this tension in Theodore, we should note that he is not really a speculative theologian. He is primarily an exegete, 'the Interpreter', as he was called, and is so even in his dogmatic writings.[35] He experiences the theology and presence of Christ as a liturgist. His speculative theology is therefore subsidiary, and not an aim in itself. His philosophy stands even further in the background. It makes itself felt primarily in his anthropology. We must give a brief account of it (see below), as Theodore, too, interprets the unity of God and man in Christ along the lines of the body-soul unity. But this is not the sole philo-

---

[34] *Manhood and Christ*, 169; Theodore M., *Hom. cat.* X, 18: ed. R. Tonneau, *Les homélies catechetiques de Theodore de Mopsueste* (ST 145), Città del Vaticano 1949, 273.
[35] Cf. R. A. Norris, *Manhood and Christ*, 125.

sophical element in his christology.[36] As with the Cappadocians, we also find unnoticed in his writings the special rôle of the analysis of the *ens physicum concretum*, i.e. the concepts of *prosopon* and *hypostasis*. *Prosopon* plays a special part in his interpretation of Christ. We must examine his achievements here.

How far did his speculation, his *intellectus fidei*, lag behind the traditional kerygma and the pre-speculative interpretation of it by the church? Is his speculative-theological inadequacy so extensive that the result is *de facto* an unorthodox picture of Christ? By what standard is this deficient orthodoxy to be measured? We feel that a preliminary look at the Council of Ephesus, held three years after his death, and even at Chalcedon itself, is no error in methodology.[37] For the whole development tends towards Ephesus and Chalcedon, and it has even been asserted, though not quite rightly, as we shall see, that Theodore already anticipated the Chalcedonian formula. Thus a further pointer as to method is not out of place. On the one hand, his· orthodoxy is insufficiently proved by reference to formulas which have an orthodox ring, but on the other hand, a heretical intent should not be assumed without further investigation. It is therefore necessary to make a careful investigation of the pattern of his thought over and above his formulas. When we do this, however, we must take the orthodox tendencies of Theodore (and of the moderate Antiochenes in general) as a starting point unless the contrary is proved, and notice the concrete situation of his christology and theology. We must therefore ask, 'How does the christological problem present itself to him, and what means of solving it are at his disposal?' From here we shall be able to estimate his objective and subjective relationship to the development of orthodox christology. We shall now attempt to discover the significance of Theodore's christology in three ways, by outlining first his significance as a critic of the Logos-sarx framework, secondly his own christological thought, and thirdly his christological formula.[38]

---

[36] R. A. Norris investigates principally this anthropology of Theodore's, but not the metaphysic of the *ens concretum* in Theodore. Norris is rather stricter in his assessment of Theodore's christology than I. Oñatibia and L. Abramowski. The study by G. Koch, mentioned above, offers a good synthesis between a positive assessment of Theodore's christology and criticism of it. See his introduction, §, 3, 14–23.

[37] U. Wickert, *Studien zu den Pauluskommentaren*, accuses me of making such an error. On the other hand, R. A. Norris, *Manhood and Christ*, 234–8, has no objection to taking the christology of Chalcedon as a norm by which to measure Theodore's orthodoxy.

[38] For Theodore's christology see (in addition to the studies already cited): H. Kihn, *Theodore von Mopsuestia und Junilius Africanus*, Freiburg 1880, esp. 171–97, 393–409; E. Amann, 'La doctrine christologique de Théodore de Mopsueste', *RevSR* 14, 1934, 160–90; id., 'Théodore de Mopsueste', *DTC* 15, 235–79; M. Jugie, 'Le "Liber ad baptizandos" de Théodore de Mopsueste', *EO* 34, 1935, 262–71 (against the article by E. Amann in *RevSR*); M. Richard, 'La tradition des fragments du Traité Περι τῆς ἐνανθρωπήσεως de Théodore de Mopsueste', *Mus* 46, 1943, 55–75; id., 'Hypostase', 21–9; R. Tonneau, *Les homélies catéchétiques de Théodore de Mopsueste* (ST 145), XV–XXXIX; R. Devreesse, *Essai sur Théodore de Mopsueste* (ST 141), Città del Vaticano 1948, 109–18; M. V. Anastos, 'The immutability of Christ and Justinian's condemnation of Theodore of Mopsuestia', *DOP* 6, 1951, 123–60; K. McNamara, 'Theodore of Mopsuestia and the Nestorian Heresy', *ITQ* 19, 1952, 254–78; 20, 1953,

(i) The critic of the 'Logos-sarx' framework

Theodore's principal opponents in christology are, in addition to the Manichaeans and the Gnostics, the Arians and the Apollinarians (*Hom. Cat.* V, 8: ed. Tonneau, 111–13). The combination of the two last groups is significant, and there is an intelligible reason for it. Whereas other polemic at the end of the fourth century contented itself more or less with merely stressing the church's tradition of the soul of Christ and the soteriological importance of the taking of it by the Logos, Theodore succeeded in making a more searching criticism of the Logos-sarx relationship in the teaching of his opponents and, following Didymus, managed to make the soul of Christ a theological factor. We also find him challenging the basic presupposition of the narrower Logos-sarx christology, namely the vital, dynamic influence of the Logos on the flesh of Christ. Within the Logos-sarx framework, this Stoic idea of the Logos as ἡγεμών is far more decisive than the oversight of the soul of Christ. It is, in fact, the real source from which the whole pattern of a christology without a soul of Christ (whether as a theological or as a physical factor) has developed. At this point, therefore, criticism had to begin.

Theodore takes up the endeavours of Didymus of Alexandria, apparently forgotten in Alexandria itself.[39] In the *Fifth Catechetical Homily*, one of the most important documents for the interpretation of his teaching, he challenges Eunomius and the Arians. There is no mistaking the progress which has been made.

> The disciples of Arius and Eunomius say that he (Christ) took a body but not a soul; the divine nature, they say, takes the place of the soul. And they lower the divine nature of the Unique (Son) to the point (of saying) that he declines from his natural grandeur and performs the actions of the soul, by enclosing himself in the body and accomplishing everything to make it 'subsist'. Consequently, if the divinity takes the place of the soul, it (*sc.* the body) had neither hunger, nor thirst, nor was it tired, nor did it have need of food; for all this happens to the body because of its weakness and because the soul is not equipped to satisfy the needs which it has save according to the law of the nature which God has given it.[40]

This text is best understood if we begin from the Apollinarian hypostasis-concept, which includes the giving of physical life by the Logos. There is *one* physis, *one* hypostasis in Christ because the Logos alone performs all actions. Here, the Logos is combined with the body in a vital unity. But in Theodore's view, such a *symbiosis* contradicts Christ's true

---

172–91; F. A. Sullivan, *The Christology of Theodore of Mopsuestia*, Rome 1956; on this F. McKenzie, *TheolStud* 19, 1958, 345–73; F. A. Sullivan, *TheolStud* 20, 1959, 264–79; P. Galtier, 'Théodore de Mopsueste, sa vraie pensée sur l'Incarnation', *RSR* 45, 1957, 161–86, 338–60.

[39] But there seems to be no immediate dependence of Theodore on Didymus in christology. Cf. L. Doutreleau, 'Vie et survie', 33–92. Doutreleau does not mention Theodore. Nevertheless, Didymus' works were read in Antioch, ibid. 44.

[40] Ibid. V, 8, translated in Norris, *Manhood and Christ*, 150. See the whole text, Tonneau, 109–29; V, 7–19.

nature. Had the eternal Godhead in fact taken the place of the soul, he says, then the body could have lacked nothing, for all inadequacies result from the natural weaknesses of the human life-principle. If, then, Christ was hungry, thirsty, and suffered in other ways, this can only have been possible because the functions of life are performed by a human soul and thus come from a finite source. If this soul is to help the body to 'subsist' at all, it needs the help of a 'perfect' body. If anything is lacking, it can no longer fulfil its part of the task and will itself be drawn into a community of suffering. Eventually it will even be compelled to separate from the body. But if the Godhead had taken over the place of the soul, it would have been so powerful that it would of necessity also have taken over the role of the body, and those who denied the reality of Christ's bodily nature would be right. Both body and soul, however, had to be assumed because it was necessary to make good the death of the body and the sins of the soul. The sins (as the cause of death) had first to be taken away so that death itself might finally be conquered. Now the sins themselves happened in the soul. 'Therefore Christ had to assume not only a body but also a soul; or rather vice versa, first the soul had to be assumed and then the body because of the soul' (ibid., V, 11). It was only possible to save the body through the spiritual soul. 'Now this was only possible if (Christ) made the soul immutable and delivered it from the movements of sin, since we will only be freed from sin when we have acquired immutability' (ibid.). It thus came about that Christ assumed a soul and by the grace of God brought it to immutability and to a full dominion over the sufferings of the body (ibid., V, 14: Tonneau, 119). For this reason he also had to appropriate a human understanding, as a human soul cannot but be rational. Redemption was won by the grace of God gaining dominion over a man with whom God has clothed himself.

Our holy Fathers also said 'who was incarnate' so that you would understand that it was a perfect man that he took. . . . And he took not only a body, but the whole man, composed of a body and an immortal and rational soul. He assumed him for our salvation and through him he won salvation for our life (ibid., V, 19: Tonneau, 127).

The difference between this picture of Christ and the other, that of the Logos-sarx christology, is quite apparent. The human nature of Christ regains its real physical-human inner life and its capacity for action. After Didymus, Theodore had to do this work again. In the stress on the immutability of the soul, of course, we again have a Hellenistic element which could easily conceal the soteriological significance of Christ's soul. But it none the less remains the fact that the created soul provides the life for the body of Christ and is also the principle of the acts decisive for our redemption. Against Apollinarius, Theodore shows the activity of the assumed man:

Moreover (the divine Son) furnished his co-operation in the proposed works to the one who was assumed. (Now) where does this (co-operation) entail that the Deity had replaced the (human) nous (*sensus*) in him who was assumed? For it was not his wont to take the place of the nous in any, whoever they were, to whom he accorded his co-operation. And if moreover he accorded to the one who was assumed an extraordinary (*praecipuam*) co-operation, this does not mean (either) that the Deity took the place of the nous. But suppose, as you would have it, that the Deity took the role of the nous in him who was assumed. How was he affected with fear in his suffering? Why, in the face of immediate need, did he stand in want of vehement prayers—prayers which, as the blessed Paul says, he brought before God with a loud and clamorous voice and with many tears? How was he seized of such immense fear that he gave forth fountains of sweat by reason of his great terror?[41]

Apollinarius and Theodore reached diametrically opposed conclusions but still agree on an important point. Both see redemption achieved in the complete moral integrity, in the immutability of the spiritual principle in Christ, but the Laodicean holds to the immutability of the Logos himself, his opponent to the immovability of the created soul of Christ which is achieved by the grace of the spirit.[42] Now man is the *victor* over sin[43] and death, though with God's grace only. In comparison with the Logos-sarx framework, the picture of Christ is clarified in one important, decisive point: the redeeming sacrifice is seen as an act of Christ's 'human decision'.[44] Theodore's theological insight regained what others had lost. Here, of course, the question of the person of Christ arises.

(ii) *Christological thought*

When the complete manhood of Christ is stressed so decisively, it follows that the idea of the distinction of the natures in Christ must come right into the foreground. The question of the interpretation of the unity then becomes all the more burning.[45] In fact, everywhere in the interpretation of Christ built up by Theodore we have the impression of a loosening of the unity in Christ. Here the whole character of the 'Word-man' framework seems to put it at a disadvantage. The lack of the idea of a vital, dynamic unity of life makes itself felt. Theodore can offer

[41] Swete, *Theodori Episcopi Mopsuesteni in Epistolas B. Pauli Commentarii*, Cambridge 1880-2, II, 315; here, mostly with R. A. Norris, *Manhood and Christ*, 204. The other texts translated by N. ought also to be considered. See ibid. 202-7, 190-7.

[42] See R. A. Norris, op. cit., 186-9.

[43] See Theodore Mops., *Hom.cat.* V, 10: ed. Tonneau, 115; Swete II, 311; R. A. Norris, op. cit., 206.

[44] Theodor. Mops., *Hom. cat.* XV, 16: ed. Tonneau, 487: 'and as sacrifice he offers nothing other than himself—(a sacrifice) in which he delivers himself up to death for all.' With Hebrews, Theodore strongly stresses the heavenly sacrifice without, however, misunderstanding the earthly one and transferring it to the Logos *qua* Logos. Cf. ibid., nos. 17, 19, 21: ed. Tonneau, 491, 495, 497. See F. J. Reine, *The Eucharistic Doctrine and Liturgy of the Mystagogical Catecheses of Th. of M.*, Washington 1942; I. Oñatibia, 'La vida cristiana . . .', *Scriptorium Victoriense* 1, 1954, 18–23.

[45] Theodore Mops., *In Ps.* 8, 1: ed. R. Devreesse, *Le Commentaire de Théodore de Mops. sur les Psaumes* (ST 93), Città del Vaticano 1939, 43; *Hom. cat.* III, 6: ed. Tonneau, 61: 'En deux mots, ils nous apprirent les deux natures; par la distinction des noms, ils nous enseignèrent la distinction des natures. Ceux qui de l'unique personne (prosopon) du Fils dirent ces deux choses, nous apprirent la conjonction exacte des deux natures.' Further texts in R. Devreesse, *Théodore Mops.*, 115.

nothing comparable in its place—as long as he does not transcend the level of a merely accidental, moral conjunction in his interpretation of Christ and move on to the idea of a substantial unity. Does he ever manage to do this?

At this stage we need not object to the *indwelling framework*, as this occurs both in the biblical tradition and among the representatives of the Logos-sarx idea. Origen and Athanasius could speak in just the same way as Theodore.[46] But the *homo assumptus* formula seems inevitably to put Theodore's christology on the accidental level. It was precisely because of it that he had to swallow the greatest insults, so that he was regarded as a *Paulus (Samosatenus) redivivus*, as a proponent of an anagogic christology, teaching two persons and two sons, in short of the adoptionist christology which was seen to be embodied in Paul of Samosata. Theodore's language, in fact, all too often gives the impression that the union in Christ was achieved by the assumption of an already self-sufficient man.

Le Fils unique de Dieu, Dieu le Verbe, voulut bien, seul pour notre salut a tous, assumer (l'un) d'entre nous, afin de la ressusciter d'entre les morts; il le fit monter au ciel, se l'adjoignit et l'établit à la droite de Dieu' (*Hom. cat.* XVI, 2: Tonneau, 537).

It may nevertheless be said with some justification that he had at least dimly guessed at the idea of an ontic unity in Christ, even though he lacked the right concepts to show the metaphysical level on which it was achieved. He also sees what is involved in the key passage for the Logos-sarx framework, John 1. 14, and shows this in his explanation of the clause 'He became man' in the Nicene creed:

He became man, they (the 318 Fathers) said. And it was not through a simple providence that he lowered himself, nor was it through the gift of powerful help, as he has done so often and still (does). Rather did he take our very nature; he clothed himself with it and dwelt in it so as to make it perfect through sufferings; and he united himself with it (*Hom. cat.* VII, 1: Tonneau, 161).

This formula is extremely valuable. We can see from it that Theodore intended more than a pure moral union in grace, even though his real theological grounds are still insufficient for the purpose. He would distinguish the 'assuming' of the human nature, the 'being clothed' with it, and the 'union' with it from a merely accidental relationship between Word and humanity such as happens, for example, in the action of grace upon the prophets. For this reason he does not dissociate himself from the language of 'incarnation', which has its foundation in John and was

46 Theodore Mops., *In Ps.* 44, 9a: ed. Devreesse, 290[13-15]: Σμύρνα ... ἀπὸ τῶν ἱματίων σου. Ἱμάτιον αὐτοῦ καλῶς ἐκάλεσε τὸ σῶμα, ὅπερ ἔξωθεν ἦν περικείμενον, ἔνδον οὔσης τῆς θεότητος κατὰ τὸν τῆς ἐνοικήσεως λόγου. *In Ps.* 2, 6: ed. Devreesse 11[15-16]: 'susceptus itaque homo ius super omnia dominationis accipit ab inhabitatore suo, Verbo suo.' *Hom. Cat.* III, 5: ed. Tonneau, 59: 'Seul Seigneur, qui est de la nature divine de Dieu le Père, laquelle pour notre salut se revêtit d'un homme, habita en lui et fut manifesté par lui.'—*Hom. cat.* VIII, 5: ibid., 193: 'Et Dieu est celui qui habite, mais homme est son temple, dont lui-même, qui l'a édifié, fait aussi sa demeure.'

canonized by the Fathers of Nicaea. He sees no opposition between becoming man and assuming a man:

> And for our salvation he took upon himself to become man and to manifest himself to all. And he took to himself all that (belongs) to the nature of man . . . (ibid., V, 5: Tonneau, 107). 'Human form' in fact means nothing other than that he became man. . . . Our holy Fathers (of Nicaea) then rightly said, 'who was incarnate and was made man' to show that he became man, after the witness of blessed Paul. . . . (ibid., V, 7: Tonneau, 109).

In this sense, when commenting on Rom. 9. 5, Theodore can make an excellent observation, though in the same context the limitations of his picture of Christ emerge. Paul said:

> (Jesus Christ) *who is God over all* (Rom. 9. 5), to show the glory of Christ which comes from God the Word, who assumed him and united him to himself, for him cause and master of all. And because of this exact conjunction which this man has with God the Son, the whole creation honours him and even worships him. Blessed Paul could doubtless have said '*in whom* is God over all', but he avoids this (way of speaking) and says '*who is God over all*', because of the exact conjunction of the two natures (ibid., VI, 4: Tonneau, 137).

Theodore is here expressing, or at least guessing at, the idea of a complete unity of subject. In noting a point of language he sees that Paul here goes beyond a mere indwelling-relationship and expresses a single subject in Christ. In particular he establishes that Holy Scripture emphasises the union of the natures as much as their distinction and in such a way that both divine and human expressions are spoken 'as of one'.

> '. . . when they (the Scriptures) say *as of one* that which belongs to either one of them (the natures), we understand what a wonderful and sublime conjunction is effected (between them)' (ibid., VIII, 10: Tonneau, 201). In Rom. 9. 5, Paul teaches the duality of the natures: 'But he takes this teaching *as of one* in that he says . . .' (the scriptural quotation follows). John 6. 62 ('if you should see the Son of man ascending where he was before') gives rise to similar considerations. Theodore notices that a 'man' claims for himself a life in pre-existence: 'And had this not been as we have said, he (the Lord) would have had to say "if ye should see the Son of man ascending where *he who is in him* was before you would understand the greatness of the divine nature which dwells in me"' (ibid., VII, 11: Tonneau, 203. See 12). Finally, the exegesis of John 14. 25 has a fully orthodox ring: '. . . speaking of himself as man he moved on to his divine nature to give a clear revelation of his greatness' (*Comment. in Joh.* 14, 25: ed. Vosté, 198). The one 'I' in Christ stands above the two natures and calls them both his own.

Of course this often-repeated 'as of one' has a suspicious sound about it. Theodore seems to suggest that what is at stake is still not a real unity, but a real duality (of persons). Still, it should be noticed that the passages cited above all show a positive tendency to uphold the unity in Christ. To explain it, though, Theodore would have had to make clear the difference in the planes on which unity and, similarly, duality in Christ are to be sought. But who in Greek theology had yet put this in clear concepts? The search was still on everywhere. Theodore, too, is vigorously involved. Did he know the ideas of the two Gregories? A text from the *Commentary on the Psalms*, in which the traditional formula of '*unus atque idem et Deus Verbum . . . et homo*' stands alongside the hotly disputed ἕτερον μὲν . . . τὸν θεὸν λόγον, ἕτερον δὲ τὸν ἄνθρωπον is typical (*In Ps.* 8. 5: Devreesse, 46). Moreover, he expressly stresses that the duality pertains '*ad naturae distinctionem*'. Of course he finds himself in difficulties where he has to give the grounds for unity. His almost Chalcedon-like formula should not deceive us in this respect: '. . . *honoris eminentiam per coniunctionem personae homo Deo unitus accipit*' (ibid., 8. 1: Devresse 43). But what he chiefly lacks is the recognition, rooted so deeply in Alexandrian intuition, that in Christ the 'Logos' is the one 'I' and the one subject. The human nature is quite subordinate to this one 'I'. Theodore seems to put this one 'I' as a third element over and above the two natures, which results from them. In the *Commentary on John*, when referring to Rom. 7, Theodore speaks of this unity of the 'I' in Christ. In Rom. 7, Paul spoke of two natures and of two different things; nevertheless he joins the pronoun '*ego*' to both members and thus speaks of 'one', i.e. of one person. He could do this because of the unity of body and soul. 'So our Lord, when he spoke of his manhood and his Godhead, referred the pronoun "I" to the common person (*parṣôpâ*)'.[47]

What is this common *prosopon*? It is not easy to reach an understanding of the term. Friends as well as opponents of Theodore often misinterpreted it by looking for either too much or too little in it. In Theodore, as also later in Nestorius and in Theodoret, before Chalcedon, the word *prosopon* should not simply be rendered 'person', giving the word the strictly ontological content which it had later. *Prosopon* here should not be interpreted in the light of the definition of person in Boethius or Leontius of Byzantium. At this stage we must also exclude the full Chalcedonian sense of *prosopon*. The Antiochene concept of *prosopon* derives from the original meaning of the word *prosopon*, 'countenance'. *Prosopon* is the 'form in which a physis or hypostasis appears'. Every nature and every hypostasis has its own proper *prosopon*. It gives expression to the reality of the nature with its powers and characteristics. Now as Theodore stresses the reality and completeness of the two natures in Christ it follows naturally that he must allow such a mode of appearance for each of the two natures. But here he makes a distinction, as did Cyril of Alexandria later, between the real condition of the two natures in Christ and the way in which they should be regarded theoretically. This should not be overlooked. Thus,

---

[47] Theodore Mops., *Comment. in Joh.* 8. 16: ed. Vosté, 119. Cf. ibid. on John 14. 13: ed. Vosté, 193³⁶–94⁷: '*Utrobique, sive de divinis sive de humanis agatur, ponit pronomen "ego" ita ut sensus dictorum cognoscatur e contextu, differentia autem naturarum e differentia verborum. Ex eo vero quod utrobique tamquam de uno loquitur de semetipso, manifestat adhaesionem personae; quod nisi esset verum, neque honoris aliquid foret et qui est assumptus, quemadmodum evidenter in omnibus partem habet propter habitantem in eo.*'

according to Leontius of Byzantium, a fragment from Theodore's work on the incarnation reads:

> For when we distinguish the natures, we say that the nature of God the Word is complete, and that (his) *prosopon* is complete (for it is not correct to speak of an hypostasis without its *prosopon*); and (we say) also that the nature of the man is complete, and likewise (his) *prosopon*. But when we look to the conjunction, then we say one *prosopon*.[48]

But how are we to understand this 'one *prosopon*'? Surely not as a third 'mixed *prosopon*' in addition to the two other *prosopa* of the two natures. Theodore has in fact been wrongly understood to mean this. Fragments of Theodore of doubtful tradition recognize two *prosopa*, the divine and the human, which are said to achieve their union through the one common third *prosopon*. But the authentic Theodore always speaks only of one *prosopon* in two natures.[49] Now this one *prosopon* is produced by the Logos giving his own *prosopon* to the 'assumed man'. Theodoret, as we shall see later, is the clearest interpreter of the ideas which underlie this approach. Theodore himself begins from the indwelling of the Logos in the man Jesus of Nazareth. This indwelling forms the basis for the complete, indissoluble and inexpressible union of Logos and man in Christ. The union is made manifest by the Logos-*prosopon* becoming the means of showing forth Christ's human nature. The one divine *prosopon* permeates and at the same time shapes the humanity of the Lord. For this reason the humanity also receives the 'honour' due to the Godhead. In the miracles, the human nature becomes the instrument of the Logos:

> It means that in coming to indwell, he (the Logos) united the assumed (man) as a whole to himself, and made him to share with him in all the dignity in which he who indwells, being Son by nature, participates; so as to be counted *one prosopon* according to the union with him, and to share with him all his dominion (ἀρχῆς); and thus to work everything in him, just as through him he will exercise judgement upon all and bring about the second coming. And here, of course, the difference in the characteristics of the natures is not overlooked.[50]

This interpretation is confirmed by a newly discovered and hitherto unknown quotation from Theodore's work *Contra Eunomium*, which is preserved only in Syriac:[51]

[48] Leontius, frag. VI, in Swete, op. cit., II, 299: translated Norris, 228–9. There is a Syriac parallel in cod. Brit. Mus. Addit. 14669, with a Greek retroversion in M. Richard, *Mus* 56, 1943, 64f.

[49] R. Devreesse, *Theodor. Mops.*, 249; M. Richard, *Mus* 56, 1943, 63–6; id., 'Hypostase', 23–4. The index for *prosopon* in R. Tonneau, *Hom. cat.*, gives only passages in which *one prosopon* is mentioned. Thus it would seem that in the genuine works of Theodore there is no teaching of two *prosopa* and a third common one. J. Montalverne does not seem to have noticed this fact in his otherwise good study, *Theodoreti Cyrensis doctrina antiquior de Verbo 'inhumanato'*, Romae 1948, 73.

[50] Theodore M., *De Incarnatione* VII: Swete II, 296, cf. Norris, 221.

[51] Luise Abramowski, 'Ein unbekanntes Zitat aus *Contra Eunomium* des Theodor von Mopsuestia', *Mus* 71, 1958, 97–104; cf. id., 'Zur Theologie Theodors von Mopsuestia', *ZKG* 72, 1961, 263–6; *A Nestorian Collection of Christological Texts*. Edited and translated by Luise Abramowski and Alan E. Goodman, Volume I: Syriac Text, Volume II: Introduction, Translation and Indexes, Cambridge 1972: for the text cited here see Vol. I, 180 (Syr.); Vol. II, 107 (translation). The sentence in square brackets is regarded by Luise Abramowski as a later gloss.

This, together with many other things, the blessed Theodore, also, speaks in the 18th book against Eunomius (Cambridge University Library Or. 1319, fol. 91r.), as follows:

Prosopon is used in a twofold way: for either it signifies the hypostasis and that which each one of us is, or it is conferred upon honour, greatness and worship; for example 'Paul' and 'Peter' signify the hypostasis and the *prosopon* of each one of them, but the *prosopon* of our Lord Christ means honour, greatness and worship. For because God the Word was revealed in manhood, he was causing the glory of his hypostasis to cleave to the visible one; and for this reason, '*prosopon* of Christ' declares it (*sc.* the *prosopon*) to be (a *prosopon*) of honour, not of the ousia of the two natures. [For the honour is neither nature nor hypostasis, but an elevation to great dignity which is awarded as a due for the cause of revelation.] What purple garments or royal apparel are for the king, is for God the Word the beginning which was taken from us without separation, alienation or distance in worship. Therefore, as it is not by nature that a king has purple robes, so also neither is it by nature that God the Word has flesh. For anyone who affirms God the Word to have flesh by nature (predicates that) he has something foreign to the divine ousia by undergoing an alteration (fol. 91v) by the addition of a nature. But if he has not flesh by nature, how does Apollinarius say that the same one is partially homoousios with the Father in his Godhead, and (partially) homoousios with us in the flesh, so that he should make him composite? For he who is thus divided into natures becomes *and is found (to be) something composite by nature.*[52]

This important text deals with the *prosopon* of Christ. According to Theodore, *prosopon* can be identical with hypostasis, i.e. with the concrete individual nature of an individual being, a man like Peter or Paul, or with the second person of the Trinity, the Logos. In this man or even in the Logos, the hypostasis has the *prosopon* that is proper to its nature. In other words, *prosopon* here is the expression of a nature, ultimately of an ousia, which is, however, termed hypostasis, because it is a concrete, individual nature. If we speak of the *prosopon* of Christ, this does not mean that behind this *prosopon* there is a new composite 'Christ-nature', as is Apollinarius' view. Rather, this *prosopon* of Christ is to be interpreted in the light of the unique relationship into which the divine hypostasis of the Logos enters with the human nature which it takes. This taking is not a combination of the natures of Logos and flesh to form a new nature, but an equality of honour, of greatness, of worship, which is now shared equally by Christ's human nature and the hypostasis of the Logos. Theodore uses an analogy: the king wears purple robes to express his position. But they are not his by nature; they do not grow together with him to become one nature or substance. So, too, Christ's human nature does not grow together with the Logos into one ousia, but receives the same honour and worship as the Logos. The *prosopon* of Christ is thus the ultimate expression of the close conjunction which exists between Christ's humanity and the hypostasis of the Logos. The example of the royal robes would be

52 L. Abramowski makes a correction to the German translation of the last sentence of this fragment in *Mus* 71, 1958, 101 and in *ZKG* 72, 1961, 264. I am grateful for this information. Cf. A. E. Goodman, 'An Examination of some Nestorian Kephalaia (Or. 1319, University Library, Cambridge)', in *Essays and Studies presented to Stanley A. Cook* (Cambridge Oriental Series 2), 1950, 73–83.

appropriate to represent this conjunction as external, accidental. But Theodore emphatically stresses that it is a quite unique conjunction: indestructible, inalienable, not separated by distance. The conjunction with the hypostasis of the Logos is so close that precisely in this man Jesus the Logos is worshipped, and the man Jesus as the Logos. Christ's humanity, then, receives the *prosopon* of the Logos, not on the basis of a natural conjunction, but through another conjunction, the nature of which Theodore does not describe more closely. He merely paraphrases its peculiar characteristics. We have seen in the Cappadocians that with this analysis we no longer move merely in the realm of the moral and the accidental, but in the realm of an analysis of being. We can see clearly enough what Theodore is aiming at: on the one hand he would exclude the natural synthesis of the Apollinarians, and on the other seek an essential unity such as exists between hypostasis and *prosopon*.

In this way, then, Theodore posits *one prosopon* in Christ, and this *one prosopon* is achieved by the Logos giving himself to the human nature which he unites to himself. But this self-giving is not understood as a '*unio in hypostasi et secundum hypostasim*' in the sense of later theology.

Nevertheless, Theodore's christology is not simply opposed to later understanding of the union in Christ. He falls just short of it, but is open to a unity of person in the Chalcedonian sense. He has already clearly seen the problem of finding in Christ a basis for a strict union between the Logos and manhood which is not a confusion between two natures. He seizes any chance left to him to stress the uniqueness of this unity in Christ, which lies in the fact that both natures are left entire. He uses the analogy of the unity of husband and wife, 'who are no longer two *prosopa* but one, though it is evident that the natures are distinct' (Swete II, 299). It should be noticed that here Theodore is primarily concerned with the saying in Matthew, 'So that they are no longer two, but one flesh' (Matt. 19: 6).

Theodore even introduces the famous body-soul analogy. It is put most clearly in a fragment of Theodore's fourth book *Adversus Apollinarem*, preserved by Facundus of Hermiane:

> According to us, man is said to consist of a soul and a body, and we say that these—soul and body—are two natures, but that one man is composed out of both. Is it proper, in order to assure that the two are one, that we confound the natures and say by conversion that the soul is flesh and the flesh, soul? And because the soul is immortal and rational, but the flesh mortal and irrational, shall we convert and say that the immortal is mortal and the irrational, rational? . . . The division of natures persists: the soul is one thing, the flesh, another. The one is immortal while the other is mortal; the one is rational, but the other, irrational. Yet the two are one man, and one of the two (natures) is never absolutely and properly said to be 'man' in itself—unless perhaps with some added qualification, such as 'interior man' and 'exterior man'.[53]

[53] Swete II, 318f., quoted here in the translation by R. A. Norris, *Manhood and Christ*, 151–2.

Body and soul make up one man, though—considered independently and in a condition of separation—each has its own physis and hypostasis.[54] 'In the same way (τὸν αὐτὸν δὴ τρόπον) the unity of *prosopon* in Christ is achieved.'[55] In agreement with his Neo-Platonic contemporaries, Theodore asserts the substantiality or the hypostatic nature of the human soul as being different from that of animals (*Hom. cat.* V, 15) and stresses that it is incorporeal, immortal and essentially rational, so that Apollinarius' trichotomism is excluded. He does not assume the Platonist doctrine of 'parts' of the soul nor does he allow the soul to be conceived of as pre-existent or remove it in its highest 'part' from the visible world-system. Spirit and body in Theodore's thought are more closely combined than in the Platonism of other Fathers or in Origenism. His own position is:

> ... both similar and dissimilar to that of the Neo-Platonic teachers. Theodore's final observation clearly rejects the Neo-Platonic view that the soul is the man. He insists, as we should have expected, that the corporeal frame is a constitutive part of human nature. On the other hand, he insists upon the substantiality of the soul, and refuses to subordinate soul in any way to its body. Soul is united to body, but it is not an attribute of body, nor is it inseparable from body, nor is its essential nature as immortal and rational affected by its union with 'flesh'. What is missing in this passage is any indication of the *manner* in which soul and body, as two distinct 'natures', are united.[56] ... As he sees it, body and soul are plainly two different 'things' which are brought into a peculiarly intimate relation without either's nature being essentially altered in the relation. To this extent he rejects the Peripatetic account of the body-soul union. It is noticeable, however, that he makes no reference to a doctrine of 'mixture'—even in its Platonic form; and the effort to discern in Theodore's writings parallels to the quasi-voluntaristic doctrine of body-soul union which Nemesius takes over from Ammonius and Porphyry fails for lack of sufficient evidence. It may be again, that Theodore was not interested in the question: and if so, this fact must clearly have a bearing on the way in which his christology is to be understood.[57]

By all accounts, if we take this soul-body analogy seriously, we have here the expression of a unity which transcends any mere functional union (i.e. one based on the moral behaviour and proving of the man Jesus). Leontius of Byzantium ought to have noticed this in his criticism of Theodore, yet in his selection from Book VIII of the *De Incarnatione* it was just this extract which he left out.[58] Only the 'in the same way' (see above) is left to indicate that it once stood there.

This, then, is the way in which Theodore is to be understood when he says over and over again that it is his purpose to express a strict union, an ἄκρα ἔνωσις in Christ, even though he has insufficient grounds for it. Any analogies suggested by him which seem to express a merely 'accidental' union in Christ should not be isolated. In particular, what has been called

[54] Swete II, 299, see *Mus* 56, 1943, 64f. For the following see R. A. Norris, op. cit. 149–59, 125–36.
[55] Swete II, ibid.
[56] R. A. Norris, op. cit., 152.
[57] Ibid., 153.
[58] Cf. *Mus* 56, 1943, 64f.

his '*Bewährungslehre*' (that is, the theory that Christ earned his exaltation to Sonship through his obedience and virtue) is itself simply a product of the 'unity of *prosopon*', or, more accurately, of just one aspect of this unity. The *prosopon* of the Logos moulds the whole moral character of Christ as that of the man who lives before God. In this context Theodore surpassed all his predecessors in writing a theology of 'grace' and 'freedom'. If, as a result, he is regarded as a heretic, this is first because of the isolation of statements which, while being in themselves dangerous, must nevertheless be given their place in the general context of Theodore's christological and theological expression; secondly, because no notice has been taken of the positive trend of his christology, which, while stressing the two natures firmly, is open for an indication of the true unity in Christ, and finally, because the peculiar situation of his theology has not been appreciated. He challenges Arianism and Apollinarianism, which *de facto* predicate of Christ a '*unio in natura et secundum naturam*'. If this is rightly to be rejected, a means of union in Christ must be demonstrated which preserves what is positive and rejects what is false in the repudiated theology. But this only became possible with the conceptual distinction of physis and hypostasis at Chalcedon.

We must also note that it was at just this point that the discussion of the so-called *communicatio idiomatum* in Christ began in earnest. The time had come to give a theological criticism and vindication of a way of speaking which had hitherto been merely traditional and had been employed since the apostolic age without further thought. It had been explained wrongly as a natural unity by both Arians and Apollinarians. Theodore therefore should not simply be measured by the yardstick of the '*communicatio idiomatum*' without it being said at the same time that in his time it had to be demonstrated afresh that the '*communicatio idiomatum*' was, in fact, a valid standard. Right up to the Council of Chalcedon, none of the strictly orthodox theologians succeeded in laying the foundations for such a vindication in the form of a speculative analysis. They quite rightly accepted the traditional '*communicatio idiomatum*'. But as long as Apollinarius too could use statements taken straight from tradition as a basis for his heresy we should condemn no attempt aimed at depriving Apollinarianism of this basis. The danger to this '*communicatio idiomatum*' is a consequence of Theodore's inadequate speculative theology and the polemical situation, not simply a rejection of tradition. Theodore would only have become a formal heretic had he rejected a doctrine of the '*communicatio idiomatum*' which had been clarified by further theological development and decisions of the church. But this was historically not the case, nor can it be assumed from the general trend of this theology. He would have seized any opportunity of justifying a 'strict unity' in Christ wherever it was not incompatible with the equally important duality of the natures,[59] but such an opportunity presented itself only when the Council of Chalcedon had made the distinction between nature and person.

Incomplete though Theodore's christology may be, we should not overlook its positive elements. Faced with the predominance of the one-sided Logos-sarx framework in fourth-century Greek theology, he emphasizes the full manhood of Christ and especially his soul, and the physical and moral activity of this soul as a theological factor. And if he is not alone in so doing, at least he achieves the deepest theological level. In his picture of Christ, the significance of the human acts of the redeemer and the spiritual life of Jesus have a secure place. This enables him to bring to light a feature in the inner life of the Lord which, if the Logos-sarx christology was to be consistent, either had to disappear, or, at the least, could not be assigned its proper place: 'grace' and its operation in the work of the redeemer. And if Theodore went on to attach a disproportionate importance to this 'grace', it was, of course, because his presentation of the unity in Christ was too weak and uncertain. He needed it as a bond of union. But to make him an adoptionist as a result would be as false as to overlook the limitations of his interpretation of Christ.

(iii) Christological formula

In this context of Theodore's christological thought we must now examine the formula in which he summed it up. The one explains and supports the other. If we look at his terminology against the background of this thought, the deficiencies of which we already know, we must, of course, concede that the *wording* of the formula stands closer to the Council of Chalcedon than the ideas to which it gives expression.

Without doubt, the most significant aspect of Theodore's terminology is his use of the word *prosopon*. With this word he explains the effect of the union of Logos and man. But another important term, *hypostasis*, also appears. He took it over from Apollinarius,[60] but had to interpret it in his own way. The special characteristics of the Apollinarian concept have been sufficiently stressed. A hypostasis is a self-moving power. There is

---

[59] We may therefore try (with P. Galtier, *RSR* 45, 1957, 357) to understand even those of Theodore's expressions which speak of a dialogue between the 'assumed man' and the 'assuming Logos'. These passages are quoted by T. Camelot, *Chalkedon* I, 217ff. We should not look behind them for any metaphysics of an explicit two-persons doctrine.

[60] For what follows cf. M. Richard, 'Hypostase', 21-9; R. Tonneau, *Hom. Cat.* introd., XVIII-XXV. M. Richard makes a special investigation of the fragment from *De Incarn.* VIII, 62 (see p. 438 below) because of which Theodore was charged with teaching two persons. In spite of strong testimony, this text is, in Richard's opinion, not at all trustworthy. In particular, the parenthesis οὐδὲ γὰρ κτλ. is suspicious. Fortunately, we have a Syriac translation of this fragment preserved in Codex Brit. Mus. Addit. 14669; ed. E. Sachau, *Theodori Mops. fragmenta syriaca*, Leipzig 1869, 69. In Richard's translation, 'Hypostase', 24, the decisive parallel text runs: 'Car lorsque nous distinguons les natures, nous concevons la nature divine dans sa propre hypostase et la nature humaine (dans sa propre hypostase). Mais lorsque nous considérons la conjonction, nous disons une personne et une hypostase.'

only *one* hypostasis and *one* physis in Christ because there is only *one* αὐτοκίνητον—the Logos. Theodore completely dissociates himself from this approach. The *Catechetical homilies* show that he opposed a more static concept of hypostasis to this dynamic one. This is the case in the homily in which he defends the reality of the soul and the perfection of Christ's human nature against the Arians (*Hom. Cat.* V, 15: Tonneau, 121–3). He makes a distinction between the soul of a human being and that of an animal. The latter has no hypostasis, whereas the soul of a human being is one (*qnomâ*). This can be seen from the fact that the human soul can exist in separation from the body and the animal soul can exist in separation from the body and the animal soul cannot, as it goes into the ground with the blood. The criterion of distinction is, then, the respective possibility or impossibility of separate existence. Now, if we look at Christ we see that both natures are capable of separate existence. We must therefore assign a hypostasis, i.e. a real existence, to each nature. Are there, then, two hypostases in Christ? Certainly, so long as we are considering the distinction of the natures:

> But if we consider the conjunction, we speak of *one* person [and *one* hypostasis]. When we divide the nature of man, we in fact say that the nature of the soul is different from that of the body. For we know that both have their (own) hypostasis and nature, and believe that the soul separated from the body remains in its own nature and hypostasis and that for each of the two there is a nature and hypostasis. (For we have learnt from the apostle to speak of the inner and the outer man [2 Cor. 4. 16] and we name that which distinguishes them from what is common by adding the words 'outer' and 'inner' so as not to give them the simple title [man]); but if they are united in one we say that they are *one* hypostasis and *one* person and name them, the one as the other, with *one* name. In the same way we also say here (of Christ) that there is the divine nature and the human nature and that—understanding the natures in this way—the person of the union is one. If then we try to distinguish the natures we say that the man is perfect in his hypostasis and the God perfect in his. But if we want to consider the union, we say that *both the natures are a single person [and hypostasis]* and acknowledge that because of its union with the Godhead the flesh receives honour beyond all creatures and the Godhead fulfils everything in him.[61]

Two natures and a single person and hypostasis! If we may count on the authenticity of the statement about the 'one hypostasis', we have the Chalcedonian formula here for the first time in Eastern christology. There remain serious doubts as to the authenticity of this expression 'one hypos-

---

[61] Theodore Mops., frag. from *De incarn.* VIII, 62: ed. Sachau, 69; Greek retroversion in M. Richard, *Mus* 56, 1943, 64–5; French: id., 'Athanase', 24. On this R. Tonneau, *Hom. Cat.*, introduction, XXIV, n. 6; R. Devreesse, *Théodore de Mops.*, 46. More recently, H. Diepen O.S.B., 'L'*assumptus homo* a Chalcédoine', *RevThom* 51, 1951, 573–608; 53, 1953, 254–86 would explain the 'one hypostasis' as an interpolation; similarly F. Sullivan, *Christology*, 58–98; in support of M. Richard, J. L. McKenzie, *TheolStud* 18, 1958, 347–55. But the new fragment of the 18th book against Eunomius quoted above now shows quite clearly that Theodore does not speak of one hypostasis in Christ. Cf. Luise Abramowski, 'Zur Theologie Theodors v.M.', *ZKG* 72, 1961, 264: 'It is once again clear that Theodore sought to describe the unity of the two natures in Christ with the help of the word πρόσωπον and not with the word ὑπόστασις. . . .' We must therefore put 'one hypostasis' in brackets, that is in so far as it is applied to Christ.

tasis'. Elsewhere, Theodore always puts physis and hypostasis side by side. *Prosopon* is distinguished clearly from them. A being has a *prosopon* in so far as it is a physis and a hypostasis. The duality in Christ is to be sought on the side of the physis and the hypostasis, and the unity is on the side of the *prosopon*.[62]

There is still a hard road before we have a clear terminological distinction between what is of the 'person' and what is of the 'nature'. It would be wrong to misunderstand Theodore's contribution to the Chalcedonian formula. With him, the debate over the interpretation of the person of Christ as we have it in Arianism and Apollinarianism has swung right over to the opposite pole. Here the Logos-anthropos christology stands quite clearly over against the Logos-sarx christology. It is not a matter of formulas here, but of the ultimate explanation of the relationship between God and the world as it is given in the incarnation and the redemption through Christ. Since the time of Justin, there has necessarily been controversy about christology, as about the other problems of Christian monotheism. Theodore has still not found the right balance. The decisive crisis still lies ahead.

[62] J. L. McKenzie stresses the significance of the body-soul comparison which would also give Theodore grounds for speaking of 'one hypostasis,' art. cit., 349f.

PART THREE

KERYGMA—THEOLOGY—DOGMA

Ephesus and Chalcedon (431–451)

INTRODUCTION

WE are now at the beginning of the conciliar epoch of patristic christology. The main events are played out in the East. The West is merely a subsidiary setting as far as external events are concerned, though it also intervenes decisively in what happens in the East. This epoch begins with the Council of Ephesus (431) and ends with the Third Council of Constantinople against Monothelitism (680–1), which had a twofold prelude in Rome, with the First Lateran Council of 649 and the Synod of Rome under Pope Agatho (680). The Council of Chalcedon (451) is the most important point in this period. This is clear from further developments, which stretch from the much disputed Second Council of Constantinople (553) to the year 681, and even beyond. Of course, one could put the beginning of the conciliar epoch of christology as early as Nicaea (325) and even bring in a number of particular synods before and after Nicaea, such as the Synod of Antioch (268) and the Synod of Alexandria (362). In the fourth century, however, Nicaea, because of the pressure of the Arian struggles, was considered with reference to *trinitarian* doctrine. Its significance for the doctrine of the *incarnation* only begins with the dispute over Nestorius. Finally, in the Monophysite struggles of the fifth and sixth centuries, it becomes a real authority which both Monophysites and Chalcedonians claim for themselves.[1]

The christological content of the creed of Nicaea is, then, brought into consciousness in the struggle against Nestorius. In essentials, it makes no new advances beyond the early Christian creeds. Nevertheless, the church's doctrine of the incarnation was made to depend on it, above all else, as on a fixed point. This was because the creed of Nicaea stresses more strongly than its ancient predecessors the consubstantiality of the Son (Logos) with the Father and his Godhead, and then goes on to predicate the incarnation and the whole *oikonomia* of just this Son. The acknowledgement of the unity of the God-man is thus rooted in the creed and as a result Nicaea becomes a rallying point against Nestorius.[2]

Nestorius, too, will refer to Nicaea, also to read from it the unity of Christ, but of course in his own way. Finally, Cyril of Alexandria, the Councils of Ephesus and Chalcedon, Monophysites and Chalcedonians all read their christological framework from this council. Theirs is a christology centred on the Logos, in which, of course, Christ's humanity has received different degrees of emphasis. This Logos-christology finds one-sided expression in Cyril's formula of the 'one nature of the Logos made

---

[1] See *Chalkedon* III, Index, s.v. 'Nikaia'.

[2] H. Denzinger–A. Schönmetzer, *Enchiridion Symbolorum*, Freiburg 1963 (cited hereafter as DS), 125 and 40–60, esp. 55.

flesh'. The Council of Chalcedon will compensate for the bias, but without bringing peace. The partisans of Cyril regard the Chalcedonian picture of Christ as a Nestorian secularization. The Chalcedonians, on the other hand, select only the words 'one nature' from the *mia physis* formula of Cyril and his Monophysite supporters and see the humanity of Christ engulfed, as it were, in the fire of the Logos. In reality, Nestorius and Cyril, Chalcedonians and Monophysites, are much nearer together than they themselves know.

The new christological epoch is first of all shaped by two theologians, Nestorius and Cyril. The former, as Patriarch of Constantinople (428–431), intervened in a dispute which had arisen in the city over the attribution of the title 'Theotokos' to Mary. He quickly vanishes from the theological scene and his supporters are banished from the Byzantine realm. After 451 the debate and the struggle is carried on only between supporters of Cyril and Chalcedonians. Nevertheless, Nestorius' real concern is represented in this conversation, that is, the concern of the Nestorius who wanted to hold fast to tradition and saw a real problem. This is the new element in his writing, that more than anyone else before him he utilized an insight the method of which was correct, in that he looked for the unity and the distinction in Christ on different levels, the unity on the level of the prosopon and the distinction on the level of the natures. True, he had his predecessors, the Cappadocians and Theodore of Mopsuestia. But it is only with him that we see how the insight which in them is found more or less incidentally becomes the centre of theological considerations, particularly in the *Liber Heraclidis*. The christological definition of Chalcedon is on the line of his search, but in it there is some compensation for his dangerous weaknesses. With some justification, the Monophysites later detect a 'Nestorian' flavour in the Chalcedonian Definition. F. Nau sees a recognition of the orthodoxy of Nestorius in this identification of his writings with Chalcedon.[3]

Cyril, on the other hand, suffers just as much as Nestorius in the straits of the christological problem. But he does not attempt to solve it by distinguishing the two levels, one for the unity and one for the distinction in Christ. His solution is rather the '*mia physis*' and the picture of Christ which that produces. Nestorius lets himself be guided by concepts and proceeds by way of meandering and repetitious *analyses*. Cyril is possessed by an *intuition* which rests on John 1. 14 and the Nicene creed. With this he exercises a magical influence for centuries to come. Nestorius primarily stresses the distinction, without wishing to deny the unity in Christ, as has been supposed. Cyril puts the unity in Christ in first place without being able to interpret the distinction, as would have been a necessary step towards finding a solution to the problems then current.

[3] F. Nau, *Le Livre d'Héraclide de Damas*, Paris 1910, 370.

Chalcedon is here, in fact, the *via media*. Nestorius is the more modern theologian, but he does not have the same religious force as his counterpart, who thinks in more archaic terms. Chalcedon takes over from Cyril and from the whole tradition the firm acknowledgement of the one[4] Christ, but dares to stress the distinction in him more strongly, as did the Antiochenes. The council thus goes the way demanded by developments, though without bringing this demand into full consciousness. Now was the time to make plain to the responsible theologians and pastors of the church that a clear decision had to be made about the areas of unity and distinction which were to be recognized in Christ. Because this happened with too little deliberation, even though it happened *de facto*, Cyril's intuition could press more and more strongly upon the solution of Chalcedon. This explains the confusion and embarrassment which predominated in the church's christology from Ephesus right up to the Monothelite dispute.

The epoch of christology from Ephesus to Chalcedon is thus characterized by various features:

(1) It is no longer felt most important, as in the fourth century, to stress the full realities in the person of Christ, whether of the true Godhead or of the perfect manhood.[5] It is now the *manner* of the union that comes more decisively into the foreground. The discussion therefore no longer takes place over the 'Logos' and the 'man' in Christ, and as a result it is no longer expressed in terms of Logos-sarx and Logos-anthropos. For the full Godhead and full manhood of Christ are acknowledged on both sides. The chief concern is with the relationship of the one to the other.[6]

(2) The more progressive trend of theology applies itself decisively to the question of the manner of the unity in Christ and does so by marking out the levels on which unity and distinction are to be sought in Christ.

(3) This movement, which lies in the logic of the development, is, however, held up and diverted by Cyril of Alexandria and his supporters. They see in the christological efforts, above all of the Antiochenes, only a danger to the unity of Christ. They therefore create an emphatic 'unitive' christology and do so by centring it decisively on the Logos. Their op-

---

[4] It is remarkable how the formula Πιστεύομεν . . . καὶ εἰς ἕνα(!) Κύριον Ἰησοῦν Χριστόν finds its way into the creeds comparatively late (c. 325). Cf. DS, nos. 40–51.

[5] Cf. Nestorius' observation in *Liber Heraclidis*: B, 432; N, 276–7; DrH, 314.

[6] We would stress once again that the problematic of the fourth century was primarily determined: (1) By the question of the divine and full human reality in Christ. It is precisely because of this that the christological discussion of this century can be approached through the contrast between 'Logos-sarx' and 'Logos-anthropos'. (2) There was already considerable thought in this period about the manner of the unity of Christ. The late-Arian and Apollinarian christologies are at least *de facto* already an interpretation of this question. But we find the question of the manner of the unity under more or less *explicit* consideration in Gregory of Nyssa, Nemesius and Theodore of Mopsuestia. A. Gesché, *La christologie du 'Commentaire sur les Psaumes' découvert à Toura*, Gembloux 1962, does not therefore give a full assessment of fourth-century developments when he does not allow the opposition between 'Logos-sarx' and 'Logos-anthropos' as a factor in these developments and does not feel that the question of the manner of the union is yet raised.

ponents see this (wrongly) as a return to the late-Arian and Apollinarian positions which were held only by a few extremists.

(4) As a result, a modern and an archaic way of posing the problem stand side by side. The difference between them will be recognized only with difficulty, and not at all accurately. Formula is put against formula, and these are judged by the opposing side in the light of its own pre-suppositions. The one formula which is sanctioned at Chalcedon meets the demands of the problem of the day and paves a way to the explanation of the manner of the unity in Christ. The other formula, that of Cyril, merely sharpens the expression of the 'fact' of the unity and leaves the question of its character as it was before. Thus the result of the church's struggle against Apollinarianism can no longer be taken so lightly, as will later become apparent in the opposition in the pictures of Christ drawn by the supporters of Severus and those of Leo.[7] Only now are the classical types of 'Alexandrian' (i.e. Cyrillian) and 'Antiochene' christology con-trasted. The pattern by which we attempted to interpret fourth-century developments, 'Logos-anthropos' against 'Logos-sarx', is no longer applicable, clear as the lines which lead back to it still are. We shall con-sider the history of classical Antiochenism and Alexandrianism only for the years between 429 and 451.[8]

(5) The *kerygma Christi* of the apostolic and post-apostolic period is thus put into a dogma formulated in Hellenistic terms which has been prepared for by the theology of three centuries. We seem to have come a long way from the Bible. Nevertheless, it is remarkable how the content of so decisive a concept as hypostasis is determined precisely by the way it is used in Heb. 1. 3.

The concepts themselves, however, give no indication of fidelity or infidelity to the Bible. What matters is the way in which the person of Jesus Christ is understood. The church's dogma is meant to protect and to maintain the *biblical* kerygma of Jesus Christ and to do so against rational-istic and mysticizing solutions, whether or not these actually existed. Granted, it seems as though the church's consciousness of Christ is limited to what can be expressed in a formula. But this is true only of theological discussion, and even here only for the more apologetic works of the Fathers. As exegetes and liturgists, as preachers and as pastors of their congregations, they possessed the fullness of faith in Christ as they had always done. By showing in sharper outline so to speak the point of union of Godhead and manhood in the traditional picture of Christ, they put the whole picture of their faith in a clearer light.

[7] For this cf. J. Lebon, *Chalkedon* I, 555.

[8] For the later fortunes of these parties see the masterly articles by J. Lebon and C. Moeller in *Chalkedon* I, 425–580; 637–720 and the proposed continuation of the present work. See now A. de Halleux, *Philoxène de Mabboug*, Louvain 1964.

THE SCANDALUM OECUMENICUM
OF NESTORIUS AND
THE COUNCIL OF EPHESUS

INTRODUCTION: ECCLESIASTICAL KERYGMA, THEOLOGY AND THE ORTHODOXY OF NESTORIUS

IT is not strictly our task to decide the question of Nestorius, the deposed Patriarch of Constantinople. Nevertheless, an accurate description of his role in the evolution of the christological tradition may be an immediate contribution to his theological rehabilitation. The more we can show the orthodoxy of his thought, the more ecumenical contact will be possible with the Nestorian church of today, though Nestorius himself would probably not claim to be the father of a new community. In his letter to the inhabitants of Constantinople, he expresses his disapproval of the teaching of his more extreme followers, a fact which is not usually noticed: 'leur enseignement et le nôtre n'est pas le même'.[1]

As our survey on Nestorius in the light of dogmatic teaching and historical research[2] shows, two different positions may be adopted in passing judgement on the case of the Patriarch. A stand may be made, first, on the kerygma or dogma of the church; secondly, on the researches of theological scholarship. We shall attempt a brief definition of the relationship between these two positions.

1. NESTORIUS AND THE KERYGMA (OR DOGMA) OF THE CHURCH

The kerygma of the church is the presentation of the beliefs held by the church at the time in question. This kerygma confessed Mary as 'Mother of God' (*Theotokos*) and spoke of the 'suffering God' (*Deus passus*) as an expression of the fact that the true Son of God was born, as man, from Mary and died on the cross. This kerygma was not the result of theological speculation, but of the belief and confession of the church according to the apostolic tradition. Nestorius, though his own intentions were good, made the mistake of halting a kerygmatic evolution whose age and

---

[1] Nestorius, *Lettre aux habitants de Constantinople*, tr. F. Nau, *Le Livre d'Héraclide de Damas*, Paris 1910, 374, nos. 6 and 8.
[2] See the appendix, which is presupposed here, particularly in connection with the literary question.

theological value he did not fully appreciate.[3] In the great confusion[4] caused on the kerygmatic level, the church's reaction followed the laws of the kerygmatic tradition. This remains true, even if we have to complain of Rome's inaccurate information and the passionate feelings of Cyril of Alexandria. The Nestorian criticism of the use of *Theotokos* was felt by those who knew the tradition of the church to be an unjust rejection of a legitimate kerygma and a σκάνδαλον οἰκουμενικόν[5]. The faithful were σκανδαλιζόμενοι.[6] In other words, a central feature of the faith and preaching of the church had been attacked in the sight and hearing of simple believers and their bishops. Matters were the more serious because *Theotokos* was a key word for faith in the incarnation.[7]

We now know that this state of alarm was created on Nestorius' side by his imprudence and lack of clarity in theological thought, and on that of Cyril largely by personal, church-political and terminological concerns, while Pope Celestine had insufficient knowledge of the true situation and the intentions of the Patriarch of Constantinople.

> If Nestorius and Cyril could have been compelled to discuss their differences calmly and to define their terms with precision, under the supervision of a strict and impartial arbiter who could have kept them under control until they had explained themselves clearly, there is little doubt that they would have found themselves in substantial agreement theologically, though separated *toto caelo* as far as the prestige of their respective archiepiscopal sees was concerned.[8]

But, unfortunately, history does not always take the shortest path to the solution of its difficulties.

In this state of alarm, the Nestorian rejection of *Theotokos* was considered by the church in the context of all its possible systematic or

---

[3] This Nestorius did so to speak *ex cathedra*, that is on the kerygmatic level, as bishop of his church. But he himself was more moderate than some of his followers, e.g. the Antiochene presbyter Anastasius whom he permitted to preach against the title 'Theotokos'. Cf. Socrates, HE 7, 32: PG 32, 808–9. According to Cyril of Alexandria, the most excessive follower of Nestorius was the Bishop Dorotheus, who in full assembly cried: 'If anyone says that Mary is *Theotokos*, let him be anathema' (ACO I, 1, 5, p. 11, no. 3). But even here we may presume that *Theotokos* in the abusive sense of the Apollinarians is meant. The mistake was to attribute this sense to all uses of the title. Only in the course of the dispute did Nestorius come to see more and more the orthodox sense of *Theotokos*. He was then ready to allow it, but mostly with reservations caused by his anti-Arian and anti-Apollinarian attitude. Thus explicitly in *Ep.* 3 *ad Celest.*: F. Loofs, *Nestoriana* 181[17–20]. In his 'Second Homily on the Temptations of Jesus' he even uses this title without explanation. See F. Nau, *Le Livre d'Héraclide de Damas*, Paris 1910, 345[7]; Milton V. Anastos, 'Nestorius was orthodox', *DOP* 16, 1962, 122, n. 6. Nestorius did not know the full tradition of *Theotokos*. Otherwise he could not have affirmed that *Theotokos* is not to be found in the Fathers (*Liber Heraclidis*: ed. P. Bedjan, *Le livre d'Héraclide de Damas*, Paris–Leipzig 1910, 220). Cf. the testimonies quoted by Socrates, HE 7, 32: PG 67, 812 AB, who censures the ignorance of the Patriarch (809B) about the writings of the Fathers.
[4] See the colourful account by Socrates, who describes this confusion of the parties and compares it with a battle in the darkness (ibid.).
[5] Cyril Al., *Ep.* 2 *ad Nestor.*, ACO I, 1, 1, p. 24[23–4].
[6] Ibid. 24[25]; similarly *Ep.* 8: PG 77, 60B.
[7] E. Schwartz, 'Zur Vorgeschichte des ephesinischen Konzils. Ein Fragment', *HZ* 112, 1914, 249 calls *Theotokos* a 'cult-word.' It would be better to speak of a liturgical use of the title.
[8] Milton V. Anastos, art. cit., *DOP* 16, 1962, 120.

historical consequences, even if only *grosso modo*. An investigation was made to discover all the consequences which this denial might *objectively* have (a doctrine of two sons, of two persons in Christ). All possible lines were drawn to other heresies of earlier periods (adoptionism, Judaism). In this way an objective, impersonal picture of heresy was formed, which was then assigned to Nestorius as its originator.[9] All this results in a 'popular' image of a heresy and a heretic which chiefly corresponds with the demands of the church's preaching rather than with those of historical accuracy. The church reacts to the *impia kerygmata* of the Bishop of Constantinople, which are felt to disturb the faith of the 'oikoumene', and does so by affirming her own kerygma, *'ex cura pastorali'*.[10] In the belief of his contemporaries, the condemnation of Nestorius removed an 'ecumenical scandal'. A αἵρεσις was eradicated by a καθαίρεσις.

2. The Position of Historical Research

It is the task of theological scholarship to take into consideration all factors which could serve to explain the case of Nestorius. These factors include not only the psychological, philosophical and theological presuppositions of Nestorius and of his opponents, but also the circumstances of civil and ecclesiastical politics. Scholarship may rightly put the question, 'Was Nestorius a Nestorian?' and show a concern for his person. It must therefore make good the neglect of his contemporaries and undertake a detailed analysis of the christological concepts and intentions of Nestorius and his opponents. At the time of the Council of Ephesus, the church did not possess a theological method which would make possible a scientific judgement on the kerygmata of Nestorius. There was neither the ability nor the inclination to investigate the Patriarch's basic ideas and concepts.[11] Modern scholarship is on the way towards filling this gap[12]

---

[9] Against this method of procedure already Socrates, HE 7, 32: PG 67, 809BC. He does not find these crimes in Nestorius, with the exception of his rejection of 'Theotokos'.

[10] Cf. Celestin., *Ep. ad. Nestor.* (Summer 430, after the Synod of Rome): ACO I, 2, 9[27]: '*Ubi est diligentia pastoralis?*' For the importance of this term *diligentia* and, consequently, of the objection contained in the question, see: H. Jaeger, 'La preuve judiciaire d'après la tradition rabbinique et patristique' in: *La Preuve* (Recueils de la Société Jean Bodin pour l'Histoire Comparative des Institutions 16) *I. partie: Antiquité*, Bruxelles 1965, 415–594. Nestorius sincerely acted out of pastoral care, though in an imprudent manner. The accusation of 'imprudence'—as in the case of Eutyches—would have applied better to the action of Nestorius than the accusation of negligence. Cf. Socrates, loc. cit.

[11] Socrates himself is an example of objective research into the case of Nestorius. But even he does not investigate the speculative presuppositions of Nestorius' doctrine. Cf. HE 7, 32: PG 67, 809BC.

[12] See the appendix. What follows is based on: L. I. Scipioni, *Ricerche sulla cristologia del 'Libro di Eraclide' di Nestorio. La formulazione teologica e il suo contesto filosofico* (Paradosis 11), Fribourg 1956; A. Grillmeier, 'Das Scandalum oecumenicum des Nestorius in kirchlich-dogmatischer und theologiegeschichtlicher Sicht', *Schol* 36, 1961, 321–56; Milton V. Anastos, 'Nestorius was orthodox', *DOP* 16, 1962, 119–40, and esp. on: Luise Abramowski, *Untersuchungen zum Liber Heraclidis des Nestorius* (CSCO 242, Subsidia 22), Louvain 1963. See now especially the monograph by L. I. Scipioni, *Nestorio e il concilio di Efeso*, Milano 1974. For further aspects of Nestorius' christology see H. Chad-

and is performing an 'ecumenical' task now vigorously inculcated by the Second Vatican Council.

wick, 'Eucharist and Christology in the Nestorian Controversy', *JTS*, NS 2, 1951, 145–64, being careful to exclude the spurious texts of the *Liber Heraclidis*. A. Houssiau, 'Incarnation et communion selon les Pères grecs', *Irénikon* 45, 1972, 457–68, esp. 463–7 (eucharist in Nestorius and Cyril of Alexandria). Cf. also R. L. Wilken, 'Tradition, Exegesis, and the Christological Controversies', *Church History* 34, 1965, 123–45; id., *Judaism*, 201–21 (Cyril and Nestorius).

CHAPTER ONE

THE LANGUAGE AND THOUGHT OF NESTORIUS AT EPHESUS

IN order to obtain an accurate picture of historical developments we shall refer here first only to those writings of Nestorius which are directly connected with the Council of Ephesus, though we do not find in them a systematic treatise of his christology. The *Liber Heraclidis* will be discussed when we examine the dispute after the Council. Only supplementary references will be made to it at this stage.

It appears that when Nestorius became bishop of Constantinople he found that a dispute over the title *Theotokos* had already started:

> When I came here, I found a dispute among the members of the church, some of whom were calling the Blessed Virgin Mother of God, while others were calling her Mother of man. Gathering both parties together, I suggested that she should be called Mother of Christ, a term which represented both God and man, as it is used in the gospels.[1]

Thus it was not Nestorius who set the *Theotokos* question in motion. He allowed himself to be drawn into the dispute in order to act as mediator. It was his purpose to stand between the parties, one of which wanted to describe Mary as the Mother of God (θεοτόκος), the other merely as Mother of man (ἀνθρωποτόκος). On both sides he saw a mistake which he might eliminate. As an ardent persecutor of heretics of all descriptions[2] he allowed himself to be drawn into a struggle for which the theological means at his disposal were not adequate. This struggle consisted in a defence against real or alleged heresies and the calumniation of his own person. Over and above this he strove to clarify his own teaching, in which—to make the point at this early stage—no essential development is recognizable, even in his later writings.

I. DEFENCE

Nestorius directs his remarks principally against the Arians and Apollinarians.[3] Among the latter he includes even Cyril of Alexandria. He

[1] F. Loofs, *Nestoriana*, Halle 1905 (cited hereafter as *Nestoriana*), 185²⁻¹⁰ (*Ep. ad. Ioann. Antioch.*, December 430); similarly in the *Tragoedia, Nestoriana*, 203; cf. also *Liber Heraclidis* (from this point the following editions will be cited: P. Bedjan, *Le Livre d'Héraclide de Damas*, Leipzig 1910 = B; F. Nau, *Le Livre d'Héraclide de Damas*, Paris 1910 = N; G. R. Driver-L. Hodgson, *The Bazaar of Heraclides*, Oxford 1925 = DrH) B, 151; N, 91; DrH, 99. A good deal of the *Nestoriana* is now available in new editions: in ACO, in CSCO (edition of Severus of Antioch by Lebon and Hespel). See L. Abramowski, *Untersuchungen zum L.H.*, 213, n. 13.

[2] Cf. F. Nau, *Nestorius d'après les sources orientales*, Paris 1911, 13f. Apprehension at the intolerance of Nestorius is not the least cause of the sharp reaction against Nestorius on the part of the bishops present at Ephesus.

[3] See F. Loofs, *Nestorius and his place in the History of Christian Doctrine*, Cambridge 1914 (cited hereafter as *Nestorius*), 67, n. 1; A. Grillmeier, *Schol* 36, 1961, 330–2.

rightly observes that in denying the soul of Christ the Arians and Apollinarians give a special significance to the title *Theotokos*. Because in their
christology the Logos enters into a physical, natural unity with the flesh,
he is also involved in whatever happens to the body, such as birth,
suffering and death. The Arians seek to spread the title *Theotokos* so as to
have the opportunity of attacking the very divinity of Christ.[4] Nestorius
sees the abolition of this title as the only way out. But here he also comes
into conflict with historical truth and orthodox christology.

First, he identifies the teaching of Cyril of Alexandria and his adherents
with Apollinarianism. Secondly, he attacks the traditional doctrine of the
communicatio idiomatum, to which the church gave particular expression
in the title 'Mother of God' and the phrase '*deus passus*'. He should not be
blamed for giving an Apollinarian interpretation to Cyril's formula, 'one
nature of the Word made flesh', for we now know that Cyril in fact took
over this pointed form of expression from the '*fraudes Apollinistarum*'.
Cyril understood this formula in an orthodox way (see below), but it
nevertheless needed special consideration and careful qualification to protect it from a heretical interpretation. Other expressions of Cyril could
cause quite understandable difficulties, as is clear from a letter of Nestorius
to Theodoret:

> For what does he (Cyril) say? 'Even if the distinction of the natures is not misunder-
> stood, from which (ἐξ ὦν), as we say, an inexpressible union is achieved.' This ἐξ ὦν
> (sounds) as though he were speaking of the natures of the Lord in either case as being
> parts which together made up one. For he should not have said 'from which' (ἐξ ὦν)
> but '*of which* an inexpressible unity, as we say, is achieved'. For this inexpressible unity is
> not made up from the natures, but it is an inexpressible unity *of* the natures.[5]

As is well known, this ἐξ ὦν was rejected at Chalcedon and a solution
was found similar to that proposed by Nestorius. The Chalcedonian 'in
two natures' corresponds in content and, indeed, almost in wording with
the formula of his quoted above. Before we come to this, however, we
must first determine the further interpretation given by Nestorius and its
relationship to Chalcedon. It may be remarked in passing that there is
some occasion for mistaking Cyril's language for that of the Apollinarians.
But as well as criticizing the Alexandrian formula, Nestorius also rejects
the traditional *communicatio idiomatum*.

Nestorius and his opponents do, however, have one starting point for
understanding the person of Christ in common, which both affirm in
the same way: the Nicene creed, which in the view of the orthodox is
the pattern for the possibility of the *communicatio idiomatum*. For this
creed predicates of one and the same subject, the eternal Lord and Son,

---

4 *Nestoriana*, 273⁶⁻¹³.   5 *Nestoriana*, 197f. (XII).

eternal procession from the Father and a temporal birth in the incarnation; and as well as the birth, the suffering, the resurrection and the whole of the historical career of Jesus (cf. D, 54; DS, 125). In the Nicene creed itself it is clear enough that there is 'one and the same' subject to whom these two sets of expressions refer. This 'one' is the Son, in so far as he subsists in the Godhead. We may therefore substitute the 'Logos' instead, although the Nicene creed does not use this word, in contrast, perhaps, to the creed of Eusebius of Caesarea.

Stress is laid first only on the relationship between this Son and the Father within the Godhead. Only then is there mention of his descent in the incarnation. Thus the Logos is the one subject of two sets of sayings, which contain both the divine and the human elements. The temporal events of the incarnation are also ascribed to the eternal Son. At this stage, such a definition of the subject of the christological statements is still far removed from a well-considered interpretation; but there is no doubt that the starting point is the Logos as subject. This is the explanation given by Cyril and those who advance the *communicatio idiomatum* in the strict sense, predicating both divine and human of the one subject (each in accordance with the difference of the natures). In exoneration of Nestorius, however, we must point out his actual position in the history of dogma.

We can distinguish three stages, so to speak, in the development of some dogmas: first, the unconsidered thesis, given in the light of the sources of revelation; secondly, the stage of careful examination and discussion; thirdly, the final ratification by the church. Now in the period under consideration, the *communicatio idiomatum* was still in the second stage, that of criticism, which had begun with Eustathius of Antioch. The misuse of the *communicatio idiomatum* in Arian and Apollinarian christology made it necessary for statements about Christ which had been customary from as early as the time of Ignatius of Antioch to be verified in this way. By the time of Nestorius, the question has still not been solved, as the whole christological problem (the distinction of the unity and the duality in Christ) is in need of further clarification.

But how does Nestorius interpret the christology of the Nicene creed? It appears that from Cyril onwards his interpretation has usually been wrongly understood. Readers of Nestorius have failed to note that he sometimes gives *semantic* explanations and sometimes makes *ontological* statements. If all that he says is taken as a christological ontology, the following picture of his teaching emerges.

In order to be able to give both human and divine predicates of 'one and the same', he speaks of the 'Logos' as little as possible, preferring 'Christ' or the 'Son' or the 'Lord'. For him, these titles depict an additive subject which contains within itself both the divine and the human properties. F. Loofs has a paraphrase of Nestorius' views in his discussion with Cyril:

> You start in your account with the creator of the natures and not with the πρόσωπον of the union. It is not the Logos who has become twofold; it is the one Lord Jesus Christ who is twofold in his natures. In him are seen all the characteristics of the God-Logos, who has a nature eternal and unable to suffer and die, and also all those of the manhood, that is a nature mortal, created and able to suffer, and lastly those of the union and the incarnation.[6]

Referring to the Nicene creed, Nestorius indeed expressly observes:

> Notice how by putting 'Christ', the indication of the two natures, (the Fathers) did not first of all say, 'We believe in the one God-Logos', but chose a name which describes the two.[7]

So the subject of all expressions should be 'Christ'. Thus Nestorius would seem not to see fully the metaphysical structure of this word 'Christ'. He does not show that the Logos is subject as the bearer of both the divinity and the humanity. Instead, he regards 'Christ' superficially only as the sum of the two natures and sees these in turn merely as a collection of qualitative expressions. In so far, then, as 'Christ' is the sum of the properties of Godhead and manhood, Nestorius ventures to make both eternal and temporal expressions about him. He thus reduces the subject 'Christ' to the sum of the two natures and only rarely leaves room to consider the bearer, the subject of these natures. This preference of Nestorius for 'nature' instead of 'subject' or 'person' seems to be decisive. Wherever he says 'God' or 'man' in his discussion of the *communicatio idiomatum* we must read 'Godhead' or 'manhood':

> If you will, take a closer look at the statements (of the Nicene creed) and you will find that the choir of Fathers did not say that the consubstantial Godhead is capable of suffering, nor (did they say) that the (nature) coeternal with the Father was 'newborn', nor that that (the Godhead) was raised which itself raised the destroyed temple. . . . See how they put first 'Lord' and 'Jesus' and 'Christ' and 'Only-begotten' and 'Son', the names common to the Godhead and the manhood as a foundation, and thus they build on it the tradition of the incarnation, the passion and the resurrection.[8]

Christ is thus 'the common name of the two natures' (ibid., 175[18-19]). It therefore seemed logical to say that Nestorius takes as his subject a pure qualitative or adjectival sum of properties and therefore that for him birth and death cannot be predicated of the Logos *qua* Logos. Paul had already spoken in this way ἵνα μὴ τὸν θεὸν λόγον ἐντεῦθέν τις παθητὸν ὑπολάβῃ, τίθησι τὸ 'Χριστός' (ibid., 176[4-5]; cf. 196[24]-197[11]).

> And even if you make your way through the whole of the New (Testament) you will nowhere find death attributed to God (τῷ θεῷ = the Godhead), but either to Christ or the Son or the Lord. For (the designation) 'Christ' and 'Son' and 'Lord' applied by Scrip-

[6] F. Loofs, *Nestorius*, 79f., with references (from the *Liber Heraclidis*).
[7] *Nestoriana*, 295[7-9].   [8] *Nestoriana*, 174[26]-175[11].

ture to the Only-begotten is an expression of the two natures (τῶν φύσεων ἐστί τῶν δύο σημαντικόν) and reveals now the Godhead, now the manhood, now both.[9]

But at this very point, just where we seem to have an ontological analysis, Nestorius explicitly remarks that he is concerned with semantics and does not mean to make ontological statements. There is a further instance immediately afterwards, when he explains the names *Theotokos, Anthropotokos* and *Christotokos* ('Mother of God', 'Mother of man', 'Mother of Christ').[10] Once this fact has been noted, it is clear that he in fact defines the one subject of the incarnation more adequately than has hitherto been supposed. The credit for this recognition is to be given to L. I. Scipioni. Nevertheless, there is still some tension between Nestorius and the language generally used in the church.

Just as Nestorius believes on his presuppositions that he must reject the traditional christology of the *communicatio idiomatum*, so too he guards himself against the interpretation of his rejection put forward by the orthodox side. The starting point for the latter is *their* understanding of the structure of the statements about Christ; they find in Nestorius a denial of the true unity of God and man in Christ, i.e. a teaching of two persons. But as far as Nestorius in fact sees the difference or distinction in Christ on the level of the natures, he cannot be accused of teaching such a doctrine of two persons in the strict sense, at least, not as he himself intends it. So he says in a sermon preached in 430:

I did not say that the Son was one (person) and God the Word another; I said that God the Word was *by nature* one and the temple *by nature* another, one Son by conjunction.[11]

In these words he repudiates the teaching of two sons with which he was so often charged. For 'Son' is to him in fact just one of the names which expresses the unique subject.[12] In asserting his belief in the unity of the Sonship in Christ he writes one of the best pages of his christology:

Even before the incarnation the God-Logos was Son and God and together with the Father, but in the last times he took the form of a servant; but as already previously he was a Son both in name and in nature, he cannot be called a separate Son after taking this form, otherwise we would be decreeing two sons.[13]

---

9 *Nestoriana*, 269[14-20]; similarly 273[13-17].

10 Cf. *Nestoriana*, 312–13 (Sermon of 430): 'puta, qui dicit θεοτόκος si et ⟨άνθρωποτόκος dicat⟩, Χριστοτόκος dicat, quod nomen sit duarum significatio naturarum ... est quidem, ut dixi, vox ista, id est Χριστοτόκος significativa duarum naturarum, et deitatis et humanitatis. quando autem cum simplicior-ibus agitur, opus est voce manifestiore. quod impedit intellecto Χριστοτόκος dici et θεοτόκος et άνθρωποτόκος? sicut, qui dicit, "Christus", confitetur, quia deus et homo, sic et θεοτόκος et άνθρωποτόκος si dicas, utrumque confessus est.' Cf. ibid., 181f., 185, 203–4, 247[5-6], 252[10], 167[19-20]: si quis autem hoc nomen theotocon propter natam humanitatem coniunctam deo verbo ... proponet ... ferri tamen potest.

11 *Nestoriana*, 308[8-11].

12 Cf. *Nestoriana*, 275[1-9]; ibid., 283, 299[19-21]; ... naturae duplices, sed filius singularis; 335[25-27]; 336[1-4, 17-24].

13 *Nestoriana*, 275[1-5].

Nestorius here has an inkling of the true unity of subject in Christ. The designation 'Son' already refers to the pre-existent Logos who takes flesh in the incarnation. The name 'Son' permits no division. The distinction lies on the side of the natures. The significance of the words quoted above has recently been emphasized strongly by L. I. Scipioni.[14] According to him, Nestorius does not want to make a real distinction between the 'Logos' on the one hand and 'Son', 'Lord', 'Christ' on the other. The Antiochene simply gives these words different terminological significances: 'Logos' denotes the Son, considered in his divine nature; 'Son' stands for the designation of the 'person' of the Logos as the subject distinct from the Father. 'Christ' is the same person in the status of the incarnation.

It is clear that it is always a matter of *the same person*, except that the term 'Logos' sees this (same) person in his *divine nature* as such, whereas 'Son', 'Lord' and Christ see him directly as a person. For this reason Nestorius can predicate of the person existence in both natures, human and divine.[15]

Thus we must concede that Nestorius cannot describe the 'Word' or the 'Logos' as the sole subject or the sole bearer of the two natures, because 'Word' is a purely quidditative designation of the divinity of the Son. But he does not remain on the level of *nature*.[16] For him, 'Son' denotes the person as such, the second person of the Trinity.

Volendo in tutti i casi usare un sinonimo bene accetto a Nestorio, si potrebbe dire che il soggetto attributivo unico delle due nature è la seconda Persona della Trinità in quanto Persona e non in quanto natura. Ed è qui che si diparte l'intero discorso cristologico di Nestorio.[17]

Nestorius therefore is seriously concerned to maintain the traditional unity in Christ. For this reason he opposes the expression 'ἀνθρωποτόκος' from the moment he takes office as bishop. He will never have it that Christ is a 'mere man' (ψιλὸς ἄνθρωπος).[18] He intends to remain on traditional ground and to keep his picture of Christ in harmony with the Nicene creed (*Nestoriana*, 284).

The question, however, remains whether he can produce a convincing expression of this intention in the *positive* exposition of his christology so that he can justifiably reject the charges made against him.

[14] See L. I. Scipioni, *Nestorio e il concilio di Efeso*, 386–92. Scipioni criticizes my remarks in *Schol* 36, 1961, 332–5 (and in CCT¹, 1965, 379). Note also the remarks of T. Šagi-Bunić, '*Deus perfectus et homo perfectus*' a Concilio Ephesino (a. 431) ad Chalcedonense (a. 451), Freiburg 1965, 104–19 (see also the index of this work s.v. 'Nestorius').
[15] L. I. Scipioni, op. cit., 390–1.
[16] Ibid., 391 with reference to *L.H.*, p. 362 (232); and Scipioni, *Ricerche*, 57–9.
[17] Scipioni, *Nestorio e il concilio di Efeso*, 392.
[18] Cf. *Nestoriana*, 182; 248¹⁻⁹; 249⁴; 259¹⁶⁻¹⁷; 299 (against Paul of Samosata); 354. Socrates, HE 7, 32, 8 also defends Nestorius: 'But I read his writings and I will say the truth; he did not hold the same opinions as Paul of Samosata and Photinus nor did he at all regard the Lord as a mere man, only he abhorred the term θεοτόκος as a bugbear.'

2. The Christ of the Patriarch Nestorius

The chief concern of the Bishop of Constantinople is to provide for a clear distinction of the natures in the face of the heretical tendencies of his time, whether real or only supposedly so. At one point he says, 'In every respect remember the many words in which I have made a distinction between the two natures of the Lord Christ.'[19] But the distinction of the natures is the easier part of the christological problem. It is harder to explain the unity which he means to maintain: one Christ, one Son, one Lord. Nestorius indubitably supposes this unity as a matter of fact and is in search of a foundation for this unity; he is not simply, as he is so often represented, a theologian whose slogan is 'division at any price'. Indeed, some of his formulas come near to displaying an understanding which is presupposed by the traditional *communicatio idiomatum*:

> But I say this for you to learn how close a conjunction existed between the Godhead and the flesh of the Lord visible in the child. For the same (person) was both child and Lord of the child.[20]

Nestorius even has command of the password of traditional christological understanding, the εἷς καὶ ὁ αὐτός which occurs over and over again in the Chalcedonian Definition:

> (c) . . . one and the same which is seen in the uncreated and in the created nature. (e) Therefore he who is recognized as one Christ in two natures, the divine and the human, the visible and the invisible, will hold the future judgement. . . . (f) For the oneness of the Son is not damaged by the distinction of the natures. But in the same way as the perishable body is one thing and the immortal soul is another, yet both go to make up *one* man, so too (one is made up) from the mortal and the immortal, from the perishable and from the imperishable, from that which is subject to a beginning and from the nature which has no beginning. That means that I confess God the Logos *one* πρόσωπον of the Son.[21]

If we take these formulas as they stand, independently of any further explanation by Nestorius, they could compete with any christology of their time. We even find the famous comparison of the unity in Christ with the unity of 'body and soul' in a human being—the very comparison from which the Arian and Apollinarian interpretation of Christ takes its start. From all this we see that even Nestorius works with a certain store of traditional formulas and concepts—an impression which is further strengthened by the *Liber Heraclidis*.

[19] *Nestoriana*, 354, IVb.
[20] *Nestoriana*, 292[1–4]: ἦν γὰρ ὁ αὐτὸς καὶ βρέφος καὶ τοῦ βρέφους δεσπότης. Similarly ibid., 328[3–9]: καὶ τὸ βρέφος γὰρ θεὸς αὐτεξούσιος . . . Γνωρίζωμεν τοίνυν τὴν ἀνθρωπότητα τοῦ βρέφους καὶ τὴν θεότητα . . . τὸ τῆς υἱότητος τηροῦμεν μοναδικόν. . . . Between them, of course, stands the sentence: 'We acknowledge the difference of the natures in the indivisible power of worship.' Cf. also 327[4]; 299[19–21]: *unus enim filius quod visibile est et invisibile, unus Christus et iste, qui utitur, et id, quo utitur; naturae duplices, sed filius singularis.*
[21] *Nestoriana*, 330–31. For ibid., a–e see Severus of Antioch, *C. imp. Gramm.*; J. Lebon, CSCO 94/Syr. 46 V., 20, 120, 171, 181.

Nestorius only begins to go his own way where he tries to give a positive explanation of the unity of God and man in Christ. Here some of his traditional formulas are again called in question, as the texts quoted above suggest in their different ways. For this reason we must go behind his formulas and attempt to reach the understanding of Christ which lies at the root of them. In thus struggling over his own interpretation, Nestorius shapes formulas which represent a sharpening of the Antiochene approach while at the same time being the occasion of his condemnation as a heretic.

Nestorius' particular difficulty arises from the fact that in interpreting Christ he is not dealing with two abstract natures, but with an individual, concrete human nature and the Godhead which subsists in the Logos. Godhead and manhood in Christ are concrete realities. To describe them he uses the expressions *ousia* (essence), *physis* (nature) and *hypostasis* (actual concrete reality).

We need not say much here about the first two expressions, *ousia* and *physis*. There will be an opportunity for that when we come to the *Liber Heraclidis*. They have there the same significance as in the Ephesine period of Nestorius. The fact that the term *hypostasis* already comes to be used in christology in 431 is, however, of some interest for the preliminary history of the Chalcedonian Definition. Hypostasis is Nestorius' term for designating the three persons in the Trinity.[22]

Christological use of it is rare and only starts after the beginning of the dispute, probably after Nestorius had received Cyril's letter of anathemas.[23]

If Nestorius spoke of the three hypostases of the Trinity in contrast to the one nature and, in the sermon of 25 March 431, of the 'two hypostases of the natures', this would prove alarming. In the Latin of Marius Mercator the suspect sentence becomes rather more pacific: '*Coniunctionis igitur confiteamur dignitatem unam, naturarum autem substantias duplices.*'[24] *Substantia* stands for *hypostasis* here and means no more than the reality and concrete particularity of the divine and human nature in Christ. It would be wrong to read a strict doctrine of 'two persons' in the dogmatic sense into this text at this stage. Nestorius is merely rejecting the confusion of two natures in one. Hypostasis is also to be taken in this sense in a fragment from the *Hypomnemata*, i.e. the *First Apology* of Nestorius, which has been handed down only by Severus and says:

[22] See L. Abramowski, *Untersuchungen zum L.H.*, 213-17. We would draw attention to the important text-critical observations made there and merely excerpt some important passages which show us the significance of the word hypostasis.

[23] Ibid., 214f.

[24] F. Loofs, *Nestoriana*, 340¹⁷ᶠ. Whereas M. Richard contests this text, L. Abramowski, op. cit., 215, n. 18, accepts it, referring to Severus, *Ctr. Gram.* III, 20.

If we say 'one ousia', the 'hypostasis of the God Logos' becomes confused with the 'changeableness of the fleshly (hypostasis)'.[25]

In speaking of the 'hypostasis of the human nature' of Christ, Nestorius only means to stress its concrete, unconfused reality.[26]The three extant texts containing the word *hypostasis* from the time before the *Liber Heraclidis (Second Apology)* are also to be taken in this sense.

The two natures of Christ are joined in *synapheia*, which rests on the unity of the *prosopon*. So, for example, Nestorius congratulates Cyril on the promising insight through which he has come to the 'distinction of the natures into the divine and the human and their conjunction in one *prosopon* (εἰς ἑνὸς προσώπου συνάφειαν)' (*Nestoriana*, 176[15-17]).

So after the distinction we have the conjunction of the two natures (φύσεις διπλαῖ),[27] the *synapheia* or *coniunctio*. This is Nestorius' favourite expression; only rarely does he speak of union, of ἕνωσις.[28] For behind that he again suspects the 'one nature' of the Apollinarians. The concept of *synapheia* in Nestorius has not yet acquired such a philosophical determination that we can conclude from it alone whether it describes a purely accidental unity in Christ or a deeper, substantial one.[29] Nestorius therefore defines *synapheia* by various additions which are meant to show the quality of the union. The most important definition is given in the formula quoted above, the unity of *prosopon*. As already with Theodore of Mopsuestia, so too with Nestorius we are not to take this to be the 'unity of person' in the Chalcedonian sense. This is true least of all of the Nestorius of the time of Ephesus. We therefore leave the word *prosopon* untranslated. F. Loofs gives a good description of the use of *prosopon* in the writings of Nestorius:

For Nestorius, who in this respect was influenced by the manner of speaking common at that time, the main thing in his notion of πρόσωπον according to the etymology of the word and to the earlier history of its meaning, was the *external undivided appearance*. . . . In not a few places in Nestorius, it is true, the meaning of πρόσωπον coincides with our understanding of the term *person*, e.g. 'these πρόσωπα' means these persons, and εἷς καὶ ὁ αὐτός and ἓν πρόσωπον may be used alternately. Nevertheless, before we go further, I must lay stress on the fact that the notion of πρόσωπον in Nestorius grew upon another soil and, therefore, had a wider application than our term *person*.[30]

25 Severus, *Ctr. Gramm.* II, 32, cited in L. Abramowski, ibid., 216 and n. 19.
26 This is also true of the passages from the *Theopaschites*, F. Loofs, *Nestoriana*, Syr., 369[3-12]; in a bad translation, 209-10; for corrections see L. Abramowski, 216.
27 This expression figures only in the *Nestoriana*, not in *L.H.* See L. Abramowski, *Untersuchungen zum L.H.*, 214.
28 T. Camelot has a brief selection in *Chalkedon* I, 223, n. 1.
29 But M. Jugie, *Nestorius et la controverse nestorienne*, Paris 1912, 107-12 would seek here a heretical intent in Nestorius, though he grants the possibility of an orthodox interpretation: 'Sans doute, les termes συνάφεια, συνάπτειν n'ont pris en eux-mêmes, rien d'hérétique. On les trouve chez beaucoup de Pères dont l'orthodoxie est incontestable; mais sous la plume du condamné d'Ephèse ils sont révélateurs' (ibid., 112). For Jugie, the doctrine of two distinct persons in Christ is unquestionably to be assumed for Nestorius. See H.-M. Diepen, 'L'assumptus homo patristique', *RevThom* 63, 1963, 230, n. 1; A. Grillmeier, *Schol* 36, 1961, 348, n. 67 (Gregory of Nyssa).
30 F. Loofs, *Nestorius*, 76f. See 74-94.

According to Nestorius, each nature has its own prosopon, its own characteristics, its own appearance, through which it is characterized in its individuality. For Nestorius the *prosopon* is the last point in the analysis of a concrete nature. He stops at the *'notae individuantes'* and assigns them a special role in the interpretation of the unity of Christ. As is well known, the later metaphysical definition of the concept of person goes beyond 'individuality', to look for the decisive element of the concept of person in the καθ' ἑαυτὸν εἶναι, the *incommunicabilitas absoluta* of a complete rational nature. Chalcedon opened the way to this by its practical distinction between nature and hypostasis.

Even here, however, we still have no definition of the term person, and it is that which led to the complicated entanglements of the period after Chalcedon. Within his own terminology and conceptuality, Cyril found his way to the idea of the ultimate unity of subject in Christ, but he did this without being able to grasp the concept of person as such. Now in that Nestorius stands by the 'individuality' of the natures and stresses this to an extraordinary degree, he obstructs the way to a speculative solution of the christological problem as far as one is possible at all. But we should not overlook one positive point. By building the unity of Christ completely on the idea of *prosopon*, Nestorius transcends all attempts to envisage this unity as a *unio in natura et secundum naturam*. This was the way of the Arians and the Apollinarians; but even some speculative attempts by orthodox Fathers came near to this natural unity. The idea of a distinction between nature and person came only slowly. It first appeared in christology in the time of Gregory of Nyssa. But as for Nestorius a concrete nature consists only of the physis as such and the individual characteristics, there remains only this realm of the individual (the *prosopon*) to interpret the unity in Christ, as the union cannot be *in natura et secundum naturam*. He seeks to draw from his *prosopon* theology everything that it seems to contain towards an interpretation of the unity in Christ.

Nestorius' concept of *prosopon* is largely determined by the Bible and then, above all, by the approach made by the Cappadocians in distinguishing nature from hypostasis in trinitarian theology. The *Liber Heraclidis* will make this latter point clearer. Nestorius is fond of referring to Phil. 2. 5-8.[31] 'Form of God' and 'form of a servant' suggest what he means by a prosopon: the mode of appearance of a concrete nature. Thus he makes Christ, the 'only-begotten' (not the Logos), say:

Being in the form of God I am clothed in the form of a servant; although I am God the Logos, I am visible in the flesh; although I have rule over all things I take upon myself

[31] See *Nestoriana*, index, 394; also on Heb. 1. 3 (ἀπαύγασμα, χαρακτήρ !).

the *prosopon* of the poor for your sake; although I am visibly hungry, I give food to those who hunger.[32]

To be 'in the form of a servant', to be 'visible in the flesh' and to 'take upon himself the prosopon of the poor' are equivalent. Nestorius begins with this idea of the 'countenance' to make his unity of prosopon comprehensible. In this, the whole is to be seen as the appearance of the divine in human form. The whole countenance represents Christ. But in the countenance there are two eyes, the divine and the human nature unconfused:

Christ is indivisible in that he is Christ, but he is twofold in that he is both God and man; he is one in his Sonship, but he is twofold in that which takes and that which is taken. In the πρόσωπον of the Son he is individual, but, *as in the case of two eyes*, he is separate in the natures of manhood and Godhead. For we do not acknowledge two Christs or two Sons or Only-Begottens or Lords, not one Son and another Son, not a first Only-Begotten and a new Only-Begotten, not a first and a second Christ, but one and the same, who has been seen in created and uncreated nature.[33]

Everything that can be found in a concrete being over and above the physis as such is counted as an element in the *prosopon*: the state of human nature, induced by the fall of Adam, belongs to the *prosopon* of this nature; so, too, do dignity and honour, cult and worship, desire and will. *Prosopon* is a collective term for all that pertains to the characteristics of a nature, inwardly and outwardly. The *prosopon* is the appearance, the way in which a thing is seen and judged and honoured; it is also the way in which it acts and exists. In other words, Nestorius gathers together all the characteristic properties (*idiomata*), the physical appearance and condition, the moral attitude, the spiritual actions and functions, and finally the reactions which they summon up in man. Each nature realized in concrete existence has its natural *prosopon*.[34] Just as each concrete *ousia* is a *hypostasis*,[35] so too it has a *prosopon* of its own.

The *prosopon* is now the basis on which the unity in Christ is realized, or better, revealed.

The divine Logos was not one (ἄλλος) and another (καὶ ἄλλος) the man in whom he came to be (ἐν ᾧ γέγονεν). Rather, one was the *prosopon* of both in dignity and honour, worshipped by all creation, and in no way and no time divided by otherness of purpose and will.[36]

---

[32] *Nestoriana*, 358[1-4]; cf. L. Abramowski, *Untersuchungen zum L.H.*, 217, where the expression πρόσωπον τῆς φύσεως is explained, a forerunner of the expression πρόσωπον φυσικόν of the *L.H.* In the three places where it occurs, 'prosopon of nature' means the historical, concrete form of existence or appearance of our (fallen) human nature, e.g.: *Christus debentis suscepit personam naturae et per eam debitum tanquam Adae filius reddidit* (*Nestoriana*, 255[20f.]); *personam enim eiusdem naturae suscepit* (ibid., 256[19]). Nestorius does not say *naturam suscepit*; the *prosopon* of the nature is the immediate object which is taken.

[33] *Nestoriana*, 280[5-16].   [34] See L. Abramowski, ibid.

[35] Nestorius, *Theopaschites*, frag. apud Sever. Ant., *Ctr. Gramm.* II, 32, tr. J. Lebon, CSCO 112, p. 192[9-13]: *Nam confessus es a uobis statui Christum esse unam naturam ex incorporalitate et corpore, atque hypostasim uninaturalem* τῆς θεοσαρκώσεως. *Id autem est confusio duarum naturarum quod naturas spoliat hypostasibus propriis, cum inter se confunduntur.*

[36] *Nestoriana*, 224[12-15].

The two natures have *one* Lordship (αὐθεντία) and *one* power (δύναμις) or might (δυναστεία) and *one* prosopon in the *one* dignity (ἀξία) and in the same honour (τιμή).[37]

Throughout his whole career, indeed his whole life, Nestorius takes pains to explain this unity of *prosopon* in itself and as the exclusive basis of unity in Christ. In the *Liber Heraclidis* we see that he is making even greater efforts in this direction. We shall find there the idea of the compensation of *prosopon*, an idea which was not yet developed in the period between 429 and 436. The unity of *prosopon* is based on the fact that the *prosopon* of the Logos makes use of the *prosopon* of Christ's manhood as an instrument, an *organon*. The whole is the union of the two natures, of an invisible and a visible element. But the realities are in a special relation to each other, as in action and passion:

unus enim filius quod visibile est et invisibile, unus Christus et iste qui utitur et id quo utitur.[38]

A strange case: we are reminded of the Alexandrian idea of the humanity of Christ as the *organum divinitatis*, but it is in a specifically Nestorian context and approach. This use does not happen in the Apollinarian sense of a *vital symbiosis*; it is only on the level of the *prosopon*. Is the sentence just quoted, *iste qui utitur et id quo utitur*, the explanation of the preceding sentence: *unus enim filius quod visibile est et invisibile*? That is, would the human nature of Christ be the instrument for making visible his invisible nature? The opposition 'visible-invisible' is frequent in Nestorius' writings.[39] The idea of the manhood of Christ as the *prosopon* which reveals the hypostasis of the Logos seems to be near at hand.[40] In the opposition 'invisible-visible', Nestorius lays stress more on the kenosis than on the revelation or *epiphaneia*.

Nevertheless, even he writes a *theologia gloriae*. The Godhead becomes transparent in the manhood, '*manente naturarum inconfusione*'. The flesh has its own glory, which, in the relation to the Godhead, is more a kenosis than a revelation; but the hidden divinity gives the flesh a higher glory, which reveals and proclaims the union with this hidden nature.[41]

Whatever the relation of the active and passive elements in this 'use' may be, as a whole the idea shows quite an orthodox conception of the incarnation. The active part is the Godhead of Christ, the passive the manhood. There is no place for any merit by which the man Jesus would earn the honour of Sonship.

---

[37] *Nestoriana*, 196[15-17]; cf. 354 IV b.

[38] Ibid., 299[19-20]; L. Abramowski, *Untersuchungen zum L.H.*, 222, n. 29, with a fragment of Severus, *Philalethes*, CSCO 133, 284[22-6]: . . . c'est lui qui, en venant sans être pécheur pour avoir accompli (?) le précepte (Heb. 10. 7), est *apparu* comme *organe* de la divinité, dont il n'est aucunément séparé. . . .'

[39] L. Abramowski, op. cit., 222f.

[40] Ibid., for the question of Ps.-Nestorius in the *L.H.* see the appendix.

[41] Nestorius, *Theopaschites*, frag. apud Sever. Ant., *Ctr. Gramm.* III, 36: CSCO 101, p. 222[14-19]: 'gloria enim carnis visibilis superior visibili clamat unionem naturae quae tegebatur'. See the comments by L. Abramowski, *Untersuchungen zum L.H.*, 223f. We are quite near to the idea of the compensation of *prosopa* proposed in the *L.H.*

Thus we can see clearly that Nestorius is seeking a speculative analysis of the unity of Christ. He also attempts to root this unity in the ontic sphere. We may not make the references to the moral unity of God and man in Christ in the writings of Nestorius into the real and exclusive means of the *synapheia* in Christ. We may not isolate the moral element from the other *idiomata* by which an ousia is made a hypostasis and receives its *prosopon*. The *prosopon* is 'appearance', the collection of qualities in which a thing, or better, a spiritual nature, exists, is seen and judged and honoured; it is also the manner in which it acts. In other words, Nestorius gathers all the possibilities of grounding the unity of natures in Christ on an ontic basis apart from taking as this basis the physis *qua* physis. But the only sphere of ontic reality given in a concrete being apart from the physis or ousia is for him the sphere of individual properties. He can rightly claim to have found an ontic basis for the discussion of the unity of Christ. For the *idiomata* are part of the *ens concretum physicum*. Nestorius must therefore leave each of the natures in Christ its own *prosopon* with the result that he sometimes speaks of two *prosopa*, sometimes of one *prosopon* in Christ.[42] But the fundamental weakness of his solution emerges when the unity itself is to be explained. He takes refuge in the idea of the 'use' of the *prosopon*. As he feels that this theory is not sufficient, he introduces into the *Liber Heraclidis* the further one of a 'double use' or the 'compensation' of *prosopa*. He cannot succeed, as his metaphysical starting point is wrong. But we must acknowledge that his intention was sound.

In the time of Nestorius, it is everywhere apparent that no adequate metaphysic of the substantial union of spiritual beings had yet been evolved. More than all others, however, Nestorius saw the problem of finding such a substantial union which would leave intact the physis *qua* physis. This clear insight into the problem, together with his inadequate solution, explains his inability to justify his own theological positions and to think himself into others. All the traditional difficulties come to a head in his writings. We understand how he could be condemned if the consequences of his false premises were drawn. But we can recognize just as clearly that he need not have been condemned had attention been paid to his care for tradition and to the new problem which he posed, despite his speculative 'impotence' (G. L. Prestige) to solve it.

Before we discuss the Nestorius of the *Liber Heraclidis*, we must examine the debate over him in Rome and at Ephesus.

---

[42] On the numerical relationship of the two different expressions, see F. Loofs, *Nestorius*, 77f.; L. Abramowski, *Untersuchungen zum L.H.*, 217–24.

CHAPTER TWO

THE NESTORIUS QUESTION AND ROME

THE oral and written propaganda of the Patriarch of Constantinople in the question of the *Theotokos* is first echoed in his immediate surroundings and in Alexandria.[1] The latter place was attacked in a special way by the theses which Nestorius advanced. Nevertheless, the first act of the 'tragedy' which now opens takes place in the West, in Rome. Nestorius himself put his views before Pope Celestine I (422–432) in several letters and in copies of a number of his sermons. Thus the bishop of Rome, who had had no dealings with christological heresy since the days of Pope Damasus, was unexpectedly confronted with a great new problem immediately after the easing of the Pelagian disputes. Now would have been the opportunity for Latin theology to show the *via media* between Constantinople (Antioch) and Alexandria in the light of its own traditions. Of course, for a really successful conclusion to the Eastern dispute, not only a dogmatic decision but also a new step forward in the theological interpretation of the incarnation was needed. Is Rome up to the task?

1. THE CASE OF LEPORIUS

Augustine was still alive at the beginning of the Nestorian dispute in the East. It would have been a good opportunity for him to have gained special importance in the christological sphere as well, while at the same time coming into closer contact with the East than hitherto.[2] But his death came too soon. What Augustine might have meant in the Nestorian question can be seen, however, from his intervention in the case of Leporius, the forerunner of Nestorius in the West. It was not least because of the tact and skill of Augustine that this matter did not become a *scandalum oecumenicum* like that of Nestorius, of whom Cassian says that he was *praeclarae urbis contaminator ac sanctae plebis gravis et exitiosa contagio*.[3] Leporius was won over not by the promulgation of a verdict on him, but

---

[1] For Constantinople: the *contestatio* of Eusebius of Dorylaeum (Winter 428–9), ACO I, 1, 1, pp. 101–2. He is the first to draw the parallel between Nestorius and Paul of Samosata. For the historical significance of this *contestatio* see M. Tetz, 'Zum Streit zwischen Orthodoxie und Häresie an der Wende des 4. zum 5. Jahrhundert. Anfänge des expliziten Väterbeweises', *EvTh* 8, 1961, 354–68. For the parallel between Nestorius and Paul of Samosata see similarly Marius Mercator, *Commonitorium.* no. 18: ACO I, 1, 5, p. 28. Socrates passes a more sober judgement, HE 7, 31, 32: PG 67, 809–12 (see Cassian below). Proclus too preaches against Nestorius: ACO I, 1, 1, pp. 103–7. For Alexandria: Cyril, Easter Festal Letter 17 to the bishops and *Ep.* 1 to the monks of Egypt; First and Second Letters to Nestorius (*Epp.* 2 and 4).

[2] For the relationship between Augustine and the East see the numerous articles by B. Altaner, listed in 'Bibliographie B. Altaner', *HistJb* 77, 1958, 576–600.

[3] Cassian, *De incarn.* VII, 30, no. 3: CSEL 17, 389.

by the resolution of his theological doubts.[4] These were in fact the same as those of Nestorius in the East. This is clear from a report which Augustine, along with other bishops, sent to the bishops of Gaul in the years 418–21. Leporius did not agree with the traditional *communicatio idiomatum*. He was perplexed by references to a 'born and crucified God':

> He did not wish to confess that God was born of a woman, that God was crucified or had suffered in a human way, fearing that the Godhead might be believed to have been changed into man or to have been corrupted by being mingled with man; *a pious fear but an incautious mistake*. In his piety he saw that the Godhead could not be changed, but incautiously he presumed that the Son of man could be separated from the Son of God so that each was different, and one of them could be Christ and the other not, or Christ could be twofold.[5]

The monk of Gaul did not really mean heresy. He merely wished to protect the traditional dogma of the divinity of Christ in his own fashion against doctrines which really or supposedly confused the natures. Cassian is thus unjust in fathering on Leporius an explicit heretical intent, by making the monk a strict adoptionist and a Pelagian in christology (*De incarn.* I, 2, nos. 4–6: CSEL 17, 238–45). Like Nestorius, Leporius stresses the distinction of the natures. In this he is successful, but can no more give an adequate expression of the unity in Christ than can Nestorius. This was the most acute theological problem of the time. The Bishop of Marseilles, however, replied to Leporius' affirmations with excommunication. Thereupon Leporius fled to Africa and there found the right man to show him a way out of his difficulties. Augustine taught the monk to see from the Latin tradition the levels on which duality and unity are to be sought in Christ. True, it was still only a very formal and summary distinction, but it was sufficient to enable Leporius to make his way back into the communion of the church. Even Chalcedon at a later date will not have a great deal more to offer. We have Augustine's solution in the *libellus emendationis* which the monk Leporius had to read in the presence of a number of bishops, among them Augustine, at Carthage, and to which, along with them, he had to subscribe.[6] It has been called 'une première ébauche du Tome à Flavien'.[7] It states that the incarnation is to be regarded as a conjunction of human nature with the *person* of the Word and not with the divine *nature*:

[4] For Leporius: the sources are collected in P. Glorieux, *Prénestorianisme en Occident*, Tournai–Paris–Rome–New York 1959, 5–38; for his christology see E. Amann, 'Leporius', *DTC* IX, 324–440; id., *RevSR* 23, 1949, 227–30; A. Trapé, 'Un caso de nestorianismo prenestoriano en Occidente resuelto por San Agustín', *Ciudad de Dios* X 155, 1943, 45–67; cf. H.-M. Diepen, 'L'*assumptus homo* patristique', *RevThom* 63, 1963, 225–45, 363–88; 64, 1964, 32–52; J. Mehlmann, 'Tertulliani liber de Carne Christi ab Augustino citatus', *Sacris Erudiri* 17, 1966, 269–89; id., 'Tertulliani liber de Carne Christi a Leporio Monacho citatus', ibid. 17, 1966, 290–301.

[5] Augustine, *Ep. CCXXIX ad Eppos. Galliae*: CSEL 57, 431; Glorieux, op. cit., 12f.

[6] Leporius, *Libellus emendationis*: PL 31, 1221–30; Glorieux op. cit., 14–25.

[7] M. J. Nicolas, *RevThom* 51, 1951, 610.

Thus the flesh served the Word and not the Word the flesh; and yet the Word was most truly made flesh. But as we have said, this happened only *personally* and not by nature, with the Father or with the Holy Spirit.[8]

Because person and nature are distinct in the Trinity, it is possible to refer the incarnation to the person of the Logos and to allow Godhead and manhood to be unconfused. Under the guidance of Augustine, Leporius learnt the right grasp of the subject of the incarnation. The incarnation is the 'descent of the Logos' and not a gradual 'ascent of a mere man'. There is *one person* in Godhead and in manhood, and so both the human and the divine can be predicated of this one person:

For God the Father was not made man, nor was the Holy Spirit, but the Only-Begotten of the Father. Thus one person is to be accepted of both the flesh and the Word so that we may believe faithfully and without any doubt that one and the same was inseparably God the Son, a giant of twofold substance. In the days of his flesh he truly and always acted as man, and truly and always had the attributes of God; for he was crucified in weakness, but lives through the virtue of God. For this reason we are not afraid to talk of God being born from man, of God suffering as man, of God dying, and so on; but we are proud to say that God was born and that God suffered as man—for I am not ashamed of the gospel. . . .[9]

It is Augustine who speaks in this *libellus*, particularly in the formula *gigas geminae substantiae*, which was to be repeated so frequently in the Middle Ages.[10] Augustine surely also inspired the idea of the separation of the Godhead from the body of Christ in death, while it remains united with the soul. For because in the view of Augustine (as of Origen) the conjunction of Godhead and manhood took place *mediante anima*, the separation of the soul of Christ from the body also represented the parting of the Godhead from it.[11] In a fine formula shaped on the lines of the creed, Leporius—surely again with Augustine's help—at last finds the way out of the labyrinth of his doubt:

Therefore I believe and confess that according to the great sacrament of piety my Lord God was born in the flesh, suffered in the flesh, died in the flesh, was raised in the flesh and was glorified in the flesh; and I believe that he will come in the same flesh to judge both the living and the dead; and from him each one will have his eternal reward according to his merits.[12]

In the East, however, the basic presuppositions which helped to resolve the case of Leporius with so little friction were available neither to Nestorius nor to his opponents. To be an Augustine to the Patriarch of Constantinople would surely have been a difficult, though a useful task.

[8] PL 31, 1224Df.: Glorieux, op. cit., 17.
[9] PL 31, 1225Df.: Glorieux, op. cit., 18f.
[10] The formula comes from Ambrose in connection with Ps. 18. 6; Augustine, *Contra sermonem Arianorum* ch. 8: PL 42, 689; cf. id., *Ctr. Maximinum* II, 10, 2: PL 42, 765. For the Middle Ages, see L. Ott in *Chalkedon* II, 907f.
[11] See A. Grillmeier, *ZkTh* 71, 1949, 52.
[12] PL 31, 1229B: Glorieux, op. cit., 23.

Unfortunately, there was no such person even in Rome when his case was initiated there.

2. THE CASE OF NESTORIUS AT ROME

As has already been remarked, from the end of 428 Nestorius tried, through his own propaganda, to acquaint East and West with his christological ideas. He himself informed Pope Celestine I, first by his letter *Fraternas nobis invicem.*[13] In this he asks the Pope for information about the Pelagian errors, hitherto unknown to him. He also describes his own struggle against the christological 'heresies', in particular that which he describes as *cuiusdam contemperationis confusio*. It is taught by the Arians, Apollinarians and their adherents. He also militates against the title *Theotokos*, as this is not in accordance with the Nicene creed. He feels that it is false *Mariam cum Deo quodam modo tractare divine*. He puts forward his basic ideas on the incarnation in a very incomplete sketch. Pope Celestine answers only on 10 August 430, evidently after several more letters from Nestorius have already reached Rome and the struggle is already at its height (cf. ACO I, 2, 14, no. 1). The delay was caused by the lack of translators for the Greek original (ibid., 7, no. 3). There is now abundant material in Rome; in addition to the letters mentioned, there is the collection of expositions and homilies which Cyril also received.[14] But because the translation of a whole set of writings is no easy matter, moves are made towards Alexandria, to obtain from there more speedy information about the contents of Nestorius' writings (cf. Cyril, *To Nestorius*, ACO I, 1, 1, no. 3, p. 24).

This is a significant step. In the Rome–Alexandria–Constantinople triangle which is now being formed, the first two points combine more and more clearly against the third. In the summer of 430, an envoy of Cyril, the Deacon Posidonius, comes to Rome to bring a formal complaint against the Bishop of Constantinople (ACO I, 1, 5, 10–12). In the closing words of this letter (ibid., 12) Cyril says that he is sending to Celestine in a Latin translation extracts from the writings of Nestorius[15] and of the Fathers. The theme of the complaint is that by Nestorius δυσφημεῖται Χριστός (ibid., 12³). In a special instruction by Posidonius, Nestorius' teaching is interpreted as pure adoptionism, as a doctrine that the man Jesus, by his own merit, earned acceptance as Son and that consequently Christ was two sons (I, 1, 7, 171). However intense the conjunction between

---

[13] ACO I, 2, 12–14; Loofs, *Nestoriana*, 165–8. Nestorius also included in the sphere of his propaganda Macedonia, which belonged to eastern Illyria and was thus dependent on Rome (cf. ACO I, 1, 5, 11³⁰⁻³³). On what follows see the article, already mentioned, by E. Amann, 'L'affaire Nestorius vue de Rome', *RevSR* 23, 1949, 5–37, 207–244; 24, 1950, 28–52; L. I. Scipioni, *Nestorio e il concilio di Efeso*, Milano 1974, 149–200 (L'intervento di Roma).

[14] ACO I, 2, 85; cf. Liberatus, *Breviarium* c. 4: ACO II, 5, 1024⁻⁷.

[15] Contained in the *Collectio Palatina*, no. 29: ACO I, 5, 55–60.

the Logos and the man Jesus (κατὰ μείζονα συνάφειαν), it was still only the kind of conjunction which existed between God and Moses and the prophets. In this way a particular interpretation of the christology of Nestorius was brought from Alexandria to Rome.

A verdict on the Bishop of Constantinople was sought from yet a third side. Leo, the Archdeacon of Rome, asked the Abbot of St Victor in Marseilles, *John Cassian* (born *c.* 360, died *c.* 435), as one well acquainted with the East, for some guidance in this difficult question. For this purpose Cassian surely obtained the documents at the disposal of the Roman Curia, though in his writing *De Incarnatione Domini contra Nestorium Libri VII* there are only a few extracts from them.[16] It is amazing how little Cassian, who probably came from Scythia Minor, the present Dobrogea, and had long remained in the East, could sympathize with Eastern theology. He himself is no great theologian. Unfortunately he does not recognize the need of the hour, to take the questions raised by Leporius in the West and Nestorius in the East as the occasion for a deeper consideration of the adequacy of the christological terms and concepts used hitherto. He sees in the teaching of Nestorius only an explicit heresy similar to the adoptionism of Paul of Samosata and the doctrines of Pelagius.[17] Christ was a *solitarius homo*.

Thus it was not the intention of the monk of St Victor to recognize the difficulties of his opponent and to cure them, but to oppose what seemed to him to be an already established heresy with the tradition of the church. He is not a doctor, like Augustine, but a judge. He himself betrays some uncertainty in his christology. Some of his formulas and ideas contain a strong stress on the Godhead and on the divinization of the manhood of Christ (cf. above on Hilary). Christ can no longer properly be called 'man', as the Godhead lays claim to all that is in him (III, 3, no. 2, p. 265). According to Paul in 2 Cor. 5. 16, we may 'no longer know Christ after the flesh'. For the nature of the flesh has been completely taken up into the spiritual substance (i.e. the Godhead) (*natura enim carnis in spiritalem est translata substantiam*). What was once of man has now been made completely of God (*quod fuerat quondam hominis, factum est totum dei*). What was before in twofold substance (*quidquid fuerat prius substantiae duplicis*) has become one power (*factum est virtutis unius*), Christ now lives only '*ex maiestate divina*' (III, 3, no. 5, 264f.). In the transfigured Christ upon whom

---

[16] Cf. F. Loofs, *Nestoriana*, 51–7; E. Schwartz, *Konzilstudien I. Cassian u. Nestorius*, Strassburg 1914. Both authors give a list of contents of the dossier of Nestorius from which the quotations of Cassian are taken. Cf. E. Amann, *RevSR*, 1949, 231–2 (those utilized are the *First Letter of Nestorius to Celestine* and 4 *Sermons of Nestorius*). For the work of Cassian see PL 50, 9–272: CSEL 17, 233–391, ed. M. Petschenig. It was written before the summer of 430. Our quotations follow the pages of CSEL. See now V. Codina, *El aspecto cristológico en la espiridualidad di Juan Casiano* (OCA 175), Rome 1966. Codina stresses the influence of Origen, which reached Cassian direct and through Evagrius.

[17] Cf. Cassian, *De incarn.* I, 3; V, 1, 2, 4, 14: CSEL 17, 239f.; 302f., 306, 323. In VII, 21, no. 4, Nestorius is called '*Pelagianae haereseos spinosa suboles*'. The same is true of Leporius. This connection between Nestorius and Pelagius must have weighed particularly heavily with Rome.

Saul looked it was no longer possible to distinguish what was flesh and what was God (*quid sit caro et quid sit deus*). Cassian emphatically exclaims:

> For I cannot here separate one from the other. . . . What room is there here for division and separation? . . . How can we help believing that in one and the same substance God and Jesus exist?[18]

Further sentences have a certain Monophysite undertone:

> Understand then without any doubt that Christ is God; and when you see that the substance of God and Christ is altogether inseparable, admit also that the person cannot be severed.[19]

Even the Archdeacon Leo may have shaken his head when reading such sentences. He is to use different language later, in his Tome, at the inspiration of the old Latin tradition. But even Cassian has expressions which Nestorius could have written.[20] At first one gains the impression that Cassian developed a similar speculative interpretation of the incarnation—as far as we can speak of this—to Nestorius himself (in the *Liber Heraclidis*). He evidently sees the union of Godhead and manhood in Christ brought about by a mutual interpenetration or *perichoresis* of the natures. This leads to the strong emphasis on the divinization of the human nature which has already been described. For this reason, too, we have the remark that there is no distance between 'Christ' and the Word (*nullam penitus inter Christum et verbum esse distantiam*),[21] a phrase which we shall meet again in Nestorius' *Liber Heraclidis*. Indeed, Cassian sometimes expresses himself more unskilfully than his opponent by representing 'Christ' and 'Word' as the two realities which are united in the incarnation, whereas for Nestorius 'Christ' is always the union of Logos and man(hood):

> . . . and so since Christ and the Word were united in the mystery of the incarnation, Christ and the Word of God became one Son of God in either substance.[22]

So at first sight it appears that Cassian is less able to define the subject of the incarnation than Nestorius. But as his work progresses, he discovers better and better formulas and makes continually closer contact with the Latin tradition. Some of it already anticipates Leo's *Tomus ad Flavianum*. Beginning with the creed of Antioch, which Nestorius, too, once recognized, he arrives at the crucial point of christological expression: both that which belongs within the Godhead (the Godhead of the consubstantial Son, his relationship to the Father and his mediation in creation) and that

---

[18] Cassian, *De incarn.* III, 6, nos. 3–4; p. 267.

[19] Ibid., III, 7, no. 3, p. 270; cf. 7, nos. 1–2, p. 269.

[20] He describes Christ as *homo unitus Deo* or as *homo susceptus* (II, 3, no. 3, p. 250; no. 4, p. 251). He speaks of *Filius Dei* and the *homo suus* (VII, 17, no. 3, p. 373).

[21] Ibid., IV, 5, nos. 2–3, pp. 290f.

[22] Ibid., IV, 4, nos. 2–3, p. 290; cf. also the very awkward formulas in IV, 5, no. 1, p. 290; especially V, 9, no. 4, p. 316. But Cassian has a definition of the name of Christ which occurs in almost the same words in Nestorius: '*Christus omnia est* (i.e. God and man) *et nomen illius significatio est utriusque naturae*' (VI, 22, no. 6, p. 349). Cf. below on the *L.H.*

which belongs to the worldly history of the incarnation, are predicated of the one *Verbum*, the Word.[23] Gal. 4. 4 also finds a good application here (VI, 8, nos. 1–4). If the consubstantial Son of God is to come into the world he cannot do it in his Godhead, but must take the way of an incarnation in history. Where Nestorius had started from the Nicene creed, Cassian finds in the creed of Antioch a good basis for the *communicatio idiomatum*: 'deum utique natum, deum passum, deum resurrexisse'.[24] Expressions can suddenly appear which recur in the Chalcedonian Definition. He is stimulated to this by Nestorius' requirement: *homoousios parienti debet esse nativitas*. Even Nestorius could have accepted the answer:

> Next, if you say that the child born ought to be of one substance with the parent, I affirm that the Lord Jesus Christ was of one substance with his Father, and also with his mother. . . . For according to his divinity he was of one substance with the Father; but according to the flesh he was of one substance with his mother.[25]

Because there is thus in Christ a true unity of God and man, the reality of the redemption is at the same time safeguarded. Nestorius, as a 'mimic of the Pelagian', is said to make Christ a 'mere man' (*solitarium hominem*) and thus a mere moral example and tutor, not a real redeemer (*eruditorem humani generis magis quam redemptorem*). Christ would then give to mankind not the redemption of their life (*redemptionem vitae*) but just an indication of the right way to live. So salvation would only be reached by a pure imitation or discipleship of Christ: that is the result of Nestorius' interpretation of Christ (VI, 14, no. 1, p. 341). It is evident that this is a false interpretation of Nestorius.

Cassian's expert judgement, requested by Leo, opens up no new perspectives on the theological questions of the time. His own christology is by no means a unity, and is extremely unclear in parts. Nor does it offer any basis for founding a christology of the manhood of Christ. True, the natural and historical reality of the manhood of Jesus is fully assured by the double *homoousios* which is predicated of Christ. But Cassian makes no attempt, say, to show the content of the full humanity of Christ (in evaluating Christ's human nature and its power in understanding and will). He has, moreover, an incomplete, even false, idea of the relation of the Godhead of Christ to his human nature. The whole complex of the biblical-messianic spirit-christology is something which he will not recognize as such (cf. VII, 17, nos. 1–7, pp. 372–5). He will not concede that Jesus as a man needs to be filled with the Holy Spirit, because in this way Christ is represented as weak and in need of help. There is a considerable share of the Pelagian idea of grace in this, despite the fact that he

[23] The text of the creed: VI, 3, no. 2; 4, no. 2; 6–10 passim.
[24] Ibid., VI, 9, no. 2, p. 336; cf. the good formulas for the incarnation in VI, 17, no. 2, p. 345. In VI, 19, nos. 2–4, p. 346 we have the asseveration of the identity of the subject of the incarnation on the basis of the creed.
[25] Ibid., VI, 13, nos. 1–2, pp. 340f.

accuses Nestorius of such Pelagianism:

> The whole of your blasphemy then consists in this: that Christ had nothing of himself: nor did he, a mere man, as you say, receive anything from the Word, i.e. the Son of God; but everything in him was the gift of the Spirit.[26]

Although Scripture speaks quite clearly of the grace of the Spirit (for example in the baptism scene), Cassian interprets this as a direct emanation of the Godhead of the Word on to the manhood of Christ. True, he also has the phrase in Col. 2. 9 which speaks of the indwelling of the fullness of the Godhead in Christ (VII, 7, no. 2). But does Paul mean by this what Cassian reads out of it? In any case, Cassian refuses to accept a further special endowment of grace given to Christ's human nature alongside the divinity of Christ as such. It is superfluous:

> How far then from him was it to need being filled with righteousness, as he himself filled all things with righteousness, and for his glory to be without righteousness, whose very name justifies all things. . . . not because we are to believe that in all these things which he himself did, the unity and co-operation of the Spirit was wanting—since the Godhead is never wanting to itself, and the power of the Trinity was ever present in the Saviour's works—but because you will have it that the Holy Ghost gave assistance to the Lord Jesus Christ as if he had been feeble and powerless: and that he granted those things to him, which he was unable to procure for himself.[27]

Through fear of teaching two persons, he assigns to the divinity of Jesus everything that falls within the sphere of the biblical-messianic grace of the Spirit (VII, 20, nos. 1–3, pp. 377f.). In so doing Cassian draws a very empty picture of the humanity of Jesus. It is only with the greatest difficulty that he can assent at all to the famous phrase of the *Tomus ad Flavianum*, which has become the standard of Western christology: *Agit enim utraque forma cum alterius communione quod proprium est* (see below). But some phrases still open up a glimpse of a richer theology of the manhood of Christ, as, for example, the Augustinian idea of the *caro uxor (sponsa) verbi*, which Cassian appropriates: the Son of God left Father and 'mother', i.e. the God of whom he is born and the heavenly Jerusalem which is the 'mother' of us all (cf. Gal. 4. 26), to cleave to human flesh as his bride (*et adhaesit humanae carni quasi uxori suae*).[28] Cassian also sees the connection between incarnation and church (*quia et caro ecclesiae caro Christi est . . . quia sacramentum quod in carne Christi creditur etiam fide in ecclesia continetur*).[29]

Thus Posidonius and Cassian were the men who interpreted the case of Nestorius to the Roman Curia. At the beginning of August 430, Celestine

---

[26] Ibid., VII, 17, no. 2, p. 373. [27] Ibid., VII, 18, no. 3 and 17, no. 7, pp. 375, 374.
[28] Ibid., V, 12, nos. 3–4, pp. 321–2. In this context it is also suggested that the hypostatic union takes place *mediante anima*. There are also hints here of the idea advanced at the *Concilium Toletanum* XV (688) that there are three substances in Christ, *deus—anima—caro* (nos. 2–4; cf. Denzinger, *Enchiridion Symbolorum*, 295: DS, 567).
[29] Ibid., no. 5, p. 322. Here we have Cassian's concrete idea of Christ. The flesh is the temple in which the Godhead dwells together with the soul: *sicut caro illa habitatorem habuit in se deum, ita animam quoque in se cohabitantem deo* (nos. 4–5).

I now held a synod at Rome to show his own position.[30] Nestorius was condemned because to the public scandal of the Word of God he taught contrary to the common faith and because the honour of the *virgineus* (*virginalis*) *partus* was violated.[31] Celestine does not give a very detailed picture either of the teaching of Nestorius or of his own attitude. He says that the Bishop of Constantinople teaches the division of the two natures. Now he makes Christ a mere man, now he lets him dwell in communion with God in so far as God condescends to this.[32] Let Nestorius explain that this *virgineus partus* has given to the world not a *solitarius homo*, but the true Son of God, who thus assures our salvation (cf. ACO I, 2, 21, no. 4). So the case of Nestorius is treated in a purely defensive and conservative way. The real significance of the problem raised by the whole development of christology from Apollinarius onwards is not recognized. Celestine and the Synod of Rome are unable to realize adequately the christological problems raised by Nestorius. So they also do not recognize the necessity of giving a theological basis to the *communicatio idiomatum* and of creating a formula which expresses simultaneously both the unity and the difference in Christ. Gennadius, of course, judges from a later standpoint, when he sums up the result of the Synod of Rome of 430 in this way:

> Celestine, bishop of Rome, addressed a volume to the churches of the East and West, giving an account of the decree of the Synod against the above-mentioned Nestorius and maintaining that while there are two complete natures in Christ, the person of the Son of God is to be regarded as single. The above-mentioned Nestorius was shown to be opposed to this view.[33]

Even Nestorius would have been content with this formula. Unfortunately, the atmosphere between Constantinople and Alexandria was by now so inflamed that the search for such a clarificatory formula had no chance right from the beginning. Ephesus solves the point at issue in a conservative and dogmatic way and so indeed performs a necessary work. But the synod omits to open up a theological speculative way towards solving the existing tensions. This is at the expense of the peace and unity of the church.

[30] The verdict of the synod of 10 August 430 is in the *Coll. Veronensis*, ACO I, 2, 20[23]; see also Celestine's letter in the same collection. Cf. E. Amann, *RevSR* 24, 1950, 28–44. Along with Garnier, Amann is of the opinion that the tractate of Cassian was used at the Synod (38, n. 1).

[31] ACO I, 2, 8[9] and 9[2]; 15, no. 2: Nestorius teaches falsely *de virgineo partu et de divinitate Christi*.

[32] ACO I, 2, 15, no. 2. E. Amann is wrongly of the opinion that the charge of 'psilanthropisme' against Nestorius does not occur in the writings of Celestine (art. cit., 39).

[33] Gennadius, *Vir. inl.*, n. 54 (189) éd. Bernouilli, 80. Here cited after E. Amann, *RevSR* 24, 1950, 31, n. 2. Cf. also Arnobius iun., *Conflictus* II, 1: PL 53, 289B–290B.

CHAPTER THREE

CYRIL OF ALEXANDRIA, THE ADVERSARY OF NESTORIUS

WHILE Rome, together with Cyril of Alexandria, exerted a decisive influence in the case of Nestorius, it did so more in a church-political and dogmatic respect than through an original contribution to the theological side of the question. Only with Leo the Great is there added to the teaching authority and church-political influence of Rome a theological interpretation of the picture of Christ which is to be influential for a long time. The immediate counterpart to the christology of Nestorius is Cyril of Alexandria and his christological doctrine. The latter achieved its historical importance precisely through its opposition to Nestorius, so acute that even Leo was held by Cyril's supporters to be on the side of Nestorius.[1]

1. CYRIL AND APOLLINARIUS

Hitherto we were able to establish a connection of Cyril only with orthodox Alexandrian Logos-sarx christology as it was embodied in Athanasius and Ps. Basil, *Ctr. Eunom. IV-V*. His contact with this type of christology is to become closer and more fateful. *Apollinarian formulas* find their way into Cyril's theological language. In 429-30, Cyril devotes himself to a deeper theological study so as to be able to enter the field against Nestorius, the repudiator of the title *Theotokos*. Certain circles seem to have used this moment to send the Patriarch of Alexandria a number of works, among them some which bore the names of the Roman Popes Julius and Felix. Here Cyril reads the words and formulas which are to become a matter of dispute to theological factions for centuries. From now on, his terminology and ideas become sharper. The most decisive feature, however, is his acceptance of the central formula of the Apollinarian Logos-sarx christology, the μία φύσις formula, alongside which may be placed the other, that of the μία ὑπόστασις.[2] As a result, Cyril's picture of Christ demands comparison with the Christ of the Bishop of Laodicea.[3] The mere fact that the Patriarch of Alexandria takes over the key formula of Apollinarian christology in his contest with Nestorius shows the decision he has faced and the difficulties he has to put before his

---

[1] See L. I. Scipioni, *Nestorio e il concilio di Efeso*, Milano 1974, 94-148.

[2] A brief review of the occurrences of hypostasis may be found in M. Richard, 'Hypostase', 242-5. For the *mia-physis (hypostasis)* formula, cf. J. van den Dries, *The Formula of S. Cyril of Al.* μ.φ.τ.Θ.Λ.σ., Rome 1939; for hypostasis and physis cf. *Chalkedon* I, 170, n. 15.

[3] H. M. Diepen, *Douze Dialogues*, 13-24 (Cyrille et Apollinaire); 25-48 (where the Apollinarian texts are given).

opponent. We must therefore attempt to discover Cyril's inner approach so as to be able to establish his real difference from Apollinarius.

The decisive element in the Apollinarian picture of Christ—we stress this once again because of its importance—is the vital, dynamic relationship between Logos and flesh, the constant flow of energy and of all lifegiving power from the Logos to his flesh and his instrument. There is only 'one' physis in Christ because in him there is only 'one' all-animating source of life and movement, the Logos. The μία φύσις formula of Apollinarius has a clearly vitalistic sense; while the personal element is not, of course, lacking in it, it is developed on a completely false foundation. We must judge the relationship between Cyril and Apollinarius in the light of this vital dynamism, and not from the standpoint of the distinction between nature and person. The point in question is thus the vital, dynamic character of the physis concept. If Cyril is to integrate this Apollinarian physis formula into the theology of the church, he must make a complete breakdown of the decisive element and in so doing achieve an inward transformation of the physis concept. This he does. Once he has recognized the soul of Christ he is no longer in a position to take over the dynamism of Apollinarius, at least within the physical, natural sphere of Christ's humanity. But he does not achieve his end simply by recognizing the 'soul'. He has to see its significance for the concrete approach of the physis concept and, above all, to find in it a theological factor for interpreting the whole picture of Christ. Did Cyril arrive at this sort of basic approach? His opponents and their criticism brought him to it.

The decisive evidence for this is the *Second Letter to Succensus*. Here we read four objections to Cyril's μία φύσις formula.[4] The fourth objection is particularly interesting, as it puts Cyril's formula where it belongs in the history of dogma, that is within the area of the Logos-sarx christology. Succensus quite rightly begins with the crucial point and wants to show that it cannot be claimed that Christ suffered only after 'the flesh' and that there is only one physis in the incarnate Word. Anyone who wants to avoid Apollinarianism must grant that Christ also suffered in his 'rational soul' as well as in the flesh. But given this, it follows logically that there are two physeis in the incarnate Christ. One is the Logos. The other is formed of the flesh and the rational soul.[5] Here Succensus hits the nail right on the head. He knows why Apollinarius was able to speak of the μία φύσις; it was because he had removed any possibility of the human nature of Christ being called a 'nature'. Now if Cyril, in contrast to

---

[4] For the christological standpoint of the objectors see A. van Roey, 'Deux fragments inédits des lettres de Succensus', *Mus* 55, 1942, 87–92; C. Moeller, 'Un représentant de la christologie néo-chalcéd., Nephalius d'Alexandrie', *RHE* 40, 1944–5, 111; G. Jouassard, *RSR* 44, 1956, 239 with n. 16.

[5] Cyril Al., *Ep. 46 ad Succens.* 2, 5: ACO I, 1, 6, 161–2; PG 77, 245A.

Apollinarius, has to assume a rational soul in Christ, his concept of physis is in immediate need of correction. Cyril cannot deny the conclusiveness of this argument and in fact concedes that Christ's human nature also is an αὐτοκίνητον, a self-moving principle, a physis.

The other objection put forward by Succensus also concerns the whole pattern of Cyril's Logos-christology.

> I (Cyril) know that they have in mind something more in addition to this (καὶ ἕτερόν τι πρὸς τούτοις ἐστὶ ζητούμενον). For he who says that the Lord suffered only in the flesh (i.e. and not in the soul) makes the suffering irrational and not endured by the will (ἀκούσιον); but if anyone says that he suffered with rational soul, so that the suffering was of free will, there is no objection to saying that he suffered in his human nature. But if this is true, how are we not to grant that the two natures exist (ὑφιστάναι) without separation after the union?[6]

The choice, then, is restricted to this: either the 'two natures' formula is to be accepted or the whole human psychology of Christ and the redemptive act accomplished by his soul will be lost. If we see these questions against the background of the Eastern Logos-sarx christology, the progress which Greek theology has now made is unmistakable. The theological relevance of the soul of Jesus Christ is sketched out with exceptional clarity and an account is given of its relationship to the μία φύσις formula. The first objection had already been framed in similar terms, though it did not lead so deeply into the problem: 'If there is only one physis in Christ then the suffering must be predicated of the *divine* physis.'[7]

Cyril answers all this with a clear recognition of the soul of Christ. This is made the 'natural principle of suffering', the principle which once Athanasius and even Cyril himself in his earlier writings had failed to stress, though it would have been the one decisive answer to the difficulties caused by the Arians.[8] Cyril will now admit the validity even of language about the 'two natures', though his recognition of the complete human nature does not prevent him from keeping his μία φύσις formula. It is not immediately plain here where Cyril differs from Apollinarius; the difference can only be worked out in the light of the vital, dynamic physis concept of the Laodicean. In this way, however, Cyril can be acquitted of all suspicion of an Apollinarian, Monophysite tendency—a suspicion which has occasionally been raised against him in recent times. So we find that the Logos-sarx christology has now finally been super-

---

6 Ibid., ACO I, 1, 6, 161[19-25]: PG 77, 244D.

7 Ibid., no. 2: ACO I, 1, 6, 158[8-10]: PG 77, 240A.

8 Ibid., ACO I, 1, 6, 158[27-28]: PG 77, 240C: τὸ πεφυκὸς ὑπομένειν τὸ πάθος. τὸ πεφυκὸς πάσχειν. But both body and soul belong to this natural principle of suffering: ibid., 158[13-18]. They form a ἑτεροφυές over against the Logos, in other words, precisely what Apollinarius wanted to exclude by his μία φύσις. Cf. *Quod unus sit Christus* (PG 75, 1289D); body and soul are emphasized along with the μία φύσις: μίαν αὐτοῦ φύσιν εἶναί φαμεν, κἄν εἰ ἐν προσλήψει γενέσθαι σαρκὸς ψυχὴν ἐχούσης τὴν νοεράν. See G. Jouassard, op. cit., 240, n. 20.

seded on Alexandrian soil. The Cyril of the Nestorian controversy recognizes a real human psychology in Jesus Christ. Suffering is transferred to the soul, as well as the body,[9] and above all, the significance of the human obedience and sacrificial action of Christ is seen.[10] For the Alexandrians, too, the soul of Christ has become a theological factor.

The right thing now would have been for Cyril to give up the 'Apollinarian' language of the μία φύσις formula once and for all. Had he done this, without doubt the further development of christological dogma would have been preserved from much confusion. The whole complex of this formula belongs to the sphere of the one-sided Logos-sarx christology and with it should have vanished from the theology of the church. But the Apollinarian forgers had disguised their work admirably. Cyril's consciousness that this was a formula sanctioned by the church prevented him from giving it up. But these formulas were not all that continued to associate him with the Logos-sarx christology, even though he had transformed them inwardly. There is also his doctrine of ζωοποίησις and the ὄργανον concept. Cyril, too, continues to make the bond between Logos and sarx as close as possible. As in the writings of Athanasius—and also Apollinarius—we see in Cyril's picture of Christ the divine ἐνέργεια of the Logos flowing directly into the body. The body of Christ is conjoined with the life itself and is therefore also itself life-giving.[11] But here, too, a clear dividing line may be drawn. One thing clearly distinguishes Cyril from Apollinarius—the giving of the *natural* life which the body needs is no longer derived from the Logos *qua* Logos, but is attributed to the soul. So although he uses the same language and terminology, the content of Cyril's writings is far removed from that of the writings of Apollinarius.

The one positive element which Cyril took over from the Athanasian and Apollinarian Logos-sarx christology is therefore not to be underestimated. From it he formed the new Alexandrian christology, which was the deepest expression of Christ that Greek theology was able to offer. A feature of it is the recognition of the unity of subject in Christ, the Logos. Whereas among the Antiochenes 'Christ' seems to emerge alongside the Logos as a new subject of christological expressions, in Alexandrian theology all expressions are directly orientated on the Logos.

This results in the clear consciousness of the unity in Christ. The Logos

---

[9] Cyril Al., *Or ad Augustas* 44: ACO I, 1, 5, 58³⁰⁻³⁶–59⁵: PG 76, 1413B; see R. A. Norris Jr, *Manhood and Christ*, Oxford 1963.

[10] Cyril Al., *Scholia de incarn. Unig.* 8: PG 75, 1377A–C: it was necessary that the soul should suffer united with its own body; it had to weep and lament and bow an obedient neck to God. Act of sacrifice: *Or. ad Augustas* 23: ACO I, 1, 5, 40⁴⁻⁸,¹¹: ἱερατεύειν ἀνθρωπίνως; ibid., no. 32: ACO I, 1, 5, 50³⁶–51¹: ἀνθρωπίνως μὲν λεγόμενος λειτουργεῖν, ἱερατεύων δὲ τῷ πατρὶ τὸ ἴδιον σῶμα (PG 76, 1369B, 1396B). Cf. F. M. Young, 'Christological Ideas' (see p. 418, n. 15 above).

[11] Cyril Al., *Ad dominas* 3: ACO I, 1, 5, 63¹⁹ (PG 76, 1205A): λόγος . . ., ἡ πάντα ζωογονοῦσα φύσις; ibid., no. 120: ACO I, 1, 5, 91³⁹⁻⁴² (76, 1273); no. 133: 957⁷⁻¹² (76, 1283); no. 192: 111³⁵⁻³⁶ (76, 1230B): εἰ γὰρ καὶ γέγονε σὰρξ ὁ λόγος, ἀλλ' ὡς θεὸς ἐνεργεῖ μετὰ τῆς ἰδίας σαρκός, ἐχούσης

'is' flesh without being changed into flesh. If such a statement can be made, it rests on the inner insight into the substantial unity of God and man in Christ. Cyril without doubt contributed to the final acceptance of the idea of this unity in Christ, though he did not succeed in expressing it in clear terms. Apollinarius had reached his consciousness of the substantial unity in Christ through his idea of the vital symbiosis of Logos and sarx. Cyril maintains the closeness of the connection, but gives it another basis. This, of course—to make the point yet again—he was hardly able to make clear in its ontological nature, and indeed for many he concealed it again through his ambiguous terminology.

The fruits which Cyril, along with Athanasius, was finally able to reap for the church from the ideas of the Logos-sarx christology may be summed up in the key formula: 'God the Logos did not come into a man, but he "truly" became man, while remaining God'.[12] Before the beginning of the Nestorian controversy, Cyril had used the 'indwelling formulas' unconcernedly with the rest of the tradition. After 429 they are either repudiated or expanded.[13] Wherever he still allows them, they are associated with a distinction. According to Cyril, Nestorius defends one form of indwelling. It establishes only an accidental relationship and remains an 'ordinary', 'simple' indwelling.[14] If such a relationship is spoken of, there must be a 'true, substantial' relationship between Logos and human nature.[15] In any case, 'incarnation' is something quite different from being 'conjoined' with a man.[16] The substantial character of the union immediately becomes clear. Now if Cyril, and with him the orthodox church tradition, acknowledged the 'Word-man' framework and none the less held firm to the essential and substantial character of the incarnation, his christology represents a synthesis of two christological types, the best elements of which he has combined. Cyril's special contribution is that he preserved this consciousness of the deep substantial nature of the conjunction of God and man in Christ. When this consciousness is combined with the clear terminology of Leo the Great, we shall be on the way to a fruitful synthesis.

To many of his contemporaries and successors, however, Cyril's theology appeared not as a 'synthesis' but as intolerable one-sidedness.

αὐτῆς δι' αὐτὸν τὴν δύναμιν; no. 136: 967⁻⁸ (76, 1284); no. 145: 98¹⁰⁻¹⁴ (76, 1288); no. 147: 98²⁸⁻³¹ (76, 1289)—Or. ad Augustas 45-6: ACO I, 1, 5, 59-60 (76, 1416-17); cf. J. Gross, La divinisation du chrétien d'après les Pères Grecs, Paris 1938, 282-5.

[12] Cyril Al., Or. ad Dominas 31: ACO I, 1, 5, 73¹⁻²: PG 76, 1228C.

[13] Cyril Al., Ad Monach.: PG 77, 24C; Scholia de incarn. Unig. 17: PG 75, 1391D; De recta fide ad Theodos.: PG 76, 1169A; Or. ad Augustas 2: ACO I, 1, 5, 53²⁷⁻²⁸: PG 76, 1401C; Ctr. Nestor. 1: ACO I, 1, 6, 21-2: PG 76, 33A. Further passages in N. Charlier, Thesaurus de Cyrille, 60, n. 1.

[14] Cyril Al., Ctr. Nestor. 1, 8: ACO I, 1, 6, 30³⁷⁻⁸: σχετικὴ κατοίκησις; 31¹⁻²: ἁπλῆ ἐνοίκησις (PG 76, 56).

[15] Ibid., 30³⁰: ἀληθινήν τε καὶ καθ' ὑπόστασιν.

[16] Cyril Al., Quod unus sit Christus: PG 75, 1329B: οὐκ ὡς ἄνθρωπον ἑαυτῷ συνάψας . . . ἐν αὐτῇ δὲ μᾶλλον αὐτὸς γεγονώς.

Even the Fathers of Chalcedon made some distinction in their verdict on his christological language. If we wish to understand the relationship of the council to Cyril and Cyril's contribution to the formula of Chalcedon we must obtain from Cyril himself the means of making this distinction.

2. AMBIGUOUS LANGUAGE

The dividing line between the Orientals on the one side and Cyril and his adherents on the other was the μία φύσις formula and similar expressions, especially as they were expressed in the much-disputed anathematisms. We must ask how Cyril stood towards this whole group of formulas to see how far he could also allow and approve another terminology. As a result, it will be possible to judge how near his christology comes to the formula of Chalcedon. Our chief starting-point will be the μία φύσις formula.

When Cyril used the expression 'φύσις' without qualification and inflexibly, he could never allow it for the humanity of Christ. Apollinarius could make no concessions here, as his whole system was rooted in the formula. But once Cyril had rejected the idea of the nature of Christ which lay at the root of the Apollinarian formula, he could no longer raise any objections in principle to the application of the physis concept to the humanity of Christ. It can, in fact, be shown that he does describe the humanity of the Lord with this term and does so not only when he is quoting the language of his opponents but also in his own terminology, both before and after Ephesus.[17] Of course, he is not fond of using the expression, for two reasons: first, because Holy Scripture prefers the term 'sarx', and secondly, because he sees in the expression the danger of a concession to the division taught by Nestorius. Nevertheless, the Patriarch does not repudiate the mention of Christ's ἀνθρωπίνη φύσις or φύσις τῆς ἀνθρωπότητος as such, but only in so far as this use of physis introduces a 'division' into Christ. This surely emerges from the interesting Letter to Succensus in which the question is put whether one is to recognize 'one' or 'two' physeis in Christ.[18] Cyril will allow the expression 'Christ suffered φύσει τῆς ἀνθρωπότητος', and will even concede that we can speak of a twofold physis in Christ. But the possibility of misinterpretation makes him cautious. He is not even satisfied with the addition of an 'ἀδιαιρέτως', as there is a quite different kind of 'indivisibility', i.e. a physical and a moral

---

[17] Cyril Al., In Lev.: PG 69, 576B: 'who came to us εἰς δύο μὲν φύσεις, which remain distinct.' Scholia de incarn. Unig.: PG 75, 1381A: 'the physeis or hypostaseis remain unconfused', ibid., 1385C: '. . . we say that there is the one and the same Jesus Christ, acknowledging at the same time the distinction of the natures (τὴν τῶν φύσεων διαφοράν) and preserving them unconfused from each other'.
[18] Cyril Al., Ep. 46 ad Succens. 2: ACO I, 1, 6, 161–2: PG 77, 245A.

one.[19] Cyril would protest against this kind of a division of the natures, but not against the acceptance of two physeis *per se*.

A similar conclusion may be drawn from the question: 'Did the Alexandrian reject the Nestorian δύο φύσεις formula as such, and absolutely, because by itself without a special addition it implies two persons?' Had Cyril been of this opinion, his μία φύσις would have been so necessary that he could have tolerated no variation in his language. But is it correct that the Patriarch is against the δύο φύσεις formula as such? The question can also be put in another way. For Cyril, does the δύο φύσεις language of itself already contain the notion of division, or is it only Nestorius who introduces the idea of division into it?[20] The answer can probably best be given by an extract from the letter to Acacius in which Cyril makes a distinction between the heresy of Nestorius and Antiochene christology and sees the decisive difference not in the use of the physis formula in itself, but in the definition of the relationship between the two natures.

> He (Nestorius) says: 'God is indivisible from the visible (= the man in Christ), therefore I do not divide the honour of that which is indivisible; I divide the natures, but I unite (one thing) the worship.' But the Antiochene brethren (= those who subscribed to the reunion of 433) accept that of which Christ is thought to be (composed), only merely in thought; true, they speak of a distinction of the natures (for, as has been said, Godhead and manhood are not the same thing in their physical characters) but recognize one Son and Christ and Lord and speak of the one prosopon in him as of one in reality; in no wise do they divide that which is united. Nor do they accept the physical division (φυσικὴ διαίρεσις), as has befallen the originator of these unfortunate discoveries.[21]

This extract is surely not concerned with the δύο φύσεις formula as such, for Cyril will allow the Antiochenes to speak, as he himself does, of the distinction of the natures, that is of the hypostaseis.[22] A *distinction* of the natures is necessary, a *division* is reprehensible. To speak of δύο φύσεις makes a distinction, but does not of itself divide; it only has the latter effect if a reprehensible intention to divide is associated with it. This is expressed still more clearly in the *Letter to Eulogius*:

> Some criticize the confession of faith which has been formulated by the Orientals and say, 'Why did the Bishop of Alexandria tolerate and praise those who speak of two natures?' ... Against those who blame us for this our answer is that we must not flee from or shudder at all that the heretics say, for they acknowledge much of what we ourselves acknowledge. ... That is even the case with Nestorius when he says that there are two natures signifying the distinction between the flesh and God the Word (i.e.

[19] Cyril acknowledges an ἀδιαίρεσις φυσική, his opponents the ἀδιαίρεσις τῇ ἰσοτιμίᾳ, τῇ ταυτοβουλίᾳ, τῇ αὐθεντίᾳ; *Ep.* 46 *ad Succens.*: ACO I, 1, 6, 162¹⁹⁻²²: PG 77, 245C. *Ctr. Nestor.* 1, 3: ACO I, 1, 6, 37–8; PG 76, 73–6.

[20] The Nestorian formula is particularly evident in *Ctr. Nestor.* 1–3: ACO I, 1, 6, 13–75: PG 76, 9–168; *Apol. ctr. Theodoret.* 3: ACO I, 1, 6, 116–20: PG 76, 401–9; *Ep.* 4 *ad Nestor.*: ACO I, 1, 1, 26–7: PG 77, 45C.

[21] Cyril Al., *Ep.* 40 *ad Acac. Melit.*: ACO I, 1, 4, 27: PG 77, 193D–196A.

[22] Ibid., 26²⁵⁻²⁶; PG 77, 193B; *Proem. Ctr. Nestor.* 2: ACO I, 1, 6, 34: PG 76, 64B, 65A; *Apol. ctr. Theodoret.*: ACO I, 1, 6, 119¹⁹: PG 76, 408B.

another is the physis of the Logos and another that of the flesh). But he does not join us in acknowledging the union (ἕνωσιν).[23]

In contrast to Nestorius' real division, [24] however, Cyril will speak of two natures only in 'the realm of thought'. If this limitation is absolute, it follows that he knows only *one* content of the term φύσις which must be defined still more closely so that there can be no question of a 'double language'. Nevertheless, the μία φύσις formula, together with some related expressions, has a certain special place and might be termed 'ambiguous language'.

As the above-quoted letters to Succensus and Eulogius further show, Cyril can at the same time both write in the style of the Anathemas and yet refrain from the extreme formulas. Here he seems to have adjusted himself to his audience. The events of the Union of 433 and the correspondence with the Antiochenes at all events show that Cyril knew an account of his own christology in terms which could match Antiochene language. The Fathers of Chalcedon perceive this distinction and therefore make a selection from his letters which avoids all extreme formulas. If, then, we look merely at the wording of the Chalcedonian Definition, Cyril's immediate contribution to it is really very small. But the few words which Cyril was able 'personally' to contribute to the Chalcedonian Definition are not the only decisive factor for his relationship to the Council. So powerful was his influence that the whole subsequent history of the Council of 451 is no more than a confrontation of the Chalcedonian Definition with his account of the dogma of the incarnation. Of course, men were no longer merely concerned with—and alienated from—just the Cyril of the Union of 433, but with the Cyril of the anathematisms.[25] But the church outgrew this too by preferring Cyril's christological *idea* to his *formulation* of it. Now this idea is the Alexandrian inner view of the unity in Christ.

3. Cyril and the Concept of Person

Cyril occupies a position midway between Apollinarius and Nestorius. We must take note of this if we are to be able to recognize and evaluate a twofold tendency in his christological idea and language. In contrast to Apollinarius, he has to be careful to ascribe to Christ's humanity the character of a full working-principle, a *physis*. In contrast to Nestorius,

[23] Cyril Al., *Ep.* 44 *ad Eulog.*: ACO I, 1, 4, 35: PG 77, 224D/225A. Explanations of this passage by writers vary. Some assume that Cyril agreed to a change in his terminology in 433. They rely on Cyril's phrase συνεχωρήκαμεν αὐτοῖς, which refers to the Antiochenes: ACO I, 1, 4, 35[21]. But this phrase does not mean a concession in terminology. It merely demonstrates that the thought of the moderate Antiochenes and the language in which they express it implies no real separation.
[24] Cf. the further passages *Ep.* 45 *ad Succens.*, 1: ACO I, 1, 6, 151[14], 153[17]: PG 77, 229A, 232CD; *Ep.* 46 *ad Succens.* 2: ibid. 162[5]: PG 77, 245A; *Ep.* 50 *ad Valer.*: ACO I, 1, 3, 97[27]: PG 77, 269C.
[25] For Cyril and Chalcedon see below.

he continually emphasizes the 'one *physis*' in Christ. In this there is some contradiction. But without doubt opposition to Nestorius predominates in Cyril's christology from 429. All his thought is directed towards expressing the *unity* in Christ, though at the same time he does not in any way neglect to *distinguish* between Godhead and manhood. The key problem in these struggles is, then, the development of an approach by which both the unity and the distinction can be maintained in Christ, and to find clear linguistic means for expressing this approach. It is well known where Cyril's difficulty lies, despite the depth and clarity of his ideas. It results from the Apollinarian μία φύσις formula, which causes him to limit the content of the term *physis*[26] and to use it in the sense of an 'individual, existent substance'. Thus he can express the unity in Christ well, but is somewhat obscure about the distinction.

Physis primarily means the 'essence' of a thing, ὁ τοῦ πῶς εἶναι λόγος, as the Patriarch puts it.[27] In this sense he could also speak of the ποιότης φυσική.[28] So the concept *physis* contains not only the idea of simple essence, but also the notions of 'actuating' and giving life (see *Ep. 46 ad Succens.* 5). In the end, however, a *physis* can actuate only if it is 'rounded off', if it is a hypostasis. Now this hypostasis is primarily equated with the idea of existence and reality. ὑφιστάναι is to produce from nothing, to root in being.[29] 'The basis needs to be built up in a *physis*, φύσις ὑφεστῶσα, which as such again bears the title ὑπόστασις.'[30] In any case, the concept of existence, of reality, is first in the significance of hypostasis and last in that of *physis*. So Cyril can also use the expression hypostasis for the complete *physis*, in the same way as he can speak of an ἀνυπόστατος μορφή, i.e. of an unreal, human nature of Christ with which he reproaches his opponents.[31] Both terms, *physis* and hypostasis, are thus not so much synonymous as associated one with another. The contents which they express elaborate each other, so that the one requires the other. But the basic meaning of hypostasis from which Cyril begins is existent, real substance. In this sense Cyril can even equate hypostasis with πρᾶγμα, reality.[32]

If we now seek to interpret the famous *mia physis* (*hypostasis*) formula from this standpoint, we see that *physis-hypostasis* is qualified by three

---

[26] J. van den Dries, *Formula of S. Cyril*, 9–41, gives a survey of different interpretations.

[27] Cyril Al., *Ctr. Nestor.* 2: ACO I, 1, 6, 42³³: PG 76, 85A; J. N. Hebensperger, *Die Denkwelt des hl. Cyrill von Al.*, Augsburg 1927, 85–6.

[28] Cyril Al., *Ep. 40 ad Acac. Melit.*: ACO I, 1, 4, 26²⁶: PG 77, 193B.

[29] *Thesaurus* 20: PG 75, 341B: ὑπόστασις = ἡ εἰς τὸ εἶναι παραγωγή = ὕπαρξις. Ibid. 356A, 364B. ὑφιστάναι = create, produce, make: *Thesaurus* 10, 21, 13: PG 75, 137A, 357D, 220B, 224D. Very clear and important is *Apol. ctr. Theodoret.*: ACO I, 1, 6, 112¹⁴⁻¹⁷: PG 76, 396C: οὐ γὰρ ὁμοιότητες ἁπλῶς ἀνυπόστατοι (= unreal) καὶ μορφαὶ συνέβησαν ἀλλήλαις καθ' ἕνωσιν οἰκονομικήν, ἀλλὰ πραγμάτων αὐτῶν ἢ γοῦν ὑποστάσεων γέγονεν σύνοδος. Cyril means to stress the reality of the two natures.

[30] J. N. Hebensperger, *Denkwelt*, 95, refers to *Ep. 46 ad Succ.* 2: ACO I, 1, 6, 162¹⁻²: PG 75, 245AB.

[31] Cyril Al., *Apol. ctr. Theodoret.*: ACO I, 1, 6, 113²²⁻³: PG 76, 397C.

[32] Ibid., 112¹⁵⁻¹⁶: PG 76, 397C.

words, μία—τοῦ θεοῦ λόγου—σεσαρκωμένη or σεσαρκωμένου.[33] Now *physis-hypostasis* itself means here the 'divine substance'. When 'of the God-Logos' is added, this names the subject, the personal bearer, to whom this *physis-hypostasis* belongs. Only the whole φύσις τοῦ θεοῦ λόγου produces a 'natural prosopon' and designates the substance with its bearer. Now is it possible to explain the addition 'incarnate' on this interpretation without having to accept a confusion of the natures? If we consider Cyril's own ideas about the unity of the divine-human being, no particular difficulty presents itself. Cyril would root the fleshly nature of Christ as deeply as possible in the divine reality of the Logos, in his substance, in his hypostasis. This substance is described as 'incarnate' in so far as the human nature of Christ has its hypostasis, i.e. its ground of existence and being, in the Logos. If in this context Cyril stresses that Godhead and manhood preserve their character, their ποιότης φυσική, the 'unity of hypostasis' represents that unity which takes separate existence from the human nature of Christ. So in the end the formula of the one *physis-hypostasis* necessarily leads to the idea of a unity of person, even if Cyril does not bring the element of person sufficiently into play, and in particular does not distinguish it either in language or concept from the concept of nature. But if we look beyond the *mia-physis* formula to the rest of Cyril's language, we see that he has a series of expressions which express not only the unity of person but also the distinction of the natures.[34] From all this, then, it is clear that Cyril in fact transfers the unity in Christ into the '*personal*' realm while ascribing a duality to the *natures*. Here he has anticipated the distinction of the Council of Chalcedon and has helped to lay its theological foundations. He has a greater depth of idea, just as the Antiochenes have the greater clarity of formula. The synthesis of the church will combine the two.

Should we now wish to survey Cyril's christological formula as a whole, we can make no better summary than in the sentences which M. Richard ('Hypostase', 245–52) selects as essential:

(1) The ὑποστάσεις or φύσεις of Christ may not be divided after the union.

(2) The ἰδιώματα may not be divided between two persons or two hypostases (or two independent *physeis*), but they must all refer to a single person, to the μία ὑπόστασις (φύσις) τοῦ θεοῦ λόγου σεσαρκωμένη.

(3) The Logos is united καθ' ὑπόστασιν[35] to the flesh which he has taken.

---

[33] J. van den Dries, *Formula of S. Cyril*, 113–67. It is impossible, however, to agree with all his interpretation.

[34] Cyril Al., *Ctr. Nestor.* 2, 6: ACO I, 1, 6, 43¹: PG 76, 85B: Nestorius fails εἰς ἰδικὴν ἑτερότητα διιστὰς ἄνθρωπον καὶ θεόν. *Scholia de incar. Unig.*: PG 75, 1385C: Οὐ διοριστέον οὖν ἄρα τὸν ἕνα κύριον Ἰησοῦν Χριστόν, εἰς ἰδικῶς ἄνθρωπον, καὶ εἰς θεὸν ἰδικῶς . . ., τὴν τῶν φύσεων εἰδότες διαφοράν, καὶ ἀσυγχύτους ἀλλήλαις τηροῦντες αὐτάς. *Apol. ctr. Theodoret.*: ACO I, 1, 6, 112¹⁴⁻¹⁷: PG 76, 396C is very significant.

[35] M. Richard investigates the derivation of this type of language. Ps. Ath., *Ctr. Apollin.*: PG 26,

These formulas become the great point at issue in the coming discussions. According to this explanation, the last-mentioned formula is meant to describe the unity in Christ in an emphatic way:

> In fighting against his (Nestorius') teaching we were compelled to say that the union took place καθ' ὑπόστασιν. The addition of καθ'ὑπόστασιν merely means that the nature or hypostasis of the Logos, that is, the Logos himself, is understood to be and in reality is a single Christ, the same God and man, as he has truly united himself with a human nature without any alteration or confusion.[36]

Afterwards, Cyril no longer attaches any great weight to this formula. Only post-Chalcedonian theology will again take up the expression after it has already had a long currency with the Monophysites. The Council of Constantinople in 553 will give it official character.

1113B, has been mentioned. But the text is not clear, not well dated and of uncertain derivation. The *unio* καθ' ὑπόστασιν is finally attested in Marcus Eremita, *Ctr. Nestor.* (cf. J. Kunze, *Marcus Eremita*, Leipzig 1895, 13); further in Marcus, *Melchisedech*: PG 65, 1124BC. But here, too, there is no satisfactory solution to the question of the date. At all events, Theodoret finds Cyril's formula new: cf. in Cyril Al., *Apol. ctr. Theodoret.*: ACO I, 1, 6, 114[11]: PG 76, 400A. Cyril himself seems to concede this: ibid., 115[12-16]: PG 76, 400D-401A. See *RevThom* 56, 1956, 688f.

[36] ACO I, 1, 6, 115[12-16].

CHAPTER FOUR

THE COUNCIL OF EPHESUS

WHAT direct contribution did the Council of Ephesus make to the development of the christological formula? The question can be answered quickly if we take it quite literally. The Fathers of the Synod of 431 made no new formula of belief, and did not even discuss a formula or a concrete statement as such. The focus of attention proved rather to be a dogmatic idea which was known already to have been expressed in other documents and which was seen to be endangered by the teaching of Nestorius. It was through this idea that the council was to acquire its special significance. That is, the synod which was assembled round Cyril of Alexandria and which was recognized by the envoys of the Pope and by the whole church. Nevertheless, one can speak of a 'creed of Ephesus'. The group of bishops assembled round John of Antioch, apart from Cyril, originated a credal formula[1] which, with a few alterations, was to become the *Formulary of Reunion* of 433. From here it had a direct influence on the Chalcedonian definition.[2] This 'creed of Ephesus', if we may call it that, thus stands between the Third General Council and Chalcedon and forms the link between the two synods.

The Council of 431 was therefore not concerned either with the composition of a new formula of belief or with the wording of particular sentences. The concrete formula as such faded right into the background, even if it could not be left out of consideration altogether. Instead, the centre of attention was the dogmatic 'content' of the church's dogma of the incarnation and the denial of this in the Nestorian kerygma. But even if no direct contribution towards the creation of a christological formula was made at Ephesus—it was because of this omission that Chalcedon became necessary—there are none the less a number of 'formula-making' elements in all the proceedings of the Fathers in council. First, there is their reference back to the formula of Nicaea and their special stress on this ecumenical council; in the view of the Synod of Ephesus, Nicaea framed the decisive formula on the incarnation. Secondly, there is their declaration that this dogma of Nicaea is expressed in the second letter of Cyril to Nestorius. The whole method of theological reasoning adopted by the Fathers of 431 must be seen as a third element in the history of christological formulas. We will examine these three points together.

Juvenal of Jerusalem gave the lead at the decisive session of 22 June 431: first of all, he proposed, the declaration of belief (πίστις) put forward by

---

[1] Theodoret., *Ep.* 151 *ad mon. orient.*: PG 83, 1420A.
[2] Text: ACO I, 1, 4, 17: PG 77, 176C–177B.

the 318 holy Fathers and Bishops who assembled at Nicaea should be read out so that the *sermones de fide* (περὶ πίστεως λόγοι), which were the points at issue, could be compared with it. Whatever corresponded with Nicaea was to be accepted, and whatever differed was to be rejected.[3] The reading took place. Peter of Alexandria, the chief notary, thereupon proposed that Cyril's second letter to Nestorius should be read.[4] This was accepted. After the reading Cyril rose and asked the Fathers to state whether the letter corresponded with the creed of Nicaea. Thereupon the Fathers one after the other solemnly asserted the inner unity of the two documents of the faith (ACO I, 1, 2, 13–31).

Now the second part of Juvenal's proposal was carried out. Palladius of Amaseia proposed that Nestorius' reply to this letter should be read, and this was done. Again Cyril rose (ibid., 31) and put the same question as he had with his own letter, its relationship to the creed of Nicaea. In turn, the bishops gave their verdict in the negative (ibid., 31–5), though Nestorius too had referred to this council (ACO I, 1, 1, 29).

The reading of these two letters and the verdict of the council upon them is the decisive dogmatic act of the Synod. The rest of the proceedings, where they have any connection with dogma at all, are no more than a repetition and an extension, a postlude to these first events, and in later approval of evidence by no means the same exalted tone prevailed.[5] At all events, the attitude of the council towards Cyril's third letter to Nestorius, which contained the much-disputed anathemas, is not what it was towards the second letter. Although the Fathers were convinced that here too there is complete accord with Nicaea, no voting followed. Cyril's third letter to Nestorius, like that of Pope Celestine, rated only as evidence and was included in the Acts (ACO I, 1, 2, 36[19-20, 26]). This is still truer of the patristic anthology which was read on the proposal of Flavian of

---

[3] ACO I, 1, 2, 12: cf. E. Honigmann, 'Juvenal of Jerusalem', DOP 5, 1950, 221–5. The proceedings of Ephesus ought to be examined with reference to contemporary legal procedure. H. Jaeger, Paris, drew my attention to Harald Schmidt, Der Einfluss der Rhetorik auf das Recht der Papyri Ägyptens, Diss. Erlangen 1949, dactylogr., where stress is laid on the distinction between 'pistis atechnos' and 'pistis entechnos', according to Pap. Lips. I, 32. The reading of a law proving a certain right is legal evidence for the fact of a pistis atechnos, i.e. a material proof, as opposed to a proof reached by rhetorical argument. For the following see P.-T. Camelot, Éphèse et Chalcedoine (HCO II), Paris 1962; in a German edition: Ephesus und Chalkedon (GÖK II), Mainz 1963; COD, 1973, 37–74; L. I. Scipioni, Nestorio e il concilio di Efeso, Milano 1974, 149–298. Scipioni is very critical of the contribution of the Council of Ephesus: 'In fact, because of Cyril, the Council of Ephesus failed completely in its aim, and gave the ambiguity of the mia physis an ulterior helping hand' (summary, 430).

[4] ACO I, 1, 2, 13: Text I, 1, 1, 25–8: PG 77, 44–9.

[5] J. Lebon would include the following part of the session under the rubric 'procedural details', 'Autour de la définition de la foi au concile d'Éphèse (431)', EphThLov 8, 1931, 393–412. Thus the council sought a precedent for 'procedural matters' in the letter of Celestine of Rome: ACO I, 1, 2, 36, no. 49; text ACO I, 1, 1, 77–83. See now H. M. Diepen, Douze Dialogues de Christologie ancienne, Roma 1960, 49–66 (les XII Anathematismes), 67–94 (la déposition de Nestorius). Diepen wants to demonstrate that the anathematisms of Cyril were already canonized at Ephesus (in the juridical sense, which would include a dogmatic verdict). This thesis is not proven. Cf. T. Šagi-Bunić, 'Documentatio doctrinalis Ephesino-Chalcedonensis', Laurentianum 3, 1962, 499–514; M. V. Anastos, DOP 16, 1962, 123, n. 8.

Philippi. It was in the hands of the chief notary, Peter of Alexandria (ibid., 39–45). As a counterpart, extracts were read from the writings of Nestorius (ibid.; 45–52). It was concluded that Nestorius was at fault and must be condemned. This condemnation was expressed and confirmed by signature (ibid., 54–64). The tenor of the καθαίρεσις was as follows:

> The holy synod which, by the grace of God, in conformity with the ordinance (θέσπισμα, properly means 'oracle') of our pious and Christ-loving kings, is assembled at Ephesus, to Nestorius, the new Judas! Know that because of your godless teachings (κηρύγματα) and disobedience towards the canons, in accordance with the decree of the statutes of the church on the 22nd of the current month of June you are condemned by the Holy Synod and dispossessed of any dignity in the church.[6]

So for the Fathers of 431 Nicaea provided the really authoritative christological formula, the simple wording of which was once again no more than a re-presentation of the apostolic faith and the tradition of the primitive church.[7] The dogmatic idea which the Fathers found in it was this:

> One and the same is the eternal Son of the Father and the Son of the Virgin Mary, born in time after the flesh; therefore she may rightly be called Mother of God.

The whole discussion with Nestorius turned on this point. This was the *dogma of Ephesus*, which was thus that of Nicaea. Divine life with the Father, descent to the earth, incarnation and humanity must be predicated of one and the same subject, the Logos who is ὁμοούσιος with the Father. The formula of 433 will similarly stress precisely this 'one and the same' which will also be included in the Chalcedonian Definition. This reference to the simple formula of 325 is significant for the stage of development which we have now reached. The continuity of christological proclamation is thus guaranteed in a special way. The creation of a formula by the church always means a return to the beginnings of the proclamation.[8]

Cyril's second letter to Nestorius, however, was considered by the Fathers to be the official expression of the teaching of Nicaea. Few documents concerned with the doctrine of the incarnation have been approved with such ceremony;[9] the Council of 431 itself emphasizes the agreement of the letter with the creed of 325. In 450, Leo the Great expressed himself to the same effect.[10] Finally, the Council of Chalcedon

---

[6] ACO I, 1, 2, 64; Latin I, 3, 83.

[7] Nicaea 325: ACO I, 1, 2, 13: τὸν δι' ἡμᾶς τοὺς ἀνθρώπους καὶ διὰ τὴν ἡμετέραν σωτηρίαν κατελθόντα καὶ σαρκωθέντα, ἐνανθρωπήσαντα. Cf. I. Ortiz de Urbina, El Simbolo Niceno, Madrid 1947, 224–44; id., Nicée et Constantinople (HCO I), Paris 1963, 69–92; J. N. D. Kelly, Creeds, 205–30.

[8] Pius XI, Encycl. 'Lux veritatis', II: AAS 23, 1931, 506–7.

[9] P. Galtier, 'Unité ontologique et unité psychologique dans le Christ', BLE 41–2, 1940–41, 161–75, 216–32; esp. 169.

[10] Leo M., Ep. 67 ad Ravennium episc. Arelat.: PL 54, 886A–887A; Ep. 69: PL 54, 891A: 'Sanctae memoriae Cyrilli Alexandrini episcopi epistolam qua Nestorium corrigere, et sanare voluit, pravas praedicationes ipsius arguens, et evidentius fidem Nichaenae definitionis exponens, quamque ab eo missam apostolicae sedis scrinia susceperunt. . . .' He is talking about Cyril's second letter to Nestorius.

established just this point (ACO II, 1, 2, 79, no. 12; 80, no. 18). So the authority of the letter is vouched for in a unique way. Of course only the agreement of its doctrine of the incarnation with the dogma of Nicaea was defined, but this extended *de facto* to the doctrine of the unity of subject in Jesus Christ described above. This does not mean that at this stage any individual formula or even any concept was sanctioned. The occurrence in the letter of the expression ἕνωσις καθ' ὑπόστασιν[11] clearly creates a certain precedent for Chalcedon and facilitates a definitive acceptance of the term ὑπόστασις into the proclamation of the Christian faith. But we should surely not look for a philosophical definition in this expression, which occurs for the first time as a christological formula in Cyril. The phrase 'union by hypostasis' is merely meant to express the reality of the union in Christ in contrast to a purely moral and accidental interpretation which the synod presumed to be the teaching of the other side (ibid., 26⁹–27¹); it is thus to be contrasted with a ἕνωσις κατὰ θέλησιν μόνην or κατ' εὐδοκίαν or a unity which is only achieved by the assumption of the external mode of appearance of another *prosopon*.

Thus the influence of the Council of Ephesus on the history of the formula lies in its having given a central significance to the Council of Nicaea[12] and in its canonization of the second letter of Cyril to Nestorius as the authentic interpretation of this council. In this way a precedent was made for the Council of Chalcedon both in the mode of procedure and the choice of evidence, so that it was to choose the same method as that employed at Ephesus and was once again to refer to the same evidence. To these documents read in 431, however, one other was to be added, Cyril's *Laetentur* letter, which contains the *Formulary of Reunion* of 433. This in turn has as its chief constituent the *Symbolum Ephesinum* of the Antiochenes.[13] These basic outlines of the dogmatic procedure at Ephesus were comparatively simple, but they produced considerable complications for the church. These complications result not least from Cyril's other letter, the third letter to Nestorius, with its anathematisms, and from one particular kind of language used by the Patriarch of Alexandria which gave new life to the terminology of the Logos-sarx framework. A more profound reason for all the confusion is, however, to be sought in the failure hitherto to determine and express in clear concepts the metaphysical levels on which unity and distinction are to be sought in Christ.

11 ACO I, 1, 1, 26²⁷; 27¹⁰⁻¹¹: ἐνώσας ἑαυτῷ καθ' ὑπόστασιν.
12 Cf. H. de Manoir, S.J., 'Le Symbole de Nicée au concile d'Ephèse', *Greg* 12, 1931, 104–37.
13 For further details see below. On the whole matter cf. also: A. D'Alès, *Le dogme d'Ephèse*, Paris 1931; P. Galtier, *L'unité du Christ*, Paris 1939, 13–88; T. Šagi-Bunić, art. cit.

SECTION TWO

FROM EPHESUS TO CHALCEDON

CHAPTER ONE

THE REACTIONS OF THE ANTIOCHENES

In November 430, envoys from Cyril had delivered to Nestorius, the Patriarch of Constantinople, the letters of Pope Celestine (of 11 August 430) and with them the twelve anathematisms of the Patriarch of Alexandria. The latter, together with the Pope's writings, were to be signed by the person to whom they were sent. Nestorius, however, sent these *Capita* on to John, the Patriarch of Antioch. They became the great stumbling block to the Orientals, even to the moderate group, which, after the Council of Ephesus, recognized the Reunion of 433 and finally even consented to the condemnation of Nestorius. The discussion which was thus initiated became particularly significant for the shaping of the christological formula. We must therefore begin first of all with the documents which are concerned with the anathematisms. At the request of Nestorius, John of Antioch handed on the task of refuting the twelve *Capita* to Theodoret, Bishop of Cyrus, and his brother in office, Andrew of Samosata. Only part of their work has been preserved. In addition, there is a third document of the struggle, the author of which is unknown. Its text has been transmitted in a Latin translation; in content it resembles the work of Theodoret, so that some have supposed him to have written it.[1]

1. THEODORET OF CYRUS[2]

Before the beginning of Lent 431 Theodoret, one of the noblest figures in the intellectual struggles of the Eastern church, sent off his refutation of

[1] M. Richard, 'Hypostase', 253–8. There is a useful survey of the events between 431 and 449 and the relevant sources in: Luise Abramowski, 'Der Streit um Diodor und Theodor zwischen den beiden ephesinischen Konzilien', *ZKG* F. IV, T. 67, 1955–56, 252–87; also A. Schönmetzer, *Chalkedon* II, 946ff. (chronological table).

[2] For the earlier christology of Theodoret: there is good information on sources and literature in H. G. Opitz, 'Theodoret', *PWK* II R., 5, 1791–1801; J. Montalverne, *Theodoreti doctrina* XXI–XLI. His thesis of the basic orthodoxy of Theodoret's christology, even before 433–5, is to be maintained against A. Bertram, *Theodoreti eppi. Cyrensis doctrina christologica*, Hildesiae 1883, and against C. da Mazzarino O.F.M.Cap., *La dottrina di Teodoreto di Ciro*, Roma 1941, etc. On the question of Theodoret's development see K. Jüssen, 'Die Christologie des Theodoret v. C. nach seinem neuveröffentl. Isaias-Kommentar', *TG* 27, 1935, 438–52; M. Richard, 'Notes sur l'évolution doctrinale

the anathematisms,[3] along with a letter in which he accused the Bishop of Alexandria of Apollinarianism.[4]

From this root (i.e. the Apollinarian heresy) there grew the 'one nature of the flesh and of the Godhead' and the 'attribution of suffering to the Godhead of the only-begotten' and whatever else has become an object of contention to priest and people.[5]

Cyril himself, says Theodoret, is the inventor of this unity καθ' ὑπόστασιν in Christ, as such an expression is to be found neither in scripture nor in the Fathers.[6]

Now Theodoret evidently takes both terms, ὑπόστασις and φύσις, as synonyms and understands them to mean 'substance', 'nature'. So for him a 'union by nature or substance' is inevitably Monophysitism, a mixing (κρᾶσις) of the natures.[7] Does Theodoret himself then acknowledge 'two hypostases' in Christ? In his criticism of the Third Anathema, he does in fact sound as though he would accept and defend this way of speaking. He even shows that Cyril must grant it if he is to recognize as complete and intact both the hypostasis of the Godhead and that of the humanity in Christ. It is indeed for this reason that Cyril himself also speaks of a division of 'hypostases' (i.e. in the plural). 'Therefore there is nothing strange and illogical in speaking of two united hypostases or natures.'[8] But Theodoret has not used this term before.[9] There is, however, some progress in the third dialogue of the *Eranistes*. Here πρόσωπον and ὑπόστασις are virtually identical. In the interpretation of the sacrifice of Abraham, there is, in fact, a reference to the two natures of Christ, which are symbolized in Isaac and the ram. But this comparison may not be understood to imply a division, but only a distinction of natures in Christ. Thus picture and reality do not coincide:

de Théodoret', *RSPT* 25, 1936, 459–81; M. Brok, 'Touchant la date sur le Psautier de Théodoret de Cyr', *RHE* 44, 1949, 552–6; J. McNamara, 'Theodoret of Cyrus and the Unity of Person in Christ', *ITQ* 22, 1955, 313–28; see also M. Richard, 'L'activité litt. de Théodoret avant le concile d'Ephèse', *RSPT* 24, 1935, 83–106; M. Mandac, 'L'union christologique dans les oeuvres de Théodoret antérieures au concile d'Ephèse', *EphThLov* 47, 1971, 64–96; G. Koch, *Strukturen und Geschichte des Heils in der Theologie des Theodoret von Kyros*, Frankfurt 1974.

[3] For the chronology see J. Montalverne, *Theodoreti doctrina*, 42–3.
[4] Theodoret, *Reprehensio*: in Cyril Al., *Apol. ctr. Theodoret*.: ACO I, 1, 6, 107–46: PG 76, 389A–452; *Ep.* 150: ACO I, 1, 6, 107–8: PG 83, 1413A–1416B = PG 76, 389A–392A; *Ep.* 151 *ad monach. orient.*: PG 83, 1416B–1433A; *Ep.* 169 *ad Alexandrum Hierap.*: PG 83, 1473B–1476A: ACO I, 1, 7, 79–80. Up to the Council of Chalcedon the anathematisms remain Theodoret's great concern. In *Ep.* 112 *ad Domnum* of the year 449 (PG 83, 1309 CD), he describes the whole of his earlier attitude towards them. He speaks of more than 50 *Synodica* which were made against the *Capitula*. In fighting against the anathematisms, the Orientals at Ephesus in 431 put even the question of the person of Nestorius in the background (G. Bardy, 'Acace de Bérée et son rôle dans la controverse nestorienne', *RevSR* 18, 1938, 24, n. 3).

[5] Theodoret, HE V, 3: ed. Parmentier, 280[18–21]: PG 82, 1199D.
[6] Theodoret, *Repreh.* in Cyril Al., *Apol. ctr. Theodoret*.: ACO I, 1, 6, 114[10–14]; PG 76, 400A. We are concerned with the christological use of this term, as Theodoret knows it in a trinitarian usage: *De incarn.*: PG 75, 1429D–1432A.
[7] ACO I, 1, 6, 114[15–16]: PG 76, 400B: ἀνάγκη γὰρ τῇ κράσει ἀκολουθῆσαι τὴν σύγχυσιν· εἰσιοῦσα δὲ ἡ σύγχυσις ἀφαιρεῖται τὴν ἑκάστης φύσεως ἰδιότητα.
[8] Ibid., 117[17–18]: PG 76, 404B.
[9] M. Richard, 'Hypostase', 253: 'En réalité le mot hypostasis ne faisait pas partie de son lexique christologique.'

Isaac and the ram correspond to the original (= Christ) as far as the difference of natures is concerned, but do not in respect of a division of the separate 'hypostases' (κατὰ δὲ τὸ διῃρημένον κεχωρισμένων τῶν ὑποστάσεων οὐκ ἔτι). For we acknowledge such a union of Godhead and manhood that we perceive an indivisible person and know him to be both God and man.[10]

At all events, this passage would make no sense if Theodoret had not in practice accepted an identification of prosopon and hypostasis, even if because of the situation he perhaps did not dare expressly to acknowledge *one hypostasis* in Christ.[11] In the light of his trinitarian language he could have found no special difficulty in making the content of the term hypostasis rather more specific in his christology, too, (i.e. making it synonymous with prosopon) and in distinguishing it as such from οὐσία and φύσις.[12] But a direct transference of trinitarian language to christology did not take place immediately, though after 430 Theodoret finally brought about an assimilation of the two kinds of language. Only at the Council of Chalcedon does the word ὑπόστασις acquire a positive significance for the christology of the Bishop of Cyrus. This is clear from his letter to John of Aegea, a Nestorian opponent of the Council.[13] In any case, the light in which he saw the history of the word hypostasis immediately after the synod is particularly interesting. Now he even produces *scriptural proof* of the use of the word—a possibility which he had once disputed for Cyril's καθ' ὑπόστασιν. True, his silence in the other post-Chalcedonian works (e.g. the *Haereticarum fabularum compendium*) raises doubts about the authenticity of otherwise sufficiently attested fragments of the letter. But we can understand how because of the newness of this term and its association with the christology of the opposition Theodoret needed time to make it his own. Only in the sixth century is a satisfactory basis created for the further history of the expression. Theodoret himself seems no longer to have had the strength to incorporate the new formula fully into his theology. He does, however, already have two elements which are important for later developments: he attempts a scriptural proof and establishes the connection between the Chalcedonian doctrine of the incarnation and trinitarian theological terminology.[14]

While Theodoret had a hard struggle to clarify the term hypostasis, οὐσία and φύσις presented him with no special problems. Both concepts were already synonymous for him before the Nestorian controversy, and

---

[10] Theodoret, *Eranistes* 3: PG 83, 252C.   [11] M. Richard, 'Hypostase', 264.

[12] Cf. Theodoret, *Expositio* 3: ed. De Otto, *Corp. Apologet*, t. 3 v. 4, 6–10; *Eranistes* 1: PG 83, 36AC. The assertion of J. Montalverne, *Theodoreti doctrina*, 104, n. 55, that in *Eranistes* 1: PG 83, 33ff. Theodoret allows mention of the one hypostasis in Christ, cannot be substantiated.

[13] Theodoret, *Ep. ad. Joannem Aeg.*: PO 13, 190–1. Cf. M. Richard, 'Un écrit de Théodoret sur l'unité du Christ après l'incarnation', *RevSR* 14, 1934, 34–61; id., 'La lettre de Théodoret à Jean d'Egées', *SPT* 2, 1941–2, 415–23; C. Moeller, *Chalkedon* I, 658f.

[14] Note, too, how according to PO 13, 191, Theodoret rejected the expression ὑπόστασις σύνθετος, a formula which was to be an object of dispute in the sixth century.

meant the condition of a nature or its essence.[15] His use of these expressions to represent the duality of the natures in Christ is Theodoret's strength and that part of his christology which most furthered developments towards the Chalcedonian Definition. It is sufficient to point to the Formulary of Reunion of 433, a good measure of which seems to derive from the Bishop of Cyrus himself. The argument with which he rejects the ἕνωσις φυσική and Cyril's *mia physis* formula is worth noting. In a natural conjunction, like that between body and soul, he sees a *necessary* conjunction, which, moreover, unites parts which are on the same level of being, i.e. whose being is similarly limited in time, created, and subject to slavery.[16] But in Christ there is a unity which is completely subject to the *ordinance of grace* and therefore stands not under the law of necessity, but under that of freedom.[17]

> For 'nature' means something necessary and unconnected with the will, as, for example, if I say that we hunger by nature—a case where we do not suffer of our own free will, but under compulsion.[18]

This objection does not, of course, meet Cyril's thought, but at the same time it shows that a 'union of well-pleasing' (ἕνωσις κατ' εὐδοκίαν) must not be condemned out of hand as an accidental conjunction. Theodoret is merely concerned to stress the freedom of the incarnation. He himself always acknowledges a real, substantial unity in Christ.

To describe this unity, however, Theodoret had no other term at his disposal than πρόσωπον, so beloved of the Antiochenes. It occurs for the first time with a christological significance in his work on the Trinity and the incarnation,[19] in which he acknowledges the 'distinction of the natures and the unity of the prosopon'. The Bishop later also vigorously acknowledged *one* prosopon in Christ,[20] not that mixed prosopon for which the Antiochenes have been censured. Of course, if we look behind the terminology, which already sounds quite Chalcedonian, for his christological idea proper, we can find some inadequacies in Theodoret, too. At all events, it would be a mistake to look in his writings for our concept of 'person' with its ontological content. For Theodoret, prosopon still has much of its original significance of 'countenance'.[21] His view can be seen

---

[15] J. Montalverne, *Theodoreti doctrina*, 77–8.

[16] Theodoret, *Eranistes* 2: PG 83, 145A: φυσικὴ τῶν ὁμοχρόνων, καὶ κτιστῶν, καὶ ὁμοδούλων ἡ ἕνωσις.

[17] Theodoret, *Eranistes* 2: PG 83, 145A: ἐπὶ δὲ τοῦ δεσπότου Χριστοῦ τὸ ὅλον εὐδοκίας ἐστί, καὶ φιλανθρωπίας, καὶ χάριτος. That is therefore at least a theological idea in the ἕνωσις κατ' εὐδοκίαν of the Antiochenes. They wish by it to stress the quality of grace in the union in Christ such as Theodoret surely acknowledged, even if his basis for it was insufficient.

[18] Theodoret, *Repreh. in Cyril Al., Apol. ctr. Theodor.*: ACO I, 1, 6, 116[19-21]; 117[3-6]: PG 76, 401–4.

[19] Theodoret, *De incarn.* 21, 31, 32: PG 75, 1456A, 1472C, 1473B; cf. J. Montalverne, *Theodoreti Doctrina* 78, n. 3, 103–6.

[20] Cf. *Eranistes* 3: PG 83, 280D, where the two *prosopa* are expressly rejected.

[21] M. Nédoncelle, 'Prosopon et persona', 277–84: original meaning of *prosopon* = countenance.

in his comments on Ezek. 11. 22–3. The prophet sees how the glory of the Lord leaves the city of Jerusalem and descends upon the Mount of Olives. This Theodoret interprets of the ascension of the Lord:

> But he stood on the mount of Olives over against Jerusalem. This mountain is the mount of Olives from which our Lord was received up into the heavens after the flesh. Rightly he went then, when he had appeared in human form and had *displayed the two natures in one prosopon* (καὶ τὰς δύο φύσεις ἑνὶ δείξας προσώπῳ), intimating the divine by fire and manifesting the human through the amber . . . on to this mountain and thence ascended into heaven.[22]

Following the description in Ezek. 1. 27–8, the bishop sees in Christ a figure of light which makes the divine and the human natures visible in one mode of appearance. Theodoret begins with the basic meaning 'countenance', and by prosopon means the visible and tangible representation of the unity of God and man in Christ. He also speaks of it as a 'showing'. To understand the idea expressed by this we must introduce the 'indwelling framework', which is surely a basic presupposition of his christology. The unity and the being of 'Christ' are brought about by the dwelling of the Godhead of the Only-Begotten in all its fullness in the manhood of Jesus.[23] But because this indwelling framework at root means a loosening of the conjunction of God and man, Theodoret also feels compelled to balance the expression. It is because of this that he emphasizes with such striking frequency that the Godhead and manhood in Christ unite themselves in *one combined appearance*. The Godhead is visible in the manhood of Christ and so illuminates the 'one countenance' of Christ. Theodoret certainly intends this formula of the one 'countenance' in Christ, as he explains when discussing 2 Cor. 4. 6:

> The 'in the countenance of Jesus Christ' (ἐν προσώπῳ Ἰησοῦ Χριστοῦ) has this meaning: as the divine nature is invisible, it becomes visible in its inwardness through the manhood that is taken, for this is illuminated with divine light and sends out lightnings.[24]

This is the picture of Christ in a theology which tries to explain the unity in Christ not so much with metaphysical concepts as with the help of similes and analogies. Eustathius had already laid the foundation for such an interpretation and Theodore of Mopsuestia had carried it further. The 'shining, transfigured Christ' is the image in which Theodoret can see

---

[22] Theodoret, *In Ezek.* 11. 22–3: PG 81, 901CD. The commentary was probably written before 436. But the same expression 'showing the one *prosopon*' still occurs in *Ep.* 83 *ad Dioscorum*, written in 448.

[23] We have come across the reference to the fullness of the indwelling over and over again from the time of Justin. Theodoret, *Comment. in Is.* 11. 2–3: ed. Möhle, 59[22–52]; *Expositio*: ed. De Otto, *Corp. Apologet.* t. 3. v. 4, 62–4; *Repreh. in Cyril Al. Apol. ctr. Theodoret*, ACO I, 1, 6, 126; *In Col.* 2. 9: PG 82, 608CD. In all these texts Theodoret contrasts the fullness of the indwelling in Christ with the 'partial grace' (μερικὴ χάρις) of other men, even of the prophets. In this context Theodoret also describes Christ as a θεοφόρος ἄνθρωπος. Basil spoke in a similar way: *In Ps.* 59. 4: PG 29, 468A; *Ep.* 261, 2: PG 32, 969C.

[24] Theodoret, *In II Cor.* 4. 6: PG 82, 401B.

divinity and manhood together as 'in one countenance'.[25] The impression of a real unity in Christ is to be given through the emphatic description of mutual interpenetration. It is clear that the Antiochene 'analogy' does not approach the essential Alexandrian expression of the unity in Christ.[26] But though the picture of Christ given by the two groups is so different, it is nevertheless in both the picture of the transfigured Christ.

We may, however, also observe in Theodoret a real struggle to arrive at a substantial inward interpretation of the divine-human figure of Christ. If (with L. I. Scipioni, see on Nestorius) we may correctly interpret the Antiochene prosopon doctrine along the lines of the Stoic teaching of krasis, then Theodoret too would be nearer to the Chalcedonian christology than has hitherto been assumed. Of course, the decisive weakness of his christology is evident precisely here. His concept of prosopon does not aim at emphasizing the hypostasis of the Logos as the one and only one, although he surely meant a unity of person. This prosopon is constituted by the union of Word and manhood—one might almost say by making the two of equal status. In Cyril's view, on the other hand, the being of Christ is centred in the hypostasis of the Logos.

Despite all Theodoret's stress on the pre-eminence of the Godhead, his picture of Christ is built up too symmetrically and is not constructed clearly enough round the hypostasis of the Logos. For him, the common subject of the sayings is 'Christ' (as the conjunction of the two natures), so that here the divine and human expressions are really justified, as of one subject. On the other hand, he will not make the Logos the common subject of the divine and the human sayings. The reason for this refusal lies in the fact that he cannot distinguish the two kinds of saying: that which ascribes something to the Logos as the possessive and effective subject, and the other which expresses something of the Logos as of his essential nature. For him 'the Logos has suffered' means: the Logos has suffered in his divine nature. Therefore up to 448–9 he still found difficulty in recognizing the title *Theotokos*.[27] Originally he still wanted to add ἀνθρωποτόκος with the older Antiochene tradition.[28] For example, when the anathematisms of Cyril came to Antioch along with the reply of Nestorius, Theodoret for a while believed that the honorific title 'Mother of God' needed some explanation.[29] Mary was Mother of God 'by the

25 Cf. his account of *Ezek.* 1. 27–8: PG 81, 836B. There is a similar idea in *Or. de divina et sancta caritate*: PG 82, 1517D. The relationship with the passages quoted above might be a reason for assuming the much-disputed authenticity of this letter. Cf. *In Ps.* 95. 6: PG 80, 1645D–1648A; *In Col.* 2. 9: PG 82, 608D–609A.

26 *In Hebr.* 3. 4: PG 82, 697D is also to be interpreted in this sense. For the idea of mutual interpenetration see *Ep.* 145: PG 83, 1387–1389A.

27 Theodoret, *De unitate Christi*: PG 83, 1437C. On this cf. M. Richard, 'Un écrit de Théodoret sur l'unité du Christ après l'incarnation', *RevSR* 14, 1934, 34–61; J. Montalverne, *Theodoreti doctrina*, 105–17.

28 Theodoret, *Ep. ad monach. orient.*: PG 83, 1429B–D, 1437BC.

29 Theodoret, *Repreh. in Cyril Al., Apol. ctr. Theodoret.*: ACO I, 1, 6, 109²⁶⁻²⁹, 110¹⁻⁵: PG 76, 393C. Cf. M. Richard, 'L'activité litt. de Théodoret', 97.

union' (τῇ ἑνώσει), but Mother of man 'by nature' (τῇ φύσει), a distinction which Diodore of Tarsus had already used.[30] Eventually even this addition vanishes, as *Ep.* 16 shows.[31]

It is also clear from Theodoret's often repeated distinction in the exegesis of John 2. 19, 'Destroy this temple', that he was not wholly successful in distinguishing the 'personal unity' from a 'natural unity' and making the hypostasis of the Word visible as the only subject of the metaphysical 'I' in Christ. Christ did not say 'Destroy me', 'for he clearly taught that it was not God who was destroyed but the temple'.[32] Christ could only have said 'Destroy "me" ' had he been composed in accordance with the Logos-sarx framework of the Apollinarians.[33] We found a deeper recognition of this 'I' in Christ in the writings of Theodore of Mopsuestia, though at the same time this 'I' appears to be the weakest point of his christology.

The incomplete, symmetrical conception of Christ, in which the hypostasis of the Logos does not come fully into its own, does not, however, seem to have been the last stage in Theodoret's development. In two letters which were written in 449 during his internment, his concept of prosopon was given a yet deeper interpretation. The unity of subject and of person in Christ is very finely and very clearly expressed:

> So the body of the Lord is indeed a body, but incapable of suffering, incorruptible and immortal. . . . For it is not separated from the Godhead and belongs to none other than the Only-begotten Son of God himself. And it shows us no other person (prosopon) than the Only-Begotten himself, who is clothed with our nature.[34]

In these almost Athanasian expressions, the idea of the central place of the hypostasis of the Logos is quite clearly expressed. This becomes still more clear in the following letter. In it, Theodoret proves from Paul that Christ is identical with the Only-begotten of the Father, 'that our Lord Jesus Christ is no other person of the Trinity than the Son'.[35] Despite the

---

[30] According to Eutherius of Tyana to Alexander of Hierapolis: ACO I, 4, 216[17-20]. See now M. Tetz, *Eine Antilogie des Eutherios von Tyana* (PTSt 1), Berlin 1964, 62; for the doctrine of Eutherius himself see the excellent index by M. Tetz.

[31] Theodoret, *Ep.* 16 *ad Iren.*: PG 83, 1273C. On this M. Richard, 'Théodoret sur l'unité', 34–61.

[32] Theodoret, *Ep.* 151 *ad monach. orient.*: PG 83, 1420B.

[33] Theodoret, *De trinitate et incarn.* 18: PG 75, 1452AB; cf. PG 83, 1420B. The same significant argument occurs in the *Pentalog.* (Frag.): ACO I, 5, 166[19-20]. We should not, however, read a duality of persons out of the repudiation of this 'me'. Here Theodoret's sole concern is not to permit the destruction of the Godhead as such and to exclude the Apollinarian Logos-sarx framework. Here, of course, he clearly lacks the right insight into the nature of the church's *praedicatio idiomatum*. Cf. *Eranistes* 2: PG 83, 145A–148B; 3: ibid. 264A–280D, where the formula of suffering is contested.

[34] Theodoret, *Ep.* 145: PG 83, 1389A: οὐδὲ γὰρ ἕτερον ἡμῖν ἐπιδείκνυσι πρόσωπον, ἀλλ' αὐτὸν τὸν μονογενῆ τὴν ἡμετέραν περικείμενον φύσιν. The relatively numerous passages of a similar kind which M. Mandac (n. 7 above) has collected in *EphThLov* 47, 1971, esp. 81–95, should also be noted. See e.g. *Expositio* 10–11: PG 6, 1224C–1225C: De Otto, 34–6, 40: 'Le Logos . . . avant revêtu le temple selon la plus profonde union, est sorti (de la Vierge) à la fois Dieu et homme (θεὸς ὁμοῦ καὶ ἄνθρωπος) . . .; le Fils étant (ὑπάρχων) Dieu et homme (θεὸς καὶ ἄνθρωπος) . . . en tant que Dieu (θεός) (il est) du (ἐκ) Pere . . . en tant qu'homme (ἄνθρωπος) il est de la (ἐκ) Vierge' (88).

[35] Theodoret, *Ep.* 146: PG 83, 1393B.

difference in terminology, even in idea, the aspirations of the Bishop of Cyrus are also those of Cyril of Alexandria—a mediatory theology which avoids the division of Christ into two persons as much as it avoids the confusion of natures. He even recognizes that between himself and the Cyril of the Reunion of 433 there is no difference of ideas, with the result that he eventually comes round to supporting his own christology with quotations from Cyril. It is a theological precedent which the Fathers of the Council of 451, and in their turn the supporters of the Council of Chalcedon, will follow in their struggle over the Council.[36]

2. Andrew of Samosata

Three documents are of prime importance for the assessment of the christological formula of Andrew of Samosata: his refutation of Cyril's anathemas, a letter to Rabbula of Edessa and a fragment conserved by Anastasius Sinaita. His reply, like the *Reprehensio* of Theodoret, has been preserved for us in the framework of Cyril's answer.[37] Andrew does not go so far as to accuse the Alexandrian of open error. He labours first to point out contradictions and inaccuracies to him. In so doing, he eventually wants to show that Cyril—contrary to his own assertion—acknowledges two hypostases in Christ. And here he puts himself in the wrong:

> But we must not assign the sayings to two persons or hypostases or to two Sons, dividing the union, that is the one Son; for the complete unity and the one Son cannot be divided and are inseparable in every respect and way and view.[38]

In his criticism of the third anathema, Andrew certainly seems to take the two concepts physis and hypostasis as synonymous and as a result to accuse Cyril of speaking of 'one hypostasis' in Christ.[39] But here—in the context of the third anathema—Cyril has hardly reproduced the whole personal thought of his opponent. (He makes the extract begin with an 'again', the relevance of which is very hard to define.) So we may probably assume that Andrew himself allowed the expression 'one hypostasis'. As he speaks clearly elsewhere of 'two natures', we already have *de facto* the Chalcedonian distinction of the one hypostasis (the one prosopon) and the two natures. True, according to the extant evidence the Bishop of Samosata does not seem to have made further use of the formula.[40] In these very

---

[36] M. Richard, 'Evolution doctrin. de Théodoret', 459–81, investigates the rest of Theodoret's terminology in respect of the change from the concrete to the abstract account of the natures. As the anonymous writer mentioned above uses the terms *hypostasis* and *physis* in a similar way to Theodoret we will be content with this reference (ACO I, 5, 288–94; M. Richard, 'Hypostase', 253).

[37] Cyril Al., *Apol. ctr. Orient.*: ACO I, 1, 7, 33–65: PG 76, 316A–385A.

[38] Andreas Samosat., in Cyril Al., *Apol. ctr. Orient.*: ACO I, 1, 7, 419[9–12]: PG 76, 333A.

[39] Ibid., ACO 386[6–7]: PG 76, 325D, where Andrew refers to Cyril's letter to the Egyptian monks (ACO I, 1, 1, 17[22–4]; PG 77, 25D; after M. Richard, 'Hypostase').

[40] See his letters to Rabbula of Edessa and to Alexander of Hierapolis. The former is preserved in *Cod. Vatican.* syr. Borgian. 82 (p. X) fol. 317v–322v, ed. F. Pericoli-Ridolfini, 'Lettera di Andrea

documents the Antiochene character of the formulas again comes through strongly without, of course, contradicting the essentials of what Andrew affirmed in his criticism of the anathemas.[41]

Our attention has recently been drawn to a new fragment from the works of Andrew which Anastasius Sinaita produces in his *Hodegos*, ch. 22 (PG 89, 292C–293B).[42] Andrew here discusses the beginning of Cyril's fourth anathema.

This text does not come from Andrew's refutation of the anathemas which was composed at the same time as Theodoret's refutation of the anathematisms. Here Andrew refers not only to Cyril's Apologia for the anathemas against Theodoret . . . but also to the *Scholia de incarnatione*. . . . The *Scholia* were certainly composed after 431. The polemical tone of our passage shows that the reconciliation of 433, in which Andrew joined, had not yet taken place. We have a renewed discussion between Andrew and Cyril over the christology of the anathematisms and the writings which were later produced to defend them.[43]

There is more mention of hypostasis in the fragment quoted than in the whole of the letter to Rabbula. We have here a discussion of concepts such as we hardly find anywhere else at this period. Andrew returns to Cyril's trinitarian terminology and compares it with his christological concepts. By doing this he hopes to point out to Cyril contradictions in both spheres. He begins from the equation *physis = hypostasis*, but *hypostasis = prosopon*. Now for the Trinity this means three natures and three persons, but in Christ two natures and two prosopa. If Cyril then says 'from two natures', or 'two hypostases' or 'two prosopa' (ἐκ δύο φύσεων, ἤγουν ὑποστάσεων, ἤτοι προσώπων . . . εἶναι Χριστόν) this means that Christ was already in existence (and thus a hypostasis or person) before the union in the womb. In his writing *De sancta et consubstantiali Trinitate, ad Hermiam*, on the other hand, Cyril draws a distinction between hypostasis (person) and physis (cf. *OrChr*, art. cit., 57). It is interesting that

di Samosata a Rabbula di Edessa', *RSO* 28, 1953, 153–69 (with Italian translation). The translation offered below comes from G. Brandhuber. Cf. A. Baumstark, 'Ein Brief des Andreas von Samosata an Rabbula von Edessa und eine verlorene dogmatische Katene', *OrChr* 1, 1901, 179–81; Luise Abramowski, 'Zum Brief des Andreas von Samosata an Rabbula von Edessa', *OrChr* 41, 1957, 51–64. See also her brief but important additional remarks in 'Peripatetisches bei späten Antiochenern', *ZKG* 79, 1968, 358–62. The other letter, to Alexander of Hierapolis, is in ACO I, 4, 86–7.

[41] Some of these formulas may be quoted here in G. Brandhuber's translation: '*Et dico factam esse coniunctionem* (συνάφειαν) *naturae divinae et humanae et Unigenitum a Patre sibi coniunxisse in unitate* (ἐν ἑνότητι *vel* ἑνώσει) *illam naturam, quam assumpsit ex semine David, ut essent duae naturae, in deliberatione* (λογισμός) *autem una persona* (πρόσωπον) *propter coniunctionem, cum Deus Verbum usus esset illo corpore ut templo et ut instrumento actionis . . . cum una persona percipiatur in coniunctione naturarum, dividimus cogitatione et verbo nequaquam naturas sed quae proprie habet unaquaeque ex naturis . . . videmus Deum et hominem nobis praedicantem scripturam et divisionem naturarum in una persona sine confusione nos docentem. . . . Ego autem etiam nequeo intelligere, quo modo possibile* (sit) *ut non utamur divisione simul retenta coniunctione*' (Cod. Borg, syr. 82. fol. 318v., 319r. v., 320v.–321r.). Cf. F. Pericoli-Ridolfini, *RSO* 28, 1953, 154–9, 163–6. If the 'one hypostasis' formula does not occur in this letter, no more does 'two hypostases' language.

[42] Cf. L. Abramowski, *OrChr* 41, 1957, 55–60 with the text. She is indebted to M. Richard for the reference.

[43] *OrChr*, art. cit., 57–8.

Andrew now suggests to his opponent a new definition of hypostasis so that he can avoid the accusation of teaching two persons. The ὑποστάσεις may be said to be ὑπάρξεις τινὰς πραγμάτων ἐνουσίων, i.e. 'the forms in which substantial things exist' (OrChr, art. cit., 58f.). In this way he could distinguish between prosopon and hypostasis. So, too, he could also speak of two hypostases in Christ without having to speak of two prosopa. By excluding this definition, however, Cyril is closing the way to a further apologia. Andrew therefore appears to have in mind two solutions to the conceptual confusion of his time: first, to take prosopon (person) with hypostasis and to distinguish them both from physis (as Cyril does in De sancta et consubstantiali Trinitate), or, to contrast prosopon with the other concepts of physis and hypostasis (and make a new definition of the latter). He gives no hint in this text of the solution which he himself favours. But everything goes to show that he takes hypostasis and prosopon together and opposes them to physis.

Andrew for his part really seems to cling to the equation of hypostasis and person made in trinitarian terminology. We have heard above of the πρόσωπον of the Logos . . . in the Letter to Rabbula we read of the 'nature of the hypostasis (of the Logos)'—such statements are not made about the manhood. The Logos, as hypostasis, is thus, in fact, the centre on which the person of Christ is formed. The *natures* occupy a somewhat different position; they are both present in the one person of Christ and are to be carefully distinguished from one another.[44]

So—to judge from Andrew of Samosata and Theodoret—the Oriental bishops were already to some extent prepared for the Chalcedonian Definition, and were therefore able to accept it at the council without any particular difficulty.[45]

The discussion surely brought the opponents, the Antiochenes and Cyril of Alexandria, closer together. The Reunion of 433 is the visible expression of this. A short account of how this Reunion came about may be given in the words of R. V. Sellers:[46]

In the following year (432), the Emperor (Theodosius II) made another effort to heal the schism. Acting on the advice of Maximian and the clergy at the Capital that peace would be forthcoming if only John (of Antioch) and his following would cease being contentious and confirm the deposition of Nestorius and Cyril . . . would forgive the

---

[44] L. Abramowski, OrChr 41, 1957, 60.

[45] M. Richard, 'Hypostase', 255. Isidore of Pelusium should be added to the pre-Chalcedonian evidence which Richard produces for the history of 'hypostasis'. He speaks both of δύο φύσεις (Ep. I, 236; cf. I, 42: PG 78, 328D; 208D–209A) and of one hypostasis: εἰς ἓν σὺν αὐτῇ γεγονὼς πρόσωπον καὶ μίαν προσκυνουμένην ὑπόστασιν (Ep. I, 360: PG 78, 388A). See A. Schmid, Die Christologie Isidors von Pelusium, Freiburg/Schw. 1948, 81–2. It may be noted that Isidore has neither the δύο ὑποστάσεις, δύο πρόσωπα nor the μία φύσις and μία οὐσία language, but ἓν πρόσωπον, μία ὑπόστασις. In this the great Egyptian monk and adviser of Cyril already anticipates the formula of Chalcedon. T. Šagi-Bunić, 'De Dyophysitismo extra Scholam Antiochenam', Laurentianum 4, 1963, 231–51.

[46] R. V. Sellers, The Council of Chalcedon, London 1953, 15–17. See the thorough analysis of the proceedings and texts in T. Šagi-Bunić, 'Deus perfectus et homo perfectus' a Concilio Ephesino (a. 431) ad Chalcedonense (a. 451), Freiburg 1965, 19–73, which is utilized in what follows.

harm done to him at Ephesus, he wrote to Acacius of Beroea and the venerated Simeon Stylites, requesting their help, and appointed the tribune and notary Aristolaus to act as his representative. Aristolaus went first to Antioch, and, as a result of his visit, John and his bishops, together with Acacius, assembled in synod (April 432) and drew up their six propositions.[47] In the first of these—the rest have not reached us—they declared that they firmly adhered to the faith of Nicaea and received only that exposition of it which the holy and blessed Athanasius had written against Apollinarius in his *ad Epictetum*; but they flatly rejected *quae vero nuper superintroducta sunt dogmata, vel per epistolas vel per capitula.* Clearly, what they were striving after as a *modus vivendi* was a return to the position which obtained before Cyril drew up his anti-Nestorian writings. The Propositions of the Orientals, together with a letter from Acacius of Beroea, Aristolaus then took to Alexandria. But Cyril was adamant. What he had written against the heresy of Nestorius was in accordance with Scripture, and could not be withdrawn; moreover, as he understood the imperial commands, the Orientals should first anathematize the heresiarch and then (*et tunc*) approach the Alexandrian see; at the same time he was ready to offer an explanation of his writings, which, he considered, would satisfy them.

Thus any possibility of an understanding appeared to have vanished. The extreme supporters of the Antiochene party under the leadership of Alexander of Hierapolis did not wish to proceed further until Cyril had gone back on his anathemas. John of Antioch, however, was prepared to make a step towards peace. He arranged with Acacius that Paul of Emesa should be the messenger of peace to Alexandria. To him he gave a letter in which he expressed the hope that Cyril's declarations as contained in his letter to Acacius would remove the disunity over the anathematisms (*Capitula*). At the same time Paul had with him the Formula drawn up by the Orientals in August 431 which was to become the *Symbolum Unionis*. Its text ran as follows:[48]

(After an introductory paragraph, in which the Orientals state that in a few words they declare their doctrine 'concerning the Virgin *Theotokos* and the manner of the incarnation of the Only-begotten Son of God', as they have 'received it both from the divine Scriptures and from the tradition of the holy Fathers' and that they 'make no addition at all to the Creed of the holy Fathers put forth at Nicaea. . . .')

We confess, then, our Lord Jesus Christ, the only-begotten Son of God, perfect God and perfect man, consisting of a rational soul and body, begotten of the Father before the ages as to his Godhead, and on the last days the Same, for us and for our salvation, of Mary the Virgin as to his manhood; the Same *homoousios* with the Father as to his Godhead, and *homoousios* with us as to his manhood. For there has been a union of two natures (δύο γὰρ φύσεων ἕνωσις γέγονε); wherefore we confess one Christ, one Son, one Lord.

[47] ACO I, 4, 92f.: PG 84, 658Cf.
[48] Here in the translation by R. V. Sellers, op. cit., 17. A distinction should be made between (1) the Ephesine Redaction (RE) of this Antiochene creed (SA), which is contained in the letter of Count John to Emperor Theodosius II: ACO I, 1, 7, p. 70[15-22]; (2) the Antiochene redaction (RA) worked out at Antioch in the year 432, which was brought to Alexandria by Paul of Emesa, inserted in the letter of John of Antioch to Cyril of Alexandria: ACO I, 1, 4, pp. 8–9, no. 3 (this text has been slightly expanded in comparison with RE); the RA was taken over by Cyril of Alexandria in his famous *Laetentur* letter: ACO I, 1, 4, p. 17 (nos. 4–5 with Preface); COD, 69–70; *Ep. Ioann. Ant. ad Sixtum papam*: ACO I, 1, 7, p. 159[20-32]. Further comments in Šagi-Bunić, op. cit., 19f., n. 7.

In accordance with this thought of the unconfused union, we confess the holy Virgin to be 'Theotokos', because the divine Logos was incarnate and made man, and from the very conception united to himself the temple that was taken of her.

And with regard to the sayings concerning the Lord in the Gospels and Apostolic [writings], we know that theologians take some as common, as relating to one person, and others they divide as relating to two natures (τὰς δὲ διαιροῦντας ὡς ἐπὶ δύο φύσεων) explaining those God-befitting in reference to the Godhead of Christ and those lowly in reference to his manhood.

As the preface to the SA indicates (it is only reproduced briefly here), the intention of its author was to exclude any Apollinarian misunderstanding from the interpretation of the person of Jesus Christ and so make it possible for the Antiochenes to accept the title '*Theotokos*' for Mary. In all, the biblical tradition, taken over by the Fathers and especially by the Council of Nicaea, is to provide the real basis for the confession. Apollinarianism is excluded by the confession of 'Jesus Christ, the Son of God, perfect God and perfect man, consisting of a soul and body'. It must be allowed that the chief accent of the SA lies on this duality in Christ. If one isolates this formula, Christ appears almost to be the *sum* of perfect Godhead and perfect manhood, in typical Antiochene fashion. This is especially the case when one considers it against the background of the *static* treatment of the natures among the Antiochenes. But the indications of a dynamic historical perspective must not be overlooked. 'One and the same' is first born of God and then 'on the last days' born as man from Mary. The result is the twofold *homoousios* in him, which has dogmatic significance, as the further history of christology is to show. Be this as it may, in this dynamic-historical perspective one can see a good beginning which could lead the Antiochenes to a more profound grasp of the unity of the subject in Christ. Of course this was achieved only after changing fortunes and a lengthy struggle. But it is already expressly said in the SA that the '*God Logos*' became flesh and that therefore Mary may be called mother of God. Nevertheless, it remains the case that the 'unmixed distinction of Godhead and manhood in Christ' is better expressed among the Antiochenes than the unity. Yet in his *Laetentur* letter and in the inclusion of the SA in this document, Cyril recognized the orthodoxy of the formula, while at the same time being able to give an Alexandrian point to the Antiochene basis by means of a carefully chosen formulation in the explanation which he added. It is probable that he was hesitant over the juxtaposition of 'perfect God and perfect man'. Even if, in these concrete expressions, 'God' is to be translated 'Godhead' and 'man' is to be translated 'manhood', there is too little safeguard for Cyril against a duality of subjects. So he introduces his dynamic historical view into the more static Antiochene perspective by a simple but significant linguistic change in the '*deus perfectus–homo perfectus*'.

Starting from John 3. 13 ('No one has ascended into heaven but he who descended from heaven, the Son of Man'), he says:

But since God the Word who came down from above and from heaven 'emptied himself, taking servant's form' (Phil. 2. 7), he was called 'Son of Man', though still remaining what he was, that is, God. (For he is immutable and unalterable by nature); but because [also in respect of the incarnation] he is understood as one, he is said to have come down from heaven in his own flesh; so he is also called 'man from heaven' (cf. 1 Cor. 15. 47): *the same* perfect *in Godhead* and perfect *in manhood*, and conceived of as in one prosopon. For the Lord Jesus Christ is one, although the difference of the natures is not ignored, from both of which we say that the inexpressible union has been brought about.[49]

By his changing of the juxtaposed nominatives 'perfect God' and 'perfect man' into 'the same perfect in Godhead and perfect in manhood', Cyril has tautened the saying to express better the unity of subject in Christ. This is all the more the case, since the starting point or subject of the whole process of the incarnation is the 'God Logos'. In the SA, all statements are attached to the designation 'Jesus Christ, the only begotten Son of God', to which is immediately added, 'perfect God, perfect man . . .'.[50]

Here, then, we can see quite clearly the basic framework of two christologies, which can be alike in substance, but quite different in their tendencies. Cyril accepted this formula and interpreted it in his own terms. He did not need to withdraw his twelve anathematisms. But while Cyril himself can from then on to some extent suit his language to his audience, and refrains from the more extreme formulas when addressing those who support the Union, these for their part distinguish between the Cyril of the *Laetentur* letter (and the Symbol of Union), and the Cyril of the anathemas. This too will be the attitude of the Council of Chalcedon (see below). But Chalcedon derives its decisive statement from the interpretation of the SA by Cyril as outlined above, and not from the text of the SA itself, a fact which will also concern us. Cyril, too, for his part, could be in agreement with the doctrinal development among moderate Antiochenes, as indeed he defended the Formulary of Reunion against the

---

[49] Cyril Al., *Ep. ad Ioann. Ant. de pace (Laetentur)*: ACO I, 1, 4, p. 18[22]–19[1]. The last sentence ends: τέλειος ὢν ἐν Ἰεότητι καὶ τέλειος ὁ αὐτὸς ἐν ἀνθρωπότητι καὶ ὡς ἐν ἑνὶ προσώπῳ νοούμενος (p. 18[25]–6).
[50] Ibid., p. 17[10–11]. T. Šagi-Bunić, op. cit., 75–94, has drawn attention to this difference. But he is too stern in his criticism of the moderate Antiochenes who composed and accepted the SA. One cannot simply assign the RA a '*tendentia dualistica*' (p. 22). The sentence on pp. 35f. is also too sharp: '*in toto textu SA nihil invenies, unde concludere liceret, Christum symboli unionis esse unum idemque subiectum quod aeque spectaretur in alterutra natura*'. Šagi-Bunić here introduces the problems of the *Western logical* analysis of Eastern texts, which approach the question of the unity and distinction in Christ from an *ontological* perspective. Moreover, in the SA, Nestorianism is clearly excluded by the justification for the title *Theotokos*. Even Cyril did not require more of the Antiochenes. For further discussion of the problems of the Antiochenes and Cyril (albeit with the reservations made above), see Šagi-Bunić, op. cit., 36f., nn. 32 and 33. See further vol. II of the present work (in connection with Boethius).

charge of Nestorianism and in so doing acknowledged the orthodoxy of
its supporters.[51]

3. NESTORIUS AND HIS 'LIBER HERACLIDIS'

As well as the Antiochenes already mentioned, Nestorius, too, played a
part in theological developments after his deposition (431) and exile (436–
451),[52] though—apart from the influence of his writings and his supporters—he exerted no direct influence upon them. If we may still assign
the *Theopaschites* (431–5) and the *Tragoedia* (= *First Apologia*) to the
period about Ephesus, only the *Liber Heraclidis* (the *Second Apologia*) and
the '*Letter to the inhabitants of Constantinople*'[53] are relevant for the period
of his exile. This last, written after the 'Robber Synod' of 449, shows that
Nestorius declared himself in agreement with the christology of Flavian
of Constantinople and of the *Tome* of Leo I to Flavian. The *Liber Heraclidis*
also confirms the fact that Nestorius had knowledge of this important
writing of Leo's.[54] If he describes the document as the expression of his
view it is certainly not useless to investigate the extent of the development
of the christological thought and language of Nestorius after the Ephesine
period and their relation to the last phase of the pre-Chalcedonian development. We shall first examine the general position of the *Liber Heraclidis*
and then its christological formula and ideas.

In her significant study, *Untersuchungen zum Liber Heraclidis des Nestorius*,
Louvain 1963, Luise Abramowski had put forward the thesis that the first
part of the *L.H.* (B, 10–25; N, 5–81) was not to be assigned to Nestorius
but to a post-Chalcedonian author who wrote between 451 and before

---

[51] Cyril Al., *Ep.* 40 *ad Acac. Melit.*: ACO I, 1, 4, 20–31: PG 77, 181–201; *Ep.* 44 *ad Eulog.*:
ACO, ibid., 35–7: PG 77, 224–8; *Ep. ad Dynat. Nicop.*: ACO, ibid., 31–2: PG 77, 249–53; *Ep. ad
Valerian.*: ACO I, 1, 3, 90–101: PG 77, 256–77. This is the historical context of the valuable passage
contained in *A Collection of Christological Texts. Cambridge Library Ms. Oriental 1319*, edited and
translated by Luise Abramowski and Alan Goodman, vols. I and II, Cambridge 1972: I, 130–46
(Syr.); II, 75–88 (English). An anonymous writer produces a refutation of Cyril's twelve
anathematisms, which recur three times in the collection, with two forms of text. The refutation
largely consists in a patristic anthology. Both are probably reproduced in abbreviated form in the
collection. Various elements betray an archaic christology, which fits well into the period before
433, e.g. the reservation of the term 'hypostasis' for the Trinity. At the end there is a kind of creed
which is particularly reminiscent of the Symbol of Union of 433 because of its '*perfectus deus et
perfectus homo*' (cf. II, 88). It is interesting that the anthology offered here only has parallels in
Theodoret's *Eranistes*, and that was not written until 448. The editors therefore refer in II, XLIf.,
to Theodoret's lost *Pentalogus adv. Cyrillum* (432), the fourth book of which contained an anthology
which has been preserved for us (in whole or in part?) by Pope Gelasius, *De duabus naturis*. The
admonition to peace which is added at the end of the creed, with Heb. 12. 14, is also reminiscent of
433.

[52] According to Nau, PO IX, 586, n. 1, the date of the exile would be 434. But see L. Abramowski,
Untersuchungen zum L.H., 68, n. 61. For what follows see the literature mentioned on p. 449, n. 12
above and in the appendix.

[53] French translation in F. Nau, *Le Livre d'Héraclide de Damas*, Paris 1910, 373–4. Cf. M. Jugie,
Nestorius et la controverse nestorienne, Paris 1912, 70f.

[54] *L.H.*: B, 473, 514; N, 302f., 327; DrH, 345f., 374f. Henceforward we cite all texts of *L.H.*
according to these three editions, but quote the English text of DrH with some alterations which
will be indicated.

539/40 (i.e. the date of the translation of the text of *L.H.* into Syriac which we now have). In his new work *Nestorio e il concilio di Efeso*, Milano 1974, 299–361, L. I. Scipioni discusses this thesis at length and comes to a quite different conclusion over the authenticity of this first part. The starting point must be that of the Syriac (and Greek) tradition, that this first part is authentic. Special attention should be paid to the observation of the Syriac translator, which runs:

> 'Le présent livre . . . doit être lu après ces deux autres livres faits par le saint (Nestorius) à savoir *Theopasqitos* et *Tragaedia* qu'il á ecrit comme une apologie contre ceux qui le blâmaient d'avoir demandé un concile' (Nau, 3).

Given the fragmentary character of the text and all the observations of a redactional nature that are made, Scipioni adopts the simple hypothesis of a 'double composition' (doppia composizione), which is to be assigned to the hand of Nestorius himself. According to the witness of Severus of Antioch, the *Theopasqitos* was a tractate written in the form of a dialogue. In it an 'orthodox' (i.e. a supporter of the doctrine of 'two natures') discussed with a 'Theopaschite' (i.e. a representative of the doctrine of the *communicatio idiomatum*, which was the subject of the polemic between Nestorius and Cyril). This writing probably represents an answer from Nestorius to Cyril's polemical writings, perhaps to one of the first christological dialogues of the Patriarch of Alexandria. According to Severus, the *Tragaedia*, on the other hand, is an *apologia* of Nestorius, '*de iis quae in synodo Ephesina evenerunt, deque causa, quae eam congregavit*' (quoted 306). How can the two writings be in the *L.H.* that we now have?

The two writings begun between 431 and 435 were hardly finished before Nestorius' banishment to Egypt. So it is understandable that Nestorius wanted to write an even more extensive treatise on the problems which occupied him. For this new plan he will have gone back to the *Theopaschites*, using it as a basis for an answer and a counterpart to Cyril's last writings, *Quod unus sit Christus* (probably 437), and the dialogue *De incarnatione*. Because Cyril regarded his two writings as an exhaustive account of the faith and a sketch of the most important christological heresies, after 437/8 (the date of the appearance of the dialogue *De incarnatione* and the tractates against Diodore and Theodore), Nestorius had to attempt something similar and act in the same way as Cyril. A further reason for writing may have been the summoning of the Council of Chalcedon. Probably at the urging of his friends, Nestorius wrote a second apology, which goes back to the *Tragaedia* composed earlier and represents an attempt either to revise the *Tragaedia* completely or to enlarge it in part by a report on the events which had taken place since its first composition. However, Nestorius did not succeed in his final treatment of the two parts and in joining them together in a harmonious whole. On his death he left behind the two treatises for his followers, the Dialogue and the Second Apology. A devoted disciple sought to combine them in one book, but the joins remained obvious. Or perhaps the two texts were simply put side by side and a later glossator attempted to combine them in an appropriate fashion. The result was the *L.H.* in its present form, both parts of which do in fact come from the hand of Nestorius. The new work is the reason why the two treatises which preceded it, the *Theopaschites* and the *Tragaedia*, did not come down to us, although they were known to contemporaries and to subsequent historians. They were superseded by the new work.

A significant factor in respect of the 'Dialogue' is the relationship with Irenaeus and his *Adversus Haereses*, especially Book III, which has been worked out in detail by Scipioni. This offers new perspectives for interpretation and helps to clarify many obscure passages in the Dialogue. Nestorius here proves to be particularly concerned with soteriology. Here the concept of the 'mediation' of Christ is central, and is also significant for an understanding of the human nature of Christ in Nestorius (cf. B, 85–8; N, 55–7). The Christ of the 'Dialogue' is mediator of both creation and redemption, and also revealer. From this there follows in turn the theme of Christ, as the 'archetype' with a contrast between the first and second Adam, the first and second creation and finally the idea of recapitulation. The incarnation can be understood as the God Logos forming for himself his 'own', perfect, specific human nature, which is to have for its prosopon the prosopon of the 'Son'. The Logos has as its own both the divine and the human nature. Each of the two natures has its corresponding 'physical prosopon' (πρόσωπον φυσικόν), but they only present 'a single prosopon', the prosopon of the Son. For the Son makes the physical prosopon of the man his own and gives the man his own physical prosopon. In his account of the unity in Christ, Nestorius is always fighting against the 'physical' or the 'hypostatic union' of Cyril's teaching. It damages the integrity of the natures in Christ.

After the publication of the *Tomus ad Flavianum* by Leo I, a new situation arose for Nestorius. Now he had to show that his own christology was in accord with that of the Tome, which in historical terms amounted more to an incrimination of the Tome than a justification of Nestorius. But as a result he had an opportunity to develop the whole structure of his christology and to ground it in individual details. We have the result of this in the second part of the *L.H.* So whereas Luise Abramowski wants to regard the *Dialogus* as a work of subsequent reflection on the second part of *L.H.*, Scipioni sees it as a writing which was written before the appearance of Leo's Tome. In contrast to the Second Apology, it had a strong soteriological orientation, but already presupposed the essential ontological elements which were then developed in detail on the basis of the new situation created by the Tome in the second part of *L.H.* We now turn particularly to this second part.

(a) Theology of two natures

In the *Liber Heraclidis*, too, there are numerous indications that Nestorius wanted to preserve the basic lines of the church's christology. Here, too, of course, he forms his verdict on orthodoxy and heresy on his own speculative presuppositions:

> I have not renounced the just course of the orthodox nor shall I renounce it until death; and although they all, even the orthodox, fight with me through ignorance and are unwilling to hear and to learn from me, yet the times will come upon them when they will learn from those who are heretics, while fighting against them, how they have fought against him who fought on their behalf.[55]

As ever, he is intent on maintaining that Christ is 'one and the same', although he has in himself two natures, as Cyril also concedes.[56] Christ is only 'one thing and another, because Christ is God the Word and of humanity by union' (ibid.). He means to have the duality in Christ always expressed on the level of the *natures*:

> If then I said 'Christ' and 'God the Word another, apart from Christ', or 'Christ apart from God the Word', you have said well. . . . Now I have said that the name 'Christ' is indicative of two natures, of God indeed one nature [and of man one nature].[57]

'Nature' as a purely factual, qualitative expression of being remains for Nestorius the constant starting point and the principle of duality in Christ. It is on this that he bases the distinction between 'Logos' (divine nature) and 'Christ' (unity of divine and human nature). He also uses it to regulate christological expressions. This, moreover, explains his misunderstanding of the title *Theotokos* and the *Communicatio idiomatum*:

> By one nature on the one hand . . . he was born of God the Father; by the other, on the other hand, that is [by that] of the humanity, [he was born] of the holy virgin. How then canst thou name her 'Mother of God' when thou hast confessed that he was not born of her?[58]
>
> . . . that the 'Only begotten Son of God created and was created the same but not in the same (*ousia*); the Son of God suffered and suffered not, the same but not in the same (*ousia*); for [some] of these things are in the nature of the divinity and [others] of them in the nature of the humanity. He suffered all human things in the humanity and all divine things in the divinity.[59]

---

[55] B, 137; N, 88; DrH, 95.　　　　　　　　　　　　　　[56] B, 293; N, 186; DrH, 209f.

[57] B, 292 (and 356ff.); N, 185 (and 229ff.); DrH, 209 (and 257ff.); cf. L. I. Scipioni O.P., *Ricerche sulla cristologia del 'Libro di Eraclide' di Nestorio*, Fribourg 1956, 104.

[58] B, 408; N, 262; DrH, 296; cf. B, 358f.; N, 230; DrH, 259.

[59] B, 204; N, 122f.; DrH, 138. Moreover, Cyril's teaching too is regarded as a mixing of the natures or substances. Cyril says 'that the *ousia* of the child and the *ousia* of the Maker of the child exist in the same *ousia* of God the Word' (B, 322; N, 205; DrH, 231). Thus Cyril acknowledges in Christ 'not [one] *prosopon* but [one] *ousia* indeed' (B, 323; N, 206; DrH, 232).

In the *Liber Heraclidis*, too, Nestorius keeps to his definitions of 'Christ' and 'Logos' and their different relationships to the two natures in Christ. 'Therefore the two natures belong unto Christ and not unto God the Word' (B, 248; N, 150; DrH, 170). Word or Logos is here an expression of the 'nature'. To predicate two natures of the Logos is for Nestorius synonymous with assigning two substances to the nature of the Logos. But he sees quite clearly that two complete natures unite in 'Christ'. This is the constantly repeated *Leitmotif* in his *Liber Heraclidis*, the real opponents of which are, in fact, Apollinarianism and Arianism (as a christological doctrine: B, 150; N, 91; DrH, 98f.):

> For every union which results by a natural composition in the completion of the nature results from incomplete natures, but that which [results] from complete natures results in one *prosopon* and subsists therein. For God the Word did not make use of a bodily frame without soul nor of a soul without will and without mind, nor of a bodily frame and of a soul instead of a soul and an intelligence. But thereby is distinguished the church of the Arians and [that] of the Apollinarians, which does not accept the whole natures which have been united.[60]

Nestorius here rightly puts forward the old Antiochene demand which insists so strongly on the completeness of Christ's human nature. But by stressing the completeness of the two natures in Christ is he not also in danger of speaking of an 'independence' of these natures? Does not the *natura completa* threaten to become *persona*?

> Two natures [result in] one Christ, which are self-sustaining (*ntírín*) in their natures and do not need for the support of one another that they should be supported by the union: but they have established the dispensation on our behalf.[61]

We may see in this 'self-sustaining' no more than the content of the term *substantia* or *natura completa*. We may not seek in it a 'personality' in the Chalcedonian sense and in the precision of a later time. For Nestorius takes only the *natura completa* or *individualis* as the final limit of his analysis. This analysis of concrete being is very important if we are to form a judgement on the final scope and intent of Nestorius' christology. He has clearly recognized that it must be the aim of christological speculation to show the levels on which the unity and distinction in Christ are to be sought. If he is concerned to lay the foundations of the *distinction* in Christ, he refers to the essence (*ousia*), the nature (*physis*), the *hypostasis* and finally to the *prosopon*. If it is necessary to demonstrate the unity in Christ he only refers back to the *prosopon*. In its primary meaning 'nature' (*physis*, *kyânâ*) is simply equivalent to reality as opposed to the 'phantasmagorical, illusory, unreal'. Now a nature can be incomplete and complete. 'For every complete nature has no need of another nature that it may be and live, in

---

[60] B, 431f.; N, 276f.; DrH, 313f.   [61] B, 414²⁻⁴; N, 265; DrH, 300f.

that it has in it and has received (its whole) definition that it may be' (B, 418; N, 268; DrH, 304). For Nestorius, body and soul are incomplete natures, 'man' is a complete nature. A nature becomes complete through its properties, differences and characteristics. These are something real and are what first make a nature 'recognizable' and distinguishable from another nature. Thus, say, a human nature is distinct from other natures through reason and free will, and also through bodily experiences such as birth, growth, upbringing and development. Like 'nature', so too 'essence' (*ousia, îtûtâ*) has a primary meaning of 'reality', 'real entity' as opposed to 'phantasmagorical, illusory'. By taking these concepts in practice as synonymous, Nestorius further narrows down the concept of 'essence' (*ousia*) to mean the 'essential content' or 'specific being' of the nature.

The first addition to the nature (*kyânâ, physis*) or essence (*ousia*) is the 'form' (μορφή). Nestorius often speaks of the 'likeness of the nature', of the *schema* and of the appearance of the *ousia* (cf. B, 443; N, 284; DrH, 322). The analysis of concrete being in the writings of the Stoics has usefully been quoted as a parallel.[62]

Now in the Stoic writings the *ousia* is in the first place determined by the κοινὴ ποιότης, the specifying quality. It thus becomes a species, a κοινῶς ποιός, that is, say, 'horse', 'man'. If the ἰδία ποιότης is then added it becomes ἰδίως ποιός, i.e. the individual, Socrates, Diogenes. So too Nestorius knows a twofold determination of *ousia*: first, through the 'natural property'[63] (*dîlâyâtâ da-kyânê*: B, 284[5], 302[12]); then through the 'property of the hypostasis' (χαρακτὴρ τῆς ὑποστάσεως: B, 229[3-4], 233, 252, 302, 304-5, 442), which represents the final determining of the individual being. The *hypostasis* is thus the *ousia* in so far as it is determined

[62] So L. I. Scipioni, *Ricerche*, 45–67. We are indebted to this study in the following pages. Of course Scipioni can demonstrate no direct use of Stoic writings by Nestorius. The Stoic material had already entered the thought-world of the Fathers before his time. For the Antiochenes, see P. Canivet, *Histoire d'une entreprise apologétique au Vᵉ siècle*, Paris 1957, 308–15. Scipioni could have pointed out to the Cappadocians here. Nestorius seems most like Basil and Gregory of Nyssa in his view of the relationship between *physis, hypostasis* and *prosopon*. See above, pp. 370–8. Nestorius finds his idea of concrete being in a number of scriptural passages which occur in his writings again and again, especially Phil. 2. 5–11 (μορφή, σχῆμα) and Heb. 1. 3 (χαρακτὴρ τῆς ὑποστάσεως αὐτοῦ = the form of his *hypostasis*. See B, 229; N, 138; DrH, 156. This passage is especially discussed.) It is interesting that Basil also develops his trinitarian doctrine of person on Heb. 1. 3. A closer investigation must be made of this sequence Stoa–Cappadocians–Nestorius, but that is impossible here. A brief reference may, however, be made to the other patristic sources used by Nestorius in *L.H.* He has only a small collection of constantly recurring passages from the Fathers which are taken from the Acts of the Council of Ephesus: Athanasius, *C. Arian.* 3, 13; *Ad Epictet.* 2 and 7: ACO I, 1, 2, 40; Gregory of Nazianzus, *Ep.* 101 *ad Cledon.*: PG 37, 180–181, 177BC; Gregory of Nyssa, *Or.* 1 *de Beatitud.*, ACO I, 1, 2, 44[21-2]; Theophilus Alex., *Ep. pasch.* 6, ACO I, 1, 2, 41; Ambrose, *De fide* 1, 94; 2, 77–78, ACO I, 1, 2, 42–3; the Syriac text, B, 146, of the *L.H.* does not reproduce accurately the Greek text which Nestorius read in the Acts. In addition there is again, as in the period of the Council of Ephesus, the Nicene creed which Nestorius still interprets in the same way as before. Nestorius' knowledge of the Fathers is not great, otherwise he could not affirm that the Theotokos title did not occur in them (B, 220; N, 132; DrH, 149). Even the acts of the Council of Ephesus contained a passage from Gregory of Nazianzus which he must have read (ACO I, 1, 2, 43[18] = PG 37, 177C). Cassian, *De incarn. Dei ctr. Nestor. libri* VII can therefore easily find a counterproof, VII, 24–31: CSEL 17, 382–91.

[63] I.e. the property which constitutes the nature.

by the whole complex of properties. Nestorius calls this complex of properties the *prosopon*. The *Liber Heraclidis* knows this word in the meaning of 'role,' 'function' (B, 111, 279, 284; N, 72, 176, 179; DrH, 76, 199, 203) but also as signifying 'human individual' (B, 195, 197, 364; N, 117, 117, 234; DrH, 132, 133, 264, etc.).

In christology, however, a different meaning presses into the foreground: *prosopon* as the form, image, appearance of a nature. In this significance the *Liber Heraclidis*, too, speaks of two 'natural *prosopa*' in Christ. For each of the two natures has its permanent individual determination, the Godhead in the natural *prosopon* of the Son, the manhood in what Nestorius describes as the *'forma servi'*. The 'natural *prosopon*' has its reality from the reality of the nature whose mode of appearance it is. But without the natural *prosopon* the natures are incomplete, unrecognizable and indistinguishable. Thus the 'natural *prosopon*' is the complex of the properties, the differences and the characteristics by which a nature is differentiated, limited and finally determined. If two natures no longer preserve their *prosopon naturale*, in their union they are no longer differentiated but mingled. Thus 'nature' in its 'natural *prosopon*' is the 'hypostasis'. In fact, *hypostasis* coincides with *natura completa*, but formally it describes the completeness of the *natura completa*. We can already see that in his analysis of concrete being or concrete nature Nestorius distinguishes different strata, each of which he adduces in accordance with its character to interpret the unity and distinction in Christ. *Ousia* and *hypostasis* (= concrete reality) clearly belong to the principles which condition the distinction in Christ. He seeks to explain the unity from the *prosopon*, i.e. from that sphere which makes the *ousia* the *hypostasis*, the *natura completa*. But here he makes a distinction: as far as the *prosopon* must be described as a 'natural *prosopon*' it is to be included among the principles of differentiation. Here his insight was correct, as developments after Chalcedon have shown. For even in the union, the human nature of Christ remains a *natura completa individualis*. Nevertheless, he is determined to maintain the *prosopon* as the principle of the union. For this purpose he forms the concept of the *'prosopon* of union'. We must now investigate what he has achieved by this. For our aim, however, it is necessary to make a survey of the christological formula of the *Liber Heraclidis*.

(b) The christological formula of the Liber Heraclidis

The natures are merely the object of the union in Christ. The union of God and man in Christ takes place not in the sphere of *ousia* or nature or *hypostasis*, but in the sphere of *prosopon*, as Nestorius says with almost scholastic exactitude:

> . . . the union did not take place according to the *ousia* and the nature but according to the *prosopon*. Or, . . . when we speak of the *prosopon*, we say that the Son of God is adored,

concerning also the flesh as united with him; but in discussing the natures and speaking of two natures, we say that the humanity is adored with the divinity which is united with it.[64]

Nestorius has an approach to his formula which is significant for the understanding of it; he reaches it by reversing the trinitarian formula. True, in some respects Gregory of Nazianzus had already anticipated him here.[65] But Nestorius more than anyone else makes full use of the comparison. In so doing he raises the whole process of reflection to the level of a metaphysical analysis. He finds the opportunity for a closer comparison of *prosopon* and *hypostasis*, and of these two terms with others, *physis* and *ousia*. Even though he does not exploit the opportunity to the full, the mere fact of this parallelism and differentiation of trinitarian and christological concepts shows that Nestorius is striving for a doctrine of incarnation within an orthodox framework:

> But further, as in the Trinity, [there is] there one *ousia* of three *prosopa*, but three *prosopa* of one *ousia*; here [there is] one *prosopon* of two *ousiai* and two *ousiai* of one *prosopon*.[66]

That is in practice the current orthodox formula both for Trinity and for incarnation. In both cases Nestorius prefers the contrast of *ousia* and *prosopon*. Interestingly enough, however, in some places he uses the other term '*hypostasis*' instead of '*prosopon*' for the trinitarian formula. In the Trinity the δυναστεία and the ἐνέργεια are common, the difference is μόναις ὑποστάσεσιν (*qnomê*).[67] It is significant that by doing this he comes near to the identification of *prosopon* and *hypostasis* in christology as well. He is at least for a moment conscious of this possibility, though, of course, he does not exploit it fully and consistently. This happens in the setting of a criticism of Cyril's formula ἕνωσις καθ' ὑπόστασιν.

Nestorius argues that he can only understand Cyril's phrase ἕνωσις καθ' ὑπόστασιν if Cyril uses ὑπόστασις to express what Nestorius calls πρόσωπον ... it would seem that Nestorius regularly uses ὑπόστασις as practically equivalent to οὐσία and in Trinitarian doctrine would himself speak of three πρόσωπα in one ὑπόστασις (or οὐσία). But Cyril has the later usage in which the two are distinguished and so speaks of three ὑποστάσεις in one οὐσία. Nestorius evidently appreciates this difference of terminology in Trinitarian doctrine and tries to find in it a clue to the understanding of Cyril's christology, asking whether after all Cyril always means by ὑπόστασις what he calls πρόσωπον.[68]

---

[64] B, 231 and 317; N, 139 and 202; DrH, 158 and 228.

[65] Greg. Naz., *Ep.* 101 *ad Cledon.*, PG 37, 180B: in the incarnation: λέγω δὲ ἄλλο καὶ ἄλλο, ἔμπαλιν ἢ ἐπὶ τῆς Τριάδος ἔχει. 'Εκεῖ μὲν γὰρ ἄλλος καὶ ἄλλος ἵνα μὴ τὰς ὑποστάσεις συγχ᾿ωμεν. οὐκ ἄλλο δὲ καὶ ἄλλο, ἓν γὰρ τὰ τρία καὶ ταυτὸν τῇ θεότητι. Nestorius explicitly refers to Gregory's trinitarian teaching (B, 317; N, 202; DrH, 228). Cf. above on Andrew of Samosata.

[66] B, 342; N, 219; DrH, 247, cf. B, 143; N, 167f.; DrH, 189f.; B, 361f.; N, 232; DrH, 261f.; B, 425f.; N, 272f.; DrH, 308f.

[67] B, 326; N, 207f.; DrH, 234. Cf. also the text of Nestorius read at Ephesus: Loofs, *Nestoriana*, 225: Κοιναὶ γὰρ αἱ τῆς Τριάδος ἐνέργειαι καὶ μόναις ὑποστάσεσιν τὴν διαίρεσιν ἔχουσαι. DrH, 234, n. 4, says on this: 'This use of ὑπόστασις is quite unusual in Nestorius.... The curious thing is that, whilst the Syriac above (i.e. the Syriac version of the text read at Ephesus) represents Nestorius' regular usage, this passage accurately represents the Greek text....' Cf. further B, 335f.; N, 213f.; DrH, 242 (*hypostasis*!).

[68] DrH, 156, n. 2.

So he demands of Cyril:

Say therefore [what] the *hypostatic* union [is]. Dost thou wish to regard a *hypostasis* as a *prosopon*, as we speak of one *ousia* of the divinity and three *hypostases* and understand *prosopa* by *hypostases*? Thou callest therefore the *prosopic* union *hypostatic*; yet the union was not of the *prosopa* but of the natures. ... But I am not persuaded of any other hypostatic union with other natures nor of anything else which is right for the union of diverse natures except one *prosopon*, by which and in which both the natures are known, while assigning their properties to the *prosopon*.[69]

Nestorius therefore makes this juxtaposition of *prosopon* and *hypostasis* in his own sense and within the framework of his doctrine of union. He still does not see what we to-day understand by hypostatic union, i.e. unity in the 'person'. But it is certain that he repudiates what is known as a doctrine of two persons, i.e. he does not make Christ a unity from two pre-existent persons *in actu secundo*. For this reason he says: 'yet the union was not of the *prosopa* but of the natures' (loc. cit). He is ready to allow the validity of the expression 'hypostatic union' provided that it is understood in his sense:

Understandest thou (by hypostatic union) the one *prosopon* of Christ, or the *hypostasis* of the *ousia* and of the nature as the form of his *hypostasis* (χαρακτὴρ τῆς ὑποστάσεως αὐτοῦ Heb. I. 3) and sayest thou with hypostatic union the union of the natures? But I say that; and I praised thee for having said it and having made a distinction of the natures according to the divinity and to the humanity and the coherence of these in one *prosopon*.[70]

In other words, he allows the validity of the expression 'hypostatic union' if *hypostasis* here means exactly the same as *prosopon*, i.e. the *forma qualificans* (as ἰδίως ποιόν) of the *ousia* or *physis*, as is in his view the case with the trinitarian formula: μία οὐσία (φύσις)—τρεῖς ὑποστάσεις (τρία πρόσωπα). But Nestorius does not exploit this possibility further to give a new interpretation to Cyril's hypostatic union. This new interpretation would only have made sense had he been able to go one step further. Then this juxtaposition of *prosopon* and *hypostasis* could have been of the greatest use to Nestorius. It would have led him both to an understanding of Cyril's formula and also to a solution of his own difficulties. One step further and the Chalcedonian identification of *prosopon* and *hypostasis* and the differentiation of them from *physis* (*ousia*) would have been anticipated. In addition, of course, the Chalcedonian sense of *hypostasis* and *prosopon* would have had to have been discovered, i.e. the metaphysical significance of 'person' (even at Chalcedon it is only given *per modum intuitionis* and not yet *per modum definitionis*). Cyril has already come very near to this meaning with his formula of the hypostatic union. Did

[69] B, 229f.; N, 138f.; DrH, 156f. Both before and afterwards, then, the hypostatic union remains for Nestorius a union of incomplete natures. So it is impossible for him to use this term. Cf. L. I. Scipioni, *Ricerche*, 74–7.

[70] B, 229; N, 138; DrH, 156, partly changed by us. For the use of Heb. I. 3 in this whole controversy cf. also F. M. Young, 'Christologica Ideas', see p. 418, n. 15 above.

Nestorius make this discovery? In practice he in fact anticipates the 'formula' of Chalcedon. Could not the formula in time also lead him completely to the goal, i.e. to the Chalcedonian understanding? More than once he says that Christ is *'in two natures'* or *'one prosopon in two ousiai'*.[71] Thus the Chalcedonian ἐν δύο φύσεσιν is literally repeated and the second formula, quoted above, would have been allowed by the Fathers of Chalcedon as a parallel to their own. Indeed, Nestorius is one with these Fathers in opposing his formula to Cyril's ἐκ δύο φύσεων (οὐσιῶν), as we have already established in the earlier texts of the Ephesine period. Sometimes he even reveals complete agreement between himself and Cyril:

> Thou sayest therefore that very thing which I also [say], commending [it]: that the divinity exists united with the humanity and the humanity exists in nature and united to the divinity.[72]

But it is clear that such agreement can only be expressed in very general formulas. We are faced with the question whether the already almost Chalcedonian formulas mentioned above are the fruit of an understanding itself characteristic of the Fathers of Chalcedon; in other words, whether Nestorius was on the right way to a speculative solution of the christological difficulties then pending. Does Nestorius seek the solution of the christological problem in a sphere in which the later theology of the church is also active?

(c) Christological formula and thought

Nestorius maintains that *prosopon* is the 'appearance' (μορφή) of the *ousia*: 'the *prosopon* makes known the *ousia*' (B, 321; N 139; DrH, 158). If body and soul unite, the result is a 'natural union' (ἕνωσις φυσική) and a single (!) *prosopon* (and that a natural *prosopon*) corresponding to this unity. As incomplete natures, body and soul have no individual *prosopon* of their own (B, 240; N, 145; DrH, 164). In Christ, on the other hand, the 'one' *prosopon* does not belong to a nature or hypostasis which arose through the 'natural union' of Godhead and manhood, but to the unity of the two unconfused natures:

> When he [Christ] speaks as from his own *prosopon* [he does so] by one *prosopon* which appertains to the union of the natures and not to one *hypostasis* or [one] nature.[73]

It is this that is the 'common *prosopon* of our Lord Jesus Christ' (B, 250; N, 151; DrH, 171). Each of the essences (*ousiai*) in Christ has its *hypostasis*, i.e. its reality, and thus also its appearance, i.e. its 'natural' *prosopon*. But in addition, each of the natures in Christ makes use of the natural *prosopon* of the *other* nature. So there arises the *one* prosopon of the union:

---

[71] E.g. B, 249, 324, 328; N, 150, 206, 209; DrH, 170, 233, 236. Here Nestorius refers to Gregory of Nazianzus, Ambrose and Athanasius.

[72] B, 274–5; N, 173; DrH, 195.   [73] B, 239; N, 144; DrH, 163.

... the natures subsist in their *prosopa* and in their natures and in the *prosopon* of the union. For in respect to the natural *prosopon* of the one the other also makes use of the same on account of the union; and thus [there is] one *prosopon* of the two natures.[74]

All depends on the interpretation of this *prosopon* of the union. It belongs to each of the two natures which have their respective *prosopa*: 'one *prosopon* which belongs to the natures and to the *prosopa*' (B, 340; N, 218; DrH, 246). This one *prosopon* is the result of the union of God and man and not of itself the way or the means to it. Now this one *prosopon*, and with it the unity in Christ, is achieved in a twofold way; through the compensation of the *prosopa* and through the mutual interpenetration or *perichoresis* of these *prosopa*.

This idea of the *compensation of prosopon* seems to be peculiar to Nestorius as opposed to the other Antiochenes. From it he derives his understanding of the incarnation: 'since the incarnation is conceived (to consist) in the mutual use of giving and taking' (B, 362; N, 233; DrH, 262). It is the weakest point of his christology, almost a cul-de-sac into which he has found his way. He believes that it is possible to derive his idea from Phil. 2. 5–11:

... so that the likeness[75] of a servant which was taken should become the likeness of God, and God the likeness of a servant, and that the one should become the other and the other the one in *prosopon*, the one and the other remaining in their natures.[76] For he made use of the likeness (*dmutâ* = μορφή) and of the *prosopon* of a servant, not the *ousia* nor the nature, in such wise that he was by nature in them both, as being Christ.[77]

In Nestorius' view, then, the incarnation takes place as follows: the divine *prosopon* of the Son uses the *prosopon* of the manhood as its representation or form, whereas the *prosopon* of the manhood obtains the divine form of glory (in the exaltation). This exchange is strictly limited to the *prosopa* which are exchanged, while the divine and human substances are untouched by the exchange:

But in the *prosopa* of the union, the one in the other, neither by diminution nor by suppression nor by confusion is this 'one' conceived, but by taking and by giving and by

---

[74] B, 305; N, 194; DrH, 219.

[75] J. F. Bethune-Baker, *Nestorius and his Teaching*, Cambridge 1908, 152, n. 1, says on this expression 'likeness': 'The Syriac word *d'mûtha* is the natural equivalent for the two Greek words ὁμοίωσις (Gen. 1. 26) and μορφή (Phil. 2. 6–7). When, therefore, there is reference to the passage in Gen. we should understand that it translates the former Greek word, when to Phil. 2, the latter. Now all through this work Nestorius appears to use μορφή in a strongly theological sense which is practically equivalent to the sense he gives to φύσις (*kyânâ*, 'nature'), ὑπόστασις (*q'nômâ*) and οὐσία (*ousia*). This is certainly so whenever there is a reference to Phil. 2.' Cf. DrH, 89, n. 1. The last remark is not quite correct. Here Nestorius takes *prosopon* as synonymous with μορφή, form, figure, appearance, just as in the trinitarian formula: one *physis*, three *hypostaseis*, or three χαρακτῆρες τῆς ὑποστάσεως αὐτοῦ (Heb. 1. 3). With this he contrasts the christological formula: two *physeis*, two *hypostaseis*, but *one* 'form of his substance' (χαρακτὴρ τῆς ὑποστάσεως).

[76] B, 267; N, 167; DrH, 183.

[77] B, 216; N, 130; DrH, 147. Phil. 2 is also used when Nestorius is describing the incarnation under the image of the king, who puts on the garment (*schema*) of the servant (B, 130f.; N, 84; DrH, 90f.).

use of the union of the one with the other, the *prosopa* give one another, but not the *ousiai*.[78]

Thus Nestorius stresses two things: that it is the *prosopa* and not the *ousiai* which are involved in the exchange, so as to avoid monophysitism, and that it is 'mutual compensation'. Both these Cyril denied. He explains the incarnation purely from the *ousia* and not from the *prosopon* and, moreover, from the divine *ousia* alone and not from the human *ousia* as well. Thus there is no longer any possibility of compensation: 'thou takest away the compensation from the union of the two *ousiai*' (B, 349; N, 224; DrH, 252). Is there any possibility of this compensation of *prosopon* contributing anything to the interpretation of the incarnation?

It is open to two objections: first, the basis of this compensation appears to be only external to the two natures, i.e. the compensation does not appear to make possible an ontic, substantial union because it only concerns something peripheral in the natures; secondly, the compensation itself appears to be achieved through a sort of moral attitude, so that the result is only a 'unity of attitude' (ἕνωσις σχετική) (corresponding to *Bewährungslehre*, the theory that Christ earned exaltation through obedience). From ancient times this has been the usual interpretation of Nestorian christology.

We saw that in order to avoid the confusion of natures or essences Nestorius transfers the unity in Christ into the realm of the *prosopon*. In his writings, however, the *prosopon* may not be interchanged with the accidents of a nature. It is indeed the realm of the ἰδίως ποιόν, as it were the last and external stratum in an essence or nature. But it is at the same time the realm of substantial completion of individuality. Here in christology *prosopon* does not mean merely 'role' or pure 'figurative representation', just as, for example, an ambassador takes the place of the '*prosopon*' of the sender or a picture reproduces merely the external form of what is depicted without containing the entity itself (cf. B, 83f.; N, 54; DrH, 57—a passage which belongs to a part of the *Liber Heraclidis* excluded by L. Abramowski). For Nestorius the *prosopon* is rather something substantial; so much so in fact that his unity of *prosopon* cannot fully avoid the charge of becoming a *unio in naturam et secundum naturam*. In any case, it comprises the complex of characteristics which belong to the substance and go to define the substance itself. In the light of this, therefore, we cannot complain that Nestorius has a purely accidental unity in Christ. He seeks only to apply to christology the concept of *prosopon* then current.

But does he perhaps finally come to grief in his interpretation of the action of the 'compensation' itself? Does not everything here remain in the realm of an accidental or moral unity? According to Nestorius, this compensation consists in the fact that on the ground of his unity with

<hr />

[78] B, 348; N, 223; DrH, 252.

manhood God can reveal himself and work as a human *prosopon*, just as the manhood of Christ, by virtue of its acceptance by the Godhead, can present itself as a divine *prosopon*. We can understand this compensation most easily if we begin with a passage which is conceived on the lines of the 'indwelling framework':

> ... thou oughtest not have accused me and calumniated me as not confessing one *prosopon* in two *ousiai* or as defining them individually (literally 'by parts,' or 'in parts') in distinction and in division, as things which are distant from one another. For I have called the 'dweller' one who by all means dwells in the nature; and the dweller is he who dwells in him in whom there is dwelling, and he has his (DrH 'a') *prosopon*, while he in whom there is dwelling has the *prosopon* of him who dwells. So by the use of their *prosopa* as though they were making use of their own authoritatively, the one is the other and the other the one, the one and the other abiding just as they are in their natures.[79]

The *prosopon* of the Godhead has made the manhood its temple and has given to this manhood its *prosopon*, its characteristics, its mode of appearance, i.e. all that belongs to the natural prosopon of the Son. On the other hand, the manhood itself, indeed the *prosopon* of the manhood, serves as a representation of the divine *prosopon*. This also leads to a community of will and action:

> And because also the *prosopon* of the one is the other's and that of the other the one's, and the one (comes) from the other and the other from the one, the will belongs to each one of them.[80]

Just as the will and desire of the human nature are now appropriated by the divine *prosopon* and the divine will stands at the disposal of the human *prosopon*—for this reason Nestorius has been described as a Monothelite— so too the human *prosopon* receives divine honour and worship while the divine *prosopon* clothes itself in the lowliness of human existence. Community of will and of honour—both points were the occasion for Nestorius' compensation of *prosopon* being qualified as a purely moral-accidental unity:

> And he (Cyril) accuses me of these things as if I were dividing Christ and making (him into) sundry parts, the divinity by itself and the humanity by itself while making use of (the words) 'honour' and 'the equality of one' and in such wise that they (= honour and equality) tend to bring together in love and not in the *ousiai* things far apart.[81]

The charge contained in these words is usually made under the term 'Bewährungslehre', i.e. that the man Jesus first had to merit acceptance on the part of the Godhead through his love and his obedience. The unity of Christ is said to be purely nominal. The man Jesus can only be called God because the divine name, divine honour and worship is lent to him on the basis of grace. Let us allow Nestorius to answer these charges. Let us try to grasp his idea of the incarnation as a whole. For it is only because his

[79] B, 324; N, 206; DrH, 233.   [80] B, 239; N, 144; DrH, 163.
[81] B, 142; N, 167; DrH, 189.

individual ideas have been isolated that they could be so dangerously misinterpreted. The pattern of the compensation of *prosopon* first conceals the fact that Nestorius does not understand the incarnation purely symmetrically. The incarnation is not an act of the human *prosopon* of Christ, as it were something earned or won by merit, but is clearly a divine act. The divine *prosopon* appropriates Christ's human nature. It is plainly an action 'from above': 'And the *ousia* of the divinity makes use of the *prosopon* of the humanity' (B, 440; N, 282; DrH, 320). This divine grasping does not just take place from time to time as is the case with a moral relationship; it is a definitive condition. This grasping does not take hold of an already pre-existent and personal manhood, but is at the same time an *actus creativus* which creates this manhood as a temple of the Godhead. Nestorius finds his interpretation in Phil. 2:

> He took the likeness of a servant: and the likeness of the servant was not the *ousia* of a man, but he who took it made it (his) likeness and his *prosopon*. 'And he became the likeness of *men*', but he became not the nature of *men*, although it was the nature of a *man* which he took; he who took it came to be in the likeness of *man*, whilst he who took and not that which was taken was found in *schema* as man; for that which was taken was the *ousia* and nature of man, whereas he who took was found in *schema* as man without being the nature of man.[82]

To the divine 'taking', which is at the same time a kenosis or a veiling, there corresponds a happening on the human side, the exaltation, which, however, is a 'happening' and not a human 'action':

> ... the *prosopon* of the divinity and the *prosopon* of the humanity are one *prosopon*, the one on this hand by *kenosis*, the other on that by exaltation.[83]

So in Nestorius, too, the 'mutual compensation of *prosopa*' is on the one hand active and divine and on the other passive and creaturely, as is shown by Phil. 2. 'That which took' is contrasted with 'that which was taken' (B, 290; N, 184; DrH, 208). It is because the very act of taking a human nature comes from above that Nestorius lays so much stress on its freedom and character of grace. The incarnation is not a necessary natural fact, a ἕνωσις κατὰ φύσιν, but a free disposal by the divine dispensation (οἰκονομία). Christ is therefore a ἕνωσις κατ᾽ οἰκονομίαν, or κατ᾽ εὐδοκίαν, or κατὰ χάριν. This is the proper sense of these expressions which have been expounded to fit a '*Bewährungslehre*'.[84] They are not meant to loosen the unity in Christ; they merely stress the divine freedom in the work of the incarnation. In none of this is the human freedom of Christ a matter of concern. From Christ's Godhead finally come the

---

[82] B, 241; N, 156; DrH, 165.   [83] B, 341; N, 218; DrH, 246.
[84] Nestorius sees in Cyril's physical union a confusion of the two *physeis* after the manner of a necessary natural unity, as is given in the unity of body and soul. But Cyril means by it a substantial, ontic unity with no confusion of the natures. Nestorius too is falsely judged if this ἕνωσις κατ᾽ οἰκονομίαν is understood as an accidental-moral unity.

honour (τιμή), glory (δόξα) and worship which are also bestowed on the man in Christ. Nestorius does not make this equality of honour, worship and grace the ground of the unity in Christ; the equality follows from the fact of the taking of human nature by God in Christ:

... nor do I speak of an adhesion through love and through proximity, as though it were between those which are far apart [and] those united by love and not in the *ousiai*; nor again do I speak of a union in equality of honour and in authority but of the natures and of whole natures, and in the combination of the *ousiai* I concede a union without confusion; but in respect to one honour and to one authority I predicate the union of the natures and not of the honour and of the authority ... [I spoke] not of the proximity nor the equality of honour nor of the dignity, but I said that I separate not God the Word himself in his nature from the visible nature, and by reason of God who is not to be separated I separate not even the honour; ... for he is one thing and his honour is another, and his *ousia* is another and whatsoever belongs to the *ousia* is another. But, although I have said that I distinguish the natures and unite the adoration, I have not said that I separate the natures from one another by a separation of distance, as thou accusest me in thy calumniation.[85]

Nestorius does not fully feel the weight of this accusation, but he does feel that he has not been rightly and fully understood. Cyril is aiming at the decisive point, that Nestorius assumes no substantial and essential unity in Christ, but merely a moral, accidental unity on the basis of the same honour and worship of Godhead and manhood in Christ. The Bishop of Alexandria always sees first in Christ the 'one nature', the 'one subject' of the divine Logos and then the act of incarnation (μία φύσις τοῦ θεοῦ λόγου σεσαρκωμένη). To Cyril, Nestorius appears to place an equivalent human subject (person) alongside the God-Logos. Between the two, Logos and man, there is only the bond of mutual love, whereas each of the two natures is fully independent. Nestorius singles out this last charge and interprets it in his own way. His opponents should not think that he leaves the two natures separate from each other, the God-head in heaven and the manhood on earth. He does not produce the unity merely through reciprocal acts of these, so to speak, 'locally' separated natures. No, the essences themselves are brought together and mutually interpenetrate each other. So we come to a further attempt to make the unity in Christ as close as possible without destroying the duality of the natures.

The 'mutual compensation' is expanded through the idea of the 'mutual compenetration' of the two natures in Christ. That which takes and that which is taken enter into each other, a process which the Greeks describe with the word *perichoresis*.

... we understand neither that which took nor that which was taken in distinction but that which was taken *in* that which took.[86]

[85] B, 432–3; N, 277; DrH, 314. The above translation has been altered in a number of places from that of DrH.
[86] B, 290; N, 184; DrH, 208.

This idea of mutual compenetration has both a theological and a philosophical side, both of which are important for its evaluation. The theological significance of the christological perichoresis of Nestorius is clear from its parallelism with the trinitarian perichoresis:

Confess then the taker as he took and the taken as he was taken, wherein [each is] one and in another, and wherein [there is] one and not two, *after the same manner as the manner of the Trinity.*[87]

Thus Nestorius does not merely limit himself to a terminological approximation of the christological formula to the trinitarian one, as we have seen above; he also makes use of this analogy for a christological ontology. This is an incontrovertible proof that he is concerned with a substantial unity in Christ. Just as in the Holy Trinity the three *prosopa* are joined through the one *ousia* and thus penetrate each other in essence, so in Christ the two *ousiai* penetrate each other without confusion to form the unity of one *prosopon*. On the presupposition, then, that the two *ousiai* or *physeis* remain unconfused, Nestorius will exploit any possibility of a substantial basis to the unity of Christ. Even the well-known 'indwelling-doctrine' of Nestorius which he has read out of Scripture (Col. 2. 9) and has in common with a considerable tradition (B, 324; N, 206; DrH, 233), may be taken in this sense of an inward compenetration. It was strongly stressed to distinguish the natures, and, with the theological misunderstandings already indicated, was interpreted as a doctrine of two persons.[88] With an image used by Cyril himself,[89] Nestorius rejects the charge laid against him by Cyril of letting the Godhead and manhood of Christ exist apart from each other.[90] This is the analogy of the burning bush (Exod. 3. 1–5):

---

[87] B, 289; N, 183; DrH, 207.

[88] The 'clothing' framework should be regarded in a similar way (cf. B, 304; N, 193; DrH, 218), as, too, the idea that the manhood of Christ is the instrument of the Godhead (*First speech against 'Theotokos'*: Loofs, *Nestoriana*, 252; further 247, 205, 260).

[89] Cyril Al., *Hom. pasch.* 17, PG 77, 781C. Even M. Jugie, *Nestorius et la controverse nestorienne*, Paris 1912, 111 admits: 'Cette dernière comparaison exprime une union plus intime; certains Pères orthodoxes en ont employé d'approchantes.' As for example the image of the fire in the iron, the drop of vinegar in the sea. But Jugie will not be convinced, for he continues: 'mais il faut se souvenir que Nestorius maintient deux personnes distinctes, deux *prosopons* naturels, comme il dit.' Jugie does not suspect that this comparison could in any way express the unity of Christ in Nestorius. For him *prosopon* is 'person' in the classical, dogmatic sense.

[90] Nestorius cites (B, 233; N, 141; DrH, 159f.) a sentence from Cyril's letter to him which was read at Ephesus: ACO I, 1, 1, 288⁻¹⁰. Here Cyril asserts that if one does not accept the hypostatic union (τὴν καθ' ὑπόστασιν ἕνωσιν) one must necessarily describe the man in Christ 'by himself' (ἰδικῶς) as Son (in honour) and the divine Logos by himself as Son (by nature), i.e. there are then two subjects (= persons). Nestorius does not understand the ἰδικῶς rightly. He thinks that Cyril prevents him from acknowledging the essential difference of the two natures: 'How sayest thou that the nature of man cannot be understood "properly" (= ἰδικῶς, i.e. in its own reality) especially apart from the *ousia* of God the Word . . .?' It is once again clear here that Nestorius has no thought at all of a teaching of two persons. The idea of person has not come to him at all. In order to show how despite the difference of the natures there is still an inward unity in Christ, he produces the example of the bush quoted above, in which an 'unconfused unity' is expressed: 'If then the distinctions of the natures have not been annulled, the nature of the flesh appertains solely to the nature

... as the fire was in the bush and the bush was fire and the fire bush and each of them was bush and fire and not two bushes nor two fires, since they were both in the fire and they were both in the bush, not indeed in division but in union.[91]

Here Nestorius so to speak jumps over his own shadow, so inward would he have the conjunction of the natures in Christ to form the unity of *prosopon*. But it is the mutual penetration of the two natures in respect of the *prosopon* which he takes as the ground of this unity. Nestorius thus means to give an ontological basis to this unity, i.e. to assume an ontic unity along with the difference of the natures. Just as he here accepts an Alexandrian illustration, so, too, he even takes over a daring concept to interpret the incarnation which properly belonged to his opponents. He took it over unthinkingly only because he found it in the writings of Gregory of Nazianzus; it is the saying about 'mixture', σύγκρασις:

Read, O man, what thou hast among thy testimonies and contend not with a shadow: 'two natures indeed, God and man, but not two sons; for one thing and another are those things whereof our Saviour [is formed]; yet [he is] not one and another—far from it!— but one in the mixture (ἐν τῇ συγκράσει); God who was made man and man who was made God.'[92]

In his attack on Cyril's *Twelve Capita*, Theodoret vigorously rejected such expressions as κρᾶσις and σύγχυσις.[93] If Nestorius accepts them, this is evidence of his purpose to make his union of prosopon as close as possible. Unfortunately he does not speak of his philosophical idea of κρᾶσις here.[94]

It is impossible to deny that Nestorius in all seriousness seeks a substantial unity (a *unitas ontica*) in Christ. In view of the position of the then current metaphysic of *ens concretum* he cannot achieve more than he actually did. Once he has recognized that the two *ousiai* in Christ must remain unconfused, all that is in question is the sphere of the *notae individuantes*, of the ἰδίως ποιόν which makes the *ousia* the *hypostasis*. This is the *prosopon*. Once, too, that he has rightly recognized that each of the two natures in Christ is to be taken concretely and in its individuality, he concludes quite logically from his standpoint that the unity in Christ can only come about by means of a compensation of *prosopon*. Unfortunately he had no idea of going beyond the individuality of the concrete nature and asking for a deeper analysis of the independence of

of the humanity. But that which is Son consubstantial with God the Father and with the Holy Spirit uniquely and solely appertains to the divinity; for by the union the flesh is Son and God the Word is flesh' (B, 234; N, 141; DrH, 160).

[91] B, 234f.; N, 141; DrH, 160. The same analogy is used by Babai the Great. See L. I. Scipioni, *Ricerche sulla cristologia del 'Libro di Eraclide' di Nestorio*, Fribourg 1956, 149.

[92] B, 359f.; N, 231; DrH, 260, cf. 224. Cf. Greg. Naz., *Ep.* 101 *ad Cledon.*: PG 37, 180A. Nestorius often speaks of this passage in Gregory and of its context.

[93] Theodoret, in Cyril Al., *Apol. cap. XII c. Theodoret.*, ACO I, 1, 6, 114, no. 19.

[94] L. I. Scipioni, *Ricerche*, here makes use of a reference to the teaching of Babai the Great, cf. 35–44, 110–158. Babai, with the Fathers, frequently uses the analogy of the fire that is in the glowing iron.

the concrete spiritual being. To solve the problems pending, Nestorius would have had to be an innovator in the metaphysical sphere. Now, while a man may be blamed for not having made full use of knowledge which has already been developed by someone else, he cannot be blamed for not being an innovator. In some sense, of course, Nestorius failed on the first count, as the theological position of current christology could have shown him that his metaphysical analyses did not fully succeed in doing justice to tradition. We mean the doctrine of the *communicatio idiomatum*, of which the famous Theotokos was the expression. It already contained a metaphysical intuition that the Logos was the final subject in Christ. Cyril's christology was governed by this intuition, even if he expressed it in misleading formulas.

We must therefore in the end fault Nestorius for not having taken the tradition of the *communicatio idiomatum* seriously enough and not having thought it through sufficiently. This is a 'theological' omission. But at the same time we must again remember that Nestorius was concerned with the Apollinarian and Arian misuse of the *communicatio idiomatum* which he saw even in Cyril's formulas. This tradition had to be justified all over again. But that was a speculative concern. Nestorius took part in clarifying the task in his own way. But here his 'philosophical' inadequacy emerged and prevented him from giving full value to the old tradition of the *communicatio idiomatum*. This tradition should have spurred him to reconsider his speculative presuppositions. But he was more inclined to measure the tradition by his own speculative framework than vice versa.[95] Nevertheless, he meant to keep its substance. If he misunderstood a part of this tradition it was only in good faith to save another part. His opponents isolated the negative part of his affirmations from his positive insights and paid no attention to his philosophical background.

Taken exactly as he is, the Nestorius of the *Liber Heraclidis* does not belong to the extremists, but may be numbered among the 'moderate Antiochenes'. Just as at the beginning of his episcopate, despite all his impetuosity, he wanted to play the mediator between two extremes, so, too, even after his deposition he rejected the extreme positions of certain supporters. His letter to the inhabitants of Constantinople is evidence of this.[96] As his formulas and his joyful welcome of the Tome of Leo show, he stood at the very gateway of Chalcedon. Only a little, but vital, assistance in speculative theology and the door could have opened for him. It was the tragedy of the man that this assistance was accorded to him neither in the years surrounding Ephesus nor later. So he remained for ever trapped in his old patterns of thought, whether they were of a philosophical or a theological nature. He could only have fully understood and accepted even the Chalcedonian Definition had he been able to trans-

---

[95] As is shown by his attitude to the *Theotokos*.   [96] Translated Nau, 374.

form these patterns. It is essentially the Cappadocian narrowness of the relationship between nature and *prosopon* that he was unable to transcend. For this reason no essential development may be observed in his writings between the Council of Ephesus and the *Liber Heraclidis*. Nestorius did not point the way into the future. Nevertheless, we shall find his conceptual and metaphysical starting-point in the sixth century, not only amongst the Nestorians, but also amongst the Chalcedonians and even the Monophysites.[97]

[97] For further sources of Antiochene christology see C. Baur, 'Drei unedierte Festpredigten aus der Zeit der nestorianischen Streitigkeiten', *Trad* 9, 1953, 101–26, and esp. M. Tetz, *Eine Antilogie des Eutherios von Tyana* (PTSt 1), Berlin 1964.

CHAPTER TWO

THE EVE OF CHALCEDON

DESPITE all the differences, we can see that the moderate Antiochenes, including Nestorius, and Cyril of Alexandria were moving towards one and the same goal, the expression of Christ as truly *one* (εἷς καὶ ὁ αὐτός) in the distinction of his Godhead and manhood. Andrew of Samosata shows us that the speculative attempts of the Antiochenes, too, could already open a way towards defining the unity and distinction in Christ in more technical terms, thereby solving the burning problem of their time. The concept of 'hypostasis' comes more and more into the foreground. We shall first refrain from evaluating this development and limit ourselves to a consideration of its course.

The word 'hypostasis' was finally to find a way into the Chalcedonian Definition and thus into church terminology generally through two Bishops of Constantinople. *Proclus* and *Flavian*, the Patriarchs of Constantinople, passed it on.[1] They deliberately sought a *via media* between the two opposing terminologies as embodied in Cyril and his Antiochene opponents.

1. PROCLUS

Proclus, consecrated Bishop of Cyzikus in the year 426 but not accepted there, and Patriarch from 434–46, belongs among the opponents of Nestorius in Constantinople. In his sermon of 25 March 431,[2] the most famous sermon on the Virgin Mary in ancient times, he composes a series of well-chosen formulations of belief in the incarnation. In the presence of the Patriarch Nestorius, he lets an acknowledgement of the *Theotokos* slip out at the close of the sermon almost of its own accord (107²⁵). For Proclus, Mary is the 'workplace of the union of the natures' (τὸ ἐργαστήριον τῆς ἑνότητος τῶν φύσεων, 103¹³). From her was born neither 'the pure Godhead' nor 'a mere man' (θεὸς οὐ γυμνός—ἄνθρωπος ψιλός, 103²³⁻⁴).

---

[1] The following after M. Richard, 'Hypostase', 258–65, and C. Martin, 'Un florilège grec d'homélie christologique des IVᵉ et Vᵉ siècles sur la nativité (Paris gr. 1491)', *Mus* 54, 1941, 17–57. See now F. J. Leroy, S.J., *L'homilétique de Proclus de Constantinople. Tradition manuscrite, inédits, études connexes* (ST 247), Città del Vaticano 1967, with the edition of homilies which can be assigned to Proclus anew (173–256); according to Leroy, the homily edited by D. Amand is also to be assigned to Proclus. Cf. D. Amand, 'Une homélie grecque inédite antinestorienne du cinquième siècle sur l'Incarnation du Seigneur', *RevBen* 58, 1948, 223–63; J.-M. Sauget, 'Une homélie de Proclus de Constantinople sur l'ascension de Notre-Seigneur en version syriaque', *Mus* 82, 1969, 5–33; M. Aubineau, 'Bilan d'une enquête sur les homélies de Proclus de C.', *RevEtGrec* 85, 1972, 572–96.

[2] ACO I, 1, 1, 103–7. The date given follows M. Richard, 'Hypostase', 256f. For Nestorius' gentle answer, see ACO I, 5, 37–9; F. Loofs, *Nestoriana*, 336–41. In the following we rely only on certainly genuine documents. See B. Altaner, *Patrology*, Freiburg–London 1960, 395f.

'We do not proclaim a divinized man, but we acknowledge the incarnate God' (104²³⁻⁴). 'One and the same is with the Virgin and of the Virgin' (106²¹). Christ and God the Logos are not distinct as 'one and the other' (ἄλλος . . . καὶ ἄλλος, 106²³). In him 'the natures have come together and yet the union remains unconfused' (συνῆλθον αἱ φύσεις καὶ ἀσύγχυτος ἔμεινεν ἡ ἕνωσις, 107³⁻⁴). This is already the language of the Fathers of Chalcedon.

Proclus deliberately chooses the mean between the sharp Alexandrian and the pointed Antiochene terminology. Unlike Theodoret, he also avoids speaking against the 'Deus passus' formula. It would be quite possible from his point of view, though the famous, much disputed Theopaschite formula which runs 'One of the Trinity has been crucified' may hardly be ascribed to him.[3] Thus the Chalcedonian mean is already achieved and anticipated in the dialectic of the different theological views. This is primarily evident in an important terminological decision which has already been mentioned. Had Nestorius paid close attention, he could already have found the solution to his difficulties in Proclus.

Earlier research into Proclus indicated only two passages where the term 'hypostasis' is used as opposed to 'physis', a short homily, the so called *Sermo de Dogmate Incarnationis*,[4] and the famous *Tomus ad Armenios* of the year 435.[5] In the homily we read this important sentence:

> There is only one Son, for the natures are not divided into two hypostases, but the awesome economy of salvation has united the two natures in one hypostasis.[6]

Meanwhile, however, as a result of the clarification of the extent of Proclus' homilies, the sources available have been shown to be much richer.[7] This has increased the degree of certainty that Proclus uses the term 'hypostasis'. After Apollinarius, Cyril (Theodore of Mopsuestia?), Isidore of Pelusium and Andrew of Samosata, his is now a new name which is significant for the christological use of hypostasis. Though the formula is common to them all, the inner differences in their theological positions

---

[3] So M. Richard, 'Proclus de Constantinople et le théopaschisme', *RHE* 38, 1942, 303–31.

[4] For the history of its tradition see C. Martin, op. cit., 17–30. Edition ibid., 40–57. Latin trans. from the Syriac, PG 65, 841–3.

[5] For the literature see V. Grumel, *Les Regestes des Actes du patriarcat de Constantinople*, vol. 1: Les Actes des patriarches, fasc. 1: Les Regestes de 381 à 715, Kadiköy 1932; a new edition has now been prepared by J. Darrouzès, Paris 1972, no. 78, p. 37.

[6] Proclus, *Sermo de dogmate incarn.*: frag. in *Doctrina Patrum*: ed. F. Diekamp, 49. Cf. C. Martin, 'Florilège grec.', 46. This text comes from Homily 23, which has been preserved in full, though the εἰς has been omitted in the mention of the 'Son'. However, Leroy, op. cit., 214, n. 185, points to another text from Vatic. 1633f. 50 r, where it can be read.

[7] F. J. Leroy, op. cit., 215, says of the formula 'one hypostasis in two natures' in the introduction to Hom. 30: '. . . le prédicateur revient plusieurs fois sur la formule ⟨une seule hypostase en deux natures⟩ (§4, 5, 9, 13; "une seule hypostase complète en deux natures complètes" 14), tandis que plusieurs autres passages insistent sur l'unité du Fils: "Le Fils (ou Christ), unique en deux natures" (§4 deux fois et 5; un seul Dieu Fils en deux natures, 8; un seul Fils en deux natures dans l'unité, 11, 14; un seul Christ en deux natures et un seul mediateur entre les deux côtés, 14; un seul Fils, notre Seigneur Jésus Christ qui est confessé et adoré en deux natures, 29).' See the translation of Homily 30, which has been handed down in Arabic, op. cit., 271–23.

should not, of course, be forgotten. But from whom did Proclus inherit the term? Cyril of Alexandria seems a likely source.[8] But if the duality of the natures is expressed along with the unity of hypostasis, Proclus just as clearly departs from Cyril's formula and makes a concession to the Antiochenes, by whom, of course, 'prosópon' was preferred to 'hypostasis'. Feeling the tension between the Johannine and Pauline formulas of the incarnation (John 1. 14; Phil. 2. 5-7), he tries to find a synthesis between both of them, as his *Tomus ad Armenios* shows us (cf. ACO IV, 2, 190$^{3-16}$).

When Proclus became Patriarch of Constantinople in 434, he soon had an exceptional opportunity of taking up a position on the question of the doctrine of the incarnation.[9] In 435, the Armenian priests Leontius and Abel, without the knowledge of the highest Armenian church leaders but ostensibly in their names, arrived with an inquiry about the teaching of Theodore of Mopsuestia.[10] A number of extracts from Theodore's works were brought. The answer was the much-cited *Tomus ad Armenios* of Proclus,[11] to which in turn were added a number of *Capitula* arising out of the collection made by the Armenians. At no stage in all this was the name of Theodore mentioned. Restraint and a tendency to mediate characterize the document throughout. Antiochenes and Alexandrians could each detect certain features of their own teaching, though the extreme formulas of both sides were avoided. The word 'hypostasis' had meanwhile become so accepted that it could appear even here:

> For knowing only one Son and having thus been taught in all piety, I acknowledge only one hypostasis of God the Word made flesh.[12]

Cyril's formula is here altered in a small, but probably not unintentional way: instead of μία ὑπόστασις τοῦ θεοῦ λόγου σεσαρκωμένη it reads μία ὑπόστασις τοῦ θεοῦ λόγου σαρκωθέντος. True, Cyril also knew the other form which referred the word 'incarnate' to the Logos. But it had remained very rare. We may see in Proclus' formula a clarification in the

---

[8] M. Richard, 'Hypostase', 260, would exclude Theodore of Mopsuestia, whom he supposes to have the formula, because of the attitude displayed by Proclus in the dispute about him at the time of the Armenian affair in 435. We might also conclude that Proclus would be more inclined to listen to Cyril than to Theodore from his conduct in the Nestorius and Theotokos questions. M. Richard tries to establish that he could already refer to Cyril by determining the date of the *Sermo de dogmate incarnationis*. He conjectures 25 December 430 for the *Sermo de Nativitate* and 28 February or 1 March 431 for the *Sermo de dogmate incarnationis*.

[9] On the prehistory and history of the *Tomus ad Armenios*: literature in V. Grumel, *Regestes*, 37, ed. Darrouzès, 63f.; R. Devreesse, *Théodore de Mopsueste*, 125–52; M. Richard, 'Proclus de Constantinople et le théopaschisme', *RHE* 38, 1942, 303–31; id., 'Acace de Mélitène, Proclus de Constantinople et la Grande Arménie', *Mémorial L. Petit*, Bucharest 1948, 393–412, with Latin translation of the correspondence between Acacius of Melitene and Sahak, the Patriarch of the Armenians (394–400); V. Inglisian, 'Die Beziehungen des Patriarchen Proklos von Konstantinopel und des Bischofs Akakios von Melitene zu Armenien', *OChr* 41, 1957, 35–50.

[10] ACO IV, 2, XXVII–XXVIII. Text of this inquiry in a Greek translation from the Syriac by E. Schwartz.

[11] ACO IV, 2, 187–95: PG 65, 856–73.

[12] ACO IV, 2, 191^{20}: PG 65, 864D: Ἐγὼ γὰρ ἕνα εἰδώς τε καὶ διδαχθεὶς εὐσεβῶς υἱόν, μίαν ὁμολογῶ τὴν τοῦ σαρκωθέντος θεοῦ λόγου ὑπόστασιν.

meaning of 'hypostatic' or 'personal', whereas Cyril's own formula, used most often, understood hypostasis more in the sense of substance. Thus hypostasis has its Chalcedonian sense. The Tome of Proclus, which, as the signature itself testifies,[13] had been written in 435, was to play yet a further role three years later when the Patriarch sent on his Tome with the *Capitula* to the Antiochenes and required their subscription, together with the rejection of the extracts from Theodore.[14] The Orientals naturally recognized the derivation of the anonymous text immediately and offered resistance to the demands of the Patriarch of Constantinople. The Tome itself they accepted without opposition. Even though it still contained no express acknowledgement of a definite, circumscribed christological formula, it had nevertheless already laid a good foundation for the final acceptance of one by the Antiochenes.

2. THE TRIAL OF EUTYCHES AND THE FORMULA OF FLAVIAN OF CONSTANTINOPLE[15]

Flavian, the successor of the Patriarch Proclus, who died in 446, saw at the beginning of his term of office a resurgence of the dogmatic struggles to which he himself was to fall victim. The opposing parties were *Eutyches*, the monophysitically inclined Archimandrite, and *Theodoret of Cyrus*. We have the basic dogmatic elements of this controversy in the latter's *Eranistes*, while in his letters we can trace the seriousness of the position in the Eastern church. The powerful *Dioscorus*, with all his supporters from Egypt to Constantinople, entered the dispute, in which the emperor *Theodosius* II showed an uncertain attitude. What was the significance of a couple of concepts, in this tremendous battle which was soon to shake the whole of Christendom? On 8 November, 448, the so-called σύνοδος ἐνδημοῦσα, i.e. the synod of bishops who happened to be in the capital, met at Constantinople. Bishop *Eusebius of Dorylaeum* rose and instituted a *libellus* against the Archimandrite Eutyches, the contents of which were no less than a charge of heresy. Canonical proceedings were demanded. The trial, so significant for church history, in fact took place in seven sessions, from 12–22 November. We have sufficient details of the course of the proceedings.[16] Only in the last session did the accused himself appear in court. In the first session, after the charge made by Eusebius, Cyril's second letter to Nestorius and the *Formulary of Reunion* of 433 were read out, thus bringing before the assembly the formula ἕνωσις καθ᾽

13 ACO IV, 2, 205.   14 R. Devreesse, *Théodore de Mops.*, 143–52.
15 Cf. E. Schwartz, 'Der Prozess des Eutyches', *SBMünchAk*, 1929, H. 5, 1–93. M. Richard, 'Hypostase', 264–5; H. Bacht, 'Die Rolle des orientalischen Mönchtums in den kirchenpolitischen Auseinandersetzungen um Chalkedon (431–519)', *Chalkedon* II, 197–231; T. Šagi-Bunić, '*Deus perfectus et homo perfectus*' a *Concilio Ephesino* (a. 431) ad *Chalcedonense* (a. 451), Freiburg 1965, 169–80 (Eutyches); 180–7 (Flavian).
16 ACO II, 1, 1, 100–45.

ὑπόστασιν.[17] After a few words by Eusebius, in which he represented any deviation from these norms as an attack upon the faith,[18] Flavian rose and read a confession of faith which contained an important formula:

> We acknowledge that Christ is from two natures after the incarnation, in one hypostasis and one person confessing one Christ, one Son, one Lord.[19]

With this confession Flavian stands, probably deliberately, on a central line between Alexandrian and Antiochene christology. There are two important points.

(a) First of all there is the concept *physis*. With the ἐκ δύο φύσεων, so important for what is to follow, there reappears for the first time an expression which Flavian seems to derive immediately from Cyril's letter *Laetentur coeli*: '*Unus enim Dominus Jesus Christus, quamvis non ignoretur differentia naturarum, ex quibus ineffabilem unionem dicimus factam.*'[20] Still intended rightly by both Flavian and Cyril, it became the slogan of the Monophysites. Flavian's formula was self-explanatory, as 'after the incarnation' was added to the words '*from* two natures'. It therefore meant the same as '*in* two natures'. In the discussion, then, the opponents of Eutyches also fluctuate between two, albeit little-used, formulas, and thus adopt the same line.[21] So both acknowledge two natures. The Synod of Flavian thus reaches the final verdict of the Patrician Florentius: 'Whoever does not say "from two natures" and "two natures" does not believe rightly.'[22] Eutyches, however, only accepted the formula 'from two natures' under pressure[23] and gave it a twist which prevented his opponents from using the expression and set it up as a Monophysite catchword: 'I acknowledge that the Lord was "from two natures" before the union, but after the union I acknowledge only "one nature".'[24] By distinguishing the two disputed expressions *secundum prius et posterius* he introduced into the

---

[17] ACO II, 1, 1, 104–11.   [18] Ibid., 113, no. 270.

[19] Ibid., 114⁸⁻¹⁰: καὶ γὰρ ἐκ δύο φύσεων ὁμολογοῦμεν τὸν Χριστὸν εἶναι μετὰ τὴν ἐνανθρώπησιν, ἐν μιᾷ ὑποστάσει καὶ ἑνὶ προσώπῳ ἕνα Χριστόν, ἕνα υἱόν, ἕνα κύριον ὁμολογοῦντες. Cf. Flavian's formula to the emperor, ACO, ibid., 35, where the *mia physis* formula is also acknowledged.

[20] Cf. ACO II, 1, 1, p. 110, 5–7 (no. 246): εἷς γὰρ κύριος Ἰησοῦς Χριστός, κἄν ἡ τῶν φύσεων μὴ ἀγνοῆται διαφορά, ἐξ ὧν τὴν ἀπόρρητον ἕνωσιν πεπρᾶχθαι φαμέν. On this see T. Šagi-Bunić, O.F.M.Cap., '*Deus perfectus et homo perfectus' a concilio Ephesino (a. 431) ad Chalcedonense (a. 451)*, Freiburg 1965, 184, n. 247. Only in the second line reference should be made to *Ep. 45 ad Succens*. 1: ACO I, 1, 6, 153, 21; PG 232D. But now see the text of the monk Marcian (above, p. 335, n. 27), where we already have 'a single Son from two natures', in defence against an Apollinarian interpretation.

[21] ACO II, 1, 1, 117²², 118², 120⁹⁻¹¹, 121⁹. For the history of the two formulas see the good collection in A. Schmid, *Christologie Isidors*, 56–64. After Cyril's prelude, they occur alongside each other for the first time in 448 and are eventually used in contrast. So A. Schmid rightly (56–8) against W. M. Peitz S.J., *Liber Diurnus, Fides Romana I. Das vorephesinische Symbol der Papstkanzlei*, Rome 1939, 40–1, 73–98; E. Weigl, *Christol. v. Tode d. Ath.*, 69, 79, n. 1, who would make Gregory of Nyssa the creator and Proclus the advocate of ἐν δύο φύσεσιν. Schmid further points out (60–4) that Isidore himself did not use the two formulas. True, they occur in four passages of his letters (*Ep.* 23, 303, 323, 405: PG 78, 197, 357–60, 369, 409), but these may be Monophysite and Diphysite forgeries.

[22] ACO II, 1, 1, 145⁵⁻⁶.   [23] Ibid., 140²²⁻²⁴.

[24] Ibid., 143¹⁰⁻¹¹: ὁμολογῶ ἐκ δύο φύσεων γεγενῆσθαι τὸν Κύριον ἡμῶν πρὸ τῆς ἑνώσεως, μετὰ δὲ τὴν ἕνωσιν μίαν φύσιν ὁμολογῶ.

phrase 'from two natures' the temporal and genetic connotation which eventually debarred the Diphysites from further use of the formula. Although *Dioscorus* dissociated himself from the teaching of Eutyches, he still used at Chalcedon the same distinction as the Archimandrite: 'I accept the "from two (natures)", but the "two (natures)" I do not accept.'[25]

(b) So Flavian was ill-advised with his coinage 'from two natures' and had unwittingly helped to provide the Eutychians with a useful propaganda slogan. He had greater success, on the other hand, with his reference to the *'one* hypostasis and the *one* prosopon' in Christ. He had inherited this formula from Proclus and he now became its decisive mediator to the Council of Chalcedon. Pope *Leo the Great* was also initiated into the proceedings and was himself able to inspect the Acts of the trial of Eutyches, as Flavian sent them to Rome.[26] Flavian's first formula recurs in the covering letter and Eutyches is represented as denying it.[27]

If we now look at the general position of christological formulas at this all-important Synod of Constantinople in 448, we see that the acknowledgement of the 'two natures' found unqualified approbation, while the phrase 'one hypostasis' was still only accepted with considerable restraint. Only Basil of Seleucia had spoken of a 'hypostatic union'. Also associated with him was a presbyter, John, and the accuser of Eutyches, Eusebius of Dorylaeum.[28] This caution was understandable, as the new christological language had not yet become the common usage of the Greek bishops, and one thing above all was still missing, the distinction between hypostasis and physis. Chalcedon is to make a considerable alteration in the language of Flavian's formula of 448, but it will still take 'the one hypostasis and the one prosopon' into the church's theological terminology for ever.

Before this, however, the year 449 brought another bitter set-back. The Second Synod of Ephesus (449) naturally took over the 'one hypostasis' language, but derived its total christological formula exclusively from the language of Cyril's anathemas. The two bishops Basil of Seleucia and Seleucus of Amasea now revoked the acknowledgement of the natures which they had professed in 448.[29] The tactical proceedings of Dios-

---

25 Ibid., 120[14]: τὸ ἐκ δύο δέχομαι· τὸ δύο οὐ δέχομαι.

26 ACO II, 1, 1, 36–7.

27 Ibid., 37[10–11]: Eutyches says: '... τὸν Χριστὸν μὴ δεῖν ὁμολογεῖσθαι ἐκ δύο φύσεων μετὰ τὴν ἐνανθρώπησιν ἐν μιᾷ ὑποστάσει καὶ ἐν ἑνὶ προσώπῳ παρ' ἡμῶν γνωριζόμενον. The *unio* καθ' ὑπόστασιν is mentioned here (37[12–13]).

28 ACO II, 1, 1, 124[29], 140[18–19].

29 ACO II, 1, 1, 179[14–21], 181[17–12]. But as early as the first session of Chalcedon, 8 October 451, Basil once again acknowledged the old formula and asserted that he had been put under pressure at Ephesus (ACO, ibid., 93[17–39]). For the role and significance of Basil of Seleucia in the period before and after Chalcedon, cf. B. Marx, 'Der homiletische Nachlass des Basileios von Seleukeia', OCP 7, 1941, 329–69; T. Šagi-Bunić, op. cit. (above, p. 524), 188–204, is especially important, with critical comments on Marx, op. cit., 195; M. van Parys, 'L'évolution de la doctrine christologique de Basile de Seleucie', Irénikon, 493–514. See below, p. 548. M. Aubineau gives a critical edition of

corus had won a victory which was, however, only of short duration. The confusion which he had caused could only be reduced to order by a statement from the whole church and by the combined efforts of both church and state. The hour had come when the decisive word about Christ had to be spoken by the church.

3. LEO THE GREAT AND HIS 'TOMUS AD FLAVIANUM'

In the Nestorius affair Leo I (440–61) appeared on the scene only fleetingly, when as archdeacon he asked the abbot Cassian for his expert opinion in the case. Now, however, the time has come for him to make a decisive intervention in the christological struggle himself. There now appears the most important christological document of its kind which the Latin church produced. The impulse for it came from the East.

Eutyches was by no means inclined to come to terms with the verdict of the Home Synod of 448.[30] Instead, he launched a systematic campaign to avenge himself on his opponents and lead the Alexandrian cause to victory. He entered a formal protest against the judgement and appealed 'to the holy council of the Bishops of Rome, Alexandria, Jerusalem and Thessalonica' (ACO II, 1, 1, 175, no. 818). He sent letters all over the world, of which that to Pope Leo is still extant.[31] The letter seeks to arouse the sympathy of the Bishop of Rome. Despite his extreme age and his serious illness Eutyches had been compelled to appear before the tribunal. The *libellus fidei* which he had wished to present had not been incorporated in the acts. Required to acknowledge the 'two natures' in Christ, he had

Basil's *Homily on the Holy Pascha* and an introduction to his literary work in *Homélies Pascales* (SC 187), 167–277. We shall be returning to Basil in the second volume of the present work. For the moment, however, it may be remarked that both Basil and the Patriarch Flavian could accept the orthodoxy of the *mia physis* formula. For Flavian, see his *professio fidei* presented to the Emperor: ACO II, 1, 1, 35–6.

[30] For the following see H. Bacht, *Chalkedon* II, 197–231.

[31] We have it in two versions of a Latin translation: ACO II, 4, 143, no. 108 and II, 2, 1, 33f. Eutyches had also written to Peter Chrysologus of Ravenna; the answer is preserved in ACO II, 1, 2, 45–6 and II, 3, 1, 6. For comments see P. Batiffol, *Le Siège Apostolique*, Paris 1924, 445–6. We shall select just a few terminological peculiarities from the christology of the Bishop of Ravenna, e.g. the use of 'persona'. Christ is the new Adam who takes the 'persona' of the old Adam: 'Hic est Adam, qui suam tunc in illo cum fingeret imaginem collocavit. Hinc est quod eius et personam suscipi t et nomen recepit ne sibi quod ad suam imaginem fecerat deperiret' (PL 52, 520B); cf. F. Loofs, *Nestoriana*, 225²⁰ᶠ· 'Personam suscipere' means the taking of human nature. We should not look for Nestorianism here. Chrysologus is far more in danger of explaining the unity in Christ by way of a confusion: 'Deus unus constat in Christo: quia quidquid est et deitate et humanitate Deus unus est. Desiit in Christo substantiarum diversitas, ubi caro coepit esse quod spiritus, quod homo Deus, quod nostri corporis et deitatis una maiestas' (Serm. 59: PL 52, 363C–364A). We could assume that *substantia* here means the same as the Greek *hypostasis* in its Chalcedonian significance. Chrysologus would then be speaking of the unity of person or hypostasis in Christ. But this is not the thought of the Bishop. He maintains that in Christ the properties of the human nature are changed into Godhead. This does not imply a dissolution of the human nature, as his *Sermons on the Creed* (57–62), discussing the 'Ascendit ad coelos' and 'Sedet ad dexteram Patris', show. For the christology of Chrysologus, see Robert H. McGlynn, *The Incarnation in the Sermons of Saint Peter Chrysologus*, Mundelein, Illinois 1956. This dissertation gives the most important texts, but does not go into the question of their authenticity. Cf. Dom A. Olivar, *Sacris Eruditi* 6, 1954, 327–42.

had to refuse to add anything to the decisions of Nicaea and Ephesus. Instead he had asked that the Bishop of Rome be allowed to give his decision on the question—though Flavian in his letter to Leo does not allow this to be the case (ACO II, 2, 1, 24). Far from doing this, however, his accusers read out a condemnation which had already been prepared for some time. Even his life had been in danger. He had escaped safely only through Leo's intercession and the help of the soldiers which he had brought along with him as a precaution. In closing, Eutyches supplicates the Pope for his authentic decision and for protection from the calumny of his opponents.

Together with this letter, Eutyches sent copies of the charges made to the Home Synod by Eusebius of Dorylaeum, his own *libellus fidei*, which had been rejected by Flavian, and an anthology of passages from the Fathers which also included the well-known Apollinarian forgeries with the *mia physis* formula (cf. ACO II, 2, 1, 34–42, nos. 7–12). Leo I at first adopted a waiting attitude until he had received the necessary information about the case (*Ep.* 24 *ad Theodosium*: ACO II, 4, 3–4). Eutyches was meanwhile spreading vigorous propaganda in the East. Posters were put up to interest the people in his case. Above all, however, he worked on the emperor Theodosius through his protectors at court, the chief of whom was Chrysaphius. Theodosius interceded for the Archimandrite in a letter to Leo, accusing the opposing party of Nestorianism. Leo answered this in his *Ep.* 24, mentioned above. At the instigation of the Archimandrite, the emperor arranged an official investigation of the acts and the verdict of the Home Synod of 448. Eventually he even condescended to rehabilitate the monk and call a general council to clarify the disputed questions. The decree of 30 March 449, for the summoning of the council, and the rescripts to the Patriarch Dioscorus of Alexandria and the Archimandrite Barsumas in Syria which followed, show quite clearly that the purpose of the new synod was already established—the utter defeat of Nestorianism, the rehabilitation of Eutyches, and the condemnation of the Patriarch Flavian and his supporters (ACO II, 1, 1, 68, no. 24; 71, nos. 47, 48). The presidency of the new synod was entrusted not to the bishop of the capital but to his rival, Dioscorus of Alexandria. Theodoret, as the member of the opposition most to be feared, was prohibited from taking part in the synod.

While the emperor, the Patriarch of Alexandria and the powerful party of monks were making these preparations for the new synod to suit themselves, Flavian found help only from Leo I. His fears and his desires can be seen in his second letter to Rome (ACO II, 1, 1, 39–40). Leo became alarmed. On 13 June 449 a papal legation left for Constantinople. It consisted of Bishop Julius of Puteoli, the presbyter Renatus (who died on the way) and Hilary the deacon, later to become Pope. In a number of letters Leo sought to stress that no synodal ruling was necessary in the Eutyches dispute. But he had no success. On 8 August 449 the synod assembled at Ephesus. Apart from about 140 bishops who had appeared, the scene was dominated by groups of monks who had been brought by Eutyches from Constantinople and by Barsumas from Syria. Dioscorus had brought along an escort of monks and sturdy *parabalani*[32] as well as his twenty suffragans. The papal envoys had nothing but the dogmatic letter of Leo, the so-called *Tomus ad Flavianum*, which he had entrusted to them.[33] It was his purpose that this letter should be read at the new synod to clarify the dogmatic disputes. But in the first session Dioscorus immediately began proceedings about Eutyches. The latter was allowed to read out his writing to the Synod, teeming, as it was, with misrepresentations. The repeated demand of the Roman delegates that Leo's letter should be heard before the reading of the acts of the earlier proceedings did not, on the other hand, meet with any success. Eutyches managed to thwart it by casting doubt on the impartiality of the legates. He pointed out that they had already been entertained by his opponent, Flavian. This proved effective.

The monk was now declared orthodox by 113 of the Fathers present at the council and rehabilitated as priest and Archimandrite. On the other hand, Flavian and Eusebius of Dorylaeum were deprived of their office. They were charged with having violated the ruling made at Ephesus (431) that no addition was to be made to the Creed of Nicaea (Actio VI of 22 July 431: ACO I, 1, 7, 105f.). The Roman deacon Hilary tried in vain to protest. Knowing no Greek, he shouted his Latin κοντραδίκιτουρ (*contradicitur*) at the excited assembly. To intimidate the antagonistic oriental bishops, Dioscorus gave a sign for soldiers, monks and *parabalani* to burst in. The synod became a scene of wild uproar, so that Leo was able later to coin the famous phrase *in illo Ephesino non iudicio sed latrocinio* (so in *Ep. 95 ad Pulcheriam Aug.* of 20 July 451: ACO II, 4, 51).

Dioscorus' victory was complete when in a further session (of 22 August; the exact number is not known) Ibas of Edessa, Theodoret of Cyrus and Domnus of Antioch had been deposed and exiled.[34] The Antiochenes were excluded and the Formulary of Reunion of 433 had lost its significance. Juvenal, bishop of Jerusalem, was the first to cast his vote for the orthodoxy of Eutyches. So the way seemed open for 'Monophysitism' in the East.

[32] These *parabalani* were an organized band of sick attendants who were at the Archbishop's disposal in Alexandria. Cf. H. Bacht, *Chalkedon* II, 227, n. 40.
[33] We use here the edition of the *Tome* by C. Silva-Tarouca, TD, ser. th. 9, Rome 1932, and would draw attention to the *Introductio*. There is an English translation of the Tome in E. R. Hardy, *Christology of the Later Fathers* (Library of Christian Classics III), London–Philadelphia 1954, 359–70 (W. Bright).
[34] Cf. J. Flemming, *Akten der Ephesinischen Synode vom Jahre 449* (Syriac), AbhGöttGW NS 15, H. 1, 1917.

Meanwhile, from Rome, Leo I was doing all he could to reverse the decisions of the 'Robber Synod'. Immediately after the session of the synod on 22 August the deacon Hilary returned in haste to Rome. Flavian was able to entrust to him a further letter of appeal in which he called for Leo's help in the desperate situation (ACO II, 2, 1, 77–9). He asked the Pope to begin widespread propaganda in reply, with the church in this dangerous position. The Emperor, the clergy and the monks of the Eastern capital were to be won over by letters (ACO II, 2, 1, 79). Leo acceded to this request. On 13 October 449, a number of letters were sent to the East in the name of the Roman synod of 29 September–13 October, to Pulcheria, to her imperial brother, to the clergy and people of Constantinople and to four important Archimandrites. Pulcheria, the clergy and people, and two of the Archimandrites replied at the beginning of March 450. The Emperor, however, remained unswervingly on the side of Dioscorus. In November 449, he had appointed as successor to the deposed (and already deceased?) Patriarch Flavian the Alexandrian *apocrisiarius* Anatolius. At first the latter stood alongside Dioscorus, but he soon became concerned for the pre-eminence of his own see.[35]

On 16 July 450, Leo sent a Roman delegation to the East to give events a new turn by direct negotiations. To this delegation Leo again gave his *Tomus ad Flavianum*, this time with an anthology of extracts from the Fathers and his *Epp.* 69–71. The expected change came, however, not through the efforts of the delegation but with the sudden death of the emperor Theodosius (28 July 450) and the accession of the empress Pulcheria. The delegation was immediately able to reap the fruits of the new situation, as the Tome of Leo was now received with great reverence and carefully translated into Greek along with the extracts from the Fathers. In this form it was promulgated at a synod of Constantinople in October 450. One of the first measures of the new Empress was the deposition of Eutyches' protector, the intriguer Chrysaphius. With this the fate of Eutyches and of the synod of 449 was sealed. On 25 August, Pulcheria took as her consort and co-regent a vigorous and capable officer, the Thracian Marcian. Even in the notice of his election to Leo, the new Emperor expressed his readiness to join with the Pope in restoring the shattered peace of the church by a new General Council (*inter Ep. Leon.*, *Ep.* 73). In Marcian, who both spoke and thought in Latin, and in Pulcheria, Leo found the help necessary for ordering the church of the empire and

---

[35] See H. Chadwick, 'The Exile and Death of Flavian of Constantinople: a Prologue to the Council of Chalcedon', *JTS*, NS 6, 1955, 17–34. Chadwick is inclined to date the death of Flavian in February 450, and not in August 449. Anatolius would then have been nominated during the lifetime of Flavian. Chadwick is further of the opinion that in that case Anatolius could have had an interest in the removal of his predecessor, as Leo (according to *Ep.* 50 of 13 October 449, Silva-Tarouca TD ser. th. 15, 39) would withhold his approval of any bishop appointed in Flavian's lifetime. So it would be quite possible that Anatolius had some hand in Flavian's death on his way to exile.

clarifying christological belief. Leo's own contribution was expressed in his *Tomus ad Flavianum*. It is now our task to describe the christological content of this writing.[36]

In the *Tomus ad Flavianum* we have virtually a synthesis of what Leo had to say on the christological question before the Council of Chalcedon. This is also clear from the text of the *Tomus* itself. Even if it could be demonstrated that as Papal Secretary Prosper of Aquitaine played a large part in the redaction of the Tome,[37] as redactor he worked directly with texts taken from Leo's own addresses.[38] We shall now attempt to give a short sketch of the christological thought of the Tome of Leo and of the pre-Chalcedonian sermons and letters.[39] We shall then examine the way in which this thought is expressed and the contribution made by Leo to the development of the formulas of the church.

(a) Leo's christological thought in the pre-Chalcedonian period

It will be useful to give a brief survey of the construction of the Tome (following the verse numeration made by C. Silva-Tarouca):

vv. 1–15: Introduction (Eutyches' disregard of scripture and creed in which he shows himself to be *multum inprudens et nimis inperitus*).

vv. 16–53: 1. The origin of the two natures in Christ shown in creed and scripture.

vv. 54–93: 2. The co-existence of the two natures of Christ in the unity of person.

vv. 94–120: 3. The mode of operation of the two natures.

vv. 121–76: 4. The *communicatio idiomatum*.

vv. 177–205: Conclusion (the *inprudentia hominis inperiti*, Eutyches, who was insufficiently censured at the synod of 448).

(1) It is thus remarkable how Leo builds his christology on the Apostles' creed and bases it on the sentence: *(Credo) in Deum Patrem omnipotentem— et in Christum Iesum filium eius unicum dominum nostrum qui natus est de Spiritu sancto et Maria virgine*. By these three sentences the machinations of almost all heretics are destroyed (*omnium fere haereticorum machinae destruuntur*; v. 15). One and the same, who is everlastingly born of the everlasting Father, was also born of the Holy Spirit and the Virgin Mary

---

[36] For Leo's christology see: P. Kuhn, *Die Christologie Leos des Grossen in systematischer Darstellung*, Würzburg 1894; M. J. Nicolas, O.P., 'La doctrine christologique de saint Léon le Grand', *RevThom* 51, 1951, 609–70; P. Galtier, 'Saint Cyrille d'Alexandrie et saint Léon le Grand à Chalcédoine', *Chalkedon* I, 345–87.

[37] J. Gaidioz, 'Saint Prosper d'Aquitaine et le Tome à Flavien', *RevSR* 23, 1949, 270–301.

[38] The edition by C. Silva-Tarouca (in TD, ser. th. 9), which divides Leo's text into verses, puts the sources of the Tome in bold type. Verses 54–176, which represent the *corpus doctrinale* of the Tome, in particular make wide use of Leo's sermons, 21–4: *De Nativitate*, 51, 54. According to M. J. Nicolas, *RevThom* 51, 1951, 610, the *Libellus emendationis* of Leporius is 'comme une première ébauche du Tome à Flavien'.

[39] Leo's pre-Chalcedonian letters have been made conveniently available in C. Silva-Tarouca's edition, *S. Leonis Magni epistulae contra Eutychis Haeresim, Pars prima: Epistulae quae Chalcedonensi Concilio praemittuntur* (AA, 449–51), Pont. Univ. Gregoriana, TD ser. th. 15, Romae 1934. The *Sermones* of Leo are appearing in four volumes in SC; Vols. 1–3 have so far been published (nos. 22, 49 and 74 in the series); in addition there is A. Chavasse, *Sancti Leonis Magni Romani Pontificis Tractatus Septem et Nonaginta* (CCL cxxxviii et cxxxxviii A), Turnholti 1973. We shall pay special attention to the *Sermones* in the second volume of the present work.

(*Idem vero sempiterni genitoris unigenitus sempiternus natus est de Spiritu Sancto et Maria virgine*; v. 21). God had himself to be born in human nature so as to destroy death, the work of the devil. Christ's human nature could not be overcome by sin and death, as it had been raised above sin by virtue of his birth from the Virgin through the Spirit (vv. 25–9)—a clear echo of the Augustinian doctrine of original sin. Even if Eutyches was incapable of understanding the creed, he should at least have learnt from Scripture (Matt. 1. 1; Rom. 1. 1–3; Gen. 22. 18; Gal. 3. 16; Matt. 1. 23; Isa. 9. 6; Luke 1. 35) that Christ's human birth, while being truly miraculous, was none the less really human (vv. 30–53: *fecunditatem virgini sanctus Spiritus dedit, veritas autem corporis sumpta de corpore est*, vv. 49, 50).

(2) The first result of the demonstration of the reality of the twofold birth of Christ is the fundamental sentence:

> *Salva igitur proprietate utriusque naturae,*
> *Et in unam coeunte personam,*
> *Suscepta est a maiestate humilitas, a virtute infirmitas,*
> *Ab aeternitate mortalitas* (vv. 54–6).

Each of the two natures is preserved in its characteristics. The true God was born in the complete and perfect human nature (v. 61), *totus in suis, totus in nostris* (v. 62). This section (vv. 54–93) is thus concerned with the co-existence of the two natures in the one Christ. Here Leo is in his element. This theology of the two natures might almost have been made for his predilection for antitheses and rhythmic parallelism. In one clause he speaks of the divine properties, in the other of the human nature. The rhythm of his language swings to and fro like a pendulum, from the divine side to the human side, from the transcendence of God to the immanence of our earthly history. The latter should be noted. Despite all his predilection for a static treatment of the nature of Christ, corresponding to the doctrine of two natures, Leo again and again shows his love for a salvation–historical approach. His christology serves as a support for a soteriology. But alongside Irenaeus and Athanasius he is one of the most significant representatives of the so-called 'mystic doctrine of redemption', i.e. that doctrine which sees the foundation of redemption already laid in the *being* of Christ, not merely in his *acts*. The being of Christ already represents redeemed man (cf. vv. 62–84). With more and more new phrases Leo illustrates the matter in accordance with a phrase formulated by Gregory of Nazianzus (*Ep.* 101 *ad Cledon.*), but already current from the time of Irenaeus, Tertullian and Origen: *Quod non est assumptum, non est sanatum.* The doctrine of two natures becomes a doctrine of the divinization of man, even though Leo is here far more restrained than, say, Athanasius:

> *Et ad resolvendum condicionis nostrae debitum*
> *Natura inviolabilis naturae est unita passibili;*

Ut quod nostris remediis congruebat
unus atque idem mediator Dei et hominum homo Christus Iesus
et mori posset ex uno et mori non posset ex altero (vv. 57–60).

The Augustinian predilection for the *mediator Dei et hominum* joins in one a static doctrine of two natures with a dynamic soteriology.[40] Leo's picture of Christ here displays considerable tension. But this is the very way in which he means to refute Eutyches. For Eutyches—at least as Leo understands him—destroys the *mysterium Christi* by denying the reality of the human nature.[41] Such a denial does away with the God-man tension, which must be maintained:

Qui enim verus est Deus, idem verus est homo . . .
sicut enim Deus non mutatur miseratione,
ita homo non consumitur dignitate (vv. 91–93).

One and the same is God and man, twofold in nature but one in person. This unity of person is the point on which the pendulum of Leo's diphysite approach swings. This 'person' in Christ is not a third element which only results from the union of the two natures, even if the sentences cited above (vv. 54 and 55) appear to suggest this:

Salva igitur proprietate utriusque naturae
et in unam coeunte personam.

For the analysis of the Apostles' creed in the Tome shows that he who becomes man is the Son of the Father who has already existed from eternity and is thus pre-existent as a person. A new person does not come into being when the human nature is taken, nor does this result in two persons. Leo stresses this again and again in his letters and sermons when he is speaking against Nestorius (whose name does not occur in the Tome).

The struggle against the two christological extremes of Nestorianism and Eutychianism is a supplement to Leo's positive christology. He is fond of contrasting Nestorius and Eutyches as diametrical opposites:

And greatly as Nestorius fell away from the truth, in asserting that Christ was only born man of his mother, this man also departs no less far from the catholic path who does not believe that our substance was brought forth from the same Virgin: wishing it of course to be understood as belonging to his Godhead only; so that that which took the form of a

---

[40] Augustinian, too, in Leo is the idea that Godhead and soul unite in Christ more easily than body and soul in a human being. Cf. Aug., *Ep.* 137 *ad Volusianum*, no. 11: PL 33, 520; Leo M., *Ep.* 35 *ad Julian. Choens.*, TD, ser. th. 15, 15[51-7]. Behind this there stands the idea, influenced by neo-Platonism, that the union in Christ takes place *mediante anima*. Cf. also the *libellus emendationis* of Leporius and his interpretation of the death of Christ (ed. Glorieux, 22–3) which is cited in Leo's *Exemplaria testimoniorum* under the name of Augustine (together with *Ep.* 165 sent to the emperor Leo: PL 54, 1182).

[41] For Eutyches' christology see: R. Draguet, 'La christologie d'Eutychès d'après les Actes du synode de Flavien (448)', *Byz* 6, 1931, 441–57; also T. Camelot, 'De Nestorius à Eutychès', *Chalkedon* I, 213–42. R. Draguet would acquit Eutyches of the charge of heresy. T. Camelot, however, stresses the one-sidedness of Eutyches' christology.

slave, and was like us and of the same form, was a kind of image, not the reality of our nature.[42]

This interpretation of the heresies is in accordance with Leo's systematizing disposition and his predilection for antithetical formulas. We have already shown that in the case of Nestorius the Pope's view did not do justice to the historical reality. Just as he makes Nestorius the adoptionist *par excellence*, equally decisively he stamps Eutyches a docetist and a Manichaean. In this case, however, he does not want to judge lightly. At first he feels himself insufficiently informed and waits for further information about the Archimandrite before passing judgement.[43] But in the Acts of the Home Synod of 448 he reads, to his astonishment, a sentence of Eutyches which appears to him impossible:

> *Confiteor ex duabus naturis fuisse Dominum nostrum ante adunationem, post vero adunationem unam naturam confiteor* (vv. 178f. of the Tome).

The Pope is scandalized that Flavian did not firmly reject this statement. How surprised he would have been, had he known that both Flavian himself and Cyril held this ἐκ δύο φύσεων, though in a rather more carefully formulated form (see above). In any case, Leo is unable to think himself into Cyril's understanding of the unity in Christ, which would avoid any danger of a division of Christ and so prefers to say ἐκ δύο φύσεων εἰς instead of the formula ἐν δύο φύσεσιν. As understood by Cyril and Flavian, however, this formula is not meant to imply a temporal succession, i.e. first of all a separate and independent existence of the two natures by themselves and then their dissolution in a unity. The formula ἐκ δύο φύσεων εἰς on the one hand acknowledges the reality of the two natures of Christ and on the other hand lays decisive stress on the state of oneness. Christ is *ex duabus (naturis) unus*.[44] If we are to understand how Eutyches could arrive at his obviously clumsy formula, we must take into account the whole of Cyril's christology and his idea of physis and of the act of the incarnation. Presented in the Latin language, viewed in the light of the Latin understanding of *natura*, the formula of Eutyches must in any case lead to an absurd heresy which Leo could rightly repudiate. It was impossible for him to enter into the spirit and the final trend of the christology of Cyril and of the Alexandrians by the exchange of purely official documents. This was only to be corrected in the period after Chalcedon. We shall have to concede that Leo the Great had a tendency to simplify and at the same time to exaggerate Nestorianism and Euty-

[42] Leo M., *Ep.* 30 *ad Pulcheriam Aug.*: TD, ser. th. 15, 6; cf. also *Ep.* 35 *ad Julian. Choens.*: TD, ibid., 14; *Ep.* 84 *ad Pulcheriam Aug.*: TD, ibid., 68f.; *Ep.* 90 *ad Marcianum*, TD, ibid., 77.

[43] Cf. Leo M., *Ep.* 23 *ad Flavianum*; *Ep.* 34 *ad Iuvenal. epp. Hieros.*; *Ep.* 24 *ad Theodosium Aug.*: TD, ser. th. 15. 2–4, 18. 1–2.

[44] Cf. the excellent observations of J. Lebon in *Chalkedon* I, 510–34, on ἐκ δύο (φύσεων) in the Monophysite writings. Cyril intends to show by his formula ἐκ δύο φύσεων 'que sa doctrine n'a rien de commun avec celle des apollinaristes et des phantasiastes de tout genre' (art. cit., 516).

chianism. He did this with honourable intent and with the clarity of Latin conceptuality and thus became a clarifying influence. But his method of simplification still unnecessarily forced into contradiction much that could have been gained by a more sympathetic approach, provided, of course, that the necessary psychological presuppositions were present.[45] But how can we ask of a Latin like Leo something that the East failed to achieve among themselves, as is clear from the contrast between Antioch and Alexandria? Did not Eutyches himself fall victim to a formula of Cyril which was both hard to understand and historically suspect?

(3) Leo's view of the divine-human working of Christ shows that Leo was inwardly a long way from the Alexandrian conception of the unity in Christ. It is precisely here that the Tome is of value in showing the way forward. Maximus Confessor did not refer to it without reason in the Monothelite disputes (PG 91, 96f.). The third section of the Tome begins in v. 94 with a bold statement:

Agit enim utraque forma cum alterius communione quod proprium est. Verbo scilicet operante quod Verbi est et carne exsequente quod carnis est.

Even firm supporters of Leo might here raise a warning finger and advise a more careful approach. To the Severians these words were anathema:

Reconnaître, comme le veut Léon, à chaque nature *l'opération* de ce qui lui est *propre* ce serait, aux yeux de Sévère, lui attribuer une activité *séparée* qui lui appartiendrait *exclusivement* et à laquelle l'autre 'forme' ne participerait pas en réalité, quoi qu'en dise, mais par une pure rélation accidentelle.[46]

There are, in fact, also considerable differences over the question of the work of Christ between Leo and Chalcedonian theology on the one side and the approach of Cyril and Severus on the other.[47] While Severus of Antioch, following Cyril, merely considers the *principium quod* (to use our theological language) of the activity and works of Christ, Pope Leo goes further and distinguishes the *principium quo*, i.e. the duality of the natures. Whereas Leo allows the two natures to strive, each in its own way, to the term of their activity (the *terminus actionis*) and so can acknowledge two activities (*activitates*), Severus sees only 'une chose mue' and consequently only one working movement (mouvement opératoire, κίνησις ἐνεργετική), only *one* activity.[48] The strict Cyrillians do not dare to speak of a duality

---

[45] See further my remarks in *Chalkedon* II, 4–6, and the study instigated by them: Suso M. Klehr O.P., *Leo der Grosse in der Auseinandersetzung mit der Häresie*, Lektoratsthese an der Albertus-Magnus-Akademie, Walberberg 1963, dactylogr., with a full documentation.

[46] J. Lebon in *Chalkedon* I, 553.

[47] J. Lebon, op. cit., 555, draws attention to 'la différence immense qui sépare, en cette question des activités, la pensée de Sévère et des monophysites de celle de saint Léon et les chalcédoniens'. Here Lebon regards the Severians merely as consistent supporters of Cyril, i.e. as orthodox.

[48] So J. Lebon, op. cit.

in Christo, but only *extra Christum*, i.e. with reference to the *effects* of his activity, both divine and human. Leo, on the other hand, boldly speaks of the duality of the natures and the principles of action (the *forma*). Each of the two natures in Christ remains true to the laws of its being: '*Et sicut Verbum ab aequalitate paternae gloriae non recedit, ita caro naturam nostri generis non relinquit*' (vv. 96, 97).

Little as we may suspect Cyril's idea of the work of Christ, we may still say that Leo provides an easier approach to the understanding of it and could, had he so ventured, have laid a broader foundation for a theology of the humanity of Christ. This is evident, say, from his stress on the duality of will in Christ. For him this is virtually proof of the duality of the natures: 'In the form of God he and the Father are one (John 10. 30), but he came in the form of a servant not to do *his* will but the will of him who sent him (John 5. 30)' (*Ep.* 165, 8: PL 54, 1176C). Leo's interpretation of the suffering in Gethsemane is quite different from that of Athanasius. The latter ascribes the victory in Gethsemane to the divine will of Christ, while the weakness of the flesh asks to be freed from suffering (PG 26, 441BC; see above on Athanasius). Leo sees in the struggle of Christ the *manifesta distinctio* of the nature that takes and the nature that is taken and shapes a clear dyothelitic formula long before the Monothelite dispute: '*Superiori igitur voluntati voluntas cessit inferior*' (*Serm.* 56, 2: PL 54, 327B).

Thus the human will of Christ is the means by which he is proved before God. But this will or mind (*mens*) rules the flesh, in which there was no opposition to the spirit because of original sin, in union with the divine will of Christ:

> For he had no opposition in his flesh, nor did the strife of desires give rise to a conflict of wishes. His bodily senses were active without the law of sin, and the reality of his emotions being under the control of his Godhead and his mind, was neither assaulted by temptations nor yielded to injurious influences.[49]

Here there are certainly the first cautious hints at a theology of the freedom of Christ. But Leo's Christ stands as a man in free decision before God.

The unity of the two modes of action is stressed as much as the distinction of the divine and the human activity: *agit enim utraque forma cum alterius communione*. True, the human nature of Christ acts by virtue of the powers which lie within it; but it is not in them that its redeeming force lies. This is based rather on the conjunction of the human activity (preserved unconfused) with the Godhead. Each nature works what is proper to itself in community with the other. But in what does this *communio* or *connexio* consist (*Serm.* 54, 1: PL 54, 319B: *Exprimit quidem sub distinctis actionibus veritatem suam utraque natura, sed neutra se ab alterius connexione*

---

[49] Leo M., *Ep.* 35. 3 *ad Iulian. Choens.*: TD, ser. th. 15, 17.

disiungit)? Leo at first leaves open what he understands by it, though he often stresses it:

> Such unity is the result of the union that whatever of Godhead is there is inseparable from the manhood; and whatever of manhood is indivisible from the Godhead (*Serm.* 28, 1: PL 54, 222A).

We are, however, compelled to ask whether Leo's interpretation of the activity of Christ does not in fact make this *communio* too loose. A Cyrillian is immediately shocked by the '*utraque forma agit*'. The '*forma*', i.e. the nature, is here made the subject of the actions. If we are not to misinterpret these words to mean a Nestorian separation we must remember Leo's immediate concern, his struggle against the Eutychian confusion. He really wants only to accentuate the distinction of the natural principles of the actions (the *principia quo*, as they are later termed). This difference is not removed by the unity of person:

> *Quamvis enim in Domino Iesu Christo Dei et hominis una persona sit*, aliud *tamen est unde in utroque communis est contumelia*, aliud *unde communis est gloria* (*Tome*, vv. 122, 123).

The choice of the neuter shows that the recognition of the nature as the principle of action does not in any way claim for it the character of a person. So for Leo the *communio* or *connexio* between the divine and the human activity is achieved through the unity of person.[50]

(4) The so-called *communicatio idiomatum* arises as of its own accord from the position of the idea of person in Leo's work:

> Accordingly, on account of this unity which is to be understood as existing in both the natures, we read on the one hand that 'the Son of Man came down from heaven' (John 3. 13), inasmuch as the Son of God took flesh from that Virgin of whom he was born; and, on the other hand, the Son of God is said to have been crucified and buried, inasmuch as he underwent this, not in his actual Godhead, wherein the Only begotten is co-eternal and consubstantial with the Father, but in the weakness of human nature. Wherefore we all, in the very Creed, confess that 'the only-begotten Son of God was crucified and buried' according to that saying of the apostle, 'For if they had known it, they would not have crucified the Lord of Majesty' (1 Cor. 2. 8).[51]

The almost symmetrical juxtaposition of the two natures in Christ and their firm anchorage in the one person give Leo his certainty in the use of the *communicatio idiomatum* or exchange of predicates. This is only possible because his concept of person is not so suspect as that of the Antiochenes and of Nestorius in particular. With the Latin tradition behind him, Leo already had *de facto* the true Chalcedonian content of the word 'person'. He would, of course, have been as hard put to define the word as any of his contemporaries.

---

[50] It is only possible to assess Leo's concept of person once the pre- and post-Chalcedonian documents have been considered. See the continuation of the present work (in preparation).

[51] Leo M., *Tomus ad Flavian.*, vv. 126–32; trans. W. Bright in: Edward R. Hardy, *Christology of the Later Fathers*, 366.

(b) Christological formula

Leo, who was not really creative in the sphere of christological doctrine
—his greatest achievement was the interpretation of the twofold *actio* in
Christ—was likewise unproductive in the sphere of linguistic formulas.
He did, however, leave his own particular mark on the existing tradition
by his sense of rhythm and his love of antithetical formulas. In his repudiation of Nestorius and Eutyches he felt compelled to search for a still
clearer account of the ancient christological dogma. But all this took place
within the limits of already existing possibilities. Before the outbreak of
the dispute with Eutyches, the Pope was sometimes quite unconcerned
in his language. He even used the language of a christology which confused the natures in order to stress the unity in Christ. This was because
Nestorius stood on the other side:

> For this wondrous child-bearing of the holy Virgin produced in her offspring one
> person which was truly human and truly divine, because neither substance so retained
> their properties that there could be any division of persons in them; nor was the creature
> taken into partnership with its Creator in such a way that one was the in-dweller and the
> other the dwelling; but so that the one nature was *blended* with the other.[52]

Leo, like the Cappadocians, speaks here of a mingling of the two
natures, and in this mingling—as opposed to a mere indwelling of the
Godhead in the manhood—he sees the unity in Christ. Indeed, he ascribes
the possibility of the unity of person to the fact that the two substances in
Christ did not preserve their properties so as to constitute two persons.
This is a very incomplete and unclear idea of unity of person. What does
each of the two substances forfeit to make unity possible? Leo does not
say. In fact he says immediately afterwards: '*Tenet enim sine defectu
proprietatem suam utraque natura*' (ibid., 2: PL 54, 201A). So he imagines
the union in Christ as a *circumincessio* of the two natures. Other Fathers
too, even Nestorius, had tried this solution.

But this confusion-terminology and thought is rare. It disappears of its
own accord as the controversy progresses. In the dialectic of the Eutychian
and Nestorian heresies, Leo develops his peculiar skill in formulations
which show clearly the levels at which unity and duality are to be sought
in Christ:

> He is not twofold in person nor confused in substance; in his power he is incapable
> of suffering, but in his weakness he is mortal (*Serm.* 69, 3).

The divine and the human are so united 'that that which is proper to each
is not taken away and yet the person is not twofold' (*Serm.* 65, 1; *Ep.*
124, 6). The Word is 'one and the same nature with the Father and the
Holy Spirit, but in taking man is not of one substance but one and the
same person' (*Ep.* 35. 2; *Ep.* 165. 6).

[52] *Serm.* 23, 1: PL 54, 200A.

Thus the unity in Christ is one of 'person', while the duality is one of 'substance' or of 'nature'. Leo, moreover, is fond of using this word 'substance' in his sermons, while the *Tomus ad Flavianum* consistently avoids the expression *'substantia humana'*.[53] This is all the more strange, as a reply to the heresy of Eutyches really requires this formula of 'two substances', because he denied that Christ is *con-substantialis* (Greek of course ὁμοούσιος) with us. In the Latin translation of the First Letter of Flavian to Leo (ACO II, 1, 22[17]) we read that Eutyches allows Christ to be *'unius substantiae'*. In the Second Letter of Flavian it is said that according to Eutyches *'ex Maria corpus factum Domini non esse nostrae substantiae'* (ACO II, 2, 1, 23[17]). If, then, the word *substantia* is avoided in the Tome as a description of the human nature of Christ, this must be attributed to the redactor. He can be none other than Prosper of Aquitaine, for this linguistic feature of the Tome occurs in just the same way in his writings.

Prosper d'Aquitaine, lorsqu'il aborde la christologie, ne dit jamais que le Christ est de notre substance ou de la même substance que sa mère. Jamais il ne parle de la substance humaine du Christ. Il multiplie cependant les affirmations concernant la réalité de l'humanité du Christ; il ajoute aux citations d'Augustin des parenthèses pour insister sur la vérité du corps du Christ et répéter que le Christ a pris vraiment notre nature. Les occasions en face d'Eutychès étaient nombreuses de dire que le Christ avait pris notre substance: jamais Prosper ne le fait.[54]

Prosper, then, seems to have had certain scruples about using the word 'substantia' to describe the human nature of Christ. Is he perhaps conscious of the difficulties which had arisen between Greeks and Latins through the different use of *hypostasis* and *substantia* in trinitarian doctrine? Be this as it may, the Tome as edited by Prosper went a long way towards producing the formula of Chalcedon. The words *'salva igitur proprietate utriusque naturae'* (v. 54) of themselves immediately removed the difficulty which could have arisen from the acknowledgement of one *hypostasis* in Christ. Had Prosper left the text of Sermon 21 unaltered, the Latin *substantia* and the Greek *hypostasis* would have clashed in the Chalcedonian Definition and would have meant different things. As things were, it was possible to distinguish between *physis* and *hypostasis* without causing

---

[53] J. Gaidioz gives the evidence in *RevSR* 23, 1949, 282–8. He shows that in three passages of the Tome which have been taken over from earlier sermons of Leo the word *substantia*, which formerly occurred, has been replaced by the word *natura*. This word is also avoided at other places in the Tome, although it was present in the original text of the passages which have been incorporated. 'De la sorte, pas une seule fois dans la lettre à Flavien, ne se rencontre le terme "substantia", jamais il n'est question de la substance humaine du Christ' (op. cit., 283). V. 54 of the Tome is the most significant: *Salva igitur proprietate utriusque naturae*, where the original sermon reads *utriusque substantiae* (PL 54, 192A). Migne's text of the Tome (PL 54, 763A) wrongly combines the two: *utriusque naturae et substantiae*. So too the English translation mentioned in n. 33 above.

[54] J. Gaidioz, *RevSR* 23, 1949, 285f. G. has developed this further in his thesis *Christologie de Saint Prosper d'Aquitaine*, Lyon 1947 (inaccessible to me). We also find in the Tome Prosper's habit of supporting his statements by testimonia from the scriptures. Sermon 21, quoted in vv. 54–60, is further expanded in a way typical of Prosper. Paul's saying, originally quoted incomplete, about the one mediator between God and man (1 Tim. 2. 5), is expanded *homo Christus Iesus*, a phrase which Prosper is fond of using. Some other sections of the Tome also reflect his style.

translation difficulties for the Latins and without giving rise to terminological confusion. The deacon Rusticus then later translated the Greek *hypostasis* with Rufinus' *subsistentia*, so that the Latin text of the Chalcedonian Definition, which had incorporated Leo's phrase from the Tome (v. 54) ran on smoothly: *magisque salva proprietate utriusque naturae, et in unam personam atque subsistentiam concurrente*. With Leo's old text (from Sermon 21) and with an unfortunate translation of *hypostasis* by *substantia* there would have been a contradiction: *salva proprietate utriusque substantiae et in unam personam atque substantiam concurrente*.[55] We shall return once again in our analysis of the Chalcedonian Definition to the contribution of the Tome of Leo to its formula. From his side, Leo had already anticipated the decisive solution in Latin. How rarely elsewhere East and West could meet in their theology!

[55] Cf. ACO II, 1, 2, 129f. and 3, 2, 156, where E. Schwartz in fact lists three codices which translate *hypostasis* by *substantia*.

SECTION THREE

THE COUNCIL OF CHALCEDON

THE early history of christological doctrine now reached its climax at the Council of Chalcedon, which was held in October of the year 451.[1] It was the purpose of those who were responsible for the synod to put an end to the bitter internal disputes which had occupied the period after the Council of Ephesus. For Ephesus had left unfulfilled a task which by this stage of development was long overdue: that of creating a dogmatic formula which made it possible to express the unity and the distinction in Christ in clear terms. Only in this way could both Nestorianism and Monophysitism in the long run be countered. But even the new synod of 451 only bore fruit after a long period. First of all, it too meant a new dispute, indeed even a division of Christendom. But more than any other synod of the early church, it also spurred on theological reflection, the work of which is not yet completed even today. Thus Chalcedon has a twofold significance; first in the context of the formulation of the doctrines of the church, and secondly in the history of narrower theological speculation or reflection.

[1] On what follows, cf. M. Goemans, 'Chalkedon als "Allgemeines Konzil" ', *Chalkedon* I, 251–89; I. Ortiz de Urbina, 'Das Symbol von Chalkedon', ibid., 389–418; A. Schönmetzer, Zeittafel nos. 111–37: *Chalkedon* II, 950–2; R. V. Sellers, *The Council of Chalcedon*, London 1953, 207–53; P.-T. Camelot, *Ephèse et Chalcédoine* (HCO 2), Paris 1962, 79–182; in a German edition: *Ephesus und Chalkedon* (GÖK 2), Mainz 1963, 179–222. See P. Smulders, 'De ontwikkeling van het christologisch dogma', *Bijdragen* 21, 1961, 357–422; T. Šagi-Bunić, ' "Duo perfecta" et "duae naturae" in definitione dogmatica Chalcedonensi', Roma, *Laurentianum* 5, 1964.

CHAPTER ONE

THE DOGMATIC FORMULA OF CHALCEDON

It was only under constant pressure from the emperor Marcian that the Fathers of Chalcedon agreed to draw up a new formula of belief. Even at the fourth session of the council, on 17 October 451, the delegates of the emperor heard the synod once again endorse its purpose to create no new formula over and above the creeds of Nicaea and Constantinople. Ephesus had adopted the same attitude. But if, it was argued, a new account of the faith was already necessary, then it was to hand in the letter which Leo sent in condemnation of Nestorius and Eutyches (ACO II, 1, 2, 93, no. 6). Nevertheless, the Acts do testify to some striving towards a new formula of belief. That put forward by thirteen Egyptian bishops remained without significance for the synod. All the more important is the work of a special commission, which had assembled on 21 October under the patriarch Anatolius. This commission had prepared a creed, the text of which is unfortunately no longer extant (cf. ACO II, 1, 2, 123, no. 3). But we see from the subsequent discussion that it had a predominantly Cyrillian tendency. For it evidently avoided the emphatic diphysitism of Leo's letter and used instead the disputed formula ἐκ δύο φύσεων (ACO II, 1, 2, 123f., esp. no. 13). Anatolius himself was the driving force behind it. But the imperial commissioners—together with the Roman delegates—brought about the turning point. The letter of Leo, they held, must be used in the new formula, for the council had already accepted it and subscribed to it, whereas Dioscorus of Alexandria had been condemned. Why, then, still the ἐκ δύο φύσεων?

Leo or Dioscorus? Faced with this dilemma, the bishops gave way and expressed themselves agreeable that a committee, to be formed at the Emperor's pleasure, should work out a new formula in accordance with Leo's formula of the two natures (ACO II, 1, 2, 124f., nos. 22–8). Thereupon twenty-three bishops assembled with the imperial commissioners in the oratory of St Euphemia. When they returned to the full assembly, they were able to put before the synod a long declaration of faith, which was finally greeted with shouts of approval on 25 October. The Acts cite first of all quite a lengthy preamble, which is followed by the creeds of Nicaea (325) and Constantinople (381). After a long transition we then read the text which may be described as the 'Chalcedonian creed'. A *clausula* finally lays stress on the significance and binding character of this document of the faith. We are here concerned with this 'Chalcedonian

Definition' proper:[1]

Following, then, the holy Fathers, we all with one voice teach that it should be confessed that our Lord Jesus Christ is one and the same Son, the Same perfect in Godhead, the Same perfect in manhood, truly God and truly man, the Same [consisting] of a rational soul and a body; *homoousios* with the Father as to his Godhead, and the Same *homoousios* with us as to his manhood; in all things like unto us, sin only excepted; begotten of the Father before ages as to his Godhead, and in the last days, the Same, for us and for our salvation, of Mary the Virgin *Theotokos* as to his manhood;

One and the same Christ, Son, Lord, Only begotten, made known in two natures [which exist] without confusion, without change, without division, without separation; the difference of the natures having been in no wise taken away by reason of the union, but rather the properties of each being preserved, and [both] concurring into one Person (*prosopon*) and one *hypostasis*—not parted or divided into two persons (*prosopa*), but one and the same Son and Only-begotten, the divine Logos, the Lord Jesus Christ; even as the prophets from of old [have spoken] concerning him, and as the Lord Jesus Christ himself has taught us, and as the Symbol of the Fathers has delivered to us.

As the whole psychological attitude of the Fathers at the council already shows, the task of the special committee must necessarily have been to construct its own exposition of the tradition. Otherwise it could not expect its work to be recognized. An analysis of the Chalcedonian creed shows that it is anticipated almost clause for clause in other documents. The documents which are chiefly used are the second letter of Cyril to Nestorius, Cyril's letter to the Antiochenes with the Formulary of Reunion of 433 (*Laetentur* letter), and the Tome of Leo to Flavian. Finally we must also add Flavian's *professio fidei*, which had been read out at the Council of Chalcedon in the context of the acts of the trial of Eutyches. One clause even seems to hint at a letter of Theodoret.[2] Here, as in almost no other formula from the early councils, all the important centres of church life and all the trends of contemporary theology, Rome, Alexandria, Constantinople and Antioch, have contributed towards the framing of a common expression of faith. It would be a mistake to understand Chalcedon merely as a reaction to the 'Cyrillian' Council of Ephesus.

The decision arose from the necessity of countering both Nestorianism and Eutychianism. Because Monophysitism now represented the greater danger, the pointed Alexandrian formulas, which had been so fateful for Eutyches, had to be relegated to the background. Their place was taken by the Tome of Leo, and the Antiochenes played a special part with the Formulary of Reunion of 433. The Chalcedonian creed, in agreement with tradition, was to serve the acute needs of the proclamation of the faith. For this reason it was taken by the Fathers along with the declarations of faith made at Nicaea and Constantinople, which as such offered a survey of the whole of saving truth. Chalcedon sought to discover the solution

[1] ACO II, 1, 2, 129-30; Latin ACO II, 3, 2, 137-8. We quote the text in the English translation by R. V. Sellers, *The Council of Chalcedon*, 210f., cf. COD, 83-7.
[2] Cf. the detailed analysis in I. Ortiz de Urbina, *Chalkedon* I, 398-401.

of just *one* disputed question: *how* the confession of the '*one Christ*' may be reconciled with belief in the '*true God and true man*', '*perfect in Godhead, perfect in manhood*'.

The historical significance of Chalcedon is that it tackled this problem, which had troubled the theologians of the church really since the time of Eustathius of Antioch, with two conceptual distinctions. At first sight this seems a very meagre reason for assembling several hundred bishops from all over the world. A few abstract concepts occupied the centre of the discussion. Was this to be the climax of the early church's belief in Christ? True, the discussion was over a few concepts. But these concepts were to become the vessel and the expression of the church's central dogma of the person of Jesus Christ, which now, at the height of the fifth century, had become the critical question of theological debate. Although the specialist theologians usurped this formula more and more, it was not made for them alone. It was intended to give expression to the faith of the whole church.

This was the purpose for which the Fathers of Chalcedon worked. Even now we find among them no 'theologians', in the sense of mediaeval or modern theological techniques. There is no attempt at a philosophical definition or speculative analysis! In theological method Chalcedon is no different from any of the earlier councils. Even if abstract concepts find their way in, the theological method here consists only in 'listening to' the proven witnesses of the Christian faith. True, the formulas are carefully developed, but only in connection with an already formed tradition. The work of the Fathers of Chalcedon is really 'dogmatic'. Moreover, their grasp of the content of their expressions is more intuitive than speculative. They produce formulas as witnesses to the Word and not as scholars. None of them could even have given a definition of the concepts with which they had now expressed christological dogma. This had the disadvantage of leaving much unclear, but at the same time the advantage —in view of the world-wide significance of the statement—of leaving open the expression of much about which the Fathers could not as yet think explicitly. To a Christian of the time, the formal terms of Chalcedon did not sound so formal as they might seem to a theologian of the nineteenth or the twentieth century.[3] They were meant to express the *full reality* of the incarnation. Marcian and Pulcheria emphasized this in several post-Chalcedonian letters to calm inflamed passions:

proinde duas naturas audientes perturbatas vestras animas fuisse docuistis veluti quadam novitate auribus vestris inlata, quapropter scitote quia vobis quidem harum rerum examinationem

---

[3] In the judgement of Harnack, for example, the church of the East was 'robbed of its faith'. 'The four bleak, negative definitions (ἀσυγχύτως, etc.), which are meant to express everything, are to the sensibility of the classical Greek theologian highly irreligious' (*Dogmengeschichte* 2, Tübingen 1931, 395 and 396). This verdict does no justice to the actual dogmatic and theological significance of Chalcedon.

facere non congruit, dum subtilitatem huius rei intellegere nequeatis, nos autem patrum suscipientes doctrinas naturam *intellegimus* veritatem.[4]

How, then, is the dogmatic solution of pending theological questions achieved? First of all, belief in the unity in Christ is expressed in accordance with tradition (*sequentes igitur sanctos patres*). This is done first in quite simple periphrastic expressions: 'we confess that our Lord Jesus Christ is one and the same Son'. This εἷς καὶ ὁ αὐτός occurs twice in this double formula and four times as a simple αὐτός. It reaches far back into the early patristic period, say to Ignatius of Antioch (*Ad Eph.* 7. 2), whose christological framework is built in such a way as to predicate the divine and the human of one and the same subject. The Nicene concern is again taken up, just as it had been interpreted in Ephesus: that it is one and the same Logos who dwells with the Father and 'who for us men and for our salvation came down from heaven, and was incarnate and was made man'. By first choosing a formula so easily understandable by the people and by not laying down particular expressions of any theological trend to express recognition of the unity in Christ, the Council of Chalcedon created the possibility of once again reconciling the conflicting terminologies. For in this simple formula Alexandrians and Antiochenes, who otherwise appeared to be irreconcilably divided through the dilemma of 'one *physis*' or 'two *physeis*', could meet.[5]

In an equally understandable way, stress is now laid on the distinction in the God-man, as it was on the unity:

> The Same perfect in Godhead, the Same perfect in manhood, truly God and truly man, the Same [consisting] of a rational soul and a body.

This formula has been chosen very carefully. Its significance can only be seen from a comparison with the Symbol of Union of 433 and Flavian's *professio fidei* of 12 November 448. Flavian took over the following formula from Cyril's *Laetentur* letter:

> *Dominus noster Iesus Christus, filius Dei unigenitus, Deus perfectus et homo perfectus ex anima rationali et corpore.*[6]

In the creed which he composed at the command of the emperor, however, he altered the 'Antiochene' character of this formulation by a more careful version: we proclaim Christ '*deum perfectum et eundem hominem perfectum in assumptione animae rationalis et corporis*'.[7] It has rightly been pointed out that here Flavian moves from a '*unitio duarum perfectarum quidditatum*' to a stronger stress on the one subject in Christ.[8] It makes a difference in fact whether I say 'perfect God and perfect man of a rational

---

[4] Marcian, *ad Archimandrit. et Monach.*: ACO II, 5, 6[2-6]; cf. Pulcheria, ibid. 7-8.
[5] Cf. Cyril Al., *Or. ad Dominas* 79: ACO I, 1, 5, 82[29-30]; Theodoret., *Ep.* 21: PG 83, 1201BD.
[6] ACO II, 1, 1, p. 114[4-5]; see T. Šagi-Bunić, op. cit., 182.
[7] ACO II, 1, 1, p. 35[15-16]; Šagi-Bunić, ibid., 186.   [8] T. Šagi-Bunić, ibid., 187.

soul and body' (as does the Symbol of Union) or 'one and the same perfect in Godhead and in manhood', as Cyril had already done in his explanation of the Symbol of Union in the *Laetentur* letter.[9] The Council of Chalcedon exchanged Cyril's formula for the Antiochene one, as the sentence quoted above indicates.

The one Christ, the one incarnate Son of God is truly and perfectly God and man! Motifs recur from an earlier period, the time of the struggle against Gnostics and docetists. The Arian and Apollinarian denial of the completeness of Christ's human nature is also refuted: Christ has a rational soul and a truly human body. Nothing may be taken away from the human nature of Christ to explain his unity. Here once again the first theological attempt to interpret the unity of the God-man by positing a strict unity of Logos and sarx is repudiated. Along with the anti-Apolinarian theology of the church of the fourth century, Chalcedon takes upon itself the responsibility of showing a way of explaining the unity in Christ commensurate with this recognition. Its chief concern, however, is to express both the distinction and the completeness of Godhead and manhood. To do this, the most disputed word of the fourth century, the *homoousion*, is recalled, this time to be used of both the Godhead and the manhood:

> *Homoousios* with the Father as to his Godhead, and the Same *homoousios* with us as to his manhood; in all things like unto us, sin only excepted; begotten of the Father before ages as to his Godhead, and in the last days, the Same, for us and for our salvation, of Mary the Virgin *Theotokos* as to his manhood.[10]

This return to the keyword of Nicaea is surely made because of Eutyches, for while conceding this *homoousios* for Mary in her relationship to us, he did not allow it for Christ.[11] His flesh was not of the same substance as ours. To this Eutychian trend towards Monophysitism is opposed the emphatic diphysitism of the Council of Chalcedon. It gives the Definition its distinctive stamp. We find traces here especially of the Formulary of Reunion of 433, Theodoret and Leo the Great.

[9] ACO II, 1, 1, p. 110[4-5]: τέλειος ὢν ἐν θεότητι καὶ τέλειος ὁ αὐτὸς ἐν ἀνθρωπότητι.... Quoted in Šagi-Bunić, op. cit., 211. The interpretation of the formula '*Deus perfectus et homo perfectus*' in terms of '*duo perfecti*' is now excluded. Once Cyril's formula has been adopted, it is merely a question of the '*unus perfectus*'. Nevertheless, there is a difference between Cyril and Chalcedon, which Šagi-Bunić characterizes in the following way: '*Apud Cyrillum unus perfectus affirmatur et extollitur, duplicitas autem perfectionis agnoscitur et cointelligitur tamquam veritas ex qua in favorem unicitatis illius qui perfectus est argumentatur. In definitione (Chalcedonensi), a contrario, formaliter duplicitas perfectionis unius eiusdemque Christi affirmatur et extollitur, unus perfectus autem* (in the statement quoted above) *simpliciter supponitur sive implicite affirmatur*' (op. cit., 213). Cf. further T. Šagi-Bunić, O.F.M., Cap., *Problemata christologiae chalcedonensis. Continuitas doctrinalis et drama conscientiae episcoporum qua fidei iudicum*, Roma–Laurentianum 1969, 6–43.

[10] For the historicity and significance of the double 'homoousios' cf. M. F. Wiles, 'ΟΜΟΟΥΣΙΟΣ 'ΗΜΙΝ, *JTS* 16, 1965, 454–65; but above all B. Studer, 'Consubstantialis Patri. Consubstantialis Matri. Une antithèse christologique chez Léon le Grand', *RevEtAug* 18, 1972, 87–115 with further literature. In the second volume of this work, we shall see in connection with Timothy Aelurus how significant this double *homoousios* became even for the Monophysites, a fact which hitherto has not sufficiently been noted.

[11] Cf. ACO II, 1, 1, 142, no. 516; T. Camelot, *Chalkedon* I, 237.

So in clearly comprehensible language, separation and confusion are excluded from an understanding of Christ and unity and distinction are acknowledged in just the same way. The Fathers of Chalcedon must still, however, take into consideration the state of theological discussion and the formulas which are used in it. Otherwise the acute doctrinal problem cannot be solved.

It had now become necessary to find the formula which like a hidden entelechy had accompanied the wearisome struggles of centuries to interpret the *mysterium Christi*. The Fourth Council could only consider that its task as had been fulfilled if it had stated in clear terms *how* both the unity and the distinction in Christ were to be understood. True, Latin, Antiochene and finally even Constantinopolitan theology had already prepared all the elements of a solution. The time had now come to make from them the right choice that would do justice to all claims. But was this at all possible? The Alexandrians were shouting μία φύσις, the Antiochenes δύο φύσεις. Chalcedon made its choice and said: Christ is one and the same Son, Lord, only-begotten, but ἐν δύο φύσεσιν! Christ is one in 'two natures'. For the supporters of Dioscorus this sounded like a declaration of war. It was to be the tragedy of the Fourth General Council that it led to a long war and a division in the church. This was not the fault of the church Fathers.

It has convincingly been shown that the formula 'in two natures' could have been achieved by an exact interpretation of Cyril's saying *'perfectus existens in deitate et perfectus idem ipse in humanitate'*, which has already been cited. This is particularly clear in the case of Basil of Seleucia, if one begins with a 'confession' which he made in the Synod against Eutyches in 448 and which was again read out in the first action of the Council of Chalcedon:

Adoramus unum Dominum nostrum Iesum Christum in duabus naturis *cognitum* (γνωριζόμε-νον). *Hanc enim habebat in semetipso ante saecula* (προαιώνιον) *tamquam splendor gloriae Patris existens; hanc autem, tamquam qui ex matre propter nos natus est, ex ipsa assumens sibi univit secundum hypostasim; et* perfectus Deus (ὁ τέλειος θεός) *ac filius Dei vocatus est etiam* perfectus homo (τέλειος ἄνθρωπος) *ac filius hominis; omnes nos salvare volens in eo quod factus est nobis in omnibus similis, praeter peccatum.*[12]

Basil read Cyril's saying quoted above as though it were written: *'unus et idem existens* in perfecta deitate *et* in perfecta humanitate'. From that point, the following consideration would be possible for Basil: the *duo perfecta* are the 'divinity' and the 'humanity' of Christ. But because according to one paragraph of the Second Letter to Nestorius 'divinity' and 'humanity' are the *naturae diversae* which have been conjoined in the unity, without their difference being 'removed' or becoming 'unrecog-

---

[12] ACO II, 1, 1, p. 117²²⁻⁸. Cf. Šagi-Bunić, *'Deus perfectus et homo perfectus'* (above, p. 540), 191. We summarize here briefly the argument of pp. 188–204.

nizable', I would immediately conclude that 'the one Christ can be recognized in two natures'. This would then build a bridge for the Alexandrians between Cyril and the 'in two natures' of Chalcedon. Unfortunately, this connection remained hidden and unrecognized.

This ἐν δύο φύσεσιν introduces the section of the Chalcedonian Definition which, with its pregnant formulation, was intended to accommodate the theological questions of the new period. 'In two natures' and not 'from two natures'! So the unity in Christ is not to be sought in the sphere of the natures (not *in natura et secundum naturam*). For the natures as such remain preserved. This is still further stressed with a threefold variation: 'without confusion . . . the difference of the natures having been in no wise taken away by reason of the union, but rather the properties of each being preserved' (σωζομένης δὲ μᾶλλον τῆς ἰδιότητος ἑκατέρας φύσεως). Thus the nature is the unimpaired principle of the distinction in Christ. The Fathers were probably not conscious of the significance of their decision as it is expressed in the following sentences, and of what it was to mean for future generations of theologians. Otherwise they would have given still stronger expression in the formula to the opposition which is present in its content. As it is, the statement of the unity of person or hypostasis, which in fact represents the contrast to the stress on the duality of the natures, is added without either being emphasized: 'and [both] concurring into one person (*prosopon*) and one *hypostasis*—not parted or divided into two persons (*prosopa*), but one and the same Son and Only-begotten, the divine Logos, the Lord Jesus Christ. . . .' So even in these words, the Fathers do not have the feeling that they are saying something completely new. They merely associate their authority with a formula which in fact already existed beforehand. We have been shown this by the immediate preliminaries to Chalcedon. What has been prepared by pre-Chalcedonian theology obtains an ecumenical significance from the dialectic of Nestorianism and Eutychianism and through the decision of the Council. Two brief formulas may be extracted from the longer Chalcedonian Definition, which from now on are to determine christology: Christ 'without confusion' and 'without division' (ἀσυγχύτως-ἀδιαιρέτως)—'one person or hypostasis, in two natures' (ἓν πρόσωπον, μία ὑπόστασις, ἐν δύο φύσεσιν).

Even though the concepts of *hypostasis* and *prosopon* have not yet been defined, the sense of the dogma of Chalcedon is quite clear. The Fathers mean to say that while there is a real distinction between the natures of Godhead and manhood, Christ is still to be described as 'one', as 'one person or hypostasis'. This statement could be made even independently of any exact definition of the metaphysical content of these concepts. It is not the task of councils to produce metaphysics, but to serve the church's proclamation of revelation. The formula of the council states only the bare essentials of what was needed to resolve the difficulties of the time, which were, of course, the result of a long development. It was not at that time the intention to draw out all the consequences of the complete distinction of the natures in Christ. The words taken from the Tome of Leo (*magisque salva proprietate utriusque naturae*) point forward the furthest. But had it been possible to look into the future, it would have been easy to have inserted a safeguard against Monothelitism and Monergism. The need for stating all the particular implications of the abstract concept 'in two natures' had yet to be recognized. The Fathers thought that these implications were quite clear from Holy Scripture. From the time of Ignatius of Antioch, the two sets of expressions had been taken from there to describe the Godhead and the manhood in Christ. The *'proprietates utriusque naturae'* in the Chalcedonian Definition are meant in this concrete biblical sense. Here we have an indication that the apparently abstract and formal concepts of this Definition must always be supplemented from Holy Scripture. It is intended to explain just one definite question of the church's christology, indeed the most important one. It does not lay claim to having said all that may be said about Christ.

So the dogma of Chalcedon must always be taken against the background of scripture and the whole patristic tradition. It is not to no purpose that the Definition itself points to the prophets and the sayings of Christ himself (even as the prophets from of old [have spoken] concerning him, and as the Lord Jesus Christ himself has taught us) and finally to the creed of the Fathers, i.e. to Nicaea, indeed beyond Nicaea to the two succeeding councils and to the letters of Cyril, received with such solemnity, and the Tome of Leo. Few councils have been so rooted in tradition as the Council of Chalcedon. The dogma of Chalcedon is ancient tradition in a formula corresponding to the needs of the hour. So we cannot say that the Chalcedon Definition marks a great turning point in the christological belief of the early church. To apply a kind of Hegelian dialectic to the relationship between Ephesus and Chalcedon is as misguided as Harnack's above-mentioned lament over the downfall of the true Greek faith in Christ.

CHAPTER TWO

CHALCEDON AND THE HISTORY OF THEOLOGY

THOUGH the dogma and dogmatic formula of Chalcedon represent no real innovation in the Christian tradition, the Fourth General Council, along with Nicaea, is the ancient synod which did the most to spur on theological reflection. Terms like *homoousios, hypostasis, physis* and *prosopon* found their way into dogmatic formulas not with an exact technical meaning, but with a content which had hardly been determined pre-scientifically, or even by popular science. This content was sufficient for the Fathers to express their dogmatic truth, in this case, that there is only one person in Christ despite the unimpaired duality of the natures. What they wanted to say was not unskilfully expressed by the frequently repeated 'one and the same'. So Chalcedon did not need to give an exact metaphysical analysis of the concepts of *prosopon* and *hypostasis*. Nor did it need to adopt a particular philosophical system in which such concepts could acquire a special significance. This is true for the sphere of dogma proper. But in so far as the concepts employed in the expression of this dogma also had a more exact philosophical content, it was at the same time possible to make a speculative theological analysis of the dogmatic expressions, in which, of course, the character of analogy in the use of the concepts was to be noted.

But what possibilities were there for such a speculative analysis at the time of Chalcedon? We have already seen that they were very few. The only significant attempt at giving a theory of the incarnation had been made by Nestorius on the basis of the Stoic-Cappadocian analysis of *physis* (*ousia*) and *hypostasis*. Our investigation has shown that one particular concept played a special part in this theory which was also used by Chalcedon, the concept of *proprietas*, ἰδιότης. The *hypostasis*, the *prosopon*, comes into being by the addition of the ἰδιότης to the *ousia*. Is it possible to arrive at a tolerable speculative interpretation of the Chalcedonian Definition with these Stoic-Cappadocian presuppositions? To this question we must give a negative answer. If we have as a basis the Cappadocian conception of *hypostasis* the result is, in fact, a contradiction between the expressions *magisque salva proprietate utriusque naturae* and *et in unam personam atque subsistentiam concurrente*. On one hand it is said that each nature keeps that which makes it a *hypostasis*, and yet at the same time it is said that there is only one *hypostasis* or *prosopon*. It follows from this that the Chalcedonian Definition already points into the future. For its speculative understanding it requires a different metaphysical idea of *hypostasis* and *prosopon* from that recognized hitherto. It also follows that while Nestorius might well have accepted the dogmatic formula of Chalcedon, he could not have vindicated it in a speculative analysis. He need not be faulted for this; Chalcedon provided new motives for christological reflection too, and, in addition, impulses for the working out of the concept of person and its differentiation from the concept of nature. The stimulus provided did in fact have some effect, and after careful work first produced some results in the course of the sixth century. All possibilities have not been exhausted even today.

The position of the Chalcedonian Definition in the history of theology is determined not merely by the concepts which it contains but also by its basic christological framework, i.e. by the particular way in which it gives a theological interpretation of the person of Jesus Christ. The character of the Chalcedonian framework may best be defined in the light of its contrast with the antithesis of the chief formula of Cyril of Alexandria, 'The one nature of the Word made flesh'. It is a characteristic of this formula to define Christ from the *physis* of the Logos. The Logos is mentioned first. This *physis* is not symmetrically opposed to the *physis* of the manhood. Instead, we hear of a historical event which has happened to the *physis* of the Godhead of the Logos, namely that it has taken flesh. This is really John 1. 14, ὁ λόγος σὰρξ ἐγένετο, with a closer interpretation of the subject and a stress on his unity. In Cyril's interpretation, the complete human nature of Christ is meant to be expressed by the one word σεσαρκ-ωμένη(ου).

In contrast to this, the Chalcedonian Definition looks symmetrical and undynamic because of the juxtaposition of the divine and the human natures. Even if the two natures are said to '*concurrere*', there is no thought of capturing the act of incarnation in an historical perspective. But whereas the *mia physis* formula can only express a 'katagogic' christology, the Chalcedonian form is also capable of providing a basis for an 'anagogic' christology. In other words, it is possible to advance from the human reality of Jesus into the depths of the divine person. At the same time, Chalcedon leaves no doubt that the one Logos is the subject of both the human and the divine predicates. We can trace quite clearly in the Chalcedonian Definition the wish of the Fathers to take the Nicene framework as their starting point: *ante saecula quidem de Patre genitum secundum deitatem, in novissimis autem diebus eundem propter nos et propter salutem nostram ex Maria Virgine Dei genetrice secundum humanitatem*. . . . In the view of Chalcedon, Christ is not just a '*homo deifer*' or a human subject, *habens deitatem*, but the God-Logos, *habens humanitatem*, or rather, *habens et deitatem et humanitatem*. The person of Christ does not first come into being from the concurrence of Godhead and manhood or of the two natures, but is already present in the person of the pre-existent Logos. Thus the Chalcedonian picture of Christ, too, is drawn in the light of the Logos. But now the features of Christ's manhood are depicted with unmistakable clearness, even though only in outline. It will be the task of later developments both in preaching and theology to let the 'fullness of Christ' shine out even through the sober language of Chalcedon. It is no coincidence that in the Monergistic and Monothelitic disputes recourse will be had to Chalcedon in particular, to think further into the completeness of the human nature of Christ and its capacity for action. All future discussion on the will, knowledge and consciousness of Christ belong in the end in that area of christological problems which was marked out by Chalcedon.

Theological reflection about Christ was given special impetus by the Fourth Council and above all by the contrast of ἀσυγχύτως–ἀδιαιρέτως, or by the four characteristics of the hypostatic union in Christ, regarded with such distrust by Harnack: ἀσυγχύτως, ἀτρέπτως, ἀδιαιρέτως, ἀχωρίστως. 'Without confusion' and 'without separation' represent the two extreme poles of christological tension. These concepts (along with the other two) had already found a firm footing before the Council of Chalcedon.[1] But now they are given a new emphasis, indeed to some extent they are put in a new order. For now the 'without confusion', directed against Eutyches, is put in the first place, which at Ephesus had been occupied by 'without separation'. Both are given the same weight, though in the history of christology now one and now the other had to come further into the foreground. Unity of person and distinction of natures may be thought through right to the limit, to the establishment of a theological law which acquires the weight of an equation: 'Union as far as distinction.' Maximus Confessor has already put it like this: 'For there is evidently a union of things in so far as their physical distinction is preserved.'[2] The christological unity contains its own tension.

If the person of Christ is the highest mode of conjunction between God and man, God and the world, the Chalcedonian 'without confusion' and 'without separation' show the right mean between monism and dualism, the two extremes between which the history of christology also swings. The Chalcedonian unity of person in the distinction of the natures provides the dogmatic basis for the preservation of the divine transcendence, which must always be a feature of the Christian concept of God. But it also shows the possibility of a complete immanence of God in our history, an immanence on which the biblical doctrine of the economy of salvation rests. The Chalcedonian Definition may seem to have a static-ontic ring,

---

[1] Cf. I. Ortiz de Urbina, *Chalkedon* I, 408-9. The ἀτρέπτως belongs to ἀσυγχύτως, while the ἀχωρίστως belongs to ἀδιαιρέτως. The word ἀχωρίστως has a twofold significance. It rejects (1) a separation of Christ into two persons and (2) a temporary separation of the Logos from the body of Christ at death such as can be seen from the history of the *descensus Christi*. Cf. A. Grillmeier, 'Der Gottessohn im Totenreich', *ZkTh* 71, 1949, 23-53, 184-203.

[2] Maximus Conf., *Opusc. th. polem.* 8: PG 91, 97A; cf. J. Ternus, *Chalkedon* III, 107.

but it is not meant to do away with the salvation-historical aspect of biblical christology, for which, in fact, it provides a foundation and deeper insights.[3]

[3] See John A. T. Robinson, *The Human Face of God*, London 1973.

CHALCEDON—END OR BEGINNING?

WE have been concerned to outline the development of belief in Christ from its beginning to its first climax in a council of the church. We cannot claim to have given a full and exhaustive description, or the only correct interpretation of this course. Because of the lack of literary sources, important periods of the history of christology lie in almost total darkness, particularly the time from Origen to the Council of Nicaea and beyond. More attention must be given to the whole period from Origen to the Council of Ephesus than has been possible here. A full account of the characteristic theological ideas of the fourth century and their significance for Christian tradition has by no means as yet been given. Even the history of the heresies of this period still requires intensive investigation. The ecumenical concern of today calls for a full historical explanation of the divisions which were produced by the Councils of Ephesus and Chalcedon.

The pre-Chalcedonian phase of belief in Christ took place almost exclusively within the countries bordering on the Mediterranean sea and, in the last stages, even within the narrower sphere of the Byzantine Roman empire. We have continually been dogged by the question of the Judaizing, the Hellenizing and the Latinizing of the preaching of Christ. Here, too, we cannot claim to have said the final word. Nevertheless, we believe that to a certain extent we have made it clear that the simple, original proclamation of Christ, the revealer and bringer of salvation, the proclamation of Christ the Son of God can be heard in undiminished strength through all the *philosophoumena* of the Fathers.

These *philosophoumena*, these technical concepts and formulas (though their 'technical' character should not be exaggerated), are not an end in themselves. They have a service to perform for the faith of the church. They are intended to preserve the Christ of the gospels and the apostolic age for the faith of posterity. In all the christological formulas of the ancient church there is a manifest concern not to allow the total demand made on men's faith by the person of Jesus to be weakened by pseudo-solutions. It must be handed on undiminished to all generations of Christendom. On a closer inspection, the christological 'heresies' turn out to be a compromise between the original message of the Bible and the understanding of it in Hellenism and paganism. It is here that we have the real Hellenization of Christianity. The formulas of the church, whether they are the *homoousios* of Nicaea or the Chalcedonian Definition, represent the *lectio difficilior* of the gospel, and maintain the demand for faith and the stumbling-block which Christ puts before men. This is a sign that they hand on the original message of Jesus. Nevertheless, the Hellenistic element in them, too, needs a thorough examination and demarcation.

Now these formulas clarify only one, albeit the decisive, point of belief in Christ: that in Jesus Christ God really entered into human history and thus achieved our salvation. If the picture of Christ is to be illuminated fully, these formulas must always be seen against the whole background of the biblical belief in Christ. At the same time, they represent a way forward pursued by the church. They prove the church's desire for an ever more profound *intellectus fidei*, which is not to be a resolution of the *mysterium Christi*. None of the formulas, once framed, should be given up. Yet not one of them can claim to be the church's last word on a divine revelation. Even Chalcedon is, as Karl Rahner has so finely put it, not an 'end', but a 'beginning':

Work by the theologians and teachers of the church bearing on a reality and a truth revealed by God always ends in an exact formulation. That is natural and necessary. For only in this way is it possible to draw a line of demarcation, excluding heresy and mis-understanding of the divine truth, which can be observed in everyday religious practice. But if the formula is thus an end, the result and the victory which bring about simplicity, clarity, the possibility of teaching and doctrinal certainty, then in this victory everything depends on the end also being seen as a beginning.[1]

The church must regard the *mysterium Christi* as a reality which is con-tinually to be thought through afresh. It is Christ's promise that his Spirit will lead the church more and more profoundly into all truth (cf. John 16. 13).

This insight comes primarily from a deeper surrender of the church, in faith, to the message of Jesus. But it will also be gained by reflection, with the help of philosophical concepts and approaches. This has been the practice of the Fathers since the early Christian period, and indeed even some writers of the Old and New Testaments already follow the same course. Little as the act of faith may be confused with rational insight,[2] the conjunction of the biblical proclamation with the problems of a de-veloped *Weltanschauung* demands a disciplined mind. But in the end, human understanding will never be able to unveil the *mysterium Christi*.

Finally, for each age the task of proclaiming the traditional picture of Christ within the framework of the current ideas and language still remains. Has our age already succeeded in fulfilling this task, as the Fathers did for their time? Bultmann has made us painfully aware of the difficulty of relating the original message of Christ to the modern men-

---

[1] K. Rahner, 'Chalkedon—Ende oder Anfang?', *Chalkedon* III, 3.

[2] Cf. B. Lonergan, *De Verbo Incarnato*, Rome 1961², 2–16; id., *Insight, A Study of Human Under-standing*, London–New York 1958²; 731–48; id., 'Theology and Understanding', *Greg* 35, 1954, 630–48; id., *Method in Theology*, London 1973.

tality, and has energetically sought a remedy for this state of affairs. But does his proposal indicate the right course for us to follow? While the Fathers, too, started from his problem, they would vigorously challenge his solution in so far as it passes judgement on the church's picture of Christ in the patristic period. Pope John XXIII, in his opening address to the Second Vatican Ecumenical Council, made a similar appeal to that made by Bultmann. But Pope John called for a synthesis. The church is to speak the language of the modern age, but in such a way that the substance of tradition is preserved. But he does concede that linguistic garb, conceptual representation and the content of the message of revelation are not the same thing.

What does this imply for the Chalcedonian Definition? We cannot yet answer the question here—it still calls for a great deal of consideration. But the demand for a complete reappraisal of the church's belief in Christ right up to the present day is an urgent one. Here we are once again brought up sharply against the problems of a biblical hermeneutic and a theory of the development of dogma. One thing, however, is quite clear: a biblical hermeneutic must be designed to reveal more and more the fullness of the faith of the Old and New Testaments, and not to conceal it. Anyone who believes, on hermeneutical grounds, that the bridges with Christian tradition must be broken and whole periods of the church's tradition must be written off, must examine both his hermeneutic and his understanding of the content of the christological tradition. For perhaps he has made for himself a picture which does not correspond with the real understanding of the Fathers. At all events, the Fathers believed that they were fighting for the pure picture of Christ, as it was drawn by the Bible.

THE NESTORIUS QUESTION IN MODERN STUDY

As no agreement has been reached upon the verdict to be passed on Nestorius it is necessary to outline in brief the position of modern study. When we come to a theological assessment of Nestorius it is, of course, significant that the condemnation expressed at Ephesus has in later times frequently been confirmed:[1] by Pope Hormisdas in his *Libellus professionis fidei* of 517; by the Second and Third Councils of Constantinople in 553 and 680/1; by the Lateran Council under Martin I in 649; by Eugenius IV in the Decree for the Jacobites (4, II, 1442; 1441 *stilo Florentino*); by Benedict XIV in the constitution *'Nuper ad nos'* of 1743; in most recent times by the Ephesus encyclical of Pope Pius XI, *'Lux Veritatis'* (AAS, 1931, 493–517); and finally by the Chalcedon Encyclical of Pope Pius XII, *'Sempiternus Rex Christus'*(AAS, 1951, 625–44). These documents deliberately contain no scholarly discussion of the teaching of Nestorius. Indeed, this could only begin once the sources had been made available. For this reason we are to expect no essential change in the verdict on Nestorius even from the Reformers, though this change has been said to be noticeable as early as Luther (J. C. L. Gieseler, *Lehrbuch der Kirchengeschichte* I, 2, Bonn 1845, 153; cf. F. Loofs, *Herzog-Hauck PRE* 13, 3, Leipzig 1903³, 736, and especially C. W. F. Walch, *Entwurf einer vollständigen Historie der Kezereien, Spaltungen und Religionsstreitigkeiten*, Bd. V, Leipzig 1770, 826–30; this last, however, with qualifications). Luther finds the chief error of Nestorius in his denial of the *communicatio idiomatum* and finally says of the Decree of Ephesus: 'Es hat auch dis Concilium viel zu wenig verdampt an dem Nestorio'; in other words, this council dealt with Nestorius far too lightly (*Luther-Werke* T. 50, Weimar 1914, 590; ibid., 581–92). In his *De duabus naturis in Christo*, Chemnitz too does no more than arrive at the traditional verdict on Nestorius.

Only in the seventeenth century was a new basis for scholarship laid by Johann Garnier in his naturally very disordered and incomplete edition of *Marius Mercator* (two volumes), Paris 1673. The edition of the so-called *Synodicum adversus tragoediam Irenaei*, Louvain 1682, by Christian Lupus (died 1681) is important. The *Annotationes* of this posthumous work are incomplete. Baluzius re-edited *Marius Mercator* in 1684. At the same time criticism of the traditional verdict on Nestorius begins. For the first time the question 'Was Nestorius a Nestorian?' is asked. Walch gives an excellent survey of this in his *Historie* mentioned above, vol. V, 817–37. The work of the Calvinist J. Bruguier of Lille is particularly important; in a book published anonymously in Frankfurt in 1645 he sets out to prove Nestorius orthodox and Cyril as the heretic (*Disputatio de supposito, in qua plurima hactenus inaudita de Nestorio tamquam orthodoxo et de Cyrillo Alexandrino aliisque episcopis Ephesi in Synodum coactis tamquam haereticis demonstrantur* . . .). Walch ascribes the work to David Derodon (op. cit., 830–2).

[1] See A. Grillmeier, *Schol* 36, 1961, 325–6.

The Catholic authors maintain a negative attitude, in particular Dionysius Petavius, who, in the sixth book of his Treatise on the Incarnation, attacks the anonymous work (*Dogmata Theologica*, ed. Fournials, T. VI, 1–105). He refers to other well-known authors of his time. Lenain de Tillemont, too, reaches the same conclusion in the fourteenth volume of his *Memoires pour servir à l'histoire ecclésiastique des six premiers siècles*, Paris 1709, although he knows of 'un grand nombre de questions & de difficultez qu'on pourroit faire sur le dogme de Nestorius' (p. 309). For this he refers once again to Petavius and Garnier. The extensive work by the Jesuit Louis Doucin, *Histoire du Nestorianisme*, Paris 1698, which traces this history down to 553, is of no particular value. For him, Theodoret is as suspect as Nestorius himself. He has no sense of history. All that matters are the purely dogmatic viewpoints of a later period, especially those of the Second Council of Constantinople. The *Annali Ecclesiastici* of Baronius, T. I, Roma 1683 (for the year 428 and after) sharpen the tone against Nestorius. Richard Simon draws attention to the oriental sources (*Critique de la Bibliothèque des auteurs Ecclésiastiques . . . du Elies Du-Pin* T. I, Paris 1730, 171–3; posthumous). On the other hand, Walch's *Historie*, mentioned above, 838–936, gives an example of a theoretical and practical endeavour towards a new understanding of Nestorius and points to similar attempts. According to Walch both Nestorius and Cyril teach rightly, but both should have tempered their language (861). But the author still has insufficient means at his disposal to criticize the term *prosopon* in Nestorius. This tendency of Walch is still followed by J. A. Dorner, *Entwicklungsgeschichte der Lehre von der Person Christi*, T. II, Berlin 1853, 60–86. He is inclined to attribute a teaching of two persons to Nestorius (p. 63).

With the end of the nineteenth and the early years of the twentieth century a new phase in the study of Nestorius begins. This is concerned with two fields of research:

(1) *The editions of the text.* F. Loofs in *Nestoriana*, Halle 1905, gathers together the texts known up to his time, thereby taking up once again the work of Garnier. But the most significant event was the discovery and publication of the so-called *Liber Heraclidis*, the (second) apology of Nestorius preserved in a Syriac translation. F. Loofs in *ThLZ* 51, 1926, 193–201, and Luise Abramowski, *Untersuchungen zum Liber Heraclidis des Nestorius* (CSCO 242, Subsidia 22), Louvain 1963, 1–4, give a report of the find and the two primary and four secondary transcripts made from it. Paul Bedjan, *Nestorius, Le livre d'Héraclide de Damas*, Paris–Leipzig 1910, arranged an edition of the whole Syriac text by using one primary and two secondary transcripts (the latter derive from the second primary transcript). F. Nau (1910) provided a French translation (with the assistance of P. Bedjan and M. Brière); on this see J. Lebon in *RHE* 12, 1911, 513–19; P. Peeters in *AnalBoll* 30, 1911, 356–60 with improvements on Nau. We have an English translation in *The Bazaar of Heracleides, newly translated from the Syriac and edited with an Introduction, Notes and Appendices* by G. R. Driver and L. Hodgson, Oxford 1925 (for criticism see F. Loofs, loc. cit.). In the study mentioned above, L. Abramowski took up a long overdue task by making a completely fresh investigation into the literary-historical testimony to the *Liber Heraclidis* (=*LH*), in Ebed-Jesus, the Life of

Bar-Edta and in Evagrius Scholasticus, ibid., 4–15. At the same time the question of the predecessor of the *LH* (Second 'Apologia'), the *Tragoedia* (First 'Apologia') of Nestorius, is raised. This is associated with the *Tragoedia* of Irenaeus of Tyre. The fragments of this *Tragoedia* of Nestorius have been recently discovered in Irenaeus of Tyre, Evagrius Scholasticus, in cod. add. 12156 of the British Museum and in Severus of Antioch (ibid., 27–32). But the principal user of the *Tragoedia* proves to have been Barhadbešabba, the Nestorian church historian. In her literary-critical analysis of Barhadbešabba's church history, L. Abramowski shows that chs. 20–28 and 30 have made use of the 'Apologie' (*Tragoedia*) of Nestorius in far more than the literal quotations which had already been recognized by R. Abramowski (ibid., 33–73). Long sections, not explicitly said to be quotations, have been inserted into the continuous text. Moreover, catchwords and leading thoughts of Nestorius have been incorporated into the description given by the historian. Nestorius' (First) Apology and his *LH* are chiefly concerned with a report of and polemic against the Council of Ephesus. Just an accurate comparison with the *LH* made it possible to recognize the 'hidden' quotations made by Barhadbešabba from the (First) Apology. 'It should, however, be noticed that all the parallels of content, style and language which could be indicated at no time touch on the dialogue at the beginning of the *LH*' (L. Abramowski, *Untersuchungen zum literarischen Nachlass des Nestorius*, Dissertation, Bonn 1956, dactyl., 115 f.). This led the writer to make a literary-critical investigation of the *LH* itself (*Untersuchungen zum Liber Heraclidis des Nestorius*, see above, which was a part of the dissertation just quoted). The literary-critical analysis of the *LH* results in the following picture, cf. ibid., 119:

(*a*) The bulk of the book derives from Nestorius (B, 126–521; N, 81–332; DrH, 85–380).

(*b*) At its conclusion this text has suffered not only the one interpolation which has already been recognized by Loofs, but several others. The interpolator is to be located in Constantinople and can be dated quite accurately, between 451 and 470 (one of the inserted texts which perhaps does not come from the same hand has the year 455 as a *terminus post quem*). The interpolations are:

B	N	DrH
495^{18}–506^{19}	316^{28}–323^3	362^{13}–369^{21}
507^6 –507^{19}	323^{12}–323^{26}	370^3 –370^{19}
510^{14}–512^3	325^7 –326^{10}	372^{12}–373^{15}
519^{16}–519^{18}	330^{30}–330^{33}	378^{31}–378^{34}
520^2 –520^{16}	331^2 –331^{16}	379^2– 379^{19}

(*c*) The text of Nestorius has been given a Nestorian introduction (B, 10–125; N, 5–81; DrH, 7–86) which is written in dialogue form (the division into chapters is secondary, as Nau already recognized). The author of this introduction L. Abramowski names 'Ps.-Nestorius'.

As far as the authenticity of B, 10–125 par. is concerned, these results are now challenged by L. I. Scipioni, *Nestorio e il concilio de Efeso*, Milano 1974, 299–361 (Ch. 6, 'Il periodo dell'esilio'). Scipioni sums up his criticism in English, as follows: 'We feel that the above-mentioned arguments are based on philological elements which are too narrow to be decisive, and do not take into account the obvious adherence and continuity of the contents that exist between the part in question and the remains of Nestorius' earlier preaching activity, besides the large number of points of contact with the part of the same text held to be authentic. Moreover, it is anachronistic when it considers the first part as being of later date, since its contents are certainly less elaborate and more informal, and therefore of earlier date than those of the authentic part which are a true development and a firmer explanation. The break between the two parts of the text, noted by the critics, is explained by us with the hypothesis of two drafts at different dates, corresponding to the twofold typology found in Nestorius' previous writings: the *Theopaschitos* and the *Tragoedia*, whose disappearance we thus explain. The first part isolated by the critics and which we have called *Dialogue* is apparently a recast of the *Theopaschitos* meant to give an organic reply to Cyril's last christological dialogues, with which there are several things in common. In this part, Nestorius is seen to have the same themes which dominated his initial theology, and the interest remains predominantly soteriological. There is, however, a development in the necessity to defend and explain the nature of the union *en prosopo monadiko* which he sets up against Cyril's *en physei mia*. The line of exposition is a result of the opposition proclaimed by Cyril (between the *henosis* of his own doctrinal formula and the *synapheia schetike* attributed to Nestorius), when explaining the Symbol of Union of 433. The evolution lies not in the christological formula (δύο φύσεις, ἓν πρόσωπον)—which Nestorius already held before the controversy with Cyril—but in the necessity he felt of clarifying the nature and the characteristics of the union in the prosopon which Nestorius, right from the start, had forcefully set up against the *physike* or *hypostatike* (*henosis*) of the Apollinarians, and taken up, in his view, by Cyril' (op. cit., 430f.).

Here a further important step has been taken in Nestorius scholarship, the significance of which is only made clear by the controversy indicated here.

Knowledge of Nestorianism after Chalcedon has been substantially furthered by the edition by Luise Abramowski and Alan E. Goodman, *A Nestorian Collection of Christological Texts, Cambridge University Library Ms. Oriental 1319*, Vols I and II, Cambridge 1972, which has already been mentioned several times. The edition is based on the copy of a manuscript probably coming from the late eighth or early ninth century, which contains excerpts of Nestorian theology from the sixth to eighth centuries. It probably goes back to an earlier collection of the kind. The aim of the collection is to provide the reader with the necessary armoury to refute the adherents of that theology who do not follow the compiler in confessing 'two natures, two hypostases and one prosopon (person)' in Christ. This formula (two hypostases) was only taken up in the official teaching of Nestorianism in 612. The opponents are the Monophysites, the Chalcedonians and the Neo-Chalcedonians (cf. op. cit., II, XVIIIf.). The collection contains some well-known passages but also some new passages. In their excellent edition, Abramowski and Goodman have carefully added all the available information about the authors, the works, the sources and the historical background. A particularly valuable passage in this volume is excerpt VI, which relates to the time of peace between the Antiochenes and Cyril of Alexandria (432/3). We have already mentioned it in connection with the

Symbol of Union. The work will occupy us further in our account of post-Chalcedonian christology.

In this context the investigations into the councils carried out by E. Schwartz should also be mentioned. His work, of course, is concerned more with clarifying the text and editing it, and elucidating the politics of church and state, rather than describing the theological implications. Schwartz is thus inclined to overestimate the (church) political element. For Nestorius, the following studies are relevant: (1) 'Die Reichskonzilien von Theodosius bis Justinian', in *ZSavignyStiftg* 42, kan. Abt. 11, 1921, 208–53; see now E. Schwartz, *Gesammelte Schriften* 4, Berlin 1960, 111–58; (2) 'Die Konzilien im 4. und 5. Jahrhundert', *HZ* 104, 1910, 1–37: *Konzilstudien I. Cassian und Nestorius*, Strasbourg 1914; (3) 'Die sogenannten Gegenanathematismen des Nestorius', *SbMünchAk, Phil.-hist. Kl.*, 1922, H. 1 (these 'anathemas' are explained to be spurious); (4) 'Zur Vorgeschichte des ephesinischen Konzils. Ein Fragment', *HZ* 112, 1914, 237–63. For Schwartz Nestorius is no heretic, ibid., 257. The textual presuppositions of the Nestorian question are now improved by a new study on Eutherius of Tyana, one of the most faithful friends of Nestorius. In the time of the Ephesian quarrels he wrote a sharp pamphlet against Cyril of Alexandria and his followers. This writing was handed down under the name of Athanasius of Alexandria. M. Tetz studied the question within the frame of the tradition of the Athanasian corpus. He is able to publish the first complete edition of the *Antilogia*—a title chosen by the editor according to indications in Eutherius' introductory letter (M. Tetz, *Eine Antilogie des Eutherios von Tyana*, *PTSt* 1, Berlin 1964, p. 4[18]). Hitherto a special form of the *Antilogia* was known under the title *Confutationes quarundam propositionum*. Tetz proves that this text is a secondary abbreviation of the original writing of Eutherius which left out four chapters (ibid., ix). The *Antilogia* seems to have been preserved from destruction by the library of the Acoimetes in Constantinople, who were strict defenders of the Council of Chalcedon. Indeed, the formulas of Eutherius are very close to the Chalcedonian conception of Christ.

(2) *The new description of Nestorius' teaching*. A further twentieth-century contribution to the study of Nestorius is the repeated attempts at a new description of his teaching. Even before the *LH* had been made available, J. B. Bethune-Baker began, with the help of a transcript of the work placed at his disposal, to vindicate the teaching of Nestorius: *Nestorius and his Teaching, A fresh examination of the evidence*, Cambridge 1908. The main chapter deals with the terms presumed to have been used by Nestorius (ousia, hypostasis, prosopon), with the repudiation of the title 'Theotokos' and above all with the question 'Did Nestorius postulate two persons in Christ?' (82–100). Bethune-Baker thinks that the unity of prosopon in Nestorius represents no merely moral unity. Nestorius' *Bewährungslehre* (that is, the theory that Christ earned his exaltation to Sonship through his obedience and virtue) is given a very positive assessment (121–39). His teaching on the incarnation is then compared with that of Cyril by means of two lengthy quotations from the *LH* (148–70). Nestorius is to be shown as a defender of the orthodox teaching which was then defined at the Council of Chalcedon (189–96). Cyril is blamed for one or two objectionable expressions which would, however, be capable

of an orthodox interpretation. This is principally clear from the analysis of the formula of the 'hypostatic union' (171–88).

With this work, Bethune-Baker introduces the second epoch of efforts to rehabilitate Nestorius. Whether in so doing he has been influenced by the results of earlier scholarship cannot be seen from his work. More restrained in his judgements, but nevertheless strongly dependent upon Bethune-Baker, is L. Fendt in his Strasbourg dissertation *Die Christologie des Nestorius*, Kempten 1910. In considering the position of scholarship we can give wide recognition to the conclusions of Fendt (the pupil of Albert Ehrhard), at that time still a Roman Catholic. With him, Catholic scholarship too begins to adopt a milder approach to the Nestorius question. Of course, it was for this reason that J. B. Junglas, *Die Irrlehre des Nestorius*, Trier 1912, was subject to severe censure. In seeking a partial vindication of Nestorius he argued that the heretical element in his work was not so much in the prosopon doctrine as in the *Bewährungslehre*. This might result in an unfortunate shifting of accent. In judging the case of Nestorius we must begin with the prosopon concept; this is the point from which the *Bewährungslehre* is to be judged. The parts of the acts which were read out at the Council before the condemnation of Nestorius do not speak of this *Bewährungslehre*, but of the unity in Christ as it is expressed in the *communicatio idiomatum*. Several more Catholic theologians move in the direction of a deeper desire to understand Nestorius and towards at least a partial vindication of his person and his theology, especially I. Rucker, *Das Dogma von der Persönlichkeit Christi und das Problem der Häresie des Nestorius. Die Quintessenz der syr. Nestorius-Apologie, genannt Liber Heraclidis (Damasceni)*, Oxenbrunn 1934. This attempt to work out a new and yet correct interpretation of the christology of Nestorius did not, however, succeed (cf. A. Deneffe, *Schol* 10, 1935, 548–60).

E. Amann gives a better groundwork for the solution of this problem. His article 'Nestorius', *DTC* XI, 1, 76–157, with great care seeks to explain the positive and the negative, the psychological and doctrinal elements in the Nestorius case. In these pages we have the best description and interpretation of Nestorius hitherto. Less balanced, but still worth noting because of the material it contains, is the study of the same author, 'L'affaire Nestorius vue de Rome', in *RevSR* 23, 1949, 5–37, 207–44; 24, 1950, 28–52, 235–65. As the title states, an attempt is made here to explain the handling of the Nestorius affair by Rome. E. Amann advances many important documents and important matter for their interpretation. But his tendency to rehabilitate Nestorius and to attack Cyril and his party, now more emphatic in comparison with his earlier work, did not remain uncontradicted. Cf. L. Ciccone, *DThP* 54, 1951, 33–55. It should be noted that the article did not receive a last revision.

The latest advances from the Catholic side towards the solution of the Nestorius question have been made by L. I. Scipioni, O.P., in his work *Ricerche sulla Cristologia del 'Libro di Eraclide' di Nestorio. La formulazione e il suo contesto filosofico*, Fribourg 1956, and by the writer in the paper already quoted: *Schol* 36, 1961, 312–56. Similarly, from the Orthodox side, we have Milton V. Anastos, 'Nestorius was orthodox', *DOP* 16, 1962, 119–40. Scipioni's problem is not whether Nestorius was a Nestorian; his purpose is to go beyond earlier scholarship in giving an analysis of the whole of the *LH* rather than merely giving an investigation of individual theological terms. Unfortunately he did not see the necessity of first making a complete literary–critical analysis, a task now fulfilled in his new study (see above). The important things about his work are the new emphasis on Nestorius' insistence on the unity of Christ, 'the firm and undiscussed starting-point' of his christology (170), stress on Nestorius' anti-Apollinarianism and an account of the philosophical background of his doctrine. L. I. Scipioni holds that the prime contributory factor was the Stoic teaching of *krasis*. We largely follow his interpretation, adding a separate inquiry on the Nestorius of the time between 429–436 and recalling the Cappadocian background. In putting forward this theme Scipioni had already been anticipated by R. Arnou, 'Nestorianisme et Néoplatonisme. L'unité du Christ et l'union des "Intelligibles"', *Greg* 17, 1936, 116–31. Whereas I. Rucker (op. cit.) and also H. A. Wolfson, *The Philosophy of the Church Fathers* I, Cambridge, Mass. 1956, 451–63, had made Nestorius an Aristotelian, R. Arnou stamps him as a Neo-Platonist. But by recourse to the Stoa, L. I. Scipioni was able to show that the unity of prosopon in Nestorius lies not so much in the moral as in the metaphysical realm. His investigation is limited to the *LH* as 'a systematic treatise, in which Nestorius has attempted an organic presentation of his thought' (13). While he here rightly concedes to Nestorius a more or less full approximation to orthodoxy, he leaves on one side the Nestorius of the documents which were condemned at Ephesus (13). Does Scipioni thus concede a development in the teaching of Nestorius? R. Seeberg had already made such a distinction between an earlier and a later Nestorius in the second edition of his *Lehrbuch der Dogmengeschichte, Band 2*, Leipzig 1910, 202. Such a development is, of course, possible, but is not easy to define, especially as Nestorius in the *LH* is given to referring back to earlier propositions and expressions of his own. There seems to be no substantial progress, especially if the interpolations in the *LH* are excluded. Abramowski gives an accurate description of this evolution (ibid., 213–24) and we have tried to do the same (see Part Three).

Here, too, the study by L. I. Scipioni, mentioned above, affords further clarification. Scipioni stresses that Nestorius remained completely faithful to himself in his teaching. 'However, there is a further evolution consisting above all in a more meticulous rectification of the ideas and contents. This is after a decisive event: Pope Leo's intervention in the current Monophysite controversy in the *Tomus ad Flavianum*. It is decisive for Nestorius because the Pope's intervention represents, in his view, the "just verdict" he had in vain sought so long from the Council of Ephesus. Leo had at last re-established the true faith for which Nestorius had suffered so much. Now, like old Simeon, he could intone his *Nunc Dimittis* and close his eyes in peace. But he was asked to give a clarification and he could not circumvent this request. This is the reason for the text, and marks a decisive metaphysical turn in the christological problem, putting into the background the soteriological aspect which up to this point had been prevalent in Nestorius' writings. Nestorius sets to work, as never before, on the Cyrillian terminology, measuring himself against the notions of *ousia, hypostasis, henōsis, kath'hypostasin*, etc., trying to define them, analysing, comparing, re-examining his own formulas and terminology, which are in effect those of the Antiochene tradition, but which here for the first time take on new and more definite meanings. Finally, we have analysed this terminology and thought; it is an analysis which tends to restore Nestorius' true importance. We are able to conclude that Nestorius had, in fact, anticipated the formula of Chalcedon' (op. cit., 431f.).

In one place or another, different words might be possible or necessary (cf. the remarks above on the immediate preliminaries to the Chalcedonian Definition); nevertheless, Scipioni's study covers the whole of Nestorius' christology. The results are also significant for ecumenical dialogue between the churches.

In contrast to these studies, which have a more or less marked tendency to seek to understand or to vindicate Nestorius, two other writers are concerned to expound the traditional view of the relationship between Cyril and Nestorius. So especially M. Jugie, *Nestorius et la controverse nestorienne*, Paris 1912; id., *Theologia dogmatica christiana orientalis*, Tome V, Paris 1935, 76–211; id., 'Nestorio e Nestorianismo', *Enciclopedia Cattolica* VIII, 1952, 1780–4. Jugie finds a firm starting-point for his criticism of Nestorius in the later dogmatic concepts such as person and hypostasis, and finds in his writings an explicit doctrine of two persons and two hypostases. In dealing with the later Nestorius, however, he makes particular reference to the 'Counter-anathemas' which from the time of E. Schwartz have no longer been accepted as genuine (*Die sogenannten Gegenanathematismen des Nestorius*, SBMünchAk Phil.-hist. Kl., 1922, Heft 1). The study of C. Pesch, *Nestorius als Irrlehrer. Zur Erläuterung einer wichtigen theologischen Prinzipienfrage*, Paderborn 1921, employs a similar method and arrives at the same results. According to Nestorius, God and man are joined only in a moral union 'which is based on mutual love and knowledge' (91[21]). P. Bedjan and F. Nau had already passed judgement in this way in the introductions of their editions of the *LH*; the latter also in his study *Nestorius d'après les sources orientales*, Paris 1911, and 'S. Cyrille et Nestorius', *RevOrChr* 15, 1910, 355–91; 16, 1911, 1–51.

In Anglican theology most writers have concurred in the verdict of J. F. Bethune-Baker, in particular R. V. Sellers, *Two Ancient Christologies*, London 1940: 'From all this it seems clear that Nestorius is hardly deserving of the title "Nestorian", and that this is a legitimate conclusion is borne out by statements of his which show that for him Jesus Christ is very God incarnate' (164). The same author makes a similar attempt to draw together Nestorius and Cyril in his work *The Council of Chalcedon*, London 1953. In his work *Fathers and Heretics*, London 1948, 120–49, G. L. Prestige also puts forward compelling arguments for a better assessment of Nestorius. He sees clearly the limitations of the christology of Nestorius: 'the unorthodoxy of Nestorius was not a positive fact but a negative impotence; like his master Theodore, he could not bring within the framework of a single, clearly conceived personality the two natures of Christ which he distinguished with so admirable a realism. . . . The orthodoxy of Nestorius was positive: with his peculiarities of presentation once for all eliminated, the substance of his doctrine was accepted as the faith of Christendom at the Council of Chalcedon in 451' (143f.). According to G. L. Prestige there are only small differences within the Antiochene school.

For Aubrey R. Vine, *The Nestorian Churches*, London 1937, 21–36, it was really Theodore of Mopsuestia who formed the Antiochene christology as it was condemned in Nestorius. It is correctly said that Nestorius never fully understood the idea 'which *"communicatio idiomatum"* was meant to convey' (35). J. W. C. Wand, *The Four Great Heresies*, London 1955, 89–109, sees both the positive element and the inadequacy in Nestorius' christology: 'Nestorius was right, of course, in asserting a singularity of person, but wrong in saying that it could be made up of an earlier duality of persons, for two persons who were *ex hypothesi* already perfect and complete could not without diminution make a third' (98f.).

The modern Protestant approach to the 'Nestorius affair' found most pointed expression in the four lectures which F. Loofs gave at the University of London in 1913 and published under the title *Nestorius and his place in the History of Christian Doctrine*, Cambridge 1914. First of all he describes the newly awakened interest in Nestorius and the tragedy of his life (26–60), going on to outline his teaching (60–94) and finally his place in the history of dogma (94–130). For Loofs, Nestorius is orthodox by the standard of the Council of Chalcedon but not by the standard of the Second (553) and Third (680/1) Councils of Constantinople. Nevertheless, in his teaching Nestorius stands in a better and more complete tradition than Cyril. Loofs then describes this dogmatic background with his own particular terminology and insight; it is formed by a general christological framework common to all Christians and occurring in both East and West. This framework presupposes no mystic, immanent doctrine of the Trinity and no ἕνωσις κατὰ φύσιν with their mythologies, but is economic (viz. temporarily) -trinitarian and monotheistic. Here Loofs, of course, supports his positions with constructions which have not gained wide acceptance. For this reason this attempt represents no solution of the Nestorius question. Loofs also defends the orthodoxy of Nestorius in his article in *PRE* 13, 736–49, which has already been mentioned. In comparison with this he is very restrained in his *Leitfaden zum Studium der Dogmengeschichte* 37 (ed. K. Aland, Tübingen 1959⁶, 227–35). A .v. Harnack, *Lehrbuch der Dogmengeschichte*, II, 1, Tübingen 1931⁵, 355–68, and W. Koehler in his *Dogmengeschichte*, Zürich–Leipzig 1938, 158f. speak quite moderately on the Nestorius question. In his *Lehrbuch der Dogmengeschichte* II³, Erlangen–Leipzig 1923, 210–42, R. Seeberg, elsewhere so concerned to reach a balance, passes a very sharp verdict. In his view, 'Nestorius offered a presentation of the Antiochene christology which is the clearest, simplest, and nearest to the church's understanding that we possess. There is nothing "heretical" in his thought. . . . None of the great "heretics" of the history of dogma bears this name as undeservedly as Nestorius' (219f.). Of course, R. Seeberg overlooks the role of Theodoret and the other moderate Antiochenes. Other historians have still more pointed expressions (cf. H. Ristow, 'Der Begriff ΠΡΟΣΩΠΟΝ in der Theologie des Nestorius', in *Aus der byzantinistischen Arbeit der Deutschen Demokratischen Republik* I, Berlin 1957, 218–36; the survey of the position of Nestorius scholarship given there on 219–21 is very defective. Cf. also C. Pesch, 'Zur neueren Literatur über Nestorius', 115, in the additional volume to the *Stimmen aus Maria Laach*, Freiburg 1914). All these assessments of Nestorius and the Nestorius question given by the Protestant side are developed and surpassed by the excellent passage 'Zur Christologie des Nestorius in der *Zweiten Apologie* und in den übrigen *Nestoriana*', which occurs in the study of L. Abramowski, often quoted here: *Untersuchungen zum LH*, 208–29. We may expect a survey of more recent discussion from the publication of papers from the Sixth International Conference on Patristic Studies, Oxford 1971. See especially H. E. W. Turner, 'Nestorius Reconsidered' (cf. L. I. Scipioni, *Nestorio e il concilio di Efeso*, 389, n. 47).

BIBLIOGRAPHY

THE following bibliography is restricted to recent books and articles of special interest for the problems examined here; for further literature and details of patristic texts readers are referred to the footnotes, and for earlier studies, to my article in *Das Konzil von Chalkedon* I, Würzburg 1973[4], 5–202, and to the bibliography of A. Schönmetzer, ibid. III, 825–65, 877–9.

Abramowski, L., 'Der Streit um Diodor und Theodor zwischen den beiden ephesinischen Konzilien', *ZKG* 67, 1955/56, 252–82.
—— 'Zum Brief des Andreas von Samosata an Rabbula von Edessa', *OrChr* 41, 1957, 51–64.
—— 'Ein unbekanntes Zitat aus *Contra Eunomium* des Theodor von Mopsuestia', *Mus* 71, 1958, 97–104.
—— 'Zur Theologie Theodors von Mopsuestia', *ZKG* 72, 1961, 263–93.
—— *Untersuchungen zum Liber Heraclidis des Nestorius* (CSCO 242, Subsidia 22), Louvain 1963.
Abramowski, L.–Goodman, Alan E. (eds.), *A Nestorian Collection of Christological Texts*, Vol. I: Syriac Text, Vol. II: Introduction, Translation and Indexes, Cambridge 1972.
Abramowski, R., 'Untersuchungen zu Diodor von Tarsus', *ZNW* 30, 1931, 234–61.
—— 'Der theologische Nachlass des Diodor von Tarsus', *ZNW* 42, 1949, 19–69.
Aeby, G., *Les missions divines de saint Justin à Origène* (Paradosis 12), Freiburg 1958.
Amann, E., 'L'affaire Nestorius vue de Rome', *RevSR* 23, 1949, 5–37, 207–44; 24, 1950, 28–52, 235–65.
Anastos, M. V., 'Nestorius was orthodox', *DOP* 16, 1962, 119–40.
Andresen, S. C., *Logos und Nomos*, Berlin 1955.
—— 'Zur Entstehung und Geschichte des trinitarischen Personbegriffes', *ZNW* 52, 1961, 1–39.
Armstrong, G. T., *Die Genesis in der Alten Kirche* (BGBH 4), Tübingen 1962.
Athanase d'Alexandrie, *Sur l'incarnation du Verbe*. Introduction, Text-critique, Traduction, Notes et Index par C. Kannengiesser (SC 199), Paris 1973.
Auf der Maur, H., *Die Osterhomilien des Asterios Sophistes als Quelle für die Geschichte der Osterfeier* (Trierer Theol. Studien 19), Trier 1967.
Bacht, H., 'Die Rolle des orientalischen Mönchtums in den kirchenpolitischen Auseinandersetzungen um Chalkedon (431–519)', *Chalkedon* II, 193–314.
Barbel, J., *Christos Angelos* (Theophaneia 3), Bonn 1941.
—— *Gregor von Nazianz. Die fünf Theologischen Reden* (Testimonia III), Düsseldorf 1963.
Barnard, L. W., *Athenagoras. A Study in Second Century Christian Apologetic* (Théologie historique 18), Paris 1972.
Bauer, W., *Orthodoxy and Heresy in Earliest Christianity*, Philadelphia 1971 and London 1972.

Baur, C., 'Drei unedierte Festpredigten aus der Zeit der nestorianischen Streitigkeiten', *Trad* 9, 1953, 101–26.

Baus, K., 'Das Gebet zu Christus beim heiligen Hieronymus', *TThZ* 60, 1951, 178–88.

—— 'Das Gebet der Märtyrer', *TThZ* 62, 1953, 19–32.

—— 'Die Stellung Christi im Beten des heiligen Augustinus', *TThZ* 63, 1954, 321–39.

—— *Von der Urgemeinde zur frühchristlichen Grosskirche* (Handbuch der Kirchengeschichte, ed. H. Jedin, Vol. 1), Freiburg–Basel–Wien 1962.

Baus, K.-Ewig, E., *Die Reichskirche nach Konstantin dem Grossen*, Erster Halbband: *Die Kirche von Nikaia bis Chalkedon* (Handbuch der Kirchengeschichte, ed. H. Jedin, Vol. 2), Freiburg–Basel–Wien 1973.

Bavel, T. J. van, *Recherches sur la Christologie de Saint Augustin* (Paradosis 10), Freiburg 1954.

Benoit, A., *Saint Irénée. Introduction à l'étude de sa théologie*, Paris 1960.

Beskow, Per, *Rex Gloriae. The Kingship of Christ in the Early Church*, Uppsala 1962.

Bienert, W. A., *'Allegoria' und 'Anagoge' bei Didymus dem Blinden von Alexandrien*, Berlin–New York 1972.

Bietenhard, H., *Die himmlische Welt in Urchristentum und Spätjudentum*, Tübingen 1951.

Birdsall, J. N.-Thomson, R. W. (eds.), *Biblical and Patristic Studies. In Memory of Robert Pierce Casey*, Freiburg 1963.

Bizer, C., *Studien zu den pseudathanasianischen Dialogen. Der Orthodoxos und Aetios* (Diss. Bonn 1966), Rotaprint 1970, revised.

Blackman, E. C., *Marcion and his influence*, London 1948.

Boismard, M.-E., *St John's Prologue*, London 1957.

Bouchet, J. R., O.P., 'Le vocabulaire de l'union et du rapport des natures chez saint Grégoire de Nysse', *RevThom* 68, 1968, 533–82.

—— 'La vision de l'économie du salut selon s. Grégoire de Nysse', *RSPT* 52, 1968, 613–44.

Boularand, É., *L'hérésie d'Arius et la "Foi" de Nicée* I–II, Paris 1972.

Braun, R., *'Deus Christianorum', Recherches sur le vocabulaire doctrinal de Tertullien* (Publications de la Faculté des Lettres et Sciences Humaines d'Alger XLI), Paris 1962.

Brière, M., 'Fragments syriaques de Diodore de Tarse réédits et traduits pour la première fois', *RevOrChr* X (XXX), 1946, 231–83 (with Syriac text by P. de Lagarde).

Bultmann, R., 'Ignatius and Paul', in *Existence and Faith*, ed. S. M. Ogden, London 1960, 267–77.

Buytaert, E. M., 'L'authenticité des dix-sept opuscules contenus dans le ms. T 523 sous le nom d'Eusèbe d'Emèse', *RHE* 43, 1948, 5–89.

—— *L'héritage littéraire d'Eusèbe d'Emèse* (Bibl. du Muséon vol. 24), Louvain 1949.

—— *Eusèbe d'Emèse. Discours conservés en latin. Textes en partie inédits.* T.I. *La collection de Troyes.* T.II. *La collection de Sirmond* (Spic. Lov. 26,27), Louvain 1953, 1957.

Camelot, T., O.P., *Ephèse et Chalcédoine* (HCO 2), Paris 1961; German edition; *Ephesus und Chalcedon* (GÖK 2), Mainz 1963.

Canivet, P., *Histoire d'une entreprise apologétique au Ve siècle*, Paris 1957.

Cantalamessa, R., O.F.M.Cap., *La Cristologia di Tertulliano* (Paradosis 18), Freiburg 1962.

—— 'Méliton de Sardes. Une christologie antignostique du IIe siècle', *RevSR* 37, 1963, 1–26.

—— *L'omelia 'In S. Pascha' dello Pseudo-Ippolito di Roma. Ricerche sulla teologia dell'Asia minore nella seconda metà del II secolo* (Pubblicazioni dell'Università Cattolica del Sacro Cuore, Contributi, serie terza, Scienze Filolog. e Lett. 16), Milano 1967.

Capelle, B., O.S.B., 'Le Logos Fils de Dieu dans la théologie d'Hippolyte', *RTAM* 9, 1937, 109–24.

—— 'Hippolyte de Rome', *RTAM* 17, 1950, 145–74.

Cerfaux, L., *Le Christ dans la Théologie de Saint Paul*, Paris 1951.

Charlier, N., 'Le *Thesaurus de Trinitate* de saint Cyrille d'Alexandrie. Questions de critique littéraire', *RHE* 45, 1950, 25–81.

Codina, V., *El aspecto cristológico en la espiridualidad di Juan Cassiano* (OCA 175), Roma 1966.

Colpe, C., *Die religionsgeschichtliche Schule. Darstellung und Kritik ihres Bildes vom gnostischen Erlösermythos* (FRLANT, NF 60), Göttingen 1961.

Crouzel, H., *Théologie de l'Image de Dieu chez Origène*, Paris 1956.

—— 'Origène devant l'incarnation et devant l'histoire', *BLE* 1960, 81–110.

—— *Origène et la 'connaissance mystique'*, Paris 1961.

—— *Origène et la philosophie*, Paris 1962.

Cullmann, O., *The Christology of the New Testament*, London 1963².

Daniélou, J., *Origen*, London 1955.

—— *The Theology of Jewish Christianity*, London 1964.

—— *Gospel Message and Hellenistic Culture*, London 1973.

Denhard, H., *Das Problem der Abhängigkeit des Basilius von Plotin* (PTSt 3), Berlin 1964.

Denzinger, H.–Schönmetzer, A., *Enchiridion Symbolorum*, Freiburg 1963.

Devreesse, R., *Essai sur Théodore de Mopsueste* (ST 141), Città del Vaticano 1948.

Diepen, H. M., O.S.B., 'L'assumptus homo à Chalcédoine', *RevThom* 51, 1951, 573–608.

—— *Douze dialogues de Christologie ancienne*, Roma 1960.

—— 'L'assumptus homo patristique', *RevThom* 63, 1963, 225–45, 363–88; 64, 1964, 32–52.

Dörries, H., *De Spiritu Sancto. Der Beitrag des Basilius zum Abschluss des trinitarischen Dogmas* (AbhGöttGW, 3F, No. 39), Göttingen 1956.

—— *Das Selbstzeugnis Kaiser Konstantins* (AbhAkWissGöttGW, Phil.-hist. Kl., 3F, No. 34), Göttingen 1954.

Doutreleau, L., 'Le *De Trinitate* est-il de Didyme l'Aveugle', *RSR* 45, 1957, 514–57.

—— 'Vie et survie de Didyme l'Aveugle', *Les Mardis de Dar El-Salam: Sommaire 1956–57*, Paris 1959, 33–92.

—— *Didyme l'Aveugle. Sur Zacharie I–III* (SC 83–5), Paris 1962.

Eltester, W., *Eikon im Neuen Testament* (BZNW 23), Berlin 1958.

Elze, M., *Tatian und seine Theologie*, Göttingen 1960.

Farina, R., *L'Impero e l'Imperatore Cristiano in Eusebio di Cesarea. La prima teologia politica del Cristianesimo*, Zürich 1966.

Favale, A., S.D.B., *Teofilo d'Alessandria* (Biblioteca del Salesianum 41), Torino 1958.

Fierro, A., *Sobre la Gloria en San Hilario* (AnalGreg 144), Rome 1962.

Fondevilla, J., *Ideas trinitarias y cristologicas de Marcelo de Ancyra*, Madrid 1953.

Fortin, E. L., A.A., *Christianisme et culture philosophique au cinquième siècle. La querelle de l'âme humaine en Occident*, Paris 1959.

Gaidioz, J., 'Saint Prosper d'Aquitaine et le Tome à Flavien', *RevSR* 23, 1949, 270–301.

Galtier, P., 'Théodore de Mopsueste: sa vraie pensée sur l'Incarnation', *RSR* 45, 1957, 161–86, 338–60.

—— *S. Hilaire de Poitiers*, Paris 1960.

Geiselmann, J. R., *Jesus der Christus*, Stuttgart 1951.

Gerhardsson, B., *Memory and Manuscript. Oral Tradition and Written Tradition in Rabbinic Judaism and Early Christianity* (Acta Sem. Neot. Upsal. 22), Uppsala 1961.

—— *Tradition and Transmission in Early Christianity* (Coniectanea Neotestamentica XX), Lund-Copenhagen 1964.

Gesché, A., 'L'âme humaine de Jésus dans la christologie du IVᵉ siècle', *RHE* 54, 1959, 385–425.

—— *La christologie du 'Commentaire sur les Psaumes' découvert à Toura*, Gembloux 1962.

Glorieux, P., *Prénestorianisme en Occident*, Tournai–Paris–Rome–New York 1959.

Goppelt, L., *Typos*, Gütersloh 1932.

—— *Christentum und Judentum im ersten und zweiten Jahrhundert. Ein Aufriss der Urgeschichte der Kirche*, Gütersloh 1956.

Grass, H.–Kümmel, W. (eds.), *Jesus Christus. Das Christusverständnis im Wandel der Zeiten* (Marburger Theologische Studien 1), Marburg 1963.

Greer, R. A., *Theodore of Mopsuestia. Exegete and Theologian*, London 1961.

—— 'The Antiochene Christology of Diodore of Tarsus', *JTS* 17, 1966, 327–41.

Grillmeier, A., S.J., 'Der Gottessohn im Totenreich', *ZkTh* 71, 1949, 1–53, 184–203.

—— *Der Logos am Kreuz*, München 1956.

—— 'Hellenisierung-Judaisierung des Christentums als Deuteprinzipien der Geschichte des kirchlichen Dogmas', *Schol* 33, 1958, 321–55, 528–58.

'Christologie', *LThK* II, 1958, 1156–66.

—— 'Vom Symbolum zur Summa', in J. Betz–H. Fries (eds.), *Kirche und Überlieferung*, Freiburg–Basel–Wien 1960, 119–69.

—— 'Das *Scandalum oecumenicum* des Nestorius in kirchlich-dogmatischer und theologiegeschichtlicher Sicht', *Schol* 36, 1961, 321–56.

—— *Le Christ dans la tradition chrétienne. De l'âge apostolique à Chalcédoine (451)*, Paris 1973.

—— *Cristologia antica e Ermeneutica moderna*. La discussione attuale sulla cristologia calcedonese, Brescia 1974.

—— *Mit ihm und in ihm. Christologische Forschungen und Perspektiven*, Freiburg 1975.

Grillmeier, A.–Bacht, H. (eds.), *Das Konzil von Chalkedon I–III*, Würzburg 1973[4], 1962[3], 1959[2], 1951–54.

Gruber, G., *ZWH. Wesen, Stufen und Mitteilung des wahren Lebens bei Origenes* (MüThS II 23), Munich 1962.

Guillaumont, A., *Les 'Kephalaia Gnostica' d'Evagre le Pontique et l'histoire de l'Origénisme chez les Grecs et chez les Syriens* (PS 5), Paris 1962.

Gutwenger, E., *Bewusstsein und Wissen Christi*, Innsbruck 1960.

Hanson, R. P. C., *Allegory and Event*, London 1959.

Harkins, Paul W., 'Chrysostom the Apologist: on the Divinity of Christ', *Kyriakon* I, 441–51.

Harl, M., *Origène et la fonction révélatrice du Verbe Incarné* (PS 2), Paris 1958.

—— (ed.) *Écriture et culture philosophique dans la pensée de Grégoire de Nysse. Actes du Colloque de Chevetogne (22–26 September 1969)*, Leiden 1971.

Hay, C., 'St John Chrysostom and the Integrity of the Human Nature of Christ', *FrancStud* 19, 1959, 290–317.

Hayes, W. M., *The Greek Manuscript Tradition of (Ps.) Basil's ADVERSUS EUNOMIUM Books IV–V*, Leiden 1972.

Hegermann, H., *Die Vorstellung vom Schöpfungsmittler im hellenistischen Judentum und Urchristentum* (TU 82), Berlin 1961.

Hennecke, E.–Schneemelcher, W.–Wilson, R. McL., *New Testament Apocrypha* I, London 1963; II, London 1965.

Henry, P.–Hadot P., *Marius Victorinus, Traités Théologiques sur la Trinité I–II* (SC 68, 69), Paris 1960.

Holl, K., *Amphilochius von Ikonium in seinem Verhältnis zu den grossen Kappadoziern*, Tübingen–Leipzig 1904.

Holte, R., *Logos spermatikos. Christianity and Ancient Philosophy according to St. Justin's Apologies* (Studia Theologica 12), Lund 1958.

Houssiau, A., *La christologie de S. Irénée*, Louvain 1958.

—— 'Incarnation et communion selon les Pères grecs', *Irénikon* 45, 1972, 457–68.

Hübner, R., *Die Einheit des Leibes Christi bei Gregor von Nyssa. Untersuchungen zum Ursprung der 'physischen' Erlösungslehre*, Leiden 1974.

—— 'Gregor von Nyssa als Verfasser der sog. Ep. 38 des Basilius. Zum unterschiedlichen Verständnis der οὐσία bei den kappadozischen Brüdern', *Epektasis*, 463–490.

—— 'Gregor von Nyssa und Markell von Ankyra', Harl, M. (ed.), *Écriture et culture philosophique* (see above), 199–229.

Jarry, J., *Hérésies et factions dans l'Empire Byzantin du IVe au VIIe siècle* (Publications de l'Institut Français d'Archéologie Orientale du Caire. Recherches d'Archéologie, de Philologie et d'Histoire, T. XIV), Le Caire, 1968.

Iersel, B. M. F. van, *'Der Sohn' in den synoptischen Jesusworten*, Suppl. *Novum Testamentum* 1961.

Jervell, J., *Imago Dei* (FRLANT 58), Göttingen 1960.

Jonas, H., *Gnosis und spätantiker Geist: I Die mythologische Gnosis* (2nd ed.); II, 1 *Von der Mythologie zur mystischen Philosophie* (FRLANT NF 33 & 45), Göttingen 1954.
—— *The Gnostic Religion*, Boston 1958.
Jouassard, G., 'Un problème d'Anthropologie et de Christologie chez saint Cyrille d'Alexandrie', *RSR* 43, 1955, 361–78.
—— 'Saint Cyrille d'Alexandrie et le schéma de l'Incarnation Verbe-Chaire', *RSR* 44, 1956, 234–42.
Käsemann, E., 'Kritische Analyse von Phil. 2, 5–11', *ZThK* 47, 1950, 313–60; in *Exegetische Versuche und Besinnungen* I, Göttingen 1960, 51–95.
Karpp, H., *Textbuch zur altkirchlichen Christologie. Theologia und Oikonomia*, Neukirchen–Vluyn 1972.
Kelly, J. N. D., *Early Christian Creeds*, London 1972³.
—— *Early Christian Doctrines*, London 1960².
Koch, G., *Die Heilsverwirklichung bei Theodor von Mopsuestia*, München 1965.
—— *Strukturen und Geschichte des Heils in der Theologie des Theodoret von Kyros. Eine dogmen- und theologiegeschichtliche Untersuchung* (Frankfurter Theologische Studien 17), Frankfurt 1974.
Köster, H. *Synoptische Überlieferung bei den Apostolischen Vätern* (TU 65), Berlin 1957.
Kraft, H., *Kaiser Konstantins religiöse Entwicklung* (BHistTh 20), Tübingen 1955.
Kruijf, T. de, *Der Sohn des lebendigen Gottes. Ein Beitrag zur Christologie des Matthäusevangeliums* (AnalBibl 16), Rome 1962.
Laurentin, A., *Doxa. Problèmes de Christologie. Études des Commentaires de Jean 17,5 depuis les origines jusqu'à S. Thomas d'Aquin* I–II, Paris n.d.
Lebon, J., *Le moine saint Marcien. Étude critique des sources, édition de ses écrits*, ed. A. van Roey (Spicilegium Sacrum Lovaniense 36), Louvain 1968.
Léon-Dufour, X., *The Gospels and the Jesus of History*, London 1968.
Liébaert, J. *La doctrine christologique de saint Cyrille d'Alexandrie avant la querelle nestorienne*, Lille 1951.
—— *Christologie* (HDG III 1), Freiburg–Basel–Wien 1965.
Lohse, B., *Epochen der Dogmengeschichte*, Stuttgart 1963.
Loi, V., *Lattanzio nella storia del linguaggio e del pensiero pre-niceno*, Zürich 1970.
Lubac, H. de, *Histoire et Esprit. L'intelligence et l'Ecriture d'après Origène* (Théologie 16), Paris 1950.
Marcus, W., *Der Subordinatianismus als historiologisches Phänomen. Ein Beitrag zu unserer Kenntnis von der Entstehung der altchristlichen 'Theologie' und Kultur unter besonderer Berücksichtigung der Begriffe Oikonomia und Theologia*, München 1963.
Mandac, M., 'L'union christologique dans les oeuvres de Théodoret antérieures au concile d'Ephèse', *EphThLov* 47, 1971, 64–96.
Martin, J. P., *El Espiritu Santo en los origenes del Cristianismo. Estudio sobre I Clemente, Ignacio, II Clemente y Justino Mártir* (Biblioteca di Scienze Religiose 2), Zürich 1971.
Massaux, E., *L'influence de l'Evangile de saint Matthieu sur la littérature chrétienne avant saint Irénée*, Louvain–Gembloux 1950.

McGlynn, R. H., *The Incarnation in the Sermons of St Peter Chrysologus*, Munde-lein, Illinois 1956.

McHugh, J. F., *The Exhaltation of Christ in the Arian Controversy. The Teaching of St. Hilary*, Shrewsbury: Pont. Univ. Gregoriana 1959.

McNamara, J., 'Theodore of Mopsuestia and the Nestorian Heresy', *ITQ* 19, 1952, 254–68; 20, 1953, 172–91.

—— 'Theodoret of Cyrus and the Unity of Person in Christ', *ITQ* 22, 1955, 313–28.

Meijering, E. P., *Orthodoxy and Platonism in Athanasius. Synthesis or Antithesis?*, Leiden 1968.

Minutes and Papers of Consultations on Chalcedon:

    (1) 'Geneva, Faith and Order Commission 1969', *The Ecumenical Review* XXII, 1970, No. 4.

    (2) 'Geneva 1970–Addis Ababa 1971', *GOTR* 16, 1971, Nos. 1 and 2.

    (3) 'Pro Oriente, Vienna in Austria', *Wort und Wahrheit*, Supplementary Issue, No. 1, December 1972.

Montalverne, J., *Theodoreti Cyrensis doctrina antiquior de Verbo 'inhumanato'* (Studia Antoniana 1), Romae 1948.

Morgan, A., *Light in the Theology of Saint Ambrose* (Diss. Pont. Univ. Gregori-anae), Rome 1963.

Mühlenberg, E., *Apollinaris von Laodicea* (Forschungen z. Kirchen- u. Dogmen-geschichte 23), Göttingen 1969.

Nautin, P., *Hippolyte et Josipe*, Paris 1947.

—— *Hippolyte, Contre les hérésies, Fragment*, Paris 1949.

Nédoncelle, M., 'Prosopon et persona dans l'antiquité classique', *RevSR* 22, 1948, 277–99.

Neusner, J., *Aphrahat and Judaism* (Studia Post-Biblica 19), Leiden 1971.

Nicolas, M. J., O.P., 'La doctrine christologique de saint Léon le Grand', *RevThom* 51, 1951, 609–70.

Norris, R. A., Jr, *Manhood and Christ. A Study of the Christology of Theodore of Mopsuestia*, Oxford 1963.

Norton, M. A., 'Prosopography of Pope Damasus', *Folia* 4, 1950, 13–51; 5, 1951, 33–55.

Oñatibia, I., 'La vida cristiana tipo de las realidades celestes', *Scriptorium Victoriense* I, 1954, 100–33.

Orbe, A., S.J., *Estudios Valentinianos* I–III, V (AnalGreg, 99–101, 65, 113, 83), Roma 1955–58.

Ortiz de Urbina, I., *El Símbolo Niceno*, Madrid 1947.

—— *Nicée et Constantinople* (HCO 1), Paris 1963.

Otis, R., 'Cappadocian thought as a coherent system', *DOP* 12, 1958, 95–124.

Pade, P. B., Λόγος Θεός. *Untersuchungen zur Logos-Christologie des Titus Flavius Clemens v. Alexandrien*, Rome 1939.

Pannenberg, W., 'The Appropriation of the Philosophical Concept of God as a Dogmatic Problem of Early Christian Theology', *Basic Questions in Theology* II, London 1971, 119–83.

Pellegrino, M., *La catechesi cristologica di S. Clemente Alessandrino*, Milano 1940.

Pericoli-Ridolfini, F., 'Lettera di Andrea di Samosata a Rabbula di Edessa', *RSO* 28, 1953, 153–69.

Perler, O., 'Pseudo-Ignatius and Eusebius von Emesa', *HistJb* 77, 1958, 73–82.

Plagnieux, J., 'Le grief de complicité entre erreurs nestorienne et pélagienne d'Augustin à Cassien par Prosper d'Aquitaine', *RevEtAug* 2, 1956, 391–402.

Plinval, G. de, *Pélage. Ses écrits, sa vie et sa réforme*, Lausanne 1943.

—— 'Pelagio e Pelagianismo', *Enciclopedia Cattolica* IX, Rome 1952, 1071–7.

—— 'Points de vue récents sur la théologie de Pélage', *RSR* 46, 1958, 227–36.

—— 'L'heure est-elle venue de recouvrir Pélage?', *RevEtAug* 19, 1973, 158–162.

Prestige, G. L., *God in Patristic Thought*, London–Toronto 1956².

—— *St Basil the Great and Apollinaris of Laodicea*, London 1956.

Pruche, B., 'Didyme l'Aveugle est-il bien l'auteur des livres contre Eunome IV et V attribués à Saint Basile de Césarée?', *StudPat* X (TU 107), 151–5.

Quasten, J., *Patrology* I–III, Utrecht–Brussels–Antwerp 1950, 1953, 1963 (cont.).

Quispel, G., *Die Gnosis als Weltreligion*, Zürich 1951.

Rahner, H., *Greek Myths and Christian Mystery*, London 1962.

Refoulé, F., 'La christologie d'Evagre et l'origénisme', *OCP* 27, 1960, 221–66.

Richard, M., 'Un écrit de Théodoret sur l'unité du Christ après l'incarnation'. *RevSR* 14, 1934, 34–61.

—— 'L'activité littéraire de Théodoret avant le concile d'Ephèse', *RSPT* 24, 1935, 83–106.

—— *Asterii Sophistae Commentariorum in Psalmos quae supersunt. Accedunt aliquot homiliae anonymae* (SymbOslFascSuppl XVI), Oslo 1956.

—— 'Notes sur l'évolution doctrinale de Théodoret', *RSPT* 25, 1936, 459–81.

—— 'L'introduction du mot "hypostase" dans la théologie de l'incarnation', *MSR* 2, 1945, 5–32, 243–70 (='Hypostase').

—— 'Théodoret, Jean d'Antioche et les moines d'Orient', *MSR* 3, 1946, 147–56.

—— 'Saint Athanase et la psychologie du Christ selon les Ariens', *MSR* 4, 1947, 5–54 (='Athanase').

—— 'Malchion et Paul de Samosate', *EphThLov* 35, 1959, 325–38.

Richard, M.–Hemmerdinger, B., 'Trois nouveaux fragments de l'*Adversus Haereses* de Saint Irénée', *ZNW* 53, 1962, 252–5.

Ricken, F., 'Nikaia als Krisis des altchristlichen Platonismus', *TheolPhil* 44, 1969, 321–351.

Riedmatten, H. de, O.P., 'Some neglected aspects of Apollinarist christology', *DomStud* 1, 1948, 239–60.

—— *Les Actes du procès de Paul de Samosate. Etude sur la christologie du IIIe et IVe siècles* (Paradosis 6), Freiburg 1952.

—— 'La correspondance entre Basile de Césarée et Apollinaire de Laodicée', *JTS*, NS 6, 1955, 199–210; 7, 1956, 53–70.

—— 'La christologie d'Apollinaire de Laodicée', *StudPat* II (TU 64), Berlin 1957, 208–34.

Ritter, A.-M., *Das Konzil von Konstantinopel und sein Symbol*, Göttingen 1965.

Robinson, John A. T., *The Human Face of God*, London 1973.

Roldanus, J., *Le Christ et l'homme dans la théologie d'Athanase d'Alexandrie. Etude de la conjonction de sa conception de l'homme avec sa christologie* (Studies in the History of Christian Thought IV), Leiden 1968.

Rondeau, Marie-Josèphe, 'Le "Commentaire des Psaumes" de Diodore de Tarse' I–III, *RevHistRel* 176, 1969, 5–23, 153–88; 177, 1970, 5–33.

Rudolph, K., *Die Mandäer*. I. *Das Mandäerproblem*, II. *Der Kult* (FRLANT NF 56, 57), Göttingen 1960/1961.

Rüther, T., *Die sittliche Forderung der Apatheia in den beiden ersten christlichen Jahrhunderten und bei Clemens von Alexandrien*, Freiburg 1949.

Šagi-Bunić, T., 'Documentatio doctrinalis Ephesino-Chalcedonensis', *Laurentianum* 3, 1962, 499–514.

—— 'De dyophysitismo extra scholam Antiochenam', *Laurentianum* 4, 1963, 231–51.

—— ' "Duo perfecta" et "duae naturae" in definitione dogmatica Chalcedonensi', *Laurentianum* 5, 1964 (extract).

—— '*Deus perfectus et homo perfectus*' a concilio Ephesino (a. 431) *adCh alcedonense* (a. *451*), Rome 1965.

—— 'Problemata christologiae Chalcedonensis: Continuitas doctrinalis et drama conscientiae episcoporum qua fidei iudicum', *Laurentianum* 8, 1967; 9, 1968 (extracts).

Sagnard, F. M. M., O.P., *La Gnose Valentinienne*, Paris 1947.

Samuel, V. C., 'One incarnate Nature of God the Word', *GOTR* 10, 1964–65, 37–53.

Sansterre, J.-M., 'Eusèbe de Césarée et la naissance de la théorie "Césaropapiste" ', *Byz* 42, 1972, 131–95, 532–94.

Schendel, E., *Herrschaft und Unterwerfung Christi*. 1 *Korinther* 15, 24–27 *in Exegese und Theologie der Väter bis zum Ausgang des 4. Jahrhunderts* (BGBE 12), Tübingen 1971.

Schenke, H.-M., *Der Gott 'Mensch' in der Gnosis*, Göttingen 1962.

Schiltz, E., 'La christologie de S. Augustin', *NRT* 63, 1936, 689–713.

Schlier, H., 'Das Denken der frühchristlichen Gnosis', *Neutestamentliche Studien für Rudolf Bultmann* (BZNW 21), 1957[2], 67–82.

Schmid, A., *Die Christologie Isidors von Pelusium* (Paradosis 2), Freiburg 1948.

Schneemelcher, W., 'Zur Chronologie des arianischen Streites', *ThLZ* 79, 1954, 393–400.

Schoeps, H. J., *Theologie und Geschichte des Judenchristentums*, Tübingen 1949.

—— *Urgemeinde, Judenchristentum, Gnosis*, Tübingen 1950.

—— *Vom himmlischen Fleisch Christi*, Tübingen 1951.

—— *Aus frühchristlicher Zeit*, Tübingen 1956.

Schweizer, E., *Ego Eimi*, Göttingen 1939.

—— 'Zur Herkunft der Präexistenzvorstellung bei Paulus', *EvTh* 19, 1959, 65–70.

—— *Lordship and Discipleship* (SBT 28), London 1960.

Scipioni, L. I., *Ricerche sulla cristologia del 'Libro di Eraclide' di Nestorio. La formulazione teologica e il suo contesto filosofico* (Paradosis 11), Freiburg 1956.

—— *Nestorio e il concilio di Efeso. Storia dogma critica* (Studia Patristica Mediolanensia 1), Milano 1974.

Seibel, W., *Fleisch und Geist beim hl. Ambrosius*, München 1958.

Sellers, R. V., *Eustathius of Antioch and his Place in the Early History of Christian Doctrine*, Cambridge 1928.

—— *Two Ancient Christologies*, London 1940.

—— *The Council of Chalcedon*, London 1953.

Simonetti, M., *Studi sull'Arianesimo*, Rome 1965.

Sirinelli, J., *Les vues historiques d'Eusèbe de Césarée* (Université de Dakar, Publications de la Section de langues et littérature 10), Dakar 1961.

Spanneut, M., *Recherches sur les écrits d'Eustathe d'Antioche*, Lille 1948.

—— *Le stoïcisme des Pères de l'Eglise de Clément de Rome à Clément d'Alexandrie* (PS 1), Paris 1957.

Stead, G. C., 'The Platonism of Arius', *JTS* 15, 1964, 16–31.

—— 'Eusebius and the Council of Nicaea', *JTS* 24, 1973, 85–100.

Strecker, G., *Das Judenchristentum in den Pseudoklementinen* (TU 70), Berlin 1958.

—— *Der Weg der Gerechtigkeit. Untersuchung zur Theologie des Matthäus* (FRLANT 82), Göttingen 1962.

Studer, B., *Zur Theophanie-Exegese Augustins. Untersuchung zu einem Ambrosius-Zitat in der Schrift De videndo Deo* (Ep. 147) (Studia Anselmiana 59), Rome 1971.

—— '*Consubstantialis Patri-Consubstantialis Matri*: Une antithèse christologique chez Léon le Grand', *RevEtAug* XVIII, 1972, 87–115.

Sullivan, F. A., *The Christology of Theodore of Mopsuestia*, Rome 1956.

Tetz, M., 'Eudoxius-Fragmente?', *StudPat* III (TU 78), 1961, 314–23.

—— *Eine Antilogie des Eutherius von Tyana* (PTSt 1), Berlin 1964.

—— 'Zur Theologie des Markell von Ankyra':

(I) 'Eine Markellische Schrift "De Incarnatione et contra Arianos"', *ZKG* 75, 1964, 217–70.

(II) 'Markells Lehre von der Adamssohnschaft Christi und eine pseudo-klementinische Tradition über die wahren Lehrer und Propheten', *ZKG* 79, 1963, 3–42.

(III) 'Die pseudathanasianische Epistula ad Liberium, ein Markellisches Bekenntnis', *ZKG* 83, 1972, 145–94.

—— 'Markellianer und Athanasios von Alexandrien. Die markellische *Expositio fidei ad Athanasium* des Diakons Eugenios von Ankyra', *ZNW* 64, 1973, 75–121.

Thomson, R. W., *Athanasius Contra Gentes and De Incarnatione Edited and Translated* (Oxford Early Christian Texts), Oxford 1971.

Tonneau, R.–Devreesse, R., *Les homélies catéchétiques de Théodore de Mopsueste* (ST 145), Città del Vaticano 1949.

Trapé, A., 'Un caso de nestorianismo prenestoriano en Occidente resuelto por San Agustin', *Ciudad de Dios* 155, 1943, 45–67.

Turner, H. E. W., *The Patristic Doctrine of Redemption*, London 1952.

—— *The Pattern of Christian Truth. A Study in the Relations between Orthodoxy and Heresy in the Early Church*, London 1954.

Verbeke, G., *L'évolution de la doctrine du pneuma du stoïcisme à saint Augustin*, Paris–Louvain 1945.

Verhoeven, L., *Studien over Tertullianus' Adversus Praxean*, Utrecht–Amsterdam 1948.

Vögtle, A., and others, 'Jesus Christus', *LThK* V, 1960, 922–64.

Völker, W., *Der wahre Gnostiker nach Clemens Alexandrinus* (TU 57), Berlin 1952.

—— *Gregor von Nyssa als Mystiker*, Wiesbaden 1955.

Vööbus, A., 'Aphrahat', *JAC* 3, 1960, 152–5.

Wallace-Hadrill, D. S., *Eusebius of Caesarea*, London 1960.

Warkotsch, A., *Antike Philosophie im Urteil der Kirchenväter. Christlicher Glaube im Widerstreit der Philosophien*, Munich–Paderborn–Wien 1973.

Weber, A., *APXH. Ein Beitrag zur Christologie des Eusebius von Caesarea*, München 1964.

Weigandt, R., *Der Doketismus im Urchristentum und in der theologischen Entwicklung des zweiten Jahrhunderts*, Diss. Heidelberg 1961.

Weischer, B. M., 'Der Dialog "dass Christus einer ist" des Cyrill von Alexandrien. Nach Hss. in Berlin, Cambridge, London, Paris und Tübingen zum ersten Mal im äthiopischen Text hersg. und mit deutscher Übersetzung versehen', *OrChr* 51, 1967, 130–85.

Werner, M., *The Formation of Christian Dogma*, London–New York 1957.

Wickert, U., *Studien zu den Pauluskommentaren Theodors von Mopsuestia*, Berlin 1962.

Wiles, M. F., 'In Defence of Arius', *JTS* 13, 1962, 339–47.

—— 'The Nature of the Early Debate about Christ's Human Soul', *JEH* 16, 1965, 139–51.

Wilken, R. L., 'Tradition, Exegesis, and the Christological Controversies', *Church History* 34, 1965, 123–45.

Wilson, R. McL., *The Gnostic Problem*, London 1958.

Wlosok, Antonie, *Laktanz und die philosophische Gnosis* (AbhHeidAkWiss 1960, 2), Heidelberg 1960.

Wölfl, K., *Das Heilswirken Gottes durch den Sohn nach Tertullian* (AnalGreg 112), Rome 1960.

Wolfson, H. A., *The Philosophy of the Church Fathers* I, Cambridge, Mass. 1956.

—— 'Philosophical implications of Arianism and Apollinarianism', *DOP* 12, 1958, 3–28.

Young, F. M., 'Christological Ideas in the Greek Commentaries on the Epistle to the Hebrews', *JTS* 20, 1969, 150–63.

Zemp, P., *Die Grundlagen heilsgeschichtlichen Denkens bei Gregor von Nyssa* (MünchTheolStud II, 38), München 1970.

INDEX OF SUBJECTS

INDEX OF ANCIENT AUTHORS

INDEX OF BIBLICAL REFERENCES

Old Testament

New Testament

INDEX OF MODERN SCHOLARS

CPSIA information can be obtained at www.ICGtesting.com
Printed in the USA
LVOW08s0341040614

388455LV00001B/83/P